Volume III
From the Jinggangshan to the Establishment of the Jiangxi Soviets
July 1927–December 1930

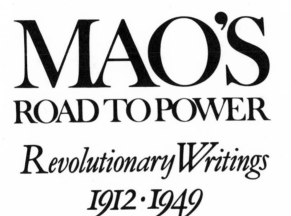

MAO'S
ROAD TO POWER
Revolutionary Writings
1912·1949

This volume was prepared under the auspices of
the John King Fairbank Center for East Asian Research,
Harvard University

The project for the translation of Mao Zedong's pre-1949 writings has been supported by a grant from the National Endowment for the Humanities, an independent federal agency.

The Cover

Volumes I and II of this edition each display on the cover a sample of Mao's calligraphy for the period in question. It is our wish to follow this precedent throughout the whole series, but we have been unable to locate a single document from Mao's hand for the three and a half years from July 1927 to December 1930. There are several poems from this period which Mao copied out in the 1960s, but such a text would not have constituted an emanation of his personality during the years spent in Jiangxi. Fortunately, we have been able to obtain a copy of a document that Mao wrote in August 1931, and it is a passage from this which appears on the cover of the present volume.

The text in question is that of an order to the First Front Army drafted by Mao in Xingguo *xian*, Jiangxi Province, on August 8, 1931, in the context of Chiang Kaishek's third "Campaign of Encirclement and Annihilation." The portion reproduced on the cover corresponds to the second page of Mao's manuscript. A printed text of the order appears in *Mao Zedong junshi wenji*, Vol. 1, pp. 245-46. The whole of this document will, of course, be translated in Volume IV of our edition.

Volume III
From the Jinggangshan to the
Establishment of the Jiangxi Soviets
July 1927–December 1930

MAO'S
ROAD TO POWER
Revolutionary Writings
1912 · 1949

Stuart R. Schram, Editor

Nancy J. Hodes, Associate Editor

An East Gate Book

M.E. Sharpe
Armonk, New York
London, England

An East Gate Book

Translations copyright © 1995 John King Fairbank Center for East Asian Research

Introductory materials copyright © 1995 Stuart R. Schram

Maps copyright © 1995 Stephen C. Averill

Translation of "Xunwu Investigation," on pp. 296–418, copyright © 1990
Board of Trustees of the Leland Stanford Junior University.

Library of Congress Cataloging-in-Publication Data

(Revised for vol. 3)

Mao, Tse-tung, 1893–1976.
Mao's road to power.

"East gate book."
Includes bibliographical references and index.
Contents: v. 1. The pre-Marxist period, 1912–1920—
v. 3. From the Jinggangshan to the Establishment of the
Jiangxi Soviets, July 1927–December 1930.
I. Schram, Stuart R.,
II. Title.
DS778.M3A25   1992
951.04   92-26783
ISBN 1-56324-049-1 (v. 1 : acid-free); ISBN 1-56324-457-8 (pbk; acid-free)
ISBN 1-56324-439-X (v. 3 : acid-free)
CIP

Printed in the United States of America

The paper used in this publication meets the minimum requirements of
American National Standard for Information Sciences—
Permanence of Paper for Printed Library Materials,
ANSI Z 39.48-1984.

∞

BM (c)   10   9   8   7   6   5   4   3   2   1

Contents

Acknowledgments

Major funding for this project has been provided by the National Endowment for the Humanities, from which we have received four generous grants, for the periods 1989–1991, 1991–1993, 1993–1995, and 1995–1997. In addition, many individual and corporate donors have contributed substantially toward the cost-sharing element of our budget. These include, in alphabetical order: Mrs. H. Ahmanson; Ambassador Kwang S. Choi; the Dillon Fund; John Guth, on behalf of the Fairbank Center Committee; the Harvard-Yenching Institute; James R. Houghton, the CBS Foundation, the Corning, Inc. Foundation, J.P. Morgan & Co., and the Metropolitan Life Foundation; Dr. Alice Kandell and the Kandell Fund; and James O. Welch, Jr., RJR Nabisco, and the Vanguard Group.

Translations of the materials included in this volume have been drafted by many different hands. Our team of translators has included, in alphabetical order, Hsuan Delorme, Gu Weiqun, Li Jin, Li Yuwei, Li Zhuqing, Lin Chun, Pei Minxin, Shen Tong, Su Weizhou, Tian Dongdong, Wang Xisu, Wang Zhi, Bill Wycoff, Ye Yang, Zhang Aiping, and Zheng Shiping.

Nancy Hodes, Research Assistant since mid-1991, and associate editor of the series, has been involved in all aspects of the work on the present volume. She has played a major role in the revision and annotation of the translations, and in checking the final versions against the Chinese originals. She has also drafted some translations, as has Stuart Schram. In particular, she has prepared the initial drafts of all Mao's poems, which were then revised in collaboration with Stuart Schram. Final responsibility for the accuracy and literary quality of the work as a whole rests with him as editor.

We are particularly grateful to Professor Stephen C. Averill of Michigan State University for the many-sided assistance he has offered us in the revision of this book. During the spring and summer of 1995, when he was in Cambridge as a visiting scholar at M.I.T. and Harvard, he kindly read the entire set of proofs very carefully. Professor Averill made many valuable comments and suggestions from his perspective as a specialist in the period in the history of Chinese Communism covered by this volume, and prepared the two maps. He also brought to our attention important sources published in Jiangxi Province, containing a number of additional texts which have enabled us to expand substantially the coverage of Mao's writings, especially during the latter half of 1930.

Thanks are also due to Mr. Shum Chun of the Yenching Library Rare Books Room, who transcribed for us the record of a Politburo Meeting on July 4, 1927, which constitutes the source for the first text in this volume. The copy of this document available to us is barely legible. Mr. Shum deciphered virtually all of it and transformed it into a neat computer printout which greatly facilitated our task of translation.

This project was launched with the active participation of Roderick MacFarquhar, Director of the Fairbank Center until June 30, 1992. Without his organizing ability and continuing wholehearted support, it would never have come to fruition. His successors, Professor James L. Watson and Professor Ezra Vogel, have both taken a keen and sympathetic interest in our work.

The general introduction to the series, and the introduction to Volume III, were written by Stuart Schram, who wishes to acknowledge his very great indebtedness to Benjamin Schwartz, a pioneer in the study of Mao Zedong's thought. Professor Schwartz read successive drafts of these two introductions, and made stimulating and thoughtful comments which have greatly improved the final versions. For any remaining errors and inadequacies, the fault lies once again with the editor.

GENERAL INTRODUCTION

Mao Zedong and the Chinese Revolution, 1912-1949

Mao Zedong stands out as one of the dominant figures of the twentieth century. Guerrilla leader, strategist, conqueror, ruler, poet, and philosopher, he placed his imprint on China, and on the world. This edition of Mao's writings provides abundant documentation in his own words regarding both his life and his thought. Because of the central role of Mao's ideas and actions in the turbulent course of the Chinese revolution, it thus offers a rich body of historical data about China in the first half of the twentieth century.

The process of change and upheaval in China which Mao sought to master had been going on for roughly a century by the time he was born in 1893. Its origins lay in the incapacity of the old order to cope with the population explosion at the end of the eighteenth century, and with other economic and social problems, as well as in the shock administered by the Opium War of 1840 and further European aggression and expansion thereafter.

Mao's native Hunan Province was crucially involved both in the struggles of the Qing dynasty to maintain its authority, and in the radical ferment which led to successive challenges to the imperial system. Thus on the one hand, the Hunan Army of the great conservative viceroy Zeng Guofan was the main instrument for putting down the Taiping Rebellion and saving the dynasty in the middle of the nineteenth century. But on the other hand, the most radical of the late nineteenth-century reformers, and the only one to lay down his life in 1898, Tan Sitong, was also a Hunanese, as was Huang Xing, whose contribution to the Revolution of 1911 was arguably as great as that of Sun Yatsen.[1] In his youth, Mao profoundly admired all three of these men, though they stood for very different things: Zeng for the empire and the Confucian values which sustained it, Tan for defying tradition and seeking inspiration in the West, Huang for Western-style constitutional democracy.

---

1. Abundant references to all three of these figures are to be found in Mao's writings, especially those of the early period contained in Volume I of this series. See, regarding Zeng, pp. 10, 72, and 131. On Tan, see "Zhang Kundi's Record of Two Talks with Mao Zedong," September 1917, p. 139. On Huang, see "Letter to Miyazaki Tōten," March 1917, pp. 111–12.

Apart from Mao's strong Hunanese patriotism, which inclined him to admire eminent figures from his own province, he undoubtedly saw these three as forceful and effective leaders who, each in his own way, fought to assure the future of China. Any sense that they were contradictory symbols would have been diminished by the fact that from an early age Mao never advocated exclusive reliance on either Chinese or Western values, but repeatedly sought a synthesis of the two. In August 1917, Mao Zedong expressed the view that despite the "antiquated" and otherwise undesirable traits of the Chinese mentality, "Western thought is not necessarily all correct either; very many parts of it should be transformed at the same time as Oriental thought."[2] In a sense, this sentence sums up the problem he sought to resolve throughout his whole career: How could China develop an advanced civilization, and become rich and powerful, while remaining Chinese?

As shown by the texts contained in Volume I, Mao's early exposure to "Westernizing" influences was not limited to Marxism. Other currents of European thought played a significant role in his development. Whether he was dealing with liberalism or Leninism, however, Mao tenaciously sought to adapt and transform these ideologies, even as he espoused them and learned from them.

Mao Zedong played an active and significant role in the movement for political and intellectual renewal which developed in the aftermath of the patriotic student demonstrations of May 4, 1919, against the transfer of German concessions in China to Japan. This "new thought tide," which had begun to manifest itself at least as early as 1915, dominated the scene from 1919 onward, and prepared the ground for the triumph of radicalism and the foundation of the Chinese Communist Party in 1921. But though Mao enthusiastically supported the call of Chen Duxiu, who later became the Party's first leader, for the Western values incarnated by "Mr. Science" and "Mr. Democracy," he never wholly endorsed the total negation of Chinese culture advocated by many people during the May Fourth period. His condemnations of the old thought as backward and slavish are nearly always balanced by a call to learn from both Eastern and Western thought and to develop something new out of these twin sources.

In 1919 and 1920, Mao leaned toward anarchism rather than socialism. Only in January 1921 did he at last draw the explicit conclusion that anarchism would not work, and that Russia's proletarian dictatorship represented the model which must be followed.[3] Half the remaining fifty-five years of his life were devoted to creating such a dictatorship, and the other half to deciding what to do with it, and how to overcome the defects which he perceived in it. From beginning to end of this process, Mao drew upon Chinese experience and Chinese civilization in revising and reforming this Western import.

To the extent that, from the 1920s onward, Mao was a committed Leninist, his

---

2. Letter of August 1917 to Li Jinxi, Volume 1, p. 132.
3. See his letter of January 21, 1921, to Cai Hesen, Volume 2, pp. 35–36.

understanding of the doctrine shaped his vision of the world. But to the extent that, although he was a communist revolutionary, he always "planted his backside on the body of China,"[4] ideology alone did not exhaustively determine his outlook. One of Mao Zedong's most remarkable attributes was the extent to which he linked theory and practice. He was in some respects not a very good Marxist, but few men have ever applied so well Marx's dictum that the vocation of the philosopher is not merely to understand the world, but to change it.

It is reliably reported that Mao's close collaborators tried in vain, during the Yan'an period, to interest him in writings by Marx such as *The 18 Brumaire of Louis Bonaparte*. To such detailed historical analyses based on economic and social facts, he preferred *The Communist Manifesto*, of which he saw the message as "*Jieji douzheng, jieji douzheng, jieji douzheng!*" (Class struggle, class struggle, class struggle!) In other words, for Mao the essence of Marxism resided in the fundamental idea of the struggle between oppressor and oppressed as the motive force of history.

Such a perspective offered many advantages. It opened the door to the immediate pursuit of revolutionary goals, since even though China did not have a very large urban proletariat, there was no lack of oppressed people to be found there. It thus eliminated the need for the Chinese to feel inferior, or to await salvation from without, just because their country was still stuck in some precapitalist stage of development (whether "Asiatic" or "feudal"). And, by placing the polarity "oppressor/oppressed" at the heart of the revolutionary ideology itself, this approach pointed toward a conception in which landlord oppression, and the oppression of China by the imperialists, were perceived as the two key targets of the struggle.

Mao displayed, in any case, a remarkably acute perception of the realities of Chinese society, and consistently adapted his ideas to those realities, at least during the struggle for power. In the early years after its foundation in 1921, the Chinese Communist Party sought support primarily from the working class in the cities and adopted a strategy based on a "united front" or alliance with Sun Yatsen's Guomindang. Mao threw himself into this enterprise with enthusiasm, serving first as a labor union organizer in Hunan in 1922-1923, and then as a high official within the Guomindang organization in 1923-1924. Soon, however, he moved away from this perspective, and even before urban-based revolution was put down in blood by Chiang Kaishek in 1927, he asserted that the real center of gravity of Chinese society was to be found in the countryside. From this fact, he drew the conclusion that the decisive blows against the existing reactionary order must be struck in the countryside by the peasants.

By August 1927, Mao had concluded that mobilizing the peasant masses was not enough. A red army was also necessary to serve as the spearhead of revolu-

---

4. Mao Zedong, "Ruhe yanjiu Zhonggong dangshi" (How to study the history of the Chinese Communist Party), lecture of March 1942, published in *Dangshi yanjiu* (Research on Party History), No. 1, 1980, pp. 2–7.

tion, and so he put forward the slogan: "Political power comes out of the barrel of a gun."[5] In the mountain fastness of the Jinggangshan base area in Jiangxi Province, to which he retreated at the end of 1927 with the remnants of his forces, he began to elaborate a comprehensive strategy for rural revolution, combining land reform with the tactics of guerrilla warfare. In this he was aided by Zhu De, a professional soldier who had joined the Chinese Communist Party, and soon became known as the "commander-in-chief." These tactics rapidly achieved a considerable measure of success. The "Chinese Soviet Republic," established in 1931 in a larger and more populous area of Jiangxi, survived for several years, though when Chiang Kaishek finally devised the right strategy and mobilized his crack troops against it, the Communists were defeated and forced to embark in 1934 on the Long March.

By this time, Mao Zedong had been reduced virtually to the position of a figurehead by the Moscow-trained members of the so-called "Internationalist" faction, who dominated the leadership of the Chinese Communist Party. At a conference held at Zunyi in January 1935, in the course of the Long March, Mao began his comeback. Soon he was once again in effective charge of military operations, though he became chairman of the Party only in 1943.

Mao's vision of the Chinese people as a whole as the victim of oppression now came decisively into play. Japanese aggression led in 1936 to the Xi'an Incident, in which Chiang Kaishek was kidnapped in order to force him to oppose the invader. This event was the catalyst which produced a second "united front" between the Communists and the Guomindang. Without it, Mao Zedong and the forces he led might well have remained a side current in the remote and backward region of Shaanxi, or even been exterminated altogether. As it was, the collaboration of 1937-1945, however perfunctory and opportunistic on both sides, gave Mao the occasion to establish himself as a patriotic national leader. Above all, the resulting context of guerrilla warfare behind the Japanese lines allowed the Communists to build a foundation of political and military power throughout wide areas of Northern and Central China.

During the years in Yan'an, from 1937 to 1946, Mao Zedong also finally consolidated his own dominant position in the Chinese Communist Party, and in particular his role as the ideological mentor of the Party. Beginning in November 1936, he seized the opportunity to read a number of writings by Chinese Marxists, and Soviet works in Chinese translation, which had been published while he was struggling for survival a few years earlier. These provided the stimulus for the elaboration of his own interpretation of Marxism-Leninism, and in particular for his theory of contradictions. Another of the main features of his thought, the emphasis on practice as the source of knowledge, had long been in evidence and had found expression in the sociological surveys in the countryside which he himself carried out beginning as early as 1926.

---

5. See below, the texts of August 7 and August 18, 1927, pp. 31 and 36 of this volume.

In 1938, Mao called for the "Sinification of Marxism," that is, the modification not only of its language but of its substance in order to adapt it to Chinese culture and Chinese realities. By 1941, he had begun to suggest that he himself had carried out this enterprise, and to attack those in the Party who preferred to translate ready-made formulas from the Soviet Union. The "Rectification Campaign" of 1942-43 was designed in large measure to change the thinking of such "Internationalists," or to eliminate them from positions of influence.

When Mao was elected chairman of the Politburo and of the Secretariat in March 1943, the terms of his appointment to this second post contained a curious provision: Mao alone, as chairman, could out-vote the other two members of the Secretariat in case of disagreement. This was the first step toward setting Mao above and apart from all other Party members and thereby opening the way to the subsequent cult. At the Seventh Party Congress in April 1945 came apotheosis: Mao Zedong's thought was written into the Party statutes as the guide to all work, and Mao was hailed as the greatest theoretical genius in China's history for his achievement in creating such a remarkable doctrine.

In 1939-1940, Mao had put forward the slogan of "New Democracy" and defined it as a régime in which proletariat (read Communist Party) and bourgeoisie (read Guomindang) would jointly exercise dictatorship over reactionary and pro-Japanese elements in Chinese society. Moreover, as late as 1945, when the Communists were still in a weaker position than the Guomindang, Mao indicated that this form of rule would be based on free elections with universal suffrage. Later, when the Communist Party had military victory within its grasp and was in a position to do things entirely in its own way, Mao would state forthrightly, in "On People's Democratic Dictatorship," that such a dictatorship could in fact just as well be called a "People's Democratic Autocracy." In other words, it was to be democratic only in the sense that it served the people's interests; in form, it was to exercise its authority through a "powerful state apparatus."

In 1946, when the failure of General George Marshall's attempts at mediation led to renewed civil war, Mao and his comrades revived the policy of land reform, which had been suspended during the alliance with the Guomindang, and thereby recreated a climate of agrarian revolution. Thus national and social revolution were interwoven in the strategy which ultimately brought final victory in 1949.

In March 1949, Mao declared that though the Chinese revolution had previously taken the path of surrounding the cities from the countryside, henceforth the building of socialism would take place in the orthodox way, with leadership and enlightenment radiating outward from the cities to the countryside. Looking at the twenty-seven years under Mao's leadership after 1949, however, the two most striking developments—the chiliastic hopes of instant plenty which characterized the Great Leap Forward of the late 1950s, and the anxiety about the corrupting effects of material progress, coupled with a nostalgia for "military communism," which underlay the Cultural Revolution—both bore the mark of rural utopianism. Thus Mao's road to power, though it led to total victory over the Nationalists, also cultivated in Mao himself, and in the Party, attitudes which would subsequently engender great problems.

Revolution in its Leninist guise has loomed large in the world for most of the twentieth century, and the Chinese revolution has been, with the Russian revolution, one of its two most important manifestations. The Bolshevik revolution set a pattern long regarded as the only standard of communist orthodoxy, but the revolutionary process in China was in some respects even more remarkable. Although communism now appears bankrupt throughout much of the world, the impact of Mao is still a living reality in China two decades after his death. Particularly since the Tiananmen events of June 1989, the continuing relevance of Mao's political and ideological heritage has been stressed ever more heavily by the Chinese leadership. Interest in Mao Zedong has been rekindled in some sectors of the population, and elements of a new Mao cult have even emerged.

Though the ultimate impact of these recent trends remains uncertain, the problem of how to come to terms with the modern world, while retaining China's own identity, still represents perhaps the greatest challenge facing the Chinese. Mao did not solve it, but he boldly grappled with the political and intellectual challenge of the West as no Chinese ruler before him had done. If Lenin has suffered the ultimate insult of being replaced by Peter the Great as the symbol of Russian national identity, it could be argued that Mao cannot, like Lenin, be supplanted by a figure analogous to Peter because he himself played the role of China's first modernizing and Westernizing autocrat. However misguided many of Mao's ideas, and however flawed his performance, his efforts in this direction will remain a benchmark to a people still struggling to define their place in the community of nations.

INTRODUCTION

The Writings of Mao Zedong, 1927–1930

The texts from 1912 to November 1920 contained in Volume I of this edition shed light primarily on the life and intellectual development of the young Mao. Though several of the more important documents emanate from organizations, such as the New People's Study Society or the Cultural Book Society, Mao's imprint on these bodies was so profound that the views expressed there can legitimately be taken as corresponding in substantial measure to his own thinking. Volume II, which covered the period December 1920—June 1927, introduced a new dimension: Mao's activity as a member of two parties, the Chinese Communist Party and the Guomindang, neither of which he led or controlled. As a result, the constraints of party orthodoxy shaped what he wrote to some degree, and to the biographical perspective of the first volume was added a new domain: that of "party history."

In Volume III, Mao's life and thought, as well as the history both of the Chinese Communist Party and of the Guomindang, continue to be important topics. At the same time, however, another theme makes its appearance: that of military tactics and military history. This concern with military affairs manifests itself in several different ways. First, in line with Mao's statement, in August 1927,[1] that "political power is obtained from the barrel of a gun," the central role of armed force in the Chinese revolution is a basic postulate in virtually everything he wrote during these three years, and indeed during the ensuing two decades. Second, Mao took an increasing interest in military tactics for its own sake and began, during the period covered here, to develop his own distinctive ideas in this domain. He did so of necessity, because fighting had become a large part of his life. Finally, the form which should be taken by armed struggle, and its place in the overall strategy of the Chinese Communist Party, became in 1928—1930 a key issue in the interaction between Mao Zedong and his supporters, on the one hand, and the central Party leadership, on the other. In other words, military history and Party history are intricately intertwined during the period covered by this volume.

Another important qualitative change in the context within which Mao operated from mid-1927 onwards, as compared to the period covered by Volume II, concerns the locus of his actions. During the First United Front, he had been close to the center of things, serving for a time as secretary of the Communist Party's Central Bureau, and as acting head of the Guomindang Propaganda Department. Even when his role was less prominent, he was in direct contact with the

---

1. See below, his remarks at the August 7 Emergency Conference.

leaders of both parties. Now he would find himself geographically isolated, and excluded from the major decision-making bodies of the Chinese Communist Party.

In this situation, he was perpetually engaged in a struggle on two fronts, seeking on the one hand to persuade the Central Committee to accept his point of view regarding the strategy which should be followed, and on the other hand to impose his authority over the various military and political entities claiming allegiance to the Chinese Communist Party scattered about the countryside. A primary function of the introductions to the volumes in this series is to present and analyze the documents they contain. Unfortunately, there are few texts in the present volume addressed even by implication to lower levels of the Party. Many documents do, however, deal very concretely with the problems confronting Mao at various times. This is particularly true of the many military orders signed by Mao Zedong and Zhu De for the latter half of 1930. As a result, this introduction focuses in the first instance on Mao's interaction with those in authority over him, but also seeks to provide some background regarding the situation in which he and his forces found themselves.

From the United Front to Armed Struggle
in the Countryside

Volume II of this edition ended in June 1927, when the Guomindang "center," represented by Chiang Kaishek, had already broken with the Communists, and the "united front" between the Chinese Communist Party and the "Left Guomindang" in Wuhan was under extreme strain. On July 15, Wang Jingwei and the Wuhan Left effectively put an end to the "bloc within" by expelling Communists from the Guomindang. Already, in the context of a meeting of the Standing Committee of the Politburo, called to discuss the situation in Hunan, Mao had argued that if the Communists did not possess their own army, they would be helpless in case of such an emergency. Foreshadowing the course he was to follow three months later, he declared that, by "going up the mountains," the foundation for a real military force could be laid. [2]

On July 20, 1927, Mao participated in drafting a circular of the Chinese Communist Party Central Committee regarding the tactics of the peasant movement which reiterated the same point about "going up the mountains." All the "present so-called revolutionary armies," asserted the circular, were in fact led by "reactionary officers who represent the landlord class." It therefore called for the peasants to "arm themselves," while recognizing that for the time being, it was "not possible for peasant armed forces to exist openly," except in the mountains. [3]

At about the same time, a group of Communist leaders, with the support of Soviet emissaries, were planning a military insurrection in the city of Nanchang

---

2. See below, "The Hunan Problem," July 4, 1927.
3. See below, "The Overall Tactics of the Peasant Movement at Present," July 20, 1927.

in northern Jiangxi, if possible with the support or tacit acceptance of General Zhang Fakui and his Second Front Army. This uprising, which took place on August 1, was initially successful, but the insurgents soon found themselves under attack by greatly superior Guomindang forces, and retreated toward Guangdong, under the leadership of He Long, the commander of the Twentieth Army, and Ye Ting, who commanded the Twenty-fourth Division of the Eleventh Army.

On the very day when the Nanchang Uprising was launched, Mao Zedong signed for the last time, in his capacity as an alternate member of the Guomindang Central Executive Committee, a document emanating from that party. In this declaration of August 1, on which his name appeared alongside that of Sun Yatsen's widow, Song Qingling, he called for "loyal commanders and soldiers . . . to summon up the unflinching courage of the Director General and thus make it impossible for those who have usurped the name of the Party to make use of even one soldier." To suggest that the magic name of Sun Yatsen would suffice to wrest control of the Guomindang armies from Chiang Kaishek and Tang Shengzhi was, however, scarcely a viable policy.[4]

Barely a week later, the so-called August 7 Emergency Conference met in Hankou, to discuss the strategy which should be adopted after the break with the Guomindang, and to install a more radical Party leadership. On this occasion, Mao began to sketch out a solution to the dilemma in which the Communists found themselves caught:

> [W]e used to censure Sun Yatsen for engaging only in a military movement, and we did just the opposite, not undertaking a military movement, but exclusively a mass movement. Both Chiang Kaishek and Tang Shengzhi rose by grasping the gun; we alone did not concern ourselves with this. At present, although we have paid some attention to it, we still have no firm concept about it. The Autumn Harvest Uprising[5] . . . is simply impossible without military force. . . . From now on, we should pay the greatest attention to military affairs. We must know that political power is obtained from the barrel of the gun.[6]

Ten days later, at a meeting of the Hunan Provincial Committee, Mao elaborated on the same theme:

> If we wish to create and unleash [the Autumn Harvest] Uprising, it will not do to rely on the power of the peasants alone. There must be military support. With the help of one or two regiments, the uprising can take place; otherwise it will fail in the end.

---

4. See below, "Declaration of Members of the [Guomindang] Central Committee," August 1, 1927.

5. The uprising in Hunan, scheduled to take place in September, in which Mao was to play a leading role as special commissioner sent to the province in mid-August with a mandate to reorganize the Provincial Party Committee. See below, the text of August 9, 1927, and the notes thereto.

6. See below, Mao's "Remarks on the Report of the Representative of the International at the August 7 Emergency Conference."

> The development of the uprising must lead to the seizure of political power. If you want to seize political power, to try to do it without the support of military forces would be sheer self-deception. Our Party's mistake in the past has been that it neglected military affairs. Now we should concentrate 60 percent of our energies on the military movement. We must carry out the principle of seizing and establishing political power on the barrel of a gun.[7]

At the end of August, replying to criticism from the Central Committee directed against his plan to use the two regiments at his disposal to "shield the development" of the worker-peasant uprising he was organizing, Mao declared bluntly: "When you say that we here are engaging in military adventurism, . . . this truly . . . constitutes a contradictory policy which pays no attention to military affairs, while at the same time calling for an armed uprising of the popular masses." [8] In other words, it is irresponsible to ask the ill-armed and unorganized masses to rise up against disciplined armies and be shot down.

In his August exchanges with the Central Committee, Mao also seized enthusiastically on what proved to be a distorted rumor to the effect that the International[9] had decided to break once and for all with the Guomindang and call for the establishment of soviets in China. The Guomindang banner, he said, had already become "nothing but a black flag," and Communists should raise high the red banner of their own Party.[10] In fact, at that time Moscow was still insisting on the maintenance of nominal collaboration with the ultraleftist rump of the Guomindang, but within a month Stalin finally came to realize that this was an illusion and changed his policy. The difference regarding the role of organized armed forces in the next phase of the revolution did not similarly evaporate.

The Struggle on the Jinggangshan

In a Politburo discussion on August 9, Mao had stated that the military force of one division which he proposed to establish in southern Hunan should be able to occupy five or six xian, but if it were defeated, this force could "go up the mountains."[11] At the end of October 1927, Mao Zedong effectively led the remnants of the forces that had carried out the Autumn Harvest Uprising to what was to become the Jinggangshan base, a remote mountainous area astride the Hunan-Jiangxi border.

---

7. See below, the record of the meeting of August 18, 1927.

8. See below, "Letter from the Hunan Provincial Party Committee," August 30, 1927. It appears from the November 14, 1927, resolution of the Central Committee, discussed below, that this letter was signed by the secretary of the Hunan Provincial Committee, Peng Gongda, but since Mao was said to have constituted the "heart" or "core" (*zhongxin*) of the Provincial Committee, he may well have written, and certainly endorsed, this text.

9. In his August 20, 1927 letter, Mao refers to the Communist International simply as "the International," and that is the usage commonly followed in this volume, though to avoid monotonous repetition the contraction "Comintern" is also used on occasion.

10. See below, "A Letter from Hunan to the Central Committee," August 20, 1927.

11. See below, "Hunan Is Important," August 9, 1927.

In late September 1927 Mao learned that there were two "local armed forces" on the Jinggangshan, under the leadership of Wang Zuo and Yuan Wencai. In 1936, talking to Edgar Snow, Mao characterized these men simply as "two former bandit leaders." According to many recent accounts, they had by this time rallied to the revolutionary cause, and Yuan Wencai had joined the Communist Party as early as 1926. In any case, Mao met with Yuan at the beginning of October and came to an understanding with him, and on October 24, 1927, Mao's army ascended the mountain and was welcomed by Wang Zuo. In November, Zhu De and Chen Yi, who were then in southern Jiangxi, sent Mao's youngest brother Mao Zetan to make contact with him, and by December 1927, regular liaison had been established between the forces of Mao and Zhu.[12]

Unfortunately, no substantial texts are available to us from September 1927 to May 1928, though the *Nianpu* includes brief citations or paraphrases from several speeches and letters of this period. No doubt Mao was too busy struggling for survival during these eight months to spend much time writing down his thoughts. Some sources indicate that he sent reports to the Hunan Provincial Committee and the Central Committee in January and March 1928, but these were apparently not received and may have been lost.[13]

In its "Resolution on Political Discipline" of November 14, 1927, the Central Committee had enumerated various errors in the conduct of the uprising in Hunan, including not only the "military opportunism" denounced in August, but failure to distribute the land to the peasants and to carry out the "policy of massacring the local bullies and bad gentry." All these points were integral parts of the radical and terrorist line adopted at this time by the Central Committee, headed by Qu Qiubai.[14] Though the secretary of the Hunan Committee, Peng

12. Pang Xianzhi (ed.), *Mao Zedong nianpu 1893–1949* (Chronological Biography of Mao Zedong, 1893–1949) (hereafter *Nianpu*) (Beijing: Zhongyang wenxian chubanshe, 1993), Vol. 1, pp. 220–29. Mao's statement of 1936 appears in Edgar Snow, *Red Star over China* (London: Gollancz, 1937), pp. 165–66.

13. Regarding the reports sent in January and March 1928, see the chronology in Gui Yulin, *Jinggangshan geming douzheng shi* (History of the Revolutionary Struggles on the Jinggangshan) (Beijing: Jiefangjun chubanshe, 1986), pp. 269, 271 (hereafter, Gui Yulin, *Jinggangshan*). A recent and detailed study of Mao's career down to 1935 by Ma Yuqing and Zhang Wanlu, *Mao Zedong gemingde daolu* (Mao Zedong's Revolutionary Way) (Xi'an: Shaanxi Renmin chubanshe, 1991) (hereafter, Ma and Zhang, *Mao's Way*), states categorically (p. 192) that the document of May 2, 1928, translated below, was "the first report received directly by the Central Committee from the Jinggangshan base."

14. Qu Qiubai (1899–1935), a native of Jiangsu, studied Russian at Beijing University and went to Moscow as correspondent for the Beijing *Morning News* in October 1920. While in Soviet Russia, he joined the Chinese Communist Party and attended the Third and Fourth Comintern congresses. Returning to China, he occupied important posts both in the Guomindang and in the Communist Party. During the summer of 1926, he lectured at the Peasant Movement Training Institute in Guangzhou while Mao was the principal. Elected to the Politburo of the Chinese Communist Party at its Fifth Congress, in May 1927, he became the dominant figure in the Party following the August 7 Emergency Conference. He left for Moscow in April 1928 to attend the Sixth Congress of the Chinese

Gongda, was severely criticized, "the most serious responsibility" for this disobedience was attributed to Mao Zedong, who, as special commissioner in charge of the Autumn Harvest Uprising, had "in fact been the heart of the Hunan Provincial Committee." Both Mao and Peng were dismissed from their positions as alternate members of the Politburo and as members of the Hunan Provincial Committee.[15] Mao learned explicitly of this demotion only in March 1928, though he must have been sufficiently aware of the line currently being pursued by the new Party leadership to realize that he was not acting in accordance with it.

Throughout most of the period covered by this volume, Mao Zedong confronted serious problems in his relations with the Central Committee, but during the first half of 1928, when he was dealing with Qu Qiubai, these problems were different in character from those he faced subsequently in the case of the next strongman in the Party, Li Lisan. In Li's case, personal rivalry would play a major role in his attitude toward Mao. There is, in contrast, no indication that Qu Qiubai was in any way hostile to Mao, who had been one of his strongest supporters before and during the August 7 Emergency Conference. The differences between him and Mao appear to have been essentially ideological, though they ran very deep.

These divergences regarding ideology and tactics are clearly evident from a comparison of Mao's own statements, translated below, with the available documentation regarding the position of the Central Committee. One crucial issue was that, already emphasized, of the role of military force in the revolutionary struggle. Thus the Central Committee's Circular No. 28 of January 12, 1928, regarding the tactics of armed uprisings, began its list of "erroneous attitudes" common among local Party organizations with the following item:

> 1) Not trusting in the strength of the masses—for the reason that they do not trust in the strength of the masses, but lean toward **military opportunism**,[16] they draft their plans in terms of military forces, planning how to move this or that army unit, this or that peasant army, this or that workers' and peasants' rebel-suppressing army, how to link up with the forces of this or that bandit chieftain, how to organize this or that guerrilla detachment, and in this way to unleash an "armed uprising" by a plot calling itself a plan. Such a so-called armed uprising has no relation whatsoever to the masses. For example, last year's Autumn Harvest Uprising in Hunan . . . saw the mobilization of military force alone.[17]

This passage manifestly echoes the criticism of Mao two months earlier, in the resolution of the November 1927 plenum. On the one hand, it is rooted in the

Communist Party, which met in the Soviet capital in June 1928. The Congress removed him from his leading position, but re-elected him to the Politburo.

15. For the text of this resolution, see *Zhonggong zhongyang wenjian xuanji* (Selected Documents of the Central Committee of the Chinese Communist Party), Vol. 3 (1927) (Beijing: Zhonggong zhongyang dangxiao chubanshe, 1989), pp. 478–84 (hereafter, *Central Committee Documents*).

16. These words are emphasized in the original by the use of dots under the characters.

17. *Central Committee Documents*, Vol. 4 (1928), p. 57.

view that guerrilla warfare is "one form of the armed uprising of the peasant masses in its initial stage," and that the peasants themselves can create military forces capable of fighting the landlord militias and other "counterrevolutionary armies."[18] But at the same time, the reference to "linking up with bandit chieftains" (as Mao had effectively done on the Jinggangshan) raises the issue of the class purity of the revolutionary forces. In a striking formulation, the circular attacks the view that "guerrilla warfare constitutes the whole of the peasants' armed uprising" and argues that war waged by "guerrilla units" (in quotation marks), in isolation from the masses, represents "not the proletarian party showing itself capable of leading the peasants and the declassed poor, but the proletarian party being led by vagrant-style deproletarianized 'tactics.' "[19]

The fact that such ideological differences between Mao and the Central Committee existed does not mean that the local Party leaders in Hunan, with whom Mao had to deal directly, were not actuated rather by considerations of personal prestige. Personal rancor, or personal ambition, was in fact blatantly in evidence in the behavior of the representative of the Southern Hunan Special Committee, Zhou Lu, who showed up on the Jinggangshan in early March 1928 to announce Mao's disgrace. Not content with telling Mao Zedong that he had been removed from the Politburo and the Hunan Provincial Committee, Zhou falsely claimed that Mao had been deprived of his Party membership. Only when he saw the text of the resolution in April did Mao learn that this was not true. Meanwhile, Zhou Lu had abolished Mao's Front Committee and replaced it by a Divisional Committee headed by He Tingying.[20]

---

18. Ibid., p. 61.

19. Ibid., p. 65. The terms translated "declassed poor" and "deproletarianized vagrant-style" are, respectively, *feijiejihuade pinmin* and *feiwuchanjiejihuade youminshi*.

20. When he came to the base area, Zhou Lu was head of the Military Department of the Southern Hunan Special Committee. For Mao's own brief account of this episode, and of the defeats which resulted when he and his men were led away to southern Hunan by representatives of the Southern Hunan Special Committee, see below, section II of the "Report of the Jinggangshan Front Committee" of November 25, 1928. Zhou Lu was, in the end, the victim of his own initiative; he was captured and executed following the failure of the expedition to southern Hunan which he had promoted. The channels of communication at this time between the Central Committee in Shanghai and Mao in the border area remain somewhat obscure. Probably, in the chaotic situation then obtaining, the Central Committee sought to use all possible avenues for conveying its instructions to the grass roots. The "Letter to the Three Provinces of Hunan, Hubei, and Jiangxi," March 10, 1928 (*Central Committee Documents* [1928], pp. 159–67), states: "As for the disposition of Mao Zedong's army, this should be agreed between the two special committees [of Eastern Hunan and Southwest Jiangxi]." References to the Southern Hunan Special Committee in a letter of January 20, 1928, to Li Weihan are extremely uncomplimentary; comrades on the committee are said to have "incorrect and unproletarian political tendencies." (See *Central Committee Documents* [1928], pp. 71–75.) Li Weihan (1896–1984), also called Li Hesheng, pseudonym Luo Mai, had been a friend of Mao's during his student days, active in the New People's Study Society. At the August 7 Conference he had been elected to the Politburo and

Apart from the fact that Mao was no longer even a member of this committee, the scope of its activity was limited strictly to military matters, and it had no power over political work in the base area. Mao was thus reduced to the status of an army commander. The first text of 1928 translated here, Mao's letter of May 2, 1928, was written in this essentially military capacity, but it urged very strongly the establishment of a special committee to take overall charge of Party affairs in the border area. The report was forwarded by the Jiangxi Provincial Committee to the Central Committee on May 19, 1928, and presumably reached Shanghai fairly promptly.[21] Meanwhile, the Jiangxi Provincial Committee, dissatisfied at the contradictory information it was receiving, decided to send someone to Ji'an to find out what was actually happening.[22]

On or about April 20, 1928, Mao Zedong and Zhu De met for the first time in Lingxian, in the aftermath of the failed uprising in southern Hunan ordered by Zhou Lu. A few days later, they combined their forces on the Jinggangshan.[23] On May 20, Mao Zedong convened a conference at Maoping in Ninggang *xian*, at which a Special Committee was set up, with Mao as temporary secretary, and Zhu De as a member. Shortly afterward, Mao and his comrades learned that the actions taken at the Maoping conference had been approved retrospectively by the Jiangxi Provincial Committee.[24]

The next message emanating from higher authority reached Mao at the end of

---

made head of the Organization Department, and from then on he was, with Qu Qiubai, one of the two most powerful figures in the Party. In its letter of January 20, the Central Committee invited him to go to Hunan and "rectify" the Southern Hunan Special Committee.

21. This, and other materials emanating, in particular, from the Hunan and Jiangxi Provincial Committees, can be found in three major documentary collections. The earliest of these is *Jinggangshande wuzhuang geju* (The Armed Independent Régime on the Jinggangshan) (Nanchang: Jiangxi renmin chubanshe, 1979), pp. 120–121 (hereafter, *The Jinggangshan Régime*). The second is *Jinggangshan geming genjudi shiliao xuanbian* (Selected Historical Materials on the Jinggangshan Revolutionary Base) (Nanchang: Jiangxi renmin chubanshe, 1986), pp.29–30 (hereafter, *Jinggangshan Historical Materials*). The second collection has been compiled by the Jiangxi Provincial Archives and should in principle be more accurate, but in some cases details missing from the texts which appear in it can be found in the earlier source. The third collection is *Jinggangshan geming genjudi* (The Revolutionary Base on the Jinggangshan), 2 vols., (Beijing: Zhonggong dangshi ziliao chubanshe, 1987) (hereafter *The Jinggangshan Revolutionary Base*).

22. Letter of May 10 and report of May 13 from the Jiangxi Provincial Committee to the Central Committee, *Jinggangshan Historical Materials*, pp. 25–28.

23. *Nianpu*, Vol. 1, pp. 238–39. Much detailed and precise information regarding the origins and characteristics of the various armed forces that joined together on the Jinggangshan to form what came to be called the Fourth Red Army, and the organizational changes that took place during the ensuing two years, can be found in the memoirs of Xiao Ke, *ZhuMao hongjun ceji* (Perspectives on the Zhu-Mao Red Army) (Beijing: Zhonggong zhongyang dangxiao chubanshe, 1993), especially pp. 3–13 (hereafter, Xiao Ke, *The Zhu-Mao Red Army*).

24. The report of Du Xiujing dated June 15, 1928, discussed in the following paragraph, confirms that a letter from the Jiangxi Provincial Committee along these lines had been forwarded by the the Western Jiangxi Special Committee.

May, when an emissary from the Hunan Provincial Committee, Du Xiujing, arrived in the border area.[25] In addition to presenting an oral report, Du read out a letter from the Hunan Provincial Committee stressing that it was "completely wrong to burn whole cities."[26]

A month later, on June 30, 1928, two representatives of the Hunan Provincial Committee arrived on the Jinggangshan almost simultaneously. Mao's account, in his report of July 4, 1928, translated below, says they arrived "at the same time," but in fact they did not travel together. Mao found the letters they brought him blatantly contradictory. Yuan Desheng had left first, with letters dated June 19, 1928, indicating that Mao could continue to build his base on the Jinggangshan.[27] Du Xiujing, for his part, brought a letter and directive dated June 26, 1928, containing substantially different instructions. These documents would have made plain to Mao that the unpalatable orders thus presented to him were largely the work of Du himself. After his visit to Ninggang at the end of May, Du had submitted a rather critical report to the Hunan Provincial Committee.[28] Mao, Du wrote, was doing his best, but was trying to cope with too many things at once. The Provincial Committee in turn acknowledged its debt to "Elder Brother Du" in the second letter of June 19, and the letter of June 26 clearly reflected the opinions expressed in his report.[29] Yuan and/or Du also brought Mao a resolution from the Central Committee regarding work in Hunan.[30]

The letter dated June 26 ordered Mao to "leave with the army" for southern Hunan. The Divisional Committee created in March was to be abolished and

---

25. Du Xiujing (1907-??) was a Hunanese, who had joined the Chinese Communist Party in 1925. In March 1928, he was secretary of the Anyuan City Party Committee, and a member of the Eastern Hunan Special Committee. He lost contact with the Hunan Provincial Committee in 1929, and abandoned the Chinese Communist Party, but rejoined the Party in 1985.

26. For a summary of the report and the letter, see *Nianpu*, Vol. 1, p. 243. For Du's own account of his first meeting with Mao in late May, after two earlier attempts to reach the Jinggangshan had failed, see Du Xiujing, "Si shang Jinggangshan" (Four trips up the Jinggangshan), in *The Jinggangshan Revolutionary Base*, Vol. 1, pp. 419–25.

27. Yuan Desheng (1894–1934), a native of Hunan, worked as a coal miner at Anyuan, where he joined the Communist Party in 1923. After participating in the Nanchang Uprising of August 1, 1927, he was sent back to Anyuan. For the texts of the letters he brought, see *The Jinggangshan Régime*, pp. 131–39.

28. The version of Du Xiujing's report which appears in *The Jinggangshan Régime*, pp. 124–30, is dated June 15, 1928. The Hunan Provincial Committee's second letter of June 19 suggests that the report was delivered orally.

29. For these two letters, see *The Jinggangshan Régime*, pp. 135–42.

30. See below, Mao's "Report to the Hunan Provincial Committee," July 4, 1928. The document from the Central Committee cannot have been that dated June 4, which reached Mao, according to his November 25 report, only on November 2, 1928. It may have been the letter of March 10, addressed to the Provincial Committees of Hunan, Hubei, and Jiangxi, which contained a section on Hunan stressing the need to move in the direction of Wuhan. See *Central Committee Documents* (1928), pp. 159–67.

replaced by a Front Committee, of which Mao was appointed secretary. Du Xiujing was, however, to remain as "inspector" (*xunshiyuan*) of the Provincial Committee, "to help the Front Committee in its work." Yang Kaiming (who had accompanied Du to the Jinggangshan) was appointed secretary of the more powerful Special Committee.[31] Thus both the newcomers were set over Mao. Ironically, in view of the repeated criticisms of Mao Zedong for his intimacy with bandits and lumpenproletarians, the former bandit chieftain Yuan Wencai was also to be appointed to the Special Committee and was to be in charge of the Jinggangshan base during the absence of the main force. Yang and Du, the letter concluded, would explain everything face to face; the "former emissary," Yuan Desheng, was to return to the Provincial Committee.

Mao immediately called a meeting, on the evening of June 30, at which Du and Yuan were present, together with Zhu De, Chen Yi, and the other principal leaders of the Jinggangshan base area. There the decision was taken to reject the "erroneous" ideas of the Hunan Provincial Committee. Mao then proceeded to draft the report of July 4, translated below, to justify this action. Yes, he argued, we will go to southern Hunan, but not just now. We must first consolidate our position here and wait until a new war between the warlords breaks out.

Not surprisingly, Mao was unable to maintain this position. Apart from the opposition of Du and Yang, who outranked him in the Party, he had to contend with the attitude of the Twenty-ninth Regiment, composed of peasants from southern Hunan, who found the Jinggangshan a very poor and lonely place, and wanted to return home. In fact, after the arrival of Zhu De and his forces in April, there were no longer one or two thousand troops, but over ten thousand in the base area, and the economy of the Jinggangshan really could not support them. Mao had agreed, therefore, that some of the units from Hunan could return there, but in mid-July, the peasants of the Twenty-ninth Regiment insisted on going there too, without adequate preparation. Zhu De was opposed to their action, but went along with them because he was afraid that without him, things would be even worse. Thus in the end, the bulk of the Red Army participated in this expedition, and suffered a disastrous defeat. Du Xiujing, who had supported this action in mid-July, argued in a report written subsequently that the fault lay entirely with the Hunan Provincial Committee, and not with the Border Area Special Committee, which had opposed this adventure.[32]

---

31. Yang Kaiming (1905–1930), a native of Hunan, joined the Chinese Communist Party in 1926, after working at the Peasant Movement Training Institute in Guangzhou. In 1928 he was secretary of the Hunan Provincial Party Committee. He was arrested at the end of 1929, and executed in Changsha in February 1930.

32. For Du's July letter, see *Jinggangshan Historical Materials*, pp. 42–46. In memoirs written half a century later, Du accepted that, applying the "wrong decisions" of the Hunan Provincial Committee, he had borne a large measure of responsibility for the disaster. See Du Xiujing, "Bayue shibai" (The August defeat), *The Jinggangshan Revolutionary Base*, Vol. 2, pp. 521–29.

In mid-August, Yuan Desheng turned up again, armed with a copy of the Hunan Provincial Committee's letter of July 20, asserting that the strategy of advancing on eastern Hunan, in order to link up with the workers at Anyuan, was "absolutely correct."[33] Mao immediately called an emergency meeting of the Special Committee, at which Yuan read out the letter, and Mao criticized the erroneous views of the Provincial Committee. News of the disastrous defeat just suffered by Zhu De and the Red Army in southern Hunan arrived during the meeting and tipped the balance against going to eastern Hunan. On August 23, at a meeting in Guidong, the Front Committee organized in July on the orders of the Hunan Provincial Committee was dissolved and replaced by an Action Committee with Mao as secretary. It was decided to leave Du Xiujing behind in southern Hunan as the secretary of the Southern Hunan Special Committee and to return to the base on the Jinggangshan.[34]

The letter which Mao proceeded to write at the end of August to the Hunan Provincial Committee explaining the situation was a masterpiece of diplomacy. He referred to the meeting on May 30, addressed by Du Xiujing, and declared that the Provincial Committee's letter read out on that occasion was accepted "without reservation." Thus Mao glossed over the fact that he and his allies had accepted neither the letter of June 26 nor that of July 20, emphasizing rather how much they agreed with the earlier directive. "We will," he wrote, "make great efforts to transform the army and cleanse it of the lumpenproletariat." He promised faithfully never again to commit the mistake of burning cities, though in doing so his forces, and those of Zhu De, had merely been responding to the urgings of the Qu Qiubai leadership.[35]

The main forces of the Fourth Red Army, led by Mao, Zhu De, and Chen Yi, finally arrived back at the main base on September 26, 1928. Mao proceeded to carry out a purge in the base area. The ostensible end was the elimination of unreliable elements who had been admitted to the Party during a period of excessively rapid and indiscriminate recruitment in the summer of 1928, though Mao undoubtedly took advantage of this occasion to get rid of some of his adversaries. Yang Kaiming, who disappeared from the scene at this time, did suffer from illness, but Mao must have been pleased at the opportunity to replace him.[36] At the Second Congress of *xian* Party organizations in the border area in October 1928, Mao was re-elected to the Special Committee, but only as the

33. In many sources this letter is dated July 30, but the text in both the documentary volumes cited here bears the date of July 20, 1928. See *The Jinggangshan Régime*, pp. 148–50, and *Jinggangshan Historical Materials*, pp. 56–58.

34. See Gui Yulin, *Jinggangshan*, p. 280; *The Jinggangshan Régime*, p. 311; and Mao's own account in section II of the November 25, 1928, report.

35. See below, "Letter of the Special Committee of the Hunan-Jiangxi Border Area to the Hunan Provincial Committee," August 1928.

36. See below, the discussion of this change in the Jinggangshan Report of November 25, 1928. Tan Zhenlin (1902–1983), who took his place as secretary of the Hunan-Jiangxi Border Area Special Committee, was a native of Youxian, Hunan, who had joined the Chinese Communist Party in 1926.

fifteenth in a list of nineteen members. Finally, the Central Committee letter of June 4 reached the Jinggangshan on November 2, 1928, and Mao was able to re-establish the Front Committee, with himself in charge.

Meanwhile, the political context to which Mao had been striving to adapt throughout the summer and autumn had changed significantly. Qu Qiubai had left for Moscow in April 1928 to attend the Sixth Congress of the Chinese Communist Party, and while there had been removed from his post as secretary general of the Party because of his ultraleftist errors. Xiang Zhongfa, who had been appointed in his place, was essentially a figurehead, and most of the other members of the Standing Committee of the Politburo had little influence. Real power was in the hands of Li Lisan and Zhou Enlai.[37] Li and Zhou were still in Moscow when the June 4 letter, which restored Mao to control of the border area, was written, and it is not clear exactly who in Shanghai drafted it. Within half a year, however, Mao found himself confronted, not with the diffuse and contradictory signals from higher levels which had marked the period we have just been discussing, but with a much more sharply focused position regarding the theory and strategy of revolution.

Mao's dialogue with and struggle against his old friend Li Lisan looms large in this volume.[38] Before we turn to the unfolding of this relationship in 1929 and 1930, however, more needs to be said about the texts of the autumn of 1928. To the extent that these deal with political and military history, Mao tells his own story vividly, though not always with perfect clarity, and the brief summary of events provided above, together with the notes, should suffice to make these documents intelligible. Some points of political doctrine and practice ought to be noted, however, both for the sake of their own inherent interest and because they provide the background for Mao's confrontation with the "Li Lisan line."

The two most important texts are the resolution of October 5, 1928, and the

---

37. For a biographical sketch of Zhou Enlai, and a discussion of the role he played from the Sixth Congress until the end of 1930, see below the section of this Introduction entitled: "Toward the Li Lisan Line."

38. Li Lisan (1899–1967), original name Li Longzhi, was a native of Liling, Hunan Province, also known under the aliases of Bai Shan and Li Minran. Li Lisan had met Mao Zedong during his student days, but Mao remarked later to Edgar Snow that their friendship "never developed." After studying at the Changjun Middle School in Changsha, Li went to France in 1919 on the work-study program. There he was an active sponsor of the Socialist Youth League and was deported by the French government in 1921 for related activities. In 1922, Mao Zedong, then in charge of the labor unions in Hunan (see his writings in this capacity in Volume II), sent Li Lisan to Anyuan to organize the workers there. Li played a major role in the May Thirtieth movement of 1925 in Shanghai. In 1926, he lectured on the workers' movement at the Peasant Movement Training Institute while Mao was principal there. He was elected to the Politburo at the Fifth Congress of the Chinese Communist Party in 1927 and was one of the principal organizers of the Nanchang Uprising in August 1927. After a period as Party secretary in Guangdong, he returned to Shanghai at the end of 1928 to work on the Central Committee. For further details, see below, the note to Mao's letter to him, November 28, 1929.

report of November 25, 1928. Both of these are well known because they are included, in revised form, in the *Selected Works*, though more than half of the October resolution is omitted from that edition. As in the case of the "Analysis of All the Classes in Chinese Society" and the "Report on the Peasant Movement in Hunan" in Volume II, significant variants between the current official versions and the texts as Mao originally wrote them are shown in the notes and through the use of italics. (For details regarding the way this is done, see the "Note on Sources and Conventions," which follows this Introduction.)

Both of these documents endorse the view of the International according to which the Chinese revolution is still in the "bourgeois-democratic stage," without indicating precisely when this formulation was laid down. The reference (which Mao did give in the briefer text of December 16, 1928, also translated below) is in fact to the resolution on the Chinese revolution adopted by the Ninth Plenum of the Executive Committee in February 1928. This document had been distributed by the Central Committee on April 30, 1928, and probably reached the Jinggangshan in the late summer or early autumn. It contained a stern condemnation of the view put forward by the Qu Qiubai leadership in November 1927 regarding "permanent revolution" in China, and was accompanied by a circular of the Central Committee explaining rather lamely that this term really meant only that the *bourgeois-democratic* revolution was steadily moving forward.[39]

Discussing this issue in section IA, the resolution of October 5, 1928, likens the defeat of the bourgeois-democratic revolution in China to "that of the Russian Revolution in 1905." This, like many other parallels to Soviet experience throughout Mao's works, has been eliminated in the *Selected Works* version.

The October 5 resolution has been given the title, in the *Selected Works*, of "Why Is It That Red Political Power Can Exist in China?" Mao's answer is well known, from this and other texts: because China is a "semicolony," in which the various imperialist powers can be played off against one another, and because it has a "localized agricultural economy," not a unified capitalist economy. Consequently, small areas of soviet power can emerge in China, but their long-term survival will be impossible unless the revolution continues to move forward in the country as a whole. A "fairly long period" of stagnation, "as in the case of Russia from 1905 to 1917," would be fatal to them. Mao concluded that this would not happen, because the revolution in China was continuing to develop, thanks to "the continuous splits and wars within the ranks of the domestic bourgeoisie."

Independent régimes under Red political power could therefore be created and maintained, but only if there were "a regular Red Army of adequate strength." Moreover, Red Army units must be concentrated so they could deal with enemy threats, and not scattered, in an attempt to take the offensive in several directions at once. Consequently, the Central Committee's recommenda-

---

39. *Central Committee Documents* (1928), pp. 174–77.

tion, in the June letter, that "guerrilla warfare should be extended to an excessively wide area" was casually brushed aside, as one of two minor points in the letter reflecting a lack of understanding of "concrete circumstances" in the base area.

The long second section of this resolution, which has only recently become available, surveyed the achievements of the Party in the Border Area since the foundation of the Special Committee four months earlier, and put forward recommendations for improvement. The organizational defects there stigmatized, such as reliance on the army rather than the masses, failure to stress class backgrounds in the appointment of cadres, and overconcentration of authority, amounted in many respects to a criticism of Mao himself. It cannot, however, be assumed simply for this reason that Mao did not take responsibility for the second half of the resolution. The document summed up the conclusions reached at the meeting, and Mao was obliged to accept these points, whether or not he actually wrote every word. This portion of the resolution also included an eloquent section on struggle in the rural areas, calling for the massacre of landlords and despotic gentry in the context of a pitiless Red terror. Only thus could political power be seized in the countryside.

The links between the fate of the base areas and the progress of the revolution in China as a whole would remain a major topic of controversy in Mao's dealings with the new Central Committee elected by the Sixth Congress, as would the role of the Red Army. Two other important issues, which likewise carried over from one period to the next, were agrarian policy and the role of the vagrants or vagabonds in the countryside.

On the land problem, Mao adopted at this time a very radical policy, which is spelled out in section IVB of the November report. Lumping together all the owner-peasants (not just the "rich peasants" as in the *Selected Works* text) with the small landlords as the "intermediate class" (*zhongjian jieji*), he treats this whole category as an even more troublesome enemy than the big landlords. Such an approach was understandable in an area such as the Jinggangshan, which was so poor that there were hardly any real landlords, and land had to be taken from less privileged strata if there was to be any reform at all. Not only was all land confiscated without exception, but it was distributed in a totally egalitarian manner on the basis of the number of people in each household. Following receipt of the Central Committee letter on November 2, this principle was combined to a limited extent with distribution on the basis of labor power, which favored the richer peasants. Mao, as indicated in section IVB7 of the November report, had reservations about such a policy and asked the Central Committee and the two Provincial Committees of Hunan and Jiangxi to instruct him regarding the methods used in Soviet Russia in dealing with the rich peasants. Meanwhile, the Land Law of December 1928, translated below, reflected this provisional compromise. Mao, in a note of 1941, declared that it contained "mistakes of principle," meaning leftist mistakes.

Logically, hostility toward even moderately privileged social strata went together with a tolerant attitude toward those at the bottom of the social scale. Consequently, while disputing the claim of the Hunan Provincial Committee that the whole of his army was made up of vagrants, Mao declared that it was entirely appropriate to have a great many of them, since they were "after all particularly good fighters." The solution, he added, lay in intensifying political training, "so as to effect a qualitative change in these elements."[40]

Before turning, now, to the development of Mao Zedong's policies and ideas in the course of 1929, it is appropriate to summarize the changes in the Soviet line at this time and the relation between Stalin's views and those of the leadership of the Chinese Communist Party. As already noted, Qu Qiubai's apocalyptic visions of "permanent revolution" had been repudiated by the Ninth Plenum of the Executive Committee of the International in February 1928. The Comintern's message on that occasion was, however, somewhat convoluted. It was necessary to discourage further "putschist" uprisings, while expressing qualified approval for the "Guangzhou (Canton) Commune" of December 1927, which Stalin had personally encouraged. The activities of Mao Zedong and others in the countryside could not be condemned, for they at least had the merit of existing, but at the same time it was stressed that such "spontaneous demonstrations by peasant partisans" could become the starting point for a victorious national uprising "only on condition that they are linked with the new upsurge of the tide of revolution in the proletarian centers."

The new orientation was spelled out in greater detail, and in some respects modified, at the Sixth Congress of the Chinese Communist Party and the Sixth Congress of the Communist International, both of which took place in Moscow in the summer of 1928. It has often been assumed that these two congresses were contemporaneous, or in any case convergent. In fact, the first was held in June and July, and the second in August and September. In the rapidly evolving situation within the Soviet leadership, the passage of a few weeks meant that the line adopted on these two occasions was in fact significantly different. Stalin had allied himself with Bukharin at the end of 1927 in order to defeat the "Left opposition" of Trotsky and Zinoviev. Now, in the summer of 1928, as he prepared to move toward a policy of forced industrialization and rapid collectivization, he was ready to break with the supporters of a more lenient policy toward the Russian peasantry.

Thus, while Bukharin had played the central role at the Sixth Congress of the Chinese Communist Party, his standing had been greatly weakened by the time the Comintern congress met two months later. He still gave the opening report, but exercised little real influence over the proceedings. Stalin's shift to the left

---

40. See below, section IVA3 of the November 1928 report. In the *Selected Works* version, both the praise of the *youmin* as "particularly good fighters" and the idea of effecting a "qualitative change" in them have disappeared.

was symbolized by the fact that Qu Qiubai, though he had been removed as secretary general of the Chinese Party, was extremely influential in the discussion of the resolution on the national and colonial question. At the end of the congress, while acknowledging that the previous "adventurist" moods had led to disastrous defeats, it was proclaimed that the present period in China must be "a phase of preparation of mass forces for an upsurge of revolution." And though "permanent revolution" had been repudiated, Lenin's formula of the "growing over" (*pererastanie*) of the democratic revolution into the socialist revolution was adopted, and this process was said to be "inevitable." In other words, the guidelines thus laid down for the new leadership of the Chinese Communist Party encouraged a further drift toward the left, though not necessarily in the way Li Lisan and Zhou Enlai actually went about it. [41]

Toward the Li Lisan Line

The long delays in communication between Moscow and Shanghai, and especially between the Central Committee of the Chinese Communist Party in Shanghai and Mao Zedong in the hinterland, have led to considerable confusion in the literature about which directives from whom Mao was responding to at various times. As already indicated, the November 25, 1928, Report of the Jinggangshan Front Committee, though written after Li Lisan had begun to place his stamp on the Chinese Communist Party, was in no sense a response to Li Lisan's policies, about which Mao had as yet no knowledge. The same applies to the texts, translated below, for the first three months of 1929.

On December 10, 1928, Peng Dehuai led his Fifth Red Army to Ninggang to join forces with the Fourth Red Army.[42] The resolutions of the Sixth Congress of the Chinese Communist Party reached the Jinggangshan at the beginning of January 1929, and on January 4, Mao called a meeting at which they were explained and discussed. At the same time, it was decided that the main force of the Fourth Red Army, led by Mao Zedong and Zhu De, would seek to establish a new base in southwestern Jiangxi, while the two regiments making up the Fifth Army remained on the Jinggangshan under the command of Peng Dehuai. The Bailu Conference of January 4, 1929, marked an important turning point in Mao's rural revolution. As Mao stated frankly in his report of March 20, 1929, his main reason for leaving the Jinggangshan was that he and his comrades "had

---

41. For a clear and authoritative discussion of the political situation in Moscow in 1928, and of the contrast between the two congresses, see E. H. Carr, *A History of Soviet Russia: Foundations of a Planned Economy 1926–1929*, Vol.3, Part III (London: Macmillan, 1978), especially pp. 856–87 (hereafter, Carr, *Foundations*, Vol. 3-III).

42. Peng Dehuai (1898–1974) was, like Mao, a native of Xiangtan *xian*, Hunan. A former regimental commander in the Guomindang National Revolutionary Army, he joined the Chinese Communist Party in April 1928. In July 1928, he led an uprising at Pingjiang, and created the Fifth Red Army, of which he assumed command.

no way out economically." In other words, the Jinggangshan area was so poor, backward, and isolated that it could not serve as a viable base for further expansion and development of the Red forces. The decision to leave the Jinggangshan was, however, also the result of the blockade imposed by Guomindang forces, and of the pressure of constant enemy attacks. Another assault by the White forces was imminent at the time Mao and Zhu left, and Peng Dehuai may not have been happy at the prospect of staying behind to face it on his own.

Mao and Zhu set out on January 14. During the march, the "Notice of the Fourth Army Headquarters" and the "Manifesto of the Communist Party," which constitute the first two texts for 1929 translated below, were issued.[43] The "Official Fund-Raising Letter" of February 13, 1929, and the two communications of March 16, 1929, addressed to merchants and intellectuals, and to soldiers in the Guomindang armies, represented an attempt to adapt the Red Army's appeal to the wider and more complex society into which it was now penetrating.

The Report of March 20, 1929, to the Fujian Provincial Committee and to the Central Committee contained news of a recent victory at Tingzhou and outlined plans for "carrying out guerrilla warfare within an area of more than twenty *xian* in southern Jiangxi and western Fujian," establishing "independent régimes under soviet power," and linking these to form a larger independent régime "in the Hunan-Jiangxi border area as a whole." Mao obviously hoped that the Party leaders would be pleased and impressed by what he had to tell them. The Central Committee's letter of February 7, addressed to Mao Zedong and Zhu De and received on April 3, 1929, was written in ignorance, not only of these recent developments but of Mao's report of November 25, 1928, which had not yet reached Shanghai. Even so, Mao must have been taken aback by the conclusion that "the problem is . . . how to avoid the annihilation of our armed forces by the enemy."[44]

The letter of February 7 began on a rather petulant note with a complaint about Mao's silence:

> In the half year since the new Central Committee elected at the Sixth Congress returned to China and began work, we have several times sent people and letters to you, but from beginning to end we have been unable to obtain a reply. This is truly worrisome.

Although the letter went on to note that the Western Jiangxi Special Committee had confessed to having lost a letter from the Jinggangshan which they were

---

43. See Gui Yulin, *Jinggangshan*, pp. 286–87; *The Jinggangshan Régime*, pp. 320–21; Ma and Zhang, *Mao's Way*, pp. 245–49.

44. For the text, see *Central Committee Documents* (1929), pp. 29–37. Extracts in translation can be found in Tony Saich (ed.), *The Rise to Power of the Chinese Communist Party: Documents and Analysis, 1920–1929* (Armonk, N.Y.: M.E. Sharpe, 1996), Doc. C.23, pp. 471–74 (hereafter Saich, *Rise to Power*).

supposed to transmit to the Central Committee, Li Lisan and his comrades still seemed to blame Mao for the difficulties in communication. After reiterating the line of the Sixth Congress regarding the nature of the revolution, which was "bourgeois-democratic," but would "necessarily be transformed into a socialist revolution," and the "main task," which was "winning over the masses," the letter spelled out the implications for the role of the Red Army:

> If our Party cannot unite around itself the broad worker and peasant masses, especially the masses of industrial workers, then however favorable the objective political circumstances may be for us, however much the workers' and peasants' struggles may develop, or however much it may even continue to be possible to set up soviet areas in the countryside, and however much Red Army organizations such as those you lead can survive in other areas, it will not be possible to push forward the high tide of this revolutionary wave. . . . Hence, the main work of the Party at present is to establish and develop the Party's proletarian basis (chiefly the branches of industrial workers), and lead the worker and peasant masses in their struggle for their daily living. . . . Consequently, the armed forces you lead must also be evaluated anew in the light of this nationwide political situation and the Party's tasks.

"In accordance with the directives of the Sixth Congress, the Central Committee long ago informed you," the letter stated with some asperity, that "you should divide up the Red Army's armed forces into small . . . units, and scatter them in all the villages of the Hunan-Jiangxi Border Area, to carry on and deepen the agrarian revolution." Such a policy of avoiding concentration would provide fewer targets for the enemy and "would be advantageous for the provisioning and survival of your troops. But either this directive did not reach your organization, or you did not accept it or put it into practice." Mao had, of course, not received the directive in question.[45] This renewed injunction to divide up his forces was rendered even less palatable because it was accompanied by a brusque order to leave the army and come to Shanghai:

> In the light of present circumstances, the Central Committee has decided that it is necessary for Comrades Zhu and Mao to leave the army and come to the Center. You two comrades have been working in the army for more than a year, and you may, of course, be disinclined to leave it. The thing is that the Central Committee, on the basis of objective investigations and subjective necessity, is profoundly convinced that it is necessary for Comrades Zhu and Mao to leave the army at present. . . . If Comrades Zhu and Mao remain with the army, the target will be extremely great, and if the enemy is paying more attention it will be harder to divide up our forces.

---

45. The reference is manifestly to the directive of September or October 1928 to the Hunan-Jiangxi Border Area Special Committee and the Commander of the Fourth Army, in *Central Committee Documents* (1928), pp. 661–81; the passage on dispersing the Red Army appears on p. 671.

The concluding remark that Zhu and Mao, when they came to the Center, could "make their precious experience of more than a year of struggles of the armed popular masses available to the whole country and the whole revolution" did not suffice to make the proposal acceptable. The document closed with the order to leave the army "immediately" and "come quickly to the Center." Mao's reply, dated April 5, 1929, explained in detail why he did not agree with the Central Committee's assessment of the situation. Though he made a tactical concession by agreeing in principle to leave the army "for another assignment," he made it brutally plain that he would not comply with the order to break up the army.

Before analyzing Mao's response, it is important to ask who was speaking in the name of the Central Committee and what were his, or their, motives. Li Lisan is commonly assumed to have been the most powerful figure in the leadership from the Sixth Congress until his disgrace at the end of 1930, but in fact it can be argued that at this time Zhou Enlai exercised greater influence. In any case, it was he who drafted the February 7 letter.[46]

Zhou, who had returned to China in early November 1928, was a member of the Politburo and also head of the Organization Department of the Central Committee. In this capacity, it was natural that he should deal with a matter of this kind. The content of the letter was dictated in part by the position of the International, which had recently advised the dispersal of the Red Army and recommended that Mao and Zhu should spend some time in "study."[47] It was also the case, however, that at the Sixth Congress of the Chinese Communist Party, Zhou (who used the name Moskvin or "Comrade M") had spoken disparagingly of Mao Zedong in his report on organization. Mao, he said, had a considerable armed force at his disposal, but was "continually flying from place to place," and his troops had "a bandit character."[48]

Both Li Lisan and Zhou Enlai were more thoroughly schooled in Marxism than Mao and had devoted more time to the workers' movement. Thus, on grounds of both ideology and experience, they were more inclined to stress the

---

46. See Jin Chongji, *Zhou Enlai zhuan 1898–1949* (Biography of Zhou Enlai, 1898–1949) (Beijing: Zhongyang wenxian yanjiushi, 1989), pp. 192–93 (hereafter, Jin, *Zhou Enlai*).

47. See ibid., p. 192.

48. Quoted in Carr, *Foundations*, Vol. 3-III, p. 867. Zhou Enlai (1898–1976), *zi* Xiangyu, was born in Jiangsu. After graduating from Nankai Middle School in Tianjin in 1917, he studied in Japan for a year and a half, returning to China at the time of the May Fourth Movement. After a year at Nankai University, devoted mainly to work with the student movement, he went to France under the work-study program in November 1920. He joined the Chinese Communist Party in 1922. On his return to China in 1924, he became head of the Political Department of the Huangpu (Whampoa) Military Academy. He was elected to the Central Committee at the Fifth Congress in May 1927. In the reorganization of July 12, 1927, he became a member of the Provisional Standing Committee of the Politburo. At the Sixth Congress in June 1928, he was again elected to the Central Committee.

role of the urban proletariat in the Chinese revolution. This was, of course, also the attitude of Moscow, as documented in a whole series of Comintern directives from the late 1920s and early 1930s. But at the same time, Stalin was impressed with the achievements of the Red Army in China, at a time when victories were scarce on the world scene. As a result, it had been laid down at the two congresses of the summer of 1928 that, while placing primary emphasis on the cities and the working class, the Chinese Communist Party must take full account of the possibilities offered by the struggle in the countryside.

It had been logical for Qu Qiubai to advocate dividing up the Party's forces in the rural areas and using small detachments to ignite the flames of revolution, since he really believed that a nationwide revolutionary conflagration was imminent. Such a strategy seems less natural on the part of a Central Committee which had been told by Moscow *not* to expect revolution too soon. To explain Li Lisan's behavior, Richard Thornton has advanced the hypothesis that Li—who could not violate Moscow's injunction to support the Red Army, but did not want to build up a rival with an independent power base in the countryside—sought to give the appearance of supporting the rural soviets, while in fact undermining their leaders.[49] There is undoubtedly some substance to this argument, though when this first letter from the new Central Committee was written in February 1929, on the basis of fragmentary information about the situation in Jiangxi, Mao must have appeared less powerful, and therefore less threatening, than he subsequently became.

In any case, Mao Zedong, having achieved the victories chronicled in his March 20 report, felt himself to be in a strong enough position to defy the Central Committee. The plan for preserving the Red Army by dispersing it to arouse the masses he characterized as "a kind of ideal view (*yizhong lixiang*)," meaning that it was the invention of theorists far removed from reality, if not a figment of the imagination.

The weightiest passage in the letter of April 5, 1929, was undoubtedly that regarding the relation between the cities and the countryside. Mao began by stating and accepting the whole of the orthodox Marxist position on this matter and then went on to argue that his own strategy was, in fact, entirely compatible with this orthodoxy:

> Proletarian leadership is the sole key to the victory of the revolution. Building up the Party's proletarian basis and establishing Party branches in industrial enterprises in key areas are the greatest organizational tasks for the Party at present. But at the same time the development of the struggle in the countryside, the establishment of soviets in small areas, and the creation and expansion of the Red Army are prerequisites for aiding the struggle in the cities and

49. See Richard C. Thornton, *The Comintern and the Chinese Communists 1928–1931* (Seattle: University of Washington Press, 1969), especially pp. 76–79 (hereafter, Thornton, *The Comintern and the Chinese Communists*).

hastening the revolutionary upsurge. The greatest mistake would therefore be to abandon the struggle in the cities and sink into rural guerrilla-ism. But in our opinion, it is also a mistake—if any of our Party members hold such views—to fear the development of the power of the peasants lest it outstrip the workers' leadership and become detrimental to the revolution. For the revolution in semi-colonial China will fail only if the peasant struggle is deprived of the leadership of the workers; it will never suffer just because the peasant struggle develops in such a way as to become more powerful than the workers. The Sixth Congress has pointed out the mistake of neglecting the peasant revolution. . . .

The parenthetical remark about the error of fearing the power of the peasants, "if any of our Party members hold such views," was ironic to the point of provocation; Mao knew very well that many of those in Shanghai did. Most people in Moscow did also, but Mao chose to ignore that fact, and evoke nonetheless, in conclusion, the authority of Moscow, where the Sixth Congress had been held, in support of the importance of what he was doing. By "the leadership of the workers," Mao meant, of course, the leadership of the Party of the proletariat and, more concretely, his own leadership.

As it happened, at the very moment when Mao was composing his letter, the Central Committee in Shanghai was revising its attitude somewhat, in the light of information received about the victories in Jiangxi. On April 4, Zhou Enlai declared, at a meeting to discuss the problem of the Fourth Army, that the instruction to Mao and Zhu to leave the army was "correct in principle," but that account should be taken of current reality. A new letter was therefore sent on April 7, to the effect that if Mao and Zhu "could not come for the time being, the Central Committee would like to see the Front Committee send a capable comrade to discuss the matter."[50]

An important dimension of the confrontation between Mao Zedong and Li Lisan was the agrarian question, and in particular the attitude which should be adopted toward the rich peasants. The letter of September or October 1928 to Mao Zedong contained the following passage on this theme:

> The general line of the work in the countryside is the struggle of the peasants against the landlord class. At present, the **landlord class is the principal enemy of all the peasants**[51] (including the rich peasants, the middle peasants, the small peasants, and the semi-small peasants), and the party must rally the whole body of the peasants to oppose the oppression and feudal exploitation of the landlords and despotic gentry. . . . On the basis of the overall strategy of opposing the landlords, we must unite with the rich peasants; deliberately to accentuate the struggle against the rich peasants is wrong, for this serves to confuse the principal contradiction between the peasants and the landlord class.

---

50. This letter is not included in *Central Committee Documents*. It is cited in Jin, *Zhou Enlai*, p. 193.

51. Emphasis in the original.

This statement was qualified by the proviso that, when class struggle between the poor peasants and the rich peasants took place, the Party should, of course, stand on the side of the poor peasants.[52] The overall position of the Central Committee toward the rich peasants was, nevertheless, rather indulgent. Mao, as we have seen, took a very different line toward the "intermediate classes" in his report of November 25, 1928. This letter did not reach Mao for some time, but a copy was received in Moscow, where it aroused grave misgivings.

During the first half of 1929, the leftward trend in Stalin's economic policies which had manifested itself in the summer of 1928 took new and harsher forms, culminating in the removal of Bukharin from his position as chairman of the Executive Committee of the International on July 3, 1929. In this context, even the qualified sympathy of the Chinese Communist Party for the rich peasants was totally unacceptable, and on June 7, 1929, the International sent an extremely blunt letter on the peasant question to the Chinese comrades. Singling out for criticism the passage cited above, the International declared that "some leading comrades" were "still permitting serious errors in decisions on the peasant question." These errors, the letter said, dated back to the Sixth Congress of the Chinese Communist Party (i.e., before Stalin's turn to the left at the Sixth Comintern Congress), when the "kulaks" had been included among the peasantry as allies of the proletariat. This "opportunist interpretation" of Lenin's position was extremely harmful at a time when the "kulak elements" were going over to the side of reaction in China.[53]

The Central Committee of the Chinese Communist Party apparently did not receive this Comintern letter during its Second Plenum, in June-July 1929. Circular No. 40 of July 9, 1929, outlining the decisions of the Plenum, asserted once again: "At the present stage of the rural struggle, it is still a mistake to oppose rich peasants unconditionally." When this document was published in the Party organ *Buersaiweike* (Bolshevik) on August 1, 1929, there was, however, a note to this passage reading: "This erroneous sentence has already been corrected by the Central Committee of the Chinese Communist Party on the original resolution, following receipt of the directive letter from the Communist International."[54]

---

52. *Central Committee Documents* (1928), p. 680.

53. For the complete text of this letter, see P. Mif (ed.), *Strategiya i Taktika Kominterna v Natsional'no-kolonial'noy Revolyutsii na Primere Kitaya* (The Strategy and Tactics of the Comintern in the National-Colonial Revolution, on the Basis of the Chinese Example) (Moscow: Izdanie Instituta MKh i MP, 1934), pp. 236–44 (hereafter, Mif, *Strategy and Tactics*). A conveniently available English translation, which is somewhat abridged and omits the reference to the directive to Mao, can be found in Jane Degras (ed.), *The Communist International 1919–1943: Documents*, Vol. III, 1929–1943 (London: Oxford University Press, 1965), pp. 31–36 (hereafter, Degras, *Communist International*, III).

54. For the text of the circular, see *Central Committee Documents* (1929), pp. 342–57, which also contains (p. 357) a note regarding the change made on August 1. For a translation, see Conrad Brandt, Benjamin Schwartz, and John K. Fairbank (eds.), *A Documentary History of Chinese Communism* (Cambridge, Mass.: Harvard University Press, 1952), pp. 166–79 (hereafter, *Documentary History*). A partial translation of the lengthy resolution of the Second Plenum itself appears in Saich, *Rise to Power*, Doc. C.14, pp. 386–400.

This Comintern rebuke, which was a source of embarrassment to Li Lisan, must have brought joy to Mao, for it was entirely in line with his own position and could be seen as strengthening his hand in dealings with the Central Committee. In his Jinggangshan Land Law of December 1928, translated below, he had been obliged to make one concession to the Party leadership, accepting the distribution of land according to labor power (which favored the wealthier elements among the peasantry) as a possible alternative to the equal distribution to every individual, which Mao himself regarded as the only correct principle. In the Xingguo Land Law of April 1929, also translated below, he had made a second concession, replacing the confiscation of all land by the confiscation of public land and that of the landlord class alone. In 1941, when the Xingguo Land Law was first published, Mao added a note stating that this change was "a correction of principle,"[55] as compared to confiscating the land of all the peasants. Nonetheless, this provision, which allowed not only poor peasants but rich peasants to keep their land, cannot have been to his liking. Encouraged by the June letter from Moscow, he soon moved forward, not only to a new land law of February 7, 1930, more in harmony with his own ideas, but to the extremely harsh directive of June 1930 "On the Problem of the Rich Peasants."

Meanwhile, Mao himself suffered something of an eclipse from June to November 1929, when an attack of malaria coincided with a temporary weakening in his political standing.[56] In April and May, the Red Army, as indicated in the brief report of June 1, 1929, translated below, had been fighting, with mixed fortunes, in southern Jiangxi and then in western Fujian. At the same time, disagreements had developed within the Party and the Red Army themselves, and there was considerable tension in the relations between Zhu De and Mao Zedong.

On broad questions such as the importance of base areas, and of military force, the two men were in agreement. Differences had arisen, however, about the control of military operations, the nature of military planning, and the political role of the army. Zhu De did not oppose overall Party leadership, but he thought the Party, and Mao as secretary, were trying to run too many things directly. He agreed that plans were necessary, but in view of the need to cope with the immediate military threat, he thought Mao was too much inclined to spend time devising overall, long-term plans. And while Mao wanted the army to engage in propaganda, as well as in fighting, Zhu De thought fighting was the army's main task. In sum, Zhu De was conscious of the fact that he had much experience of warfare, and Mao, although he was learning fast, did not know so

---

55. Mao Zedong, *Nongcun diaocha* (Rural Investigations) (Yan'an: 1941), p. 127.

56. His illness has been variously reported in the literature as malaria and tuberculosis. The fact that he was suffering from malaria is confirmed in *Nianpu*, Vol. 1, pp. 281–90, *passim*. His withdrawal because of a mysterious ailment accounts for the well-known incident of the publication of an obituary of Mao Zedong in early 1930 attributing his death to a "a long-standing disease of the lungs." (See *International Press Correspondence* for March 20, 1930.)

much about military strategy. Zhu De's feeling that he should be in charge of strictly military matters was further accentuated by the fact that the troops he had brought with him to the Jinggangshan significantly outnumbered those of Mao and his bandit allies, and by the fact that the Twenty-Eighth Regiment, under Zhu's own command, was the best fighting force in the Red Army.

The situation was aggravated when, in early May 1929, the Military Department of the Central Committee sent Liu Angong to join the Fourth Army, with instructions that he should be given a leading position.[57] In accordance with orders from the International, Liu became head of the Political Department of the Front Committee, and secretary of the newly-created provisional Army Committee of the Fourth Army. He immediately sought to expand the role of the Army Committee, and to limit that of the Front Committee. Liu, freshly arrived from Moscow with no knowledge of the Red Army at all, saw in grossly simplified fashion two factions—one for and one against the Central Committee and the International. Zhu De, he said, supported the directives of the Central Committee; Mao Zedong, who had invented his own system, opposed the Center.[58]

According to accounts recently published in China, while Liu Angong was thus attacking Mao, Lin Biao did his best to exacerbate the conflict by setting Mao against Zhu De. In a letter sent to Mao only a few hours before an enlarged meeting of the Front Committee held in Baisha on June 8, 1929, Lin denounced the overweening ambitions of "certain comrades," meaning Zhu De, and their attempts to ingratiate themselves with the rank and file.

The text of Lin's letter of June 8 is not available, but Mao's long reply of June 14, 1929, recently published in Beijing and translated below, provides a comprehensive overview of the situation as Mao saw it at this time. Evoking a struggle which had been going on "for over a year," and had only recently been exposed, Mao asserted, "When controversy arises over questions within the Party, this represents progress for the Party, not retrogression."

The first and most important point taken up in this letter was that of individual leadership and Party leadership. At first glance it may appear somewhat paradoxical that Mao, often perceived as a dissident guerrilla leader who resisted the orders of the Central Committee, should have come down unequivocally on the side of Party leadership. In fact, it was entirely logical that he should do so, since within the Fourth Army he was resolved that the Party organization should maintain supremacy over individual military leaders bent on carrying out heroic exploits. A second crucial theme, among the fourteen points discussed by Mao in this letter to Lin Biao, was that of attacks on the "patriarchal system within the Party in the Fourth Army,"

---

57. Liu Angong (?–1929), was a native of Sichuan, who had spent a period in the Soviet Union studying military affairs. He was killed in combat in October 1929.

58. See Jin Chongji, *Zhu De zhuan* (Biography of Zhu De) (Beijing: Zhongyang wenxian chubanshe, 1993), pp. 175–80 (hereafter, Jin, *Zhu De*), and also *Nianpu*, Vol. 1, pp. 274–77.

by which critics meant the concentration of authority in the Party secretaries and other leading organs of the Party, and above all Mao's own authority.[59]

At the Baisha meeting, Mao complained bitterly that, because of the role taken by the Army Committee, the Front Committee had to assume responsibility, but was unable to exercise effective leadership. Mao also requested that a new secretary of the Front Committee be appointed immediately, so that he could escape from this ambiguous situation.[60] Mao's general point about organization was accepted. By a large majority, the meeting voted to abolish the Army Committee, and to replace Liu Angong by Chen Yi as head of the Political Department of the Front Committee. If, as seems probable, Mao's offer to resign, echoed in his letter to Lin Biao, was intended to strengthen his own position, that gambit was not successful.

When the Seventh Congress of Party Representatives from the Fourth Red Army met a week later, on June 22, 1929, at Longyan in Fujian, it was chaired by Chen Yi, who presented the main report, though Mao Zedong and Zhu De also spoke during the debates. The resolution adopted by the congress reviewed the ideological debates within the Fourth Army since its formation. While declaring that the overall trend had been correct, the resolution criticized as erroneous the view, which Mao had caused to be adopted in early May 1929 at a conference in Yudu, according to which it would be possible to conquer the whole of Jiangxi Province within one year.

Regarding the controversies which had taken place immediately before the Seventh Congress, the resolution asserted that while there had been a tendency toward "patriarchalism," it was too one-sided to speak of a "dictatorship of the secretary" [of the Front Committee]. In other words, Mao's style of leadership had been authoritarian, but not excessively so. At the same time, Mao's complaint at the Baisha meeting regarding the paralysis of the Front Committee was dismissed as unfounded, and his ideological stance and work style were rigorously criticized. Zhu De's work style was likewise censured, and both Liu Angong and Lin Biao were denounced for attacking the Party from outside.

Although Mao remained a member of the new Front Committee of thirteen members elected by the congress, he was replaced as secretary by Chen, thus losing his leading position in the Fourth Army. The rationale behind this decision was that, since Mao and Zhu De were continually quarreling, it was better to put the third main leader of the Fourth Army, Chen Yi, in control. Mao, at his own request, was permitted to go to a Red Army hospital in western Fujian for treatment; while there, he would also direct the work of the Western Fujian Special Committee.[61]

---

59. See below, "A Letter to Lin Biao," June 14, 1929.

60. *Nianpu*, Vol. 1, p. 278.

61. This account of the congress is drawn in the first instance from Xiao Ke, *The Zhu-Mao Red Army*, pp. 88–102. See also *Nianpu*, Vol. 1, p. 281, and *Zhongguo gongchandang huiyi gaiyao* (A Summary Account of Chinese Communist Party Meet-

On July 29, 1929, at an emergency meeting of the Front Committee, Mao agreed that Chen Yi should go to Shanghai, in the role of the "capable comrade" asked for by Zhou Enlai in his letter of April 7 cited above. During the month of August, the Central Committee met several times to discuss the decisions of the June 22 conference, and Mao's letter of June 14 to Lin Biao. A committee of three, consisting of Li Lisan, Zhou Enlai, and Chen Yi, was appointed to draft a directive to the Fourth Army. Zhou Enlai made the final revisions on September 28, and Chen Yi carried the resulting document back to Jiangxi.[62]

This directive letter asserted that "at present, when the reactionary political setup is in the process of collapse, but the nationwide revolutionary high tide has not yet arrived," the Red Army's strategy of guerrilla warfare in the Guangdong-Hunan-Jiangxi-Fujian border areas was correct. At the same time, it urged Mao and his comrades to make greater efforts to rouse the masses. In carrying out guerrilla actions, they should constantly move about and not follow a conservative strategy of staying in one place. The experience of the Jinggangshan had shown that it was impossible to survive for long in a poor and backward place. On the other hand, to envisage (as Mao had done in his April letter) conquering the whole of Jiangxi in one year was also wrong.

A whole section was devoted to the "Zhu-Mao problem." So much time and energy had been consumed by this matter, the letter said, because it had not been dealt with in terms of a clear political line which would have indicated "who was right and who was wrong." Criticisms of Zhu and Mao had also been made in an "idealist" fashion, without "investigating their mistakes from a political standpoint." Moreover, Zhu and Mao themselves had often been suspicious of each other on personal rather than political grounds. The Front Committee should therefore "correct (*jiuzheng*) their errors and restore their prestige among the masses." They could, however, retain their leadership functions, and Comrade Mao should remain secretary of the Front Committee.[63]

On October 22, Chen Yi wrote Mao sending him a copy of the September letter, and inviting him to resume a leading role in the Front Committee of the

---

ings) (Shenyang: Shenyang chubanshe, 1991), pp. 88–90 (hereafter, *Party Meetings*). Jiang Hua, who was at this time secretary general of the Political Department of the Fourth Army, and who personally delivered Lin Biao's letter of June 8, 1929, to Mao, categorically rejects the widely accepted view that Mao willingly gave up his post as leader of the Front Committee because he was ill. Mao, according to Jiang, became ill only after he went to Fujian. See Jiang Hua, "Guanyu hongjun jianshe wenti de yichang zhenglun" (A controversy regarding the problem of building a Red Army), *Dangde wenxian* No. 5, 1989, pp. 36–40.

62. *Nianpu*, Vol. 1, pp. 284–86.

63. For the text of this letter, see *Central Committee Documents* (1929), pp. 473–90. Zhou Enlai's role in preparing this letter is explained in detail in a note to the text as it appears in his works, but in that version section 8, on the Zhu-Mao problem, is missing. See *Zhou Enlai xuanji* (Selected Works of Zhou Enlai), Vol. I (Beijing: Renmin chubanshe, 1980), pp. 29–43 (hereafter, Zhou, *Works*).

Fourth Army. Zhu De and Chen Yi both wrote to Mao again on November 18 urging him to return immediately to lead the Front Committee, and on November 26, Mao met with Zhu and Chen and agreed to accept this invitation.[64]

On November 28, Mao sent to the Central Committee a letter formally notifying them of his recovery, and of the fact that he was resuming his functions as secretary of the Front Committee. At the same time, he wrote in a more personal vein to his old friend Li Lisan. The concern he expressed about his family was undoubtedly sincere, even though he had been living for some time with another woman, He Zizhen, who formally "became his revolutionary companion" in June 1928, a year and a half before his wife, Yang Kaihui, was executed in February 1930.[65] How sincere he was in asking for Li's "excellent guidance" is another matter.

On December 28, 1929, the Ninth Congress of Party organizations in the Red Army met in Gutian (in Shanghang *xian*, Fujian), under the chairmanship of Chen Yi. Mao presented the political report, translated below as the "Draft Resolution of the Ninth Congress of the Chinese Communist Party in the Fourth Red Army." Only the first section of this important document appears in the *Selected Works*, under the title "On Correcting Mistaken Ideas in the Party." This portion of the report took up some of the issues which, according to the Central Committee's September letter, called for rectification, such as "ultrademocracy." The full report went on to deal at length with problems of organization, training, and propaganda.

Meanwhile, a letter from Moscow dated October 26, 1929, which arrived in Shanghai in early December, had altered fundamentally the context in which Li Lisan must elaborate his strategy, in ways which would have a decisive impact on the relationship between Li and Mao. On July 10, 1929, Chinese authorities in the Northeast had taken over the telegraph installations of the Chinese Eastern Railway, closed the Soviet trade delegation in Manchuria, and arrested the Soviet manager of the railway. This action had been taken on the orders of Zhang Xueliang, who in December 1928 had accepted nominal subordination to Chiang Kaishek's Nanjing government, and the matter was pursued aggressively by Chiang. In the end, after a Soviet military offensive on the border in November 1929, the Chinese government was obliged to back down and restore the status quo. Meanwhile, however, Moscow saw the crisis over the Chinese Eastern

---

64. *Nianpu*, Vol. 1, pp. 289–90.

65. See *Nianpu*, Vol. 1, p. 247. One account, based on the recollections of numerous eyewitnesses, argues the view that Yuan Wencai and Wang Zuo played an important role in pushing Mao into this relationship with He Zizhen, a native of the area, in order to secure his loyalty to the people of the Jinggangshan. See Liu Xiaonong, "Mao Zedong dierci hunyin neiqing" (Inside Information on Mao Zedong's Second Marriage), *Jizhe xie tianxia* (Reporters Write about the World), No. 21, May 1992, pp. 4–11. Whether or not Yuan and Wang actually arranged the match, it seems clear that they supported and encouraged it.

Railway as yet another aggressive imperialist plot against the Soviet Union, and the letter of October 26 was, in effect, a call to the Chinese Communist Party to throw all its weight into the struggle to frustrate this design. In order to encourage them in this, the Comintern suddenly discovered that the "revolutionary wave" in China was beginning to rise. The consequences of this directive were to prove exceedingly far-reaching.[66]

Carrying Out the Li Lisan Line

On December 8, 1929, the Central Committee issued Circular No. 60, in which the previous position regarding the tactics of the Red Army was completely reversed. This document advocated concentration rather than dispersal of forces, and linked the armed struggle of the masses in the countryside to that in the cities. "The previous tactics of avoiding the capture of major cities must be changed," the directive stated. "Provided only that there is a possibility of victory and the masses can be aroused, attacks should be launched on the major cities." These tactics, "if coordinated with the workers', peasants', and soldiers' struggle in the whole country," could "promote the great revolutionary tide."[67]

This circular has long been regarded as marking the first stage in the elaboration and application of the "Li Lisan Line." At the same time it must be emphasized that, as noted earlier in this Introduction, Zhou Enlai's influence in the Central Committee was at least as great as that of Li Lisan, and this document could not have been issued without his agreement. In fact, both Li and Zhou adopted at this time an exceedingly radical position. There were, however, differences between them. Zhou Enlai saw a revolutionary high tide in China; Li Lisan believed such a tide was rising in the whole world. Li Lisan wanted immediate action; Zhou Enlai wanted to prepare first. Nonetheless, they were the joint protagonists of the leftward impulse which asserted itself beginning in December 1929.

The new view of the relation between the rural and urban struggles stated in Circular Number 60 was not too far removed from that of Moscow. The Comintern letter of October 26 asserted: "One distinctive characteristic of the national crisis and the revolutionary upsurge in China is the peasant war." But although the movement in the countryside (in which the Comintern lumped together the soviets under Mao's leadership and the activities of traditionalistic organizations such as the Red Spears) was "in the process of becoming one of the courses along which the mighty upsurge of the all-Chinese revolution will continue to develop,"

---

66. For an abridged translation of this directive, see Degras, *Communist International*, III, pp. 84–89. For a concise account of the Chinese Eastern Railway crisis, see Carr, *Foundations*, Vol. 3-III, pp. 895–910.

67. For the text of this directive, see *Central Committee Documents*, Vol. 5 (1929), pp. 561–75. The extracts quoted here are from section 8, pp. 570–71.

the "truest and most substantial indication of the swelling upsurge" was "the animation of the workers' movement, which has emerged from its depressed state following the heavy defeat of 1927." In other words, guerrilla warfare in the countryside was a legitimate and valuable part of the revolutionary effort, under Chinese conditions, but the more conventional and less exotic activities of the workers in the cities were not only more fundamental, but would, in the end, be decisive.

For his part, Li Lisan had long been far more skeptical than the Comintern regarding the significance of anything which took place in the countryside. After the turnabout of December 1929, however, as he began to lay his plans for a great offensive the following summer, Li concluded that that Red Army could provide an extremely useful auxiliary force, which would complement the action of the workers' movement and ultimately permit victory through a two-pronged attack from the cities and the countryside.

Previously, Mao Zedong had been reluctant to throw his forces against Guomindang strongpoints, thus risking both the future of the revolution and the foundations of his own power. No doubt this reticence on his part stemmed from an acute awareness of the shortcomings of the Red Army, which he openly acknowledged in the Gutian Resolution of December 1929. These included not only "incorrect ideas" (treated in the portion of this text included in the *Selected Works*) but serious organizational weaknesses and "feudal" practices such as the beating of soldiers by the officers. By early 1930, however, Mao himself had become extremely sanguine regarding the prospects for rapid victory. In his letter of January 1930 to Lin Biao, translated below, he criticized Lin for his undue pessimism about the coming of the high tide and declared that though the time limit of one year he had himself set in April 1929 for the conquest of all of Jiangxi had been "mechanical," such an achievement was not far off.

On the issue of the relative weight of the cities and the countryside in the Chinese revolution, Mao Zedong and Li Lisan remained in 1930 at opposite extremes, with Moscow occupying a position somewhere in the middle. On two other points, the time-scale of the revolution and the central role of China in the world revolution, Mao and Li stood in many respects close to one another, and in opposition to Moscow.

If Circular No. 60 of December 8, 1929, was the first expression of the Central Committee's new orientation, Circular No. 70 of February 26, 1930, formulated that line more systematically. This directive, too, like the February 1929 letter to Mao, was in fact drafted by Zhou Enlai. At a Politburo meeting in Shanghai on February 17, 1930, Zhou declared that the Party's present task, in the light of circumstances such as the continuing struggles of the warlords, was to "create a direct revolutionary situation and seize political power." Thereupon, he was entrusted with the task of drafting Circular No. 70.[68]

---

68. On Zhou's role, see Jin, *Zhou Enlai*, pp. 209–10. The full text of Circular No. 70 can be found in *Central Committee Documents*, Vol. 6 (1930), pp. 25–35.

This new document called for organizing political strikes of the workers, local insurrections, and uprisings of the soldiers in the White armies, as well as expanding the Red Army, in order to achieve "preliminary victory in one or several provinces." If the Party pursued these policies resolutely, "a direct revolutionary situation in the whole country" could be brought about. Criticizing Zhu and Mao by name for their "persistent attitude of hiding and dispersion," the directive called for urban leadership of insurrections, in order to eliminate all such tendencies rooted in "peasant consciousness and banditism."

While he can scarcely have appreciated the renewed criticism of his peasant or bandit mentality, Mao's general outlook at this time did not differ sharply from that enunciated by Zhou Enlai. His radicalism, and his chiliastic expectation of a rapidly rising revolutionary tide, are vividly illustrated by the texts of February 1930 translated below. On February 6–9, 1930, Mao presided over a joint meeting of the Front Committee of the Fourth Red Army, the Western Jiangxi Special Committee, and the Army Committees of the Fifth and Sixth Red Armies held at Pitou (in Ji'an *xian*, not far from the town of Donggu). This conference adopted a land law calling for the confiscation of owner-peasants' land, as well as that of the landlords. Mao also maintained his own egalitarian criterion of the number of mouths, rather than the Central Committee's criterion of labor power, as the preferred basis for redistribution.[69]

As for broader political and strategic issues, a recent authoritative Chinese publication states that the assessment by the Pitou conference was "excessively optimistic."[70] The proclamation issued on February 14 in the name of the presidium of the joint conference called on the Red Army to encircle Ji'an, demoralize the defenders, and take the city. Such a directive could assuredly be regarded as optimistic in view of the fact that the West Jiangxi Special Committee had been calling for the seizure of Ji'an since the previous November, but the two attacks already launched against it had been unsuccessful, and future attempts also failed.[71]

Order No. 1 of the newly established joint Front Committee (of which Mao was the secretary) conjured up even wider vistas. "With the movement of the imperialists to attack the Soviet Union," this document asserts, "a high tide of world revolution will burst out, the high tide of the Chinese revolution will arrive very soon, Chinese soviets will appear as successors to the Russian soviets, and they will become a powerful branch of the world soviets." Here, and in the letter of January 1930 to soldiers of the Guomindang Army, also translated below, the need to make revolution in China in order to defend the "state of the proletariat"

---

69. See below, the Land Law of February 7, 1930.

70. See *Party Meetings*, p. 104.

71. See Stephen C. Averill, "The Origins of the Futian Incident," (in Tony Saich and Hans van de Ven [eds.], *New Perspectives on the Chinese Communist Revolution* [Armonk, N.Y.: M.E. Sharpe, 1995]), p. 92. (Hereafter, Averill, "Futian Incident.")

is strongly underscored. At the same time, this text holds out the prospect of a revolutionary upsurge in the whole country which will "bury the ruling classes completely." Thus, the promotion of a revolutionary high tide was seen not simply as the internationalist duty of the Chinese Communist Party but as an enterprise which would rapidly lead to victory, first in Jiangxi and then in several other provinces.[72]

In early March, shortly after the adoption of Circular No. 70, the Central Committee sent Zhou Enlai to Moscow to report to the International.[73] Consequently, during the crucial period in the summer of 1930 when the Central Committee actually ordered the Red Army to attack the cities, Li Lisan was virtually in sole control of Party policy. Zhou Enlai, who had joined enthusiastically in formulating the radical and offensive line from December 1929 to March 1930, did not approve of the steps toward immediate action taken by Li Lisan in the spring and summer of 1930. Thus these policies can, after all, legitimately be called the "Lisan Line."

In recent years, Mao Zedong's attitude toward the Li Lisan line has been the subject of a wide-ranging debate among Chinese scholars enjoying access to the relevant sources. Although some of these authors still adhere to the view laid down in the resolution of 1945 on Party history, according to which Mao never agreed with Li's plan to attack the cities and carried it out only because discipline required obedience to orders, others argue that Mao Zedong was won over to this strategy by the winter or spring of 1930 and followed it spontaneously and enthusiastically.[74]

As noted above, the texts translated in this volume provide solid evidence that, beginning in January 1930, Mao did believe a revolutionary tide would soon sweep across China. That does not, of course, mean that Mao and Li agreed in all respects, or that their interests were convergent. On April 3, 1930, the

---

72. See below, the documents of February 14 and 16, 1930. It is confirmed in *Nianpu*, Vol. 1, p. 298, that Mao, as one of three members of the presidium of the Pitou Conference, shared responsibility for the proclamation of February 14. As secretary of the new Front Committee, he must also have endorsed the notice of February 16, whether or not he wrote it himself.

73. Jin, *Zhou Enlai*, pp. 210–13. The immediate reason for sending him was a dispute between the Chinese Communist Party and the "Eastern Bureau" of the Comintern, which served as the agency for transmitting Moscow's orders.

74. For articles illustrating a range of views on this issue, see the contributions to the authoritative inner-Party journal *Dangshi yanjiu* (Research on Party History, hereafter *Party History*) by Lin Yunhui, "Lue lun Mao Zedong tongzhi dui Lisan luxian de renshi he dizhi" (A Brief Account of Comrade Mao Zedong's Understanding of and Resistance to the Lisan Line), *Party History* 4, 1980, pp. 51–59; Tian Yuan, "Zai lun Mao Zedong tongzhi dui Lisan luxian de renshi he dizhi" (More on Comrade Mao Zedong's Understanding of and Resistance to the Lisan Line), *Party History* 1, 1981, pp. 65–71; and Ling Yu, "Mao Zedong tongzhi he Lisan luxian de guanxi taolun zongshu" (A Summary of the Discussion Regarding Comrade Mao Zedong's Relationship to the Lisan Line), *Party History* 3, 1982, pp. 78–80.

Central Committee sent a letter to the Front Committee of the Fourth Army stating that the Red Army was "one of the forces directly contributing to an initial victory in one or several provinces." It was, however, an "extremely erroneous" conservative attitude to assume that this meant (as Mao had said in his letter of April 1929) "taking the whole of Jiangxi in one year." Taking Jiangxi was possible, but only in the context of a nationwide revolutionary upsurge, and only if the Fourth Army overcame its tendencies toward dispersion and recruited the broad masses to form a truly powerful Red Army. The immediate destination should be Jiujiang, which would serve as a guarantee of victory in Wuhan. Finally, Mao was told that he absolutely must obey the order to come to Shanghai for a conference of delegates from the soviet areas which the Central Committee would soon hold.[75]

Neither Mao's actions nor those of Li Lisan can be interpreted purely in terms of their rivalry with each other as Richard Thornton tends to argue. Both of them did, after all, seek victory for the Party and the revolution. There can be no doubt, however, that at the very least, Li hoped in this way to kill two birds with one stone: to make use of Mao's military strength in achieving his own goals and to assert his control over Mao Zedong.[76] Mao, for his part, obviously had no intention of risking his freedom, or his life, by going to Shanghai. Further appeals from Li Lisan went unanswered, and at the end of May, Li was obliged to hold the conference of soviet areas without the leader of the most important of them. Mao's rival Li Wenlin, a leader of the revolutionary organizations in Southwest Jiangxi, did attend, and used the occasion to build up his own standing.[77]

The political resolution adopted on this occasion repeated the view that, while the Red Army could help achieve victory in one or several provinces, such a prospect was inseparable from a nationwide revolutionary upsurge. To imagine that the soviet areas could preserve their conquests over a prolonged period of time

---

75. For the text of this letter, see *Central Committee Documents* (1930), pp. 57–60.

76. See Thornton, *The Comintern and the Chinese Communists*, pp. 121–38, especially p. 130.

77. Li Wenlin (1900–1932), a native of Jiangxi, was a graduate of the Huangpu Academy who had participated in the Nanchang Uprising. In 1928, he was sent to reorganize the Party near his home in Jishui *xian*, Jiangxi. Mao encountered him there on the way down from the Jinggangshan in February 1929. On that occasion, Li gave substantial aid to Mao's forces, and the two men established good relations. As late as January 5, 1930, Mao underscored his positive attitude toward Li Wenlin by including him in the list of four exemplars of the "correct" policy of setting up revolutionary bases which appears in the letter of that date to Lin Biao, translated below. Editing his *Selected Works* in 1950, however, Mao removed Li's name from this enumeration, for by the spring of 1930 Mao and Li had come into conflict regarding the control of the revolutionary organizations and of the armed forces in Western Jiangxi. See Yung-fa Ch'en, "The Futian Incident and the Anti-Bolshevik League: The 'Terror' in the CCP Revolution," *Republican China*, Vol. XIX, No. 2, April 1994, pp. 1–51, Averill, "Futian Incident," p. 100, and the discussion below in this Introduction.

without a victory of the revolution in the entire country was "a great mistake."[78]

Meanwhile, Mao was busy conducting an investigation of social, economic, and political conditions in Xunwu, where his forces spent a fortnight in May 1930. As pointed out above, in the General Introduction, an emphasis on practice as the source of knowledge had long been characteristic of Mao Zedong's thought, and he had frequently carried out social surveys since his student days.[79] The Xunwu investigation, presented below in Roger Thompson's meticulous translation, contains a wealth of information about many aspects of life in that area, including not only agrarian relationships and the history of the land struggle but the types of food and other consumer goods available in the *xian* town, culture, and relations between men and women.

It was in the course of the Xunwu investigation that Mao first met Gu Bo, who soon became one of his close personal associates, and played an active role in the Futian affair, discussed below in the concluding section of this Introduction.[80]

From mid to late June 1930, Mao convened a Joint Conference of the Red Fourth Army Front Committee and the Western Fujian Special Committee, which constituted in effect his response to Li Lisan's May conference of the soviet areas.[81] This conference, which met first at Nanyang in Changting *xian*, and then in Tingzhou City, adopted an extremely harsh line toward privileged strata in the countryside. The International had already warned Li Lisan against his kindness to the rich peasants, and at the May conference of the soviet areas Li called for confiscating "all land of counterrevolutionary kulaks."[82] Mao, for his part, needed no guidance from Moscow to stiffen his hostility to the rich peasants. As noted earlier, his report of November 25, 1928, had adopted a wholly negative attitude toward the "intermediate classes," and the land law of February 7, 1930, had called for the confiscation of the land of owner-peasants.

The June resolution "On the Problem of the Rich Peasants" began by extend-

---

78. Thornton, *The Comintern and the Chinese Communists*, p. 142, quoting from the Russian-language proceedings of the May conference. (These materials are absent from *Central Committee Documents*.)

79. See, for example, the text of March 1927, "An Example of the Chinese Tenant-Peasant's Life," in Volume II of this edition, pp. 478–83.

80. Gu Bo (1906–1935) was a native of Xunwu in Jiangxi Province. He joined the Chinese Communist Party in December 1925, and participated in the Guangzhou uprising of 1927. In October 1929, he became secretary of the Xunwu Party Committee. In May 1930, he provided considerable assistance to Mao Zedong in conducting the investigation in Xunwu of which the report is translated below. Thereafter, he worked for some time in the First Front Army, and was closely associated with Mao. For a detailed account of his career, see Roger Thompson's monograph: Mao Zedong, *Report from Xunwu* (Stanford: Stanford University Press, 1990), especially pp. 9–30 *passim*.

81. On this gathering, see *Nianpu*, Vol. 1, pp. 310–11, and also Ma and Zhang, *Mao's Road*, pp. 327–29.

82. Thornton, *The Comintern and Chinese Communists*, p. 145, citing the documents of the conference.

ing the definition of this category to include not only "feudal" rich peasants with extra land to rent out, and "capitalist" rich peasants with the resources to hire others to work the land for them, but "newly enriched" peasants who had surplus grain every year, though they relied on their own labor. Such people were regarded by many in the Party as "middle peasants," but Mao in this text characterized their "semifeudal exploitation" as even crueler than that of the landlords. In his preface to the Xunwu investigation, written in February 1931, Mao acknowledged that in May 1930 he "still did not completely understand the problem of China's rich peasants" and deplored the absence, in the Xunwu investigation, of a separate discussion of the landholdings of rich, middle, and poor peasants. His self-proclaimed ignorance of the rich peasants did not, however, inhibit him from urging that they be pitilessly expropriated. Mao's continuing faith in a rapid and total victory of the revolution found expression in the statement that land redistribution could be completed in two weeks, after which the Party could begin immediately to criticize the limitations of individual ownership in the countryside and urge the peasants to move forward toward socialist collective cultivation.[83]

The Nanyang conference also adopted a resolution on the vagabonds which treats these people as generally counterrevolutionary and "capable of turning traitor at any time." It is, read the text, particularly necessary to purge them from the ranks of the Red Army "at this time, when the high tide of revolution is approaching swiftly, and preparations for a general uprising in the whole country to achieve nationwide victory are ever more urgent."[84] This may well have reflected an attempt on Mao's part to make himself appear more orthodox in the eyes of the Central Committee, which was constantly accusing him not only of "peasant consciousness" but of associating with bandits and other riffraff. It is, in any case, unlike most of Mao's other writings regarding such marginal elements in Chinese society.

Mao was not, of course, investigating these matters merely out of idle curiosity. On the one hand, a knowledge of social relationships was obviously important to someone who wished to manipulate them in order to make revolution. But, on the other hand, Mao considered that the concrete knowledge he had acquired by engaging in such surveys gave him unique qualifications for leading the revolution.

This point is driven home in the text which appears, below, immediately after the Xunwu investigation: "Oppose Bookism." After enunciating at the outset his famous aphorism "Without investigation, there is no right to speak," Mao went on to spell out the obvious implications of this view for his relationship with Li Lisan and others in Shanghai. "Surprisingly," he wrote, "when problems are discussed within the Communist Party, there are also people who say, whenever

---

83. See below, "On the Problem of the Rich Peasants," June 1930.
84. See below, "The Problem of Vagabonds," June 1930. This text was drafted by Deng Zihui, but Mao revised and endorsed it.

they open their mouths, 'Show me where it's written in the book.' " Even Marxist books, he added, though they should be studied, "must be integrated with our actual situation." Plainly this was aimed at those who had learned about Marxism in Moscow, or in Paris, but did *not* know or understand the realities of rural China.

In "Oppose Bookism," Mao also wrote: "To carry out directives blindly without discussing and examining them in the light of the real conditions, simply because they come from 'higher levels,' is a formalistic attitude which is quite wrong." Mao Zedong had, as we have seen, refused a year earlier to commit this error of blind obedience. And yet, in mid-June, when Li Lisan, having determined that the moment had arrived to put his line into practice, ordered the Fourth Army to attack major cities, Mao immediately agreed to do so.

On June 11, 1930, Li put through the Politburo a resolution declaring that the Chinese revolution could set off the world revolution and bring about the final victory over imperialism.[85] At about the same time, a resolution was adopted calling for the reorganization of the Red Army in four army groups. The First Army Group comprised the forces of Zhu and Mao, the Second those of He Long in Hunan, the Third those of Peng Dehuai in the former Jinggangshan base area, and the Fourth the guerrilla bands in areas north of the Yangzi. All these forces were to be placed under a single command, with Zhu De as commander in chief and Mao Zedong as political commissar. No doubt Li Lisan believed that he could control Mao more effectively if he were directly subordinated to the Central Committee.[86]

On June 15, Li addressed a letter to the Front Committee denouncing the previous behavior of the Fourth Army in the bluntest possible terms and demanding that they change their ways. Mao and his comrades, said Li, understood nothing of the changed political situation brought about by the contradictions in the reactionary camp and were therefore incapable of comprehending the orders of the Central Committee, which they had persistently disobeyed. These points were repeated like a refrain in every paragraph. Li also taunted Mao with being "terrified of imperialism" and having for this reason rejected earlier instructions to take the offensive in directions where the imperialists were strong. Once again, Mao was accused of "peasant consciousness," which led him to regard rural work as primary and urban work as secondary. He did not understand, said Li, that the land revolution could be carried through only if the rule of the Guomindang were overthrown in the whole country. "Your viewpoint regarding independent régimes," Li wrote, "is a peasant viewpoint."[87]

---

85. The resolution of June 11, 1930, can be found in *Central Committee Documents* (1930), pp. 115–35. For a slightly abridged translation, see *Documentary History*, pp. 184–200.

86. This view has been put forward by Thornton, *The Comintern and Chinese Communists*, p. 157.

87. For the text of the letter dated June 15, 1930, see *Central Committee Documents* (1930), pp. 137–41.

This rude and insulting missive did not, in fact, reach Mao until October.[88] Meanwhile, however, Li Lisan sent an emissary, Tu Zhennong, to inform Mao of the substance of the Central Committee's recent decisions. Tu arrived at the headquarters of Zhu and Mao in Changting on June 21, 1930, and gave a report lasting two days.[89]

In the context created by Li Lisan's order to launch an offensive against the cities, Mao was led to devote a great deal of his time to military matters. This volume contains nearly fifty orders and directives, signed by Zhu and Mao, for the six months from June 22 to December 29. Many of these deal in fine detail with routes and schedules for the movement of various units belonging to the First Army Group,[90] but they also contain Mao's observations on the overall strategy of the revolution. This dimension of his thinking is developed more systematically in nine or ten letters, telegrams, reports, and resolutions dating from the second half of 1930. Taken together, these materials provide a far more concrete and vivid account of Mao's role in the implementation of the Li Lisan Line than has previously been available.

The day after Tu Zhennong came to report on Li's new strategy, Zhu and Mao issued an order stressing that the situation "was opening up a good deal" because of the conflict between Chiang Kaishek and his rivals, so that the First Route Army, "in concert with the masses of workers and peasants," could "seize Jiujiang and Nanchang so as to establish political power in Jiangxi.[91] Three days later, Mao produced a telegram which echoed in fact, with exemplary fervor, all the key points of the Li Lisan line. "The reactionary rule," Mao wrote, "is already headed toward collapse." He confirmed that the First Army Group would advance on Nanchang and regroup at Wuhan with the Second and Third Army Groups. They would "seize victory first of all in the provinces of Hunan, Hubei, and Jiangxi, in order to push forward the nationwide revolutionary high tide." But at the same time, the telegram called for political strikes by the workers, local uprisings by the peasants, and revolts by the troops of the White armies. It looked forward not only to the complete overthrow of the Guomindang but to the "final decisive battle against the Guomindang warlords and the imperialists," adding that the victory of the Chinese revolution would raise the curtain on the world revolu-

---

88. This fact is stated by Mao himself in the letter of October 14, 1930, to the Central Committee, translated below. It is confirmed by Jin Chongji, *Zhu De*, p. 205.

89. Jin, *Zhu De*, p. 205. For information regarding Tu Zhennong, see the note to the report of September 17, 1930.

90. As explained below, in the "Note on Sources and Conventions," we have placed at the head of this volume two maps showing the area in which these military actions took place. It has not seemed appropriate to annotate all the names of places and individuals which appear in these orders, but the full texts have been translated as background to the writings of a more general character referred to below.

91. See below, "Order to the First Route Army of the Red Army to Set Out from Western Fujian and regroup at Guangchang," June 22, 1930.

tion. "Our red flag," proclaimed Mao, "will fly throughout the entire world."[92]

It might be argued that Mao responded in this way because he had been persuaded by Tu Zhennong's report, or simply because he had no alternative but to obey. In the light of all the available sources, however, it seems more likely that, sharing as he did much of Li Lisan's revolutionary optimism at this time, he saw an opportunity to strengthen his own position by falling in with Li Lisan's strategy, just as Li Lisan was bent on using and controlling him. Though Mao still believed in the fundamental importance of the countryside, and Li stressed rather the leading role of the urban workers, the prospect of an imminent revolutionary conflagration in the whole country appeared to offer wide scope for the simultaneous implementation of both these strategic visions.

What was Moscow's position regarding the issues raised by Li Lisan's new policies? The picture is somewhat obscured by the fact that communications between China and the Soviet Union were poor, so that letters often took several months to reach their destination. As a result, Shanghai and Moscow were frequently responding to positions which had long since been abandoned. (The same, as we have just seen, was true of communications between Mao and the Central Committee.)

To take only one example, the Comintern letter of June 1930 (commonly dated July 23 in Chinese sources because that is when it was received in Shanghai) was drafted in Moscow in May in response to what was known there of the policy adopted by the Chinese Communist Party in February (that laid down in Circular No. 70).[93] In this letter, while noting that an objective revolutionary situation still did not exist throughout the country, because the "waves of the workers' movement and the peasants' movement" had not merged into one, the Comintern predicted that the revolutionary situation would shortly encompass "if not the whole of Chinese territory, then at least the territory of a number of key provinces." Nonetheless, though the Comintern expected the decisive battles in China to take place in the near future, they did not agree with Li Lisan that the time for an offensive had already come. Moscow therefore explicitly refused to sanction Li's decision to order attacks on Wuhan, Changsha, and other cities, and

---

92. See the "Telegram of the Chinese Revolutionary Military Commission on Attacking Nanchang and Regrouping at Wuhan," June 25, 1930, signed by Mao as chairman of the commission, and by all the other principal commanders, including Zhu De, Peng Dehuai, Lin Biao, and Chen Yi.

93. In recent years, these matters have been clarified by the publications of Soviet scholars, based on the Comintern archives. Perhaps the most authoritative of these is the book by A. M. Grigor'ev, *Revolyutsionnoe Dvizhenie v Kitae v 1927–1931 gg.* (The Revolutionary Movement in China in the Years 1927–1931) (Moscow: Izdatel'stvo "Nauka," 1980) (hereafter, Grigor'ev, *The Revolutionary Movement in China*). Chapter 4 of this work is devoted to the elaboration and implementation of the Li Lisan line. Grigor'ev's argument is summarized in his article "The Comintern and the Revolutionary Movement in China under the Slogan of the Soviets (1927–1931)," in *The Comintern and the East*, ed. R. A. Ulyanovsky (Moscow: Progress Publishers, 1979), pp. 345–88.

for coordinated uprisings in those places, arguing that both the Red Army and the workers' movement should first be further strengthened.[94]

Although Li Lisan received this letter four days before Peng Dehuai's Third Army Group attacked and occupied Changsha on July 27, 1930, he chose to ignore it and to conceal it from others in the Party. He probably felt that he had no choice but to go forward. Victory, which he still believed possible, would justify him in the eyes of the International; defeat would be scarcely a greater disaster than ignominious retreat.

Peng's forces were able to take Changsha, thanks to the "chaotic struggles among the warlords" to which Mao repeatedly referred. In the context of the war between Chiang Kaishek and the Guangxi faction, Governor He Jian had sent most of his forces to pursue the troops of Zhang Fakui and Li Zongren, thus greatly weakening the garrison at Changsha. Despite this initial victory, however, the workers' uprising central to Li Lisan's strategy did not materialize. As a result, the Red Army was obliged to evacuate the city ten days later, on August 6, 1930.

Meanwhile, at the end of July, the First Army Group of Zhu and Mao approached Nanchang, as promised in the June 25 telegram. Some of the cadres wanted to attack the city, but Mao Zedong and Zhu De were skeptical about the prospects, and sent Luo Binghui to reconnoiter. Luo reported back that the enemy forces were extremely strong and their positions were well fortified. It was therefore decided to limit the action to taking a railroad station across the river from Nanchang, and shooting off guns to commemorate the third anniversary of the Nanchang uprising on August 1.[95]

These events provide the context for Mao's poem, dated July 1930, "From Tingzhou to Changsha." It is suggested in the notes to our translation that this was written after the first onslaught on the cities had ended in defeat. The exact date of composition is uncertain, and it could also have been written on the way, but in the awareness that the enterprise on which Mao and his comrades had embarked was hazardous indeed.

In mid-August, despite the difficulties and defeats already encountered, Mao proclaimed his intention of taking Changsha, and advancing on Wuhan. At the same time, he asked the Central Committee to send him reinforcements—if possible, as many as thirty thousand.[96] On August 23, 1930, the First Army Group of Zhu and Mao, having gone to Hunan to participate in the new attack on Changsha, joined together with Peng Dehuai's Third Army Group to establish

---

94. See Grigor'ev, "The Comintern and the Revolutionary Movement in China," pp. 369–73. Substantial extracts from the June 1930 directive can be found in Degras, *Communist International*, III, pp. 114–20.

95. See below, the "Order to Seize the Niuhang Railway Station," and also *Nianpu*, Vol. 1, pp. 312–13,

96. See below, "Letter to the Southwest Jiangxi Special Committee, for Transmission to the Central Committee," August 19, 1930.

the First Front Army. A majority of the Front Committee was in favor of the attack, so despite their own growing reservations, Zhu and Mao issued the "Order to Advance Toward Changsha" of August 24, 1930, translated below. On August 31, another order was issued, of which the content is sufficiently indicated by the title: "Order to Lure the Enemy out of Their Fortifications, Destroy Them, and March into Changsha on the Heels of Victory." This was followed on September 10 by yet another order for an assault on Changsha. In carrying it out, the Red Army suffered heavy losses. On September 12, Zhu and Mao finally issued the order to abandon the attack.[97]

Five days later, in a report to the Central Committee, Mao summed up the reasons for the defeat at Changsha, but then went on to put forward once more the objectives of attacking Nanjing, taking Wuhan, and establishing political power in the whole country. The immediate objective was, however, to take Ji'an.[98] Although, as noted above, the attempts to take this small but important city in the spring of 1930 had been unsuccessful, Ji'an seemed on the face of it a reasonable objective. In fact, the direction thus given to the action of the "Zhu-Mao Army" had violent and no doubt unforeseen consequences.

In the wake of the Pitou Conference of February 1930, the Western Jiangxi and the Southern Jiangxi Special Committees had been merged to form the Southwest Jiangxi Special Committee. Despite the fact that Mao had played a key role in setting up this organization, the Southwest Jiangxi Special Committee soon fell under the control of a faction hostile to Mao and the First Front Army on multiple grounds. Not only were the leading figures, including Li Wenlin, supporters of the Li Lisan line. They were natives of Jiangxi, who resented being taken over by a Hunanese-dominated "guest army." Moreover, many of the leaders of the Southwest Jiangxi Special Committee were themselves of elite origins, naturally concerned with the interests of the rich peasants.[99]

The resulting tensions manifested themselves progressively during the last four months of 1930. The rhetoric of the first order announcing the new strategy, issued on September 13, was calculated to dispel any impression that Mao and his comrades were giving up their revolutionary objectives. It called for "destroying . . . reactionary rule in Jiangxi, . . . attacking Nanjing to the right, and securing the seizure of Wuhan to the left, to facilitate . . . the seizure of political power in the whole country." Four days later, in a report of September 17, 1930, to the Central Committee, Mao sounded a soberer note. The attack on Changsha,

---

97. See below, the translations of these two documents. The order of September 12 referred explicitly only to "postponing" the assault on Changsha until a more opportune moment, but its significance was clear.

98. "Report to the Central Committee," September 17, 1930.

99. Regarding the extremely complex interrelation between ideology, regional and provincial differences, economic interests, and political organizations in Jiangxi at this time, see the previously cited article by Stephen C. Averill, "The Origins of the Futian Incident," pp. 79–115, especially pp. 100–102.

Mao argued, while it had cost the Red Army heavy losses, had "demolished the prestige" of more than thirty Guomindang regiments, and in that sense constituted a great victory.[100]

On September 29, Zhou Yili, an emissary from the Yangzi River Bureau of the Central Committee, came to the headquarters of the First Front Army in Yichun (now Yuanzhou) with a letter from the Central Committee dated August 29 ordering yet another attack on Changsha. Mao succeeded in convincing him that this was not feasible, and Zhou accepted the plan for taking Ji'an put forward by Mao and Zhu. The ensuing military orders dated September 29, October 2, and October 3 contain little of general interest, but trace the progress of the offensive against Ji'an. As stipulated in the orders of October 2 and October 3, the final attack took place on October 4, and the Red Army occupied the city on that day.

A resolution dated from Ji'an on October 7, 1930, refers to the existence of "a revolutionary situation in the whole world, in the whole country, in all provinces," and concludes: "In the course of this revolutionary 'high tide' [*gaochao*] . . . soviet power must undoubtedly burst upon the scene in the whole country and in the whole world."[101] This language echoes the telegram of June 25, 1930. The same tone continues three weeks later, in the resolution of October 26, 1930, on the political situation, which states that the "revolutionary high tide in China will soon take the form of a general outburst."

Toward a Strategy of Protracted War

The disastrous failures of the summer and early autumn of 1930 led, understandably, to a sharp struggle within the top leadership of the Chinese Communist Party, in which the Communist International ultimately played a decisive role. This, in turn, changed the context in which Mao Zedong was operating, creating both opportunities and threats. But before turning to these aspects of the situation in late 1930, some of Mao's writings of this period merit a brief comment.

Among the most interesting of these are his rural investigations. Both while his army was occupying Ji'an and during the retreat from that city, Mao continued the practice of summoning meetings everywhere he went to collect data regarding social and economic conditions which he had inaugurated in May 1930 with the Xunwu investigation. The most important of these exercises in late 1930 was the Xingguo investigation of October 1930. This text, translated below, is only slightly over half as long as that regarding Xunwu. It

---

100. See below, the translations of these two texts.

101. The full text of this resolution is not currently available. The passages cited here were quoted by Qu Qiubai in an article in *Shi hua* (True Words), no. 2 (December 9, 1930), pp. 3–4. Qu was, of course, seeking to justify himself by criticizing the leftist errors of others, but these extracts are undoubtedly authentic.

contained, however, as Mao noted in his preface, more analysis than did the Xunwu survey regarding the differing attitudes of the various classes toward land reform. This substantial document, and the briefer notes regarding Dongtang, Mukou Village, and other places underscore Mao's continuing commitment to the axiom he had laid down in May 1930: "No investigation, no right to speak."

Particular importance attaches to Mao's attitude toward the rich peasants, since this was one of the main points of divergence between him and Li Lisan. We have already noted Mao's continuing sharp hostility to this class, from the Jinggangshan Report of November 1928 to the February 7, 1930, land law, to the June 1930 conference which produced the resolution "On the Problem of the Rich Peasants." Generally speaking, this attitude continues in the materials of the second half of 1930, though it is perhaps slightly attenuated. Thus, in the Xingguo investigation, Mao stigmatizes the rich peasants as, with the landlords, one of the "truly exploiting classes" (see Section II, "The Old Land Relationships in this District"), but adds that, in one district, five out of twelve rich peasant families had in fact joined the revolution (Section III, "The Various Classes in the Struggle"). In the same text, he declares that the *youmin*, or vagrants, "generally favor the revolution" (Section III, par. 8). His sweeping denunciation of similar elements in the text of June 1930, "The Problem of Vagabonds," may thus have been something of an aberration.

In defending his own policy of equal redistribution on the basis of the number of family members versus the criterion of labor power, Mao Zedong several times attacked the Southwest Jiangxi Special Committee, which had adopted the latter principle at its Second Plenum of July 1930.[102] The tension between this body and the First Front Army has already been mentioned above. The Southwest Jiangxi Special Committee was to be Mao's adversary in November and December 1930 in one of the most savage inner-Party struggles in which he was ever involved: the so-called Futian Incident.

During the months leading up to this clash, Li Lisan's position in the Party was significantly weakened, but he by no means lost all influence. The Third Plenum of the Central Committee met in Shanghai from September 24 to 28, 1930.[103] Zhou Enlai, who had been sent to Moscow by Li in March 1930 to explain his new line, was sent back to China by the International to participate in this gathering, as was Qu Qiubai, who chaired the meeting. Stalin's intention was that on this occasion Li Lisan should be sternly condemned, but the Plenum was, in fact, largely a whitewash. Li was found guilty only of individual tactical mistakes, but not of a systematic error of "line."

---

102. See, in particular, "The Mistakes in the Land Struggle in Jiangxi," November 14, 1930, translated below.

103. Most earlier studies, including serious monographs such as that of Thornton (*The Comintern and the Chinese Communists*, p. 187), indicate that the meeting took place in Lushan, but it has now been revealed that this statement in the contemporary documents was a deliberate distortion for security reasons.

This development can be understood in part as an effort by the leftists Qu and Zhou to protect their fellow leftist Li Lisan, in order to safeguard their own position vis-à-vis the rightists such as Zhang Guotao and Cai Hesen.[104] It should also be noted, however, that Moscow did not begin denouncing "errors of line" by the Chinese Party until it was learned that Li Lisan was calling for uprisings in Mongolia, and talking about "world revolution." Such a perspective, which implied the involvement of the Soviet Union in a worldwide civil war, was wholly unacceptable to Stalin. The International therefore sent a letter in November utterly condemning the Third Plenum. "The peasant movement," stated the letter, "has far outpaced, in speed and scope, the movement of the industrial workers." When Li Lisan proposed an armed uprising in Wuhan, the letter noted, the Chinese Communist Party had only two hundred members there. To attack the major centers, tightly controlled by imperialism, would only bleed white both the urban working class and the Red Army.[105]

Toward the end of November, the Comintern's China expert, Pavel Mif, arrived in China, and at a Politburo meeting on December 14, he obtained the agreement of the Chinese leadership to the convening of a Fourth Plenum. This meeting, which took place on January 16, 1931, finally and definitively repudiated the Li Lisan line and installed a new leading group headed by Chen Shaoyu (better known under his pseudonym, Wang Ming). Zhou Enlai, who at the December 14 meeting had wholeheartedly endorsed Mif's position and denounced Li Lisan, remained a member of the Politburo chosen at the Fourth Plenum. Li Lisan had already been sent to Moscow for a "trial" before Comintern interrogators. Qu Qiubai lost influence in the Party and was assigned to cultural work. Otherwise, the leadership was entirely made up of Mif's pupils and protégés known as the "Twenty-eight Bolsheviks."

Information regarding the Third Plenum reached the First Front Army only in December.[106] In any case, on reading it, Mao could only have concluded that Li Lisan remained a powerful figure whose influence constituted a threat to his policies. Of the Comintern letter of November 16 and Li's subsequent disgrace, Mao presumably knew nothing.

Whatever his understanding of the situation in Moscow and Shanghai, Mao Zedong was also involved, as already noted, in a complex set of relations with those who exercised power in the Party at the local level. The conflict was particularly acute with the Jiangxi Provincial Action Committee and the Southwest Jiangxi Special Committee, dominated at this time by Li Wenlin. Despite the tensions between them, Mao's General Front Committee and Li Wenlin's

---

104. Perhaps the most cogent argument for this view is that of Thornton, *The Comintern and the Chinese Communists*, pp. 188–200.

105. For extracts from the Comintern letter of November 16, 1930, including the passages cited here, see Degras, *Communist International*, III, pp. 135–41.

106. *Nianpu*, Vol. 1, p. 317.

Jiangxi Provincial Action Committee held a "Joint Conference" in Luofang from October 25 to November 1, 1930. The "Resolution on the Land Problem" of October 19, 1930, endorsed on this occasion, asserted that the Southwest Jiangxi Special Committee was filled with AB Corps elements.[107] (The initials "AB" are commonly thought to stand for "Anti-Bolshevik"; in any case, this body had been formed in 1925–1926 to fight the Communists.)

The Southwest Jiangxi Special Committee had, in fact, waged a major campaign from May to September 1930 against AB Corps infiltration of the Party, in response to prompting from Moscow and the Central Committee. The reference to this phenomenon in the October 19 resolution was thus, in itself, widely acceptable. Indeed, another resolution adopted at the Luofang Joint Conference called for a struggle against the AB Corps in the First Front Army as well.[108] There was, however, disagreement both about the nature of the AB Corps and about the reasons for the excesses committed in the course of the campaign in Southwest Jiangxi.[109]

At the Luofang Conference, Li Wenlin had criticized the principle of "luring the enemy deep," which Mao regarded, together with the strategy of a "protracted war," as one of the two cornerstones of his military thought.[110] In November, Mao therefore judged that the time had come to take forceful action against his opponents in Jiangxi. In the course of the ensuing confused struggles, the real policy differences became intertwined with reciprocal accusations of association with the AB Corps, on the basis of tenuous evidence, or no evidence at all save for confessions under torture. In November 1930, some 4,000 of the 40,000 officers and men in the First Front Army were arrested as AB Corps members, and about half of them were executed.

In late November, Mao arrested Li Wenlin on the same charge. Thereafter, Mao sent his fellow Hunanese, Li Shaojiu, a member of his political staff, to carry out a purge in Futian and then in Donggu, in which many cadres were arrested, tortured, and executed or threatened with execution. It was in the context of these actions that the events known as the "Futian Incident" or the "Futian Rebellion" took place.

This whole episode is so confusing and controversial that it is difficult to summarize the facts with confidence, but a few points are agreed on by all the

---

107. See below, the translation of this resolution.

108. See below, "The Present Political situation and the Tasks of the First Front Army and of the Party in Jiangxi," October 26, 1930.

109. See Yung-fa Ch'en, "The Futian Incident and the Anti-Bolshevik League,", pp. 4–10, and also Yu Boliu and Chen Gang, *Mao Zedong zai zhongyang suqu* (Mao Zedong in the Central Soviet Area) (n.p.: Zhongguo shudian, 1993), pp. 166–73.

110. On "luring the enemy deep," see below,"Investigations in Dongtang and Other Places," November 8, 1930. The strategy of a "protracted war" is outlined in Section III of "Eight Great Conditions for Victory," December 22, 1930, translated below, which also discusses "luring the enemy deep."

conflicting accounts.[111] In the aftermath of Li Shaojiu's exactions, Liu Di, a battalion political commisar, turned against him on December 11, seized control in Donggu, made a forced march to Futian and there attacked the prison, releasing some twenty members of the Southwest Jiangxi Action Committee. More than a hundred of Mao's supporters were killed in the course of these events.[112]

The men freed in Donggu and Futian thereupon declared that, although hostile to Mao, they were loyal to the Party and to the Central Committee. They appealed to the three military leaders, Zhu De, Peng Dehuai, and Huang Gonglue, to detain Mao and join them in resisting his policies. Zhu De, as noted above, had earlier clashed with Mao on some issues, but Zhu and Peng now agreed with Mao's military strategy. Their support ultimately enabled Mao to assert his authority once again. A highly polemical but rather detailed overview of the inner-Party polemics in December 1930, and of the role of Zhu De and Peng Dehuai, is provided by the "Letter of Reply by the General Front Committee" of December 1930, translated below. Although it is not signed by Mao, he was the secretary of this committee, and the letter may therefore be presumed to reflect his views.

There followed a period of confused military and political struggle, which was not pursued wholeheartedly by either side because each was waiting to hear more about what had happened to Li Lisan and his line. The worst killings by Mao's supporters took place in early 1931, after news of the final overthrow of Li Lisan at the Fourth Plenum had reached the area, in the context of a campaign to "suppress counterrevolutionaries."

Meanwhile, despite the disruption thus caused, the forces of Mao Zedong,

---

111. Among the earlier studies, some of the most detailed and interesting are that of John Rue, in his *Mao Tse-tung in Opposition 1927–1935* (Stanford: Stanford University Press, 1966), pp. 218–35, (hereafter, Rue, *Mao in Opposition*), sympathetic but not uncritical; Hsiao Tso-liang, *Power Relations within the Chinese Communist Movement, 1930–1934* (Seattle: University of Washington Press, 1961), pp. 98–113, (hereafter, Hsiao, *Power Relations*), hostile to Mao but balanced and well documented; and, for a critical Soviet perspective, Grigor'ev, *The Revolutionary Movement in China*, pp. 223–27. The most authoritative recent overview is that, already cited, of Stephen Averill, "Futian Incident." Basing himself on recently published Chinese studies and a wide range of primary sources, Averill stresses the importance of local conditions and especially of the tensions between cadres from Jiangxi and Mao's largely Hunanese army in bringing about the incident. Yung-fa Ch'en, in his article already cited, while recognizing the significance of this factor, emphasizes rather the political conflict between Mao and Li Wenlin resulting from the fact that Li was a fervent partisan of the Li Lisan Line, which both Mao and Li still believed to correspond in large measure to the position of the Central Committee.

112. See Averill, "Futian Incident," especially pp. 100–08. Some authors have argued that the AB Corps had ceased to exist in Jiangxi by 1930, but Averill offers convincing evidence that such a group did exist within the Guomindang. That does not mean, of course, that those denounced by Mao, or by his rivals in the Jiangxi Provincial Action Committee, were actually members of this organization, or even that their accusers sincerely believed they were.

Zhu De, and Peng Dehuai defeated the Guomindang troops sent against them by Chiang Kaishek in the first "Campaign of Encirclement and Annihilation," in late December 1930 and early January 1931.

Although Mao had thus won a substantial military victory, and the role of Li Lisan was greatly diminished, he would soon find himself faced with an even more powerful faction in the Central Committee, supported by the Soviet Union. Those developments, like the further unfolding of the struggle symbolized by the Futian Incident, belong to the period covered by Volume IV of our edition and will be illustrated by the materials published there.

Note on Sources and Conventions

This edition of Mao Zedong's writings in English translation aims to serve a dual audience, comprising not only China specialists, but those interested in Mao from other perspectives. In terms of content and presentation, we have done our best to make it useful and accessible to both these groups.

Scope. This is a complete edition, in the sense that it will include a translation of every item of which the Chinese text can be obtained. It cannot be absolutely complete, because some materials are still kept under tight control in the archives of the Chinese Communist Party. The situation has, however, changed dramatically since Mao's death, as a result of the publication in China, either openly or for restricted circulation (*neibu*), of a number of important texts.

Although the *Zhongyang wenxian yanjiushi* (Department for Research on Party Literature), which is the organ of the Central Committee of the Chinese Communist Party responsible for the publication of Mao's writings, has always disclaimed any intention of producing his complete pre-1949 works, it appeared at one time that an edition containing a very full selection was in fact on the way, at least for a part of his early career. An advertising leaflet dated December 20, 1988, announced the appearance, in the spring of 1989, of two volumes, *Mao Zedong zaoqi zhuzuo ji* (Collected Writings by Mao Zedong from the Early Period), and *Jiandang he da geming shiqi Mao Zedong zhuzuo ji* (Collected Writings by Mao Zedong during the Period of Establishing the Party and of the Great Revolution [of 1924-1927]), and invited advance orders for both volumes. The events of June 4, 1989, led first to the postponement of publication, and then to the decision to issue only the first of these volumes, for internal circulation, under the new title of *Mao Zedong zaoqi wengao, 1912.6-1920.11* (Draft Writings by Mao Zedong for the Early Period, June 1912-November 1920).

Prior to June 1989, further volumes in a similar format were in preparation. These plans have now been set aside, and no complete Chinese edition can be expected unless there is a radical change in the political situation. But, as forecast in Volume I, the corpus of available materials has now been substantially expanded by the publication in Beijing in December 1993 of two major series to commemorate the hundredth anniversary of Mao's birth. These are the *Mao Zedong wenji* (Collected Writings of Mao Zedong), of which the first two volumes, for the period 1921-1942, have now appeared, and the third volume is in press; and a six-volume edition of Mao's military writings, *Mao Zedong junshi wenji* (Collected Military Writings of Mao Zedong). We have therefore resumed the publication of our edition, after the pause for the centenary announced in Volume I.

Sources. Since there is no complete, or nearly complete, Chinese edition of Mao's writings from December 1920 onward, this and all subsequent volumes of our edition must be drawn from a variety of materials.

The twenty volumes of the *Mao Zedong ji* (Collected Writings of Mao Zedong) and the *Mao Zedong ji. Bujuan* (Collected Writings of Mao Zedong. Supplement), edited by Professor Takeuchi Minoru and published in Tokyo in the 1970s and 1980s still constitute the most important single collection of Mao's pre-1949 writings available outside China. (For details on this, and other sources cited below, see the Bibliography at the end of this volume.) Apart from the *Selected Works* of the 1950s (discussed below), other official Chinese editions of Mao's works, especially the two centenary series described above, contain a number of important new items. The various specialized volumes issued in the 1980s to commemorate Mao's ninetieth birthday also provide useful materials from the pre-1949 period. Those drawn on in this volume include *Mao Zedong nongcun diaocha wenji* (Collected Writings by Mao Zedong on Rural Surveys), published in 1982, and *Mao Zedong shuxin xuanji* (Selected Correspondence of Mao Zedong), which appeared in 1983.

As already indicated, all of these recent publications of the Party center are selective. Fortunately, we have been able to supplement them with materials drawn from an extremely wide range of sources, including contemporary newspapers and periodicals of the 1920s and 1930s, individual texts published in China for restricted circulation, and facsimiles of handwritten materials. Particularly important, for the period covered by this volume, is the series *Jiangxi dangshi ziliao* (Materials on Jiangxi Party History), published in Jiangxi Province, which contains the texts of many orders and letters signed by Mao that are not available elsewhere.

Information regarding the source we have followed is given in an unnumbered footnote at the beginning of each text. We have also included in these source notes information about the first publication, or the earliest known version, of the writing in question, whenever available. To avoid ambiguity, all works referred to in these notes are designated by their Chinese titles, sometimes in a shortened version. (For indications regarding short titles, and for full bibliographical details regarding all works cited, including those mentioned above, see the Bibliography at the end of this volume.)

Other things being equal, we have generally referred the reader who wishes to consult the Chinese text to the *Mao Zedong ji* and the *Bujuan* whenever the item in question appears there, because this series offers the convenience of a large quantity of materials in compact form. There are, however, instances in which the version contained in recent official Chinese publications is more accurate or more complete, and we have accordingly taken it as the basis for our translation. In such cases, the nature of the more significant differences is indicated in notes to the text in question, but we have not sought to show the variants systematically. That has been done only in dealing with changes made in the original text of Mao's writings when they were revised for inclusion in the official edition of his *Selected Works*.

Variants. While there are some differences between the various versions of texts by Mao published in the 1930s and 1940s, these are on the whole minor. Systematic revision of his pre-1949 writings was undertaken only from 1950 onward, in preparing the four-volume edition of the *Mao Zedong xuanji*, translated into English as the *Selected Works of Mao Tse-tung*. This problem did not arise in our Volume I, because its coverage ended in 1920, and the earliest item in the *Selected Works* is the "Analysis of All the Classes in Chinese Society," written in 1925. Apart from this text, Volume II contained the well-known "Report on the Peasant Movement in Hunan" of February 1927. The present volume includes four items of this kind, two from late 1928, one from December 1929, and one from January 1930.

Much ink has been spilled regarding the question of which version of the texts included in the official canon is more authentic, or more authoritative. Despite the passions formerly aroused by this issue, the answer seems rather obvious. For purposes of the historical record, only the text as originally written (when it is available) can tell us what Mao actually said in the 1920s and thereafter. For the study of Mao Zedong's thought, both versions have their uses in documenting how his ideas evolved over time. For purposes of defining ideological orthodoxy under the People's Republic, the *Selected Works* version is, of course, the ultimate standard.

In any case, the purpose of this edition is not to lay down which was the "real" Mao, but to enable the reader to distinguish between what Mao wrote at any given moment in his life, and the revised texts which were produced in the 1950s under Mao's close supervision, and often with his own active participation. We have endeavored to do this in the following manner:

1. The translations that appear here correspond to the earliest available version of the text in question.
2. Words and passages from this original version that have been deleted in the *Xuanji* are printed in italics.
3. Substantive and significant changes in the text, including additions made by Mao, or under his authority, in the 1950s, are shown in the footnotes. The *Mao Zedong ji* indicates meticulously *all* changes, including those that involve only matters of punctuation or style (such as the frequent replacement of the somewhat more literary conjunction *yu* by the more colloquial *he*, both meaning "and.") We have shown in the English version only those changes that appeared to us to have a significant impact on the meaning of the text. Any such judgement is, of course, in some degree subjective. We have sought to err on the side of showing too many variants, rather than too few, even when there was monotonous repetition in the changes, but we have not hesitated to leave out of account variants we regarded as trivial.

In footnotes of this kind, the words that appear *before* the arrow reproduce enough of the original text to identify what has been changed. The words that appear *after* the arrow correspond to what has been added or revised in the *Xuanji*. Because, in the rewriting of the 1950s, sentences and whole passages have often been substantially recast, it would take up far too much space, and make our text unreadable, to show every variant in detail. In some instances, it has been possible to show the new version in the form of complete sentences, but frequently we include only enough of the new wording to make plain the main thrust of the changes.

Because the official translation of the *Selected Works* has been available for four decades, and has been widely quoted in the literature, we have taken this version as our starting-point whenever it corresponds to the original Chinese text, but have modified or corrected it as we judged appropriate. As indicated above, in the Introduction, we have incorporated Roger Thompson's translation of the Xunwu investigation of May 1930 into this volume. In those few instances where other materials in this book had already been published in English, we have made our own translations, comparing them subsequently with existing versions.

Annotation. So that any attentive reader will be able to follow the details of Mao's argument in each case, we have assumed no knowledge of anything relating to China. Persons, institutions, places, and events are briefly characterized at the point where Mao first refers to them. Some individuals of secondary importance, especially those who appear only as names in a long list, are not included in the notes. We have also ruled out, with rare exceptions, annotations regarding people or events in the West. Despite these limitations, the reader will soon discover that the personages who appear in these pages are as numerous as the characters in a traditional Chinese novel.

To keep the notes within reasonable compass, we have generally restricted those regarding Mao's contemporaries to their lives down to the period covered by each volume. To make it easier to locate information, a number of references have been inserted indicating where the first note about a given individual appears in the volume. In a few instances, notes about Mao's contemporaries have been split into two, so that the reader will not be confronted in reading a text regarding the late 1920s with information relating to events of the 1930s which might themselves require explanation.

In most biographical notes dates of birth and death, separated by a hyphen, are given immediately after the name. A blank following the hyphen should, in principle, signify that the person in question is still living. In the case of individuals born in the 1870s and 1880s, this is obviously unlikely, but in many instances even the editors working in Beijing have not been able to ascertain the facts. We have done our best to fill these gaps, but have not always succeeded. Sometimes a Chinese source ends with the word "deceased" (*yigu*), without giving the date of death. Here we have inserted a question mark after the hyphen, and have mentioned the fact in the note. It should not be assumed that all those born in the 1890s for whom no second date is given are already dead; some of them are in fact very much alive as of 1995.

Beginning in 1928, the geography of the areas in Jiangxi, Hunan, and Fujian where the forces of Mao Zedong and Zhu De were operating figures extensively in the texts of Mao's writings. This is especially true for the latter half of 1930, where many of the orders translated here chronicle the progress of the Red Army from day to day, and even from hour to hour. To annotate all of the place names mentioned would have imposed an intolerable burden on the printer, and on the reader. We have therefore provided notes regarding geography, or the terrain, only in exceptional cases. In order to facilitate the understanding of the text, we have, however, included two maps, one of South-central China, and the other showing, on a larger scale, the principal localities in the base areas mentioned by Mao. These appear immediately after the present "Note on Sources and Conventions."

The introductions, including that to the present volume, should be considered in a very real sense as an extension of the notes. These texts will, we hope, help readers unfamiliar with Mao Zedong, or with twentieth-century China, find their *own* way through Mao's writings of the early period. Any controversial or provocative statements which they may contain are intended to stimulate reflection, not to impose a particular interpretation on the reader. This is a collection of historical source material, not a volume of interpretation.

Use of Chinese terms. On the whole, we have sought to render all Chinese expressions into accurate and readable English, but in some cases it has seemed simpler and less ambiguous to use the Chinese word. These instances include, to begin with, *zi* (courtesy name) and *hao* (literary name). Because both Mao, and the authors he cited, frequently employ these alternative appellations instead of the *ming* or given name of the individual to whom they are referring, information regarding them is essential to the intelligence of the text. The English word "style" is sometimes used here, but because it may stand either for *zi* or for *hao*, it does not offer a satisfactory solution. The Chinese terms have, in any case, long been used in Western-language biographical dictionaries of China, as well as in Chinese works.

Similarly, in the case of second or provincial-level, and third or metropolitan-level graduates of the old examination system, we have chosen to use the Chinese terms, respectively *juren* and *jinshi*. The literal translations of "recommended man" and "presented scholar" would hardly have been suitable for expressions which recur constantly in Mao's writings, nor would Western parallels (such as "doctorate" for *jinshi*) have been adequate. We have also preferred *xian* to "county" for the administrative subdivision which constituted the lowest level of the imperial bureaucracy, and still exists in China today. Apart from the Western connotations of "county," there is the problem that *xian* is also often translated "district" (as in the expression "district magistrate"), and "district" itself is ambiguous in the Chinese context. We have also preferred to use the Chinese word *li* rather than to translate "Chinese league" (or simply "league"), or to give the equivalent in miles or kilometers.

Approximately one-third of this entire volume consists of the investigations of local conditions to which Mao attached such importance. The most important of these are the Xunwu investigation of May 1930, reproduced here from Roger Thompson's monograph Mao Zedong, *Report from Xunwu* (Stanford: Stanford University Press, 1990), and the Xingguo investigation of October 1930. For obvious reasons, Mao employed in these texts many different units of measurement, which it has seemed on the whole preferable to leave untranslated, in order to avoid ambiguity. Each such unit is explained and defined at the point of its first occurrence. To make it easier to find the relevant footnotes, they have been included in the index, under the Chinese name of the unit in question.

Monetary units are, if possible, the source of even greater confusion than units of weight or volume. Generally speaking, the Chinese term for "dollar," *yuan*, has been left untranslated. It was, however, used in the 1920s and 1930s in two different senses: to designate 1 *yuan* silver coins, and the corresponding banknotes, and to refer to 10-cent or 20-cent silver coins totaling 1 *yuan*. This fractional currency did not enjoy its full face value, but was discounted by varying amounts depending on the time and place. To avoid ambiguity, whole-*yuan* coins or banknotes were commonly referred to as *da yang*, or "big foreign [dollars]," while the smaller coins and notes were called *xiao yang* or "small foreign [dollars]." As in Volume II of this edition, where this problem occurs in Mao's report of May 1926 on propaganda (p. 373 and note 3), we have translated *da yang* as "big foreign dollars." *Xiao yang*, in contexts where Mao explicitly discusses the relation between the two units, is translated "small foreign dollars." Where *yuan* appears without any further indications, it can be assumed that it almost certainly stands for fractional silver currency with a face value of one dollar. More information about monetary units is contained in the notes to the Xunwu and Xingguo investigations. (See also Appendix A to Roger Thompson's *Report from Xunwu*.)

In one other instance, we have used an English translation instead of a Chinese term. The main subdivisions in older writings, commonly referred to by their Chinese name of *juan*, are here called simply "volume" (abbreviated as "Vol."). Readers who consult the Chinese texts should have no difficulty in determining when this refers to the physically-separate volumes of modern editions, and when it means *juan*.

Presentation. As already indicated, we have tried to turn Mao's Chinese into good English. At the same time, since this is a work of reference, we have sometimes followed Mao in directions which do not accord with English usage. Mao frequently emphasized words or phrases by placing dots or circles next to each of the characters involved. In this edition, the corresponding text has been set in bold. Usually we have also added a note explicitly pointing this out, but it should be clearly stated that all such highlighting is Mao's, not ours. Also, some of the Chinese texts we have translated contain omissions, because the editors in Tokyo, or even those in Beijing, did not have access to a complete version of the document in question, or could not read a few characters. When the number of missing characters is small, each one is commonly represented in the printed Chinese text by a hollow square occupying the space which would normally be taken up by a single character. In our English version, each such square has been represented by the symbol [X], so the reader of the translation can see how much is missing. Where the gap is a long one, we have dispensed with this procedure, and conveyed the necessary information in a footnote.

Finally, like many Chinese writers, Mao tended to produce very long paragraphs, sometimes extending to several pages. Although this may seem monotonous to the English reader, we have generally followed his paragraphing exactly, because it must be presumed to reflect Mao's own sense of where the crucial turning-points in his argument are to be found. We have even, with the agreement of Roger Thompson, introduced the same practice into the translation of the Xunwu investigation, but we have not done so rigidly. In several instances, Professor Thompson has turned massive blocks of text containing figures and other data into tables which are much easier to follow, and we have retained this more accessible presentation. For the most part, however, the translations in this volume seek to reproduce Mao's original in form as well as in substance.

About the Maps

As explained above, in the Note on Sources and Conventions, the two maps which appear here have been included in order to aid the reader in following Mao's often minutely detailed account of the geography of battles and of political events. The different symbols employed indicate the importance of the towns in question. On Map No. 1, the solid squares designate provincial capitals; the hollow squares represent other major centers. Since Map No. 2 does not include any provincial capitals, solid squares are used there for the biggest cities shown. On both maps, the larger round dots correspond to *xian* administrative centers. The small dots are used for lesser localities prominently mentioned in the materials included in this volume. Since the aim of the maps is to illustrate the text, rather than to achieve cartographic precision, the location of the various dots may not always be mathematically exact.

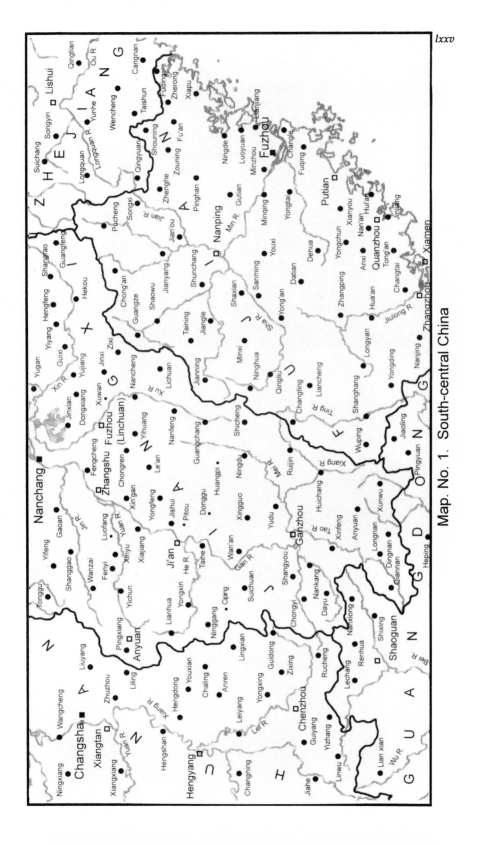

Map. No. 1. South-central China

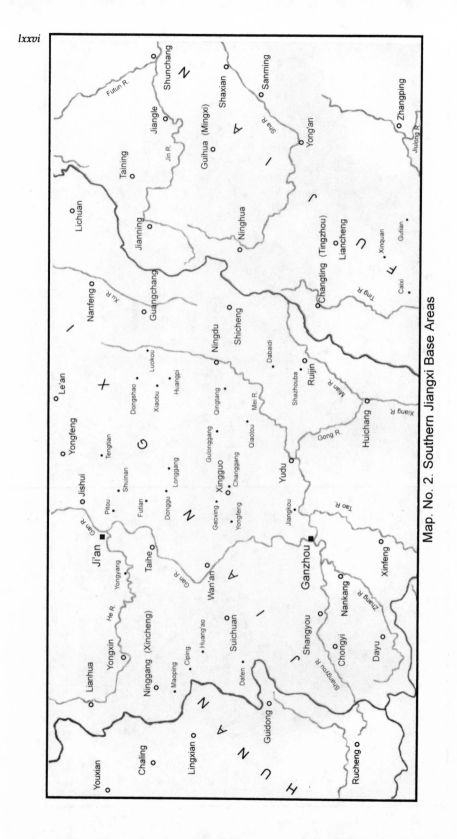

Map. No. 2. Southern Jiangxi Base Areas

Volume III
From the Jinggangshan to the
Establishment of the Jiangxi Soviets
July 1927–December 1930

MAO'S
ROAD TO POWER
Revolutionary Writings
1912 · 1949

—————————————1927—————————————

The Hunan Problem

(July 4, 1927)

Zhong,[1] Luo,[2] Mao, Zhong,[3] He,[4] Liu,[5] Zhou,[6] Shuzhi,[7] Teli.[8]

This text consists of a portion of the stenographic record of a meeting of the Standing Committee of the Politburo of the Chinese Communist Party. Our source is a photocopy of the handwritten text contained in *Mao Zedong junshi shengya* (Mao Zedong's Military Career), edited by the Chinese People's Revolutionary Military Museum (Beijing: Renmin chubanshe, 1993), p. 29. A passage from these minutes is reproduced in an article by Sun Gang, "Mao Zedong 'shangshan' sixiang de tichu" (How Mao Zedong Put Forward the Idea of "Going up the Mountains"), *Dangde wenxian*, no. 1, 1988, p. 78. Although the copy we have followed is not entirely clear, we believe that our translation renders the content with reasonable accuracy. Our source breaks off rather abruptly, but no fuller version is available to us.

1. Zhongfu was the *zi* of Chen Duxiu, who at this time was still secretary general of the Party. (On July 12, 1927, he was dropped from these functions, and from the Politburo, on the orders of the International.) For details regarding Chen, see below, the relevant note to the letter of November 28, 1929, to Li Lisan.

2. Luo stands for Luo Mai, pseudonym of Li Weihan (1896–1984), also known as Li Hesheng, a native of Hunan. After studying at the First Normal School in Changsha, Li had visited in France on the work-study program. He had been secretary of the Hunan Provincial Committee of the Chinese Communist Party from April 1923 until April 1927. At the Fifth Congress, he was elected to the Politburo, and on July 12, 1927, he became a member of the new temporary Standing Committee of the Central Committee.

3. This Zhong stands for Deng Zhongxia (1894–1933). Regarding Deng, see the note in Volume II of this edition, p. 115.

4. He stands for Cai Hesen (1895–1931), alternative name Cai Linbin, a native of Hunan who had been Mao's close friend since his student days. He had played an important role in convincing Mao that China should follow a Leninist path. (On this, see Mao's letter to him of January 21, 1921, in Volume II, pp. 35–36.) At this time he was a member of the Standing Committee of the Politburo; he was relieved of that responsibility in the reorganization of July 12, 1927.

5. Liu stands for Liu Zhixun (1898–1932), alternative name Keming, a native of Changsha, who had been secretary of the Hunan Provincial Peasant Association, and would shortly participate in the August 1 Nanchang Uprising.

6. Zhou stands for Zhou Enlai. For information on Zhou and his role from 1927 to 1930 see above, the Introduction to this volume.

7. Shuzhi is Peng Shuzhi (1895–1983), a native of Hunan, who had joined the Communist Party in 1921 and had served as an editor of the Party journal *Xiangdao*.

8. Teli is the *zi* of Zhang Guotao (1897–1979), a native of Jiangxi. After studying at Beijing University, he was elected a member of the Central Committee at the First Congress of the Chinese Communist Party in 1921, and thereafter played a major role in the Party. At this time, he was a member of the Standing Committee of the Politburo, and he remained on the new temporary Standing Committee of the Central Committee after July 12.

Hesen: There has been a clash between He[9] and Tang.[10] The forces of He are extremely isolated, and that being the case, He is the one who is making use of repression in the present incident.

Mao: The Changsha incident[11] is actually a case of He usurping Tang's political power. Tang has left, and he wanted us to join forces with him to restore [his power], but saw that we were not strong. Now he himself has recovered, but he still needs our help. Because we are not strong, Tang launched an attack on He, and tried to win over He's subordinates. Consequently, he is unable to attack Xu[12] immediately. This proves that the strength of the He faction in Hunan is very great. Tang truly needs our assistance, but because we are not strong he does not know where to start. Tang might be determined to get rid of He.

---

9. He Jian (1887–1956), *zi* Yunqiao, *hao* Rongyuan, was a native of Liling in Hunan. In October 1926 he had participated, under the command of Tang Shengzhi, in the capture of Wuchang. In April 1927 he had spoken out against radical land policies, arguing that many of the officers in his army were landlords. The regiment under Xu Kexiang which carried out the massacre in Changsha discussed in the following paragraph was part of his Thirty-fifth Army.

10. For a detailed note on Tang Shengzhi, see Mao's "Hunan Peasant Report" in Volume II, p. 430. As indicated there, Tang (who was commander-in-chief in Wuhan) was regarded by Mao in early 1927 as a "revolutionary military man," and he was elected to the provisional executive committee of the All-China Peasant Association on March 30, 1927. At the end of May, Tang, who was at the front of the Northern Expedition, was called upon to investigate the massacre that had just been carried out by his subordinates, and his own attitude began to change. In a telegram of June 26, published on June 29, he placed the primary blame on the peasants. Five days later, at the time of this meeting, the Communists were still hoping against hope that he would not break with them.

11. The reference is to the events of May 21, 1927, in Changsha and its environs, described below in the note regarding Xu Kexiang.

12. Xu is Xu Kexiang (1890–1967), a Hunanese, who was garrison commander in Changsha. On May 21, 1927, his forces violently repressed the labor unions and peasant associations in what came to be known as the "Horse Day Massacre" (this date being, according to the Chinese cyclical system, a day of the horse). The killing of Communists and peasant activists continued for many days in central Hunan, and the number of victims was very large. A document of June 13, 1927, "Latest Directive of the All-China Peasant Association," translated in Volume II of this edition, pp. 514–17, contains a graphic account of the atrocities committed on this occasion.

Zhong: He is linked to Feng[13] and Chiang.[14] Tang is on the side of the left wing. Wang[15] spoke about how to deal with Tang, and said our method was so careless that wasn't it natural Tang should be upset? Instead of opposing him, can we comfort him? For the sake of opposing Chiang we do not oppose him, but since four people have already been killed, we cannot make a public statement.

Wasn't the clash between Tang and He supposed to end in a compromise? Recently, however, Tang has indicated that he was against He, but where are the differences?

He does not have enough strength to resist Tang. The question is whether or not Tang is determined to finish off He. If we are really out to punish Chiang, in Wuhan at present we should encourage Tang to get rid of He.

Luo: Get in touch with Tang directly.

---

13. Feng is Feng Yuxiang (1882–1948), *zi* Huanchang, a native of Hebei, who rose through the ranks to become commander of the Sixteenth Mixed Brigade, which played a key role in the defeat of Zhang Xun's attempt at monarchical restoration in 1917. In 1924, Feng participated in a conspiracy against Wu Peifu which led to Wu's dismissal. He then reorganized his army as the First Army of the Guominjun (National People's Army), a title which he continued to use thereafter. In 1926, on his return to China after spending three months in the Soviet Union, Feng made a public declaration of allegiance to the Guomindang. By the spring of 1927, his troops occupied Shaanxi and northern Henan, and held an important position between the rival régimes in Wuhan and Nanjing. After discussions with Chiang Kaishek from June 19 to 21, 1927, Feng rallied to Nanjing, and began to purge Communists in areas under his control, thus decisively weakening the Wuhan government.

14. Jiang Jieshi (1887–1975), school name Zhongzheng, is (with Sun Yatsen) one of two persons referred to in these volumes by the Cantonese form of his name, in the spelling long used in the West, Chiang Kaishek. A native of Zhejiang, he received military training in Japan, where he joined the Tongmenghui in 1908. In 1923 he was appointed chief of staff in Sun's headquarters in Guangzhou, and in 1924 he became commandant of the Huangpu (Whampoa) Military Academy. In the summer of 1925, he took command of the newly formed National Revolutionary Army, and soon established himself as one of the top leaders of the Guomindang. In May 1926 he acted to curtail the influence of the Communists in the Guomindang. After the victorious advance of the Northern Expedition had further consolidated his power, he turned decisively against the Left and massacred the workers in Shanghai in April 1927, thus laying the foundation for his own preeminence in the régime subsequently established in Nanjing.

15. The reference is to Wang Jingwei (1883–1944), *zi* Jixin, a native of Guangdong. He joined the Tongmenghui in 1905 and was closely associated with Sun Yatsen from that time forward. It was he who drafted the testament which Sun signed on his deathbed in 1925. Though he ended his life as the premier of the Japanese puppet government in Nanjing, he was a leading figure in the Guomindang Left in 1925–1927. It was on his recommendation that Mao became acting head of the Propaganda Department of the Guomindang in 1925–1926. Many of the texts translated in Volume II reflect Mao's positive attitude toward him at that time.

Mao: Zhou[16] and Cao[17] said that they had their own difficulties. He is ferocious and insatiable—if you give an inch he wants a foot, he uses gold to bribe his opponents. Last time Cao said that we were pressing too hard. We think that the He faction is too weak.

Zhong: Our policy is to oppose Chiang, ally ourselves with Tang, and finish off He.

Shu: He forced Li[18] to dissolve the special Party headquarters in the Second Division of the Eighth Army; He's strength in Wuhan is very great.

Mao: Apart from promoting the dissension which already exists between Tang and He, we should draw Tang to our side, so that Wang [Jingwei], Deng,[19] and Zhang[20] will be able to exert some kind of influence. In addition to the decision by the Thirty-sixth [Army] to oppose Chiang, the Second Front [Army] has decided to oppose Chiang as well, and so has the Eighth Army. Ye Qi's division has links with Kaixin.[21]

Luo: Regarding the consultations between Tang and Feng.

Mao: If Feng's telegram is authentic,[22] Feng is sure to attack Wuhan; then the situation in Wuhan will be like that [X][X][X][X].

---

16. The reference is presumably to Zhou Lan (1891–1953), *zi* Shuqi, a native of Hunan, deputy commander of the Thirty-sixth Army. Tang Shengzhi, as military governor of Hunan, had sent him to Changsha as special commissioner to resolve the problems created by the Horse Day Massacre.

17. The reference may be to Cao Bowen (1893–1971), a native of Changsha, who was at this time a member of the Hunan Provincial Government.

18. The reference is to Li Pinxian, the commander of the Eighth Army, which had disarmed the picket corps of the Wuhan General Labor Union on June 18, 1927, while He Jian's Thirty-fifth Army occupied the headquarters of labor unions in Hankou and Hanyang.

19. Deng is Deng Yanda (1895–1931), *zi* Zesheng, a native of Guangdong. In 1924 he had helped create the Huangpu Academy, and at the Second Congress of the Guomindang in 1926 he was elected an alternate member of the Central Executive Committee. During the Northern Expedition he served as director of the General Political Department of the National Revolutionary Army. At the Third Plenum in March 1927, Deng had sided firmly with the Wuhan leftists against Chiang Kaishek, and he was at this time head of the Guomindang Peasant Department.

20. Zhang is Zhang Fakui (1896–1980), *zi* Xianghua, a native of Guangdong. After rising steadily in rank in the military forces supporting Sun Yatsen, he distinguished himself in 1926 as a divisional commander in the Northern Expedition. In the summmer of 1927 he led Wuhan's Second Front Army in a campaign against Chiang Kaishek.

21. Ye Qi (1882–1935) commanded the First Division under Tang Shengzhi. Ye Kaixin (1887–1937), *zi* Jingqiu, a native of Hunan, was at this time the commander of the Fifth Army.

22. The reference is to Feng's telegram of June 21, 1927, to Wang Jingwei and Tan Yankai, following his meeting with Chiang. It demanded that Borodin be immediately sent back to the Soviet Union, and that the leadership of the Nanjing government be accepted.

Teli: The problem now is linked to the maneuvers of the third party, which opposes Chiang, and also opposes the Communists.[23] I am afraid that Tang is already resolved to wipe out the Communists. As to whether he gets rid of He or reaches a compromise with him, that's his own affair.

Mao: It's a question of money.

He: I do not agree with Teli's view that the Hunan Incident concerns only Tang. As yet, Tang cannot go over to the third party.

Teli: That is not all. Even Wang has given in to the third party, and this has been made public by Zhang.

Zhong: It is impossible that Wang should surrender to Chiang.

He: Let us decide upon our policy and act on it.

Zhongfu: Tang has retreated to the second line, following the neutral line of Wang. We should push him toward Wang; it may not succeed, but we should not push him to He's side.

Decision: Support Tang and oppose Chiang.

Zhongfu: We continue to need the peasant association in Henan. Our masses are neither rich peasants nor rifraff, they are sharecroppers. We should use the slogan of reducing rent to lead their struggles.

. . .[24]

Weihan: The secret activities of the peasant movement in the countryside should be made public. We must also make use of the organizations of the popular masses.

Zhongfu: The central theme of the peasant associations is to get close to the sharecroppers. The sharecroppers should constitute the heart [of the peasant

---

23. Deng Yanda had already envisioned the possibility of a third force between the Communist Party and the Guomindang, but he did not publicly call for establishing a "provisional action committee of the Guomindang" until November 1927, and such an organization did not formally come into existence until 1930. This body, commonly known at the time as the Third Party, adopted a stand so critical not only of the Communists, but of Chiang Kaishek, that Chiang had Deng Yanda, who headed it, executed for treason in November 1931. In these discussions, *disan pai* (third party or faction) refers not to such a truly independent political tendency, but to the attitude of figures from the former Wuhan Left who claimed to occupy an intermediate position, but who in July 1927 were progressively aligning themselves with Chiang Kaishek.

24. There are suspension points here in the Chinese text, indicating that a passage of indeterminate length has been omitted.

associations], and we should use them to fill up the peasant associations. The slogan of confiscating the land will not have much effect in the countryside.

Weihan: The peasants do not want to turn the land over to the state; instead they want to own it themselves.

Zhongfu: At present, the slogan of rent reduction should be put forward in the countryside.

Hesen: The peasant movement in Hunan can get in touch with Deng Yanda.

Zhongfu: The Peasant Department of the Central Committee should send someone to reorganize the peasant associations.

Mao: It will be best to send a left-wing comrade.

Weihan: One of the big shortcomings in Hunan is that there are no Party comrades in the countryside.

Hesen: What should we do about the developments in the countryside? We should penetrate it if we can.

Hesen: (1) Quickly develop the Party in the rural areas; (2) the peasant self-defense army should go up the mountains; (3) the rent reduction movement [should be pursued].

Weihan: I do not agree with Hesen's second point, because if that happens the peasant army is sure to turn into a bandit force. They may think that guns can be hidden, but it will be better if they can be changed into a pacification corps.

Zhongfu:[25] The provincial Party headquarters should pay particular attention to the problem of recruitment by the various armies. If they want to run labor unions or peasant associations, we need not stand on ceremony in sending the masses to them in large numbers, but we must maintain our links with the peasant associations, in order to preserve their class nature and revolutionary nature. So every call for recruits should be made in conjunction with the peasant association, for we have people in every army political department. In this way, we will be able to see to it that the the peasants are turned into an armed force [*wuzhuang hua*]; otherwise, we will merely be engaging in empty talk about arming the peasants.

---

25. Beginning here, through the statement "Hesen and Teli: Agree with the previous speaker," this portion of the minutes is reproduced in the article by Sun Gang cited in the source note, and we have been able to check our transcription against this printed text.

Mao: There are two tactics for the Provincial Peasant Association: (1) They can transform themselves into a pacification force [*anfu jun*] with a legal existence, but this is really difficult to do. (2) Apart from this, there are two lines: (a) go up the mountains, or (b) join the army. By going up the mountains, we can create a foundation for a real military force, and supplies can be obtained by selling guns.

Teli: In my opinion, they can go up the mountains, but they need not have any links with the Communist Party. They can rob the rich and help the poor.

Zhongfu: We can't do that. Those who are unable to hide their guns can go up the mountains. The provincial Party headquarters should do their utmost to recruit soldiers.

Mao: If we do not maintain a military force, then in future, as soon as an emergency arises, we will be helpless [*wu banfa*].

Hesen:[26] Those who can remain should remain. (1) Send them to join the army, (2) preserve them as they are, (3) go up the mountains.

Mao: As regards the question of a training course, [X] [X] some comrades want to join the army.

Weihan: That can be postponed temporarily.

Zhongfu: The best thing is to become soldiers.

Hesen, Teli: Agree with the previous speaker.

Zhongfu: We may find a mutually beneficial method.

Weihan: There is a very good secret society in Hunan (the Red [X] Society),[27] they [X][X][28] us to be bandits.

---

26. This observation by Cai Hesen, and Mao's response to it, are omitted from Sun's article.

27. The Chinese is *Hong hui*, with a clear gap between the two words. We assume that the person taking notes on the meeting was uncertain about the name of this society, and therefore omitted the middle character. The reference may well be to the Red Spear Society (Hongqianghui), a peasant self-defense organization of a hybrid character which was active in the countryside in Hunan and elsewhere at this time. It is also possible, however, that the reference was to the Hongjianghui or Hong River Society, an organization formed by radical students from the members of various secret societies in Liuyang and Liling in eastern Hunan, and Pingxiang across the border in Jiangxi, to play a leading role in the uprising which took place there in 1906, and which still existed in both Hunan and Jiangxi.

28. As we have not been able to decipher these characters, it is not clear whether the peasant associations would teach the secret society to be bandits, or vice versa.

Mao: Guo Liang[29] can do secret work.

Zhongfu: Guo cannot survive, he should come out immediately and go to Shanghai to do work with the labor unions. More than a hundred people have already gone back. Though Wu Hongqian, Wu Hengqi, Dong Ziyuan and other left-wing leaders were attacked, we were not blamed.

Zhongfu: These people can be turned over to Wang, Deng and the other leftists. We should organize left-wing organizations.

Mao: We should try our best to preserve left-wing leaders in Hunan.

Zhongfu: Now the leftists have two doubts about the issue of left-wing organizations: (1) whether it will arouse the rightist . . . .

---

29. For a note regarding Guo Liang, see below, the "Guidelines on the Movement in Southern Hunan," August 1, 1927.

The Overall Tactics of the Peasant Movement at Present

Central Committee Circular,[1] Peasant Series, No. 9

(July 20, 1927)

1) The development of the peasant movement in recent years has already shown that the Chinese revolution has entered a new stage, the stage of agrarian revolution. The agrarian revolution is, quite simply, a process. The development of this process requires a democratic political power of the workers, peasants, and petty bourgeoisie led by the proletariat and an armed force of the workers and peasants. At present, this revolution has encountered a setback in China. The reasons are that (a) the leadership of the proletariat is not yet firmly established; in other words, the subjective organizational capacity of the proletariat is not sufficient for leading this revolutionary alliance of workers, peasants, and petty bourgeoisie; (b) an armed force of the workers and peasants has not been established; (c) our Party has made the mistake of having wavering and uncertain policies; (d) the class nature of the Wuhan Central Committee of the Guomindang, the

---

We have translated this document from *Zhonggong zhongyang wenjian xuanji* (Selected Documents of the Central Committee of the Chinese Communist Party), Vol. 3 (1927) (Beijing: Zhonggong zhongyang dangxiao chubanshe, 1989), pp. 216–22. There the source is given as the original mimeographed text in the Party archives, corrected in one instance on the basis of the version that appeared in the *Shaanxi shengwei tongxun* (Bulletin of the Shaanxi Provincial Committee), No. 6, March 10, 1928. Neither of these early publications is available to us. The text followed here is slightly more complete and accurate than one published in 1983, which is reproduced in the *Mao Zedong ji. Bujuan*, Vol. 9, especially as regards section (7).

1. Volume II of this edition ended with a series of documents illustrating Mao's role during the period of active collaboration between the Communists and the "Left Guomindang" in Wuhan, from March to June 1927. On July 15, 1927, at an enlarged session of the Standing Committee of the Central Executive Committee, the Wuhan Guomindang resolved to exclude Communists from their party, and this decision was made public on the following day. The present circular outlines the tactics laid down by the Central Committee of the Chinese Communist Party, and by the Peasant Department of the Central Committee, in response to the situation thus created. It was probably not drafted by Mao Zedong, but he was involved in the Peasant Committee, and undoubtedly made a contribution to shaping this text. His influence is reflected, in particular, in subsection d.iii of paragraph 6, which echoes his call of July 4, 1927, for "going up the mountains," translated above.

National Government, and the so-called revolutionary army is that they are the representatives of the landlord class and cannot shoulder the new historical task, the agrarian revolution. They have gone from restricting the worker and peasant movements to the completely counterrevolutionary stance of opposing and killing the workers and peasants. This betrayal is historically inevitable and shows that the deepening of the revolution is in no way surprising. The duty of our Party can consist only in waging resolute struggles against this new counterrevolution, gathering together all revolutionary forces, and carrying out the revolution in its new stage, the agrarian revolution. This is the objective situation of the revolution at present, which requires us to give an answer in the form of new tactics.

2) The peasants of the whole country are now gasping for breath under the new and old warlords. The burdens of over ten years of wars among the new and old warlords and the economic aggression of imperialism have been imposed mainly on the poor peasants. In the north, heavy taxes and levies have already made the majority of peasants abandon their land, so they cannot earn a living. In the various provinces of the south, the sufferings of the peasants are no different from those of the peasants in the north. Such freedoms as were won after repeated struggles have been completely taken away again. Whether in the south or in the north, the majority of the poor peasants (tenant peasants, semi-owner peasants, farm laborers, unemployed peasants, and the majority of owner-peasants[2]) who suffered excessive oppression have already awakened and are fighting their enemies everywhere. Especially in the south, since the killings by Li Jishen[3] and Tang Shengzhi,[4] the peasants' resistance and struggle have become more heroic and resolute. At the same time, new and old warlords, because of the conflicts among them and their internal contradictions, cannot establish a unified reactionary political regime. On the contrary, they now continue to collapse rapidly one after another. Therefore, the national revolutionary tide, though seemingly at a temporary low ebb, is actually rising. The present counterrevolutionary situation is only a reflection of the class conflicts at a time when the revolution has entered the period of solving the land question. Only by taking a resolute stand on behalf of this agrarian revolution can our Party lead the advance of this revolutionary tide. How can we develop the tide of the agrarian revolution? This goal can be reached only by quickly grasping the objective conditions, seizing every opportunity, raising appropriate slogans, and leading the broad masses to continue the struggle without interruption.[5] At present, the

---

2. *Zigengnong*, literally, "peasants who cultivate their own land."

3. Li Jishen (1886–1959), *zi* Renchao, a native of Jiangsu, was at this time military governor of Guangdong.

4. On Tang Shengzhi, see the relevant note to the text of July 4, 1927.

5. *Buduan de douzheng*. The adverb used here is the same as that in the Chinese translation of Trotsky's "permanent revolution" (*buduan geming*). It reflects the general climate in the Party in the autumn of 1927, when the Central Committee, headed by Qu Qiubai, called for *wujieduan geming*, "uninterrupted revolution."

impetus for promoting the agrarian revolution should come from slogans such as "refuse to hand in heavy taxes and supplementary levies," "refuse to pay in money and grain in advance," "reduce rent by 25 percent," "abolish usury," "confiscate the land of big landlords, local bullies and bad gentry, and counterrevolutionaries," "take over ancestral halls and monasteries and all other public land," "carry out [the policy of] land to the tiller," "down with greedy officials and corrupt bureaucrats," "down with the local bullies and bad gentry," "down with new and old warlords," "implement revolutionary democracy,"[6] "establish the political power of the peasants' associations in the countryside," "elect *xian* governments," "disarm the reactionary armies," "restore the peasants' associations," "arm the peasants," "peasants have the freedoms of assembly, association, speech, publication, and resisting rent and taxes."

3) In the various northern provinces such as Zhili, Shandong, Shanxi, and Henan, owner-peasants and semi-owner peasants account for the majority. They are increasingly bankrupt under the misery of harsh taxes and levies and become bandits or flee to other provinces. In these places, we should regard the owner-peasants, poor peasants, tenant peasants, and farm laborers as the center in uniting all the impoverished popular masses in the countryside, together with the small landlords, in a fighting alliance to oppose all heavy taxes and miscellaneous levies and advance payments of money and grain, oppose all requisitions in time of war, and reduce rent by 25 percent. At the same time, following on from the development of these struggles, we should move forward to seize political power in the countryside, seize weapons, and even confiscate the land of all ancestral halls, monasteries, despotic gentry and big landlords, and counterrevolutionaries, and redistribute it among the peasants and tenants[7] without compensation.

In the southern provinces of Hunan, Hubei, Jiangxi, and Guangdong, tenant peasants are the majority, followed by owner-peasants and semi-owner peasants. Tenant peasants are exploited by the landlords' heavy rent, while owner-peasants and small landlords are exploited in the extreme by the taxes and levies of the warlords. We should immediately, under the slogans of reducing rents "by 25 percent," and of resisting vexatious levies and taxes and taxation in advance, carry out rent and tax strikes. On the one hand, this will serve to lay bare the hypocritical features of the Wuhan and Nanjing governments' reduction of rent and taxes. On the other hand, it will enable us to unite all the impoverished popular masses in the countryside, including the small landlords, around the

---

6. Literally, "people's rights" (*minquan*), the second of Sun Yatsen's "Three People's Principles," a term commonly used at this time by Mao and others to convey the idea of democracy.

7. The term which appears here in our source is *dizhu*, "landlord." A note indicates that this is probably wrong, but offers no guess as to what the correct character might be. The version in the *Bujuan* has *dihu*, or "rural household." "Tenants" seems as good a solution as any, but the situation remains obscure.

nucleus of tenant peasants, owner-peasants, and poor peasants, in order to deal heavy blows to the local bullies and bad gentry, greedy officials and corrupt bureaucrats, to seize political power and arms in the countryside, under the peasants' associations, and even to confiscate all land belonging to despotic gentry and big landlords, counterrevolutionaries, and all ancestral halls and monasteries, in order to promote the agrarian revolution. This is the slogan which we should now propagate with all our might, concentrating the forces of the peasant masses in order to realize it.

Everywhere without exception, the struggle to oppose usurious loans with annual interest exceeding 20 percent should be carried out thoroughly, because this is the common demand of all the oppressed popular masses.

4) The agrarian revolution is simply a process, and the struggle for political power is a main characteristic of this process. Only through a struggle to seize political power can the rule of the feudal landlords in the countryside be overthrown, can the explosion of the land question be accelerated, and can a powerful organ be provided to resolve this issue. In various southern provinces such as Guangdong and Hunan, though the main characteristic of the peasant movement has already become the expropriation of the big landlords, it is in fact impossible to solve the land question on its own if the peasants have not grasped political power. According to the experiences in Hunan and Guangdong, this analysis is absolutely correct.

What is called the struggle for political power means establishing the revolutionary democracy of the peasants, or in other words, establishing the political power of the peasants' associations. In the history of the peasant movement in China, the peasants' associations are no longer an occupational organization, but are rural political alliances with the poor peasants as the backbone. The reason is that in fact the peasants' associations have united not only the ordinary peasants (those who cultivate the land and those who are unemployed), including handicraft workers, primary school teachers, and small merchants, but also those small landlords who have freed themselves from the influence of the big landlords and expressed sympathy for the peasants' associations. Therefore, the peasants' associations are currently the revolutionary political alliance of the poor peasants with the rest of the petty bourgeoisie in the countryside, the political power of the peasants' associations. This is a correct form of political power in the countryside, and we must begin realizing it everywhere in practice.

5) In light of the experience of the peasant movements in the two provinces of Hunan and Hubei, a few points for special attention regarding the organization of peasants' associations should be stated:

    a) In every province, the peasant movement should concentrate our human and financial resources in the areas that are important from a political, military, or communications standpoint, so as to set up central bases for leading the movement in the whole province. It is better to deepen the movement in these areas, at the expense of a temporary delay in expansion; we must absolutely not pursue expansion alone and forget the work in the central bases.

b) In addition to uniting ordinary peasant masses, handicraft workers, primary school teachers, and small merchants, the peasants' associations have also included small landlords under certain conditions. We must, however, pay attention to the composition of the leading organs of the peasants' associations at all levels. Generally speaking, small landlords are not admitted to the leading organs. In addition, tenant peasants, poor owner-peasants, and unemployed peasants should each make up at least one-fifth of the members of the executive committees of district associations. It is necessary to elect primary school teachers to the executive committees of district associations.[8]

c) The peasants' associations at all levels should set up women's departments and youth departments. The children's movement and children's organizations are completely under the direction of the youth department of the peasants' associations. Female peasants are to join the peasants' associations, and a separate body for women is not to be organized.

6) Only if there is a revolutionary armed force can victory be assured in the struggle of the peasants' associations for political power and in the agrarian revolution. But the present so-called revolutionary armies are in fact led by reactionary officers who represent the landlord class and are slaughtering the peasants everywhere. Armed clashes have already become an extremely widespread phenomenon in the peasant movement and are therefore a most serious and urgent issue at the present stage of the peasant movement. Any participant in the peasant movement who has neither given 120 percent of his attention to this issue, nor sought a correct answer to it, has in fact not prepared for the victory of the peasant revolution. The Party headquarters at all levels should use all sorts of methods to provide military training to the peasants and to enable them to arm themselves. We now point out a few important ways of doing this:

a) Using various methods to seize weapons from the landlord class and all counterrevolutionaries and to arm the peasants with them.

b) Brave and trained members of the peasants' associations may join the armies in an organized way to receive military training and to carry out the work of undermining the army organizations and seizing their weapons by various methods.

c) The above methods may be also adopted with regard to the military forces of the landlord class, such as the militia headquarters [*tuanfangju*] and the local militia [*baoweituan*], when it is impossible to take over their arms immediately.

---

8. This recommendation may not be unrelated to the fact that Mao himself had been a primary school teacher and the principal of a primary school.

d) At present, it is not possible for peasant armed forces to exist openly, under names such as "peasants' self-defense army" or "peasant army." Such forces can exist only in the following three forms: (i) under legal names such as "household militia" [aihutuan], "local militia" [bao-weituan], and "united village association" [lianzhuanghui]; (ii) training in a dispersed and secret way in peacetime and concentrating forces when battles occur; (iii) in case both methods are impossible, "going up the mountains."

e) In the case of armed groups in the north such as the Red Spear Society and the Big Sword Society,[9] the Party should send suitable comrades to mix with their lower-level masses and lead them to fight for their own interests, so as to win their trust, thus enabling them gradually to free themselves from their reactionary leaders and become a revolutionary armed force. It is absolutely impermissible to begin by attacking their reactionary leaders, or by proposing changes in the form of their organizations, or doing away with superstition. Such mechanical and hasty methods cannot win the support of the masses. At the same time, the past methods of only contacting their leaders or borrowing the names of military leaders to inspire them are also ineffective.

In the south, the secret societies [huifei] who generally use the slogan of "robbing the rich to help the poor" have, during the high tide of the peasant revolution, introduced the slogans of "down with the local bullies and bad gentry" and "down with greedy officials and corrupt bureaucrats." They have also been capable in their actions of drawing close to the peasants' associations, or even of joining an alliance under the peasants' associations. Originally, most of them were unemployed peasants or peasants on the brink of bankruptcy. Their economic slogans, such as "robbing the rich to help the poor," are close to the slogan of "confiscating the land of big landlords." Naturally they are the enemies of the landlord class, and the opponents of the reactionary armies in cities (before they are sold out by their reactionary leaders). If they can be led to take the correct revolutionary road, they will certainly become forceful allies of the agrarian revolution. Their lives and environment are, however, altogether abominable. Most of their leaders are waiting for the opportunity to become warlords. Therefore, they cannot obtain correct political leadership in taking the revolutionary road and fighting consistently for certain goals. On the contrary, they regard "looting and pillaging" as their normal way of life. Their ideas and actions follow those of their leaders completely. Consequently, we must understand the active role of the

---

9. The Big Sword Society was a secret society of the traditional type; the Red Spear Society, which had been praised by Li Dazhao in an article of 1926, was a hybrid organization, halfway between a secret society and a peasant association. In its letter of June 7, 1929, to the Chinese Communist Party regarding the peasant problem, the Comintern would stress the importance of making use of such forces to promote the revolution.

secret societies in the peasant revolution on the one hand, but at the same time we must understand that they may turn toward reaction. Our goal is to strengthen their revolutionary spirit and revolutionary training, so that they will turn into forceful supporters of the agrarian revolution under the leadership of the peasants' associations. The methods are basically the same as those discussed above.

7) In the past, the Party's organizations among the peasants were unable to fulfill their leadership responsibilities properly. In many places, although there were struggles involving hundreds of thousands of peasant masses, usually only a few comrades were active there, and the Party organizations there did not carry out their leadership responsibilities. In some places, although there were organizations of the Party, they did not go deeply among the masses (remaining at the level of district associations and not reaching township associations). In some cases, even though there were organizations, they played no role. In others, the comrades responsible for the peasant movement ignored the collective leadership of the Party and were accustomed only to individual actions. Consequently, all the work of our Party in the countryside often appears to be a case of "Let there be men and the government will flourish; but without the men, their government decays and ceases."[10] If our Party cannot actively fulfill its organizational responsibilities in time of peace, then in [X][X] time,[11] there is naturally even less hope that it can become the sole leading core of the struggle of the masses. If the leadership of our Party is to be set up properly among the peasantry, then first, the Party branches should be able to reach down to township level and truly become the leading core of the mass struggle. Second, the Party's guidance of the peasants must go through the Party and the [Youth] League (correcting the past mistakes of [X][X] leaders). Both the Party and the League must submit absolutely to the direction of the Party. Third, peasant departments should [X][X] be set up in the Party headquarters of every province, to supervise and [X][X] the effective implementation by Party headquarters at all levels of the plans which are put forward once a month or once every two months for the peasant movement of the province as a whole.

An Zhongyuan
Zong Rongming [12]

---

10. The words cited here, which the authors of this circular place in quotation marks, correspond to a slightly abridged citation from *The Doctrine of the Mean*, XX, 2 (Legge, Vol. I, p. 405).

11. The missing expression must be one meaning war or struggle.

12. In the context of the repression which followed the break with Chiang Kaishek in April and with the Left Guomindang in July 1927, the Chinese Communist Party took various security measures, including the use of code words in its written communications. Some of these involved the use of characters which sound vaguely similar to the intended meaning, but are written quite differently. This is the case of the two names which appear here. An Zhongyuan evokes Dang zhongyang, or Party Central; Zong Rongming stands for Zhong[yang] nongmin [weiyuanhui], or Central Peasant Committee.

Declaration of Members of the Central Committee[1]

(August 1, 1927)

Since the Second National Congress, when we were elected as members of the Party Central Committee, thanks to the great trust placed in us by the comrades of the whole country, we have striven for the future of the national revolution in accordance with the principles and policies of this party, and the teachings of the late Director General.[2] Thanks to the cooperation and hard work of the comrades of the whole country, the party and the state have been able to traverse several critical periods without suffering excessive damage. Now the crisis of the party and the state is even more acute than in the past, so we must inform our comrades of the whole country honestly of the true facts regarding recent events and point out the only way for them to continue the struggle. Since the March Twentieth Incident[3] last year, we have seen that in the course of the revolution, there are always a few ambitious people, with military force at their command, who are trying to collude with the counterrevolutionary forces in order to seek their own interests rather than those of the party. At that time, taking the interests of the revolution as a whole into consideration, and hoping that by promoting the Northern Expedition and developing the force of the broad masses of the people, it would be possible one day to deter the conspiracy of these careerists, for the space of a year we went so far as to bend our wills and abase ourselves by dealing with Jiang Zhongzheng[4] and the like. We could not venture to abandon the comrades of the whole country, ignore the future of the revolution, and go

---

This declaration originally appeared in the Nanchang *Minguo ribao*, August 1, 1927. Our source is the version reproduced in the *Mao Zedong ji. Bujuan*, Vol. 2, pp. 291–95, from a documentary collection published in China in 1979.

1. As will be seen from the text, the reference is to the Central Executive Committee of the Guomindang. Although Wang Jingwei and the leadership of the Wuhan Left had decided on July 15 to break with the Communists, a few individuals remained committed to the united front, the most eminent of these being Sun Yatsen's widow, whose name heads the list at the end of this document.

2. Sun Yatsen.

3. Chiang Kaishek's coup of March 20, 1926, against the Soviet military advisers, which led in May 1926 to a purge of Communists from senior positions in the Guomindang.

4. Chiang Kaishek, here called by his school name Zhongzheng.

off, claiming to be above politics and worldly considerations. From then until the spring of this year, Renegade Chiang Kaishek first sought to move the party headquarters and the government to Nanchang, in order to achieve his personal goal of exercising a reactionary autocracy; then he openly turned traitor, setting up a separatist régime in the southeast, colluding with the warlords, cruelly killing comrades, and slaughtering the masses. To ensure the survival of the party and the state, comrades of the whole country have initiated the movement to restore party rights. The Third Plenum of the Central Committee was also held and passed various resolutions for consolidating the revolutionary forces. The principles and policies of this party, and the teachings of the late Director General, are under threat and must be restored. This movement for restoring party rights depends entirely, however, on the united efforts of the comrades of the whole country. Only thus can a heavy blow be dealt to Renegade Chiang Kaishek, and the future of the revolution regained. Tang Shengzhi and other military men, however, have also seized the occasion to pursue their private interests of getting rid of Chiang and expanding their own forces, in the name of supporting this movement. We clearly know that these military men are in no way sincere about the revolution, and it is inevitable that they will endanger the party and the state in the future. Furthermore, only if our party follows the teachings of the late Director General and secures the participation of the broad peasant masses in the revolution can we consolidate the revolutionary bases. Therefore, not only do we believe that the development of the peasant movement by the broad masses of the peasants in Hunan and Hubei and their revolutionary actions to solve the land problem and to establish self-government in the villages should not be repressed; we also hold that this is precisely the result of our party's principle of "land to the tiller" being gradually understood by the broad masses of the peasants. Only when the broad masses of the peasants have such an understanding and carry out such actions can we destroy the remaining feudal forces and have a real guarantee for the revolutionary forces of this party, and for a new China of the people, by the people, and for the people. After the Second Northern Expedition began, General He Jian,[5] who is under Tang Shengzhi's command, unexpectedly began to plot betrayal. He instigated Xia Douyin and others to make a sudden attack on Wuchang,[6] and secretly ordered Xu Kexiang[7] and others to launch a revolt in Changsha. At this crucial moment, the military men and those in collusion with them, who controlled the military forces, simply sat by and watched, and were unwilling to join in putting

---

5. On He Jian, see the relevant note to the text of July 4, 1927.
6. Xia Douyin was the commander of the Fourteenth Independent Division. On May 13, 1927, he suddenly transferred his allegiance from the Left Guomindang to Chiang Kaishek and moved toward Wuhan, though his attack was beaten off.
7. On Xu Kexiang, see the relevant note to the text of July 4, 1927.

down the rebel troops. Frightened by the reactionary bluff and bluster, a few weak leaders in the Central Party Bureau became wavering and soft in their attitudes and dared not take resolute and appropriate punitive actions against the rebel troops. In the meantime, Zhu Peide[8] in Jiangxi, who was planning to compromise with Mr. Chiang, also took action to expel the revolutionaries and to halt the labor and peasant movements. This was again tolerated and regarded as natural by a few leaders of the Central Party Bureau. After Feng Yuxiang entered Henan, he even went openly to Xuzhou to meet Renegade Chiang[9] and sent a telegram to the Central Committee threatening to dismiss all the political workers in the army. Again a few leaders of the Central Party Bureau were unable to restrain this. They could not help dealing with matters and taking decisions, but they disrupted their own measures. Under the direction of these few weak leaders, the Central Party Bureau has completely lost its prestige. They are simply dependent on the pleasure of the military men and have used the sacred resolutions of the Central Committee to seek their private gains. Because of this, the military men have become even more swollen with arrogance, while the party and the government have become nothing but a tool for the military men. Since Tang Shengzhi returned to Hunan, he has arbitrarily reorganized the provincial government and the provincial party headquarters and ceaselessly applied a policy of massacre. Tens of thousands of party members and peasants who had struggled faithfully were hacked to pieces in the whole of Hunan, and five thousand in Hubei. The Central Committee in Wuhan, however, expressed the following opinions regarding the killing of these tens of thousands of comrades: first, most of them were Communists; secondly, those killed had not obeyed the orders of the Central Committee and had acted on their own; third, the principle of "land to the tiller" "should be dealt with through politics and the laws." Today the facts are obvious and can hardly be covered up. Among those killed in Hunan and Hubei, apart from a certain number of Communist Party members who were faithful to the revolution and joined this party, more than 80 percent were members of this party who had not joined any other party. These tens of thousands of party members were all engaged in arduous work

---

8. Zhu Peide (1888–1937), *zi* Yizhi, was a native of Yunnan and a graduate of the provincial Military Academy. Long associated with Sun Yatsen, he was elected to the Guomindang Central Executive Committee in 1926 and commanded the Third Army in the Northern Expedition. Because of a personal relationship with Zhu De, dating back to his days at the Yunnan Military Academy, Zhu Peide opted for Wuhan at the time of the split between Chiang Kaishek and the Guomindang Left and became governor of Jiangxi. In May 1927, however, he began to take action against the Communists in Jiangxi, even while supporting Wuhan against Nanjing. After the Nanchang Uprising of August 1, 1927, Zhu Peide played an important role in the peace negotiations among conflicting Guomindang factions.

9. On Feng Yuxiang, see the relevant note to the text of July 4, 1927.

among the masses of the workers and peasants, in accordance with our party's resolutions regarding the peasants and the workers and the teachings of the late Director General. Now they have been cruelly murdered in this way by the reactionary military men, and the Central Committee in Wuhan has even accused them of disobeying the orders of the Central Committee. Their selling out of the party and of their comrades has reached this extreme! The teachings of the late Director General state that the problem of "land to the tiller" should not be solved by politics and the law. Now the Central Committee in Wuhan uses politics and the law to protect Tang Shengzhi and the like in massacring party members, workers, and peasants. They are even going so far as to use politics and the law to solve the problem of massacring the peasants. Such [they claim] was the Director General's real intention! Tang Shengzhi, He Jian, and the like went on a rampage in Wuhan, the capital. They surrounded the Central Party Bureau, occupied the offices of the mass organizations, robbed the Central Bank, arrested the members of the Central Committee, searched the houses of Comrade Song Qingling, the widow of the Director General, and of Comrade Chen Youren,[10] the foreign minister. Intimidated by such military men, the Central Committee put forward a resolution on splitting with the Communists, in an attempt to drive all the faithful members out of the Party, so as to facilitate the counterrevolutionary schemes of the military men. They went to this extreme in their shameless betrayal of the party! The resolution on splitting with the Communists could not be put through the Standing Committee of the Central Committee. Now these people want to call for the convening of a plenum of the Central Committee on August 15. In the meantime, they have already begun to make up stories and twist the facts in Wuhan and in all the other institutions under their control. They are carrying out a big anti-Communist propaganda campaign, in an attempt to force the members of the Central Committee to pass their resolution, so as to cover their illegal acts of betrayal. While witnessing all this, we know that a few leaders in Wuhan have already willingly accepted the domination of the military men and are selling out the party and themselves. If we still suffer patiently and do not struggle against them, thus facilitating their schemes of betrayal, how will we be able to explain all this to our comrades throughout the country who have placed their great trust in us? What shall we say to the Director General and earlier martyrs of our party? We have therefore decided, for the sake of the future of the revolution and of the party, to leave Wuhan one after the other and to try our best to lead the comrades of the whole country in a struggle to preserve the revolutionary legitimacy of this party. What is more painful is that Comrade Wang Jingwei,[11] who used to hold the leading position in this party, has this time adopted a vague attitude,

---

10. Commonly known in the West as Eugene Chen.
11. Regarding Wang Jingwei, see the relevant note to the text of July 4, 1927.

has been surrounded by a bunch of bad people, and has finally yielded to the military force of the warlords. After this, he uses a glib tongue to befuddle the minds of the public. Having thus submitted, he makes confused and contradictory speeches and acts in an abnormal manner. Compared to his behavior when he first returned from abroad, all his actions now are like those of a totally different person. When the Director General was dying, he was worried that some leaders of this party might be won over by the soft tactics of the enemy. Now, less than three years after the Director General's death, more than half the old leaders of the party have been won over by the enemy. How distressing it is to think of this! When we consider the difficulties that the Director General encountered during forty years spent in building this party, and the great expectations placed in us by millions of revolutionary comrades throughout the country, we cannot sit and watch the glorious history of this party ruined by a few old leaders. We therefore solemnly declare: We have not given our consent to all the directives and resolutions recently issued by a few members of the Central Committee in Wuhan, falsely appropriating the name of the Central Party Bureau, and we will not be held responsible for them. The so-called Party Bureaus and governments in Wuhan and Nanjing have both become the tools of the new warlords. They have misinterpreted the Three People's Principles, and scrapped the Three Great Policies.[12] They are criminals, condemned by the Director General and by the national revolution. By different routes, these leaders and Chen Jiongming,[13] Yang Ximin,[14] Feng Ziyou,[15] Xie Chi, Zou Lu,[16] and their ilk are heading toward the same end. The sacrifices of the Northern Expedition should have brought about the full implementation of the testament of the Director General of our party, rescued the masses of the people from their sufferings, and liberated the workers and peasants, thus promoting the

---

12. The so-called Three Great Policies listed below in the second of the proposals put forward in this document, were advocated by Sun Yatsen in the political testament which he endorsed on the brink of death in Beijing in 1925. Their significance has been a subject of dispute.

13. Regarding Chen Jiongming see, in Volume II, p. 228, the relevant note to Mao's editorial of October 20, 1925.

14. Regarding Yang Ximin see, in Volume II, p. 264, the relevant note to "Announcement of the Chinese Guomindang to All Party Members Throughout the Country and Overseas Explaining the Tactics of the Revolution," December 4, 1925.

15. Regarding Feng Ziyou see, in Volume II, p. 263, the relevant note to the text of December 4, 1925. Although he had opposed cooperation with the Communists since 1924, Feng was discredited at this time because of his participation in the assault on, and abduction of, two prominent Guomindang members who had come to Beijing at the end of 1925 to attend the Western Hills conference and never again enjoyed significant political influence.

16. On Zou Lu and Xie Chi, both leading participants in the Western Hills conference, see in Volume II, pp. 280 and 328, the notes to Mao's articles "Zou Lu and the Revolution," December 5, 1925, and "Opposition to the Right-Wing Conference Spreads Throughout the Whole Country," January 10, 1926.

revolutionary forces. Now the old and new warlords work hand in glove with each other in massacring the workers and peasants and oppressing the popular masses. This will not only waste the sacrifices of the Northern Expedition but also result in the creation of separatist warlord régimes like those that existed before, causing war and chaos in China to come and go in endless cycles. From now on, we have no choice but to lead the comrades of the whole country in fighting all our lives to carry out the Director General's testament. We dare not hesitate, for this would adversely affect the revolutionary situation as a whole. At this moment, the comrades of the whole country should adhere to the spirit in which the Director General built this party and struggle resolutely against those who make fraudulent use of the revolutionary name of this party. We especially hope that the loyal commanders and soldiers, under the direction of this party, will be able to summon up the unflinching courage of the Director General and thus make it impossible for those who have usurped the name of the Party to make use of even one soldier. We hope they will fight to the end for the realization of the true revolutionary program of this party. At this difficult moment, all our comrades must unite closely, and fight for the following proposals:

1. Oppose the directives and resolutions issued in the name of the Central Party Bureau by a few members of the Central Committee in Wuhan.
2. Uphold the Three People's Principles for building a society of the people, by the people, and for the people, and support the Three Great Policies of allying with Russia and with the Communist Party, and assisting the workers and peasants. Oppose every attempt to misinterpret or to betray the Principles and the Policies.
3. Work hard to build a new base area, so as to convene the Third National Congress outside the spheres of the old and new warlords, to discuss the question of concentrating the revolutionary forces and continuing the revolutionary work.
4. Before the Third National Congress is convened, the representatives from the Provincial Party Headquarters will elect leaders trusted by the whole Party to form a provisional leading body for the revolution.
5. Continue to fight against the imperialists, and strive for the solution of the land problem. Totally change the weak, compromising, and excessively accommodating attitudes of a few members of the Central Committee in Wuhan. Correctly and bravely appeal to the general public with our revolutionary programs in order to arouse the masses.
6. Make every effort to abolish the exorbitant taxes and levies, to end all corrupt practices, and to realize this party's positions representing the interests of the common people.
7. Actively prepare our forces for wiping out the new-style warlords such as Chiang, Feng [Yuxiang], and Tang [Shengzhi], who represent the forces

of all the imperialists, the northern warlords, and feudal society within the country.

We believe that all these things are extremely urgent at the moment. Only if the whole Party is determined to strive resolutely and in unison for these programs will the revolutionary movement in China have a chance of success. Let all our comrades remember this!

Sun Song Qingling, Deng Yanda, Tan Pingshan, Peng Zemin, Lin Zuhan, Wu Yuzhang, Yu Shude, Yun Daiying, Enkebatu, Yang Baoan, Liu Yazi, Gao Yuhan, Xie Jin, Bai Yunti, Mao Zedong, Dong Yongwei, Jiang Hao, Han Linfu, Xia Xi, Xu Suhun, Deng Yingchao, Qu Wu.[17]

---

17. Without taking up the space which would be required to annotate each of these names, it should be pointed out that, of the nine full members of the Central Executive Committee listed here, seven (Tan Pingshan, Peng Zemin, Lin Zuhan, Wu Yuzhang, Yu Shude, Yun Daiying, and Yang Baoan) were Communists. Mao, Xia Xi, Deng Yingchao (Zhou Enlai's wife), and many of the alternate members were also Communists. Several of the others, including prominent figures such as Song Qingling and Deng Yanda, were strongly sympathetic to collaboration with the Communist Party. By issuing this declaration as a Guomindang document, Mao and his comrades were faithfully obeying Stalin's orders, rescinded only in mid-September, that the "Guomindang flag" should still be used in China.

General Guidelines of the Hunan Provincial Committee of the Chinese Communist Party on the Movement in Southern Hunan

(August 1, 1927)[1]

1) The center of the special movement in southern Hunan should be Rucheng *xian*, and from this center, four or five *xian* such as Guidong, Yizhang, Chenzhou, and others should be occupied next, to create a political situation and organize a revolutionary leading organ like a government which will carry out the agrarian revolution, oppose the Tang [Shengzhi] government in Changsha, and establish liaison with the anti-Tang forces in western Hunan. Such a government in southern Hunan has three functions:

a) To destabilize further the already unstable rule of Tang in Hunan, and promote the rapid disintegration of Tang's subordinates.

b) To serve as the vanguard of the peasant uprising in the whole province.

c) To create centers of revolutionary force for the purpose of overthrowing the Tang government.

2) The military aspect:

a) The Central Committee is requested to order Comrade Peng Pai not to move the peasant army of Guangdong now in Rucheng to other places.[2]

This text has been translated from *Mao Zedong junshi wenji*, Vol. 1, pp. 4–5, which states that it has been taken from a handwritten copy in the Party archives.

1. This document was drawn up by Mao in late July and approved by the Standing Committee of the Central Committee on August 1, 1927.

2. Regarding the revolutionary career of Peng Pai, who had begun organizing peasant associations in his native province of Guangdong as early as 1921, see Fernando Galbiati, *P'eng P'ai and the Hai-lu-feng Soviet* (Stanford: Stanford University Press, 1985). Peng himself was, at this time, about to embark on the retreat from Nanchang toward Shantou (Swatow) and was nowhere near Rucheng, which is located in the southeastern corner of Hunan, on the edge of what would later become the Jinggangshan base area. The reference is apparently to the Haifeng peasant army under Wu Zhenmin, which had undertaken an expedition northward toward Hunan after the failure of an uprising in Haifeng and Lufeng in May 1927.

b) The one thousand troops in Liu[yang] and Ping[jiang] should immediately leave for Rucheng under the command of Guo Liang.[3]

c) One regiment of the Jiangxi revolutionary army should be dispatched to Rucheng.

Since these three units have the strength of approximately one division, with the regiment of the revolutionary army as the core, they can certainly occupy at least five *xian* or more.

3) Southern Hunan must come under the orders of the Jiangxi revolutionary leading organ. After the founding of the revolutionary Guangdong government,[4] it will come under the orders of the Guangdong government and supply all its needs. The Central Committee should order the Jiangxi side to implement this plan.

4) The Party's Southern Hunan Special Committee should come under the orders of the Hunan Provincial Committee, but may act independently when communications are interrupted.

---

3. Guo Liang (1901–1928), also known as Guo Jingru, a Hunanese from Changsha *xian*, had been a fellow student of Mao's at First Normal School and a member of the New People's Study Society. He played a leading role in the labor movement in the 1920s and was elected to the Central Committee of the Chinese Communist Party at the Fifth Congress. In August 1927, after participating in the Nanchang Uprising, he was, like Peng Pai, retreating southward through Jiangxi and Fujian. On August 3, 1927, in the context of a program for peasant uprisings in the four provinces of Hunan, Hubei, Guangdong, and Jiangxi, the Central Committee proceeded to appoint the Southern Hunan Special Committee mentioned in paragraph (4) of this document. (See below, the note to the text of August 9, 1927.) Guo was one of the four members, together with Mao Zedong, and it was no doubt in that capacity that he was to take charge of the two regiments located near Pingjiang and Liuyang. In early 1928, Guo was appointed secretary of the Hunan-Hubei-Jiangxi Special Committee, but was soon arrested and was executed in Changsha on March 29, 1928.

4. I.e., after the success of the uprising that Peng Pai launched in Haifeng and Lufeng at the end of October, which was expected to spread to all of Guangdong.

Remarks on the Report of the Representative of the International at the August 7 Emergency Conference

(August 7, 1927)

The whole of the Comintern representative's report is very important.[1] First, the issue of the Guomindang has long been a problem for our Party and has not yet been resolved. There was, in the first place, the issue of joining it, and then there emerged the question of what kind of people were supposed to join it, i.e., that industrial workers should not join it. In fact, we did not make up our mind whether we should instruct the peasants to join it or not, let alone the industrial workers. At that time, a fundamental idea of ours was that the Guomindang belonged to others. We did not realize that it was an empty house waiting for people to move in. Later, like a maiden getting into the bridal sedan chair, we reluctantly moved into this empty house, but we never made up our mind to play the host there. I think this was a big mistake. Afterward, some of our people argued that industrial workers should also join it. I heard that in Hubei a decision was made to that effect, but it was merely empty words on paper which were never carried out. In the past, there were some among the masses who, disregarding the orders of the Center, seized some lower-level organs of the Guomindang and played the host in the house. But this ran counter to the opinion of the Center. It is only now that we have changed our tactics, so as to let the workers, peasants, and masses enter the

---

We have translated this text from *Baqi huiyi* (The August 7 Meeting) (Beijing: Zhonggong dangshi ziliao chubanshe, 1986), pp. 57–58. According to the preface to this volume, most of the documents it contains were there openly published for the first time. Mao's remarks regarding Lominadze's report had, however, been copied down at the Museum of the History of the Revolution and included in the *Mao Zedong Ji. Bujuan*, Vol. 2.

1. The reference is to Besso Lominadze, a protégé of Stalin, who had replaced M. N. Roy as Comintern representative to the Chinese Communist Party in late July 1927. (Borodin, who left China at about the same time, had been representative to the Guomindang.) For a translation of Lominadze's report, see Saich, *Rise to Power*, Doc. C.3, pp. 308–13.

Guomindang to play the host there. Second, the issue of the peasants. The peasants want a revolution, Party [members] close to the peasants also want a revolution, but the upper level of the Party is a different story. Before I arrived in Changsha, I had no reason to oppose the Party's decision, which sided entirely with the landlords. Even after arriving in Changsha, I was still unable to answer this question. It was not until I had stayed in Hunan for more than thirty days that I completely changed my attitude. I made a report in Hunan expressing my opinion, and simultaneously also sent a report to the Center.[2] This report had its impact in Hunan, but it had no influence whatever on the Center. The broad masses inside and outside the Party want revolution, yet the Party's guidance is not revolutionary; there really is a hint of something counterrevolutionary about it. I have established these views under the guidance of the peasants. Formerly, I thought the opinion of the leading comrades was right, so I didn't really insist on my own views. Thus my opinions, which they said were unreasonable, did not prevail. So the Party's opinion went in the direction of Xu Kexiang.[3] It was really strange that even Tang's[4] troops admitted that only eight households of military officers had been destroyed; and yet our Party seemed to accept that no one knew how many households had been destroyed. In sum, the influence of the masses over the Party leadership was far too small in the past. Third, as regards military affairs, we used to censure [Sun] Yatsen for engaging only in a military movement, and we did just the opposite, not undertaking a military movement, but exclusively a mass movement. Both Chiang [Kaishek] and Tang [Shengzhi] rose by grasping the gun; we alone did not concern ourselves with this. At present, although we have paid some attention to it, we still have no firm concept about it. The Autumn Harvest Uprising, for example, is simply impossible without military force.[5] Our conference should attach great importance to this issue. The members of the Standing Committee of the new Politburo should take a firmer stand and pay attention to this issue. The failure in Hunan this time can be said to have resulted entirely from pedantic and subjective mistakes. From now on, we should pay the

---

2. The first of these was the celebrated "Hunan Peasant Report," intended primarily for the Guomindang, which appears in Mao's *Selected Works*; the second, more forthright assessment of the situation, prepared for the Central Committee of the Chinese Communist Party, has only recently become accessible in Chinese and is translated for the first time in Volume II of this edition, pp. 425–28.

3. I.e., in the direction of commanders troubled by the disorders and attacks on landlords brought about by the revolution. Regarding Xu Kexiang, the prime mover of the "Horse Day" incident, see above, the note to the text of July 4, 1927.

4. The reference is to Tang Shengzhi.

5. Because he sought to make maximum use of the small number of troops under his command when he led this uprising in Hunan a few weeks later, Mao would subsequently be censured by the Party leadership for his "military deviationism."

greatest attention to military affairs. We must know that political power is obtained from the barrel of the gun.[6] Fourth, the issue of organization. From now on, higher authorities should listen attentively to reports from the lower levels. Only then can the nonrevolutionary be transformed into the revolutionary.

---

6. Mao's enunciation of this axiom has long been thought to date from 1938, but in fact he first put it forward in 1927. The Chinese formulation is slightly different, but the essential idea is the same. Here the wording is: *"Zhengquan shi you qiangganzi zhong qude de."* In November 1938, at the Sixth Plenum of the Sixth Central Committee, he put forward the formula: *"Qiangganzi limian chu zhengquan,"* which can be rendered "Political power grows (or comes) out of the barrel of a gun." (For the context, see the *Selected Works*, Vol. II, pp. 224–25.)

Mao Zedong's Statement Regarding the Resolution on the Struggles of the Peasants

(August 7, 1927)

1. A criterion must definitely be fixed for big and medium landlords. Otherwise, we will not know who is a big or medium landlord. In my opinion, we could take fifty *mu* as the limit; above fifty *mu*, whether the land is fertile or barren, it should all be confiscated.

2. The question of small landlords is the central problem of the land question. The difficulty is that, if we do not confiscate the land of the small landlords, then since there are many localities where there are no big landlords, the peasant associations would have to cease their activity. Hence, if we wish basically to abolish the landlord system, we must have a certain method for dealing with the small landlords. At present we must resolve the small landlord question, for this is the only way we can satisfy the people.

3. The problem of owner-peasants. The land rights of rich peasants and middle peasants are not the same. The peasants want to attack the rich peasants, so we must adopt a clear orientation.

4. The bandit problem is an extraordinarily great problem. Because such secret societies and bandits are uncommonly numerous, we must have tactics [for dealing with them]. There are some comrades who hold that we can simply use them; this is [Sun] Zhongshan's[1] method, which we should not follow. It suffices that we carry through the agrarian revolution, and then we will certainly be able to lead them. We must definitely regard them as our own brothers, and not as strangers.[2]

This text has been translated from *Baqi huiyi*, p. 73. Unlike Mao's comments on Lominadze's report, these remarks on the peasant problem do not appear in either of the other volumes cited in the source note to the previous document.

1. Sun Yatsen.

2. *Keren*. The usual meaning is "guest," but here "stranger" seems more apt.

Hunan Is Important

(August 9, 1927)[1]

D:[2] We have all read the report on the problem of Hunan (by Meyer[3]). From this report we can draw three conclusions: (1) The plan for the insurrection by He Ye of the Provincial Committee is erroneous; we should not organize a division in Hunan to take Guangdong together with the military forces from Nanchang, but should form a broad basis in Hunan, and extend it to include the whole province. (2) The Provincial Committee is not strong, there is not a single worker or peasant element, and it is the same with the C.Y.[4] Judging by the way he talks, the secretary wants to protect the interests of the small landlords; this secretary is unsuitable, and the Provincial Committee should be reorganized. People close to the masses must join the Provincial Committee and guide the work there, and there should be five or six worker and peasant elements. (3) Their acceptance of the International's decisions is insincere, so they do not have a firm attitude toward the Party's position. At present, we should send capable comrades such as Dong[5] to explain things in detail, and to support resolutely the views of the [August 7] Emergency Conference.

Dong: To organize a division to go to Guangdong is wrong. All of us should not look only at Guangdong; Hunan is also very important. The organization of the

This document has been translated from the extracts quoted in the article by Sun Gang in *Dangde wenxian*, no. 1, 1988, cited in the source note to the first text in this volume. Mao's own remarks are conveniently available in *Mao Zedong junshi wenji*, Vol. 1, p. 6, but without Lominadze's introductory statement, which provides the context.

1. The text translated below is an extract from the record of a meeting of the Politburo of the Central Committee held on this date.

2. Lominadze, the Comintern representative.

3. Meyer was the Soviet consul in Changsha, and concurrently a representative of the International. His report was highly critical of the Hunan Provincial Committee.

4. The Communist Youth League.

5. Mao Zedong. As indicated above, in a note to the text of August 1, 1927, the Central Committee decided on August 3 that a Southern Hunan Special Committee of four members, including Mao Zedong, should be set up right away, to direct operations there. (See the plan for the Autumn Harvest Uprising in the four provinces of Hunan, Hubei, Guangdong, and Jiangxi in Saich, *Rise to Power*, Doc. C.6, pp. 317–19.) Resolutions adopted at the Politburo meeting of August 9 stipulated that Mao Zedong and Peng Gongda were entrusted with the compilation of the list of the nine members of the new Provincial Committee, of whom at least three must be workers or peasants. Peng Gongda was appointed provincial party secretary. (See the letter of August 9, 1927, to the Hunan Provincial Committee transmitting these decisions, in Saich, *Rise to Power*, Doc. C.7, pp. 319–21.)

popular masses in Hunan is even more extensive than that in Guangdong. What is lacking is military force, and now that the time for an uprising is at hand, military force is even more necessary. Not long ago, I drafted a plan, which has been approved by the Standing Committee,[6] for establishing a military force of one division in southern Hunan, to occupy five or six *xian*, and create a political base, in order to develop the agrarian revolution in the whole province. Even if it should be defeated, this force ought not to move to Guangdong, but should go up the mountains. The present Provincial Committee has been trying to pick up the pieces in the tragic situation following the emergency.[7] It was set up less than two months ago, and it has established some merit for itself in restoring the Hunan organization. It is very true that in the future, the Provincial Committee should add worker and peasant comrades to the leadership. Previously, the masses within the Party were dissatisfied with the Party leaders.

---

6. See above, the document dated August 1, 1927.

7. By "emergency" (*shibian*), Mao is referring to the situation created by the Horse Day Massacre of May 21, 1927, and the subsequent repression.

Views Expressed at the First Meeting of the Hunan Provincial Committee of the Chinese Communist Party

(August 18, 1927)

I. The Peasant Question (the land question)

(A) Zedong's views:

(1) There must be targets for land confiscation. In China there are only a few big landlords, but quite a number of smaller landlords. If we confiscate only the big landlords' land, few landlords will be affected, and the amount of land confiscated will be extremely small. The number of poor peasants demanding land is very great, and if we confiscate the land of the big landlords alone, we cannot satisfy the demands and needs of the peasants. If we want to win over all the peasants, we must confiscate the land of [all] the landlords and distribute it among the peasants.

(2) The method of land confiscation should be that the revolutionary committee (our Party) lays down a land policy, and the whole procedure is carried out by the peasant unions or by the revolutionary committees.

(3) This land confiscation policy must include suitable arrangements for the landlords whose land has been confiscated. I therefore propose that those landlords who are unable to work, or whose labor power is deficient, that is to say, those who are old and weak, should be provided by the peasant unions with equal rations of agricultural produce from the proceeds of the agricultural tax.

(4) We should proclaim the abolition of all the unreasonably heavy taxes for the peasants; an agricultural tax should be levied.

[passage omitted]

This summary of views put forward on August 18 is an excerpt from Peng Gongda's report of October 8, 1927, on the course of the uprising. (For an almost complete English version of the whole report, see Saich, *Rise to Power*, Doc. C.8, pp. 322–31.) Our source for the extracts translated here is *Mao Zedong ji. Bujuan*, Vol. 2, pp. 299–300, which has taken them from Vol. 3 of *Zhonggong dangshi cankao ziliao* (Reference Materials on the History of the Chinese Communist Party). The Soviet consul, Meyer, mentioned above in the text of August 9, also spoke on this occasion, and presented a summary of the decisions taken at the second meeting of the new Politburo.

II. The Question of the Uprising

(A) Zedong's and Lirong's[1] views:

(1) The development of the Autumn Harvest Uprising in Hunan will solve the land problem for the peasants. Nobody can deny this. But if we wish to create and unleash this uprising, it will not do to rely on the power of the peasants alone. There must be military support. With the help of one or two regiments, the uprising can take place; otherwise, it will fail in the end.

(2) The development of the uprising must lead to the seizure of political power. If you want to seize political power, to try to do it without the support of military forces would be sheer self-deception. Our Party's mistake in the past has been that it neglected military affairs. Now we should concentrate 60 percent of our energies on the military movement. We must carry out the principle of seizing and establishing political power on the barrel of a gun.[2]

[balance omitted]

---

1. Lirong is Yi Lirong (1898–), Mao's longtime friend and comrade from the New People's Study Society, who is still living today in Beijing. For details, see the note to Mao's letter to him dated November 1920, in Volume I of this edition, p. 611.

2. Here Mao has put the idea he had first enunciated on August 7 in different words: "... zai qiangganzi shang duoqu zhengquan, *jianshe zhengquan.*"

Report of the Hunan Provincial Committee to the Central Committee of the Chinese Communist Party[1]

On the Methods for Carrying out the Autumn Harvest Uprising in Hunan

(August 19, 1927)

Dear Brother Shirong:[2]

At present, in terms of objective circumstances, the Hunan Autumn Harvest Uprising has indeed come at a most opportune time. We here have now decided on the following methods:

1. The Hunan Autumn Harvest Uprising should start from Changsha, and southern and western Hunan should rise up simultaneously. We should resolutely seize all of Hunan, in order to carry out a land revolution, and set up a worker-peasant-soldier soviet régime.
2. The uprising in Changsha will have the workers and peasants as its main force. It has been decided to move Chen Lie's and Li Longguang's regiments forward to kindle the flames of the uprising, so if only we employ to the greatest possible extent all other methods for smashing the reactionary government, the uprising can be carried through.
3. Once Changsha is taken, a revolutionary committee should immediately be set up to carry out all the revolutionary measures of the political power of the workers, peasants, and soldiers.
4. Right now in Hunan, because of Xu Kexiang's rebellion against Tang Shengzhi and the fact that Tang's forces have all been sent to the front to fight against Xu, southern Hunan and Changsha are literally cut off from each other. Consequently, a separate committee has been organized in

---

Our source for this document is *Mao Zedong ji. Bujuan*, Vol. 9, pp. 321–22, which reproduces the text as published in *Qiushou qiyi* (The Autumn Harvest Uprising) (Beijing: Zhongong zhongyang dangxiao chubanshe, 1982).

1. This report was drafted at a meeting of the Hunan Provincial Committee on August 19, 1927, in which Mao Zedong participated. Mao was probably not the author, but it reflects his views on the agrarian revolution, and on the Autumn Harvest Uprising.

2. Shirong, or Wu Shirong, was another code name for the Central Committee.

southern Hunan to direct the uprising there. If it should by any chance prove impossible to take southern Hunan at present, we have decided to take the three *xian* of Donggui, Rucheng, and Zixing and set up the political power of the workers, peasants, and soldiers. The southern Hunan and the other revolutionary committees will resolutely carry out a policy of agrarian revolution.

The above are the principles we have adopted here for dealing with the Autumn Harvest Uprising in Hunan. As for the details, they will be related to you face to face by some of the more experienced friends. It is our hope that you will send a reply approving our position as soon as you have received this letter, and that you will give us all the support you can.

Xiang Caixia[3]

---

3. Xiang is pronounced like the traditional name for Hunan, though the character is quite different. The whole of the signature is presumably a code name for "Hunan Provincial Committee."

A Letter from Hunan to
the Central Committee

(August 20, 1927)

[Preceding passage omitted] ... (3) A certain comrade has come to Hunan announcing that a new instruction from the International proposes the immediate establishment of soviets of workers, peasants, and soldiers in China.[1] On hearing this, I jumped for joy. Objectively speaking, the situation in China has long since reached 1917, but formerly, everyone held that we were in 1905. This has been an extremely great error. Soviets of workers, peasants, and soldiers are wholly adapted to the objective situation, and we must therefore resolve to establish immediately the political power of the workers, peasants, and soldiers in the four provinces of Guangdong, Hunan, Hubei, and Jiangxi. As soon as it is established, this political power should rapidly achieve victory in the whole country. We expect that the Central Committee will without a doubt accept the instruction of the International and will, moreover, apply it in Hunan.

This new instruction of the International influences my view of the Guomindang, since in the period of soviets of workers, peasants, and soldiers, we should no longer use the banner of the Guomindang. We must raise high the banner of the Communist Party, to oppose the flag of the Guomindang carried by Chiang [Kaishek], Tang [Shengzhi], Feng [Yuxiang], Yan [Xishan], and other warlords. The Guomindang banner has already become the banner of the warlords, and only the banner of the Communist Party is the banner of the people. I was not very well aware of this point when I was still in Hubei. In the past few days, since I have arrived in Hunan and seen what Tang Shengzhi's provincial party committee[2] is like, and what the people's attitude toward it is, I have come to the conclusion that we really cannot use the Guomindang banner any more, and that if we do, we will

---

We have translated this document from *Mao Zedong ji*, Vol. 2, pp. 11–12, which reproduces the text published at the time in the internal Party organ *Zhongyang tongxin* (Central Correspondence), no. 3, August 30, 1927.

1. Mao is referring here to Meyer's summary of current policies at the meeting on August 18. Neither Moscow nor the Central Committee of the Chinese Communist Party had in fact called for "the immediate establishment of soviets," because Stalin still believed in the possibility of collaborating with the Left Guomindang, and abandoned that hope only in mid-September. Meanwhile, the Chinese comrades were instructed merely to explain the idea of Soviets, without actually forming any. It is not clear whether Mao or Meyer was responsible for this misunderstanding.

2. The reference is, of course, to the Guomindang party committee in Hunan. Judging by the document of August 1, 1927, which appears above, already by that date Mao had few illusions about Tang Shengzhi.

certainly be defeated again. In the past, we did not actively seize the leadership of the Guomindang, but let Wang, Chiang, Tang, and the others go on leading it. Now we should let them keep this flag, which is already nothing but a black flag, and we must immediately and resolutely raise the Red flag. As for the petty bourgeoisie, let them rally entirely under the leadership of the Red flag; objectively, they are certainly entirely under the leadership of the Red flag.

(4) The Land Question

This time, I have learned from investigations among the peasants in two areas, Qingtai Township in Changsha [*xian*] (where I went myself), and Shaoshan Township in Xiangtan [*xian*] (from which five peasants came to the provincial capital) that the Hunanese peasants definitely want a complete solution of the land question. Yesterday, I discussed the matter with some peasant comrades from the countryside, and on the basis of conclusions drawn from their opinions, I propose some guidelines for the land question, of which the most important are:

a) Confiscate all the land, including that of small landlords and owner-peasants, take it all into public ownership, and let the peasant associations distribute it fairly to all those in the village who want land, in accordance with the two criteria of "labor power" and "consumption" (in other words, the actual amount of consumption for every household, calculated on the basis of the number of adults and children in the household).

b) During the process of land distribution, the peasant association at the district level first directs its counterpart at the township level to draw up a household register. After it is finished, the township association submits the register to the district association, which then distributes the land according to the register.

c) The unit for land distribution should be the district, not the township. A township which has more people in proportion to the land may be included with a township which has fewer people in proportion to the land. This is the only way to ensure a fair distribution. As for including District A with District B, this is impossible for the time being.

d) After the land has been confiscated, there must be a method for settling the family members of the landlords (excluding the big landlords), for only thus can the people's minds be set at ease. The method distinguishes among . . . [passage omitted] four categories: 4 percent for the first category, 3 percent for the second category, 2 percent for the third category, and 1 percent for the fourth category.

Although this draft was discussed once yesterday at the meeting of the provincial Party committee, it still needs more opinions from the peasant comrades before I present it to you for a decision. The above draft is merely presented here as material for discussion. . . . [balance omitted]

Letter from the
Hunan Provincial Party Committee

(August 30, 1927)

To a certain superior [organ]:[1]

Your letter, Hunan series no. 5, has been received. With regard to the two mistakes pointed out in the letter, neither facts nor theory are at all compatible with what you say. Our reply is as follows:

1) In terms of their overall revolutionary significance, both the seizure of Changsha and the Autumn Harvest Uprising are meant to promote the agrarian revolution; they are one and the same thing. The uprising in Changsha will serve as the starting point for the Autumn Harvest Uprising, and the development of the Autumn Harvest Uprising will lead to agrarian revolution and the seizure of political power. According to our plan, the principal fighters in taking Changsha will be the workers and peasants. The purpose in deploying a certain two[2] regiments in the attack on Changsha is to compensate for the insufficiency of the worker-peasant forces. They are not the main force, they will serve to shield the development of the uprising. They are not the only important component in this uprising. When you say that we here are engaging in military adventurism, and order us to cancel the plan for the uprising in Changsha, this truly reflects a lack of understanding of the situation here, and constitutes a contradictory policy which pays no attention to military affairs, while at the same time calling for an armed uprising of the popular masses.

2) You say that we pay attention only to the work in Changsha and neglect other places. This is absolutely untrue. It is an error on our part that we did not

---

Our source for this document is *Mao Zedong ji*, Vol. 2, pp. 13–14, which reproduces the text from *Zhongyang tongxin* no. 5, September 20, 1927.

1. The salutation actually reads, "To a certain elder brother" (*moumou xiong*). "Elder brother" was, however, a common locution at the time for referring to a hierarchical superior. Since Mao was in Hunan as the special commissioner entrusted directly by the Central Committee with organizing the Autumn Harvest Uprising, it may be assumed that the organ addressed here was the Central Committee. This follows also from the fact that the letter to which he is replying was "Hunan Series no. 5" [*Xiangzi wuhao*]. Only the central Party authorities would have a separate series for Hunan.

2. Once again, for security reasons the names of the regiments, presumably those indicated in the document of August 19, are replaced by "certain" (*moumou*).

inform you earlier of the considerable preparations that have been made in various areas. (See the plan for the uprising in central Hunan.) With regard to the work in southern Hunan, we have one more thing to add. That we take the uprising in Changsha as the starting point in no way implies that we will abandon southern Hunan. We do not use Hengyang as a second starting point simply because our force is sufficient only for a rising in central Hunan. If we launched an uprising in every *xian*, our force would be dispersed, and we fear that even the plan for the uprising in central Hunan could not be carried out. For this reason, we have decided not to use Hengyang as a second starting point. Nevertheless, every *xian* in southern Hunan has already been ordered to make preparations in an organized way according to plan for the uprising, and every *xian* has already done so. As soon as the uprising starts in Changsha, every *xian* will rise up at the same time.

Autumn Harvest Uprising

(To the Tune of "Moon over the West River"[1])

(1927)

Ours is called the Workers' and Peasants' Revolutionary Army,
Ours is the flag of the sickle and axe.[2]
We won't linger among Lushan's peaks;
We'll advance directly to the rivers of Hunan.[3]

Landlords inflict every manner of oppression,
The peasants hate them one and all.
In the autumn harvest season, gloomy clouds at dusk;
With a clap of thunder, the uprising takes place.

This poem was first published "unofficially" in the periodical *Jiefangjun wenyi* (People's Liberation Army Literature and Art), no. 7, 1957, where it was cited in an article on the poetry of Mao Zedong. We have translated it from *Mao Zedong shici duilian jizhu* (Annotated Edition of Mao Zedong's Poems and Couplets) (Changsha: Hunan wenyi chubanshe, 1991), pp. 21–22, which remains, as in previous volumes of this edition, our source for all of Mao's poems.

1. As noted in Volume II of this series, much of Mao's poetry makes use of the convention of "tune title" (*cipai*), a label traditionally attached to this form of classical poetry. The conventional "tune title" relates to technical matters of meter and rhyme, but has nothing to do with the theme or expressions in the particular poem.

2. According to the editors of the *Mao Zedong shici duilian jizhu*, at the time this poem was written, the hammer on the flag of the Communist Party was commonly mistaken for an axe.

3. When this poem was first published, instead of Lushan and the rivers Xiao and Xiang in Hunan, Mao gave specific local place names indicating the route of march of the troops that took part in the uprising.

Report on Arrival at Anyuan[1]

(September 1927)

As soon as he arrived at Anyuan, Comrade Mao immediately called together the comrades and reported on the proceedings of the August 7 meeting, and the changes in the new policies, such as the reorganization of the Hunan Provincial Committee, his return to Hunan, and the decision to launch the Autumn Harvest Uprising. He said the decision to launch an Autumn Harvest Uprising in Hunan and Hubei was made while I was at the Central Committee [meeting]. The commanding organ of the Hunan uprising is divided into two parts. One is the Front Committee, with Mao Zedong as secretary and various responsible military persons as members. The other is the Action Committee, with Comrade Yi Lirong as secretary and responsible comrades from the various *xian* as members. The uprising at Changsha should use rickshaw workers and the peasants of the suburbs as the main force and may also organize about five hundred wounded soldiers. Every *xian* has already prepared to launch peasant uprisings, and preparations have already been made to cut the electric lines and railroads in all areas. I have also brought with me a letter of introduction from the Central Committee which requires He and Nie[2] to deploy two regiments of their armies to serve as the military force of the uprising. They are now taking a roundabout route along the border of Fujian. If they can come, it will be all the better. I hope that Comrade Pan

---

This text is translated from *Mao Zedong ji. Bujuan*, Vol. 9, p. 323, which reproduces it from *Qiushou qiyi*.

1. This is an extract from the report of Pan Xinyuan (mentioned in the last sentence of the text) to the Central Committee, dated July 2, 1929.

2. The reference is to He Long (1896–1969), original name Wenchang, a native of Hunan, and Nie Rongzhen (1899–), a native of Sichuan, who had been respectively commander-in-chief and secretary of the Front Committee during the Nanchang Uprising of August 1, 1927. After the retreat to Shantou in August and September 1927, both of them fled to Hong Kong. He Long returned to China in November, and by March 1928 he was engaged in guerrilla warfare in the Hunan-Jiangxi border area. Nie Rongzhen had gone to France and Belgium on the work-study program. He later studied at the Red Army Academy in Moscow and, on his return to China in 1925, served as a political instructor at the Huangpu Academy. From Hong Kong, he went to Guangzhou, where he participated in the uprising of December 1927. Thereafter, he worked underground in Hong Kong, Tianjin, and Shanghai until 1931.

Xinyuan[3] will make a detailed report on the situation of the armies, and meetings will be held to discuss the work related to the dispositions for the uprisings in all areas of Ping[jiang], Liu[yang], Li[ling], and An[yuan].[4]

---

3. Pan Xinyuan (1903–1931), alias Pan Qingquan, a native of Liuyang, Hunan, joined the Chinese Communist Party in 1923. In 1927, he was Party representative in the Second Regiment of the First Division of the Workers' and Peasants' Revolutionary Army, and in this capacity participated in the Autumn Harvest Uprising. In 1930 he was a political commissar in the Fourth Red Army during its assault on Changsha; in August 1931, he was captured and executed.

4. This brief and optimistic document represents the last contemporary word from Mao himself about the Autumn Harvest Uprising in Hunan, but on September 16 and 17, the Soviet consul and emissary of the International, Meyer, under the pseudonym of Ma Kefu, produced two letters and a report to the Central Committee containing savage criticism of Mao and Peng Gongda. These materials, which helped prepare the ground for Mao's disgrace in November 1927, first appeared in the internal Party organ *Zhongyang tongxin*, no. 6, September 30, 1927. For a translation, see Hyobom Pak, *Documents of the Chinese Communist Party 1927–1930* (Hong Kong: Union Research Institute, 1971), pp. 103–11. Meyer denounced the decision to postpone the attack on Changsha, originally scheduled for September 15, as "extremely shameful treachery and cowardice," and "an evil instance of Chinese-style philistinism," and demanded that the Central Committee send a plenipotentiary to reorganize the Hunan Provincial Committee.

—————————1928—————————

Report to the Jiangxi Provincial Party Committee and to the Party Central Committee

(May 2, 1928)

To the Central Committee:

Here we present the report by Comrade Mao Zedong forwarded from Ji'an:

Dear Elder Brother Yulin:[1]

Enclosed is Comrade Zedong's letter to you people, and to the Central Committee. It is important that you forward the letter to the Central Committee after you read it. Comrade Zedong's report is as follows:

 1) After the defeat,[2] we retreated from southern Hunan to the Jiangxi border (our troops did not suffer heavy losses, but the organs of political power in southern Hunan and Chaling were destroyed). What is outrageous is that the *xian* Party Committees and *xian* governments of Hunan brought a large group of peasant troops along with us.[3] Now there are eighteen thousand troops here.

 2) We have occupied the three *xian* of Yongxin, Ninggang, and Suichuan, and we will soon be able to expand our territories.

 3) Yang Ruxuan's division, which had pursued Mao's troops, ended up being driven away by Mao's troops to the border of Jiangxi. Its Eighty-first Regiment was put to flight at Wudoujiang in Suichuan. One battalion of the Seventy-ninth Regiment was previously disarmed by Mao's troops. Now this regiment has also

---

We have translated this document from *Jinggangshande wuzhuang geju* (The Armed Independent Régime on the Jinggangshan) (Nanchang: Jiangxi renmin chubanshe, 1979), pp. 120–21 (hereafter, *The Jinggangshan Régime*). The text is conveniently reproduced from this source in *Mao Zedong ji. Bujuan*, Vol. 2, pp. 301–03.

 1. Once again, the term "elder brother" is used to address a hierarchical superior in the Party. Yulin ("Jade forest") is probably a code name for the Jiangxi Provincial Committee.

 2. The reference is to the defeat of March 1928 in southern Hunan, where Mao had been ordered to go by the Southern Hunan Special Committee, after the Front Committee which constituted the basis of his own power had been abolished. See the Introduction to this volume.

 3. Presumably Mao's objection was that these peasant troops were, as indicated under point (6) of this report, "messy" and undisciplined. By their requirements for food, they also placed a heavy logistic burden on his army, and they were in any case ill-trained and ill-armed. Subsequently, as indicated in the report of November 25, 1928, translated below, they further disrupted operations because of their desire to return home to southern Hunan.

been put to flight by Zhu's[4] troops at Yongxin. The Thirty-first Regiment of Mao's troops is now coming from Ninggang, and the enemy troops from Yongxin have retreated to Ji'an. This time, we have captured three hundred rifles.

4) The reason we did not go directly to Ji'an is that we have adopted a strategy of deepening our work both internally and externally. By keeping Yongxin as the center, and by organizing insurrections in the nearby *xian*, internally we can establish a Party army, raise money, and make clothes. Externally, we can help the localities launch worker and peasant uprisings, establish the political power of the workers and peasants, and distribute the land. We have, therefore, decided that it will be much more significant to devote our efforts to this work than to launch an attack on Ji'an.

5) The Hunan Special Committee decided previously that the troops of Zhu and Mao should be combined into the Fourth Red Army, with Zhu De as military commander and Mao Zedong as Party representative. Zhu's troops have been organized as the Tenth Division, and Mao's troops as the Eleventh Division. The peasant troops from the *xian* of southern Hunan were incorporated into these two divisions. Zhu is concurrently commander of the Tenth Division, with Wan Xixian as Party representative. Mao is concurrently commander of the Eleventh Division (a post which was originally held by Zhang Ziqing, but because he has been wounded, Mao acts as commander concurrently), with He Tingying as

---

4. The reference is to Zhu De (1886–1976), *zi* Yujie, a native of Sichuan. In 1909 Zhu had entered the Yunnan Military Academy, where he joined both the Guomindang and the secret society known as the Gelaohui. After participating in the 1911 revolution under the command of Cai Ao and receiving important commands, he drifted into warlord ways, and became addicted to opium. In 1922, he made a clean break with this past, putting himself under medical care to overcome the opium habit and going to Germany to study. In Berlin, he met Zhou Enlai, who sponsored him for membership in the Chinese Communist Party, and also joined the Guomindang. Expelled from Germany in July 1925 for his revolutionary activities, he spent a period in the Soviet Union studying military affairs. After returning to China at the end of 1926, he renewed his friendship with Zhu Peide, who had been his student at the Yunnan Military Academy (see above, the relevant note to the Declaration dated August 1, 1927), and thus became chief public security officer in Nanchang. In this capacity, he played a significant, though not dominant role in the Nanchang Uprising. In the course of the retreat from Nanchang toward Shantou, his troops, which constituted the rear guard, were far less severely mauled by the enemy than the main force under Ye Ting and He Long, and he was thus able to maintain their existence as a small but effective fighting unit. In January 1928, Zhu De set up a short-lived soviet in Yichang in southern Hunan. From there he made his way to the Jinggangshan, meeting up on the way with Mao Zedong, who had been ordered to go to Hunan in March by the Southern Hunan Special Committee.

Regarding He Long, see above, the relevant note to the report of September 1927. Ye Ting (1896–1946), *zi* Xiyi, was a native of Guangdong. He joined the Guomindang in 1919, and thereafter held various military commands. In August 1927, he played a leading role in the Nanchang Uprising in his capacity as commander of the Eleventh Army. After the retreat to Shantou, and a brief sojourn in Hong Kong, he was sent by the Party to Guangzhou to exercise military leadership during the Canton Commune. After that uprising was defeated, he left China for Europe, returning only in 1937 at the beginning of the Anti-Japanese War.

Party representative. We also have a training corps, commanded by Chen Yi.[5] We are equipped with a few machine guns. The Twenty-eighth Regiment of Zhu's division, and the Thirty-first Regiment of Mao's division, have relatively high combat capability and can beat off some relatively mediocre enemy troops.

6) A mass of ten thousand messy people with very poor discipline (except for a certain portion of them) are quite a burden. Now we are trying hard to strengthen discipline, and the situation is improving daily.

7) The Party is improving daily, as the army, divisional, and regimental Party Committees and each Party branch have started Party training classes.

8) Feeding the troops is a big and difficult problem. In the past month, most people received only three cents[6] a day for rice and nothing else. These days in Yongxin, however, we have been able to raise some money.

9) The border area between the two provinces covers about ten *xian*. In the past, the two Provincial Party Committees had always been unable to control them. Thanks to the efforts of our comrades, the organizational activities of the Party in these *xian* are growing every day. But since Comrade Zhou Lu (representative of the South Hunan Special Committee) came to Ninggang in March to abolish the Front Committee, the Party organizations in the *xian* have suddenly lost their center and become independent régimes. Certain unhealthy tendencies are developing among them. Already at the meeting of the Front Committee last December, it was suggested that a Border Area Special Committee be established. The Hunan Provincial Committee and the Central Committee had best send another capable comrade here to be Party secretary. Comrade Mao is responsible for work in the army and finds it very difficult to do both concurrently.

10) Our permanent mailing address is as follows:

Mr. Yuan Wencai
Ninggang

Mr. Wang Zuo[7]
The Five Big and Small Wells
Jinzhu Mountain, Suining Border

---

5. Chen Yi (1901–1972) was a native of Sichuan. In 1919–1921, he visited France on the work-study program, but was expelled because of his participation in the student occupation of the Institut Franco-Chinois in Lyon. In 1926, he joined the staff of his former comrade in Paris, Zhou Enlai, at the Huangpu Academy. After participating in the Nanchang Uprising of August 1927, he made his way to the Jinggangshan as the second in command of Zhu De's forces.

6. The Chinese here is *fen*, which was originally the name for the copper cent created in the currency reforms of 1914. By this time, these coins had depreciated by approximately one-half in terms of the silver dollar or *yuan*, and the term *fen* was commonly used for a unit of account corresponding to one-hundredth of a dollar, rather than to the actual coin. Because the meaning is vague in any case, we have translated simply "cent" in this and other texts of 1928 referring to the soldiers' pay.

7. Wang Zuo (1898–1930), *hao* Nanshan, and Yuan Wencai (1898–1930) were natives of Jiangxi. They were the two chieftains of the bandit forces which Mao had found

11) Please send us political analyses and important party documents frequently.

12) Please send us large numbers of insurgents who can no longer hold out in other districts, regardless of whether their skills are military or political, the more the better. The Front Committee had done nothing deserving of a rebuke, and yet it was rebuked. Is this not intolerable? Being unable to sleep is an unavoidable evil at present. Since receiving the letter from Ji'an, the view is that a Special Committee should be organized. What do you think? We want to receive clear and definite directives from you. As soon as such an organization is approved, we will organize it. If we thus establish an organ of political power in the Luoxiao mountain range, with Ninggang as its center, and if the Party organization is strong, the army can create a real revolutionary base area in Hunan and Jiangxi. Comrade Mao and others have put forward this argument very clearly many times in reports, which have been repeatedly forwarded by the Southern Hunan Special Committee to the Hunan Provincial Committee, and then to the Central Committee. We have, however, received no clear word of either approval or rejection. Meanwhile, in the letter from the Anyuan City Party Committee, it is mentioned in passing that the Hunan Provincial Committee has approved it. But this is not a clear directive from the Provincial Committee. Two days ago, we received a letter from the Ji'an *Xian* Committee in which it is mentioned that the Jiangxi Provincial Committee has also approved it, and Comrade Mao has been appointed to be Party secretary. But again this is not a clear directive from the Provincial Committee. How can we begin to organize such a committee? Besides, we are afraid of receiving unpalatable censure.

> With our greetings,
>
> Mao Zedong
> Secretary of the Military Commission
> Fourth Army of the Workers' and Peasants'
> Revolutionary Army
> May 2, in Yongxin City
>
> Forwarded by the Ji'an *Xian* Committee;
> transmitted by the Jiangxi Provincial
> Committee, May 19

---

occupying the Jinggangshan area when he led his troops there in October 1927. Recent official accounts assert that Wang and Yuan had already transformed their bands into a peasant self-defense force before Mao's arrival, and even that Yuan had joined the Chinese Communist Party in 1926. In any case, Mao reorganized them and made use of them.

A Report on the Current Status of the Red Army[1]

(June 16, 1928)

I) The struggle here now has been rather intense and widespread. The enemies, with ten regiments (Yang Ruxuan's four and Wu Shang's six[2]) are advancing toward us, not including, of course, the landlords' household militia.[3] The broad peasant masses from the two *xian* of Chaling and Lingxian have been suppressed. The cleanup in the countryside by the Whites has totally crushed our party organization to the point that many of our brave comrades working in Chaling have been killed, as was the leader of the Lingxian *Xian* Committee. The Eighth Army has fought against us four times, losing once and winning three times. But because of the enemy's stubborn resistance, we were obliged to withdraw completely from the two *xian*, Chaling and Youxian, which we had previously occupied. We no longer have even have one inch of land in southern Hunan. Recently, however, there has been a military victory.[4] In May, Yang Ruxuan's Seventy-ninth Regiment and one battalion of the Twenty-seventh Regiment, their engineer and artillery units, the machine-gun company, the medical unit of their division headquarters, and their transportation unit were all wiped out and most of them captured. Yang escaped to Ji'an (some said that he had been wounded), and the commander of the Twenty-seventh Regiment, Liu, was killed. We have captured seven mortars, two mountain cannons, and over twenty *Dan* of silver *yuan*. But since the enemy's two crack regiments were still in the vicinity of Yongxin *xian*, we decided not to pursue any further. The military dispositions here are that we assume a defensive posture toward Hunan and an offensive posture toward Jiangxi. But we have not yet made any move in the last

Our source for this document is *Mao Zedong junshi wenji*, Vol. 1, pp. 8–10, where it is reproduced from a copy in the Party archives.

1. This is an extract from a letter which Mao sent to the Hunan and Jiangxi Provincial Committees for transmittal to the Central Committee.

2. Yang Ruxuan was at this time the commander of the Twenty-seventh Division of the Guomindang Third Army. Wu Shang was commander of the Guomindang Eighth Army.

3. As indicated by Mao's reference to it in the Circular of July 20, 1927, para. (6), the household militia (*aihutuan*) was originally a kind of peasant military organization. "Household" referred to the compulsory participation by almost every household. After the defeat of the left in the summer of 1927, many "household militia" units were taken over by the landlords and used against the revolution.

4. This refers to the counterattack at Caoshi'ao in mid-May 1928, during the third "annihilation" campaign against the Jinggangshan base.

few days. We will decide after the situation becomes clearer. A group of lower-ranking officers in the army have not yet given up their opportunist attitude and are looking for a chance to escape to southern Jiangxi. This has become an internal party struggle. Now that the Special Committee has been set up, it is only by the orders of the Special Committee that it will be more or less possible to control them. There are three reasons for using Ninggang as our base camp: (1) This is the middle section of the Luoxiao range. The location is excellent, easy to defend and hard to attack; (2) the Party has been able to organize the masses for the first time (Red Guard units and Red guerrilla units have been formed), and it would be a shame to give them up; (3) southern Hunan and southern Jiangxi can influence only one province and can extend only to the upper reaches, whereas here we can control two provinces and extend to the lower reaches. For these three reasons, we will struggle against our enemies with all our might and never retreat or give up. But up here in the mountains, it is extremely difficult to get supplies for food, money, and medicine for the wounded. We are constantly trying to solve these problems.

II) We have learned for the first time, from a letter from Ji'an, that the Jiangxi Provincial Committee has approved the setting up of a Hunan-Jiangxi Special Committee (Chaling, Youxian, Lingxian, Ninggang, Lianhua, Yongxin, and Suichuan), and has also endorsed the congress of *xian* representatives called together on May 20 and 21, which adopted resolutions on political issues, political discipline, slogans for the uprising, and political slogans, and elected leaders (the majority of them worker and peasant elements). Wan Xixian and Mao Zedong were elected members of the Standing Committee, and Zhu De, Chen Yi and Liu Feixiao, alternate members. Mao Zedong was designated as temporary Secretary.[5] Since [I], Zedong, am studying right now, I really cannot assume these responsibilities. Later, when the two provincial committees and the Central Committee send someone here, a meeting of the worker-peasant-soldier representatives will be called to carry out elections. (1) [We must] expand the Party to include six provinces. (2) Launch a peasant uprising here. (3) Transform the army into a real Red army. (4) Establish a strong Party within the army. (5) Set up military schools and Party schools. Please send us the political news every three days via the eastern Hunan Special Committee. I read from the newspapers that in Gaolong one *xian* magistrate, two company commanders, and over fifty soldiers have been martyred, but victory was finally won when Zhu De joined in the fight. (6) The Fourth Army Committee secretary will officially take charge today.

---

5. The First Congress of the Party in the Border Area was convened in Maoping, Ninggang *xian*, on May 20, 1928. Mao Zedong, who chaired the meeting, delivered a report (of which the text is not presently available) in which he addressed the question of how long the Red régime could survive. The congress elected a Special Committee as the supreme leading organ in the border area, with a standing committee of which the membership is given in the text. Mao became secretary, with Chen Yi as secretary of the Army Committee. For the context, see the Introduction to this volume.

Report to the Hunan Provincial Committee by the Special Committee of the Hunan-Jiangxi Border Area and the Army Committee of the Fourth Red Army of the Chinese Communist Party

(July 4, 1928)

To the Hunan Provincial Committee:

Comrade Yuan and Comrade Du[1] arrived at Yongxin at the same time on June 30, and from them we have obtained the circular of the Provincial Committee and the resolution of the Central Committee regarding work in Hunan. The directives given in the two letters from the Provincial Committee are quite inconsistent. The former asks us to continue to build the organs of political power in the *xian* in the middle section of the Luoxiao mountain range as the military bases, without changing the Central Committee and Provincial Committee directives of a month ago. The latter, however, asks us to rush to southern Hunan after we capture Yongxin in order to avoid "annihilation" by the enemy and to solve the problem of economic difficulties. Here, after they defeated the troops of Yang Chisheng on June 23, most of the Fourth Red Army troops have moved toward Lianhua, Anfu, and southwest of Ji'an through Yongxin, carrying on guerrilla warfare to raise money and mobilize the masses for uprisings. On the evening of June 30, the Special Committee, the Army Committee, and Yongxin *Xian* Committee held a Joint Conference to discuss the letters from the Provincial Committee. Comrades Yuan and Du also attended the meeting, at which it was decided that the Fourth Red Army should continue to deepen the work among the masses in various *xian* in the border area of Hunan and Jiangxi to build or consolidate the bases. With such bases, moving forward toward

---

Our source for this document is *Mao Zedong ji. Bujuan,* Vol. 2, pp. 305–07, which reproduces the text from a documentary collection published in China in 1981.

1. Regarding Yuan Desheng and Du Xiujing, representatives of the Hunan Provincial Committee, and their roles at this time, see the Introduction to this volume. Mao's own views about their errors are spelled out in several documents translated below, including the resolution of October 5, 1928, and the report of November 25, 1928.

Hunan and Jiangxi, the Red Army will arrive at places with consolidated independent régimes that cannot easily be wiped out by the enemy. The reasons are as follows:

1) The life-style of the Fourth Red Army is itself much marked by the habits of roving insurgents in the past. So the troops are extremely unwilling to stay in one place for a long time and to carry on the difficult work of the mass struggle. They are still much under the influence of the Red Army's pernicious traditions of adventurism. Only after nearly a month of many-sided education to wash away these traits, and only because, at the same time, the masses in Yongxin and Ninggang *xian* have generally stood up, have the troops of the Fourth Red Army gradually given up this idea and begun to understand that the policy to build Ninggang as the general headquarters suggested last time by the Central Committee and the Hunan Provincial Committee is correct. If we suddenly change our policy now and ask the Fourth Red Army to return to its roving path, it would be even more difficult to transform this army. It is pointed out in the last letter from the Provincial Committee that the Fourth Red Army has already traveled thousands of miles and moved like roving insurgents. They should choose a place to rest, so that they can better transform themselves. This directive is extremely correct and should not be rashly changed just as it is being implemented.

2) On the enemy side, the troops of Hunan Province are very tough and have real military strength. They are not as easy to attack as the enemy troops in Jiangxi. The latter have been defeated four times in succession, and they are scared out of their wits. Besides, their soldiers' morale is much shaken because of the impact of our practice of setting the captives free. The only troops that are able to fight are those of Wang Jun's Seventh Division.[2] The First Division and its First Regiment are stationed in Pingxiang, and its Second Regiment is in Jiujiang and Nanchang. We judge that it will be difficult to move these troops to attack us. Even if they are sent here, we can also use appropriate strategies to defeat them. The situation is different for the enemy troops from Hunan. After five or six engagements with them, we could put only a small number of these troops to flight, without inflicting casualties on them, and they are as strong as they were before. It is, therefore, not appropriate to rush ahead toward southern Hunan if we are to avoid tough battles. Otherwise we may get deeply caught in the encirclement of the enemy troops and suffer the misfortune of losing our whole army. The enemy troops from southern Hunan now consist of two divisions of the Guangxi clique, the Twenty-first Army, one army of Shang Chengjie (three thousand rifles), one division of Xu Kexiang, and one army of Wu Shang.

---

2. Wang Jun (1891–1936), *zi* Zhiping, was a native of Yunnan, and received his military training there. In the fall of 1925, when the National Revolutionary Army was established, he was appointed commander of the Seventh Division of the Third Army. In September 1929, he became commander of the Third Army.

These troops are seven or eight times stronger than the enemy troops of Jiangxi. Even if our army can win battles against the troops of Shang Chengjie and Xu Kexiang, there is no way we can defeat the armies of Wu Shang and the Guangxi clique. As soon as we arrive there, we would be caught in the encirclement of Wu Shang, the Guangxi clique, Shang Chengjie, and Xu Kexiang and would face the danger of being wiped out immediately. It seems that the Provincial Committee has not taken this fact into consideration.

3) Ninggang can become the general headquarters for our military forces because it is located in a highly strategic position among the big, steep mountains, and its roads lead to the two provinces. If we are victorious, we can certainly defend it. If we lose, we can easily retreat. Moreover, there is absolutely no way for the enemy troops to encircle us. If you add to this the Party and mass base in the various *xian*, we can indeed engage in a protracted struggle against the enemy. If we now recklessly abandon Ninggang, then "a tiger on the plain may be attacked by a dog," and the Fourth Red Army would be in very serious danger.

4) Our proposal by no means reflects conservative ideas. In the past the insurrections throughout the country were at one time very vigorous, but when one day the enemy troops launched counterattacks, they were easily swept away like water flushing the river bed. All this is the result of seeking only to build up the momentum of the insurrections without attempting to consolidate the bases. At present we are trying our best to correct this mistake by building a general headquarters for the military forces on the one hand, and by consolidating the bases on the other, to prepare the way for future uprisings in the two provinces of Hunan and Jiangxi. We are working hard in Yongxin and Ninggang and making progress every day. We are also moving toward Lianhua, Anfu, and the southwest of Ji'an to deepen the agrarian revolution and to create local armed forces. After one more month's work, we will be reasonably confident of winning a victory if the enemy troops come again to attack us.

5) From the economic standpoint, because the troops of the Fourth Army are so numerous, the daily cash allowance for meals, even practicing the utmost economy, is 700 *yuan*. Apart from burning and killing in the *xian* of southern Hunan, the local economy is bankrupt, and the local bullies have taken everything. After they arrived at Leiyang in February, the troops of Zhu De were not able to raise a single cash. They could keep alive only by selling opium. It is now absolutely impossible for them to go to southern Hunan to resolve their economic difficulties. Only in the Hunan-Jiangxi border area can the present economic difficulties truly be resolved.

6) Our wounded soldiers have increased in number to five hundred. If we rush forward toward southern Hunan [with the wounded soldiers], the soldiers' morale will be shaken. But we cannot leave them behind either. This is also one of the most difficult problems.

On the basis of the above six practical reasons, we conclude that, before a new war among the warlords breaks out, we cannot leave Ninggang, Yongxin, and Lianhua for southern Hunan. As soon as the bases here are somewhat consolidated, and there are some good opportunities elsewhere, the Fourth Red Army can leave Chaling, Youxian, and Liuyang to take part in the general insurrection in Hunan. In the meantime, every effort must be made to maintain the network of communication with Hunan, so that the two sides can correspond with each other and cooperate to show our strength.

We beg the Provincial Committee to give further consideration to the above opinions and to make new decisions according to the present situation. Such is our hope. Please allow us to present the detailed reports about the army and the local situation later.

Border Area Special Committee
Army Committee of the Fourth Red Army
City of Yongxin, July 4

Letter of the Special Committee of the Hunan-Jiangxi Border Area to the Hunan Provincial Committee

(August 1928)

Hunan Provincial Committee:

1. Comrade Du [Xiujing] has arrived and we have read the letter. The Army Committee here called an Enlarged Session on May 30, at which Comrade Du made a report on the political situation and read out the letter of the Provincial Committee. The Enlarged Session accepted the letter without reservation and attached great importance to Comrade Du's report, which synthesizes the lessons of the actual struggle in various places. The things that are mentioned in the letter of the Provincial Committee and call for an explanation are as follows: A. Actual strength. . . . To pool the Red efforts in the south and east of Hunan and those in the west of Jiangxi by means of guerrilla warfare depends solely on strength, but a reconnaissance of the enemy situation should be made before arriving at a decision on the action to be taken. B. We also agree that it is a mistake to organize a small group of people with few arms into independent regiments or battalions, but this has never been practiced here. C. Our [forces] here consist of troops under Zhu and Mao and a peasant army from southern Hunan. Now the southern Hunan peasant army has gone to operate in its home area. Originally it was established as the X Division; afterward, this was changed to the X Regiment.[1] Division headquarters have now been abolished, and army headquarters set up to exercise direct command.

2. The Provincial Committee points out that it is wrong to burn cities. We shall never commit this mistake again.

3. The Party has been formally organized throughout the army, the form of organization being modeled on that of the Party in the Guomindang Revolutionary Army.

4. In the past, the Southern Hunan Special Committee instructed us to orga-

---

Our source for this document is *Jinggangshande wuzhuang geju*, pp. 156–57. The same text is reproduced in *Mao Zedong ji. Bujuan*, Vol. 2, pp. 309–10.

1. From the texts of October and November 1928 which follow, it is clear that the unit number, omitted here, was "Twenty-ninth."

nize the CY[2] in the army. Our experience of the past few months shows that this is not convenient for our work. Then the Second CY Congress of the Fourth Army made a decision to merge the two,[3] and this time the Enlarged Session again confirmed the necessity of the merger. But this cannot be done on a partial and local basis and necessarily calls for a final decision from the Provincial Committee. This position differs from that of the Liquidationists, as the CY maintains a secretariat which enables it to participate fully in the work.

5. We will make great efforts to transform the army and cleanse it of the lumpenproletariat.

6. We made a plan long ago to abolish the wage system for the soldiers, but in fact the life of the soldiers is very difficult. Soldiers who bear such hardships and stand such hard work are really hard to come by.

7. Please send a large number of Anyuan miners to serve in our army.

8. The Provincial Committee has nominated Zedong as chairman of the Army Committee which has just been established. This seems unnecessary, because local work here is in more urgent need of hands. The Army Committee has not been completely organized yet. The secretary is Comrade Chen Yi. This instruction has not been carried out.

9. The Southern Hunan Special Committee has moved with the army to Zixin and will go to Hengyang via Anren. The responsible person from Yichen has returned. . . .

---

2. Communist Youth League. As already noted, it was common at the time to use the initials of English expressions as a shorthand or code in this way.

3. I.e., the Youth League and Party organizations in the army.

Jinggangshan

(To the Tune of "Moon over the West River")[1]

(Autumn 1928)

At the foot of the mountain, our flags and banners can be seen,
At its peak our drums and bugles are heard to respond.
The enemy troops besiege us thousands strong,
We stand alone and will not be moved.

Already our defense was like a stern fortress,
Now do our united wills form yet a stronger wall.
The roar of gunfire rises from Huangyangjie,[2]
Announcing the enemy has fled in the night.

Our source for this poem is *Shici duilian*, pp. 23–25.

1. For the convention of "tune title" (*cipai*), see note 1 to Mao's 1927 poem, "Autumn Harvest Uprising."

2. A strategic access route to the Jinggangshan occupied by enemy forces in August 1928, from which they were driven after a decisive battle on August 30. For Mao's own account of this campaign, see below, Chapter III of his report of November 25, 1928.

Draft Resolution of the Second Congress of Xian Party Organizations in the Hunan-Jiangxi Border Area[1]

(Buyunshan Mountain, Ninggang *Xian*, October 5, 1928)

I. Political Problems and Tasks of the Party Organizations in the Border Area

A. The Internal and External Political Situation

The present rule of the new warlords of the Guomindang remains the rule of the comprador class in the cities and the despotic gentry in the countryside. Abroad, it has capitulated to imperialism, and at home, it has replaced the old warlords by new ones, imposing even more savage economic exploitation and political oppression on the workers and peasants. The bourgeois-democratic revolution launched from Guangdong had gone only halfway when the compradors and despotic gentry seized the leadership and immediately shifted it to the road of counterrevolution. The workers, peasants, other common people, and even the bourgeoisie of the whole country are still subject to counterrevolutionary rule and have not secured the slightest bit of political or economic emancipation.

Before the capture of Beijing and Tianjin, the four cliques of new Guomindang warlords—Chiang Kaishek, the Guangxi warlords,[2] Feng

---

We have translated this document from *Jinggangshan geming genjudi* (The Revolutionary Base on the Jinggangshan), Vol. 1 (Beijing: Zhonggong dangshi ziliao chubanshe, 1987), pp. 181–95. This is the only known source which includes Part II. The version in the supplementary volume to the 1947 Jin-Cha-Ji edition of Mao's selected works, reproduced in *Mao Zedong ji*, Vol. 2, pp. 15–23, breaks off at the end of Part I, with the indication "balance omitted," and this section does not appear in Vol. 1 of the official *Selected Works*.

1. In the *Selected Works*, this document has been given the title "Why Is It That Red Political Power Can Exist in China?" The First Congress of the Party in the border area had taken place in May 1928 (see above, the note to the report of June 16, 1928). The Second Congress met from October 4 to 6, 1928. As noted in the Introduction to this volume, it marked the first stage in Mao's return to a leading position, after the period during which he had been reduced to the role of a military commander by the emissary from the Hunan Provincial Committee, Du Xiujing.

2. The leader of the so-called Guangxi clique, Li Zongren (1890–1969), *zi* Delin, was a native of Guilin in Guangxi. In the course of the two years 1924–1925, Li, with his two

Yuxiang,[3] and Yan Xishan[4]—had concluded a temporary alliance against Zhang Zuolin.[5] As soon as these cities were captured, the alliance immediately broke up, giving way to a situation of acute struggle among the four cliques, and now a war is brewing between Chiang and the Guangxi clique.[6] The contradictions and struggles among the various warlord cliques within China reflect the contradictions and struggles among the imperialist powers. Consequently,[7] under no circumstances can there be a compromise, and all compromises can only be temporary. A temporary compromise today prepares the ground for a bigger war tomorrow.

China is in urgent need of a bourgeois-democratic revolution, and this revolution can be carried through only under the leadership of the proletariat. In the 1926[8] revolution, which started from Guangdong and spread toward the Yangzi, because the proletariat failed to exercise its hegemony resolutely, and leadership was seized by the compradors and despotic gentry, there was a change in the nature of the revolution.[9] As a result, the bourgeois-democratic revolution met with a historic[10] defeat. *Broadly speaking, this defeat was similar to that of the*

---

chief subordinates Huang Shaohong and Bai Chongxi, established control over the whole of Guangxi. In 1926, he rallied to the Guomindang, and his forces became part of the National Revolutionary Army. Li played a major role in the victories of the Northern Expedition, and in the final drive on Beijing in June 1928.

3. On Feng Yuxiang, see above, the note to the declaration of August 1, 1927.

4. Yan Xishan (1883–1960), *zi* Baichuan, was a native of Shanxi. After graduating from the Military Academy in Japan, he became an instructor in the New Army and participated in the 1911 revolution. After the death of Yuan Shikai, he established himself as the sole ruler of Shanxi, allying himself with the Anfu clique of Duan Qirui. In 1922 and 1924, he supported the Zhili faction of Cao Kun and Wu Peifu against Zhang Zuolin, but after Feng Yuxiang's coup in Beijing in 1924, Yan established good relations with him as well. In 1927, he announced his allegiance to the Guomindang, and in 1928 his forces led the drive on Beijing.

5. Zhang Zuolin (1875–1928), *zi* Yuting, was a native of Fengtian (now Liaoning). From 1919 until his assassination in 1928, he ruled the northeastern provinces as a virtually autonomous state. Volume II of our edition contains a number of discussions by Mao of Zhang's role and of his conflicts with Wu Peifu's Zhili faction. See, in particular, pp. 239–46, the text of November 27, 1925, "Propaganda Guidelines of the Chinese Guomindang in the War against the Fengtian Clique."

6. Although Li Zongren, Feng Yuxiang, and Yan Xishan had all supported Chiang's Northern Expedition against Zhang Zuolin's Fengtian faction, it is quite true that this did not signal the end of conflict among them. After the fall of Beijing and Tianjin in June 1928, Chiang, Li, Feng, and Yan met in July to discuss military reorganization, but failed to come to an agreement.

7. Here the words "as long as the situation persists in which China is divided among the imperialist powers" have been inserted in the *Selected Works* version.

8. 1926 → 1926–1927

9. There was a change in the nature of the revolution → Revolution was replaced by counterrevolution.

10. A historic → A temporary

Russian Revolution in 1905. The Chinese proletariat and peasantry suffered a heavy blow in this defeat, and the Chinese bourgeoisie (but not the compradors and despotic gentry) suffered *similar* blows. Yet in the last few months, organized strikes in the cities and uprisings in the countryside, by the workers and peasants under the leadership of the Communist Party, have developed both in the north and in the south. Hunger and cold are creating great unrest among the soldiers of the warlord armies. Meanwhile, the bourgeoisie, led[11] by the clique of Wang Jingwei and Chen Gongbo,[12] is promoting a campaign of considerable proportions in favor of nationalism and people's rights and against imperialism, warlords, and the compradors and despotic gentry,[13] everywhere in coastal areas and along the Yangzi. This campaign is a new development; *as regards its nature, it is part of the democratic revolution China urgently needs.*

China's democratic revolution, according to the instructions from the International and the Central Committee, consists in overthrowing the rule of imperialism and its warlord tools in China, so as to complete the national revolution, and carrying out the agrarian revolution, thereby eliminating the feudal exploitation of the peasants by the despotic gentry. Such a revolutionary movement has been growing daily since the Ji'nan Massacre in May.[14]

The situation in China has undergone tremendous changes in the last few months, and the same is true of the international situation. Since the two developments represented by Japan's invasion of China, and the signing of the naval treaty between Britain and France have taken place, America, on the one hand, and Britain, France, and Japan, on the other, have found themselves polarized in positions of irreconcilable opposition. The present international situation is that, on questions touching China and Europe, the United States has adopted a policy of active intervention, while Britain, France, and Japan have adopted a policy of active resistance. Thus a world war is brewing, and its outbreak is merely a matter of time.

---

11. Led → Urged on

12. I.e., by the leaders of the former Left Guomindang régime. On Wang, see, above, the declaration of August 1, 1927. Chen Gongbo (1892–1946), a native of Guangdong, was a founding member of the Chinese Communist Party who participated in the First Congress, but he soon became disillusioned and gravitated toward the Guomindang. From 1927 onward, his political fortunes were linked to those of Wang Jingwei.

13. Campaign . . . despotic gentry → Reformist movement

14. The massacre at Ji'nan (Tsinan in contemporary English-language sources) took place while Chiang Kaishek and his armies were passing through the city in the direction of Beijing, in the course of the Northern Expedition. Japan had sent troops there, ostensibly to protect her citizens residing in Ji'nan. Despite the conciliatory attitude of Chiang Kaishek, clashes occurred, and when an ultimatum from the Japanese commander was not immediately complied with, a Japanese offensive was launched on May 8. In three days of fighting, thousands of Chinese soldiers and civilians were killed, in what proved to be the first in a series of "incidents" leading to full-scale war between the two countries.

B. *Reasons for the Emergence and Survival of Soviet* [15] *Political Power in* **Various Places in Present-Day** *China*

The prolonged existence inside a country of one or more small areas under Red political power, surrounded on all sides by White political power, is something which has never occurred anywhere else in the world. There are special reasons for the emergence of this curious thing. Moreover, it can exist and develop only under certain conditions. First, it cannot occur in any imperialist country, or in any colony under direct imperialist rule. It necessarily takes place in economically backward and semicolonial China, which is under indirect imperialist rule. For this strange phenomenon can occur only in conjunction with another strange phenomenon, namely, war within the White régime. The *most* remarkable feature of semicolonial China consists in the incessant wars among the various factions of old and new warlords *within the country*, supported by the compradors and despotic gentry,[16] since the very first year of the Republic. Such a phenomenon is not to be found in any of the imperialist countries, nor in any of the colonies under direct imperialist rule. It occurs solely in China, which is under indirect imperialist rule. There are two reasons for the emergence of this phenomenon: a localized agricultural economy (not a unified capitalist economy) and the policy of the imperialist forces to divide and exploit through spheres of influence. Because of the prolonged splits and wars among the White political forces, one or several small areas of Red political power have come into existence surrounded on all sides by White political power.[17] The independent régime on the borders of Hunan and Jiangxi is one of many such small areas. In difficult and critical times, some comrades often have doubts as to the survival of such Red political power and manifest negative tendencies.[18] This is because they fail to find the correct explanation for the development and existence of such Red political power. If only we know that splits and wars among the White political forces will continue without interruption, we will have no doubts about the emergence, survival, and daily growth of Red political power. Second, the places in China where *small areas* under Red political power have come into existence and lasted for a *relatively* long time are definitely not those unaffected by the democratic revolution, such as Sichuan, Guizhou, Yunnan, or the northern provinces, but *only* regions like Hunan, Guangdong, Hubei and Jiangxi, where

---

15. Here, and throughout this text, "Soviet political power" (*suweiai zhengquan*) has been replaced by "Red political power" (*hongse zhengquan*).

16. Compradors and despotic gentry → Imperialism and the compradors and despotic gentry within the country

17. One or several small areas of Red political power have come into existence surrounded on all sides by White political power → The conditions have been created for the emergence and survival of one or more small Red areas under the leadership of the Communist Party amid the encirclement of the White political power.

18. Negative tendencies → Pessimistic feelings

the masses of workers, peasants and soldiers rose in great numbers in the course of the bourgeois-democratic revolution two years ago.[19] In many parts of these provinces, trade unions and peasant associations were organized on a wide scale, and many economic and political struggles were waged by the worker and peasant classes against the urban and rural bourgeoisie.[20] As a result, an urban soviet régime[21] lasting three days emerged in Guangzhou, while independent peasant régimes existed in Haifeng and Lufeng, in eastern and southern Hunan, in the Hunan-Jiangxi Border Area, and in Huang'an, Hubei. As for the *emergence* of the present-day Red Army, it *can only be* a split-off from the National Revolutionary Army, which underwent democratic political training and came under the influence of the masses of the workers and peasants. Armies such as those of Yan Xishan and Zhang Zuolin, which have received no political training at all and have never come under the influence of the workers and peasants, cannot possibly give rise to elements that can serve to constitute a Red Army. Third, whether it is possible for the worker-peasant-soldier soviet political power[22] in small areas to "survive for a long time" hinges on whether or not the nationwide revolutionary situation continues to move forward. If it does, then not only will the small areas under Red political power undoubtedly survive for a long time, but they will definitely become one of the many forces contributing to the seizure of overall political power. If the revolution does not continue to move forward in the country as a whole, but stagnates for a fairly long period of time, *as in the case of Russia from 1905 to 1917*, then long-term survival of the small areas under Red political power will be impossible. *What, then, is* the situation of the Chinese revolution? *In reality, it* is continuing to develop along with the continuous splits and wars within the ranks of the domestic bourgeoisie[23] and the international bourgeoisie. Therefore not only will the small areas under Red political power undoubtedly last for a long time, but they will continue to develop and gradually approach the seizure of overall political power. Fourth, the existence of a regular Red Army of adequate strength is a necessary condition for the existence of Red political power. If we had only Red Guards of a local character, but no regular Red Army, we could deal only with the household militia,[24] but not with the White armies. Consequently, even if there were the most excellent worker and peasant masses, without adequate armed forces,[25] it would still be absolutely impossible to create an independent régime, let alone a durable and constantly developing independent régime. It follows that the idea of

---

19. Two years ago → Of 1926 and 1927
20. Urban and rural bourgeoisie → The landlords and despotic gentry and the bourgeoisie
21. An urban soviet régime → A régime of the masses
22. Worker-peasant-soldier soviet political power → Political power of the popular masses
23. Domestic bourgeoisie → The compradors and despotic gentry within the country
24. On the "household militia" (*aihutuan*), see the note to the text of June 18, 1928.
25. Armed forces → Regular armed forces

"establishing independent régimes of the workers and peasants by armed force" is an important one, that must be fully assimilated by the Communist Party, and by the masses of the workers and peasants in areas under the independent régimes. Fifth, in addition to the above-mentioned conditions, there is another important prerequisite for the long-term existence and development of the Red political power, namely, that the Communist Party's organization must be strong, and its policy correct.

C. The Independent Régime in the Border Area and the August Defeat

The splits and wars among the warlords have weakened the ability of the White régime to rule. Thus opportunities have been provided for the rise of Red political power in small areas. But fighting among the warlords does not go on every day without ceasing. Whenever the White political power in one or more provinces enjoys temporary stability, the ruling class of one province, or an alliance of the ruling classes of several provinces, will surely exert every effort to destroy Red political power. In areas where all the conditions for Red political power are not completely met, it will assuredly be overthrown by them.[26] That is why Red political régimes emerging at favorable moments before last April in *many* small areas such as Guangzhou, Hailufeng, the Hunan-Jiangxi Border Area, southern Hunan, Liling, and Huang'an, were crushed one after another by the White political power. From April onward, the independent régime in the Hunan-Jiangxi Border Area was confronted with a situation in which the ruling forces in the south were enjoying temporary stability. The troops sent by the two provinces of Hunan and Jiangxi to annihilate us were always more than eight or nine regiments, and at times as many as fifteen.[27] Yet with a force of less than four regiments we fought the enemy for four long months, daily enlarging the territory under our independent régime, deepening the agrarian revolution, extending the soviet organizations, and strengthening the Red Army and the Red Guards. This was possible because the policies of the Party organizations (local and army) in the border area were correct. The policies of the Border Area Special Committee and the Army Committee of the Party at that time were as follows: Struggle resolutely against the enemy, set up political power in the middle section of the Luoxiao mountain range, and oppose escapist *defeatism*; deepen the agrarian revolution in areas under the independent régime; let the army Party organizations promote the development of local Party organizations, and let the regular army foster the development of local armed forces; concentrate the Red Army units so as to deal at opportune moments with the enemy confronting them, and oppose the division of forces to avoid being wiped out[28] one by one; adopt

---

26. In areas where all the conditions for Red political power are not completely met, it will assuredly be overthrown by them → In areas where all the necessary conditions for its establishment and persistence are not fulfilled, Red political power is in danger of being overthrown by the enemy.

27. Fifteen → Eighteen

28. Wiped out → Wiped out by the enemy

the policy of expanding the area under the independent régime in a series of waves, and oppose adventurist tactics. Thanks to the appropriateness of these tactics, to a terrain in the border area which was favorable to our struggle, and to the inadequate coordination between the troops invading from Hunan and those from Jiangxi, we were able to win victory on so many occasions in the four months from April through July. The enemy, though many times stronger than we were, was not only unable to destroy our independent régime but also lent an impetus[29] to its daily expansion, and our régime tended to exert an ever-growing influence on the two provinces of Hunan and Jiangxi. The August defeat resulted entirely from the failure to understand[30] that the period was one of temporary stability for the ruling classes and from the adoption of a strategy suited to a time of political splits among the ruling classes, dividing our troops for a rash advance, and thus bringing about a defeat both in the border area and in southern Hunan. Comrade Du Xiujing, the representative of the Provincial Committee,[31] did not investigate the actual situation and paid no attention to the resolution passed at the Joint Conference of the Special Committee, the Army Committee, and the Yongxin *Xian* Committee [on May 20, 1928]. He simply applied formalistically the orders from the Hunan Provincial Committee and fell in with the action[32] of the Twenty-ninth Regiment, which wanted to evade struggle and return home. His error was truly a grave one.[33]

D. The Role of the Border-Area Independent Régime in the Worker-Peasant Insurrections in Hunan, Hubei, and Jiangxi Provinces

The significance of the armed independent régime of the workers and peasants in the Hunan-Jiangxi Border Area, with Ninggang as its center, is assuredly not confined to the few *xian* in the border area; this régime has a very great role to play in the process of worker and peasant insurrection to seize political power in Hunan, Hubei, and Jiangxi. To extend the influence of the agrarian revolution and of the soviet political power in the border area to the lower reaches of the rivers in Hunan and Jiangxi and even as far as Hubei; constantly to expand the Red Army and to enhance its quality through struggle, so that it will be able to carry out its necessary mission in the coming general insurrection in the three provinces; to enlarge the local armed forces in the various *xian*, that is, the Red Guards and the worker-peasant insurrection detachments, and improve their quality, so that they are able now to fight the household militia and small armed units and will be capable in future of safeguarding the political power of the

29. Lent an impetus → Was unable to prevent
30. The failure to understand → The failure of some of the comrades to understand
31. Provincial Committee → Hunan Provincial Committee
32. Action → Views
33. Here the *Selected Works* text adds the following sentence: "The situation arising from this defeat was salvaged as a result of the corrective measures taken by the Special Committee and the Army Committee of the Party after September."

border area; gradually to reduce the dependence of personnel[34] on the assistance of Red Army workers, so that the border area will be completely self-reliant and will not only have its own personnel to take charge of work there but will even be able to provide personnel for the Red Army and the expanded territory of the independent régime—such are the tasks of extreme importance for the border area Party organizations, in connection with the insurrection unfolding in the three provinces of Hunan, Hubei, and Jiangxi.

E. Economic Problems

The shortage of daily necessities and cash has become a very serious problem[35] inside the White encirclement. Because of the tight enemy blockade, daily necessities such as salt, cloth, and medicine have been very scarce and dear in the territory of the independent *soviet* régime in the border area throughout the whole of the past year. As a result, the lives of the masses of the workers, peasants, and petty bourgeoisie, as well as of the masses of the soldiers of the Red Army have been disrupted, sometimes to an extreme degree. The Red Army has to fight and provision itself at the same time. It even lacks funds to pay the daily food allowance of five cents per person;[36] the soldiers are undernourished, many are ill, and the wounded in hospitals suffer even more. Such difficulties are, of course, unavoidable before the nationwide seizure of political power. It is, however, urgently necessary to overcome them to some degree, that is, to make life a little easier and, in particular, to secure more adequate supplies for the Red Army. Unless the Party in the border area can find appropriate methods for coping with the economic problems, the future of the independent régime will be filled with difficulties if the stability of the enemy forces lasts for a relatively long period. A proper solution of these economic problems truly deserves the attention of every Party member.

F. The Problem of Military Bases

There is yet another task facing the Party in the border area, namely, to consolidate the two military bases of Five Wells and Jiulong. Five Wells,[37] at the juncture of the four *xian* of Yongxin, Lingxian, Ninggang, and Suichuan, and Jiulong,[38] at the juncture of the four *xian* of Yongxin, Ninggang, Chaling, and Lianhua, both have topographical advantages; not only are they important military bases for the border area at present but they will remain *among the* import-

---

34. Personnel → Local personnel
35. Serious problem → Serious problem for the army and the people
36. Here the *Selected Works* text adds: ". . . which is provided in addition to grain."
37. Five Wells → The Five Wells mountain district
38. Jiulong → The Jiulong mountain district

ant military bases for the future insurrections in the three provinces of Hunan, Hubei, and Jiangxi. This is particularly true of Five Wells, where we have the popular masses,[39] as well as a terrain that is especially difficult and strategically important. The way to consolidate these bases is, first, to build up a system of defense; second, to store a sufficient amount of grain; and third, to set up relatively good Red Army hospitals. The Party in the border area must devote the utmost efforts to the effective completion of these three tasks.

II. The Transformation of the Party in the *Xian* of the Border Area and Some Recommendations[40]

The Special Committee of the Border Area was founded only four months ago. During this short period of time, it has done a great deal in leading the Workers' and Peasants' Red Army in tasks such as carrying out the "land revolution," "establishing the Soviets," and striking devastating blows at the old society. Nevertheless, because of the rural economic environment of the border area, because the history of the Party is very short, and because there have been very few independent struggles (since there is the Red Army to rely on), the tendency toward a peasant party marked by an opportunist heritage is frightfully apparent in every Party branch at all levels in the Border Area. It is an important responsibility of every Party branch from now on to point out all the past errors within the party, eliminate the evil legacy of opportunism within the Party, reform the Party branches at all levels, and cause the Party to take the road of true proletarian leadership.

The Party has not yet been set up in Youxian. The influence of the Party in the other *xian* can only reach most or part of those *xian*. Strong central districts[41] have not been set up, nor has the Party extended its influence to the broad masses in every direction. Hence it is also an important responsibility of Party branches in the Border Area from now on to set up a Party branch in Youxian and strong central districts in every *xian*, and establish a foundation for the Party in every *xian*.

A. The Past Mistakes of the Party

1. In the past the evil legacy of opportunism has been excessively strong in the Party in every *xian*, and we have relied on the army rather than leading an independent struggle of the masses. This has been a very great error.

---

39. Popular masses → Support of the popular masses
40. As indicated above, in the source note, Part II of this text, amounting to more than half of the whole, is omitted not only from the official *Selected Works*, but from all other previously available versions. Because this passage is so long, we have not set it in italics, as has been done in the case of all other passages deleted by Mao in 1950.
41. *Zhongxin qu*, here translated "central districts," were temporary Party organs set up in the fluid and rapidly changing circumstances prevailing at the time, in places where the strength of the Party was insufficient to justify establishing *xian*-level organizations.

2. In the past, the Party in every *xian* had strongly marked characteristics of a peasant party, and showed a tendency to evolve toward non-proletarian leadership. The Party in Yongxin wanted to break away publicly from the special committee and set up an "independent kingdom." The other *xian*, such as Ning[gang], Ling[xian], Lian[hua] and so on also paid no attention to reporting to the Special Committee and thereby forming a connection with it. These were all serious organizational errors.

3. In the past, in the early period, the Party organs were all individual dictatorships, autocracies of the Party secretary; there was no collective leadership or democratic spirit whatsoever. For instance, Mao Zedong was the only member of the Special Committee, and Liu Zhen was the only member of the Party committee of Yongxin *xian*. In practice, this led to the error that the masses knew only the individual but not the Party. This is absolutely not a Bolshevik Party. Although this mistake was forcefully pointed out at the Emergency Conference,[42] and there are always three Standing Committee members supervising the work of the Special Committee, it is still impossible to set up the various departments and the Secretariat because of the shortage of personnel. In addition, many people working for the Special Committee are ill. Politics is constantly changing, the relationship between the Party committees of the various *xian* and the Special Committee cannot become intimate, and as a result, the Special Committee itself opposes the instructions from the general headquarters at various levels, and has not tried its best to carry out the decisions of the Emergency Conference.

4. Most of the leading organs are headed by petty bourgeois intellectuals, and not enough attention is paid to promoting people of worker and peasant background to serve on the leading organs.

5. In the expansion of the Party organization in the past, attention was paid exclusively to quantitative development, rather than to improving the quality. Party and class were not clearly distinguished, and press-ganging was the only method of recruitment employed. This will ruin the Party organization, and as a result the Party will become incapable of struggle.

6. In the past the Party neglected the basic organization—the branch.

7. In the past, the Party's method of work was wrong. The authority for dealing with every problem concerning the Party should be concentrated in the Standing Committee, and in the Organization Department, the Propaganda Department . . . , and so on, which are after all the technical departments of the Standing Committee. In the Party in the Border Area, however, not only is power not concentrated in the Standing Committee, but there is not even an organization department. It is merely a matter of the autocracy of the Party secretary.

---

42. The reference is not to the August 7, 1927, conference, but to the emergency conference called by Mao in mid-August 1928 at Jiupi in Yongxin *xian*, when Yuan Desheng brought a letter from the Hunan Provincial Committee demanding that the Red Army immediately march toward eastern Hunan. (See above, the brief account of this meeting in the Introduction.)

After the Emergency Conference, things in the Special Committee itself and in the Party committee of Yongxin *xian* improved a bit (all work is decided by the standing committee). The Party organizations at various levels below the Special Committee still suffer, however, from the same defects, and have not corrected these errors at all.

8. In the past the Party in the various *xian* of the Border Area paid much too little attention to secret work, to the point where quite a large number of Party members did not understand secret work. When taking political power, they made everything public; when they lost power, they would simply "lie in ambush."

9. In our work in the past, the upper levels were always separated from the lower levels, nor did the upper levels satisfactorily inspect and supervise the lower levels. The Party only paid attention to the work in the various organs, and committed the error of separating itself from the masses.

10. In the past the Party paid very little attention to the work in the urban areas, and to the workers' movement.

11. In the past the Special Committee only paid attention to military dispositions, for example, to the work in the two *xian* of Ninggang and Yongxin. It did not take account of the whole, to the extent that it became a subsidiary of the army. If the army took a certain *xian*, it would begin to pay attention to the work there; if the army did not reach a certain *xian*, the work in that *xian* would be ignored.

12. In the past the Party slighted the work of the Youth League to an extreme degree, or even displayed a tendency to eliminate the Youth League.

B. Transforming and Building the Party From Now on

1. The Party must be thoroughly transformed, starting with the transformation of the branches, eliminating opportunist leadership both in organization and in policy.

2. The Special Committee and the *xian* committees should each have at least four inspectors. They should regularly guide the work at the lower levels, and aid in the transformation of Party organizations at all levels.

3. Do your utmost to promote as many worker comrades as possible to leading organs. Executive committees and standing committees at every level should have more than half worker and peasant comrades participating. In promoting worker and peasant elements, we should pay special attention to the significance of education.

4. The party organs at every level must be fully organized, and individual leadership must be opposed. All power should be concentrated in the standing committee, while the various departments are the technical organs.

5. In the course of transforming the Party, we must adopt a completely proletarian point of view. We must make the utmost efforts to pay attention to discussing and carrying out the new policies of the Party. We must resolutely

[distance ourselves] from the petty-bourgeois, liberal, independent, and romantic elements in the Party's past, and be strictly on guard against the tendency to form "independent kingdoms."

6. The Party should extend democratization to the highest possible degree. Every policy should be discussed enthusiastically and understood thoroughly by the Party members, so that the mass of Party members will be able to establish their work plans in accordance with the policies. The Party committee members as well as the secretaries at every level should be chosen by the method of elections.

7. Party members should consist of progressive, conscious, loyal, and courageous poor workers and peasants; strict limits should be set on petty-bourgeois elements, intellectuals, and rich peasants.

8. In the development of the Party, special attention should be paid to quality. When introducing Party members, the sponsors should do a lot of propaganda work toward, and investigation work about, those being introduced. Whenever a new comrade is introduced, he should be approved at a Party branch meeting, and then endorsed by the district committee. We oppose the press-gang method of recruiting Party members. We must make sure that every Party member is a proletarian fighter. The Party organization must not seek to become universal, but should pay special attention to creating the basis for a strong Party in the central districts.

9. The Party should pay attention to its basic organization—the branch, and put into practice the slogan "All of our work depends finally on the branch." At the same time, special attention should be paid to branch work in the urban areas, and excellent worker comrades should also be promoted to become branch Party secretaries and committee members in the rural areas, so as to increase the leadership capacity of the workers and be strictly on guard against the tendency toward a peasant party. We must choose progressive elements among the Party members in the rural areas, and give them special training, so as to prepare them to become the backbone of the Party.

10. The organization of the Party should be absolutely secret. Every Party member in every Party organization at every level should make the utmost effort to pay attention to secret work. We oppose relying on military and political strength to organize the Party. The Party should be organized secretly within the area controlled by the enemy group; fleeing and "lying in ambush" should be opposed.

11. The Special Committee should pay the utmost attention to the soundness of its own organization, as well as that of every *xian* committee. The Youxian *Xian* Committee should be set up at once, and there should be overall arrangements for the Party's work in each and every one of the *xian* in the border area.

12. "Iron discipline" is the primary trait of a Bolshevik party. Only in this way can we prevent the Party from taking a non-proletarian road. Only by wiping out opportunists and eliminating corrupt elements who refuse to struggle

can we gather together the strength of the revolutionary progressive elements and unite them around the Party, so that the Party will be strongly fortified and march in step to become a powerful fighting organization. Only thus can we enhance the leadership capacity of the proletariat. Consequently, the strict application of discipline is an important task in transforming and building the Party center.

C. The Question of the Work in Every Xian

It is the responsibility of the Special Committee to discuss the detailed plan for the work in every *xian*.

D. The Question of the Struggle in the Rural Areas

1. In the past, the struggle in the rural areas did not carry out the "land revolution" at all resolutely. The so-called redistribution of the land wholly failed to satisfy the thoroughgoing demands of the impoverished farm laborers. Instead it was an equal distribution based on the compromising standpoint of the rich peasants, middle peasants, and poor peasants. This is a great mistake which has been made in the past.

2. In the past, while carrying out the "land revolution," we entirely failed to impose a severe Red terror, and to massacre the landlords and despotic gentry as well as their running dogs (this was done somewhat better in Lianhua and Chaling).

3. In the past, under the Red political power in the rural areas, we largely neglected the class struggle between the rich peasants, the middle peasants and the poor peasants in the countryside. As a result there was no unity and strength of the poor peasants under the White terror, the rich peasants defected, and the middle peasants wavered.

4. Our overall strategy in the rural struggles from now on is: unite the poor peasants; pay attention to the middle peasants; plunge into the land revolution; strictly impose Red terror; massacre the landlords and the despotic gentry as well as their running dogs without the slightest compunction; threaten the rich peasants by means of the Red terror so that they will not dare to assist the landlord class.

5. On the basis of this strategy, we should immediately organize the following: (1) A farm laborers' union (poor sharecroppers should join this organization), which will serve to unite the farm laborers, enhance their strength, and make them the backbone in the countryside. (2) Red execution teams or insurrection teams, which should be organized under the White terror from the bravest workers and peasants. Each Red execution team should consist of five to seven persons. They should carry out guerrilla attacks in the dead of night to create a Red terror in the countryside. When political power has been seized, the Red execution team can be changed into Red Guards. (3) Select the brave elements from among the workers and peasants, and organize them into insurrection teams to develop the insurrection in the countryside and seize political power there.

E. The Question of the Workers' Movement

1. Workers are the vanguard of all the toiling masses, they are the leaders of all the toiling masses. In the past we paid no attention to the workers' movement, let alone leadership by the workers. As a result, the tendency toward a peasant party emerged. This is a very serious crisis for the Party.

2. Our Party should make a great effort to organize unions among the handicraft workers in the countryside, as well as among the workers in the urban areas, lead the workers from fragmentary economic struggles to armed uprising, and correct our past mistake of ignoring the workers' movement.

3. Party headquarters and soviets at every level should make great efforts to promote workers, so that they will be able to assume leadership positions and lead the struggle.

F. The Question of the Soldiers' Movement

The reason the Chinese Communist Party advocates the policy of "armed uprising to seize political power" is that in carrying out this policy it is necessary to coordinate very well the three forces represented by the workers, peasants, and soldiers, for only then will a victorious uprising be possible. Because China's "democratic revolution" has not yet been carried out, the warlords, despotic gentry, and comprador class are able to make use of feudal relationships to fool the workers and peasants and make mercenaries of them, claiming that [the warlord armies] are instruments for protecting them. As a result, the majority of those now serving as soldiers feel quite at ease living a hungry and bitter life under the command of their class enemies (some soldiers in the enemy armies have not received any pay for years). Before the Guomindang turned traitor, the National Revolutionary Army had, however, received some kind of propaganda regarding "class struggle." As for those who gravitated to the military camps after the incident[43] (employees of the peasants' associations or the labor unions), they are naturally endowed with even more consciousness. Under great pressure and close watch from the reactionary officers, it is not easy for these conscious elements to find leaders, so they do not dare rashly to conduct propaganda and organizational work in the reactionary military camp. In reality, however, they are filled with revolutionary sentiments, and are very willing to defect. This serves to demonstrate that the possibility of a soldiers' movement already exists objectively. Moreover, the success of this kind of movement has been proven a reality in Hunan, Guangdong, and other provinces. The present obstacle of reactionary force depends entirely on the several millions of as yet unawakened soldiers of the National Revolutionary Army. If we do a good job with our

---

43. *Shibian*, i.e., the rupture of the Guomindang with the Communist Party in the spring and summer of 1927.

soldiers' movement, reactionary rule will quickly collapse. If, on the other hand, we ignore the soldiers' movement and concentrate exclusively on work with the peasants instead, the Chinese revolution will never succeed.

The Party organizations at all levels in the Border Area have always paid little attention to work with the soldiers, and concentrated on the peasant movement alone. (Some Party organizations have nothing but peasant work.) We should bear in mind that many of our experiences of failure in the past can be attributed mainly to the absence of participation by the soldiers' movement in the insurrection. (The uprising in Guangdong at the end of last year, the repeated failure of uprisings in Hunan . . . [are examples of this].)[44] If we continue to pay no attention to this, then future failures can be predicted. It is very evident that if we now rely solely on the subjective force in the Border Area, it will be impossible to entertain vain hopes of carving out a kingdom for ourselves, or to set up a bigger independent régime. Therefore Party organizations at all levels must make great efforts to develop the soldiers' movement. We must never forget that the policy of "an armed uprising to seize political power" can only be carried out if the three forces of the workers, peasants, and soldiers are coordinated.

1. At the present the soldiers' movement is as important as the workers' and peasants' movements. Every *xian* should select a large number of worker and peasant comrades, in a planned and organized way, and send them to the reactionary army to become soldiers, porters, cooks, and so on, and thus play a role within the enemy's forces. Special attention should be paid to this work in Yongxin, Chaling, Suichuan and other *xian* where large numbers of enemy troops are concentrated.

2. Strengthen the propaganda work directed toward the enemy soldiers.

3. Send some people to the interior of the enemy forces to organize the Party. Do not organize soldiers' committees, so as to avoid organizational complexities, and the risk of discovery by enemy officers.

4. Use inconspicuous comrades, and women in the rural areas, to conduct oral propaganda and agitation.

5. Spread rumors and instigate terror, in order to shake the morale of the enemy, thus leading to wavering and ultimately to collapse.

G. The Question of Propaganda

1. In the past the Party organizations in all the *xian* of the Border Area paid no attention at all to propaganda, imagining that they could establish a kingdom with nothing but a few rifles. They did not know that the Communist Party can

---

44. The reference is to the Guangzhou commune of December 1927, the Autumn Harvest Uprising of September 1927 in Hunan, and the uprising in the spring of 1928 in southern Hunan. Mao may also have been thinking of events in the early summer of 1927 documented in Volume II of this edition.

overthrow the enemy only by holding propaganda pamphlets in its left hand and rifles and bullets in its right hand. Meanwhile in none of their work (such as organizing soviets and insurrection teams, redistributing the land, organizing the Party and so on) did they make propaganda about their methods and their significance. They made use only of military and political strength to force others to do things, [saying] "If you don't obey, we will kill you." This was an extremely serious mistake.

2. We must find a way to perfect propaganda departments in the Special Committee as well as in the *xian* Party committees. Every week, slogans and a propaganda outline should be sent out on time. The daily wall newspaper should also be distributed to the Party organizations at every level for them to copy and post. Whenever a guerrilla unit sets out on a guerrilla mission, there should be good propaganda (mass assembly—speeches in makeup, propaganda team, and individual propaganda).

3. In the future, the work reports of subordinate Party organizations to their superior Party organizations must include a report on propaganda work. When inspecting and investigating the work of lower levels, the higher levels should also pay attention to the inspection and examination of their propaganda work. The Special Committee as well as the *xian* Party committees should distribute their propaganda outlines to all lower-level Party organizations on a weekly basis.

4. For the present, we should try our best to make a political analysis of the internal clashes among the warlords, and pay attention to propaganda work directed against the chaotic struggles among warlords. At the same time, we should make extremely forceful propaganda about the great strength of the workers, the peasants, and the Communist Party, explaining that in the end the chaotic struggles among the warlords will be wiped out by a worker and peasant insurrection.

5. At present, our propaganda toward the worker and peasant masses as a whole should forcefully expose the policies of the warlords and despotic gentry for cheating the workers and peasants, and forcefully propagate the views of our Party.

6. The soviets, the agrarian revolution, communism, the Red Army, and the insurrection teams should all be the subject of specialized propaganda outlines. We should intensify this propaganda, and cause it to penetrate deeply into the minds of the masses.

7. Right now we should analyze in detail for our comrades and for the masses the political and economic contradictions and clashes within the ruling class. We should do our best to make propaganda about the strength of the workers and peasants themselves, as well as the forces of insurrection in various regions, and shatter the defeatist view that there is no hope of recovery. At the same time, we should also shatter among our comrades and the masses the passive view of relying solely on the army. (Of course we do not

deny the strength of the army in launching uprisings, and in assisting the workers and peasants to launch uprisings).

H. The Question of Training

1. In the past, the reason why the local Party organizations were not strong was that Party members lacked training, even to the extent that there was no ceremony of admission into the Party. Now every Party member must receive training in the basic theories of the Party.

2. The Special Committee will organize an education and propaganda committee, compile training materials, and plan the weekly training work.

3. The Special Committee should organize regular training classes. Every *xian* should also run as many short-term training classes as possible, in order to produce people qualified to be cadres.

4. At the Party organization meetings at various levels, and in the course of actual work, we should try our best to promote worker and peasant elements, and train these workers and peasants as people qualified to be cadres.

5. At present, basic training work should strive to eliminate the opportunist, feudal, and petty-bourgeois thought of the ordinary comrades, and establish among them the revolutionary outlook on life of the proletariat.

6. Raise the level of literacy and political education of our comrades. At the same time, we should also launch a literacy drive, so as to raise the "writing" and "reading" ability of our worker and peasant comrades.

I. The Question of the Soviets

1. In the past the politics of the soviet was really nothing but a metamorphosis of the peasant association, so its work was monopolized by the secretary general and chairman. Some of the governments were even controlled by rich peasants and became magistrate's yamens. These so-called soviet governments should all without exception be reorganized.

2. The Special Committee should enact a law regarding soviet organization, and all *xian*, district, and township soviets should be organized according to this organization law.

3. The soviets must have workers, poor peasants, and revolutionary soldiers as their main force. They must oppose the control of rich peasant secretaries general, and put into practice "all political power to the Soviets."

4. The government of the Hunan-Jiangxi Border Region must once again be thoroughly transformed.

5. The relationship between Party organizations and soviets at all levels should be clarified, to eliminate the evil of equating the Party with the government. The Special Committee must issue a circular regarding the difference between the Party and the government, and the Party organizations at various levels should conduct extensive propaganda.

J. The Land Question. We Accept the Central Committee's Circular Regarding the Land Question, and Will Hand It Over to the Special Committee for Discussion before Making a Final Decision.

K. The Question of the C.Y.

1. The Youth League is a political organization of the Party among the worker and peasant masses. In the past many of the League headquarters at various levels in the border region were unclear about the political tasks of the Youth League. In the various *xian* of the Border Area, the Youth League only carried out a few cultural movements intended to expand its influence. In reality it became a subordinate organ of the party, and this led to an even more serious mistake by the Party organizations at various levels in the Border Area—they advocated eliminating the League.

2. At present, all the *xian* of the Border Area should engage in the work of building the Youth League. Since, however, the strength of the League itself is deficient, and it can scarcely shoulder this responsibility alone, the Party organizations at various levels must set aside part of their strength [for this purpose], and constantly pay attention to Youth League work. They should help it to establish League branches in every *xian* in the Border Area, expand League organizations, and perfect the leading organs of the Youth League.

3. The budget of the League should be independent, so that it will be able to do what it wants as far as its operations are concerned, and avoid budgetary dependence of the Youth League on the Party.

4. Paying attention to the work of the Youth League is a responsibility which must be assumed by the Party organizations at all levels. From now on, the reports of Party organizations at all levels to their superiors must include a section entitled "the work of the Youth League." While investigating the work at various levels, inspectors from higher levels must also pay attention to Youth League work.

5. Most of the Party organizations and League organizations at various levels have not understood the relationship between the Party and the League, and as a result, there has been a tendency for each to go its own way.

Report of the Jinggangshan Front Committee to the Central Committee[1]

(November 25, 1928)

Hunan Provincial Party Committee: Please forward this report to the Central Committee.

I. About the Letter from the Central Committee

The June 4 letter from the Central Committee passed through the hands of the Jiangxi Provincial Committee and the Ji'an Xian Committee and did not reach the Jinggangshan till December 2.[2] This is an excellent letter. It has corrected many of our mistakes and resolved many controversial issues here. As soon as it arrived, we sent copies to Party committees at all levels, both in the army and in the localities. Troops which had set out for Suichuan gathered in Jinggangshan on November 6, and the Special Committee called a meeting of over thirty people to discuss the letter from the Central Committee. Participants were Special Committee members and activists in the army and in the localities. (Those who attended included Zhu De, Chen Yi, He Tingying, He Changgong, Yuan Wencai, Wang Zuo, Tan Zhenlin,[3] Deng Ganyuan, Li Quefei, Chen Zhengren,

---

Our source for this document is *Mao Zedong ji*, Vol. 2, pp. 25–66, which reproduces the text as published in the supplementary volume to the 1947 Jin-Cha-Ji edition of Mao's selected works.

1. The title in the *Selected Works* is "The Struggle on the Jinggangshan." None of the headings in this text, at whatever level, are numbered in the revised version. To avoid confusion, we have not set the numbers alone (whether in roman numerals, letters, or arabic numbers) in italics to show that they have been deleted. Words and phrases omitted from the headings have, however, been set in italics—or in roman, where the heading itself is in italics. As indicated by the use of italics, the whole of Section I has been omitted from the *Selected Works*.

2. December 2 is a misprint; the correct date, given in a number of sources, is November 2. For the full text of the letter, see "Zhongyang zhi Zhu De, Mao Zedong bing qianwei xin" (Letter of the Central Committee to Mao Zedong and Zhu De, and to the Front Committee), in *Central Committee Documents*, Vol. 4, pp. 239–57.

3. Tan Zhenlin (1902–1983) was born in Yuxian in Eastern Hunan, not far from the Jinggangshan. He worked in bookstores and in the printing trade from the age of 12 and joined the Communist Party in 1926. He participated in the Autumn Harvest Uprising

Wang Zuonong, Xiao Wanxia, Liu Huixiao, Xie Chunbiao, Liu Di, Xiong Shouqi, Yang Kaiming, Cao Shuo, Deng Jiuting, Mao Zedong, Song Qiaosheng, and Peng Gu. The representative of the Hunan Provincial Committee, Yuan Desheng, also participated.) It was recognized that, apart from one or two points relating to concrete circumstances (such as [the recommendations] that guerrilla warfare should be extended to an excessively wide area, and that the system of Party representatives should be abolished),[4] *all the principles and strategies embodied in the letter were extremely appropriate to the current situation, and we should act accordingly. A Front Committee was also immediately organized as the Party's supreme organ [in the border area].*[5] *In accordance with the letter, the Front Committee now comes under the jurisdiction of the Jiangxi Provincial Committee, because it is in Jiangxi at the moment. When it moves to Hunan, it comes automatically under the jurisdiction of the Hunan Provincial Committee. At the same time, it can request direct instructions from the Central Committee through these two provincial committees. Unfortunately, of the four appendices to the letter from the Central Committee, we have decoded only two. The two that have been converted into plain texts are "Confiscate the Land and Establish the Soviets" and "The February Resolution of the International." We are unable to decode two other documents, "Military Work" and "Organizational Problems." We need them badly. Please send us as soon as possible the deciphering code, or send us another copy.*

II. The Independent Régime in the Border Area and the August Defeat

The phenomenon of the emergence of one or more small areas under Red political power, surrounded on all sides by a White régime, is to be found[6] only in China. When we analyze the reasons for its appearance, we find that they lie in the incessant splits and wars within the comprador and despotic gentry classes. So long as these splits and wars continue, the existence and development of the armed independent régime of workers and peasants will continue. *Under such circumstances of splits and wars within the comprador and despotic gentry*

---

under Mao's leadership in September 1927 and thereafter accompanied Mao to the Jinggangshan. He was one of the five members of the new Front Committee organized at the beginning of November 1928, following the receipt of the Central Committee's June 4 letter.

4. The June 4, 1928, letter of the Central Committee stressed very heavily the importance of continued and rapid expansion of the area controlled by the forces of Zhu and Mao, by using the Red Army to mobilize the masses and bring about an insurrection patterned on that of Guangzhou. For Mao's opinion about the Central Committee's recommendation on the abolition of Party representatives in the army, see Section IVA5 of this report.

5. I.e., at the meeting on November 6, in obedience to the direct order contained in the letter, the Special Committee was abolished and replaced by the Front Committee.

6. Is to be found → Is to be found in today's world

classes, the existence and growth of the independent soviet régime[7] depend on the following concrete conditions: (1) excellent masses; (2) an excellent Party; (3) a fairly strong Red Army; (4) a favorable terrain for military operations; (5) sufficient economic strength to provide for subsistence. In addition, the independent régime has different strategies toward the ruling classes which surround them on all sides, depending on whether the ruling classes are stable[8] or split up. For example, during the war between Li and Tang[9] in Hunan and Hubei, and the war between Zhang and Li[10] in Guangdong, we could adopt a comparatively adventurous strategy, and the area carved out by military means could be relatively extensive. We must, however, still take care to establish a firm foundation in the central districts, so that we shall have something secure to rely on when the White terror comes. When the ruling classes[11] are stable (relatively speaking), as was the case in the southern provinces after April of this year, our strategy must definitely be one of gradual advance. In military affairs, the thing most to be avoided is to divide our forces in reckless advances; in mass work[12] (such as land distribution, the establishment of soviets,[13] organizing[14] the Party, and organizing local militia), the thing to be avoided most is scattering our personnel and neglecting to establish a solid foundation in the central districts. The defeats of many small Red régimes in localities *all over China* have resulted either from the absence of objective prerequisites or from subjective mistakes in tactics. *Subjective* mistakes in tactics have been made solely because of failure to distinguish clearly between periods of *temporary* stability and periods of splits in the political power of the ruling class. In a period of *temporary* stability, *some comrades* advocated in military affairs dividing up our forces for an adventurous advance and even proposed using the Red Guards as the sole force to defend large areas *of the independent soviet régime*, as though quite unaware of the fact that the enemy could attack not only with the household militia, but even in concentrated operations with regular troops. In mass work, they utterly neglected to *issue instructions to* lay a solid foundation in the central districts and sought boundless expansion without taking account of the limitations on our subjective capacities. Anyone[15] who called for a policy of gradual expansion in the military domain, and for concentrating our manpower[16] in mass work[17] on laying a solid

---

7. Soviet régime → Armed régime of the workers and peasants
8. Stable → Temporarily stable
9. Li and Tang → Li Zongren and Tang Shengzhi
10. Zhang and Li → Zhang Fakui and Li Jishen
11. Ruling classes → Régime of the ruling classes
12. Mass work → Local work
13. Soviets → Political power
14. Organizing → Expanding
15. Anyone → If they encountered anyone
16. Manpower → Strength
17. Mass work → Local work

foundation in the central districts, so as to secure an invincible position, they labeled a "conservative." This is[18] the root cause of the August defeat in the border area and the simultaneous defeat of the Red Army in Hunan.[19]

Work in the border area[20] began in October of last year. At the outset, Party organizations no longer existed in any of the *xian*. The local armed forces consisted only of the two units under Wang and Yuan[21] in the vicinity of the Jinggangshan, each having sixty rifles in bad repair. The arms of the peasants' self-defense corps in Yong, Lian, Cha, and Ling[22] *xian* had all been handed over to the despotic gentry, and the revolutionary sentiments of the masses had already been completely repressed. By February of this year, *xian*[23] committees had been established in Ninggang, Yongxin, Chaling, and Suichuan, Lingxian had a special district,[24] and in Lianhua *xian*, there were the beginnings of a Party organization, which had begun to establish connections with the Wan'an *xian* committee. All *xian* except Lingxian had a few local armed units. In Ninggang, Chaling, Suichuan, and Yongxin *xian*, especially in the latter two, there were a good many guerrilla uprisings to massacre[25] the despotic gentry and mobilize the masses; they did a great deal of work, and did it fairly well.[26] During that period, nothing at all was done[27] to deepen the agrarian revolution. The organs of political power were called *the "Assembly of Workers', Peasants', and Soldiers' Representatives,"* or the *"People's Committee,"* or Government of the Workers, Peasants, and Soldiers *for short. The term "soviet" was not used as yet.* Soldiers' Committees were set up in the army, *and the system of soldiering for pay was abolished.* When *guerrilla* units went on missions,[28] action committees were set up to direct them. *These simple methods were partly the product of our own invention and were partly copied from reports of the December 11 uprising in Guangzhou[29] as we had read about it in the newspapers (for example, People's Committees). This was because all communication with the Provincial Committee had been cut off since late November, and we knew nothing at all about the Party's positions and policies. The resolution of the November Enlarged Plenum of the Central Committee, which is of momentous significance in the history of the Chinese*

---

18. This is → Their wrong ideas were
19. The Red Army in Hunan → The Fourth Red Army in southern Hunan
20. Border area → Hunan-Jiangxi border area
21. I.e., of Wang Zuo and Yuan Wencai's bandits.
22. Yong, Lian, Cha, and Ling → Yongxin, Lianhua, Chaling, and Lingxian
23. *Xian* committees → *Xian* Party committees
24. Special district → Special district committee
25. Massacre → Overthrow
26. They did a great deal of work, and did it fairly well → All were fairly successful.
27. Nothing at all was done → Nothing was done as yet
28. Missions → Separate missions
29. I.e., the "Guangzhou Commune" of 1927.

revolution,[30] *exerted an influence on Party organizations in the border area only after Comrade Zhu De and others brought a copy from Hunan this April.* At this time, the leading organ[31] was the Front Committee (with Mao Zedong as secretary), which had been appointed by the Hunan Provincial Committee during the Autumn Harvest uprising. The Front Committee was abolished in early March at the suggestion[32] of the Southern Hunan Special Committee and reorganized as the Divisional Committee (with He Tingying as secretary). It thus became an organ responsible for Party affairs in the army alone, with no influence over local party organizations. *This had great drawbacks.* Moreover, at the suggestion[33] of the Southern Hunan Special Committee, Mao's men were transferred to Hunan.[34] As a result, the border area was abandoned[35] for more than a month. At the end of March came the defeat in Hunan,[36] and in April, the forces of Zhu and Mao, together with the Southern Hunan Peasants' Army, withdrew to Ninggang and began to re-establish the independent régime in the border area.

From April onward, when the independent régime in the Hunan-Jiangxi Border Area was confronted with the temporary stability of the ruling forces in the south, the number of regiments sent by the two provinces of Hunan and Jiangxi to suppress us[37] was at least eight or nine, and at times reached eighteen. Nevertheless, with a force of less than four regiments, we fought the enemy for four whole months, daily expanding the territory of the independent régime, deepening the agrarian revolution, extending the soviet organization,[38] and expanding the Red Army and the Red Guards. All this was possible because the policies of the Party (the Party organizations in the army and in the localities) in the border area were correct. The policies of the Special Committee[39] (with Mao Zedong as secretary) and the Army Committee (with Chen Yi as secretary) were as follows:

Fight the enemy resolutely, create a political power in the middle section of the Luoxiao mountain range, and oppose flightism *in the case of defeat*;

Deepen the agrarian revolution in regions controlled by the independent régime;

Let the army Party organizations help promote the development of the local

---

30. As noted in the Introduction to this volume, the Plenum of November 1927 adopted a radical leftist line of "permanent revolution" and removed Mao Zedong from the Politburo because of his "military deviation."

31. Leading organ → Highest organ of the Party

32. Suggestion → Demand

33. Suggestion → Demand

34. Hunan → Southern Hunan

35. Abandoned → Occupied by the enemy

36. Hunan → Southern Hunan

37. To suppress us → The reactionary troops sent to "suppress" us

38. Soviet organization → Political power of the popular masses

39. Special Committee → Border Area Special Committee

Party organization, and let the army help promote the development of the local armed forces;

Be on the defensive against Hunan, with its comparatively strong ruling power, and take the offensive against Jiangxi, with its comparatively weak ruling power;

Devote great efforts to building up Yongxin, create an independent régime of the popular masses, and make arrangements for a long-term struggle;

Concentrate the Red Army to fight the enemy, confronting them when the time is opportune, and oppose the division of forces so as to avoid being destroyed one by one;

In expanding the area under the independent régime, adopt the policy of advancing in a series of waves, and oppose the policy of rash advance.

It is only thanks to the appropriateness of these tactics, as well as to the terrain of the border area, which was advantageous to our struggle, and to the imperfect coordination of the invading forces from Hunan and Jiangxi, that we were able to win all the victories during the four months from April to July and expand the independent régime of the popular masses. Although the enemy was several times our superior in numbers, he was not only unable to destroy our independent régime but created a situation in which it grew day by day.[40] The influence of the independent régime on Hunan and Jiangxi provinces was also constantly increasing. The August defeat resulted entirely from the failure[41] to understand that the period was one of stability[42] for the ruling classes, and the adoption, on the contrary, of a policy suited to a period of splits within the ruling classes, dividing our forces for an adventurous advance toward southern Hunan, thus leading to defeat both in the border area and in southern Hunan. The representative of the Hunan Provincial Committee, Du Xiujing, and the secretary of the Special Committee[43] appointed by the Provincial Committee, Yang Kaiming,[44] took advantage of the fact that Mao Zedong, Wan Xixian, and other strong dissenters were far away in Yongxin. Without examining the actual situation at the time, or taking into account the resolution of the Joint Conference of the Army Committee, the Special Committee, and the Yongxin *Xian* Committee expressing opposition to the views of the Hunan Provincial Committee, they

---

40. Created a situation in which it grew day by day → Could not prevent it from developing
41. Failure → Failure of some of the comrades
42. Stability → Temporary stability
43. Special Committee → Border Area Special Committee
44. Yang Kaiming (1905–1930), a native of Changsha, had received a mandate from the Hunan Provincial Committee to supplant Mao as secretary of the Special Committee for the border area. See below, Mao's account of changes in the Special Committee in Section IVD6 of this report.

could think of nothing better than mechanically to apply the order of the Hunan Provincial Committee to march to southern Hunan, and fell in with the action of the Twenty-ninth Regiment (made up of peasants from Yizhang) who fled,[45] and wanted to return home. The result was defeat both in the border area and in southern Hunan. *This was truly an extremely great error.*

In mid-July, the Eighth Army invaded the Jiangxi border area, but retreated without achieving anything.[46] The main force of the Red Army, which was attacking Ling and Cha,[47] changed its plans[48] and turned toward southern Hunan. Forces from Jiangxi,[49] *amounting to eleven regiments in all* (five regiments[50] commanded by Wang Jun and Jin Handing, and six regiments of the Sixth Army commanded by Hu Wendou), launched an offensive against Yongxin. At this point, our army had only one regiment (*led by Mao Zedong*) in Yongxin. Under the cover provided by the great *Red* masses, it pinned down these eleven regiments within a radius of thirty *li* of the *xian* town for twenty-five days, by means of guerrilla attacks from every direction. In the end, because the enemy *had learned our real situation, and* launched a fierce assault, we lost Yongxin, and then Lianhua and Ninggang. At that moment, internal dissensions flared up suddenly within the Sixth Army; it hurriedly withdrew[51] and engaged Wang Jun's Third Army at Zhangshu. The remaining five Jiangxi regiments then hastily withdrew to the *xian* town of Yongxin. If our main force had not gone to southern Hunan, there is no doubt whatsoever[52] that, *aided by the power of the masses,* we could have put this enemy force to flight and extended the territory of the independent régime to include Ji'an, Anfu, and Pingxiang and link it up with Pingjiang and Liuyang. As the main force was away, and the one regiment we had was utterly exhausted, we decided to leave part of these men to defend the Jinggangshan in cooperation with the two units under Yuan Wencai and Wang Zuo, and Mao Zedong was ordered to[53] lead one battalion[54] to Guidong to meet the main force and invite it back. By that time the main force bound for

---

45. Fled → Fled the struggle
46. The Eighth Army invaded the Jiangxi border area, but retreated without achieving anything → The Eighth Army from Hunan, under Wu Shang, invaded Ningkang, penetrated to Yongxin, sought battle with us in vain (our men tried to attack them from a side road but missed them), and then, being afraid of the masses who supported us, hurriedly retreated to Chaling via Lianhua.
47. Which was attacking Ling and Cha → Which, precisely at this time, was advancing from Ninggang to attack Lingxian and Chaling
48. Changed its plans → Changed its plans on reaching Lingxian
49. Forces from Jiangxi → Moreover, enemy forces from Jiangxi
50. Five regiments → Five regiments of the Third Army
51. Sixth Army; it hurriedly withdrew → Enemy forces from Jiangxi, and the Sixth Army under Hu Wendou hurriedly withdrew
52. There is no doubt whatsoever → It is entirely possible
53. Mao Zedong was ordered to → That I should
54. One battalion → The rest

southern Hunan had already suffered defeat and was retreating[55] to Guidong, and on August 23 we joined forces there.

The enemy's Eighth Army from Hunan under Wu Shang invaded Ninggang, and subsequently advanced to Yongxin, but they could not engage us in any way. (It was not worthwhile to ambush them.) When, fearing our masses, they left Yongxin to retreat back to Chaling via Lianhua, the enemy's Eleventh Regiment from Jiangxi occupied the town of Yongxin the next day. At this time, the main force of the Red Army (*led by Zhu De*) launched an offensive from Ninggang against Chaling and Lingxian. When they reached Lingxian,[56] some soldiers (the whole of the Twenty-ninth Regiment), suffering from homesickness,[57] wanted to return to Hunan;[58] some others[59] opposed going to southern Hunan and wanted to go to southern Jiangxi, but did not want to go to Yongxin *to fight the enemy* either. Du Xiujing encouraged these tendencies,[60] and the Army Committee was unable to prevent *these harmful actions,* so the main force set out on July 17 from *Miandu in* Lingxian for Chenzhou *via Zixing.* Our troops engaged forces[61] under Fan Shisheng[62] in Chenzhou city on July 24. Initial victory was followed by defeat, and the troops retreated at dusk[63] *and lost their way.* Thereupon,[64] the Twenty-ninth Regiment fled toward Yizhang; part of it was annihilated by Hu Fengzhang[65] at Lechang, and the remainder was scattered in the Chenzhou-Yizhang area, and no one knows what has become of it. Only about one hundred rifles were mustered that evening. Fortunately, our main force[66] suffered only small losses, and on August 18, it occupied Guidong. When they were joined by *Mao Zedong and others* from the Jinggangshan on the 23rd, it was resolved to return to Ninggang.[67] *In the afternoon of the same day, two regiments under Wu*

---

55. The main force bound for southern Hunan had already suffered defeat and was retreating → The main force was retreating from southern Hunan

56. When they reached Linxian → had arrived in Lingxian in mid-July

57. Some soldiers (the whole of the Twenty-ninth Regiment), suffering from homesickness → The officers and men of the Twenty-ninth Regiment, who were wavering politically

58. Hunan → Southern Hunan

59. Some others → The Twenty-eighth Regiment

60. These tendencies → The mistaken ideas of the Twenty-ninth Regiment

61. Forces → Enemy forces

62. Fan Shisheng, a native of Yunnan, had been acquainted with Zhu De when both men were serving as soldiers in that province. At this time, he was commander of the Guomindang Sixteenth Army in Guangdong. During the retreat from Nanchang and Shantou, Zhu De's troops were given shelter and rations by Fan, on the pretext that they were still under the Guomindang banner as a unit of Fan's army. This opportunistic alliance came to an end in January 1928, when Zhu De moved into southern Hunan and took Yizhang.

63. Retreated at dusk → Withdrew from the battle

64. Thereupon → Thereupon, acting on its own,

65. Hu Fengzhang → Hu Fengzhang's bandits

66. Main force → Main force, the Twenty-eighth Regiment

67. Return to Ninggang → Return to the Jinggangshan by way of Chongyi and Shangyou

Shang in Lingxian launched a sudden fierce attack on Guidong. The ferocious battle lasted for half a day and resumed the next morning. Casualties on our side were rather heavy (the enemy's losses were even greater), so we retreated into Jiangxi. While the army was marching from Miandu to southern Hunan, the original Army Committee was disbanded and was replaced by the Front Committee appointed by the Hunan Provincial Committee, with Chen Yi as secretary. After we were defeated and evacuated Guidong, the Front Committee was dissolved, and an Action Committee was organized to take command, with Mao Zedong as secretary. The army arrived at the foot of the Jinggangshan on September 8, after passing through Chongyi, Shangyou, and Suichuan. There were six factors that led to the failure of our assault on Chenzhou: *(1) Some soldiers and officers were so homesick that they lost their combat capability; it was also against the inclination of some of the officers and soldiers to go to southern Hunan, against the sentiments of the masses. (2) The soldiers got tired on long expeditions in the summer heat. (3) The army advanced recklessly for several hundred* li *from Lingxian, thus cutting itself off from the border area, and becoming an isolated force. (4) The worker and peasant masses in southern Hunan had not yet been aroused, so our action constituted a mere military adventure. (5) We did not know the enemy's situation. (6) Preparations were inadequate, and the officers and men did not understand the significance of the campaign.* When the campaign failed,[68] Battalion Commander Yuan Chongquan defected with an infantry company and an artillery company. Although the two companies were subsequently brought back, Regimental Commander Wang Erzhuo lost his life in this action, *and the significance of this loss was considerable.* On August 30, units of the Hunan army under Wu Shang and units of the Jiangxi army under Wang Jun, four regiments in all,[69] seized the opportunity offered by the fact that our forces *had been defeated in Guidong and* were seeking to return but had not yet reached their destination to launch a *fierce* assault on our Jinggangshan. We had less than a battalion of soldiers, but we fought back, taking advantage of the favorable terrain at Huangyangjie (the route leading from Ninggang to the Jinggangshan), and repulsed the enemy after fighting from noon till night. *The enemies suffered very great casualties. This battle* saved our last base,[70] *and struck a blow at the morale of our enemies. Since then, they have not dared to look down upon the Communist Army any more. This battle has become one of the best-known encounters in the border area.*

While in Hunan, the Army (the Front Committee) organized xian *Party Committees in Guidong and Rucheng, which it passed through going and coming. A Special Committee was also set up to take charge of the existing* xian

---

68. When the campaign failed → When we reached Chongyi

69. Units of the Hunan army under Wu Shang and units of the Jiangxi army under Wang Jun, four regiments in all → Enemy units from Hunan and Jiangxi

70. Our last base → This base

committees in Zixing and Chenzhou. Du Xiujing was the secretary, and the address was Gate 12, Longxia, Zixing. Eighty guns were distributed to arm the newly established Red Guards in Zixing, Guidong, and Rucheng xian. In Chenzhou there were Red Guards at Yaoling, with forty to fifty guns. Things were unclear in xian such as Leiyang and Yongxing. The Thirtieth and Thirty-third Regiments of the Peasants' Army, which returned to southern Hunan in May, have long since been dispersed, and the enemy has captured most of the three to four hundred guns. The broad masses in southern Hunan, who were mobilized by the Red Army in the spring, had been totally repressed by the enemy. On this occasion, the Red Army again mobilized part of the local masses while passing through Zixing, Rucheng, and Guidong xian, organized soviets, and divided up the land in Shatian in Guidong. We do not know what conditions have been created there at present. Because of the communications blockade, we have received no correspondence as yet from the recently organized Southern Hunan Special Committee.

III. The Independent Régime from September to the Present[71]

Since April of this year, the area under the independent régime[72] has been gradually extended. On June 23, in the battle of Longyuankou (on the border of Yongxin and Ninggang) we defeated the enemy troops from Jiangxi for the fourth time. After this, the independent régime reached the peak of its development, embracing the whole of Ninggang, Yongxin, and Lianhua *xian*, small portions of Ji'an and Anfu, the northern part of Suichuan, and the southeastern part of Lingxian. Most of the land[73] had already been distributed, and the remainder was in the process of distribution. Soviets[74] were set up everywhere in the districts and townships. Ninggang, Yongxin, and Suichuan had *xian* soviets,[75] and a border area soviet[76] was established. Everywhere in the villages, workers' and peasants' insurrectionary detachments, *armed with spears,* were organized, and at the district and *xian* levels, Red Guards, *armed with rifles,* were organized. In July the Jiangxi enemy launched an attack, and in August the Hunan and Jiangxi enemy forces jointly attacked Huangyangjie.[77] All the *xian* towns and the plains in the border area were occupied by the enemy. Abetting the evildoers, the peace preservation corps *(armed with rifles)* and the household militia *(armed with spears)* ran amuck, inflicting White terror throughout the

---

71. The Independent Régime from September to the Present → The Current Situation in the Area under the Independent Régime
72. Area under the independent régime → Red area
73. Most of the land → In the Red areas, most of the land
74. Soviets → Organs of political power
75. Soviets → Governments
76. Soviet → Government
77. Huangyangjie → The Jinggangshan

towns and the countryside. The majority of the Party and government organizations collapsed. The rich peasants and the opportunists in the Party went over to the enemy in droves. It was not until the battle of Huangyangjie[78] on August 30 that *the enemy realized there was no hope of overcoming the natural barrier of the Jinggangshan*, and the enemy troops from Hunan retreated to Lingxian, while the enemy troops from Jiangxi continued to occupy all the *xian* seats, and the towns and villages[79] *in the plains area*. From beginning to end, however, the enemy could not seize certain places:[80] the western and northern districts of Ninggang; the Tianlong, Xiaoxijiang, and Nannianshan[81] districts in the northern, western, and southern sections of Yongxin, respectively; Shangxi district in Lianhua; Jinggangshan district in Suichuan; and the Qinshigang and Dayuan districts in Lingxian. During the two months of July and August, the Red Army (*about* a regiment) and the Red Guards of the various *xian* fought scores of battles, large and small. *Although they were defeated,* they lost no more than *about* thirty guns, before retreating finally into the mountainous areas. *The enemy went all out to invade and finally launched an offensive against our Jinggangshan base with the combined forces of the two provincial armies. They were not successful in a single encounter and finally gave up and retreated. We triumphed over combined forces sent to suppress us at Huangyangjie on August 30. Our army returned to the Jinggangshan on September 9 after its campaigns in the south, and this marked the beginning of the new phase from September onward.*

As our army was marching back to the Jinggangshan via Chongyi, Shangyou, and *Suichuan*, the Independent Seventh Division under Liu Shiyi from western[82] Jiangxi, *taking advantage of the fact that we were the remnants of a defeated army,* pursued us *with five battalions* all the way to Suichuan. On September 13, we launched an attack on Liu Shiyi with four battalions and defeated him at the town of Suichuan, capturing two hundred fifty rifles.[83] *We also took prisoners, including one battalion and one company commander, three or four platoon leaders, and some two hundred soldiers. The Action Committee (with Mao Zedong as secretary) commanding the army and the Suichuan Xian Committee jointly administered the affairs of the masses of Suichuan and provided for the maintenance of the army. The army sent columns in four directions toward four townships to wage guerrilla warfare, each branch setting up its own Action Committee to take command. The branch heading east pushed as far as Wan'an*

---

78. Huangyangjie → The Jinggangshan
79. The towns and villages → Most of the villages
80. Certain places → The mountain areas
81. Nannianshan → Wanshan
82. Western → Southern
83. On September 13, we launched an attack on Liu Shiyi with four battalions and defeated him at the town of Suichuan, capturing two hundred fifty rifles → On September 13, we defeated Liu Shiyi, captured several hundred rifles, and took Suichuan.

and established liaison with the Wan'an Xian Committee. On September 24, Li Wenbin's regiment of the Jiangxi army arrived from Taihe, and the Independent Seventh Division arrived from Gangzhou and attacked the town of Suichuan. Our forces were not concentrated, and we could commit only two battalions to the battle. Although we could not sustain the fight and withdrew, the morale of the soldiers remained intact. Our troops returned to the Jinggangshan on September 26. On October 1 at Ninggang, we engaged *the Twenty-seventh Regiment of* Zhou Hunyuan's brigade, which was part of Xiong Shihui's army.[84] *We captured one battalion commander, one company commander, two platoon leaders, one hundred soldiers, and a hundred and ten rifles. We drove the remaining enemies to Yongxin and* recovered the whole of Ninggang *xian. Li Wenbin's regiment thought that we would attack Ninggang. Consequently, it left Suichuan, taking an indirect route through Taihe and Yongxin to bring reinforcements. Suichuan was left in the hands of the Independent Seventh Division (the weakest in manpower) alone. Since we expected that the masses in Suichuan would be very highly mobilized, and since our army was hard pressed for supplies, we recaptured Suichuan on October 13. The Independent Seventh Division fled without firing a shot. The Suichuan Action Committee in command of the troops (with Zhu De as secretary) joined the Suichuan Xian Committee in planning the work in Suichuan. They decided to establish five guerrilla columns, distribute the land, establish a soviet, expand the Party organization, and raise funds.* At that time, 126 soldiers of the Third Division of the Eighth Army[85] under Yan Zhongxing stationed in Guidong came over to us. They were formed into a special task battalion, with Bi Zhanyun (who had served under Xiang Chenjie before being placed under Yan Zhongxing) as commander. *On November 2, two regiments of the Twenty-first Brigade of the Jiangxi enemy (commanded by Li Wenbin), together with a segment of the Independent Seventh Division, launched a new offensive against us at Suichuan. In order to avoid a direct clash, our army gave up Suichuan, intending to fall on the enemy with the suddenness of a thunderbolt at Ninggang and Yongxin, where his forces were relatively weak, thus breaking the siege.* On November 9, we routed the Twenty-seventh Regiment[86] of Zhou's brigade at the *xian* town of Ninggang and at Longyuankou. *We captured 160 guns, killed one enemy battalion commander and several dozen enemy soldiers, and took prisoner two deputy battalion commanders, one company commander, one platoon leader, and over one hundred soldiers. On the morning of* the next day, we launched an attack on Yongxin[87] *to fight the*

---

84. Xiong Shihui (1893–1974), a native of Jiangxi, had participated in the Northern Expedition. He had been commander of the Fifth Division of the Guomindang armies since August 1928.

85. Third Division of the Eighth Army → Hunan enemy forces

86. The Twenty-seventh Regiment → One regiment

87. We launched an attack on Yongxin → We advanced and occupied Yongxin, but withdrew to Ninggang shortly afterward

Twenty-eighth Regiment of Zhou's brigade and the remnants of the Twenty-seventh Regiment. It was not until three o'clock in the afternoon that we forced the enemy to retreat, and our vanguard occupied the town of Yongxin. Unexpectedly, the enemy was reinforced by the Thirty-fifth Brigade from Hongtianhe (between Ji'an and Yongxin), so we retreated toward Ninggang for fear of a disadvantageous battle. Although the enemy suffered heavy casualties that day, we, too, had over a hundred casualties. This was the biggest battle after we returned to the border areas. The Red Guards and the Insurrection Teams participated in both these campaigns, although their strength was not very great. Present circumstances in the border area are as follows: the Fourteenth Brigade of Zhou Hunyuan and the Fifteenth Brigade of Liu Shiyi are stationed on the Jiangxi border. Both have already been defeated by us and are in the process of reorganization. The Twenty-first Brigade of Li Wenbin and the Thirty-fifth Brigade (commander unknown) are our most powerful opponents. Wu Shang's Eighth Army is still occupying Chaling, Lingxian, and Guidong xian *on the Hunan border.* At present, the area of the Red Independent Régime[88] extending from the southern slopes of the Jinggangshan to the border of Lianhua *xian* in the north, embraces the whole of Ninggang, parts of Suichuan, Lingxian, and Yongxin, forming a narrow unbroken stretch from north to south. *In addition,* there are also regions such as the Shangxi district of Lianhua, and the Tianlong and Wannianshan districts of Yongxin, which are not firmly linked with this unbroken stretch, *but are controlled by the Red Independent Régime.* The enemy is attempting to *encircle the entire territory of the independent régime,* and by military attacks and economic blockade to eradicate this "den of Communist bandits."[89] The difficulty and intensity of the struggle are going to increase with every passing day. We cannot afford a moment's repose.

IV. Existing Problems

A. Military Problems

1. The Military Period.[90] The struggle in the border area is *almost* purely military. Consequently, the Party and the masses must both be militarized. How to deal with the enemy and how to wage war *have become important items on the daily agenda of the army, and of the local Party organizations at all levels, and fighting* has come to constitute our daily life.[91] What we call an independent

---

88. The area of the Red Independent Régime → Our area

89. This "den of Communist bandits." → Our base area, and we are now preparing to defeat his attacks.

90. This heading is missing in the revised version, as are subheadings nos. 4, 6, 7, 8, 9, 12, and 13 below. We have therefore set the whole of these heading in italics. Changes in the other eight headings of this group are indicated by notes and italics in the usual way.

91. Our daily life → The central problem in our daily life

régime must be armed. Wherever such an area may be located, if it is unarmed or insufficiently armed, or if, *although it has arms,* wrong tactics are used in dealing with the enemy, the White armed forces (the White army, the peace preservation corps, and the household militia) will immediately snatch away our territory.[92] As the struggle is getting fiercer every day, our problems have become extremely complex and serious.

2. Origins of the Red Army.[93] *Broadly speaking, the soldiers may be divided into the following six categories:* (a) troops formerly under Ye and He in Chaozhou and Shantou;[94] (b) the Wuchang Guards Regiment; (C) the Peasants' *Army* from Liuyang and Pingjiang; (d) the Peasants' *Army* from southern Hunan and workers from Shuikoushan; (e) soldiers we have captured from the armies of Xu Kexiang, Tang Shengzhi, Bai Chongxi, Zhu Peide, Wu Shang, and Xiong Shihui; (f) *workers and* peasants from various *xian* in the border area. *The first four groups form the backbone of the Red Army.* After more than a year of *endless* battles, however, the troops formerly under He and Ye, the Guards Regiment, and the Peasants' Army from Liuyang and Pingjiang *have lost two-thirds of their men* and have been reduced to *only* one-third of their original strength. *Even* the Red Army[95] from southern Hunan has suffered heavy losses in killed and wounded *in the eight-month struggle in the border area.* Consequently, although the first four groups, *because of their superior quality,* constitute the mainstay of the Fourth Red Army, their number is much smaller than that of the last two categories. Of the last two groups, prisoners of war are most numerous. If we were deprived of reinforcements from this source, we would have serious problems finding soldiers for the Fourth Army. Despite[96] *the existence of these reinforcements, of which the quality is inferior to the former groups (though quite a few among them are good soldiers),* enlistment still cannot keep up with the increase in rifles. The rifles, once their number has increased, are seldom lost; soldiers may be lost *at any time* through casualties, sicknesses, and desertion. *(A few soldiers desert every time we are defeated.) Moreover, few of the peasants in the border area are willing to serve as soldiers. As soon as the land is divided up, everyone goes to till it. Now the soldiers of peasant or working-class origin in the Fourth Army in the border area constitute an extreme minority. Thus the problem is still very great.* The Hunan Provincial Committee promised to send us workers from Anyuan, and we hope this will be done very soon.

---

92. The White armed forces (the White army, the Peace Preservation Corps, and the Household Militia) will immediately snatch away our territory → It will be immediately occupied by the enemy

93. Red Army → Red Army in the Border Area

94. Chaozhou and Shantou were places traversed by the forces under the command of Ye [Ting] and He [Long] in their retreat after the Nanchang uprising of August 1, 1927.

95. Red Army → Peasants

96. Despite → Despite this

3. Composition.[97] One part consists of workers and peasants, and the other of vagrants.[98] *(So it is not true to say, as the Hunan Provincial Committee does, that they are all vagrants). It is urgently necessary to replace this contingent of vagrants by workers and peasants, but workers and peasants are hard to come by.* On the one hand,[99] fighting is going on every day, and the vagrants are after all *particularly good* fighters. *At the same time*, casualties continue to mount. *Consequently, not only can we not diminish the vagrants now in our ranks but* it is difficult to find more for reinforcements. Under the circumstances, the only solution is to intensify political training, *so as to effect a qualitative change in these elements.*

4. *Nature.* The majority[100] of the soldiers are men from the mercenary armies who have been transformed. Once they join the Red Army, the mercenary system is abolished.[101] Hitherto, there has been no system of regular pay, but only an allowance for food and pocket money.[102] As for the distribution of land to the officers and soldiers of the Red Army,[103] *apart from those from the various* xian *of the border area, whose families have been allotted land according to the regulations,* it is rather difficult to allot land to those from distant places. *First of all, the independent régime is small, and much of it is mountainous, so local peasants themselves barely have enough land to share, and there is no surplus. Secondly, the outcome of battles is unpredictable, and the independent régime does not have a stable territory. Yesterday, the land was distributed by the Red power, but today the White power seizes it back and demands that the peasants pay the rent to the landlords. Consequently, not only do the officers and soldiers of the Red Army have no notion of sharing out the land themselves but many, even among the peasants, do not consider the distribution of the land as necessarily final. This is the result of the overwhelming strength of the White Power and of the incessant and fierce struggles between Red and White. It is, however, our unwavering principle that the Red Army soldiers should get land, and we are continuing to discuss methods for implementing this principle.*

5. Political training.[104] *In general*, the Red Army soldiers are all endowed with class consciousness. They have acquired basic *political* knowledge about such things as land distribution, establishing soviets,[105] and arming the workers

---

97. Composition → Composition of the Red Army

98. Here the *Selected Works* version adds the parenthetical remark: (Of course it is inadvisable to have too many of the latter.)

99. On the one hand → But because

100. The majority → The majority of the Red Army soldiers

101. Is abolished → Is abolished, making the men feel they are fighting for themselves and for the people and not for somebody else

102. An allowance for food and pocket money → Grain, money for cooking oil, salt, firewood and vegetables, and a little pocket money

103. Red Army, → Red Army, land has been allotted to all those who are natives of the border area

104. Political training → After receiving political education

105. Soviets → Political power

and peasants. They *already* know that they are fighting for themselves, and for the workers and peasants. Consequently, they can endure even this miserable life and these fierce struggles[106] without complaint. Soldiers' Committees have been organized in companies, battalions, and regiments. *The function of the committees is to supervise the officers,* to represent the soldiers' interests, *and to participate in army administration.* They also carry out political training *in the army,* and mass movements[107] outside the army. *Once the Soldiers' Committee has been fully established, the Political Department can be abolished. Its staff members can all be taken into the Soldiers' Committee and work there. This would be better than having a separate Political Department. Before April this year, all the armies here had Political Departments. Then they were abolished because of the unfavorable influence they exerted. Whenever there is a Political Department, the officers and soldiers, as well as the masses, are led to think that political work rests only with the few people in the Department, and that the job of all the rest is merely to fight. Only if we abolish the Political Department, so that everyone will have to fight and everyone will also have to do political work (political training and mass movement), can the purely military mentality be smashed.* The system of Party representatives[108] *has developed from experience, and in our opinion it* cannot be abolished *yet. Party representatives at the army and divisional levels (here there is no such thing as a division; the regiment is directly subordinated to the army) can be abolished. At the regimental, battalion, and company levels,* especially in the company, *they must not be abolished now.* Because Party branches are organized on a company basis, the company Party representative[109] has to supervise the soldiers' committee of the whole company in carrying out political training and guiding the movement of the popular masses. He is, at the same time, secretary of the Party branch. Experience demonstrates that companies which have a relatively good Party representative are *somewhat* sounder than the others.[110] Because casualties among the lower cadres are heavy *at present*, soldiers captured from the enemy are often made platoon leaders or even company commanders overnight. Some of those captured in February and March this year are already battalion commanders. It is a gross error to imagine that we no longer need Party representatives simply because our army is now called the Red Army. Zhu's forces[111] abolished Party representatives in southern Hunan at one time, but later *felt this was not a good idea and could not be maintained. When they reached the border area,* they

---

106. Miserable life and fierce struggles → Bitter struggle

107. Mass movements → Mass work

108. The system of Party representatives → Experience has demonstrated that the system of Party representatives

109. Representative → Representative is particularly important, and

110. Others → Others, and that the company commander can hardly play this important political role

111. Zhu's forces → The Twenty-eighth Regiment

restored the system. If we change the name to political instructor, this would lead to confusion with the Guomindang political intructors, who are sincerely hated by *most* captives. In addition, to change the name does not change the nature of the system. Therefore, we have decided to make no change. Casualties among Party representatives are very heavy, and while we have started training classes, we hope that the Central Committee and the two Provincial Committees will send us at least thirty men capable of serving as Party representatives.

6. *Military training.* Other people's[112] soldiers need six months' to a year's training before they go into battle. Our soldiers, recruited only yesterday, have to fight today with virtually no training. *Consequently, part of the middle- and lower-ranking cadres, as well as many soldiers,* know very little about the art of war and rely only on their bravery. *This is very dangerous.* Since it is impossible to have long periods of rest and training, the only thing to do is to see whether we can avoid battle,[113] and thus obtain time for *rest* and training. As for training lower-level officers, we now have an instructional corps of 150, and we intend to continue this on a regular basis. We hope the Central Committee and the two Provincial Committees will send a minimum of thirty[114] officers, from platoon leader and company commander upwards, to the border area.

7. *Problems of Supply.* The Hunan Provincial Committee has asked us to pay attention to the material life of the soldiers and to make it at least better[115] than that of the average worker or peasant. At present, the very reverse is the case; *no doubt few people's lives are so miserable as that of the Red Army soldiers. Because of the shortage of funds,* each man gets only five cents a day for food, apart from rice *(which is supplied by local sources),* and often even this rate is hard to maintain. *The common saying of the soldiers, "Overthrow the capitalists, and eat pumpkin every day," reflects their misery. Probably there are not many in this world who suffer more bitterly than the Fourth Army.* The monthly cost of food[116] alone, *other items being provided for by the provincial [committee],* is more than 10,000 *yuan,* which is obtained entirely from expropriating the local bullies. *But first of all, you can expropriate only once in a given locality; afterward, there would be nothing to take. Second, we are tightly surrounded by the enemy, and in order to get at the local tyrants, we often have to break through the enemy's lines, so we cannot go too far. Third, the hostile armies must be taken seriously, and one or two battalions would not be able to raise funds on their own. We need many soldiers in order to raise funds, so the problem is not a simple one.* We now have cotton padding enough to make winter clothing for the whole army of five thousand men *(the regular Red Army),* but we still do not

---

112. Other people's → Ordinarily
113. Battle, → Some battles,
114. A minimum of thirty → More
115. Better → A bit better
116. Food → Cooking oil, salt, firewood, and vegetables

have the cloth, *and we do not know when this problem can be resolved.* Cold as the weather is, many of the soldiers are still wearing only two layers of thin clothing. Fortunately, we are accustomed to hardship. Besides, everybody puts up with the same hardship: from the army commander to the cook, everyone has five cents for food.[117] And when pocket money is dispensed, no one gets more than the other: everyone has his twenty or forty cents. *Everybody realizes that he is "suffering on behalf of the proletariat,"* so there is no animosity toward anyone. *Despite this, financial problems have been and remain very serious.*

8. *Problems of the sick and wounded.* After every engagement there are wounded. Because of malnutrition, cold and other factors, many[118] are ill. We have founded a *Red Army* hospital *on the Jinggangshan,* which employs both Chinese and Western medicine for diagnosis and treatment, but we are short of both medicine and doctors, *and the problem is very serious. In September, we had over two hundred sick and wounded soldiers, and after the recent battle at Yongxin, the number increased.* At present, the number of people in the hospital *(including staff)* is over eight hundred. *If we do not take care of the sick and the wounded, the morale of the army will be shaken. If we want to take good care of them, we face truly great difficulties getting medical equipment and supplies.* The Hunan Provincial Committee promised us drugs *a long time ago,* but we have still not seen any. We still hope the Central Committee and the two Provincial Committees will send us a few Western doctors, and some iodine tablets.

9. *Democracy*[119] in the Army. Apart from the role played by the Party, the reason why the Red Army can hold out despite such miserable material conditions and continuous fierce battles lies in its thorough implementation of democracy.[120] The officers do not beat the soldiers; officers and men *have the same food and clothing, and* receive equal treatment; soldiers enjoy freedom of assembly and speech; overelaborate formalities have been abolished; all financial transactions are completely open; *and the soldier's representatives inspect the accounts.* The soldiers handle the mess arrangements, and although there is only five cents a day for food, they manage to save some for pocket money (about sixty or seventy cash per person per day). All these methods give great satisfaction to the soldiers. The newly captured soldiers in particular feel that the camp of today and the camp of yesterday[121] are worlds apart. They feel that, although

---

117. Food → Food, apart from rice

118. Many → Many officers and soldiers

119. Here Mao employs to convey the idea of democracy the term *minquanzhuyi,* derived from *minquan* or "people's rights," the second of Sun Yatsen's "Three People's Principles." As can be seen from many of the texts in Volume II of this edition, this usage was common on Mao's part in the 1920s.

120. Throughout this paragraph, the term *minquanzhuyi* has been replaced in the *Selected Works* by *minzhuzhuyi.*

121. The camp of today and the camp of yesterday → Our army and the Guomindang army

materially they are worse off in the Red Army than in the White army, spiritually they have been liberated. *Therefore, they are reasonably content.* The fact that the same soldier fights more bravely in the Red Army today than he did for the enemy army yesterday reflects the influence of this democracy. The Red Army is like a furnace, in which all captured soldiers are melted down and transformed the moment they come over; *that is a fact.* In China, not only do the masses of workers and peasants[122] need democracy, but the army needs it too, *even more urgently.* The thorough implementation of democracy in the army will, in future, be an important policy for destroying the feudal mercenary army *in China. For the life of a soldier in the feudal mercenary army is simply more than any human being can bear.*

10. The Party in the army.[123] At present, it comprises four levels, the company branch, the battalion committee, the regimental committee, and the army committee. There is a branch in the company, with a small group in each squad. An *extremely* important reason why the Fourth Army[124] is still able to hold together after many difficult battles is precisely that "The Party branch is organized on a company basis." Two years ago, our organizations within the Guomindang armies wholly failed to take hold among the soldiers. Even among Ye Ting's troops there was only one branch to each regiment, a truly preposterous situation.[125] At present, the proportion of Party members to nonmembers in the army is about one to three, or an average of one Party member to every four soldiers. Recently, it was decided to recruit more Party members among the combat soldiers, so as to reach the goal of a fifty-fifty ratio. At present, the company branches are short of good secretaries, so we ask the Central Committee to send us a number of activists from among those who can no longer function where they are now, *to serve as Party representatives in the companies.* Party workers from southern Hunan are almost all doing Party work in the army *(and political work at the same time).* Some of them were scattered to a certain extent during the retreat in southern Hunan last August, so we have no people to spare at present. *In the seven months since the armywide conference of representatives last April elected the Army Committee (Party Committee in the Army), we have held in all six armywide representatives' conferences. The Sixth Congress was held on November 14 and 15, after we received the letter from the Central Committee. Decisions were reached on political, military, organizational, and propaganda matters, which all represented progress as compared to the previous five conferences. A twenty-three-member Army Committee was set up, with Zhu De as secretary (as designated by the Central Committee).*

---

122. Masses of workers and peasants → People
123. The Party in the army → The Party organization
124. Fourth Army → Red Army
125. A truly preposterous situation → That is why we could not stand up to any serious test

Within [the army] it serves as the highest organ of Party power in the army and is subordinate to the Front Committee. Outside [the army] it serves as the Army Committee of the border area soviet, in command of the Red Army and the local militia. The model of the Party within the army has broadly taken shape already. Some of the Party members are resolute in their revolutionary outlook, but the majority still lack a good education, and in the future we must pay attention to this.

11. Local armed forces. They are divided into the Red Guards and the worker and peasant insurrectionary detachments. The insurrectionary detachments are armed with spears and shotguns. They are organized on a township basis, with one detachment to every township, its strength being proportional to the size of the township. Their task is to suppress the counterrevolution, to defend the township government, and to assist the Red Army or the Red Guards in combat when the enemy comes. The insurrectionary detachments started in Yongxin, and originally they were secret *organizations for carrying out the uprising.* After we seized power in the whole *xian,* they came out into the open. Subsequently, this system spread to the whole of the border area, but the name was not changed. The Red Guards use five-shot, nine-shot, and single-shot guns, *mostly five-shot.* The number of guns in the various *xian* is *roughly* as follows: 140 in Ninggang, 220 in Yongxin, 43 in Lianhua, 50 in Chaling, 90 in Lingxian, 130 in Suichuan, and 10 in Wan'an, totaling 683. Most of these have been supplied by the Red Army, but a few were captured from the enemy by [the Red Guards] themselves. Most of the Red Guards from the various *xian* are constantly fighting with the armed forces of the despotic gentry, the peace preservation corps, and the household militia, and as a result their *marksmanship and* ability to fight are increasing all the time. Before the Horse Day Incident,[126] the peasants' self-defense corps[127] had 300 guns in Youxian, 300 in Chaling, 60 in Lingxian, 50 in Suichuan, 80 in Yongxin, 60 in Lianhua, 60 in Ninggang (Yuan Wencai's men), and 60 on the Jinggangshan (Wang [Zuo's] men), totaling 970. After the Horse Day Incident, apart from Yuan and Wang's men, who kept their arms, only six guns were retained in Suichuan, and one in Lianhua, all the rest having been seized by the despotic gentry. The fact that they had no control *at all* over the situation was *entirely* the result of the actions of the former opportunist Party.[128] Even now the Red Guards of the various *xian* still have far too few rifles. The despotic gentry have more guns than the Red Guards, so the Red Army must continue to help the *xian* with arms. So long as this effort does not damage the Red Army itself,[129] it must do everything possible to assist the local

---

126. Regarding the "Horse Day Massacre" of May 21, 1927, see above, the note to the declaration of August 1, 1927, regarding Xu Kexiang.

127. The peasants' self-defense corps → All the *xian* in the border area had peasants' self-defense corps, whose rifles numbered

128. Actions of the former opportunist Party → Opportunist line

129. Damage the Red Army itself → Lower the Red Army's fighting capacity

armed forces,[130] *and to make them stronger every day.* It has been laid down *by the armywide conference* that the Red Army[131] should adopt a four-company system, with seventy-five rifles to every company. (Adding to this the rifles of the special task company, machine-gun company, mortar company, regimental headquarters, and battalion headquarters, each regiment will have 1,075 rifles.) Additional guns captured in action should be used as much as possible to arm the local *workers and peasants.* The commanders of the Red Guards should be people who have been sent from the *xian* to the Red Army training corps and have finished their training. The number of people sent by the Red Army from outside areas to command local forces should be gradually reduced. Zhu Peide is also stepping up *greatly* his effort to arm the peace preservation corps and the household militia. The armed forces of the despotic gentry in the various *xian* of the border area are of considerable size and fighting capacity. Consequently, it is extremely urgent to expand our local Red armed forces in the border area.

12. The Strategy of the Red Army and the Red Guards. Besides adhering to the principles laid down (annihilate small enemy forces swiftly with our main forces; make use of the masses to combat large enemy forces; do not launch foolhardy attacks), the principle for the Red Army should be concentration, while that for the Red Guards should be dispersion. At the present time, when the bourgeois[132] political power is stable,[133] and the enemy is capable of massing huge forces to attack the Red Army, dispersion is *extremely* disadvantageous for the Red Army, *while concentration is advantageous.* In our experience, the dispersion of our forces has led almost every time to defeat, while concentrating our forces to attack smaller, equal, or even slightly larger enemy forces has frequently led to victory. The Central Committee has instructed us to wage guerrilla warfare in an area extending several thousand *li* in all directions. This is much too vast, probably because of an overestimation of our strength. *(The Hunan Provincial Committee is already informed regarding the number of guns in the possession of the Fourth Army. Comrade Yuan Desheng has been asked to brief you on this in person, so it is excluded from this report.)* As for *the strategy* of the Red Guards, dispersion is most advantageous, and they are all using this method in their operations in all the *xian.*

13. Regarding organization. At present, we are still following the old methods of organization of the Guomindang. We are unable to decode the Central Committee's "Resolution on Military Work" and are unable to guess at the organization of the army of the Taiping Heavenly Kingdom.[134] Please prepare

---

130. Assist the local armed forces → Arm the people
131. The Red Army → Each battalion of the Red Army
132. Bourgeois → Reactionary
133. Stable → Temporarily stable
134. The letter of June 4 declared that the forces of Zhu and Mao were "still a Guomindang-type army," which needed to be transformed from a mercenary to a volunteer basis. They were instructed to abolish the system of Party representatives in the army,

another copy of the document and send it to us, so as to facilitate discussion.

14. Propaganda aimed at the enemy forces. The *two* most effective methods are releasing captured soldiers, and giving medical care to wounded *enemy* soldiers. When we capture enemy soldiers, battalion and company commanders, and platoon leaders, we conduct propaganda among them, and then divide them into those who want to go and those who want to stay. Those who want to leave are given money for their traveling expenses and set free. This *concrete propaganda* immediately knocks the bottom out of the enemy propaganda that "The Communist bandits kill everyone and anyone on sight." No wonder Yang Chisheng's *Ninth Division Ten-Day Review* exclaimed, regarding this method, "How insidious!" The Red Army soldiers are extremely enthusiastic in welcoming and comforting[135] the prisoners, and the prisoners reciprocate with warm gratitude in their speeches at every "Farewell Meeting for New Brothers." Giving medical care to the wounded enemy soldiers also has a very great effect. Some of the more intelligent among our enemies (such as Li Wenbin) are copying our methods. They stopped killing our prisoners and started to treat our wounded. But *after staying in the enemy camp when captured or wounded,* our soldiers returned nevertheless, guns and all. This has happened twice already. *Very few Red Army soldiers have been captured by the enemy, since the Red Army has suffered few defeats in the border area.* We are also doing our utmost to carry out written propaganda, for example, by painting slogans. We cover the walls with slogans wherever we go. We are, however, lacking in people skilled in painting, and we request the Central Committee and the two Provincial Committees to send us a few.

15. Military bases: Our first base is the Jinggangshan, situated at the junction of Ninggang, Lingxian, Suichuan, and Yongxin *xian*. At its northern foot lies Maoping in Ninggang; at its southern foot lies Huang'ao in Suichuan. The distance between the two points is 90 *li*. At its eastern foot lies Nashan in Yongxin; at its western foot lies Shuikou in Lingxian. The distance between the two is 180[136] *li*. The circumference measures 550 *li*, stretching from Nashan to Longyuankou (both in Yongxin *xian*), Xincheng, Maoping, Dalong (all in Ninggang), Shidu, Shuikou, Xiacun (all in Lingxian), Yingpanxu, Daijiapu,

---

which (as Mao himself indicates here) was modeled on the Guomindang, establish a Political Department (*zhengzhibu*), and apply the "Taiping Heavenly Kingdom pattern of organization." Directive No. 51 of the Central Committee, entitled "Outline of Military Work," May 25, 1928 (presumably the one Mao had been unable to decode), spelled out this point. It recommended adapting the organization of the Red Army to the available arms, including old-fashioned guns, swords, and so on. The "three-five system" was to be used: twelve men to a squad, three squads to a platoon, five platoons to a company, five companies to a regiment, and five regiments to a division, each division to have 4,500 men. "This system," asserted the directive, "adopts the spirit of the Taiping system and seeks to adapt it to the needs of guerrilla warfare." See *Central Committee Documents* (1928), pp. 222–38, especially p. 233.

135. Welcoming and comforting → Comforting and sending on their way
136. 180 → 80

Dafen, Duiziqian, Huang'ao, Wudoujiang, Che'ao (all in Suichuan), and back to Nashan. In the mountains there are paddy fields and villages at Dajing, Xiaojing, Shangjing, Zhongjing, Xiajing,[137] Ciping, Xiazhuang, Xingzhou, Caoping, Bainihu, and Luofu. Formerly, all these places were dens of bandits and deserters.[138] The population is, however, under two thousand, and the rice production is less than 10,000 *shi*. All the grain required by the army must be supplied from Ninggang, Yongxin, and Suichuan *xian*. All the strategic passes in the mountains are *strongly* fortified. The *Red Army* Hospital, bedding and clothing workshops, ordnance department, and regimental rear offices are all up here. At present, grain is being transported to the mountains from Ninggang. Provided that we have sufficient supplies *(grain and money, the most important being money)*, the enemy can never break in. *There is a Defense Committee in the camp, in charge of defense, with Wang Zuo as chairman.* The second base is Jiulong,[139] at the juncture of Ninggang, Yongxin, Lianhua, and Chaling *xian*. It is less important than the Jinggangshan, but serves as the rearmost base for the local armed forces of the four *xian*, and has also been fortified. Since the Red régime is surrounded on all sides by the White régime, a military base in the mountains is indispensable.[140] *Because the enemy is present on all four sides, and we must defend ourselves on all four sides, it would be extremely difficult for the Red Independent Régime to survive for long when the bourgeois political power is stable without taking advantage of the natural barriers to make up for occasional deficiencies in manpower (for instance, when the enemy's overwhelming numbers present grave dangers).*

B. The Land Problem

1. The Land Situation in the Border Areas. Broadly speaking, over 60 percent of the land was in the hands of the landlords, and less than 40 percent in the hands of the peasants. *If we distinguish among the different cases,* in the border areas of Jiangxi, Suichuan showed the highest concentration, with about 80 percent of the land belonging to the landlords. Yongxin came next, with the landlords owning about 70 percent. There were more owner-peasants in Wan'an, Ninggang, and Lianhua. *Apart from Wan'an, for which we do not have the results of any direct investigations, there are a fair number of owner-peasants in Ninggang and Lianhua,* but nevertheless the landlords held the greater part of the land, the proportion being about 60 to 40. The situation in Chaling and Lingxian

---

137. The preceding five place names mean, respectively, Big Well, Small Well, Upper Well, Middle Well, and Lower Well.

138. Bandits and deserters → Bandits and deserters, but they have now been turned into our base area

139. Jiulong → The Jiulong Mountains

140. A military base in the mountains is indispensable → It is essential to make use of the strategic advantages offered by mountains

xian in the Hunan border area was rather similar, with the landlords holding some 70 percent of the land.

2. The Problem of the Intermediate Class. Under the circumstances outlined above, we can win the support of the majority of people for confiscating and redistributing all land. Roughly speaking, there are three classes in the countryside: the *despotic gentry class, who are* big or middle landlords, the intermediate class of small landlords and owner-peasants,[141] and also the class of the poor peasants.[142] *Within the intermediate class,* the interests of the owner-peasants[143] are often interwoven with those of the small landlords. The owner-peasants[144] account for a small proportion of the total land, but when their holdings are combined with the land held by small landlords, the total is considerable. This is probably more or less the case throughout the country. The policy in the border area is to confiscate all land, and redistribute it thoroughly, so that in the areas of Red *political power,* the class of the despotic gentry and the intermediate class are both under attack. Such is our policy, but in applying it we have encountered considerable obstruction from the intermediate classes. In the initial stage of the revolution, the intermediate classes pretended to capitulate to the poor peasant class, but in reality they *were plotting to* take advantage of their former social status and clan influence to *spread rumors* and to intimidate the poor peasants, so as to delay the distribution of the land. When *higher-level political authorities put pressure on them until* they could no longer delay things, they either concealed their actual holdings or retained the good land and gave up the poor land to others. During this period, the poor peasants, having long been trampled down, and because[145] the victory of the revolution was not assured, were often tricked by the intermediate classes and did not dare to act resolutely. Vigorous action is taken against the intermediate classes in the countryside only when the revolution is on the upsurge, for example, when political power has been seized in one or several *xian,* when the reactionary armies have suffered several defeats, and when the Red Army has repeatedly demonstrated its prowess. For example, it is in the southern section of Yongxin *xian,* where the intermediate classes are most numerous, that delays in distributing the land and cheating in reporting land-holding were most flagrant. Only after the Red Army won its great victory at Longyuankou on June 23, and only after the district government killed[146] several people for delaying distribution, was land actually distributed there. But since the feudal family system is widespread in every *xian,* and all the families in a village or group of villages often have the same surname, a fairly long time will be required for class polarization to take place in the villages and for clan

---

141. Owner-peasants → Rich peasants
142. Poor peasants → Middle and poor peasants
143. Owner-peasants → Rich peasants
144. Owner-peasants → Rich peasants
145. Because → Because they felt that
146. Killed → Dealt with

ideology to be overcome. *In the countryside, where clan organizations prevail, the most troublesome are not the despotic gentry, but the intermediate classes. This is the biggest problem.*

3. The Defection of the Intermediate Classes under the White terror: The intermediate classes had been under attack during the high tide of revolution, so they defected as soon as the White terror arrived. It was none other than the small landlords and owner-peasants[147] in the two *xian* of Yongxin and Ninggang who led the reactionary army to burn the homes of the revolutionary peasants there. They were very bold about burning down houses and arresting people at the direction of the counterrevolutionaries. When the Red Army returned to the area around Ninggang *(in September),* Xincheng, Gucheng, and Longshi, several thousand peasants who had heard and believed the reactionary propaganda that the Communists would kill them fled with the counterrevolutionaries to Yongxin. Only after we had conducted propaganda to the effect that "Peasant defectors will not be killed," and "Peasant defectors are welcome to come back to harvest their crops," did some of these peasants slowly return.

4. When the revolution is at low ebb in the country as a whole, the most difficult problem in the areas ruled by the independent régime is keeping a firm grip on the intermediate class. This class rebels mainly because it has received excessively heavy blows from the revolution. When there is a revolutionary upsurge in the country as a whole, the poor peasant class has something to rely on and becomes bolder, while the intermediate class has something to fear and dares not create a disturbance. When the war between Li Zongren and Tang Shengzhi spread to Hunan,[148] the small landlords in Chaling sought to placate the peasants. Some of them gave pork to the peasants as a New Year's gift (at that time the Red Army had withdrawn from Chaling toward Suichuan). But when the war was over, nothing was heard of such things again. Now that there is a high tide of counterrevolution in the whole country, the intermediate classes which have suffered our blows have gone over almost completely to the despotic gentry, and the poor peasant class has become isolated. This is truly a serious problem.

5. The Pressure of Daily Life as a Cause of the Defection of the Intermediate Class: The Red independent régime and the White areas are now facing each other like two countries at war. As a result of the enemy's tight blockade, and our unduly harsh treatment of the petty bourgeoisie, trade between the two areas has almost entirely ceased. Necessities such as salt, cloth, and medicines are scarce and costly, and agricultural products such as timber, tea, and oil cannot be

---

147. Owner-peasants → Rich peasants

148. In September 1927, Tang Shengzhi opposed the formation of a Central Special Committee to function as an interim government, with the aim of reconciling the Nanjing and Wuhan factions of the Guomindang. Thereupon, Nanjing launched a punitive expedition against him in October 1927, with Li Zongren as commander-in-chief. Tang was obliged to abandon Wuhan, and Li came to control both Hubei and Hunan.

shipped out. As a result, cash income[149] is cut off, and the people as a whole are affected. The poor peasant class is better able to bear such hardships. The intermediate class, when it can bear them no longer, will go over to the despotic gentry. *This economic problem is extremely serious.* Unless the splits and wars within the despotic gentry and among the warlords in China continue, and unless a nationwide revolutionary situation develops, the small fragmentary Red régimes will come under extreme economic pressure, and their long-term existence will be called into question. For not only is such economic pressure unbearable for the intermediate classes but a time may well come when even the worker and peasant classes[150] and the Red Army will not be able to endure it. In Yongxin and Ninggang *xian* there was no salt for cooking, and supplies of cloth and medicines were completely cut off, not to mention other commodities. Now, *because it is not the extreme high tide* [of counterrevolution], salt can be had again, but it is extremely expensive. Cloth and medicines are still unattainable. Timber and tea-oil, which are produced abundantly in Ninggang, the western part of Yongxin, and the northern part of Suichuan (all currently part of our areas) still cannot be shipped out. *The shortage of cash is extremely acute. If the captured despotic gentry do not send us money, we have no money to use. All this poses an enormous problem.*

6. Criteria for Land Redistribution: *In a given region,* the township serves as the unit for distribution. In mountainous areas where arable land is scarce, such as Xiaojiang District in Yongxin, three or four villages were sometimes taken as a single unit for land distribution, but such cases were very rare. The human criterion used to be that everyone, male or female, old or young, got an equal share. Now we have switched to the method of the Central Committee, which takes labor power as the criterion. The able-bodied get twice as much as those who cannot work.

7. The Question of Concessions to the Owner-peasants: As yet, this has not been discussed in detail. The rich peasants among the owner-peasants have put forward the demand that productive capacity should be taken as the criterion, so that those with more manpower and capital (farm implements, etc.) would get more land. The rich peasants feel that neither equal distribution nor distribution according to labor power are advantageous to them. Their idea is that, as regards manpower, they are willing to work harder, and that if, *in addition,* account is taken of their capital, they can raise bigger crops. If they receive the same allocation as everyone else, and their special efforts and extra capital are ignored (left unused), they will not like it. Here we are still applying the method of the Central Committee. But this question must be discussed further, and when conclusions have been reached, we will submit another report. On the one hand, we request the Central Committee and the two Provincial Committees to instruct us

---

149. Cash income → The peasants' cash income
150. Worker and peasant classes → Workers and poor peasants

as soon as possible regarding the methods (the concrete methods, not merely the broad policy) used by Soviet Russia in dealing with the rich peasants, especially during the democratic revolution, when the Soviet government was surrounded by the White régime. As for not confiscating the land of owner-peasants, the whole of it has already been confiscated on the territory of the independent régime in the border area, so of course the problem will not arise again. When opening up new territories, we will adopt a no-confiscation policy in the initial stage. In this way, we can make use of the strength of the owner-peasants to support the poor peasants, and to attack the despotic gentry.

8. The Land Tax. The rate in Ninggang is 20 percent, or 5 percent more than that set by the Central Committee. Since the tax is already being collected, we cannot very well make a change now, but the rate will be reduced next year. Apart from this, there are portions of Suichuan, Lingxian, and Yongxin under the independent régime which are situated in mountainous areas where the peasants are so poverty-stricken that they should not be taxed at all. For the expenses of the government and of the Red Guards we rely on expropriating the despotic gentry in the White areas. As for the provisioning of the Red Army, rice is obtained for the time being from the land tax in Ninggang, but in this case too, cash is obtained entirely from expropriating the despotic gentry. During our guerrilla operations in Suichuan in October, we collected more than ten thousand *yuan*. This will last for some time; we will give the matter more thought when it has been spent.

C. The Problem of the Soviets[151]

1. Soviets[152] *in the Border Area* at the *Xian*, District, and Township Levels. *Soviets* have been organized everywhere at each of these levels, but more in name than in reality. *The majority of the worker and peasant masses, and even of Party members, have not yet understood the idea of a soviet.* In many places, there is no such thing as the council of workers', peasants', and soldiers' representatives. The executive committees of the soviets[153] at township, district, or even *xian* level have all been elected by the masses.[154] But mass meetings called on the spur of the moment can neither discuss questions nor offer political training,[155] and they can easily be manipulated by intellectuals or opportunists. *The greatest error regarding the organs of political power in many localities in the border area consists in ignorance of what is meant by a soviet, ignorance of the fact that the council of workers', peasants', and soldiers' representatives is the supreme permanent organ of power, and the executive committee is merely*

---

151. The Soviets → Political Power
152. Soviets → People's political power
153. Soviets → Governments
154. By the masses → At a mass meeting
155. Training → Training for the masses

the organ in charge of day-to-day affairs when the council is not in session. Some places do have a council, but it is regarded as nothing more than a temporary body for electing the executive committee. Once the election is over, all power is monopolized by the committee, and the council is never mentioned again. It is not *at all* the case that there are no soviet organizations[156] worthy of the name; it is simply that there are very few of them. The reason lies in the *great* lack of propaganda and education regarding this new political system called the soviets.[157] The evil habits of the arbitrary despotism of the feudal era are deeply ingrained in the minds of the masses, and even of ordinary Party members, and cannot be eradicated all at once. When something happens, they seek the most convenient solution and have no liking for this troublesome democratic system. Democratic centralism can be widely and genuinely established in mass organizations only when its efficacy is demonstrated in the revolutionary struggle, and the masses understand that it is the best method for mobilizing their forces and is extremely advantageous for their struggle. We are presently engaged in drafting a detailed law (based on Central Committee's outline) for the organization of the soviets[158] at all levels, in order gradually to correct previous mistakes. *Soldiers' soviets* (conferences of soldiers' representatives at all levels) are now being established in the Red Army on a permanent basis, so as to correct the previous mistake of having only *permanent* soldiers' committees, and not *permanent* conferences of soldiers' representatives.

2. *Executive Committees at All Levels.* At present, the masses of the people are all familiar with the *"soviet* government of the workers, peasants, and soldiers" at various levels. *In Ninggang, the popular masses call it the* "ai[159] *government" for short (In the dialect of settlers from other provinces we use the same character; the* ai *government means "our government"). In some other places, it is known in a truncated form as the* "su *government."* What they call by this name is actually the executive committee, because they are still unaware of the powers of the council and think that the executive committee alone is the real power. *Such an attitude is not universal.* An executive committee without a council of representatives, *or a properly constituted council of representatives,* behind it, often deals with matters without taking account of the views of the masses. Everywhere there are instances of hesitation and compromise on the confiscation and redistribution of land, of squandering or embezzling funds, and of recoiling before the White forces or fighting only half-heartedly. In addition, the committee seldom meets in full session, all business being decided and handled by its standing committee. In the district and township governments

---

156. Soviet organizations → Councils of workers', peasants', and soldiers' deputies
157. Soviets → Councils
158. Soviets → Councils
159. In other words, they refer to it by the third of the characters *su-wei-ai* used in the Chinese phonetic transcription of the word "soviet."

even the standing committee rarely meets, and business is decided and handled separately by the four individuals who work in the office, namely the chairman, secretary, treasurer, and commander of the Red Guards (or insurrectionary detachment). Thus democratic centralism has not become a regular practice even in the work of the government.

3. The Problem of Petty Bourgeois Control of Government Committees. In the early period, small landlords, rich peasants, *and intellectuals* vied with one another to get on the government committees, especially at the township level. Wearing red arm sashes and feigning great enthusiasm, they wormed their way into the government committees by trickery and seized control of everything, relegating the poor peasants to a supporting role. They can be thoroughly cleared out only when they are unmasked in the course of struggle, and the poor peasant class rises up. Although such a state of affairs is not universal, it has occurred in a number of places.

4. The Relationship between the Party and the Government Organs. Although the Party does not order the government organs around, neither does it realize the importance of respecting the independence of government organs. The Party enjoys extremely great prestige and authority among *Party members and* the masses, the government much less. The reason is that, for the sake of convenience, the Party handles many things directly and brushes the government organs aside. This is a common mistake in many places. In some places, there are no Party or Youth League leading groups; in other places, they exist, but are not functioning properly. In the future, the Party must act as back-stage boss.[160] With the exception of propaganda, the Party's policies and the measures it recommends must be carried out through the mass[161] organizations. We need to avoid the Guomindang's error of running the government directly.

5. The Supreme Soviet. We proclaimed "The Soviet Government of Workers, Peasants, and Soldiers in the Hunan-Jiangxi Border Area" as early as May, but because of the pressure of time, it was far from perfect. We have now decided to reshuffle the border soviet and its committee, which will be the highest organ of political power in the border area.

D. The Present State of the Party in the Border Area[162]

1. The Course of the Struggle against Opportunism. It may be said that around the time of the Horse Day Incident,[163] the Party organizations in every *xian* of the border area were *entirely* opportunist.[164] As a result, when counter-

---

160. Act as back-stage boss → Carry out its task of leading the government

161. Mass → Government

162. The Present State of the Party in the Border Area → Questions of Party Organization

163. Regarding the "Horse Day Incident" of May 21, 1927, see the note to section IVA11.

164. Opportunist → Dominated by opportunism

revolution set in, there was very little resolute struggle. In October of last year, when the Red Army (the First Regiment of the First Division of the First Army of the Workers' and Peasants' Revolutionary Army) arrived in the *xian* of the border area, only a few *individual* Party members who had gone into hiding were left, and the Party organization had been entirely destroyed. The four months from November of last year to April of this year were a period of rebuilding the Party. The period since May has been one of rapid expansion. During the past year, manifestations of opportunism have been widespread within the Party. Some Party members have no stomach for fighting and *have turned into ambushists* (when the enemy comes, they hide in the remote mountains, calling this lying in ambush). Others are filled with activism, but have turned into idealist insurrectionists.[165] Both tendencies are the result of petty bourgeois consciousness.[166] This situation has finally changed only after a long period of tempering in practice and inner-Party struggle.[167] During the same period, this kind of stupidity resulting from petty bourgeois consciousness[168] has existed *for a long time* in the Red Army as well. When the enemy comes, they advocate either desperate resistance or flight. This sort of desperationism or flightism often existed side by side in the views put forward by the same individual regarding a given situation.[169] This opportunist ideology has been gradually corrected through prolonged inner-Party struggle and through lessons learned from actual events, for instance, from the losses incurred in reckless battle and the reverses suffered during precipitate flight.

2. Localism. The economy in the border area is *not only* agricultural, it is still[170] in the age of the mortar and pestle. (In the mountainous areas, mortar and pestle are still in general use for husking rice, while in the plains there are many treadle-operated stone pestles.) Everywhere the unit of social organization is the clan organization, consisting of people with the same surname. As regards Party organization in the villages, because of the way people live together, Party members with the same surname often make up a branch, and the branch meeting is simply[171] a clan meeting. In these circumstances, it is very difficult indeed to build a "militant Bolshevik Party." Such people do not really understand that

---

165. Turned into idealist insurrectionists → Resorted to blind insurrection

166. Result of petty bourgeois consciousness → Expression of petty bourgeois ideology

167. Tempering in practice and inner-Party struggle → Tempering through struggle and inner-Party education

168. Stupidity resulting from petty bourgeois consciousness → Petty-bourgeois ideology

169. This sort of desperationism or flightism often existed side by side in the views put forward by the same individual regarding a given situation → Often both ideas emanated from the same individual in the course of the discussions on what military action to take

170. It is still → In some places it is still

171. Simply → At the same time

the Communist Party does not distinguish between countries and provinces, nor do they understand that a sharp line should not be drawn between *xian*, districts, and townships. Localism exists to a serious extent in the relations between *xian*, and it is deeply rooted also in the relations between districts and townships within the same *xian*. In modifying such localism, *subjective* reasoning alone can at best produce only limited results. For the most part, it takes White oppression, which is by no means localized (such as joint suppression campaigns by the two provinces), in which people share a common lot in the course of their struggles, gradually to induce them to abandon their localism. Amid many such objective lessons, localism is gradually weakened.

3. The Problem of the Native Inhabitants and the Settlers.[172] There is another peculiar feature in the border area, namely the division between the native inhabitants and the settlers. A profound gulf has long existed between the native inhabitants and those who came here as colonists from Guangdong and Fujian[173] hundreds of years ago. Their traditional feuds are deep-seated, sometimes erupting in violent *"national"* struggles. From the Guangdong[174] border, all the way along the border areas of Hunan and Jiangxi, up to southern Hubei, there are probably several millions of such settlers. These settlers occupy the mountainous areas, are oppressed by the native inhabitants who live in the plains, and have never had any political rights. They all, without exception, welcomed the national revolution of last year and the year before, thinking that the day had come for them to raise their heads. But unexpectedly the revolution turned into a counterrevolution,[175] and the settlers continue to be oppressed by the native inhabitants as before. Within our *independent* border area, the problem of the native inhabitants and the settlers exists in Ninggang, Suichuan, Lingxian, and Chaling, but it is in Ninggang that it is most serious. Last year and the year before, the revolutionaries among the native inhabitants joined together with the settlers, under the leadership of the Communist Party, overthrew the political power of the native despotic gentry, and took control of the whole *xian*. Last June, the government of Zhu Peide turned counterrevolutionary. In September, the despotic gentry served as guides for Zhu Peide's army in its suppression

---

172. Mao refers here to the "native inhabitants" and "settlers" respectively as *tuji* and *keji*. These designations correspond to *bendi* and *kejia*, commonly represented in English-language sources by their Cantonese transcriptions, Punti and Hakka. A convenient survey of the relations between these two ethnic groups since the nineteenth century can be found in S. T. Leong, "The Hakka Chinese of Lingnan: Ethnicity and Social Change in Modern Times," in *Ideal and Reality: Social and Political Change in Modern China, 1860–1949*, ed. David Pong and Edmund S. K. Fung (Lanham, Md.: University Press of America, 1985), pp. 287–323. Leong's article includes brief biographies of eight Hakkas who began their Party careers during the period of the Jiangxi soviet, and played important roles after 1949.

173. Colonists from Guangdong and Fujian → Migrants from the north

174. Guangdong → Guangdong and Fujian

175. Turned into a counterrevolution → Failed

campaign against Ninggang, in a war which still continues.[176] In theory, this kind of schism should not extend to the oppressed workers and peasants, let alone to the Party. In reality, however, by force of long *historical* tradition, the division between the native inhabitants and the settlers still leaves considerable traces.[177] For example, after the August defeat in the border area, when the native despotic gentry returned to Ninggang, bringing the troops[178] with them, they conducted large-scale propaganda claiming that the settlers were going to massacre the native inhabitants. As a result, most of the native peasants defected, put on white ribbons, and led the army[179] to burn down houses and comb the mountains. And when, in October and November, the Red Army *twice* defeated the White army, the native peasants fled with them, and the settlers hastened to confiscate the *pigs, cattle, clothes, and other* property of the native peasants. When reflected in the Party, this sort of historical residue[180] takes the form of pointless arguments.[181] The way to settle this is to proclaim to the masses that "peasants who have defected will not be killed" and that "peasants who have defected will also get their share of land when they return," thus leading them to shake off the influence of the despotic gentry, and return home without misgivings. *(Many of them have already done so.)* At the same time, the *xian* soviet[182] must compel the settlers to return confiscated *cattle and property* to the original owners, and notices must be posted stating that native peasants will be protected. Within the Party, *the causes of differences should be eliminated*, and education should be intensified in order to achieve unity.

4. The Defection of the Opportunists. During the revolutionary upsurge (in June), many opportunists took advantage of open recruitment to make their way into the Party. In a very short time, the number of Party members in the border area jumped to more than ten thousand. Branch leaders, and even district committee leaders were mostly new Party members, who had not been able to receive a good inner-Party education. As soon as the White Terror struck, the careerists defected. *In many places,* they led the reactionaries to hunt down our comrades. As a result, the majority of Party organizations in White territory collapsed.

5. *Party Purification and the Establishment of Underground Organizations.* Since September, the Party has carried out a drastic purge and has set strict class qualifications for membership. Party organizations in Yongxin and Ninggang *xian* were completely dissolved, and re-registration was carried out. Re-registration has been completed in Yongxin, and Ninggang will soon follow. Although the number of Party members has been greatly reduced, the Party's

---

176. In a war which still continues → And once again stirred up the conflict between the native inhabitants and the settlers
177. Still leaves considerable traces → Still exists
178. Troops → Reactionary troops
179. Army → White army
180. Historical residue → Situation
181. Arguments → Struggles
182. Soviet → Government

fighting capacity has, on the contrary, increased. Formerly, the Party's organization relied on open political power,[183] *almost completely neglecting the importance of secret work.* Since September, we have carried out the work of building[184] a *complete* underground organization.[185] At the same time, we have made every effort to penetrate deeply into the White regions, in order to exercise an influence in the enemy camp. *In some areas, this has begun to show some results.* In the towns,[186] however, we still have no foundation at all. The reasons are, first, that the enemy is relatively strong in the towns, and second, we had harmed the interests of the *petty* bourgeoisie in the cities too much, *business is slow, the craftsmen have ceased to work,* and as a result we can scarcely find a foothold. We are now correcting our *former* mistakes and striving to establish our organizations in the cities, but so far without much success.

6. Leadership Organs[187] at All Levels. The branch executive council has been renamed the branch committee. The branch is under the district committee, and the district committee is under the *xian* committee. Where there are special circumstances, a special district committee has been organized between the district committee and the *xian* committee. Cases in point are Beixiang Special District and Southeast Special District in Yongxin *xian*. In the border area there are five *xian* committees in all: Ninggang, Yongxin, Lianhua, Suichuan, and Lingxian. There used to be a *xian* committee in Chaling, but because the work there did not take root, most of the organizations established last winter and spring were smashed by the *powerful* White forces. For the past six months, we have been able to work only in a narrow band of mountainous territory in the vicinity of Ninggang and Yongxin, so the *xian* committee was changed to a special district committee. We have sent people to Youxian and Anren, both of which can be reached only via Chaling, but they have returned without accomplishing anything. The Wan'an *Xian* Committee was cut off for more than six months after the joint meeting with the former Front Committee[188] in Suichuan in January. It was not until September, when the Red Army reached Wan'an in a guerrilla operation, that we resumed contact. *According to a letter from the Wan'an Xian Committee, it lost its previous nine district committees and all its 120 guns. At present, our organizations exist only in the Guards Regiment. Our comrades there have taken some of the guns. One battalion of the Red Army guerrilla forces reached a point close to the Wan'an* xian *town, and then returned, after the responses previously arranged from within the city and from other places totally failed to materialize.* Eighty revolutionary peasants followed

---

183. Relied on open political power → Was entirely open
184. Carried out the work of building → Built
185. Organization → Organization, so as to prepare the Party for carrying on its activities when the reactionaries come
186. Towns → Nearby towns
187. Leadership organs → Organs of Party leadership
188. The former Front Committee → Us

[our troops] to the foot of the Jinggangshan and were organized into a *detachment of* Wan'an Red Guards, *with ten guns.* There is no Party organization in Anfu. Ji'an borders on Yongxin, but *for all this time our independent régime has been in existence,* the Ji'an *Xian* Committee has been in touch with us only twice and has given us no help at all. This is truly strange. In the Shatian area of Guidong, land distribution was carried out twice, in March and August. Party organizations have been established and are *currently* under the jurisdiction of the Southern Hunan Special Committee, with its center at Shiertong in Longxi. All the *xian* committees are placed under the Special Committee of the Hunan-Jiangxi Border Area. On May 20, the First Party Congress of the border area was held at Maoping in Ninggang and elected twenty-three people as members of the First Special Committee, with Mao Zedong as secretary. In July, the Hunan Provincial Committee sent Yang Kaiming here, and he became acting secretary.[189] In September, Yang fell ill, and Tan Zhenlin took his place. In August, when the main force of the Red Army went to southern Hunan, and the White forces were pressing hard on the border area, an emergency meeting was held in Yongxin. In October, after the Red Army returned to Ninggang, the Second Congress of the border area was called together, once again at Maoping. The congress started on October 4[190] and lasted for three days. It adopted resolutions on political problems, the tasks of the Party in the border area, *problems of organization, problems of propaganda, and the land problem.* It also elected nineteen people as members of the Second Special Committee (Tan Zhenlin, Zhu De, Chen Yi, Long Chaoqing, Zhu Changkai,[191] Liu Tianqian, Yuan Panzhu, Tan Sicong, Tan Bing, Li Quefei, Song Yiyue, Yuan Wencai, Wan Zuonong, Chen Zhengren, Mao Zedong, Wan Xixian, Wang Zuo, Yang Kaiming, He Tingying), and five standing committee members, with Tan Zhenlin (a worker)[192] as secretary and Chen Zhengren (an intellectual) as deputy secretary. On November 14, the Sixth Party Congress of the Red Army elected twenty-three people to constitute the Army Committee, with a five-member standing committee and Zhu De as secretary. The Special Committee and the Army Committee are both subordinated to the Front Committee. In accordance with the directives of the Central Committee, the Front Committee was set up[193] on November 6 and consisted of five members: Mao Zedong, Zhu De, the local Party secretary (Tan Zhenlin), a worker comrade (Song Qiaosheng), and a peasant comrade (Mao Kewen), with Mao Zedong as secretary. For the time being, the Front Committee has set up a secretariat, a propaganda section, an organization section, a labor movement committee, and a

---

189. I.e., as noted above, he replaced Mao.
190. 4 → 14. According to *Nianpu*, Vol. 1, p. 254, the date of October 4 is correct.
191. Zhu Changkai → Zhu Changjie
192. Tan had had only three years' schooling and had worked briefly in the labor movement in 1926.
193. Set up → Reorganized

military affairs commission *(i.e., the one elected by the Red Army Congress mentioned above).* *Now that it has been established,* the Front Committee will supervise local party organizations *in every xian.* The Special Committee still has its raison d'être, since the Front Committee is often on the move.[194] The problem of the leading role of proletarian consciousness[195] in the Party is extremely important. *It can almost be said that* the Party organization in all the *xian* of the border area is entirely a peasant party. If they do not receive leadership[196] from the *urban* proletariat, they are bound to develop erroneous tendencies. Besides correcting previous mistakes and paying active attention to the workers' movement in the *xian* seats and in other large towns *in the countryside,* it is also extremely necessary to increase worker representation in the soviets[197] *and to have Party members from among the workers, poor peasants, and soldiers join all levels of leadership in local Party and military organs. We have paid attention to this point during the past year, and the proportion of workers and peasants in local Party leadership has gradually increased. Soldier participation in Red Army organs at all levels is also relatively satisfactory. The only thing we need to do is further to increase their quantity and pay attention to their quality, so that they may take "real control," and gradually divest themselves of petty bourgeois consciousness, becoming truly pure.*

E. The Problem of the Character of Revolution

1. We agree completely with the International's resolution on China: at present, China is definitely still at the stage of bourgeois-democratic revolution. Carrying through[198] a thoroughgoing democratic revolution in China comprises, externally, the overthrow of imperialist *privileges,* in order to achieve complete national liberation *and unification*; internally, it comprises the elimination of the power and influence of the comprador class in the cities, the abolition of feudal relationships in the countryside, the completion of the agrarian revolution, and the overthrow of the warlord system,[199] *which is a metamorphosed form of the political organization of the despotic gentry.* Only in *the process of* such a democratic revolution can a genuine foundation for workers' political power[200] be formed, so as to advance to the socialist revolution. In the past year we have fought in many places and are acutely aware that the revolutionary tide is ebbing daily in the country as a whole. Although Red political power has been established in a few tiny spots, ordinary democratic rights do not yet exist throughout

---

194. Often on the move → Often on the move with the army
195. Consciousness → Ideology
196. Leadership → Ideological leadership
197. In the soviets → In the leading organs of the Party at all levels
198. Carrying through → The program for
199. The warlord system → Warlord power
200. Workers' political power → The transition to socialism

the country as a whole. Neither workers, nor peasants, nor even the democratic faction among the bourgeoisie have freedom of speech or assembly. The Communist Party[201] is the most heinous crime. Wherever the Red Army goes, people are cold and aloof, and only after we have conducted propaganda do the masses gradually come forth.[202] Whatever enemy units we face, they all fight stubbornly, and there are hardly any cases of mutiny or desertion to our side. This holds true even for the Sixth Army, which recruited the greatest number of "rebels" after the Horse Day Incident. *This cannot be called an insurrection, it is merely contending for the country.*[203] This method of contending for the country cannot succeed. The reason for this is that there is absolutely no revolutionary high tide in the country as a whole. The whole country is suffering the ruthless feudal domination of the despotic gentry, and the vast forces of the oppressed classes have not yet been set in motion. So we are reduced to contending for the country in this cold atmosphere. We have an acute sense of our isolation, which we keep hoping will end. Only by launching *and carrying through* a democratic revolution[204] in the political and economic domains, with the participation of the petty bourgeoisie,[205] can we turn the revolution into a seething high tide that will engulf the entire country. *Consequently, the resolution of the International is entirely correct.*

2. Policy toward the Petty Bourgeoisie. Up to February of this year, this matter was handled well in the border area. In March, the representative of the Southern Hunan Special Committee, Zhou Lu, arrived in the border area. He criticized us[206] for not burning and killing enough, for not carrying out the policy of "turning the petty bourgeois into proletarians and then forcing them to make revolution." Thereupon,[207] the policy underwent a transformation. In April, after the whole of our army arrived in the border area, there was still not much burning and killing, but the expropriation of the middle merchants in the towns and the collection of compulsory contributions from the small landlords and rich peasants in the countryside were rigorously enforced. The slogan of "All factories to the workers," put forward by the Southern Hunan Special Committee, was also given wide publicity. This excessive[208] policy of attacking the petty bourgeoisie drove most of them to the side of the despotic gentry, with the result that

---

201. The Communist Party → Joining the Communist Party

202. Come forth → Arise

203. *Da jiangshan*, literally "fighting for the rivers and mountains" (i.e., for the land of China). The use of this expression implies an attempt to conquer the country in an old-fashioned way, like the aspirants to the imperial throne who set out in the past from a limited territorial base.

204. Revolution → Struggle

205. Petty bourgeoisie → Urban petty bourgeoisie

206. Criticized us → Criticized us for being too rightist

207. Thereupon → Thereupon, the original leadership of the Front Committee was changed, and

208. Excessive → Ultraleftist

they put on white ribbons and opposed us. Recently, with the gradual change in this policy, the situation has been steadily improving. Especially in Suichuan, *relatively* good results have been achieved. The *small* merchants in the *xian* town and other market towns no longer avoid us and quite a few speak well of the Red Army. The fairs at Gelin and Shangfeng (the fair is held at noon every three days) attract twenty thousand people, more than ever before. This shows that our policy has already changed.[209] As for the overthrow of the feudal exploitation of the despotic gentry (in Suichuan the Pacification Guards imposed extremely heavy taxes; there are five tax posts on the seventy *li* from Huang'ao to Caolin, which collect tax on every kind of produce), the peasants and small merchants are all in favor of it.[210]

3. The Central Committee wants us to issue a political program taking account of the interests of the petty bourgeoisie. We, for our part, propose that the Central Committee work out a program for the entire democratic revolution, taking account of workers' interests, the agrarian revolution, and national liberation, *and that they also decide on a slogan,* to be followed everywhere.

4. A peculiarity of the revolution in China, a country with a predominantly agrarian economy, is the use of military action to develop insurrection. We recommend that the Central Committee devote great effort to military work. *The most important form of military activity is within the enemy armies. The development of the Red Army remains secondary at present.*

F. The Problem of the Independent Régime

The area stretching from northern Guangdong along the Hunan-Jiangxi border into southern Hubei lies entirely within the Luoxiao mountain range. We have traversed the whole range, and a comparison of its different sections shows that the middle section, with Ninggang as its center, is the most suitable for our independent régime.[211] The northern section has terrain which is less suitable for our taking either the offensive or the defensive, and it is too close to the enemy's big political centers. Unless we plan a quick seizure of Changsha or Wuhan, it is very dangerous to station large forces in and around Liuyang, Liling, Pingxiang, and Tonggu. The southern section has better terrain than the northern section, but our mass base there is not so good as in the middle section, and from a political standpoint, we cannot exert as much influence on Hunan and Jiangxi as we can from the middle section. The middle section has the following advantages: (1) A mass base, which we have been cultivating for over a year. (2) A fairly good basis for the Party.[212] (3) Local armed forces which have been well tempered in

---

209. Has already changed → Is correct

210. The peasants and small merchants are all in favor of it → When we crushed the Pacification Guards and abolished these tolls, we won the support of all the peasants as well as of the small and middle merchants.

211. Independent régime → Armed independent régime

212. Party → Party organizations

battles, having been built up for more than a year—a rare achievement. With the support of the Fourth Red Army, they will prove indestructible in the face of any enemy force. (4) We have an excellent military base in Jinggangshan, and every *xian* has its own local military bases. (5) [The middle section] can exert influence on both provinces and on the lower valleys of their rivers. This endows it with much more political importance than that possessed by southern Hunan or southern Jiangxi, each of which can influence only its own province or at most the upper river valley and the hinterland of its own province. The defect of the middle section is that, since it has long been under the independent régime, and faces large enemy encirclement and suppression forces, its economic problems, especially the shortage of cash, are extremely difficult.

Within a few weeks in June and July, the Southern Hunan Special Committee[213] changed its mind three times about the policy[214] we should adopt here. First Yuan Desheng *brought a letter and* approved the plan to establish political power in the middle section.[215] Then Du Xiujing and Yang Kaiming came *with a letter* advocating that the Red Army move toward southern Hunan without the slightest hesitation, leaving only two hundred rifles to defend the border area, together with the Red Guards. They stated, moreover, that this was an "absolutely correct" policy. The third time Yuan Desheng came again, barely ten days later, carrying a letter which, apart from abusing us at great length, proposed that the Red Army go to eastern Hunan. Once again, it was stated that this was the "absolutely correct" policy and should be carried out "without the slightest hesitation." These rigid directives put us in a truly difficult position, because failure to comply would verge on insubordination, while we knew very clearly that compliance would mean defeat. When the second letter arrived, the Army Committee, the Special Committee, and the Yongxin *Xian* Committee held a joint meeting. Considering that it would be dangerous to move toward southern Hunan, they decided not to carry out the Provincial Committee's instructions. A few days later, however, Du Xiujing and Yang Kaiming, holding to the views of the Provincial Committee, and taking advantage of the homesickness of the Twenty-ninth Regiment, *which in turn used the Provincial directive as an excuse*, dragged the Red Army off to attack Chenzhou, thus bringing defeat both to the border area and to the Red Army. The Red Army lost about half its fighting strength.[216] Countless houses were burned down, and countless people were killed in the border area. One *xian* after another fell to the enemy, and some of them have not been recovered even now. As for going to eastern Hunan, it was certainly not advisable for the main force of the Red Army to do so at a time

---

213. Southern Hunan Special Committee → Hunan Provincial Committee

214. Policy → Plan of action

215. The middle section → The middle section of the Luoxiao mountain range.

216. Regarding these events of June and July, and the letters brought by the emissaries from the Hunan Provincial Committee, see also the Introduction to this volume.

when there was as yet no split within the political power of the despotic gentry *class* in Hunan, Hubei, and Jiangxi. Had we not advanced on southern Hunan in July, we would not only have avoided the August defeat in the border area; we could have taken advantage of the fighting at Zhangshu[217] between Cheng Qian's[218] Sixth Army and Wan Jun, routed the enemy troops in Yongxin, and swept through Ji'an and Anfu, thus enabling our vanguard to reach Pingxiang and make contact with the Fifth Army in the northern section. Even if all that had happened, the proper place for our general headquarters would still have been Ninggang, and only guerrilla forces should have been sent to eastern Hunan. Since war had not broken out among the despotic gentry, and powerful enemy forces were still present in Pingxiang, Chaling, and Youxian on the Hunan border, if the main force had moved north, the enemy would certainly have taken advantage of it. The Central Committee told us to go to eastern or to southern Hunan, but either course was very dangerous. Although the decision to go to eastern Hunan was not carried out, we do have the experience of southern Hunan. *One false move, and the whole chess game is lost. The Fifth Army suffered defeat for loss of contact between the border area in southern Hunan and Pingxiang and Liuyang. Anyuan also suffered setbacks.* We should always remember this painful experience.

We are now in a period when the despotic gentry class is not yet split, and the suppression forces of the enemy deployed around the border area number more than ten regiments. If we can continue to find ways of getting cash (food and clothing no longer constitute a big problem), then with the foundations for our work established in the border area, we shall be able to cope with these enemy forces, or even with larger ones. As far as the border area is concerned, it would at once suffer devastation, just as it did in August, if the Red Army moved away. Although not all our Red Guards would be wiped out, the Party and our mass base would receive a crippling blow. Apart from *bandit-style* bases in the mountains, of which the independent régime could still maintain a few, in the plains we would all have to go underground as we did in August and September. If the Red Army remains, it can expand gradually in all directions from its current base, and the prospects will be very bright. If we want to enlarge the Red Army, the only tactic is to engage the enemy in a prolonged struggle in the vicinity of the Jinggangshan (that is to say, in the four *xian* of Ninggang, Yongxin, Ling-xian, and Suichuan), where we have a good mass base. We must take advantage in this struggle of the conflicting interests of the enemy troops from Hunan and Jiangxi, and of their inability to concentrate their forces because they must defend themselves on all sides, and wage a long-term struggle against the enemy. We must employ advantageous[219] tactics, fight no battle unless we can win it, be victorious every time we fight, capture arms and men, and thus gradually expand

217. Zhangshu → Zhangshu in Jiangxi Province
218. Cheng Qian's → The Guomindang's
219. Advantageous → Correct

the Red Army. Considering the preparatory work that had already been done among the masses of the border area between April and June, there is not the slightest doubt that the Red Army could have been enlarged in August if its main force had not gone off to southern Hunan. Despite that mistake, the Red Army has returned to the border area, where the terrain is favorable and the people well disposed, and our prospects are still not bad. In a place like the border area, it is only by being resolved to fight, and by fighting with indomitable courage, that the Red Army can expand its arsenal and train good soldiers; *apart from this, there is no other effective method.* The red flag has already been flying in the border area for a year now. Although it has incurred the bitter hatred of the despotic gentry class in Hunan, Hubei, and Jiangxi, and indeed in the whole country, it has gradually aroused hope among the workers, peasants, and soldiers of the neighboring provinces. As regards the soldiers, the warlords are treating "bandit suppression" as a matter of major importance and are putting out propaganda *favorable to us* such as "a year has been spent and a million *yuan* used up in the effort to eradicate the bandits" (Lu Diping), or even "they have twenty thousand men and five thousand guns" (Wang Jun). Because of this *propaganda favorable to us,* the attention of enemy soldiers and of junior officers with no prospects is gradually being drawn to us, and more and more of them will defect to our side, thus providing another source of recruitment for the Red Army. The uninterrupted presence of the Red flag on the border is an indication not only of the strength of the Communist Party but also of the bankruptcy of the ruling class, and is of great nationwide political significance. *Therefore, our contingent plan to use "southern Jiangxi as a retreat" will not be put into effect unless our economic situation worsens to such a degree that southern Jiangxi becomes the only place where we could survive. We might have to go there some time; but it would be entirely for economic rather than political reasons. Politically speaking,* we have held from the very beginning that the strategy of creating and expanding political power in the middle section of the Luoxiao mountain range is absolutely necessary and correct.

G. Communications and Other Matters

1. It is of crucial importance to establish an organ in charge of communication. Two hundred yuan (four liang[220] of gold) has been entrusted to Comrades Yuan and Xiao, who will be in full charge of establishing this organ. Necessary expenses will be met by us. The organ will be located in Pingxiang. Another such organ is also required in the Ji'an area; the Jiangxi Provincial Committee will be responsible for it.

2. When we had almost finished writing this letter, we received a letter from the Central Committee. The copy from Hunan includes Notice No. 47 (on secret organizations), although it still does not contain the resolution on military affairs. In addition, there is also Comrade Runxian's August 15 letter, stating that a

---

220. One *liang* or Chinese ounce (sometimes referred to as a *tael*) is equivalent to approximately 1.3 ounces avoirdupois.

messenger had been sent to deliver the Central Committee's letter and notice, but we have never received either of them. We did not receive the three poems either.[221]

3. We have ready access to newspapers now. We are a lot happier than before, when we could not get hold of a paper for two or three months at a stretch. We still hope, however, that you will regularly send us analyses of the political situation.

4. The August southern expedition army held a representatives' conference on arrival at Shatian in Guidong. It resolved to ask the Provincial Committee to punish Du Xiujing for his mistakes, since he is the representative of the Provincial Committee.

5. The Front Committee approves completely Mao Zedong's long letter of August to the Provincial Committee, which is to be forwarded to the Central Committee.[222] *Comrade Yuan will again be the messenger.*

6. It is only now that Comrade Yuan Desheng is returning to the Provincial Committee, because he was waiting for the completion of the discussion of the letter from the Central Committee and our reply.

7. We earnestly request that future directives from higher levels[223] *should be based on our reports, rather than on inspectors' biased reports.*[224] *The inspector who came here in June, Du Xiujing, made his report to the Provincial Committee from a completely false standpoint (two hundred guns plus the Red Guards were enough to defend the independent régime in the border area; the Red Army at that time was conservative, and so on), and since the Provincial Committee decided to act in accordance with that kind of report, defeat was sure to follow. In addition, future directives from higher levels regarding military action must, above all, not be too rigid. The Central Committee's letter is the most appropriate and leaves us room for maneuver, as it orders us to take independent decisions based on current situations. Even more disastrous was that the Hunan Provincial Committee and Southern Hunan Special Committee believed in the*

---

221. The letter of August 15 from "Comrade Runxian" (code name for the Hunan Provincial Committee), and the three poems mentioned here, are not included in the available documentary collections. Circular No. 47, on reorganization of the Party under the White terror and developing secret work, can be found in *Central Committee Documents* (1928), pp. 200–208. It stresses that secret work is carried out, not to shield the Party from danger, but to enable it to fulfill more effectively its mission of leading the masses. More than 80 percent of Party members in the countryside should be farm laborers, sharecroppers, and handicraftsmen. Owner-peasants and intellectuals should be kept under observation.

222. This letter appears above, in this volume.

223. The Chinese term *xiongchu*, literally "elder-brother department," was commonly used at the time for any hierarchical superior; here, the reference is in the first instance to the Central Committee.

224. In fact, by the time Mao produced this report, the Central Committee had already sent, in September or October 1928, another letter to him and Zhu De asserting that, despite some errors of detail, the instructions of the Hunan Provincial Committee, including the order to march to southern Hunan, had all been "extremely correct." For further text, see *Central Committee Documents* (1928), pp. 661–81.

rumors spread by Su Xianjun (a regimental commander expelled from the Party by us, who was a criminal army deserter and informer who later arrested Guo Liang) and He Jie (chief of staff, responsible for the burning and massacre at Chenzhou). Please do not listen to any more irresponsible words in the future.

8. Yang Kaiming is seriously ill. Wan Xixian is kept here by important tasks and cannot come to southern Hunan.

9. The Special Committee of the Youth League will report to the Provincial Committee regarding the state of the Youth League. We will not weary you with it here.

10. There are three copies of this letter. The Hunan Provincial Committee is to forward one to the Central Committee and one to the Jiangxi Provincial Committee. The Ji'an Xian Committee is to forward one copy to the Jiangxi Provincial Committee, which is to forward it to the Central Committee. Thus one copy should certainly arrive.

Front Committee

Mao Zedong, Secretary

Resolutions of the Sixth Congress of Party Representatives from the Fourth Red Army

(December 6, 1928)

I) Minutes of the Congress:

Six months of hard struggles have gone by since the Fifth Congress of the Fourth Army, which was held in May of this year in Ninggang New City. The Preparatory Meeting for the Sixth Congress took place on November 13. The congress met officially on November 14 and adjourned on the 15th. Seventy-nine representatives were present. All the army branches were represented except for one battalion of the Thirty-second Regiment, which was stationed at Yongxin and could not send its delegation in time. The delegations had brought with them over thirty motions. After the initial sorting of these motions, they were put into seventeen categories. During the congress, we discussed various important political, military, and party-related questions. In particular, a long time was devoted to the discussion of the nature of the Chinese revolution. This was a characteristic of the Sixth Congress. As far as the various motions are concerned, since all the representatives had important responsibilities and needed to get back to their posts as soon as possible, we could not go over each of them during the congress. In the end, we decided that they would be discussed and executed by the new Army Committee. In the election of this committee, a list of forty-nine candidates was initially put forward by the congress presidium, and of these twenty-three were selected by the congress as members of the Sixth Army Committee. Their task was to form an Executive Committee and to carry out all the work. The congress was adjourned on the 15th. Since all the resolutions of this congress have an extremely important bearing on the future of the Red Army, and on the development of the border area, they are recorded briefly below.

Editor, New City
December 1928

II) Political Resolutions:

1) On the Nature of the Chinese Revolution. In accordance with the February resolution of the International on the Chinese revolution, we consider that the

---

Our source for this document is *Jingganshan geming genjudi*, vol. 1, pp. 199–204. The same text appears in *Jinggangshande wuzhuang geju*, pp. 167–71, and is reproduced in *Mao Zedong ji. Bujuan*, Vol. 2, pp. 311–18, except that the date at the end is December 16 instead of December 6.

Chinese revolution is still in the bourgeois-democratic phase.[1] The leader of this revolution is the proletariat; as regards external affairs,[2] its content consists in overthrowing the warlords and completing the agrarian revolution, in order to demolish the relations of feudal exploitation and bring democracy and freedom to the oppressed masses of China. Only then can there be a socialist future for the Chinese revolution. If we deny this democratic phase of the revolution, thinking that the Chinese revolution has already entered the phase of socialist revolution, this misunderstanding will be extremely harmful to the Chinese revolution. The correctness of this view of the International has been demonstrated in the course of our past struggles. Ever since the Guangzhou uprising,[3] the widespread arson and random killing which have taken place everywhere display a total incomprehension of the nature of the Chinese revolution. The Fourth Red Army in ... bitter experience. Our action from now on will be to lead the worker-peasant-soldier masses and the petty bourgeoisie, to enlarge the movement for democratic revolution, to deepen the agrarian revolution, and to overthrow the extremely reactionary situation prevailing at present. The Red Army must proclaim a concrete political program for the cities and act forcefully to correct the former policy of unrestricted confiscation of military supplies.

2) The World Situation. Ever since the revival of German and Austrian capitalism, the Franco-British naval agreement, the American war treaties, Italy's assertion of its rights over the Mediterranean Sea, Japan's invasion of China, America's conclusion of a unilateral treaty with China, and so on, the conflicts within international imperialism have intensified day by day. This is an opportune moment for a forward surge of the world revolution!

3) The Domestic Situation. Recently the various factions of warlords within the Guomindang have formed a united government. On the surface, they advocate perpetual peace, but in reality, it is the dictatorship of Chiang Kaishek's faction trying to bring others together to gain some temporary peace. From the standpoints of military-political, financial, and party affairs, there are extremely complicated rivalries within the Guomindang. The weakness of this "united gov-

---

1. The first sentence of the "Resolution on the Chinese Question" adopted by the Ninth Plenum of the Executive Committee of Comintern on February 25, 1928, reads: "The current period of the Chinese revolution is a period of the bourgeois-democratic revolution. ... " The term for "democratic" used in the official Chinese translation of this resolution is Sun Yatsen's *minquan*, which Mao consistently employed at this time. See *Central Committee Documents* (1928), pp. 757–63.

2. The only available text reads here *dui wai*, or "toward the outside." The editors of the Tokyo edition have queried this, and it is obviously an error. Presumably it should read *dui nei*, or "as regards internal affairs." The first paragraph of the Comintern resolution, which Mao and his comrades take as their text, says that "in the economic domain, the democratic revolution has not yet been completed (the agrarian revolution and the elimination of feudal relations). ... "

3. I.e., the Canton or Guangzhou Commune of December 1927, already mentioned several times in earlier texts.

ernment" can be seen in particular from the bandit disasters in the north and the worker-peasant-soldier insurrections in the south. China is a semicolony, and her ruler is international imperialism. Because international imperialism is not united, the warlord government under its protection is naturally coming apart. Therefore the relative tranquillity of China's current political situation is merely the lull before a large-scale, complicated war among the warlords.

4) The Birth and Existence of the Soviet Government. One of the characteristics of the Chinese revolution is that a soviet régime can be brought forth in China under White rule, and the situation permits it to survive. Because China is a semicolony, and the ruling class of a semicolony is basically split and cannot be unified, a soviet régime can be born and develop in the midst of these divisions. So long as these splits within the ruling class continue, the soviet régime can continue to exist. The truth of this statement is attested by the emergence of the soviets everywhere during the past year. The independent régime in the border area during the past year also demonstrates that in order for a soviet régime to survive, the following four conditions must be fulfilled: (1) A Communist Party capable of resolute struggle; (2) large and organized masses of workers and peasants; (3) relatively strong and well-armed Red Army and Red Guard Units; and (4) a strategic terrain which enables a smaller force to defeat a larger one.

5) Our Immediate Political Tasks. Within the territory of China, Hunan and Jiangxi have gone through extremely turbulent revolutionary currents in the past, and therefore there is a relatively deep foundation among the masses. The independent régimes in the border area are, moreover, destined to influence the revolutionary movement in these two provinces. Thus the task of the Party in the Fourth Red Army is to establish a Bolshevik Party, to lead the masses in expanding the movement for the democratic revolution, to deepen the agrarian revolution in the areas the Red Army has entered, and to carry out an effort everywhere to accelerate the crumbling of the ruling class.

III) Resolutions Concerning Party Affairs:

1) It is not appropriate for Party organizations at all levels in the Red Army to deal openly with matters of all kinds. Efforts should be made to restore conditions of secrecy. Party organs can be established within the Soldiers' Committees at all levels. Responsible Party comrades should concurrently be staff members of the Soldiers' Committees. Outwardly the power of the Soldiers' Committees should be strengthened, and a Party body should be established to exercise leadership over them. Military organs should also be strengthened, so they will have the capacity to exercise the Party's revolutionary leadership over military affairs. We need to correct the previous mistake of direct intervention by the Party organization in day-to-day affairs and of regarding the military organs and Soldiers' Committees as nothing but empty shells.

2) The Fifth Army Committee decided to strengthen each regimental com-

mittee. Since the Army Committee is responsible only for political supervision, it has no understanding of the conditions at lower levels. The various regimental committees also exercise independent authority, so it is getting harder and harder to maintain coordination. From now on, we should strengthen the Army Committee, which should frequently check on the work of the branches.

3) Since the Red Army has experienced large-scale warfare, many cadres of the Party Committees have been almost wiped out by casualties. From now on, the Army Committee must hold periodic training programs to prepare people for Party work.

4) We must recruit Party members among the combat soldiers. The proportion should be at least one-half.

5) The Company Branch Executive Committee should be called the Company Branch Committee. The number of committee members should be increased so that a majority of comrades may take part in the supervisory work. We should effectively make the Company Branch Committees the core of the Red Army. The number of the committee members should be five to seven.

6) Since the Company Branch Committees are the core of the Party's work in the Red Army, the Party representatives should be in charge of this core and, at the same time, assume as their open task the planning and supervision of political work. In reality, the current system of Party representatives should not be abolished.

IV) Military Resolutions:

1) Establishing Military Bases. (a) Build strong fortifications in the big and small Five Wells districts; (b) Accumulate food supplies in the bases; and (c) build hospitals, barracks, and Red Army memorial halls.

2) The Military Establishment. Each company is given seventy-five long-barreled guns. There should be four companies in a battalion. Each regiment should have a special task company which will be allotted the same number of long-barreled guns as an infantry company. Each regiment may have machine-gun companies and mortar companies. Each of these companies may have forty long-barreled guns. The regiment dispatch platoon may be allotted eight long-barreled guns and the battalion headquarters, four. The army headquarters may establish special task battalions, which will be organized the same way as the regular battalions.

3) All the guns and bullets belong to the army headquarters. The regiments, battalions, and companies may not acquire them at will.

4) Each company may be allotted no more than six handguns; each battalion, no more than three; each regiment, no more than five; and the army headquarters, no more than six.

5) The tactics of the Red Army are: when encountering a small enemy force, eliminate it quickly with our main forces. When encountering a large enemy force, make use of the masses to surround them on all sides, tire them out, and

then eliminate them with our main forces. The Red Army should make the greatest efforts to avoid hard-fought battles.

6) Military skills need to be strengthened. Moreover, attention should be paid to the ways and means used to supervise the lower-ranking cadres in order to strengthen the fighting capacity of the Red Army.

7) Within the military organizations, scout units, medical units, and stretcher units should be strengthened. In each battalion, there should be a stretcher platoon. New accounting methods should be adopted in financial management and reporting.

8) A history of the Red Army and biographical sketches of fallen comrades should be compiled. Their wills and belongings left behind should be collected as souvenirs.

9) In Red Army political training, the following points need to be considered: (a) strengthening the Soldiers' Committees so that they may truly represent the soldiers, participate in the management of the army, preserve army discipline, promote the soldiers' political education, and be involved in the mass movement outside the army; (b) conducting literacy classes periodically for the soldiers; (c) arousing the soldiers' class consciousness so that they may understand the main issues involved in the revolution and be equipped with general knowledge in politics; (d) organizing entertainment and encouraging the soldiers to play an active role in it, so that they may enjoy the arts; (e) establishing in every company a propaganda unit composed of at least three members who are dedicated to propaganda full-time whether in war or in peace; (f) posters and slogans should be regulated and issued by the Military Committee so that they are coordinated and do not cause confusion.

10) Party organs at all levels should be constantly engaged in planning work and work aimed at destroying the enemy.

11) In order to expand the Red Army, we need to recruit workers, peasants, and revolutionary elements.

12) The Army Committee should begin to build up the first battalion of the Thirty-second Regiment.

V) Resolution on Economic Problems:

The supplies office of the army headquarters and the impedimenta units of the regiments need to submit detailed monthly economic reports to the Committee of Soldiers' Representatives for examination and approval and later making public to the masses.

Economic matters concerning the Red Army must be completely open.

VI) Resolution on the Problem of Discipline:

During the Red Army's campaigns in New City and Yongxin on November 10, the Ninggang No. 4 district Red Guard unit and some peasants, instead of going to the front to engage in fighting, seizing the enemy's guns, and assisting in transportation, first aid, and searching the mountains, and other such activities, were busy confiscating oxen and other odds and ends. Such conduct violated revolutionary discipline and encroached on the peasants' interests. This congress should call the Ninggang *Xian* Committee and the *xian* government to account. It is hoped that nothing like this will happen again in the future. As for the oxen that have been taken away, they should all be returned, and a public statement should be made to explain these mistakes to the masses.

VII) Motions Brought up at the Congress:

1. To strengthen the stretcher units;
2. To strengthen the reconnaissance troops;
3. To strengthen military political schools;
4. To give preferential treatment to the enemy forces;
5. To recruit new privates;
6. To purchase ammunition and Western medicines;
7. To dispatch personnel to contact the Fifth Army;
8. To strengthen discipline both in the army and in the Party;
9. To accumulate food supplies in the rear;
10. To proclaim the political program of the democratic revolution;
11. To forbid random arson and killing;
12. To protect middle-level and petty merchants' interests;
13. To restore the Luoxiao Range régime and to expand northward;
14. The Red Army should copy the military organization of the Taiping Heavenly Kingdom;
15. To tabulate the Red Army personnel and weapons immediately;
16. No private trading is allowed in the army;
17. To strengthen the Soldiers' Committees.

Because it was necessary to adjourn the congress earlier than planned, the above seventeen motions were not discussed thoroughly at the congress. They have been given to the new Army Committee for discussion and execution.

Issued on December 6, 1928

Jinggangshan Land Law

(Adopted in December 1928 on the Jinggangshan)

1. Confiscate all land, and turn ownership over to the soviet government, which should use the following three methods to redistribute it:

   a) distribution to the peasants for them to cultivate individually;
   b) distribution to the peasants for them to cultivate in common;
   c) organization by the soviet government of model farms to cultivate the land.

Of the above three methods, the first is to be the primary one. Under special circumstances, or when the soviet government is strong, the second and third methods may also be employed.

2. The sale and purchase of all land, once it has been confiscated and redistributed by the soviet government, are to be prohibited.

3. After the land is redistributed, except for the old, the young, and the sick, who are unable to till the land, and except for those performing public service, the rest of the population must be compelled to work.

4. The quantitative criteria for land redistribution are:

   a) using the number of people as the criterion and redistributing an equal amount of land to men, women, the old, and the young;
   b) using labor power as the criterion and giving twice as much land to those who can work as to those who cannot.

Of the above two criteria, the first is to be the primary one. In places where special circumstances prevail, the second criterion may be applied. The reasons for adopting the first criterion are:

   i) before the facilities for caring for old people and children are in place, the old and the young, if they are given too little land, will certainly not be able to make a living;
   ii) it is relatively simple and convenient to use the number of people as the criterion for land redistribution;
   iii) very few families do not have old people or children. At the same time, although the old and the young are not capable of tilling the land, local

---

Our source for this resolution is *Mao Zedong ji*, Vol. 2, pp. 67–69, where it has been taken from the 1944 edition of *Mao Zedong xuanji*, Vol. 3.

governments should, after land redistribution, also assign them appropriate public services to perform, such as communication duties.

5. The administrative criteria for land redistribution are:

a) using the township as the unit for land redistribution;
b) using several townships as the unit for land redistribution (as was done in Xiaojiang District in Yongxin [*xian*]);
c) using the district as the unit for land redistribution (as was done in Huang'ao District in Suichuan [*xian*]).

Of the above three criteria, the first is to be the primary one. Under special circumstances, the second and third criteria may be used.

6. The methods of redistributing wooded and hilly lands are:

a) Hills where tea-oil plants[1] are grown and firewood-producing hills are to be redistributed according to the same method used for the land, taking the township as the unit; they are to be redistributed equally for cultivation and use;
b) Bamboo forests shall become the property of the soviet government. Peasants may, however, enjoy the use of the bamboo after obtaining permission from the soviet government. Permission for [cutting] fewer than fifty stalks of bamboo should be obtained from the township soviet; for fewer than a hundred stalks, permission must be obtained from the district soviet government; for more than a hundred stalks, permission must be obtained from the *xian* soviet government.
c) All bamboo is to be sold by the *xian* soviet government; the proceeds from such sales will be allocated by the soviet government at a higher level.

7. The collection of land tax:

a) Three rates of land taxes are set according to production conditions: (a) 15 percent; (b) 10 percent; (c) 5 percent. Of the above three rates, the first is to be the primary one. Under special circumstances and after permission is obtained from the soviet government at a higher level, the second and third rates may be used.
b) In the event of natural disasters or other special circumstances, exemption from land tax may be granted after petitioning to and obtaining approval from the soviet government at a higher level.

---

1. Chashan, literally "tea mountains," refers to hills where the plant producing *chayou*, or "tea-oil," was grown. This oil was in fact pressed from the seeds of the camellia. It was an important item in the rural economy of Jiangxi, as attested by Mao's "Xunwu Investigation" of May 1930, which appears below.

c) Land tax is to be collected by the *xian* soviet governments and turned over to higher-level soviet governments for allocation.

8. Rural artisans, if they themselves wish to receive redistributed land, may each get half the amount of land given to every peasant.

9. Officers and soldiers of the Red Army and the Red Guards, as well as all those serving in the government or in other public agencies, should all receive the same amount of redistributed land as given to peasants. The soviet government will hire people to cultivate it for them.

Note:[2] This land law was enacted in the winter of 1928 on the Jinggangshan (the soviet border region of Hunan and Jiangxi). This was the summary of the experience of the land struggle during one whole year, from the winter of 1927 to the winter of 1928. Before this, there had been no experience whatsoever. This land law contained several mistakes: (1) confiscation of all land, instead of only the land of landlords; (2) the ownership of the land was vested in the government, rather than in the peasants, who had only the right of use; (3) sale and purchase of the land were prohibited. These were all mistakes of principle and were later corrected. As for why it was declared that cultivation in common, and using labor power as the criterion for land redistribution should not be used as the primary methods, but that private farming and using the number of people as the criterion for land redistribution should be used as the primary methods, the reason is that at the time, although it was felt that the former method was inappropriate, quite a few comrades advocated it. A decision was therefore taken in this sense, but afterward this was changed and only the latter method was used. The practice of hiring people to farm the land of Red Army personnel was later changed to mobilizing the peasants to farm for them.

---

2. This note was added by Mao Zedong himself when the text was first published in the 1941 edition of *Rural Investigations*.

——————————1929——————————

Manifesto of the Communist Party

(January 1929)[1]

At present, the Chinese revolution remains at the stage of democratic revolution. The democratic revolution aims at overthrowing the two biggest enemies, namely, foreign imperialism and the domestic landlord class. For several decades, China has suffered the invasion of various imperialist countries such as Britain, the United States, France, and Japan. They bring foreign goods into China and ship Chinese agricultural products overseas, causing the Chinese peasants to suffer great losses; they open factories, exploiting Chinese workers; they operate banks, absorbing Chinese capital; they manage the customs, dominating China's lifeline; they establish churches, rearing running dogs for themselves; using the concessions as bases, they deploy their gunboats around the important coastal and river ports—Shanghai, Hankou, Tianjin, and Guangzhou—and station their armies in Beijing, Tianjin, and Shanghai. They have quite simply turned China into their colony. Given such oppression by the imperialists, the hundreds of millions of Chinese workers, peasants, soldiers, and petty bourgeois have no choice but to rise up and resist. Still less does the Communist Party have any alternative but to stand in front of the masses and lead them in courageous battle. Moreover, the Guomindang, which represents the despotic gentry and the capitalist class, has turned traitor halfway. Not only has it abolished the slogan "Down With the Imperialists" but it has colluded with the imperialists, betraying the country and fawning on foreign powers in the manner of Wu Peifu and Sun Chuanfang. Since the bourgeois Guomindang has turned against the revolution, the workers, peasants, soldiers, and petty bourgeoisie have no choice but to shoulder the responsibility of overthrowing imperialism. Only when imperialism is overthrown can China be unified, industry be expanded, and the whole Chinese people be liberated. This is the number one responsibility of the Chinese Communist Party. China's present system of land ownership is a semifeudal system. The peasants are exploited by high rents, high

---

Our source for this text is *Mao Zedong ji. Bujuan*, Vol. 3, pp. 13–15, which has taken it from two documentary collections published in China, one in 1979 and one in 1982. No earlier version is known to exist.

1. As noted in the Introduction to this volume, the decisions of the Sixth Congress of the Chinese Communist Party of June 1928 had reached the base area only at the beginning of January 1929. This manifesto, drafted by Mao around January 10, was intended to convey the line of the Sixth Congress, as Mao and his comrades understood it.

interest, and high taxes, and the land is concentrated in the hands of the land-lords. In nearly every *xian* within China's borders, seven-tenths of the land is in the hands of landlords, and the peasants have very little land. Out of a hundred households in a given village, seventy are poor peasants without adequate food and clothing, no more than twenty are middle peasants with just enough food and clothing, and no more than ten are rich peasants with surplus money and food. The vast majority of people in the villages have a very hard life; only a few local bullies who collect rents in grain and collect interest enjoy prosperity. The bu-reaucrats and warlords in the towns are simply representatives of the local bul-lies. On one hand, they exact heavy taxes and levies, exploiting the peasants and the petty bourgeoisie; on the other hand, they collude with the imperialists in their exploitation of China. Land revolution is the main content of the Chinese democratic revolution. If the landlords, bureaucrats, and warlords are not elimi-nated, the Chinese peasants will be unable to obtain land, and the democratic revolution cannot be considered successful. Therefore, the second responsibility of the Chinese Communist Party is to overthrow feudal exploitation and solve the land problem. As stated above, the two main goals of the democratic revolu-tion are to eliminate imperialism and to overthrow feudal exploitation. But the Guomindang has already betrayed the democratic revolution. The new warlord factions such as Chiang, the Guangxi clique, Feng, Yan, and the Fengtian clique[2] have become representatives of the landlord class and lackeys of imperialism. Therefore, in order to wipe out imperialism and overthrow feudal exploitation, it is indispensable to overthrow the warlord Guomindang government and establish a worker-peasant-soldier representative (soviet) government. This is the third responsibility of the Chinese Communist Party. The tasks that the Red Army, led by the Chinese Communist Party, has come here to carry out at this time are the three tasks mentioned above. At the same time, the tasks that the Chinese Com-munist Party has led the worker-peasant-soldier masses to carry out all over the country are these same three tasks as well. In order to implement these three tasks, and in accordance with the directives of the Sixth Chinese Communist Party Congress, we proclaim a political program with the following ten points:

1) Overthrow imperialist rule in China;
2) Confiscate all factories, stores, ships, mines, and banks set up with foreign capital;
3) Unify China and acknowledge the right to self-determination of the Man-chu, Hui, Tibetan, Miao, and Yao nationalities;
4) Overthrow the warlord Guomindang government;

---

2. The reference is to Chiang Kaishek, Li Zongren, Feng Yuxiang, Yan Xishan, and Zhang Xueliang. Regarding Li, Feng, and Yan see the notes to the resolution of October 5, 1928. Zhang Xueliang had become leader of the Fengtian faction following the assassina-tion of his father, Zhang Zuolin, in June 1928.

5) Establish a government of councils of worker-peasant-soldier representatives;

6) Establish an eight-hour work day for workers, and increase their wages and benefits such as unemployment assistance, social security, and so on;

7) Confiscate the land of the entire landlord class and distribute it among the peasants who have no land or very little land;

8) Improve the living conditions of soldiers, and give them land and work;

9) Abolish all taxes and levies exacted by the [central] government, the warlords, and the local governments, and adopt a system of uniform, progressive taxation;

10) Unite with the proletariat of the whole world, and with Soviet Russia.

These ten points of the political program are concrete measures to achieve the three goals. Workers, peasants, soldiers, all the impoverished masses, and all oppressed members of the petty bourgeoisie, let us quickly unite under the leadership of the Chinese Communist Party to struggle against the imperialists, the landlord class, and the Guomindang new warlords!

> Fourth Army Headquarters of the Red Army
> of the Chinese Communist Party

Notice Issued by the Fourth Army Headquarters of the Red Army[1]

(January 1929)

The aim of the Red Army is democratic revolution,
Our western Jiangxi First Army's reputation has spread far
    and wide.
The present plan is to move forward by divisions.
Be they officers or foot soldiers,
All must obey commands.
Be fair in dealings with the people,
Thus proving ourselves trustworthy.
Wanton burning and killing
Must be strictly forbidden.
All over the nation,
Oppression is unbearable.
The workers and the peasants
Endure bitter sufferings.
Local bullies and bad gentry
Are tyrannizing over villages and towns.
High interest and heavy taxes
Rouse everyone's anger.
White Army soldiers
Go hungry and cold.
The petty bourgeoisie
Pays extremely heavy taxes.
The more imported goods there are,
The harder it is to sell domestic ones.
As for imperialism,
Who is there that doesn't hate it?

Our source for this document is *Mao Zedong wenji*, Vol. 1, pp. 52–53, where it has been reproduced from a lithographed copy in the Party archives. No such contemporary text is available to us.

1. This notice or proclamation, drafted by Mao, was issued sometime in the second half of January, after the main force of the Red Army began its descent from the Jinggangshan toward southern Jiangxi on January 14. To enhance its popular appeal and make it easy to remember, it is cast in the form of a poem with four-character lines.

The Guomindang bandit party
Is completely reactionary.
It says one thing and means another,
They can't be too strong.
Chiang, Gui, Feng, and Yan[2]
Share a bed but not their dreams.
Conflicts have arisen among them,
The warlords will meet their fate.
Food is what alleviates hunger,
Medicine is what cures disease.
What the Communist Party advocates
Is exceedingly just.
The fields of the landlords
Should be given to the peasants to till.
Debts need not be paid back,
Rents need not be paid.
An increase in workers' wages
Must be borne by the bosses.
Eight hours of work a day
Is just the right amount of time.
The way the troops are treated
Urgently requires improvement.
In distributing the land,
Soldiers are entitled to a share.
Enemy officers and their soldiers
Must be allowed to switch sides.
What they've done in the past
Will not be held against them.
The method of progressive taxation
Is by far the most suitable.
All exorbitant taxes and levies
Must be thoroughly swept away.
As for merchants in the cities,
They have hoarded bit by bit.
As long as they are obedient,
The rest does not matter.

---

2. A reference to the four major factions within the Guomindang at this time. Chiang refers to Chiang Kaishek and his supporters; Gui to the Guangxi warlords, Li Zongren and Bai Chongxi; Feng to Feng Yuxiang and his National People's Army; and Yan to the Shanxi warlord Yan Xishan. The other three had all supported Chiang's Northern Expedition against Zhang Zuolin's Fengtian faction, which ended with the fall of Beijing and Tianjin in June 1928. This did not, however, mark the end of conflict and rivalry among the various military leaders.

The treatment meted out to foreigners
Must be exceedingly strict.
Their factories and their banks
Must be confiscated and taken over.
Foreign investments and foreign debts
All are declared null and void.
Foreign troops and foreign ships
Are not allowed to enter our borders.
Overthrowing the big powers
Will bring joy to everyone's heart.
Overthrowing the warlords
Means a thorough purging of evil.
Unifying the whole of China
Is reason for the nation to rejoice.
As for Manchus, Mongols, Hui, and Tibetans,
They will determine their own statutes.
The Guomindang government
Is nothing but a pack of scoundrels.
Uniting to get rid of them,
We thoroughly purge the corrupt régime.
The workers and peasants of the entire nation
Are swift as the wind and powerful as thunder.
The day when we will seize political power
Is not far away.
The success of revolution
Depends on the popular masses alone.
Let this be proclaimed on every hand,
And everyone be roused to action.

> Commander of the Army: Zhu De
> Party Representative: Mao Zedong

An Official Fund-Raising Letter

(February 13, 1929)[1]

The Red Army is an army that strives for the well-being of the workers and peasants. It also makes every effort to protect the merchants. It exercises strict discipline and does not encroach upon anyone. Because of the current shortage of food supplies, we are writing to you now to request that you kindly collect on our behalf 5,000 big foreign dollars for the soldiers' pay, 7,000 pairs of straw sandals and 7,000 pairs of socks, 300 bolts of white cloth, and 200 laborers. It is urgent that these be delivered to our headquarters before eight o'clock this evening. We hope that you will do as we request without delay. If you ignore our requests, it will be proof that the Ningdu merchants are collaborating with the reactionaries and are out to make things difficult for the Red Army. In that case we will be obliged to burn down all the reactionary shops in Ningdu as a warning against your treachery. Do not say that we have not forewarned you. The above message is communicated to all the gentlemen in charge of the Ningdu *Xian* Reception Center.

> Fourth Red Army
> Zhu De, Commander-in-Chief
> Mao Zedong, Party Representative

We have translated this document from a brief article by Xue Feng in *Wenwu tiandi*, no. 3, 1983, p. 4, which includes a barely legible reproduction of the original manuscript. The article transcribes verbatim the greater part of the text, and explains the circumstances in which the letter was written. The version which appears in *Mao Zedong ji. Bujuan*, Vol. 9, p. 325, has been excerpted from this source.

1. In Xue Feng's article, the text of the letter is introduced by the following passage:

    In mid-January 1929, Comrades Mao Zedong, Zhu De and Chen Yi led the main forces of the Fourth Red Army in its march from the Jinggangshan to southern Jiangxi. They reached the Ningdu *xian* capital on February 13. The local people welcomed the arrival of the Red Army enthusiastically, and even the bigwigs of the chamber of commerce had set up a "Ningdu Reception Center."

    That afternoon, the Political Department of the Fourth Red Army delivered an official fund-raising letter to the Ningdu Reception Center. Its contents were as follows:

2. The last sentence of the text of the letter, the signatures, and the date have been added on the basis of the facsimile of the handwritten original which accompanies the article in *Wenwu tiandi*. After transcribing the letter, Xue Feng adds: "Before eight o'clock in the evening, the staff of the Reception Center delivered the funds and laborers to the military supply section of the Fourth Red Army Headquarters. This fund-raising task was thereby successfully completed." The author also notes that beginning in 1931, when the soviet areas were better established, contributions were replaced by taxation as the method for obtaining funds from merchants.

Notice to Merchants and Intellectuals

(March 16, 1929)

Fellow-merchants:
Fellow-intellectuals:

1) The Red Army led by the Communist Party has come to where you are. How is the Communist Party going to deal with you? How are you going to deal with the Communist Party? How are you going to deal with the revolution?

2) The revolution led by the Communist Party at the present time is called the democratic revolution. It aims to overthrow three counterrevolutionary things. The first aim is to overthrow imperialism. Foreigners should not be allowed to perpetrate violence in China. China should be managed by Chinese, and foreigners should not be allowed to control it. The second aim is to overthrow the landlord class. The rent collection system should be abolished, and land should be fairly distributed among the peasants. The third aim is to overthrow the Guomindang government and establish a worker-peasant-soldier government. These are the three great tasks in the struggle the Communist Party is now leading.

3) You should not be terrified at the enunciation of these three tasks. Not only should you not be terrified but you should welcome them wholeheartedly. The worker and peasant classes long for the accomplishment of these three tasks, and you will derive great benefit from it as well. Do you understand your position? You are the petty bourgeoisie in a semicolony. Imperialism is oppressing China, and foreign goods are constantly imported, so that Chinese industry and commerce have been unable to develop. Can you imagine how great the benefits to you will be when the imperialists are overthrown? The land has been concentrated in the hands of the semifeudal class who exact heavy rents and interest, so that the peasants are extremely poor and the people in the countryside do not have money to buy goods in the city. Consequently, the industries and businesses in the city cannot develop fully. If the landlord class is overthrown, and the tenancy system eliminated, the peasants will have the entire harvest, and their buying power will be greatly increased. Just think, won't business in the cities enjoy great development? The Guomindang and its government are lackeys of

---

This document has been translated from *Mao Zedong ji. Bujuan*, Vol. 3, pp. 17–20, which has taken it from three documentary collections published in China between the years 1979 and 1981. No contemporary text appears to be available.

the imperialists, and they represent the landlord class. If the Guomindang and its government are overthrown, the imperialists will lose their running dogs, and the landlord class will have no one to represent them. When the worker-peasant-soldier government seizes political power, then there will be hope for the success of the democratic revolution (the revolution that eliminates imperialists and the landlord class). Don't you think this would benefit you?

4) The Communist Party's policy on the cities is to abolish exorbitant taxes and levies and protect the commercial dealings of the merchants. During the revolution, only the big merchants, not the small merchants, will be requested to help raise funds to provide military supplies. The possessions of the reactionaries in the cities (the running dogs of the warlords, the corrupt bureaucrats, leading Guomindang officials, scabs, and renegade peasants and students[1]) will be confiscated. The same thing will happen to local bullies who exact rents and heavy interest in the countryside while they themselves reside in the cities. As for ordinary merchants and the petty bourgeoisie, their possessions will remain untouched. But these ordinary merchants and the petty bourgeoisie in general should support the worker-peasant revolution, accept the leadership of the worker and peasant classes, and strive together to accomplish the three great tasks of overthrowing imperialism, the landlord class, and the Guomindang government. Do not be two-faced, paying lip service but harboring enmity within. You must know that the democratic revolution led by the Communist Party is bound to succeed and will succeed quickly. If you disobey now, you will embark on the counterrevolutionary path and will assuredly have no place to stand in the future.

5) The only way out for intellectuals is also to join the worker-peasant revolution. If the intellectuals are willing to take part in the revolution, the worker-peasant classes will always accept them, and they will be given more or less important work, in accordance with their talents. The Red Army Political Department is recruiting a great number of political workers. Those students, teachers, and staff members who are willing to endure hardships and dare to struggle may all join the Red Army and do political work.

6) War between Chiang Kaishek and the Guangxi faction has already broken out in Hunan and Hubei. The new nationwide war among the warlords has already been initiated. The Guomindang, which deceives the popular masses, has completely disintegrated. The Three Principles of the People are absolute rubbish,[2] and the unification of the whole country is stinking talk. The running dogs of the Americans, the Chiang and Feng [Yuxiang] factions, the running dogs of the British, the Guangxi faction, and the running dogs of the Japanese, the Fengtian and Yan Xishan factions, have begun a confused struggle against one

---

1. *Gongzei, nongzei, xuezei.* The first of these three terms is the standard expression for scab or strikebreaker. The other two compounds are not commonly used, but obviously have the same sense of renegade, traitor to one's class, and so on.

2. *Goupi*, literally, "dog fart."

another purely for selfish gains. The collapse and defeat of the Guomindang national government and the new warlords of various factions is imminent. The revolutionary régime of the workers and peasants will soon emerge everywhere in the country to take the place of the counterrevolutionary régime. Merchants and students, all you of the oppressed petty bourgeoisie, rise quickly and help the worker and peasant classes to engage in this historic revolutionary struggle!

Let the merchants arise and help the worker and peasant classes!

Let the students arise and help the worker and peasant classes!

In order to accelerate the development of business, the merchants cannot but support the land revolution so as to increase the peasants' productivity and buying power!

In order to accelerate the development of business, the merchants cannot but overthrow imperialism and stop the import of foreign goods!

In order to accelerate the development of business, the merchants cannot but overthrow the Guomindang government and support the worker-peasant-soldier government!

As long as the merchants support the revolution, the Communist Party will not confiscate their property and will protect their freedom of trade.

Let the revolutionary intellectuals join the ranks of the worker-peasant revolution!

Let the revolutionary intellectuals join the Red Army's Political Department!

Long live the democratic revolution!

Long live the liberation of the oppressed classes of the whole country!

> Army Party Department
> Fourth Army of the Communist Party Red Army

A Letter to Our Brother Soldiers Throughout the Country

(March 16, 1929)

Dear Brother Soldiers All Over China:

We have seven things to tell you. Please think them over carefully after you have read them.

First, soldiers come from poor worker and peasant families. Who among us soldiers is not of worker or peasant origin? Where can we find a soldier who is the son of a landlord or a capitalist? Back home, if we were tillers, we had no land to till, and if we were workers, we had no work to do. Even if we did have land to till, the harvest wasn't enough for us to pay rent to the landlords and taxes to the officials. So we had to borrow money, but with interest added to interest, we were unable to pay back our debts. No longer able to live at home, then, we had no choice but to become soldiers. Some of us were workers fired by factory owners or shopowners. Unable to make a living, and with nowhere to turn, we had to sell our own lives for a few dollars a month.

Second, to be a soldier in the White army is to undergo extreme misery and suffer much oppression. We didn't know at first what life would be like in the army. We just followed the rich and the powerful, only thinking to join the army to become soldiers and be able to pick up a gun and kill to our hearts' content and wreak vengeance on our enemies. We didn't know that we had gone wrong and had walked into the camp of this thing called the National Revolutionary Army. The primary target of their revolution seems to be us soldiers. Haven't they treated us harshly, severely cursed us, beat us up, and even shot some of us? If we make even a minor mistake, we are rewarded with blows from truncheons or whips, slaps in the face, or kicks. This has become commonplace. As for pay, they just say they have no money, and sometimes we go for seven or eight months without pay. Every so often they get generous and give us a little money, with some government bonds thrown in. But as for the regimental and divisional commanders, if you looked into it you would find that they have at least a few thousand, or tens of thousands, or hundreds of thousands of silver dollars in the

Our source for this letter is *Mao Zedong ji. Bujuan*, Vol. 3, pp. 21–25, which has taken it from two documentary collections, one published in 1979 and the other in 1982. No contemporary text appears to be available.

bank. What about the new warlord, Chiang Kaishek? He has even more. The money he has sent to the United States alone amounts to tens of millions of *yuan*. He has his Western-style house built in the concessions. According to the newspapers, it cost his wife, Song Meiling, 30,000 *yuan* to have a coat tailor-made by a big company in Shanghai. But what about us? What kind of housing are we living in and what kind of clothing do we wear? Even among those regimental and divisional commanders, does any of them lack a Western-style house in which to live? You live in either thatched huts or dilapidated houses. How about the officers' clothes compared with your ragged military uniforms? They enjoy feasts and choice foods at western restaurants. How about your food? Don't you get six dollars' worth of food each month? Don't you only have one dish at each meal? After several years of fighting, many officers have been promoted and accumulated great wealth. How about you? Many of our brother soldiers have been killed in strange places thousands of miles from home, and alas, some of their mothers and wives haven't even been told of their deaths. Some of them hadn't even been able to get married!

Third, we soldiers ought to be clear about who are our friends and brothers and who are our foes and enemies. We should not help our foes and enemies to kill our friends and brothers. Let's all take a look. Are the local bullies and bad gentry, landlords, and capitalists truly our "friends"? Absolutely not. They are our mortal foes and archenemies. How about the workers who make tools and build houses, and the peasants who provide us with food and clothing? Are they our enemies? Absolutely not. They are our friends and brethren. Among the workers and peasants, many are actually our own fathers, uncles, brothers, and relatives. Can we kill our own relatives and friends at the command of our enemies? No, we cannot and we should not. But many of our brother soldiers have not realized this. They have been deceived by the new warlord Guomindang, and go around killing their own friends and brothers for the local bullies and bad gentry, landlords, and capitalists. How distressing this is! Do you not believe it? Chiang Kaishek claims to be most "revolutionary," but during the first Northern Expedition, when he arrived in Jiangxi he killed the head of the General Workers' Union in Ganzhou; when he went to Shanghai, he disarmed the workers' inspection corps, which had opened Shanghai to him and helped him to force Sun Chuanfang out, and he shot to death a large number of workers. The number of workers and peasants killed by Xu Kexiang in Hunan, He Jian in Hubei, and Li Jishen in Guangdong totaled several hundreds of thousands. Don't they all talk about "making revolution"? Upon whose lives are they actually making revolution? Those of the workers and peasants. But aren't we ourselves, the soldiers, the ones who have been deceived and used by them to kill the workers and peasants? So many soldiers were killed during the two Eastern Campaigns and two Northern Expeditions and the war between Chiang Kaishek and the Guangxi faction! The result was a new emperor, Chiang Kaishek. How much blood have we soldiers shed only to fatten these man-eating beasts? How many of our soldiers' corpses have been cast aside only to build a throne for the new warlord? Enough! We've had enough deception from them! Brother soldiers in the Guomindang armies! Come to your senses right now! You ought to know for sure who our enemies are. Don't be deceived by them any more! They have deceived you with [the slogan] "No fear of death and no need for money," but they hide themselves in the rear, raking in piles and piles of money. You are the only ones who end up dead! They "love the country and love the people," but sold the Ji'nan Massacre to Japan[1] and aviation rights to the United States. Hundreds of thousands of slaughtered workers and peasants have been "loved" by them this way. All the nation's rights have been sold out because of their love. Who can deny it? Brother soldiers, wake up!

Fourth, let's ask ourselves, what have we got after several years of fighting? Ever since Chiang Kaishek betrayed the revolution, the warlords have been fighting against one another for territories and privileges. As far as they are concerned, no matter who wins and who loses, they can still be promoted and get rich. All we can do is scale mountains and ford streams, endure the hardships of arduous journeys, and be sent to the battlefields to die. Even the small amount of compensation has gone into the officers' pockets. Those who didn't die are disabled and can no longer run around for the warlord, so they are laid off in batches and sent off to repair roads. Those who cannot work on the roads have no recourse but to beg. Across numerous mountains and countless rivers, without any money to their names, how can any of them make it home? And, because of incessant fighting between the warlords, taxes and levies have grown heavier and the rents and interest exacted by the local tyrants have steadily increased so that our parents, wives, and brothers are dying of hunger and exposure. In short, the soldiers fight for the warlords, the warlords keep getting promoted and getting rich, and the soldiers who don't get killed end up being dismissed!

Fifth, the Red Army soldiers fight for their own liberation. Brother soldiers! If you want to find a way out, to make a living, to avoid suffering, to be rescued from slavery, to gain benefits for your families, the only way is to come to your senses, to unite and kill the counterrevolutionary warlord officers, to replace them with officers elected among yourselves, to set up a Soldiers' Committee to take part in managing the armies, to unite with the workers and peasants to overthrow the local bullies and bad gentry who have oppressed us, to confiscate the land from the landlord class and distribute it among the peasants. Only then can we be assured of a bright future. Only when we have overthrown the Guomindang government and established our own government of the councils of worker-peasant-soldier deputies will we have true and long-lasting happiness. Our Red Army is our soldiers' own army and the workers' and peasants' army. It is also an army led by the Communist Party. It is not subject to oppression and

---

1. Regarding the Ji'nan Massacre, see above, the relevant note to the text of October 5, 1928.

exploitation by officers; officers and soldiers receive equal pay; they wear the same clothes and eat the same food, and the army is managed by the Soldiers' Committee. It is authorized also to shoot counterrevolutionary officers, to wipe out local tyrants and distribute their land, to overthrow the Guomindang government, to set up a worker-peasant-soldier government, to eliminate the warlords, and to expel imperialist forces from China. This is a true revolutionary army.

Sixth, the Fourth Red Army has struggled with the counterrevolutionaries for several years now and has eliminated many despotic gentry and warlords. On August 1 two years ago, Chiang Kaishek had defected to imperialism and started protecting local bullies, bad gentry and capitalists; workers and peasants were being killed, and he wanted us to protect our enemies and kill our own brothers, the workers and peasants. At that time, therefore, we of the Fourth Red Army did not forget the revolution and would not be deceived by him into killing our own brothers and friends. Under the leadership of the Communist Party, an insurrection erupted in Nanchang, and we started fighting against the counterrevolutionary warlords. For the last two years, we have been moving and fighting in Hunan, Jiangxi, Fujian, and Guangdong provinces and have overthrown many local bullies and bad gentry, eliminated many new warlords, and set up many worker-peasant-soldier governments.

Seventh, soldiers in the Red Army welcome White army soldiers to join the Red Army and take part in the revolution. Brother soldiers, let us all unite and jointly attack our class enemies! Wake up! We welcome you. Brothers, arise. Let us raise the bright Red banner and loudly shout, "Comrades! Come quickly and build our working people's Republic. The working class must be the masters of the world, only then will mankind enter into the Great Harmony. We are the revolutionary vanguard of the workers and the peasants. We are the revolutionary vanguard of the workers and the peasants." Finally, let us loudly shout:

1. Brother soldiers all over the country, turn your guns around and kill the counterrevolutionary officers!
2. Let soldiers throughout the land rise up in rebellion and eliminate the new and old warlords!
3. Let soldiers throughout the land rise up to organize their own Red Army!
4. Workers, peasants, and soldiers, unite!
5. Strike at the local bullies and distribute the land!
6. Overthrow the Guomindang government.
7. Down with imperialism.
8. Establish a worker-peasant-soldier government.
9. Long live the success of the Chinese revolution.
10. Long live the success of the world revolution.

Soldiers' Committee, Fourth Red Army

Letter from the Fourth Red
Army Front Committee to the
Central Committee

(March 20, 1929)

To the Fujian Provincial Committee, and to be forwarded to the Central Committee:

1) We (the Fourth Red Army) captured Tingzhou on March 14.[1] Guo Fengming (commander of the Second Fujian Brigade) was killed, and his body exposed in Ting City for three days.[2] We have captured about five hundred rifles (the single-shot ones and nine-shot ones are of no use to the soviet Red Army), seven or eight carbines, three mortars, and several hundred rounds of shells. The remnants of Guo's brigade retreated toward Shanghai and Hangzhou.

2) The Tingzhou masses are excellent. After we had distributed the grain and property of the local bullies and the reactionaries and carried out extensive propaganda, the workers, and the peasants from the vicinity of the town, rose up in a big way. In the ensuing days we have been carrying out basic organizing work for peasant associations and workers' unions (both underground and open). Within a day or two a provisional organ of political power, the revolutionary committee, will be set up. For the present,[3] the political department will replace the organ of political power.

3) In view of developments in the current situation (we have read the March 3 Shanghai newspaper, the March 13 . . . , and the Zhangzhou and Chaozhou newspapers), as for western Fujian and southern Jiangxi, we hope that the Cen-

---

Our source for this document is *Mao Zedong junshi wenji*, Vol. 1, pp. 53–57, which cites a handwritten copy in the Party archives. This report also appears in *Mao Zedong ji. Bujuan*, Vol. 3, pp. 31–35, where it has been taken from a documentary collection published in 1982. No earlier text appears to be available.

1. Tingzhou (now known as Changting) is located in southwestern Fujian, just across the border from Ruijin in Jiangxi.

2. Guo Fengming (1892–1929), a native of Fujian, had been commander of the Second Fujian Brigade since 1928. As indicated by Mao, he was killed in battle on March 14, 1929.

3. Taking *zixia* to be a typographical error for *muxia*.

tral Committee will notify us of overall plans. We are especially anxious to receive speedy direction as to actions the Red Army should take![4]

4) Here are our opinions on the overall plans: We must act vigorously to win over the masses throughout the country. At this time, no matter what factions try to deceive the masses, nothing will be able to win out over the facts regarding our Communist Party. Besides workers and peasants, it is also very important for us to win over the masses of the soldiers. Our views regarding the center of gravity of the work as a whole are: in Jiangsu and Zhili, the number of Red Army small soviet areas should be increased. Not only in places such as Hunan, Jiangxi, Guangdong, and Fujian but also in northern Jiangsu, northern Anhui and Hubei, southern Henan, and Zhili, Red Armies, as well as small soviet areas, should also be established.

5) The Front Committee has decided on plans of action for the Fourth and Fifth Armies and for the [independent] Second and Fourth Regiments of the Red Army in Jiangxi. At the initial stage of our fight against the Guomindang, there should be guerrilla warfare within an area of more than twenty *xian* in southern Jiangxi and western Fujian. From mobilizing the masses we should proceed to the open establishment of independent régimes under soviet power, and then connect these independent areas to form an independent régime in the Hunan-Jiangxi border area as a whole.

6) The Jiangxi Red Army's independent Second Regiment (Li Wenlin's unit) has about four hundred guns. It is strong in combat effectiveness and is now stationed at the juncture of Xingguo, Taihe and Ganzhou. The independent Fourth Regiment (Duan Yuequan's unit) has over three hundred guns. It is still weak in combat effectiveness and is now stationed at the intersection of Xingguo and Yudu.[5] Peng Dehuai's Red Army unit has about three hundred guns (and the

---

4. Two weeks after sending this report, Mao and his comrades received the Central Committee's letter of February 7, 1929. As will be seen from Mao's reply of April 5, 1929, translated below, this long-awaited communication was scarcely welcome when it finally arrived.

5. These two units had originally been local forces from Donggu and elsewhere in Ji'an *xian*, put together by Communist Party cadres from bandit gangs, remnants of peasant associations, and miscellaneous other elements. Li Wenlin (1900–1932), original name Zhou Jintang, was a native of Jishui *xian* in Jiangxi. (See above, the note to the Introduction regarding him.) In September 1928, as representative of the West Jiangxi Special Committee, he had been responsible for forming the Second Independent Regiment, and had become its commander and political commissar, with Duan Yuequan as executive officer. Duan Yuequan (more commonly known as Duan Qifeng), a former farm laborer and martial arts master, was an influential leader of the Three Dots Society in the area who had been persuaded to join the revolution with his band. In the winter of 1928–1929, he became commander of the newly formed Fourth Independent Regiment. Both these men were later identified with the Southwest Jiangxi Special Committee, fell under suspicion during the Futian Incident (see below, "A Letter of Reply by the General Front Committee," December 1930), and were eventually executed, Li in 1932 and Duan in 1933. For more details see Stephen C.

remnant troops from the Jinggangshan) and is stationed at the intersection of Yudu and Xinfeng. On March 7, Peng's unit attacked the remnants of Liu Shiyi's unit and captured over a hundred rifles, one water and one land machine gun, and seven *Dan*[6] of bullets. For about the next ten days, the Red Fourth Army will operate on the Fujian border; afterward, it will wage guerrilla warfare around Ruijin and Ningdu on the Jiangxi border. At that time, the action to be taken will be determined with reference to the battle situation in Hunan and Jiangxi, according to the best interests of the development of the Red Army and the development of the worker-peasant masses. We will either return to the Fujian border, or conduct guerrilla warfare in southern Jiangxi for a longer period, or move closer to the Guomindang battle zone near Ji'an. The only plan that certainly must be carried out is to mobilize the masses within the regions of western Fujian and southern Jiangxi to the point of publicly establishing an independent régime. This plan should not be discarded, as it is the basis for progress.

7) The Fujian Provincial Committee should immediately send a special commissioner for western Fujian to supervise the work concerning the eight *xian* belonging to Tingzhou. The Tingzhou Party units are extremely weak and are incapable of assuming the responsibility for establishing political power. The principal tasks at present are to expand the Party organization and the mass organizations, to establish organs of political power, and to build up the western Jiangxi Red Army (at this time there is still no one to collect the guns). We hope that the Provincial Committee will pay special attention to our needs.

8) The armed forces of the ruling class throughout Fujian and Zhejiang, and in eastern and southern Jiangxi, are exceptionally weak (compared to those in the country as a whole). We wonder whether or not the Central Committee has already discussed plans to target these three localities for the open establishment of separate régimes. Since the ruling forces in these three places are relatively weak, and they are all near the sea, they are worthy of our attention.

9) We left the Jinggangshan on January 14, mainly because we had no way out economically. On the 20th, we were defeated in a battle at Dayu with Li Wenbin,[7] so we walked around Nanxiong on the Guangdong border and into southern Jiangxi. We encountered pursuing troops three times, at Xinfeng, Anyuan, and Xunwu, retreating as we fought. On February 1, we arrived at the

---

Averill, "The Origins of the Futian Incident," in Tony Saich and Hans van de Ven (eds.), *New Perspectives on the Chinese Communist Revolution* (Armonk: M. E. Sharpe, 1995), pp. 79–115 (hereafter Averill, "Futian Incident").

6. A unit of weight which varied according to circumstances, but corresponded roughly to 50 or 60 kg. In this volume, we capitalize this term to distinguish it from another character, also pronounced *dan*, which represents a unit of volume. For more details see below, the relevant note to the Xunwu Investigation of May 1930.

7. Li Wenbin (1902–1939) was a native of Heilongjiang. At this time, he was commander of the Twenty-First Brigade of the Seventh Division of the Guomindang First Army Group.

juncture of Fujian, Guangdong, and Jiangxi provinces, Luofuzhang, and rested there for one day. All along the way were places without Party organizations and without mass support, and the pursuing troops of the Fifth Regiment followed us closely with the help of the reactionary militia. It was truly a most difficult time for our army. After we arrived at Luofuzhang, in order to make arrangements for the wounded, to find a place to rest where there was a Party organization and mass support, and to aid our troops on the Jinggangshan, we decided to go to Donggu (at the juncture of Ningdu, Xingguo, and Ji'an [xian], belonging to Ji'an). On February 11, arriving at Dabodi in Ningdu, we fought against an advance party of the pursuing troops, Liu Shiyi's Fifteenth Brigade, and inflicted a severe defeat on them.[8] The morale of our army was thereby greatly raised. We captured over two hundred rifles, six amphibious machine guns, and a large number of enemy soldiers. The rest of their troops retreated to Ganzhou. By the time the rest of the pursuing troops, Li Wenbin's unit (three regiments), arrived, we had already left for Donggu, where we rested for a week, met with the Jiangxi Red Army's Second and Fourth Regiments, and also made contact with the Special Committees of Jiangxi and southern Jiangxi (at Yudu) and took care of the wounded. When Li Wenbin (whose troops are the very best of the Jiangxi Army) followed us to Donggu, we decided to give up the policy of openly setting up independent régimes in fixed areas and adopt a policy of flexible guerrilla warfare (the policy of circling around), to counter the enemy's policy of vigorous pursuit. On February 25, we left Donggu, went through Yongfeng, Le'an, Guangchang, and Shicheng, then entered Rentian City, between Ningdu and Ruijin. The rear guards were only one li from us, and that is why we left Rentian city for Tingzhou. Zhang's brigade turned back abruptly; because of the outbreak of the war in Hunan, the Chiang faction needed to concentrate its troops, and hence Zhang's brigade was recalled.[9] Then we had a chance to concentrate on dealing with Guo Fengming. Twice, on the 13th and 14th, we defeated Guo's unit, and the Red Army's Second and Fourth Regiments were also able to evolve in the region of Xingguo and Yudu. Since we started out from the Jinggangshan, we have lost a total of over two hundred guns and six hundred men. The greatest loss was that of cadres. This is most unfortunate! The hardship we encountered this time was the greatest in the history of the Red Army. Only by expending all our energy were we able to deal with these hardships and gain the present victory. The reasons we were able to overcome these difficulties are solid internal unity (even during the most difficult times, very few soldiers defected, and among

---

8. Liu Shiyi (1891–1982), zi Renfu, was a native of Jiangxi, who had studied military science in Japan. At this time, he was deputy commander of the Fifth Division of the Guomindang First Army Group, and concurrently commander of the Fifteenth Brigade.

9. The reference is to the Thirty-fifth Brigade of the Twelfth Division of the Guomindang First Army Group, commanded by Zhang Yuren.

the cadres, Yuan Wencai[10] and a handful of others left the ranks), and correct guidance by the Party.

10) The highest Party organization in the army is the Front Committee appointed by the Central Committee (as required by the actual situation, aside from the list of names appointed by the Central Committee, a few more have been added). Except for a portion of it remaining in the Hunan-Jiangxi Border Area, the Fourth Army has been reorganized into three sections totaling three thousand men, fifteen hundred guns, and very little ammunition. As the result of frequent battles, we have lost many old cadres, and combat effectiveness is no longer what it was. But the state of exhaustion and defeat in which we left the Jinggangshan has been dissipated, and morale is high once again. As a result of losses suffered on two occasions, the shortage of officers and political workers has reached an extreme. We hope very much that the Central Committee will send us replacements. At the very least, they should send several military instructors and several political instructors, so that training schools may be opened here.

11) Over the past two years, because of difficulties in communications, we have received only two documents from the Central Committee. The first was the long letter of last June, which we received in October on the Jinggangshan; the other was the Resolutions of the Sixth Congress (political, military, land, political power, peasants, and the Congress . . . a total of six), which we received in Yongxin in January of this year.[11] The letters we have sent to the Central Committee include: a long letter by Mao Zedong written last August in care of the Hunan Provincial Committee and a detailed report from the Front Committee written in November in care of the Provincial Committees of Hunan and Jiangxi, which recounted the struggles in the Hunan-Jiangxi Border Area in the last two years and the current plans of the Red Army. We don't know whether or not they were received.[12]

12) The resolutions adopted at the Sixth Congress are extremely correct, and we accept them with great joy. Previously, we had already mimeographed over five hundred copies to distribute to the Party organizations along the way here from the Jinggangshan. Now we have printed another thousand lithographic copies to be used in expanding the organizations in western Fujian and southern Jiangxi. The only things that are missing are the three resolutions on organiza-

---

10. The nature and behavior of the two bandit chieftains, Wang Zuo and Yuan Wencai, and the reasons why they were ultimately killed by the Communists themselves, have been the subject of many contradictory statements since Mao's first interviews with Edgar Snow in 1936. For a brief discussion of this problem, see the Introduction to this volume.

11. This statement does not appear to be entirely accurate. Apart from the two items mentioned here, Mao himself refers in texts translated above to several other documents which had reached him during the year 1928.

12. For a fuller statement regarding communications which Mao had sent, see below, the letter of April 5, 1929.

tion, propaganda, and trade unions. Could we please ask you to send them to complete the set?

13) A Western Fujian Special Committee needs to be set up quickly. The Southern Jiangxi Special Committee is far away from the Jiangxi Provincial Committee, but has been in close contact with the Front Committee; since its establishment last May, the Hunan-Jiangxi Border Area Special Committee has had a close relationship with the Hunan Provincial Committee, but has little contact with the Jiangxi Provincial Committee. Of all the Party organizations in southern Jiangxi, Yudu and Donggu are the best, followed by Xingguo, Xinfeng, Ningdu, Anyuan, and Xunwu; Ruijin, Huichang, and Shicheng have no organizations as yet. Changting is beginning to develop one. The best of them all, at Yongding, is more than 300 *li* from us, and because of having to deal with events in Jiangxi, the Red Army cannot go there now. Comrade Ruan Shan's Red Army needs to come to Tingzhou. Only thus, when we leave for Jiangxi, can the Tingzhou régime continue to exist, and to have close contact with us. After Guo Fengming died, there was no one to rule Tingzhou. The center for activities in the eight *xian* should be in Changting. We hope the Provincial Committee will give this careful consideration!

14) In calculating strength, the Central Committee must not overestimate us.

The Front Committee

A Letter from the Front Committee to the Central Committee[1]

(Ruijin, April 5, 1929)

To the Central Committee:

On April 3, at Ruijin, we received your letter of February 7, which had been forwarded to us by the Fujian Provincial Committee.[2] The Central Committee's letter makes too pessimistic an appraisal of the objective situation and of the subjective forces. The third "suppression" campaign against the Jinggangshan represented the high water mark of the counterrevolutionary tide. But there it stopped, and since then the counterrevolutionary tide has gradually receded, while the revolutionary tide has gradually risen. Although our Party's fighting capacity and organizational strength have been weakened to the extent described by the Central Committee, they will be rapidly restored, and the passivity among comrades in the Party will quickly disappear as the counterrevolutionary tide gradually ebbs. The masses will certainly come over to us. Butcherism[3] only serves to "drive the fish into deep waters," and reformism no longer has any appeal to the masses. The illusions of the masses about the Guomindang will assuredly be soon dissipated. In the circumstances which will arise, no other party will be able to compete with the Communist Party in winning over the masses. The political line and the organizational line laid down by the Sixth Congress are entirely correct: the current stage of the revolution is democratic and not socialist, and the present task of the Party is to win over the masses and not to stage immediate armed insurrections. Nevertheless, the revolution is de-

---

We have translated this text from *Mao Zedong wenji*, Vol. 1, pp. 54–63. There the source is given as a handwritten copy in the Party archives. This letter was first published in the 1941 edition of the internal documentary collection *Liuda yilai* (Since the Sixth Congress).

1. Large portions of this text were quoted by Mao in his letter of January 5, 1930, to Lin Biao, translated below. We have used the same wording in both cases for the passages which overlap.

2. The Central Committee's letter of February 7, 1929, has long been known only from Mao's references to it and from other secondary sources. The full text has now been published in *Central Committee Documents* (1929), pp. 29–37. As explained in the Introduction to this volume, it was drafted by Zhou Enlai.

3. I.e., the adversary's policy of massacring the population.

veloping swiftly, and we should adopt a positive spirit in our propaganda about, and preparations for, armed insurrection. In the present chaotic situation we can lead the masses only if we have positive slogans and a positive spirit. Only by having such a spirit can the Party recover its fighting capacity. We feel that the Party committed the error of adventurism in the past, and now it has a rather marked liquidationist tendency in some places. The Party branches in the localities that we have passed through in western Fujian and southern Jiangxi had very low combat morale and had lightly let go many opportunities for battle. The masses are vast, and also revolutionary, but the party branches are not taking the lead. The examples of western Fujian and southern Jiangxi make us wonder whether there are similar phenomena elsewhere. So we have to oppose the evil tendency toward adventurism and commandism, but we must also energetically guard against the tendency toward liquidationism and immobilism. Proletarian leadership is the sole key to the victory of the revolution. Building up the Party's proletarian basis and establishing Party branches in industrial enterprises in key areas are the greatest organizational tasks for the Party at present. But, at the same time, the development of the struggle in the countryside, the establishment of soviets in small areas, and the creation and expansion of the Red Army are prerequisites for aiding the struggle in the cities and hastening the revolutionary upsurge. The greatest mistake would therefore be to abandon the struggle in the cities and sink into rural guerrilla-ism. But in our opinion, it is also a mistake—if any of our Party members hold such views—to fear the development of the power of the peasants lest it outstrip the workers' leadership and become detrimental to the revolution. For the revolution in semicolonial China will fail only if the peasant struggle is deprived of the leadership of the workers; it will never suffer just because the peasant struggle develops in such a way as to become more powerful than the workers. The Sixth Congress has pointed out the mistake of neglecting the peasant revolution. In this letter from the Central Committee, the idea "develop a vast struggle everywhere in the rural areas" represents the only correct view.

The Central Committee asks us to divide our forces into very small units and disperse them over the countryside and to withdraw Zhu De and Mao Zedong from the army, thus concealing the major targets, all this with the aim of preserving the Red Army and arousing the masses.[4] This is a kind of ideal view. In the winter of 1927–1928, we did start to plan to disperse our forces over the countryside, with each company or battalion operating on its own and adopting guerrilla tactics in order to arouse the masses while trying not to present a target for the enemy; we have tried this many times, but have failed every time. The reasons are: (1) Most of the soldiers of the Red Army come from other areas and have a background different from that of the local Red Guards. The peasants in Ninggang and other *xian* of the Hunan-Jiangxi Border Area are willing to serve

---

4. Such were, in fact, the orders of the Central Committee. See also the discussion in the Introduction to this volume.

only in the local Red Guard units but not in the Red Army. Therefore, in the Red Army, one can hardly find any peasants from the Hunan-Jiangxi Border Area. The Red Army is made up of veterans from the National Revolutionary Army,[5] the peasant army from Liuyang, Pingjiang, and southern Hunan, and prisoners of war from the past. (2) Division into small units results in weak leadership and organization and inability to cope with adverse circumstances, which easily lead to defeat; (3) The units are liable to be crushed by the enemy one by one. (Because of the division of forces, the Fifth Army in Pingjiang and Liuyang *xian* and the Fourth Army in the border area and in Hunan have been defeated five times.) (4) The more adverse the circumstances, the greater the need for concentration and for the leaders to be resolute in struggle, because only thus can we have internal unity to resist the enemy. Only in favorable circumstances is it advisable to divide our forces for guerrilla operations, and it is only then that the leaders need not stay with the ranks all the time, as they must in adverse circumstances. This last time when we left the Jinggangshan and marched toward southern Jiangxi and western Fujian, because our troops were centralized, and the leading organ's (the Front Committee) and the leaders' (Zhu and Mao) attitudes were unwavering, not only was the enemy unable to do anything to us but their losses were greater than their gains, and our gains were greater than our losses. Our two victories in Ningdu and Tingzhou *xian* completely wiped out the combat effectiveness of the local bullies, Guo's and Liu's brigades, resulting in the current mass mobilization in southern Jiangxi and western Fujian.[6] Without the centralization of the army and sound leadership, this could not have been done. The tactics we have derived from the struggle of the past three years are indeed different from any other tactics, ancient or modern, Chinese or foreign. With our tactics, the masses can be aroused for struggle on an ever-broadening scale, and no enemy, however powerful, can cope with us. Ours are guerrilla tactics. They consist mainly of the following points:

> "Divide our forces to arouse the masses, concentrate our forces to deal with the enemy."

> "The enemy advances, we retreat; the enemy camps, we harass; the enemy tires, we attack; the enemy retreats, we pursue."[7]

> "To extend stable base areas, employ the policy of advancing in waves; when pursued by a powerful enemy, employ the policy of circling around."

---

5. I.e., the Guomindang army.

6. Regarding the battles with Guo Fengming and Liu Shiyi, see above, Mao's report of March 20, 1929.

7. This terse summary of the Red Army's tactics, known in Chinese as the "sixteen-character formula" because each of its four clauses consists of four characters, had been coined by Mao Zedong and Zhu De in May 1928. It appeared for the first time in written form in the present letter, and soon came to be regarded as the definitive formulation of Mao's guerrilla principles.

"Arouse the largest numbers of the masses in the shortest possible time and by the best possible methods."

These tactics are just like casting a net; at any moment we should be able to cast it or draw it in. We cast it wide to win over the masses and draw it in to deal with the enemy. Such are the tactics we have used for the past three years. When we were in the Hunan-Jiangxi Border Area, once we had pulled the forces together and defeated the enemy, we were able to scatter and work for two to three weeks (in several big teams, and then each big team could again be subdivided), until the enemy once more marshaled his forces to attack us, at which point we would get together again to defeat the enemy, then scatter again to work. This time when the enemy pursued us, we used the spiral guerrilla tactics and went through a vast area and mobilized vast masses. Whenever we came to a place, we would stay a minimum of half a day and a maximum of five days. First, we conducted propaganda on a large scale. (The press propaganda team and oral propaganda teams, under the Political Department, are based on the company; two teams per company and three people per team. Along the march and wherever we went, propaganda was immediately conducted everywhere.) Then we distributed money and goods (grain, clothing, and tools owned by big landlords and reactionary elements), and we went ahead with organizing (Party branches, underground workers' unions, and underground peasants' unions). Our techniques of working with the masses have greatly improved. The Red Army now is not purely a combat force; its main function is, rather, to mobilize the masses. Combat is only a means. The time we spend on combat as compared with the time we spend on mass work stands in a proportion of 1 to 10. The army today is different from that in the days of Ye and He.[8] The only occupation of the army of Ye and He was to fight. This would not work today. It would not have survived. At no time can the Red Army survive without a united leading organization for the Party and the army; otherwise, it will fall into anarchy and will certainly fail.

At present the Party's leading organ is the Front Committee, with Mao Zedong as secretary, and the military commanding organ is the headquarters, with Zhu De as chief of the army. If the Central Committee needs Zhu and Mao for other assignments, please send us capable replacements for them. We think Comrade Liu Bocheng can take over the military post and Comrade Yun Daiying can take over the Party and political work. If they can both come, they will be able to do better work than we can. Last June in a letter from the Central Committee, it was mentioned that Comrade He Long would be sent here to inspect our work, but we don't know why he has not yet arrived. Now it is very convenient to come here from Fujian. We hope that you will send people to inspect our work at any time.

Since Liu's and Guo's brigades were wiped out, it may be said that we have

---

8. The reference is to the forces of Ye Ting and He Long, at the time when these commanders were leading them on the retreat from Nanchang.

no more enemies in western Fujian and southern Jiangxi. The armies of Chiang Kaishek and the Guangxi warlords are approaching each other in the vicinity of Jiujiang, and a big battle is imminent. Henceforth, the rule of the Guomindang will disintegrate, and the revolutionary high tide will arrive very quickly. As for how our work should be arranged under these circumstances, we feel that, so far as the southern provinces are concerned, the armed forces of the compradors and landlords in Guangdong and Hunan Provinces are too strong, and that in Hunan, moreover, we have lost almost all the masses, inside as well as outside the Party, because of the error of the Party's adventurist policies. In the three provinces of Fujian, Jiangxi, and Zhejiang, however, the situation is different. First, the military forces are weakest there. In Zhejiang, there is only a small provincial defense force under Jiang Bocheng.[9] In Fujian, although there are five groups of enemy troops totaling fourteen regiments in all, Guo's troops have already been smashed; the troops under Chen and Lu[10] are bandits of small fighting capacity; the two brigades of marines stationed along the coast have never seen action and their fighting capacity is undoubtedly not great; Zhang Zhen[11] alone can put up some sort of a fight, but according to an analysis made by the Fujian Provincial Committee, even he has only two good regiments. In addition, Fujian is now in a state of complete anarchy and disunity. In Jiangxi, there are sixteen regiments under the two commands of Zhu Peide and Xiong Shihui; they are stronger than the armed forces of either Fujian or Zhejiang, but far inferior to those of Hunan. (When they have fought with us, apart from Li Wenbin's brigade, we have defeated them all.) Secondly, fewer adventurist mistakes have been made in these three provinces. We are not clear about the situation in Zhejiang, but the Party's organizational and mass base is somewhat better in Jiangxi and Fujian than in Hunan. Take Jiangxi, for example. In northern Jiangxi we still have some bases in De'an, Xiushui, and Tonggu; in western Jiangxi the Party and the Red Guards still have some strength in Ninggang, Yongxin, Lianhua, and Suichuan; in southern Jiangxi the prospects are still much brighter, as the Second and Fourth Regiments of the Red Army are steadily growing in strength in the *xian* of Ji'an, Yongfeng, and Xingguo; in eastern Jiangxi, the Red Army's Third Regiment under Fang Zhimin has by no means been wiped out. All this places us in a position to close in on Nanchang. We hereby recommend to the Central Committee that during the period of prolonged and chaotic warfare among the Guomindang warlords, we should contend with Chiang Kaishek and the Guangxi clique for Jiangxi Prov-

---

9. Jiang Bocheng (?–1951), a native of Jiangxi, was commander of the local defense forces.

10. Lu Xingbang (1880–1945) and Chen Guohui (1895–1933) were both natives of Fujian. Each of them had spent several years as a bandit, before pursuing a military career. At this time, Lu was commander of the Guomindang's newly organized Second Division; Chen was commander of the First Mixed Brigade of the Fujian forces.

11. Zhang Zhen (1884–1963), a native of Fujian, had participated in the Revolution of 1911. At this time, he was commander of the Guomindang's Temporary First Division, with responsibility for the campaign against the Red Army in Fujian.

ince, and at the same time for western Fujian and western Zhejiang. In these three provinces we should enlarge the Red Army and create an independent régime of the masses, with a time limit of one year for accomplishing this plan.

During this one year, we must lay the foundations for the struggle of the proletariat in Shanghai, Wuxi, Ningpo, Hangzhou, Fuzhou, Xiamen, and other places, so that they can lead the peasant struggles in Zhejiang, Jiangxi, and Fujian. The Jiangxi Provincial Committee must be soundly established, and efforts must be made to build a basis among the workers in Nanchang, Jiujiang, Ji'an, and on the Nanchang-Jiujiang Railroad.

We came to Tingzhou on March 14, after we had defeated Guo's brigade and shot Guo Fengming. Then we found out about the rift between Chiang Kaishek and the Guangxi faction, and how a chaotic struggle within the Guomindang will soon come. As for our present arrangements, we have decided that during the initial stage of the fighting within the Guomindang, with the twenty-odd *xian* of western Fujian and southern Jiangxi as our sphere of action, we should mobilize the masses with our guerrilla tactics, in order that the masses may openly establish an independent régime. We must deepen the land revolution and establish worker-peasant political power, and then join this régime to the one in the Hunan-Jiangxi Border Area to form a strong force, which will be the foundation for future development. Therefore, we did not go down to Hangyong or to Longyan. After working in Tingzhou for seventeen days, we came to Ruijin on April 1. We plan to enter and occupy Yudu on April 8. When we get to Yudu, we will call a big meeting to discuss our action plans with the Southern Jiangxi Special Committee and with Comrade Luo Shounan sent by the Military Department of the Central Committee. The masses in western Fujian and southern Jiangxi are extremely well disposed. Several thousand had come together to seize grain from the local tyrants at Changting *xian* seat, Xinqiao, Hetian, and other places. At Tingzhou, we organized twenty underground peasants' unions and five underground workers' unions, and also established the trade union federation. The party organization has doubled in size. One Red Guard unit was also organized, but since it could not stand on its own, it has followed the army to Ruijin. The first organ of political power was a provisional revolutionary committee, appointed by the Political Department. After several workers' unions and peasants' unions had been organized, a representative assembly was called together to elect the formal revolutionary committee. Both the provisional and the formal revolutionary committees issued political programs. On arriving in Ruijin, we planned for four days' work. The army was scattered to work in the *xian* town, Rentian City, Xijiang, and Jiubao, and in each place each team was divided into subteams. The headquarters are in the *xian* capital. The masses of Ruijin have risen like a raging fire to welcome us. They have fought very bravely against the landlords. Unfortunately, there was formerly no organization, not a single comrade, and no local leading organizations. Since the work was done in a rush, it was not well done, especially in the *xian* town. After we get to Yudu, we will spend about one week there working in the *xian* capital and the four cities. Later we may march toward Ningdu and

Guangchang, or toward Wan'an and Taihe, depending on the circumstances. We will engage in guerrilla warfare for a while in southern Jiangxi before we move to western Fujian. Then we will take on the remnants of Guo Fengming's and Lu Xingbang's and Chen Guohui's units. The Fujian Provincial Committee must make efforts to prepare for this.

As for the situation in the army, except for a small portion which has been left in the border area, we have with us in the main force of the Fourth Army a total of three thousand six hundred men and eleven hundred guns. We lost two hundred guns and six hundred men at Dayu, Xinfeng, and Xunwu (most of the men lost contact during the fighting). Only a few score guns and a little more than one hundred men were actually taken by the enemy. The shocking reports in the newspapers were all lies of the enemy. After the Ningdu and Tingzhou battles, we have not only recovered but even gained a little. The army is now organized as the first, second, and third columns, each of which is in charge of two detachments (equivalent to battalions), and each detachment is in charge of three groups [da dui] (equivalent to companies). Each column has about five hundred guns and over twelve hundred men. When we divide the forces to wage guerrilla warfare, we use the columns as units, spread them out, and then divide them again into detachments. It is very convenient to divide the forces and bring them back together again. Eight hundred men and five hundred guns from Comrade Peng Dehuai's Fifth Army came to the Jinggangshan. Of those, six hundred men and four hundred guns are now at Ruijin. They have been reorganized as the Fifth Column of the Fourth Army. Comrade Peng Dehuai is now in command, with the title of deputy army commander. Within the next few days, we need to return to the Hunan-Jiangxi Border Area to rally the old troops, to restore political power, and to restore contact with southern Jiangxi, which is still under the Front Committee. Political departments have been established. The army has a political department, and each column has its own political department within which there are the Secretariat, Propaganda, Organization (which includes sections for staff members, peasants, and Party affairs) and Political Security divisions. At the levels of detachments and companies there are Party representatives. We plan to abolish the Party representatives at levels higher than columns and have only the head of the Political Department. At Tingzhou, we have had new clothes made for the whole army, and each man was given four *yuan* as spending money. Provisions are no problem, and morale is high. Two other armies from eastern Jiangxi and Lichuan (near Guangchang) want to join us. One consists of five hundred men who have defected from Jin Handing with more than three hundred guns. They have been reorganized as the Fourth Column, with Tian Guiqing as its commander. The other one is composed of over three hundred bandits with more than two hundred guns. They had been battered from all sides and could not find a way out. Now they have been reorganized as an independent battalion with Hu Zhusheng as its commander. Both of these armies will arrive in Ningdu after April 14 to be reorganized and trained. The Second and the Fourth Regiments of the Jiangxi Red Army are now stationed in Xingguo and have good contact with us. The Hunan-Jiangxi Border Area has been defeated once, but now is the opportunity for its recovery. In that area, there are, in addition to Wang Zuo's forces, with two hundred guns, which belongs to the Fourth Red Army, the Red Guard units of the six *xian*, Ninggang, Yongxin, Lianhua, Suichuan, Lingxian, and Chaling, with a total of eight hundred guns. At a time when the warlords are engaged in chaotic warfare and are incapable of paying attention to other matters, these two units can not only defend themselves but also move outward. When Comrade Peng leads his army back there, they will be even more capable of this. The secretary of the Hunan-Jiangxi Border Area Special Committee is Comrade Deng Qianyuan. In Hunan, since the uprising failed last March, the foundation of the Party has been completely wiped out under the reign of adventurism. The arms of the peasants have also been seized by the despotic gentry, and the masses suppressed. Last August, when the Red Army attacked Bing [*xian*], we organized three *xian* committees at Zixing, Rucheng, and Guidong, three armed Red Guard units of the peasants, and a Special Committee over them with Du Xiujing as its secretary. But according to a recent report, they have again been sacrificed to adventurism. In Liling, since last spring's uprising, when the Party organization was broken up and the armed forces wiped out, they have obtained seventy guns from the Fourth Army during the summer and were fully recovered by fall at Huangtuling at the juncture of Youxian and Liling. This proves how difficult it is for a small armed force to survive independently.

The commanding organ for the Party in the Red Army is the Front Committee appointed by the Central Committee. The letter from the Central Committee dated June 4 of last year said: "As for the commanding organ for the front, the Central Committee considers that it is necessary to organize a committee. The appointees are as follows: Mao Zedong, Zhu De, one worker comrade, one peasant comrade, and the local Party secretary of wherever the Front Committee may be located, with Mao Zedong as the secretary. In addition, a Trade Union Committee must be set up, with the worker comrade on the Front Committee as its secretary, as well as an Army Committee, with Zhu De as its secretary. The members of the Army and Trade Union Committees will be determined by the Front Committee. The limits of jurisdiction will be determined according to the circumstances. The work within all areas of jurisdiction will be supervised by the Front Committee. When the Front Committee is in Jiangxi, it will be under the direction of the Jiangxi Provincial Committee; when in Hunan, it will come under the Hunan Provincial Committee. The Provincial Committee in question, upon receiving reports from the Front Committee, should respond immediately and submit both the Front Committee reports and the Provincial Committee's responses to the Central Committee promptly." We feel this directive from the Central Committee concerning organization is entirely appropriate and meets the needs of the struggle. The Red Army, which transcends local characteristics, should not be subjected to the leadership of the *xian* and Special Committees, nor even of a particular provincial committee. The Fifth Army in Pingjiang and Liuyang, and the Fourth Army in Hunan and in the Hunan-Jiangxi border area, have been defeated many times under the command of localism. The Red Army, which transcends locality, must be under the direct command of the Central Committee. Only thus can it adapt itself to the needs of the revolutionary environment and not suffer harm from the evil influence of localism.

Since August of last year, we have submitted three reports to the Central Committee. One was a long letter written by Mao Zedong after our defeat in the border area, discussing questions such as the independent régime and the policies of the Hunan Provincial Committee to be forwarded by the Hunan Provincial Committee.[12] The original draft of the first letter has been lost. Another was a report of the Front Committee, written last November just after we first received your June letter, and just before the Red Army had to return to the Hunan-Jiangxi Border Area. It contained an historical account of the struggle in the Hunan-Jiangxi Border Area and also discussed policies and plans concerning the setting up of independent régimes, and was forwarded by the Hunan and Jiangxi Provincial Committees.[13] The original draft of this letter is still here and I am enclosing a copy of it again. The third was a letter sent by the Front Committee at Changting on March 20, to be submitted to you via the Fujian Provincial Committee.[14] Have you received it? Another copy is enclosed. For three years, we have not received a single one of the publications of the Central Committee until we got to Tingzhou, where we finally saw *The Young Pioneer*, Nos. 3 and 4, *The Chinese Worker*, No. 3, *The People's Voice*, No. 2, published in Beijing, and *The Outpost*, No. 2, put out by Tingzhou comrades in Shanghai. In the Hunan-Jiangxi border area, because of the enemy blockade, we were unable to read any newspapers for two to three months. Since last September, we have been able to buy newspapers from Ji'an and Changsha, but it is still very difficult. Since we came to southern Jiangxi and western Fujian, the convenience of the postal services allows us to read newspapers every day from Nanjing, Shanghai, Fuzhou, Xiamen, Zhangzhou, Nanchang, and Ganzhou. Since we have come to Ruijin *xian*, we can read He Jian's official paper and Changsha's *Republican Daily*. It is like being able to see the sky again through the clouds, and our joy is indescribable! We hope that the Central Committee will write to us once a month, and we will submit at least one report to the Central Committee every month. We also hope that you will find a way to send us Central Committee publications.

---

12. This must be the letter "written last August" referred to above, in the Report of March 20, 1929. If so, not only the "original draft," as indicated in the text, but all copies appear to have been lost. Presumably the content paralleled to some extent that of the report of October 5, 1928, translated above.

13. This clearly refers to the well-known report of November 28, 1928, also translated above.

14. This document is also translated above.

Order of the Military Department of the Fourth Army

(Yucheng, 8 A.M., April 10, [1929])

The position of assistant Party representative of this corps, left vacant by the commander of this corps, Lin Jun, is to be filled by the appointment of Wang Tingying. Please note and respect this order.

The Changting Red Guards

Army Commander, Zhu De
Political Commissar, Mao Zedong

Our source for this text is *Mao Zedong ji. Bujuan*, Vol. 3, p. 47.

[Xingguo Xian *] Land Law*

(April 1929)

1. Confiscate all public land and all land belonging to the landlord class, and turn ownership over to the government of the congress of workers, peasants, and soldiers of Xingguo, which should redistribute it to the landless peasants and peasants with little land, for them to cultivate and use.

2. Further purchase and sale of all public land and land belonging to the landlord class are prohibited once it has been confiscated and redistributed by the government of workers, peasants, and soldiers.

3. The quantitative criteria for land redistribution are:

a) using the number of people as the criterion, and redistributing an equal amount of land to men, women, the old, and the young;

b) using labor power as the criterion and giving twice as much land to those who can work as to those who cannot.

Of the above two criteria, the first is to be the primary one. In places where special circumstances prevail, the second criterion may be applied. The reasons for adopting the first criterion are:

i) before the facilities for caring for old people and children are in place, the old and the young, if they are given too little land, will certainly not be able to make a living;

ii) it is relatively simple and convenient to use the number of people as the criterion for land redistribution;

iii) very few families do not have old people or children. At the same time, although the old and the young are not capable of tilling the land, local governments should, after land redistribution, also assign them appropriate public services to perform, such as communication duties.

4. The administrative criteria for land redistribution are:

a) using the township as the unit for land redistribution;

b) using several townships as the unit for land redistribution (as was done in Xiaojiang District in Yongxin [*xian*]);

c) using the district as the unit for land redistribution.

Our source for this document is the 1941 edition of *Nongcun diaocha*, pp. 125–27. The text also appears in *Mao Zedong ji*, Vol. 2, pp.73–75.

Of the above three criteria, the first is to be the primary one. Under special circumstances, the second and third criteria may be used.

5. The methods of redistributing wooded and hilly lands are:

a) Hills where tea-oil plants are grown and firewood-producing hills are to be redistributed according to the same method used for the land, taking the township as the unit; they are to be redistributed equally for cultivation and use;

b) Bamboo forests are the property of the soviet government. Peasants may, however, enjoy the use of the bamboo after obtaining permission from the soviet government. Permission for [cutting] fewer than fifty stalks should be obtained from the township soviet; for fewer than a hundred stalks, permission must be obtained from the district soviet government; for more than a hundred stalks, permission must be obtained from the *xian* soviet government.

c) All bamboo is to be sold by the *xian* soviet government; the proceeds from such sales will be allocated by the soviet government at a higher level.

6. The collection of land tax:

a) Three rates of land taxes are set according to production conditions: (i) 15 percent; (ii) 10 percent; (iii) 5 percent. Of the above three rates, the first is to be the primary one. Under special circumstances and after permission is obtained from the soviet government at a higher level, the second and third rates may be used.

b) In the event of natural disasters or other special circumstances, exemption from land tax may be granted after petitioning to and obtaining approval from the soviet government at a higher level.

c) Land tax is to be collected by the *xian* soviet governments and turned over to higher-level soviet governments for allocation.

7. Rural artisans, if they themselves wish to receive redistributed land, may each get half the amount of land given to every peasant.

8. Officers and soldiers of the Red Army and the Red Guards, as well as all those serving in the government or in other public agencies, should all receive the same amount of redistributed land as given to peasants. The soviet government will hire people to cultivate it for them.

Note: This law was issued four months after the enactment of the previous land law [of December 1928], when the Red Army arrived from the Jinggangshan in Xingguo in southern Jiangxi. One important substantive change was made, consisting in the replacement of "confiscate all land" by "confiscate all public land and all land belonging to the landlord class." This was a correction of principle. All other provisions remained unchanged, however, and were modified only in 1930. These two land laws are preserved in order to show how our understanding of the land struggle developed.[1]

---

1. This note, like that to the Jinggangshan land law of December 1928, was added to the text by Mao himself when it was first published in the 1941 Yan'an edition of *Rural Investigations*. For a brief discussion of the relation between this land law, that of December 1928, and that of February 1930, and the reasons for the changes, see the Introduction to this volume.

Report of Mao Zedong, Secretary of the Front Committee of the Fourth Red Army, to the Central Committee

(Sent on June 1, 1929, from Huleishi, Yongding, in Fujian)[1]

To the Central [Committee]:

1. Our army (the first and second columns of the Fourth Army), coming from Ruijin and without attacking Tingzhou, took the route leading directly to Longyan. On May 24, we reached the town of Longyan and its environs, where, in Toushi, we took unawares two battalions of Chen Guohui's forces, one special task company, and one machine gun company, disarming most of them, and obtaining two machine guns, more than two hundred rifles, and thirty thousand cartridges and capturing one battalion commander and more than two hundred soldiers.

2. Because Guo Fengming's forces and Huang Yuepo's regiment were located in Yongding, it was necessary to crush them speedily, so on May 26 we attacked Yongding. Huang's regiment retreated to Shanghang without a fight.

3. Our army is now at Yongding. The troops have been split up and sent to various *xian* towns, such as Hulei and Jinfeng, to carry out guerrilla actions and to assist the revolutionary masses in the work of organizing the masses. They have also gone to new districts to launch the mass struggle and to wipe out the forces of the militia,[2] and they are engaged in this right now.

After five days, they will then move on to other *xian* (such as Longyan and Shanghang). The Party has a fair base in western Fujian, and the masses are good, too. The struggle is developing daily in every *xian*, and hopes for the future are very high. Most of the forces of Zhang Zhen, Chen Guohui, and Lu Xinming have gone into Guangdong, leaving a vacuum in western and southern

---

We have translated this report from *Zhonggong zhongyang wenjian xuanji*, Vol. 5 (1929), pp. 681–87. The version in *Mao Zedong ji. Bujuan*, Vol. 3, pp. 55–56, consists only of brief extracts.

1. The heading of this document, as printed in *Central Committee Documents* (1929), adds that the report reached the Fujian Provincial Committee on June 25 and the Central Committee on July 1, 1929.

2. *Mintuan*, the landlord militia.

Fujian. The three remnant forces of Zhang Zhen, Chen Guohui, and Lu Xinming (replacing Brigade Commander Guo) total five thousand men, so the present time offers a particularly favorable opportunity for guerrilla operations in the whole of western Fujian. We hope the Provincial Committee will give more leadership to this dimension of the work.

4. On April 1, we withdrew from Tingzhou to Ruijin. In the five *xian* of Ruijin, Yudu, Ganzhou (Dongxiang), Ningdu, and Xingguo, we carried out the work of annihilating the reactionary military forces, in order to unleash and organize the masses. This went on for forty-five days in all, and the line [of march] was from Ruijin to Yudu to Dongxiang in Ganzhou to Xingguo to Ningdu. On May 15, we returned again to Ruijin. Every time we reached the territory of a *xian* or of a locality, we split the troops up and spread them around to every township. In each township, the troops were then once again split up into smaller units. With this kind of concentration and dispersion, it is easy to develop in tandem our plans both for winning over the masses and for dealing with the enemy, rather than stressing one aspect or the other. This corresponds to the directive of the Central Committee to "disperse your forces for guerrilla attacks, under a unified command." This is the situation now in western Fujian.

5. In southern Jiangxi, during these forty-five days of guerrilla action, Zhu Peide has again been pursuing the bandit suppression campaign,[3] sending one brigade from Ganzhou to attack Yudu and one brigade from Taihe to attack Xingguo. The troops that advanced together from Fuzhou to Ningdu, and to Ruijin from Fuzhou, were those of Wang Jun's division and of Li Wenbin's forces. In Ruijin, we did not, however, launch guerrilla attacks [on them]. When we were approaching Longyan, they had already entered Tingzhou. At this time, when the warlords have just launched chaotic struggles in the whole country, these units of enemy forces may be unable to pursue us again. This cannot, however, be determined with certainty and is under investigation. Toward such armies with powerful fighting capacities, we will certainly adopt the policy of moving around in circles, and will definitely not fight with them until all the conditions exist (for example, in terms of terrain and the masses) for a sure victory. So, in the end, the enemy will have no way to deal with us.

6. In southern Jiangxi, the base of the Party and the masses is relatively better in Yudu, Xingguo, and Dongxiang in Ganzhou. Anyuan. . . .[4] Ningdu are not as good, and Ruijin is just beginning. In *xian* such as Shicheng, Guangchang, and Nanfeng, there is no organization at all. As for the newly reorganized Southern Jiangxi Special Committee, in Yudu in southern Jiangxi they are extremely short-handed. In some places adventurism prevails, and in most places it is still opportunism (immobilism). The Provincial Committee gives them very little leadership. The three *xian* of Yudu, Xingguo, and Ningdu all have organs of political

---

3. I.e., the "Campaign to Encircle and Annihilate the [Communist] Bandits."
4. All ellipses in this text follow those in the Chinese original.

power (revolutionary committees of the workers, peasants, and soldiers); under the revolutionary committees are the peasant associations and labor unions. The landlord forces are very weak in all the *xian* of southern Jiangxi. Previously, the two local armies of Liu Shiyi and Lai Shicong (the younger brother of Lai Shihuang) were truly threatening, but the Red Army attacked and defeated Liu's brigade twice, and he sent what was left of his troops to Shanghai and Zhejiang. When the Red Army attacked and defeated Lai's troops at Ningdu on April 30, they, too, were completely destroyed (Lai Shicong was made prisoner, and more than a hundred rifles—some good, some bad—were taken). Since these two units no longer exist, and the troops of Zhu Peide will certainly not dare to stay long in the remote areas of southern Jiangxi, the future of southern Jiangxi also looks extremely promising. Because developments in southern Jiangxi may also allow the establishment of contact with the Jinggangshan in western Jiangxi (six *xian*, including Ninggang), and with the forces of Fang Zhimin in eastern Jiangxi,[5] we request that the Central Committee send a circular to the Jiangxi Provincial Committee asking them to pay attention to the work in these two localities.

7. From January 26 to January 29 on the Jinggangshan, the two companies of soldiers under Comrade Peng Dehuai successfully resisted a very large force engaged in encirclement for four days and four nights, but were defeated by them in the end. The Red Detachments in the various *xian*, together with Wang Zuo's battalion, are still in the border area and have not suffered great losses. Comrade Peng then withdrew to southern Jiangxi, having obtained more than a hundred rifles from Liu Shiyi's troops. On April 1, they joined forces with the Fourth Army in Ruijin. The Front Committee decided that Comrade Peng's forces and Wang's forces should be reorganized as the Fifth Column of the Fourth Army (there is no Fourth Column), with Wang Zuo as column commander, and that the Red Guards of the Hunan-Jiangxi Border Area should constitute the Sixth Column of the Fourth Army, with Comrade He Guozhong as column commander. In all, they have fourteen hundred rifles, and the fighting strength of these two columns is considerable. These two columns are under the orders of Comrade Peng in his capacity as deputy commander-in-chief of the Fourth Army (internally, Peng is known as the secretary). The Hunan-Jiangxi Border Area Army Committee comes under the Front Committee. When the Front Committee is unable to exercise command directly, they are subject to the

---

5. Fang Zhimin (1899–1935) was born in Yiyang *xian* in eastern Jiangxi, and joined the Chinese Communist Party in 1924. Following the break with the Guomindang, he returned in the autumn of 1927 to his native place, and spent the remainder of his life building what came to be known as the Fujian-Zhejiang-Jiangxi base area. Though at the outset he had no military training or experience, the forces under his control became, as indicated above in the letter of April 5, 1929, the Third Regiment of the Red Army, and were then reorganized in July 1930 as the Tenth Red Army. In Mao Zedong's letter of January 5, 1930, to Lin Biao, Fang was cited, together with Zhu and Mao, He Long, and Li Wenlin, as one of four exemplars in setting up base areas.

Hunan-Jiangxi Border Area Special Committee. The heart of the guerrilla zone is Ninggang. All the *xian* of the border area that have extensive forces can be considered battle areas, and attention is paid to maintaining links with Jiangxi and Fujian. On April 14, Comrade Peng's forces set out from Yudu, in the direction of the four border areas of Xinfeng, Nankang . . . and Suichuan. Subsequently, they went from . . . to . . . , and their activity. . . . The Second Independent Regiment and the Fourth Regiment of the Jiangxi Red Army, under the leadership of the Jiangxi Provincial Committee, have between them about a thousand rifles (the Fourth Army gave them a supplement of five hundred, half good and half bad), and the combat capacity of these two regiments is fairly good. The Fourth Regiment, which has been set up only recently, is somewhat inferior, but its internal organization is fairly sound, and the Party is very capable of exercising influence in military matters. Their sphere of guerrilla activity is in Ji'an . . . Taihe, Wan'an and Xingguo. . . . In all these *xian*, their method of work is inferior compared to that mentioned earlier, but under the influence of the Fourth Army there has been some progress. When the Fourth Army was carrying out guerrilla activities in southern Jiangxi, they were subject to the orders of the Front Committee (their relations with the Front Committee have not changed), and in concert with the Fourth Army they carried out the work of unleashing and organizing the struggles of the masses. Their sphere of responsibility was the forces of of Xingguo and Ningdu. After the Fourth Army came to western Fujian, they carried out guerrilla attacks on various *xian* in all directions, with Xingguo as their center.

9.[6] While we were in Ningdu, the Special Committee of the East River Area[7] sent us a letter, saying that the East River was preparing an armed uprising, and they wanted the Red Army to send troops to help out. The Front Committee sent them a letter in reply stating that it did not approve of carrying out a general uprising at this time; that at present we could only launch guerrilla warfare; and that the Red Army really could not send troops to assist, because the reactionary forces there were very strong, and troops could not be sent over very long distances. After arriving in western Fujian, we sent them another letter, urging them to carry out mass work, and adding that after the Red Army had worked for a time in western Fujian, it might possibly come to the East River area to carry on guerrilla actions for a while. There is liaison between the East River Special Committee and the Western Fujian Special Committee, but hitherto there have been no links with the Southern Jiangxi Special Committee. In accordance with the progress of the work, it is necessary for all the special committees to have close links and for leading organs to be set up in the territories along the borders between the various

---

6. The Chinese original contains no section number 8. Either this portion of the text is missing or section 7 (which contains several gaps indicated by ellipses) has been combined with section 8.

7. In Guangdong.

provinces, or for the Front Committee to make permanent arrangements there. We anticipate that the Central Committee will discuss this and give direction.

10. At the time when the First, Second, and Third Columns of the Fourth Red Army withdrew to southern Jiangxi after the defeat at Dayu, the number of men had fallen from three thousand six hundred to three thousand, a loss of six hundred (this includes over a hundred wounded or sick, who are now in Donggu recuperating, so the number of losses is actually two hundred).[8] Fortunately [losses] were made up[9] in the battle of Dabodi on the sixth[10] against Liu's brigade, but because there were no soldiers to carry them, all the rifles were handed over to the Second Regiment of the Jiangxi Red Army.[11] During the past three months, the number of men has increased by one thousand six hundred. The number of rifles has increased by five hundred (in the four campaigns of Tingzhou, Ningdu, Longyan, and Kanshi, a total of eight hundred rifles were gained, of which over three hundred relatively inferior ones were given to the local Red Guards), which together with what we originally had makes a total of two thousand. As regards ammunition, three months ago we had, on average, fewer than forty rounds for each rifle. This, too, has now doubled. Such is the real strength of our army. Propaganda for outside consumption gives numbers far in excess of these. For example, the Party organs in various places go so far as to say that Zhu and Mao have twenty thousand men, and ten thousand rifles. When the situation is so unclear, mistakes are bound to occur in the estimates. At present, there are three forces under the command of the Front Committee, or which have relations with it. One consists of the First, Second, and Third Columns of the Fourth Army, with two thousand rifles. This is the main force. Another is the troops in the Hunan-Jiangxi Border Area, with one thousand four hundred rifles, and the third consists of the Second and Fourth Regiments of the Jiangxi Red Army, with one thousand rifles, making in all four thousand five hundred rifles. Broadly speaking, all three of these components are regular army units with fairly good fighting capacity. They have all been created during the most difficult high tide of the counterrevolution.[12]

---

8. Here two hundred may be a misprint for five hundred; if so, the figures would balance.

9. From the context, it appears that this must mean losses in matériel, not the losses in men discussed in the previous sentence.

10. As indicated in a note to the Chinese original in *Central Committee Documents* (1929), there is a problem here, since the report of March 20, 1929, translated above, states that the victorious battle against Liu Shiyi's brigade took place on February 11. (See paragraph 9 of the March 20 document.)

11. In the Chinese text, a closing parenthesis appears here, but since there is no indication as to where the opening parenthesis should be, we have omitted this one.

12. The text of this report that appears in the *Bujuan* is made up of fragmentary extracts, so in general there would be no point in indicating the variants. It might be noted, however, that the abbreviated version contains at this point the following curious passage: "The most important thing at present is to get the popular masses themselves to rise up. Only then can the Red Army join forces with them and fight, so as to win final victory."

11. The detailed circumstances of the Party in the Red Army have already been recounted in the copy of last year's November report sent on April 1 from Ruijin, which has been transmitted upward by the Fujian Provincial Committee and which you have undoubtedly perused already. Before November of last year, the whole army had an Army Party Bureau. After the November directive of the Central Committee,[13] we organized this Front Committee. The Front Committee set up Army Committees to deal with the Party bureaus at various levels (such branches included regimental committees, battalion committees, and company committees). In addition, as regards local Red Guards, the Front Committee, in addition to leading the Red Army, also provides leadership for the local Party offices. In January of this year, when the Fourth Army set out from the Hunan-Jiangxi Border Area to the Fujian-Jiangxi Border Area, marching or fighting battles every day, it found itself in a special situation. In these circumstances, and in order to deal with them, it was felt that the system of army committees was too cumbersome, so the decision was taken that the army committees should temporarily cease to function, power was concentrated in the Front Committee, and committees were organized under the direct control of the Front Committee. Now, because the time has grown longer, and the size of the Red Army has grown greatly as compared with what it was previously, and the Front Committee cannot keep track of everything, it has been decided to organize a supreme Party office for the army, with Comrade Liu Angong as secretary and head of the Political Department. Some defects which had manifested themselves within the army are now in the process of being progressively improved.

Now let us report that as of May, the important statistics for the First, Second, and Third Columns of the Fourth Red Army, and for those military units directly subordinated to the Party in the army, are as follows:

a) Number of Party members, 1,329.

b) Total number of personnel: officers, 330; combatant soldiers, 734; noncombatant soldiers, 188; support personnel, 68.

c) Statistics on comrades being developed: officers, 9; combatant soldiers, 99; noncombatant soldiers, 9; support personnel, 10.

d) Statistics regarding age: below the age of 18, 95; from 19 to 23, 544; from 31 to 40, 179; under 48, 48.

e) Statistics regarding social origins: workers, 311; peasants, 626; small merchants, 106; students, 192; others, 95.

These statements manifestly correspond rather to the viewpoint of Li Lisan than to Mao's position at this time. Perhaps they were mixed up with Mao's own words when portions of his report were quoted in communications of the Central Committee.

13. Although the Chinese text here speaks of a "November Directive," what is actually meant is "after the receipt, on November 2, of the Central Committee letter of June 4, 1928." As indicated above, in the Introduction, it was then that Mao was able to re-establish the Front Committee, with himself in charge.

f) Statistics regarding punishment of comrades: exhortation, 29; warning, 96; placed under investigation, 10; dismissed, 31; total, 166.

g) Statistics regarding activists: members of branch committees, 65; group leaders, 123; group members, 200; total, over 500.

h) Statistics regarding comrades wounded and killed: officers, 6 wounded and 3 killed; combatant soldiers, 9 wounded and 5 killed.

Since submitting our previous letter, we sent another letter on April 1 from Ruijin, enclosing with it a letter from Comrade Peng and a copy of the detailed report of November of last year. We do not know whether these have all been received by the Central Committee or not. On reaching Yudu,[14] we learned of the Central Committee's letter to all the comrades, and Central Circulars Nos. 15 and 20.[15] While we were in Xingguo, we produced several thousand lithographed copies of these and distributed them to the Red Army and to the Party bureaus in various localities. Comrade Liu Angong has not yet begun work, but we have heard a detailed oral report. On May 20 in Ruijin we received a letter from the Central Military Commission to the Front Committee, and on reaching Longyan, we also received Central Circular No. 34,[16] a small pamphlet from the World Trade Union Movement, and the Central Committee's "Declaration to the Masses Regarding the Wars between Chiang and Guangxi."

Apart from this, we have also received a small pamphlet from the Fujian Provincial Committee "On the Political and Economic Situation in Western Fujian and the Party's Policy Now and in the Future," and periodicals such as *Liehuo* (Fierce Fire). For a long time we have been in the remote mountains and inaccessible valleys, and our communications with the outside world have been cut off. It has truly been an unexpected pleasure to receive recently the various directives from the Central Committee and the Fujian Provincial Committee. Only the Jiangxi Provincial Committee has not had a single word for us during the past three years. The last two times we have come to southern Jiangxi, when Comrade Luo Shounan has brought documents to us from the Central Committee, he arrived empty-handed, because the documents had been retained by the Jiangxi Provincial Committee. This is an extremely bad situation, and we request the Central Committee to instruct the Jiangxi Provincial Committee that they absolutely must correct it.

13. What was reported in the newspapers about how we killed people and burned places down runs totally counter to the facts. For example, during our

---

14. The Chinese text here reads *Yubu* instead of *Yudu*. We assume this to be a typographical error.

15. The reference is to Circular No. 15 of November 8, 1928, "The Current Political Situation and Mass Work," and Circular No. 20, issued in early December 1928, "The Imperialist Invasion of China. . . . " The texts of these can be found in *Central Committee Documents* (1928), pp. 689–94 and 723–46.

16. Circular No. 34, "Guidelines for the Work of Opposing the Warlord Wars," April 10, 1929, can be found in *Central Committee Documents* (1929), pp. 110–25.

seventeen days in Tingzhou, we have raised only 20,000 [*yuan*] from the big merchants and 30,000 from the despotic gentry and landlords. Their propaganda said that we collected several hundred thousand. Only five people were killed, all of them most reactionary (from the camp of Guo Fengwu). The Changting Revolutionary Committee burned four, and the Red Army burned one, but their propaganda said that more than five hundred houses had been burned. Only three or four of Guo Fengwu's diehard followers were killed, but their propaganda said that more than a thousand people were killed. In sum, this is all nonsense and unworthy of credence. It has already become an article of faith that in order to kill people and burn houses, there must be a mass basis. It can be said that there has been no burning or killing by the army on its own.

14. At present the most pressing need in the Red Army is for personnel. Because of the long period of struggles, our losses have been very great, and officers and political workers are severely lacking at all levels. Our only hope is that the Center will send us some. We now request that the Central Committee send, within a very short time, a hundred middle- and lower-ranking officers and a hundred lower-level political workers, as well as several doctors and several bomb-makers. We also need five higher-ranking officers and five high-level political workers within the next month. Comrades Zhu and Mao can leave the ranks at any time; we must simply ask the Central Committee to send replacements.[17] The people who come can be escorted here by the Fujian Provincial Committee.

15. We request that the Fujian Provincial Committee take responsibility for setting up an organ for communication in Xiamen,[18] with exclusive responsibility for transmitting [messages] between the Front Committee and the Central Committee. The expenses for setting up this organ are being sent in the form of

---

17. As noted in the Introduction, this had been the peremptory demand of the Central Committee in its February 1929 letter to Mao and Zhu. In his initial reaction to this order, while rejecting the Central Committee's other idea of breaking up the Red Army into small units and scattering them in all the villages, Mao had indicated his willingness, and that of Zhu De, to leave the army if "capable replacements" could be sent. (See above, the translation of Mao's letter of April 5, 1929.) Perhaps he only reiterated here his readiness to accept reassignment because by this time he had received the Central Committee's letter of April 7, mentioned in the Introduction, indicating that this sacrifice would not be required of him "for the time being." On the other hand, he returned to this theme two weeks later, stressing not only his "lack of wisdom," but his physical weakness. (See below, the letter to Lin Biao of June 15, 1929.) Moreover, as indicated in the Introduction, Mao proceeded to spend five months recuperating in a hospital for an ill-defined illness, from late June to late November, though he continued to direct the work of the Western Fujian Special Committee during this interlude. Though the problem remains obscure, one point can be asserted with confidence: in the long term, Mao had no intention of giving up control of the army he had helped create.

18. Xiamen, commonly called Amoy in English-language sources, is located on the coast of Fujian not very far from the localities in which the Red Army was operating at this time.

10,000 *yuan* worth of opium, to be transmitted by the Longyan *Xian* Committee. As to how it is to be transported, kindly instruct the Longyan Committee.

16. Because the Red Army has been fighting for a long time, not only are the officers and the political workers extraordinarily starved for knowledge, but they also display mental fatigue. In order to alleviate the fatigue of the Red Army and prepare personnel for the future, the Fourth Red Army has designated twenty-two people to study in Russia, who will set off as soon as replacements are sent by the Central Committee. These twenty-two have already been selected by the Front Committee, as listed in a separate letter, to which we hope for a speedy reply!

We will report subsequently on the situation regarding propaganda!

Mao Zedong, Secretary of the Front Committee

Proclamation of the Fourth Red Army Headquarters and Political Department

(June 1929)

To be publicly announced. Our Red Army, under the guidance of the Communist Party, carries out the three great tasks of the democratic revolution, to overthrow imperialism, to overthrow the landlord class, and to overthrow the Guomindang government, under the guiding principle of helping the workers and peasants and all oppressed classes to attain liberation. Today the Guomindang is rent by disunity, chaotic warfare among Chiang Kaishek, the Guangxi faction, Feng Yuxiang, and Yan Xishan is going on all over the country, and the reactionary government has been shaken to its foundations. Throughout the country, workers, peasants, soldiers, and the oppressed petty bourgeoisie are joining together to make revolution, in increasing numbers and increasing strength. In every province and every *xian*, every village and every town, there is a great deal of activity, of soldiers organizing Red armies, of workers organizing labor unions, of peasants organizing peasant associations. Our army has come to this place, knowing that the people are suffering bitterly, that the price of grain is very dear, that interest rates are very high, that rents are very heavy, and that there are a multitude of harsh fees. The local bullies and bad gentry control everything, using the clan temples and public associations to cheat and oppress all poor people of all families. These local bullies and bad gentry are no more than a few out of every hundred people. The great majority of the people should join together and overthrow these despotic gentry, for the benefit of the majority of the people. The most urgent things that must be done now are listed below.

1. In the case of large landlords who receive rents of 200 *Dan* or more, all their household grain and public association grain (except for that of the welfare granary) shall be confiscated without compensation and distributed among the poor peasants. The small landlords with rental incomes of less than 200 *Dan* must sell their household grain at a reduced price, to be fixed at one-half the original price per *Dan*. (Grain that merchants have imported from other places, however, shall not be included under this item.)

2. All debts that workers and peasants owe to landlords shall be canceled

---

Our source for this proclamation is *Mao Zedong ji. Bujuan*, Vol. 3, pp. 57–58, where it is taken from documentary collections published in 1979 and 1982.

without repayment. (Debts incurred among merchants, or among workers and peasants, shall not be included under this item.)

3. Beginning this year, ownership of the fields shall revert to the peasants who till them, and rent shall no longer be paid to landlords.

4. Eliminate all harsh fees, miscellaneous taxes, *lijin*,[1] and land taxes.

5. The labor unions organized by workers, the peasant associations organized by peasants, and the revolutionary committees organized by workers and peasants together, shall seize the guns of the counterrevolutionaries and organize worker and peasant Red Guard units.

6. All local bullies and bad gentry who regularly oppress the workers and peasants, or obstruct the revolution, or who have not accounted for public funds that have passed through their hands, can be arrested by the peasant associations, and in accordance with the severity of their crimes, may be sentenced to punishments such as death, imprisonment, physical punishment, fines, parading in public, or writing a confession of their sins.

The above six items shall be implemented immediately upon being posted. If there are those who object, and who seek some personal gain for themselves and obstruct the public interests of the great majority of the people, they are counterrevolutionaries, and these evil persons should be rooted out without mercy. Heed this proclamation.

> Commander of the Army: Zhu De
> Party Representative: Mao Zedong
> Head of the Political Department: Chen Yi
> June [X], 1929

---

1. The transportation tax on goods moved within the country, commonly transcribed *likin* in English-language sources of the period.

Letter to Lin Biao[1]

(June 14, 1929)

Comrade Lin Biao:

1. I am greatly moved by your letter,[2] and my courage is strengthened because you are bravely moving forward. I will work with you and all the comrades who are for the unity of the Party and the advancement of the revolution against all harmful views, habits, and systems. The question under dispute at present is not a question which concerns one individual or a particular moment. It is a question concerning the entire Party of the Fourth Army and the struggle which has been going on for a year. Previously, it was, however, concealed for various reasons, and it has been exposed only recently. In fact, the past concealment was wrong, and the current exposure is the only proper course. When controversy arises over questions within the Party, this represents progress for

---

We have translated this letter from *Mao Zedong wenji*, Vol. 1, pp. 64-75, where the source is given as a mimeographed copy in the Party archives. It does not appear to have been published previously.

1. Lin Biao (1907–1971), original name Yuyong, was a native of Hubei. After graduating from middle school in 1925, he joined the Communist Youth League in Shanghai and thus gained admission to the fourth class at the Whampoa Military Academy. After participating in the Northern Expedition under the command of Ye Ting, he joined, in August 1927, in the Nanchang Uprising, of which Ye was one of the principal leaders. In the course of the retreat from Nanchang, he followed Zhu De and Chen Yi to the Jiangxi-Guangdong-Hunan Border Area at the end of 1927 and went up the Jinggangshan with Zhu De in the spring of 1928. Earlier in 1929, he had played a role in the battles at Dabodi and Shanghang, described by Mao in texts translated above. At this time, he was commander of the First Column of the Fourth Red Army.

2. Serious tensions had developed at this time between Mao Zedong and Zhu De, and according to accounts recently published in China, Lin Biao did his utmost to exacerbate the conflict. The letter to which Mao is responding here had been sent by Lin Biao only a few hours before the Baisha meeting of June 8, 1929. The text of Lin's letter is not available to us, but its main theme was the overweening ambitions of "certain comrades," meaning Zhu De. See Jin Chongji, *Zhu De zhuan* (Biography of Zhu De) (Beijing: Zhongyang wenxian chubanshe, 1993), pp. 175–80 (hereafter Jin, *Zhu De*). At the Baisha meeting, the Army Committee was abolished, leaving the Front Committee in sole control, and this decision was confirmed two weeks later at the Seventh Congress of Party Representatives from the Fourth Red Army. On the latter occasion, however, Mao lost his leading position as secretary of the Front Committee. For more details regarding these events, see the Introduction to this volume.

the Party, not retrogression. It is retrogression only if one compromises, muddles through, and erases the line between the two sides, thereby reducing important matters to insignificance in a vulgar way. I think this time it will not lead to fearful and evil consequences. Only a few days after the Baisha conference,[3] the question has already been hotly debated among the masses in the Party. I think our comrades will definitely demand a thorough clarification of this question and will definitely refuse to compromise, sit on the fence, and be blind to the distinction between right and wrong. They will certainly be able to choose and support a view that promotes the unity of the Party and the advancement of the revolution. There is absolutely no doubt that through this the work of transforming the Fourth Army can be completed, and as a result the Party of the Fourth Army can make extremely great progress.

2. One cannot understand the origins of the current debate without knowing the history of the struggle in the Fourth Army. Without an understanding of this origin, one cannot understand the nature of the entire problem in the struggle between two different systems of thought since the initiation of the Fourth Army. Among the key points of this problem are the following: (1) individual leadership and Party leadership; (2) the military point of view and the political point of view; (3) cliquism and anti-cliquism; (4) the roving rebel mentality and the anti-roving-rebel mentality; (5) the question of political power in the middle section of the Luoxiao Mountain Range; (6) the question of local armed forces; (7) urban policy and the question of Red Army discipline; (8) the assessment of the current situation; (9) the defeat in southern Hunan; (10) the question of a scientific approach,[4] and of regularization; (11) the question of military skills in the Fourth Army; (12) formalism and utilitarianism; (13) the separation of powers and the concentration of power; (14) other decadent ideas. Let me speak about them below.

3. The main question for the Party of the Fourth Army is that of individual leadership and Party leadership. To discuss this question, we must first of all remember that the greater part of the Fourth Army was born out of the old army. Moreover, it was brought forth in an environment of defeat. If we remember these two points, we can then understand why all the ideas, habits, and systems are so difficult to change and why Party leadership and individual leadership are always in opposition,[5] and have long been in a state of conflict. Since the Red Army emerged from the transformation of the old army, it brought with it a conflict between supporters of all the old ideas, old habits, and old systems and some who fight against these ideas, habits, and systems. This is the first reason why up to now it has not yet been possible to establish absolute Party leadership

---

3. The conference of June 8, 1929, mentioned above, which was held in Baisha, Shanghang *xian*, Fujian.

4. *Kexuehua*, literally, making scientific.

5. Here eight or nine characters are missing from the mimeographed text held in the Party Archives in Beijing.

in the Fourth Army. Moreover, the greater part of the Fourth Army emerged in an environment of defeat (this was in 1927), and the Party organization that put it together was the one from before the defeat, which was extremely weak in the first place and lost the leadership completely in the course of the defeat. It can be said that survival at the time depended nine times out of ten solely on the leadership of the individual. It is this which created the enormous power of the individual leader. That is the second reason why it has not been possible to establish absolute Party leadership in the Fourth Army. Having understood these two causes, if we then look again at the history of the Fourth Army since it was organized, we can understand the central factor in the ebb and flow of the struggle between the individual and the Party. Since the Fourth Army was established, the Party has established a basis everywhere at the company level and above. Now that the policy of the higher leading bodies (the Special Committee of the Hunan-Jiangxi Border Area and the Fourth Army's Army Committee and Front Committee) is correct, and with the establishment of local Party branches in the various *xian* of the border region, and the development of the mass struggle, the role of the individual has been gradually reduced, and the leadership of the Party has been strengthened. In general, this can be divided into three periods. The first period is from the creation of the Fourth Army to September of last year, when we returned to the border area. It includes the victories in a series of battles in the border area and the defeat in southern Hunan. In this period, the Party was unable to wield the absolute power of command. Cliquism existed widely and was on the rise. The Party dared not attempt to allocate and transfer the guns. There were clashes between the principle of giving attention to all aspects of the rear area of the Red Army and the selfish departmentalism of a minority of Red Army comrades. It was not possible to establish a system of military supplies or regulations regarding the organization of the army. Individual control over politics and weapons was common. From the company to the corps, the Party as it existed at that time was in reality in a subordinate position, and regarding certain issues, it was absolutely obliged to accept the orders of an individual.

The second period was from last September, when we returned to the border area, to March 14 [1929], when we took Tingzhou. During this period, the Party was first able to criticize[6] cliquism theoretically (even though it still could not really do it). A system of military supplies was set up. The system of seventy-five long-barreled guns per company was set up.[7] But it did not yet extend to short-barreled guns.[8] It was not so difficult as in the first period to transfer guns to the localities. In this period, a minority of comrades tried hard to bow their heads, and the Party was really in a commanding position. This was so in general

---

6. The Chinese text here reads *jianshe* (establish), but the editors in Beijing regard this as an obvious typographical error for *piping* (criticize).

7. After this clause, seven or eight characters are missing from the original.

8. Here approximately thirty characters are missing.

from the Party branch to the Front Committee. There were several obvious characteristics during this period: First, in the situation created by the Hunan defeat and the flight of most of the remaining forces, the individual did not manifest much effective leadership. At the same time, unlike the first period, when there was a series of military victories, now there was the possibility of collapse if we did not rely on Party leadership. This is the first reason why Party leadership gained ground. Second, during this period, as compared to the first period, there was indeed some progress in Party organization, as well as in the political consciousness and experience of struggle among the comrades. It was more difficult for the incorrect words and actions of a minority of comrades to gain support from the rank and file. As a result, these people had to restrain themselves somewhat. This is the second reason why Party leadership gained ground. Third, in this period, we encountered two fresh friendly forces: the Fifth Army[9] and the Second and Fourth Regiments.[10] The Fifth Army could not influence the Fourth Army much, but it did provide some stimulus to the Fourth Army in smashing cliquism. Particularly at the Bolu Meeting,[11] in discussing the merging of the Fourth and Fifth Armies, Comrade Peng Dehuai's indignant remarks dealt quite a blow to the minority of comrades. As for the Second and Fourth Regiments, the comrades of the Fourth Army were truly ashamed to see them. Their political instructors exercised authority over the officers. In the first five registers,[12] the names of the officers were placed after those of the political instructors. They cannot allocate one bullet without asking the Party. They have absolute Party leadership. This can also be identified as a factor which helped to strengthen the leadership of the Party in the Fourth Army.

The third period is from Tingzhou to the present. During this period, the Party and the Red Army have truly progressed in all areas as compared to the previous situation. Because of the establishment of the First, Second, and Third Columns, cliquism really began to weaken. The column committees were somewhat more effective than the Front Committee. Party branches at all levels could discuss various issues without misgivings. The number of short-barreled guns could also be regulated. The establishment of the Political Department also limited the authority of the Headquarters. These are the organizational aspects. As far as the political line is concerned, an effort could be made in their work to carry out the

---

9. The Fifth Army, under the command of Peng Dehuai, reached the Jinggangshan base and joined forces with the Fourth Army in December 1928.

10. The Second and Fourth Independent Regiments of the Jiangxi Red Army joined forces with the Fourth Army in Ji'an in February 1929.

11. The reference is to a meeting convened in Bolu, Ninggang *xian*, January 4–7, 1929, with the participation of the Front Committee of the Fourth Red Army, the Border Area Special Committee, the Army Committees of the Fourth and Fifth Armies, and the various *xian* committees of the border area.

12. Here the Chinese has *ce*, meaning "roll" or "register." The Beijing editors suggest that the reference is to *huamingce*, "muster roll."

political tasks delineated at the Sixth Congress.[13] Urban policy was somewhat better applied. Progress was made in propaganda. They learned the tactics of large-scale guerrilla warfare. As a result of the development of the situation, the organization of the Red Army was also expanded. But because the will of the Party was very greatly extended, the will of the individual underwent unprecedented suffering. Then there were several military victories in a row, and a formalistic theory arrived from afar. These three factors combined to bring about the outbreak of the current dispute. The focal point of the controversy is whether we still need the Party branch in the present-day army. Because a minority of comrades firmly insisted on having an army committee, they had to attack the Front Committee. This in turn impinged on the question of the Party organization itself. The slogans of their attack were "the Party runs too many things" and "power is too much concentrated in the Front Committee." When, in the course of the controversies, the discussion touched on the work of the Party branch, some said that the branch should be concerned only with the education of the comrades. This also arose from the question of the sphere of the Party's authority. Because they advocated that the sphere of the Party's interference should be restricted, they had to demand limits on the work of the Party branch as well. With the expansion of the will of the Party, and the restriction of the will of the individual, all questions had to be the subject of resolutions by Party meetings at various levels. Only then could the Party members as individuals carry out their work according to those resolutions. Thus the individual did not enjoy the freedom of the hero.[14] As a result, their demand for considerable freedom found expression in such slogans as "Do we have to ask the Party even about one gun?" and "Should the Party take care of the groom when he runs out of things to eat?" deriding the work of the Party bureaus regarding minute details. Such are the views they expressed at the Hulei meeting of the Front Committee.[15] Although the questions under discussion were divided into three (the scope of the Party's power, the work of the Party branch, and the lack of freedom for the individual), the spirit was the same throughout. This is the concrete manifestation of the struggle for supremacy between Party leadership and the leadership of the individual. Since the recent controversies emerged, some comrades have felt that the Party in the Fourth Army has arrived at a crisis. If the individualist leadership exercised by a minority of comrades is victorious, the result, as you said in your letter, will inevitably be that the close unity of the Party will be disrupted and the future prospects of the revolution will be harmed. But I am confident it will not

---

13. I.e., at the Sixth Congress of the Chinese Communist Party, held in Moscow in June 1928, of which word had reached Mao and his comrades in January 1929.

14. This comment cannot fail to call to mind Mao's advocacy in earlier years, inspired by Nietzsche, of the idea of the hero. See especially, in Volume I of this edition, his comments on Paulsen, pp. 263–64.

15. This was a meeting of the Front Committee of the Fourth Army held at the end of May 1929 in Hulei, Yongding *xian*, Fujian.

come to this, because the Party of the Fourth Army at present has made obvious progress since the first and second periods. The foundations of the various columns can no longer be shaken. Decisions based on the selfish desires of the individual will be rejected by the masses. We need only look at the fact that at a meeting attended by forty-one people,[16] the Army Committee which a minority of comrades obstinately insisted on establishing was abolished by a vote of thirty-six to five in order to see that the majority will definitely not support their demand, which is "harmful to solidarity and harmful to the revolution." The struggle between individualism and anti-individualism, that is to say, between individual leadership and Party leadership, is the main thread that runs through the history of the Fourth Army. Generally speaking, on the following questions (each one of them), there are none on which there are not diametrically opposed viewpoints. Let us simply try to list them.

4. Some comrades in the Fourth Army have always been partial to the military viewpoint and are at odds with those who adopt a political viewpoint, that is to say, a mass viewpoint. This is a serious problem concerning the political line. Thanks to long-term experience of struggle, and the influence of the worker-peasant masses, the brains entertaining this simplistic viewpoint have been gradually washed clean to some extent. The simplistic mentality of "fighting big battles" and "taking dozens of *zhou* and *xian*" has become less common, but has not been completely eliminated. It raises its head at every opportunity. Particularly at times of military defeat, [such people hold that] everything else can be eliminated, and it is all right as long as you keep the guns. At meetings, what these comrades hate most is the discussion of questions of propaganda and organization. In guerrilla work, they try to develop military influence alone, not political influence. The cliquism left over from the warlord armies is one of the problems that does the most harm to the Red Army. And yet a minority of comrades are not only unwilling to strive vigorously to eliminate cliquism but even have a tendency to encourage it. If we do not eliminate cliquism, it will be impossible to have completely collective leadership by the Party as they do in the Second and Fourth Regiments, and then the Red Army will be nothing but a fine-sounding name!

The mentality of roving rebel bands has always been very powerful in the Red Army. Its source is to be found in the component of vagrants in the Fourth Army. The Party has already waged many struggles against this mentality, but a remnant of it still exists today, and even now those who formerly represented this mentality cannot be said to have abandoned it. The most striking political manifestation of this mentality of roving rebel bands lies in the dissident views on the problem of political power in the middle section of the Luoxiao Mountain Range. We must not forget that the unanimity within the Party in the Fourth Army regarding the question of the independent régime in the Hunan-Jiangxi Border Area is merely superficial. In their hearts, some of the comrades are constantly prepared to abandon the struggle in the border area. Whenever there is

---

16. I.e., the Baisha meeting referred to in note 2 above.

a crisis, these comrades immediately. . . . [17] All those who have participated in the struggle in the Hunan-Jiangxi Border Area understand this. The question of establishing a military force in the Hunan-Jiangxi Border Area has always ended in a struggle because it involves transferring guns from the Red Army. This is a manifestation of opposing views coming out of two different political lines—that of the military viewpoint and that of the mass viewpoint. The component of vagrants in the Red Army produced the mentality of roving rebel bands. At the same time, it has affected urban policy and the discipline of the Red Army. It is also evident that responsible comrades have put forward different views. According to one view, it does not matter much if military discipline is disrupted to some extent, or a city is smashed up a bit. The other view is just the opposite. As regards the matter of disrupting military discipline, some comrades feel that it would be better not to have this recent victory than to have our discipline broken. Other comrades do not feel so concerned and merely dismiss the matter with a sigh of regret. This is only the most recent example. In the past, there were many such instances. The question of military discipline is a big political question for the Red Army, but because one group of people advocates rigor while another group advocates laxity, the result is rather negative. As regards the psychology of the masses, the effect is rather harmful, because the majority behave [badly], and only a minority behave well.

On the assessment of the current situation, too, there have always been divergent views. As a result, views regarding the actions of the Red Army also differ. This was particularly striking when we were in the border area. Most comrades do recognize that it was a mistake for the greater part of the forces of the Fourth Army to go to southern Hunan in July of last year. The meeting of delegates at Shatian also recognized this. Who could have predicted that a bizarre view would arise recently among a minority of comrades saying that it was right to go to southern Hunan and that it was, in contrast, wrong to stay in the border area? This is another example of diametrically opposing views.

A Communist really must be a bit more scientific in his thinking and actions. Yet some comrades place themselves in direct opposition to the scientific attitude, so that we can find many contradictions in a single speech or a single action. When they speak, they are wholly unconcerned about the effect of what they say. They just shoot off their mouths at random, paying no attention to right and wrong. "Say whatever you like. They only understand so much." What an unscientific attitude! An army that wants to progress even a little must regulate itself. We can only regard a "messy rotten" situation such as that which formerly prevailed in the Red Army as a phenomenon characteristic of primitive ranks of vagrants. We must struggle against it with the utmost force. Yet it is clear that some of the comrades, intentionally or unintentionally, support such a phenomenon, or at least they do not have the resolve to fight against it. This has hitherto

---

17. Here three or four characters are missing in the original.

made it impossible for the Red Army to establish a pattern. It lags far behind the bourgeois armies, and that is truly a sad phenomenon.

"Rotten cowhide is not rotten cowhide. Spoiled bean curd is not spoiled bean curd." These are the angry words Comrade Zhu Yunqing[18] used to describe the grossly deficient military skills of the Fourth Army. Of all those who have sojourned in the Fourth Army, there is probably no one who does not recognize that the military skills in the Fourth Army are highly deficient. But some comrades do not want to pay attention to their own main task of officer training, but engage in some political agitation every day, uttering strange words like "What is there to do if we cannot attack the despotic gentry?" If this situation does not change, there is no way the problem of poor military skills in the Fourth Army can be solved.

5. In recent days, the most obvious manifestation of the two opposing views has been the controversy regarding the Army Committee. A minority of comrades insist on having an Army Committee. What they really want is to have a leading Party organ in their hands, in order to provide scope for the manifestation of their long-suppressed ambitions (which represent yet another guiding line, different from that of the past). Yet they give grave and ceremonious reasons, which unfortunately are merely formalistic. They say "if the name is the Fourth Army, there should be an Army Committee." "To complete the organizational system requires an Army Committee." Is this not an utterly formalistic mode of expression? At present, we have only a small army of somewhat more than four thousand. We do not have many "armies," as the Central Committee has many provinces under it. Moreover, the guerrilla period, in which the army is often on the march, is quite unlike the period of the border area, when the army was often garrisoned, and demands swift and centralized army command. A minority of comrades do not consider these practical reasons at all. They are just obstinately resolved to insert formalistically an Army Committee between the Front Committee above and the Column Committee below. Everyone knows we don't really need it, when the people are the same and the work is the same. Yet a minority of comrades have exerted their utmost efforts,[19] insisting that it must absolutely be set up. What actually is the reason for all this? If you want to search out a reason, I can only say that this is the synthesis of all the wrong lines practiced by a minority of comrades in the past and the final struggle between two guiding lines. We can easily understand the true meaning of this debate if we have a clear understanding of the history of the Fourth Army.

To set up a new leading organization, the Army Committee, they had to dig out the old reasons to attack the old leading organizations, the Front Committee and the Party branches. The most specific arguments put forward in their attack

---

18. Zhu Yunqing (1907–1931), a native of Guangdong, was a graduate of the Whampoa Military Academy. He joined the Chinese Communist Party in 1925 and served on the Jinggangshan. At this time he was chief political adviser to the Fourth Army.

19. Literally, "have exerted the force of nine oxen and two tigers."

are: (1) that the Party has replaced the mass organizations; (2) that there is a patriarchal system within the Party in the Fourth Army. But these attacks, too, lapse completely into formalism. From the very beginning of the Party in the Fourth Army, it has been strictly forbidden to replace the mass organizations with those of the Party. As regards the worker and peasant organizations under the leadership of the Front Committee, there has never been an instance in which a Party branch has replaced a workers' or peasants' association. As for the soldiers' organizations, there has never been an instance in which the Party branch of any company replaced the soldiers' committee of that company. Everyone in the Fourth Army who has eyes has seen all this. As for a Party bureau or organ replacing a mass organ or an administrative organ, for example, the replacement of the Column Soldiers' Committee, the Column Headquarters, or the Column Political Department by the Column Committee, or the replacement of the Army Soldiers' Committee, the Army Headquarters, or the Army Political Department by the Front Committee, these things have never happened, either. But here also the formalism of a minority of comrades has manifested itself. They say that even though the organs of the Party bureau have not replaced the mass organs or the administrative organs, the Column Headquarters, in fact, rarely report to the Army Headquarters and that the Army Headquarters is now treated lightly. This minority of comrades does not understand that this represents the difference between formalism and utilitarianism. The leadership of the Column Committee and the Front Committee having been strengthened, all questions (whichever ones they want to raise) can be raised at the meetings, discussed, and resolved. Afterward, the responsible comrades in the administrative organs will be notified and will carry out these resolutions. Otherwise, it can be called acting on one's own (as in the arbitrary allocation of financial resources, guns and ammunition, and so on). This sort of thing is an example of the strengthening of Party leadership. We have to admit that this represents progress. At every meeting, the responsible comrades from the administrative organs are always present and voice their opinions. Moreover, many questions can be discussed only if they are raised by these responsible comrades (for example, battle plans, training plans for officers and soldiers, etc.). Everybody has participated in the discussion and voting on these questions, and afterward the decisions are carried out. As a result, it is felt that the administrative organs have become somewhat simpler and freer. In reality, what is so bad about that? The army commander is not so busy, but the Party representative (who is quite distinct from the secretary of the Party committee) has even less to do, because the Party representatives at the lower levels do not send reports to him. The Column Headquarters sends few reports to the Army Headquarters, but the Political Department of the column sends even fewer reports to the Political Department of the army. Not taking into account the comparison between the recent situation and the arbitrary allocation which prevailed earlier in the administration; not considering whether the present system leads to more results in the work and is more convenient for struggle than in the earlier period of frenzied activity—the first stage of the Hunan-Jianxi Border Area when there were many more reports; judging not on the basis of practical needs, but on the basis of mere outward forms—what kind of Communist attitude is this? Let me just ask, if it does not work in practice, no matter how much better it looks in terms of form, what use is it? As for the accusations against the Action Committee of the Hunan-Jiangxi Border Area, they do not consider how many results the system of the Action Committee achieved in the border area, they merely opine in formal terms that the Party organization replaced the administrative organ and that this was a bad thing. This is another formalistic error. If this formalism continues to develop, in all matters the results will not be considered, but only the form, and this will be unspeakably dangerous. Everyone who has eyes to see understands that the Action Committee system achieved very great results in the struggle in the border area. Moreover, the Action Committee functions, on the one hand, as an internal Party bureau and, on the other hand, as an open administrative office. Why would this in any way hamper the system of administrative organs?

As for the attack on the patriarchal system within the Party in the Fourth Army, this is also a formalistic observation. Here we must first ask what a patriarchal system is. Only then can we know if there is such a system in the Fourth Army. Otherwise, casual and thoughtless comments will assuredly not correspond to the facts. The definition of a patriarchal system is that there are only orders from individuals, no collective discussion; there are only appointments from above, not elections by the masses. If everyone agrees with this definition, let us see if there exists within the Party of the Fourth Army what this definition describes. We will then know whether there is a patriarchal system or not. Collective discussion in the Party of the Fourth Army, from the Party branch to the Front Committee, has always existed. At Party meetings at every level, particularly the two levels of the Front Committee and the Column Committee, whether it is a general meeting or a meeting of the members of the standing committee, on virtually every occasion there are present, besides the committee members who are required to be there, comrades in responsible positions who are not committee members. If some comrades of the minority are forgetful, they can check the minutes of the meetings of all the columns (the Third Column has a complete set of minutes since May of last year; not a single one is missing) and of the Front Committee (the minutes are available starting with this year, and none are missing). On the important questions, such as the discussion about leaving the Jinggangshan, the separation of our forces in Donggu, or the current debate and the separation of forces, we have always sought the opinions of the masses. There are simply no grounds for saying that within the Party of the Fourth Army there are only orders by individuals and no collective discussion. As for the process by which the various leading organs were created, from the detachment[20] committees to the col-

---

20. A detachment at this time was a guerrilla unit roughly comparable in size to a battalion in the Chinese regular army.

umn committees and the Front Committee, they were appointed by the Central Committee. But this is no proof that a patriarchal system exists within the Party of the Fourth Army. In fact, one cannot find a patriarchal system within the Party of the Fourth Army. Why do the comrades of the minority use this excuse? What is the objective origin of this kind of talk? It is true that in the Fourth Army there is the system which allows the Party secretary to serve concurrently as the Red Army Party representative. Some comrades do not distinguish clearly that the Party representative and the secretary are two different things as regards their functions. Because the spheres of competence of the Party representatives and of the military commanders have never been fully clarified, the problem of a struggle for power frequently arises. This has led some muddle-headed people to regard the Party representative working in a certain place as the Party secretary working there. This is why comrades in several companies of the Third Column called the Party secretary of their company "boss." This mistake can be eliminated only by separating the Party representative from the Party secretary. This can be done by searching for people from within, on the one hand, and by looking at the same time for more people from the outside, on the other. (The concurrent posts in the past were the result of the fact that we had very few qualified people. Everyone knows this.) The source of formalism lies in idealism. Idealism comes from individualism that originates in the categories of the vagrants, the peasantry, and the petty bourgeoisie. This is based on the same line as cliquism, the roving rebel mentality, the purely military viewpoint, and so on. All these are one and the same thing. Another aspect of the development of this kind of thinking will assuredly lead to the doctrine of the separation of powers—another way of thinking which represents the vagrants, the peasantry, and the petty bourgeoisie. This is completely incompatible with the fighting organizations of the proletariat, whether it be the class organization—trade unions—or the vanguard organization of the class—the Communist Party—or its military organization—the Red Army. This is why the form of separation of powers should not be allowed to exist in the Army Committee and the Front Committee.

Vaingloriousness, boasting, the ideology of the hero, and other decadent ways of thinking all have their origin in individualism.

6. We are historical materialists. To get at the truth regarding any matter whatsoever, we have to investigate it both from the perspective of history and from the perspective of the circumstances. I have now raised the various aspects of the historical questions since the Fourth Army came into being to prove that the current question (the question of the Army Committee, but it is a question of principle) is merely a historical theme, the last struggle of a wrong ideological line in history. We should never forget the origins and composition of the Red Army. According to the statistics for May, of the 1,324 Party members in the Army, there are 311 workers, 626 peasants, 100 small businessmen, 192 students, and 95 others. The ratio of workers to nonworkers is 23 percent to 77

percent. When we discuss the thinking of an individual, we should not forget his class origin, his educational background, and his work history. This is the attitude toward research of a Communist. Manifestly, there exists in the Party of the Fourth Army an incorrect ideology based on the peasants, the vagrants, and the petty bourgeoisie. This ideology is harmful to the solidarity of the Party and the future of the revolution. It runs the risk of deviating from the proletarian revolutionary standpoint. We must fight against this ideology (it is mainly a question of thought, the rest is a small matter)[21] and overcome this ideology in order to pursue the thoroughgoing transformation of the Red Army. We should oppose without hesitation everything that hampers the elimination of old, decadent thinking and the transformation of the Red Army. This is the goal for which our comrades will struggle now and in the future.

As for my request to leave the Front Committee,[22] this does not mean I am passive and will not participate in this struggle. There are the following reasons:

1) I have done everything within my ability in the last two years to fight against the incorrect ideas within the Party. Now, after I have recounted the content of this question yet again, the majority of the comrades will be impelled to struggle ceaselessly. Only this will make it possible to achieve final victory.

2) I have stayed for too long in the Fourth Army. The effect produced by a certain historical position can be most unfavorable. This is the main reason I want to point out.

3) I myself am too weak physically and too poor in my wisdom and knowledge, so I hope that the Central Committee can send me to Moscow to study and rest for a while. Before receiving the permission of the Central Committee, the Front Committee can send me to do some work in the localities, so that I can improve myself with the change of environment.

4) The Party of the Fourth Army already has a relatively solid foundation. My departure will certainly not have any negative effect. Now that the split and the struggle in the ideology of the Party have begun, my departure can on no

---

21. Here seven or eight characters are missing from the original.

22. As indicated in the Introduction to this volume, Mao Zedong had received orders from the Central Committee in February 1929 to leave the army and come to Shanghai. In his letter of April 5 and in his report of June 1, translated above, Mao had agreed in principle to comply, though he probably had no intention of actually doing so. Here Mao goes a step farther than in his two previous communications, not only accepting the necessity of a transfer but suggesting that he himself had actually requested it. This may have been merely an attempt to save face, but he did suffer from illness at this time, as suggested in point 3 below, and went to a hospital to rest shortly after writing the present letter.

account prevent the goal of victory from being attained. So the worry expressed in the last section of your letter is excessive. Naturally, I can only express my views regarding my work. The decision will be made by the Party Bureau. Every day that I remain here will be a day on which I will fight with all of you in the ideological struggle!

C. salutations![23]

Mao Zedong
June 14, at Xinquan

---

23. Mao here uses the Roman letter C to stand for "Communist" in the Chinese text.

The War between Chiang Kaishek and the Guangxi Warlords

(To the Tune of "Clear Calm Music")[1]

(Autumn 1929)

A sudden shift in wind and clouds,
And the warlords have renewed their conflicts.
Scattering only enmity upon the world,
Yet another yellow millet dream is dreamt.[2]

Red flags have leapt across the Ting River,[3]
Straight down to Longyan and Shanghang.[4]
A piece of the golden cup[5] has been restored,
Now we are truly busy sharing out the land.

This poem was first published in *Renmin wenxue*, May 1962. We have translated it from *Shici duilian*, pp. 26-28.

1. When this poem was first published (along with five others) in *People's Literature*, each *ci* had a "tune title" but no subject title (for the convention of "tune title" [*cipai*], see note 1 to Mao's 1927 poem, "Autumn Harvest Uprising"). Under the general heading for all six poems, there appeared an "author's note," as follows: "These six *ci* were composed by humming them out on horseback between 1929 and 1931, and then were all forgotten. The comrades of the editorial board of *People's Literature* have collected them and sent them to me, wishing to publish them. I have made minor changes in them. April 27, 1962."

2. "Yellow millet dream," meaning something like "a pipe dream," comes from a popular story of the Tang dynasty in which a poor scholar who complains to a Daoist of his misfortunes is given a pillow upon which to lay his head and sleep. When he wakes from a dream of great fortune, the millet put on to cook before his nap is not yet done.

3. Tingzhou, which the Red Army had captured on March 14, 1929 (see, in particular, the report of March 20, 1929), is located on the Ting River in Fujian.

4. Longyan and Shanghang are *xian* in Fujian Province taken by the Red Fourth Army in May and June, 1929.

5. The image of a golden cup is used to signify the territorial integrity of the nation. (This metaphor is attributed to the first emperor of the Liang dynasty, during the period of the Northern and Southern dynasties.) Mao's idea is that, by setting up a soviet régime, he and his comrades had reclaimed at least a small fragment of the country for the real China.

Double Ninth Festival

(To the Tune of "Picking Mulberries")[1]

(October 1929)

Men grow old; heaven ages not,
Year after year comes the Double Ninth.
Today is Double Ninth again,
On the battlefield, yellow flowers[2] most fragrant.

Once a year comes the relentless autumn wind,
Resembling not the glories of spring.
And yet more glorious than spring,
River and sky a vast expanse, ten thousand leagues of frost.[3]

This is another of the six poems first published in *Renmin wenxue*, May 1962. We have translated it from *Shici duilian*, pp. 29–30.

1. The Double Ninth Festival occurs on the ninth day of the ninth month of the lunar calendar (in 1929 it fell on October 11) and is traditionally celebrated with feasting, mountain climbing, and chrysanthemum viewing.

2. I.e., chrysanthemums.

3. An allusion may be intended here to the chrysanthemum, for which one name is *shuangxia jie*, "hero under the frost."

Letter to Li Lisan[1]

(November 28, 1929)

Brother Lisan:

I haven't been in touch with you for quite a while. Only with Comrade Chen Yi's arrival[2] did I learn of your situation. I have been very ill for three months, and although I am better now, my spirits are not yet fully recovered. I often think of Kaihui, Anying,[3] and the others, and would like to communicate with them, but I don't know their mailing address. I've heard that Zemin[4] is in Shanghai. Please get in touch with him for me and ask him to tell me Kaihui's mailing address and to write to me.

I am terribly starved for knowledge. Please send me reading materials often, and if you can spare the time, I would be so grateful if you'd write me a letter with your excellent guidance.

We have translated this letter from *Mao Zedong shuxin xuanji*, pp. 28-29, where it is taken from a handwritten copy in the Party archives. It does not appear to have been published previously.

1. On Li Lisan, see the relevant biographical note to the Introduction to this volume. At the time, he held the positions of member of the Standing Committee of the Politburo, and chairman of the Propaganda Department of the Central Committee of the Chinese Communist Party, and was the dominant figure in the Party.

2. Chen Yi had been to Shanghai to report to the Central Committee and had been given both oral briefings and a directive dated September 28, 1929, addressed to the Front Committee of the Fourth Red Army. (For the text, see *Central Committee Documents* [1929], pp. 473–90.) Section 8 of this document, entitled "The Zhu-Mao problem," severely criticizes the political and ideological errors of Zhu De and Mao Zedong, as well as their defects in work style and their tendency to quarrel with one another, but concludes that, once they have "sincerely accepted the directive of the Central Committee," they should remain members of the Front Committee, and Mao should continue as its secretary.

3. The reference is to Mao's wife, Yang Kaihui, and their son, Mao Anying.

4. Mao Zemin (1896–1943), Mao's younger brother, was at this time in charge of the publications department of the Central Committee of the Chinese Communist Party.

Duxiu's recent actions are truly outrageous. The Central Committee documents denouncing him have arrived here, and we should make them widely known.[5]

A Communist salute to you,
Mao Zedong

Post Office Box " "[6]

---

5. The reference is to Chen Duxiu (1879–1942), *zi* Zhongfu, the former chairman of the Party. Regarding his background and earlier activities, see the various texts about him, or signed jointly by him and Mao, in Volumes I and II of this edition. After his disgrace at the "August 7 Emergency Conference" of 1927, he had remained a member of the Party and continued to put forward views at odds with those of the leftist faction which had assumed control of the organization. In the summer of 1929, when conflict erupted between China and Russia following Zhang Xueliang's seizure of the Chinese Eastern Railway, Chen Duxiu sent a letter to the Central Committee arguing that, by aligning itself completely with Moscow, the Party was placing the interests of the Soviet Union above those of China. It is presumably Chen's conduct in this matter which is here stigmatized as "truly outrageous," though Mao may also be referring to the sympathy for Trotsky and Trotskyism which Chen Duxiu had openly expressed. Li seized upon the pretext of Chen's line regarding the railway to announce his expulsion from the Party on November 15, 1929. If "the Central Committee documents denouncing" Chen Duxiu, presumably brought by Chen Yi, included this circular, communication between Shanghai and the soviet area had in this case been remarkably rapid. Mao's later comments regarding the affair of the Chinese Eastern Railway (see below, the note to the "Letter . . . to the Soldiers of the Guomindang Army," January 1930) suggest that he did actually agree with the Central Committee on this issue, but in any case it would have been politic for him to say so, in the light of his own increasingly tense relations with Li Lisan.

6. On the only available text, the return address is shown thus, with the box number missing.

To the Central Committee of the Chinese Communist Party

(November 28, 1929)

To the Central Committee:

I have recovered from my illness. On November 26, the observer from the Fujian Provincial Committee, Comrade Xie,[1] and I arrived in Tingzhou from Jiaoyang and met with the Fourth Army, to work on the Front Committee, in compliance with the directive of the Central Committee. The Fourth Army attack on Mei *xian* was not successful, and although the losses suffered were not small, morale is still high, and for the immediate future we are working within the borders of Fujian. Western Fujian already has 800,000 Red masses, who are able to provide cover for the Red Army. The situation created by the joint offensive of Liu (Heting), Jin (Handing), and Zhang (Zhen)[2] is not a serious matter. It has now been decided that the only way out is, after a period of getting things in order, to mount an attack on Liu and Zhang to break up their joint offensive. We are now in the process of preparing one month's provisions.

There is absolutely no problem in uniting the Fourth Army Party under the correct guidance of the Central Committee. Comrade Chen Yi has already arrived, and the intent of the Central Committee has already been fully achieved. The only problem is that the basic theoretical knowledge of Party members is too low, and we must quickly carry out education. In addition to requesting that the Central Committee send us Party publications (such as *The Bolshevik, Red Flag, The Essentials of Leninism,* and *History of the Russian Revolutionary Movement,* none of which we have received yet), we also request a sum of money for purchasing books (about 100 *yuan,* individual books to be sent separately). The address for requesting or sending payments is "   ." We are absolutely starving for books and newspapers, so please do not put this aside as an unimportant matter. I shall make a detailed report on behalf of the Front Committee.

Mao Zedong
November 28, 1929
Tingzhou

We have translated this letter from *Mao Zedong shuxin xuanji,* pp. 26-27, where it is taken from a handwritten copy in the Party archives. It does not appear to have been published previously.

1. Xie Hanqiu.

2. The parentheses around this and the preceding two given names appear in the Chinese original.

Draft Resolution of the Ninth Congress of the Chinese Communist Party in the Fourth Red Army

(December 1929, at the Gutian Congress in Western Fujian Province)

I. The Problem of Correcting Erroneous and Nonproletarian Ideological Tendencies in the Party[1]

Various kinds of nonproletarian consciousness[2] are *very strongly* present in the Party of the Fourth Army and are an extremely great hindrance to *the application of* the Party's correct line. Unless they are thoroughly corrected, the Fourth Army definitely cannot shoulder the tasks imposed on it by China's broad[3] revolutionary struggle. The *overall* source of the various incorrect tendencies[4] in the Party of the Fourth Army lies, of course, in the fact that its basic units are composed largely of peasants and other elements of petty bourgeois origin; yet the failure of the Party's guiding organs to wage a concerted and determined struggle against these incorrect tendencies[5] and to educate the members in the Party's correct line is also a major cause of their existence and growth. Basing itself on the spirit of the September letter of the Central Committee, this congress points out the sources, manifestations and methods of correction of various *erroneous tendencies toward* nonproletarian consciousness in the Party of the Fourth Army and calls upon comrades to eliminate them thoroughly.

Our source for this resolution is *Mao Zedong ji*, Vol. 2, pp. 77-125, where it has been taken from the 1944 edition of *Mao Zedong xuanji*, Vol. 3.

1. Only this first of the nine sections making up the original Gutian Resolution is included in the *Selected Works*, under a modified version of the original section title: "On Correcting Mistaken Ideas in the Party."

2. Here, and in similar contexts throughout this text, *yishi* ("consciousness" or "mentality") has been replaced in the *Selected Works* by *sixiang* ("ideas" or "thought").

3. Broad → Great

4. Tendencies → Ideas

5. Tendencies → Ideas

A. The Purely Military Viewpoint [6]

1. The sources of the purely military viewpoint:

a. Low political level. In consequence, failure to realize the importance of political leadership and the fundamental differences between the tasks of the Red Army and those of the White army.

b. Remnants of the ideas of mercenary armies. Especially since many enemy soldiers were captured in previous battles and these elements have joined the Red Army, they have brought with them strongly marked mercenary ideas, thus providing a foundation for the purely military viewpoint at the lower levels.

c. The above two reasons have given rise to a third reason, namely placing excessive faith in military strength, and not trusting in the power of the masses.

d. The fact that the Party has neither actively paid attention to military work nor discussed it is another cause for the formation of the purely military viewpoint in some comrades.

2. The purely military viewpoint is very highly developed among some of the comrades in the Red Army. It manifests itself as follows:

a. These comrades regard military affairs and politics as opposed to each other and refuse to recognize that military affairs are only one means of accomplishing political tasks. Some even say, "When military work is well done, political work will naturally be well done; when military work is not well done, political work cannot be well done either." This is to go a step further and recognize military work as leading politics.

b. They think that the task of the Red Army, like that of the White army, is merely to fight. They do not understand that, *in terms of the significance of its task,* the Red Army is an armed group for carrying out the political tasks of the class.[7] *As regards its work,* especially *its work* in China now, it should certainly not confine itself to fighting; besides the one type of work which consists of fighting,[8] it should shoulder such important tasks as doing propaganda among the masses, organizing the masses, arming the masses, and establishing revolutionary political power.[9] The Red Army fights not just for the sake of fighting but *entirely* for the purpose of conducting propaganda among the masses, organizing the masses, arming the masses, and establish-

---

6. This and the other main headings regarding types of deviation are emphasized by the use of dots opposite the characters in the original Chinese version.

7. Class → Revolution

8. The one type of work which consists of fighting → Fighting to destroy the enemy's military strength

9. Establishing revolutionary political power → Establishing revolutionary political power and setting up Party organizations

ing political power.[10] Apart from these objectives, fighting *completely* loses its meaning, and the Red Army loses the *basic* reason for its existence.

c. Hence, organizationally, these comrades subordinate the departments doing political work to those doing military work and put forward the slogan of letting Army Headquarters handle outside matters. If this line[11] is allowed to develop, it would involve the danger of estrangement from the masses, monopoly[12] of the government by the army and departure from the class stand[13]—it would take the path of the Guomindang army.[14]

d. At the same time, regarding propaganda, they overlook the important task of *the work of* propaganda teams. On the question of mass organization, they neglect the organizing of soldiers' committees and the organizing of the worker and peasant masses. As a result, both propaganda and organizational work are abandoned.

e. They become conceited when a battle is won and dispirited when a battle is lost.

f. Selfish departmentalism *of the Fourth Army*—they think only of the main force[15] and do not realize that it is an important task of the Red Army to arm the localities.[16] This is cliquism in a magnified form.

g. Unable to see beyond their limited environment in the Fourth Army, a few comrades believe that no revolutionary forces exist beside theirs. Hence their extreme addiction to the idea of conserving strength and avoiding action. This is a remnant of opportunism.

h. Some comrades, disregarding the subjective and objective conditions, suffer from the malady of revolutionary impetuosity; they will not take pains to do minute and detailed work among the masses but, *full of idealist illusions*, want only to do big things. This *again* is a remnant of adventurism.

3. The methods of correction are as follows:

a. Raise the political level in the Party by means of education, destroy the theoretical roots of the military viewpoint, be clear on the fundamental difference between the Red Army and the White army; at the same time, eliminate the remnants of opportunism and adventurism, and break down the selfish departmentalism of the Fourth Army.

b. Intensify the political training of officers and men and especially the education of ex-prisoners *at the time of their enlistment.* At the same time, as

---

10. Establish political power → Establish revolutionary political power
11. Line → Idea
12. Monopoly of the government → Control of the government
13. Departure from the class stand → Departure from proletarian leadership
14. Take the path of the Guomindang army → Take the path of warlordism like the Guomindang army
15. The main force → The Fourth Army
16. To arm the localities → To arm the local masses

far as possible let the local governments select workers and peasants experienced in struggle to join the Red Army, thus organizationally weakening or even eradicating the purely military viewpoint.

c. Arouse the local Party organizations to criticize the Party organizations in the Red Army and the organs of mass political power *(the soviets)* to criticize the Red Army itself, in order to influence the Party organizations and the officers and men of the Red Army.

d. The Party must actively attend to and discuss the military aspect of the work. All the work must be discussed and decided upon by the Party before being carried out through the mass line.[17]

e. Draw up Red Army rules and regulations which clearly define its tasks, the relationship between its military and its political apparatus, the relationship between the Red Army and the masses, and the powers and functions of the soldiers' committees and their relationship with the military and political organization.

B. Ultrademocracy

1. Since the Party of the Red Army[18] accepted the directives of the Central Committee, there has, *indeed,* been a great decrease in the manifestations of ultrademocracy. For example, Party decisions are now carried out fairly well; and no longer does anyone bring up such slogans as "applying democratic centralism from the bottom to the top" or "letting the lower levels discuss all problems first, and then letting the higher levels decide." *These are facts.* Actually, however, this decrease is only superficial[19] and does not *in any way* mean that ultrademocracy has already been fundamentally eliminated *from the ideas of ordinary party members*. In other words, the *pernicious* root of ultrademocracy is still deeply planted in the hearts of many comrades. Various expressions of reluctance to carry out Party decisions are a proof.

2. The methods of correction are as follows: First, in the sphere of theory, eliminate the roots of ultrademocracy. To begin with, it should be pointed out that the danger of ultrademocracy lies in the fact that it damages or even completely wrecks the Party organization and weakens or even completely undermines the Party's fighting capacity, rendering the Party incapable of fulfilling its fighting tasks and thereby *inevitably* leading to the defeat of the revolution. *At the same time, it actually helps prolong the reactionary life of the ruling class.* Next, it should be pointed out that the source of ultrademocracy resides in the individualistic aversion to discipline of the petty bourgeoisie *(small peasant production and small-scale capitalism in the cities).* When this individualistic

---

17. Carried out through the mass line → Carried out by the masses
18. The Party of the Red Army → The Fourth Army of the Red Army
19. Only superficial → Only temporary and superficial

aversion to discipline is transmitted into the Party, it develops into ultra-democratic thought in the political and organizational domains. Such thought is utterly incompatible with the fighting tasks of the proletariat. *Objectively, it is really a kind of counterrevolutionary thought. Unless we work hard to correct it and to prevent it from developing freely, people with such ideas will certainly take the road of counterrevolution.*

Second, in the sphere of organization, rigorously enforce democracy under centralized guidance. This should be done along the following lines:

a. The leading organs of the Party must offer a correct line of guidance and find solutions when problems arise, in order to establish themselves as centers of leadership.

b. The higher organs must be familiar with the situation in the lower organs, and with the life of the masses, so as to provide the social source[20] for correct guidance.

c. No Party organ at any level should make casual decisions. Once a decision is reached, it must be firmly carried out.

d. All decisions of any importance made by the Party's higher organs must be promptly transmitted to the lower organs and to the mass of Party members. The method is to call meetings of activists or general membership meetings of the Party branches or even of the columns (when circumstances permit) and to assign people to make reports at such meetings.

e. The lower organs of the Party and the mass of Party members must discuss the higher organs' directives in detail, in order to understand their meaning thoroughly and decide on the methods of carrying them out.

C. Lack of Organizational Consciousness[21]

The lack of organizational consciousness in the Party organization in the Fourth Army *has many manifestations in various aspects. The most salient ones are the following three kinds:*

1. Failure of the minority to submit to the majority

For example, when a motion is voted down,[22] they *become very annoyed* or even do not sincerely carry out the Party resolutions. *All [such behavior] is an example of this type [of mistake].*

The methods of correction are as follows:

a. At meetings, all participants should be encouraged to voice their opinions as fully as possible. *It should be clearly understood that* the rights and wrongs in any controversy should be clarified without compromise or gloss-

---

20. Social source → Objective basis

21. Lack of Organizational Consciousness → On Views Incompatible with Organization

22. When a motion is voted down → When a minority finds its motion voted down

ing over. In order to reach a clear-cut conclusion, what cannot be settled at one meeting should be discussed at another, provided there is no interference with the work.

b. One requirement of Party discipline is that the minority should submit to the majority. If the view of the minority has been rejected *at the first Party meeting*, it must support the decision passed by the majority *until the convening of the next meeting*. It can bring up the matter for reconsideration at the next meeting, but apart from that it must not act against the decision in any way.

2. Criticism made without regard to the organization

a. Inner-Party criticism is a weapon for strengthening the Party organization and increasing its fighting capacity. In the Party organization of the Red Army, however, many people are not clear about this significance of criticism[23] and wrongly use it for personal attacks. As a result, it damages the Party organization as well as individuals. This is *entirely* a manifestation of petty bourgeois individualist *consciousness*. The method of correction is to help Party members understand that the significance of criticism is to increase the Party's fighting capacity in order to achieve victory in the class struggle and that it *absolutely* cannot be used as a means of personal attack.

b. Many Party members make their criticisms not inside, but outside the Party. The reason is that *the political significance of the Party organization has not yet become part of the thinking of* Party members in general, *and they therefore* do not understand the importance of the Party organization (its meetings and so forth), and see no difference between criticism inside and criticism outside the organization. *The consequences of this fact alone will be enough to lead the Party onto the road of destruction.* The method of correction is to establish the political significance of Party organization in the thinking of ordinary Party members.[24] *This is the only way to eliminate fundamentally all irresponsible criticisms that have adverse influences on the masses and that disregard Party organizational discipline.*

3. *Special treatment of some Party members. Some Party members do not come to Party branch meetings or small group meetings, do not present work reports even if they come to the meetings, and detach themselves in many ways from ordinary Party members, on the pretext that they are busy. The fact is that*

---

23. Many people are not clear about this significance of criticism → Criticism is not always of this character

24. To establish the political significance of Party organization in the thinking of ordinary Party members. → To educate Party members so that they understand the importance of Party organization and make their criticisms of Party committees or comrades at Party meetings.

they do not want to get close to the masses, and also fear the criticism of the masses. The result is that they become separated from the masses, and separated from the Party. As regards this matter, responsible persons in Party branches, instead of rectifying the situation, have shown signs that they are intimidated by these special Party members.

The causes of this phenomenon: First, the Red Army has always suffered from a major mistake, namely, that Party organs pay very little attention to the discussion of work relating to military affairs. Consequently, they do not urge comrades responsible for military affairs regularly to submit plans for military affairs (such as training, management, battle, and other plans) and reports to Party meetings. As a result, discussions in the Party are divorced from military affairs and comrades responsible for military affairs also forget that they should be guided by the Party and should report to the Party. As a result, the military work of the Red Army has become a special area of work that is not understood by Party organs and ordinary Party members. This is not merely a major obstacle to the task of the militarization of Party members, it will also separate the Party from military affairs, creating the danger of the inability of the Party to guide military affairs. Second, because of the above-mentioned major serious mistakes concerning the tasks of the Party, some comrades responsible for military affairs have become a special group in the Party. At the same time, many comrades responsible for other work have also turned into special persons who do not want to come to Party branch meetings and do not speak even if they come. This is one reason why the life of Party branches in the Red Army is as abnormal and unhealthy as it is at present.

Methods of correction: First, Party meetings at various levels (from Party branches to the Front Committee) must all put plans and reports of military work on the agenda for discussion and decision. Second, all Party members, regardless of their fields of responsibility, must attend general meetings of Party branches and small group meetings and submit work reports, and may be absent only for good reasons.

D. Absolute Egalitarianism

1. Absolute egalitarianism was extremely serious in the Red Army at one time. *After many struggles, it has certainly declined to a large extent, but there still exist many remnants.* For example, on the matter of allowances to wounded soldiers, there were objections to differentiating between light and serious cases, and the demand was raised for equal allowances for all. When officers rode on horseback, it was regarded not as something necessary for performing their duties but as a sign of inequality. Absolutely equal distribution of things was demanded, and objections were raised to somewhat larger allotments in special cases. In the hauling of rice, the demand was made that all should carry the same load on their backs, irrespective of age or physical condition. Equality was demanded in the allotment of billets, and the headquarters would be abused for occupying large rooms. Equality was demanded in the assignment of fatigue duties, and there was unwillingness to do a little more than the next man. It even went so far that when there were two wounded men but only one stretcher, neither could be carried away because each refused to yield priority to the other. All *the above* examples demonstrate that absolute egalitarianism[25] has not been fundamentally eradicated from the heads of the masses. What is called getting rid of it to some extent is only partial or formal, and nothing more.

2. Absolute egalitarianism *is actually*, like ultrademocracy in political matters, the product of a handicraft and small peasant economy. The only difference is that the one manifests itself in the political sphere, while the other manifests itself in the material aspect.

3. The method of correction: We should point out *in theory* that before the abolition of capitalism, absolute egalitarianism is a mere illusion of peasants and small proprietors, and that even in the period of a socialist *economy*, there can be no absolute equality, for material things will then be distributed on the basis of the needs of individuals and their work[26]. The distribution of material things in the Red Army must be as equal as possible, as in the case of equal pay for officers and men, because this is required by the present circumstances of the struggle. But absolute equality[27] beyond reason must be opposed because it is not required by the struggle; on the contrary, it hinders the struggle.

E. Idealist Views[28]

1. Idealist views are very strong among Party members of *the Red Army*. They constitute a great obstacle to the analysis of the political situation, the guidance of the work, *and the organization of the Party*. The reason is that idealist analysis of a political situation and idealist guidance of work is inevitably *accompanied by* and results in either opportunism or adventurism. As for *the spirit* of idealist criticism *in the Party*, loose and groundless allegations, or mutual suspicion, the consequence is often unprincipled and *meaningless* disputes *in the Party* and the disruption of the Party organization.

Another point that should be mentioned in connection with inner-Party criticism, *apart from the spirit of idealist criticism*, is the spirit of nonpolitical criti-

---

25. Absolute egalitarianism → Absolute egalitarianism is still very serious among officers and soldiers of the Red Army

26. On the basis of the needs of individuals and their work → On the basis of the principle of "from each according to his ability, to each according to his work," as well as on that of meeting the needs of the work.

27. Absolute equality → Absolute egalitarianism

28. Idealist Views → On Subjectivism. Throughout this section, "idealist" (*weixin*) has been replaced by "subjective" (*zhuguan*) in the *Selected Works*.

cism.[29] They do not understand that the main task of criticism is to point out political mistakes, and *that* pointing out organizational mistakes *is only a secondary task*. As for shortcomings in personal *life* and *minor technical points*, unless they are *closely* related to political and organizational mistakes, there is no need to be overcritical and to embarrass the comrades concerned. Moreover, once technical criticism develops, the greatest danger is that *the attention of the* Party members will concentrate entirely on routine technical aspects,[30] and everyone will become timid and overcautious and *inevitably* forget about the Party's political tasks. This is the greatest danger. *Like the spirit of idealist and nonscientific criticism, the spirit of technical and nonpolitical criticism in the Party of the Red Army will certainly lead to (and has already led to) the worst consequences.*

2. The only method of correction[31] is to politicize and make scientific[32] the thinking of Party members and the life of the Party. To this end we must: (1) teach Party members to apply the Marxist method[33] in analyzing political situations and appraising the class forces, instead of making a subjective analysis and appraisal; (2) direct the attention of Party members to social and economic investigation and research, so as to determine the tactics of struggle and methods of work and help comrades to understand that without the investigation of actual conditions they will fall into the pit of fantasy and adventurism; and (3) in inner-Party criticism, eliminate the idealist and the technical spirit; statements should be based on facts and discussion of work should focus on its political significance.[34]

F. Individualism[35]

1. Individualism in the Red Army manifests itself in the following ways:

a. Retaliation. Some comrades, after being criticized inside the Party by a soldier comrade, look for opportunities to retaliate outside the Party, and one way is to beat or curse the comrade in question. *There are many such cases. Besides,* they also seek to retaliate within the Party. You have criticized me at

---

29. The spirit of nonpolitical criticism → Some comrades ignore the major issues and confine their attention to minor points when they make their criticism.

30. Routine technical aspects → Minor faults

31. The only method of correction → The main method of correction is to educate Party members so that

32. *Zhengzhihua, kexuehua.*

33. The Marxist method → The Marxist-Leninist method

34. Eliminate the idealist and the technical spirit; statements should be based on facts and discussion of work should focus on its political significance → Guard against subjectivism, arbitrariness and the vulgarization of criticism; statements should be based on facts and criticism should center on politics.

35. Individualism → On Individualism

this meeting, so I'll find some way to pay you back at the next. *There are also quite a few such cases.* Such retaliationism[36] arises from purely personal considerations; it is oblivious of the interests of the class and of Party life as a whole. *Such people are only aware of their own existence.* Their target is not the enemy class, but individuals in our own ranks. This is a corrosive agent which *greatly* weakens the organization and its fighting capacity.

b. Small group mentality. Superficially, it is an enlargement of individualism,[37] but in reality it is still the narrowest kind of individualism and has a strong corrosive and centrifugal effect. Small group mentality used to be rife in the Red Army, and although a great deal has been eliminated as a result of hard struggle, there are still remnants, and further efforts are needed *in the course of struggle.*

c. The employee mentality. Some comrades do not understand that the Party and the Red Army constitute an instrument for carrying out the tasks of the class,[38] and they are part of it. They do not realize that they themselves are the main force in the struggle,[39] but think that *the struggle has nothing to do with them,* their responsibility is merely to their superior officers, or *to organs at Party headquarters,* and not to the revolution. This mentality of an employee of the revolution is quite developed and explains why there are not many activists who work unconditionally.[40] Unless it is eliminated, the number of activists will not grow and the heavy burden of the revolution will remain on the shoulders of a few people, much to the detriment of the struggle.

d. Pleasure-seeking. In the Red Army there are also quite a few people whose individualism finds expression in pleasure-seeking. They always hope that their unit will march into big cities. They want to go there not to work but to enjoy themselves. The last thing they want is to work in the Red areas where life is hard. *The consequence of pleasure-seeking is to care only about personal interests and not to care about the revolution as a whole, or about group actions.*

e. Passivity and going slow on work. Some comrades become passive and stop working whenever anything goes against their wishes. The *basic* reason

---

36. *Baofuzhuyi.*

37. Superficially, it is an enlargement of individualism, → Some comrades consider only the interests of their own small group and ignore the general interest. Although on the surface this does not seem to be the pursuit of personal interests

38. The tasks of the class → The tasks of the revolution

39. The main force in the struggle → The makers of the revolution

40. This mentality of an employee of the revolution is quite developed in the Red Army and explains why there are not many activists who work unconditionally. → This passive mentality of an "employee" of the revolution is also a manifestation of individualism. It explains why there are not very many activists who work unconditionally for the revolution.

for going slow on work certainly lies in individualism and lack of a genuine and clear understanding of one's class tasks,[41] *but there are also objective reasons arising from improper handling of affairs,* assignment of work or enforcement of discipline *by the Party and the army.*

f. The desire to leave the army. The number of people who ask for transfers from the Red Army to local work is on the increase. The reason for this, too, does not lie entirely with subjective individualism.[42] In addition, there are causes residing in *objective circumstances,* such as: (1) the material hardships of life in the Red Army, (2) exhaustion after long struggle, and (3) the handling of affairs,[43] assignment of work, or enforcement of discipline.

2. *The source of individualism lies in influences ranging from small peasant thinking to bourgeois thinking within the Party.* The method of correction is primarily to make use of[44] education to rectify individualism ideologically. Next in importance is to conduct affairs, make assignments, and enforce discipline in a proper way. In addition, methods must be found to improve objective conditions.[45]

G. The Ideology of Roving Rebel Bands

1. *The sources of the ideology of roving rebels in the Red Army are as follows: (1) The immediate cause is that* the vagrants account for the majority in the Red Army;[46] (2) *A more remote cause is* the existence of a broad mass of vagrants in the whole country and in various southern provinces in particular. *These two immediate and remote causes have resulted in* roving-rebel-style[47] political ideology *and plans of action* in the Red Army. *However, large-scale actions of roving insurgents in the style of Huang Chao,*[48] Li

---

41. The basic reason certainly lies in individualism and lack of a genuine and clear understanding of class tasks → This results mainly from lack of education, but there are also cases when it is caused by the way leaders handle problems

42. Lie entirely with subjective individualism → Lie entirely with individuals

43. The handling of affairs → The leadership's handling of problems

44. Make use of → Strengthen

45. Ways must be found to improve objective conditions. → Ways must be found to improve the material life of the Red Army, and every available opportunity must be utilized for rest and rehabilitation in order to improve material conditions. In our educational work we must explain that in its social origin individualism is a reflection within the Party of petty bourgeois and bourgeois ideas.

46. The vagrants account for the majority in the Red Army → The proportion of vagrants is large

47. *Liukouzhuyi,* literally, "roving-rebel-ist"

48. Huang Chao (?–884), a native of Shandong, who had started life as a salt merchant, became in 875 the leader of a rebel band. In 880, he succeeded in capturing Chang'an and proclaimed himself emperor, but by 884 he had been utterly defeated and committed suicide. His wide-ranging campaigns lasting nearly a decade constituted one of the most famous peasant wars in Chinese history.

Chuang,[49] and Hong Xiuquan[50] are impossible in imperialist-controlled China, and especially in a modern China where advanced weapons (hand grenades, steel cannons, machine guns, etc.), advanced methods of communication (telephones and radios for military use), and advanced means of transportation (automobiles, ships, and railways) have already been introduced. So the ideology of roving rebel bands naturally cannot become the final forceful program of action of the Red Army. However, its influence still manifests itself strongly in all fields. For example, (1) Some people want to increase our political influence only by means of roving guerrilla actions, but are unwilling to increase it by undertaking the arduous task of helping the masses build up political power;[51] (2) In expanding *the organizational line of* the Red Army, some people follow the line of *expanding the Red Army by* "hiring men and buying horses" and "recruiting deserters and accepting mutineers,"[52] rather than the line of expanding the local Red Guards and the local troops and thus developing nonlocal forces of the Red Army;[53] (3) Some people lack the patience to carry on arduous struggles together with the masses and only want to go to the big cities to eat and drink to their hearts' content. All these manifestations of roving-rebelism[54] seriously hamper the Red Army in performing the tremendous tasks imposed on it by the revolution.[55] Consequently, the eradication of roving rebel ideology is an important objective in the ideological struggle within the Party in the Red Army.[56]

---

49. Li Zicheng (1606–1645), a native of Shaanxi, turned brigand at an early age and called himself General Chuang (the character *chuang* means "impetuous" or "daredevil"). In 1644, he proclaimed himself emperor and took Beijing, where the last Ming emperor hanged himself in consequence. Subsequently, he was defeated by Wu Sankui, a Ming general who had gone over to the Manchus, and driven south to Hubei, where he was killed by local militia.

50. Hong Xiuquan (1814–1864) was the principal leader of the Taiping Heavenly Kingdom. In view of the fact that, as noted above, Li Lisan and the Central Committee had repeatedly urged Mao to make use of the Taiping model of military organization, because it was particularly suited to guerrilla warfare, this reference may constitute a veiled attack on Li.

51. Unwilling to increase it by undertaking the arduous task of helping the masses build up political power → Unwilling to increase it by under taking the arduous task of building up base areas and establishing the people's political power.

52. These two set phrases evoke the indiscriminate recruitment of followers by some rebels in Chinese history.

53. Developing nonlocal forces of the Red Army → Developing the main forces of the Red Army

54. Roving-rebelism → Roving rebel ideology

55. Seriously hamper the Red Army in performing the tremendous tasks imposed on it by the revolution → Seriously hamper the Red Army in performing its proper tasks

56. In the Red Army → In the Red Army. It must be understood that the ways of roving rebels of the Huang Chao or Li Chuang type are not permissible under present-day conditions.

2. The methods of correction are as follows:

a. Transform the incorrect ideas *that have their basis in* the vagrants in the Party through education,[57] and eradicate the ideology of roving rebel bands.

b. Intensify education among the basic sections of the Red Army and among recently recruited captives to counter the vagabond outlook.

c. Attract activist workers and peasants experienced in struggle to the ranks of the Red Army so as to change its composition.

d. Create new army units from among the masses of workers and peasants who are involved in struggle.

H. *The Remnants of Adventurism*

1. Relatively great efforts have been made in the struggle against adventurism in the Party organization in the Red Army, but these efforts cannot be described as already adequate. *So, though many ideas and actions of adventurism in the Red Army have been overcome,* some remnants still exist. *The source of adventurism lies in a combination of lumpenproletarian and petty bourgeois consciousness.* Its manifestations include the following: (1) blind action regardless of subjective and objective conditions; (2) inadequate and irresolute application of the Party's policies for the cities; (3) slack military discipline, especially in moments of defeat; (4) acts of house-burning at the expense of the mass base exist to some extent in all units;[58] and (5) the practices of shooting deserters and of inflicting corporal punishment, of which *some aspects* also result from adventurism.

2. The methods of correction are as follows:

a. Eradicate adventurism theoretically.[59]

b. Correct adventurist behavior through rules, regulations, and policies.

II. On the Problem of Party Organization

The matter of Party organization in the Red Army is now in an extremely grave period. In particular, the quality of Party members is so poor and the organization is so lax that they are very greatly affecting the leadership of the Red Army and the implementation of policies. The congress has made a special detailed analysis of this issue, and taken decisions on it. Comrades should stand by the spirit of the congress and work hard to transform the organization of the

---

57. Transform the incorrect ideas *that have their basis in* the vagrants in the Party through education → Intensify education, criticize incorrect ideas

58. Acts of house-burning at the expense of the mass base exist to some extent in all units → Acts of house-burning are still carried out by some units

59. Theoretically → Ideologically

Party. Success can be achieved only if the Party organization is truly capable of assuming the Party's political tasks.

A. The Organizational Line of the Party

1. The line for developing Party members takes combat soldiers as its main object. At the same time, noncombat soldiers such as laborers and orderlies should not be neglected either.

2. One of the important principles of Party organization in the Army is to set up a branch in every company and a small group in every squad. In case the number of Party members is too small among the troops and it is impossible to set up a small group in every squad, platoons may temporarily serve as the unit to set up small groups which assign group members to various squads in a planned manner. It must, however, be clearly understood that this is a transitional method.

3. The original method for setting up small groups in the Red Army, which consists in mixing cadres and ordinary members, intellectuals and laborers, is very correct. But the various elements, whose work and capacities are different, have not yet been well integrated in a planned way. In the future, this point should be given more attention. It is impermissible simply to organize cadres into small groups.

B. The Issue of Laxity in Party Organization

1. The present status of the Party organization in the Fourth Army:

a. It has been too easy to join the Party. Many people who are not qualified as Party members have also been pulled into the Party. Officers, in particular, are all dragged into the Party without any conditions whatsoever. As a result, the quality of the Party has become very poor.

b. The Party headquarters at all levels have resolved problems, but completely forgotten the task of educating comrades in their work. There are extremely few meetings of a training nature, such as assemblies of activists, joint meetings of party secretaries and members responsible for propaganda and organization, joint meetings of Party committees and groups, branch meetings, assemblies of Party members at the levels of columns and detachments.

c. General laxity in discipline. Especially when one is responsible for important work and cannot be replaced by others, one can muddle through making mistakes and not be called to order. If one person is treated in this way, others have to be treated likewise. So discipline becomes generally lax.

d. As all officers are Party members, the consequence is that the staff members of all military and political organs pay very little attention to the work of their social professions, and all believe that the work of their social professions is the same as the Party's work and the two cannot be separated. For example, work conferences on military affairs at various levels and work conferences on political affairs at various levels are almost nonexistent, and it is held that all affairs can be easily decided by the Party. There is almost no mention of the fact that Party members should play core roles in social and professional work.

e. The relations between lower- and higher-level organs are not close. The reports of lower-level organs are seldom approved, replied to, or dealt with by instructions from higher-level organs. Higher-level organs rarely send people to attend the meetings of lower-level organs. This is certainly due to the imperfections of the organization of the higher-level organs, but the unenthusiastic attitude of higher-level organs toward work is also one of the reasons why lower levels receive no instructions, or no detailed instructions. This is the case especially regarding instructions on practical work. For example, when an army unit issues working instructions on guerrilla warfare and so forth, it generally gives no specific instructions. There are certain army units that do not even give general instructions.

f. Many branch assemblies or small group meetings are not held on time.

2. The Line for Correcting [These Errors]

a. The old basis should be rigorously eliminated. For instance, all those who have erroneous political views, take opium, enrich themselves, gamble, and refuse to mend their ways despite repeated warnings should be expelled from the Party, regardless of whether they are cadres or not.

b. Qualifications for new members who join the Party in the future:

i.   They should have no errors in their political views (including class consciousness);

ii.   They should be loyal;

iii.   They should have the spirit of sacrifice and be capable of working actively.

iv.   They should not be bent on enriching themselves.

v.   They should not take opium or gamble.

Only those who meet the above five qualifications may be presented for membership in the Party. Those who recommend them should first investigate whether or not those they are introducing genuinely meet the above qualifications. When they have been recommended and joined the Party, new Party members should be told in detail about branch life (including the secret work) and about key points that Party members must observe. The introducers should take considerable responsibility for those they recommend. Branches should appoint people to talk to those who will soon join the Party and review their qualifications for joining the Party.

3. The Party headquarters at all levels do not exist merely to resolve problems and direct the practical work. They also have the weighty responsibility of educating comrades. All sorts of conferences for training comrades, as well as other training methods, such as training courses and discussion meetings, should be organized in a planned way.

4. Discipline should be strictly enforced, and all manifestations of laxity in discipline abolished.

5. The nature of Party members' social and professional work should be distinguished from that of their Party work. Every Party member (except professional revolutionaries who have important or special tasks inside the Party) must have one social profession. At the same time, he should do Party work in his social profession.

6. The work attitude of Party headquarters at all levels should be more active than before. The lower levels should present more thorough analyses to the higher levels, and the higher levels should conduct thorough discussions of these reports and make specific replies and also do their best to send people to attend the meetings at the lower levels. Neither shortage of staff members, weak capacity for work, nor insufficient work time can be used as a pretext to cover up their own lack of enthusiasm and neglect of this work.

7. Branch committees and Party headquarters above the branch level should decide every month the materials to be discussed by branch and small group meetings in a planned way, determine the time of meetings, and closely supervise and promote the holding of these meetings.

C. How to Create Interest on the Part of Party Members in Attending Meetings

1. The reasons for the lack of interest on the part of Party members in attending meetings:

a. Not understanding the significance of the meetings. The first important purpose of branch meetings is to solve problems. All problems relating to the struggle, and to internal affairs, must be resolved through concentrated discussions at meetings. Those who do not attend meetings or do not actively express their opinions at the meetings they attend lack understanding of the political significance of meetings, or in other words lack interest in the struggle. All those who are enthusiastic about the struggle are definitely eager to come to the meetings and to speak at them. The second purpose is to educate comrades. Meetings not only resolve problems but, in the process of solving problems, require us to observe the context of problems and study the instructions of higher levels, thus stimulating the mental capacities of comrades. The politicization and actualization[60] of meetings will politicize and actualize the

---

60. *Shijihua.*

head of every comrade. If every comrade is politicized and actualized, the fighting force of the Party will become very much greater. This is the educational significance of meetings. The fact that Party members in the Red Army do not understand this significance is the first reason why they dislike going to meetings or show little interest even if they come.

b. The interest in discussions declines as resolutions are adopted but never applied, and the requests made of higher levels are not responded to for a long time.

c. Responsible persons do not prepare properly in advance. They fail to prepare agendas, understand the contents and contexts of the issues, or prepare any comments on ways to resolve the issues.

d. The chairmen casually stop Party members from speaking. When Party members occasionally digress from the subjects under discussion, they are stopped immediately, so they feel frustrated and become silent. When they make mistakes in their speeches, they are not only stopped but derided.

e. A feudal style, rigid and devoid of any liveliness, is applied in conducting meetings. Attending meetings is like being imprisoned.

2. Methods of Correction: First, meetings should be politicized and actualized. Second, comrades, especially new Party members or Party members who lack enthusiasm in work, should be reminded often of the great significance of meetings. Third, resolutions should not be made in a careless and rash way, and once resolutions are decided upon, they should be carried out resolutely. Fourth, higher-level organs should be prompt in answering questions from the lower levels. Putting off replies for too long may cause loss of enthusiasm. Fifth, responsible persons should prepare agendas beforehand and make items of the agenda concrete. Prior investigation of the content and context of problems should be conducted carefully, and some thought should be given in advance to ways of resolving them. Sixth, chairmen should adopt good practices in conducting meetings. They ought to guide the tide of the masses' discussion to focus on a certain problem. But digressions that constitute significant developments should not be stopped in a discouraging fashion; on the contrary, the gist of these developments should be grasped and introduced to all, and new items of agenda should be formulated. These are the only ways to make meetings interesting, truly to resolve problems, and truly to realize the educational significance of meetings. Seventh, feudal procedures for conducting meetings must be abolished. The meetingplace of a Communist Party should reflect the positive, lively, and straightforward spirit of the proletariat and incorporate it into the pattern of meetings.

D. The Youth Organization within the Red Army and Its Work

1. In the army, the interests of youth cannot be distinguished from those of adults, and the League does not have special objectives for its work. Moreover, the Party's method for setting up small groups, taking the squad as the unit, is

most advantagous for the struggle. Consequently, there is no need to set up small groups of the League within Party branches.

2. Since those Party members who are young have sentiments different from those of adult members, they need to receive special education, apart from receiving the Party's general training. Furthermore, because winning over the masses of young workers and peasants is one of the important tasks of the Party, there must be special organizations to carry out this work. Consequently, a Party branch should single out those Party members who are under twenty (except special cases, such as being responsible for important Party tasks) to form a youth work conference. Such conferences may be held regularly by brigades as a unit in a planned way, but detachments and columns themselves should also decide on the times to hold such meetings in light of their respective conditions.

3. In order to plan for the education of young Party members, and for methods of winning over the masses of young workers and peasants, and to guide youth work conferences, the Front Committee and column committees may set up five-member commissions on youth work, and each detachment committee and branch committee should have one youth commissioner working under the direction of Party headquarters at various levels.

E. The Relationship between Political Commissars and Inner-Party Work

In principle, the Party secretaries at the two levels of brigades and columns do not serve concurrently as political commissars. But in units that are short of staff members, they may serve in the two positions at the same time temporarily. Higher-level Party headquarters may, on the basis of their observation of the situation and under appropriate conditions, appoint political commissars who are not Party secretaries to be special representatives of the Party. These special representatives have the task of directing the Party's work at specific levels.

F. The Issue of the Highest Party Headquarters of the Directly Attached Units

All directly attached units of the army and various columns may organize Party committees as their highest Party headquarters. The number of committee members ranges from five to seven.

G. The Issue of the Party and the League in Soldiers' Associations

The soldiers' associations of companies do not form Party and League organizations, and the work is directed by branch committees. The soldiers' associations of columns should set up Party and League organizations that are under the leadership of column Party committees.

III. The Problem of Inner-Party Education

A. *Significance*

The most urgent issue within the Party in the Red Army is the issue of education. The strengthening and expansion of the Red Army and the fulfillment of the tasks of the struggle must all start with inner-Party education. Without raising the inner-Party political level and eliminating various deviations within the Party, it is absolutely impossible to strengthen and expand the Red Army, and even more impossible to shoulder the important tasks of the struggle. Therefore, systematically carrying out inner-Party education, and correcting the past situation of having no plans and letting things take their own course, is one of the major tasks of the Party. The congress decides to use the following materials and methods to educate Party members. The leading organs of the Party should hold more detailed discussions and then proceed to carry out this task.

B. *Materials*

1. Political analysis;
2. Discussion of notices from higher-level leading organs;
3. The organizational ABCs;
4. Correction of the eight erroneous ideas within the Party in the Red Army;
5. Discussion of the issue of opposing opportunism and the Trotskyist opposition;
6. Tactics and techniques of mass work;
7. Social and economic investigations and studies of the guerrilla regions;
8. Study of Marxism-Leninism;
9. Study of social and economic science;
10. The question of the present stage and future of the revolution.

All the above ten items, except some (such as study of Marxism-Leninism) which are, in fact, applicable only to cadres, are applicable to ordinary Party members.

C. *Methods*

1. Party newspapers;
2. Political bulletins;
3. Editing various types of pamphlets for educating comrades;
4. Training courses;
5. Organized assignment of readings;
6. Reading books and newspapers to illiterate Party members;

   7. One-to-one talks;
   8. Criticism;
   9. Small group meetings;
10. Branch assemblies;
11. Joint meetings of branch committee members and group leaders;
12. Assemblies of activists above the level of group leader, taking columns as the unit;
13. Assemblies of activists above the level of branch committee secretaries in the army as a whole;
14. Assemblies of Party members, taking the column as the unit;
15. Joint meetings of secretaries, committee members responsible for propaganda, and committee members responsible for organization, taking columns as the unit;
16. Joint meetings of secretaries, committee members responsible for propaganda, and committee members responsible for propaganda above the level of detachments in the whole Army;
17. Political seminars;
18. Appropriate assignment of Party members to participate in actual work.

IV. The Problem of Propaganda Work by the Red Army

A. The Significance of the Propaganda Work of the Red Army

The task of the propaganda work of the Red Army is to expand political influence and win over the broad masses. Only by accomplishing this propaganda task can the overall tasks of the Red Army, such as organizing the masses, arming the masses, establishing political régimes, destroying the reactionary forces, and promoting the revolutionary upsurge be fulfilled. The propaganda work of the Red Army is therefore first-priority work for the Red Army. To neglect this work is to abandon the main tasks of the Red Army and amounts to helping the ruling class weaken the force of the Red Army.

B. The Present Status of the Propaganda Work of the Red Army

1. Shortcomings in the content of propaganda:
   a. No concrete political program has been issued (The political programs issued in the past, such as the Four Character Proclamation,[61] were not concrete);
   b. Propaganda and agitation regarding the daily struggles of the masses have been neglected;

---

61. The reference is manifestly to the Notice (*bugao*) dated January 1929, signed by Mao and Zhu De, written in lines of four Chinese characters.

c. The achievements of the urban poor have been neglected;

d. Propaganda addressed to the masses of women has been neglected;

e. There is inadequate propaganda addressed to the masses of young people;

f. There is inadequate propaganda addressed to the lumpenproletariat;[62]

g. There is all too little propaganda aimed at disrupting the armed organizations of the landlord class (such as the militia and the Pacification and Protection Corps);

h. Propaganda does not take account of time and place.

2. Shortcomings in the techniques of propaganda:

a. Inadequacies of propaganda teams

i.   The number of propaganda team members has declined from five for each brigade to three. Some brigades only have one or two propaganda team members, some only have one, and a few units have none at all.

ii.   The backgrounds of propaganda team members are highly deficient. There are captives, cooks and grooms, and opium addicts. Some people suspected of desertion have been disarmed and forced into the propaganda teams; some have been sent to propaganda teams after they proved incapable of serving as clerks; some are thrust into propaganda teams because they are disabled and are rejected by other work units. Propaganda teams at present have quite simply become reception centers and are completely incapable of carrying out their tasks.

iii.   Almost all officers and soldiers reject propaganda teams (at the same time, the dissatisfaction of ordinary people results from the fact that the backgrounds of team members are too bad, and the achievements of their work are too few). "Idlers" and "peddlers of fake plasters" are the names given to propaganda team members by the ordinary people.

iv.   Propaganda teams do not have enough propaganda funds.

v.   There are no plans for the training of propaganda team members. At the same time, the supervision of their work is also inadequate. Consequently, the work of propaganda teams is really done any old way, and no one cares whether they do it or not.

b. Handbills, proclamations, manifestos, and the like are old and outdated, and the methods of distributing and mailing them are incorrect.

c. Wall newspapers are seldom put up. The political bulletins have very brief content, are rarely published, and have small characters that are barely readable.

---

62. *Liumang wuchanjieji,* literally "the vagabond proletariat," instead of the term usually employed by Mao, *youmin wuchanjieji,* which we translate as "the vagrant proletariat."

d. Revolutionary folksongs are quite simply nonexistent.

e. Only a few pictorials are published.

f. There is almost no propaganda in makeup.[63]

g. No clubs that serve the dual purpose of entertaining soldiers and getting close to the worker and peasant masses have been set up.

h. Oral propaganda is poor in quantity and quality.

i. Red Army discipline[64] is a kind of practical propaganda to the masses. Now discipline is lax in comparison with the past, and this has a bad influence on the masses.

j. Putting back the doors [taken down to sleep on], bundling up the straw [used for bedding], sweeping floors, talking politely, paying fairly for what you buy, returning everything you borrow, and compensating for damage are all a form of Red Army propaganda work. At present these things, too, are done inadequately.

k. There are few mass rallies, and those held are not well organized.

l. The methods for propaganda addressed to the soldiers of the White armies are not good.

C. The Way to Correct These Defects

1. Regarding the Content of Propaganda:

a. A concrete political program should be published and called the Political Program of the Red Army.

b. Propaganda should be in harmony with the fighting spirit of the masses. Apart from issuing general slogans regarding the uprising, there should also be slogans related to daily life that are appropriate in places where the fighting spirit of the masses is low, which can be used to mobilize for daily struggles and link them to the slogans about uprisings.

c. The urban poor (medium-size and small merchants and students) are a considerable force in the process of the democratic revolution. To neglect to win over this force is the same as handing it over to the despotic gentry and the bourgeoisie. In the future, in-depth propaganda work should be conducted among the masses of medium-size and small merchants and students in the cities, with the purpose of winning them over.

---

63. I.e., propaganda by soldiers who put on makeup and perform sketches. For more details on this, see, below, paragraph IVC2f.

64. The reference is, in particular, to the "Three Main Rules of Discipline" mentioned below in paragraphs VA4 and VB7, and which, together with the "Eight Points for Attention," came to define the Red Army's work style. The three rules went through various formulations, but in substance remained: (1) to obey orders, (2) to take nothing from the masses, and (3) to turn in everything captured. The "eight points" (at this time, there were only six or seven of them) are listed in the following paragraph. For a more detailed account of this matter, see below, the relevant note to the "Order on Rectifying Military Bearing and Discipline," March 21, 1930.

d. Women account for half the population. The economic position of working women, and the special exploitation suffered by them, prove not only that women have an urgent need for revolution but also that they are a force that will decide the success or failure of the revolution. In the future, there should be practical slogans for women, and widespread propaganda should be carried out among them.

e. The masses of young toilers make up over 30 percent of the population. They are also the bravest and most resolute in the struggle. Therefore, propaganda aimed at winning over the masses of young people is a significant task in propaganda work as a whole.

f. If the broad masses of vagrants in China stand on the side of the revolutionary classes, they become instruments of the revolution. If they stand on the side of the reactionary classes, they become the instruments of counter-revolution. So, to win over the masses of vagrants from under the influence of the reactionary classes is one of the tasks of the propaganda of the Party. In conducting the work of propaganda, the different life-styles and characters of various groups of such masses should be noted and different propaganda should be carried out accordingly.

g. Destroying the armed organizations of the landlord class and winning over the masses under their influence is one of the conditions for the victory of the agrarian revolution in the countryside. In the future, the propaganda work among the members of the militia and Pacification and Protection Corps should be given special attention.

h. Wherever one goes, one should have propaganda slogans and agitation slogans appropriate to that place. Furthermore, there should also be different slogans that are formulated for different times (for example, the Autumn Harvest Festival, New Year's days, the war between Chiang Kaishek and the Guangxi clique, and the struggle between Chiang Kaishek and Wang Jingwei).

2. Regarding the Techniques of Propaganda
   a. The question of propaganda teams
      i. Significance: The propaganda teams of the Red Army are important instruments of the propaganda work of the Red Army. If propaganda teams are not well organized, a large part of the propaganda work of the Red Army is wasted. Therefore, the problem of reorganizing and training propaganda teams is one of the tasks to which the Party must devote greater efforts at present. The first step in this work is to correct, from a theoretical standpoint, the attitude of looking down on propaganda work and propaganda teams, which is widespread among officers and soldiers. From now on, strange names such as "idlers," and "peddlers of fake plasters" should be abolished.

ii.   Organization: Detachments constitute units, and troops directly under the army or columns constitute units. Every unit organizes a propaganda team with one leader, one deputy leader, sixteen propagandists, one porter (carrying propaganda materials), and two persons running errands. The propagandists of each team are divided into several branches (the number of branches is determined by the number of brigades or other units and organs). Every branch has one branch leader and three propagandists.

The propaganda teams of all detachments are under the command of detachment political commissars. When various brigades are scattered in the course of guerrilla warfare, every brigade should dispatch a propaganda team branch to accompany them in their work under the command of the brigade political commissar. The propaganda teams of directly attached troops are under the leadership of the head of the propaganda sections of the political department. All propaganda teams of the whole columns are directed by the propaganda sections of the political departments of the columns. The propaganda teams of the whole Army are led by the propaganda section of the army political department.

The expenses of propaganda teams are paid by political departments, and sufficient funds should be provided.

Ways to transform the composition of propaganda team members: Apart from asking local governments to select and send progressive elements to join the propaganda teams of the Red Army, outstanding elements (so far as possible, not squad leaders) from the soldiers of various armed units may be chosen as propaganda team members. Political departments should frequently make plans for training propaganda teams, specifying training materials, methods, times, teachers, and so on, in an active effort to improve the quality of propaganda team members.

b. The old handbills, bulletins, declarations, and other propaganda materials should be reviewed, and new ones should be drafted quickly.

The appropriateness and effectiveness of the distribution of propaganda materials must be an important aspect of the problem of propaganda techniques. Whether to mail propaganda materials by inserting them in packages for mailing, or by stamping propaganda and agitation slogans on the packages, is a matter to which political organs should pay attention and which should be dealt with properly.

c. Wall newspapers are one of the important ways to carry out propaganda among the masses. The army and the columns serve as the units to run wall papers. The propaganda sections of political departments are responsible for them and the name of all the papers should be *Current Affairs Bulletin*. The contents are, first, international and domestic political news; second, the situation of the mass struggle in the guerrilla regions; third, the situation of the work of the Red Army. There should be at least one issue every week. The papers should be all written on large sheets of paper and do not need to be mimeographed. Each time, as many pages as possible should be produced. In editing and printing the political news bulletin, attention should be paid to the following points: 1. it should be put out quickly; 2. it should be rich in content; 3. the characters should be a bit bigger and clearer.

d. The various political departments are responsible for collecting and editing revolutionary folksongs that express the different sentiments of the masses. The editorial committee of the army political department has the responsibility for supervising, promoting, and investigating this work.

e. The art unit of the propaganda section of the army political department should be fully developed and should publish lithographed or mimeographed pictorials. In order to strengthen the art unit of the army, the painting talents of the whole army should be concentrated and work together.

f. Propaganda in makeup is the most concrete and most effective method of propaganda, and all propaganda teams of various detachments and various directly attached troops should establish makeup propaganda units to organize and direct the makeup propaganda toward the masses.

g. With the company as the unit, soldiers' associations may set up their own clubs.

h. Propaganda teams should have oral propaganda units and written propaganda units to study and direct oral and written propaganda techniques.

i. The three points of discipline should be strictly observed.

j. The political departments or propaganda teams should hold various kinds of mass rallies in a planned and organized way. The order of rallies, speakers, subjects of speeches and speaking times should be decided in advance.

k. Propaganda directed at the White soldiers and lower-ranking officers is extremely important. In the future, attention should be given to the following methods:

i. The language of propaganda should be simple and concise, to enable them to finish reading in an instant, and should be epigrammatic, so as to leave an impression on them.

ii. Apart from writing, in a planned way, slogans appropriate to the reality of certain armed units along the two sides of roads where the enemy often passes, handbills should be stored with the party headquarters and mass organizations along the roads and be distributed to the enemy troops ingeniously when they pass.

iii. The names of enemy officers and soldiers and the numbers of the enemy units to which they belong may be learned from the captured officers and soldiers and from the inspection of the mail. Propaganda materials should then be mailed to them, or letters should be written to them.

iv.   Considerate treatment of captured enemy soldiers is an extremely effective method for conducting propaganda directed at enemy troops. Methods of considerate treatment of captured soldiers include: First, there should be no body searches for money and other objects. The past practice of body searches of captured soldiers for money and goods by Red Army soldiers should be resolutely abolished. Second, captured soldiers should be warmly and enthusiastically welcomed, to make them feel happy in their minds. Any humiliation of the captured soldiers by word or deed should be opposed. Third, captured soldiers should enjoy the same material treatment as the old soldiers. Fourth, if they do not want to stay, they will be let go with travel expenses after they have been exposed to propaganda, so that they may spread the influence of the Red Army in the White army. The practice of forcibly keeping those who are unwilling to stay in order to satisfy the greed for more soldiers should be opposed. All the above points are entirely applicable to captured officers, except in special circumstances.

v.   Providing medical treatment for wounded enemy soldiers is also a very effective method for conducting propaganda directed toward the enemy troops. The medical treatment of wounded enemy soldiers and the money issued to them should be exactly the same as those of the wounded soldiers of the Red Army. Advantage should be taken of all possible circumstances to send the enemy wounded back to the enemy army after they are given medicine and money. The treatment of the wounded enemy officers is also the same.

V. The Problem of the Political Training of Soldiers

A. *The problem of materials*

Textbooks should be very artistically compiled on the following topics, to be used as training materials for soldiers:

1. Analysis of the current political situation and the tasks and plans of the Red Army;
2. Various aspects of the agrarian revolution;
3. Armed organizations and their tactics;
4. The reasons for developing the Three Main Rules of Discipline;
5. Roll call slogans for mornings and evenings;
6. The literacy movement;
7. How to carry out mass work;
8. Item-by-item explanations of Red Army slogans;
9. The correction of various deviations;
10. The Soviet Russian Red Army;

11. The present stage of the revolution, and its future;
12. Comparison between the Red Army and the White armies;
13. Comparison between the Communist Party and the Guomindang;
14. Revolutionary stories;
15. Stories of social evolution;
16. Hygiene;
17. Basic knowledge of the geography, politics, and economy of the guerrilla areas;
18. Revolutionary songs;
19. Pictures and newspapers.

B. Methods

1. Attending political courses

a. The courses are divided into ordinary, special, and cadres' courses. There are two kinds of ordinary courses: When the whole detachment is in one place, the detachment constitutes the unit for attending courses, and the political commissars of detachments serve as course directors. The political commissars of companies serve as teachers of different courses. Apart from combat soldiers who should take the courses, messengers, orderlies, permanent laborers, grooms, and cooks should all come to class. The objective of the ordinary courses is to enable ordinary soldiers to gain elementary political knowledge.

b. A special course is formed with the detachment as a unit by selecting through examination fifty soldiers from various brigades who have some degree of literacy and a little basic political knowledge. Detachment political commissars serve as head teachers, and brigade political commissars teach various classes. The objective of special courses is to produce talented people with political knowledge higher than that taught in ordinary courses, so that in future they may be promoted to serve as lower-ranking cadres.

c. Cadre courses are formed with columns as a unit. Troops directly attached to armies may also constitute a unit. Cadre courses are composed of company commanders, deputy company commanders, squadron commanders and deputy squadron commanders, junior officers at all levels, and other designated persons. The objective is to raise the existing political level of the lower-ranking cadres to enable them to lead the masses and to become middle-ranking cadres in the future. The teachers are the political commissars, heads of the political departments of columns, column commanders, and other capable persons.

d. Committees on political training should be organized with detachments as the unit. The organizers are those political commissars and military commanders of detachments who are capable of acting as political instructors. The political commissars of detachments should be the directors. The task is to discuss various issues about the political training of soldiers within the detachments.

e. Political training in the troops directly attached to armies and various columns should be conducted by the committees on political training organized by the political propaganda sections of the army and various columns.

f. Methods of teaching:
    i.   Stimulating methods (abolish stuffing methods);
    ii. Proceed from near to far;
    iii. Proceed from the easy to the difficult;
    iv. Speak in popular language (new words should be explained in an easily understandable way);
    v. Speak clearly;
    vi. Speak with humor;
    vii. Gesture to assist speaking;
    viii. Review previously learned concepts;
    ix. Prepare outlines;
    x. Cadre courses should adopt the form of discussions.

2. Speeches at roll call in the mornings and evenings
   a. Speeches are limited to no more than half an hour at a time.
   b. Materials:
    i.   Report political news;
    ii. Criticize daily life;
    iii. Explain political slogans of the week.

3. Speeches at assemblies
   a. Once every week for detachments; once every half month for columns; those for the whole army are flexible.
   b. The content of every speech must be decided, speakers must be appointed, and the times of speeches must be apportioned through discussion between political work organs and military affairs organs.
   c. Everyone must attend all talks, except those on duty.
   d. Lower-level political organs must report to higher-level political organs about the influence of the content of each speech on the masses.

4. One-to-one talks
   a. One-to-one talks must be conducted with the following types of people:
    i.   Those who have erroneous tendencies;
    ii. Those who have been punished;
    iii. Wounded soldiers;
    iv. Sick soldiers;

      v.   New soldiers;
     vi. Captured soldiers;
   vii. Those who do not like their work;
  viii. Those who are ideologically vacillating;

    b. Before making speeches, the psychology and environment of the objects of talks should be investigated.

    c. During the talks, one should take a comradely position, and speak to the person sincerely.

    d. After the talks, the gist and impact of the talks must be recorded.

5. Recreational activities

    a. With companies as units, the work of the entertainment department of soldiers' associations should be strengthened by carrying out the following recreational activities:

      i.   Hide and seek, etc.;
     ii. Soccer;
    iii. Music;
    iv. Martial arts;
     v.   Flower drum tunes;
    vi. Old operas;

    b. Every propaganda team should set up a makeup propaganda troupe.

    c. The equipment expenses of recreational activities are paid with public funds (the expenses of brigades are approved by the political departments of columns).

6. Improve treatment

    a. Resolutely abolish corporal punishment;

    b. Abolish insults and curses;

    c. Preferential treatment of wounded soldiers;

    d. Restore the system of issuing 0.4 *yuan* in silver every month for straw shoes;

7. How to conduct special education for new soldiers and captured soldiers

    a. Inform new soldiers and captured soldiers of the customs of life in the Red Army, such as: 1. equality between the lives of officers and soldiers (there are only differences of duties but no differences of class between officers and soldiers, and the officers are not the exploiting class and the soldiers are not the exploited class); 2. the Three Main Rules of Discipline and their rationale; 3. the significance and functions of soldiers' associations; 4. the economic systems in the Red Army (economic resources, managerial and economic organizations, economic openness, and the system of inspection by soldiers); 5. the management of company messes, submesses and their surpluses by economic committees; 6. abolishing physical punishments and insults; 7. considerate treatment of captured soldiers.

b. Explain in outline the history of the Red Army.

c. The guiding principles of the Red Army: 1. The differences between the Red Army and the White army should be explained in detail to captured soldiers; 2. the difference between the Red Army and bandits; 3. the three great tasks of the Red Army.

d. Explain the organizational systems of the Red Army.

e. Basic political knowledge, such as: 1. The Guomindang and the Communist Party; 2. the aggression against China by the three big imperialist countries of Britain, Japan, and the United States; 3. the fighting among various factions of warlords under the direction of imperialism; 4. redistribution of land; 5. the soviets; 6. the Red Guards.

VI. Special Education for Young Soldiers

A. The political departments of various columns are responsible for compiling literacy textbooks for the young (using as reference materials the primary school textbooks of the Commercial Press, *The Common People's Thousand-Character Textbook*, the textbooks compiled by the Longyan Cultural Association, etc.).

B. Every column should set up an internal school of young soldiers with three to four classes. Every detachment forms one class and every directly attached unit has one class. The number of students for each class should not exceed twenty-five persons. The director of the political department should be the principal of the school, and the head of the propaganda section should be the dean. Each class has a head teacher and should complete ninety hours of instruction as one semester.

C. Paper, pen, ink, and other accoutrements shall be purchased with public funds and issued to students.

VII. The Problem of Abolishing Corporal Punishment

A. The Effects of Using Corporal Punishment in the Red Army

The units that have the severest beatings are hated by soldiers the most and have the most numerous deserters. The most obvious examples are the following: A certain officer of the Eighth Detachment of the Third Column liked to beat people. As a result, not only did all the dispatchers and cooks run away but the quartermaster sergeant and the adjutant also ran away. For a time, there was a company commander in the Twenty-fifth Brigade of the Ninth Detachment who took extreme pleasure in hitting people and was called blacksmith by the masses. Consequently, the soldiers felt that they had no way out and were full of resentment and hate. Only when this company commander was transferred elsewhere were the soldiers liberated. The beatings in the Third Company of the Special Task Detachment led to the desertion of four cooks, a head of the special task force, and two squad leaders with long experience of struggle. One of the squad leaders by the name of Xie Wencheng left behind a letter before he went away, explaining that he was not a counterrevolutionary and fled only because he could no longer stand the oppression. In the early period of the founding of the Fourth Column, the column commanders transferred from the Second and Third Columns were bent on beating soldiers brutally. As a result, the soldiers deserted one after another, and finally these officers themselves could not maintain their foothold there and had to leave the Fourth Column. The Second Column has more deserters than any other column. Although there is more than one cause, one of the most important is that the majority of lower-ranking officers of the Second Column have the worst habit of beating people up. In the Second Column, there have been three cases of suicide (one platoon leader and two soldiers). This is the biggest blemish on the Red Army and has the gravest significance. It must be acknowledged that this results from the particular prevalence of the practice of beating people in the Second Column. The outcry of the ordinary soldiers in the Red Army now is "Officers do not beat soldiers, but they beat them to death"! Such expressions of the masses' anger, resentment, and hatred truly deserve our most serious attention.

B. The Origin of Corporal Punishment and the Reasons for Abolishing It

In order to maintain their feudal exploitation, the feudal classes have to use the cruelest punishment as a tool to suppress the resistance and rebellion of the oppressed. This is the reason why corporal punishment is a product of the feudal era. As the economy develops and progresses to the capitalist system, liberalism must be put forward to promote the individuality of the masses of workers, peasants, and soldiers, to strengthen their capacity to work and fight, and to create the conditions for capitalist development. Therefore, all capitalist states have generally abolished corporal punishment, and the strange phenomenon of beating people has long ceased to exist in their armies. As the economy develops to the birth of socialism, and the class struggle intensifies, the worker and peasant classes will overthrow the political authority of the ruling class and the exploitation based on this authority. Only by mobilizing the forces of the broad masses of their own classes can they win victory in this struggle. The soviet political régime is the political régime of the most advanced classes. No remnants of feudal systems should exist under it. Therefore, not only has the Soviet Union long since eliminated corporal punishment in the Red Army, but all of its laws strictly prohibit the use of corporal punishment. The Fourth Army of the Red Army is a product of a China that still has not eliminated the feudal system. Its main components are in large part transformed elements from feudal and warlord armies. The general ideas and habits of the feudal system are still widespread among ordinary officers and soldiers. So the habit of beating people and the conventional idea that fear can be instilled only through beating are still similar to the habits of feudal warlord armies. Although the slogan of officers not beating soldiers and the stipulations of soldiers' associations on the right to complain were put forward a long time ago, they are simply not effective. Consequently, distances between officers and soldiers have been created, the spirits of soldiers and officers have been depressed, the number of deserters is increasing daily, resentment and hatred permeate the army, and incidents of suicide have even occurred. This situation runs completely counter to the Red Army's tasks of struggle. If it is not corrected quickly, there will be indescribable dangers.

C. Methods of Correction

1. Resolutely abolish corporal punishment.
2. A movement for abolishing corporal punishment should be launched. This movement should be carried out among both officers and soldiers, so as to disseminate widely the significance of the saying that "to abolish corporal punishment serves precisely to assist the struggle" among the masses of officers and soldiers. Only thus can officers be made to feel not only that they will still be able to lead the soldiers after the abolition of corporal punishment, but that abolition can further benefit management and training. On the side of the soldiers, they will not become more mischievous because of the abolition of corporal punishment. On the contrary, their fighting spirit will be higher as a result of the abolition. The elimination of the misunderstandings between officers and soldiers will lead to conscientious acceptance of management, training, and general discipline.
3. After the abolition of corporal punishment, some wrongdoing may occasionally occur because of past habits. We should, therefore, strengthen our sense of duty and try to give play to the spirits of persuasion and voluntary observance of discipline in order to overcome this feudal system, which is most contradictory to the tasks of the struggle. A few instances of wrongdoing should never be a pretext for covering up the habit of beating people derived from the feudal system. All those who oppose the abolition of corporal punishment under the pretext of occasional wrongdoing, or go slow in the movement to abolish corporal punishment, are objectively obstructing the development of the revolutionary struggle and are in fact assisting the ruling class.
4. Legal procedures of the Red Army in abolishing corporal punishment: (1) The rules and regulations of the Red Army on punishment shall be amended. (2) The supreme military and political organs shall jointly issue a notice abolishing corporal punishment and promulgate new rules and regulations of the Red Army on punishment. (3) After the notice is issued, the military and political organs should, on the one hand, convene meetings of officers to explain thoroughly the

reasons for abolishing corporal punishment and to enable all the officers to support the important reform embodied in the notice and try hard to implement it in their units. (4) On the other hand, soldiers' associations should convene representative conferences of soldiers to support this reform and to demand conscientious observance of discipline in the future. In addition, the disciplinary sanctions by the masses should be strict for the purpose of achieving good results after the abolition of corporal punishment.

VIII. On the Question of Granting Considerate Treatment to Wounded Soldiers

A. The Sufferings of Wounded and Sick Soldiers and Their Impact

1. The medical units of all forces of the whole army are not well established, with few medical officers and little medicine, insufficient stretchers and equipment, and few and incompetent staff members. Therefore, at times many wounded and sick soldiers cannot obtain adequate treatment or even general preliminary treatment.

2. The military and political organs of the whole army have not given enough attention to wounded and sick soldiers. For example, (1) Utmost efforts have not been made to develop medical units and, moreover, absolutely no attention has been paid to this issue. Meetings of all kinds rarely discuss the issue of health. (2) Officers fail to do all they possibly can to comfort wounded and sick soldiers at all times, such as bringing them tea, covering them with quilts, and visiting them frequently. These and other habits are almost nonexistent in the Red Army. The officers adopt an attitude of ignoring wounded and sick soldiers or even of loathing them. (3) During marches, officers and even soldiers show absolutely no sympathy toward wounded soldiers who fall out of ranks. Not only do they fail to find ways to help the wounded but they angrily curse them or drive them away ruthlessly.

3. Supplies and funds for seriously wounded and sick soldiers are insufficient. Seven or eight days after being wounded, the soldiers still have no clothes into which to change. The wounded officers have money for recuperation, but wounded soldiers have none.

4. The shortcomings of Jiaoyang Hospital: (1) a state of anarchy; (2) severe shortage of medical officers and medicine; (3) medical officers selling medicine illegally; (4) unhygienic; (5) lack of winter clothes; (6) too few nurses; (7) poor food supplies; (8) lack of living space; (9) a poor relationship with the local masses. All this makes wounded and sick soldiers regard the hospital as a prison and dislike staying in the rear.

The above-mentioned ill treatment of wounded and sick soldiers has the following impact: (1) Soldiers are dissatisfied with the Red Army. The opinion "the Red Army is fine so long as one is not wounded or sick" is very prevalent among the entire body of soldiers and lower-ranking officers. (2) The discontent of soldiers and officers will further increase the misunderstandings between them. (3) Soldiers and officers are all afraid of being wounded, thus weakening the fighting force of the Red Army. (4) More deserters. (5) The masses of workers and peasants are influenced, and their courage to join the Red Army is diminished.

B. Methods for Resolving the Problem

1. Military and political organs should never behave as they did in the past and pay no attention to the issue of health, and future meetings should discuss the issue of health.

2. The organization of medical units should be made particularly sound. Competent staff should be recruited, and those who are not wanted elsewhere should not be stuffed into medical units. The number of staff members should be increased to provide adequate care. The problem of lack of doctors and medicine should be resolved by all means. With regard to doctors, attention should be paid to urge them to examine patients carefully and to avoid rashness.

3. Officers, especially those at company level, who are close to the soldiers, should frequently visit wounded soldiers, bring them tea to drink, and cover them with quilts at night. If they feel cold, solutions should be found for them, such as borrowing from others or increasing clothes for them. The above methods of taking care of the wounded should become a system, and everyone should carry it out, for this is the best method to win support from the masses.

4. Concerning wounded soldiers who fall behind the ranks during marches: (1) They are not allowed to be cursed furiously or sneered at. (2) They should be kindly persuaded and not forced aside with one push when asking them to make way. (3) No matter which forces or units they are in and whether they are combat or noncombat soldiers, all those who fall behind the ranks because of sickness or wounds should be taken care of by sending a person over. If they are seriously wounded or sick, the best efforts should be made to hire helpers to carry them. (4) In every march, the rear guard should be patient and bring up the wounded and sick soldiers who have fallen behind and carry back guns and ammunition for them whenever necessary.

5. In issuing pocket money to wounded soldiers, consideration should be given to the severity of their wound or sickness. More money should be given to the seriously wounded or sick than to the slightly wounded or sick. The very seriously wounded or sick should be given money for recuperation in light of their condition regardless of whether they are officers, soldiers, or laborers.

6. Concerning the issue of clothes and quilts to wounded and sick soldiers, besides those provided by the units in the best way they can, requests for donations should be intiated among officers and soldiers in all units. This not only serves to increase the pocket money of the wounded but is also a good method for arousing the spirit of mutual assistance and aiding those in hardship.

7. The many shortcomings of Jiaoyang Hospital in the rear should be corrected systematically. Furthermore, a request for donations (clothes, quilts, cash, and grain) should be launched among the masses of workers and peasants in western Fujian to strengthen the link between the masses of workers and peasants and the Red Army.

IX. On the Problem of the Relationship between the Military System and Political System of the Red Army

A. Before the establishment of high-level local political organs, the political and military organs of the Red Army work on an equal footing under the guidance of the Front Committee.

B. The relationship between the Red Army and the masses:

1. All items that have significance for the whole Army, such as the issuance of political programs, should be put out by the military and political organs jointly.

2. Before the establishment of local political organs, the guidance and supervision of mass work such as propaganda to the masses, organization of the masses, the establishment of political régimes, confiscation, administration of justice, punishment, fund raising, and disaster relief shall be the responsibility of the political department.

3. In areas where no political organs have been established, the political department of the Red Army should substitute itself for local political organs until such organs are established. In the areas where local political organs have already been established, the principle of enabling the local political organs to handle all matters independently and of consolidating the belief of the masses in them should be adhered to. Only in areas where local political organs are not well established, and on issues that concern both the Red Army and the localities, may the method of handling matters jointly by local political organs and the Political Department of the Red Army be employed.

4. Assisting the establishment and development of local armed forces is the responsibility of the Political Department, and assisting peacetime military training and wartime combat command of local armed forces is the responsibility of Headquarters. In both cases, the channel passing through local political organs needs to be used as much as possible and direct handling should be avoided as much as possible.

C. Inside the Red Army, the military and political systems have independent channels for dealing with personnel and administration. When they have contacts such as transfer of personnel and exchange of information, they should interact through official letters on an equal footing.

D. With regard to courtesy and administration of military discipline, both the military and political systems in their mutual relationships should abide by the principle of submitting themselves to the class[65] and should not go slow or disobey orders in any way on the pretext that the systems are different.

E. On matters such as supplies, hygiene, marches, combat, and taking up quarters, the political system should be under the command of the military system. On matters concerning political training and the work of the masses, the military system should be under the command of the political system. But the only way to command is by direct guidance of the subordinate units in the opposite system (the general affairs section or the adjutant's office).

F. All matters concerning the guidance of fund-raising and the determination and spending of funds for political work in the Red Army are under the jurisdiction of the Political Department and should not be interfered with by military organs. (The procedure of withdrawing funds is that the Political Department makes direct contact with the military supplies section.) The expenditure for the party headquarters should be apportioned by the Political Department.

G. Regarding all orders of military organs, apart from those that must be countersigned by the political commissar, the director of the Political Department does not need to sign them. All orders of political organs are executed by the Political Department independently and the political commissar does not need to countersign them.

---

65. I.e., of subordinating themselves to the interests of the working class.

———————————1930———————————

New Year's Day[1]

(To the Tune of "Like a Dream")

(January 1930)

Ninghua, Qingliu, and Guihua,[2]
Paths are narrow, forests deep, moss slippery.
Whither shall we go today?
Straight to the foot of Wuyi Mountain.
At the foot of the mountain, the foot of the mountain,
The wind unfurls our red banner like a picture.

This poem was first published in *Shikan*, January 1957. Our source is *Shici duilian*, pp. 31–32.

1. This refers to the first day of the lunar new year, which fell in 1930 on January 30.

2. Names of three *xian* in Fujian Province, through which Mao led his Red Army troops at the beginning of 1930.

Letter to Comrade Lin Biao

(January 5, 1930)

Comrade Lin Biao:

Several days have gone by since New Year and I still have not replied to your letter. One reason is that some things have kept me busy, and another is that I have been wondering what I should actually write to you. Do I have anything good to offer you? After racking my brain, I still could not find anything suitable, so I put it off. Now I have thought of a few things. Although I do not know whether they really apply to your situation, the few things I have to say are indeed about an important problem in the present struggle. Even if it does not apply to your particular circumstances, it is still a crucial general problem, and that is why I am bringing it up.

What is the problem that I want to raise? It is the problem of how to evaluate the current situation and what actions we should take in consequence.[1] *I felt quite strongly in the past, and to some extent I still feel now, that your evaluation of the situation is rather pessimistic. This viewpoint of yours was most obvious at the meeting on the evening of May 18 last year in Ruijin.* I know that you[2] believe that a revolutionary high tide will inevitably arise, but you[3] do not

---

This text first appeared in the 1947 Jin-Cha-Ji edition of Mao's works, *Mao Zedong xuanji*, compiled by the Central Bureau of the Chinese Communist Party for the Jin-Cha-Ji Border Area, *Xubian* (Supplement) (Xinhua shudian, 1947), and we have translated it from that source. It was about to be similarly published in the two-volume 1948 edition compiled by the Jin-Ji-Lu-Yu Central Bureau of the Party, when Lin Biao made a plea to the Central Committee that a document so critical of him should not be reproduced yet again. The relevant pages were therefore cut out of the books, which had already been printed, and the title blotted out in the table of contents. All references to Lin were subsequently removed in the official version published in 1951 in the *Selected Works*, under the title "A Single Spark Can Start a Prairie Fire." The fact that Lin Biao was the target is indicated in the second Chinese edition of the *Xuanji*, published in 1991, but the new title has been retained. The extensive passages quoted by Mao in this text from his letter of April 5, 1929, are reproduced here as in the translation which appears above under that date. Variants introduced by Mao in 1951 are indicated in the usual way.

1. The problem of how to evaluate the current situation and what actions we should take in consequence → Some comrades in our Party still do not know how to evaluate the current situation and what actions we should take in consequence.
2. I know that you → Although they
3. Here, and in the balance of this paragraph, you → they.

believe it could possibly come quickly. Consequently, *as far as action is concerned,* you do not approve of the plan to take Jiangxi *in one year* and approve only of guerrilla actions[4] in the three areas on the borders of Fujian, Guangdong, and Jiangxi; at the same time, you do not have a deep understanding of what it means to establish Red political power in the three areas and, therefore, do not have a deep understanding of the idea of accelerating the nationwide revolutionary high tide through the consolidation and expansion of Red political power. *Judging from your belief in the policy of * * * style mobile guerrilla actions,*[5] you seem to think that, since the revolutionary high tide is still remote, to undertake the arduous work of establishing political power would be to labor in vain. Instead, you want to extend our political influence through the easier method of roving guerrilla actions and wait until the masses throughout the country have been won over, or more or less won over, before launching a nationwide insurrection[6] which, with the participation of the Red Army, would become a great nationwide revolution. Your theory that we must first win over the masses everywhere on a nationwide scale, and then establish political power, is not, *in my opinion,* applicable to the Chinese revolution. *As I see it,* this theory derives mainly from your failure to understand clearly that China is a semicolonial country for which imperialism is contending in its final stages.[7] If you clearly recognized this, then you would understand, first of all, why, in the whole world, the strange phenomenon of chaotic warfare within the ruling class is found in China alone, why this warfare is steadily growing fiercer and more widespread, and why there can at no time be a unified political power. Second, you would understand the grave significance of the peasant problem[8] and hence why rural insurrections have developed on the present nationwide scale. Third, you would understand the *absolute* correctness of the slogan of workers' and peasants' political power.[9] Fourth, you would understand another strange phenomenon, which follows from the first (that in China alone there is chaotic warfare within the ruling class), namely, the existence and development of the Red Army and guerrilla forces, and together with them, the existence and development of small areas of Red political power[10] *(the soviets)* encircled by the White régime. (This

---

4. Guerrilla actions → Roving guerrilla actions

5. It is not clear whether the words, or the name, omitted here by the editors of the 1947 edition refer to a historical personage, to one of the leaders of the Red Army at the time, or more generally to something like "peasant-rebel style." The missing name might possibly be that of the Taipings, persistently held up by Li Lisan at this time as a model for the organization of a guerrilla army; perhaps Mao was accusing Lin of shifting his allegiance to Li.

6. Insurrection → Armed uprising

7. Imperialism is contending in its final stages → Many imperialist countries are contending

8. The grave significance of the peasant problem → The gravity of the peasant problem

9. Workers' and peasants' political power → Workers' and peasants' democratic political power

10. Small areas of Red political power → Small Red areas

strange thing does not exist outside China.) Fifth, you would understand that the expansion of the Red Army, the guerrilla forces and the Soviet areas[11] is the highest form of the peasant struggle in a semicolony, and the form toward which the semicolonial peasant struggle must move.[12] *Sixth, you would understand that they (the Red Army and the peasants' soviet) are undoubtedly the most significant allied forces of the proletarian struggle in the semicolonial countries. (The proletariat must step forward to lead them)*, and that they are important factors[13] in promoting the revolutionary high tide throughout the country. And seventh, you would also understand that the policy which merely calls for roving guerrilla actions cannot accomplish the task of promoting this nationwide revolutionary high tide, while the kind of policy adopted by Zhu and Mao, *He Long, Li Wenlin*, and Fang Zhimin is undoubtedly correct—that is, the policy of establishing base areas; of systematically setting up political power; *of close coordination, organization, and training of the Red Army, the guerrilla troops, and the broad peasant masses;* of deepening the agrarian revolution; of expanding the armed forces[14] by a comprehensive process of building up first the township insurrection troops,[15] then the district Red Guards, then the *xian* Red Guards, then the local Red Army troops, all the way up to non-local Red Army troops;[16] and of spreading political power by advancing in a series of waves. Only thus is it possible to build the confidence of the revolutionary masses throughout the country, as Soviet Russia[17] has built it throughout the world. Only thus is it possible to create tremendous difficulties for the ruling classes,[18] shake their foundations, and hasten their internal disintegration. Only thus is it really possible to create a Red Army which will become *one of* the important instruments[19] in the great revolution of the future. In short, only thus is it possible to promote the revolutionary high tide.

Now, I would like to say more about what I feel are the reasons for your rather pessimistic evaluation of the situation. I feel that your evaluation is the exact opposite of the evaluation by the faction within the Party who suffer from revolutionary impetuosity. Comrades who commit the error of revolutionary impetuosity overestimate the subjective forces and underestimate the objective

---

11. The expansion of the Red Army, the guerrilla forces, and the Soviet areas → The development and expansion of the Red Army, the guerrilla forces, and the Red areas
12. The highest form of peasant struggle in a semicolony and the form toward which the semicolonial peasant struggle must move → The highest form of peasant struggle in semicolonial China under the leadership of the proletariat and the inevitable outcome of the growth of the semicolonial peasant struggle.
13. Important factors → The most important factors
14. The armed forces → The people's armed forces
15. The township insurrection troops → The township Red Guards
16. Nonlocal Red Army troops → The regular Red Army troops
17. Soviet Russia → The Soviet Union
18. The ruling classes → The reactionary ruling classes
19. One of the important instruments → The chief instrument

forces.[20] Such an appraisal stems mainly from idealism,[21] and in the end undoubtedly leads to the *erroneous* path of adventurism. *You have not made this mistake; but your shortcomings seem to be of another kind,* namely, underestimating subjective forces and overestimating objective forces to a certain extent. This would also constitute an improper appraisal and be certain to produce bad results of another kind. You acknowledge the weakness of subjective forces and the strength of objective ones, but you do not seem to recognize the following key points:[22]

1. Although the subjective forces of the revolution in China are weak, so also are all organizations (organs of political power, armed forces, political parties, etc.) of the ruling classes, resting as they do on the fragile social and economic structure[23] of China. This helps to explain why revolution cannot break out at once in the countries of Western Europe, where, although the subjective forces of revolution are much stronger[24] than in China, the forces of the ruling classes are many times stronger. In China the revolution will undoubtedly move toward a high tide more rapidly than in Western Europe, for although the subjective forces of the revolution at present are weak, the objective forces are weak, too.

2. The subjective forces of the revolution have indeed been greatly weakened since the defeat of the Great Revolution.[25] The remaining *subjective* forces are very small, and if one judges by form,[26] this naturally makes the comrades (those comrades who have this way of looking at things) feel pessimistic. But if we judge by reality, it is quite another story. Here we can apply the old Chinese saying, "A single spark can start a prairie fire." In other words, our forces, although small at present, will grow very rapidly. In the conditions prevailing in China, their growth is not only possible but indeed inevitable, as the May Thirtieth movement and the Great Revolution which followed have fully proved. When we look at a thing, we must examine its essence and treat its form merely as an usher at the threshold, and once we cross the threshold, we must grasp the

---

20. Overestimate the subjective forces and underestimate the objective forces → Overestimate the subjective forces of the revolution and underestimate the forces of the counterrevolution. As indicated by this emendation of 1951, Mao refers to the forces of revolution as "subjective," because they are within the control of the Communist leadership, and the forces of counterrevolution as "objective," because they constitute an external reality with which the Communists must deal. There is little doubt, however, that in this letter he is also talking more broadly about the importance of subjective factors and "conscious action," which he had stressed since his earliest youth.

21. Idealism → Subjectivism

22. You acknowledge the weakness of subjective forces and the strength of objective ones, but you do not seem to recognize the following key points: → Therefore, in judging the political situation in China it is necessary to understand the following:

23. The fragile social and economic structure → The backward and fragile social and economic structure

24. Are much stronger → Are perhaps now somewhat stronger

25. The Great Revolution → The revolution in 1927

26. Form → Appearances alone

essence of the thing *and throw away the form that serves as an usher;* this is the only reliable and scientific method of analysis *that has revolutionary significance.*

3. Similarly, in appraising the objective forces,[27] we must never look merely at their form, but should examine their essence. In the initial period of our independent régime in the Hunan-Jiangxi Border Area, a few comrades, *under the influence of the incorrect appraisal of the Hunan Provincial Committee at that time,* genuinely believed the words of[28] the Hunan Provincial Committee and regarded the class enemy as altogether worthless; the two descriptive terms, "thoroughly shaky" and "utterly panic-stricken," which are standing jokes to this day, were used by the Hunan Provincial Committee at the time (from May to June the year before last) in assessing the Hunan ruler Lu Diping. Such an assessment necessarily led to adventurism in the political sphere. But during the four months from November the year before last to February last year (before the outbreak of the war between Chiang Kaishek and the Guangxi warlords), when the largest and the third[29] "joint suppression expedition" was approaching the Jinggangshan, some comrades expressed doubts, saying, "How long can we keep the Red flag flying?" As a matter of fact, the struggle in China between Britain, the United States and Japan had by then become quite open and a state of tangled warfare between Chiang Kaishek, the Guangxi clique and Feng Yuxiang was taking shape; hence it was actually the time when the counter-revolutionary tide had begun to ebb and the revolutionary tide to rise again. Yet a pessimistic mentality[30] was to be found not only in the Red Army and local Party organizations; even the Central Committee was misled by the superficial *objective* situation[31] and adopted a pessimistic tone. Its February 7 letter is evidence of the pessimistic analysis made in the Party at that time.

4. The objective situation today is still such that comrades who see only the form[32] and not the essence of what is before them are liable to be misled. In particular, when our comrades working in the Red Army are defeated in battle or encircled or pursued by strong enemy forces, they often unwittingly generalize and exaggerate their momentary, specific, and limited situation, as though the situation in China and the world as a whole gave no cause for optimism and the prospects of victory for the revolution were remote. The reason they brush aside the essence[33] in their observation of things is that they have no scientific understanding[34] of the essence of the overall situation. The question of whether there will soon be a revolutionary high tide in China can be decided only by making a

---

27. In appraising the objective forces → In appraising the counterrevolutionary forces
28. The words of → The incorrect appraisal made by
29. The largest and the third → The enemy's third
30. Mentality → Ideas
31. Situation → Appearances
32. The form → The superficial appearance
33. Brush aside the essence → Seize on the appearance and brush aside the essence
34. They have no scientific understanding → They have not made a scientific analysis

detailed examination to ascertain whether the contradictions leading to a revolutionary high tide are developing. If we correctly recognize that[35] contradictions are developing in the world between the imperialist countries, between the imperialist countries and their colonies, and between the imperialists and the proletariat,[36] *it follows that* the need of the imperialists to contend for the domination of China becomes more urgent. While the imperialist contention becomes more intense, both the contradiction between imperialism and the whole Chinese nation and the contradictions among the imperialists themselves develop simultaneously on Chinese soil, thereby creating the tangled warfare which is expanding and intensifying daily and giving rise to the continuous development of the contradictions among China's ruling classes.[37] In the wake of the contradictions among the rulers—the chaotic warfare among the warlords—come ruthless increases of taxation,[38] which steadily sharpen the contradiction between the broad masses of taxpayers and the rulers.[39] In the wake of the contradiction between imperialism and China's capitalism[40] comes the failure of the Chinese bourgeoisie[41] to obtain concessions from the imperialists, which sharpens the contradiction between the Chinese bourgeoisie and the Chinese working class, forcing the Chinese bourgeoisie to increase exploitation of the working class.[42] In the wake of imperialist commercial aggression, merchant-capitalist extortions, heavier burdens of taxation, and so on, comes the deepening of the contradiction between the landlord class and the peasantry, that is, exploitation through rent and interest is aggravated.[43] Because of the pressure of foreign goods, the exhaustion of the consumer power[44] of the worker and peasant masses, and the increase in government taxation, more and more dealers in Chinese-made goods and independent *small* producers are being driven into bankruptcy. Because of endless expansion of armies and constant extension of the warfare under the condition of lack of provisions and funds, the masses of soldiers are in the daily misery of suffering from hunger and cold, flight, and casualties.[45] Because of the growth in

---

35. If we correctly recognize that → Since

36. The proletariat → The proletariat in their own countries

37. Among China's ruling classes → Among the different cliques of China's reactionary rulers

38. Ruthless increases of taxation → Heavier taxation

39. The rulers → The reactionary rulers

40. China's capitalism —→ China's national industry

41. The Chinese bourgeoisie → The Chinese industrialists

42. Forcing the Chinese bourgeoisie to increase exploitation of the working class. → With the Chinese capitalists trying to find a way out by frantically exploiting the workers and with the workers resisting.

43. Exploitation through rent and interest is aggravated → Exploitation through rent and usury is aggravated and the hatred of the peasants for the landlords grows

44. Consumer power → Purchasing power

45. In the daily misery of suffering from hunger and cold, flight, and casualties → In a constant state of privation

government taxation, the rise in rent and interest demanded by the landlords, and the daily spread of the disasters of war, famine and banditry are everywhere and the peasant masses and the urban poor can hardly keep alive. Because the schools have no money, students fear that their education may be interrupted; because production is backward, graduates have no hope of employment. Once we understand all these contradictions, we shall see in what a desperate situation, in what an anarchic state,[46] China finds herself. We shall also see that the high tide of revolution against the imperialists, the warlords, and the landlords is inevitable and will come very soon. All China is spread with dry faggots which will soon be aflame. The saying "A single spark can start a prairie fire" is an apt description of the present situation.[47] We need only look at *the development of the national situation, in which* the strikes by the workers, the uprisings by the peasants, the mutinies of soldiers, and the strikes of *merchants and* students are taking place everywhere, to see that they are no longer just "sparks" and that the time of a great "prairie fire" is undoubtedly not far off.

The gist of the above was already contained in the letter from the Front Committee to the Central Committee on April 5, 1929, which reads in part:

> The Central Committee's letter (dated February 9)[48] makes too pessimistic an appraisal of the objective situation and of the subjective forces. The three "suppression" campaigns[49] against the Jinggangshan represented the high water mark of the counterrevolutionary tide. But there it stopped, and since then the counterrevolutionary tide has gradually receded, while the revolutionary tide has gradually risen. Although our Party's fighting capacity and organizational strength have been weakened to the extent described by the Central Committee, they will be rapidly restored, and the passivity among comrades in the Party will quickly disappear as the counterrevolutionary tide gradually ebbs. The masses will certainly come over to us. Butcherism serves only to "drive the fish into deep waters," and reformism no longer has any appeal to the masses. The illusions of the masses about the Guomindang will assuredly be soon dissipated. In the circumstances which will arise, no other party will be able to compete with the Communist Party in winning over the masses. The political line and the organizational line laid down by the Sixth Congress[50] are *entirely* correct: the current stage of the revolution is democratic and not socialist, and the present task of the Party[51] is to win over the masses and not

---

46. Anarchic state → Chaotic state

47. Of the present situation → Of how the current situation will develop.

48. February 9 → February 9 of last year. (The correct date for the Central Committee's letter to which Mao had responded on April 5, 1929, is February 7. Both the Jin-cha-ji edition of Mao's writings and the 1951 *Selected Works* have here February 9; this error is corrected in the 1991 second edition of the *Xuanji*.)

49. The three "suppression" campaigns → The Guomindang's three "suppression" campaigns

50. The Sixth Congress → The Party's Sixth Congress

51. In this instance, instead of modifying the text, Mao in 1951 inserted, after the word "Party," a parenthetical note reading: "Here the words 'in the big cities' should have been added."

to stage immediate *armed* insurrections. Nevertheless, the revolution is developing[52] swiftly, and we should adopt a positive spirit[53] in our propaganda about, and in preparations for, armed insurrection. In the present chaotic situation we can lead the masses only if we have positive slogans and a positive spirit. Only by having such a spirit can the Party recover its fighting capacity. *We feel that the Party committed the error of adventurism in the past, and now it has a rather marked liquidationist tendency in some places.* . . . Proletarian leadership is the sole key to the victory of the revolution. Building up the Party's proletarian basis, and establishing Party branches in industrial enterprises in key areas are the greatest organizational tasks[54] for the Party at present. But, at the same time, the development of the struggle in the countryside, the establishment of soviets [55] in small areas, and the creation and expansion of the Red Army are prerequisites[56] for aiding the struggle in the cities and hastening the revolutionary upsurge. The greatest mistake would therefore be to abandon the struggle in the cities *and sink into rural guerrilla-ism.* But in our opinion, it is also a mistake—if any of our Party members hold such views—to fear the development of the power of the peasants lest it outstrip the workers' leadership[57] and become detrimental to the revolution. For the revolution in semicolonial China will fail only if the peasant struggle is deprived of the leadership of the workers; the revolution itself will never suffer just because the peasant struggle develops in such a way as to become more powerful than the workers.

The letter also contained the following reply on the question of the Red Army's operational tactics:

The Central Committee asks us to divide our forces into very small units and disperse them over the countryside and to withdraw Zhu De and Mao Zedong from the army, thus concealing the major targets—all this with the aim of preserving the Red Army and arousing the masses. This is a kind of ideal view.[58] In the winter of 1927–1928, we did start to plan[59] to disperse our forces over the countryside, with each company or battalion operating on its own and adopting guerrilla tactics in order to arouse the masses while trying not to present a target for the enemy; we have tried this many times, but have failed every time. The reasons are: 1. Most of the soldiers of the Red Army[60] come from other areas and have a background different from that of the local Red Guards . . . ; 2. Division into small units results in weak leadership *and*

---

52. Is developing → Will develop
53. Spirit → Attitude
54. The greatest organizational tasks → Important organizational tasks
55. Soviets → Red political power
56. Prerequisites → Essential prerequisites
57. The workers' leadership → The workers' strength
58. Ideal view → Way of thinking which does not correspond to reality
59. We did start to plan → We did plan
60. Most of the soldiers of the Red Army → Most of the soldiers in the main force of the Red Army

organization and inability to cope with adverse circumstances, which easily lead to defeat; 3. The units are liable to be crushed by the enemy one by one . . . ; 4. The more adverse the circumstances, the greater the need for concentration and for the leaders to be resolute in struggle, because only thus can we have internal unity to resist the enemy. Only in favorable circumstances is it advisable to divide our forces for guerrilla operations, and it is only then that the leaders need not stay with the ranks all the time, as they must in adverse circumstances. . . . [61]

The weakness of this passage is that the reasons adduced against the division of forces were all of a negative character, and this is altogether insufficient. The positive reason for concentrating our forces should be[62] that only concentration will enable us to crush[63] comparatively large enemy units and occupy towns. Only after we have crushed comparatively large enemy units and occupied towns can we arouse the masses on a broad scale and set up political power extending over several adjoining *xian*. Only thus can we make a widespread impact (what we call "extending our political influence") and contribute *somewhat* effectively to speeding the day of the revolutionary high tide. For instance, both the régime we set up in the Hunan-Jiangxi Border Area the year before last and the one we set up in western Fujian last year were the product of this policy of concentrating our troops. This is a major principle.[64] But are there not times when our forces should be divided up? Yes, there are. The letter from the Front Committee to the Central Committee spoke of guerrilla tactics for the Red Army, including the division of forces within a short radius. *The main points are as follows:*

The tactics we have derived from the struggle of the past three years are indeed different from any other tactics, ancient or modern, Chinese or foreign. With our tactics, the masses can be aroused for struggle on an ever-broadening scale, and no enemy, however powerful, can cope with us. Ours are guerrilla tactics. They consist mainly of the following points:

"Divide our forces to arouse the masses, concentrate our forces to deal with the enemy."

"The enemy advances, we retreat; the enemy camps, we harass; the enemy tires, we attack; the enemy retreats, we pursue."

"To extend stable base areas, employ the policy of advancing in waves; when pursued by a powerful enemy, employ the policy of circling around."

"Arouse the largest numbers of the masses in the shortest possible time and by the best possible methods."

---

61. The suspension points here are Mao's but we have added the indication that points (1) and (3) of the April 5 letter are quoted above in abridged form.

62. Should be → Is

63. To crush → To wipe out

64. A major principle → A general principle

> These tactics are just like casting a net; at any moment we should be able to cast it or draw it in. We cast it wide to win over the masses and draw it in to deal with the enemy. Such are the tactics we have used for the past three years.

Here, "to cast the net wide" means to do so within a short radius. For example, when we first captured the *xian* town of Yongxin in the Hunan-Jiangxi Border Area, we divided the forces of the Twenty-ninth and Thirty-first Regiments within the boundaries of Yongxin *xian*. Again, when we captured Yongxin for the third time, we once more divided our forces by dispatching the Twenty-eighth Regiment to the border of Anfu *xian*, the Twenty-ninth to Lianhua, and the Thirty-first to the border of Ji'an *xian*. And we again divided our forces in the *xian* of southern Jiangxi last April and May, and in the *xian* of western Fujian last July. *These are all appropriate examples.* As for dividing our forces over a wide radius, it is possible only on the two conditions that circumstances are comparatively favorable and the leading bodies fairly strong. For the purpose of dividing up our forces is to put us in a better position for winning over the masses, for deepening the agrarian revolution and establishing political power, and for expanding the Red Army and the local armed units. It is better not to divide our forces when this purpose cannot be attained, or when, on the contrary, the division of our forces would *even* lead to defeat and to the weakening of the Red Army, as happened in August two years ago when our forces were divided on the Hunan-Jiangxi border for an attack on Chenzhou. But there is no doubt that, given the two above-mentioned conditions, we should divide our forces, because division is then more advantageous than concentration. *As for dividing our forces in order to preserve our real strength and avoid the concentration of targets under grave circumstances, I am in principle opposed to this, as explained in the letter of the Front Committee to the Central Committee quoted above. Apart from this, will there be times when the division of forces to carry out the work is necessary, because the economic situation does not permit concentration? Perhaps there will be. But I cannot draw definite conclusions about it, since we have no concrete experience of such circumstances.*

The Central Committee's February letter was not in the right spirit and had a bad effect on a few Party comrades[65] in the Fourth Army. *It seems that even you were influenced by it to some extent.* At that time the Central Committee also issued a circular stating that war would not necessarily break out between Chiang Kaishek and the Guangxi warlords. Since then, however, the appraisals and directives of the Central Committee have, in the main, been *entirely* correct. It has already issued another circular correcting the one containing the wrong appraisal. (*In fact, only a part of the circular was wrong.*) Although it has not made any correction of the letter to the Red Army, its subsequent directives have been completely devoid of those pessimistic sentiments and its views on the Red

---

65. A few Party comrades → Some Party comrades

Army's operations now coincide completely with those of the Front Committee. Yet the bad effect which this letter had on some comrades still persists. *Although the Front Committee's letter replying to the Central Committee was distributed within the Party at the same time as the Central Committee's letter, it does not appear to have had any great influence on these comrades, because the letter of the Central Committee met their taste exactly. The many correct directives issued later by the Central Committee regarding the situation have, on the other hand, either been ignored by these comrades or have not been able to wash away their earlier impression.* Therefore, I feel that it is still necessary to give some explanation.

As for the plan to take Jiangxi Province within one year, it was also proposed last April by the Front Committee to the Central Committee, and a decision to that effect was later made at Yudu. The reasons for this were given in the letter to the Central Committee, *and I reproduce them here*:

> The armies of Chiang Kaishek and the Guangxi warlords are approaching each other in the vicinity of Jiujiang, and a big battle is imminent. Henceforth, the rule of the Guomindang will disintegrate, and the revolutionary high tide will arrive very quickly.[66] As for how our work should be arranged under these circumstances, we feel that, so far as the southern provinces are concerned, the armed forces of the compradors and landlords in Guangdong and Hunan provinces are too strong, and that in Hunan, moreover, we have lost almost all the masses, inside as well as outside the Party, because of the error of the Party's adventurist *policies*. In the three provinces of Fujian, Jiangxi, and Zhejiang, however, the situation is different. First, the military forces[67] are weakest there. In Zhejiang, there is only a small provincial defense force under Jiang Bocheng. In Fujian, although there are five groups of enemy troops, totaling fourteen regiments in all, Guo's troops have already been smashed; the troops under Chen and Lu are bandits of small fighting capacity; the two brigades of marines stationed along the coast have never seen action and their fighting capacity is undoubtedly not great; Zhang Zhen alone can put up some sort of a fight, but according to an analysis made by the Fujian Provincial Committee, even he has only two good regiments.[68] In addition, Fujian is now in a state of complete anarchy[69] and disunity. In Jiangxi, there are sixteen regiments under the two commands of Zhu Peide and Xiong Shihui; they are stronger than the armed forces of either Fujian or Zhejiang, but far inferior to those of Hunan. . . . Secondly, fewer adventurist mistakes have been made in these three provinces. We are not clear about the situation in Zhejiang, but the Party's organizational and mass base is somewhat better in Jiangxi and Fujian than in Hunan.

---

66. Henceforth, the rule of the Guomindang will disintegrate, and the revolutionary high tide will arrive very quickly → The resumption of mass struggle, coupled with the spread of contradictions among the ruling reactionaries, makes it probable that there will soon be a high tide of revolution.

67. The military forces → The military forces of the enemy

68. Good regiments → Relatively strong regiments

69. Complete anarchy → Complete chaos

Take Jiangxi, for example. In northern Jiangxi we still have some bases in De'an, Xiushui, and Tonggu; in western Jiangxi the Party and the Red Guards still have some strength in Ninggang, Yongxin, Lianhua, and Suichuan; in southern Jiangxi the prospects are still *much* brighter, as the Second and Fourth Regiments of the Red Army are steadily growing in strength in the *xian* of Ji'an, Yongxin, and Xingguo; moreover, the Red Army under Fang Zhimin has by no means been wiped out. All this places us in a position to close in on Nanchang. We hereby recommend to the Central Committee that during the period of prolonged and chaotic warfare among the Guomindang warlords, we should contend with Chiang Kaishek and the Guangxi clique for Jiangxi Province, and at the same time for western Fujian and western Zhejiang. In these three provinces we should enlarge the Red Army and create an independent régime of the masses, with a time limit of one year for accomplishing this plan. *During this one year, we must lay the foundations for the struggle of the proletariat in Shanghai, Wuxi, Ningpo, Hangzhou, Fuzhou, Xiamen, and other places, so that they can lead the peasant struggles in Zhejiang, Jiangxi, and Fujian. The Jiangxi Provincial Committee must be soundly established, and efforts must be made to build a basis among the workers in Nanchang, Jiujiang, Ji'an, and on the Nanchang-Jiujiang Railroad.*

This proposal to take Jiangxi *within one year* erred only in *mechanically* setting a time limit of one year. *In my understanding*, taking Jiangxi also implied, apart from conditions within the province itself, that a nationwide revolutionary high tide would soon arise. For unless we had been convinced that there would soon be a high tide of revolution, we could not possibly have concluded that we could take Jiangxi in one year. The defect of the proposal was that it should not have *mechanically* set a time limit of one year, thus giving a flavor of *rigidity and* impetuosity to the word "soon" in the statement "there will soon be a high tide of revolution." *Your failure to believe in taking Jiangxi in one year results, however, from your overestimate of objective forces and underestimate of subjective forces. That is why you do not believe in the rapid arrival of a revolutionary high tide, and why you reach this conclusion.* As to the subjective and objective conditions in Jiangxi, they very much merit our attention. Apart from subjective conditions, which are still as described above,[70] *and about which I have no new opinions to add*, three points can now be clearly made regarding objective conditions. First, the economy of Jiangxi is mainly one of feudal *remnants, or of exploitation through land rents*, the merchant-capitalist class is relatively weak, and the armed forces of the landlords are stronger[71] than in any other southern province. Second, Jiangxi has no provincial troops of its own and has always been garrisoned by troops from other provinces. Sent there for the "suppression of Communists" or "suppression of bandits," these troops are unfamiliar with local conditions, their interests are much less directly involved than if

---

70. Described above → Described in the letter to the Central Committee
71. Are stronger → Are weaker

they were local troops, and they usually lack enthusiasm. And thirdly, unlike Guangdong which is close to Hong Kong and under British control in almost every respect, Jiangxi is comparatively remote from imperialist influence. Once we have grasped these three points, we can understand why rural insurrections[72] are more widespread and the Red Army and guerrilla units more numerous in Jiangxi than in any other province.

I have more or less finished what I want to say to you. I have been long-winded and perhaps have said too much. But I feel that our discussion of the problem has been beneficial. If indeed the issue that we have been discussing is resolved correctly, it will have a very substantial impact on the actions of the Red Army. That is why I have been very glad to write this piece.

Two last points must still be clarified. First, how then should we interpret the word "soon" in the statement "there will soon be a high tide of revolution"? This is a question shared by many comrades. Marxists are not fortune-tellers. They should, and indeed can, only indicate the general direction of future developments and changes; they should not and cannot fix the day and the hour in a mechanistic way. But when I say that there will soon be a high tide of revolution in China, I am emphatically not speaking of something which in the words of some people "is possibly coming," something illusory, unattainable, and devoid of significance for action. It is like a ship far out at sea whose masthead can already be seen *at the horizon* from the shore; it is like the morning sun in the east whose shimmering rays are visible from a high mountain top; it is like a child about to be born moving restlessly in its mother's womb. *Second, when I say that you want to use the method of mobile guerrilla actions to extend political influence, I do not mean that you have a purely military viewpoint or the ideology of roving rebel bands. Manifestly, you have neither of them, for these two kinds of ideas are devoid of any concept of winning over the masses and you, on the contrary, have proposed to "go all out to mobilize the masses." Not only have you advocated this but you have been carrying it out in practice. What I disapprove of is your lack of an incisive concept for building political power. Consequently, the task of winning over the masses and promoting a revolutionary high tide can definitely not be successfully accomplished as you have imagined in your mind. The main purpose of my letter is to make this point.*

Please correct me where I am wrong.

> Mao Zedong
> At Shanghang, Gutian

---

72. Insurrections → Uprisings

Letter from the Fourth Army of the Chinese Red Army (the Red Army of Zhu and Mao) to the Soldiers of the Guomindang Army

(January 1930)

Brother soldiers of the Guomindang army!

1. The warlords are now opening fire again!

The warlords are now fighting again. On the one hand, the imperialist allies are attacking the Soviet Union (Russia), and the Chinese warlord Chiang Kaishek is their loyal running dog; on the other hand, Chiang Kaishek, having usurped all power over the central government, has aroused the opposition of warlords big and small throughout the nation. The first kind of war, the attack on the Soviet Union, is a worldwide war of all counterrevolutionary forces attacking the revolutionary forces, while the latter is a contest among the Chinese warlords, representing imperialist interests, to seize the central government's territorial sphere of control. The outbreak of both these wars has aggravated the suffering of the workers, peasants, and soldiers, especially our brothers who are soldiers, who are tragically sacrificed directly for the warlords and imperialists. Since the situation has become this serious, you must absolutely think, brothers, about what is the way out for us soldiers!

2. Listen to the views of the Red Army:

We are China's Red Army. Two years ago a portion of our comrades fighting to the death for the national revolution, struggling bitterly, saw with their own eyes old brothers and new brothers, one group after another, become cannon fodder for the army commanders and division commanders of the Guomindang high command. Not one iota of the slogans that the Guomindang addressed to the workers and peasants and soldiers was actually carried out. Moreover, they defended the mounting oppression of the people by the local bullies and bad gentry. Especially detestable was their murder of leaders of the workers and

---

Our source for this text is *Mao Zedong ji. Bujuan*, Vol. 3, pp. 61–68, where it has been taken from two documentary collections published in China, one in 1979 and the other in 1982.

peasants associations and of Communist Party members. It was not until the black plot of this phony revolution was exposed that we really understood that the Guomindang was a counterrevolutionary thing. It was only then that we got our comrades together and with our rifles went into the countryside to join the workers and peasants to carry out the land revolution. In the last two years, the counterrevolutionary national government, using military forces from three provinces, has attacked us several times, but in the end has not been able to hurt the Red Army in the slightest. On the contrary, we thank them for sending us reinforcements which have served to make the Red Army stronger. The fact that today the Red Army is appearing everywhere throughout the nation is full proof that the strength of the worker and peasant masses is growing day by day. We are people who have been deceived by the Guomindang, and as the day of this battle approaches we think of the suffering of our brothers, and we specially and very sincerely offer an opinion to our brothers!

3. Why do we want to support the Soviet Union?

Brothers! First, we must realize the danger that the imperialist attacks on the Soviet Union pose to those of us who are soldiers. Today the entire world is divided into two fronts, one of which is the front of imperialist capitalism, of countries like Great Britain, the United States, Japan, and France, which specialize in oppressing the proletariat and the weak and small nations. Since coming to power in Nanjing, Chiang Kaishek has shamelessly surrendered to the imperialists, because he is both a capitalist and a warlord and, therefore, acts as a running dog of the imperialists. The other is the front of the proletariat, of those like the Soviet Union and the impoverished workers, peasants, and soldiers of various countries. More than ten years ago, the Soviet Union overthrew the Russian emperor and established a government of the workers, peasants, and soldiers that swept away all the capitalists, landlords, and so on. When the workers, peasants, and soldiers themselves administer their own country, they attain true freedom and equality. As the proletariat of the entire world come to see that the Soviet Union has done as well as this, they will all rise up in revolution and join with the Soviet Union. For example, China had a great revolution between 1925 and 1927, which did indeed receive help from the Soviet Union. If the Guomindang had not turned against the revolution, if the revolution had not failed, the workers, peasants, and soldiers would long ago have gained political power and would long ago have established the second Soviet Union. It has now been two years since the Guomindang turned traitor, but the revolution still has not been destroyed. Furthermore, it is again gradually raising its head. This is true of China, and it is also true of other countries. The Soviet Union has become the elder brother of us workers, peasants, and soldiers, leading millions of wretched people to overthrow imperialism and the warlords. This has aroused extreme fear among the imperialists, who have no choice but to join together to attack the Soviet Union in order to suppress all the revolutionary forces. Under the direction of the imperialists, Chiang Kaishek has been loyally and bravely going out to attack the Soviet Union, creating the agitation of these past several months regarding the Chinese Eastern Railway.[1] This is plainly and clearly the beginning of the imperialist attack on the Soviet Union.[2] When one morning war erupts, you will see that the imperialists and the Chinese warlords will want to move tens of thousands or hundreds of thousands of troops into the battle. Indeed, they intend to use our toiling worker and peasant masses to strike at the toiling worker and peasant masses. How vicious! Brothers! We must make sure that we are not cheated. We must defend the Soviet Union, defend the state of the proletariat, and turn our rifles around and shoot at the Chinese warlords!

4. We must rise up and overthrow the warlords.

Brothers! Second, we must realize that the senseless wars of the Chinese warlords add to the sufferings of those of us who are soldiers and to that of the workers and peasants. The Chinese warlords, creatures such as Chiang Kaishek, Zhu Peide, Tang Shengzhi,[3] Feng Yuxiang, Yan Xishan,[4] Zhang Fakui,[5] Zhang

---

1. Diplomatic relations between China and the Soviet Union, established by the treaty of March 14, 1924, between Moscow and the Beijing government, had been officially broken off in December 1927, in the wake of Chiang Kaishek's conflict with the Chinese Communists, but de facto contacts continued. In particular, the agreement regarding joint control of the Chinese Eastern Railway was still observed. In May 1929, on the grounds that the Soviet-dominated railway administration was conducting subversive propaganda in the northeast, the Chinese authorities closed the Soviet consulate in Harbin and seized a large quantity of documents. The tension rose rapidly until, in July 1929, railway traffic was interrupted and all Soviet personnel arrested and expelled. In retaliation, the Soviet Far Eastern Army attacked and occupied several Chinese cities near the border. The undeclared war lasted until December, despite attempts by the United States to mediate, in the name of the Kellogg-Briand Pact. On December 22, 1929, a Sino-Soviet protocol was, however, concluded in Khabarovsk with Zhang Xueliang, leading to the reopening of the railway. A Sino-Soviet conference, originally scheduled for January 25, 1930, finally met in October, but was soon adjourned following the occupation of Northeast China by the Japanese. See Jürgen Domes, *Vertagte Revolution. Die Politik der Kuomintang in China, 1923–1937* (Berlin: Walter de Gruyter, 1969), pp. 375–80 (hereafter Domes, *Vertagte Revolution*).

2. In this and the previous sentence, Mao follows very closely the language of a Comintern statement of July 18, 1929, regarding the dispute, of which the relevant sentence reads: "Chiang Kaishek, the executioner of Chinese workers and peasants, acting on the orders of world imperialism, is openly provoking a fresh war against the Soviet Union." See Degras, *Communist International,* III, p. 74.

3. For a note on Zhu Peide see above, the declaration of August 1, 1927. For a note on Tang Shengzhi, see above, the Central Committee Circular of July 20, 1927.

4. Regarding Yan Xishan, see above, the note to the draft resolution of October 5, 1928.

5. For a note on Zhang Fakui, see above, the Jinggangshan Report of November 28, 1928.

Xueliang,[6] and others, are sometimes peaceable, sometimes the opposite, and when they start fighting, today it's Nanjing attacking Wuhan, tomorrow it's Wuhan striking at Nanjing. Sometimes Guangdong attacks Guangxi, and sometimes Guangxi attacks Guangdong. This happens several times a year, to the point that we soldiers become dazed and confused. Every time they go to war, we soldiers must die by the hundreds of thousands, while the warlords, whether they win or lose, always strip the land to the extent of hundreds of thousands and into the millions in some cases.[7] As for the common people, at least several provinces if not the entire nation suffer catastrophe! Ai! Why should such wars be fought? Do not Chiang Kaishek, Feng Yuxiang, Yan Xishan, and the others all belong to the same Guomindang? Are they not all comrades loyal to the same Three People's Principles? Do they not all pay the same kind of lip service to making revolution? All this turns out to be completely false. The Guomindang is a skin-the-people party[8] of the warlords, in which [the principle of] nationalism means capitulation to Great Britian, France, the United States, and Japan, people's rights means forbidding people from holding meetings, and people's livelihood means raising rents and increasing fees and taxes. The Guomindang warlords understand only fighting over territory, stripping the land, getting rich on foreign money, capitulating to the imperialists and relying on their patronage, and defending the interests of the imperialists. The imperialists aid the warlords with money and bullets, so the warlords' fighting will never stop, and it will never overthrow imperialism. Brothers! Because the territory was distributed unevenly after the overthrow of the Guangxi faction, Chiang Kaishek, Yan Xishan, Feng Yuxiang, Zhang Fakui, and the others are fighting again! This war must inevitably further aggravate the suffering of the soldiers and add to the exploitation of the people. Soldier comrades should rise up to oppose this, and everyone should refuse to fight for the warlords. Let the soldiers on both sides turn around and overthrow the warlords and seek their own way out!

5. What are the sufferings of us soldiers?

Brothers! Third, we must realize the source of our own suffering and also our way out. Brothers! We were not born soldiers, nor was it fated that we should be

---

6. Zhang Xueliang (1898–), *zi* Hanqing, a native of Liaoning, was the eldest son of Zhang Zuolin. After graduating from the Fengtian Military Academy, he served in his father's army, and by 1919 had attained the rank of colonel. He played an active role in the first and second Fengtian-Zhili wars of 1922 and 1924, in which he held important commands. As noted above, he became ruler of Manchuria following the assassination of his father on June 4, 1928. Having learned that the Japanese army was responsible for Zhang Zuolin's death, he turned against Japan and, in December 1928, pledged his allegiance to the Guomindang government in Nanjing. In early 1930, Chiang Kaishek, on the one hand, and Yan Xishan and Feng Yuxiang, on the other, were both seeking his support.

7. These figures may refer to amounts of income to be gained from the land.

8. This is a pun on the name of the Guomindang. The Chinese for "skin-the-people party" is *guamindang*.

soldiers. It's just that at home we had no clothes to wear, no food to eat, so we had no choice but to run off and become soldiers. Why is it that we had no clothes to wear and no food to eat? First of all, it's because the imperialists invaded China and used foreign goods to make money from China. The vast market for foreign goods made it impossible to sell local products, so local production had to stop. As a result, tens of millions of workers and peasants inevitably lost their jobs. To this was added the successive years of warlord fighting, oppression by greedy bureaucrats and corrupt officials, local bullies and bad gentry, and exploitation by harsh fees and miscellaneous taxes. All these things together left our common people with no way of making a living. Having nowhere to turn, anyone who didn't become a bandit had no alternative but to serve as a soldier. After we joined the army, we first entered an army camp, where every day we had three drills and two lectures, seven beatings and eight scoldings, from hitting the palms of our hands to beatings on the buttocks, being locked up tight, expelled, and even used for target practice. These ways of treating us are a matter of course to the warlords! The main idea is to cultivate in us a slavishness of character so that we dare not rebel. And the soldier's clothing? At most two sets of clothing to wear, too long, too short, clothes that don't fit at all, so that when we go out people laugh at us. Bedding? Just a bed or two of old blankets, too heavy in summer and too light in winter, full of big holes, which might as well be a base camp for bedbugs. And living quarters? The army officers are leeches and refuse to spend money for repairs. With the wind blowing and the sun scorching, they treat the soldiers worse than prisoners in a jail. The army salaries that aren't paid for several months or years go into their pockets. The money for food is never given out, and the warlords skimp on food by providing terrible meals of rice gruel and cabbage every day, all with no oil and no salt. This is the clothing, food, and housing for soldiers. If one is wounded in battle and taken to the hospital for wounded soldiers, there are even stranger things to be seen—men who are blind, crippled, or have broken backs, lying on cots unable to move. Over there someone sobbing, over here another screaming, no funds, no medicine, the nasty stench of yellow pus running from wounds. A wounded soldier can only die a painful death. So everyone hopes for the relief of one last bullet, to end the torture of living. Ai! Compare these conditions with the Western-style houses of the warlords, playing mah-jongg, eating Western food, sleeping with several mistresses apiece, with millions in the bank—is any of them worth it? There are also warlords who deliberately embezzle money from the soldiers' salaries, so that the soldiers are totally impoverished, and then even say to our brothers: Don't worry, the war starts soon. When the war reaches a big place, our brothers can take a lot of things. Ai! This is the evil plot of the warlords! They embezzle from the army's salaries and command us to go into battle to steal. They really want us to risk our lives for them. Some brothers are happy when they hear that they are going to fight, thinking that this will be their chance to get rich, and every time they rush forward to steal wildly. This is part of the the warlords' poisonous plot. Think about it. Every time the fighting reaches a city, the warlords have long before announced that the big stores and banks are to be protected. Who would dare touch them? To get rich you could only go to the small merchants and the suffering common people, but they, like us, are suffering! Think about it again. The soldiers have fought several hundred wars for the warlords, from Guangdong to Beijing, with the result that there has been a reduction in troop size, keeping the strong and healthy and getting rid of the maimed. Let me ask you, has any soldier ever gone home with money in his pocket? The warlords' statement that you can get rich by fighting is nothing but one of their poisonous schemes to get us to risk our lives for them! Brothers, you must not let them cheat you! Ai! Brothers! At home, the oppression of the imperialists, warlords, and despotic gentry forced us to run out and join the army, and after joining the army we are still oppressed by the imperialists and, furthermore, become the tools for defending the oppression of the people by the imperialists, warlords, and despotic gentry. Without us soldiers, the imperialists, warlords, and despotic gentry could not be as cruel as this; without us soldiers, the workers and peasants and toiling common people would not suffer or be oppressed like this. We soldiers are ourselves oppressed, and we act as running dogs for others, oppressing our own wretched compatriots, getting nothing out of it for ourselves, just helping the warlords to get rich. Ai! How stupid this is! It's not worth it! Do we still not understand?

6. What alternative do we have?

Brothers! In the past, some of our brothers in the Red Army were, like you, very obedient to the warlord officers, and did not understand that the warlords are detestable. Afterward, the facts allowed them to see through the dark curtain of the warlords' oppression of the soldiers. Only then did they fully understand that the workers, the peasants, and the soldiers are of the same flesh and blood, that they should join together, so only then did they resolve to leave the warlords and come over to the side of the Red Army. Brothers! Do you want to know what the advantages of the Red Army are?

7. The Red Army is the army of the revolution of the workers and peasants.

First of all, the Red Army is the army of the worker and peasant revolution. The brothers of the Red Army cannot be separated from the workers and peasants. Worker and peasant comrades, shouldering rifles and making up the ranks— these are the Red Army. Red Army comrades, putting down their rifles and going out into the fields and into the factories—these are the workers and peasants. This is why, when the Red Army reaches a location, the workers and peasants form a crowd to welcome us, cook rice and make tea, kill pigs and slaughter sheep, to welcome us. Those local bullies and bad gentry who flee run away; those who are caught are fined, or else they are brought to trial and sentenced by a meeting of the workers, peasants, and soldiers. All their lands and property are disposed of by decision of a big meeting of the workers, peasants, and soldiers. It is for this reason that the Red Army and the workers and peasants, joining together as one, divide the lands, and with their own government for governing themselves, create a world of true freedom and equality. For example, Red Armies exist today in many places, in Guangdong, Fujian, Jiangxi, Hunan, Hubei, Henan, and Sichuan. All these are organized by the workers and peasants themselves!

8. The Red Army is an army of the soldiers themselves.

Second, the Red Army is an army of the soldiers themselves. The Guomindang army hangs out the label, National Revolutionary Army, but in its bones it is an army of the warlords. The officers have authority; the soldiers have no authority. The relationship between officers and troops in the Red Army is like that between teacher and student, like the bond of affection between older and younger brothers. Clothing, food, and living quarters are managed jointly by representatives elected by the soldiers, and are provided by the government of the workers, peasants, and soldiers. Thus in the Red Army the officers, the soldiers, and the laborers all dress, eat, and are paid the same. In the Red Army, there are only different tasks; there are no class distinctions. The commanding officer does not beat the soldiers; the soldiers respect the commanding officer; finances are open and public; and the representatives of the soldiers have the right to ask questions. How much the entire army has and how much it uses is clear and open. There is absolutely no such strange thing as the private pocketing of funds for salaries or food allotments. If an inequity occurs, a meeting can be called to raise and question it, and it will be dealt with immediately and fairly. That is why only the Red Army is a real army, based on the interests of the troops, with absolutely no oppression.

9. The Red Army supports the Communist Party in uniting the forces of the world revolution.

The Red Army supports the Communist Party in uniting the forces of the world revolution. The forces of imperialism and of the warlords are extremely great, and they have, moreover, a worldwide union. Our revolution of the workers, peasants, and soldiers must assuredly also have a worldwide union if we are to be able to overthrow them. The Communist Party is the guiding organ of the worldwide revolution and has very good organizations in various countries. The Red Army must necessarily support the Communist Party, for only thus can it attain unity with the world revolution. The political views and military plans of the Communist Party are all extremely correct and enlightened. Under the leadership of the Communist Party, the Red Army and the masses of the workers and peasants can definitely attain success, step by step. At the same time, the Communist Party is in no sense a special organization. It is simply that portion of comrades from among the workers, peasants, and soldiers who are the bravest, the most clear-headed, who have organized successfully, whose discipline has been especially strict, and who have worked especially hard. Any worker, peasant, or soldier who strives for revolution, and demonstrates this in his work, is qualified to join the Communist Party. Thus, the Communist Party is the party of the workers, peasants, and soldiers themselves. It is definitely not like the Guomindang, which is an organ only of a few warlords, capitalists, and despotic gentry, which crushes the workers, peasants, and soldiers under its feet.

Brothers! It is precisely for the above three reasons that the Zhu-Mao Red Army has been able to extend the battle to four provinces, and the counterrevolutionary factions have not been able to do anything about it. This proves that it is only when we soldiers go over to the Red Army that we shall be able to enjoy the support and welcome of the workers and peasants, that it is only when we accept the guidance of the Communist Party that we can avoid taking the wrong road, that we can avoid being beasts of burden for the warlords. Brothers! Today war has already broken out. On the one hand, it again increases the oppression that we workers and peasants and soldiers suffer at the hands of the imperialists and warlords, but on the other hand, when the imperialists and warlords fight, it is really a good opportunity for us workers, peasants, and soldiers to unite. If there is to be hope for the victory both of the world revolution and of the Chinese revolution in the near future, it will depend solely on the unity and efforts of the workers, peasants, and soldiers.

10. Come over to the side of the Red Army! Brothers! Rise up! Be no longer the beasts of burden, the slaves, of the warlords. Quickly bring your rifles and join the Red Army. The broad masses of the workers and peasants, and of the Red Army throughout the nation, warmly welcome you. Understand clearly that you were born into the worker-peasant proletarian class. Understand clearly that the enemies oppressing you are the imperialists and the warlords. Understand clearly that the workers and the peasants are your good friends. Understand clearly that the Red Army is the open road to your own self-liberation. Leave hell, rise up to heaven. Come quickly!

11. Our common revolutionary slogans:

1. Oppose the imperialist attacks on the Soviet Union!
2. Oppose the wars of the Chinese warlords!
3. Soldier masses of the entire country, unite!
4. Don't go to the front; don't fight for the warlords! Don't be cannon fodder for the warlords!

5. Make the warlords pay back wages; demand a soldier's wage of 20 *yuan* per month!
6. Brother workers and peasants do not fight brother workers and peasants; soldiers do not fight soldiers!
7. Support the Red Army; come over with your rifles to the Red Army.
8. Carry out the work of the land revolution, of distributing land to soldiers!
9. Workers, peasants, and soldiers unite!
10. Support the government of the workers, peasants, and soldiers.
11. Support the Communist Party, overthrow the Guomindang!
12. Long live the success of the Chinese revolution!
13. Long live the success of the world revolution!

Land Law

(February 7, 1930)[1]

Chapter One: Confiscation and Redistribution of Land

Article 1. After the political power of the despotic gentry and landlord class has been overthrown by an armed uprising, all land, hills, woods, ponds, and houses owned by the despotic gentry and landlord class, as well as by ancestral halls, temples and societies, must be immediately confiscated, turned over to the soviet, and redistributed by the soviet to impoverished peasants, and other categories of people in need of land. Where there is only a peasant association, and a soviet has not yet been set up, the peasant association can also carry out confiscation and redistribution.

Article 2. Of the land, hills, woods, ponds and houses belonging to owner-peasants, if there is a surplus in excess of what is needed for self-support, after the majority of local peasants demand its confiscation, the soviet should approve the peasants' demand, confiscate the surplus portion and redistribute it.

Article 3. The families of the despotic gentry, landlords, and reactionaries, after undergoing investigation by the soviet and receiving permission to reside in the countryside, may receive an appropriate amount of land when they have no other means of supporting themselves.

Article 4. Officers, soldiers, and porters of the Red Army currently in military service and those engaged in revolutionary work shall also receive redistributed

---

Our source for this text is *Mao Zedong ji. Bujuan*, Vol. 3, pp. 69–74, where it is transcribed from a documentary collection published in China in 1982.

1. This law was adopted at a conference in Pitou village, Donggu district, Ji'an *xian*. (Regarding this gathering, see below, the "Front Committee Notice No. 1" of February 16 and the notes thereto.) While many paragraphs in this text are identical to provisions in the law dated August 1930, there are significant differences. The most notable point is the harsher attitude toward relatively well-to-do peasants. Thus, apart from landlords, paragraph 2 of this law (which does not appear in the August 1930 law) authorizes the confiscation and redistribution of land belonging not only to rich peasants, but to other owner-peasants, if they have more than the minimum required to support their families. On the other hand, paragraph 10 of this law calls only for "drawing on the plentiful to make up for the scarce," while the August law adds the principle of "drawing on the fat to make up for the lean," in other words, of taking the more productive land of well-to-do peasants and giving it to the poor peasants. For a discussion of Mao's evolving position on agrarian problems during 1930, see the Introduction to this volume.

land; moreover, the soviet shall assign people to help their families farm the land.

Article 5. Rural residents who can make a living through other lines of work, such as industry, commerce and education, shall not receive redistributed land. Those who cannot make ends meet may receive a suitable amount of redistributed land, no more than enough to make up the shortfall in their incomes.

Article 6. Farm laborers and unemployed vagrants, if they are willing to receive redistributed land, should be given land. But those vagrants who receive redistributed land must rid themselves of evil addictions, such as to opium and gambling, otherwise the soviet will take back their land.

Article 7. Those who have traveled to other areas and do not live in their native villages shall not receive land.

Article 8. There are two criteria for land redistribution as regards administrative subdivisions:

a. Using the township as the unit; the peasants of a certain township pool together the land they farm in their township and in neighboring townships and redistribute it jointly.

b. Using several townships as the unit. For example, three or four townships are adjacent to each other, and some of them have more land while the others have less land; if land is redistributed taking each township as the unit, the townships with less land cannot support themselves, nor do they have any other form of production to support themselves. In this case, three or four townships may be combined into one unit to carry out the redistribution. Of the above two methods, the first is widely applicable. Under special circumstances, the second method may be used after the township soviets have made a request and received permission from the district soviet.

Article 9. The quantitative criteria for land redistribution:

a. In order to meet the demands of the majority of the people and enable peasants to receive land quickly, land should be redistributed according to the number of people in the countryside; men, women, the old, and the young should receive equal shares.

b. In places with special circumstances, after the township soviets make the request and receive permission from the district soviet, the criterion of labor [power] may be used. Those who can work get twice as much land as those who cannot work (those between fourteen and sixty who can do farm work each constitute one labor unit).

Article 10. In order to destroy the feudal forces swiftly, land redistribution should follow the principle of drawing on the plentiful to make up for the scarce. It is not permitted to distribute the land a second time, applying the principle of absolute egalitarianism. After the land has been redistributed, the soviets shall make wooden markers and place them in the fields to mark the yield of the plot and the name of its current tiller.

Article 11. All land deeds of the despotic gentry, landlords, common land owned by ancestral halls, and temples must be surrendered to the township soviets or township/district peasant associations within a specified period to be burned in public. The deeds of the land owned by owner-peasants should also be burned if the majority of peasants so demand.

Article 12. After land is redistributed, the *xian* soviets or district soviets are to issue cultivation permits.

Article 13. The redistributed land of all those in the countryside who have died, changed their occupations, or gone elsewhere will be taken back by the soviets to be redistributed once more. As for newcomers and newborn babies, the soviets should find a way to give them land, but only after the harvest.

Article 14. When land is redistributed following an armed uprising, if the peasants have already sown the seeds, the crops harvested in this season belong to the peasants who previously farmed the land; others are not allowed to harvest these crops.

Article 15. Dikes and large ponds that are not easy to redistribute are placed under the management of the soviet for public use by the people; [the soviet] also supervises people to repair and maintain them.

Article 16. Large hills and forests that are not easy to redistribute are placed under the management of the soviet. When people need to cut bamboo, they must obtain permission from the soviets according to the following rules. Permission for cutting fewer than twenty stalks may be obtained from the township soviets; permission for cutting more than twenty and fewer than fifty stalks may be obtained from the district soviets; permission for cutting more than 50 stalks may be obtained from the *xian* soviets.

Article 17. The products of large hills and forests, aside from those supplied to meet the needs of the people, are to be marketed by the soviet; the proceeds are used to pay the expenses of the soviet. Higher-level soviets determine the proportions of the proceeds to be received by the soviets at each level.

Article 18. As for hills covered with camphor, China fir, and bamboo, which cannot easily be redistributed individually, several families should form one group and obtain [the rights] of cultivation from the soviet, making available the products of these hills for the use of the members of the group.

Article 19. In order to meet the demands of the impoverished peasants, all confiscated land should be completely redistributed to them. The soviet need not keep any back, but it should keep some of the confiscated houses to be used for public purposes.

Chapter Two: Cancellation of Debts

Article 20. No debts owed by workers, peasants, and poor people to the despotic gentry and landlords shall be repaid. Notes and debt certificates must be turned over to the soviet or peasant associations within a specified time to be burned.

Article 21. Debts owed by the gentry, landlords, and merchants to the government, workers, peasants, poor people, or the petty bourgeoisie must be repaid in full regardless of whether these debts are old or new.

Article 22. Debts owed by workers, peasants, and poor people to businessmen that arise out of commercial transactions and are not commercial high-interest loans must still be repaid; but only the principal, and not other types, will be repaid; debts owed for a long period of time will not be repaid, either.

Article 23. The debts owed between workers, peasants, and poor people themselves before the revolution should be repaid in full, reduced, or written off. Township and district soviets will make appropriate regulations according to concrete circumstances. Debts incurred after the revolution should be repaid in full.

Article 24. As for articles and houses pawned or mortgaged by workers, peasants, and poor people to the despotic gentry, landlords, and dishonest pawnbrokers, all collateral will be returned unconditionally.

Article 25. As for articles and houses pawned or mortgaged by workers, peasants, and poor people to the petty bourgeoisie, part, or none, of the collateral may be returned; this is to be determined by township and district soviets according to the economic circumstances of both sides.

Article 26. As for money and grain paid in advance by workers, peasants, and poor people to the gentry, landlords, and dishonest businessmen in credit unions and grain associations, the persons who take over the credit unions and grain associations should return the money and grain to their members and dissolve the organizations. As for money and grain taken in advance by workers, peasants, and poor people from the gentry, landlords, and dishonest businessmen, the persons who take over the credit unions and grain associations need not return the money and grain to their contributing members; these organizations are also to be dissolved.

Article 27. Usurious loans are banned under the soviet régime; *xian* soviets set appropriate interest rates according to local financial conditions. These rates must not exceed the amount of returns obtained by ordinary capital under normal local economic conditions.

Chapter Three: Land Taxes

Article 28. To meet the needs of overthrowing the counterrevolutionaries (for example, maintaining and expanding the Red Army and the Red Guards and maintaining the organs of political power) and to increase benefits for the masses (for example, setting up schools and clinics, providing relief to the handicapped, old, and young, and repairing roads and river embankments), the soviet must collect land taxes from peasants.

Article 29. Land taxes may be collected only after the soviet has been established, the masses have received actual benefits, and permission is granted by higher-level soviets.

Article 30. Land taxes are to be collected progressively according to the quantity and quality of the land redistributed to peasants:

1) Those who receive, per person, land that yields less than 5 *Dan* of rice are exempted from tax.

2) A tax rate of 1 percent is levied on those who receive, per person, land that yields 6 *Dan* of rice.

3) A tax rate of 1.5 percent is levied on those who receive, per person, land that yields 7 *Dan* of rice.

4) A tax rate of 2.5 percent is levied on those who receive, per person, land that yields 8 *Dan* of rice.

5) A tax rate of 4 percent is levied on those who receive, per person, land that yields 9 *Dan* of rice.

6) A tax rate of 5.5 percent is levied on those who receive, per person, land that yields 10 *Dan* of rice.

7) A tax rate of 7 percent is levied on those who receive, per person, land that yields 11 *Dan* of rice.

8) A tax rate of 8.5 percent is levied on those who receive, per person, land that yields 12 *Dan* of rice.

Each additional yield of 1 *Dan* of rice is accompanied by an increase of 1.5 percent in the land tax rate.

Article 31. Land tax revenues are distributed among the soviets at various levels according to the following proportions: Fifty percent to the township soviet; 20 percent to the district soviet; 20 percent to the *xian* soviet; 10 percent to the provincial soviet.

Article 32. No taxes are levied on the products of hills and forests that are enough only to provide for consumption by the people and leave no surplus. If there is a surplus in addition to personal consumption, the soviet levies taxes on the surplus portion of the sale value at appropriate rates.

Chapter Four: Wages

Article 33. Rural artisans, workers, and hired laborers whose previous wages were too low should get a raise. Future wages are to be set by the soviet according to two criteria: fluctuation in the cost of living and fluctuation in the peasants' harvests. Wage rates set by township and district soviets must be approved by the *xian* or provincial soviets.

On Occupying Ji'an and Establishing a Jiangxi Soviet Government

Proclamation Number 1 of the Joint Conference of the Front Committee, the Western Jiangxi Special Committee, and the Army Committees of the Fifth and Sixth Armies[1]

(February 14, 1930)

Resolution of the Joint Conference on plans for the first actions to be taken in the struggle in Jiangxi:

I. To make basic plans in accordance with the resolution of the Joint Conference concerning the political situation and the Party's tasks.

II. The overall objective and central slogans for present actions: the overall objective for present actions is to attack and take Ji'an, and the following six slogans are the central slogans for the present.

1. Take Ji'an and eliminate all reactionary forces.
2. Take Ji'an and set up a western Jiangxi soviet government.
3. Take Ji'an and completely redistribute the land.
4. Take Ji'an and further develop the arming of the workers and peasants.
5. Take Ji'an and put a stop to the indiscriminate fighting of the warlords.
6. Take Ji'an and give armed support to the Soviet Union.

All army groups, political organs, and mass organizations should immediately and publicly raise and widely disseminate the above six slogans among workers, peasants, and soldiers, and among other oppressed groups of people (medium and small merchants and students). (For workers, peasants, and poor townspeople, they should be written all over every wall. For soldiers, these should be the slogans shouted out during morning and evening roll call.) This is the only way

---

Our source for this text is *Mao Zedong ji. Bujuan*, Vol. 3, pp. 75–81, which reproduces it from a documentary collection published in China in 1982.

1. This public proclamation states Mao's vision of rapid revolutionary success more prudently than the inner-Party "Notice No. 1" which follows.

to mobilize the broad masses and achieve the political task of opposing the undermining of political objectives and subversive propaganda.

III. Estimation of the enemy's situation and the significance of the attack to take Ji'an.

1. The enemy's situation: The war in Guangxi and Guangdong continues undecided; a coup d'état has broken out in Fujian; military action is being taken against Zhou Lan and Wu Shang in Hunan; in Hubei there is a struggle between the Hubei faction (Xia Douyin and Xu Yuanquan) and the Chiang Kaishek faction; there is a stalemate between the old Guangxi faction (Li Shiqiao and Li Yixuan) and the Chiang Kaishek faction; Chiang Kaishek and Yan Xishan are actively cooking up a great war between north and south; the struggle of the workers, peasants, soldiers, poor people, and vagrants is developing everywhere. Given the situation outlined above, the Chiang Kaishek faction cannot possibly increase its troop strength in Jiangxi within a short period of time, and in eastern and northern Jiangxi, [we] can pin down at least three of Zhang Huizan's regiments (two eastern Jiangxi regiments and one northern Jiangxi regiment), and Zhang can deploy only three regiments of troops to deal with western Jiangxi. Tan Daoyuan's single division is unable to return, and Jin Handing has been pinned down by the workers and peasants in western Fujian.[2] At the same time, he also has to participate in the fight for territory in Fujian, so for the time being it will not be easy for him to get to western Jiangxi.

The deployment in western Jiangxi of the two regiments of the Cheng [Guangyao] brigade, the one regiment of the Zhu [Yaohua] brigade, and the pacification defense corps is as follows: at Ji'an, the two battalions of the pacification defense corps have a hundred and fifty rifles protecting the *xian* capitals of Fenyi, Yuanzhou, and Xinyu, altogether forming one battalion, plus one roving guerrilla company, and in addition Fenyi has a pacification defense corps of thirty rifles; at Yuanzhou the merchant defense corps and pacification defense corps have three hundred rifles; at Xinyu the pacification defense corps has sixty rifles; Xiajiang has the Yi regiment headquarters and seven companies of troops and also a pacification defense corps with eighty-five rifles and has fortifications; Sanqutan has one battalion doing guerrilla work between Ji'an and Sanqutan, Jishui has two companies (newly deployed) and a pacification defense corps with sixty-eight rifles; Xin'gan has only a pacification defense corps with thirty-five rifles; and Xingguo and Wan'an each have pacification defense corps protecting the towns. The enemy troops and the ruling classes of the above *xian* are all in a state of great panic.

2. Our situation: In western Jiangxi, the *xian* of Xingguo, Yudu, Ningdu, and Nanfeng have a total of 1.15 million Red masses. The six *xian* towns of Ninggang, Yongxin, Lianhua, Yongfeng, Le'an, and Ningdu are all ours. In

---

2. Tan Daoyuan (1888–1946), a native of Hunan, was at this time the commander of the Fiftieth Division of the Second Column of the Guomindang Ninth Route Army. Jin Handing (1891–1967), a native of Yunnan, was the commander of the Twelfth Division of the Guomindang army.

Taihe, Ji'an, and Jishui, only the *xian* towns are in enemy hands, while the four townships are in our hands. In Anfu, Xinyu, Fenyi, Xiajiang, Nanfeng, and Yudu, a part of each of them is in our hands. Most of Xingguo is Red territory. Add to this the fact that the various places to which the Fourth, Fifth, and Sixth Red Armies have gone in western Jiangxi still have a substantial number of local armed forces and fighting morale is very high.

3. Given the circumstances of the enemy and ourselves listed above, to "take Ji'an" is indeed to implement the demands of the broad popular masses. Since the past mobilizations of the broad popular masses have already shaken the enemy's foundations, this call to action is entirely correct. Our first step is not, however, to strike at the town of Ji'an, but rather to carry out an encirclement of the town of Ji'an with the objective of making life even more difficult inside the town, increasing the mental state of panic, and isolating White rule further. Afterward, we will proceed to the plan for step two (see attached).[3]

IV. Moving and deploying the troops

1. East of the Gan River: (a) The three columns of the Fourth Army and the units directly attached to Army Headquarters will all assemble at the town of Wujiang on February 13, and on the 14th the attack on Jishui city must be carried out with determination (the three columns of the Fourth Army will have completely razed the Yongfeng city walls before the 12th); (b) The Fourth Detachment of the Second Column of the Sixth Army will set out for Zhonghu on February 13, and on the 14th, in coordination with the popular masses of Zhonghu will use armed force to destroy the enemy at Shuidong and (two companies) will set up a watch over Ji'an city, in response to the Fourth Army attack on Jishui; (c) The Zhonghu soviet, in addition to sending a portion of the masses to coordinate with the attack of the Fourth Detachment on Shuidong, shall also send a portion of the masses to set out early on the 14th for Jishui city to join with the Fourth Army attack on the enemy within the city of Jishui and eliminate the enemy, with responsibility for tearing down the city walls and constructing a floating bridge; (d) The Fifth Detachment of the Second Column of the Sixth Army will arrive in Xingtian and Donggu on the 9th, and the Red Guards, under the command of Yuan Zhenya, will reach Xingtian on the 10th and join up with the Fifth Detachment, and organize an administrative committee to direct work in the Xingtian area, with Yuan Zhenya as secretary (names and responsibilities of the administrative committee separately attached); (e) The task of the Fourth Column and the Ningnan Guerrilla Corps of the Twenty-fifth Column of the Fourth Army, as set out by the Front Committee, will be to pin down Jin Handing and to raise funds in the large Red district comprising the three *xian* of Ningdu, Guangchang, and Nanfeng; (f) The significance of having the entire Fourth Army withdraw from Yongfeng and take Jishui is: to reveal the objective of the Fourth

---

3. No such plan is in fact attached to the available text of this document.

Army, by threatening Ji'an City from a point across from Ji'an, and to influence the popular masses downstream on the Gan River to rise up, and also to make the reactionary government at Nanchang focus on western Jiangxi; (g) After Jishui has been taken, the work of the Front Committee and of the Jishui *Xian* Committee will be (i) rapidly to dismantle the city wall; (ii) to set up a *xian* government; (iii) to set up a workers' organization in the *xian* town; (iv) to develop Party and Youth League work within the city and set up a regional committee.

2. West of the Gan River: (a) The activities and duties of the Fifth Army and of the border Red Guards: The Fifth Army and the border Red Guards (with at least four hundred rifles), will assemble at Yongyang by February 13 and, using Yongyang as the command center, will coordinate their action with the armed forces of the popular masses of the western district, to put pressure on the vicinity of Ji'an City, and at the same time be on the lookout for an enemy retreat from Taihe toward Ji'an and to cut them down if the occasion avails. All armed forces of the popular masses in the western district area will come under the command of the Fifth Army. (b) The First Column (originally the Second and Third Regiments) of the Sixth Army shall arrive by February 13 and assemble at Futian (if the Third Regiment cannot make it in time this may be delayed one day; the Second Regiment must arrive at the same time) and, using Futian as its command center, will coordinate its action with the armed forces of the popular masses of Xiangshui and Jintan, and the Jishui guerrilla corps, to put pressure on the three areas of Sanqutan, Ji'an, and Xiajiang. (i) A small unit from the First Column will be sent out to coordinate its action with the mass armed forces to harass the enemy at Sanqutan and make contact with the Fourth Army at Jishui; (ii) The guerrilla unit in the Xiajiang area will harass the enemy at Xiajiang City; (iii) Both inside and outside continue to have the Red Guards and the Ruxing guerrilla units assemble at Tongshuping to harass the enemy at Ji'an (harassing the enemy means to shoot at the enemy every day before dawn and in the middle of the night) and to cut the communications of the enemy at Ji'an and Sanqutan downstream, which is also a task of the First Column of the Sixth Army. All armed forces of the popular masses in the northern sector will be under the command of the First Column.

V. Rules of action and finance policies:

1. When any unit or group of the worker and peasant masses reaches a location, especially a town or city, and has not yet received orders, it must not engage in indiscriminate searches of the people or of shops.

2. When any unit reaches a location, especially a town or city, there should be planned assignments of that unit and responsible persons to split up and

search those places that should be searched and to arrest those offenders who should be arrested.

3. All confiscation of the property of reactionaries and all arrest of offenders shall be under the direction of the political department. Dealing with the search for remnants of the enemy and the confiscation of the military equipment of the reactionaries shall be under the direction and management of the headquarters command.

4. For all fines, fund-raising, confiscation, and dealing with offenders, the political department or mass organ of political power must make clear public proclamations or statements of crimes committed.

5. Schools and post offices must not be destroyed.

6. When not politically necessary, no public organs and no equipment or implements of the popular masses should be destroyed.

7. Burning and killing that has no political significance or mass basis are prohibited.

8. Financial policy: (a) The pay and provisions of the Red Army and the expenses of the political organs should be taken mainly from the despotic gentry and landlords and should not be added to the burdens of the middle and small merchants. (b) Payments shall not be exacted from shops with less than 2,000 *yuan* in capital, while those with over 2,000 *yuan* shall be required to make contributions to the army's pay and provisions according to the following scale: those with capital of 2,500 *yuan* shall contribute 30 *yuan*, and those with 3,000 *yuan* shall contribute 40 *yuan*. For each additional 1,000 *yuan* of capital, an added contribution of one percent on the total amount of capital shall be made. In the case of 4,000 *yuan* of capital, to the 40 *yuan* contribution shall be added one percent of 4,000 *yuan*, for a total of 80 *yuan*; for those with 5,000 *yuan* in capital, to the 80 *yuan* contribution is added 50 *yuan*, for a total contribution of 130 *yuan*; someone with 6,000 *yuan* in capital, in addition to the 130 *yuan* contribution shall pay another one percent on 6,000 *yuan*, or 60 *yuan*, for a total of 190 *yuan*; increased capital shall be calculated in similar fashion. (c) Payments exacted from big gentry landlords shall be called fines, while payments from merchants shall be called contributions. (d) For big gentry landlords who own shops, contributions on that portion of their capital that is in shops shall be made according to the scale, while fines shall be assessed against that portion they have as big gentry landlords. (e) Shops owned by reactionary elements, after the middle and small merchants have become sympathetic to the propaganda, may be confiscated; otherwise, they need not be confiscated. Reactionary shopowners should be arrested and fined when this is necessary because of its significance for the masses. (f) River traffic should undergo inspection as militarily necessary, but whether a certain type of boat traffic is stopped for a period of time, or boats are detained, the goods on board such boats and other property must not be confiscated.

VI. Mass mobilization inside and outside the Party.

1. A great political duty: It is only by mobilizing all the popular masses both inside and outside the Party that success has been achieved in many areas in the past, and the mistake of letting only a few responsible persons know the objectives of actions, and not letting the masses know them, should be resolutely abolished.

2. When this announcement reaches any location, various kinds of Party meetings and mass meetings and assemblies should be convened immediately, to report in detail on the political situation, on the situation of the crumbling of the reactionary forces and the high tide of the revolutionary forces internationally, nationally, in Jiangxi and in western Jiangxi, on the future of the struggle (the outbreak of the revolution in which workers and peasants will take over Jiangxi) and on the objectives of present actions (six central slogans), and also to announce the rules (the various rules of action). The Red Army and the organs of political authority should also post flyers to enable the popular masses to understand fully what it is we want to do.

3. Mobilizing within the Party: (a) The leading organs at all levels of the Party shall hold meetings to discuss this announcement and all successive announcements. (b) Hold a large meeting of activists and send persons from leading party organs to give reports. For the military, the meetings shall be held at the army, column, or detachment level. Local party meetings shall be held at the district level. (c) Hold branch meetings to report on the content of announcements and to mobilize all Party members.

4. Army mobilization: (a) Hold meetings of army political workers to report on the political situation, future struggles, the objectives of actions, and on the various rules, to discuss ways of implementation, and of guiding the soldiers to positive action. (b) Hold talk sessions with the soldiers which also report on various items such as the political situation, and instill in them the courage to struggle.

5. Mobilization of worker and peasant masses: (a) Hold meetings at all levels of mass organs and of worker and peasant cadres (i.e., hold committee meetings at all levels), and at the district level hold large mass meetings. (b) Large mass meetings, to be called Such-and-such District Demonstration Meeting for the Attack on Ji'an, must be held within three days after this announcement is received. Good preparations must be made beforehand, and afterward a report of the results is to be made to the higher organ. (c) The central slogans of the large mass meetings, in addition to the six central slogans listed above, will also include the following six slogans (a total of twelve slogans).

i. Welcome the Fourth, Fifth, and Sixth Red Armies to help eliminate the reactionary forces.

ii. Welcome the Fourth, Fifth, and Sixth Red Armies to help distribute the land.

iii. Welcome the Fourth, Fifth, and Sixth Red Armies to help establish soviets.

iv. Welcome the Fourth, Fifth, and Sixth Red Armies to help expand the armed forces of the workers and peasants.

v. Welcome the Fourth, Fifth, and Sixth Red Armies to eliminate the indiscriminate fighting of the warlords.

vi. Welcome the Fourth, Fifth, and Sixth Red Armies to provide armed support for the Soviet Union.

Presidium of the Joint Conference

Conclusion of the Joint Conference and Announcement of the Establishment of the Front Committee

Front Committee Notice No. 1

(February 16, 1930)

The Joint Conference of the Fourth Army Front Committee, the Western Jiangxi Special Committee, and the Army Committees of the Fifth and Sixth Armies, held at Pitou in Ji'an, met for four days, February 6 to 9.[1] The political situation at the time of the convening of the Joint Conference was that imperialism was actively preparing war against the Soviet Union, that the world proletariat and the oppressed colonial masses were rising up together to oppose imperialism, that the confused wars among the Chinese warlords were expanding daily, that financial and economic crisis was spreading throughout the whole country, that the opposition movement of the workers, peasants, soldiers, and urban poor was developing everywhere, and especially that the Red armed struggle in several southern provinces, with Jiangxi as its center, was developing on a large scale, with over three million workers, peasants, soldiers, and members of the impoverished masses carrying the Red flag. The Joint Conference clearly recognizes that with the movement of the imperialists to attack the Soviet Union, a high tide of world revolution will burst out, that the high tide of the Chinese revolution will arrive very soon, that Chinese soviets will

---

Our source for this document is *Mao Zedong ji. Bujuan*, Vol. 3, pp. 83–85, where it is taken from two documentary collections published in China, one in 1979 and one in 1982.

1. This conference was convened by Mao in Pitou village, Donggu District, Ji'an *xian*. As indicated in the final paragraph of the present text, Mao's Fourth Army Front Committee was transformed into a General Front Committee, and assumed overall control of the operations of the Fourth, Fifth, and Sixth Armies. Zhu De, commander of the Fourth Army, Peng Dehuai, commander of the Fifth Army, and Huang Gonglue, commander of the Sixth Army, all became members of the reorganized committee. At the same time, the Western Jiangxi and Southern Jiangxi Special Committees were combined into a Southwest Jiangxi Special Committee. The conference adopted the February 7 Land Law, translated above. Regarding broader questions of strategy, it not only reaffirmed the view, which Mao had been putting forward since April 1929, that power could be seized in the whole of Jiangxi in the relatively near future, but held out the prospect, in the present document, of a victory in the whole country which would contribute to the world revolution.

appear as successors to the Russian soviets, and that they will become a powerful branch of the world soviets. Within China a Jiangxi soviet will appear first, because the objective conditions and subjective forces are more mature in Jiangxi than in other provinces. The Joint Conference clearly recognized that the armed struggle in the five provinces of Fujian, Guangdong, Zhejiang, Jiangxi, and Hunan, centered on Jiangxi, is a situation that is developing daily, that it is a fresh banner of the land revolution which affects the entire country, that it is a powerful element pushing forward the revolutionary high tide in the whole country, and also that it has worldwide significance as a powerful element providing armed support for the soviets and promoting the world revolution.

On the basis of the above political assessment, the Joint Conference determined that the major tasks of the Party are: (1) to expand the territory of the soviets, and in particular to raise the slogan of seizing the entire province of Jiangxi; (2) to deepen the land revolution; (3) to expand the armed forces of the workers and peasants. The realization of these three tasks will bring about the successive elimination, under the Red flag, of the reactionary forces in the various southern provinces, will rally the broad popular masses together around the Red flag, and will become a great force that will push forward the revolution in the whole country. The Joint Conference also told our comrades, and all those masses presently engaged in struggle, that the realization of these three tasks will not come entirely without effort, that it can be obtained only through intense and bitter struggle, and that with the advance of the revolutionary forces the struggle will become greater and more arduous than ever before. For our opponent is not just those who rule China—the bourgeoisie and the landlord class; it is also those who rule the world—the imperialists. But the future of the difficult struggle will inevitably be that the high tide of the revolution in the whole country will help the forces of revolution in the south, so the revolutionary forces in the south will merge together with the revolutionary forces in the whole country to bury the ruling classes completely.

The Joint Conference points out that there is a severe crisis in the Party in western and southern Jiangxi. It consists in the fact that the local leading organs of the Party at all levels are filled with landlords and rich peasants, and the Party's policy is completely opportunist. If we do not thoroughly clean up this situation, not only will it be impossible to carry out the Party's great political tasks but the revolution will suffer a fundamental defeat. The Joint Conference calls on all revolutionary comrades within the Party to arise, overthrow the opportunist political leadership, eliminate the landlords and rich peasants from the Party, and see to it that the Party is rapidly bolshevized.

The revolutionary land law passed by the Joint Conference rejects the gradual redistribution of land and points out that, no matter where it occurs, after an uprising has driven out the despotic gentry, their lands must be confiscated immediately and distributed to the peasants. The criterion for the confiscation of land is not limited to the despotic gentry and landlords. Provided only that the popular masses truly demand it, the lands of owner-peasants may also be confiscated.[2] As regards the distribution of land, it is pointed out that the present objective of the land revolution is to shake the foundations of feudalism and to win over the broad popular masses, and it is for this reason that every effort should be made to redistribute all arable fields, all forests, ponds, and buildings to those who need these things, and it is only those things that are not easily divided up (high mountains and large lakes) that should be managed by the soviets and will be set aside for common use by the people. The Joint Conference points out that to take an ostensibly leftist position in the present stage, and advocate the theory of so-called common production and common consumption, in reality would help the despotic gentry and support the forces of feudalism and would go against our duty to destroy thoroughly the foundations of feudalism. At the same time, as between redistribution according to labor power and dividing the land equally among men and women, young and old, the latter standard should be adopted. This is a very important tactic for winning over the broad masses of the poor peasants, and it must not be neglected. "Developing production" is not the number one criterion of our present tactics. It is "winning over the masses" that is the number one criterion of our present tactics.

In order to guide the broad armed struggle, and to guide the deepening of the land revolution, the establishment of political power, and the expansion of the organization of the armed forces within this environment of struggle, the Joint Conference has the most pressing need for a supreme leading organ. The Front Committee, which was formerly appointed by the Central Committee to guide the Fourth Army and the local work wherever the Fourth Army went, should enlarge its duties and change its organization to take on this great mission. Therefore the Fourth Army has organized an Army Committee to guide it. The members of the Front Committee are as follows: Mao Zedong, Guo Zhen, Zeng Shan, Wang Huai, Fang Zhimin, Zhu De, Pan Xingyuan, Huang Gonglue, Liu Shiqi, Peng Dehuai, Tan Zhenlin, Chen Yi, Deng Zihui, Zhang Tingcheng, Yuan Guoping, Li Wenlin, and Teng Daiyuan. Mao, Zeng, Liu, Zhu, and Pan have been appointed to the five-member standing committee, with Huang and Peng as standing committee alternates and Mao as secretary. In order to unify the leadership of southern and western Jiangxi, the Joint Conference has decided to combine the two special committees for western Jiangxi and for southern Jiangxi into one and has made up a new membership list to form the Southwest Jiangxi Special Committee. At the same time, it has made up a membership list for the Army Committee of the Fourth Army and has decided to convene a southwest-

---

2. As pointed out above, in the note to the February 7 Land Law, this provision was removed from the law half a year later.

ern Jiangxi Party congress and a Jiangxi provincial workers-peasants-soldiers congress.

In accordance with its duties as laid down by the Joint Conference, the Front Committee has already begun work. The Red Army, all levels of local Party offices, and all comrades are hereby notified.

The Front Committee

The Road to Guangchang

(To the Tune "Abbreviated Magnolia Blossom") [1]

(February 1930)

Across the broad sky all is white,
Marching in the snow adds urgency.[2]
Peaks tower above our heads,
Red banners blowing in the wind, we cross the great pass.

Where are we bound this time?
To the Gan River, shrouded in windblown snow.
Yesterday the order was given
For a hundred thousand workers and peasants to sweep down
    on Ji'an.

Our source for this poem is *Shici duilian*, pp. 33–34. It is another of the six poems first published together in *Renmin wenxue*, May 1962. Regarding the author's note which accompanied it there, see above, the note to Mao's Autumn 1929 poem "The War Between Chiang Kaishek and the Guangxi Warlords."

1. Guangchang is the name of a *xian* in eastern Jiangxi Province. The Red Army passed through it in February 1930, on the way to Ji'an in central Jiangxi. Regarding "tune titles" (*cipai*), see note 1 to Mao's 1927 poem, "Autumn Harvest Uprising." "Abbreviation" is another convention used in *ci* poetry, which involves reducing the number of syllables (or characters) used overall.

2. When the poem first appeared in 1962, this line read "Marching in the snow, no cypress green." The final three characters were later amended by Mao to read as above, while preserving the rhyme in Chinese.

The Significance of Dividing the Troops to Win Over the Popular Masses, and Our Line

Front Committee Announcement No. 3

(Issued on March 18, 1930, from Loutiling in the suburbs of Ganzhou City)[1]

1. Analysis of the Circumstances and Plan of Action

In the area of Ji'an, Jishui, and Yongfeng, there are the three brigades of Cheng Guangyao,[2] Zhu Yaohua,[3] and Deng Ying, plus the remnants of Tang Yunshan's troops. Because it is engaged in fighting Yan Xishan, the Chiang Kaishek faction cannot spare troops to send to Jiangxi, but this troop strength of over three brigades makes it impossible to advance to the north for the time being.

Jin Handing's troops have set out for Fujian, with the objective of mounting a pincer attack with Liu Heding on Lu's forces[4] and advancing to occupy Fuzhou. The vacuum in southern Jiangxi and western Fujian gives us a good opportunity to win over the popular masses and establish links between the three provinces. Western Fujian has only the troops of Zhang Zhen, and in the slightly more distant future we can take Zhangzhou, which would bring the Red territories all the way to the seacoast. At the same time, the Guangdong-Guangxi war has become more and more intense, and the troops stationed in the East River area [of Guangdong] are only one brigade more or less, and there is a possibility of

Our source for this document is *Mao Zedongji. Bujuan*, Vol. 3, pp. 87–93, where it is reproduced from three documentary collections published in China between 1979 and 1982.

1. Three weeks earlier, on February 26, 1930, Li Lisan had issued Central Circular No. 70, which explicitly criticized the "hide-and-disperse views" of Zhu De and Mao Zedong, and indicated that they should be preparing themselves to march toward China's major centers, rather than developing guerrilla bases in rural areas. (For the text, see *Central Committee Documents* (1930), pp. 25–34.) It is not clear whether this document had not yet reached Mao, or whether he chose to ignore it. On the relation between Mao Zedong's strategic concepts as a whole and those of Li Lisan at this time, see the Introduction to this volume.

2. Cheng Guangyao (1898–1950) was a native of Hunan, and a graduate of the Hunan Military Academy. In May 1927, he had been appointed commander of the Fifth Division of the Thirteenth Army of the National Revolutionary Army.

3. Zhu Yaohua (dates unknown) was a native of Changsha, who had risen through the ranks of the army in Hunan. From 1924 to 1927 he was a brigade commander, but since mid-1927 he had commanded a division. At this time, he was commander of the Eighteenth Division of the Guomindang Twenty-second Army.

4. Lu is Lu Xingbang, mentioned above, in the letter of April 5, 1929.

expanding the Red territories to the seven *xian* of the northwestern East River area. Although Ganzhou has not yet fallen, the effect on the popular masses of Ganzhou has not been small, and this has also had a considerable influence on the whole country. Any reinforcement of the defense of Ganzhou with new troops is not possible within a short period of time. Before new troops arrive in Ganzhou, there is no way that the Seventeenth Regiment of Jin's forces can leave Ganzhou.

Given the circumstances outlined above, the actions of the Fourth Army for a period of three months should be to split up in different areas for guerrilla actions, the regions for guerrilla actions being: in southern Jiangxi, the *xian* of Ganxian, Yudu, Ruijin, Huichang, Nankang, Xinfeng, Anyuan, and Xunwu; and in the East River area,[5] the *xian* of Wuhua, Xingning, Fengshun, Meixian, Pingyuan, Jiaoling, and Dapu; in western Fujian, the *xian* of Shanghang, Wuping, Changting, Ninghua, and Liancheng. The region of guerrilla actions for the Second Column of the Sixth Army, for three months, should be Wan'an, Dongxiang in Ganxian, Beixiang in Yudu, Dongxiang in Xingguo, Nanxiang in Ningdu, and the *xian* of Guangchang and Shicheng. The region of guerrilla actions for the First Column of the Sixth Army is the *xian* of Ji'an, Anfu, Fenyi, Yichun, Xinyu, Xiajiang, Jishui, Yongfeng, Le'an, and Xin'gan. The region of guerrilla action for the Third Column of the Sixth Army is Xixiang in Taihe and the *xian* of Suichuan and Wan'an. The Twenty-second Column of the Red Guards should coordinate its actions with those of the Second Column of the Sixth Army and be responsible for completing the Red districts in the whole *xian* of Xingguo, Beixiang in Yudu, and the whole *xian* of Ningdu. The Ningnan guerrilla unit is then responsible for completing the Red districts of Guangchang, Nanfeng, and Yihuang. For the Fifth Army of the Red Army, the first step should be to coordinate actions with the Second and Third Columns of the Sixth Army to complete the work upstream along the Gan River (in the *xian* of Taihe, Suichuan, Shangyou, and Wan'an), and the second step should be to return to the base territory of the Fifth Army in the border region of Hunan, Hubei, and Jiangxi, to widen the Red territories in eastern Hunan and southern Hubei, and northern Jiangxi, and also to open the roads between northern Jiangxi and western Jiangxi.

The significance of splitting up the troops for guerrilla action is to be better able to win over the popular masses, better able to redistribute the land and establish political power, and better able to enlarge the Red Army and the local armed forces. Under current circumstances, if we were to adopt the tactic of concentrated action with large forces, it would obviously be a line of purely military action, which would go against the great task of winning over the popular masses and expanding the soviet territories. After a period of dividing

---

5. The *xian* enumerated here, in the East River area of Guangdong, are located in the northeastern corner of that province, not far from the boundary with Jiangxi.

the troops for guerrilla actions, we should then concentrate our actions, because of the needs of a different kind of circumstances, and to seize southern Fujian and develop such places as eastern Jiangxi. Thus, we should oppose the idea of absolute concentration, while at the same time opposing also the idea of the absolute division of the troops.

2. Expand and Be Thorough at the Same Time

To try to expand without trying to be thorough is a line of serious opportunism. In the past, in such places as southwestern Jiangxi and the East River area, it was a grave mistake to wait a very long time before redistributing the land and establishing soviets and to overlook the organization of Red Guard units. When engaged in guerrilla actions, it is also easy for the Red Army to make this mistake of trying to expand and not trying to be thorough. In less than three to five days after reaching any location, it was on the move again, having put out a bit of propaganda and organized a few very tiny peasant-worker associations and a few immature budding armed groups. But as soon as the Red Army moved off, they immediately crumbled. This kind of organization cannot count as organization. There have indeed been places like this, in which some propaganda was carried out, but no organizational work was done, as in the *xian* of Nankang, Dayu, Huichang, Ruijin, and Shicheng. In some there originally was no organizing at all, and in some there was originally a little organizing, but only very little. In such places it would be a waste of effort to attempt to do thorough organizational work. In such places we naturally can only do some propaganda work and distribute the grain supplies of the big gentry, to make something of an impression on the popular masses, and then take off. But in other places, such as the *xian* of Ningdu, Yudu, Anyuan, Xunwu, Changting, and Wuping, the situation is entirely different. Not only do they already have Party and mass organizations, there are small areas and even large areas that are openly Red territory, that have a long experience of armed struggle. When the Red Army reaches these *xian*, it should give well-planned assistance to the Party and to the popular masses of the already existing Red territories to organize political power, to set up armed forces, to redistribute the land, to strengthen the organizational and fighting ability of the Party and other groups, to expand the original territory throughout the entire *xian,* and to push into neighboring *xian.* For example, in southern Jiangxi, we should expand in the four *xian* of Ningdu, Yudu, Anyuan, and Xunwu and make them completely Red, and in western Fujian, the *xian* of Wuping and Changting should be made entirely Red. In this way, embracing Ruijin, Huichang, and Shicheng as the center, our plans to go on and tie Fujian and Jiangxi together will be successful. The Red territory at Xunwu and the East River Red territory are already connected, so in this way these three provinces will be successfully joined. If we do not do our work thoroughly in these five or six *xian,* but merely mount a single guerrilla attack in the style of viewing the flowers from horseback, as we did during the forty-five days of work in southern Jiangxi last year, then who knows when the task of linking Fujian, Guangdong, and Jiangxi together will ever be realized. To specify that within a fixed period of time our best efforts will be concentrated in a territory, to enlarge this territory and at the same time do a thorough job in this territory, is a very effective work method. When the various units of the Red Army split up to work separately, a fixed period of time should be allocated for a specific territory. For those territories in which the work should be thorough more work time should be allocated, and for those territories in which the work is not to be thorough, less work time should be allocated. Within a particular territory (such as the Third Column of the Fourth Army in Yudu), which places are to be allocated more time and which places are to be allocated less time, should also be planned, for only then will the work be even more effective.

3. Development through Partnership

Our experience with the line of progress through partnership clearly demonstrates that work done in this way is effective. The concept of working in partnership with an existing small piece of Red territory to develop and establish a new small piece of Red territory, and then further encouraging it to develop must become fully established, for previously it did not exist. Past experience that was not like this was a complete waste of effort. The creation of the large piece of Red territory on the Hunan-Jiangxi border came about because, at the time of the Great Revolution, the mass struggle in the *xian* of Chaling, Lingxian, Lianhua, Yongxin, and Ninggang had a few remnants of Party organization. It was only by working in partnership with these already existing bases that development was possible. In Suichuan there was never any foundation, and the result of trying forcibly to fabricate one was that nothing came of it. In July, the Fourth Army split up and detached its troops for guerrilla actions in western Fujian, and the First Column from Kanshi and Lanjia crossed over and went up along the Ting River, going back and forth repeatedly in the border area of Shanghang and Yongding, always in working partnership to develop a few bases, working to "open up contact" and "connect." As a result, the work of the First Column was especially effective on that occasion. In the area of Longtan and Longmen, the Third Column operated in partnership with a region that had already undergone struggle, helping the peasants with their work, so it too achieved results. Unfortunately it had not been working very long when it abruptly went off to central Fujian, and consequently it was far less effective than the First Column. The Yanshi-Gutian area, to which the Second Column went, had no base at all, so it was a totally wasted trip, with no results to speak of. This time, when the Fourth Army came to Jiangxi and divided its troops among the four places of Ningdu, Le'an, Yongfeng and Tengtian, it was only the Fourth Column in Ningdu that was highly effective (during the twenty days in Ningdu, the Fourth Army not only enlarged the Red territory but made its principal contribution by rectifying the opportunism of the Party in Ningdu, carrying out the important tasks of redistributing the land, organizing a soviet, and establishing Red Guards). Apart from this, the other three units did not achieve any results in expanding the Red territories, because there were no existing organizations in those three places. Although the Third Column sent a small detachment to Jishui, unfortunately the Party of the Third Column had developed this region too late and was not yet able to send out very many staff members to put a lot of effort into the work there. Although we shall certainly not abandon our efforts, the above examples are quite enough to show us that the slogan "development in partnership" is undoubtedly correct. Nevertheless, we will certainly not tie the feet of the Red Army or prohibit it from taking a single step into territory that is entirely White. There are times when the army has to enter territory where there is no existing base, because of its significance for the whole country or for other unavoidable reasons, such as "influencing the situation, and solving the economic problem," or "retreating," and so on. This does not, however, correspond to the principles of our work policy. Our principle is undoubtedly "development in partnership," which is, as we have always said, "wavelike advance and expansion."

At this point something must also be said about how to deal with the problem of local Party groups and the popular masses "requesting troops." Some comrades have not taken very seriously local Party or popular mass requests for Red Army troops to fight local bullies or militia. They do not realize that when the local popular masses ask for troops this is a good work opportunity. For when the masses take charge, and all the arrangements and planning are done by the masses themselves, if the Red Army avails itself of this opportunity to help them out, the development of the struggle is exceptionally rapid. When we disregard the requests of the masses and just arrange the work subjectively, excellent opportunities to develop will be lost. This is an individualist way of working and is also incorrect.

4. Armed Peasants

A major condition for enlarging the Red districts is the armed forces of the peasants. If peasant armed forces cannot be created, the so-called task of doing thorough work is only an empty phrase. When a guerrilla unit reaches an area in which there is hope for doing thorough work, for one thing the existing armed peasant forces must not be taken over to enlarge the Red Army (only in the heart of a Red territory when part of the land struggle has already been thorough and there is less need for the use of armed forces may a portion of the local military forces be brought together in a planned way and turned into Red Army units). When conditions are such that the fighting strength of the Red Army is not large and there is a sense of having suffered losses, we must definitely still take rifles from the Red Army and use them to arm the popular masses. Not only must we give them rifles but we must sometimes even give them ammunition. Not only must we turn over ammunition to them but we must sometimes even give them military personnel. When the Red Army is not strong, and really cannot give away rifles and ammunition and personnel, every effort must be made to capture arms from the despotic gentry and from small enemy units with which to arm the peasants. On the whole, then, guerrilla units always work together with local armed forces, and anyone who does not think that arming the local populace is a most urgent task, anyone who does not take the local armed forces just as seriously as his own forces, is an opportunist who has rejected the popular masses.

5. Training Local Cadres

The experience in struggle of the Red Army party units is somewhat richer and somewhat more progressive than that of some of the local party units in agricultural regions. At the same time, as a local struggle develops, the shortage of working personnel and incorrect ways of working become increasingly apparent. Thus the guiding organs of the Red Army party units unquestionably must take on the responsibility of training people to become cadres in newly developing regions, and the idea of short training classes for Party members and training classes for leaders of the popular masses should be instituted in accordance with prior experience.

6. Local Party Actions Should Be Coordinated with Those of the Red Army

When last year the Fourth Army engaged in guerrilla actions in the area of southern Jiangxi and the East River, the southern Jiangxi Special Committee focused its attention on the daily struggle in the West River area and provided no guidance at all to the enthusiastic popular masses who were being roused by the Red Army in the East River area, letting them cool down. Mechanically holding onto the slogan of the greater Jiangxi-Guangdong area being the central territory, they ignored the political function of the Red Army in the East River area and ignored the great significance of connecting the three territories of southern Jiangxi, the East River, and western Fujian, demonstrating thoroughgoing opportunism. In various places of southern Jiangxi there were quite a few turtle-like cadres who did not stick their heads out until the Red Army had already been in their areas for quite a while, who when requested to start an armed struggle were frightened out of their wits. Some, who were a little more positive, still could not make use of the opportunity provided by the guerrilla actions of the Red Army to intensify their work for developing the struggle. The phenomenon in such places of the local party actions not being coordinated with the actions of the Red Army was the major reason for the lack of effectiveness of the work done. This phenomenon was worst in southern Jiangxi, and the Southwest Jiangxi Special Committee must correct it.

7. The Relationship between Red Army Party Units and the Local Party Units

The Army Committee of the Red Army holds joint meetings with the local special committee to resolve problems, and from the *xian* committee on down, work may come directly under the direction of the Army Committee. A Red Army column committee holds joint meetings with *xian* committees to resolve problems and may direct the work from the district committee on down. A Red Army detachment committee holds joint meetings with local district committees to resolve problems and may direct the work of the local branch offices on down. A Red Army company committee holds joint meetings with the local branch office to resolve problems. A special committee may direct the work of a column committee, but may not totally tie down the actions of those Red Army columns that are more than just local in nature. The Front Committee, at the column level, will delegate an inspection team to meet jointly with special committees to resolve problems and will have the authority to exercise direction from the *xian* committee on down.

Directive on Lessons to Be Derived from the
First Attack on Ganzhou

(March 19, 1930)[1]

This order is to be carried out. Be it known that there are only two ways to take a city—the surprise raid and the attack in force. In its recent attack on the city of Ganzhou, our army, having resolved to attack in force, employed the method of the surprise raid. Because of the influence of the shortcomings described below, it was impossible to attain the desired results, and this is truly a matter for regret. Herewith are listed, in broad outline, for future reference, the shortcomings and lessons to be learned from this battle.

1. Inaccurate Assessment of the Enemy Situation

Reports came in from various sources, some saying that there were no enemy [forces] in the city except for a local Security Guard Regiment about a hundred strong, and some saying that there was only one enemy battalion in the city. This led the commander to the erroneous conclusion that the enemy forces consisted of only one battalion, whereas in fact the enemy's entire Seventieth Regiment was in the city (consisting of three battalions, with three infantry companies and one machine-gun company in each battalion). Because of this, the allocation of forces and the plans for attacking the city were full of underestimations and inadequacies.

2. Failure to Reconnoiter the Terrain in Advance

The day before, when the First and Second Columns arrived in the vicinity of the city gates, the enemy closed the gates to engage in stubborn resistance. At the time, our side had not yet resolved to attack the city, so the senior commanders did not lead the subordinate commanders to reconnoiter the terrain on the out-

---

We have translated this document from *Mao Zedong junshi wenji*, Vol. 1, pp. 138–40, where the source is given as *Junshi wenxian* (Documents on Military Affairs), published in 1942 by the Revolutionary Military Commission of the Party. This collection is not available to us.

1. This is order No. 2 of the Fourth Red Army Headquarters, promulgated on the date indicated.

skirts of the city. As a result, when the Fourth Column arrived near the city's southern gate the next day, it was unable at the time to occupy an advantageous position, in preparation for later scaling the city walls. As for artillery and machine gun positions, the sector of fire was not selected in advance, nor were shooting distance and other measurements taken.

3. Lack of Thorough Preparation in Advance

When our army reached the area around Maodian and Dongtian, instruments for scaling the city walls (such as bamboo ladders, etc.) had not yet been prepared, and this caused great haste when the moment arrived.

4. Absence of Unanimous Resolve at Higher and Lower Levels

During battle, when the officers and soldiers of the various units suddenly discovered that there was actually a whole regiment of enemy forces inside the city, one unit wavered in its resolve to attack the city, and failed to carry out the order to attack.

5. Inaccurate Battlefield Reporting

The battlefield report is actually the basis upon which senior commanders assess the enemy situation and make decisions adapted to the circumstances, so it is inappropriate to underestimate the enemy or overestimate oneself, and also to . . . [2] During this battle, at one time it was reported that another attack was about to be launched, and then it was reported that the attack could not be made, thus chopping and changing, without any accurate . . . [3] at all, making it difficult for the commander to handle the situation.

6. Failure to Launch the General Assault on Time

According to the order to attack the city, the general assault on the city was originally to be carried out at 3:30 A.M. on the 16th. By 4:30 A.M., however, the Fourth Column had not arrived at the designated reserve position between the southern and eastern gates, thereby missing the time for the general assault. By the time firing began outside the south gate, dawn was already breaking, so that the city walls could not be scaled successfully.

7. Inappropriate Command

The commander of one unit fell into recklessness in the pursuit of victory, without giving sufficient consideration to the terrain and making a poor choice of

---

2. Six or seven characters are missing here.
3. Four or five characters are missing here.

the point of attack. Thus attacks were carried out in areas that should not have been attacked (such as the main road facing the gate tower) and at the wrong times (such as during the day instead of at night), and opportunities for attack at appropriate places and times were missed.

Only major [shortcomings] are briefly treated under the above headings. As for partial shortcomings on the battlefield on the part of the various units, each unit should call its own meeting of officers to discuss and criticize them, and a report must be made to headquarters. It is so ordered.

Army Commander Zhu De
Political Commissar Mao Zedong
March 19, 1930

Order on Rectifying Military Bearing and Discipline

(March 21, 1930)[1]

This order is to be followed. Given that the purpose of our army's work here is to win over the masses and to train ourselves, it follows that all rules regarding military bearing and discipline must be strictly observed. Even the slightest slackening will have adverse effects on the masses. We have therefore issued repeated orders in the hope that officers and men alike will follow the Three Rules of Discipline and the Six Main Points for Attention[2] in order to make widely known to the ordinary masses the spirit and principles of the Red Army. This will benefit the revolution and is also what the officers and men are happy to do. Therefore, anyone who contravenes military discipline and bearing, no matter to what degree, will be subject to thorough investigation. It is especially forbidden to prowl around in the prostitutes' quarters, to avoid contracting a pernicious disease, with all kinds of evil consequences, which does harm to one's own health as well as serious damage to the public good. Especially as it is

---

Our source for this text is *Mao Zedong junshi wenji*, Vol. 1, pp. 141–42, where it is taken from the same 1942 documentary collection cited in the note to the previous text.

1. This is order No. 3 of the Fourth Red Army Headquarters, promulgated at 5 P.M. on March 21.

2. Published accounts of the origin of these principles diverge substantially. According to the latest and most authoritative sources, Mao formulated the Three Main Rules of Discipline on October 24, 1927, as he was about to lead his forces up the Jinggangshan. The Six Points for Attention were put forward on January 25, 1928, and Mao formally promulgated the entire set of principles in April 1928. At that time, the Three Main Rules of Discipline were: (1) Obey orders in all your actions; (2) Don't take anything from the workers and peasants; (3) When attacking the local bullies, turn over [whatever you take from them]. The Six Points for Attention were: (1) Put back the doors [you have taken down for bed boards]; (2) Put back the straw [you have used for bedding]; (3) Speak politely; (4) Pay fairly for what you buy; (5) Return everything you borrow; (6) Pay for anything you damage. In January 1929, Mao added two more Points for Attention: (7) Don't bathe within sight of women, and (8) Defecate only in the latrines. In 1930, Mao formulated another principle, which replaced either the seventh or the eighth rule: Don't search the pockets of captives. The resulting Three Main Rules of Discipline and Eight Points for Attention remained in force with minor variations until 1949, and were reissued in standardized form on October 10, 1947. See Jiang Siyi (ed.), *Zhongguo gongchandang jundui zhengzhi gongzuo qishinian shi* (History of Seventy Years of Political Work by the Army of the Chinese Communist Party), Vol. 1 (Beijing: Jiefangjun chubanshe, 1991), pp. 147–48.

the beginning of spring, when all sorts of diseases break out, all officers and soldiers would do well to exercise extreme caution to preserve their health, for only with a healthy body can one shoulder the important responsibility of the revolution. Certainly it is impermissable to have one's work adversely affected by bringing illness upon oneself. Therefore, in addition to a separate order to dispatch special investigation and patrol units, we herewith issue a forthright instruction which must not be willfully disobeyed without the offender's being arrested and punished. It is urgently so ordered.

Army Commander Zhu De
Political Commissar Mao Zedong

March 21, 1930

Order on the Testing of Officers and Soldiers

(March 29, 1930)[1]

This order is to be followed. In view of the fact that the appropriateness of the appointment, demotion, promotion, and transfer of officers and their deputies directly influences victory and defeat in battle and the efficacy of the work, there should be testing and evaluation so that the higher organs of command may be apprised of the work performance of officers and their deputies at various levels and may provide guidance, rectification, and education. Moreover, during the period of guerrilla warfare, the important tasks of the Red Army are to overthrow the class enemy, to arm the workers and peasants, to help establish local governments, and to expand the Red area. To accomplish such tasks, during the period of warfare it is necessary to be able to achieve unity between officers and soldiers, to advance bravely, to annihilate the enemy, and to take his weapons to arm the peasants and workers in turn. In normal times, on the one hand, officers and soldiers must unite to engage in propaganda, mobilization, and organizational work and, on the other hand, officers in charge at all levels must train the soldiers in their own units. Therefore, given this sort of significant responsibility, the training of Red Army officers themselves and of the soldiers becomes highly important work. It has been found that the promotion and transfer of officers and their deputies in our army at present occur only after there have been sacrifices in battle, whereupon in great haste to make do, a vacancy is filled or someone is promoted from below. All of this is unplanned use of personnel. As for education, when our Red Army is not on the march engaging in battle, its forces are divided to carry out the work—as is naturally necessitated by our surroundings and our tasks. But this also makes it impossible for the army headquarters to plan systematically the education of the soldiers of the various columns. Thus planning for education of the soldiers has to be the responsibility of the officers in charge at the various levels (columns and detachments), and the army headquarters can do no more than give direction through guiding principles. Therefore, whether officers and their deputies are used appropriately, which is to say whether they have the appropriate command ability in battle, the appropriate management methods, education, and training for normal times, and particularly

Our source for this text is *Mao Zedong junshi wenji*, Vol. 1, pp. 143–47, where it is taken from the 1942 documentary collection cited in the note to the text of March 19, 1930.

1. This is order No. 5 of the Fourth Red Army Headquarters.

for mass work during guerrilla warfare, is all related to Red warfare and mass work. Among the soldiers, there are certainly many worker and peasant revolutionary elements who are brave, steady, and experienced in battle, whose ability qualifies them to be officers and deputies. In the past, however, we have never done any testing or evaluation. So there has been no plan for the appropriate appointment and transfer of officers and their deputies and no basis upon which to make promotions from the ranks, while an education plan has been even more sorely lacking. Now, with the purpose of (1) making sure that the transfer and appointment of officers and their deputies is carried out appropriately; (2) being in a position to promote and make use of rank and file soldiers who are brave, progressive, and relatively capable; and (3) achieving good results in the education and training of all the army's officers and men in a relatively planned way, the following methods have been decided upon:

1. Formulate an Educational System. In the future, [responsibility for] the education of the soldiers rests with the column. The army headquarters may only provide direction through guiding principles of education (but each column's education plan and implementation status must still be reported to the army headquarters in a timely fashion for review). [Responsibility for] the education of officers rests with the army headquarters.

2. Implement a System of Testing. From now on in education the Dalton system of testing[2] should be frequently used, to speed up the rate of progress. The method of testing is as follows:
Testing organization:
  (1) The testing of privates is done by company (with the participation of someone sent from the detachment).
  (2) [The testing of] noncommissioned officers (squad leaders and deputy squad leaders) is done by detachment (with the participation of someone sent from the column).
  (3) [The testing of] lower-level cadres (above the rank of deputy platoon commander and below the rank of company commander) is done by column (with the participation of someone chosen by the army headquarters).
  (4) [The testing of] mid-level officers and their deputies (detachment commander, deputy detachment commander, leader of units directly under the army headquarters, section chief) is done by the army headquarters.

---

2. An educational method initiated by the American Helen Huss Parkhurst at Dalton High School in Dalton, Massachusetts, in 1920. It involved eliminating lectures and requiring the students to learn independently from reference books or experiments, while the teachers acted as advisers. Students worked at their own pace, and those who progressed more rapidly could graduate earlier. By 1930, a small number of primary and middle schools in China had tried this method.

3. Create Assessment Forms for Officers and Soldiers (sample forms to be issued separately).

(1) The assessment form is divided into three parts

    a. background check

    b. test

    c. assessment

(2) Assessment of privates

    a. background check: name, age, date joined, number of times in combat and wounded (political aspects will be formulated by the Political Department).

    b. test:

        (1) knowledge: regulations, models, orders, guerrilla tactics.

        (2) skills: drill ground operations, field operations.

    c. assessment: personality, proclivities, abilities (to be evaluated and reported by the platoon leader).

(3) Assessment of noncommissioned officers

    a. background check (same as above)

    b. test (same as above)

    c. assessment: personality, proclivities, abilities in squad management skills, leadership in battle, and teaching and training in normal times (to be evaluated in detail by the company commander, the deputy company commander, and the political commissar).

(4) Assessment of cadres

    a. background check: name, age, place of origin, date when appointed to the present position, experience before joining the Red Army, experience after joining the Red Army, number of times in combat and wounded, awards and punishment received, and special skills.

    b. test: (political [aspects] will be formulated separately by the Political Department) tactical principles, the science of firing weapons, major aspects of battle formation.

    c. assessment: views (whether or not they are consistent with Red Army policy and whether or not there are other ideas when faced with an unexpected situation), management and training methods, guerrilla work, command capability and decisiveness, personality (relations with and feelings toward colleagues), implementation of orders, the degree of faith the soldiers have in the person.

(5) Assessment of mid-level officers and assistants

    a. background check: same as for cadres.

    b. test: (Political [aspects] will be formulated separately by the Political Department) the science of tactics, the science of firing weapons, topography, major aspects of battle formation.

    c. assessment: same as for cadres.

4. Education in the Various Departments and Sections

(1) Military Supplies Section: The Military Supplies section should come up with monthly examination questions to conduct Dalton-style testing on the managerial staff of the various columns. Guidance in the work should be given to the extent possible, and the method of holding meetings should be used to educate them.

(2) Medical Officers Section: The Medical Officers Section should offer, in a planned way, basic education in general medicine, pharmacology, and first aid to medical officers, nurses, medical orderlies, and stretcher bearers, and provide testing as well.

(3) Aides-de-camp Section: The Aides-de-camp Section should frequently discuss what they have learned about the administration of aides at various levels (grooms, cooks, orderlies, etc.) and give them instruction. Aides-de-camp at the column and detachment levels should frequently call together grooms, cooks, porters, and orderlies for admonitory talks.

It is imperative for all units to implement faithfully the above methods of education and to discuss implementation techniques and communicate these methods and their implications to lower levels by way of officers' meetings or unit meetings. Only in this way can the military skills of the Red Army be improved. Improvement in military skills will naturally facilitate the accomplishment of our political task. It is urgently hoped that all units will carry out this directive for the sake of the revolutionary work. It is so ordered.

Forms enclosed as below.

Army Commander Zhu De
Political Commissar Mao Zedong

March 29, 1930

Directive on Enlisting and Educating New Recruits

(March 29, 1930)[1]

This order is to be followed. Given that the Red Army is an instrument of struggle of the workers' and peasants' revolution, at this time when reactionary political power is collapsing and the revolutionary tide is rising higher every day, more loyal and brave workers and peasants should naturally be recruited to expand the Red Army, in order to crush the reactionary forces and attain final victory. It has recently been found, however, that in obtaining new recruits, the various units intend only to recruit youngsters to run errands, and to add some porters arbitrarily, but pay scant attention to strengthening their fighting forces. Some units have even enlisted men whose five senses are defective, hunchbacks and cripples, and men who suffer from tuberculosis, venereal diseases, appendicitis, bleeding hemorrhoids, and other afflictions, not realizing that those whose senses are defective, or who are hunchbacks and cripples, not only affect the impression given by the Red Army but are not at all qualified to be soldiers. The reason is that those with eye ailments are unable to aim and shoot; those who are deaf are unable to distinguish orders; those with a collapsed nose mostly have hereditary syphilis and are susceptible to contagious diseases [in general]; those who stutter are unable to carry out the communication tasks of a soldier; as for those with ailments such as tuberculosis, venereal disease, appendicitis, and bleeding hemorrhoids, not only does their weak physical condition make them unable to fight in the army, but there is also the danger of spreading their diseases to others. Taking into consideration the above-mentioned adverse effects, this commander[2] orders that attention be paid to the following when new soldiers are recruited and when they join the ranks: (1) Qualification for new recruits: must be over sixteen and under thirty years of age; height of at least 4 *chi* 2 *cun* (tailor's measure);[3] must be in good health, with no serious diseases

Our source for this text is *Mao Zedong junshi wenji*, Vol. 1, pp. 148–49, where it is taken from the 1942 documentary collection cited in the note to the document dated March 19, 1930.

1. This is order No. 6 of the Fourth Red Army Headquarters.

2. *Ben zhang*, i.e., Zhu De, who signs first as *junzhang*, or commander of the army.

3. The standard *chi*, or Chinese foot, at this time, made up of 10 *cun*, or Chinese inches, was equal to 14.1 English inches or 0.3581 meters. The minimum height stipulated here thus corresponds to 1.5 meters, or slightly less than five feet.

and no defective senses. (2) Recruitment authority and procedures for examination: All battalions may recruit new soldiers at any time, but new recruits are to be added to the ranks only upon examination and qualification by a medical officer or medical unit. When troops are operating separately in guerrilla warfare (referring to the separate operation by one detachment), [recruits] are to be examined personally by the detachment commander, the political commissar, or the deputy detachment commander and must meet the qualifications in (1) to be admitted to the ranks. (3) The education of new soldiers: The principle of education should be collectivity; where there are many new soldiers, a new recruit battalion should be set up in the column, and where there are fewer, a new recruit platoon should be set up under the detachment. Only when education and training have continued for a certain period of time and reached a certain level may [new recruits] be added to the companies. After receiving this order, it must be communicated to all subordinate units and carried out accordingly by all bodies. Should there be any further negligence or recruitment of those who do not meet the above regulations, not only will rations be denied to those whose names have been added to the ranks but the officers responsible will be punished as well. Absolutely no leniency will be granted. It is urgently so ordered.

Army Commander Zhu De
Political Commissar Mao Zedong

March 29, 1930

Directive on Building up Physical Strength and Improving Shooting Skills

(April 1930)[1]

This order is to be followed. In battle, our Red Army has neither the superior firepower to overwhelm the enemy nor chemical weaponry with which to create victory. We rely solely on our seething blood and our resolve to fight to the death in hand-to-hand combat against the enemy and to dye an area red with our blood. Thus each victory depends solely upon officers and men charging boldly forward, using our bravery to scare off the enemy. This, however, depends in turn on having great physical strength, to be able to run more than 100 *li*, take a dozen hills, and fight several fierce battles, all in one day. Even this is not enough, [for] we do not yet have our own ammunitions factory, or a fixed rear area. When we are short of bullets, we should use them very sparingly; only by shooting accurately can we kill and wound more enemies. If more than half our men fall behind when we advance on the run, the unity and the power of the charge will be lost. If, when we fire rapid volleys, not a single enemy is hit, we will be unable to destroy the enemy's fighting strength, or to shake their position, still less to screen an advance. Therefore, without good physical strength, even the highest revolutionary spirit and will are of no use. Without good shooting skills, we cannot kill and wound more enemies on the battlefield, and our own side sustains more casualties as well. Consequently, to do physical exercise in order to increase the strength of our bodies and to engage in target practice to improve shooting skills are the most important thing in the Red Army's military training at present. It is hereby ordered that in all units running during morning exercises be abolished, that [instead] calesthenics be practiced with weapons or barehanded, and that another time must be set aside for calesthenics during the weekly exercise schedule. During evening recreation hours, various exercises should be done such as foot races, soccer, maneuvers, human pyramids. . . . When there is a relatively long rest period, the idea could be considered of setting up simple equipment such as horizontal bars, hanging ropes, trapezes, swings, hanging rings, ropes for scaling walls. . . . (these kinds of equipment are

---

Our source for this text is *Mao Zedong junshi wenji*, Vol. 1, pp. 150–51, where it is reproduced from the 1942 docucmentary collection cited in the note to the order of March 19, 1930.

1. This is order No. 8 of the Fourth Red Army Headquarters.

all portable), practicing gymnastics with this equipment, erecting obstacle courses, and practicing applied gymnastics—[such methods] are superior to foot racing. All this can be done as long as there is a rest period of over a week and an appropriate place in which to do it. There is no difficulty in having the troops do these things, and they will surely be very happy to do them. In addition, in science and skills instruction, special attention should be paid to shooting instruction. More time should be spent on shooting instruction, and shooting competitions should be held. In the future, every month or two the army headquarters will hold a competition among the different columns and units directly under the army headquarters in physical strength and shooting. Contestants will be selected to participate by each unit, and awards will be given as encouragement. (The rules for competition will be made and issued at the time). Each column and each unit directly under the army headquarters should start preparing now and know that this is the most important way to improve the fighting power of the Red Army. It is expected that the officers responsible will communicate this to the rank and file and make every effort to ensure and supervise its implementation. It is so ordered.

Army Commander Zhu De
Political Commissar Mao Zedong

Guidelines for the Work of Propaganda Personnel

(April 26, 1930)

Item 1. All propaganda personnel must have a set of equipment and use white (or black) coloring material to write slogans stipulated by this office, at any time and in any place on walls that are easily seen by people traveling on the streets and roads.

Item 2. In addition to writing on walls each and every one of the slogans from the book of slogans stipulated by this office, longer slogans must be written out on colored paper and pasted up in places where they are easily seen by people traveling on the streets and roads.

Item 3. Whenever a town is reached, the main slogans stipulated by this office are to be written on sheets of red cloth and hung in the middle of the street.

Item 4. Propaganda teams must frequently designate specific personnel to take all the propaganda materials and a pot of paste, and paste the propaganda materials where they may be easily seen by people traveling on the streets and roads.

Item 5. All propaganda personnel, no matter whether with an army unit on the move or with an army unit stationed somewhere, must carry propaganda materials and distribute them in an orderly fashion whenever they encounter the masses.

Item 6. In White districts where reactionary propaganda has caused the people to flee in fear, all propaganda personnel must see to it that propaganda materials are placed so that they may be seen when the people return. For example, paste propaganda materials on the streets and roads, in schools, in factories, in shops, and in soldiers' quarters.

Item 7. From among the propaganda team, designate a certain number of propagandists who are good speakers to conduct oral propaganda. Whenever and

Our source for this text is *Mao Zedong ji. Bujuan*, Vol. 3, pp. 95–97, where it is reproduced from a documentary collection published in China in 1979.

wherever, they should hoist a propaganda banner and use various tools to attract the masses, call the masses together and address propaganda to them, and also look for those among the masses who are relatively receptive to the propaganda and talk with them individually. For example, when there is only a very small crowd, talk with them individually.

Item 8. From among the propaganda team, designate those propaganda personnel who are both artistic and good speakers to be in charge of presenting propaganda in costume, and when there is a day or more of rest, go to work in places where there are more people and also find a way to call a large mass meeting.

Item 9. When starting work [in a particular area], every propagandist should be careful to make a social survey of the area in question and should report the results of such investigations to the statistics section daily, to make up overall statistics.

Item 10. All propaganda personnel should at all times take care to examine the situation regarding the local bullies and all reactionary elements and quickly report them to the defense office to find a way to deal with them.

Item 11. When fighting the local bullies, it is essential to delegate propagandists to accompany the security section and make propaganda and also to aid the security section in its work. (As in the case of distributing confiscated grain to the poor peasants.)

Item 12. When holding large mass meetings, propagandists should take responsibility for setting up the meeting place, for calling the masses together, and for maintaining order at the meeting. Before and after holding meetings, do intensive propaganda among the masses.

Item 13. When a battle is not going well, or we are in strategic retreat because the enemy is attacking us, all propagandists must write a lot of propaganda slogans that are addressed to the enemy troops and distribute a lot of propaganda material meant for the enemy troops.

Item 14. In time of battle, all propagandists must help in carrying and attending to wounded soldiers and also hire the masses from the vicinity of the battleground to carry the wounded to the first-aid stations for treatment.

Item 15. At the end of every battle, all propagandists must focus on looking after enemy soldiers and talking with them and making propaganda to them individually.

Item 16. After hostilities are concluded, you should assist in hiring masses from areas near the battleground to bury the dead soldiers.

Item 17. All propagandists, at all times and in all places, should pay attention to maintaining troop morale.

Item 18. All propagandists, at the end of each day of work, must report the circumstances of work during that day to the team leader, to be put down as a written report and turned over to the section leader for inspection.

Issued by the Political Department of the
Fourth Army of the Red Army

Xunwu Investigation[1]

(May 1930)

Preface

The scale of this investigation is the largest of all I have done. In the past I systematically investigated seven *xian*: Xiangtan, Xiangxiang, Hengshan, Liling, Changsha, Yongxin, and Ninggang.[2] The five Hunan *xian* were done during the period of the Great Revolution (1926–1927). Yongxin and Ninggang were done during the Jinggangshan period (November 1927). I placed the materials on the Hunan investigations in the hands of my wife, Yang Kaihui. In all probability, when she was killed, these five investigations were lost. I gave the Yongxin and Ninggang investigations to a friend in the mountains when the Red Army left Jinggangshan in January 1929. These were lost when Chiang Kaishek and the Guangxi clique both attacked the Jinggangshan. I am not too concerned when I lose things, but losing these investigations (especially the ones for Hengshan and Yongxin) caused me pain. For an eternity I can never forget them. The Xunwu investigation occurred in May 1930 when the Fourth Army arrived. At this time, after the Pitou Conference (the joint conference of the Fourth Army Front Com-

---

The "Xunwu Investigation" was originally scheduled for publication in 1937, and the final chapter of the report was at one time included in the draft table of contents for Vol. 1 of Mao's *Selected Works*, which was issued in 1951, but the work did not actually appear in print until thirty years later. It first became available in *Mao Zedong nongcun diaocha wenji* (Collected Writings of Mao Zedong on Rural Investigations) (Beijing: Renmin chubanshe, 1982), pp. 41–181. A few further corrections and improvements were made in this carefully edited text when the Xunwu Investigation was incorporated into Vol. 1 of the *Mao Zedong wenji*, pp. 118–245, and it is the 1993 version which we have followed here. For details regarding the authorship of our English translation, see Note 1 below.

1. This translation of Mao's Xunwu investigation is reproduced from Mao Zedong, *Report from Xunwu*, Trans., and with an introduction and notes, by Roger R. Thompson (Stanford: Stanford University Press, 1990), with the kind permission of Professor Thompson and of the publisher. Apart from changes required in order to make the text conform to the usage employed in these volumes (for example, the replacement of "county" by "*xian*"), this excellent version has been reproduced almost verbatim. A few modifications of detail have been made after consultation with the translator. Roger Thompson's monograph contains, in the introduction and notes, a wealth of information about the history of Xunwu, conditions prevailing there in 1930, and the political context in which Mao produced this document, as well as detailed maps of the area. It would not have been appropriate to include all this material in our edition. Some of his notes have been reproduced below; they are marked at the end "RT." Those interested in local history and grass-roots revolution are strongly urged to consult Professor Thompson's original work.

2. The first five of these are in Hunan; Yongxin and Ninggang are in Jiangxi.

mittee and the West Jiangxi Special Committee held on February 7),[3] and before the Tingzhou Conference (joint conference of the Fourth Army Front Committee and the West Fujian Special Committee held in June),[4] I still did not completely understand the problem of China's rich peasants. At the same time, in the area of commerce, I was a complete outsider. Because of this I pursued this investigation with great energy. Throughout the time when I organized this investigation, I was helped by the Xunwu Party secretary, Comrade Gu Bo (Gu is a middle school graduate, the son of a bankrupt small landlord, a former primary school teacher, and former chairman of the *xian* revolutionary committee and of the *xian* soviet; he is from Huangxiang District).[5]

Several people gave me many documents and always came to the investigation meetings:

Guo Youmei. Fifty-nine *sui*,[6] owner of a general store, former president of the chamber of commerce; from Xunwu City District.

Fan Daming. Fifty-one *sui*, poor peasant, *xian* soviet official; from Xunwu City District.

Zhao Jingqing. Thirty *sui*, middle peasant, former iron-founder, former small merchant, former soldier and platoon leader under Chen Jiongming, now a *xian* soviet committee delegate; from Shuangqiao District.

Liu Liangfan. Twenty-seven *sui*, formerly involved in *xian* tax collection, now chairman of the Xunwu City suburban township soviet; from Xunwu City District.

Those who gave us some documents and who sometimes attended our meetings were:

Li Dashun. Twenty-eight *sui*, poor peasant, a former district soviet delegate.

Liu Maozai. Fifty *sui*, an old examination degree student *[tongsheng]*, once

---

3. Regarding the Pitou Conference, also called the February 7 Conference, see above, the three documents dated February 7, February 14, and February 16, 1930, emanating from it, and the notes to these texts.

4. The Tingzhou Conference refers to the joint conference of the Front Committee of the Fourth Red Army and the Western Fujian Special Committee which took place in June 1930 in Tingzhou (now Changting), in southwestern Fujian. The conference discussed political, military, and economic issues. In regard to land redistribution, it adopted a strongly leftist line, which finds expression in the resolution "On the Problem of the Rich Peasants," translated below.

5. Throughout this report, Mao tends to write extremely long paragraphs. In Roger Thompson's monograph, these are broken up to make the text more readable. In this documentary collection, we have on the whole followed Mao's own paragraphing, while deviating from this principle occasionally. In the Chinese original, the three lists of people which appear below are all run together with what goes before, making the text difficult to follow. Other similar departures are not mentioned in the notes.

6. Throughout Mao gives ages in terms of *sui*, the Chinese system that reckons age in terms of the number of calendar years in which a person has lived.—RT.

operated a gambling house and had a small business; originally a small land-lord but declined and became a poor peasant; was a delegate to the *xian* revolutionary committee; now a delegate to a district soviet.

Those who came to a few investigation meetings and who gave us a small number of documents were:

Liu Xingwu. Forty-six *sui*, peasant; had a small business; a delegate to a town-ship soviet; from Xunwu City District.

Zhou Buying. Twenty-three *sui*, student at Mei *xian* Normal School, chairman of the district government; from Shipaixia.

Chen Zhuoyun. Thirty-nine *sui*, graduate of a local self-government school, a former worker in a tailoring shop; had a small business; a former primary school teacher.

Guo Qingru. Sixty-two *sui*, a *xiucai*, participated in the imperial provincial ex-aminations, a former primary school teacher; from Xunwu City District.

Our investigation meetings involved these eleven people and myself. I was the chairman and secretary. Our investigation, which lasted over ten days, took place while the Red Army units were organizing the masses in Anyuan, Xunwu, and Pingyuan. This gave me time to organize these investigation meetings.

Xunwu *xian* is located at the junction of three provinces— Fujian, Guangdong, and Jiangxi. Since conditions in the neighboring *xian* of the three provinces are similar, conditions in Xunwu *xian* can serve as an example.

This investigation has one great defect: there is no analysis of middle peas-ants, hired hands, or vagrants. Also, in the section "Traditional Land Relation-ships," there is no separate discussion of the landholdings of rich peasants, middle peasants, or poor peasants.

February 2, 1931, Xiaobu, Ningdu *xian*

Chapter I. Administrative Jurisdictions in Xunwu

There are seven districts, which include four wards in Xunwu City and twelve *bao*.[7]

The seven districts are:

---

7. According to a map in the 1881 edition of the gazetteer for Xunwu *xian*, the area beyond Xunwu City was divided into twelve *bao* (lit., fortress) and four wards *(xiang)*. Except for Renfeng (Huangxiang) District and Shuangqiao District, the sub-*xian* districts in Republican Xunwu *xian* took their names from a consolidation of the Qing jurisdic-tions: Nanqiao *bao* and Bafu *bao* became Nanba District; Xiangshan *bao*, Yaogu *bao*, and Zixi *bao* became Jiansan (lit., unites three) District; Xunwu *bao*, Dadun *bao*, and Guiling *bao* became Chengjiang District (taking the name of the major market); and Sanbiao *bao* and Shuiyuan *bao* became Sanshui District. See *Changning xianzhi* (Gazetteer for Changning [Xunwu] *xian*) (1881), 1: 2b–3a. Until January 1914, Xunwu *xian* was known as Changning *xian*.—RT.

Xunwu City District: including East, West, South, and North wards; this is the administrative center of the *xian*.

Renfeng District[8] (or Huangxiang *bao*): there are two administrative centers in this district, Gongping and Changpu (or Huangxiang), with a bureau in each center.

Shuangqiao District (or Shuangqiao *bao*): divided into thirteen *duan* [sections], with Liuche the administrative center.

Nanba District: two *bao*, Nanqiao and Bafu, with Niudouguang the administrative center.

Jiansan District: three *bao*, Xiangshan, Yaogu, and Zixi, with Jitan the administrative center.

Chengjiang District: three *bao*, Xunwu, Dadun, and Guiling, with Chengjiang the administrative center.

Sanshui District: two *bao*, Sanbiao and Shuiyuan, with Sanbiao the administrative center.

There was no *xian* government in Xunwu before the Wanli period [1573–1620] in the Ming dynasty; Xunwu *xian* was established during the Wanli period. Before that time, part of Xunwu was under the jurisdiction of Anyuan *xian* in Jiangxi Province. This was Shiqi *bao*, which comprised the present Chengjiang, Sanshui, Renfeng, and Xunwu City districts; the other part was under the jurisdiction of Pingyuan *xian* in Guangdong Province and comprised the present Shuangqiao, Nanba, and Jiansan districts.

Chapter II. Transportation and Communication in Xunwu

Waterways

The Xunwu River originates in the Pangu'ai area of the Guiling Mountains. Passing through Chengjiang, Jitan, Shipaixia, Chetou, and Liuche, it merges into the Longchuan River, which goes down to Huizhou [in Guangdong]. The Xunwu River is a tributary of the Dongjiang [East River], and ships can go as far upstream as Chengjiang. There are three big market towns [*xu*] along the river: Chengjiang, Jitan, and Liuche, with Jitan the biggest.

Ships can also go from Shipaixia to Heling in Xunwu City District (10 *li* south of the town).

Land Routes

With Shipaixia being the hub, there are four main roads. One road goes to Yunmenling (110 *li*) via Jitan (30 *li*), Chengjiang (60 *li*), and Pangu'ai. This is

8. Renfeng District was renamed Huangxiang District after the Xunwu *xian* soviet government was established in May 1930.

the main road to Guangdong Province for Xingguo, Yudu, and Huichang *xian*. Another goes to Anyuan City (140 *li*) via Xunwu City (30 *li*), Sanbiao (60 *li*), and Taiyangguan. This is the main road to Mei *xian* for Xinfeng and Anyuan. Another road goes to Bachi in Pingyuan *xian* (45 *li*) via Zhucun and Niudouguang (20 *li*). This is the main road to Mei *xian* for Huichang and Anyuan. The roads from Huichang and Anyuan merge at Shipaixia and then go to Mei *xian* together. Another road goes to Xingning and Wuhua *xian* via Chetou (20 *li*), Liuche (35 *li*), Huangtangdu (60 *li*), and Luofu (95 *li*) and Luogang (125 *li*) in Xingning *xian*. This last road is the main way from Xunwu to Huizhou.

There are some other, smaller roads. One goes from Chengjiang to Luotang (30 *li*) in Wabujie of Anyuan, then from Luotang south to Xiaba and then north to [Yun]Menling. Another road goes from Jitan to Pingyuan (60 *li*) via Xiaotian, Chuandu, and Shuyuan. Another road goes from Xunwu City to Wuping (180 *li*) via Daluxia, Zixi, Jianxi, Liche, and Laidi. Another road goes from Xunwu City to Hushan (60 *li*) in Nanxiang in Anyuan *xian* via Shangping, then north from Hushan to Anyuan City (60 *li*), and then west to Taiping (36 *li*) and Egong (60 *li*). Another road goes from Xunwu City to Xinxu (60 *li*), then from Xinxu to Egong (80 *li*) in Dingnan, passing through Gongping (3 *li*) and Liangguangting (45 *li*), then south from Egong and then west to Dingnan City, passing through Hezi on the way to Xinfeng. The following roads are even smaller: one from Xinxu to Longchuan City (240 li) via Changpu (20 *li*) and Aipaikou; and another road from Changpu and Aipaikou to Xingning City (180 *li*).

Xunwu City is 90 *li* from Menling, 180 *li* from Wuping, 240 *li* from Mei *xian*, 240 *li* from Xingning, 110 *li* from Anyuan, 310 *li* from Longchuan, and 160 *li* from Dingnan (via Shangping, Hushan, Taiping, and Egong).

Telegraph

The Telegraph Bureau was moved from Jitan to Xunwu City in 1922. The telegraph line goes from Jitan to Xunwu City to Yunmenling and to Pingyuan.

Postal Service

There is a third-class post office in Xunwu City. One postal route goes to Menling via Jitan and Chengjiang. Another route goes to Bachi via Niudouguang and then from Bachi to Mei *xian*. Another route from Bachi goes to Pingyuan. Another route goes to Anyuan via Sanbiao. There are "postal agents" in Chengjiang, Jitan, and Niudouguang and "receiving offices" in Sanbiao and Shipaixia. There is postal service on the Menling route on the second, fifth, and eighth days of the [ten-day cycle of the] lunar calendar.[9] The Bachi route has

---

9. The thirty-day lunar month is divided into three ten-day periods. In addition to postal deliveries, periodic markets were also scheduled in terms of the lunar calendar. For example, a market town might host a regularly scheduled market on the first, fourth, and seventh days of the ten-day cycle.—RT.

service on the first, third, fifth, seventh, and ninth, and the Anyuan route on the second, fourth, sixth, eighth, and tenth. Letters to Ganzhou are sent via the Anyuan route, and those to Yudu and Xingguo via the Menling route. Usually, amounts up to 200 *yuan* can be remitted through the post office in Xunwu City. With advance notice up to 500 *yuan* can be remitted. But otherwise not.

During the March 25 uprising the year before last,[10] the director of the post office was seized and fined 500 *yuan*. This time the new director, fearing capture, fled first. The director of the Telegraph Bureau was killed during the March 25 uprising.

The Means of Land Transportation

Just as in Guangdong Province, there are no vehicles on any roads. The major means of land transportation are the shoulders of humans, and next mules and horses. There are many mules and horses on the road from Xunwu City to Mei *xian* and some on the roads from Xunwu City to Menling and Jitan, but none on the other roads. There are more mules than horses, but they are generally called "horses." The goods carried by horse are mainly salt and soybeans.

Chapter III. Commerce in Xunwu

Business from [Yun] Menling to Mei Xian

Of the goods brought from Shicheng and Ruijin *xian*, rice and soybeans are the most important, with an [annual] worth of several hundred thousand *yuan*. Tea-oil is the major item of trade from Xingguo *xian*,[11] although some rice (not much) is imported from there. No goods are brought in from Yudu or Huichang *xian*.

Four boatloads of oil come from Menling to every market in Chengjiang (the oil is carried by humans from Menling to Chengjiang and then loaded onto boats). Every boat carries 12 *Dan*[12] of oil, and each *Dan* is worth 30 *yuan*

---

10. The March 25 uprising was the *xian*-wide uprising that was organized by the Xunwu Communist Party, which led the peasants and young students on March 25, 1928.

11. *Chayou* and *muyou* refer to the oil pressed from the seeds of the tea-oil plant. They are used mainly as a foodstuff. "Tea-oil" *(chayou)* is pressed from the camellia plant.—RT.

12. The Chinese word *dan* stands for two different characters, one of them signifying a measure of capacity, and the other a measure of weight. The exact value of these units varied from place to place, or even according to the commodities being measured. Here the reference is presumably to the *dan* as a unit of weight (sometimes called a picul), variously defined as 50 kilos or 133 pounds. The other *dan*, roughly equivalent to a bushel or 1 hectolitre, was a dry volume measure used for rice. It occurs very frequently in Mao's Xunwu report as the unit in which land rents were fixed. As pointed out in a note to the volume containing the Chinese text of this document, however, Mao often uses the two terms loosely and interchangeably. For a more detailed discussion, see Appendix B, "Weights and Measures in Xunwu," in Thompson, pp. 224–25. In this volume, we have distinguished between these two characters by capitalizing the transcription when it refers to the unit of weight.

(xiaoyang).[13] Figuring a hundred markets a year, the oil traded is worth 150,000 yuan.

Most of the rice coming from Shicheng and Ruijin to Menling goes to Mei xian via Luotang, Xiaba (in Wuping xian [Fujian], at the common boundary of the three provinces), and Xinpu (in Jiaoling xian [Guangdong], 30 li from Mei xian). The amount transported is about 300 Dan a day. Rice bound for Mei xian usually does not pass through Xunwu xian, but oil and soybeans do. The amount of beans is almost double that of oil. Some Dan contain 5 dou,[14] and some contain 3 dou; the amount is not very regular. One dou is worth 1.5 yuan (xiaoyang). There are five boatloads of oil and beans at every market (one market every three days); each boat contains 14 Dan, and the value of each Dan is 6 yuan (assuming 4 dou in each Dan). So the value of the oil and beans at each market is 420 yuan, and the annual total is 42,000 yuan for the hundred markets held each year. The amount carried by porters is 20 Dan per market, for a total of 2,800 Dan annually, with a value of 16,800 yuan. So the sum of these two categories is 58,800 yuan.

Business from Anyuan to Mei Xian

Chicken

The most important good transported along this route is chicken, with oxen next, and pigs third. Most of the chickens come from Tangjiang, Nankang, and Xinfeng, although some come from Anyuan, and some even from Suichuan. The transport route for chickens runs through Wangmudu, Jinji, Xintian, and Banshi but avoids Anyuan City, passing 5 li to the north, and enters Xunwu xian on the way to Mei xian. From Mei xian, the chickens are shipped to Songkou [Jiaoling xian] and then to Shantou for export. Most of the chickens passing though Xunwu are from Anyuan, with some from Menling. Since between 100 and 300 Dan are shipped each day, if each Dan weighs 60 jin,[15] then a daily amount of 100 Dan is equal to 6,000 jin. Chicken dealers carry chickens from the Tangjiang area to Mei xian or Xinpu to sell (from Xunwu the route to Xinpu runs through

---

13. As pointed out in a note to the Chinese edition of Mao's rural investigations, the exchange rate among the three currencies mentioned by him—dayang (guangyang, zayang), xiaoyang (haoyang, maoyang), and tongyuan—varied according to time and place. For a detailed discussion of the problems thus raised, see Appendix A, "Currency and Prices in Xunwu," Thompson, pp. 221–23.

14. The dou is a unit of measure commonly translated "peck," and equivalent to approximately 1 decalitre. This sentence illustrates the point, made above, that Mao sometimes uses the two characters read dan interchangeably. Here Dan, in principle a unit of weight, plainly stands for the unit of volume.

15. A jin is a measure of weight commonly taken to correspond roughly to one pound, or 500 grams (1.1 pounds). In Xunwu, the value of the jin, and the relation between the jin and the Dan, varied widely according to the product being measured.—RT.

Dazhe; after being loaded on boats, the chickens go directly to Songkou without passing through Mei *xian*) and get a price of 0.5 *yuan* per *jin* (0.4 *yuan* in Xunwu). With 6,000 *jin* every day, the value of the chickens is 3,000 *yuan* a day or 1.08 million *yuan* each year. Since the chicken guild in Mei *xian* sells chickens in Songkou at the price of 0.7 *yuan* or more a *jin*, we can say the profit is great.

Oxen

The first day of [each ten-day] cycle is the "ox market day." The ones in November are most prosperous, with seven hundred to eight hundred oxen at each market; the ones in January and February are the next most prosperous, with one hundred to two hundred oxen at each market. Those in March, April, May, June, and July are the slackest, with three to five or ten-odd at the most for each market. The first day in August is the "opening day"; business becomes more prosperous from this day, with forty to fifty or sixty to seventy oxen sold per market. There are almost a hundred oxen at each market by September and October.

How many oxen each year?

January	100
February	100
March	60
April	no markets
May	"
June	"
July	"
August (3 fairs)	250
September (3 fairs)	250
October	300
November (3 fairs)	2,100
December (2 fairs)	160
Total	3,320

The average price of an ox is 40 *yuan*, making the total value each year 132,800 *yuan*.

Like chickens, most oxen come from Tangjiang and Xinfeng, with some from Anyuan, but none from Xunwu. The difference is that chickens only pass through Xunwu, but oxen are sold here. The ox market is held on the riverbank outside the East Gate of Xunwu City. The sellers are from Tangjiang, Xinfeng, and Anyuan; the buyers are from Mei *xian*, Wuping, Jiaoling, and Pingyuan. The middlemen (brokers) are from Xunwu. Oxen not exported through Shantou via Songkou are usually bought by ox dealers to sell to families for plowing farmland or sold to other towns for slaughter. The fee for brokers is a half *mao*[16] from both the buyer and the seller. The ox tax paid to the government by the tax farmer is 1,740 *yuan* each year. In the past "bidding" *(toubiao)* [for the post of tax farmer] took place annually, and the one who offered the most obtained the bid. But recently, the bidding has been held once every three years. The tax is figured by the head, at 0.4 *yuan* for each ox and 0.5 *yuan* for each water buffalo. The tax is called *xiang*. After the tax [is paid], the character *xiang* is burned on the hide of the ox with a lime stamp, and the buyer can lead the ox away. Besides this tax, a levy of 0.1 *yuan* per ox was added recently. The tax that the tax farmer sends to the government plus his own income totals 2,000 *yuan* or more each year. Based on a tax rate of 0.4 *yuan* per ox, more than 4,500 oxen should be sold in Xunwu each year; thus, the figure of 3,320 cited above is a low estimate.

Pigs

Most come from Xinfeng; some are from Anyuan. Pigs arrive by two routes: most come from Anyuan *xian* to Mei *xian* via Xunwu City, Niudouguang, and Bachi. Some come from Nanxiang in Anyuan *xian* to Mei *xian* via Gongping, Xinxu, Liuche, and Zhongkeng in Pingyuan *xian*. A total of five thousand pigs, valued at 225,000 *yuan*, arrives via these two routes. The average weight is 100 *jin*, and at a price of 0.4 *yuan* a *jin*, the [average] value of a pig is 45 *yuan*. The Xunwu government levies a tax of 0.2 *yuan* per pig.

Business from Mei Xian *to [Yun] Menling*

Most business is in the following five categories:

Foreign Goods. Tooth powder, toothbrushes, flashlights, rubber shoes, soaps, foreign umbrellas, lanterns, and foreign iron [tinned iron] are major trading items. Some of these items, for example, tooth powder and toothbrushes, are made in China, but are usually called foreign goods.

Sea Delicacies. Kelp, sea cucumbers, fish maw, squid, mussels, and salted fish are all major trade items.

Salt. Ten years ago it came mostly from Huizhou, but three or four years ago most of it began coming from Chaozhou. This is because merchants began using a different route. Right now most salt is again coming from Huizhou because of the blockade set up by reactionaries in Bachi and Zhongkeng against Red areas. The blockade also stops salt from arriving from Chaozhou. After arriving in Menling, most salt goes directly to Xingguo.

Kerosene. Mostly Asia Brand.

---

16. The *mao* was both a unit of account and an actual silver coin. It was defined as one-tenth of a *yuan*, though the 20-cent coin was more common than the 10-cent coin.—RT.

Textiles. Most textiles come from Xingning; a much smaller amount comes from Mei *xian*. Both places purchase foreign yarn to make into cloth. The weaving industry in Xingning is well developed, and the businesses there are generally larger than those in Mei *xian*. Foreign yarn (from foreign countries) [is also imported over this route].

A good quantity of sugar and flour is also traded.

There is no transportation service from Mei *xian* to Menling. Most goods are carried by people. All salt is carried by horses; the only transportation service is to Chengjiang by boat. Part of the flour is also carried by horses.

Porters carry a *Dan* of goods from Menling to Mei *xian* and then bring back another *Dan* of goods.

Business from Mei Xian to Anyuan and Xinfeng

The goods traded are the same as those to Menling, but in smaller amounts. The ratio is about four to six. This is because Anyuan and Xinfeng comprise a small area, whereas the goods going to Menling are sold in Ruijin, Shicheng, Yudu, and Xingguo—a very large area.

Products from Huizhou

The only major trade is in salt. Apart from a little salted fish and sugar sold to Xunwu, there is nothing else.

Xunwu's Exports

The goods listed in the sections above are imported to or pass through Xunwu. In this section exported goods are listed.

First is rice. Mei *xian* is short of rice; so it is twice as expensive there as in Xunwu, and a lot of rice is supplied by Xunwu to Mei *xian* every year. Rice from Chengjiang, Sanbiao, Jitan (in Xiangshan), and Xunwu City District is exported to Mei *xian* through Niudouguang, Bachi, and Dazhe. Rice from Longtu, Yutian, Liuche, Fangtian, and the upper half of Huangxiang District is exported to Mei *xian* via Zhongkeng. Rice from Datong, the lower half of Huangxiang District, Datian, Lantian, and Douyan, as well as from Longchuan [*xian*] is exported to Mei *xian* via Cenfeng and Shizheng. The amount carried over these three routes is almost equal—about 100 *Dan* a day or 36,000 *Dan* a year. At a price of 8 *yuan* a *Dan*, the value is 288,000 *yuan*.

The second is tea. Tea grows in Shangping and Xiaping in the West Ward, and Tuhe, Gangsang, and Ezihu in the South Ward. Tea is picked in March, April, May, July, and August. Twenty *Dan* (70 *jin* per *Dan*) are exported at each market, for a total of 2,000 *Dan* at the one hundred markets held each year. With a total of 140,000 *jin* at a price of 0.5 *yuan* per *jin*, the total value is 70,000 *yuan*. Eighty percent or more is exported to Xingning, and 20 percent or less is shipped to Mei *xian*.

When tea is being picked, the traders from Xingning come to the countryside and buy freshly picked tea shoots and process the tea themselves. Among the tea shoots, the "tea before rain" (picked before April 20,[17] also called "first spring tea") can be sold at the price of 1 *yuan* for 8 *jin*, a *jin* of tea can be made from 5 *jin* of tea shoots. This tea before rain is expensive, with a price of 1 *yuan* per *jin*. As for the "second spring tea" (picked in March and April) and "autumn tea" (picked in July and August), 15 *jin* sells for 1 *yuan*. Tea made from these tea shoots can be sold for 0.5 *yuan* per *jin*.

In the tea trade, profits can be made from the second spring tea and autumn tea, but very little money is made from the first spring tea. Some tea can be made from the tea picked in December, which is called "snow tea." The snow tea is as expensive as the tea before rain and is also sold to the same upper-class families. Not much snow tea is [produced], and traders cannot make much money from it.

Besides the Xunwu City District, some tea is also grown in Yanyangping in Shuangqiao District, although not much is produced (just over 100 *yuan* each year). The quality is very good. This is because tea plants are grown in gardens instead of on hillsides.

The third is paper. Paper is made in Huangxiang and exported to Xingning (via Luofu and Luogang), Mei *xian* (via Zhongkeng, or some via Cenfeng), and Longchuan (via Beiling). On the average 60 *Dan* is traded at each market. With a hundred markets a year, a total of 6,000 *Dan* at 8 *yuan* per *Dan* is worth 48,000 *yuan*.

The fourth is timber. It is produced in the West Ward (Shangping and Xiaping) and South Ward (Ezihu) of the Xunwu City District, Hejiao in Nanba District, Xiangshan and Gaotou in Huangxiang District, Xiaomukeng and Zhaitangkeng in Sanshui District, and Luofuzhang in Jiansan District. All the timber is exported to Dongjiang[18] except for that from Luofuzhang, which is exported to Chaozhou and Shantou. The timber shipped from Luofuzhang to Chaozhou and Shantou is very expensive, but that shipped to Dongjiang is very cheap. The total value is more than 10,000 *yuan* a year. Twenty years ago much more was produced.

As for timber exports, the traders from Longchuan make investments, assisted by the local timber merchants. They all go to the hills to check the trees and then give the money to the "mountain lord" (the money is for those trees, among the

17. The text reads *guyu*, one of the twenty-four solar periods of the Chinese solar year. This corresponds approximately to the period from April 20 to May 4.—RT.
18. Dongjiang refers to the catchment of the East River, which is fed in part by the Xunwu River. The East River passes through Longchuan and Huizhou in eastern Guangdong before entering the Pearl River estuary near Canton.—RT.

many on the hills, that they have agreed may be felled). The trader employs some workers to fell the trees, and the local merchant takes care of those trees already felled so that they will not be stolen. Most of the trees are felled in April and May, with fewer and fewer after June and none after September. The tree bark is peeled off as soon as the trees are felled; they are then laid on the ground for at least two months and dried. If, after two months, the price is good and selling is to the trader's advantage, the timber is bound together to make rafts and then transported down the river. Sometimes the timber is held for three or four years there. The position of the local merchants, relative to the lumber dealers (outside traders), is like that of workers; so they call the lumber dealers "boss," whereas the lumber dealers call them "raft chief." The profit is divided so that 90 percent goes to the boss and 10 percent to the raft chief.

The fifth is [dried] mushrooms. The most important places for production are the hilly areas in Sanbiao; places along the boundary with Anyuan like Dahudong, Xiaohudong, Zhaitangkeng, Shangba, and Xiaba; and places along the boundary between Xunwu City District and Anyuan like Shangping and Xiaping. Next is Yeziche on the boundary between Shuangqiao District and Pingyuan. The price of mushrooms is 2 *yuan* a *jin*, and an amount worth 10,000 *yuan* is produced each year. More mushrooms are produced in Anyuan than in Xunwu. Mushrooms from Anyuan are sold to Nanxiong, and those from Xunwu to Xingning. There are no traders to buy mushrooms. Rather, Xunwu natives buy them and sell them in other places.

The sixth is tea-oil. It is produced in Datong, Douyan, Huangtangdu, Lantian, and Datian in Shuangqiao District. The amount is about 15,000 *jin* a year, which, at 25 *yuan* per 100 *jin*, brings in a total of 3,750 *yuan*. Tea-oil is exported to Xingning and Mei *xian* via Luofu and Cenfeng.

Here is a list of the six products and their values (only for export):

1.	Rice	288,000 *yuan*
2.	Tea	70,000
3.	Paper	48,000
4.	Timber	10,000
5.	Mushrooms	10,000
6.	Tea-oil	3,750
	Total	429,750 *yuan*

The Major Markets of Xunwu

First is Jitan. Salt, rice, oil, and soybeans are the main trade items. The second is Niudouguang. Less salt and rice is traded here than in Jitan, but about the same amounts of oil and soybeans are handled here as in Jitan. The third is Liuche.

The major item is textiles imported from Xingning; oil and soybeans are second. The fourth is Xunwu City. The largest trade is the oxen trade, followed by oil, salt, and rice; the third is textiles. (There used to be textiles from Ganzhou, but none were brought in after 1928. This is because those textiles, made from local thread with "one ply big, another ply thin," were replaced by textiles made in Xingning and Mei *xian* from foreign thread. Those textiles from Xingning and Mei *xian* are very good, "very smooth.") The chicken business is large, but chickens are only passing through and are not traded [in Xunwu], so they do not count. The fifth market is Chengjiang. Oil, soybeans, and salt are the major goods passing through here; rice is next; there is also a large trade in opium, which comes from Xingning and Yudu. The sixth is Shipaixia, which is the general port for oil, salt, rice, soybeans; but most of these goods are only in transit. There is some trade in salt and rice. Chicken, pigs, and oxen also pass through here.

There are some small markets, such as Cenfeng (rice), Gongping (paper), Huangxiang, and Sanbiao.

Xunwu City

What Is Xunwu City?

A person who is completely ignorant of the inside story of the world of commerce is bound to fail in choosing proper tactics to deal with the mercantile bourgeoisie and in attempting to gain the support of the poor urban masses. It is extremely clear that gaining the support of the poor is deemed unimportant by some comrades, but the high-level organs of the leadership feel that it is important. However, even they have never been able to give comrades concrete tactics to follow and have particularly failed to indicate a concrete work method. Doesn't this phenomenon result from a lack of understanding of what a market town is? I have resolved to understand the town problem, but I have never been able to understand it because I have never found people who could supply sufficient data. Now in Xunwu, through Comrade Gu Bo's introductions, I found two old gentlemen, Guo Youmei and Fan Daming. Many thanks to these two gentlemen for allowing me to become like a young student and to begin to understand a bit about town commerce. I was overjoyed. If my findings can pique the interest of comrades (particularly those comrades in the rural movement and those doing Red Army work) to study the town problem and encourage them to study towns in addition to studying the rural question, then this will have been a valuable experience. Our study of the town question is the same as our study of the rural question; **we must spare no effort in studying one place thoroughly.**[19] Afterward, it will be easy to study another place and to understand general situations. If one views the flowers from horseback, like a certain

---

19. The words in bold, here and elsewhere in this document, are underscored in the original by placing dots next to the characters.

comrade's so-called "going to a place and asking questions randomly,"[20] then one cannot understand a problem profoundly even after a lifetime of effort. This study method is obviously incorrect.

Among Xunwu's many markets, because of this convenient opportunity, we can take Xunwu City's market as an example to investigate.

In speaking of Xunwu City's market, one truly longs for the past to replace the present. Compared with the present level of business in Xunwu City, twice as much was done in the past. The most flourishing years were 1901 and 1902. At that time not only did people from Chengjiang and Jitan in the northern half of the *xian* come to Xunwu City to buy things, but people from settlements in the southern half of the *xian* like Huangxiang and Liuche and even people from Bachi in Pingyuan *xian* [Guangdong] came to Xunwu City to buy things. This is because during the Qing products from Ganzhou passed through Xunwu on the way to eastern Guangdong. If the inhabitants of eastern Guangdong wanted to buy Ganzhou products, it goes without saying that those of Liuche and other places would. Because of this, the trade in Xunwu City, occupying a central position, naturally was quite well developed. But since the development of the trade in foreign-style goods in Mei *xian* and of the textile trade in Xingning, the decline of the trade in native products from Ganzhou kept people not only from eastern Guangdong and Bachi from coming to Xunwu City but also from Liuche and other places in the southern half of the *xian* from coming to Xunwu City to buy things. And in 1901 and 1902 it was still the so-called Age of the Degree Holders. The New Policies[21] hadn't yet been implemented, and the major trade in Xunwu City was in silk goods from Ganzhou. But from that time on things changed, the need for silk decreased, and the imperial degrees were abrogated in the first year of the Republic [1912]. The market for silk goods was virtually wiped out, and trade in Xunwu City declined greatly. Xunwu is the kind of place where the competition between handicraft products and capitalist products expresses the drastic force of the cycle of boom and bust. How can it not be worthwhile to pay attention? Moreover, until now [i.e., before the town was occupied by the Red forces], Xunwu City had both shops and stalls that were open every day and periodic markets on the first, fourth, and seventh days [of the ten-day cycle]. Approximately two thousand seven hundred people live either inside or just outside the stout walls of the city. The aspect of the city is quiet and deserted; only on market days does it become lively and

---

20. It is not clear to whom Mao is referring here.

21. The New Policies *(xinzheng)* were promulgated beginning in 1901. Among the reforms under this rubric were reorganizations of government administration and the military; educational reforms, including the abolition of the examination system in 1905; and attempts to establish electoral bodies at the local, provincial, and national levels.—RT.

then only for a few hours. Is not Xunwu, then, an excellent source of data?

In order to analyze living conditions and the organization of Xunwu City, we will look at all kinds of goods and services in Xunwu City.

Salt

Goods are sold mostly to people from the four wards of the city and people from Sanbiao and Shuiyuan, two *bao* in Sanshui District. People from other localities rarely come to Xunwu City to buy things. The only exception to this is salt. The greater part of the salt is sold for export to Anyuan and Xinfeng; only a small part is sold in Xunwu City District and Sanbiao. Also, because it is an item used daily, it is the number-one good traded in Xunwu City. There are five salt shops in Xunwu City. Each shop can do as much as 20,000 *yuan* of business or as little as 6,000 or 7,000 *yuan*. The five shops together can have 100,000 *yuan* of business in a year.

Salt is divided into Chaozhou salt and Huizhou salt. Chaozhou salt is good, but expensive. A *yuan [xiaoyang]* buys 10 to 11 *jin*. The color of Chaozhou salt is dark green, and since it is pure, it can prevent spoilage. The color of Huizhou salt is white, but it is less salty. Because of this, the price is relatively low; a *yuan* buys 16 to 17 *jin*. Only those who want inexpensive salt eat Huizhou salt. In the past most salt sold in Xunwu was Chaozhou salt; not much Huizhou salt was used.

Two of the shops (Huitong and Xinfachang) selling Chaozhou salt are run by natives of Xunwu; one shop is run by Han Xiangsheng, a native of Pingyuan; another is run by Zhou Yuchang, from Wan'an *xian* [Jiangxi]; and one (Wanfengxing) is run jointly by a native of Xunwu and by someone from Taihe *xian* [Jiangxi]. Huitong has 3,000 *yuan* of capital and is considered the largest. Zhou Yuchang previously had 2,000 *yuan*, but last year, because the paper trade was disrupted by bandits, he lost over 900 *yuan* of capital. Now he has only about 1,000 *yuan* left. These two businesses were started over twenty years ago. The number-three shop is Han Xiangsheng's, with capital of around 700 *yuan*; he started business some ten years ago. The number-four shop is Wanfengxing, with 200 *yuan* invested four years ago. Now its capital is 400 to 500 *yuan*. The number-five shop is Xinfachang, begun more than ten years ago. Although its owners have tried every tactic, its capital does not exceed 100 *yuan*.

The proprietor of the Huitong Shop is Zhong Zhourui. He is a landlord (among those who run salt businesses, he's the only landlord). His shop is inside the East Gate, and his family lives outside the South Gate. He owns rice paddies with rents of 220 *dan*. Every year there are two crops, and every crop yields 220 *Dan* of grain. One crop goes for the rent; one crop is kept by the peasants. His family consists of his wife, three sons, three daughters-in-law, and one bride-in-waiting (she was purchased and is now five *sui*; because she does not have a husband now and must wait for the boss's wife to bear a son, she is called a bride-in-waiting, which elsewhere is referred to as a daughter-in-law raised from childhood).[22] Including himself, there are nine people in the household [lit., nine people eat there]. He does not hire any clerks, and he directs his sons and daughters-in-law himself. He was the first "capitalist" *[zibenjia]* in Xunwu City.

Han Xiangsheng is from Bachi in Pingyuan *xian*. He supports three people: his wife, one child, and himself. He does not hire anyone, and every year he can make a little money. The owner *[zhuren]* of the Xinfachang Shop is Kuang Mingkui, a Chetou man who was a civil *xiucai* during the Qing. He opened his shop more than ten years ago and does a business of several dozen *yuan*. In his household are his wife and one child. Because he does things fairly and justly, he has twice served as president of the chamber of commerce: once for a term of two years in the Qing and again from last year until the present. He is sixty-odd *sui* and is a white-haired old man.

General Goods

There are sixteen or seventeen general stores, of which ten or so are large. The names of the thirteen largest stores and the places of origin of their owners are:

Name of business	Origin of owner
Zhicheng	Xingning
Luntaixing	Ji'an
Yitaixing	Ji'an and Xunwu
Yicheng	Xingning
Pan Yueli	Xingning
Wang Runxiang	Xingning
Pan Dengji	Xingning
Xiangxing	Xingning
Yongyuanjin	Xingning
Junyi	Began by a porter from Xunwu
Luo Jinfeng	Xunwu (with 300 *Dan* of rents, the only landlord among these owners)
Fan Shunchang	Fujian
Huang Yufeng	Fujian

Among them, the Huang Yufeng Shop's business is mainly tobacco and paper. The most important trade for the others is in textiles, followed by foreign

---

22. For a discussion of the practice of minor marriages referred to in the text, see Arthur P. Wolf and Huang Chieh-shan [Jieshan], *Marriage and Adoption in China, 1845–1945* (Stanford: Stanford University Press, 1980), pp. 1–15 (hereafter, Wolf and Huang, *Marriage and Adoption*). A report on this custom as practiced in southern Jiangxi at the turn of the century can be found on p. 7.—RT.

goods. Foreign goods of all kinds are sold in small markets. Here is a brief list of 131 items:

tooth powder*
toothbrushes*
rubber overshoes*
leather shoes*
rubber boots*
sport shoes*
slippers
pencils
pens (fountain pens)
chalk
ink sticks
writing brushes
inkstones
ink boxes (for Chinese calligraphy)
brush covers
brush racks
paste
exercise books
red paste for seals
plain paper
printing ink
textbooks (there is no separate book-store; books are sold in the general goods stores)
calligraphy and paintings
small towels
soap*
perfumed soda
toilet water
perfumed toilet water
woolen towels*
foreign socks*
foreign enamel wash basins
foreign enamel bowls
foreign enamel bowls (with a handle)*
hair oil
hair cream
gloves
rouge

mufflers*
big or small combs
cosmetics
vanishing cream
flashlights*
batteries*
matches*
cigarettes (there are many brands: Jinzi, Zhongguo, Sanpaotai, Hade-men, Shanmei, etc., with Jinzi and Zhongguo more popular)
Magu cigarettes
cigarette holders
foreign umbrellas
straw hats
formal hats
imported enamel cups
visored caps
imported felt
cotton blankets
woolen hats (for children)
nightcaps
kapok pillows
leather pillows
Zhongshan buttons
white bone buttons
black bone buttons
conch buttons
snaps
elastic
suspenders
silk belts
imported belts
talcum
undershirts
fans (black and white paper)
clocks
watches
alarm clocks
letter paper*

envelopes*
diaries
mirrors
eyeglasses
foreign knives
toys (small guns, trains, roly-polies, dolls, small rubber balls, whistles, etc.)
German razors
safety razors
shears
hair scissors (this and the three preceding items are for haircutting)
leather suitcases
rattan suitcases
indigo* (blue)
dyestuff (red, black, gray, pinkish red)*
copper locks
foreign copper locks
iron locks
foreign iron locks
copper net hooks
bone net hooks
kerosene*
storm lanterns*
rush-wick lamps*
covered lamps
enamel table lamps
lamps with lotus lids
foreign lamps
square lamps
six-cornered lamps
round flints
flat flint steel (this and the preceding item are for lighting lanterns)
bone chopsticks
lacquer chopsticks
abacuses
water pipes
pipes
nails*
copper pots (for tea)
iron pans
iron trays
iron spoons
tiles
various pieces of china*
dominoes
mahjongg tiles
jujubes
dried *longyan*
various canned foods (beef, mixed vegetables, duck, winter bamboo shoots, loquats, sand pears, lichee, *longyan,* pineapple, milk)
couplets
foreign candles
white foreign wax
raisins
foreign thread
galvanized wire
ink

These 131 products are all called "foreign goods" by the merchants, and are sold at general stores. The twenty-three asterisked items are sold the most; the items not asterisked are sold in lesser quantities. One hundred eight of the 131 items come from Mei and Xingning *xian.* Most of the goods are from Mei *xian;* only Western-style socks, mufflers, and other woven goods come mainly from Xingning. Tiles and couplets come from Ganzhou. Leather pillows, letter paper, envelopes, copper bowls, kerosene, fans, water pipes, and writing brushes— these eight items come from both Mei *xian* and Ganzhou. Most leather pillows, letter paper, envelopes, enamelware, fans, and water pipes come from Ganzhou and are of the highest quality. The stationery from Ganzhou is made of paper manufactured in China; that from Mei *xian* is made with foreign paper. Kerosene and cigarettes come mostly from Guangdong; smaller amounts come from Ganzhou. Cigarettes come from Mei *xian*, Xingning, and Ganzhou. Writing brushes come mostly from Ganzhou; only a few come from Mei *xian*.

The foreign goods of secondary importance are as described above; below I discuss the most important item traded in the general stores—textiles.

The textiles include native cotton cloth (blue, white, printed, gray, red, green, and striped cotton); glazed [i.e., shiny, smooth] cotton cloth (blue, white, gray, black, red, glazed, green, and printed); fine cotton (white, gray, black, blue, striped, and indigo blue); silk goods (all kinds of silk with patterns, all kinds of satin, brown-colored raw silk, and gambiered [i.e., dyed yellow] Guangdong gauze); woolen cloth (thick woolen cloth, rough woolen cloth, fine glazed woolen cloth); Chinese linen (white, blue, black, off-white, light green). Native cotton cloth is made from foreign yarn by Chinese. It is shipped from Xingning. Glazed cotton cloth and fine cotton are called foreign cloth and are shipped from Hong Kong via Mei *xian*. As for the silk goods, patterned silks and brown-colored raw silk come from Hangzhou via Ganzhou and Mei *xian*. Xunwu women use it to make bonnets. Every woman wears this type of bonnet. The textile business is worth some 100,000 *yuan* annually in Xunwu City. The marketing area is Xunwu City District and Sanbiao District.

General stores, in addition to the two main categories of textiles and foreign goods, also sell tobacco, pastries, incense and candles [for ancestor worship], and also a bit of [cooking] oil and salt.

In Qing times, the general goods business within Xunwu City was worth around 150,000 *yuan* annually; now it is around 120,000 *yuan*. The 120,000 *yuan* is divided among:

textiles	80,000-odd *yuan* (native cloth: 70,000 *yuan*; foreign cloth: 10,000 *yuan*, of which, woolens, 2,000 *yuan*, Chinese linen, 1,000-odd *yuan*)
foreign goods	20,000 *yuan* (each business sells at most 1,100–1,200 *yuan*; at the least 200–300 *yuan*)
tobacco	about 10,000 *yuan*
pastries	about 400 *yuan* (only two businesses sell pastries on the side)
incense,spirit money, firecrackers	about 500 *yuan* (two businesses sell incense and spirit money on the side; thirteen businesses sell firecrackers)

In order to understand general stores better, let us look at the concrete details of a few.

The shopkeeper *[dianzhu]* of the largest general store is a Xingning native, Chen Zhicheng, who owns a shop in Xunwu City, in Jitan, and in Chengjiang.

The shop in Xunwu City has capital of 3,000 *yuan*. He himself had only about 1,000 *yuan*. He borrowed the rest. The annual interest each year on 3,000 *yuan* is 900 *yuan*. Apart from paying wages, food, and fuel costs, he uses his profits for interest payments. Chen also likes to use his money for whoring and gambling.

The second-largest business is Luntaixing, whose capital, comprising three shares, is 2,000 *yuan*. After expenses, it makes profits of 300 to 400 *yuan* every year.

The third-largest business is Yitaixing, whose capital, comprising three shares, is more than 1,000 *yuan*.[23] Every year it makes a profit of 100 to 200 *yuan*.

The fourth-largest business, Luo Yicheng, is owned by one person with over 1,000 *yuan* of capital. Every year he can make 400 to 500 *yuan*. He's very economical: vegetables for food; native cloth for clothing. There are two apprentices. His family is still in Xingning. He is a Xingning native who, when he first came to Xunwu, peddled sweets from baskets he carried in Xunwu City and the four wards. For one copper cash[24] he'd break off a piece of candy. (Now a piece of candy costs one copper cent.)[25] Sometimes he exchanged candy for every type of salvage goods (hair, scrap copper, scrap iron, pig and ox bones, scraps of padded cloth). He is the kind of person who started from scratch. He came to Xunwu more than thirty years ago, made good, and opened a general store more than fifteen years ago.

Guo Yihe is the general store with the least capital, about 100 *yuan*. It sells tobacco, safety matches, eggs, red rope (red cord), silk thread, strips of embroidery (used on shoe quarters), writing brushes and ink, towels, towels made with foreign yarn, bone buttons, and other items. The store shopkeeper is Guo Youmei (he is participating in our investigation meetings), and he and his wife have clothing, food, and tax expenses each year of over 100 *yuan*. His business is barely sufficient for those expenses. He is a Wan'an native who came to Xunwu when he was twelve *sui*; he is now fifty-nine *sui*. Before he came, his uncle had traded in Xunwu for sixty years. Together these two have been in business in Xunwu for a hundred years. The store has always dealt in textiles. Business was best in 1899 and 1900; they had capital of 3,000 *yuan* and from elsewhere they received on consignment *[jiao]* (when merchants borrow goods and then sell them, it's called *jiao*) goods worth 5,000 to 6,000 *yuan*. He himself consigned to other people goods worth 4,000 to 5,000 *yuan*. So, at that time, although he had only 3,000 *yuan* of capital, he could do around 20,000 *yuan* of business. This was the number-one store in Xunwu City. Now one can go to Liuche, Bachi, Niudouguang, and Chetou to buy things, but at that time the merchants from shops in those places all came to Xunwu City to buy things. The most important

---

23. The text has "more than a string of capital," which is glossed parenthetically as "over a thousand *yuan* of capital."—RT.

24. *Mingqian* is copper cash *(tongqian)*.

25. *Tongpian, tongban,* and *tongkezi* are all copper coins *[tongyuan]*.

source of goods was Ganzhou (textiles, silk goods, paper, writing brushes and ink, straw hats, and straw mats from Suzhou); there was also trade with Ji'an (purple cloth and silk thread). At that time one could go to Ganzhou and buy 300 *yuan* of goods with only 100 *yuan* of cash and take them away. Now this is impossible. This kind of impossibility is not limited to the Guo Yihe Shop. Almost no shops consign goods. No goods are being consigned in Ganzhou or in Mei *xian* and Xingning. This is a great change in the economy. Just recently (1928), the "world went out of kilter." As for goods consigned by merchants to peasants, the peasants are exploited by heavy rents and interest, and have always been impoverished. On top of this, the year before last locusts ate the grain and there was also a drought, so the peasants could not pay the bills held by Xunwu City merchants. As a result, Xunwu City's merchants cannot pay the bills of merchants in Mei *xian* and Xingning, and Mei *xian* and Xingning merchants are nervous about consigning goods to people. In 1916 the Guo Yihe Shop suffered a great attack (the Guangfu faction led more than a thousand peasants to Xunwu City and attacked many other stores). After government troops recovered the city, they launched a great attack upon Guo Yihe and plundered more than 6,900 *yuan* worth of things. From that year until now, one year has been worse than the last, until things have reached the present state. Guo [Youmei] served two terms as president of the chamber of commerce, from 1925 to 1927.

Here I want to talk about the system of employees in general stores and look at the origins of their class connections, which are so obscure.

To become a master *[chushi]* after being an apprentice for three years in a general store, according to established practice one must help the boss for a year. At the beginning of the year, the person takes the old clothes worn during his apprenticeship that he no longer wants and exchanges all of them for new ones, because now he has some money. Moreover, his status is not the same. After helping for a year, if he is capable, the boss continues with him in place. If he is not capable, the boss dismisses him. The boss says to him: "Our store doesn't need so many people; next year you must find other work." But he can turn around and go to a new shop, where his status becomes a bit higher and the clothes he wears become a bit better, and his salary (not called wages) is increased each year. In society he is not referred to as an "apprentice" any more. Rather, people respect him as a "gentleman" *[xiansheng]*.[26] During the year that he is helping, the boss does not give him a fixed salary. Also, he does not have a "salary" label. But the boss gives him every kind of winter and summer clothing.

---

26. A more specific translation might be "articled clerk," to borrow a coinage from early nineteenth-century England. This type of clerk agreed to certain articles of apprenticeship, much as the "gentleman" in a Xunwu shop might have. This Chinese term for "gentleman" can also be used for "teacher," "sir," or "mister." In the past it could be appended to various occupations, like that of bookkeeper *(zhangfang xiansheng)* or fortune-teller *(suanming xiansheng)*. As the text makes clear, in Xunwu a "gentleman" was considered capable enough to take over the business eventually.—RT.

If he returns home to get married, the boss, besides sending more than 10 *yuan* of travel expenses (if his home is far away), must also send him more than 10 *yuan* of gifts like fruit and sea delicacies, so that when he returns home he can give a fine banquet. If he is going home not to get married but only to see his father and mother and if his home is far away, then he is given some "traveling expenses." The least amount of traveling expenses is 10-odd *yuan*, although the amount can reach 24 or 25 *yuan*. If he is someone from close by, without a doubt, he is sent 10-odd to 20-odd *yuan*. After helping for a year, he formally has a salary. The lead year he gets 40 to 50 *yuan*; the second year more than 50 to 60 *yuan*. If he does well and the shop makes money, his salary increases each year. During the Guangxu period [1875–1908] when business was good, the highest "gentleman's" salary was 120 *yuan*, but now because business is bad, the highest salary does not exceed 80 *yuan*. If a gentleman is loyal, dependable, smart, and capable, the boss may turn the business over to him completely and, in some cases, return home to live. When the profit is divided, a bonus is given to the gentlemen. In most cases it is three-tenths of the profit; in a few cases two-tenths; and in a very few cases one-tenth. When the boss of the Guo Yihe Shop, Guo Youmei, returned home to Wan'an to live, for example, he gave the business to a dependable and esteemed gentleman. There are undependable gentlemen to whom a business cannot be turned over, because of their whoring, gambling, and cheating.[27]

Oil

The third-largest business in Xunwu City is the oil trade. The oil comes from Menling and Anyuan and is sold in Xunwu City District and Huangxiang and a bit in Sanbiao. The only broker for oil is Liu Fuxing, whose capital consists of 100 silver dollars *[dayang]*. He paid a license fee for the oil monopoly. As an agent for buying or selling oil, he receives 0.2 *yuan* for each *Dan* of oil traded. Business is greatest in November and December, when a large market (first day in the market cycle) has a trade of 100 *Dan*; so in two months 600 *Dan* are traded. In the small markets (fourth and seventh days) maybe 30, 40, or 50 *Dan* are traded; so in two months 400 *Dan* are traded. From January to October the trade in each market does not exceed 3-odd *Dan*, so altogether the trade does not exceed 300 *Dan*. The total for the whole year is 1,300 *Dan*; so the brokerage fees are 260 *yuan*. Everyone has to buy oil from him since his license grants him a monopoly. This license is granted by the provincial government in Nanchang after the *xian* government sends a document stating the license was paid. Then

---

27. A parenthetical comment in the text glosses *da futou* and *da leigong* as meaning, literally, "to eat fried doughcakes" *(chi youbing)*, which the editors of *Mao Zedong nongcun diaocha wenji* explain as behavior in which one secretly gains petty advantages.—RT.

and only then is one issued. Besides the 100-*yuan* for a license, one must also pay a 5-*yuan* administrative fee. A license is good for eight years, after which it expires and a new one must be obtained. Licenses are not limited to oil brokers *[hang];* they are also required for salt brokers, [soy]bean brokers, and livestock brokers.

[Soy]beans

There is also only one broker. In the public area of the City God Temple, beans are bought and sold. He Zizhen, a leader of the reactionaries in Xunwu who was head of the Public Security Bureau and who recently become head of the police, bought a license in 1927 and opened a soybean business. Business is greatest in November and December, when there is a trade of 800 *Dan*. One thousand *Dan* of business is done a year. The broker's fee is 2 *sheng* per *Dan* (1 *Dan* = 5 *dou*; 1 *dou* = 10 *sheng*). The price of every *Dan* of beans is 7.5 *yuan* (every *sheng* is 1.5 *mao*). This figures out to 4 percent; so every year one can make 300 *yuan*. He Zizhen is a native of Xunwu City and lives outside the East Gate. He had a deprived childhood but graduated from a middle school in Pingyuan and studied two years at a Henan mining school. He returned to Xunwu and became a schoolteacher for eight or nine years; both Gu Bo and Pan Li were his students. Around the time of the Guomindang's purge of 1927, the Cooperative Society faction led by Gu and Pan clashed with the New Xunwu faction led by He Zizhen. There was a clash in April 1927. He Zizhen fled Xunwu during the March 25 uprising in 1928, but by April he had regained his power. Afterward he also became head of the Public Security Bureau and police chief. He gradually became wealthy and bought land near Xunwu City. Before 1925 and before he was struggling with the Cooperative Society faction, he represented the power of merchant capital. He organized the Society of Fellow Students Studying in Guangdong and began the Commoners Charitable School in 1921. In June 1925, when the Cooperative Society faction held a big meeting in Xunwu City and showed an increase in its revolutionary strength, he cooperated with feudal bullies and gentry and attained a leading position among the feudal faction. He Zizhen became the worst reactionary leader. This time when the Red Army came to Xunwu, he led the retreat of the Pacification and Defense Militia *[jingwei tuan]* to Xiangshan.

Butchers

There are only three butcher businesses, which are set up along the side of the street; there are no butcher shops. The three are Liu Ener, Chen Laoer, and Liu Shiwei. Liu Ener once had 100 *yuan* of capital, but now he has nothing. Chen Laoer and Liu Shiwei have no capital at all because no money is needed to buy pork [for butchering]. They take the pig on credit, butcher it, and sell the pork.

Then they pay the [pig's owner]. On the average one can butcher two pigs a day. If a pig weighs 100 *jin*, then every year the total weight of the slaughtered pigs is 72,000 *jin*. At present, a pig can be bought for 0.25 *yuan* per *jin*, and pork can be sold for 0.28 *yuan* per *jin*. So there is a profit of 0.03 *yuan* per *jin*. So every year one can make 2,160 *yuan*. This is not a bad trade. But one must pay a large slaughter tax. In the past these three men paid 100 *yuan* of taxes a month or 1,200 *yuan* a year. Recently, because business has been relatively bad, only 1,000 *yuan* has been paid; so each man pays a bit more than 300 *yuan*. Because the three men must collect the slaughter tax, no one apart from these three can sell pork or slaughter pigs, except for personal use. After the Red Army entered Xunwu City, the number of butchers increased to seven or eight, and the activity around the market increased markedly. Because no tax was collected, you earned what you got. All the butchers liked this. Before the Red Army came, the price of pork was 0.32 *yuan* but now it is 0.28 *yuan* per *jin*.

Wine

Chen Guihe, Gao Yuanli, Yuan Lizhan, Zhou Yuchang, Liu Shuangsheng, Ling Wensheng, Peng Tongfu—these are the seven largest wine businesses. Fan Guangchang, Kuang Hongsheng, and Luo Deli are the smaller businesses. The four largest businesses, with capital not exceeding 100 *yuan*, are those of Zhou Yuchang (Ji'an native), Gao Yuanli (Ji'an native), Liu Shuangsheng (Xunwu native), and Chen Guihe. Ling Wensheng (Xunwu native), Yuan Lizhan (Ji'an native), and Peng Tongfu are businesses whose capital does not exceed 40 or so *yuan*. These seven businesses all sell sweet wine made of polished glutinous rice, which is called *shuijiu*. It is also called yellow wine because of its color. Because it has a mellow taste, does not harm people, and is relatively inexpensive, peasants and the poor people in Xunwu City like to drink it. It is divided into double *[shuang]* wine and single *[dan]* wine (these terms are used only in Xunwu City; in the countryside, instead of *shuang[jiu]* or *dan[jiu],* they say "good" or "weak"). Since fermented glutinous rice wine has more fermenting agent, it has a higher proof. Wine is sold by the bottle, not the *jin*. Double wine [sells] for 18 coppers a bottle; it is the best of the yellow wine. When common people invite someone to dinner, they drink it, but they also use it for their own meals. Drunkards have to have a little at every meal, but if they have some wine, they do not even care about eating. Single wine, which is 10 coppers a bottle, is bought by poor people when they are thirsty; they drink it like tea [i.e., in great amounts]. The business in double wine is greater than that in single wine.

Fan Guangchang, Kuang Hongsheng, and Luo Deli are all run by natives of Xunwu City. Their capital does not exceed 10 *yuan*. They all sell white wine. Zhou Yuchang also sells white wine. This kind of wine is made with sticky rice. It is stronger than yellow wine. It is not sold by the bottle, but by the cup; each cup costs two coppers. A *jin* sells for 0.16 *yuan*. Yellow wine outsells white wine nine to one. Whether speaking of white wine or yellow wine, both are part of the wine business. But the purpose of these businesses is not just to sell wine. The mash that is left after making wine is fed to pigs; this is an even more important purpose. If there is too much for your own pigs, you sell the leftovers. It takes two coppers to buy one small bowl of wine. During the best season for yellow wine shops (March through August is the thirsty season), every shop can sell 5 *yuan* of wine a day. In the off-season (September to February), a wine shop can take in 2 *yuan*. Yellow wine shops can make 1,020 *yuan* a year. The seven shops together do a business of over 7,000 *yuan*. In the hot half of the year white wine shops can take in a *yuan* a day, and in the cold half of the year they can take in 0.5 *yuan* a day. So every business makes 270 *yuan* a year. Together the four businesses make around 1,000 *yuan*.

A wine tax must be paid. Depending on whether business is good or bad, the large wine shops can pay about 0.4 *yuan* a month; the small wineshops about 0.2 *yuan* a month. There are also ones that pay 0.15 *yuan*.

Marine Products

The items in the marine products stores are plentiful. "Delicacies from the hills and seas" is their slogan. The gains and losses of the marine product merchants are quite interesting. First I illustrate the categories of items sold and then observe the merchants' gains and losses.

Salted Fish. The most sales [lit., the first category]. These include mandarin fish, mackerel, seahorses, perch, skinned fish, rockfish, golden carp, sturgeon, spotted butterfish, carp, big-eyed sea bream, salamander (big body, small tail), flounder (also called *bingbeiluoshishi,* it has eyes on only one side; thus it needs to collaborate with another fish when seeking food. For this reason, occasions when people rely on one another are usually called *bingbeiluoshishi;* so this kind of fish has become a metaphor), spiny dogfish (it has two horns on its head). These salted fish all come from Chaozhou and Shantou.

Seaweed. Second in sales. It includes green seaweed and kelp. Green seaweed, also called Jiangxi seaweed, is of the highest quality and comes from Ganzhou. Compared with green seaweed, less kelp is sold, its quality is lower [lit., next], and its price is cheaper. It comes from Mei *xian* and over a thousand *jin* are sold each year. The price is 0.2 *yuan* per *jin*.

Sugar. Also carried at the marine products store; third in sales. It is divided into white sugars, brown sugars, rock candy,[28] and slabs of sugar-preserved kumquats. The white sugars include snow powder, nice-looking but not sweet, which comes from Mei *xian*; rough white sugar, very sweet, from Huizhou; and white-rice sugar,[29] a medium-quality sugar that comes from Huizhou. These three kinds are all imported sugars; one *jin* sells for 0.17 to 0.18 *yuan*. The brown

---

28. Rock sugar *[bingtang]* is a crystallized sugar formed into lumps.—RT.
29. This kind of sugar is white and looks like rice ground into small grains.—RT.

sugars are taro sugar, which is ball shaped and comes from Mei *xian*; loaf sugar, which is sold by the block, is the best, and comes from Huizhou; loose-sand sugar, which is mixed with sand, is the worst, and comes from Huizhou. In the past, brown sugar was cheaper than white sugar; now brown sugar is expensive and white sugar is cheap. Previously brown sugar was not more than 0.16 *yuan* per *jin*; now the price has risen to 0.23 to 0.24 *yuan* per *jin*. The old price for white sugar was 0.26 to 0.27 *yuan* per *jin*, and now it is only 0.17 to 0.18 *yuan* per *jin*. Brown sugar is native sugar, and white sugar is imported sugar. The annual sale in Xunwu City of white sugar is over 1,000 *jin*, and of brown sugar (available only during the winter season) 6,000 to 7,000 *jin*. Since brown sugar is sweeter [than white sugar], it sells better. Rock candy [for cooking] comes from Mei *xian*, and annual sales amount to only several dozen *jin*, at about 2 *mao* and a few *fen*[30] per *jin*. Sugar-preserved kumquats in slab form come from Mei *xian*. There are annual sales of over 20 or 30 *jin* at 0.3 *yuan* per *jin*.

Of the above sugars, loaf sugar sells the best. This is because it is an important ingredient in rice cakes. At New Year's, it does not matter whether a family lives in town or the countryside or whether it is poor or rich, every family makes rice cakes.

Bean Flour. Fourth in sales. Most of it comes from Yunmenling; some comes from other *xian*. It is made from sweet potatoes and sold in powdered form, not yet made into noodles. It is an ingredient for meatballs and the like. Annual sales are a few thousand *jin* at about 0.15 to 0.16 *yuan* per *jin*.

Pigskin. Fifth in sales. It is used in ordinary meals as imitation fish maw. It comes from Mei *xian*. Annual sales are over a thousand *jin*, 0.1 *yuan* for 3 *liang*, 0.55 *yuan* per *jin*.

Fujian Bamboo Shoots. These come from Mei *xian* and Anyuan; "Fujian bamboo shoots" is just a name. Sixth in sales. They are used not only at banquets but also at ordinary meals as well, especially during the harvest and field-weeding periods. There are some bamboo plantings in Xunwu itself. In March and April, peasants go to Mei *xian* and sell it. In July and August Xunwu people want to have some, but there isn't enough; so they buy some from Mei *xian*. Annual sales are 500 to 600 *jin*, one *jin* sells for 0.23 to 0.24 *yuan*.

Squid. It is used at banquets and at ordinary meals. Seventh in sales. It comes from Mei *xian*. The annual sales are around 300 to 500 *jin*. One *jin* costs 0.7 to 0.8 *yuan*.

Fermented Soybeans. Annual sales of about 3,000 *jin* at one *jin* for 0.14 *yuan*. The inhabitants of Xunwu can also make this and use it to make soy sauce, but the locally produced product is not sold commercially. It is a very common food; almost every household eats it. Add some oil and then steam it. One bowl of it can be served for several meals; so for frugal people this is very economical.

---

30. One *fen* was equivalent to a tenth of a *mao*. It was purely a unit of account, because the one-cent copper coin introduced in 1914 had depreciated to less than half its face value.

Mianhui. That is, flour. Coming from Mei *xian*, much of it is foreign-style flour. Buns, Chinese dumplings, noodles, and cakes are all made with it. Cakes are most popular. Egg cakes, cookies, *pang* cake (*pang* means hollow in the center), five-seed cake,[31] and lard cake are all made of flour. At 0.2 *yuan* per *jin*, annual sales are about a hundred packages.

Foreign Wax. It comes in white chunks. One *jin* costs 0.25 to 0.26 *yuan*. There are annual sales of 500 *jin* or so.

Yufen. This is also called *xifen;* it is made from sweet potatoes. It is different from bean powder because it comes in the form of noodles. It comes from Mei *xian*. All the common people eat it. At 0.1 *yuan* for about half a *jin*, there are annual sales of about 600 to 700 *jin*.

The above eleven items are used the most; those that follow are less commonly used.

Top Quality [lit., unsurpassed in the market]. This type of squid is the best and is served only when guests are invited. It comes from Mei *xian*. It is not used much; each year squid worth 200 to 300 *yuan* is sold. The common squid is called "foreign[-style] squid."

Preserved Vegetables. This is a turnip and is similar to a radish. This preserved vegetable comes from Xinfeng. There are annual sales of 200 to 300 *jin*. It is sold only after the Dragon Boat festival,[32] but after August no more is shipped in. One *jin* costs 0.2 *yuan*; it is a little more expensive than *xifen*.

Sharkfin. One *liang*[33] costs 0.4 *yuan*; it is rarely used. Annual sales amount to only 10 to 20 *jin*.

Sea Cucumbers. With annual sales of 200 to 300 *jin*, business is greater than for shark fin. One *jin* costs 2.8 to 2.9 *yuan*.

Fish Maw. Annual sales are 200 to 300 *jin*, and the price is about the same as for sea cucumbers. Normally, if a meal has sea cucumbers, you would certainly serve fish maw, and it would not be the imitation fish maw made from pigskin.

Cuttlefish. There are annual sales of only 40 to 50 *jin*. One *jin* costs 0.7 to 0.8 *yuan*, about the same as squid.

Scallops. Annual sales are about 20 *jin*; one *jin* sells for 1.2 or 1.3 *yuan*.

Dried Gongyu [lit., tribute fish]. Annual sales of about 8 to 10 *jin*. Each *jin* costs 0.2 *yuan*. About 70 to 80 *jin* used to be sold.

Big Shrimp. Annual sales are 70 to 80 *jin*. One *jin* sells for 0.6 *yuan*. "Big shrimp" are not really shrimp that are big. They are also called "dried shrimp"

---

31. Melon seeds, almonds, and walnuts are among the types of seeds and nuts used to make this cake.—RT.

32. According to the 1881 gazetteer for Xunwu *xian*, the Dragon Boat festival was held on the sixth day of the sixth lunar month, instead of the usual fifth day of the fifth month. *Changning xianzhi*, "Fengsu," p. 1b.—RT.

33. The *liang* or Chinese ounce was a unit of weight equivalent to one-sixteenth of a *jin*. One ounce or *liang* of silver (commonly referred to as a tael) was also a unit of currency, equal to approximately .72 silver dollars.—RT.

and are smaller than Chaozhou shrimp, which can weigh as much as 4 *liang* apiece.

Pressed Shrimp [lit., shrimp shells]. Tiny shrimp pressed as flat as shrimp shells are called shrimp shells. Annual sales are over 100 *jin*. During New Year's and [other] festivals, every household makes [Hakka-style] stuffed bean curd. This involves making a hole in [the middle of] a piece of bean curd, inserting ground pork, fish roe, and dried mushrooms mixed with the pressed shrimp or adding garlic and leeks. All these are diced and stuffed [into the bean curd]. One *jin* of pressed shrimp costs over 0.1 *yuan*.

Jellyfish. One *jin* goes for 0.3 *yuan*, and annual sales aren't much—20 to 30 *jin*.

Dried Mussels. The big ones are called *haoshi* [dried oyster]. They are also called *xili*. Annual sales of dried mussels are 40 to 50 *jin*, and one *jin* costs a bit over 0.3 *yuan*. No dried mussels are sold in Xunwu City.

Tianqingpu [lit., reddish-black ray]. This is a kind of marine fish, and big ones are as big as a fan. They are rarely sold in Xunwu City.

These products, from Top Quality to *tianqingpu,* are marine products that come from the Chaozhou-Shantou region.

Day Lily. Also called golden needles. Two *mao* per *jin*; annual sales of 40 to 50 *jin*.

Cloud Ears.[34] Annual sales of 50 *jin*; a *jin* costs 1 *yuan*. During the Guangxu period, these cost no more than 0.5 *yuan* a *jin*. They have since doubled in price. They come from Mei *xian*.

Dried Mushrooms. Annual sales of 100 *jin*. Winter mushrooms are better and cost 2 *yuan* per *jin*. Spring mushrooms are not as good, with one *jin* going for 1.2 to 1.3 *yuan*. They are local products.

Shredded Preserved Cabbage [lit., winter vegetables]. This canned food is made with cabbage. It used to come from Tianjin, but recently it has also been made in Mei *xian*. There are annual sales of over one hundred jars at 0.4 *yuan* a jar.

Dried Bean Curd Roll [lit., curd bamboo]. This is made of thin sheets of bean curd rolled into tubes. One *jin* costs 2 *mao* and several *fen*; annual sales are 40 to 50 *jin*. It comes from Xingning.

Doufumei [lit., bean curd mold]. This is fermented bean curd that comes from Mei *xian*. It is made from three items: soybean milk, taro, and flour. It is not made the way the dried bean curd used by the common people is made.

Pepper. For white pepper, annual sales are 10 *jin* at 1.2 *yuan* per *jin*. In the Guangxu period the price was under 0.4 *yuan*. Now the price has tripled. Annual sales of black pepper are 20 to 30 *jin*, and one *jin* costs 0.5 to 0.6 *yuan*. It used to be not more than 2 *mao* and a few *fen* per *jin* during the Guangxu period. All pepper comes from abroad.

Dried Chinese Olives. Dried Chinese olives are made by boiling fresh olives,

---

34. Cloud ears are a type of white fungus that grows on trees.— RT.

taking the seeds out, and then curing them. In Xunwu these are called *lanjiao*, and in Mei *xian* they are called *lanshi*. Annual sales are 10-odd *jin* at 2 *mao* and a few *fen* per *jin*.

Soy Sauce. Produced locally and in Menling. This is how to make soy sauce. First steam the soybeans and then dry them halfway, spread them flat and wait until they ferment, and then boil them again. Add some spices and salt to the boiling liquid, and soy sauce is the result. After boiling, the soybeans become fermented soybeans *[doushi]*. However, the quality of this type of fermented soybeans is not good. Good fermented soybeans are made by boiling down the soy sauce. Fermented soybeans and soy sauce sell well in March, June, and September. Monthly sales for fermented soybeans are 200 to 300 *jin*; annual sales are over 3,000 *jin*, one *jin* sells for 0.14 *yuan*. Annual sales of soy sauce are over 300 *jin*, one *jin* goes for 0.15 *yuan*.

Persimmons. Annual sales are about 100 *yuan*; a small one costs three coppers, two large ones cost a *mao*.

Red and Black Dates. Annual sales for both are 100 *jin* or so. Black dates cost 0.4 *yuan* per *jin*, red dates 0.2 *yuan* per *jin*.

Longyan. Annual sales of 10 to 20 *jin*. One *jin* of those with a skin costs a little over 0.3 *yuan*. Peeled ones are called *yuanrou*, cost 1 *yuan* per *jin*, and are available only in herb stores.

Lichees. This fruit is rarely sold. The price is about the same as that of longyan.

Dried Star Fruit. Annual sales are some 10 *jin*, one *jin* sells for 0.4 *yuan*.

These products, from persimmon to dried star fruit, all come from Mei *xian*.

Melon Seeds. Melon seeds come from both Xinfeng and Menling. One *jin* costs a little less than 0.3 *yuan*. Annual sales are 200 to 300 *jin*.

All thirty-nine products listed above are part of the trade of marine products shops. In addition, marine products shops also supplement sales with kerosene and tea-oil.

The general outline of marine products shops in good times and bad is related below.

The stores with the most business are Shunchang Laodian, Shunchang Xingji, Lu Quanli, Tang Yaojie, Rong Chunxiang, Luo Jieci, and Zhang Junyi. In addition, there are a number of small stalls that sell marine products. Among these stores, Shunchang Laodian and Zhang Junyi are both general stores and marine products stores.

Shunchang Xingji is a branch of Shunchang Laodian; it has the best marine products business. It has capital of 1,000 *yuan* and consigns 200 to 300 *yuan* [of goods] to Mei *xian* each year. The store proprietor, Fan Zuxian, is a native of Xunwu City and supports over twenty people in his family. Business profits are barely sufficient for living expenses and consignment fees.

Lu Quanli is the proprietor of the second-largest marine products shop. He is a Mei *xian* native, and his store has capital of 1,000 to 2,000 *yuan*. Besides marine products, he sells tong oil, tea leaves, mushrooms, and tea-oil of various kinds and ships wholesale to Xingning and Mei *xian*. His marine products business is not as good as that of Xingji, but Xingji does not engage in the side trades he does. He also consigns goods to Mei *xian*. Because he is a native of Mei *xian*, his business is very good. He has no problem doing about 1,000 *yuan* of business. He supports a wife and hires two "gentlemen" (annual salary of 60 *yuan* each). After expenses, he has at least 200 or 300 *yuan* of profits annually. In years with a good business climate, he has profits of about 1,000 *yuan*.

Tang Yaojie, a native of Jiaoling, has capital of 2,000 *yuan*. He has no hired employees. He covers consignment fees and living expenses but makes no profits. Many years ago [when there were] brokers for oil and salt, he made a lot of money; but two years ago he started losing money, so he changed to marine products.

Rong Chunxiang, a native of Xunwu *xian*, has capital of 700 to 800 *yuan*. His family has several dozen *Dan* of paddy land. He supports seven or eight people. He has no employees. As for his expenses, he uses his business profits to pay for them. The grain from the family's land outside Xunwu City is saved up. Among the marine products businesses, his was the best. After the soviet was established, one part of his land was confiscated. Needless to say, he seethed with anger. His childhood was difficult; he helped a local bully with his accounts and made some money and got a start.

The proprietor of the Shunchang Laodian is Fan Xingfu, a Xunwu City native; he has 300 to 400 *yuan* of capital. He has more than ten family members and hires one gentleman at an annual salary of 50 to 60 *yuan*. His marine products business makes just enough to supply [his family's] needs. His grandfather Fan Yuanfu was a large landlord with three children and an extended family of 140-odd people. He received 800 *Dan* of rent a year. Later their wealth declined as their land was dispersed, and Fan Xingfu's family had land with rents of only 30 to 40 *Dan*. Under the soviet's division of land, his family was eligible to receive a bit of land. But his brother Fan Laoba still received over 100 *Dan* of rent; so this year during the land redistribution most of his land was distributed. Fan Laoba does not engage in business. The Shunchang Xingji was started by his cousin. He had 40 to 50 *Dan* of paddy land and over twenty family members. When the soviet divided the land, they received some land. From the final years of the Qing through the early years of the Republic, his family and his brothers together had seven stores—Laodian, Xingji, Daji, Maoji, Junji, Hongchang, Lufeng—which dealt in silk, textiles, general goods, and marine products. Their businesses were known far and wide. They could consign to Ganzhou 4,000 to 5,000 *yuan* [of goods]. That is about what the Guo Yihe Shop could do back then. In 1922 business gradually fell off, and in 1925 they had only two businesses: Laodian and Xingji. The most important reason was the changing market—foreign [and foreign-style] goods replaced native goods. When Mei *xian* business replaced Ganzhou business, the southern half of Xunwu no longer required native goods supplied from Ganzhou. The Guo Yihe Shop declined for the same reasons. Another reason has to do with the large number of children born and raised in feudal families (large landlord and nascent mercantile capitalist families). Much whoring, gambling, feasting, and wearing of fine clothes—their ostentatious behavior impoverished their families. Before 1921, the primary school in Xunwu City (some landlords raised shares to build it; 5 *yuan* for one share) was a famous "diploma mill." The children of landlords throughout the *xian*, ostentatious but without prospects, spent money to go to this "mill" for three years, obtained a diploma, and then put on airs. They used the words "graduate of Xunwu City East Primary School" on their namecards, returned home, and swindled their ancestors. Why do we say they swindled their ancestors? First, just after they graduated, their ancestral halls, in accordance with precedent, awarded the graduates some money. This is called "grabbing the bonus." Second, every year, along with *xiucai* and *juren,* they receive an equal part of the educational allowance [lit., study grain]. Third, every year after the ancestral sacrifices are completed, they, along with the degree holders, receive a part of the sacrificial meat. The Fan family has sixty or seventy young scions who had entered that diploma mill. In addition to grabbing the bonus and obtaining grain, after they graduated, they got 100 *jin* of meat from their ancestral trusts [gongtang],[35] large and small, during the division of meat each year.

Luo Jieci, a native of Xunwu City, has 200 to 300 *yuan* of capital. He supports four people [including himself], has no employees, makes wine, and sells marine products. After expenses, he makes a profit of 100 to 200 *yuan*. His is a fine business. He liked to whore in the past, but now he has stopped on account of his wife (her brideprice was 500 *yuan*). He is honest and hardworking. He uses mash [from wine making] to feed pigs. So things have gotten better year by year, and the family now has more than 10 *Dan* of paddy land.

Zhang Junyi trades in both marine products and general goods and has 200 *yuan* of capital; the rest is borrowed. He does not hire anyone, but his children are in the trade. Every year he makes some profit. He is a native of Xunwu *xian*. Five or six years ago, he was a porter and helped Xunwu City merchants ship grain and mushrooms to Mei *xian*. From Mei *xian* he shipped back cloth and salted fish to Xunwu. He shipped things himself, and at the same time he was a head porter, a job that allows one to make a profit. Xunwu *xian* merchants gave him money to go buy things. Xunwu City merchants and Mei *xian* merchants tipped him money, and from this he became rich.

As for the marine products business carried on from stalls, no business exceeds a few dozen *yuan* of capital, or at most 100 *yuan*. These [peddlers'] goods come from Xunwu City's large marine products stores and from petty traders

---

35. *Gongtang* land refers to land owned by all types of ancestral halls, religious associations, and village associations. These lands were controlled mostly by the landlords and rich peasants.

[xiaofan]. [People in] this kind of stall trade often can get rich if they work hard. Xunwu City has many shops that began as stalls. Pan Dengji, He Xiangsheng, Luo Yisheng, Liu Hengtai, and Fan Laosi had a business but no shop. On the first, fourth, and seventh days [of the ten-day market cycle, peddlers] take goods on a pole to the market in Xunwu City; on the third, sixth, and ninth days, they take goods on a pole to the market in Jitan. [In this way] they can make some money.

Herbs

The seven herb stores in Xunwu City are Baihetang, Yang Qingren, Xin Desheng, Tian Renhe, Wang Putai, Huang Yuxing, and Fuchuntang.

Baihetang is the number-one store. The proprietor, a certain Chi, is a native of Chaozhou. But originally he was a native of Huangxiang named Liu. When he was young, his family was very poor; so his father and mother sold him to the Chi family, herb merchants from Chaozhou. Later he came to Xunwu to open an herb shop with capital of about 1,000 *yuan*. He became the boss. Guangdong merchants have a common saying: "Not afraid of difficulties; only afraid of not having progeny." Those people who are without children can certainly purchase children to carry on the family line; this is because they are "afraid of not having progeny." The need for labor power also prompts the purchase of children. When children are bought, usually the intelligent and capable ones are adopted as sons. The dull ones are kept as servants *[nugu].*[36] Baihetang's manager, who was himself purchased, had a child who died young; so he bought a son. He supports seven people [including himself]: [the son just mentioned], the two sons and two daughters he fathered, and his wife. He has also taken on three apprentices. He makes some profit. The herb business is very profitable. One buys in bulk and sells in small quantities. There are two categories of herbal medicines: common and special. The common category (water medicine) is for curing illnesses, and everyone needs them. The special [lit., delicate] kinds are used as supplements [to food], and only local bullies are able to buy them. One can bargain about the prices for special kinds, but the prices of common herbal medicines are set by the herb merchants. Among the seven herb stores, only three businesses—Baihetang, Yang Qingren, and Wang Putai—have the special types of herbs.

Yang Qingren, a native of Zhangshu, used to have capital of 500 to 600 *yuan*, but last year his son gambled away several hundred *yuan* and now he only has 200 to 300 *yuan*.

Wang Putai, who is also a native of Zhangshu, has capital of 100 *yuan*. He works hand in glove with the evil gentryman He Zizhen and the Catholic father Chen (a Mei *xian* native). Father Chen loaned him 400 *yuan*. Furthermore, he borrowed 200 *yuan* from the local prostitute Lai Fengzi. In addition to the herb

---

36. *Nugu* means "male servant" in Hakka.

shop, he also opened a foreign-goods store. Where did Lai Fengzi's money come from? She became the mistress of one of the company commanders subordinate to Lai Shihuang[37] and returned to Xunwu last year with 300 ill-gotten *yuan*. Wang Putai thought of a way to flatter Lai Fengzi in order to borrow this money. When the money was received, Wang Putai sent Lai Fengzi perfume, terrycloth towels, and many other gifts.

Xindesheng is owned by a certain Du, who is also a native of Zhangshu. It has 400 to 500 *yuan* of capital. Tian Renhe, Huang Yuxing, and [the owner of] Fuchuntang are also from Zhangshu, and all have capital of 100 *yuan*.

Annual herb sales are:

Baihetang	3,000
[Yang] Qingrentang	800
Xindesheng	600
Tian Renhe	600
Wang Putai	400
Huang Yuxing	300
Fuchuntang	300
Total	6,000 *yuan*

Wang Putai has participated in counter[revolutionary] organizations. When this faction meets, he certainly attends, although on the surface he does not appear to be an official. General goods merchant Chen Zhicheng, marine products merchant Bao Huaxiang, and the manager of the boarding house Tonglaian are all involved in local politics. When Xunwu City came under the influence of the soviet, the businesses of these four were confiscated.

Tobacco

Two shops in Xunwu City process tobacco. One shop is Huang Yufeng's, a Shanghang native whose family has operated a shop in Xunwu for two generations. In the past they had capital of 3,000 *yuan*. By selling tobacco, paper, and general goods, they made a profit of more than 10,000 *yuan*, which they took back to Shanghang to buy land. More than 1,000 *yuan* of capital was retained by the Xunwu City shop. Another shop is Yongquanhao, which also processes its own tobacco. This shop, opened by an Anyuan native the year before last, has capital of 300 to 500 *yuan*.

---

37. Lai Shihuang (1889–1927) was a native of Jiangxi, who had commanded the Guomindang Fourteenth Army in the Northern Expedition. He was shot for dereliction of duty on December 31, 1927.

Huang Yufeng has two workers, one who shaves the tobacco [blocks] and one who makes the packages. Yongquanhao hires one worker. The workers' annual salary is 60 *yuan*. They eat the boss's food. Their lot is about the same as the "gentlemen" in the general goods and herb stores. What differs is that the workers do not usually eat meat or drink wine and have a special dinner only on the first and fifteenth. The gentlemen usually have meat to eat; hence they do not have special dinners. Moreover, gentlemen usually eat at the same table as the boss. Workers, when few, eat together at the table with the boss. If there are a lot of workers, the boss and the gentlemen eat at one table and the workers eat at another. These examples all show that the status of the gentlemen is higher than that of the workers. Workers are generally not called workers, but "master workers" *[shifu]*.

Most of the tobacco in general stores and marine products stores is purchased from this type of tobacco shop.

Tailoring

Altogether there are thirteen shops with sewing machines and three shops that use hand labor. Liu Qinying, Huang Saozi, Liao Jiefang, Liu Senhe, Liu Shifu, Xie Shenbao, Fan Laizi, Xie Qilong, He Xianggu, Xie Shifu, Huang Laowu, and Huang Shangxian all use machines. Every shop has one *chezi* (sewing machine). Every shop's boss is also a worker. Every person has an apprentice to do finishing work like hemming and making buttons and hooks. The capital of this type of sewing shop is in the machine. First-quality machines cost more than 200 *yuan*; second-quality around 70 to 80 *yuan*; third-quality (secondhand) about 30 to 40 *yuan*. Before 1920 there were no sewing machines in Xunwu; without exception sewing was done by hand. In 1920 a Xingning man, He Shifu, opened the first shop with a sewing machine. He originally opened a shop in Liuche, and in 1920 he moved to Xunwu City. Because his "scissors were very sharp" (when Xunwu people want to say that the tailor steals the fabric, they don't say he steals; rather, they say his scissors are sharp), and because he also liked prostitutes and did not stay put, he took his sewing machine back to Xingning. The year before last (1928) there were still only four machines in Xunwu, but last year the number increased to thirteen. This number includes several used machines bought from other people. Among the tailors, Huang Laowu's handiwork was the best, and his business was the largest. He worked hand in glove with officials and powerful gentry and had a monopoly in making fine clothes. Because of this, he had profits that he used to buy land. During the March 25 uprising he expressed opposition, and when the revolution reached Xunwu City, he fled with the reactionary faction. [As for clothing styles,] in 1920 He Shifu started using a machine. He popularized "Shanghai-style clothes" ([shirts] cut down the center with rounded bottoms and embroidery).[38] In 1923 the Shanghai

---

38. Center-cut (*poxiong*, lit., split-the-chest) refers to shirts and jackets that buttoned down the middle rather than being fastened on the side as traditional Chinese jackets were.—RT.

style fell from favor, and a type of shirt cut down the center with a square bottom and embroidery became the style. Last year the "Canton style" (seven buttons, four pockets, cut long) became the fashion. A small number of people liked to wear this kind of clothing, but most people were still wearing the embroidered style. In the past clothing was uniformly made in the old "large lapel" [dajin] style. The new style of center-cut [shirts and jackets] coincided with the introduction of new-style education. In 1918 or 1919, this style gradually began to be worn by more and more people. But even last year, if we speak of the population of all of Xunwu *xian*, most people still wore old-style clothing. Wearers of new-style clothing were in a minority. But in the past two years, particularly after the victory of the land revolution, the wearing of new-style clothing has increased daily, especially among the young people. Young students, of course, began wearing the new-style long ago, but [now even] the majority of young peasants and young workers wear new-style clothing. Only in the case of the very poor, who lack the money for new clothes, are old-style clothes still worn. Last year in the summer, with the victory of the rent resistance movement in the southern half of the *xian*, and in the winter, when the land was divided, among the young people in the countryside under thirty *sui*, over 70 percent wore rubber-soled shoes and sport shoes. (The soles for these kinds of shoes come from Canton to Xingning. The shoes are completed in Xingning, and each pair costs around 1 *yuan*.) Cadres in the Red Guard and soviet not only, without exception, wear new-style clothing and new-style shoes but also want to use electric flashlights and wear scarves. Some want to wear pants padded with down.

There are still three hand-tailoring businesses in Xunwu City.

To compare hand sewing and machine sewing of clothes, in the time it takes to sew one item by hand, someone using a sewing machine can sew about three items. To compare prices, a pair of pants produced by hand costs 0.7 *yuan*; by machine 0.6 *yuan*. To compare quality, machine-made is better than handmade. How can machines not drive out handicraft workers?

The most important markets in the *xian* are these ten places: Jitan, Chengjiang, Shipaixia, Chetou, Niudouguang, Liuche, Huangxiang (sewing machines were used here earlier than in other places), Gongping, Huangtangdu, and Cenfeng. All these places have sewing machines. Because of this, 30 percent of the population has given up handmade clothing for clothing made by machine, especially in the southern half of the *xian*, in which the speed of mechanization has been very fast.

Umbrellas

Peng Wanhe and Li Xiangren are shops that make paper umbrellas. Peng Wanhe was from Wuping [Fujian] and opened an umbrella shop in Xunwu City more than a hundred years or three generations ago. When Peng first came to Xunwu, he had only 100 to 200 *yuan* of capital, but he gradually accumulated profits from making umbrellas. As of the year before last (1928), before the March 25 uprising, the shop's capital, including land, was 1,000 to 2,000 *yuan*. The shop-keeper, the fifth Peng brother, and his father, Peng Shengxiang, bought 60 *Dan* of paddy land in the Tianbei area outside Xunwu's South Gate. They built a new house. The fifth Peng brother's third and seventh brothers lived in Tianbei. He himself manages the business in [Xunwu] City. The Tianbei land was rented out to peasants for cultivation for 50 percent of the year's crops. His family origi-nally consisted of seven brothers, but four have died; so there are three brothers left. There are also six sons and nephews, one mother, three wives, and five daughters-in-law; so altogether he supports eighteen people. The sons attended a primary school. Among his three brothers, he is the one who manages the um-brella business. He is thirty *sui*. He employs two workers. The seventh brother is over twenty *sui* and studied at the Sun Yatsen Middle School established by the Revolutionary faction, for over twenty days. Then when the March 25 uprising occurred, the reactionary faction said he was a "thug" *[baotu]*[39] and confiscated the family property in Tianbei and burned its buildings in Tianbei. The third and seventh brothers both graduated from the East School in Xunwu City. Neverthe-less, the third brother studied at the East School during the "diploma mill" era. The seventh brother was at the East School after the school had been reformed, when it was run by the revolutionary Sun Yatsen Middle School faction. Be-cause of this, after the seventh brother graduated from the East School, he en-tered the Sun Yatsen Middle School and joined the "thugs'" forces *[duiwu]*. After the third brother graduated from the East School, he served as a teacher in an elementary school in Wuping. Now the seventh brother has fled to Wuping. The fifth brother's shop now only has 40 to 50 *yuan* of capital. In the time of his father, Peng Shengxiang (during the Guangxu period), paper umbrellas were still popular. At that time about 30 percent of the people used foreign-style umbrellas and 70 percent used paper umbrellas. From the beginning of the Republic until now, this has turned around: foreign-style umbrellas now constitute 70 percent of the market, and paper umbrellas only 30 percent. It does not matter whether one is speaking of towns or the countryside, worker or peasant, merchant or stu-dent—all young men and women almost without exception use foreign-style umbrellas that come from Mei *xian* and Xingning. Because of this, those in Liuche and Niudouguang who, during the age of Peng Shengxiang, would come to the Xunwu City shop to buy paper umbrellas always go to Mei *xian* and Xingning to buy foreign-style umbrellas. In the past the Peng Wanhe Shop made and sold three thousand paper umbrellas every year. Now yearly production does

---

39. This term of opprobrium was used by opponents of the Chinese Communist Party in the Jiangxi countryside. Western observers noted in April 1928 that Communists were allying with so-called local bandits *(tufei)*. In fact, a new compound—*gongfei*—was coined to refer to the alliance of Communists *(gongchan)* and local bandits *(tufei)*. See *North China Herald* 167 (April–June 1928): 54. This double meaning could often be obscured, with *gongfei* meaning simply Communist bandits.—RT.

not exceed twelve to thirteen hundred umbrellas. Previously (in the Guangxu period), the Peng Wanhe Shop hired six or seven workers; now it employs only two people. In the past the price of umbrellas was 0.25 *yuan*; now it is 0.45 *yuan*.

Li Xiangren, from Nankang, is over forty *sui*. He began as an umbrella craftsman and then became a boss in the early Republic. He has 40 to 50 *yuan* of capital, and every year he sells around two thousand umbrellas. He hires two workers: one carves bamboo into frames and one mounts the paper; he puts on the lacquer.

There are two kinds of foreign-style umbrellas: silk umbrellas and foreign-cloth umbrellas. All silk umbrellas are made in Japan; China cannot make them. The cloth for foreign-cloth umbrellas and the iron rods come from abroad. Chinese take the cloth and pull it tight over the umbrella frame. The price of a silk umbrella is more than 1.5 *yuan*. The price of each foreign-cloth umbrella is 1.2 to 1.3 *yuan*. The proportion of sales of paper umbrellas, foreign-cloth umbrellas, and silk umbrellas is paper and foreign-cloth umbrellas, 30 percent each, silk umbrellas 40 percent.

The umbrella business now has no apprentices. In the past ten years, no one in Xunwu City has wanted to learn how to make umbrellas for the following reasons: (1) there is no future in the umbrella business; and (2) the situation of apprentices in umbrella shops, compared to that in general stores, is much worse. The craft must be studied from the age of thirteen or fourteen *sui* and then and only then can it be mastered. The apprentices must cook meals for shop personnel and must also buy food. They also must sweep the floors and do odd jobs around the shop.

Wooden Goods

In the past there was only one business, that of Hu Donglin, a Ganzhou man who did a business of 400 to 500 *yuan*. He has been in business for over twenty years and makes every kind of wooden item for sale: desks, benches, chairs, tables, beds, foot basins, clothesracks, water buckets, cabinets, wash basins, urine buckets, serving trays, signs[40] (for religious festivals, birthdays, and congratulatory occasions), couplets, bookcases, suitcases, clothes bureaus, blackboards and other items used in schools, and boxes [suspended from carrying poles] used for sending gifts.

The carpentry trade can be considered a larger business. Hu's wooden goods were sold not only in Xunwu City District but also in each district and every *xian*. But items in his store were generally not sold to workers, peasants, and poor people. Rather, they were sold to the landlord class, midlevel merchants, and rich peasants because workers, peasants, and poor peasants cannot afford

---

40. *Bian'e*, a horizontal inscribed board.—RT.

these things except for a bride's dowry [lit., when marrying off a daughter]. Then they buy clothes bureaus and small cabinets. Hu's family was in straitened circumstances in Ganzhou. Twenty years ago he came from Ganzhou to Xunwu to help in a workshop as a carpenter. He saved some money and opened a small wood shop, which slowly developed. At its height he hired four or five workers and made profits of 1,000 *yuan*. He sent half of it back to Ganzhou and what was left—400 to 500 yuan—he used for the business. The year 1928 marked the beginning of the period when business fell off. He kept only one worker, and he himself worked. His son helped a little; he had enough to feed his family. The reason for his declining business lies in the land revolution. The northern half of the *xian* did not experience revolution, but it was influenced by the revolution. The landlord class and others who had money no longer celebrated birthdays. They also no longer celebrated auspicious occasions and festivals or held honorific gatherings. Most schools closed. How could Hu's business not have declined?

All his furniture—all that was sold to feudal landlords—is in the old style. But some of it was progressive; these were the items used by schools and churches. Because he knew Pastor Bao, the wood sections of the church and hospital built outside South Gate were done by him.[41]

His relative, a certain Xie, last year asked ten people to form a "monthly loan society." Every person contributed 5 *yuan*, and altogether 50 *yuan* was raised. Xie opened a very small wood shop at the side of the City God Temple. No workers were hired; just the father and son. In one year not only did they make no profit but they lost their capital. The business is almost dead.

The wooden items used by the workers, peasants, and poor people are sold at periodic markets. On the first, fourth, and seventh days of the ten-day market-cycle, one can buy from artisans *[jiangren]*. They are called "those who make round wooden objects." They live deep in the hills and carry their goods by pole to market. These goods are commodes, carriers, water buckets, foot basins, rice buckets, rice pots, rice scoops, water dippers, wok lids, bowl covers (to cover food bowls and cooking pots), chopping boards, cutting boards (for vegetable cutting: the round one is called a chopping board and the square one is called a vegetable board), dish-washing pots, grain buckets (to carry cut stalks to the threshing area for threshing), grain flails (to beat the grain), rice hullers,[42] and

---

41. "Pastor Bao" refers to Dr. Cyril E. Bousfield.—RT. (The correspondence of Dr. Bousfield, a medical missionary stationed in Xunwu since 1912, constitutes one of the sources for Roger Thompson's account of the area.)

42. The grinding disks for hand-operated rice-hulling mills could be made with stone, clay, or wood. The rice huller *(longpan)* mentioned in the text was made of wood. For a description, with three photographs, of this type of huller, see Rudolf P. Hommel, *China at Work: An Illustrated Record of the Primitive Industries of China's Masses, Whose Life is Toil, and Thus an Account of Chinese Civilization* (New York: John Day, 1937), pp. 91–95 (hereafter Hommel, *China at Work*). Mao's text glosses *longpan* as *tuizi* (lit.,

ladders. All are sold by these craftsmen who come out of the hills. Of course, these items are not available on every market day, but depending on the season or needs, there is a market for these things. Rice hullers must certainly be ordered. Windmills must be made by master craftsmen from Shanghang. In the whole *xian*, there are ten master craftsmen from Shanghang. Every year master craftsmen from Shanghang visit the *xian* once or twice. Waterwheels are owned by only one in a hundred peasant families in Xunwu *xian* because this *xian* has many irrigation ditches in the hills. Because droughts are rare, waterwheels are not used.

Outside the South Gate are two coffin-making shops. Each shop has only 40 *yuan* of capital. They make the "firewood" (also called *huobanzi,* or kindling) used by poor people. Landlords and capitalists and tenants and workers with even a little money usually hire a carpenter to make coffins. Only by the poorest households, or in emergencies *[doujin],*[43] will this "firewood" [coffin] be bought. Those people who have lost everything or have had things taken always curse loudly: "I hope you are wiped out and lose all your children. I hope you end up packed into a cheap coffin." This refers to coffins that are made of kindling wood and are used only by nameless people. Families with money hire carpenters to make coffins. Such carpenters, except for Xunwu natives, come from Shanghang. The master workers who make windmills also make coffins.

Boarding Houses

There are Liu Wanli, He Changlong, Liu Hongxing, Wen Deli, Pan Fali, Pan Jinli, Tang Riheng, Tonglaian, Zeng Jitao, Jiu Saozi, Dazhi Sisaozi, Gu Liufang, Liu Ener (also sells white wine) and Gu Yuchang: some ten-odd boarding places. Eighty percent of the boarders are porters; the remaining 20 percent are ox dealers, people carrying bundles wrapped in cloth (these people are traveling to look for a job), people of neighboring villages coming to Xunwu City because of lawsuits, people passing through here to Ganzhou to attend school there, acrobats and trick performers, plaster vendors, fortune-tellers, monks who beg for alms, medical practitioners, geomancers, and beggars (they sing folk songs called *lianhualuo*). Among those 80 percent of customers who are porters, most carry chickens or ducks in baskets suspended from poles on their shoulders; a few carry tobacco skin (tobacco skin is tobacco leaf).

It requires little capital investment to open a boarding place. Some old quilts, some rough mats, a little rice, and some firewood will do. The rent for the place can be paid after a few months of operation.

---

pusher). This refers to a rice huller whose grinding wheel is turned by a push-pull type of motion. A turning pole, attached to the outer edge of the top grinding disk, turns the wheel by being pushed and then pulled.—RT.

43. *Doujin* is glossed as "times of emergencies."—RT.

The profit comes from those customers with long gowns and those who carry umbrellas. They are customers who are treated to better food and a nicer quilt. However, they are charged a lot more when they check out. The porters and poor people are charged lower fuel and meal fees. They pay by the bowl of rice instead of by the meal, as does the first type of customer; this is much cheaper. One bowl of rice costs half a *mao* (people with larger appetites can consume about one and a half bowls, half a bowl is enough for people with smaller appetites). One pot of wine costs the same as a bowl of rice, for those who drink. The fuel fee for one night is three coppers, which includes fuel for lighting and wood to heat the water for bathing. In the winter it costs each customer two coppers to have a quilt. The money obtained by selling food and wine is about 40 percent of the overall profit. Essentially, the ultimate source of profit for the boarding place is pig raising, because boarding houses always have table scraps and garbage, which can be used as pig food.

The enemy of a boarding house is the police and underlings from the yamen. They often come to check customers' luggage on the pretext of investigation and thus harass the customers or steal their belongings. For example, when they come to the boarding house on the pretext of checking for opium, they steal the money that belongs to customers. During curfew, the customer might get into some unnecessary and unexpected trouble because of a reply the police do not like. Therefore, customers are afraid of coming to the boarding places in Xunwu City. They seek to find places in Huang'ao, Heling, Changju, and Xinzhai—towns that are 3 to 10 *li* from Xunwu City—long before it gets dark. This, no doubt, negatively affects the boarding place business a great deal.

Among the boarding houses, the Tonglaian Boarding House is reactionary. The owner, Chen Dengqi, comes from a poor peasant family in Liuche, where he could not keep his whole family fed. He knew some martial arts; so he taught these in the Liuche countryside. In 1918 or 1919 he went to Xunwu City and became a bailiff. In 1925 he opened the Tonglaian Boarding House and sold oil at the same time. He colluded with government officials and was friends with the evil gentryman Chen Tufeng of Liuche. During the March 25 uprising, he sheltered *xian* magistrate Xie Yin in his escape and got into Xie's good graces. After [Xie's] political power was restored, Chen was promoted to captain of the Pacification and Defense Corps. He led corp members to Shuangqiao District to kidnap people for ransom and burn down the houses of the revolutionary masses. After the *xian* magistrate left, he went back to the boarding house. This time the soviet confiscated his house.

Bean Curd

The population of Xunwu City is under three thousand, and yet there are more than thirty bean curd stores. Nine out of ten meals in this city are served with bean curd. Bean curd is popular because it is cheap and convenient. In Xunwu's villages, people also like bean curd—it constitutes half the peasants' daily diet—but it is not as popular as in Xunwu City.

One tray of bean curd is made with 2.5 *sheng* of soybeans. The cost of 2.5 *sheng* of soybeans is 0.5 *yuan*. One tray of bean curd sells for 0.65 *yuan*. The profit is 0.15 *yuan*. "One tray of bean curd" means forty-six pieces of big dry bean curd. The retail price is seven pieces for 0.1 *yuan*; one piece for three coppers. One tray of small dry bean curd contains ninety-two pieces. The retail price for fourteen pieces is 0.1 *yuan*; two pieces for three coppers.

There are four varieties of bean curd: regular soft bean curd, fried bean curd, dry bean curd, and stuffed dry bean curd. The regular soft bean curd sells the most, fried bean curd ranks second, followed by dry bean curd. Stuffed dry bean curd sells the least because it is used only for special occasions. The profit of a bean curd shop comes from the soybean residue, for it is used to raise pigs. Because the bean curd store sells an average of one tray of bean curd a day—maybe two trays when something special is going on—its profit ranges from only 0.15 to 0.3 *yuan* a day. In raising pigs, a "sow and piglet" can usually be produced twice a year. The profit is about 40 *yuan* each time. If a store raises pigs to be sold as pork, each store can raise four pigs a year, which averages 400 *jin* of pork. This makes a profit of 100 *yuan*. However, this type of pig raising requires more rice, and it is not as profitable as raising the sow and piglet.

Bean curd businesses operate out of the owner's home; people who sell bean curd also farm at the same time. It is not easy to make bean curd. It is said: Learned easily, mastered with difficulty. It is also said: Few people claim to be masters of making bean curd and liquor.

Barbers

There are eight barbershops in Xunwu City. Before 1912 all the tools were traditional ones, and the queue was the only style. In 1912, Western scissors began to be used (shears and hair scissors) and only the monk style was in fashion. In 1913 the "Japanese-style" cut started becoming popular. Large mirrors, plastic combs, and lightweight metal combs had not appeared yet. In 1917 and 1918 the "crew cut" and the "army style" were quite popular. But the tools remained those used traditionally, not the ones like the large mirror. In 1921 some of the local young men who attended school in Ganzhou returned to Xunwu and brought back with them the "Ph.D. style." In 1923 the tall, large mirror (eight or nine inches wide; thirteen inches tall) appeared, and rattan chairs replaced the four-legged bench (one foot tall). In addition, the lightweight metal comb was brought into the city. All the new-style tools were from Mei *xian*. During the great revolution of 1926–1927, plastic combs appeared. The Japanese-style cut was renamed, and the Ph.D-style cut went out of fashion. Nevertheless, crew cuts and army-style cuts, originally widespread among students and merchants, spread widely among young workers, peasants, and poor people.

New hairstyles also became popular among the petty bourgeoisie and student masses (these masses accepted capitalist culture and opposed landlord culture): the "cultured style," "American style," and "round-headed style" (Mei *xian* people laughed at this style, calling it the "Thai pomelo").[44] The cultured style was also called the "Western style." The American style is called the *huaqi* style.[45]

It spread from Southeast Asia to Mei *xian* and then from Mei *xian* to Xunwu. Nowadays, in Xunwu City and other big market towns no one wears the shaved-head style, although a large portion of the peasants in the countryside still wear this style. Only a small part of the population wears fashionable styles like the crew cut and the army-style cut. This minority, moreover, is made up of young men.

As for prices, the shaved-head style costs a *mao* whether one is shaved or sheared. All other styles cost 1.5 *mao*; a shave costs half a *mao*.

To open a barbershop requires capital of about 40 to 50 *yuan*. The master barber usually hires two people, although a few hire one or three people. The wage for half a year is at least 30 or 40 *yuan*; a regular wage is 50 to 60 *yuan*; 80 *yuan* is maximum. When business is good, each person can make a *yuan* [a day]. Normally the boss and the two workers, on the average, bring in 3 *yuan* a day; so in a year they can bring in 1,000 *yuan* or so. Except for the expense of wages of more than 100 *yuan*, the rest goes to the boss. Expenses are fuel and food (75 *yuan* for each of the four people), rent for the shop (about 30 *yuan*), and the cost of the tools (not more than 100 *yuan*). So the boss can make a profit of around 400 *yuan* (including his own wage). How is this money used up? For whoring and gambling by the boss.

Very few barbers and tailors, whether workers or bosses, save up enough money to become rich. The reason is that these two types of people, though generally bright and capable, indulge in whoring and gambling and are fond of fine food and nice clothing. Why are they like this? It is probably because their social position is low. During the Qing dynasty, barbers were regarded by society as one of the "nine low classes." As elsewhere, the social position of tailors is also very low. Even though they are married, tailors still frequent brothels. Eight of ten barbers do not have wives, but they do not feel miserable at all. They are quite content to frequent brothels.

The "nine low classes" are contrasted with the "nine high classes." The nine low classes are (1) pedicurists, (2) masseuses (those who massage backs), (3) musicians (those who play drums and instruments), (4) chimney sweeps, (5) folk

---

44. The text reads *xuanluo you;* the first two characters are a classical reference to Thailand, and the last character refers to a grapefruit-type citrus known as pomelo or shaddock.—RT.

45. *Huaqi,* or checkered flag, refers to the U.S. flag, hence, "American." Other colloquialisms include "sun flag" for Japan and "rice flag" for Great Britain. The "rice flag" designation derived from the similarity of the design of the Union Jack to the character for "rice" *(mi)*. See Li Jui, *Early Mao,* p. 79.—RT.

performers [lit., tea pickers] (men and women singing tea-picking songs *[xi]* together), (6) opera singers *[changxi]*, (7) yamen clerks and runners *[chairen]*, (8) barbers, and (9) prostitutes. The nine high classes consist of (1) degree holders *[juzi]*, (2) doctors *[yi]*, (3) fortune-tellers *[kanyu]*,[46] (4) geomancers, (5) painters *[danqing]*,[47] (6) craftsmen, (7) monks, (8) Daoist priests, and (9) performing artists [lit., qin players] and chess players *[qi]*.

Blacksmiths

There are three blacksmiths: Master Ye, Master Yang, and Master Li. Master Yang comes from Anyuan, Masters Ye and Li both come from Yudu. Each of them has invested about 50 *yuan*. They make different kinds of firewood cleavers, axes, hoes, iron rake heads, weeding rakes, harrows (pulled by an ox), planes, shuttle spears (in the Xunwu dialect these are called *baozoi*, in Mei *xian tiaohaozi*, in Dongjiang *jianchuan*), kitchen cleavers (vegetable cleavers) spatulas (for frying vegetables), shovels (to ladle food out of woks),[48] fire [charcoal] tongs, fire [charcoal] shovels, hooks (for carrying water pails), iron ladles (to scoop rice and oil), all kinds of iron tools used by carpenters (various kinds of iron planes and rulers, oblique shovels, iron awls, carpenter's pincers, drills, choppers), irons (to press cotton cloth when making a shirt), knives for cutting cloth (for the tailor), sickles, sabers, and double sabers *(kazidao)*, small rakes *(xiaoba)*, iron nails, hinges (for mounting doors), and iron hoops. All items except sickles, sabers, and double sabers are household items that are sold in the city and the surrounding area. Traditional tools and methods are used to forge iron. Iron is produced in six places locally: Huangshashui in Xunwu City District's South Ward; Tiezashui and Shiduankeng in Shuangqiao District; and Chetou, Hengjing, and Dabeijiao in Nanba District. Every place has furnaces and casts iron ingots as well as woks, plowshares, and moldboards *(libi)*. The locally produced iron is also sold outside Xunwu *xian*; most of it is sold in Huizhou, Shilong, and Menling. Some of the woks are sold in Xunwu *xian*, but about half are sold in Huichang and Ganzhou, and a small number are sold in Chaozhou and Shantou. Plowshares and moldboards are sold only in Xunwu *xian*. Altogether about two hundred people are required for one furnace for casting iron. Every furnace needs those who carry the *xiangtan* (charcoal *[mutan]*; this is used in casting iron and casting woks; about twenty men are needed to carry it), those

---

46. A note to the Chinese edition of Mao's report indicates that *kanyu* is the same as *dili xiansheng* and *kan didi* [geomancers]. It refers to those who, through the use of superstitious practices, helped people select the location of a house or tomb. Usually they were called *fengshui xiansheng* or *yinyang xiansheng*.

47. *Dan* and *qing* are two pigments commonly used in Chinese painting. *Danqing* usually means painting, but refers to painters here.

48. Mao uses the compound *guotou*. *Guo*, the Mandarin pronunciation for the character for cooking bowl, is pronounced *wok* in Cantonese. This refers to the round-bottomed cooking vessel associated in the West with Chinese-style stir-fry cooking.—RT

who make charcoal (to turn wood into *xiangtan* requires three men per kiln; the charcoal from five kilns supplies one iron furnace; so fifteen men are needed altogether), those who ·transport the sand (sand for iron production comes from landslips; peasants carry it and sell it to those who run the furnaces; these workers are difficult to count), and those workers at the foundry (tall furnaces for casting pig iron require ten men; cupola furnaces for casting cast iron require twelve men;[49] casting woks requires twelve men, one man is the stoker, and three men are either managers or apprentices). Every furnace for producing iron requires capital of 1,000 *yuan* as does every furnace for making woks; so [together] the furnaces for making iron and woks require 2,000 *yuan*. The biggest expense is for sand and charcoal, the next is for the fuel, food, and wages of the workers. Some foundries are run by one family; others are joint-share operations. As for wages, the foreman *(gongtou)* gets 1.2 *yuan* a day; workers get 0.3 *yuan* and eat the boss's food and use his fuel. The managers get 70 *yuan* a year. Wages for foremen and workers are reckoned daily—they work a day and get paid for a day. A manager's salary is figured on an annual basis. There is also money for rituals, New Year's, and travel. These are all expenses paid by the boss for the workers. The status of foremen is high. If a foreman is treated poorly, he will take it easy, and the business will start losing money. A foreman can make 500 *yuan* a year. A foundry can produce [iron worth] 4,000 *yuan* a year. Six foundries yield 24,000 *yuan*. Before the Republic, foreign iron had not arrived here at all, or only in a very small amount, and wages were low. Iron production was greater than at present. Foundries could produce iron worth over 20,000 *yuan*. Although in the Qing there were only two foundries, together their production was more than 40,000 *yuan*. Now the number of furnaces has increased, and the amount of production of each foundry has decreased. The primary reasons are that labor is expensive (labor is expensive because industrial products from abroad are expensive) and that foreign iron is being imported.

The current price of iron is double that of thirty years ago (1899–1900). At that time a *Dan* (about 40 *jin*) of pig iron was, at most, 1.1 *yuan*. Now it is certainly 3.2 *yuan*, or 0.08 *yuan* per *jin* of pig iron. Three *jin* of pig iron can be made into one *jin* of cast iron, which is priced at 0.5 *yuan*.

Of the three blacksmiths in Xunwu City, two are Yudu natives; one is from Anyuan. All furnace operators in the countryside are natives of Yudu. There are many Yudu iron-founders. Since tall furnaces require four men to operate and short furnaces require three men to operate, with about three thousand seven hundred to three thousand eight hundred furnaces in operation, these iron-founders number about thirteen thousand. Not only do they make iron in Jiangxi, but they work in Fujian, Guangdong, and even Southeast Asia.

---

49. Pig iron ingots cast in sand molds from smelted iron ore, when resmelted in a cupola furnace and poured into molds, become cast iron. For a description of iron casting as observed in China in the 1920s, see Hommel, *China at Work*, pp. 28–31.—RT.

Fireworks

There is a fireworks shop whose boss is a certain Zhong, a Huichang man. With capital of several dozen *yuan*, this shop has been around for six or seven years. He himself works along with a master he has hired to help. Every year he does a business of 400 to 500 *yuan*. An old custom on the first day of the year is to set off large displays of fireworks. Even the smallest shop would spend a couple of *yuan* on fireworks. This year on the first the reactionary government announced restrictions. Firecrackers were forbidden not only on the first day of the year, but even on ordinary days. Because of this, the fireworks business has plummeted. The peasants in the areas of the insurrection in the southern half of the *xian* have completely rid themselves of superstition and do not want to use fireworks. Because of this, not only has Zhong's fireworks business in Xunwu City decreased, but also the importing of fireworks into Xunwu from Mei *xian* and Menling has ceased recently.

Jewelry

Xunwu women are the same as women in other places where the feudal economy has not completely collapsed. It does not matter whether they are workers, peasants, merchants, or poor peasants or rich peasants, they all wear jewelry in their hair or on their hands. All of it is silver except for the gold jewelry worn by women in large-landlord families. Every woman puts silver hair clasps in her hair and wears silver earrings. No matter how destitute the woman, she has these two kinds of jewelry. Also, bracelets and rings are owned even by those of the most modest means. Silver earrings are actually silver-plated tin or silver-plated copper. More than seven shops in Xunwu City make this kind of jewelry. Each shop needs only several dozen *yuan* of capital. Some of the jewelry is done to order; some is sold by peddlers carrying goods on their backs in a box and going to the countryside. Among the seven jewelry shops, four shops have a boss, a worker, and an apprentice, one shop has four people, one shop has two people, another shop only has one person. The apprenticeship system resembles the one for haircutting, but the work is harder and the clothes are a bit more threadbare.

Tinsmith

There is one shop [in this category], which is run by Liu Junji, a native of Xingning. This shop was opened in Xunwu City the year before last; there was no so-called tinned iron[50] before then. It has capital of several dozen *yuan*. The shop has three people: his wife, one apprentice, and Liu himself. The raw materi-

---

50. *Yangtie,* literally "foreign iron," the Chinese term for tinned or galvanized iron.

als are kerosene tins. It produces small tin lamps (rush-wick lamps),[51] pots for holding oil and tea-oil, ladles for scooping oil, pots for making tea, filters for oil and wine, tea canisters, all sorts of small boxes, and other household necessities. So this type of tin goods store is a social necessity. The business is also profitable. A kerosene tin costs 0.3 *yuan* and comes from general stores in Xunwu City, Jitan, Sanbiao, Chengjiang, and Niudouguang. These tins are made into tin products and sold for 0.6 *yuan*. This time when the Red Army entered Xunwu City, Liu Junji, for unknown reasons, fled with the reactionary faction.

Watch Repairing

Ye Gongchang, a native of Mei *xian*, runs the one watch repair shop. In addition to his tools, he has around 10 *yuan* of capital. He specializes in fixing watches and clocks. In addition to the business in Xunwu City, the only other such business in the whole county is in Niudouguang. These two businesses were started the year before last (1928). Xunwu *xian* has 120,000 people; 2 percent have watches and clocks. Altogether there are two thousand four hundred watches and clocks; so it is necessary to have one or two businesses that repair watches and clocks.

Periodic Markets

Xunwu City is a city whose trade is carried on in shops and in periodic markets. In Xunwu, the business in periodic markets represents the seminatural economy, and the business done by shops and stalls represents the mercantile economy. To compare the shop and stall business with the periodic market business, the shop and stall business constitutes 70 percent, and the periodic market 30 percent. It is apparent that the strength of the mercantile economy exceeds that of the natural economy by far.

The most important products sold at the periodic markets are as follows.

The first is rice. The rice trade takes place only on the first, fourth, and seventh days of the ten-day market schedule. Shops and stalls do not engage in this trade. Not only is rice desired by most people in Xunwu City (Xunwu City's peasants have their own rice), but it is also shipped to Guangdong. Mei *xian* or Dazhe people carry in a *Dan* of salt and take back a *Dan* of rice. This is called "salt coming; rice going." Because of this, the rice trade is greater than any other trade in Xunwu City. The items most traded in Xunwu City are, in order, (1) rice,

---

51. In the text "small tin lamps" is glossed *dundeng*, which, on p. 136 of the Chinese text, is itself glossed "rush-wick lamp" (*caodeng*, lit., grass lamp). These are lamps in which light is produced by the slow burning of two or three piths of rush extending from a raised dish filled with oil. Oils pressed from soybeans or rapeseeds were frequently used as fuel. This traditional type of lighting was replaced by kerosene lamps. See Hommel, *China at Work*, pp. 313–14.—RT.

(2) salt (more than 100,000 *yuan* annually), (3) textiles and foreign-style goods (100,000 *yuan*); and (4) [soy]beans (in excess of 20,000 *yuan*). In 1900, the price of 1 *Dan* (172 *jin*) of rice was 4 *yuan*; in 1912, it was 5 *yuan*; in 1927, during a drought, it was over 16 *yuan*. This year, before the Red Army arrived, it was 8.5 *yuan*; since the Red Army arrived, it has been 7 *yuan*.

The second is firewood. Charcoal, *shuitanzi*, kindling, bundled firewood, and brushwood are carried by shoulder "to the market" from rural areas. In 1900, 100 *jin* of charcoal *(xiangtan)* was worth 0.5 *yuan*. From 1912 to 1928, the price rose from 0.8 *yuan* to 1.2 *yuan*. Because it rained a lot last year, the price for 100 *jin* went up to 2.2 *yuan*, but now 100 *jin* costs 0.6 or 0.7 *yuan*. The price for a *Dan* (70 *jin*) of kindling was 0.17 to 0.18 *yuan* in 1900. It went up to 0.22 to 0.23 *yuan* in 1912, and it was 0.4 *yuan* from 1921 to 1927. It has been 0.5 to 0.6 *yuan* from 1927 until·now.

The third is pork. Those three butchers mentioned previously in the section on shops and stalls actually should have been included in the section on periodic markets because theirs is a business carried on in periodic markets.

The fourth is pigs. Piglets (two months old) and older piglets (three to four months old) are not sold by licensed brokers. They are bought and sold in periodic markets. Since each market has about thirty of them, and there are nine markets per month, altogether about 270 are traded each month. The price per *jin* for piglets now is 0.3 *yuan*, and for [older] piglets 0.2 *yuan*. Pigs with much meat cost 0.25 *yuan*. Why are older piglets the cheapest? Because the average weight for an older piglet is 50 *jin* or so. Unless he needs the cash, an owner does not want to sell it. But when an owner is forced to sell an older piglet, people [know the situation and] bargain the price down. The owner reluctantly lets it go.

The fifth is chicken and duck. Not many from this area are sold at markets—normally twenty at most. Sometimes no one wants even one. This proves the poverty of Xunwu. Around New Year's and other festivals over a hundred are sold at every market. The price per *jin* for chicken is 0.45 *yuan* and for duck 0.3 *yuan*.

The sixth is bamboo and wooden goods. Wooden goods that are sold at the periodic markets are discussed in the section on shops and stalls under the heading of wooden goods. Here I discuss bamboo goods: grain baskets, bamboo mats *[da]* for drying grain, bamboo scoops (to carry ashes and manure to the field), chicken and duck cages, pig cages, baskets, bags (for carrying rice cakes and other odds and ends), mill-turning handles, threshing sieves, sieves for sifting grain, bamboo beds (sleeping chairs), dustpans, bamboo chairs, stove scoops *[laoji]*, chopsticks, brooms, wok brushes, *duoerzi* (that is, kite scoops, smaller than bamboo scoops), small, square-bottomed bamboo baskets *[jiaoluo]* (small food baskets used by children to hold cakes), containers (fish baskets, also used when picking tea-oil seeds *[chazi]*),[52] bamboo fish traps (that is, the trap of

---

52. *Chazi, muzi, tao,* and *taozi* all mean seeds from the tea-oil plant.

"after the fish is caught, the trap can be forgotten";[53] it is called a *hao* elsewhere), tea baskets, bamboo hats (straw rainhats), vegetable baskets, and drying baskets. These are all sold at periodic markets.

The seventh is vegetables. These are leaf mustard, celery, amaranth, Chinese onion, *maizi*, Chinese kale, garlic bolt, bitter melon, winter melon, pumpkin (gourd), seasonal melon, sweet melon, cucumber, watermelon, sweet potato (cushaw), eggplant (Guangdong people called it *diaocai*), water convolvulus (also called *kongxincai, it is called *yongcai* elsewhere), taro, *puzi*,[54] turnip, leek, scallion, garland chrysanthemum, cabbage, *caitou* (main stem of leaf mustard), *dangji* (blade bean), chili, snow pea, *pengpidou* (hyacinth bean), kidney bean, *bayuejiao* (August bean), tiger bean, tree bean, mung bean, yellow soybean sprout, purslane, and celery cabbage. These vegetables are supplied by the nearby villages to the residents of this city.

The eighth is fish. There are grass carp, silver carp, variegated carp, shrimp, carp, crusian carp, yellow eel, loach, frog, prawn, soft-shelled turtle *(jiaoyu),* freshwater fish, and *"qiang."* Ordinary markets have only grass carp, silver carp, carp, crusian carp, yellow eel, loach, and frog; the rest are seldom seen. One *jin* of grass carp costs 0.25 *yuan*; 10 *liang* of yellow eel cost 0.1 *yuan*; a *jin* of loach costs 0.1 *yuan*; 7 *liang* of frog costs about 0.1 *yuan*. *Qiang* is a kind of rare big fish. A 40-*jin* *qiang* was sold in Xunwu last year. Some *qiang* found elsewhere weigh as much as 70 to 80 *jin*. Sometimes along rivers in the Huizhou area people who have drowned serve as food for this type of fish.

The ninth is candy. There is powder, glutinous paste, *nazi* (vermicelli), cakes (soft cake, *tielian* cake, *tieshao* cake, bean cake, *youguo,* sugar cake, fish cake, ramie-leaf cake, sweet potato cake, and impressed-character cake).[55] Whenever the market is open, candy vendors are there; especially during a "joyous procession" (during folk dancing or a religious festival), a lot more of them appear. The capital is only a *yuan* or two.

The tenth is fruit. Plums sell best; water chestnuts rank second. In addition, there are loquats, pomelos, red bayberries, persimmons, peaches, oranges, and tangerines. The fruit trade is not a small business.

---

53. Mao here evokes a passage from chapter 26 of the *Zhuangzi*. Watson renders the relevant sentence: "The fish trap exists because of the fish; once you've gotten the fish, you can forget the trap." See *The Complete Works of Chuang Tzu*, translated by Burton Watson (New York: Columbia University Press, 1968), p. 302.

54. *Puzi* is a local term for a type of aquatic grass known elsewhere in China as *jiaosun* or *jiaobai*. The base of the stalk swells under the action of a fungus which is attracted to the plant, and it is the resulting tubers which are eaten.

55. Impressed-character (lit., seal) cakes are fried cakes impressed with decorative designs such as flowers or Chinese characters. A hinged mold, which could be made of camphor wood, might impress, for example, the auspicious characters for "double happiness." See Hommel, *China at Work*, p. 155.—RT.

Prostitutes

There are thirty to forty brothels in this town of two thousand seven hundred people. The best known among the hard-bitten lot of prostitutes, young and old, are Chang Jiao, Yue E, Zhong Simei, Xie Sanmei, Huang Zhaokun, Wu Xiu, Run Feng, Da Guanlan, Xiao Guanlan, Zhao E, Lai Zhao, Yu Shu, Wu Feng, and Yi E. Except for Da Guanlan and Yi E, all are young prostitutes. Run Feng, Wu Xiu, Yue E, Wu Feng, and Zhaokun are the five best known.

When the civil and military imperial examinations were flourishing, there were just as many prostitutes as now. After the imperial examinations were abolished, their numbers declined. Around 1904 there were only about ten prostitutes. Later the number gradually increased; so now it is the same as during the booming period of the exams. When the land revolution in the southern half of the *xian* moved to the north and the Red Army arrived in Chengjiang, many of the prostitutes fled to the countryside. Among them it was said: "Wherever the Red Army is, not a blade of grass remains; even a broom will be snapped into two pieces." Therefore, they were frightened and ran away.

In Xunwu City most of the prostitutes are from Sanbiao. The people of Xunwu have a saying: "Prostitutes [lit., 'goods' *(huo)*] from Sanbiao; glutinous rice from Xiangshan." This means that the women of Sanbiao are very pretty.

Ten years ago, when business was flourishing, merchants visited prostitutes the most, powerful gentry were second, and the sons of powerful gentry (the "young masters") participated in this activity the least. In the past ten years the positions have changed: the powerful gentry visit prostitutes the most, their sons and brothers are second, and merchants the least. Why do merchants go whoring the least? Because business is not good now. Why do the gentry do this the most? Because they are involved in litigation and stay in brothels throughout the year. Only at New Year's and other holidays do they return home. Where does the money for this come from? In lawsuits, country folk give them 100 *yuan* when only 20 *yuan* is needed for legal fees. They pocket the 80 *yuan* and in this way are provided with the means to cover their expenses for prostitutes. Why are the young masters coming to the city for whoring much more than in the past? Because an increasing number of "diploma mills" are being established. The young masters break away from the warmth of their families when they go to town to study; so they feel quite lonely and leave a lot of footprints leading to brothels.

Fellowship of Goodness

In 1901 or 1902 the manager (boss) of the Hengfu Silk Store in Ganzhou, a certain Xiong (a native of Nanchang), came to Xunwu to start the Fellowship of Goodness.[56] He was a so-called Heavenly Grace Master. At that time the leader

---

56. The Fellowship of Goodness *[Tongshanshe]* was a religious sect which had split off from the Great Way of Former Heaven *[Xiantian dadao, also known as Xiantian dao]*

[shanzhang] of the society was Gu Hefu, a *xiucai* who lived in the city and whose family circumstances were deteriorating. Later the director of the Fellowship of Goodness was Pan Mingdian, a holder of a *bagong* degree, whose wealth was about 1,000 *yuan* and who served as a clerk in the *xian* court in Jiujiang [Jiangxi]. Guo Youmei joined the Fellowship of Goodness in 1901 or 1902 at a time when the fellowship had eighty to ninety members. Afterward many more people joined, and during the most flourishing period there were more than two hundred members of the Fellowship of Goodness. The Fellowship of Goodness originated in Sichuan, where the society sent formal letters to each provincial capital asking them to initiate Fellowships of Goodness. Once permission was granted by the government in each province, the society spread to the *xian*, where branches were set up. The Heavenly Grace Master of Ganzhou Prefecture received official approval from the provincial government in Nanchang. After he arrived in Xunwu, paid respects to the *xian* magistrate, and [secured] the magistrate's approval, the magistrate issued a proclamation protecting this society. The Fellowship of Goodness could then carry on its activities. Joining the society required approval by the gods. Pieces of paper rolled into balls, some with the word "permitted" and some blank, were placed in a bamboo container. The deity of the Fellowship of Goodness was Bodhidharma.[57] A person wanting to join the society was led by the person introducing him before the deity, to whom he kowtowed and paid respect. Then he picked a paper from the holder; if he picked one that said "permitted," he was allowed to join. If it was blank, then he was not allowed to join. One butcher drew a blank three times, and a local bully drew a blank four times. "You couldn't say there is no god; actually you could say there is a god."[58] Lin Hu[59] arrived in Xunwu City as a big-headed and ferocious man of 27 or 28 *sui*. Xu Chongzhi[60] also passed through once.

---

in 1843, at a meeting held in Hanyang in Sichuan. For a detailed account of the organization and doctrine of this whole family of sects, see Marjorie Topley, "The Great Way of Former Heaven: A Group of Chinese Secret Religious Sects," *Bulletin of the School of Oriental and African Studies*, Vol 26, part 2, 1963, pp. 362–92 (hereafter Topley, "The Great Way"). We have followed Topley in our translation of these two names, and of certain other terms used by the sects.

57. Bodhidharma, the founder of the Chan School of Buddhism in China, is referred to in the text as *Dama zushi*. *Dama* is a Chinese transliteration of the Sanskrit dharma, which refers to the teachings of Buddha. *Zushi* refers to a founder of a sect. See Werner, E.T.C., *A Dictionary of Chinese Mythology*, (Shanghai: Kelly & Walsh, 1932; reprinted New York: Julian Press, 1961), pp. 359–61; also Ch'en [Chen], Kenneth K.S., *Buddhism in China: A Historical Survey*, (Princeton, N.J.: Princeton University Press, 1964), pp. 351–53 (hereafter, Ch'en, *Buddhism in China*).—RT.

58. The incarnation of the Great Way, or of the Void, to whom these applications for membership were addressed was commonly called "Mother" in the Fellowship of Goodness. See Topley, "The Great Way," pp. 370–71.

59. Lin Hu was the brigade commander of the Jiangxi Independent Brigade.

60. Xu Chongzhi (1887–1965), *zi* Ruwei, a native of Guangdong, was a graduate of the Japanese Military Academy. He joined the Guomindang in 1912, and played an im-

Seven or eight company commanders under Lin Hu, stationed in Xunwu for over a month, joined the society. The membership fee was 1 *yuan*. Later, although not mandatory, you could contribute as much as you wanted. The Nanchang Fellowship of Goodness and the Sichuan Fellowship of Goodness asked for contributions in a letter that said, "If you contribute money, some day when you go to Nanchang or Sichuan, your name will be on the register and then you will be able to find a job." Guo Youmei contributed 3 *yuan* to Nanchang and 5 *yuan* to Sichuan. Xunwu's society had more than two hundred members, of whom thirty to forty were women. Their backgrounds were merchants 50 percent, landlords 20 percent, and peasants 30 percent. But the so-called peasants were not poor peasants. All of them had "food on the table" or were "quite independent." In 1918 or 1919 on the orders of the provincial government, the Fellowship of Goodness was closed for a year or two. Afterward Tang Shengzhi issued a directive saying: "The Bodhisattvas[61] can be worshiped; you do not have to abolish the society." Therefore it was re-established. In 1923 or 1924 a government directive ordered the society closed, and then and only then did it really cease to function.[62]

Every day you meditated three times—morning, noon, and evening. This was called "to practice." Those who were "practicing" could not sleep with women for two days, because if they slept with women they would not be effective. The Fellowship of Goodness had secret practices if you reached the fifth level. Then the Heavenly Grace Master told you some secrets. Guo Youmei had only reached the second level, so he never heard the secrets. Sichuan had a ninth-level Heavenly Blessing Master who came to Ganzhou. The Fellowship of Goodness members there contributed 2 *yuan* each for a welcoming banquet for the Heavenly Grace Master. Fang Benren[63] also came. Every year the Fellowship of

---

portant role in Sun Yatsen's Guangdong army from 1922 to 1925. In the summer of 1925, he reached the peak of his influence as minister of war in the Guangzhou national government, but he was expelled from Guangzhou on Chiang Kaishek's orders in September 1925 on grounds of collusion with Chen Jiongming. In December 1929, the Nanjing government ordered his arrest on suspicion of involvement in the various rebellions by local warlords against Chiang Kaishek which had taken place in 1928 and 1929. The visit to which Mao refers here presumably took place in Xu's heyday, in the early 1920s.

61. The text uses the abbreviation *pusa*, derived from the Chinese transliteration for the Sanskrit bodhisattva: *putisaduo*. A bodhisattva is a person destined for enlightenment who delays leaving the world so that he or she may help others attain enlightenment. See K. Ch'en, p. 13.—RT.

62. According to Topley, the Fellowship of Goodness, which opposed Guomindang ideology, was proscribed in 1927, rather than 1923 or 1924. Mao is referring here to action by the provincial rather than the central government. After 1949, this sect opposed the Communists as well. Two leaders of the Fellowship of Goodness were put on trial in Chongqing in early 1955. (See Topley, ibid., pp. 390–91.)

63. Fang Benren had been, during the years 1922 to 1925, commander of the southern Jiangxi garrison for the Beiyang warlords, director of frontier defenses in Jiangxi and Guangdong, and military governor of Jiangxi.

Goodness had two *Longhua hui*:[64] all members came and were charged 0.2 *yuan* per person when they arrived. They kowtowed toward the Bodhidharma, music was played, and they ate a vegetarian meal.

If you joined the Fellowship of Goodness, you could make friends and become an official.

The Xunwu magistrate went to the Fellowship of Goodness three times and kowtowed [to the god] together with Fellowship of Goodness members.

Status Within Population and Positions Within Administration

Having analyzed the composition of the population in Xunwu City, we know that it is a city based on agriculture and handicrafts. The percentages of the population in and around the city in various occupations are as follows.

Occupation	Number of Persons	Percentage
peasant	1,620	60%
artisan	297	11
vagrant[65]	270	10
prostitute	162	6
merchant	135	5
government	100	4
landlord	78	3
religious leader	22	<1
Total	2,684	100%

From this list, we can see that peasants and artisans *[xiao shougong]* constitute 71 percent of the population. It is apparent that agriculture and handicrafts are the major activities in the city. The majority of the residents in adjacent areas also get their livelihood from farming and handicrafts. The so-called artisans include workers, owners, and store clerks. The so-called handicraft industries include shops for tailoring, tobacco, liquor, umbrellas, firecrackers, haircutting, wooden goods, bean curd, jewelry, tinned-iron, watch repair, and slaughtering. Those twenty-two religious leaders include ten Protestants, three Roman Catho-

---

64. As indicated by Topley, "The Great Way," p. 373, the term *longhua hui* (lit., "dragon flower meetings") is taken from the name of the bodhi tree of Maitreya, whose flowers are said to resemble dragons' heads. There is a Buddhist belief he will hold three *longhua* meetings under this tree, and Great Way sectarians used the same name for the major meetings they held (normally three rather than two annually).

65. In the "Xunwu Investigation" Mao uses "vagrant" *(youmin)* in statistical references that should be interpreted to include also "vagabonds" *(liumang)*. When Mao uses the latter term, his reference is to the more active and violent element in the vagrant class.—RT.

lics, six Daoists, and three Buddhists. In Xunwu City there are twelve house-holds surviving totally on land rents. There are seventy-eight people in these households. The five merchants who are also landlords are included in the cate-gory of merchants. Merchants include people who are salt, oil, or soybean bro-kers; merchants dealing in general goods, textiles, marine products, and herbs; or those who run boarding houses. Altogether there are 135 people in this category. There are over thirty brothels, with over thirty prostitutes. These prostitutes, combined with people they support, number 162. Those vagabonds who are neither workers nor peasants nor merchants specialize in gambling, blackmail, or being running dogs for the rulers *[tongzhi]*. The total number of these people is, surprisingly, twice the number of merchants. They almost equal the total number of artisans. The number of vagrants and prostitutes is about equal to the number of merchants and artisans. This shows the stunning number of jobless people. The hundred government workers are the forty people of the new Xunwu *xian* soviet government and the Xunwu City District government along with the sixty people in the *xian* soviet's Red Guard. Here we do not mean the former govern-ment workers, although the number of them was about the same as that of the new government. When we talk about the leaders of the masses, we mean the leading segment of the ruling class in the old society. Naturally these were not the peasants, workers, vagrants, and prostitutes constituting 87 percent of the whole population. These were the people led by the ruling class. The rulers consisted only of the landlords, merchants, and Protestant pastors and Catholic priests, constituting 13 percent of the population. The chamber of commerce did not have much power. However, some of the merchants participated in the *xian*-wide government. Nevertheless, those few merchants did not speak just for the mercantile bourgeoisie. They did things at the instruction of the landlords. This is because the scale of commerce in Xunwu is very small; moreover, it has gradually been declining.

First among the merchants in political influence was He Zizhen, who was a soybean broker, having used a false name to obtain a license and then having someone else run the business. He was a teacher, director of the Public Security Bureau, head of the police *[jingcha duizhang]*, and a Guomindang deputy. His father was a tax farmer for the ox tax who exploited the ox dealers. Just after he returned to Xunwu, He Zizhen behaved as a bourgeois and was a member of the New Xunwu faction. Later, he cooper-ated with landlords. Now he has fled the *xian*. The second [in influence] was Huang Guangfu. He was the boss of the Baohuaxiang marine products store and the secretary of the chamber of commerce. He was able to influence the yamen. He fled and his store was confiscated. The third was the boss of a boarding house, Chen Dengqi. He first worked as a bailiff and later was promoted to captain of a pacification and defense corps. He hung out at the yamen. He fled. The fourth was the boss of a general store, Chen Zhicheng. He was not an official and yet consulted with the reactionary faction on all their affairs and attended their meetings. He fled, and his store was confiscated.

The following is a list of the twelve landlords who collect rent.

He Dexin. He previously collected 600 *dan* [in rent] but now collects 100 *dan*, just enough to feed his family of seven or eight members. People from the *xian* who had business with the yamen would ask him to intercede for them. His son, He Tingba, graduated from Pingyuan Middle School and is one of the main members of the New Xunwu faction.

He Chengzhi. He previously collected over 300 *dan*. With very few family members, he could sell 300 *dan* and thus became the richest landlord in the city. After he died, his widow managed household affairs. His son was purchased and cannot influence the yamen.

Liu Forong. He collected over 200 *dan* and sold some of it because his family was small. He was the second-richest landlord in Xunwu City. [He was known as] *shui jin niupi,* which means he was very stingy. He pays no attention to outside matters.

Liu Duanxuan. He collected only a few *dan* in rent and belonged to the Sun Yatsen faction. He exhausted his fortune in a lawsuit against He Zizhen. His son is still in jail in Ganzhou. His son is a graduate of Ganzhou No. 4 Middle School and is the new principal of Xunwu City East Primary School.

Fan Laoba. He collected over 100 *dan* and had a surplus. His elder brother managed the Shunchang Laodian store. He collected rent at home and did not hang out at the yamen. This time [the soviet] imposed a contribution of 300 *yuan* on him. The peasants confiscated his property.

Fan Jiasheng. He collected over 100 *dan* and had a surplus. He is about fifteen or sixteen *sui* and is a student at Sun Yatsen Middle School. He Zizhen imposed a fine on him. This time he was also assessed a contribution of 1,000 *yuan* by the soviet.

Zhang Sanyu. She collected over 100 *dan* and had a surplus. She is a widow and is in charge of household affairs. She is not interested in other things.

Kuang Sisao. She collects less than *100* dan and has a surplus. She has one son and one grandchild. She is not a reactionary.

Wu Laosi. He is dead and is survived by a wife, one son, and one grandchild. He collected over 100 *dan* and had a surplus. He did not meddle in politics. Wu Laosi was in charge of tax collection for the *xian* government during the Guangxu reign in the Qing dynasty. All the *xian* grain levies were managed by him. He died four years ago.

Fan Mingcai. He used to have a general store, but he closed it over ten years ago. He collected 80 *dan* and had some surplus. He was a head of a protection militia in 1912 and was an evil gentryman who indulged in whoring and gambling. He fled.

He Xiangsheng. He used to be a street vendor and became rich selling marine products. During the March 25 uprising, he was fined and his business was shut down. His adopted son, He Jiachang, whom he purchased, graduated from East Mountain Middle School in Mei *xian*. He Jiachang was one of the leaders of the March 25 uprising and a Communist Party member. He went to Southeast Asia and now is in Fujian.

He Xuecai. The father of He Zizhen. He worked as a clerk in the Judicial Section in the [former] *xian* government. Later he worked as a geomancer. He was a tax farmer for the ox tax and bought a piece of land that produced some 10 *dan* of income. He was a very evil member of the gentry.

These twelve households subsisted on land rents alone. Among them, He Dexin, Fan Mingcai, and He Xuecai are active reactionaries; Liu Duanxuan and Fan Jiasheng are sympathetic with the revolution; He Xiangsheng's son, He Jiachang, is a Communist Party member; the remaining six are households that "care only about making a fortune and don't want to mind other business."

The following five households have characteristics of both merchants and landlords.

Zhong Huitong. He was the first salt broker in Xunwu City. He collected over 220 *dan* and had a surplus of over 100 *dan*. He hung out at the yamen and influenced the people there.

Luo Jinfeng. The household was split into four separate households. Altogether their income was 6,000 to 7,000 *yuan*. The second child is the richest one; he had 250 or 260 *dan*. He was honest and did not try to influence the yamen. The oldest son is dead; he had over 10 *dan*. That was not enough to support his family. The third child had 30 to 40 *dan*, just enough to feed his family. The fourth child (a former president of the chamber of commerce and the main teacher at the Fellowship of Goodness) had only several dozen *dan*, just enough to feed his family.

Rong Chunxiang. He had several dozen *dan* of income. He saved all of it and made a living doing business. He did not try to influence the yamen.

Wen Rongji. He saved all of his 80 *dan* of income and made a living doing business. His third son, Wen Xichun, colluded with the New Xunwu faction.

Lin Bili. He manages a marine products business. He collected over 100 *dan* and had some surplus. He minds his own business.

These five households have characteristics of both merchants and landlords. Among them, Zhong Huitong and Wen Rongji are members of the reactionary faction. The rest of them are the "mind their own business" type. Among these five households, Zhong Huitong and Luo Jinfeng are middle landlords; the remaining three are small landlords.

Chapter IV: Traditional Land Relationships in Xunwu

Rural Population

Large landlords (receive more than 500 *dan* of rent)	0.045%
Middle landlords (receive 200–499 *dan* of rent)	0.4
Small landlords (receive less than 200 *dan* of rent)	3.0
Bankrupt families	1.0
Newly rich families	2.0
Rich peasants (have surplus grain and capital for loans)	4.0
Middle peasants (have enough to eat and do not receive loans)	18.255
Poor peasants (insufficient grain and receive loans)	70.0
Manual workers (craftsmen, boatmen, porters)	3.0
Vagrants (no occupation)	1.0
Hired hands (permanent and day laborers)	0.3

Old Distribution of Land[66]

Corporate	40%
Landlord	30
Peasant	30

Ancestral Trusts

There is much corporate land in Xunwu, a phenomenon spread throughout each district. There are many kinds of trusts *[gonghui]*. Trusts belonging to ancestral halls are mostly those of this deceased "esteemed person" or that deceased "esteemed person." As long as there are descendants and the descendants have money, each will certainly contribute a share from his own family's property to establish a trust. This method of making contributions toward establishing a trust is widespread. Generally that which is contributed as a share is land; money is not used. Furthermore, if that esteemed person is still alive, he himself can make bequests and establish a trust [in his own name or in the name of an ancestor]. This type is more prevalent than the previous type. After this type of corporate land *[gongtian]* is established, the rent is collected year after year. [After some of the] rent money is used for ancestral sacrifices, there is generally a surplus, which is set aside. Money is saved, not grain. Thus, every year the surplus grain is sold to poor people, and the money accumulates. After a certain number of

---

66. Throughout this chapter, "old distribution of land" refers to the situation before the land redistribution.—RT.

years, the savings yield a sum of money, and land is bought. In this way, the trust land gradually increases quite a bit. But using income to increase the total resources of a trust constitutes only a portion of the disbursements; there is also a portion that can be distributed to the descendants of the one [who established the trust]. When most of the descendants are poor, then and only then do they emphasize division. When the descendants are mostly well off, they do not concern themselves with division. When does the division happen? Also, what is the method of division? At New Year's and at other festivals, grain and meat are divided at the ancestral hall. The men all get a share; the women do not get any (in some lineages widows get a share). Every person gets a share of several *dou* of grain and several *jin* of meat. This grain is called the annual grain allowance *[hongding gu]*. There are four ways to distribute meat.

1. Meat for sacrifices. In the past shares were given to those who had won a *xiucai* or *juren* degree. Afterward graduates from new-style schools were added.
2. Meat for branches. Every branch [in the ancestral trust receives] one share.
3. Meat for old people. Every person over the age of seventy receives one share.
4. Meat per capita. Every male gets one share.

The order of the division is as follows. First, the meat for sacrifices [i.e., for degree holders] is distributed and then the meat for old people. Because these two types of people are quite respected, every person gets about 1 *jin*. Next is the meat for branch families. Every branch gets about 8 or 10 *jin*, but there are also ones who get as much as 20 *jin*. After this division is completed, a smaller division is made to the members of the branches. Why do some want a division of the meat by branches? This is a kind of struggle. Those in a branch with few people want to distribute the meat by branches; those in branches with many people oppose distributing the meat by branches and advocate a per capita division of the meat. But the result is that in every area most of the meat is divided by branches; thus the division occurs in accordance with the viewpoint of the branches with the fewest people. Why do the small branches prevail? Because in this kind of property trust, every branch originally had equal rights [and an equal voice]. Next is the division of the meat per capita. Not every trust makes this kind of division. Most trusts lack a per capita division of the meat, because trust monies are few or because there are too many people. A few trusts do not divide the grain and meat equally but rather in rotation. This is called "collecting in turn" or "the one in charge" *[guantou]*. That is, the members of the trust take turns collecting the ancestors' rent. When the rent is collected, every year a small part is used to pay the expenses for sacrifices to the ancestors. Most of the rent money lines the pockets of the one in charge but this certainly is not cheating, because this is the economic basis for the trust. Why? While the patriarch is still alive, he takes the family land and divides it among his children. But because he is afraid that his descendants will later take their share and sell it and there will be nothing left to eat, he takes from his land a part that cannot be divided. This becomes corporate land, forever inalienable. On the one hand, it provides sacrifice money after his death, and, on the other hand, it provides relief for his descendants in difficulties. This is called "providing security." His descendants quite approve of this method because this is their security. When most of these patriarchs are alive, no trusts are established. After the patriarch dies, the descendants, provided they are moderately well off, certainly establish a trust. Nominally this is called "sacrificing to the ancestors," but actually it is for themselves. So the practice of taking turns in receiving the rent is ostensibly collecting rent on behalf of the patriarch, but it is actually taking turns collecting rent on behalf of oneself. Under the circumstances, those poor descendants always clamor to divide the corporate land, whereas the rich descendants are opposed. This becomes a kind of class struggle within a lineage. The poor people clamoring to divide the land do not want to till the land after it is divided. They want to divide the land and sell it to obtain money to pay off loan sharks or to buy gruel for tomorrow's breakfast. In this situation, we can see the poor masses, because of their suffering and inability to get food, gradually abandoning the feudal thought associated with the sacrifices performed for ancestors. Their life compels them to dismiss such treasures.

To sum up ancestral lands, they constitute 24 percent of all land and 60 percent of corporate land.

Religious Trusts

There are six kinds of "religious trusts": god and shrine associations, village communities, temples, Buddhist monasteries, and Daoist monasteries. Every kind and type of god *[shen]* can have an association *[hui];* for example, the Duke of Zhao Association, the Guanyin Association, the Guanye Association, the Dashen Association, the Zhenjun Association, the Potai Association, the Laiye Association, the Gongwang Association, the Bogong Association, the Wenchang Association, and the like. None of these have temples.[67] In this cate-

---

67. Various types of deities are represented in this list, including Buddhist (Guanyin, Potai), extralocal deified mortals (Duke of Zhao, Guandi [Guanye], Wenchang), and apparently local deified mortals (Laiye). For a discussion of these categories, see Arthur P. Wolf, "Gods, Ghosts, and Ancestors," in *Religion and Ritual in Chinese Society,* ed. Wolf (Stanford: Stanford University Press, 1974), pp. 131–82. Several of the gods of these god associations are mentioned in the 1881 Xunwu *xian* gazetteer, in a section on shrines and temples *(cimiao)* (see *Changning xianzhi*). There appear to have been temples for Laigong (Laiye), Wenchang, the Duke of Zhao, and Zhenjun. Since Mao specifically mentions that god associations lacked temples, we must assume that temple associations, becoming divorced from their buildings, perhaps because of state-mandated secularization efforts, had become "god associations" that still controlled land resources.—RT.

gory is also a type of sacrifice association *[jiaohui]* that makes sacrifices to a god. Among the various kinds of gods described above, there are some for whom a shrine *[tan]* is established. A shrine is a place where a stone is set up or [where] several stones are placed to form a small room. Inside is an efficacious god. Because of this it is called a shrine. Whether a god or a shrine association, all associations have trust lands. Rich peasants and landlords put out the money to set up these god associations. Ninety-five percent of the property of these god associations consists of land; 5 percent consists of [contributions of] grain or money. This kind of land, grain, and money is called an association endowment. The purpose is (1) for the god, because the god can protect the health of a contributor's family and livestock and ensure the prosperity and wealth of his family and descendants, and (2) for eating. On the god's birthday, a meal is eaten. At New Year's and other festivals, there is also some meat for those members who contribute dues. Those who contributed membership dues but later become poor can give up their share. For example, if every share consists of a five-*yuan* endowment, when someone is given a five-*yuan* "replacement," he is considered to have resigned from the association. A community *[she]* has a kind of community shrine *[shetan]* that is different from a shrine association. Every village has one. Even if a village only has three families, there is a community shrine. Why do they want a community shrine? To ensure that their crops are not devoured by insects and that their livestock do not get sick, and to ensure the health of the people. Every community has an association. From the beginning of February to the end of October, there is a meeting each month. The meeting is usually scheduled for the second, but in some places it is on the sixteenth. On the day of the meeting, one person from each family in the community comes. Rich or poor, all have a share. A pig is killed and wine purchased for a big feast. After the feast, a meeting is held to discuss affairs like building terraces and water channels, prohibiting livestock from harming fields, and prohibiting careless use of wooded areas. The regulations are numerous, and everyone has his say. Also, there is no chairman; nor is any record [of the proceedings] desired. The discussions are chaotic, but there is a kind of natural order. So when the so-called elders or the enlightened ones voice a reasonable view, then everyone says their words have "been spoken well." [When this happens,] a decision has been reached. This community of the masses is totally different, even though they both believe in gods, from the shrine associations of the rich peasants and landlords.[68] The peasants run this kind of community discussion, not the bullies or

---

68. It seems that similar goals for different socioeconomic classes were met by different organizations. Those god associations whose antecedents can be found in the Xunwu *xian* gazetteer are all located within or just outside the Xunwu City walls. The village associations are discussed by Mao in a decidedly agricultural context. Mao suggests that the political and social functions of each are similar, despite differences in terms of class, economic functions, and location.—RT.

the powerful gentry. Nor is it completely run by rich peasants. The informal chairman is the person whose reasonable manner causes people to trust him. Very few community shrines have public halls. In the majority, when they hold the meeting on the second of every month (to worship the god), everyone contributes money. Each time everyone pays 2, 3, or 4 *mao*; but if a person is not going to eat, he does not have to pay. As for "temples" *[miao]*, they have rooms with images. A temple has a temple caretaker, called a temple elder *[miaolao]* in the local dialect, who is an old man who takes care of the image and tends the lamps and incense. Generally speaking, most temples have land, the rent from which is used to support the temple elder. Elders of the temples without land get their food and sundries from contributions of money and food from the masses. Among the temples are the City God Temple, Guandi Temple, Three Forces Temple, Three Sages Temple, Lailao Temple, Dragon God Temple, Guan[di] and Yue [Fei] Temple,[69] Yanggong Temple,[70] Eastern Mountain [Dongyue] Temple, and Jiangdong Temple. These temples honor "persons whose contributions or virtues caused people to worship them as gods."[71] Shrine associations are needed by landlords; the community shrines are needed by peasants; temples are needed by both landlords and peasants. The land income of the temples is low, and the rent is not enough to pay for the cost of incense, spirit money, and the needs of the temple elder. These are not places engaging in serious exploitation. "Monasteries" *[si]* are different in every respect. These caves of bonzes are places of extreme exploitation. All monastery land is derived from the "bequests" of large landlords, who are called "benefactors." Why do large landlords bequeath land to the monks? Because Buddhism is the religion of the large-landlord class. Large landlords, in order to "benefit" their sons, grandsons, and themselves, bequeath land to the monks. All the following Buddhist monasteries, convents, or temples *[heshang si]* are near the Xunwu City District: Wufu *an*, Huilong *si*, Zhengjue *si*, Guanyin *ge*, Dongbi *shan*, Dabei *ge*, Ehu *an*, Xizhu *shan*, Tiantai *shan*, Shizi *yan*, Sanjiao *dong*, Jiaogong *yan*, Fahua *an*, Xihua *shan*, Nanyang *shan*, Fanhui *si*, Ganlu *si*, and Jiulong *shan*. Daoist vegetarian halls are called "monasteries" *[guan]*; for example, Yungai *dong*, Dashan *li*, Chuantang *keng*, and others. The origin of the property of these monasteries and their exploitative characteristics are the same as those of [Buddhist] monasteries.

---

69. This temple for Guandi and Yue Fei may have been established after President Yuan Shikai's 1916 order directing the establishment of temples to both deified mortals.—RT.

70. For the Ming dynasty origins of this temple, dedicated to a local official, see below Chapter IV, the section **Exploitation**, subsection *Exploitation Through Taxes and Levies*.

71. The text puts in quotation marks a phrase found in local gazetteers that defines certain kinds of temples. For a discussion of these "ethico-political cults" of deified mortals, see C. K. Yang, *Religion in Chinese Society: A Study of Contemporary Social Functions of Religion and Some of Their Historical Factors* (Berkeley: University of California Press, 1967), pp. 158–64.—RT.

To sum up, the landholdings of religious trusts *(shen, tan, she, miao, si, guan)* constitute 8 percent of all land and 20 percent of corporate land.

Administrative Trusts

These are divided into two kinds: (1) land set aside to fund institutions connected with the traditional examination system, the Confucian Temple, and education; and (2) public works-related lands associated with bridge societies, road societies, and tax societies.

The examination hall lands *[kaopeng tian]* of Xunwu City bring in about 650 *dan* of rent. The powerful gentry *[haoshen]* managers skim off 180 *dan* for feasting, which leaves 470 *dan* for the examination hall [account].[72] The examination hall lands originated in the Qing when buildings were constructed and large landlords contributed much grain for the building. Funds not needed for construction were used to buy land, the income from which provided monies for repairs. A Shrine for Esteeming Righteousness [Shangyi ci] was built, and the names of the large landlords who contributed were put on tablets. The tablets of those who contributed the most were put at the top of the display case, and the tablets of those who contributed the least were put on the bottom of the display.

Sojourning stipend lands *[binxing tian]* were also contributed by landlords.[73] These lands are dispersed in every *bao* throughout the *xian*. Most are still managed by the original owner. Half of each year's income is given to the Xunwu City Sojourning Stipend Shrine (Binxing ci). This shrine has a branch bureau in every district to manage the property. Income from the property was used to provide travel money for those taking the provincial- and metropolitan-level imperial examinations and stipends for *juren* and *jinshi* degree holders. (Most was disbursed to provide traveling money for those going to the provincial *[xiangshi]* examinations or awards for those who won degrees at the provincial exams). These awards were also called stipends *[huahong,* lit., flower red]. The *xian* Sojourning Stipend Shrine can collect 1,500 to 1,600 *dan* of rent grain annually. The provincial examinations occurred once every three years, in the *zi*,

---

72. The text uses the compound "examination hall" *(kaopeng).* Although the funds generated from this type of public land seem to have been used in part for educational purposes, the text is not clear.—RT.

73. The term *binxing,* borrowed from the *Zhouli* (Rites of Zhou), means to "raise the virtuous and entertain them as guests at banquets." *Shengyuan* who had been selected to participate in the provincial exams might be invited to attend ceremonies in their honor, feted at a banquet, or given traveling expenses. See Chang Chung-li [Zhang Zhongli], *The Chinese Gentry: Studies on Their Role in Nineteenth-century Chinese Society* (Seattle: University of Washington Press, 1955), p. 41 and 41n166. Mao uses the term in the last sense, and hence *binxing* is translated as "sojourning stipend."—RT.

wu, mao, and *you* years.[74] Over a hundred Xunwu men took the provincial exam each time. Each person received 24 *yuan* for travel expenses. Those who won a *juren* degree received a stipend of more than 100 *yuan*. Within the Sojourning Stipend Shrine are over a hundred tablets on which are written the names of all the powerful gentry who contributed money. After the examination system was abolished, everyone who graduated from the No. 2 Normal School in Ganzhou received travel money of 30 *yuan* to travel in Jiangsu and Zhejiang [to broaden his knowledge]. Furthermore, everyone who went overseas to Japan to study received an allowance of 360 *yuan* for his trip. When Xunwu City built a preliminary normal school and an upper primary school, money from the Sojourning Stipend Shrine [account] was used.

A Confucian temple *[xuegong]* was also built with money contributed by landlords. Just like the Shrine for Esteeming Righteousness and the Sojourning Stipend Shrine, a Shrine for Loving Righteousness [Haoyi ci] was built to commemorate these contributions. Later, more than 1,000 *yuan* was donated for the annual worship of Confucius—this was in currency, not land.

Educational lands were contributed by every surname group of landlords in order to encourage the young people of their surname group to take the [Qing] examinations. Every surname group has these lands. For example, the Gu of Huangxiang contributed land that yields rent of 100 *dan*. The Kuang of Chetou gave land yielding over 200 *dan*. At the least, the contributions amounted to several dozen *dan*. Furthermore, Xunwu City District, like every other district, has a teacher salary association. Throughout every district there are also literary societies. These resemble associations for encouraging people to study for the examinations, but they are a kind of local form in which a group of families or a whole district unites together. Also, a certain landlord in the Gu family of Huangxiang (Gu Bo's paternal grandfather) contributed land yielding 100 *dan* of rent to build a Hall for Recognizing the Educated [Zunyu tang]. This rewards students from throughout the county, but this is a special case.

To sum up, land connected with education amounts to 4 percent of all land and 10 percent of corporate land.

A rather considerable amount of land is associated with public works-related organizations like bridge associations, road associations, and tax associations. Not only do large bridges and long bridges have associations, even small bridges in villages have associations. If there is a bridge, then there is land, because landlords and merchants contribute to maintain bridges. When a bridge is first built, there is little money [in the bridge fund], but year after year enough rent is

---

74. This refers to "branches" in the traditional sixty-year cycle designated by sixty unique combinations of characters taken from the ten "stems" and twelve "branches." The first, fourth, seventh, and tenth branches in the text would appear, for example, in the combinations corresponding to 1900, 1903, 1906, and 1909.—RT.

collected and saved so that land can be bought. Every year in December, an accounting is made and the bridge god is worshiped. This is called "gathering for the bridge association." The contributors all come together to eat, and afterward they divide up the pork. Actually the bridge association is an organization for exploitation. Larger bridge associations, such as the Fu Bridge Association in Liuche, have 8,000 *yuan*, and their property brings in 500 *dan* of rent each year. Smaller ones get 2 to 3 *dan* of rent—these are the smallest of the small bridges.

There are not many road associations, and no association owns much land. In the whole *xian* there are more than fifteen such associations. Each road association only takes in about 7 or 8 *dan* of grain. Why do bridge associations [have more assets] than road associations? Because, unlike a bridge, a road in disrepair is easy to fix; even if it is not fixed, it does not ever get to the point that people cannot use it.

There are only a few tax associations in the *xian*. For example, the Yan of Huangxiang have one, as do the Mei of Datian, the Kuang of Chetou, or the Liu of Chuanxia in Jitan, and each association has some land. The richest is that of the Kuang of Chetou. Their tax association has land with rents of 500 *dan*. Originally it was called "army land," but now it is called a tax association. The purpose of the tax association is to be responsible for an entire lineage's tax quota in order to counteract the government's grasping taxation of every family in the lineage. With every type of extortion and blackmail, tax collecting was harmful to all involved; to prevent this, a tax association would be established, or money would be collected from small ancestral trusts. If [a lineage] has a tax association, then the authorities collect taxes only from the tax association, and hence every family avoids harm. Without a tax association, the authorities take more than the quota. If the payment is late, then interest is computed and it is really high. Because of this, tax associations are started. When a tax association is organized, it has little money, but after several years it mounts up.

To sum up, public works-related land constitutes 4 percent of all land and 10 percent of corporate land.

Large Landlords

Above I discussed the land held by trusts. Now I turn to the land of individual landlords. The land owned by individual landlords constitutes 30 percent of all land, which is much less than the amount of land owned by the trusts. Of this land, small landlords (rents under 200 *dan*) own the greatest part; middle landlords (rents of 200 to 499 *dan*) are next; and large landlords (rents over 500 *dan*) own the least. In the whole country there are eight pre-eminent landlords:

Liu Tuyuan	Xunwu City District
Luo Hanzhang	Huangxiang District
Xie Jie	Nanba District
Kuang Wenrong	Nanba District
Mei Hongxing	Shuangqiao District
Pan Mingzheng (nicknamed "Uncle Shitcrock")	Jiansan District
Lin Chaoguan	Chengjiang District
Wang Juyuan	Chengjiang District

Each receives rents of 1,000 *dan* or more. The greatest among these is considered Uncle Shitcrock, who is from Xiangshan *bao* in Jiansan District. The value of all his holdings—land, buildings, forests, livestock, and his herb store and general store in Jitan—is 300,000 *yuan*. His land rents are about 10,000 *dan*. He is the leader of the powerful gentry throughout the *xian*. In the early Republic, his third son, Pan Mengchun (an illiterate scoundrel who did not pass the civil service exam or attend a new-style school), became chief of the *xian* Tax Collection Bureau (national taxes). In 1917 or 1918, his eldest son, Pan Yiren (a *xiucai* who is more or less literate), finished his three years as chief of the Tax Collection Bureau (local taxes, managing funds from the examination hall and Sojourning Stipend Shrine lands, the ox tax, the gambling tax, the business protection tax, and others). In 1924 or 1925 Pan Mengchun became the head of the All-*Xian* Protection Militia and controlled the militias of all seven districts. All true power was in his hands. He was head of the All-*Xian* Militia and needed money [for it]. At the same time the Beiyang Army's Deng Ruzhuo[75] came to the *xian* to ask for money, and Pan issued a lot of paper money. After these bills had been in use for several months, a middle landlord named Lai Aoxu in the provincial capital brought suit against him and only then was this practice stopped. In 1926, when the Guomindang's influence reached Xunwu, he lost his clout. But he immediately united with the New Xunwu faction, which, although it originally had the character of the bourgeoisie, was cooperating with the landlords at that time. He became a member of the Guomindang's *xian* branch. In March of this year, the powerful gentry brought down Magistrate Hu Zefan, and Pan became magistrate. When the Red Army arrived, he fled to Wuping. His seventy-odd guns were taken over by Zhong Shaokui of Wuping. Liu Tuyuan is the second great local bully, but he is not active. He is a graduate of a middle school and has no power in the *xian*. Xie Jie is a graduate of the Jiangxi Army Academy and was a division commander under Lai Shihuang. Now he is in Shanghai organiz-

---

75. Deng Ruzhuo was the brigade commander of the Ninth Mixed Brigade for the Beiyang warlord army and the division commander of the First Division between 1924 and 1925.

ing the South Jiangxi Mining Association in order to encourage [Chinese-operated] mines. He has joined the Reorganization faction [Gaizu pai] that organized the Jiangxi Self-salvation Society [Zijiuhui] and publishes the *Zijiu ribao* [Self-salvation Daily] and opposes Chiang Kaishek. He is zealous in calling for "mopping up the Communists." Wang Juyuan is a graduate of Ganzhou's No. 4 Middle School. He is influential in Chengjiang and is on good terms with the vagabonds. He has opened three shops in Chengjiang for marine products, general goods, and opium. In the back of the shops he has opened opium dens and invites the vagabonds to come and take opium for free. Because of this, he gets their support. He messes with other men's wives but if other people have no sense of propriety and go whoring, they are severely tormented by the vagabonds. Those who receive this kind of torment can be completely ruined financially.

Xunwu's large landlords (500 to 999 *dan*) number twelve.

Cao Shancheng (Tianbei, West Ward). Five hundred *dan*; his grandfather [was the one who] got rich; he is from an old rich family [lit., *laoshuihu,* or old tax family].

Qiu Shulie (Tuhe, West Ward). Five hundred *dan*; a useless person; his son is an engineer who graduated from Nanyang University and went to England for a while; now he is in Tianjin serving as an engineer for some boiler company.

Cao Yuansen (East Ward). Five hundred *dan*; a graduate of Xunwu City Upper Primary School; forty *sui*; he is a power in the East Ward.

Huang Jiabin (Changju, North Ward). Seven hundred *dan*; Guomindang member; He Zizhen wanted to use him, but he would not agree. Now he opportunistically expresses sympathy toward peasants. If they want guns, he gives them guns. If they want money, he gives them money. He said: "The Guomindang is useless. If I pay them, I still don't get protection; but if the money goes to the soviet, it can save my life."

Xie Shande (Yazimu, Sanbiao). Five hundred *dan*; he is a reader of old books and a hermit *[shanlaoshu]*.

Wang Fosheng (Aobei, Shuiyuan). Five hundred *dan*; his son Wang Weifan, a graduate of Chaoyang University in Beijing, is a Guomindang member who left and has not returned.

Lan Shaozong (Chengjiang). Five hundred *dan*; since his death, his widow has handled family affairs.

Cao Guodong (Jitan). Six hundred *dan*; in the past his was called a 10,000-*dan* family, but he used some money to build a mansion; a graduate of upper primary school; a relative of Uncle Shitcrock; cooperates with Pan Mengchun.

Yi Zhanliang (Guishixia, Shuangqiao District). More than 500 *dan*; at the beginning he was a reactionary, but his land was quickly divided and he was fined more than 1,000 *yuan*, so he became poor; not a reactionary.

Lai Pengchi (Danxi, Shuangqiao District). Called a 10,000-*dan* family; more than 500 *dan*; a Qing *fusheng;* very conservative, still has a queue, but not reactionary.

Kuang Mingjing (Jizijiao, Nanba). Six hundred *dan*; his fourth brother is a White army battalion commander; whole family has fled.

Chen Wanbao (Tingling). Six hundred *dan*; deals in pork and opium and runs a general store; he himself is not a reactionary, but his brother is a member of the New Xunwu faction and lives in the same household; his brother is very reactionary.

The above eight great landlords and the twelve second-level landlords together number twenty. When Jiangxi people speak of "10,000-dan families," they mean these people. Why have I listed them one by one? In order to study the class's political function. If we failed to mention examples, then we would not have substantive evidence. For this reason, I want to list examples of middle landlords. However, it is not easy to list small landlords because there are too many. Why do we distinguish middle landlords within the landlord class? Because not only is their political function greatly different from that of small landlords, but it is obviously different from that of large landlords.

Middle Landlords

Xunwu City District

Qiu Weiwu (Tuhe, West Ward). Four hundred *dan*; graduated from the Leather Course of the Imperial University in Japan;[76] worked as an engineer at Ganzhou Poor People's Factory for six months; returned to Xunwu in 1922 to serve as head of the Education Bureau; joined the Guomindang; one of the leaders of New Xunwu faction and helped make plans for the faction; tough guy; ran away with Xie Jiayou when the Red Army arrived in Xunwu.

Huang Jiakui (Changju, North Ward). Over 300 *dan*; Pingyuan Middle School graduate; member of Guomindang Executive Committee in Xunwu; member of New Xunwu faction (teacher at New Xunwu School); active reactionary.

Luo Songsheng (Changju, North Ward). Three hundred *dan*; runs the Luo Jinfeng General Store in the city; not very reactionary; his nephew is a

---

76. Mao may have misunderstood his informants. If we assume "Imperial University in Japan" is a reference to the Imperial University of Tokyo, which was the proper nomenclature beginning in 1897, there was no course corresponding to the "Leather Course." Of the university's six colleges (Law, Medicine, Engineering, Literature, Science, and Agriculture) in the 1910s, the most likely place for Qiu's course of study would have been the College of Agriculture. This college had five courses (Chinese: *ke*) of study: Agriculture, Agricultural Chemistry, Forestry, Veterinary Medicine, and Fisheries. See the *Calendar* (1917–18) of the Imperial University of Tokyo, pp. 202–3.—RT.

Guomindang member and a higher primary school graduate who speaks badly of the Communist Party.

He Tingba (outside North Gate). Over 300 *dan*; a graduate of Pingyuan Middle School; member of the Guomindang; major figure in the New Xunwu faction; energetically works against the revolution.

Liu Forong (outside Little East Gate). Three hundred *dan*; is not a reactionary; works as a doctor.

Sanshui District

Lei Changxiang (Changpai, Sanbiao). Three hundred *dan*; a "hermit"; useless.

Hu Enrong (Sanbiao *xu*). Three hundred *dan*; a religious vegetarian; uninterested in current events; tends to look for a few coppers and then stays at home and sleeps.

Hu Jingru (Sanbiao *xu*). Two hundred *dan*; graduate of No. 4 Middle School in Ganzhou; in his twenties; famous local strongman in Sanbiao; involved in *xian* politics.

Ling Lushi (Jingshi, Sanbiao). Over 300 *dan*; an old *xiucai*; in the past served as Tax Collection Bureau chief for many years; was a section chief of something; official in charge of examinations; after working for over ten years, he accumulated some savings; built a new house in Sanbiao; in his fifties.

Yuan Dehe (Yuanwu, Shuiyuan, the most reactionary area). Two hundred *dan* or so; middle school graduate; member of the Guomindang; counterrevolutionary.

There are many other middle landlords in Sanshui District, but it is difficult to name them all.

Chengjiang District

Lan Ziqian. Four hundred *dan*; provincial middle school graduate; owns the Lan Xietai general goods and textile store in Chengjiang; counterrevolutionary.

Xie Jiayou. Three hundred *dan*; higher primary school graduate; in his forties; was a regimental commander under Xie Jie in the Fourteenth Army; the head captain of the Xunwu militia; member of the Reorganization faction; he was the one who wiped out the First Battalion of the Fiftieth Regiment of the Red Army; graduated from the Jiangxi Army Academy.

Ling Xixian. Three hundred *dan*; a middle school graduate; member of the New Xunwu faction; member of the Guomindang; owns a store in Chengjiang Xin *xu*.

Jiansan District

Chen Yuheng (Jitan). Three hundred *dan*; graduate of Pingyuan Middle School; local strongman at Jitan; major figure in the New Xunwu faction; Uncle Shitcrock's grandson-in-law; very active.

Liu Taizang (Chuanxia, Jitan). Four hundred *dan*; a gambling boss; started as a vagabond; became rich through gambling; until 1916 he was a *dangwu* (a thief who tunnels into the walls of a house, and comes out at night, is called a *dangwu*).[77]

Pan Jindi (Xiangshan). Over 200 *dan*; graduate of Mei *xian* Normal School; a member of the New Xunwu faction; an active Guomindang member; the commander of Jitan Pacification and Defense Militia.

Pan Mingrui (Xiangshan). Four hundred *dan*; relative of Uncle Shitcrock; owns two stores in Jitan for general goods and marine products; the leader of Xiangshan reactionaries.

Pan Guanlan. Although he is a small landlord with a hundred-odd *dan* income, he is a reactionary leader; Pan Li died by his hand; graduated from Ganzhou Higher Primary School; worked as a primary school teacher for five or six years, he was not a reactionary at that time; was corrupted into a counterrevolutionary around the time of the March 25 uprising; his father was a gambling boss and made his money that way.

Pan Mingdian (Pingdi, Xiangshan). Over 100 *dan*; a Qing *bagong;* graduated from a school of law and administration during the Republican period; was a magistrate in Lufeng [Guangdong] and Huichang [Jiangxi]; was the head of the Education Bureau in Xunwu *xian* for a few years; was assigned to many other positions; known as *Shenjianjiuzhang* [one who holds many posts simultaneously]; originally was a middle landlord; has spent over 4,000 *yuan* campaigning for election to the provincial assembly but still has not been elected; was the warden of Nanchang High Court last year; this year he is a clerk in the Jiujiang High Court; a bureaucratic frame of mind; speaks well; has good calligraphy; handsome appearance; very proper; resembles Confucius.

Pan Jingwen (Dali, Xiangshan). Over 300 *dan*, a Qing *xiucai*; an old scholar.

Pan Guocai (Xiangshancun). Three hundred *dan*; also an old *xiucai*.

---

77. This parenthetical remark is part of Mao's text. The second character in *dangwu* is that for "crow," and the compound might be translated "to behave like a crow." (*Wuhe*, or "a gathering of crows" refers to a disorderly mob.) Presumably the meaning here is that before 1916 Liu was a burglar.

Pan Guoqing (Xiangshancun). Only 50 or 60 *dan*; higher primary school graduate; secretary to the bandit Ye Zishe; counterrevolutionary.

Liu Hanyuan (Jianxi). Over 200 *dan*; good for nothing.

Huangxiang District

Li Qilang (Huangxiang *xu*). Over 300 *dan*; gambling background; his son, Li Hanhui, a higher primary school graduate, is an important member of the reactionary faction.

Liu Yujie (Huangxiang *xu*). Over 200 *dan*; his son, Liu Jinyan, went to Xinyuan Middle School in Nanchang and then to Hujiang University and Shanghai University for some time, previously was close to the Cooperative Society faction.

Liu Yulin, younger brother of Liu Yujie. Four hundred *dan*; is a mute; has four or five sons who graduated from primary school; his youngest son went to middle school; all participated in the March 25 uprising; now they are counterrevolutionaries.

Lai Shoucheng (Hongtouling). Four hundred *dan*; his son, Lai Shifang, studied at East Mountain Middle School in Mei *xian*; counterrevolutionary.

Lai Aoxu (Hongtouling). Four hundred *dan*; *xiucai*; graduated from Shanghai Technical Training School; principal of the *xian* higher primary school for one year; was a teacher for five or six years; campaigned for the provincial assembly but lost; has two sons who went to middle school; one of them graduated from Beijing Normal School and is close to the Cooperative Society faction; the New Xunwu faction attacked him during the March 25 uprising, and now both sons are counterrevolutionaries.

Wang Ziyuan (Shanzixia). Two hundred *dan*; reactionary leader in Huangxiang; is a great evil gentryman *[lieshen]*; was the head of a protection militia *[baowei tuan]*; the head of an educational trust.

Liu Jingxi (Sichengcun). Over 300 *dan*; graduated from Mei *xian* Middle School; his father worked for Hu Qian and was killed by bandits; is not a reactionary.

Liu Quanlan (Sicheng). About 200 *dan*; started out as a usurer; is not a reactionary now; his son joined the peasants' association, but because of a misunderstanding he was mistakenly shot to death by the peasants.

Luo Chengtian (Xiwei). Four hundred *dan*; bargains with merchants even when purchasing a tiny bit of tobacco; a miser; values money more than life. That whole village of his is counterrevolutionary.

Luo Fushou (Xiwei). Used to have 300 *dan*; now the property has been divided; a counterrevolutionary.

Luo Peici (Xiwei). Two hundred *dan*; was Yudu *xian* magistrate; is a very cunning person; before the March 25 uprising occurred, while everybody was still preparing in secret, he spied [it coming]; he walked about the countryside urging [other landlords] to pretend to reform; "Sell your family's grain at a fair price and don't try to make money. Or give the grain to poor people with the same surname. If you don't, there's going to be real trouble." He is a reactionary leader; among the powerful gentry, he's fearsome.

Luo Lushou (Xiwei). Two hundred *dan*; his son is a member of the New Xunwu faction who likes attention.

Gu Lesan (Tangbei). Three hundred *dan* (with his brother); his older brother is a *xiucai* and was a provincial assemblyman for two terms; he [Gu Lesan] worked under Hu Qian as a commissariat officer; was a district head in Wuhua *xian* during the Chen Jiongming period; one of the reactionary leaders in the *xian*; taking 30–40 guns, he fled with Xie Jiayou.

Gu Guangrui (Tangbei). Over 200 *dan*; higher primary school graduate; reactionary.

Gu Hua'nan (Tangbei). Two hundred *dan*; is an honest man.

Gu Guanglu (Tangbei). Four hundred *dan*; stingy; likes to take advantage of other people; haggles with a vendor over small dishes; his son is a graduate of East Mountain Middle School in Mei *xian*; he is a fellow who cannot figure out much.

(The Tangbei Gu listed above are Gu Bo's relatives.)

Gu Youyu (Tangbei). Five hundred *dan*; operates a paper store; sells raw opium; runs a brothel; indulges in gambling; is a miser, indifferent to current events, cares only about making money; he is the weak one in a powerful family; his family takes advantage of him; if they ask for 50 *yuan*, they get 50 *yuan*; if they ask for 100, they get 100.

Yan Jinxiu (Gaotou). Used to be a 10,000-*dan* family; he became poor after spending too much money building his house; he now has about 300 or 400 *dan*; owns a store in Gongping; has over ten children and grandchildren; apathetic toward the world; primary concern is money; is a "hermit."

Yan Guoxing (Gaotou). Over 100 *dan*; a small landlord; main pursuit is business; runs a general store in Gongping; also sells paper; had good relations with other businesses; some merchants from Beiling and Yanxia lent him money; together with his own money he spent about 6,000 to 7,000 *yuan* when he ran for the provincial assembly; he lost and now is in debt; one of the reactionary leaders in Huangxiang District.

Yan Xibo (Gaotou). Two hundred *dan*; runs a general store in Gongping; not extremely reactionary.

(In the above list, several small landlords are mentioned because they are well known.)

Shuangqiao District

Huang Qingyun (Huangtian). Two hundred *dan*; not a reactionary.

Luo Shouhan (Huangsha). Two hundred *dan*; not a reactionary.

Zhao Shangqin (Yutian). Three hundred *dan*; Pingyuan Middle School graduate; reactionary.

Xie Youfeng (Yutian). Two hundred *dan*; not a reactionary.

Chen Dequan (Liuche). Two hundred *dan*; ran a salt store in Liuche; reactionary; the Twenty-first Column executed him.

Chen Jingri (Liuche). Two hundred *dan*; not a reactionary. His son, Chen Jiguang, participated in the March 25 uprising; Mei *xian* Middle School graduate; after the failure of the March 25 uprising, he escaped to Southeast Asia.

Chen Shanniu (Liuche). An inveterate gambler; over 200 *dan*; not a reactionary.

Chen Biaoji (Zukeng, Liuche). Used to be a 10,000-*dan* family; later was divided into four households; since his death, his son "Dunziliu" [Fatty the Sixth] has 300 *dan*; owns a marine products store in Liuche; is a reactionary leader.

Chen Guocai (Zukeng, Liuche). Two hundred *dan*; Mei *xian* Middle School graduate; reactionary.

Chen Tufeng (Zukeng, Liuche). Over 200 *dan*; an evil gentryman; one of the "Five Tigers of Xunwu." "Pan (Mingdian), Xie (Xuzuo), Chen (Tufeng), Peng (Zijing), Kuang (Tailan) are the so-called Five Tigers of Xunwu." With the rise of the two new factions, New Xunwu and the Cooperative Society, the five old tigers fell from the [political] stage. Chen, Pan, Peng, and Kuang are *xiucai*; only Xie is a graduate (Xunwu Preliminary Normal School).

Liao Honggui (Shijie). Two hundred *dan*; has a store that carries marine products, general goods, and pastries in Fengshan; not a reactionary.

Liu Junfu (Qiufang). Used to be a 10,000-*dan* family; after division, he now has 400 *dan*; his son Liu Hongxiang graduated from South Jiangxi [Gannan] Middle School; later he went to Culture University in Beijing; is incoherent and yet very reactionary; is one of the counterrevolutionary leaders in Shuangqiao District; he still is guarding the [Qiufang] stronghold with his life.

Liu Shifu. A brother of Liu Junfu's; over 200 *dan*; once donated some money to set up a primary school; is still in the stronghold.

Liu Yuanying (Qiufang). Over 200 *dan*; in the stronghold.

Liu Zuorui (Qiufang). Four hundred *dan*; his large family consists of about thirty members; participated in the revolution; the family property was divided. The reason was that earlier he competed with Liu Junfu in buying land; later they quarreled with each other because of an adultery case; some of his family members took part in the March 25 uprising; after its defeat, Liu Junfu brought a false charge against him and colluded with the bandit Ye Zishe and burned down Liu Zuorui's house. Now his nephew Liu Guoxiang is a soviet committee member. Liu Risheng is a township soviet committee member; he himself [Liu Zuorui] stays at home and cares about nothing. He graduated from the No. 5 Middle School in Mei *xian*; very honest; twenty-three or twenty-four *sui*; even younger than his nephew; the lawsuit was handled by his nephew's father, that is, his older brother.

Liu Baohua (Shibei). Three hundred *dan*; his son graduated from the Sun Yatsen Middle School in the *xian*; is involved in the revolution; is a Communist Party district committee secretary.

Liu Kaixiang (Shibei). Two hundred *dan*; higher primary school graduate; not a reactionary.

Tang Sixian (Xiaqi). Three hundred *dan*; graduated from Mei *xian* Middle School, a cadre of the New Xunwu faction; a complete reactionary.

Tang Lixian (Xiaqi). Two hundred *dan*; was a student at Whampoa Military Academy; was a head of a pacification and defense corps; member of the New Xunwu faction.

Tang Foshu (Xiaqi). Two hundred *dan*; is an evil gentryman; people called him a local strongman; graduated from the Primary School Teacher Training Institute; a lackey of the New Xunwu faction.

Zeng Chaoqun (Shangqi). Over 100 *dan*;[78] Mei *xian* Middle School graduate; not a reactionary.

Zeng Xilin (Fangtian). Three hundred *dan*; received a traditional education; makes extremely usurious loans; he and his nephew Zeng Guanghua (a primary school graduate) are extremely [lit., 120 percent] reactionary; they are besieged in the Qiufang stronghold by the peasants.

Zeng Juxiang (Fangtian). Two hundred *dan*; his nephew is Zeng Chanfeng; a higher primary school graduate; a member of the Communist Party whose house was burned down by the bandit Ye Zishe.

---

78. A note to the Chinese edition explains that Mao included Zeng Chaoqun in the list of middle peasants, even though he had less than 200 *dan* of lands, because Zeng and his brother together had owned more than 200 *dan* before the family property was split up. The figure cited here is that for Zeng Chaoqun's share after the division.

Zeng Hailan (Bogongao). Used to be a 10,000-*dan* family; recently the property was divided, and he got 200-odd *dan*; participated in the March 25 uprising; he spent 1,000-odd *yuan* in a lawsuit brought by Zeng Xilin; Bandit Ye also fined him; one of his younger brothers was fined over 600 *yuan* by Bandit Ye; not a reactionary now.

Yi Songzhou (Guishixia). Two hundred *dan*, a Qing *xiucai*; an evil gentryman; colluded with Bandit Ye; has fled.

He Ziwen (Danxi). In the past a 10,000-*dan* family; land was divided, and now he has more than 200 *dan*; not too reactionary.

Widow Zhong (Danxi). Over 200 *dan*; a reactionary; fled.

Lai Rongjun (Cenfeng). Over 200 *dan*; was a minor evil gentryman; now he is not a reactionary.

Mei Renhua (Cenfeng). Two hundred *dan*; not a reactionary.

Mei Diaoxian (Datian). *Xiucai*; 300 *dan*; member of the reactionary faction; fled.

Lai Wenlian (Datong). Three hundred *dan*; was caught by the Twenty-first Column of the Red Army and was fined 2,000 *yuan*; his land was divided and distributed; not a reactionary now.

Kuang Chunlong (Yanyangping). Two hundred *dan*; a usurer; property was confiscated; not a reactionary now.

Kuang Shiyang (Yanyangping). Two hundred *dan*; graduated from Mei *xian* Normal School; Guomindang member; very reactionary.

Kuang Yingshao (Huangqiangping). Two hundred *dan*; not a reactionary.

Kuang Lanchun (Huangqiangping). Two hundred *dan*; not a reactionary.

Chen (née Tao) Xianggu (Zukeng). Three hundred *dan*; widow who handles her own affairs; started as a gambler; counterrevolutionary.

Nanba District

Liu Huangxian (Longtu). Three hundred *dan*; counterrevolutionary; was executed by shooting.

Liu Tianyuan (Longtu). Three hundred *dan*; counterrevolutionary; surrendered after one of his sons was killed.

Liu Huantong (Longtu). Three hundred *dan*; was fined over 1000 *yuan* by the Red Army; now he is not a reactionary.

Liu Shidi (Longtu). Two hundred *dan*; a Qing *xiucai*; reactionary faction; the whole family fled.

Liu Zhenguang (Hejiao *xu*). Two hundred *dan*; his third son is a reactionary who fled; the other sons are not reactionary.

Liu Meirong (Hejiao *xu*). Two hundred *dan*; not a reactionary.

Zeng Yuehui (Hejiao *xu*). Two hundred *dan*; not a reactionary; his widow manages household affairs.

Zeng (née Lu) Fuxing (Hejiao *xu*). Two hundred *dan*; has some savings; colluded with Bandit Ye; whole family is reactionary and has fled.

Chen Erlaihe (Jizijiao). Two hundred *dan*; he, his sons, and his nephews were executed by shooting by the Red Army; were very reactionary.

Zhao Zhixiang (Chetou). Two hundred *dan*; old scholar; used to be a bit of an "evil" [gentryman]; not a reactionary.

Zhao Zan (Yanger) (Chetou). Two hundred *dan*; the whole family is reactionary; fled to the Qiufang stronghold; a gambler; his grandfather made the [family's] money.

Zhao Ener (Chetou). Two hundred *dan*; honest; engages in business; runs the Huaxing Store in Chetou, which was set on fire this year during the third attack by [militia from] the four *xian*;[79] his father was killed; not a reactionary.

Zhao Yinghua (Chetou). Two hundred *dan*; used to be a 10,000-*dan* family; he divided his land and gave half of it to his four sons, the other half is for himself and his wife; (when dividing family property, to keep a share for oneself is called *zuo zaozi*, "to sit on the stove"); not a reactionary; has temporarily given his remaining savings to the son who has the most children.

Wen Zanbiao (Qinglong). Over 200 *dan*; higher primary school graduate; not a reactionary.

Zhong Wenfa (Zhucun). Four hundred *dan*; has both a salt and a grain business; his grandfather willed him some money; not reactionary.

Zhong Bansan (Zhucun). Three hundred *dan*; has some property willed by his grandfather; used to gamble; sometimes serves as a mediator; not a reactionary.

Zhong Jishan (Zhucun). Two hundred *dan*; studied at the Mei *xian* Middle School; participated in the revolution; works for the Fifth Column of the Eleventh Army of the Red Army.

---

79. This was an attack by militia from Anyuan, Huichang, Pingyuan, and Xingning.—RT.

Zhong "Big Face" Liu[80] (Zhucun *xu*). Three hundred *dan*; old rich family; gambles; reactionary; the whole family has fled.

Zhong Yongliu (Zhucun *xu*). Two hundred *dan*; studied in Japan; was the head of the Wuxue [Hubei] police station; was a first-class section clerk, investigator, and the chief of the Industry Bureau in this *xian*; worked for Xie Jie; one of the reactionary leaders in Nanba District; fled to Pingyuan.

Peng Zijing (Gukenggang). Three hundred *dan*; a Qing *xiucai*; one of the Five Tigers in the *xian*; in the late Qing he was a police chief *[xunjian]* in Fenghuang Autonomous Subprefecture in Hunan; in the Republican period he was a member of the Xunwu *xian* Tax Collection Bureau and accepted bribes from gamblers; recently has worked as a commissariat officer in a unit of a militia *[tuan fangdui]*; has participated in every rural mop-up operation. His son, Peng Bingyi, graduated from the Mei *xian* Middle School; member of the New Xunwu faction and of the Guomindang; was the principal of the Zhichi Primary School. The whole family is extremely reactionary.

Li Zude (Gukenggang). Used to be a 10,000-*dan* family; suffered business losses; only 300 *dan* left; the whole family is reactionary; fled.

Peng Hongyun (Xialiao). Two hundred *dan*; not so reactionary; has a general store in Xialiao.

Peng Hongquan. Peng Hongyun's brother; 200 *dan*; reactionary; fled to Pingyuan.

Peng Jinhan (Xialiao). Two hundred *dan*; runs several businesses; has an herbal medicine store and a general store; very money-minded; not a reactionary.

Han Foxian (Mankeng). Two hundred *dan*; did some business and farming; honest man, but also fled to Pingyuan.

Zhong Yicai (Lintianba). Three hundred dan; higher primary school graduate; in his grandfather's time, his was a 10,000-*dan* family, but the land was divided among two families; did not accept the revolution and fled; now he is willing to be fined because he wants to return home.

Zhong Dingsi (Lintianba). Two hundred *dan*; has some property willed by his grandfather; some of his children are cultivators; not a reactionary; "worries about communal property" *[gongchan]* .

---

80. The editors of *Mao Zedong nongcun diaocha wenji* mentioned Zhong "Damian" Liu as an example of the types of puzzles presented by the text that they were able to solve during their investigations in Jiangxi. In this case, a man surnamed "Zhong" had a large face *(damian)*. "Liu," the editors found out, referred to his place in the family tree. See *Guangming ribao*, February 12, 1983, p. 3.—RT.

Zhong Shufen (Lintianba). Two hundred *dan*; he is dead; his widow manages the household; fined 200 *yuan*; not a reactionary.

Xie Ruilin (Niudouguang). Three hundred *dan*; doctor; unwilling to accept a fine; fled.

Xie Zhaofan (Niudouguang). Two hundred *dan*; member of the New Xunwu faction; graduated from the South Jiangxi Middle School; was the head of a protection militia; recently was the captain of a pacification and defense militia; after the success of the revolution in Nanba District, he worked as a secretary in the reactionary *xian* government; is one of the reactionary leaders in Nanba District.

Chen Chunrong (Tingling). Two hundred *dan*; honest; his son is a higher primary school graduate and served as a company commander in the White army; reactionary; the whole family fled to Pingyuan.

Chen Liuji (Niudouguang). Three hundred *dan*; had stores [selling] oil, grain, and soybeans in both Liuche and Niudouguang; colluded with Bandit Ye; very reactionary; the whole family fled.

Chen Zhongjun (Tingling). Two hundred *dan*; honest; his son was a head of a protection militia; not a reactionary.

Xie Peiqin (Fengshugang, Niudouguang). Four hundred *dan*; was a usurer; many inveterate gamblers borrowed money from him; his son was studying at the New Xunwu School; reactionary; fled.

Chen Anru (Tingling). Three hundred *dan*; trader of pigs and oxen; runs a boarding house; was fined; it is unlikely that he is a reactionary now.

Zeng Rensheng (Lianping). Over 300 *dan*; did farming himself; made money by gambling; did not pay his fine; fled.

Zhong Xingkui (Longhukeng, Zhucun). Two hundred *dan*; graduated from the Pingyuan Middle School; participated in Guomindang affairs; graduated from Nanchang Political Tutelage Training School; major figure in the New Xunwu faction; extremely reactionary.

Altogether there are 113 middle landlords in the seven districts of the *xian*.[81]

---

81. There are some discrepancies. The concluding statement that there are 113 middle landlords in Xunwu *xian* contrasts with Mao's earlier admission that it is "difficult to name" all the middle landlords in Sanshui District. Also, 116 middle landlords are named in the preceding list. Of that number, Pan Guanlan, Pan Mingdian, and Pan Guoqing (Jiansan); Yan Guoxing (Huangxiang), and Zeng Chaoqun (Shuangqiao) had less than 200 *dan*, the minimum amount required for the middle-landlord classification. Furthermore, the only way there could be "several small landlords" in Huangxiang, besides the clear case of Yan Guoxing, would be to assume that Luo Fushou became a small landlord after

Attitudes of Large and Middle Landlords Toward Production

The middle landlords, who receive 200 *dan* in rent or more, and the large landlords, who receive 500 *dan* or more in rent, pay no attention to production. They do not work personally and also do not organize production—their only goal is to sit around and watch the rents come in. Certainly every large and middle landlord has some land cultivated [under his direction], but his purpose is not to improve production methods or increase productivity. You cannot get rich on this. In order to avoid the dilemma of having no use for accumulated human and animal wastes and also to keep hired hands from being idle, the landlord selects the richest of his own land and cultivates land yielding 10 to 20 *dan* of grain. None cultivates enough land to yield 40 to 50 *dan*. This kind of landlord normally hires one worker. Only the large landlords of 10,000 *dan* or above and households without much manpower hire two workers. In order to make sure that workers do not loaf, landlords ask them to cultivate small plots of land in addition to doing other odd jobs.

Political Attitudes of Large and Middle Landlords

The life-styles of large and middle landlords can be divided into three categories on the basis of the situation in Xunwu. The first kind is the progressives *[xinde]*, who have been influenced the most by capitalism. Their life-style is comparatively luxurious. They spend freely and want to buy every kind of foreign-style good. The clothes they wear button down the middle, and they have Western-style haircuts. They are relatively keen on sending their sons to school or have themselves graduated from middle school or other kinds of schools. There are relatively few people of this type among the landlord class; most of them live near rivers or near markets. Most of them have merchant backgrounds. Wang Juyuan of Chengjiang is a good example. The second type is the moderates [lit., half-new, but not old]. They approve of new trends a bit, but right away criticize their weak points. They build schools and serve as heads of the Education Bureau, but the schools they establish are the traditional rotten ones. They become head of the Education Bureau in order to get power and money, not to "enlighten the people and promote education." In the past most of those who served as Education Bureau heads were in this category. The first type are too progressive for the job. The landlords in this group are not misers but they are not profligates

---

his land was redistributed and that the joint ownership of 300 *dan* by Gu Lesan and his brother meant that both men, separately, were classified as small landlords. This survey of Xunwu's middle landlords was skewed toward areas that had already been subject to land redistribution earlier in the year. There are 93 names given for landlords in the three southern districts in Xunwu: Huangxiang (20), Shuangqiao (36), and Nanba (37). There are 23 landlords listed for the four northern districts, which fell to Red Army troops in the spring of l930: Chengjiang (3), Xunwu City District (5), Sanshui (5), and Jiansan (l0).—RT.

either. Most of the large and middle landlords are like this. The basic characteristic of landlords is to preserve the old, so why do the second type want to jump on the bandwagon of moderation? In order to grasp the power to lead. Otherwise leadership would be seized totally by the People's Rights faction or the so-called New Study faction; so they must change their ways a bit. Because their economic connections still depend on feudal exploitation, they display all the characteristics of landlords. Their progressive attitude *[gexin]* is only on the surface. Qiu Weiwu of Xunwu City District, Pan Yiren of Jiansan District, and Xie Jiayou of Chengjiang District are examples of this layer. The third kind [of people] have totally feudal attitudes and life-styles. They live in the hills, far from rivers or markets. They have never ceased to hope for the restoration of the examination system; they are total monarchists. They want to use monarchical ideas to strike down ideas about people's rights, restore their political leadership, and return to the deteriorating and collapsing situation of the feudal economy. Their life-style is very rigid. Although most have adopted the shaved-head style haircut, some still follow the Qing practice. In Xunwu this kind of person makes up the smallest part of the large and middle landlords. An example is Mei Hongxing of Datian in Shuangqiao District. Among the large and middle landlords, the progressives constitute 10 percent, the moderates 70 percent, and the traditionalists 20 percent. But we cannot say that the so-called progressives, who are heading toward capitalism, are revolutionary. As a whole, the large and middle landlords oppose revolution. There is also a situation that needs to be explained. The moderate part of the large and middle landlord class is not formed only by reason of locality (near rivers or in the hills; close to markets or far from markets). There is also an age factor in these formations. Within one family, most of the old people are old-fashioned, most of the young people are reform-minded, and most of the middle-aged are moderate. The age factor reflects the times one grew up in. The old folks were deeply affected by the old system. Moreover, they are going to die soon and lack the ability to speak of progressive matters; they can only preserve the old. Young people are influenced by old ways only slightly, but because they have no future without reform, they are relatively less conservative. The middle-aged people are on both sides. For example, the large landlord Uncle Shitcrock is very conservative. His children advocated building schools, but these new-style schools are neither new nor old. His grandchildren—six or seven of them—have gone to Canton, Shanghai, Beijing, and England to study the so-called New Curriculum *[xinxue]*. Nevertheless, it does not matter what they have studied, they all are counterrevolutionary. Pan Zuoqin, a grandson of Uncle Shitcrock, graduated from medical school in England and returned. Now he is in Shantou, where he is considered the second best of the Western-trained doctors. Every day he earns 40 to 50 *yuan*; every month he can receive more than 1,000 *yuan*. When he first returned home, he refused the Xunwu Education Society Clinic's offer of 1,200 *yuan* a year because his income at Shantou was much greater.

Small Landlords

Small landlords (less than 200 *dan*) far outnumber the other two categories. Taking landlords as a whole, large landlords (over 500 *dan*) make up 1 percent, middle landlords (over 200 *dan*) 19 percent, and small landlords 80 percent. The number of large landlords is the smallest; their influence throughout the *xian* is insignificant. The center of power in the *xian* is among the middle landlords. Most of their children have gone to middle school. The administrative power of the *xian*—Tax Collection Bureau, Education Bureau, Security Militia—is mostly snagged by them, especially the monies for the spring and autumn sacrifices [*zhengchang*],[82] which are almost totally in their hands. Small landlords and rich peasants cannot interfere. But among the landlord class, small landlords are absolutely the greatest in number, and they display the following special characteristics. (1) Many have small businesses. They open small general stores and buy agricultural goods at a low price and wait until the price is dear to sell. Probably ten out of every hundred small landlords engage in this kind of small business. Some middle landlords engage in business and their businesses are larger than those of small landlords, but the proportion of middle landlords engaged in business is smaller. Most middle landlords have a life-style that is part of the feudal economy, unlike the extreme mercantilization of the small landlords. (2) Particularly indicative of the mercantilization of small landlords is that they also send their children to new-style schools. All the children of small landlords go to primary schools, and almost all go to higher primary school—at least in eight families out of ten. And three families out of ten have children in middle school. This class, compared with any other single class, has been influenced by the new culture [*xin wenhua*] quickly and in great numbers. In terms of administrative affairs, the small landlords are ruled by the middle landlord class; that is to say, they have no power. Their revolutionary demands during the first period of the revolutionary movement were expressed very stridently; their revolutionary activism advanced sharply. The Cooperative Society faction in Xunwu (Sun Yatsen Middle School faction) represents this class, but the New Xunwu faction (Young Revolutionary Comrades Society faction) represents the counterrevolutionary segment of the middle landlord class. Why does the small landlord class, influenced by capitalist culture, become so quickly infused with the revolutionary culture of the People's Rights movement, and why are its revolutionary demands and activities so intense and so fiercely advanced? This is solely because their class in general suffers, to the point of bankruptcy, from the encroachments of capitalism and from forced contributions to the government (of large and middle landlords). Because of the struggle between these

---

82. *Zhengchang* monies covered the expenses of memorial ceremonies, involving sacrifices to gods and ancestors. The type of ceremony that was held in the winter was called *zheng*, the one held in the autumn *chang*.

two strata (the small landlords and the large and middle landlords), which gives rise to the struggle between the peasant class and the landlord class, the New Xunwu faction, representing the middle landlords inclined in a capitalist direction, daily forms a counterrevolutionary battle line in cooperation with the large landlords. But the Cooperative Society faction represents the small landlords inclined toward the revolutionary People's Rights [movement], and daily they receive the guidance of proletarian ideology. They have united with the poor peasant class and risen up, creating the recent struggle for land revolution.

These comments on small landlords do not refer to all small landlords, just to a portion of them. Generally speaking, the small landlords can be divided into two parts. One part comes from the so-called old rich families. This part originates mostly in the division of property of large and middle landlords, the so-called large share becoming small. That is why so many large and middle landlord families become small landlord families. The portion of these people within the whole landlord class is 32 percent.

In terms of economic position, the small landlords can be divided into three categories.

1. Those who annually have surpluses: the percentage of these people within the whole landlord class is 0.96 percent; during the land struggle they were counterrevolutionary. Liu Hongxiang, Lai Shifang, and Liu Ruibiao of the Cooperative Society faction belong to this layer. They are all Cooperative Society members, but since the outbreak of the March 25 uprising and even after its defeat, they have incessantly displayed counterrevolutionary [actions and ideas].

2. Those who, in years with a declining standard of living, must incessantly sell land in order to survive. This group has a very miserable future ahead. There are many people in this layer—22.4 percent of the entire landlord class. They are enthusiastic for revolution. The people in the Xunwu Cooperative Society faction are mostly part of this stratum. For example, the following are members of this group.

Those leaders of the land struggle who have died:

Pan Li (Xunwu Communist Party *xian* committee secretary)
Liu Weilu (chairman of the Revolutionary Committee during the March 25 uprising)
Liu Weie (Communist Party district committee member)

Current leaders of the struggle:

Gu Bo (Xunwu Communist Party *xian* committee secretary)
Zhong Xiqiu (Red Army battalion commander)
Huang Yugui (Communist Party district committee secretary)

Those who did not participate in the Cooperative Society but have participated in the revolution:

Mei Ruhuang (Red Army group political commissar)

3. Those whose bankruptcy is quite severe and depend on loans to survive. This part constitutes 8.64 percent of all landlords. They are revolutionary, with many people participating in the struggle going on in Xunwu today.

Of the second and third parts of the small landlords, generally all the so-called old rich families whose circumstances are deteriorating participate in the revolution. To speak of Cooperative Society members, there are thirty middle-school students and a hundred upper-primary students or teachers who have participated or are participating in the revolution. All belong to those two strata of small landlords in deteriorating circumstances; most belong to the second stratum.

Besides the old rich families discussed above, another rather large stratum— 48 percent of small landlords—is the so-called newly rich. This layer, in complete contrast to the layer of the old rich, consists of peasants who get rich from farming or from small businesses. This layer is "flourishing." Its economic situation is based, on the one hand, on self-cultivation (little use of full-time hired help; mostly part-time hired help) and, on the other hand, on renting out remote arid land to others and collecting rents. They are serious about money, and their special trait is stinginess; getting rich is their central concern. They toil all day. They have surpluses every year, and, moreover, they either sell their unhulled grain or hull it and take it to market themselves, even to faraway places like Bachi in Pingyuan *xian*, in hopes of making a lot of money. They also make loans at reprehensively high interest rates—most at 50 percent. They loan out grain and oppress poor people [by making loans that] "take the first crop for the principal and the second crop for the interest." They also make "grain-money" and "oil-money" loans. What is a "grain-money" loan? When the last harvest is eaten and the new crop is still in the fields, they take advantage of this opportunity to loan money to the peasants and then are repaid in grain. Usually they loan out 2 *yuan* before harvest time and are repaid with a *Dan* of grain. But at that time the price of grain is almost 4 *yuan* per *Dan*. This is a type of 100 percent interest. "Oil-money loans" are the same; most are of the double-interest type. Loan-sharking is almost always done by the newly rich families. Large and middle landlords loan money at a 30 percent rate; very few make 50 percent loans, and these landlords do not make grain loans or oil-money loans. Also, there is the more severe "monthly interest" loan, with an interest rate of 10 percent a month; so that the annual interest rate exceeds that of the double-interest loan. To receive this kind of loan requires a mortgage; moreover, to save face, some borrow the term "society" *[hui]*, like the Dingtong Society. There is also the "chop loan society,"[83] a 10 percent per month loan at compound interest, which is more severe than the Dingtong Society. Large and middle landlords

---

83. The text reads *yinzi hui. Yinzi* can refer to the mark made by a "chop," a stone carved with the characters for a person's name and used to make ink impressions on paper. However, *yinzi* can also refer, as it does in the text, to a small loan made for a short period at a high interest rate.—RT.

usually do not make such loans. During the Qing these reprehensible loans were relatively scarce, but they have increased during the Republican period. "Now people are more greedy" is the historically significant criticism of poor people toward loan sharks. "Today the hearts of people are relatively more greedy"— this is something one hears when one goes among the poor peasant masses throughout Xunwu. Nothing is more important than money to the newly rich families. They do not waste money [on tuition]; nor do they sacrifice the labor of their children by sending them to school. Middle-school graduates among them are few, and although there are a few graduates of primary school, there are not as many as among the bankrupt layer. As for the bankrupt families, why have most of them gone to school? Because they inherited money and are not that desirous of it. Moreover, since those who depend on study and on their own ability for their livelihood lack other ways to raise their family's fortunes, most of the graduates come from this layer. Some people refer to the so-called newly rich families of small landlords discussed above, not as small landlords, but rather as rich peasants, the so-called half-landlord-like rich peasant. This half-landlord-like rich peasant class is the most evil enemy in the countryside. In the eyes of poor peasants there is no reason not to strike them down.

Rich Peasants

There is also a kind of peasant who is relatively rich, and is normally called an owner-peasant or middle peasant, but who is actually a kind of rich peasant. As for the so-called "half-landlord-like rich peasant" mentioned earlier, we did not call them rich peasants but rather small landlords. This is the viewpoint of the poor peasants. During struggles, most people do not argue for attacking the so-called relatively rich owner-peasants or middle peasants because they do not have the characteristics of half-landlord[-like rich peasants]. All their production comes from their own labor, not from the exploitation of others. Actually in the eyes of poor peasants, they are a special class. Except for not renting land to other people to till, they are the same type of high-interest exploiters because they have surplus money and surplus land. They add labor to their own agricultural produce, for example, turning unhulled grain into hulled rice, and then go to market themselves to sell it. They also carry on small hoarding activities. They raise piglets, shoats, and meaty pigs. These rich peasants have all the characteristics of half-landlord[-like rich peasants], but they are not the same as the self-sufficient middle peasants. Because of this, when the land struggle develops into a mass activity, most of the poor peasants cry out [slogans like] "equal land" and "tear up debts" in opposition to this kind of rich peasant. If the Communist Party should stop this activity of poor peasants, those poor peasants could not but hate the Communist Party. Because of this, we know that not only must we decide to strike down these half-landlord-like rich peasants, but moreover we must equalize the rich owner-peasants' land, cancel loans made by the rich owner-peasants, and divide the rich owner-peasants' grain—there is no doubt that we have to do this. We must do this, and then and only then can we win over the poor peasant masses. This is the paramount policy of the rural struggle. Only those opportunists who take the rich-peasant line oppose this policy.

Poor Peasants (The Four Layers of Poor Peasants)

What is a poor peasant? We can answer simply: a poor peasant does not have enough to eat (the reason is exploitation, that's obvious). But this is a conventional explanation. If we once again analyze the poor peasantry from within, then we know that poor peasants are certainly not a homogeneous class made up of one economic position, for the class has four different strata. The first group is the semiowner peasants. They do not have enough to eat because of insufficient land. They must rent some land from landlords. After paying all the rent, they do not have enough to eat, but among the poor-peasant masses they are the best off, because not only do they have oxen and plows, they also have some money in their hands. Moreover, there is something that manifests their special characteristic: they own a bit of land. This level constitutes 10.5 percent of the total rural population. Among the poor peasants they constitute 15 percent. The second level is made up of that group among tenants who are doing fairly well. They have oxen, plows, and some money, but not a bit of land. Their special characteristic is their oxen: most have one ox, and an extremely small number have two or three. Compared with semiowner peasants, they are poorer and have even less to eat, but compared with other parts of the poor peasantry, they are certainly better off. This level constitutes 42 percent of the rural population and 60 percent of the poor peasant population—they are **the largest mass** in the countryside. The third level is made up of tenants in dire straits. They likewise have no land. They have plows, but most are in poor shape, and they have some money, but not much. They also have a special characteristic: not every family has oxen. Several families may share an ox, or if they have an ox, it certainly is not their own. It is the landlord's, who turns it over to them in order to save on fodder costs. Only under certain conditions can they use the work power of this ox. In Xunwu, they refer to this as "getting only one hoof." Their level of insufficiency with respect to food, compared with those groups mentioned above, is more severe. They constitute 10.5 percent of the total rural population and 15 percent of the total poor peasant population. They are a mass of the same size as the semi-owner peasants. The fourth category comprises the poorest tenants. Besides having no land, they have no money—they normally borrow rice and salt. They also lack one iota of animal power. During the busy agricultural seasons, they wait until other people have tilled, and then afterward they join with other people (their relatives) and borrow or rent oxen. They cultivate several *mu* of infertile land rented at high rates. Although they have plows, they have no harrows, because to make one requires quite a bit of money. Their means are insufficient to do this. This layer constitutes 7 percent of the rural population and 10 percent of all poor peasants. They are not an insignificant mass. The clothes they wear are very ragged; they have to beg them from people. Two out of three meals they eat are *zaliang* (millet, slices of sweet potatoes). To supplement their income, they make cakes for sale, chop wood to sell for fuel, or hire themselves out as porters.

The System in the Hills

Most hill land in Xunwu is in the hands of the lineages who first homesteaded; the lineages that came later do not have any hill land or only a little, because the land had been occupied by first-comers. Therefore, the small lineages, who settled first, have hill land, while the great lineages, who came later, don't have any. The situation of hill lands differs from that of croplands. Cropland is bought and sold quickly. Through mortgaging, the land of small landlords and peasants can be transferred [zhuanyi] twice a year, and even more land is transferred once a year. Outright sales are also frequent. Generally speaking, because of its low productivity, a lineage hill (single-surname village) is managed by an ancestral trust. Within an area of 5 or 6 *li*, a system of compacts is used. The so-called prohibitions not only forbid the buying and selling of land, but also absolutely prohibit tree foraging. Apart from those "who chop down wood to build a temporary hut to cover a tomb site," permission to cut timber can be obtained only for purposes of the public good, like building roads or canals and repairing bridges. Besides this, the hills are opened only twice every three years for clearing brushwood and once every two years for timbering. The schedule for opening the hills is set by a gathering of lineage mates from a land reeve's [jinzhang, lit., restriction chief] village. When the time comes, every family supplies a worker who goes to the hill to collect brushwood and timber (thinning timberland is also called *luoka,* which means "to prune tree branches"). These are distributed to everyone. There are also cases when the whole hill is divided into lots in accordance with the production situation in the hills. The masses are called together to draw lots. Afterward, based on the lots drawn, they individually take their share. This is the "lineage system" of hill "communism." But there is also a geographical system of hill communism. In most cases, the village is taken as the unit, and each lineage elects the reeve. They strictly forbid private foraging and set a schedule for opening the hills—just as in the system of family "communism" in the hills. The number of land reeves varies from a minimum of three to a maximum of ten or more, based on the size of the village's forest—in most cases, there are five or six. The land reeves are all elected, and their terms are indefinite. Some serve for six months; others for four or five years. It all depends on whether a reeve fulfills his responsibility or not. All land reeves must be absolutely incorruptible and fairminded. "It doesn't matter if you are the old wet nurse of the emperor, if you exceed your quota of wood or licorice root, you will be punished." There was a land reeve in Longtu Township in Nanba District who came upon a woman stealing wood. The woman said to him: "I would like to chop down some wood to build a stand, you must not punish me. I am a Longtu person just like you—we are related. Why do you seem so cold-hearted?" The land reeve answered her: "Be quiet, you old liar. Even if you were my great-aunt, I would penalize you. You must know that I, Liu Shilie, am just and fair." If the land reeve does not maintain order and everyone chaotically chops trees down, not minding the public good, he must *nuanjin*. (Calling people's attention to the rules is called *nuanjin*. If anyone neglects the spirits and then once again pays respects, that is called *nuanshen* or *nuanfu*). Every year the land reeves call a Protect the Hills meeting. All the regulations for protecting the hills are decided at this meeting. Most Protect the Hills meetings are called on an ad hoc basis, but there are also "scheduled meetings." On the day when the Protect the Hills meeting is called, not only do the land reeves come, but also one person from every family in the area comes. Every person brings wine and rice and also pays 5 or 10 *fen* to buy cooked dishes and incense for worshiping "Bogong." (Bogong is Yang Dabogong. Every place has a shrine; every tree, field, and hill has one.) The "communism" of the public hills is shown in the above-mentioned systems. There is also the "capitalism" of the private hills, with mushrooms, tea-oil plants, tea, bamboo, and Chinese firs. The produce can be sold for relatively good profits. These hills were originally public hills but gradually fell into the hands of the wealthy. Large landlords probably own half of them, and small landlords who are newly rich and rich peasants own the other half. Because this kind of hill cannot be developed without capital, especially when growing mushrooms and tea, the owners must be large landlords. The rest are mostly small landlords and rich peasants who have gone capitalist. The hill lands of Xunwu are distributed as follows: lineage hills constitute 15 percent, village hills 5 percent, private hills 10 percent, and the so-called waste-hills—those that are remote from inhabited areas, inaccessible hills, and neglected hills—70 percent. There are waste-hills because in areas of low population with many hills there is no need for them. Some are delineated by lineage boundaries. Although people from other lineages might want to use such land, they are forbidden to do so by the Hill Lord. They can only let it be wasteland. This type of situation in which a person desires to develop a hill but cannot do so because of restrictions is common. After the land revolution, this kind of lineage barrier was wiped out.

Exploitation

Exploitation by Land Rent

Sharecropping. There are two ways of collecting land rents in Xunwu County: "sharecropping" and "measuring rent." In the former, the peasant goes along with the landlord to the fields when the crop is ripe, and the yield is split 50–50. Moreover, the peasant is asked by the landlord to take his share to the landlord's home. In some places the landlord first takes one *Dan* of grain before the division, and this *Dan* is not included in the rent. The landlord's reason for this is: "When I bought this land I spent a lot, and you, the tenant, did not supply the fertilizer. If I didn't take this *Dan* first, it would be too advantageous for you." But this method is not used by more than one family in a hundred. In another method, however, the peasant takes some grain first; this is called "taking seeds." The amount is one measure *[cuosuan]* out of all the land rent. The reason is that the seedlings came from someone else's land, not from the landlord's in question. The owner of the other land has no spring harvest from the seedling land and will suffer a loss. The first measure from the crop is to compensate the tenant or the other landlord for the loss. When the landlord or his agent comes to watch the dividing process, he requires a lunch with pork and fish (even duck sometimes), and the peasant has to carry the rent to the landlord's home after the lunch and the dividing of the crop. The peasant even has to put two eggs on the rent rice; this is a daily occurrence in this area. If the peasant has better relations with his landlord, he may put on seven or eight eggs.

Measuring Rent. The system of rent by measure is called "early rice six parts; late rice four parts." In Pingyuan *xian*, the split is 50–50. Why must it be "early six, late four"? Since the yield of early rice is greater and it gets a higher price, taking 60 percent of the yield as rent does not give the tenant any advantage. But late rice yields less and its value is lower, so the rent is 40 percent of the yield. At first glance it would seem that the 60–40 ratio, when applied to the two crops grown each year, comes out to 50–50, but this is not so. The landlord usually gets 56 percent to the tenant's 44 percent. Since the yields for early rice are relatively great, the landlord gets 6 *Dan* out of every 10 *Dan* of early rice, leaving the tenant with only 4 *Dan*. As for late rice, which generally yields 8 *Dan* (2 *Dan* less than early rice), the tenant hands over 4 *Dan* for rent and keeps 4 *Dan* for himself. These 4 *Dan* plus the 4 *Dan* of early rice [gives the tenant] a total of 8 *Dan* whereas the landlord gets 10 *Dan*. So the ratio is 56 to 44.

Rents based on sharecropping are figured at the Great Heat (sixth lunar month), and measuring rents are assessed during the first period of autumn (seventh lunar month). Landlords notify peasants that land rents are due; if the rent is not sent, the landlord goes to the tenant's home himself to press the tenant. If the rent is still not paid, he sends some workers to take the rent. If this does not succeed, he turns the land over to someone else. Some bad landlords even bring lawsuits against tenants and imprison them, but bad landlords of this type are few. Originally sharecropping covered 40 percent of all cases in this county, and "measuring rents" covered the other 60 percent. But recently the incidence of sharecropping has increased and that of "measuring rents" has decreased to about 50 percent. Why has share-cropping been on the rise? Because the number of poor tenant households has been increasing, and they frequently have no seed rice left after the rent is sent. Landlords, afraid that peasants cannot afford to pay the rents, often prefer to sharecrop, causing this method to increase. At the same time, because the peasants are afraid of losing the land or of involvement in lawsuits, they prefer sharecropping too.

From the Top of the Stalks to the Bottom of the Roots, There's Nothing to Eat. "From the top of the stalks to the bottom of the roots, there's nothing to eat" means that just after the harvest and payment of the rent the tenant has nothing left to eat. This occurs in almost 40 percent of the cases in Xunwu *xian*. Why is there no food to eat from the top of the stalks to the bottom of the roots? Take, for example, a piece of land yielding 20 *Dan*, of which over 11 *Dan* are paid as rent. Of the remaining 8-plus *Dan*, 2 to 3 *Dan* may be used to repay the landlord for loans of grain. These short-term (up to two years) loans, with an interest rate of 50 percent, are extended when the previous year's crop is consumed and the current crop has yet to be harvested.[84] At harvest time, tenants have to purchase fine things for entertaining landlords. And after the harvest, they buy some cooking oil and salt and in the spring some rice. When autumn comes, everything is gone. This is what "From the top of the stalks to the bottom of the roots, there's nothing to eat" and "One year's yield is all gone" mean. During the land struggle in the southern half of the *xian*, peasants and children everywhere sang this song:

> The moon is shining, as if burning.
> We bear hardship, while others are happy.
> Little to eat, little to wear.
> Year after year of work, always living in a dilapidated house.
> I've no money to obtain a pretty wife; I'll grow old alone.
> With no schooling, we're blind even though we have eyes.
> Oh, Heaven! How bitter is our lot.
> No other work to do but till the land year after year.
> The June harvest is hardly over before the landlord arrives.
> With umbrella in hand he looks over the rice sacks.
> Asking nothing but "Is the rice dry?"
> As soon as the destitute reply, "Not yet,"
> The landlord starts talking like an official.
> Every word he says is as mean as a tax collector's.
> Oh, what can we do?
> Bushel *[luo]* after bushel,[85] land rent plus interest,
> That's one year's yield, and it's all gone.

---

84. *Qinghuang bujie*, literally, "when the green and the yellow do not meet."
85. *Luo:* a square-bottomed bamboo basket.—RT.

Oh, all is gone.
Being aggrieved, let us poor brothers be united and of one heart.
Let's join the Red Army and kill our enemy.[86]

Renting Land. In Xunwu landlords require all tenants to sign a lease.[87] There are no exceptions to this. In Xunwu there are small leases for periods of five years and large leases for periods of seven years. Although no formal law governs this, this is the rule between landlords and tenants. Only bad landlords find an excuse to break this rule and try to change tenants in three to four years or seven to eight years.[88] Although no formal law governs this, this is the rule between landlords and tenants. The following items are covered in a lease:

---

86. In a note to this song Mao Zedong added the following glossary for passages in the lyrics in the Xunwu dialect:

ai	me
mao	do not have
xiang qi zuo	continue
an qing nuzi	pretty women
yang de lao	how to make a living
an hao xuetang	good school
ge ye jiu	just after harvesting
zuo zei tou	very bad, like a thief
daizi yi da kun	sacks for land rent
guo jie liu	umbrella
ma ge dou wu wen	nothing to ask
fang chu xia ma tou	like an official
shui hu tou	major landlord
a he	all gone
ai tong xin	be of one heart

Mao makes no special note of it, but there are numerous phrases scattered throughout the text that are Hakka in origin. S. T. Leong argues in "The Hakka Chinese of Lingnan: Ethnicity and Social Change in Modern Times," in *Ideal and Reality: Social and Political Change in Modern China, 1860–1949,* ed. David Pong and Edmund S.K. Fung (Lanham, Md.: University Press of America, 1985), pp. 297, 318, 324, that Xunwu *xian* was a "pure Hakka" *xian* in the core of the Hakka-dominated region of southern Jiangxi. We do know that Mao sometimes needed help from investigation meeting participants like Gu Bo, Guo Youmei, and Fan Daming in translating the information being conveyed by the people of Xunwu.—RT.

87. For an excellent short story published in 1933 concerning the issues of tenancy, tensions at harvest time, and the often harsh plight of the peasantry, see Zheng Nong's "On the Threshing Field," in Harold R. Isaacs, ed., *Straw Sandals: Chinese Short Stories, 1918–1933* (Cambridge: MIT Press, 1974), pp. 371–93. Zheng Nong, born in 1904, was the pen name of Xia Zhengnong, a native of Nanchang County in Jiangxi (ibid., pp. lxix–lxx).—RT.

88. This refers to the third or fourth year of the first term or the seventh or eighth year of the second term of a small lease.—RT.

The location and boundaries of the land are clearly stated.

The amount of rent and whether it is determined by sharecropping or by measure.

The quality and quantity of the rent payment: rent rice should be dry enough, and shorting is disallowed and can be penalized by the landlord.

Tribute: a chicken every year or two.

There are leases even for land yielding only 3 *Dan*. There are two reasons for this. First, without a lease, if a tenant does not pay the exact amount of rent, there is no proof in legal proceedings. Second, landlords are afraid that after a long period of time tenants might take over the land. A landlord never signs a lease; only tenants sign leases and give them to landlords. The following is an example of a lease:

> Leasee, Kuang Shiming, rents a piece of land from Ling Jiangui. This piece of land is called Tieliaoba, it is arable and has one large mound *[qiu]*.[89] After negotiations witnessed by a third party, an agreement was made to rent the land for six buckets *[tong]* of rent each year, which may be sent in two payments, one in autumn and one in winter. The rent is 60 percent for early rice and 40 percent for late rice and is to be sent to the [landlord's] home. The rice must be clean and dry; the quantity must be exact. If there is shorting, the landlord may rent the land to someone else, and the leasee will have no cause for complaint. Because an oral [agreement] does not constitute a lease, this lease is drawn up to establish the agreement.
>
> There will be tribute of one chicken each year.
>
> Witness: Luo Changsheng
> Written by: Xie Yulin
> Leasee: Kuang Shiming
> The sixteenth year of the Republic [1927],
> November 24.

Fees, Tribute, and Landlord Dinners. There are two kinds of fees: fees-in-money and fees-in[-kind] (a rooster). The fee-in-money is generally 0.1 *yuan* for each *dan* of rent specified in a five-year lease and 0.2 *yuan* for each *dan* in a ten-year lease. But sometimes, as in Huangxiang, the fee is 0.3 *yuan*. This fee is paid at the beginning of the lease. The fee[-in-kind requires] one rooster for one lease, whether a five-year or a ten-year lease, to be sent when the lease begins. Fees-in-money or fees-in-kind should be sent again when the lease is renewed (that is, either every five years or every ten years). In the southern part of the *xian*, most leases run for ten years. In Huangxiang and Shuangqiao, there are no five-year leases, and, although these are few in number, some leases run for decades. If a landlord sells land after it is leased, he returns part of the fee. In the northern part of the *xian*, most leases are for five years and fees are never refunded in any way.

---

89. *Qiu*, the word for "mound," also means "grave."—RT.

A chicken is sent in tribute each year. Although leases can specify a "rooster," because a rooster is bigger than a hen, most peasants still send hens. Peasants usually send one every other year—even though the leases say one rooster a year—around the time of the New Year's celebration or after the winter harvest. If a chicken is not sent, the landlord goes out and presses the peasant for payment. "Did you send the tribute rooster?" "Not yet, sir, please wait until I buy one." Or "No, sir, I can't give you one this year."

In Shuangqiao, there is a custom of landlord dinners, in which [a tenant] invites his landlord to dinner once a year. This is not common in other areas.

Grain Rent and Money Rent. Eighty percent of the rent in this *xian* is paid in grain; the other 20 percent is paid in money. About half the ancestral, religious, temple, and bridge trusts accept money because most of their tenants are members of ancestral trusts, religious associations, and so on. Because of this, the tenants can keep the rice for their own use and use money to pay the rent (figured according to the current rice price). Most of these tenants make money through small businesses or by raising chickens and pigs for market. Some ancestral and religious trusts controlled by powerful gentry may force tenants to send rice for rent in order to pursue their exploitative practices (rice can be sold later at a higher price). The tenants have no alternative but to turn over the grain and put it in the granary. For the same reason, landlords accept only rice and do not allow the peasants to pay in money except for landlords who live far from the croplands.

Fixed Rents and Variable Rents. Eighty percent of the rents in the *xian* are variable [lit., not-iron] rents. When there is a flood, drought, or other disaster, the rent can be reduced by 10 to 20 percent. If the yield is affected too much by a big disaster, landlords will accept some blighted grain *[panggu]* once they know the facts. Twenty percent of the rents in this *xian* are fixed. In such cases there is a "no rent reduction for disaster" clause in the leases. Actually, tenants rarely follow this rule. They ask landlords to come and see the disaster, so that blighted grain may be accepted as part of the rent.

Go Sleep with Someone If You Want Some Clothing. Many peasants have no food left to eat after paying the rent and their debts, and landlords who receive their rents in grain are unwilling to sell the grain. Only around New Year's time do landlords give some grain to peasants badly in need of food. But this is for loan only, not for sale. This is because the interest on grain loans is 50 percent semiannually (the interest rate was 30 percent for money and 40 percent for grain every half-year, but recently few grain loans have been let for 40 percent; most interest rates are 50 percent), and the appeal of such loans is much greater than that of selling. Landlords sell rice only in April or May, when the new crop is still in the fields and the old crop is gone. At that time the price is highest, and [in order to get a higher price] the landlords pretend to be reluctant to sell.

A peasant will come to a landlord's house and ask: "Sir, did you have your dinner?"

Landlord: "Um, yes."

Then the peasant will slowly bring up the subject of buying grain: "Could I buy a couple of *dou* of your grain?"

Landlord: "N . . . no, I don't have enough for my family."

Peasant: "Hey, if you don't have enough, then there's no water in the river. Please help me out; I'm waiting for food to eat."

Landlord: "OK, if you really need it, I can save some for you, but will you pay this high price?"

Peasant: "Sir, please do me a favor and don't charge me too much!"

The price is set according to the landlord's wishes; afterward he gives the grain to the peasant.

There is a story known all over the *xian*. The landlord Liu Fulang of Huangxiang is a famous miser who always mixes blighted grain with the good to sell at times when the new crop is still in the fields and the old one is gone. One day, a peasant came to his home to buy some rice. Liu called his daughter-in-law and daughter and said: "Go sleep with someone if you want some clothing." Peasants have spread this sentence so that it has become a famous joke in the whole *xian*. Why did this sentence become a joke? Because it is customary in Xunwu for adulteresses to be called *lao,* but *lao* also means to mix blighted grain with good grain. The landlord could not clearly tell [his daughter and daughter-in-law] in the presence of the peasant to mix blighted grain with good, so he carelessly came out with these funny words to his daughter and daughter-in-law. This story is still being told.

Corvée Labor. There is no corvée labor in the *xian* now. If there is any emergency or a wedding or funeral, a landlord may ask tenants to help him. If the landlord has some farmwork to do, he may ask tenants to help him in the busy season, but these laborers are paid.

Buying or Selling Land. According to Liu Liangfan, who was a clerk in the *xian* yamen, six hundred households sold land in this *xian* in 1925. Since some households bought the lands of more than one household, there were fewer than six hundred households buying land. Suppose there are 30,000 households in the *xian* (a population of 120,000, with four people per household). [This means that] one household out of every fifty became bankrupt. Even more mortgaged their lands—five households out of every hundred. (There are two mortgagees for every hundred households because one mortgagee may have several properties mortgaged to him.) So, in recent years 2 percent of the households in Xunwu have gone bankrupt, and 5 percent are heading toward bankruptcy.

The price of land: for every *dan* of rent, 17 to 20 *yuan* for [terraced] rice paddies *[kengtian]* and 30 to 40 *yuan* for bottomlands *[duantian];* generally 20 *yuan* for rice fields and 30 *yuan* for bottomlands. Rice fields can be mortgaged for 15 *yuan* [for each *dan* of rent] and bottomlands for 20 to 25 *yuan*.

There are two kinds of mortgages: *fiducia cum creditore [guoshou]* and *antichresis [buguoshou]*.[90] Fiducia cum creditore means that the mortgagor gives the land to the mortgagee after receiving money from him. The mortgagee either tills the land himself or leases it to someone else. The mortgagee makes all the decisions, and the mortgagor has no say. After the transfer of the land, the mortgagee does not pay rent to the mortgagor. Apart from reserving the right to buy the land back, the mortgagor loses the rights of ownership. It is almost like selling the land because most of the rights to the land are in the hands of the mortgagee.

Antichresis means that the mortgagee pays some money to the mortgagor, but the land is tilled by the mortgagor, who has to pay rent to the mortgagee every year. The rent is the same as for other rented land: for every [2] *dan* of combined yield [of the early and late crops], there is a *dan* of rent. For example, if the land price is 20 *yuan* for each *dan* of rent, the mortgagor gets 20 *yuan* but has to pay a *dan* of grain in rent. Since the grain normally sells for 4 *yuan* per *dan*, the yearly interest is 20 percent. Why is the mortgage rate lower than the interest rate on money charged by moneylenders? (Generally the interest rate for borrowing money starts at 30 percent a year.) This is because rich peasants (those who have just become rich) think that the low rates for mortgages are safer than the high interest rate for money loans. "Putting the money in the earth is very safe." Why do the rich peasants buy mortgages and not land? Because the bankruptcy of peasants and landlords occurs gradually, not suddenly. "First buy mortgages and then buy land" has become a common phenomenon. "Land belongs to rich people, mortgage means selling" is also a common phenomenon. So buying a mortgage is almost the same as buying the land. Ninety percent of the mortgages are fiducia cum creditore and only 10 percent are antichresis. Most of the antichresis mortgages are governed by fixed rents. But [in some cases], even though the land is legally transferred in the manner of fiducia cum creditore to the mortgagee, so that a lease changes the relationship of the original owner and the mortgage owner to that of landlord and tenant, the original owner still tills this piece of land. This is another layer of landlord-tenant relationships beyond the one between mortgagor and mortgagee.

---

90. The Chinese *guoshou* [lit., pass from one's hand], as described in the text, is similar to the type of transfer of ownership referred to in Roman law as *fiducia cum creditore*. The debtor is allowed to keep legal title and can be a tenant at will, but ownership is transferred de facto to the creditor. The Chinese *buguoshou* [lit., not to pass from one's hand] is similar to the Roman legal term *antichresis,* in which the possession of the land goes to the creditor but the debtor retains ownership. See *New Encyclopedia Britannica,* 15th ed., 26: 188.—RT.

Some antichresis land is mortgaged secretly. For example, when one of the young masters who "live for whoring and gambling" owes gambling debts or lacks money for whoring, he may secretly mortgage his family's land to some powerful and eminent rich peasants and landlords, and then transfer the land in the manner of fiducia cum creditore after his father is dead. Why does he mortgage land to the powerful and eminent? Because they don't fear complications. Even if the secret deal were to become known, they're confident that the father would honor the agreement.

Antichresis mortgages present opportunities for high degrees of exploitation between mortgagee *[dianzhu]* and mortgagor *[tianzhu]*. When the mortgagor cannot afford to pay the rent, the mortgagee adds interest to the unpaid part of the rent. This adds up year by year and finally the mortgagor certainly cannot pay off the mortgage for this land. The interest rate for unpaid rent is 30 percent or higher, rather than the 20 percent rate for mortgages.

Exploitation Through High Interest Rates

The Interest on Money. The ordinary rate of interest on money loans is 30 percent [in reality, 36 percent]. There are also 40 percent and 50 percent loans. Respectively, these constitute 70, 10, and 20 percent of the total money in the loan market. If a debtor has no land, all loans are secured by property, such as houses, livestock, or tea-oil fields *[muzi]*, specified in the contract. Those with extra money to lend include large and middle landlords, ancestral trusts, and the newly rich (small landlords and rich peasants who have suddenly become wealthy). In terms of the total amount of money lent, the middle landlords lend about 50 percent, the newly rich about 30 percent, and the big landlords and ancestral trusts about 20 percent. In terms of lending frequency, the newly rich are the most frequent lenders with 75 percent of the loans, and the middle landlords are next with 20 percent, followed by the large landlords and ancestral trusts with 5 percent. In terms of borrowers, as for 50 percent loans (50 *yuan* of interest per 100 *yuan* of principal per year) or 120 percent loans (a 10 percent interest charge per month, or 120 *yuan* in interest payments per year for a 100-*yuan* loan), poor peasants are the ones who usually borrow on these terms. Poor peasants seldom take out 30 percent interest loans. Such loans carry a 3 percent interest rate per month (36 *yuan* in interest payments per year for 100 *yuan* in principal). Among the total amount of money borrowed by poor peasants, 30 percent loans constitute 20 percent, 50 percent loans constitute 70 percent, and 120 percent loans make up 10 percent. Most of the creditors lending to poor peasants are newly rich, for they are willing to lend small amounts of money such as 3 to 5 *yuan* or 8 to 10 *yuan* to poor peasants bit by bit and charge compound interest. Since poor peasants have no land, they are able to use only their houses or livestock as security. Because creditors always jump at the chance to gobble up poor peasants' houses, livestock, small pieces of land, or gardens, when poor peasants stand in need of money, creditors are always eager to lend money. Later on, they seize the security if poor peasants do not meet their payments. Sometimes middle landlords do the same thing as the newly rich. For example, Gu Youyao, Gu Bo's grandfather, acquired three parcels of vegetable gardens and two houses from poor peasants in this manner. He might lend one *yuan* one day and two *yuan* the next day to a poor peasant. As the debt built up gradually, he came to possess the debtor's whole vegetable garden. He devotes much attention to occupying other people's property by this method. He cares about nothing else, for he thinks that taking care of local affairs and the ancestral trust will keep him from making money. He is a typical high-interest exploiter.

Most 30 percent loans occur between rich peasants and make it possible for rich peasants to start small businesses, such as trading in rice or livestock, or to establish a small shop in a market town. Why can rich peasants get 30 percent loans whereas poor peasants can get only 50 percent loans or 120 percent loans? There are two reasons: the first is the "bigness" of the loan amount. The amount of money lent by rich peasants is usually around 200 to 300 *yuan*, which can be used to do something big when it is repaid, whereas poor peasants usually borrow only a little money, which is too small to do anything with after it is repaid. The second reason is the security of the loan. Rich peasants use their land as security for loans, and, in addition, they borrow to make investments that always have the prospect of making money. But poor peasants have little property, and they frequently spend their money or use the money to pay another creditor; so their dependability is very low.

Middle landlords usually lend money, for the purposes of amassing land, to small landlords who are bankrupt or to peasants who are on the road to bankruptcy.

Few large landlords or lineages lend money. They hold on to their money because they prefer to enjoy life rather than increase their capital. They spend money on celebrating eightieth birthdays, building large houses, or educating their children (this is not a major purpose). A few of the large landlords who have become mercantilized are willing to invest their money in business. Therefore, there is no money left for lending. Some of the large landlords with extra money who do not have a business to invest in and who are not interested in lending to poor peasants or small landlords because of the risks and poor returns would rather dig a pit and bury their money in the ground than get interest by lending. Moreover, local warlords collect heavy customs and duties from those who have extra money to lend out; there is no escaping this. For instance, on several occasions Lin Hu and Liu Zhilu,[91] troop leaders under the command of

---

91. Lin Hu (1887–1960), a subordinate of Chen Jiongming, had been appointed commissioner in Guangdong by the Beijing government in 1924. Liu Zhilu, commander of the garrison in Chaozhou and Meixian, Guangdong Province, had also thrown in his lot with Chen Jiongming. When Chen was defeated in 1925, he rallied to Wu Peifu. For Mao's attacks on both of them in 1925, see Volume II, pp. 228–29 and 273–76.

Chen Jiongming, levied contributions totaling more than 10,000 *yuan* on large, middle, and small landlords, ancestral trusts, and religious trusts in the Huangxiang area. These levies encouraged landlords to hide their money in cellars.

Interest on Grain Loans. The interest on grain loans is much higher than that on money loans. It is the most sinister way in which rich peasants and well-off middle or small landlords exploit poor peasants. Most high-interest loans are made in December and March. Poor peasants borrow in December to celebrate New Year's and in March to sow seeds. No matter when they borrow, the loan has to be repaid in June when the early rice is harvested. The interest is 50 percent of the principal (repaying a principal of 1 *dan* with 1.5 *dan*) (three measures *[luo]*). A loan with 50 percent interest for six months or three months is a most terrible loan.

Early rice is harvested in June. After paying the rent for the use of the field and repaying the grain loan, poor peasants eat the remainder by August and have to borrow grain again from landlords or rich peasants. Poor peasants borrow 1 *dan* of grain in August and have to pay back 1.2 *dan* of grain in October. In other words, the interest is 20 percent for about two months. If a poor peasant cannot repay the loan, he has no option but to talk it over with the creditor: "I have nothing left to repay your grain loan this year. May I repay it after I harvest my early rice next June?" The creditor answers: "Well, we must calculate the interest in a different way. The 1.0 *dan* of grain borrowed last August is the principal of the loan and has a 5 *dou* interest due by next year, the 2 *dou* that is the interest for the 1.0 *dan* of principal for the period from last August through October should have 50 percent interest too: 1 *dou* by next year. So the total payment should be 1 *dan* 8 *dou* of grain by next June." (The original *dan* had interest of 2 *dou*, plus the interest of 5 *dou* to which was added 1 *dou*, together making 1 *dan* 8 *dou*.) In fact, the total interest payment is 80 percent from June of this year to June of next year. If the borrower cannot repay it the following year, the principal becomes 1 *dan* 8 *dou*, with the 50 percent interest being automatic. If the poor peasant is still unable to repay the loan at the harvest of late rice *[fanzi]*, nor the next year or in subsequent years, the total payment for the loan becomes a huge amount after ten years.

Tea-oil Loan Interest. The tea-oil loan is called "double oil" and is the most odious type of loan. The so-called double oil is found in the southern part of Xunwu *xian*, where there are many hillsides planted with tea-oil plants. There are no double-oil loans in the northern part of Xunwu *xian* because there are no hillsides of tea-oil plants there. Why is it called the double-oil loan? Because a loan of 1 *jin* of oil is repaid with 2 *jin*, 2 with 4, and 4 with 8. This is the double-oil loan. What is its time limit? It is always repaid in September when the tea-oil seeds are gathered, regardless of when the [loan] was made, whether it was made that month or up to a year earlier.

Landlords and rich peasants own hills with tea-oil plants and rent them to poor peasants to cultivate. Then they collect half the harvested tea-oil seeds as rent. The rent is 10 *jin* of oil when a poor peasant harvests 20 *jin* or 30 *jin* when 60 *jin* is harvested. After receiving the rent, landlords and rich peasants usually market 90 percent and lend 10 percent to poor peasants as double-oil loans. When a peasant borrows the tea-oil, the lender always says the tea-oil is his son's or his daughter-in-law's. Sometimes it is true that it is from his son and daughter-in-law's supply of tea-oil. In fact, young people in rich peasant families who have as yet not managed household affairs frequently have their own tea-oil. After the harvest season for tea-oil seeds is over, the youths pick up the tea-oil seeds that have fallen to the ground under the tea-oil plants and then squeeze oil out of those tea-oil seeds. This oil belongs to the youths. This makes it possible for the youths in a rich peasant family to make high-interest tea-oil loans:

"Sir, could you lend me some money?"

"No, I don't have any."

"Some grain."

"No."

"I have nothing to eat. Please lend something to me, anyway."

"How about some of my son's tea-oil."

The interest on tea-oil is so high that no poor peasant wants to borrow it. However, poor peasants have no choice but to take out a tea-oil loan, because neither landlords nor rich peasants are willing to lend them money or grain. Poor peasants can only sell the tea-oil they borrow and then use the money to buy grain to eat.

Sometimes poor peasants want to borrow tea-oil in order to eat. When they have harvested their crops and need cooking oil, they go to the landlord's or rich peasant's house with a bottle to borrow a bottle of oil. They borrow one big bottle of tea-oil in June and repay with two big bottlesful in September. Many poor peasants have no steelyard with which to weigh the tea-oil. Moreover, some poor peasants' wives and daughters-in-law do not know how to use a steelyard. Consequently, it is easier to measure the tea-oil with a bottle than with a steelyard. So they borrow one bottle of tea-oil and repay it with two bottles.

Selling Children. A loan in default for ten years, as mentioned above, is rare. In fact, a lender will seldom allow a borrower to extend his loan for ten years. The lender always forces the borrower to repay the loan as soon as possible and makes a new loan only after the old loan has been cleared up because he is worried about the peasant's ability to repay. Frequently a lender permits the borrower not to pay the interest on a loan for a couple of years, say no longer than three to five years, provided that the borrower repays the principal of the loan on time. By that time the interest has doubled. How does a lender force a borrower to repay a loan? During the harvest season the lender goes straight to the borrower's cropland with a pair of big baskets and says: "You must give me your crops as repayment for your loan." The only thing that the borrower can do is watch the lender take away his crops. During the harvest season, after paying the rent and loans, "from the top of the plants to the bottom of the roots, there's nothing to eat." In these cases, many peasants wipe their tears with their sleeves.

There is a saying in Xunwu *xian*: "You must repay your loan even if you marry off your daughter or sell your son." Lenders usually shout this out when pressing "terribly stubborn borrowers" for repayment. Their anger builds up because the borrower is unable to repay the loan. Reader, I am not exaggerating in order to expose the evil of the exploiting class in Xunwu. All my survey reports are made carefully without any overstatement. I always doubted that the description of "selling his wife or son" appearing in articles was true. So I carefully questioned peasants in Xunwu to see whether this really happens. The result was careful interviews of three peasants who participated in an investigation meeting. The following happened in their three villages. Liu Liangfan, from Fufushan in Xunwu City District (about 18 *li* from the city) said that his village consists of thirty-seven households divided into five surnames: the Liu, the Cao, the Chen, the Lin, and the Huang. Five households had sold sons *[naizi]*. (The Hakka call their sons *naizi*.) Three of the five households were from the Liu surname group and are related to Liu Liangfan, the chairman of the Xunwu City suburban township soviet. These were the households of Liu Changyu, Liu Changlun, and Liu Changchun. The other two households were those of Lin Fangting and Chen Liangyou. Liu Changyu (Liu Liangfan's uncle) is a carpenter; the other four are tenants. Liu Changyu sold three of his four sons, Liu Changlun sold one of his three sons, Liu Changchun sold one of his two sons, Lin Fangting sold two of his three sons, and Chen Liangyou sold half of his one son. All five households had become bankrupt with nothing left; consequently, they had to sell their sons to repay their debts and buy food. The buyer was either a nearby member of the gentry of the same surname as the seller or a rich peasant. There are more gentry buyers than rich-peasant buyers. The price of a boy ranges from a minimum of 100 *yuan* to a maximum of 200 *yuan*. When making this transaction neither the buyer nor the seller call this business "selling"; rather they call it an "adoption." But the world in general calls it "selling a child." An "adoption contract" is also commonly called a "body deed." An "adoption contract" might read:

> X writes this adoption contract. Because he is too poor to feed his children, who have a crying need for food, and because he cannot borrow money, on the advice of his relatives and friends, he would rather give his (first, second, etc.) son to his brother, X, as a son. The biological father will get ... *yuan* in payment for his son. After adoption, the adoptive father has all rights to teach and to control the marriage of the adopted son; he can even beat him. But the

biological father has no right to interfere. Both parties voluntarily agree, without coercion, with the contents of this contract, and no party will change his mind in the future. Because words are unreliable, we have written this contract as evidence.

Matchmaker A (signature)
B (signature)
C (signature)

Relative A (signature)
B (signature)
C (signature)

Friend A (signature)
B (signature)
C (signature)

Biological father of the boy (signature)
Biological mother of the boy (signature)
Biological older brother of the boy (signature)
Biological younger brother of the boy (signature)
Day   Month   Year

Only the seller writes up a contract; the buyer writes nothing. The so-called matchmakers are go-betweens. At most there are four or five of them [per transaction], who share a fee for services rendered amounting to 5 percent of the selling price. More than ten relatives and friends might be present and are paid a "signature fee" by the buyer. When a close relative or influential person (most are members of the gentry) signs his name to the adoption contract, the signature fee is high, from more than 10 to 20 *yuan*. But the fee paid to ordinary relatives and friends is less than 1 *yuan*. The ages of the boys sold range from three or four *sui* to seven and eight *sui* to thirteen or fourteen *sui*. After the deal is made, the matchmakers carry the boy on their backs to the buyer's house. At this moment the biological parents of the boy always weep and cry. Sometimes couples even fight with each other. The wife scolds the husband for his uselessness and his inability to feed his family, which have forced them to sell a son. Most of the spectators weep too. When Liu Changyu sold his son, for example, his nephew Liu Liangfan was one of those who wept for Liu Changyu. Now let us talk of Li Dashun's story. He was the second of our peasant friends to attend the investigation meeting. He comes from the large village of Huangsha, in Shuangqiao District, with four hundred households. He personally witnessed five cases of households in his village selling a son. Each of the five households sold one boy. When one boy was sold to someone in the Bachi area in Pingyuan *xian*, Guangdong, Li Dashun came across the father, carrying his baby on his back, going in the direction of Bachi. The father had tears on his face and was ashamed when he realized an acquaintance could see he was selling his son. Why did he sell his son to someone in the Bachi area in Guangdong? Because the price was higher. A boy could be sold for 200 or 300 *yuan* there. A child of four or five *sui* brings the highest price because such a child can easily "develop a close relationship." In contrast, the price of an older child, eight or nine *sui* or over ten *sui*, is lower, because it is difficult to develop such a relationship and the boy can easily escape from his adoptive parents. Mei Zhiping, the third of our peasant friends who attended the investigation meeting, is a peasant in Lantian Village in Shuangqiao District. The selling of children happened in his village also. His uncle, Mei Hongpo, is an extremely poor peasant. He has three sons: one went abroad to Southeast Asia, one is living with him, and the other was sold to someone in Pingyuan *xian*. In the neighboring village of Anjing, the poor peasant Mei Chuanhua sold five of his seven sons. Here were only three people—Liu, Li, and Mei—at the investigation meeting, but in their own villages so many people had sold their children. One of the three people, Liu, comes from the northern half of this *xian*; the other two come from the southern half of the *xian*. Therefore, we can easily imagine the situation in the *xian* as a whole. Based on their knowledge of the places they are familiar with, they estimate that 10 percent of the households in the *xian* have sold their sons. Liu Liangfan told us that he had seen of, or heard about, more than a hundred boys being sold in the vicinity of his village.

It is common to sell a boy, but no one has heard of wives or daughters being sold.

On hearing that a borrower has sold a son, lenders will hurry to the borrower's house and force the borrower to repay his loan. The lender will cruelly shout to the borrower: "You have sold your son. Why don't you repay me?" Why does the lender act like this? Because it is a critical point for his loan. If the borrower does not repay his loan after selling his son, the lender knows that he will never have another chance to get his loan back once the money is used up. Therefore, he considers only how to force the borrower to repay the loan without regard for anything else.

The old society was truly a society of man eat man!

Establishing a Savings and Loan Association. The purpose of establishing a savings and loan association is for mutual help, not to exploit the other members in it. A person might invite his relatives or friends to establish a savings and loan association in order to pay for wedding expenses, engage in business, pay burial expenses, or repay a debt. However, since such associations as the month association, the double-year association, and four-season association have a strong tendency to make money, the result can be exploitation of the peasants.

The one who organizes the association (association head) is seldom a person who is utterly destitute but is rather a middle peasant or a small merchant. Rich peasants do not need to take part in such associations. The utterly destitute cannot establish an association because no one will join it. Only semiowner peasants and tenants with their own draft animals and plows, owner-peasants, and small merchants not in danger of bankruptcy can invite people to join an association and have people come.

There are five kinds of associations: permanent associations, half-year associations, month associations, four-season associations, and double-year associations.

Permanent associations consist of six people, and one cycle lasts six years. Ten *yuan* is collected from every member but the organizer, who receives 50 *yuan*. In the first cycle there is "no principal but there's interest." [Interest rates are:] 30 percent for the first three years (15 *yuan* for each year, for a total of 45 *yuan* in three years); 25 percent for the next two years (12.5 *yuan* for each year, for a total of 25 *yuan* for two years); and 20 percent for one year (10 *yuan*). In the first cycle, the interest payments for six years total 80 *yuan*. The rules for the second cycle are the same as those for the first cycle, except that the interest decreases each year. For example, the recipients in the second cycle pay 30 percent interest for the first two years (15 *yuan* each year for a total of 30 *yuan*); 25 percent [for the next two years] (12.5 *yuan* for each year for a total of 25 *yuan*), and 20 percent for one year (10 *yuan*). The total interest is 65 *yuan*. The interest rate for the third cycle is much less than that for the second cycle. The saying the "first cycle loses face whereas the second cycle gets benefits" means that although the first cycle has economic advantages, the organizer has to beg people to join his association [before he gets it]. In the second cycle, however, one gets benefits, though a bit less, without begging.[92]

---

92. These savings and loan associations, also known as "rotating credit societies" or "cooperative credit clubs," provided money for unexpected large capital outlays. Each member had one chance, or turn, during the life of the association, to receive money from the others. The longer one waited, the lower the interest rate on funds received. In Mao's example, the association organizer received 50 *yuan* at the beginning of the association's existence. At the next meeting, a year later, another member would receive a sum of money provided by the others. The organizer would pay 15 *yuan*, and the others would pay the regular 10 *yuan*. Thus, the second recipient would receive 55 *yuan*. The first six-year cycle would proceed as follows (italicized figures indicate amount received):

Member	Start	Year 1	Year 2	Year 3	Year 4	Year 5	Year 6
Organizer	*50*	15	15	15	15	15	15
Member 2	10	*55*	15	15	15	15	15
Member 3	10	10	*60*	15	15	15	15
Member 4	10	10	10	*65*	12.5	12.5	12.5
Member 5	10	10	10	10	*67.5*	12.5	12.5
Member 6	10	10	10	10	10	*70*	10
							80

At the end of the first six-year cycle, the organizer, who received 50 *yuan* at the outset, had paid out 90 *yuan*. Therefore, he paid interest of 40 *yuan*, spread over six years. The last member paid only 60 *yuan*, but received 70, thus implicitly receiving interest of 10 *yuan*. The second cycle would begin with an initial fund of 80 *yuan*, which, as Mao points out, represents the total of all reinvested interest payments for the first cycle. Interest

The interest rates for half-year associations change each half-year. The number of association members can be as few as eight, nine, ten, or eleven or more than twenty. The system of "no principal but there's interest" does not work in a half-year association. Instead, accounts are cleared up among each member of the association once each six months. (No data for month associations, double-year associations, and four-season associations.)

Exploitation Through Taxes and Levies

Money and Grain:

Land Tax. The total tax revenue in the *xian* was 1,424 ounces of silver. A liability of one ounce of silver in regular taxes could be met with three silver dollars. The supplementary tax was 0.34 *yuan*. In fact, the land tax was collected in the form of rice, not money. Eight *shao* of grain were collected per *dan* of yield. (10 *shao* = 1 *ge*; 10 *ge* = 1 *sheng*.) According to the exchange rate, one *sheng* of land tax grain equals 0.642 ounces of silver and one ounce of silver equals 3.24 silver dollars, [so] 0.2 silver dollars *[dayang]* were collected from a 1-*dan* field. It was said that long ago Yang Xiaoyuan, a jail warden *[dianshi]* in Anyuan went to the capital city of Beijing to see the emperor. On meeting the emperor, he put a plate on his head and held a piece of paper in his hand. There were many liquor cups on the plate, which represented Anyuan and Xunwu *xian*, where there are many hills and mountains but few fields. On the paper he petitioned the emperor to reduce the land tax, with such words as "in ten thousand *qing* [1 *qing* = 16.5 acres] of mountains there is only a thread's width of land where it is possible for people to grow crops." The emperor flew into a towering rage and roared out: "You are such a low-ranking official that you should not be reporting directly to me. Not only do I disagree with you; I would also like to cut your head off." But after he read the paper, especially the paragraph that included "in ten thousand *qing* of mountains there is only a thread's width of land where it is possible for people to grow crops," the emperor said: "The words in the paper sound reasonable." So he approved a land tax reduction. Since then, the land tax in Anyuan and Xunwu *xian* has been lighter than in other *xian*. And to this day,

---

payments totaled 92.5 *yuan*, of which 2.5 *yuan* and 10 *yuan* were paid to members 5 and 6, respectively, and the remaining 80 *yuan* formed the initial fund for the beginning of the second cycle. See also James Dyer Ball, *Things Chinese*, 5th ed. (Shanghai: Kelley & Walsh, 1925), pp. 596–605. The associations were often identified by the periods of payment: fortnightly, monthly, quarterly, or annually (p. 597). Ball makes the illuminating remark that these associations were at once a borrowing club and a lending club (p. 601).—RT.

the landlords and rich peasants in the two *xian* still hold a memorial ceremony for Yang with incense and candles at the end of each year's harvest. You can see temples to Yang in both *xian*.[93]

State Rent. All land in Huangxiang District, part of Sanbiao District, and part of Xunwu City District is owned by the state. The land is called state land *[guantian]*. The government does not collect land tax from state land but rather "state rent" *[guanzu]*, which totals about 940 ounces of silver each year. The state rent rate is nine to ten times heavier than the land tax and is about 0.2 *yuan [xiaoyang]* per *dan*. How did this land become state land? In the Ming dynasty there was a very powerful rebel, Ye Kai, who made his base in Huangxiang District for many years and fought against the emperor. But finally the emperor overcame him through a stratagem and took over all of Ye Kai's land. This land became state land. It was illegal to buy and sell state land, and transfers could be effected only under the guise of rent, the so-called *dingtui* between tenants of state land. Ye Kai's subordinates had occupied Sanbiao District, and so the story behind the state land in Sanbiao is the same as in Huangxiang. As for the small pieces of state land in the City District, these came from the expropriations of the land of those in the town who broke the emperor's law.

Total. In total, the land tax and the state rent should yield 2,360 ounces of silver, which is equal to about 7,640 silver dollars at the exchange rate of one ounce of silver for 3.24 silver dollars. However, because of (1) natural disasters like erosion and flooding, (2) the fact that some residents have moved out and others were without offspring, and (3) the fact that some taxpayers were too poor to pay tax or rent, the local government lost 20 percent of the figure. In fact, about 6,100 silver dollars were collected.

Bitterness. As mentioned above, a sum of only about 6,100 silver dollars was collected each year. But the *xian* government needed more than 10,000 silver dollars each year for public expenditures on administration, justice, prisons, and public welfare. There was a big gap between revenue and expenses. Consequently, all those appointed as officials in Xunwu felt that life in Xunwu was very bitter and, as a result, collaborated with the local gentry to make up a variety of pretexts to oppress the poor people in the area in order to get money. The collection of the taxes on tobacco, liquor, and slaughtering was controlled directly by the provincial government, not the *xian* government. The latter was able to administer only the land tax.

---

93. The story was part of the oral and written tradition in Xunwu. A record of shrines dedicated to Yang (Yanggong ci) can be found in the 1881 edition of *Changning xianzhi,* "Yiwen," 4: 19a–2la.—RT.

Customary Fees. The Money and Grain Collection Department in the local government charged several customary fees. The first was the discount *[yinshui]* in the exchange rate; the person in charge of the Collection Department would get a cut of 5 to 10 percent of the money he handled. For example, the chief of the Collection Department might decide that one silver dollar *[dayang]* was equal to 1.25 *yuan [xiaoyang]*, when the official exchange rate was 1.2 *yuan.* So he could rake off more than 300 silver dollars when he collected a little over 6,100 silver dollars in land taxes and state rents each year. These discounts were the biggest way in which taxpayers were exploited by the Collection Department. The chief of the Collection Department had no salary at all and could survive only on discounts and other customary fees. The second fee was called the land transfer tax [lit., the after severance present] (also called the "severance grain" present). When anyone sold land, he had to pay a land transfer tax of 0.2 *yuan* to the Collection Department. Each year some six hundred households sold land. The Collection Department would get 120 *yuan* from that. The third was the [land deed] recording fee [lit., present]. When someone sold land, he had to pay not only the land transfer tax, but also the deed fee. He had to take the land deed to the Collection Department and have an official deed (issued by the Tax Collection Bureau) made. A recording fee of 0.2 *yuan* was charged to transcribe the information on the land deed onto an official deed. Each year the amount collected was the same as the land transfer tax. The fourth was the receipt fee, namely, the money collected from grain-tax receipts. The Collection Department got 0.03 *yuan [xiaoyang]* for each grain-tax receipt, or a total of 60 *yuan* from two thousand grain-tax receipts each year. All income from the four customary fees mentioned above belonged to the government *[gonggong]*, except for the discounts. When a new magistrate arrived and started his tour of duty, the chief of the Collection Department always gave him a present of twenty to thirty silver dollars. The money was called *diangui.* This meant the chief of the Collection Department hoped to be reappointed by the new magistrate. In addition, the Collection Department had to present the festival fees (for the Dragon Boat festival) and the New Year's fee not only to the magistrate but also to the section chief of the Tax Collection Bureau in the *xian* government. The former could receive things, whereas the latter received money (ten to twenty silver dollars). These expenses were derived from customary fees.

The People Who Are in Charge of the Money and Grain. Three people—Liu Shihui, Liu Meifang, and Huang Shaotang— were in charge of the Money and Grain Collection Department since the beginning of the Republic. They controlled the tax registers and worked hand in glove with the magistrate. Their position was hereditary. They voted one of their number in as chief, and the others automatically became assistants. When the Red Army attacked and occupied the town, they fled with all the books.

The Tobacco and Liquor Stamp Tax. The revenue from the taxes on tobacco and liquor in Xunwu *xian* was 60 *yuan [xiaoyang]* a month for each, or a total of 120 *yuan.* A merchant had contracted to collect the taxes and had established a tax bureau inside the North Gate. Once a month he went out and collected taxes in sixteen market towns: Chengjiang, Jitan, Sanbiao, Shipaixia, Liuche, Chetou, Niudouguang, Zhucun, Huangtangdu, Gongping, Huangxiang, Zhonghe, Cenfeng, Maoping, Longgang, and Shangping. He collected the tax from vendors selling liquor and every shop selling tobacco. He collected the taxes in accordance with the regulations from crooked vendors, but forced upright vendors to pay much more. He made 80 *yuan* each month based on the difference between the 120 *yuan* he had contracted to pay the government and the 200 *yuan* he actually collected. The tax bureau employed two clerks and one cook. The tax farmers were always from Ganzhou.

The Slaughter Tax. The collection of the slaughter tax was also contracted out. The amount that person contracted to pay the government was 80 *yuan*, but the actual money he collected was more than 150 *yuan* per month. So he could clear about 70 *yuan* each month. The slaughter tax farmer also established a bureau and employed one clerk and one cook. The clerk not only served the tax farmer, but also helped him to collect the tax. One-third of the 150 *yuan* came from the three butchers in Xunwu City. The slaughter tax farmers were also from Ganzhou. Although by law any rural resident had to pay a slaughter tax when he killed a pig for food, it was impossible for the tax farmer to uphold the law to the letter. He was actually able to collect the tax only from butchers with permanent slaughtering places in marketplaces.

Business Protection Tax. This was a local tax and was also called a sales tax. The funds for the Guomindang and the Pacification and Defense Militia came from the sales tax. Sometimes when the Public Security Bureau had a shortage of money, a certain percentage of the sales tax would be appropriated for it. The Sales Tax Bureau was under the Tax Collection Bureau and had established three branches, in Jitan, Pangu'ai, and outside the North Gate. There was a tax on all goods in transit, such as cooking oil, salt, rice, beans, chickens, ducks, oxen, pigs, sheep, dogs, marine products, general goods, and textiles. The tax payment started at 0.05 *yuan* and rose to a maximum of 0.5 *yuan*. Goods from nearby rural areas that were sold in small amounts—cakes, fruit, firewood, and [items] made from bamboo or wood—that were not being shipped elsewhere were tax free. In other words, everything shipped long distance was taxed. Since the development of the mass movement in the southern part of the *xian*, in areas like Liuche and Niudouguang, the Sales Tax Bureau was unable to open a branch there to collect the tax. Anyway, the three branches collected more than 2,000 *yuan* each month. The branch in Jitan itself once collected more than 2,000 *yuan* in a month, and the branch outside the North Gate once collected more than 800 *yuan* in a month. There used to be no branch in Pangu'ai, but a new branch was opened there recently by Xie Jiayou. Although the tax was called the "business protection tax," the merchants in fact hated it very much.

Ox Tax. This was collected only in Xunwu City. A total of 1,700 *yuan* was collected each year by a handful of people who contracted to collect this tax. No bureau [was associated with it]. One person emerged as spokesman. For four years he has been He Xuecai, the father of He Zizhen of the New Xunwu faction. Although the tax farmers paid 1,700 *yuan* to the government, they actually collected about 2,300 *yuan*. The ox tax was a local tax and was administered by the *xian* Tax Collection Bureau.

Gambling Tax. The gambling tax was called the "public interest tax" and was collected from gambling houses and brothels. It was a local tax. The gambling tax collector was appointed by the Tax Collection Bureau. (He Zishao did the job for two years.) The income from the gambling tax was 1,100 *yuan* each month from Xunwu City, although on one occasion 1,800 *yuan* was collected there. The gambling tax was also collected from other places in the *xian*. The year before last over 3,000 *yuan* was collected from the entire *xian*. At that time Liu Shiyi[94] sent some soldiers to collect the gambling tax. But Liu Shiyi received 2,000 *yuan* each month from this money, calling it a "protection tax." He did the same thing in every *xian* in southern Jiangxi. Later on, the Southern Jiangxi Native Place Association censured Liu Shiyi before the Jiangxi [provincial] government. Liu was forced to stop doing this. But the other powerful gentry kept doing the same thing as Liu had. This was but one act in the struggle between the powerful gentry and Liu. Many other *xian* had this kind of struggle.

General Income of the Tax Collection Bureau. The annual income was:

Ox tax	1,700 *yuan*
Business protection tax	24,000
Examination hall land rents	2,000
Sojourning Stipend Shrine land rents	3,000
Confucian Temple land rents	300

The total was around 30,000 *yuan* per year. This sum funded the Guomindang, the Pacification and Defense Corps, Tax Collection Bureau, Reconstruction Bureau, Education Bureau, the Rural Reform Bureau, Public Security Bureau, the New Xunwu School (established by He Zizhen and He Tingba), and the Puhua School (in Chengjiang, established by Xie Jiayou and Lan Yuqing). Generally speaking, this bankrolled the eating, gambling, whoring, and drug habits of the gentry and their lackeys.

---

94. Liu Shiyi was the division commander of the Jiangxi Seventh Independent Division and the brigade commander of the Fifteenth Independent Brigade in 1928.

Contributions and Loans. The [Jiangxi] provincial government forced this *xian* to buy 3,000 *yuan* of government bonds, 2,000 *yuan* of the 2.5 percent Surtax Treasury Bonds,[95] and 1,000 *yuan* of central government bonds, and to lend 4,000 *yuan* for other kinds of loans. In addition, more than 40,000 *yuan* was collected by the warlords who passed through the *xian*, such as Lin Hu, Liu Zhilu, Li Yibiao, Huang Renhuan,[96] Xu Chongzhi, and Lai Shihuang. The *xian* government made assessments on every district, village, and market [xu] in the *xian*. Every person in the *xian* who had either a one-*dan* field or business capital in excess of 100 *yuan* shared the responsibility. But the powerful gentry, land-lords, and large merchants with political influence, and officials at every level of government did not have to pay. Those who were exempt from collection also tried every method to reduce their relatives' and friends' obligations. Therefore, all the money was collected from the upright small landlords, rich peasants, and other merchants. Furthermore, a service fee, transportation fee, and tea fee were added to the assessments. In addition, for every 1,000 *yuan* originally required, the Tax Collection Bureau would collect 1,200 *yuan* and the district and town-ship governments would add a percentage. They all cashed in on this method. In the rare case when bonds or debts were redeemed by the *xian* from either the provincial government or the warlords, the commanders of the local militia in the towns as well as in every district would gobble it up, and the money never got back to the people. When Wang Ziyuan was general commander of the local militia, for example, he took 1,000 *yuan* that had been intended to repay a debt incurred by the army. The result was that all the lenders in Huangxiang sued him, but in the end they did not get a copper.

Culture in Xunwu

We can say that essentially no women can read, for no more than 300 women in the whole *xian* are literate. The cultural level of men is certainly not low—the southern half of the *xian* is more advanced than the northern half because of more developed transportation facilities and because of the influence of Guangdong. Based on the population of the whole *xian*, the figures are as follows:

---

95. The 2.5 Percent Surtax National Treasury Bonds were floated by Chiang Kaishek's régime in May and October 1927 in order to raise funds for military expenditures. These bonds were secured by a 2.5 percent surtax on custom duties that was being collected, by the end of 1927, in all treaty ports in China. This surtax on imports had been authorized, in the view of Chinese officials, by the Chinese Customs Tariff signed in Washington on February 6, 1922. See Stanley F. Wright, *China's Customs Revenue Since the Revolution of* 1911, 3rd ed., revised and enlarged with the assistance of John H. Cubbon (Shanghai: Inspectorate General of Customs, Statistical Department, 1935), pp. 345–52.—RT.

96. Li Yibiao was military commissioner for Guangzhou and Huizhou under the Beiyang warlords and the army commander of the Fourth Army of the Guangdong Army before 1925. Huang Renhuan was the commander of the First Division of the First Army of the Guangdong Army before 1925.

illiterate	60 %
literate	40 %
can read 200 characters	20 %
can keep accounts	15 %
can read the *Romance of the Three Kingdoms*	5 %
can write a letter	3.5%
can write an essay	1 %
lower primary students	5 % (5,000 people)
higher primary students	8 % (8,000 people)
middle school students	500 people
college students	30 people
returned students	6 people
xiucai	400 people
juren	1 person

(The above percentages are in terms of total population.)[97]

There are more higher primary students than lower primary students because most higher primary students enter directly after studying at private schools. In the whole *xian* there are not more than ten lower primary schools in each district. With seventy schools in seven districts, taking a figure of fifty students in each, there is a total of three thousand five hundred students. In addition there are eighty hybrid[98] lower primary schools that either exist on paper but not in reality or have not even put up a sign. Students in such schools number about one thousand five hundred. Together these two categories total about five thousand people.

There is at least one higher primary school in each district. Shuangqiao District normally has two, although at one time (before the March 25 uprising) it had four. Nanba District has two, but at one time (before the March 25 uprising) it had three. Xunwu City District has two schools (the East School in the city and the Cao Lineage School in Tianbei). At one time Huangxiang District had three schools (before the March 25 uprising). Xunwu City has three (excluding the East School). The whole *xian* normally has thirteen higher primary schools and at the height, that is, around the time of the high tide of the cultural movement

---

97. In order to make sense of this table, one must assume that the first three subdivisions under the general category "literate" are primary. They define different levels of reading ability, which might be characterized as "minimal," "functional," and "classical" (since the *Sanguo yanyi* [Romance of the Three Kingdoms] is written in *wenyan*), and add up to the total of 40 per cent for literate men. The other subdivisions, which relate to writing ability, schools attended, and traditional degrees obtained, overlap with the first three, and provide additional detail.

98. The expression here translated as "hybrid" means literally "half-old not-new." Mao uses it in reference to schools combining the traditional Confucian curriculum and the Western-influenced curriculum.—RT.

[wenhua yundong] (before the March 25 uprising but after China's Great Revolution), there were eighteen. Normally every school has a hundred students. The oldest have a history of twenty-odd years, from the end of the Guangxu period in the Qing to the present, with a total of about ten thousand students. Of these ten thousand, two thousand have already died. Higher primary school students, for the most part, are children of small landlords, with the children of large landlords and rich peasants each constituting a small part.

This *xian* has had four middle schools, but all have had a short life. The large landlord Uncle Shitcrock of Xiangshan established the Zhichi Middle School in Xiaohang in Xiangshan, which lasted a year. The Shangzhi Middle School (in Qiufang), which lasted half a year, was established by a group of Shuangqiao landlords. In Chengjiang [District] the publicly established Puhua Middle School (in Chengjiang) lasted two years. The Sun Yatsen [Zhongshan] Middle School established by the Revolutionary Faction (in Xunwu City) lasted two months. Together these schools had more than a hundred students, but there were no graduates. Most [current] middle school students attend schools in three places: Mei *xian*, Pingyuan *xian*, and Ganzhou City (each place has around a hundred students). All of them are children of landlords; most of them are from small-landlord families.

College students come mostly from the large- and middle-landlord class. Only five students are from the small-landlord class. Liu Weilu studied one term at Sun Yatsen University in Canton, Liu Weie studied two years at Beijing University, and Kuang Caicheng studied over a year at Beijing Normal University. These three were all Communist Party members. The two Liu were killed during the March 25 uprising. Kuang was a chief of staff of the Fiftieth Regiment of the Red Army and was tortured to death by Xie Jiayou in Chengjiang. Kuang Shifang, who studied for four years at Chaoyang University in Beijing, became ill and died—his thought was revolutionary. Ling Delu studied at Culture University in Beijing for a year and then went to Russia to study, but he did not have enough to live on so he tutored the children of the [Chinese] ambassador to Finland. His thought is revolutionary. These five were able to go to college only because their tuition was provided by their ancestral halls.

The twenty-five college and vocational students from large-landlord families are all reactionaries. The most important are:

He Zizhen: two years of study at a Henan mining school; head of the Xunwu Pacification and Defense Corps.

Lai Shiyuan: two years of study at Beijing Normal Preparatory School; participated in counterrevolutionary activities in Huangxiang.

Liu Hongxiang: two years of study in Beijing at Culture University; a leader of counterrevolutionary forces in Nanba District.

These three people are in Xunwu; the rest are elsewhere and are members of Chiang Kaishek's faction. Of the thirty people who have been to college, 80 percent studied law.

Six people have gone overseas to study:

Pan Zuoqin: a graduate of an English medical school; practices medicine in Shantou.

Qiu Lingyun: although he has been to England and back, he really cannot be considered a returned student; an engineer with a Tianjin mining company.

Qiu Weiwu: a graduate of Imperial University in Japan and a core member of the New Xunwu faction; he fled with He Zizhen.

Gu Ziping: returned to China from Japan after purchasing a diploma; a person who whores and gambles; from Huangxiang; has served as president of the Education Society; he was attacked at a stronghold in Huangxiang by the Red Army and fled.

These four all have large- and middle-landlord backgrounds.

Zeng Youlan: the first to go overseas to study; during the Guangxu period, he went to Japan and graduated from a law course; he served as a judicial official in Fengtian, Beijing, and Hubei; the Sun Yatsen Middle School faction has treated him as their nominal leader; after the defeat of the March 25 uprising, his home was burned; now he is a member of the Reorganization faction.

Kuang Mohan: studied in Japan; refers to himself as a Marxist; is dean at Culture University in Beijing; formed a transportation company in Nanjing along with the large Xunwu landlord Xie Jie.

These two people are neither of large nor of middle landlord background. Zeng is a small landlord who studied in Japan on government money; Kuang is a poor peasant, a graduate of a higher primary school who entered the Nanchang Military School, where someone saw his promise, sponsored him, and gave him money to go to Japan.

There are still four hundred *xiucai* scattered throughout the *xian*. Of the six hundred Gu in the single-surname village of Tangbei in Huangxiang, eleven are *xiucai*. This is the place where *xiucai* are most concentrated. When Gu Bo's great-great grandfather died at seventy *sui*, an imperially sanctioned memorial arch was constructed. Over the arch is inscribed "He personally saw seven generations." On each side is inscribed "His eyes saw five who held the *lingong* degree" and "Twelve *shengyuan* gathered at his knees."[99] This means that at that

---

99. These inscriptions refer to various Qing civil service examination degrees. *Shengyuan* (the official title for those referred to elsewhere in this text by the popular expression *xiucai*) are represented here by the word "collar" *(jin)*, which evokes the so-called Confucian gown worn by scholars in late imperial China. The other inscriptions quoted in the text refer to five men who held either the *linsheng* or *gongsheng* degrees. These degrees were just below the *juren* degree in prestige. Holders of the *linsheng* degree were given stipends and could become powerful and privileged members in their communities. They could compete for a *gongsheng* degree, the receipt of which, in the opinion of Chang Chung-li, marked one's arrival into the ranks of the upper gentry. They could be

time there were twelve *xiucai* among his descendants. In the whole *xian*, the old culture was richest among the Tangbei Gu. They occupied a central position in administration in the past. Among the two thousand people of Chetou Township in Nanba District are nine *xiucai*, which is a lot. Among the fourteen hundred people of Longtu Township in Nanba District are two *xiucai*, which is few. Recently most *xiucai* have not had anything to do, and in the countryside they are called *laotai*. (Within a lineage peasants call the most respected person a *laotai;* he is called *xiansheng* by the local people.) These people are mostly rent-receiving small landlords, but some teach (both old and new curricula) and others make their livelihood by practicing medicine. *Xiucai* are essentially products of the landlord class, but an extremely small number have a poor peasant background. They were nurtured by landlords, studied, and entered school. Xunwu only has one *juren* now: Gu Luping. His father was a farm laborer, and the family had nothing to eat. When he was young, Gu Luping carried small baskets of snacks (sweets, water chestnuts, and salted turnips) for sale. Later, while he was studying, a teacher saw he was bright and would not accept tuition. Thus, he really advanced in his studies. He served as a [Qing] magistrate twice and twice as a provincial assembly representative. In the countryside he is extremely smooth and everyone likes him. On the surface he supported the New Xunwu faction, but at the same time he prohibited his daughter from cutting her hair and he restricted her freedom of marriage. When the land struggle began in the southern half of the *xian*, he opposed it. This time when the Red Army entered and attacked the Gu family stronghold, he advocated surrender.

After the victory of the land struggle in the southern half of the *xian*, every township soviet has built at least one Lenin primary school. Each township usually has two, and in exceptional places (Longtu, Niudouguang) four have been built. Every school has forty to fifty students, which is more than double the number of schools and students during the old days of Guomindang schools. The children say: "If it hadn't been for the land revolution, we wouldn't be able to study." As for higher primary schools, because of a lack of money and teachers (revolutionary intellectuals are busy participating in the struggle), schools have not been opened.

Chapter V: The Land Struggle in Xunwu

The Method of Land Redistribution

There are a few methods for distributing land. The major one is equal redistribution per capita. Only 20 percent of the land in the *xian* was not redistributed. Of

---

named to educational or administrative posts. See Chang Chung-li, *The Chinese Gentry: Studies on Their Role in Nineteenth-Century Chinese Society* (Seattle: University of Washington Press, 1955), pp. 17–18, 27–29.—RT. (See also Appendix C to Roger Thompson's monograph.)

the land already redistributed, 80 percent of the land was reallotted on the basis of equal redistribution per capita, regardless of age or sex. At the beginning of the land struggle, no law existed that could be applied to this situation. The Xunwu *Xian* Revolutionary Committee (the *xian* government) suggested four methods, asking that the district and township soviets summon mass meetings to discuss and choose one method. The four methods are: (1) Equal redistribution per capita. (2) Redistribution according to labor power. Those who have more labor power receive more land and those who have less labor power receive less land. In other words, anyone over four years old and under fifty-five is regarded as one labor unit and receives one share; those who are under four or over fifty-five receive only one-half share.[100] (3) Redistribution according to financial resources. Artisans get less land, and those who do not have an occupation get more. (4) Redistribution according to soil fertility. Those who receive poorer lands receive more; those who get fertile lands get less. In the event, most places chose the first method. Later on, the Xunwu *Xian* Communist Party applied the first method to all districts and was supported by the majority of the poor peasants and the masses. At present about 80 percent of the areas that redistributed land used this method. Within these areas, regardless of age, sex, or labor power, the total amount of land was divided by the number of persons.

Some villages did not redistribute the land to people under four. From those over four all the way to the elderly, those incapable of farming got a 50 percent share or a 70 percent share; the rest received a full share. This was the method practiced in Liuche, Fengshan, Shangqi, and Datong townships, which have a population of about ten thousand.

Some areas redistributed the land equally by the number of persons and then had those who were incapable of farming return part of their share to the soviet; this land was then added to the share of those with greater labor power. (The amounts of shares returned were unequal; each person decided individually.) In the end, persons capable of greater physical labor got more land and those not as capable got less. This method is similar to the second method suggested by the *xian* government. The difference is that peasants returned some part of the land of their own accord after the land was redistributed instead of redistributing the land according to labor power from the beginning. Longtu Township followed

---

100. Although the editors of *Mao Zedong nongcun diaocha wenji* think that the text should actually read "over fourteen and under fifty-five," based on their analysis of the March 1930 "Xingguo Soviet Government Land Law," they decided to leave the text as it appears in the manuscript, i.e., reading "over four and under fifty-five." See *Guangming ribao*, February 12, 1983, p. 3.—RT. (This corresponds to the extremely prudent editorial policy of the Department for Research on Party Literature, which is reluctant to make any emendations at all in the text of Mao's writings, even when there are compelling grounds for doing so, if there is no written source to support such a change.)

this method. In another township, Huangsha, a similar situation occurred, except this time the land was not returned by the peasants of their own accord. When the government saw that some people could not farm the land they had received, it ordered them to return part of the land to the government. The peasants did not complain when asked to return part of the land unless the government forced them to return the fertile part and would not let them return the poor part; then they got upset. The combined population of Longtu and Huangsha is two thousand five hundred.

In addition, there is the free-farming method practiced in Datian Township. Whoever wants to farm can farm, and there is no limit on how much land these people should get. This is because Datian Township experienced a White terror in which nearly a hundred able-bodied men and dozens of elderly people and children were killed. In some cases, entire families were slaughtered. Some thirty people became Red Guards or went to other *xian* to participate in revolutionary work. The population of the township was reduced from eight hundred to six hundred, and much land was left uncultivated. Meanwhile, all the oxen in the township were taken away by the reactionaries. Thus, the land is open, without restriction, to anyone who wants to farm. Farming oxen were [then] fetched from rich households in other townships.

The Question of Redistribution of Hills and Forests

The hills in the *xian*, except for those in Niudouguang Township, still have not been redistributed and are being farmed by the original cultivators. In name, the soviet owns these hills and forests, and the cultivators pay land taxes to the soviet. Why were hills and forests redistributed only in Niudouguang? Because there are many people and little land in that township, and the peasants urgently asked that hill land be redistributed. Many peasants in other villages are also eager for the hills to be redistributed. For example, because the hills are owned by the ancestral trusts in some big lineages, the peasants in the areas outside Xunwu City's North Gate and South Gate and peasants from small lineages have no hill land to farm and are thus pushing to redistribute the hills.

The Question of Redistributing Ponds

The owner is the soviet, but the right of usage goes to the peasants. Pond management rotates annually among families who live around the pond. This method applies to the whole *xian*.

The Question of Redistributing Houses

There was no redistribution of houses. However, people who had fewer houses or whose houses were burned down by the reactionaries were allowed to move into the houses owned by those who have more houses. Many houses in Shuangqiao and Nanba districts were burned down by the enemy, and those who were burned out moved into the landlords' and rich peasants' houses; some also moved into middle and poor peasants' houses too. This created a problem. The owners of the houses disliked these newcomers giving birth to male infants in their houses. It is believed in Xunwu that if an outsider gives birth to a son in a house, the spirit of the family will be taken away by the newborn and the family's prosperity will decline. There was once a *jinshi* named Zeng Xingsong in Fangtian Township, Shuangqiao District. He was born in his maternal grandfather's house and later became a *jinshi* and an official. People believe that he thus took the good fortunes of his grandfather's family. This is a well-known story throughout the *xian*. After the failure of the March 25 uprising, the wife of the commander of the rebellion in Liuche, Zhong Xiqiu,[101] took refuge at her maternal grandfather's house. Her grandfather worried that she might be in labor soon and told her to leave right away. She finally escaped to a village in Longchuan *xian*, built a hut in the hills, and gave birth to a son there. Although at present most people whose houses are occupied by poor peasants and workers do not dare to oppose openly the latter giving birth to male infants in their houses, they are still resentful of this. The only solution is to change the status of "temporary residence" to "permanent residence"; in other words, to redistribute landlords' houses based on the land redistribution method. This is also a strategy to gain the support of poor peasants and thus shake the foundations of the feudal system.

The Area Standard for Land Redistribution

For two reasons, peasants like to take a small district as a unit and object to taking a large district as the unit within which land redistribution takes place. First, they are concerned that the land in their area will be redistributed to other areas. Because of this, not only will they not agree to take the district as a unit for redistributing land but they also are not inclined to take the township as a unit. What they wholeheartedly want is to take the village as a unit so that village land is redistributed to local villagers. Thus, although 85 percent of the land in Xunwu was redistributed within townships, the majority of the peasants did not support this method even though they did not strongly object. They did not actively disagree because the difference in the quantity of land owned by villages was not so great; hence the peasants suffered only a small economic loss with the application of this redistribution method. In those villages where the differences in the quantities of the land are large, or in villages that cover a large area almost equal to that of a township, the peasants strongly oppose taking the township as a

---

101. The organization of the March 25, 1928 uprising included a general command post led by Liu Weilu, with Zhong Xiqiu, Gu Bo, Liu Weie, and He Jiachang serving as assistant commanders. Six command posts were established in the *xian*.—RT.

unit. Xunwu City Suburban Township (which is divided into four villages) and Xinzhai Township (divided into two villages) of the Xunwu City District, and Zhucun Township (which is divided into six villages) of Nanba District, all took the village as a unit for redistribution. This type of area was not very common, constituting only about 15 percent of the *xian*. The other reason is that the peasants disliked moving. They did not want to move from district to district, or from township to township. "Whenever you move, you need a basket of grain" means that in moving one suffers great losses. In addition, the peasants have a blind faith in geomancy and consider it unlucky to abandon their ancestors' tombs. The peasants believe that geomancy is good for production. Peasants value familiarity with their fields and accustomed living arrangements. In leaving all this and moving to another township, they suffer a sense of loss without knowing why. Also, for geographical reasons some people are not willing to move. For example, owing to Chetou's convenient location, commerce flourishes there. People do not want to move to out-of-the-way places (even though these places are still in the same district and only a dozen or so *li* away). This can be regarded as an economic factor too. It is wrong to think that these peasants' localism is simply old-fashioned thinking, and it is also a mistake to regard this type of thinking in psychological terms instead of economic terms.

Vagrants Who Live in the Outskirts of Xunwu City Ask to Share in Land Redistribution

The peasants in Xunwu City received the least land during redistribution. Every person got land yielding 1 *dan* 8 *dou* [of grain]. This is the smallest amount of all the districts in the *xian*. There were fewer peasants than in other districts, yet many vagrants and prostitutes who did not farm also asked to share in land redistribution, thus reducing the amount of each share. Those prostitutes who had lovers ran away with them; those who did not have lovers asked to share in the land redistribution. They said, "There's no business; we will starve to death if we don't get our share of redistributed land." People criticized them for not being able to farm. They replied, "We can learn how to farm." In fact, they are farming in the fields already. Most of the vagrants and prostitutes have received some land. Among the vagrants, some have the ability to farm, whereas others have sons or a small bit of capital. Some prostitutes have husbands or sons. Those with a number of family members are even more earnest in asking for redistributed land. Without it, they might have created a disturbance. Under these circumstances, the government distributed some land to them. Those inveterate vagabonds and prostitutes who had absolutely no ability to farm still have not been given any land. In the outskirts of Xunwu City, 60 percent of the vagrants received land; the remaining 40 percent had no knowledge of farming.

The Quantity of Land Per Person and the Supplement for Living

The peasants in the suburban area got the least land. Each person got only 1 *dan* 8 *dou* per *dang.* (There are two crops a year; each crop is called a *dang.)* Peasants in the four wards of the Xunwu City District got a little more. Each person got over 3 *dan.* Shuangqiao District had the highest allotments. Each person got over 7 *dan* per *dang.* In Longtu and Hejiao, each person got 7 *dan.* In most places each person got 5 *dan* per *dang.* Daily rice consumption is 1 *jin*, or 360 *jin* a year. One hundred eighty *jin* equals 1 *dan*, and 2 *dan* of [hulled] rice equal 4 *dan* of [unhulled] grain. When redistributing the land, wet grain (that is, *maogu*) is always taken as a unit. Each *dang* produces 5 *dan* of wet grain, two *dang* a year equals 10 *dan.* Ten *dan* of wet grain yield 8 *dan* of dry grain. Four *dan* are consumed, leaving 4 *dan*, of which 3 *dan* of grain are made into rice cakes and rice wine. The rest is insufficient for daily expenses, such as clothes, oil, and salt, and for social intercourse (e.g., weddings, funerals, and festivals). In this case, how do people manage to make up the difference? Raising pigs, chickens, and ducks; growing some vegetables (in the suburbs of Xunwu City), sugarcane, bamboo, and miscellaneous crops (like sweet potatoes, taro, chestnuts, soybeans); and also making handicraft products (all kinds of articles made with rounded wood and with bamboo, such as wok lids, buckets, rice containers, foot basins, urine buckets, water dippers, bamboo chairs, straw rainhats, winnowing fans, rice sieves, bamboo scoops, fire grates, bamboo baskets, and other items. Most of the peasants do this as sideline work; very few of them do it as an occupation. Some peasants even make desks, benches, chairs, and tables). Some work as porters (carrying rice, salt, soybeans, oil, and miscellaneous crops; they all are hired by other people to carry these things, mostly rice and salt; the rest of those things being less common); run small businesses (like selling oil, salt, rice, soybeans, pigs, chickens, and even rice cakes, etc.); and also working for the capitalists (picking mushrooms and tea, making paper). Everyone does one or two of the above as sideline occupations in order to supplement his income. In general, income from land constitutes two-thirds of a family's income, and the miscellaneous income makes up the remaining third.

The Question of Whether to Have Corporate Land

There is no corporate land. During the meetings, the peasants were very eager to redistribute all the land; no one ever suggested keeping some of the land as corporate land. Because of the high population density and the scarcity of land, there is barely enough land for the peasants to feed themselves, not to mention that some of the peasants still do not have enough land. Who would agree that the government should still allow corporate land?

The Speed of Redistribution

After the uprising, land in the northern part of the *xian* was redistributed very quickly. For instance, from the insurrection and taking of Xunwu City to the completion of redistribution took the Xunwu City District only twenty days. Chetou and Longtu in Nanba District and Shangping in Sanshui District accomplished the redistribution at an even faster rate. They finished the investigation within one day, completed calculations within two days, promulgated the results for a day, and then spent the rest of the time determining the division of each share of redistributed land according to the principle of "drawing on the plentiful to make up for the scarce" [i.e., taking land away from those with more than the average share and giving it to those with less than the average share]. In such cases, it takes at least one week **because the real struggle is in using the principle of drawing on the plentiful to make up for the scarce.** This type of struggle is the peasants' struggle against landlords and rich peasants. Those who have plenty of land and need to have land taken away do not want to give away the fertile part. Those who lack land do not want to accept the poor part. Thus, it takes time to mix them well. Most of the southern part of the *xian* (except Chetou and Longtu) experienced a rather slow redistribution. Since last February [1929], there has been an armed struggle in the Shuangqiao area. However, it was not until the end of November that the *xian* Revolutionary Committee was established and the statistical forms for the land investigation were distributed. After a month the investigation was still incomplete because of improper methods. The investigation forms contained innumerable items (population, class status, cultural level, ethnicity, age, land ownership, land boundary, land area, yearly harvest), including some that did not need to be investigated. On top of that, the procedure was quite inconvenient. (The *xian* Revolutionary Committee first distributed the investigation forms to each township, and then each township returned the completed forms to the *xian* Revolutionary Committee for review.) This slowed the speed of redistribution. In January of this year the method was changed. The investigation forms contained only a few simple items: the name of the household head, total number of family members, how many family members can farm, how many make a living in commerce or industry, the quantity of land, and the quantity the household should get. The investigation procedure was as follows: the township government convened a "conference on the redistribution of land." Each household sent one delegate to discuss the method of redistributing land. Then the conference investigations began. (Many tables were set up at the conferences, and representatives from each village sat at tables and took down the information that people reported.) The forms were turned in to the township governments, which checked and ratified this information and then figured out the amount for each person by dividing the total quantity of land by the total number of persons. The results were then announced. Thus, it took only four days from the investigation to the announcement (one day for investigation, two days for checking, and one day for announcing). It remained, then, to redistribute the land. This was started on the fifth day. Each township government sent out a dozen or so political instructors *[zhidaoyuan]*, who fanned out to all the villages to investigate whether the land was fertile or infertile and to confirm whether the reports made by the peasants on the first day of the investigation were true or false. Based on the investigation, redistribution was then carried out. The most troublesome work was applying the principle of drawing on the plentiful to make up for the scarce and in determining the boundaries of the land. This is where the struggles occurred. This aspect of redistribution takes about a week to complete. Nevertheless, with the application of this method, the whole procedure of investigation and redistribution takes only two weeks. The northern part of the *xian* later applied this method.

Fairness

Frequently discussed issues at many land redistribution conferences included whether the township or the village should be taken as a unit, whether the standard of redistribution should be the number of persons or labor power, and how fishponds, gardens, and embankments should be redistributed. (There was no discussion of the redistribution of hills, forests, and houses.) Making a false report was strictly forbidden, but how should those who make a false report be punished? There was no need to discuss confiscation standards at all because, without any written orders, whenever people see the red flag, they know that confiscation has been announced. The simple question is how to redistribute this massive amount of land. Apparently, dividing the total quantity of land by the total number of persons was the most direct and equitable land redistribution. It also was supported by the majority of the masses. The minority who did not approve of this method (landlords and rich peasants) was frightened by the power of the masses and did not dare say a word. In other words, the word "fairness" contains the meanings of confiscation and redistribution.

Those People Who Resist the Fair Redistribution of Land

A small landlord named Liu in Fengshan Township, Shuangqiao District, hoarded his own fertile land and turned only poor land over to the government. When the masses tried to force him to turn over his fertile lands, he replied with indignation, "Over my dead body!" The township government could not solve the problem. The *xian* government sent someone to Fengshan to bear down on him, and then he turned over the land. There were other small landlords and rich peasants in Niudouguang, Nanba District, who failed to turn over their land. The township government was afraid of them and did not take any action. It was not until the *xian* government sent someone to summon a mass meeting that these small landlords and rich peasants were forced to give in. In Datian Township, Shuangqiao District, the house of a small landlord, Mei Yuankun, was burned down by the reactionaries. Mei considered this to be his contribution to the revolution. When the masses wanted him to distribute his land, he replied with vicious abuse, "Redistribute my land, but chop my head off first!" The masses informed the *xian* government, which had the district government arrest him. The person in charge in the district government, Mei Lisan, is a Communist who also is a member of Mei Yuankun's lineage. He covered up this mistake for him. Mei Yuankun later denied having said such a thing, and his land was redistributed. Another case involved the person in charge of the government of Huangtangdu Township, Shuangqiao District, a certain Lin, and the person in charge of the Xuxi Township government, also named Lin (he is also a Communist); both received fertile lands in the land redistribution. The masses cried, "The persons in charge got fertile lands, and we got poor lands." Being upset with this, the masses became apathetic in the land struggle. The *xian* therefore took the fertile land from those two people and redistributed it to the masses, to their satisfaction. Except for Mei Yuankun, who opposed the confiscation of his land, the others mentioned above argued over the redistribution of fertile and poor land rather than the confiscation of land. The masses did not consider confiscation of rich peasants' land an issue. It was the issue of who got fertile land and who got poor land that concerned them. And that is the heart of the land struggle, as is the struggle between the rich peasant and the poor peasant.

Total Redistribution of the Original Farming Land

The principle of "the township as a unit" was applied to the population and not to the land. The land cannot be divided by district. People from Township A farm land in Township B; Township B's people farm land in Township A; people from one township might farm land belonging to a neighboring district. The boundaries between districts, *xian*, and provinces are all crisscrossed by peasants when farming. So that when the people of one township totaled up the land they farmed in their township and in neighboring areas and then redistributed it equally, this was considered a reasonable act. The land redistribution was carried out this way too.

How to Take Care of the Land If the Insurrection Occurred After the Rice Seedlings Had Been Transplanted

There are three ways of dealing with this issue. The first one is the method being carried out in the northern part of Xunwu *xian*. (The land redistribution in the southern part of Xunwu occurred before the rice seedlings had been transplanted. Therefore, this problem did not exist.) The first crop (also called early rice) goes to the original cultivator, and the second crop (also called late rice) goes to the new cultivator. In this way, the rich peasant does not suffer a loss. However, the poor peasants with less land and those who do not farm, such as landlords and vagabonds, were not satisfied, especially because they felt that they had no financial resources. If the landlords cannot collect land rents, they have no grain. Vagabonds no longer had a means of livelihood since gambling had been abolished, and there was no one to borrow money from. The second way is to have the new cultivator reimburse the original cultivator for the first crop. This method also offers two standards for reimbursement, one of which is less than the other. The original cultivators were naturally not contented if they thought the subsidy was too little and were happy with a greater subsidy. This situation provoked general criticism among the poor peasants and vagabonds. Some even said, "There are so many big landlords who are flat broke nowadays and you are still trying to hold onto that tiny bit of property!" No written law in Xunwu recognizes this method; the peasants adopted it themselves. In the Xunwu City District, poor peasants who did not have enough to eat offered a small sum of money to the rich peasants, and demanded that they let them have a part of the first crop. This was actually quite common. The third method is that no matter what the state of the crop, whoever got the land gets the harvest. Some parts of Pingyuan *xian*, Guangdong, adopted this method.

Should Nonpeasants Get Redistributed Land?

In Xunwu City vagabonds with the ability to farm were allowed to receive redistributed land, and those who did not possess any farming ability did not get a share of land. Since districts other than Xunwu City had few vagabonds, all of them were allowed to get redistributed land. Artisans, merchants, and students without a stable income got redistributed land. In Xunwu City and in large townships, people who had a stable income did not get a share; those who did not have enough income got some part of the land as a supplementary source for their livelihood. Not only did Red Army soldiers and revolutionaries get land but the soviet also mobilized peasants to farm the land for them. Landlords shared in the redistribution if they lived in the township. Buddhist monks, Daoist priests, and Christian pastors were required to change their occupation. If they were no longer monks, priests, or pastors, they could share in the land redistribution. Otherwise, they could not. Because of the small number of fortune-tellers and geomancers, there are no regulations about them; they were generally allowed to share in the land redistribution. There are no monks, priests, pastors, fortune-tellers, or geomancers in the southern part of the *xian* anymore; all changed their occupation. When the father of the chairman of the Huangsha Township government died, the peasants opposed having the monks offer a Buddhist ceremony. There are very few geomancers in Xunwu *xian*; most of them are from Xingguo. There are about a hundred Buddhist monks in the *xian*. Xunwu City has one Protestant church with over two hundred members, and one Catholic church with over one hundred members. Huangxiang has one Protestant church with a hundred members or so; Niudouguang has one Protestant church with seventy to eighty members; Jitan has one Protestant church with about a hundred members;

Chengjiang has one Protestant church with about seventy to eighty members. In the *xian* there are five Protestant churches with about seven hundred members and one Catholic church with over a hundred members. Altogether there are over eight hundred members. The Protestant churches belong to the Americans. There was an American pastor in Xunwu City; Chinese preachers were in charge of the other four churches. The Catholic church belongs to the Germans, with one Chinese priest in charge of it. Members include widows (including poor peasants) and elderly women (landlords' wives) (30 percent); sly and capricious gentry and their families (30 percent); peasants of small and powerless lineages (20 percent—peasants belonging to big and powerful lineages do not convert); and young intellectuals of landlord origins without prospects (10 percent); the remaining l0 percent of members are of all types. These converts can be divided into two groups: the very bad and the very weak. The bad ones are not vagabonds, but they are wicked and crafty local people who want to be strongmen—the church is a means by which to accomplish this. The other group of people are the weak; their purpose is to seek shelter in the church.

The Question of Abolishing Debts

This question is divided into loans and bills of credit. The purpose in abolishing loans was to wipe out highly exploitative loans with interest rates of 20 percent or more. A bill of credit from a merchant was paid if it was made after January 1928. Since no debt carried less than a 20 percent interest rate, all debts were wiped out. Money that was lent without interest and as a favor from relatives and friends was still returned by the masses, but this happened rarely. The merchants had not extended the poor peasants credit; most of the credit was for the rich peasants and some for the middle peasants.

Land Tax

Last year, every *dan* [of yield] was taxed 2 *dou* in land taxes. This was practiced in both Shuangqiao and Nanba districts. In February of this year, the *xian* Revolutionary Committee held an expanded meeting that drew up tax regulations. The land tax was set at 10 percent regardless of the quality of the land. The tax rate is the same as the tax on land rent. This type of taxation makes no distinction about the quality of the land (it is not a progressive tax). In May, the *xian* soviet congress adopted the progressive taxation announced by the Western Jiangxi [Ganxi] Soviet.

Women in the Land Struggle

Women and men are equal partners in production in Xunwu. Strictly speaking, in terms of farming, women's duties are much heavier than those of men. Because certain tasks require physical strength, men are more likely to take charge of plowing and raking the fields and carrying the muck and grain. However, women assist men in carrying the muck and grain, transplanting rice seedlings, weeding fields, uprooting the weeds in the paths between the fields and on the edges of the fields, turning over the soil, and cutting the grain. But although men help out, women are chiefly responsible for hulling grain, polishing grain, watering gardens, transplanting vegetables, cutting wood, mowing grass, making tea, cooking meals, raising pigs and other domestic animals [tousheng] (the six domestic animals are called tousheng), washing and ironing clothes, mending clothes, making shoes, sweeping floors, and doing dishes. Besides these tasks, raising children is also a woman's duty; thus, the toil of women is harder than that of men. Women's tasks come one after another, and their work never ends. They are appendages of the male economy (that is, the economy from the feudal economy to the first stage of a capitalist economy). Although men are no longer serfs, a woman is still a man's serf or semiserf, without political rights and personal freedom. No one suffers more than women. As the land struggle developed, many local women bravely participated in it. When the Second Column of the Fourth Army attacked the reactionaries holed up in their stronghold, groups of women from Huangxiang carried wood to burn it. They also seized grain from reactionary landlords. With the victory of their struggle, these women attained self-consciousness. Soon after the establishment of township governments in every township, a number of divorce cases were received. Most of these cases were initiated by women (about 90 percent); very few were started by men (only 10 percent or so). Men were firmly opposed to divorce. A small group of men, on the other hand, became passive. "The revolution wants to get rid of everything, wives included." This is a sigh of resignation, for they cannot stop divorces from happening. This group of men was made up of mostly poor peasants. The majority of men are very opinionated. In Fangtian, the captain of the Red Guards, Zeng Jiaxun, who was married, got involved with another woman. His wife asked for a divorce. He would not agree and told her: "Never can a wife leave this family while she is alive. If you want to get a divorce, then I will kill you first." In Longtu, a rich peasant named Liu Xuesheng refused his wife's request for divorce. He told the chairman of the Revolutionary Committee: "If she wants to divorce me, I will exterminate her. After I exterminate her, I will then die without complaining." This category of men is mostly made up of rich peasants. The policy adopted by the political organs on this issue has been changed four times. The first was based on a resolution of the congress of peasants in November of last year. The resolution did not take a clear stand against a husband's having more than one wife; it allowed a married man to have a lover as long as his wife did not object; the proposed conditions for divorce were not rigid. If one spouse had a disease, if the woman was oppressed, if the husband and wife had a falling out and had not lived together for half a year, or if the man went to another area and had not been heard from for a year—these people were allowed to get divorced. The landlord class could divorce without any conditions. In addition to the legal provisions, it was explicated that no one should try to catch a person in the act of adultery. However, after this was made clear throughout the xian, much turmoil occurred between men and women in the southern part of the *xian*, especially in Longtu and Hejiao (in Nanba District). Armed fights almost broke out between groups of men and women. The reason was that groups of young men from both townships frequently assailed young women of the other township with obscenities. So the women themselves organized women's associations, and with this unity they became more liberal in their behavior when engaging in hard work. (They went to the hills in groups to cut firewood and tended to return home later than usual.) Meanwhile, love affairs between them and their young male friends (from other townships) increased, and couples had dates freely in the hills. People from these two townships are from the same lineage but from different branches. Because the masses, who were against the rule of trying to catch people in the act of adultery, intervened with the people who were involved in doing so, this almost led to an armed fight this January. In addition to this type of incident, there were married people in almost every township and village who had new lovers. The wives rallied together to oppose such affairs. Under these circumstances, the government made another law quite different from the previous one. This February, the enlarged meeting of the *xian* Revolutionary Committee came to a resolution on the "issue of fidelity": "Married men and women are prohibited from having sexual intercourse with a third party; whoever engages in illicit intercourse will be punished severely." At the same time another law was passed to regulate the "lover" issue: "Oppose polygamy and polyandry. [Estranged] husbands and wives who have yet to be divorced cannot have lovers. Those who have made mistakes in the past must separate immediately and unite with only one person." The resolution did not change the policy for divorce cases. Ever since this was promulgated, disputes have stopped. Peasants united together to face the crisis at that time and managed to break the enemy's attack. On May 2 we took over Xunwu City. At the same time, the Fourth Red Army had taken over the reactionary northern part of the *xian* and aroused the masses in Huichang, Anyuan, and Pingyuan to action. In this situation, on May 6, the first soviet congress of the whole *xian* withdrew the fidelity resolution. And even though the congress did not clearly forbid people to catch others in adultery, it no longer talked about "whoever engages in illicit intercourse will be punished severely." With regard to the "lover" issue, this congress adopted the resolution of the meeting in February and continued the policy on divorce of the previous two meetings. However, within one month, a soviet congress in a third area adopted a totally different resolution on the "lover" and divorce issues. Its slogan was "Absolute freedom in divorce and marriage." Naturally, the result is to forbid efforts to catch people in adultery and to ensure the freedom to have lovers. The district that approved this is the district that has had the longest period of struggle in all of Xunwu *xian* (from 1928 to the present) and is also the district that first had capitalism. Its struggle began with the arrival of the Fourth Army and with the development of the struggle in Huichang, Anyuan, Xunwu, and Pingyuan *xian*. When this proposal was mentioned, the person who made the proposal spoke out: "The people

from the Fourth Army said that conditiona! divorce implies feudal thought."
After this speech, the proposal was approved immediately. This [i.e., the marriage policy] is a new issue in Xunwu City District. Although the new government is less than a month old, the question of relations between the sexes has
become very turbulent. One of the townships rejected the propagandist
[xuanchuanyuan] sent by the government, saying: "Comrade, please do not give
us any propaganda. With more propaganda, the women in our township will all
run away." In fact, the propagandist had come to propagandize about "overthrowing the feudal forces" and "bringing down the village bosses and redistributing land." The divorce and marriage policy was explained according to the
regulations. Nevertheless, once the masses are aroused, just as water flows from
high hills to low plains, they cannot be reversed. In one township in Xunwu City
District, over ten women ran away. Their husbands went to the township soviet
and complained tearfully. Heeding their desperate pleas, the township soviet was
forced to put up a notice that read: "Young people have misinterpreted the
meaning of freedom and hence have run away in the dark of night in pursuit of
their lovers and are finding new lovers before divorcing their mates. These are
absurd, inappropriate, furtive doings. . . ." This official notice clearly expressed
the voice of the older husbands. However, this "incongruous" trend—the trend of
a democratic system taking the place of a feudal system—could not be halted.

Women have expressed their appreciation for the land struggle, because it can
help dissolve the restrictions on their personal freedom. Regardless of their class,
all unmarried young people support the slogan of freedom in marriage. However,
married men in the poor-peasant class generally oppose the right to divorce. But
their opposition differs from the obstinacy of the counterrevolutionaries. They
worry that they will lose their wife's labor and will not be able to farm if their
wife runs away. They sigh, "The revolution wants to get rid of everything, wives
included." They go to the township government and ask for help. Meanwhile,
although they feel annoyed with their wives, they do not dare hit them. The
attitude of adult males from the rich-peasant and small-landlord classes is completely different. Their expressed desire to kill their wives if the latter ask for a
divorce shows their tendency toward counterrevolutionary attitudes. And why do
these adult male peasants oppose the freedom to get a divorce? (They have no
objection against marriage freedom.) Apparently, it is because of labor power.

Do male peasants oppose liberating women? No, they do not. Once the whole
class is liberated, poor peasants and farm laborers will soon free their women.
The reason why they are afraid that their wives will run away is that before the
land struggle develops in depth, they cannot fully foresee the outcome of overthrowing the feudal system and exploitation, and they develop such thoughts. As
long as the land struggle is developed in depth, their attitudes toward marriage
will change greatly.

Oppose Bookism[1]

(May 1930)

I. Without Investigation, There Is No Right to Speak

If you have not investigated a certain problem, you will lose your right to speak on it. Isn't this too brutal? Not in the least. Since you have investigated neither the actual situation nor the historical circumstances of this problem, and have no detailed knowledge of it, anything you said about it could only be nonsense. Talking nonsense can solve no problems, as everyone knows, so is there anything unjust about depriving you of your right to speak? Many of our comrades keep their eyes shut all day long and go around talking nonsense. This is disgraceful for a Communist. How can someone be a Communist, and yet go around with his eyes shut talking nonsense?

This won't do!
This won't do!
Stress investigation!
Oppose talking nonsense!

II. To Investigate Is to Solve Problems

You can't solve that problem? Well, go and investigate its present situation and its history! When you have really investigated it thoroughly so that you understand it, you will have a way of solving that problem. All conclusions emerge at the end of an investigation of the circumstances, not before it. Only a dolt, alone

---

This essay was originally entitled "On the Work of Investigation"; "Oppose Bookism" was the title of an earlier and shorter piece on the same theme. After circulating the present version within the Party in 1961, Mao revised it for publication in 1964 in *Mao Zedong zhuzuo xuandu (jiazhongben)* (Selected Readings from the Works of Mao Zedong), Vol. 1, pp. 17–28. At the same time, he reverted to the title of the earlier article. Since this authorized version, which constitutes the source for our translation, is the only Chinese text available, it seems logical to give it the title which Mao bestowed on it in 1964. The text can also be found in the 1991 second edition of *Mao Zedong xuanji*, Vol. 1, pp. 109–18, and in *Mao Zedong nongcun diaocha wenji*.

1. In a note accompanying the draft when it was circulated in 1961, Mao explained that "bookism" or "book worship" (*benbenzhuyi*) was simply the term he had used in 1930 for "dogmatism" (*jiaotiaozhuyi*).

or with a small group of people, cudgels his brains to "find a way," or "come up with an idea," without making any investigation. We must know that in this way it is quite impossible to think of a good method, or devise a good idea. In other words, such persons will certainly produce wrong methods and wrong ideas.

Many of those doing inspection work, many leaders of guerrilla units, and many newly assigned cadres delight in proclaiming their political views the moment they arrive. After seeing only a little bit of the surface of things, or one minor detail, they begin to gesticulate and to say that this is not right, and that is wrong. Such purely subjective "talking nonsense" is truly detestable. Such people will assuredly mess things up, lose the support of the masses, and be unable to solve problems.

Many people in leading positions, when they encounter difficult problems, merely heave a sigh and are unable to solve them. They become annoyed and ask for a transfer, on the grounds that "their abilities are too slight, and they cannot do the job." These are the words of a coward. Just get moving on your own two legs, go to every section and locality within your area of responsibility, learn from Confucius to "ask about everything,"[2] and then, however limited your abilities, you will be able to solve problems. For when you have not left your gate, your brain is empty, but when you return it is already empty no longer, it has already brought back all sorts of material necessary for solving problems, and thus problems are solved. Must you go out? Not necessarily—you can summon those people who do know about the situation to an investigation meeting, grasp the "source" of your so-called difficult problem, clarify the "present situation," and thus this difficult problem of yours will easily be solved.

Investigation is like the "ten months[3] of pregnancy," and solving problems is like the "moment of birth." Investigation is solving problems.

III. Against Bookism

The idea that whatever is written in a book is correct persists even today among the culturally backward Chinese peasantry. Surprisingly, when problems are discussed within the Communist Party, there are also people who say, whenever they open their mouths, "Show me where it's written in the book." If we say that the directives of leading organs at higher levels are correct, it is absolutely not simply because they emanate from "leading organs at higher levels," but because their content is in accord with the objective and subjective circumstances of the struggle and corresponds to the requirements of the struggle. To carry out directives blindly without discussing and examining them in the light of the real

---

2. See the *Analects*, III, XV: "The Master, when he entered the grand temple, asked about everything." (Legge, Vol. I, p. 160.)

3. I.e., ten lunar months, approximately equivalent to nine months of the Western calendar.

conditions, simply because they come from "higher levels," is a formalistic attitude which is quite wrong. If the tactics and line of the Party do not penetrate deeply into the masses, the reason lies in the mischief caused by such formalism. To carry out the directives of the higher levels blindly, and without any apparent disagreement, is not really to carry them out, it is in fact the most artful way of opposing or sabotaging such directives.

The bookist method of conducting research in the social sciences is equally dangerous and may even lead to taking the path of counterrevolution. This is clearly demonstrated by the fact that in China there are many Communist Party members who carry out social science research exclusively by studying life as described in books, and no small number of them have turned into counterrevolutionaries. When we say that Marxism is correct, it is absolutely not because Marx was some kind of "sage," but because his theories have been proved correct in our practice, and in our struggles. We need Marxism in our struggle. If we welcome this theory, it has nothing whatsoever to do with any formalistic or even mystical notions of a "sage." Many people who have read Marxist "books" have become renegades to the revolution, while illiterate workers have often been able to grasp Marxism very well. We must study the Marxist "books," but they must be integrated with our actual situation. We need "books," but we must definitely correct the bookism which departs from reality.

How can we correct this bookism? Only by investigating the actual situation.

IV. If You Do Not Investigate the Actual Situation, You Will Be Idealist in Your Estimate of Class Forces, and in Your Leadership of the Work, and the Result Will Be Either Opportunism or Adventurism

Do you not believe in this conclusion? Facts will force you to believe in it. Just try to make an estimate of the political situation, and guide the struggle, without reference to concrete investigations. Will this not be empty idealism? Will not such empty idealism in your political estimate and leadership of the work give rise to opportunist or adventurist errors? Most certainly it will cause errors. This is not at all because the person in question has not made careful plans before acting, but because he has not taken care before making plans to understand the real conditions of society. We encounter this constantly in the guerrilla units of the Red Army. Those officers of the Li Kui type,[4] when they observe that their brother soldiers have committed offenses, hand out punishments right and left at random. The result is that the offenders are not convinced they have been fairly treated and stir up all kinds of disputes, so that the leaders lose prestige. Do we not encounter this frequently in the Red Army?

---

4. Li Kui was one of the heroes of *Shuihu zhuan* (Water Margin), the novel of rebellion in late Song China. He was good-hearted, but notoriously short-tempered and violent.

We must completely rid ourselves of the idealist spirit and prevent the emergence of every kind of opportunist and adventurist error. Only thus can we fulfill the task of winning over the masses and defeating the enemy. We must strive to make real investigations, for only thus can we rid ourselves of the idealist spirit.

V. The Aim of Social and Economic Investigations Is to Obtain a Correct Estimate of Class [Forces], and Following on from That to Decide on Correct Tactics for the Struggle

This is our answer to the question: "Why should we carry out social and economic investigations?" Consequently, the object of our social and economic investigation is the various classes of society, but not all sorts of fragmentary social phenomena. Recently, the comrades of the Fourth Army have, on the whole, all been paying attention to the work of investigation, but many people's methods of investigation are wrong. Consequently the results of their investigations are like posting a bill for dog meat, like a person from the country listening to the many strange tales told in the street, like standing on a high mountaintop and observing the people in a walled city. This kind of investigation is of little use and cannot enable us to attain our principal objective. Our principal objective is to understand the political and economic situation of the various social classes. The conclusion which should result from our investigation consists in a picture of the present circumstances of each class, as well as the history of its ups and downs. For example, when we investigate the composition of the peasantry, we must know not only the number of owner-peasants, semiowner peasants, and tenant peasants, which are distinguished from one another by rent and sharecropping relations, but also, and more particularly, the number of rich peasants, middle peasants, and poor peasants, who are distinguished from one another by class or stratum. When we investigate the composition of the merchants, we must know not only the number in each trade, such as grain, clothing, medicinal herbs, and so on; we must, in particular, investigate the number of small merchants, middle merchants, and big merchants. We must investigate not only the situation of each trade, but more particularly the class relations within it. We must investigate not only the relations among various trades, but above all the relations among various classes. Our principal method of investigation is to dissect the various social classes. Our ultimate goal is to understand the reciprocal relations among the various classes, and arrive at a correct estimate of class forces, so that we can establish correct tactics for the struggle, determine which classes constitute the main force in the revolutionary struggle, which classes constitute allies we must win over, and which classes must be overthrown. This is our sole purpose.

What are the social classes to which we should pay attention when carrying out investigations? They are listed below:

The industrial proletariat
The handicraft workers
The farm laborers
The poor peasants
The urban poor
The vagrants
The master handicraftsmen
The small merchants
The middle peasants
The rich peasants
The landlord class
The commercial bourgeoisie
The industrial bourgeoisie

When we carry out our investigations, we should pay attention to the situation of all these classes (some of them are strata). In the areas where we are working for the time being, only the industrial proletariat and the industrial bourgeoisie are absent; we constantly encounter all the others. Our tactics for the struggle are tactics toward all these numerous classes and strata. Our previous investigations have also had another very great defect: we have concentrated on the villages and not paid attention to the cities, with the result that, from beginning to end, many comrades have been confused about tactics toward the urban poor and the commercial bourgeoisie. The development of the struggle has caused us to leave the mountains for the plains, but though our bodies have long since left the mountains, our thinking is still up there. We must understand the villages, but we must also understand the cities; otherwise, we will be unable to adapt to the demands of the revolutionary struggle.

VI. Victory in China's Revolutionary Struggle Will Depend on the Chinese Comrades' Understanding of Chinese Conditions

The goal of our struggle is the transition from democracy[5] to socialism. The first step in this task is to win over the majority of the working class, rouse the masses of the peasantry and of the urban poor, overthrow the landlord class, overthrow imperialism, overthrow the political power of the Guomindang, and complete the democratic revolution. The development of this struggle will give rise in turn the task of carrying out the socialist revolution. The fulfillment of these great revolutionary tasks is neither simple nor easy. It will depend entirely on whether the tactics of the proletarian party in this struggle are correct and resolute. If the party's tactics are wrong, or wavering and irresolute, the revolution will inevitably suffer a temporary defeat. We must be aware that the bourgeois parties, too,

---

5. Once again, Mao uses *minquan zhuyi*, Sun Yatsen's term for democracy.

are constantly engaged in discussing tactics. Their problem is how to spread reformist influences among the working class, so as to deceive the working class and detach it from the leadership of the Communist Party. They are also concerned with how to get the rich peasants to put down the uprisings of the poor peasants, how to organize the vagabonds to repress the revolution, and so on. In such a situation, where class struggle at close quarters is constantly becoming more acute, the proletariat can obtain victory only by relying on the correctness and resoluteness of the tactics of struggle of its own party, the Communist Party. A Communist Party's correct and unwavering tactics of struggle can on no account be produced by a small number of people sitting in an office; they can only emerge in the process of mass struggle, that is to say, in the course of real experience. For this reason, we must at all times understand social conditions and carry out practical investigations. Those unwaveringly conservative and formalistic comrades whose heads are filled with empty optimism think that the present tactics of struggle could not be bettered. They believe that the "book of documents"[6] of the Sixth Congress[7] guarantees victory forever, and that so long as you observe the methods laid down there, you can never fail to triumph. Such thinking is totally wrong; it has nothing to do with the ideological line that Communists should create a new situation through struggle, it is a wholly conservative line. If we do not completely discard this conservative line, it will cause great losses to the revolution and will also harm these comrades themselves. Manifestly, part of our comrades in the Red Army are satisfied with the existing state of affairs, do not seek to understand things thoroughly, and are filled with empty optimism. They propagate the erroneous idea that "the proletariat is like this," eat their fill all day, sit in the bureaus dozing, and do not deign to take so much as a step to go out among the masses of society to investigate. Whenever they open their mouths, all they ever utter are those old platitudes people are really tired of hearing. Let us awaken these comrades by calling out to them:

> Change your conservative thinking in a hurry!
> Replace it with progressive and militant Communist thinking!
> Go into the midst of the struggle!
> Go among the masses and carry out real investigations!

VII. The Technique of Investigation

1) Hold investigation meetings, and carry out investigation through discussion.

This is the only way you can come close to correct [results], the only way to draw conclusions. Investigations which follow the method of holding no meet-

---

6. Mao writes here *"benben,"* in quotation marks, i.e., the same term representing the "bookism" against which he is inveighing.

7. Of the Chinese Communist Party, held in Moscow from June 18 to July 11, 1928.

ings and carrying out no discussions, but simply relying on one person re-counting his experience, can easily lead to error. Such a method of merely asking a few questions at random and not raising the basic issues at a proper meeting, where they can be debated, cannot elicit conclusions which are more or less correct.

2) What kind of people should attend the investigation meetings?

They must be people who have a profound understanding of social and eco-nomic conditions. As far as age is concerned, old people are the best, because they have a wealth of experience, and not only understand present circum-stances, but know about their causes. There must also be young people with experience of struggle, because they have progressive ideas, and are acute ob-servers. As regards occupation, there should be workers, peasants, merchants, intellectuals, and sometimes soldiers or vagabonds. Naturally, when a particular problem is being investigated, those who have nothing to do with it need not attend. For example, workers, peasants, and students need not be present when commerce is being investigated.

3) Is it better to have a large or a small number of people at an investigation meeting?

That depends on the investigator's capacity to preside over the meeting. Those who are good at this can hold a meeting of a dozen, or even twenty-odd people. A large meeting has the advantages of numbers, namely that it enables you to get relatively accurate answers in preparing statistics (for example, in finding out the percentage of poor peasants in the total peasant population), and in drawing conclusions (for example, in deciding whether equal or differentiated land distribution is better). Naturally, a big meeting also has the disadvantages of numbers; those who are not skilled at chairing meetings may find it difficult to keep order. So in the end, how many people attend will be determined by the circumstances of the investigator. There must, however, be at least three; other-wise, you will be handicapped by lack of knowledge and experience, and the information obtained will not correspond to the real situation.

4) Prepare a detailed outline for the investigation.

A detailed outline should be prepared beforehand, and the investigator should ask questions according to the outline, which those present will answer orally. Any points which are unclear or doubtful should be put up for debate. What I call the "detailed outline for the investigation" should have main headings and subheadings. For example, if "commerce" is a main heading, subheadings might include "cloth," "grain," "miscellaneous goods," and "medicinal herbs." Cloth can be further subdivided into "calico," "homespun," and "silk and satin."

5) You must participate personally.

Everyone responsible for leadership work, from the chairman of the township government to the chairman of the central government, from the detachment leader to the commander-in-chief, from the Party branch secretary to the secretary general, must definitely participate personally in the investigation of social and economic conditions, and must not rely exclusively on written reports, for these are two quite different things.

6) You must probe deeply.

Anyone who is participating in the work of investigation for the first time should carry out one or two thorough investigations, with the aim of understanding a particular place (such as a village or a city), or a particular problem (such as the problem of grain or currency). If you thoroughly understand one place or problem, this will make it easier for you to orient yourself subsequently in investigating other places or problems.

7) Take your own notes.

The investigator should not only preside at investigation meetings himself, and give appropriate guidance to those attending, he should also take his own notes and record the results of the meeting himself. To rely on others for this won't do.

Guidelines of the Fourth Red Army for Political Work at All Levels

(June 5, 1930)

In the past, the political departments of the army and columns have done some miscellaneous work of assistance, neglecting their main task, which is to direct the political work of the entire army or column.

The political departments at both the army and column levels are, at the same time, temporary organs of mass political power. In the past, this duty has not been carried out well either. For example, requests of the masses have not received a good response, and mass organizations and local political organs have not been helped to formulate well-rounded plans, so that when the Red Army left they would still be able to carry out their work effectively.

I. Guidelines for the Work of the Army Political Department

1) Grasp well the plan of Red Army political tasks for each period, and carry it out in political work. For example, as regards the task of overthrowing the western Fujian warlords and expanding Red political power in western Fujian, plans [should be made] for rousing the enthusiasm of the entire army, both officers and men, helping them understand the significance of this task, and heightening their sentiments of struggle.

2) Plan, supervise, and inspect the political training of the entire army, both officers and men. [This should include], for example, (a) special training for new recruits and captured troops; (b) special training for young soldiers (school for young soldiers); (c) general soldier training (ordinary classes); (d) lower level cadre training (special classes); (e) providing political training materials; (f) specifying slogans for the morning and evening roll call; (g) various kinds of assembly talks, and so on.

3) Guide and inspect the organization and work of the All-Army Soldiers' Association.

4) Plan, supervise, and inspect the propaganda work of the entire army. For example, (a) provide main propaganda materials; (b) inspect and also direct the propaganda materials and methods of the individual units; (c) supervise the

Our source for this text is *Mao Zedong ji. Bujuan*, Vol. 3, pp. 107–14, where it is reproduced from a documentary collection published in China in 1979.

organization and training of the propaganda teams of the various individual units; (d) organize and inspect propaganda in makeup.[1]

5) Supervise and encourage the political organs of the various units, in coordination with the military affairs organs, to uphold the three articles of discipline and proper military conduct generally.

6) Supervise and encourage the political organs of the various units, in coordination with the military affairs organs, to uphold the items on special treatment for wounded soldiers.

7) Supervise and encourage the political organs of the various units, in coordination with the military affairs organs, to uphold the various policies governing the army, such as the ban on corporal punishment, the ban on executing deserters, and so on.

8) Prepare and distribute forms for socioeconomic surveys, provide guidance for the various units in actual survey methods, and also supervise each unit in calculating the figures, and turn them over to the political department of the army to be totaled.

9) Plan and supervise mass propaganda for organizing mass organizations.

10) Plan and supervise assistance to the masses in setting up local political organs, such as revolutionary committees and soviets.

11) Plan and supervise assistance to local political organs in establishing local armed forces, such as uprising squads, Red Guards, and local Red Armies.

12) Plan and supervise the various units, or assist the local political organs, in eliminating reactionary forces.

13) Plan, and also guide and assist the mass organs in carrying out, the confiscation and distribution of land.

14) Plan, and guide the various units in running, leadership training classes for the masses.

15) Guide and supervise the various units in helping the local political organs to carry out various kinds of construction tasks such as schools, cooperatives, health clinics, and so on, so that they take root among the masses.

16) Deal with and also reply to requests from the masses.

17) Plan, and provide direction to the various units and to the highest mass organs in carrying out, the raising of money for Red Army supplies and for expenses for mass work.

18) Guide, and also supervise and encourage, the various units and mass organs in upholding well the policies toward towns and cities.

II. Guidelines for the Work of the Column Political Departments

1) Grasp well the plan of political tasks for each period, as provided by the higher levels, and carry it out in political work. For example, as regards the task

---

1. As indicated in earlier notes, this refers to propaganda carried out through the medium of skits and theatrical performances.

of overthrowing the western Fujian warlords and expanding Red political power in western Fujian, plans [should be made] for rousing the enthusiasm of the entire Army, both officers and men, helping them to understand the significance of this task, and heightening their sentiments of struggle.

2) Plan, supervise, and inspect the political training of the whole column, both officers and men. [This should include], for example, (a) special training for new recruits and captured troops; (b) special training for young soldiers (school for young soldiers); (c) general soldier training (ordinary classes); (d) lower-level cadre training (special classes); (e) providing political training materials; (f) specifying slogans for the morning and evening roll call (when detached for guerrilla actions, on work away from the army political department); (g) various kinds of assembly talks, and so on.

3) Guide and inspect the organization and work of the All-Column Soldiers' Association.

4) Plan, supervise, and inspect the propaganda work of the entire column. For example, (a) provide main propaganda materials; (b) inspect and also direct the propaganda materials and methods of the individual units; (c) supervise the organization and inspection of the propaganda teams of the various individual units.

5) Supervise and encourage the political organs of the various units, in coordination with the military affairs organs, to uphold the three articles of discipline and proper military conduct generally.

6) Supervise and encourage the political organs of the various units, in coordination with the military affairs organs, to uphold the items on special treatment for wounded soldiers.

7) Supervise and encourage the political organs of the various units, in coordination with the military affairs organs, to uphold the various policies governing the army, such as the ban on corporal punishment, the ban on executing deserters, and so on.

8) Supervise and guide workers at all levels in doing real social surveys, and also supervise each unit in calculating the figures, and turn them over to the political department of the Army to be totaled.

9) Plan and supervise mass propaganda for organizing mass organizations.

10) Plan and supervise assistance to the masses in setting up local political organs, such as revolutionary committees and soviets.

11) Plan and supervise assistance to local political organs in establishing local armed forces, such as uprising squads, Red Guards, and local Red Armies.

12) Plan and supervise the various units, or assist the local political organs, in eliminating reactionary forces.

13) Plan, and also guide and assist the mass organs in carrying out, the confiscation and distribution of land.

14) Plan, and guide the various units in running, leadership training classes for the masses.

15) Guide and supervise the various units in helping the local political organs to carry out various kinds of construction tasks such as schools, cooperatives, health clinics, and so on, so that they take root among the masses.

16) Deal with and also reply to requests from the masses (when working together with the army political department, they must be turned over to the army political department to deal with).

17) Plan, and provide direction to the various units and to the military supplies organ in carrying out, the raising of money for Red Army supplies and for expenses for mass work.

18) Guide, and also supervise and encourage, the various units and mass organs in upholding well the policies toward towns and cities.

When with the army political department, the above items should be dealt with under the direction of the army political department. When separated from the army political department, plans and decisions must be made independently, but reported to the army political department afterward.

III. Guidelines for the Work of Detachment Political Committee Members

A. Plan political training for the officers and men of the entire detachment, and also supervise and assist the various companies to put it into practice.
1) Intensify the political education of officers and men.
2) Direct the work of the All-Detachment Soldiers' Association.
3) Make strong efforts to help the officers and men of your detachment understand higher-level policy directives.
4) At all times examine and correct erroneous tendencies among officers and soldiers.
5) Train and guide the work of the propaganda team.
6) Make plans to open a school for young soldiers (supervise the selection of students in all units, the setting of class times and places, the teaching personnel, the selection of teaching materials, and so on).
7) Plan and implement special political training classes for the soldiers.
B. Oversee matters relating to the administration of the detachment as a whole.
1) Supervise officers and troops in carrying out all higher-level commands.
2) Oversee economic management.
3) Supervise the maintenance of military bearing and discipline.
C. Improve the way the troops are treated.
1) Take care to improve the methods of managing the troops.
2) Take care to improve the daily life of the troops (food, entertainment, sanitation, and so on).
3) Take care to improve the care of sick and wounded troops.
D. Expand political propaganda, and organize mass organizations.
1) Plan and direct mass meetings.

2) Direct officers and men and the propaganda team in presenting oral, written, and theatrical propaganda to the masses, at any time, any place.

3) Direct the officers and men in making social surveys and reporting to the higher organs.

4) Direct the officers and men in organizing mass organizations, and also provide guidance for their struggle methods.

5) When at war, direct the treatment of, and propaganda aimed at, captured soldiers by the officers and men.

E. Direct the tasks of eliminating counterrevolutionaries and of collecting funds.

1) Direct investigations by officers and men, and also find ways to arrest despotic gentry and all reactionaries, and report to the higher organs for handling (when on separate maneuvers, relatively far away from higher levels, handle it first independently, and then make a report).

2) Direct the investigation of local bullies by officers and men, and assist in fund-raising work.

IV. Guidelines for the Work of the Company Political Committee Members

A. Plan and carry out political training for the officers and men, to consolidate the political leadership, to unite the forces of the officers and men, and strengthen their fighting ability.

1) Intensify the political education of officers and men.

2) Direct the work of the Soldiers' Association (direct the meetings, and at the meetings discuss the various items of work, and also direct the application of the various resolutions).

3) Make strong efforts to help the officers and men of one's unit understand higher-level policy directives.

4) Take care to correct erroneous tendencies among officers and soldiers of one's unit.

5) Take care to provide special education for new soldiers and for captured soldiers.

B. Oversee matters relating to the administration of one's unit.

1) Supervise officers and troops in carrying out all higher commands.

2) Oversee economic management.

3) Supervise the maintenance of military bearing and discipline.

C. Improve the way the troops are treated.

1) Take care to improve the methods of managing the troops.

2) Take care to improve the daily life of the troops (food, entertainment, sanitation, and so on).

3) Take care to improve the care of sick and wounded troops.

D. Expand political propaganda and organize mass organizations.

1) Plan and direct mass meetings.

2) Direct the officers and men, or the propaganda branch team, in presenting oral, written, and theatrical propaganda to the masses, at any time, any place.

3) Direct the officers and men in making social surveys and reporting to the higher organs.

4) Direct the officers and men in organizing mass organizations, and also provide guidance for their struggle methods.

5) When at war, direct the treatment of and propaganda toward captured soldiers by the officers and men.

E. Direct the tasks of eliminating counterrevolutionaries and of collecting funds.

1) Investigate and also find ways to arrest despotic gentry and reactionaries, and report to the higher organs for implementation (when engaged in independent action, relatively far away from higher levels, deal with it first yourselves, and then make a report).

2) Investigate the local bullies and assist in the work of raising funds.

Issued by the Political Department of the Red Army Fourth Army

Reprinted by the Western Fujian Special Committee

On the Problem of the Rich Peasants

Resolution of the Joint Conference of the Red Fourth Army Front Committee and the Western Fujian Special Committee[1]

(June 1930)

1) Who Are the Rich Peasants

There are three types of rich peasants. The first type are the semilandlord rich peasants who work the land themselves and still have extra land to rent out. The second type are the capitalist rich peasants who do not rent out land. Some of them even rent land from other people, but hire farm laborers to cultivate it for them. The third type are the newly enriched peasants who neither rent out land nor hire farm laborers, but rely only on their own labor in working the land. However, they have sufficient land and labor and have surplus grain to sell or lend every year.

All types of rich peasants have two common ways of exploiting the im-

---

Our source for this resolution is *Mao Zedong ji. Bujuan*, Vol. 3, pp. 115–33, where it is reproduced from a documentary collection published in China in 1982. The Japanese editors also checked this text against the version printed in June 1930 by the Red Army, which can be found in the Chen Cheng Collection. (Regarding this important collection of primary source materials, see the Bibliography.)

1. This conference was Mao's answer to Li Lisan's gathering of delegates from the soviet areas, which had been held a few weeks earlier in Shanghai. It met in the middle and latter part of June, first in Nanyang, Changting *xian,* and then in Tingzhou City. For this reason, it is referred to sometimes as the Nanyang Conference, and sometimes as the Tingzhou Conference. (See *Nianpu*, Vol. 1, p. 310.) It adopted this resolution, and also the resolution on the vagabonds which constitutes the next document in the present volume. Mao did not draft either of them, but he revised and approved both. The line taken here regarding class struggle in the countryside is an extremely radical one, which did not attract universal support, as Mao himself underscores throughout the text. Already in his Jinggangshan report of November 1928, Mao had denounced what he called there "the intermediate class," corresponding in fact to the same stratum baptized here "new rich peasants," and the land law which he had drafted at the February 7, 1930, Pitou Conference likewise singled out for expropriation those "owner-peasants" who enjoyed more than the bare minimum for survival. (See above, section (B) of the Jinggangshan report, "The Land Problem," and the text of the February 7 law.) For a comparison of Mao's agrarian policy with the views of Li Lisan and of Moscow, see the Introduction to this volume.

poverished masses. The first way is through usurious loans (charging interest on loans of money, grain, pigs, cattle, and oil) and sale of grain on a commercial basis. The second way is through the particular methods of exploitation used by various types of rich peasants, namely the semilandlord rich peasants' exploitation through land rental and the capitalist rich peasants' exploitation of the labor of farmhands. Besides, among all types of rich peasants many engage in commercial businesses at the same time, running a small shop and peddling goods. Therefore, they use the methods of the commercial capitalist to exploit the impoverished masses.

2) The Reactionary Nature of Rich Peasants

Rich peasants are the bourgeoisie in the countryside. **But exploitation by Chinese rich peasants generally carries with it the cruelty of semifeudalism.**[2] In all aspects such as land rental, usurious loans, hiring laborers, or commercial capitalism, exploitation by the rich peasants is crueler than that by the landlords. Thus, the interests of this class and the interests of the poor peasants and farm laborers are diametrically opposed. **This class is reactionary from start to finish.**

Although in the initial period of the revolution the rich peasant class has a need to oppose exorbitant taxes and levies by warlords, because of their fundamental interests (land and capital) they will surely stand by the landlords and oppose the poor peasants and farm laborers as soon as the revolution is initiated by the poor peasants and farm laborers.

During the upsurge of the revolutionary tide, the rich peasants will fervently burn land deeds and divide up the land, adorn themselves with red ribbons, call each other comrade, and even sneak into the Communist Party. All such opportunist actions are **aimed at seeking social status and rights of leadership over the poor peasants and farm laborers** and attempting to save the development of rural capitalism from the crisis in its development (so as to move from the protection of family property at present to the development of capitalism in the future). This is the most serious issue in the rural struggle and deserves the full attention of our comrades.

When the rural struggle deepens, that is to say, when the poor peasants and farm laborers establish strong leadership, overthrow the political position of the rich peasants, confiscate the land, forests, and farm cattle of the rich peasants and abolish the debts owed them, what the rich peasants do is to create rumors to confuse the masses and to slow down the work.

When the revolution develops from crisis toward defeat, the rich peasants move from vacillation to accommodation and even to complete betrayal, following the reactionary line of the landlords and attacking the poor peasants and farm laborers.

---

2. This and other passages in bold are emphasized in the original by the use of dots next to the characters.

3) The Controversy over the New Rich Peasants

In the past, all sides (especially those from the East River) recognized only two types of peasants, namely the semilandlord and the bourgeois types, as rich peasants. They did not call the newly enriched peasants rich peasants, but "middle peasants." They opposed taking over the surplus land of the new rich peasants as well as abolishing the debts owed to them. They forgot that these new rich peasants were still an exploiting class. Although these people do not collect land rent or exploit farm laborers, they practice usurious loans and sell surplus grain at high prices in times of crisis. These two types of exploitation are exactly the same as those practiced by the semilandlord and bourgeois rich peasants. These rich peasants rely on the above-mentioned two types of exploitation and accumulate capital gradually, rushing toward the ranks of the other two types of bourgeois and semilandlord rich peasants. The poor peasants and farm laborers demand not only the confiscation of the land of the two types of semilandlord and bourgeois rich peasants and the abolition of debts owed to them but also the confiscation of the land of the new rich peasants and the abolition of debts owed to the new rich peasants. In all the places where the struggle has deepened, the poor peasants and farm laborers have done this. Nevertheless, this remains an unresolved issue of contention within the Communist Party. The view of the joint meeting on this issue is that the same **resolute support should be given to the masses' confiscation of land and abolition of debts owed to the new rich peasants** as that which is given to confiscation of land and abolition of debts owed to the other two types of rich peasants. Why should this policy be adopted? Because the confiscation of their land is the only reply to their cruel exploitation by selling highly priced surplus grain in times of crisis, and the abolition of debts owed to them is the only reply to their brutal exploitation by making usurious loans. These two kinds of exploitation are both of a semifeudal nature. Only through thorough elimination of these two kinds of exploitation can the peasants be completely liberated from these semifeudal relationships. It is not enough to eradicate only the exploitation by landlords and the first and second types of rich peasants.

4) The Broad Peasant Masses Have Sufficient Force to Overthrow the Rich Peasants, and Only by Establishing an Anti-Rich-Peasant Policy Can the Party Win over the Broad Masses of Poor Peasants to Accomplish Thoroughly the Tasks of the Democratic Revolution and Move Toward the Stage of the Socialist Revolution

Generally speaking, in the basins of the Yangzi River and the Pearl River, over 70 percent are poor peasants and farm laborers, approximately 20 percent are middle peasants, and less than 10 percent are rich peasants. The main forces of the rural struggle are the broad masses of poor peasants and farm laborers, and the middle peasants are the force with which alliances can be made. The rich peasants are an extremely isolated minority. Although the rich peasants necessarily have a counterrevolutionary nature, **the balance of class forces indicates that they will be overthrown by the broad masses of poor peasants.** Some people obviously exaggerate the class forces of rich peasants by saying that there are some provinces in the south where rich peasants or owner-peasants are the majority or account for large numbers (e.g., "Owner-peasants make up the majority of peasants in Jiangxi"; "Owner-peasants in Meixian and Dapu are numerous and the agrarian revolution cannot be carried out there"; "The rich peasants in Changting and Jianning, Fujian, amount to 40 percent"). They believe that the first step should be to oppose only the landlords, and that the time is not now right for attacking the rich peasants. These are not simply objective mistakes that run completely counter to the social conditions. Some are counterrevolutionary conspiracies subjectively attempting to set up the leadership of rich peasants inside the Party and among the masses, to confuse the class consciousness of the Party and the masses, and to weaken and abolish the Party's tasks of opposing the rich peasants.

The right-wing opportunist views of exaggerating the class forces of the rich peasants and maintaining that concessions should be made to the rich peasants at the time of attacking the landlords are extremely dangerous. To acknowledge the rich peasants as "an extremely isolated minority" and **not to realize the "severe cruelty of semifeudalism"** will naturally weaken and even lead to abandonment of the Party's tasks of opposing the rich peasants. This is also very dangerous. The Chen Duxius of the right opportunist opposition say that the Chinese countryside has already undergone a capitalist transformation and that feudal exploitation is a remnant of the remnants. Their conclusion is obviously to give up the democratic revolution and abandon the struggle against the landlords. If our reply does not take into consideration the nature of exploitation, but only the methods of exploitation, it will inevitably confirm that the "rich peasants are not the main enemies and the landlords are," and lead to refusal to recognize that the nature of the struggle against the rich peasants, like that against the landlords, is to combat brutal semifeudal exploitation. In this case our conclusion would also certainly lead to the weakening and abandonment of the important tasks of the struggle against the rich peasants. The abandonment of this task will fail to win over the broad masses of poor peasants in completing the democratic revolution and in marching toward the stage of the socialist revolution. On the contrary, only by understanding that the struggles against the rich peasants and against the landlords are both directed against the same brutal semifeudal exploitation can the Party's policy of opposing the rich peasants be established firmly, the broad masses of poor peasants be won over to complete the democratic revolution and turn toward the stage of socialist revolution, and the bases of the theories of the Chen Duxius be overthrown completely, stopping them from talking gibberish about the "rich peasants" controlling one region.

5) The Reasons for the Defeat of the Struggle in Hailufeng Lie in Adventurism and Hailufeng Localism, Not in the Struggle against the Rich Peasants[3]

The comrades in the East River area, drawing lessons from the defeat in Hailufeng and the counterrevolutionary actions of the rich peasants (the new rich peasants, whom they call the "middle peasants"), asked various localities not to attack the new rich peasants. Such arguments sometimes also crop up in other places. This is not very different from what happened during the Great Revolution, when comrades in Hunan and Hubei, tailing along with Tang Shengzhi and Xu Kexiang, screamed about the excesses of the peasant movement.[4] Now it is clear to everyone that the failure of the Great Revolution was not due to "excesses" but rather to "lack of excesses" (opportunism). The defeats in Hailufeng and other places are the results of adventurism, myopic localism, and the low tide of the national revolutionary situation at this time, but are not the results of opposing the rich peasants. With adventurist and localist leadership, defeats will occur at any time and cannot be avoided merely by refusing to oppose the rich peasants. At the same time, the struggle against rich peasants should never be equated with wanton burning, killing, and looting, which lead to adventurism and setbacks from which one may draw lessons for the future. On the contrary, resolute struggles against the rich peasants and establishment of absolute leadership by the poor peasants and farm laborers in the countryside are essential conditions to guarantee the victory of the revolution.

6) It Is Extremely Foolish to Refrain from Abolishing the Debts Owed to Rich Peasants in Order to Maintain the Circulation of Money

It is very wrong to obstruct the poor peasant masses' struggle to write off completely the debts owed to the rich peasants in order to "keep money in circulation," which means enabling rich peasants to lend money to poor peasants again. It would not be strange for the rich peasants to raise such slogans to deceive people, but would be most foolish if such proposals were put forward from the poor peasants' point of view. Because once order in the rural areas is disrupted, all lending and borrowing and buying and selling on credit will stop immediately. How can there be a situation in which the struggle has developed to the extent of confiscating the land, but the rich peasants are still out there circulating money? The facts in all the Red areas taught us long ago that the circulation of money could depend only on the poor peasants' organizing credit

---

3. Regarding the peasant movement in Haifeng and Lufeng (known collectively as Hailufeng) in Guangdong, under the leadership of Peng Pai, see above, the relevant note to "General Guidelines of the Hunan Provincial Committee," August 1, 1927, and also the numerous references to Peng Pai in Volume II of our edition, especially the note on p. 486.

4. See, in Volume II, pp. 425–517, the materials about events in the spring and summer of 1927.

cooperatives on their own, and on action by the soviet government to force the rich peasants to give loans at low interest. It is a total illusion to depend on the rich peasants to act generously and relieve the poor peasants on the condition that the poor peasants not attack them.

7) Confiscating All Land and Abolishing All Debts

"Confiscating all land" and "abolishing all debts" are the two central and irreplaceable slogans in the agrarian struggle in various southern provinces. The masses are implementing these two slogans widely everywhere, but the Party is acting like the tail of the masses everywhere and has affirmed the slogans "retroactively" after the masses themselves had already carried them out. Some have gone so far as to "deny" them from start to finish, thus acting not only as tails of the masses but also as opponents of the masses. Without correcting these serious mistakes, the Party will not be able to lead the agrarian struggle in various southern provinces. Undoubtedly, the two slogans of "confiscating the land of the landlord class" and "abolishing all debts" are no longer appropriate, and many localities have been used by the rich peasants and opportunist Communist Party members as tools to thwart the struggle of the poor peasants. Undoubtedly, the slogans of "confiscating all land" and "abolishing all debts" should be raised openly and straightforwardly all the time and in all places in the southern provinces. It is, of course, very wrong to "deny" them, and it constitutes tailism to "affirm retroactively." These two slogans should be used to mobilize the masses. The Party should not wait for the masses to start the struggle and then impose leadership on them. This tactic of "leading the masses only after they have risen up themselves" is still a tactic devoid of deep understanding of the land conditions in various southern provinces and thus it is a tactic of opportunist vacillation. This tactic of vacillation is unsuitable for the leadership of the imminent great struggle of the hundreds of millions of poor peasants.

8) The Two Slogans Should Be Raised at All Times

The view has been expressed that the Party's tactics toward the rich peasants should be different in the White regions and in the Red regions. In the Red regions, the rich peasants may be attacked and the slogans of confiscating all the land and abolishing all debts may be carried out. In the White regions, the slogan of confiscating the land of the landlords and abolishing the debts owed to the landlords should still prevail, in order to neutralize the rich peasants temporarily and enable the poor peasants to win the struggle against the landlords first. This opinion is wrong. If we recognize that the rich peasants (including those who are rich peasants in fact, but are generally regarded as "middle peasants") are the minority among the peasants (but more numerous than the landlords), and that this minority of rich peasants are still exploiting the poor peasants and farm laborers in the cruelest semifeudal way and are inevitably reactionary, **our tac-**

tics should from the beginning proclaim the evils of the rich peasants and treat the rich peasants in the same way as the landlords, and should in no way blur the class distinction between the rich peasants and other peasants, or give the rich peasants any chance to gain advantages. Their true features should be exposed from the beginning, so that the masses may recognize their reactionary nature. Furthermore, the rich peasants will never be "neutral." As soon as they see the poor peasants and farm laborers become united, they immediately join the front of the landlords. Where is such a thing as neutrality? This illusion of the neutrality of the rich peasants will certainly hinder the proletariat from mobilizing the poor peasants and farm laborers to launch fierce struggles and to fulfill the tasks of winning over the middle peasants as their allies. Therefore, if we fail to put forward the slogan of opposing the rich peasants from the very beginning, the poor peasants will be disappointed. This point has been proved in the struggles in various areas of western Fujian. Because the enemies of the poor peasants and farm laborers are not only the landlords but also the rich peasants. Exploitation by the landlords is certainly very severe, but exploitation by rich peasants is even more so.

9) The Two Slogans Should Be Raised in All Places

Another view holds that concessions should be made to the rich peasants in certain places. For example, if certain *xian* in a province and certain townships in a *xian* are so-called places "with a rich-peasant majority," it is all right not to follow the example of places where the poor peasants account for the majority in dividing up the land and abolishing debts. In such areas, local soviet governments may decide on a method that is different from the general method, for example, redistributing the land according to labor power and not cancelling the debts owed to the petty bourgeoisie, and so on. Higher-level soviet governments should criticize these viewpoints. Such opinions present two kinds of danger: The first danger is that the so-called "special places" may sacrifice all the interests of the poor peasants and farm laborers in order to please the rich peasants. They do not understand that the places that have many rich peasants must have even more poor peasants and farm laborers, that it is the tactic of the Guomindang to accommodate the interests of the rich peasants at the expense of the interests of the poor peasants and farm laborers, and that the Communist Party should never adopt such tactics. The second danger is the granting to the soviet governments of the special places the right to safeguard the interests of the rich people (i.e., the land would not be redistributed on an equal basis and the debts owed to the petty bourgeoisie would not be written off). In this case, the places may not necessarily be the places that have "many rich peasants" or "more owner-peasants" **(in fact, there is no such situation in any of the southern provinces and it is merely a rumor created by the rich peasant Communist Party members)**. Even though the places may have very few rich peasants and owner-peasants, as long as the rich peasants manage the soviet governments there, they can hoodwink the masses and make such demands. Consequently, the danger of these opinions is nothing less than guaranteeing the rich peasants' exploitation and oppression of the poor peasants and farm laborers. In all the southern provinces, the slogans of confiscating all the land and abolishing all debts should be put forward regardless of regions. This is the only way to avoid the danger.

10) Redistribution of the Land Not Equally, on a Per Capita Basis, But According to the Criterion of Labor Power, Is Definitely to the Advantage of the Rich Peasants[5]

To redistribute the land according to labor power, giving more land to families with more labor power, and less land to those with less labor power, favors only the rich peasants. The reason is that the Chinese rich peasants are mainly of two types, the semilandlord and the newly enriched. There are very few purely capitalist farms or agricultural companies, and hardly any in the various southern provinces. The absolute majority of Chinese rich peasants rely primarily on their own labor power. So the redistribution of land according to the criterion of labor power is greatly to the advantage of the rich peasants, because they have not only labor power but also ample draft animals, farm tools, and capital to go with it. They are not like the poor peasants, who although they have labor power, have inadequate draft animals, farm tools, and capital, or none at all. Therefore, the redistribution of land according to the criterion of labor power is advantageous to the rich peasants. Even among the poor peasants, the poor peasant families with more labor power (i.e., a family of eight with four able-bodied persons) may be better situated, thanks to the fact that they get more land, than families with fewer laborers (i.e., a family of eight with two able-bodied persons) to grow into rich peasants rapidly.

11) Winning Support from the Masses Is the First Criterion for Present Policies; Developing Production Is Not the First Criterion for Present Policies

When the outcome of the battle between the Red and White forces is still unclear, as is currently the case, **the only issue now is how to win over the broad masses to defeat the enemy and achieve the victory of the revolution.** At this time, the criterion that determines all tactics is winning over the masses, and not something called developing production. The reason is that at present the instru-

---

5. Consistently, in his land laws of December 1928, April 1929, and February 1930, Mao had included the criterion of labor power, but placed it second, and indicated that its use should be restricted. Regarding Mao's disagreements with Li Lisan and the Central Committee over this issue, see the Introduction to this volume.

ments of production (such as land) are still in the hands of the enemy, or, although they may have fallen into the hands of the people, may still be seized back by the enemy, and at such a time it is out of the question to talk about the problem of developing production. Those who raise inappropriate questions such as developing production at a time like this obviously represent the right-wing opportunist line of the rich peasants, because objectively they are not promoting production but obstructing the development of the struggle, helping the landlords to prolong their existence, and moving the revolution toward defeat.

12) Equal Distribution of Land on a Per Capita Basis Does Not Weaken Production, But Rather Serves as the Condition for Increasing Production

As mentioned above, when the struggle becomes fierce, only the redistribution of land on a per capita basis can win the support of the broad masses of poor peasants. **Even for the development of production, it is better to redistribute the land equally on a per capita basis than unequally on the basis of labor power,** and western Fujian is a very good example of this. The land in western Fujian having been divided up equally according to the number of family members, the crops there are growing very well this year. It is estimated that the output will increase by 20 percent compared with the time at the end of last year when the land had not yet been redistributed. In the past, some comrades in western Fujian worried that "the land had been divided into pieces that are too small" and that "those who did not work the land originally and who do not know how to work the land would allow it to fall into disuse after receiving their share." They are also concerned about various other dangers that may lead to a decrease in productive output. But current reality has proved that these worries are unwarranted. Instead of falling, productive output has risen. What are the reasons? Once the poor peasants and the unemployed masses have acquired land, they pour all of their energies into it. Now, moreover, all those parasites, landlords, and vagrants in the countryside who never engaged in production before will go hungry if they don't cultivate the land, so they are forced to start doing so. Among poor peasants, labor power that was unused in the past because of insufficient land is put to use once land is acquired. Therefore, productive output has risen. Another reason is that Chinese agricultural production is still at a stage of manual tilling, irrigation, and fertilization (with plant fertilizers and animal manure). In the period of landlord exploitation, the poor peasants, figuring that the land was not their own, were unwilling to work hard cultivating it. They staunchly refused to "plow deeply and weed frequently." They were also unwilling to build and maintain irrigation systems or to put much fertilizer down and did not even bother to gather manure. So the fields were increasingly neglected, and production declined greatly, creating a nationwide agricultural crisis. The peasants in western Fujian have acquired land, with every person having been given an equal share, and this has completely eliminated the phenomenon of work slowdowns. They are now willing to plough deeply; they have used a great deal of manpower in building irrigation ditches. This is very different from the period of exploitation by the landlords and rich peasants, when such irrigation ditches were not built. Without equal redistribution, it would have been impossible to use so much manpower in constructing and repairing irrigation ditches on a large scale. Grain straw is put into pigsties and cattle pens to make fertilizer. Grass roots are dug out to be composted. With nightsoil on top of this, the fertilizer problem is solved. The above are all results of equally redistributing the land and mobilizing manpower on a large scale. With these results, productive output has increased.

If they are short of cattle and cannot till the land they are given, those who used to rent cattle from the rich peasants may just confiscate these cattle and be done with it (or not pay the rental fees for the cattle and be done with it), and those who didn't even have rented cattle in the past may temporarily borrow or rent cattle from their relatives and friends.

If they are short of farm tools, they may borrow the spare farm tools of the rich peasants (once their surplus land has been confiscated, the rich peasants will have extra farm tools), or even confiscate rich peasants' extra farm tools.

As for the argument that fragmentation of the land into pieces that are too small is detrimental to production, this phenomenon affects only large-scale corporate agriculture, and agricultural corporations are extremely rare in China. What we see everywhere is small peasant production. Even the land of big landlords is rented out to many peasant families for cultivation, not leased to one peasant family. So there is no such thing as dividing up the land in a way not advantageous for production. Moreover, in agriculture we need to encourage the poor peasants to engage in collective production and move toward the socialist road, and discourage the rich peasants from moving toward capitalist production. **The poor peasants should gather together many small pieces of land and use the method of cooperatives, set up the cooperative system of production, and thus head toward socialist agricultural production. This is our sole purpose.**

During the period of revolution, the prices of agricultural produce were very low, and the scissors effect[6] developed further. The rich peasants with a lot of

---

6. The reference is to a metaphor coined by Trotsky in a speech at the Twelfth Congress of the Soviet Communist Party in March 1923, which has been widely used ever since, even though Trotsky himself soon fell out of favor. On this occasion, he exhibited a diagram showing the relation between agricultural and industrial prices during the previous year. Early in 1922, agricultural prices had been high as compared to industrial prices; the two lines intersected in September 1922, and thereafter agricultural prices declined rapidly with reference to those of industrial products. The graph thus had the appearance of an open pair of scissors. The moral was, of course, that the peasants were increasingly unable to purchase the implements and other industrial goods they needed. For a concise account of Trotsky's speech and the background to it, see E. H. Carr, *The Interregnum. 1923–1924* (Harmondsworth: Penguin, 1969), pp. 27–36.

land were not enthusiastic about cultivating it because doing so was not to their advantage, so production was actually undermined.

Production will not decline because families with fewer members able to work and more members unable to work have equal shares of land. This is because the few members in a family who are able to work are often capable of shouldering the task of providing food for the whole family. In addition, those who are said to be without labor power are not totally without labor power, so they can still help out with some of the work. As for large families in which those who cannot work greatly outnumber those who can (for example, a ratio of nine to one), this situation is rare, and such a family may return its land to the soviet government for transfer to others, so that it would not go to waste.

13) The Rich Peasants' Demand for Setting Aside Public Land and Use of the Slogan of Joint Production

The model farms of the soviet governments and cooperative-style collective production are good ways of moving toward socialization in agriculture, but in the present period of struggle, the main task of the soviet governments is to guide the struggle, not to promote production. Therefore model farms cannot be set up now. **In order to persuade the masses to expand the struggle, all land should be distributed to those who need it. It is not necessary for the soviet government to retain public land, forests, and extra buildings. Everything the masses need should be redistributed in principle.** There are those who propose not to distribute all the land, but rather to set aside some public fields, forests, and extra buildings and not redistribute them at all, because the soviet governments need money, or in preparation for having sons the following year. Others, such as Yuan Wencai of Jiangxi[7] and Fu Bocui of Fujian,[8] seem on the surface to stand on the Left and advocate what is called "socialist joint produc-

---

7. Yuan Wencai had, in fact, already been deliberately killed on February 10, 1930, together with the other former bandit leader on the Jinggangshan, Wang Zuo, in accordance with instructions of the Communist leadership in the old base area. The two were accused of returning to their bandit ways. This is now regarded as an error, resulting from the "leftist" line prevalent at the time, and the denunciation of bandits in the resolution of the Sixth Congress on soviet power. Mao is said to have disapproved at the time; he paid a visit to their widows in 1965.

8. Fu Bocui (1896–1993) was a native of Shanghang in Fujian Province, and an early participant in Sun Yatsen's Tongmenghui. He joined the Chinese Communist Party in September 1927, and was appointed secretary of a Party branch in Shanghang *xian*. In August 1928 he became a member of the Western Fujian Special Committee, and in 1929 he was elected to the Front Committee of the Fourth Red Army. In the spring of 1930, he was appointed commissar for economic and financial affairs in the Western Fujian Soviet Government, but in December 1930 he was expelled from the Party because of his resistance to land reform. Thereafter, he became a *xian* magistrate under the Guomindang, but in 1949 he rallied to the Communist cause again, and in January 1986, he rejoined the Party.

tion" (all land to be managed by the soviet governments; the peasants to work and till the fields under the command of the soviet governments; products to be distributed by the soviet governments according to number of people and need; the surplus to go to the soviet governments). All such proposals are thoroughly tainted with the rich peasants' line. They are clever and deceptive policies of the rich peasants to delay the redistribution of land by the poor peasants during the high tide of the revolution. Because what the poor peasants are busy doing is not preparing for having sons the following year, but rather getting their own nourishment the following day. Therefore, the poor peasants demand rapid redistribution of all land. From the poor peasants' point of view, it is entirely unnecessary to retain public land in preparation for having sons. As for socialist production, the poor peasants should organize cooperatives for collective cultivation after the land has been redistributed and feudal relationships have been thoroughly eliminated. The soviet governments will select places to set up farms after victory of the revolution has been won throughout the country and move toward socialism from there. The notion of directly implementing soviet management policies, without going through the process of redistribution and the process of cooperatives, is an out and out illusion of the petty bourgeoisie which objectively obstructs the agrarian struggle, leads the agrarian revolution toward defeat, and fundamentally negates the future of socialism.

14) When to Redistribute the Land and When to Reap the Harvest

In the past, the method was that if redistribution of land took place after seeds were sown, then that crop would be harvested by those who had done the sowing. Only the rich peasants were satisfied with this policy, and the poor peasants greatly resented it. According to this policy, in regions where there is only one harvest each year, the poor peasants and unemployed masses acquired land in name only, but in fact had to wait until the next autumn to harvest grain for the first time, so the poor peasants and unemployed masses were greatly dissatisfied. **The harvest should go to whoever acquires the land as soon as it is redistributed.** This way the rich peasants are displeased, but support of the poor peasants and the unemployed masses can be secured. Purchasing the crops of the rich peasants is another way of siding with the interests of the rich peasants. In light of the poor peasants' needs, it is even unnecessary to pay for the crops at all, because the poor peasants have no money to pay the price anyway.

15) Grain Can Also Be Divided Equally

When the rural struggle develops to a state of uprising, and in the struggle by the poor peasants, farm laborers, and unemployed masses to attack despotic gentry and burn land deeds, there will certainly be a struggle to divide up the grain equally, followed by a struggle to redistribute the land equally. **Therefore, di-**

viding up the grain is an important aspect of the rural struggle. A thorough struggle for redistributing the grain divides up equally not only the grain of the landlords, but also that of the rich peasants. The total store of grain in a township should be divided by the total population of the township, and then the surplus grain of all the households should be redistributed equally without compensation. If we raise the slogan of "opposing absolute egalitarianism" from the point of view of the rich peasants in this struggle, we will certainly lose the poor peasant masses. Obviously, this is wrong. Unquestionably we should side with the poor peasants, farm laborers, and impoverished masses, and launch the struggle to divide up the grain on an equal basis. In places where guerrilla warfare is going on and the régime cannot be stabilized even for a short time, the method of "seizing the grain" should be adopted. Although our purpose is to seize the grain of landlords, if the masses want to seize the grain of rich peasants, we should also completely support the actions of the masses.

16) It Is Not Adventurism to Raise Funds from the Rich Peasants

For the Red Army guerrilla groups and **the soviets to requisition funds from the rich peasants is entirely appropriate.** In the past the masses were forbidden to raise funds from the rich peasants, and such actions were considered adventurist. This is based on the position of currying favor with the rich peasants and is fundamentally wrong.

17) Drawing on the Fat to Make up for the Lean

If redistribution of land is carried out solely on the basis of "drawing on the plentiful to make up for the scarce," as with the experience of western Fujian last year, and the documents say "do not wishfully expect equalization," then the rich peasants will have an excuse to give the poor land to others and keep the rich land to themselves. Then the poor peasants will be very unhappy. This situation has occurred not only in western Fujian but in most other places as well. This is a real and important struggle within the overall agrarian struggle, which we should not neglect. On top of "drawing on the plentiful to make up for the scarce," **another principle of "drawing on the fat to make up for the lean" should be added,** and in the documents, "do not wishfully expect equalization" should be changed to "do not retain the rich lands."[9]

---

9. These two principles—"drawing on the plentiful to make up for the scarce," and "drawing on the fat to make up for the lean"— were characteristic traits of Mao's agrarian policy for several years, beginning at this time. See the Introduction to this volume. It should be recalled that the use of only the first slogan, which Mao stigmatizes here as an error committed in western Fujian, occurs in his own February 7, 1930, law as well.

18) Oppose the Rich Peasants' Slogan of Investigation and Study, and Speedily Redistribute the Land

Many rich peasant Communist Party members try to obstruct the agrarian struggle and delay the redistribution of land. Their slogan is that more investigations and studies need to be done. So in some cases, three years after the uprisings, the investigation and study are still going on, and the land still remains to be redistributed. In other cases, the investigation and study have been carried out for a year and the land is not divided up. We should fundamentally oppose this kind of empty investigation and study. On the issue of actually redistributing the land, it is simply not necessary to have the superior organs' investigation and study. After investigation by a township government, redistribution may begin at once. For the purpose of mobilizing the masses rapidly and thoroughly, and quickly spreading revolutionary influence, redistribution of land should be initiated very rapidly. **In all places where the masses have launched uprisings, redistribution should be finished within two weeks at most.**

19) Land Taxation Should Be Based on the Principle of Protecting the Poor Peasants, Allying with the Middle Peasants, and Attacking the Rich Peasants

The aim of progressive taxation on land, industry, and agriculture is to meet the financial needs of the struggle. With this aim, the principle of protecting the poor peasants, allying with the middle peasants, and attacking the rich peasants should be adopted. To meet the financial needs of the struggle, the poor peasants themselves have to pay considerable amounts of land taxes. But only very light taxes should be levied. The extremely poor peasants (those who do not have enough to eat every year) should be exempted. In comparison with the poor peasants, the middle-income peasants may pay a little more, but the principle of allying with the middle-income peasants should not be violated. In other words, the middle-income peasants should not be taxed too heavily either. The rich peasants may pay as much as 15 percent in land taxes. To fulfill the urgent needs of the struggle, the surplus grain of the rich peasants may be requisitioned without compensation.

20) Even after Equal Distribution, There Will Still Be Rich Peasants

The main objective of attacking the rich peasants now is not to eliminate them, but to **win the support of the poor peasant masses,** to expand the struggle, and to win the victory of the revolution. In reality, after being attacked, the rich peasants will not disappear altogether, because they enjoy all kinds of superior social and economic conditions. Even after their land has been redistributed, they will still have advantages over the poor peasants. The development of the rich peasants will certainly be more rapid than that of the poor peasants, and the latter will still be exploited by the former (the forms of exploitation are commercial and speculative selling and purchasing, and running small shops). Truly to eliminate rich peasants, and to free the poor peasants and farm laborers from exploitation by the rich peasants in the future, a national victory of the democratic revolution must be transformed into a national victory of the social revolution, and agriculture must be socialized. The socialization of agriculture must rely on the assistance and guidance of the workers in cities and the efforts of the poor peasants and farm laborers themselves. The capitalist production of the rich peasants will then be replaced by socialized production. At that time, all peasants will be proletarianized, and only then will there be no exploitation in the countryside. These are the common goals toward which the industrial proletariat and its vanguard, the Communist Party, want to lead the peasants.

21) Criticisms Are Intended to Encourage the Poor Peasants to Make Progress, Not to Pour Cold Water on Them

When the masses rise up enthusiastically and struggle to redistribute the land, the rich peasants and Communist Party members of rich peasant origin often use criticisms such as "wishfully expecting equalization," or "petty bourgeois illusions," and alter their meanings so as to resist the poor peasants' struggle for equal redistribution of the land. Examples of this can be seen everywhere. This amounts to nothing but pouring cold water on the emerging vigorous struggle of the poor peasants and will certainly discourage them. The criticism we originally put forward did not say equal redistribution of land was no good, but pointed out that **with regard to the countryside,** the private property system will not be eliminated, and the Communist system will not be realized, after the equal distribution of land, and exploitation of the poor peasants by the rich peasants will continue to occur. Therefore, after the equal distribution of land, the poor peasants **must take a further step forward and adopt the method of collective cultivation to move toward socialism;** only this will mark the final victory. Speaking about the whole country, the workers, after the equal redistribution of land, will still not be able to overthrow the bourgeoisie and the imperialists in conjunction with the forces of the peasants. Capitalism will not only continue to exploit the peasants but will intensify its exploitation as compared with the past. This will become the brutal scissors effect in the rural areas, where the peasants, though they have food to eat, have no clothes to wear and no goods to use. All farm produce is extremely cheap, and all cloth and goods are extremely expensive, and the life of the peasant is still most difficult. If the peasants want to be relieved from the suffering of the scissors effect, the only way is to **enlarge the Red Army, expand the struggle, and help the working class to win victories in big cities throughout the country, and overthrow the bourgeoisie and the imperialists, so that the soviets can manage the whole country. At the same** time, we must promote the high tide of world revolution and overthrow capitalism all over the world. Only then can the peasants gain assistance from the working class of the whole country and even the whole world and get rid of the sufferings caused by the scissors effect. Our comrades ought to seek all means and opportunities in every Red rural area to inform the peasants about the political and economic situations in the countryside and the whole world (as indicated above), encourage them to step forward, and absolutely never, taking the position of the rich peasants, drag them backward.

Criticism should start after the victory of the struggle for equal redistribution of the land. If such criticisms are raised in the fierce life-and-death struggle of land equalization, they may easily be distorted and used by the rich peasants, and two objectives may be posed before the masses (democracy and socialism), easily confusing their perceptions. For until the current objective has become a reality, the masses understand only this objective and do not understand the next objective. If we do not inspire the masses to strive forcefully to realize the current objective before this has been achieved, but neglect the current objective while encouraging the realization of the future objective, the masses may have doubts, and say: "Since they tell us that this is good, and that is also good, which one is really good?" If the criticism starts after the victory of the masses' struggle for equal redistribution of the land (two weeks is sufficient for completing the struggle for equal distribution), there will be no such problems.

22) Purge the Organization of Rich Peasants

a) To Guarantee the Victory of the Agrarian Revolution, Rich Peasant Elements Inside the Party Should Be Eliminated.

In order to ensure that the broad masses of poor peasants and farm laborers resolutely attack the rich peasants, establish the leadership of the poor peasants and farm laborers in the countryside, and guarantee victory of the agrarian revolution in the countryside, priority must be placed on the elimination of rich peasant elements inside the Party, and the rural Party in particular. This work is very significant, because up to now, local party organizations, especially the leading organs everywhere, have been full of rich peasant elements. The reason is that before the struggles in the rural areas started, most of those sent to work in the countryside by superior organs and those who came out and made the first contacts in the countryside were intellectuals of rich peasant and small landlord family backgrounds. These intellectuals naturally continued to introduce into the Party those of their own kind. When the time came for the struggle in the countryside to develop, most of this group of rich peasant and small landlord Party members became cadres in leading organs at Party branch level and above. The delays and superficiality of the development of the struggle everywhere have invariably resulted from the trouble stirred up by this group of people. They have blocked the instructions of high-level leading organs so they could not penetrate deeply into the masses. Only when the development of the struggle of the masses breaks through their opportunist leadership, and the tactics of the high-level leading organs against the rich peasants put pressure on them, can the anti-rich-peasant tactics of the high-level leading organs be linked up with the struggle of the masses, and the rich peasant line of various leading organs of the Party be eradicated. Almost all localities have experienced this process.

It is quite apparent that without purging the rich peasants (especially in the leading organs), **the mass struggle cannot be waged. The unconditional expulsion of rich peasants and all followers of the rich peasant line is a precondition for winning over the masses and guaranteeing the victory of the rural struggle.** How can we purge the rich peasants? By observing and discovering those who represent the rich peasant line in all types of struggle and getting rid of them as soon as they are discovered.

b) Rich Peasants Should Not Be Admitted into the Soviet Governments

Besides eliminating rich peasants from the Party, another fundamental means of establishing the leadership of the farm laborers in the countryside and prohibiting the leading role of rich peasants is to deprive the rich peasants of their voting rights. All past and present rich peasants may not participate in the soviet elections, and, of course, they are not allowed to be elected as representatives of the soviet governments or to other posts in all other government organs. This is an important link in ensuring that the revolution evolves from a democratic revolution to a socialist revolution. Neglect of this important link will certainly lead to serious mistakes.

23) Develop the Theoretical Struggle of Opposing the Rich Peasants

Apart from expelling the rich peasants from the organization, it is also very important to develop the theoretical struggle opposing the rich peasants. This theoretical struggle against the rich peasants should be greatly promoted both inside the Party and among the masses. Only by doing so can the rich peasant line be fundamentally overcome. It is not only necessary to overthrow the actual leadership of the rich peasants now, but also to make sure that it will not raise its head at any time.

The Problem of Vagabonds[1]

Resolution of the Joint Conference of the Red Fourth Army Front Committee and the Western Fujian Special Committee

(June 1930)

I. The Problem of Vagabonds Has Become a Grave Issue in the Struggle

In various localities, especially in the Red Army, the problem of vagabonds has become a very grave issue as the struggle develops. Many comrades have expressed incorrect points of view regarding this problem, saying such things as "The vagabonds know how to fight; we should not exclude them"; "People of all sorts may join, all we have to do is deal with anyone who breaks the rules"; "As long as the officers do a good job of leading, the organizational makeup of the troops is not important"; "Don't attack the vagabonds right now; it won't be too late to attack them when there are general uprisings"; and so on. Such erroneous viewpoints often crop up in the Red Army. The vagabond elements in the Red

---

Our source for this text is *Mao Zedong ji. Bujuan*, Vol. 3, pp. 135-39, where it is reproduced from a documentary collection published in China in 1982. No earlier version is known to exist.

1. The social category under discussion in this text, *liumang*, is now commonly translated and understood in China as "hooligan," but its meaning in 1930 was broader. The term might be rendered as "vagrant ruffian," but *liumang* evokes people in either of these categories, in other words those who are drifters, rogues, or both. It is difficult to find a precise English equivalent, but "vagabond," for which the *Oxford English Dictionary* gives the definition "leading an unsettled, irregular, or disreputable life," seems as appropriate as any. More commonly, Mao refers to these people as *youmin*, using an expression which has the rather similar meaning of "floating elements." This latter term is sometimes rendered as "lumpenproletariat," but we have consistently translated it in our edition as "vagrants." When, however, Mao combines *liumang* or *youmin* with *wuchanjieji* (proletariat) or *wuchanzhe* (proletarians), and speaks, for example, of *liumang wuchanjieji*, we have used Marx's term of "lumpenproletariat." Mao's approach to the problem in this text is very different from that which he had adopted earlier, especially in his essay "An Analysis of the Various Classes among the Chinese Peasantry and Their Attitudes Toward the Revolution" of January 1926, translated in Volume II, pp. 303–09. There he listed five of the same categories that he enumerates here—soldiers, bandits, thieves, beggars, and prostitutes—and concluded: "These people are capable of fighting very bravely, and if a method can be found for leading them, they can become a revolutionary force."

Army have produced many erroneous political and organizational concepts such as roving-rebelism, the purely military viewpoint, flightism, the policy of burning and killing, the policy of corporal punishment, a system of severe treatment, individual hedonism, individual heroism, small-groupism, and ultrademocracy, which are extremely harmful to the revolution. Especially at this time, when the high tide of revolution is approaching swiftly, and it is increasingly urgent to prepare for a general uprising in the whole country to achieve nationwide victory, the future of the struggle will be fraught with dangers if all forms of right opportunist vagabond consciousness are not overcome, and the vagabond elements are not cleaned out.

II. The Social Status and Role of the Vagabonds

Many comrades are very confused in their concept of vagabonds; lacking a clear understanding of vagabonds, they are unable to determine a correct policy toward them. Therefore, a detailed analysis of vagabonds is a precondition for determining a policy toward them.

A. The Origin of Vagabonds

The brutal exploitation by imperialism in semicolonial China has led to widespread bankruptcy among peasants and handicraft workers, thus creating an enormous mass of unemployed. Since there can be no large-scale national industries to absorb them, these unemployed masses have no way out, and this gives rise to large numbers of vagabonds.

B. The Social Occupations and the Characteristics of Vagabonds

Vagabonds have approximately thirty illegitimate occupations, such as: (1) bandits; (2) thieves; (3) prostitutes; (4) mercenary soldiers; (5) opera performers; (6) errand runners; (7) gamblers; (8) beggars (there are large masses of the above eight categories; the categories below contain relatively few people); (9) court henchmen; (10) *baojia* henchmen; (11) witnesses (with certain exceptions); (12) opium shop owners; (13) opium shop assistants; (14) diviners;[2] (15) fortune-tellers; (16) physiognomists; (17) geomancers (with certain exceptions); (18) jugglers or acrobats; (19) remedy and ointment peddlers; (20) martial arts demonstrators (with very few exceptions); (21) itinerant teachers; (22) hired snoops; (23) kidnappers; (24) vandals; (25) matchmakers; (26) traders in human beings; (27) monks (with certain exceptions); (28) Daoist priests (with certain exceptions); (29) witches; (30) Christian converts (with certain exceptions).

---

2. Diviners (*buguade*) foretold the future by the Eight Diagrams; the next category, fortunetellers (*suanmingde*), might do so by various methods.

What are called vagabonds in the current controversy should be limited to those in the categories listed above. They constitute a rough average of 5 percent of society's total population, there being approximately 20 million of them in the whole country.

They have the following characteristics: (1) they are divorced from production; (2) they have illegitimate and unstable occupations, and rely on "deception," "robbery," and "begging" for a livelihood; (3) they live irregular lives.

C. The Organizational Structure of the Vagabonds

To secure their survival and social status, the vagabond masses have organized many kinds of secret societies, such as the Green Gang and the Red Gang [Qingbang yu Hongbang][3] along the Yangzi River; the Three Dots Society [Sandianhui] in Fujian, Guangdong, Jiangxi, Guangxi and Southeast Asia; the Elder Brothers Society [Gelaohui] in Yunnan, Guizhou, Sichuan, Hunan, Hubei, Shanxi, and Gansu; the Attain Impartiality Lodge [Zhigongtang] in Fujian, Guangdong and Southeast Asia; the Amulet Society [Fuzihui] in Fujian; the Big Sword Society [Dadaohui] in Jiangsu, Anhui, Shandong and Henan; the Observance Society [Zailihui, also known as the Zailijiao, or Observance Sect] in the region of Beijing and Zhili; the Bearded Bandits [Hufei] in the three northeastern provinces; the Red Spear Society [Hongqianghui] and other similar groups in various northern provinces; the Three Harmonies Society [Sanhehui, commonly referred to as the Triad Society] and the Heaven and Earth Society [Tiandihui] in various southern provinces; the Society for the Restoration of the Han [Hanliuhui] on the banks of Lake Dongting; the Three Ks Party [SanKdang] in Shanghai; the Orchid Society [Lanhuahui] of Nanchang; the Green Dragon Society [Qinglonghui] south of the Xiang River; the Butterflies Plucking Flowers Association [Hudie caihuatuan] of Changsha; and so on. There are all kinds of societies everywhere, but they are very loosely organized and fragmented, and most of them are feudal in nature.

D. The Characteristics of the Vagabonds

The first is opposition to organization (opposing discipline and unity; individual freedom). The second is individual hedonism (indulging in visiting prostitutes, gambling, feasting, and spending in a big way). The third is a strongly mercenary

---

3. It does not seem appropriate to include even a brief note about each of the fifteen secret societies mentioned here by Mao. A convenient overview regarding this phenomenon can be found in the volume edited by Jean Chesneaux, *Popular Movements and Secret Societies in China 1840–1950* (Stanford: Stanford University Press, 1972). In order to facilitate reference to this or other sources, we have given here the Chinese name of each society, as well an English translation.

nature. The fourth is a destructive nature. The fifth is muddled class consciousness. The sixth is opposition to the masses. The seventh is opposition to socialism. The eighth is adventurism (wanton burning, killing, and looting). The ninth is roving-rebelism (no concept of political power). The above nine characteristics of vagabonds are not all separate from each other, but are connected, and result from their class status and social occupations.

E. The Vagabonds' Attitudes toward the Revolution

According to the above analysis, it is certain that the vagabonds have no enthusiasm for the revolution. On the contrary, in general they are full of counterrevolutionary tendencies. Under great pressure, they may join the revolutionary ranks out of opportunism, but they will vacillate from start to finish. At any time they are capable of turning traitor and becoming running dogs of the counterrevolution.

III. The Party's Tactics with Regard to Vagabonds

Once we have understood the social position of the vagabonds and their role in the revolution, we can determine the tactics to deal with them. The Party's overall tactics toward vagabonds should be: to wrench the vagabonds out from under the ruling class, provide them with land and jobs, force them to work, thus changing their social conditions, and, finally, transform them from vagabonds into nonvagabonds.

Under special circumstances they can be used temporarily so as to separate them from the ruling class. Then proper arrangements should be made for them, or their forces should be temporarily used to destroy the ruling class. But under no circumstances should the slightest political concession be made to the vagabonds.

When vagabonds harbor counterrevolutionary conspiracies, have counterrevolutionary potential, when they hinder the struggle of the masses, so that the masses cannot rise up unless the vagabonds are wiped out, or when the vagabonds, hiding behind revolutionary banners, are suppressing the masses, or when they are resolutely opposing the revolution and helping the ruling class to confront the revolutionary masses to the end, they should be eliminated without any hesitation. Not only should their leaders be eliminated, but some or all of their masses should also be destroyed whenever necessary.

The Red Army and the Red Guards are the important tools of the revolutionary masses in seizing state power and protecting it. **The components of these important tools must all be workers, peasants, and revolutionaries; no vagabonds can be allowed to penetrate into these organizations.**[4] Now the Red

---

4. This and other sentences in bold are emphasized in the Chinese original by the use of dots next to the characters.

Army and the Red Guards contain many vagabonds, who are the worst violators of discipline. Their interests are counter to that of all the fighting masses. They also behave in a cowardly fashion on the battlefields, afraid to advance. Although they sometimes demonstrate bravery, they do so for selfish interests and not to fulfill the tasks of a particular class. The adventurism and roving-rebelism in the course of guerrilla warfare are generated by them. On every occasion, they are always the ones who drag their feet or run away. Unless these elements are eliminated, and workers, peasants, and revolutionaries join the Red Army and Red Guards to take their place and transform the organization of the Red Army and Red Guards, such a Red Army and Red Guards will be very dangerous. Only by getting rid of them can the Red Army and the Red Guards be perfected so as to implement the great tasks of the class. In addition, eliminating all anti-organization and antidiscipline elements is the only way to win over the masses on a large scale and enable them to join the Red Army willingly and fulfill the task of expanding the Red Army and enlarge the scope of the struggle. This is not to say that the vagabond elements now in the Red Army must be expelled within twenty-four hours. **But the vagabonds must be systematically replaced by activists of the struggle of workers and peasants, and any inner-Party protection of vagabonds must be firmly opposed.** Criticism should be made of the illusions of "still having some hope of being revolutionary"; of the viewpoints that "all sorts of people may join the Red Army"; "the vagabonds should not be attacked during the guerrilla war, but only at the time of the armed uprising"; "as long as the officers do a good job of leading, the organizational makeup of the troops is not important"; and erroneous and strange opinions such as "if we don't want the vagabonds now, then we won't want the peasants later, and we won't want the workers in the future, and we'll be left with only the Communist Party."

Great efforts must be made to wipe out roving-rebelism, pure militarism, escapism, policies of burning and killing, the system of corporal punishment, individual hedonism, individual heroism, small-group mentality, ultrademocratism, and other erroneous political and organizational ideas of the vagabond elements. At the same time, those with only a few vagabond habits should receive appropriate education.

Inside the Party, general education and propaganda directed toward vagabonds should be stepped up among the masses, and an atmosphere of opposing vagabonds should be created. The Party, in particular, should purge vagabond elements, overcome the vagabond mentality, and recognize the fact that competing for leadership with the vagabond mentality is the most serious task in the Red Army now. This is the only way to ensure that the tool of the Red Army will be used by the worker and peasant classes, and that it will not be led astray by the vagabonds, thus causing the defeat of the revolution.

Order to the First Route Army[1] of the Red Army to Set Out from Western Fujian and Regroup at Guangchang

(June 22, 1930, at the city of Tingzhou)

1. The war between Chiang [Kaishek] and Yan [Xishan] is raging fiercely, and each has suffered casualties of more than a hundred thousand. Traitor Chiang has also been wounded, Zhang's troops and those of Guangxi have arrived in Changsha,[2] and the workers' and peasants' movement is on the rise everywhere. The situation is opening up a great deal.

2. This route army has the task of working in concert with the masses of workers and peasants in Jiangxi to seize Jiujiang and Nanchang so as to establish political power in Jiangxi. The plan is for the entire route army to move towards Guangchang and concentrate its forces there by July 5.

3. The Fourth Army (minus the Third Column) should advance towards Ninghua tomorrow (the 23rd). Upon arrival in Ninghua it should work for a week on raising funds. Fourth Army Commander Lin Biao will stay behind on important business, and the troops will be temporarily under the command of Zeng Shimao, chief-of-staff of this army.

4. The Second Column of the Sixth Army and the First Column of the Twelfth Army should advance toward Shicheng the day after tomorrow (the 24th), and work in the vicinity of Shicheng. They should also arrive at Guangchang and concentrate their forces there by July 5th, making sure to establish communication with the Fourth Army in Ninghua. This Second Column of

---

Our source for this order is Volume 6 of *Jiangxi dangshi ziliao* (Materials on Jiangxi Party History), pp. 48–49. This volume of the series, published in 1988, is a special collection dealing with "events around the time of the Luofang Conference." The document does not seem to have been published elsewhere.

1. The First Route Army [*diyi lujun*] had been formed from the Fourth Red Army of Zhu De and Mao Zedong, plus the Sixth and Twelfth Red Armies, in obedience to the orders brought from the Central Committee on June 21 by Tu Zhennong. It was shortly renamed the First Army Group [*diyi juntuan*], and is so designated in many of the documents translated below for the period beginning in July 1930.

2. Zhang refers to Zhang Fakui; Guangxi refers to the Guangxi faction and its leader, Li Zongren. In early May, these two commanders had led their armies into Hunan and driven back the troops loyal to Chiang Kaishek, occupying Changsha on May 28. Subsequently, however, they quarreled with one another, and as a result they were defeated in a counterattack. By the time Mao issued this order, Changsha had already been reoccupied by Chiang's troops on June 16.

the Sixth Army and First Column of the Twelfth Army are both under the direction of the column commander, Luo Binghui.

5. The Twenty-sixth Column should proceed tomorrow (the 23rd) to Ruijin for work, mobilizing the masses and undertaking to make uniforms for the First, Second, and Fourth Columns of the Twenty-second Army. It must also be in contact with the troops operating in Shicheng.

6. The Third Column of the Fourth Army, the Twelfth Army (minus the First Column), as well as the units directly attached to Headquarters will remain in Ting[zhou] for reconsolidation and training while awaiting orders, and then proceed via Shicheng to Guangchang to concentrate its forces.

7. The various large units of the original Fourth Army (that is, the First and Second Columns of the present Fourth Army, the First and Second Columns of the present Twelfth Army, and the espionage team of Headquarters) should each send tomorrow morning (the 23rd) one active, energetic soldier who has the rudiments of literacy, armed with one rifle and fifty rounds of ammunition, to the office of the original Fourth Army to assemble and await orders. They are to be sent to study at the Red Army School so that they may be used in future as reinforcements for lower-level Red Army cadres.

8. We are now in the city of Ting[zhou] but in the future will follow Headquarters in our movements.

Commander-in-chief   Zhu De

Political Commissar   Mao Zedong

Telegram of the Chinese Revolutionary Military Commission on Attacking Nanchang and Regrouping at Wuhan[1]

(June 25, 1930)

From the Central Committee of the Chinese Communist Party, for transmittal to Party branches everywhere, from the All-China General Labor Union for transmittal to Red labor unions everywhere, to the revolutionary mutual-relief societies and revolutionary student associations in all provinces, to the soviet governments in all localities, and to the Red armies in all army districts. To the *Shanghai Daily*, the *Hong Kong Daily*, the *Shanghai Red Flag*, the *Western Fujian Red Report*, and Red newspapers everywhere, for transmittal to the workers, peasants, soldiers, and toiling masses of the entire nation:

Since 1927, the Guomindang has betrayed the revolution and surrendered to the imperialists, and the various factions of the Guomindang have all become the loyal running dogs of the imperialists, with the result that the imperialist forces in China have grown day by day and the attacks of capital have been extremely severe. This has caused an evil trend of ever-deepening colonialization in China, the decline of industry, depression in the cities and bankruptcy in the villages, creating extreme panic in the Chinese economy. In particular, the sharpening conflicts and contradictions between the imperialists and the Guomindang warlords have created the continuous and

---

Our source for this document is the text published in *Dangshi ziliao*, no. 3, July 1978, as reproduced in *Mao Zedong ji. Bujuan*, Vol. 9, pp. 327–29.

1. As noted above, Li Lisan had enunciated in February 1930 a radical strategy aimed at achieving the rapid victory of the revolution in all of China. After calling a meeting of delegates from the various soviet areas, which finally met in Shanghai at the end of May, even though Mao had twice refused to obey a direct order to attend, Li produced, in the shape of a Politburo resolution of June 11, the definitive formulation of what has become known as the "Li Lisan line." (For the text, see *Central Committee Documents* [1930], pp. 115–35.) These events, and the relation between Mao's position, Li Lisan's position, and the line of the Communist International are discussed in the Introduction to this volume. As stated in the letter of October 14, 1930, translated below, the text of the resolution of June 11 did not reach the Red Army until early October. Mao had, however, learned about the substance of the new policies from an emissary of the Central Committee, Tu Zhennong, who arrived on June 21. (Regarding Tu, see the relevant note to the text of September 17, 1930.)

expanding tragic and confused wars of the warlords. All this proves that reactionary rule is already headed toward collapse. On the other hand, the revolutionary forces are moving toward balanced development, and with the intensifying struggle of the workers, the deepening of the land revolution of the peasants, the rapid expansion of the soviet districts and of the Red Army, the daily increasing revolutionization of the soldiers, the fact that the poor people and petty bourgeoisie of the towns and cities are daily moving further toward the Left, all the objective conditions for the victory of the revolution in the whole country are fully mature, and the revolutionary high tide is already before us. Given this political situation, the present task of the revolutionary masses is to concentrate all the revolutionary forces, to overthrow reactionary politics root and branch, to seize political power throughout the whole country, and to win nationwide victory for the revolution. In compliance with the resolution of the First National Conference of the Soviet Districts to complete the task of the revolution, this committee, in command of the First Army Group of the Red Army, will advance toward Nanchang and regroup at Wuhan with the Second and Third Army Groups.[2] They will seize victory first in the provinces of Hunan, Hubei, and Jiangxi, in order to push forward the nationwide revolutionary high tide, and will call upon the workers, peasants, soldiers, and the masses of poor people to rise up together, for the workers to carry out political strikes, for the peasants to carry out local uprisings, for the soldiers of the White armies to carry out troop insurrections, and turn the wars among the warlords into a revolutionary class war. We believe that only the force of the broad revolutionary masses is capable of thoroughly overthrowing all reactionary warlord forces. We are persuaded that only by overthrowing completely the reactionary rule of the Guomindang can China be unified and the workers, peasants, soldiers, and impoverished masses obtain liberation. In order to liberate themselves, and in order to seek the victory of the revolution throughout the country, the toiling worker, peasant, and soldier masses must resolutely and courageously stand with the Red Army on the battlelines, for the final decisive battle against the Guomindang warlords and the imperialists. We further believe that the victory of the Chinese revolution can assuredly raise the curtain on the world revolution. The victory of the Chinese revolution will not only be the death of the Chinese reactionary rulers and the Guomindang warlords; it will also mark the eve of the collapse of imperialism. This, our decisive war, is the decisive war in which our China will be liberated from beneath the iron heel of the imperialists and warlords.

---

2. The Shanghai conference of soviet areas had been invoked by Li Lisan to provide added authority for the Politburo's June 11 resolution on revolutionary strategy, a point which Tu had no doubt made in his lengthy report to Mao and his comrades. Tu also conveyed a directive from the Central Committee stipulating that the former Red armies should be combined into army groups, and that the First, Second, and Third Army Groups should join forces at Wuhan, as stated here.

The gunpowder of the revolution is already exploding, and the light of the dawn of the revolution will quickly arrive. Our Red flag will fly throughout the entire world. Workers, peasants, soldiers, and impoverished masses, arise as one, and shatter the shackles that the imperialists and the Guomindang warlords have placed on us.

Chinese Revolutionary Military Commmission

Chairman   Mao Zedong

Members   Zhu De, Zeng Shan, Li Wenlin, Liu Shiqi,
Deng Zihui, Huang Gonglue, Peng Dehuai,
Wang Huai, Lin Biao, Peng Qingquan,
Wu Zhonghao, Tan Zhenlin, Chen Yi,
Duan Yuequan, Fang Zhimin, Shao Shiping

June 25, 1930

From Tingzhou to Changsha

(To the Tune "Butterflies Court the Flowers")

(July 1930)

In June the heavenly troops[1] smite the corrupt and evil,
Seeking with ten-thousand-*zhang*[2] ropes to bind the *kunpeng*.[3]
Across the River Gan a patch turned red,
Thanks to Huang Gonglue's wing.[4]
A million workers and peasants eagerly rise together,
Rolling up Jiangxi like a mat, striking straight at Hunan and Hubei.
The solemn strains of the *Internationale* are heard,
A raging tempest falls upon us from the heavens.[5]

This is another of the poems first published together in the May 1962 issue of *People's Literature*. (For the author's note accompanying it, see Mao's autumn 1929 poem "The War between Chiang Kaishek and the Guangxi Warlords.") Our source is *Shici duilian*, pp. 35–37.

1. Here the Chinese term is *tianbing*, traditionally used to mean the emperor's army, or the army "with Heaven on its side."

2. The *zhang* is a measurement of length equal to 10 Chinese feet, or 3.3 meters.

3. This mythical creature appears in the opening passage of chapter 1 of the *Zhuangzi* (translated in Angus Graham, *Chuang-tzu. The Seven Inner Chapters and Other Writings from the Book* Chuang-tzu [London: Allen & Unwin, 1981], pp. 43–44). The bird called *peng* (usually translated as roc) is presented there as a metamorphosis of a giant fish called the *kun*. Here the composite name *kunpeng* is used to evoke the image of a giant, ever-changing, predatory force.

4. Huang Gonglue (1898–1931), a native of Hunan, joined the Chinese Communist Party in 1927 and was a leader in the Pingjiang Uprising of 1928. In June 1930, his Sixth Army, which had already set up a base area (the "patch of red" of the poem) on the western bank of the Gan River, became part of the First Army Group under the command of Zhu and Mao. Huang was killed in action on September 15, 1931.

5. Mao's last two lines appear to be patterned on a poem by Du Fu, the first of "Seven Songs of a Sojourner in Tonggu *xian* in 759." William Hung translates Du Fu's concluding lines: "Oh! Just this first song is sufficiently sad: A bitter wind blows on me from high above." (William Hung, *Tu Fu: China's Greatest Poet* [Cambridge: Harvard University Press, 1952], p. 157.) The character *bei* (sad, melancholy) appears in both poems; Mao applies the adjective to the *Internationale*, and in that context we have rendered it as "solemn"; Du Fu's last line speaks of a *bei feng*, translated by Hung as a bitter wind. Mao's perception of the *Internationale* was colored by the fact that, though it is a song of victory, he was hearing it (or thinking of it) in defeat. Unlike virtually all previous Chinese commentators on this poem, the editors of the *Mao Zedong shici duilian jizhu* refer (p. 37) to the last two lines as "obscurely conveying the author's complicated feelings at the time, solemn and resolute, and at the same time a mixture of grief and anger [*beizhuang er beifen*]."

Order to the First Army Group of the Red Army to Change Its Route and Advance on Chongren

(July 20, 1930, in the afternoon, at General Headquarters in the city of Yongcheng)

1. The situation of the enemy is as before.

2. On the basis of its original task, this army group will change its route and advance on Chongren. It has been decided that we will set off from here in three groups on the 21st of this month, and arrival at the *xian* seat of Chongren is to be on the 22nd.

3. The order of battle and the plans for the movement of the troops:[1]

Date	Place of Encampment		
	Left route (Fourth Army, Commanding Officer Lin Biao)	Middle route (Twelfth Army, General Command Headquarters)	Right route (Third Army, Commanding Officer Huang Gonglue)
First day, July 21	Daifang, 80 *li*	Around Zhongxiqiao and Pengzhou, 80 *li*	Arrive at Chongren (40 *li*) via Niutian (60 *li*), Le'an (50 *li*) and Gongpo (40 *li*). Arrive at *xian* town of Chongren within 3 days (on July 23). Fix own marching plan
Second day, the 22nd	Gongpo, 55 *li*	The area around Jianglei, Majiadu, and Xiawan(?)[2]	
Third day, the 23rd	Chongren, 40 *li*	Chongren	

Our source for this text is *Jiangxi dangshi ziliao*, Vol. 6, pp. 57–60.

1. The figures on this chart manifestly indicate the distances in *li* from one point to another.

2. A question mark appears in parentheses here in the original text, possibly indicating that the distance is unknown.

Addendum:

a. General Command Headquarters and directly attached units follow the Revolutionary Military Commission in marching along the middle route. A detailed marching plan is to be fixed separately.

b. Detailed marching plans for the left and right routes are to be fixed separately by the commanders of each route.

4. We will lead the General Headquarters and march with the Revolutionary Military Commission along the middle route.

Addendum:

a. For all army routes, the troops that arrive first at the *xian* seat of Chongren will be in charge of allocating encampment sites for the entire Army Group (the Third, Fourth, and Twelfth Armies), and for posting sentries and sending out scouts in all directions.

Chart of marching plans for the second period of the northward advance of the Right Route Army of the Red Army's First Army Group

Date	21st	22nd
Marching order	1. Twelfth Army 2. Espionage team of General Headquarters, Front Committee of General Command Headquarters, espionage team of the Front Committee, transportation team, baggage of units directly attached to the army 3. Third Army	Same as previously
Departure time	Leave at 1:00 A.M. Get up at 1:00 A.M., leave at 2:30 after the Twelfth Army, leave at 3:00 A.M. following the baggage of the units directly attached to General Headquarters	Same as previously
Places passed	Leave this town via the north gate, pass 10 Lusiping —20 Xianlieqiao—20 Liuyuan (50 *li*)	40 *li*
Encampment sites	Camp along the way near Liuyuan	Lixie

Marching order	Follow the order as above: espionage team of General Headquarters, General Headquarters, Front Committee, espionage team of the Front Committee, transportation team, the baggage of the directly attached units, and the 102nd Army
Time of departure	Get up at 1:00, leave at 2:00, leave at 2:30 Get up at 1:30, leave at 2:30, leave at 3:00
Places passed	Chudong 5 Lingxiali 5 Upper and Lower Luzhou 10 Jiangkou 10 Xiapo 5 Kengkou 15 Guangganyu 10 Qian 6 Zhongxiqiao 15 Pengzhou
Encampment sites	Area around Zhongxiqiao and Pengzhou; area around Matiwan, Xiawan, and Guofang

Addendum:

1. All units must set their clocks accurately and keep strictly to schedules so as not to interfere with the marching of the other units.

2. While on the march, the vanguard is to be dispatched by the Twelfth Army, and the rearguard is to be dispatched by the Third Army. While encamped, sentries are to be posted by the Twelfth Army on the way out, and by the Third Army on the way back. For unusual situations there will be separate orders.

3. The matter of setting up camp will be directed by the chief of the Adjutants' Section of the Twelfth Army, Yang Zhicheng.

4. For the departure of troops directly attached to the General Headquarters tomorrow (the 21st), the place of assembly will be on the lawn in front of the transportation team's encampment (that is, at the rear entrance to General Headquarters).

5. Upon setting out tomorrow morning, the Fourth Army must rapidly get onto the main road, so as to avoid crossing paths with the Twelfth Army.

Commander-in-chief   Zhu De

Political Commissar   Mao Zedong

Order to the First Army Group of the Red Army to Set Out from Yongfeng

(July 20, 1930, 7.30 P.M. at General Headquarters in the city of Yongfeng)

1. The overall situation of the enemy is as before.

There are at present no White troops in Xin'gan. It is said that there is one regiment of enemy troops in Xiajiang, or that it has already set out for Jishui.

2. This army group has decided to go northward according to the original plan. The plan for advancing during the second period is to divide into two routes, to set out from here (the city of Yongfeng) tomorrow (the 21st), to march for two days, and to be sure to arrive at Maixie (90 *li* from the city) and concentrate forces. A chart of the plans is as below.

Chart of the Red Army First Army Group's plans for the second period of advancing northward (setting out from Yongfeng *xian* to Maixie for concentration of forces):[1]

date	units and places of encampment	
First day: July 21	left route (the Fourth Army): via Wangjia 15 Hanshanqiao 5 Muyuan 5 Zhangjia 5 Wangjia Encamp in the vicinity of Zhangjia, Wangjia	right route (General Headquarters plus Third and Twelfth Armies): 10 Luosiping 20 Xianningqiao 20 Encamp at Liuyuan
Second day: July 22	20 Nabu 25 Maixie Encamp at Maixie	40 Maixie Encamp at Maixie

3. A detailed marching plan for the left route is to be drawn up by the Fourth Army itself. A marching plan for the right route is to be issued in a separate chart.

4. After setting out, our position will be that of the General Headquarters.

Our source for this order is *Jiangxi dangshi ziliao*, Vol. 6, pp. 55–56.

1. The numbers in the columns marked "place of encampment" on this chart presumably indicate distances in *li* from one location to another.

Addendum: Upon setting out tomorrow morning, the Fourth Army must rapidly get onto the main road so as to avoid crossing paths with the Twelfth Army.

Commander-in-chief   Zhu De
Political Commissar   Mao Zedong

Order to the First Army Group of the Red Army to Attack Zhangshu[1]

(July 22, 1930, 7:00 P.M. at General Headquarters in Maixie)

1. At present, there are no enemy troops in the town of Zhangshu. The town of Nanchang has one battalion each of artillery and espionage, and one regiment each of garrison and reserves. There is the possibility of their advancing to Zhangshu and stubbornly resisting our forces.

The rest of the intelligence about the enemy is as reported today by the staff office of this General Headquarters; there is no enemy in Xin'gan.

Today our Fourth Army has already dispatched troops that have taken the town of Xin'gan.

2. This army group has decided to launch an assault and take Zhangshu, according to the original third period plan for northward advance.

3. As the left wing forces, the Fourth Army should enter Xin'gan by tomorrow morning and clearly ascertain the enemy situation in Zhangshu. If it is true that there are no enemy forces, they should all advance toward the town of Zhangshu and take it (as soon as it is taken, sentries should be posted to Nanchang, and a way should be found to block the public road between Nanchang and Zhangshu; a floating bridge should be quickly built leading to Gaoan, or boats should be gathered). If it is found that there are enemy troops in Zhangshu, then [the Fourth Army] is to advance from Xin'gan to the area around Xiazhuang, Liuzhuang, and Huangzhuang, which are on the right of Yongtaijie, encamp, and wait for the order to attack.

The rest constitute the main force of the right wing army, and their distribution is as follows:

a. The Third Army should dispatch one column as the vanguard, to set out tomorrow promptly at 1:00 A.M. from its present encampment, march to

---

Our source for this order is *Jiangxi dangshi ziliao*, Vol. 6, pp. 61–62.

1. Zhangshu was a market town in Qingjiang *xian*, located some 50 miles southwest of Nanchang on the Gan River. Generally speaking, in the orders from the summer and autumn of 1930 which appear below, Zhangshu refers specifically to the town, and Qingjiang to the *xian* as a whole, or to its administrative center. Subsequently, Zhangshu increased in importance until it became an urban district which swallowed up the whole of Qingjiang *xian*, so only this name will be found on recent maps.

the Yanghuzhuang area by way of Mixiang, Miaoxia, Hepo, Zhangshuxia, Lijiang, Yujiafang, Sangzhuang, and Tanjiafang, and encamp there (60 *li*).

b. The rest constitute the main force of the right wing army, to advance according to the following order: the Third Army (minus one column, to set out tomorrow at 1:20 A.M. from its present location and follow after the vanguard), the General Command Headquarters and its espionage team, the espionage team of the Front Committee, the transport team (to arise at 1:20 A.M. tomorrow, and to assemble and set out at 2:20 from the mouth of the street here), and the Twelfth Army (minus one column, to set out tomorrow at 2:50 A.M.), plus the baggage of the right wing army (to advance according to the marching order of the troops).

c. The Twelfth Army is to dispatch one column as rear guard to march after the baggage and provide protection.

d. Yang Zhicheng, chief of the Adjutants Section of the Twelfth Army, is in charge of all matters relating to setting up camp for the right wing army.

e. As for the baggage of the right wing army, the main person in charge is Fan Shude, head of the baggage team of the Sixth Army's second column, and second in command is Yang Lisan, chief of the supplies section of the Twelfth Army. Each unit's baggage is to follow its own personnel in the marching order designated.

4. While marching, we will be at the head of this unit.

Addendum:

1. When setting out tomorrow morning, each unit must be strictly punctual.

2. Prior to departure, each unit must be clear about the road out, so as to avoid crossing paths with other forces.

3. Wounded and sick soldiers are to advance along with the large baggage.

4. If there is no way to gather together the baggage of all the troops, it should be stopped at the side of the road and wait until all the personnel of the unit in question have passed before being moved ahead. The person in charge of baggage in each unit is to be held fully responsible.

5. The left wing troops must be in close touch with this unit.

Commander-in-chief	Zhu De
Political Commissar	Mao Zedong

Order to the First Army Group of the Red Army About All Stipulated Arrangements for Crossing the River

(July 25, 1930, at General Headquarters in the town of Zhangshu)

Our stipulations for crossing the river at this point are hereby laid down as shown below; every unit must strictly observe them.

1. The order for crossing the river is as follows: (a) Fourth Army; (b) General Headquarters and its directly attached units; (c) Twelfth Army; (d) given this order for the three army units, we must first get across the horses, mess supplies, and large and small baggage, after which the people are to cross in the aforementioned order.

2. Security for the river crossing: the northern shore of the Gan River is the responsibility of the Fourth Army, which must dispatch one column as security forces to cross the river first at 3:00 P.M. and deploy security guards along the northern shore. The Third Army is responsible for the deployment of security guards along the southern shore the Gan River, and the guards should be dispatched at 5:00 P.M. Each unit of security forces must occupy a stronghold along the major roads on land (Qingjiang Road on the northern shore, and Nanchang Road, Fuzhou Road, and Xin'gan Road on the southern shore), and keep a close watch on them. In addition, each security force is to dispatch sentries to keep watch as far as 20 *li* in the direction under surveillance. West of the river it is necessary to set up machine guns to protect the river area so as to prevent enemy interference by steamer or small warship.

3. Dock routes
There are three docks in this area, and the routes leading to them are as follows:

Number 1 dock (there are two routes): a. Xiaogong Temple—Manzhou Street—and Suxian Street—to number 1 dock. b. Bus station—Men Street—Pingchang Street—Xianyu Street—Yufu Street—to number 1 dock (General Headquarters will cross the river here).

Number 2 dock
Bus station—East Gate—Denglong Street—Yugu Miao—to number 2 dock.

Our source for this order is *Jiangxi dangshi ziliao*, Vol. 6, pp. 63–66.

Number 3 dock

Bus station—Zijing Lane—Zhongshipai—the sportsground—Sanwang-
gong—Yangong Lane—Dade Gate—to number 3 dock.

4. Distribution of docks

a. The espionage team of the Revolutionary Military Commission, General
   Headquarters, and its directly attached units board boats and cross the
   river at number 1 dock via the second route.

b. The Fourth Army can board boats at any dock except the one at which
   General Headquarters makes the crossing.

c. The Twelfth Army should board boats and make the crossing at number 1
   dock via both routes leading to it.

d. The Third Army should board boats at docks numbers 2 and 3, and at
   number 1 dock via the second route leading to it.

(Each unit should still try on its own to come up with short cuts to the
boarding places, and have the adjutants make signs.)

5. Times for the river crossing

a. Security forces (one column of the Fourth Army) at 3:00 P.M.

b. Horses and mess supplies for each unit between 3:00 and 5:00 P.M.; crossing must be completed within two hours.

c. The Fourth Army and the Revolutionary Military Commission, plus the
   directly attached units of General Headquarters (minus one column) between 5:00 and 8:00 P.M.

d. The Twelfth Army between 8:00 and 12:00 P.M.

e. The Third Army between 12:00 P.M. and 4:00 A.M. tomorrow. (The security forces of the Third Army will be the last to cross the river, and its
   signal to withdraw sentries will be determined on its own.)

6. The number of people on each boat

Each large boat may carry approximately 80 to 90 people (about one company).

Each small boat may carry 30-odd people.

7. Stipulations regarding the crossing of horses and baggage

All horses are to be taken across the river in small open boats.

Baggage and mess supplies may be carried across the river in large boats, but
when loading, each unit must dispatch one adjutant to direct the operation so as
to avoid crowding. After landing they should be assembled and led to designated
rest areas.

8. Escort personnel

The Fourth Army is to dispatch one company to be responsible for escorting
the boats, with one soldier assigned to each boat (there are about 80-odd boats).

9. Illumination during the river crossing

When crossing the river at night, lighting on the docks is to be provided by the Adjutants Section of General Headquarters, and on the boats each unit is to carry its own lantern.

10. Safety during the river crossing

The chief of the Adjutants Section of the Fourth Army is to designate several small boats (a minimum of six), choose twenty-odd boatmen who are good swimmers, put them on the small boats (four to a boat), and situate them down river from the point of crossing, so as to provide rescue in case of emergency.

11. Points for attention when crossing the river

a.   Obey orders, and do not vie with each other for position or crowd each other.
b.   Keep quiet, do not make unnecessary noise.
c.   Do not light matches or smoke on the boat.

12. Command during the crossing

During the time when each unit is making the crossing, that unit should designate capable officers to direct the crossing at each dock. The units directly attached to General Headquarters will be commanded by General Headquarters chief adjutant Chen Yezhen.

13. Places to rest after the river crossing

After the river crossing has been completed, the Fourth Army will advance to Jinglouyu (resting on the road leading to Gaoan), the units directly attached to General Headquarters and the Twelfth Army will rest in the area around Zhujiadu and Yangjialing, and the Third Army will choose its own place to rest.

Commander-in-chief   Zhu De
Political Commissar   Mao Zedong

Order to Seize the Niuhang Railway Station[1]

(July 29, 1930)

1. One regiment of Dai Yue's forces[2] proceeded from Xinyu to Xin'gan on the 25th; the 107th Regiment of Zhu Yaohua's forces[3] proceeded from Chongren to Zhangshu on the 26th; the 108th Regiment has also received orders from Zhang Huizan[4] to proceed to the provincial capital and appears disposed to march into Nanchang in haste so as to defend against us. According to a report from someone who came from Zhangshu today, the 103rd and 107th Regiments, led by Zhu Yaohua, and one regiment from the Thirteenth Division (Deng Ying)[5] are proceeding from Zhangshu to Nanchang by boat.

2. On the basis of the original task of our army group, we intend to occupy the Nanchang-Jiujiang Railroad on August 1, International Day of Anti-Imperialist Demonstrations and anniversary of the Nanchang Uprising, in order to spread [our] political influence. A plan of operation has been decided on, according to which as a second phase of the second step in the march northward, the

---

Our source for this document is *Mao Zedong junshi wenji*, Vol. 1, pp. 152–54, where it is stated that the text has been reproduced from the original document in the Party archives.

1. This is an order of the First Army Group issued by Mao Zedong and Zhu De from Gaoan in Jiangxi. On June 25 Mao Zedong, in his capacity as chairman of the Revolutionary Military Commission, had issued a telegram, translated above, expressing agreement with Li Lisan's line of attacking major cities and announcing that the First Army Group would advance toward Nanchang. Entering Jiangxi from Changting in western Fujian, the forces under Mao Zedong and Zhu De proceeded on July 24 to attack and capture Zhangshu in Qingjiang *xian*, to the southwest of Nanchang, destroying part of the Guomindang's Eighteenth Division. At this point, a conference of cadres from the First Army Group convened by Mao and Zhu decided not to attack Nanchang, but to limit their aims to taking the Niuhang Railway Station, across the Gan River from Nanchang, where they could shoot off guns as an "August 1" demonstration to commemorate the third anniversary of the Nanchang uprising.

2. The reference is to the Fifty-second Brigade of the Eighteenth Division of the Guomindang Ninth Route Army, commanded by Dai Yue (1888–1971), a native of Hunan.

3. This regiment was part of the Fifty-fourth Brigade of the Eighteenth Division of the Guomindang Ninth Route Army; Zhu Yaohua was the brigade commander.

4. Zhang Huizan (1884–1931), a native of Hunan, was, at this time, the commander of the Eighteenth Division of the Guomindang Ninth Route Army. He was defeated and captured by the Red Army on December 30, 1930.

5. Deng Ying, a native of Hubei, was at this time the commander of the newly established Thirteenth Division of the Guomindang Ninth Route Army.

entire army group will proceed on the 30th to the area of Wanshougong and Shiziling, and wait for an opportunity to seize the Niuhang Railway Station.

3. The Twelfth Army should proceed in the direction of Nanchang after noon today (the 29th), and choose a place to encamp about 30 *li* from the city. Tomorrow (the 30th) one column should be sent to seize Shengmijie and wait for an opportunity to occupy the Niuhang Railway Station. The remaining [troops] should proceed to Wanshougong (Twelfth Army Acting Commander Luo[6] shall delegate encampment [personnel] and security forces at Wanshougong).

The Third Army should set out from here tomorrow (the 30th) by way of Yangjiafang, Licun, and Chitujie, and arrive in the vicinity of Shiziling on the 31st, to rest there and await further orders.

The units under the direct command of General Headquarters will set out from here tomorrow (the 30th) along with the Revolutionary Military Commission and the Fourth Army, and proceed by way of Xiangfuguanjie and Liangcun to Wanshougong, where they will encamp, and rest and await further orders on the 31st.

4. Upon arrival at its destination, each military unit should immediately set about mobilizing the masses and making efforts to raise funds.

5. As for the troops delegated by the Twelfth Army to take Shengmijie, as soon as Niuhang Railway Station has been taken, they should immediately set about destroying the Nanchang-Jiujiang Railroad line (pay attention to destroying the iron bridge) and the nearby telegraph lines.

6. When on the move, all movements should follow those of General Headquarters.

It is so ordered.

Addendum:

1. Departure time and order of march for General Headquarters and the Fourth Army tomorrow (the 30th) is as follows:

   a. Departure time for General Headquarters and units under its direct command, and the espionage team of the Revolutionary Military Commission is: rise at 1:30, set out at 2:30.

     The Fourth Army sets out at 3:00.

   b. When on the march, the order of the ranks is: General Headquarters espionage team, General Headquarters, Revolutionary Military Commission and its espionage team, transportation team, and the Fourth Army. The baggage of the units under the direct command of the General Headquarters are to follow behind the transportation team.

---

6. Luo Binghui (1897–1946) was a native of Yunnan. A former Guomindang general who had participated in the Northern Expedition, he went over to the Red Army in November 1929. At this time, he was, as indicated by Mao, commander of the Twelfth Division.

c. The Fourth Army should assign a rear guard to provide security during the march.

2. The route to Wanshougong is as follows:

   Starting from this city, passing through Lengcun—Wangcun—Wukouqiao—Zuojiashan, Xiangfuguanjie—Xiongboqiao—Guloupu — Shaoshan—Liangcun—Wanshougong.

3. The route to Shiziling is as follows:

   Starting from this city—Lianchengqiao—Xiejialing (Songjia)—Yangjiafang—Xiaogang (Beiyi)—Hucun—Licun —Chitujie—Luowa—Shiziling.

4. The Third Army should pay attention to finding out clearly the marching route, so as not to cross paths with the Fourth Army.

Order to Withdraw to Anyi and Fengxin for Rest and Reconsolidation

(August 1, 1930)

1. The Hundred and third and Hundred and fifth Regiments have both arrived at the Nanchang Railway Station, and they appear to be taking a solid defensive stand while waiting for reinforcements.

The troops we sent out have begun their attack on Nanchang from around the Nanchang Railway Station today (August 1) as an armed demonstration to commemorate the August 1 holiday.

2. In order to accomplish rapidly the task of marching northward, this army group has decided to lure the enemy out of its den and destroy him. It is planned to arrive at Anyi *xian* and Fengxin *xian* tomorrow (August 2) to rest, consolidate, work, and raise funds.

3. The Twelfth Army should proceed tomorrow morning (the 2nd) at 3:00 to Anyi and keep a close watch on Jiujiang (sending some [troops] in the direction of Wanjiafu and Nanxi for guerrilla [warfare]), setting out from here (excluding the First Column) and passing by way of Wushanpu, Luowa, Lianglukou (crossroads), and Shibijie to the Anyi *xian* seat. Its First Column, sent to Guofangling, should begin to withdraw after five o'clock tomorrow morning, procede to Anyi via shortcut, and rejoin the main forces (it would be best for this army to arrive and encamp at Shibijie on the first day).

The Third Army should set out from its original place of encampment (Shiziling) at two o'clock tomorrow morning, pass through Luowa, Lianglukou (making sure to go through Lianglukou on time and rapidly, so as not to cross paths with the Twelfth Army), Liujia, and Guangfuqiao, and arrive at the Fengxin *xian* seat (60 *li*). Its First Column sent to Guofangling can proceed tomorrow as far as a few *li* beyond Wanfuqiao and choose a place to encamp, and rejoin the main forces at Fengxin the day after tomorrow (the 3rd).

The Fourth Army (excluding the Second Column) should set out from its original encampment (Caoshan) at three o'clock tomorrow morning (the 2nd), pass through Liangcun, Tangjia, Tangjiafang, and Guangfuqiao, and arrive at the Fengxin *xian* seat. Its Second Column should set out at 4:30 tomorrow morning, following the directly attached unit of the General Headquarters, pass through

---

Our source for this document is *Mao Zedong junshi wenji*, Vol. 1, pp. 155–56, where it is stated that the text has been reproduced from the original document in the Party archives.

Wushanpu, Luowa, and Lianglukou, and arrive at and encamp in the vicinity of Guangfuqiao. It should begin its work there, mobilize the masses, and make efforts to raise funds, and at the same time keep a close watch over the direction of Nanchang.

The espionage team of General Headquarters, the General Command, the Revolutionary Military Commission, and the espionage division and transportation division should rise at three o'clock tomorrow morning, muster and set out at this crossroads in order at four o'clock, following behind the Twelfth Army, pass through Wushanpu, Luowa, Lianglukou (there is a crossroads here), Liujia, and Guangfuqiao, to the Fengxin *xian* seat (60 *li*), and encamp (the baggage of the directly affiliated units follows behind the transportation division).

4. As for communications between the troops in Anyi (the Twelfth Army) and General Headquarters in Fengxin, a squad of signalmen will be sent by the transportation division of General Headquarters to install telephone lines.

5. During the march, we are in the position of General Headquarters.

Addendum:

1. Huang Gonglue, army commander of the Third Army, shall be responsible for all matters of encampment at the Fengxin *xian* seat.

2. The Third Army is to send people to set up an appropriate marker at the crossroads in Lianglukou near Luowa.

3. Officers in each unit must inform all soldiers and porters in their units of the direction of movement and the destination, to prevent those who fall behind from taking the wrong route.

4. As for telephone wires, poles, and so forth, located where all troops pass through or are encamped, it is forbidden to destroy them arbitrarily without orders, to avoid difficulties arising when our army comes to install telephone lines.

Order to the First Army Group of the Red Army to Advance from Fengxin to Yifeng

(August 6, 1930, 7:00 P.M.,
at General Headquarters in the town of Fengxin)

1. In accordance with the original plan, the troops directly attached to this General Headquarters, together with the Third Army, will march toward Yifeng along with the [Revolutionary] Military Commission tomorrow (the 7th).

2. The Third Column of the Third Army should set out promptly at 3:00 A.M. tomorrow (the 7th) via the west gate of this town, march toward Yifeng by way of Liuchiqiao and Bailuyu, and find an opportunity to encamp at Cunqian (70 *li*). The General Headquarters and its espionage team, as well as the Revolutionary Military Commission and its espionage team and transportation team, should rise at 3:00 tomorrow morning. At 4:00 they should cross the bridge outside the west gate to assemble and set out, march behind the Third Column, find an opportunity to encamp at Cunqian, work in Cunqian the day after tomorrow (the 8th), arrive at Tangpu (30 *li*) on the 9th, and arrive at the town of Yifeng (40 *li*) on the 10th. The baggage of the troops directly attached to General Headquarters is to proceed following the transportation team, and it is under the command of this unit's adjutant.

3. The Third Army (minus the Third Column) should set out following the baggage of the troops directly attached to General Headquarters at 4:30 A.M. tomorrow (the 7th), and encamp in the vicinity of Bailuyu. The day after tomorrow (the 8th) it should dispatch one column to take another road and advance to Yifeng by way of Huaqiao. It should arrive in the city of Yifeng on the 10th; the rest are to enter Xinyu on the 8th, arrive in the vicinity of Banqiao and Chengtang on the 9th, and enter the city of Yifeng on the 10th.

4. During the march our position will be with General Headquarters.

It is so ordered.

General Headquarters espionage team:
Team leader   Chen Shuxiang
Political Commissar   Chen Xiping

Our source for this order is *Jiangxi dangshi ziliao*, Volume 6, pp. 74–75. The document does not appear to have been published previously.

Revolutionary Military
Commission espionage
team leader   He Jinyun

Revolutionary Military
Commission adjutant   Xiao Gangde (acting)

Transportation team:
Acting team leader   Yang Zaikui
Political Commissar   Feng Wenbin

Chief adjutant of
this Headquarters   Chen Yezhen

Commander-in-chief   Zhu De
Political Commissar   Mao Zedong

Order to the First Army Group of the Red Army to Leave Yifeng and Concentrate Its Forces in Wanzai

(August 10, 1930, at Yifeng)

1. After our troops carried out a demonstration at the Niuhang railway station on the August 1 holiday, Nanchang was greatly shaken.[1] The reactionary government was at a loss, and hurriedly ordered two regiments of Li Baobing's forces to Nanchang (they were moved immediately on the Tianjin-Pukou railway line). Moreover, it ordered Jiang Kunchuan[2] to come to Nanchang to assist in the defense, and also ordered Tan Daoyuan's division to Jiangxi. One unit of the Thirteenth Division in Ji'an was also moved to Zhangshu on the 12th, and it seems that it is going to come back to the provincial capital to reinforce the defenses.

2. This army group has made a change, and decided to complete the concentration of its forces at the *xian* town of Wanzai before the 15th of this month.

3. The vanguard forces of this army group (led by Lin Ye, the chief of staff of this army) should begin advancing from this town (Yifeng) toward Wanzai after noon today (the 10th). The time of their arrival at Wanzai has been fixed for the 12th. (Upon arrival, they must allocate camp sites for the whole army group.)

The rest of the troops (led by acting army commander Luo) should arrive at Wanzai by way of short cuts and complete the concentration of their forces before the 15th.

4. The Third Army will be responsible for the work on the front from this town (Yifeng) to Wanzai. Its army headquarters should lead one company of troops and accompany the General Headquarters in the occupation of the town of Wanzai.

5. On receiving this order, the Fourth Army should move continually forward

---

Our source for this text is *Jiangxi dangshi ziliao*, Vol. 6, pp. 76–77. No earlier versions are available to us.

1. Regarding the attempt, on August 1, the International Day of Anti-Imperialist Demonstrations and the anniversary of the Nanchang Uprising, to seize the Niuhang railway station rather than attacking Nanchang itself, see above, the order dated July 29, 1930.

2. The personal name "Kunchuan" which appears in the only available text may be a misprint. The individual in question was probably a local or middle-ranking Guomindang military commander. No information is available about him.

from Shanggao *xian* to the town of Wanzai, and it must concentrate its forces at the town of Wanzai before the 15th.

6. The unit attached to the General Headquarters should follow the Revolutionary Military Commission in setting out from here tomorrow (the 11th), and is scheduled to arrive at the town of Wanzai on the 12th.

7. We are now at the position occupied by the General Headquarters on Shangkui Street at the east gate inside the town. When the advance begins, all our movements will be coordinated with those of the General Headquarters.

> Commander-in-chief   Zhu De
> Political Commissar   Mao Zedong

Order to Attack Wenjiashi

(August 18, 1930)

1. Approximately three regiments of the remaining forces under He Jian are now entrenched along the line of Wenjiashi (approximately two regiments) and Sunjiaduan (approximately one regiment). There are also enemy communications forces in Qingjiang, between Wenjiashi and Sunjiaduan.

2. [As this] army group has as its objective to eliminate the remaining forces of this enemy division and then attack and take Changyue, the plan is to eliminate the enemy first along this line.

3. The Fourth Army should leave here tomorrow (the 19th) and proceed by way of Cihua and Qingshuitang to encamp at Tongmu. On the next day (the 20th) it should set out from Tongmu at one o'clock in the morning, and its main forces should proceed by way of Xiawan, Lishu'ao, Shizhaoshang, Niantang, Juntian, Shayekeng, Upper and Lower Jinjiawan, and Xiaojiawan, and sweep across the enemy's security forces along the main road, then turn toward Wenjiashi to surround and attack it. The line along Sanfengjian and Yanjiatan in the northwest of Wenjiashi is also the responsibility of the same army, so it should act accordingly in sending attacking and occupying forces.

4. The Third Army (excluding the Third Column) should advance tomorrow (the 19th) via Cihua to encamp at Qingshuitang, and at 2:00 A.M. the next day (the 20th) set out from Qingshuitang and, via Dougu'an, Baizhu'ao, Shanghuayuan, Zhonghuayuan, Xiahuayuan, Dalingshang, and Longtouwan, advance to attack the enemy strongholds in Gaoshengling and Guancailing.

5. The Third Column of the Third Army should set out from here after noon tomorrow (the 19th) via Fozikou and Tieyan, to encamp near Yanqian (taking care to conceal its forces). At 3:00 A.M. the next day (the 20th) it should set out from Yanqian and, via Huaihuaduan, Baimazhou, Bishuiling, Shiniutan, Wushenling, Heishizui, and Heliantang, advance to attack Wenjiashi.

6. General Headquarters will not be on the main road to Yanqian and Wenjiashi until the morning of the day after tomorrow (the 20th).

7. The Twelfth Army (attacking the enemy in Sunjiaduan) should set out from its present location tomorrow (the 19th), and proceed via Wangjiachang, Qiaoxia, Fengshu'ao, and Wanyangqiao to encamp along the line of Datuli and Songshu'ao. After completing preparations, it should advance the next day (the

---

Our source for this document is *Mao Zedong junshi wenji*, Vol. 1, pp. 157–59, where it is stated that the text has been reproduced from the original document in the Party archives.

20th) toward Sunjiaduan to attack. After wiping out the enemy at that location, it is to press on toward Qingjiang and find a way to establish contact with General Headquarters, as well as pay close attention to [the situation in] the direction of Jiangfujiang.

8. The time for the general offensive along the entire front is set at dawn on the 20th (around five o'clock).

9. Each unit's baggage is to move along with the unit itself.

10. After wiping out the enemy at that location, those of the troops attacking Wenjiashi who arrive first should vigorously pursue the remnant enemy forces to make sure that they are thoroughly destroyed.

11. Upon arrival at the preparatory position for attack (i.e., Tongmu, Qingshuitang, Yanqian, Songshu'ao, etc.), each unit must at once begin acting in concert with the local Red Guards.

Addendum:

1. At each offensive stronghold each unit must maintain close communication with its neighboring forces.

2. Each unit must conserve its forces and, when necessary, must offer mutual support to its neighboring units.

3. During the attack, the baggage of the Third Army's Third Column must be halted at Yanqian and then advanced together after the baggage of General Headquarters has arrived.

Letter to the Southwest Jiangxi Special Committee, for Transmission to the Central Committee, on the General Situation with Regard to All New Military Operations of Our Army in Western Jiangxi

(August 19, 1930, at Huangmao)

To the Southwest Jiangxi Special Committee, for transmission to the West Fujian Special Committee and the Central Committee:

At the beginning of this month from Fengxin, I sent a brief letter to the Special Committee, reporting our past operational experiences and future operational plans, and I wonder whether or not it has been received. The First Army Group set out from Xingguo, and by way of Jishui (because of the difficulty in crossing the river, which delayed us, we were unable to carry out our plan of attacking in the dark, and in the end did not take the town of Jishui), Yongfeng, and Xin'gan (we did not engage in any fighting at all on the way, the bandit-suppression troops[1] in Xin'gan and Yongfeng simply fired a few shots and fled), attacked Zhangshu at daybreak on July 24. Two battalions of the enemy's Hundred and eighth Regiment were routed, nearly two hundred rifles were captured, and more than a hundred enemy soldiers were taken prisoner. At this time there were two enemy regiments in Fuzhou, and it appeared as though the forces at Daiyue would cross the river at Xin'gan and move to Zhangshu. If we went to attack Fuzhou, the enemy in Fuzhou would surely flee without our being able to inflict damage on them. If the enemy continued to advance, we did not know either when we would be able to finish them off. If we marched directly to Nanchang, then the enemy's main forces would not have been wiped out, but would actually have been behind our army. In addition, Nanchang is surrounded by water on all four sides, and this would have put us in an unfavorable situation. Therefore, we took the opportunity to cross the river, marched in the direction opposite to Nanchang,

---

We have translated this letter from *Jiangxi dangshi ziliao*, Vol. 6, pp. 80–82. No earlier source appears to be available.

1. The term *jingfei* here refers to the White forces engaged in suppressing the Communist "bandits."

and took as our objective an attack on the Niuhang Railway Station in order to hold an August 1 demonstration. By way of Gaoan, we arrived on July 30 in the area of Wanshougong, Shiziling, and Shengmijie, about 30 *li* from Nanchang. On August 1, two columns were sent across the river from Nanchang to attack the Niuhang Railway Station. The enemy forces in Nanchang did not fire a single shot or send out a single soldier, and at this time we were unable to find any enemy to fight. Since we could not attack Nanchang, and we had fulfilled our task of holding an August 1 demonstration, we scattered in the area around Fengxin and Anyi to conduct our work, mobilize the masses, raise funds, make propaganda, and so on. We were afraid that if we waited too long for the enemy but they did not come, once the enemy did assemble enough troops and begin to attack us we would be put in a difficult situation. Moreover, at the time it was reported in the newspapers that He Jian was marching toward the Fifth Army. In order to wipe out the enemy, aid the Fifth Army, and open up broader prospects in the border region of Hunan, Hubei, and Jiangxi, our army decided to march to Liuyang to attack the enemy, and go directly to take Changsha. On our way back we would take the Zhu[zhou]-Ping[xiang] railway[2] to attack the enemy in Jiangxi (at that time we predicted that the enemy had already concentrated enough forces and was about to attack us), take Ji'an, and then come back along the Nanchang-Jiujiang Railroad and attack Wuhan. When we arrived at Wanzai we learned that the Third Army Group had taken Changsha. When leaving Fengxin, we received the July 30 and August 1 telegrams from Shanghai and learned that our troops had taken Changsha (but we did not know how it had been taken). This seizure was achieved not by a sudden attack. Instead, it was done by defeating the enemy first and then taking the city while He Jian was hesitating greatly. (The campaign started on the 23rd and did not stop until our troops moved into Changsha on the 27th, during which time we defeated six regiments of enemy troops, took two thousand to three thousand captives, and captured more than four thousand rifles and countless bullets, as well as many cannons and machine guns. Until August 5, because of our inaccurate estimation of the enemy, we underestimated the enemy and thought he did not have enough strength for a counterattack, so we did not make preparations. In addition, we did not adequately guard against the hidden counterrevolutionaries in Changsha, so that we were attacked by the enemy—the enemy surrounded us on all four sides but we were unaware of this until the enemy had already entered the streets of Changsha. As a result, the Third Army Group suffered great casualties and losses during this battle.) It is our estimation that the present situation represents a turning point. After suffering a huge defeat imposed by our Third Army Group, He Jian will certainly waver even more. It is imperative that our First Army Group (which is now operating in the Tonggu area, where we have already sent

---

2. The railway from Zhuzhou, southeast of Changsha in Hunan, to Pingxiang, just across the border in Jiangxi.

people to get in touch with it) wipe out the enemies one by one, take Changsha and Yuezhou, attack Wuhan and Jiujiang, open up bigger prospects in the three provinces, and promote a nationwide general uprising. With Jiujiang under attack, the enemy forces on the southern bank of the Yangzi River will have to move to the lower reaches and advance toward Jiujiang, so that Ji'an will be taken without a fight.

2. At present He Jian has a force of more than ten regiments that are concentrated in Liuyang and are marching toward our Third Army Group. The right route forces, about ten regiments, are scattered in the two points of Wenjiashi and Sunjiaduan. The left route is situated in the Hudongmenshi area. Yesterday we arrived here—in Huangmao (100 *li* from Wanzai, 30 *li* from Wenjiashi) and decided to finish off the enemy in Wenjiashi and Sunjiaduan tomorrow, and then to attack the enemy's left route. We require that the Third Army Group attack from Pingjiang, so as to wipe out the enemy's main force, and go directly to Changsha. This time the enemy has penetrated deeply into the Red area, and they still do not know that we are in front of them. In addition, the enemy has suffered repeated defeats, and we are confident that this enemy can be eliminated.

3. Given this increasingly intense revolutionary situation, the expansion of the Red Army is an extremely urgent matter, and we hope that the Special Committee will have Comrade Wu Zhonghao[3] bring the thirty thousand reinforcements for the First Army Group as originally decided upon, or that at the very least, ten thousand will arrive at Pingjiang and Liuyang by the middle of September. Because of the needs of the Red Army, Comrade Bao Ping, who remained behind in Donggu to provide medical treatment for Comrade Wu Zhonghao, must come together with Comrade Wu Zhonghao. To meet the needs of developing the three provinces of Hunan, Hubei, and Jiangxi, Comrade Deng Zihui should immediately lead the Red Army School northward, and Comrade Liu Shiqi should also be prepared to go north.

Secretary of the Front Committee   Mao Zedong

---

3. Wu Zhonghao (1905–1930), a native of Hunan, had joined the Chinese Communist Party in 1924. In 1927, he had participated in the Autumn Harvest Uprising, and had followed Mao up the Jinggangshan. In 1930 he was commander of the Twenty-first Western Fujian Red Army.

Order to the First Army Group of the Red Army to Advance on Xiaohe and to Continue to Attack Zhangjiafang

(August 20, 1930, at Wenjiashi)

1. The enemy's situation is as reported today by the staff office.

2. To achieve the objective of wiping out He Jian's forces, the army group has decided to continue the attack on the enemy in Zhangjiafang (Chen Guangzhong's independent Seventh Brigade[1]), and to advance toward Xiaohe (70 *li*) tomorrow morning (the 21st).

3. The Third Army will advance along the right route, and it should set out from the present location at 3:00 A.M. tomorrow and progress toward Xiaohe via Baimazhou, Jiaobanchong, Yaowangmiao, Caipaiao, Xiaokeng, Lishu'ao, and Hechang, encamping at Xiaohe upon arrival.

4. The rest should advance along the left route and progress toward Xiaohe via Qingjiang, Sunjiaduan, and Pendou, in the following order:

   a. The Twelfth Army is to allocate enough troops as a vanguard, and the entire army should complete its departure from here promptly at 3:30 A.M. tomorrow.

   b. General Headquarters, the espionage team of General Headquarters, the Revolutionary Military Commission, the Revolutionary Military Commission's espionage company and transportation team, as well as [those in charge of] the baggage of the units directly attached to General Headquarters should all get up at 2:30 tomorrow morning, and assemble at 3:30 at the eastern end of this city for departure (everyone carrying his lunch).

   c. The Fourth Army is to dispatch the rear guard. Its vanguard unit should set out at 4:30 A.M. tomorrow and advance following the baggage of the units directly attached to General Headquarters.

Our source for this order is *Jiangxi dangshi ziliao*, Vol. 6, pp. 83–84. No earlier source is available to us.

1. Chen Guanzhong (1897–1949) was a native of Hunan. As indicated, he was at this time the commander of the Guomindang's Seventh Independent Brigade.

5. During the march our position will be that of General Headquarters.

Addendum:

1. The commander of the troops that arrive first at Xiaohe (Twelfth Army or Third Army) should allocate camp sites for the entire army group.

2. The right route troops should pay attention to the roads to the city of Yonghe and to Shiwan.

Commander-in-chief	Zhu De
Political Commissar	Mao Zedong

Order to the First Army Group of the Red Army to Leave the Town of Yonghe and Concentrate Its Forces in Guanzhuang

(August 24, 1930, in the town of Yonghe)

1. The enemy's situation is as before.
2. Following orders from the Front Army, the army group is to set out from here tomorrow (the 25th) and advance in two separate groups to arrive at the Jingqian and Xijingqiao line, to arrive at the Zhoujiaping and Guanyin'ge line on the 26th, and arrive at Guanzhuang on the 27th and concentrate its forces there.
3. The Fourth Army is to advance along the right route. It should set out from here around 4:00 A.M. tomorrow and arrive in the vicinity of Xijingqiao by way of Gaoping, Shentong, Hujiatan, Liujiaao, Lingjiachong, and Dafoling. On the 26th it should choose its own route and procede to Guanyin'ge, arriving at Guanzhuang and concentrating its forces there on the 27th.
4. The rest should advance along the left route in the following order:
   a. The Twelfth Army (responsible for dispatching a vanguard) should complete its departure from here by 3:30 tomorrow morning (the 25th), and go via Shiwan and Tingziling to the vicinity of Jingping and encamp there.
   b. General Headquarters, the espionage team of General Headquarters, the Workers' and Peasants' Revolutionary Committee, and the baggage of the Military Commission's espionage team, transportation team, and directly attached units should leave here at 3:30 tomorrow morning and follow behind the Twelfth Army.
   c. The Third Army (responsible for dispatching a rear guard) should set out from its present location at 4:00 A.M. tomorrow, take a short-cut directly to the main road, and follow behind the directly attached units.
   d. The entire left route should arrive at the Zhoujiaping line by way of Fengshupu, Dayaopu, Tuoxishi, Jin'gangtou, and Jinpenling on the 26th, and arrive at Guanzhuang by way of Xikeng, Zhuangshuichong, Shuangjiangkou, Yanshanchong, and Zhujiawan on the 27th and concentrate its forces there.
5. During the march our movements will follow those of General Headquarters.

Commander-in-chief   Zhu De
Political commissar   Mao Zedong

We have translated this order from *Jiangxi dangshi ziliao*, Vol. 6, pp. 95–96.

Letter to the Southwest Jiangxi Special Committee, for Transmission to the Central Committee

(August 24, 1930, in the town of Yonghe, Liuyang)

To the Southwest Jiangxi Special Committee, to be copied and transmitted to Comrades Chen Yi and Wu Zhonghao, and to the Western Fujian Special Committee, with the request to copy it and transmit it to the Central Committee:

1. Under the command of He Jian, four divisions are attacking the Ping[jiang] and Liu[yang area]. Approximately fourteen regiments have reached the Pingjiang-Liuyang area, and the Third Army Group has retreated toward Changshoujie in Pingjiang.

2. The First Army Group went to the Niuhang Railway Station, but because the enemy in Jiangxi is very obstinate and perverse, we could not find them and make them fight. The masses in central Jiangxi also failed to rise, so it was decided to proceed towards Hunan with the objective of taking Changsha and attacking Wuhan. On August 20 we attacked the enemy in Wenjiashi from three directions. Without suffering large losses (seven hundred officers and soldiers were killed or injured, many officers at the two levels of battalion and company were injured, and Comrade Ke Wudong died in battle), our forces totally eliminated three regiments, one battalion, and one machine-gun company of enemy forces, and captured over eleven hundred enemy officers and soldiers, including one brigade commander and two regimental commanders. Approximately a thousand enemy officers and soldiers were killed or wounded. We captured fourteen hundred rifles, twenty water machine guns, seventeen portable and light machine guns, more than a hundred Mauser pistols, and a large supply of bullets.

3. The enemy forces that entered Liu[yang] constitute a total of five units, all of which have previously done battle with the Red Army and have a rather strong fighting capacity. They are [the forces of] Dai Douyuan (three regiments), Chen Guangzhong (three regiments), Li Jue (three regiments), and Peng Changren (two regiments).[1] In addition, there is a motley collection of other

---

We have translated this letter from *Jiangxi dangshi ziliao*, Vol. 6, pp. 97–98.

1. Dai Douyuan (dates unknown) was at this time commander of the First Division of the Guomindang Thirty-fifth Army. Chen Guangzhong (1897–1949), a native of Hunan, had begun life as a bandit. In June 1928 he had become commander of the Seventh

troops such as those of Guo Bushi, with a total force of approximately four regiments. One quarter has been wiped out by our army, and the other three quarters are still in the midst of their attack. These are the main forces of He Jian, and once they are eliminated, political power in Hunan will be in our hands. In addition, the Red Army will be greatly expanded, and we will be able to count on taking Wuhan, although inevitably at a considerable price.

4. On August 23 our army fought all the way to the town of Yonghe in eastern Liu[yang], and Tao Guang and Chen Guangzhong had fled toward the town of Liuyang the day before. At the same time the Third Army Group (the Fifth Army and the Eighth Army) had arrived from Changshoujie for the purpose of concentrating their forces. The morale of the Third Army Group was very high, and it had seven thousand guns, which is comparable to what the First Army Group had coming to the front. Tomorrow is the time set for the advance on Changsha, and it should be possible to take Changsha after an intense campaign.

5. The reserve army in southwestern Jiangxi must send ten thousand men to Changsha within two weeks after receiving this letter, and another twenty thousand within a month after receiving the letter. In a word, the sooner the better. The first group should be led here by Comrade Wu Zhonghao, and the second group should be brought by Comrade Chen Yi. This is a matter of extreme importance, and it is urgently hoped that efforts will be made to bring it about. Comrade Bao Ping must come.

6. It is hoped that the Central Committee will give its guidance on taking Wuhan, that it will prepare to establish organs of political power and a Red Army General Headquarters, and that it will send a responsible person to southern Hubei.

Mao Zedong

Independent Brigade. Li Jue (1898–1987), likewise a Hunanese, had graduated from the Baoding Military Academy, and had participated in the Northern Expedition. In 1930, he was deputy commander of the Nineteenth Division.

Order to Advance Toward Changsha[1]

(August 24, 1930)

1. According to reports, the enemy's main forces under the command of He Jian are retreating from Liuyang toward Changsha via [the village of] Pujishi, the unit (approximately four regiments) in Pingjiang under Luo Lin[2] is also retreating to Yong'anshi, and this enemy appears to be shortening its defense lines at Yong'anshi, Zhongsigang, Longtoupu, and Zhuzhou to resist our army.

2. The goal of this division of our army being to wipe out He Jian's troops and occupy Changsha, it has been resolved to advance toward Changsha along three routes. The First Army Group takes the left route, and the Second Army Group (excluding the Sixteenth Army) takes the central route. Setting out tomorrow (the 25th) from their present location, they should advance the first day along the Gugang, Jingxiqiao, and Jingping line, the second day along the Liuyang, Guanyin'ge and Zhoujiaping line, on the third day along the Pujishi and Guanzhuang line, and the fourth day along the Baixianqiao and Yangjiaqiao line, attacking the Zhongsigang and Zhuzhou line on the fifth day.

3. Commander-in-Chief Peng Dehuai and Political Commissar Teng Daiyuan[3] of the Third Army Group will lead their forces, the Third Army Group (excluding the Sixteenth Army) plus the masses in Liudong, and as a main force advance to attack from their present location along the Liuyang, Pujishi, Baixianqiao line toward Longtoupu. They must arrive in the vicinity of Gugang on the 25th, occupy the town of Liuyang on the 26th, occupy Pujishi on the 27th, advance upon Baixianqiao on the 28th, and attack the enemy along the Longtoupu and Zhongsigang line on the 29th.

4. Under the joint leadership of the present commanders, the First Army

---

Our source for this document is *Mao Zedong junshi wenji*, Vol. 1, pp. 160–63, where it is stated that the text has been reproduced from the original document in the Party archives.

1. This is an order to the First Front Army of the Red Army. It was issued by Mao Zedong and Zhu De at 11 P.M. on August 24, 1930, from the town of Yonghe in Liuyang *xian*, Hunan.

2. At this time, Luo Lin (1892–?), a native of Hunan, was the commander of the Guomindang's newly established Twenty-second Division.

3. Teng Daiyuan (1904–1974) was a native of Hunan, who had joined the Chinese Communist Party in 1927. In 1928 he served as a member of the Hunan-Guangdong Border Area Special Committee; in December of that year he accompanied Peng Dehuai up the Jinggangshan. He had been appointed political commissar of the Third Army Group in June 1930.

Group and the masses in Liunan will advance in attack from the present location along the Fenglinpu, Guanzhuang, Yangjiaqiao line to Zhuzhou. It is necessary to arrive at the Jingxiqiao and Jingping line on the 25th, the Guanyin'ge and Zhoujiaping line on the 26th, and occupy Guanzhuang on the 27th. On the 28th the main forces should advance to the vicinity of Yangjiaqiao, and attack Zhuzhou on the 29th.

5. Commanding his troops and in cooperation with the masses in Pingjiang, Army Commander of the Sixteenth Army Kong Hechong is to chase Luo Lin, seek an opportunity to attack Yonganshi, and gain control over this enemy, so that it will be easier for the troops south of the Liuyang River to advance.

6. After setting out, the area to the south of the line formed by Gaoping, Luojiachong, Guanyin'ge, Waziping, Xiaojiapo, Shiweili, Shihuizui, Meiziyuan, Xinsi, and Hetangpu (including these places themselves) is to be the fighting zone of the First Army Group, and the area to the north of this line (not including these places themselves) is to be the fighting zone of the Third Army Group.

7. If enemy forces take and hold the line formed by Yonganshi, Pujishi, and Guanzhuang, the Sixteenth Army, on the right, should continue to carry out its tasks as listed in item 5; the First Army Group, on the left, should quickly eliminate the enemy in Guanzhuang and send its main forces towards Zhentoushi to help the Third Army Group, in the front, to attack the enemy in Pujishi, to make sure that the entire enemy is thoroughly destroyed.

If the enemy uses its main forces to defend the southern end of the Zhongsigang and Zhuzhou line (around Longtoupu and Zhuzhou), then the Third Army Group should at once send its main forces southward along the railway line via Jiaochongpu, Youmachong and Yijiawan to attack the enemy's flank and rear.

If the enemy's main forces are at the northern end of this line (around Baiheqiao and Zhongsigang), then the First Army Group should use its main forces to take Yijiawan at once and attack the enemy's flank and rear along Tiaomajian.

If the enemy's main forces withdraw to the city of Changsha, then the Sixteenth Army, on the right, should promptly occupy the region along the railway line in Dongtundu to the north of Changsha, and the Third Army Group, in the middle, proceeding along Baiheqiao, Tiaomajian, and Guitang, should attack the Xiaowu and Liuyang Gates of Changsha. The First Army Group, following the railway, should then attack the southern suburbs of Changsha.

If the enemy gives up the railway line on the eastern bank of the Xiang River and withdraws to Xiangtan, then the Sixteenth Army, on the right, should act in concert with the masses to occupy the city of Changsha. The main forces of the Third Army Group should immediately advance on and occupy Yijiawan and cross the river there and attack Xiangtan. At the same time, it should send one unit of its forces to the vicinity of Liuputang for a feigned crossing of the river toward Xiangtan, as a cover for its main forces crossing at Yijiawan. The First

Army Group is to ford the river rapidly in the vicinity of Zhuzhou and attack Xiangtan along the left bank of the Xiang River, ensuring the thorough elimination of the enemy.

8. The troops of the Hunan-Jiangxi Border Area Red Guards located in Liuyang should be divided into two parts, attached to the First and Third Army Groups, respectively, and put under the command of the general commanders and political commissars of these army groups, to take charge of matters in the rear such as liaison, communications, transportation, and so on.

9. We ourselves will operate along with the First Army Group.

Points for Attention:

1. Discipline—in every place that troops pass through, it is imperative that discipline be strictly obeyed. Above all, it is forbidden to take property from workers and peasants without authorization; confiscation of property and burning of houses can be carried out only on orders. In particular, the masses following the army must be led to act this way.

2. Communication—all units should report daily to General Headquarters (temporarily incorporated within General Headquarters of the First Army Group) and maintain close communication with one another as well.

3. Sabotage of transportation and communication [equipment]—As for transportation and communication equipment (such as railways, bridges, trains, automobiles, steamboats, electrical cables, radio stations, etc.) there should be no unauthorized sabotage of it without orders from senior officers. Violators will be severely punished.

Commander-in-chief	Zhu De
Political Commissar	Mao Zedong

Order to the First Front Army of the Red Army to Attack Changsha

(August 28, 1930, 9:00 P.M., at Zhentou)

1. It is reported that upon hearing about our army's advance, the enemy's main forces fled in disorder to the vicinity of Langlishi and Dongshan, where it appears they will seek to offer stubborn resistance to our army. A floating bridge has been erected on the Xiang River in the direction leading toward Mount Yuelu.

The bandits of the Liuyang household militia[1] and the Changsha garrison troops who were decimated here (in Zhentoushi) by us today retreated to the area around Bojiashan and Dutoushi.

Controlled by the Sixteenth Route Army of our right route, Luo Lin's forces retreated again to Pingjiang.

Around the area of Wumeiling, Huangtuling, and Houzishi near the southeast of Changsha, there are some simple fortifications. It is said that there is a small number of enemy troops in Jiaozhongpu and Longtoupu.

2. The objective of this front army is still to take Changsha and destroy He Jian's forces. It has been decided to occupy the Fengshuhe, Xinqiao, Luoxiaping, Jiaozhongpu, and Longtoupu line tomorrow (the 29th), and press our attack forward toward Changsha.

3. The First Army Group is to switch to the middle route, and tomorrow (the 29th) it should occupy the line from Fengshuhe (30 *li* from Changsha), to Xinqiao and Luoxiaping, and quickly establish contact with the Third Army Group, after which its main forces should advance towards Changsha along the area of Dongsigang, Baimaotang, Dongshan, and Yanziling. After breaking through the enemy's stronghold in Wumeiling, it is to launch an immediate attack on Xiaowu Gate in the city of Changsha and its northeastern area.

4. The Third Army Group is to switch to the left route, and tomorrow (the 29th) it should occupy the Baiheqiao, Jiaozhongpu, and Longtoupu line (if there are enemy forces along this line they should be rapidly swept away and [the area] occupied), and quickly establish contact with the First Army Group. Thereupon, its main forces should advance toward Changsha along the area of

---

Our source for this order is *Jiangxi dangshi ziliao*, Vol. 6, pp. 99–100.

1. For an earlier reference to the *aihutuan* or household militia, which had become an instrument of the landlords, see above, the report of June 16, 1928.

Tiaomajian, Zhujialing, Zhongjiawan, and Huangnitang. After breaking through the enemy's stronghold near Huangtuling, it should launch an attack on Liuyangmen and that area.

5. The area to the left of the line that runs along Zhentoushi, Nanshanpu, Tiaomajian, Zhongjiawan, and Dongjingpu to the main road leading to the city of Changsha (including the line itself) is the battle zone of the Third Army Group. To the right of the line (excluding the line itself) is the battle zone of the First Army Group.

6. The composition and the marching position of the general reserve forces will be announced at a later date.

7. After setting out our position will be that of First Army Group General Headquarters (in Xinqiao tomorrow). During battle it will be the position of the general reserve forces.

Attention:

1. When the Third Army Group has occupied the Jiaozhongpu and Longtoupu line, it should immediately send troops to sabotage the nearby railway between Yijiawan and Zhuzhou. In the future attention should always be paid along the way to destroying the nearby railway, and guards are to be posted along the Xiang River.

2. After arriving at its designated destination tomorrow, each unit should immediately prepare knives, axes, hoes, and so on, and confiscate the water buffalo of the local bullies, or lay out money to buy the water buffalo of the peasants, so as to be prepared to launch an attack on the barriers around the enemy's strongholds.

3. After arriving at their designated positions tomorrow, all units should immediately establish contact with the other units. Neighboring units to the First Army Group and Third Army Group are to pay particular attention to this point.

Commander-in-chief   Zhu De
Political Commissar   Mao Zedong

Order to the First Army Group of the Red Army to Occupy the Line from Fengshupu and Xinqiao to Luoxiaping

(August 28, 1930, 9:00 P.M., at Zhentou)

1. An order has been received from Commander-in-chief Zhu and Political Commissar Mao of the Front Army as follows:

. . . (Omission)[1]

2. In accordance with the order, this army group will occupy the Fengshupu, Xinqiao, and Luoxiaping line tomorrow.

3. The Fourth Army is to be the right wing of this army group (middle route), and it should leave here tomorrow morning and advance toward Fengshuhe (10 *li*) by way of Baijiashan (25 *li*), Dutou (5 *li*), and Tuantouhe (a total of 45 *li*). Upon arrival at Fengshuhe it should encamp and await orders to attack Changsha.

4. The Twelfth Army is to be the left wing of this army group, and it should leave here at 3:00 A.M. tomorrow and advance toward Xinqiao (15 *li*) by way of Qijiachong (3 *li*), Jiutiaolong (2 *li*), Tuqiao (6 *li*), Zhangqiao (5 *li*), Shijiaduan (4 *li*), and Maguomiao (15 *li*) (a total of 45 *li*), encamp (straight across to Guandaopu is 5 *li*), and await orders to attack Changsha.

5. Units directly attached to General Headquarters are to follow the Workers' and Peasants' Revolutionary Committee, set out at 3:30 after the Twelfth Army, and advance to encamp at Xinqiao.

6. The Third Army is to be the reserve force of this army group, to set out from here at 4:00 A.M. tomorrow, and march after the units directly attached to General Headquarters to encamp near Xinqiao.

7. During the march we will be at the position of General Headquarters.

Addendum:

1) When the Twelfth Army arrives in Xinqiao tomorrow, if there are enemy troops in Dongsigang it should immediately aid the Fourth Army in surrounding and destroying them.

2) Acting Army Commander Luo of the Twelfth Army is in charge of allocating camp sites and posting guards in the vicinity of Xinqiao tomorrow.

Commander-in-chief	Zhu De
and	
Political Commissar	Mao Zedong

We have translated this order from *Jiangxi dangshi ziliao*, Vol. 6, pp. 101–102.

1. An omission is indicated in this manner in the original text.

Order to the First Front Army of the Red Army to Exterminate the Enemy at Yijiawan and Take Advantage of the Victory to Occupy Changsha

(August 29, 1930, 8:00 P.M.,
at Xinqiao General Headquarters)

1. According to reliable reports, yesterday and today the enemy's main forces have been moving in succession toward Yijiawan, and it appears that they have in mind to use a small portion of their forces to pin down our army by relying on the battlefield fortifications in the area of Houzishi, Shimapu, Litang, Huangtuling, and Wumeiling in the vicinity of Changsha, and have their main forces leave Yijiawan by railway and attack our army from the flank.

2. It has been decided that the Front Army should first wipe out the enemy forces in Yijiawan tomorrow (the 30th), and take advantage of the victory to make a forceful surprise attack on Changsha.

The Third Army Group is hereby ordered to use all its strength to attack the enemy forces in Yijiawan tomorrow. After succeeding in this, it should immediately dispatch a portion of its forces to attack and advance toward Changsha along the motor road. The remaining portion of its forces should attack the enemy's strongholds and advance towards Shimapu and Huangtuling by way of Tianxinqiao, Yangjiachong and Laodian. After taking them, its main forces must concentrate in the Huangtuling area and have one unit enter the city through the southern outskirts to pursue and destroy the remnants of the enemy.

3. The Twelfth Army of the First Army Group is hereby ordered to take a short cut and arrive near Datuopu before 7:00 A.M. tomorrow to intercept the routed enemy from Yijiawan (if the fighting in Yijiawan has not come to an end, then apart from posting one unit as sentries in the direction of Changsha, this army's main forces should immediately assist the Third Army Group in destroying the enemy in Yijiawan). After accomplishing this task it should rapidly advance to attack the enemy in Wumeiling and Xiaowumen by way of Linjiazui, Dongjingpu, and Guitang. After accomplishing this it should concentrate its troops around the Wumeiling area and await further orders.

Our source for this order is *Jiangxi dangshi ziliao*, Vol. 6, pp. 103–104.

The Fourth Army should leave its present location (Dongsigang) before 7:00 A.M. tomorrow, take a short cut, advance to the Zhoujiati and Zhongjiawan line, and then stop and post guards in the direction of Changsha. When the Third Army Group and the Twelfth Army advance toward Changsha, said army should rapidly attack and advance along Tianjiling and Xujiachong towards Erliting and Jingwumen in front of Litang Lake. After accomplishing this, apart from using one unit to leave through the north gate at Xinhe to cut off the enemy's path of retreat, it should mass its main forces near Erliting.

The Third Army shall constitute the general reserve force, and it should dispatch one column at 3:30 tomorrow morning to advance to Baitianpu following General Headquarters by way of the main road of Tiaomajian. The rest should set out before 7:00, follow General Headquarters, arrive near Baitianpu, and await further orders.

4. During the attack on Yijiawan, we and the general reserve forces will be near Baitianpu, and during the attack on Changsha we will be on the main road between Baitianpu and Dongjingpu.

Attention:

1) If the enemy forces we eliminated at Yijiawan were not their main forces, then the Third Army Group should only advance as far as the Shipailing and Shirenchong line, the Twelfth Army as far as the Dongjingpu and Yanziling line, and the Fourth Army only as far as the Xujiachong line. General Headquarters and the general reserve forces will then stop at places on the main Longjiawan road and await further orders.

2) As for the large baggage of General Headquarters, the Twelfth Army (except for a small number of this army's cooking utensils that can go along with it), and the Third Army, the Third Army should use its discretion to assign troops to protect it. They are to stop tomorrow after dawn 10 *li* behind the general reserve forces, and are to be under the command of Fan Shude.

Commander-in-chief   Zhu De
Political Commissar   Mao Zedong

Order to the First Front Army of the Red Army Regarding Extermination of the Attacking Enemy

(August 30, 1930, afternoon, at Baitianpu)

1. The enemy did indeed seek to launch a sudden attack on our flank (see report of the staff office for details).

2. The plan is for the Front Army first to lure out and destroy the attacking enemy, and then to take advantage of the victory to launch an attack on Changsha.

3. The Third Army Group should move all its forces to the Huangchong, Xitangchong, and Longshantang line by tonight and hide there. They should also dispatch capable spies to places such as Tianxinqiao and Xujiaqiao, wait until the enemy in Banshigang on the western bank of the Xiang River (the Seventh Independent Brigade) is halfway across the river, and then attack and eliminate them. After accomplishing this they should swiftly advance toward Changsha along the railway and motor roads to attack. If by then the battle by the First Army Group is not yet over, they should exert all their strength to help.

4. The Twelfth Army remains at its present location near Dongjingpu, and it should send out guerrilla troops at 2:00 A.M. to launch a feigned attack on the enemy stronghold in Lannichong. Its battle zone tomorrow morning is the line extending from the main road near Huangnitang to Shipailing. It is to join with the right wing of the Fourth Army, and cooperate with the Fourth Army in attacking the enemy forces which we have lured out from Houzishi (the Thirty-first Division). Its main attack route is from Laodian to Shirenchong to block off the enemy's line of retreat, and it must make sure to destroy the said enemy. After this is accomplished, it should pursue the routed enemy along the motor road and take the enemy strongholds in Houzishi. After these have been taken, its main force should move to the right to sweep across the defensive forces in the enemy's strongholds in such places as Huangtuling, Yuhuating, and Wumeiling, and then attack and advance toward Liuyangmen. The rest of the main forces shall go along the motor road straight toward the city walls of Changsha.

5. The Fourth Army remains at its present location, and it should send out troops to investigate and occupy the battlefield to the north of West Station at

---

We have translated this order from *Jiangxi dangshi ziliao*, Vol. 6, pp. 105–106.

Longjiawan. It should separately send a guerrilla detachment to arrive in the vicinity of the enemy's stronghold in Houzishi by 2:00 A.M. tonight, and mount a fierce feigned attack on it so as to lure the enemy out to launch an offensive from Houzishi. When the enemy's main forces have penetrated deep into the vicinity of Shipailing they should link up with the Twelfth Army's left wing and together with the Twelfth Army launch a sudden and fierce attack on the enemy forces near Shipailing and destroy them. After this is accomplished they should advance along the motor road, and take the enemy stronghold in Houzishi. When this has been occupied the main forces should also shift toward the right and attack and advance in the direction of Huangtuling, Wumeiling, and Liuyang-men.

6. The Third Army should immediately dispatch a force of one column to the vicinity of Dongjingpu to replace the Twelfth Army in the task of pinning down [the enemy] to the right of Shimapu and Shiba. In addition it should promptly dispatch troops at 2:00 A.M. tonight along that line (Shimapu and Shiba) to launch a fierce feigned attack on the enemy stronghold there. It should also establish firm liaison with the Seventh Regiment of our Liuyang Red Guard Forces in Dongshan and Dongsigang, and when the Twelfth Army in the front and the Fourth Army on the left wing have broken through the enemy's strong-holds in Houzishi and Huangtuling, this column will attack and advance in the direction of Shimapu, Shiba, Huqian, and Jingwumen. The rest will be the general reserve forces, and will take up a position where they now are (Baitianpu), stop, and await further orders.

7. The general clinic for wounded soldiers is in the Tongrenqin and Banzhutang area (each army must send someone to take responsibility).

8. We are at the position of the general reserve forces at Baitianpu.

Attention:

a. The guerrilla forces dispatched by each army of the First Army Group (Third, Fourth, Twelfth) at 2:00 A.M. tonight should be at least one company, must arrive promptly at the enemy's stronghold, and must fire as many shots as possible.

b. Tomorrow morning all units must finish breakfast and complete all preparations before 4:00 A.M.

c. Our Liuyang Red Guard forces have already built two raft bridges in Dongsigang and Dongshan so as to establish liaison with the Sixteenth Army.

Commander-in-chief	Zhu De
Political Commissar	Mao Zedong

Order to the First Front Army of the Red Army About Mobilizing the Masses to Force the Enemy in the Area Northeast of Changsha to Submit

(August 30, 1930, 8:00 P.M., at Baitianpu)

1. He Jian's reactionary armies are still waging stubborn resistance against us, relying on fortifications in such places as Houzishi, Lannichong, Shimapu, Shiba, Yuhuating, Huangtuling, Wumeiling, Erliting, and so on.

It has been reported in the newspapers that the armies of Zhang and of Guangxi[1] have indeed reached Wugang, and that the enemy in Xinning and Hengbao (approximately three regiments) may retreat to Xiangtan.

2. Led by commander-in-chief He,[2] our Second Army Group has already arrived at the Gong'an and Shishou line, and is now pushing forward toward Xiangyuan.

Our Third Army Group of the left route and First Army Group of the middle route are now in the region from Yijiawan and Dongsigang to the south of the city of Changsha, and are in the middle of surrounding and attacking the provincial capital.

3. Your army will remain as the left wing and be stationed along the Huaixidu, Dongtundu, and Shanmudu line, and should start at once to mobilize the masses along this line to connect with the Red Area in Ping[xiang] and Liu[yang], and pin down the enemy forces in the northeast section of the city of Changsha, seize an opportunity to cross the river and fight a way through, and establish firm contact with our Liu[yang] Seventh Regiment in Dongshan.

It is so ordered.

Sixteenth Army

Commander	Kong Hechong
Political Commissar	

Commander-in-chief	Zhu De
Political Commissar	Mao Zedong

We have translated this order from *Jiangxi dangshi ziliao*, Vol. 6, p. 107.

1. As indicated in a note to the text of June 22, 1930, Zhang refers to Zhang Fakui, and Guangxi to the forces of the Guangxi faction and of its leader, Li Zongren, which were combatting Chiang Kaishek in Hunan.

2. He is He Long.

Order to Lure the Enemy out of Their Fortifications, Destroy Them, and March into Changsha on the Heels of Victory

(August 31, 1930)[1]

1. Relying on their fortifications, the enemy forces in Changsha continue to wage stubborn resistance against us. The enemy in Banshigang has gathered many boats and appears to be preparing a secret crossing between Datuopu and Yijiawan.

Two regiments of the enemy's troops under the command of Gong Bingfan[2] arrived in Changsha from Yuezhou[3] on the 24th.

It is also said that the enemy troops in Hengbao[4] (approximately three regiments) have marched into Xiangtan.

2. The Front Army is still planning to lure the enemy forces out of their fortifications, destroy them, and march into Changsha on the heels of victory.

3. The Third Army Group (excluding the First Division of the Fifth Army) is still located around Linjiadan, Yangjiachong, Longshantang, Xitangchong, and Huanghuchong, and they will wait until after the enemy in Banshigang has crossed the river to attack and annihilate them. After accomplishing this they will carry out their original task of attacking and advancing along the railways and highways toward the southern outskirts of Changsha.

4. The First Division of the Fifth Army is still located in the vicinity of Mojialong. Tonight it should send troops to make a feigned attack on the enemy's position in Houzishi, and before dawn it should occupy a position immediately behind Shipailing. It should be able to destroy very rapidly the enemy coming from Houzishi, and at the same time to support through coordinated action the left wing of the First Army Group (Twelfth Army) and the right

Our source for this document is *Mao Zedong junshi wenji*, Vol. 1, pp. 164–66, where it is stated that the text has been reproduced from a documentary collection published in 1942.

1. This order to the First Front Army of the Red Army was issued by Mao Zedong and Zhu De on the afternoon of August 31 from Baitianpu in the southern suburbs of Changsha.

2. Gong Bingfan (1902–1982), a native of Shaanxi, was the commander of the Fifth Division of the Guomindang Ninth Route Army.

3. Yuezhou is now called Yueyang.

4. Hengbao was the collective designation for Hengzhou and Baojing, which were the old names for the towns now called Hengyang and Shaoyang.

wing of the Third Army Group (primarily supporting the Twelfth Army).

5. The Twelfth Army remains at its present location (around Laomiao and Dongjingpu). Tonight it should send troops to make a feigned attack on the enemy's positions in Shiba, Shimapu, and elsewhere. It should leave patrols along the line of Yanziling, Jingwanzi, and Laomiao, which will be in charge of attacking Guitang, Shiba, Shimapu, and other places (including the Guitang highway) when the enemy launches an offensive.

6. The Fourth Army should immediately withdraw to the north end of Liaojiachong and Zhoujiaba. Before dawn tomorrow it should occupy a position to the south of Tianjiling, from which it should be able to launch a fierce assault on the enemy attacking us from the right wing, and destroy them. Tonight it should send forward patrols to the vicinity of Xujiachong, in order to establish a link with our Seventh Regiment of the Liuyang Red Guards Army, and with the Twelfth Army in Yanziling. When the enemy strikes, this army should connect with the right wing of the Twelfth Army and carry out the attack on the area to the right of the Guitang highway (not including the highway).

7. The Third Column of the Third Army should withdraw tonight to the area around Duanjialong and rejoin its main forces.

8. The entire Third Army is located around Duanjialong and Baitianpu as the general reserve forces.

9. The heavy baggage and the station for wounded soldiers of the First Army Group remain in the original location.

10. We ourselves are with the general reserve forces in Baitianpu.

Attention:

1. At night it is necessary to watch out for enemy harassment.

2. There must be mutual exchange of personnel among all units in order to establish links, and any intelligence should be shared among them.

Commander-in-chief	Zhu De
Political Commissar	Mao Zedong

Land Law

Promulgated by the
Chinese Revolutionary Military Commission

(August 1930)[1]

Chapter One: Confiscation and Redistribution of Land

Article 1. Following the overthrow of the political power of the despotic gentry and landlord class through armed uprising, all land, hills, woods, ponds, and houses owned by all private individuals or groups—the despotic gentry, landlords, ancestral halls, temples, societies, and rich peasants—must be immediately confiscated, turned over to public ownership by the soviet government, and redistributed by the soviet to landless peasants, peasants with little land, and other needy people for their use. Where there is only a peasant association, and a soviet has not yet been set up, the peasant associations can also carry out confiscation and redistribution.[2]

Article 2. The families of the despotic gentry, landlords, and reactionaries, after undergoing investigation by the soviet and receiving permission to reside in the countryside, may receive an appropriate amount of land when they have no other means of supporting themselves.

Article 3. Officers, soldiers, and porters of the Red Army currently in military service and those engaged in revolutionary work shall also receive redistributed land; moreover, the soviet shall assign people to help their families farm the land.

Article 4. Rural residents who can make a living through other lines of work, such as industry, commerce, and education, shall not receive redistributed land. Those who cannot make ends meet may receive a suitable amount of land, no more than enough to make up the shortfall in their income.

Our source for this text is *Mao Zedong ji*, Vol. 2, pp. 179–84, where it is reproduced from a collection of captured Communist documents published by the Guomindang in 1931.

1. On the relation between this land law and that of February 7, 1930, see above, the Introduction to this volume. In assessing the evolution of Mao's agrarian policy during the summer and autumn of 1930, the resolution of June 1930 on the problem of the rich peasants should also be consulted.

2. The relative moderation of Mao's line at this time is underscored by the omission, in this text, of the article in the February 7 law providing for the distribution of the land of owner-peasants if the poor peasants demanded it.

Article 5. Farm laborers and unemployed vagrants, if they are willing to receive redistributed land, should be given land. But those vagrants who receive redistributed land must rid themselves of evil addictions such as to opium and gambling, otherwise the soviet will take back their land.

Article 6. Those who have traveled to other areas and do not live in their native villages shall not be given land.

Article 7. Land shall be redistributed taking the township as the unit. The peasants of a given township pool the farmland they till in their township and in neighboring townships, and redistribute it jointly. If three or four townships are adjacent to each other, some of them having more land and the others less, and if circumstances are such that when land is redistributed using one township as the unit, the townships with less land cannot support themselves, and have no other form of production to support themselves, three or four townships may be combined into one unit to carry out the redistribution. The township soviets must, however, make a request, and obtain the approval of the district soviet.

Article 8. In order to meet the demands of the majority of the people and enable peasants to receive land quickly, land should be redistributed according to the number of people in the countryside; men, women, the old, and the young should receive equal shares. The method of distribution taking labor power as the criterion shall not be adopted.

Article 9. In principle urban businessmen and workers are not eligible to receive redistributed land. However, unemployed workers and members of the urban poor who request redistributed land may be given an appropriate amount of land when circumstances permit.

Article 10. In order to destroy the feudal forces rapidly, and strike a blow at the rich peasants, land redistribution should follow the principles of drawing on the plentiful to make up for the scarce, and drawing on the fat to make up for the lean.[3] Landlords and rich peasants are not allowed to conceal their land and not declare it, nor to retain fertile land. After the land has been redistributed, the soviets shall make wooden markers and place them in the fields to mark the yield of the plot and the name of its current tiller.

Article 11. All land deeds of the despotic gentry, landlords, common land owned by ancestral halls, and temples must be surrendered to the township soviets or township/district peasant associations within a specified period to be burned in public.

---

3. As indicated in the note to the law of February 7, 1930, above, that law provided only for quantitative equalization of landholdings, through "drawing on the plentiful to make up for the scarce," i.e., taking from those who have ample land to give to those who do not have enough. This law adds a prescription for qualitative equalization, "drawing on the fat to make up for the lean," i.e., taking good land from the more affluent peasants to complement the generally inferior land of the poor peasants. These two slogans are characteristic of Mao's approach to land reform; he restated them frequently from this time forward.

Article 12. After land is redistributed, the *xian* soviets or district soviets are to issue cultivation permits.

Article 13. The redistributed land of all those in the countryside who have died, changed their occupation, or gone elsewhere will be taken back by the soviets for further redistribution. As for newcomers and newborn babies, the soviets should find a way to give them land, but only after the harvest.

Article 14. When land is redistributed following an armed uprising and after sowing by the peasants, the crops harvested belong to the peasants to whom the land has been redistributed; the original tillers are not allowed to lay claim to the harvest.[4]

Article 15. Vegetable gardens, dikes, and uncultivated land (which can be used to grow miscellaneous cereals)[5] should be redistributed. Large ponds that are not easy to redistribute are placed under the management of the soviet, or leased out by the soviet at a fixed price.

Article 16. Hills on which bamboo and Chinese catalpa grow must be converted into land units according to the yield of their products and redistributed together with fields. But if hired labor was previously employed, and manufacturing facilities were previously established there, thus giving them an industrial capitalist character, they may be leased out in their entirety by the soviet and need not be redistributed.

Article 17. Pine and China fir forests are to be managed or leased out by the soviet government. However, when people of the township need lumber to repair dams and irrigation canals, build public properties and houses, or repair the houses burned down by the reactionaries, they may make use of them upon obtaining permission from the district soviet government.

Article 18. Large firewood-producing hills shall be closed or opened to the public [for collection of firewood] by the soviet government.

Article 19. In order to meet the demands of the impoverished peasants, all confiscated land should be completely redistributed to them; the soviet need not keep any. Under certain circumstances, however, the soviet may use the undistributed portion to establish model farms, or lease it out on a temporary basis. At the same time, the soviet shall reserve some houses to be used for public purposes.

Chapter Two: Cancellation of Debts

Article 20. No debts owed by workers, peasants, and poor people to the despotic gentry, landlords, and rich peasants are to be repaid. Notes and debt certificates must be turned over to the soviet or to the peasant associations within a specified time to be burned.

Article 21. Debts owed by the despotic gentry, landlords, and merchants to

---

4. For an extended discussion of this point, see below, the text of November 15, 1930, "The Problem of Dividing up Green Crops and Renting Land."

5. I.e., crops other than the staple foods of rice and wheat.

the government, or to workers, peasants, poor people, or the petty bourgeoisie must be repaid in full regardless of whether they are old or new.

Article 22. Old debts owed by workers, peasants, and poor people to merchants as a result of commercial transactions occurring before the armed uprising are not to be repaid regardless of whether they are commercial high-interest loans or merely principal.

Article 23. In principle, debts incurred between workers, peasants, and poor people themselves before the armed uprising are also not to be repaid. Only interest-free loans made for the sake of friendly assistance and willingly repaid by the borrower are exempt from this rule.

Article 24. As for articles and houses pawned by workers, peasants, and poor people to the despotic gentry, landlords, and pawnshop owners, the collateral must be returned unconditionally.

Article 25. Credit unions and grain associations are to be abolished without exception.

Article 26. Usurious loans are banned under the soviet régime; *xian* soviets set appropriate interest rates according to local financial conditions. These rates must not exceed the amount of returns obtained by ordinary capital under normal local economic conditions.

Chapter Three: Land Taxes

Article 27. In order to meet the needs of overthrowing the counterrevolutionaries (for example, maintaining and expanding the Red Army and the Red Guards, and maintaining the organs of political power) and increase the benefits for the masses (for example, setting up schools and clinics, providing relief to the handicapped, old, and young, and repairing roads and irrigation canals), the soviet must collect land taxes from peasants.

Article 28. The principle of levying land taxes is to protect the poor peasants, build ties with the middle peasants, and attack the rich peasants. They may be collected only after the soviet has been established, the masses have received actual benefits, and permission is granted by higher-level soviets.

Article 29. Land taxes are to be collected progressively according to the quantity of rice harvested by the peasants each year from redistributed land:

1) Those who receive, per person, land that yields less than 5 *Dan* of rice are exempted from tax.
2) A tax rate of 1 percent is levied on those who receive, per person, land that yields 6 *Dan* of rice.
3) A tax rate of 1.5 percent is levied on those who receive, per person, land that yields 7 *Dan* of rice.
4) A tax rate of 2.5 percent is levied on those who receive, per person, land that yields 8 *Dan* of rice.

5) A tax rate of 4 percent is levied on those who receive, per person, land that yields 9 *Dan* of rice.

6) A tax rate of 5.5 percent is levied on those who receive, per person, land that yields 10 *Dan* of rice.

7) A tax rate of 7 percent is levied on those who receive, per person, land that yields 11 *Dan* of rice.

8) A tax rate of 8.5 percent is levied on those who receive, per person, land that yields 12 *Dan* of rice.

Each additional yield of 1 *Dan* of rice is accompanied by an increase of 1.5 percent in the land tax rate.

Article 30. Land tax revenues and expenditures are subject to the unified control of higher-level soviet governments. Lower-level governments are not authorized to collect taxes or to make expenditures at their discretion. The scale of expenditures is determined by higher-level governments according to the amount of tax revenues and the degree of urgency of the needs of the governments at various levels.

Chapter Four: Wages

Article 31. Rural artisans, workers, and farm laborers whose previous wages were too low should get a raise. Future wages are to be set by the soviet according to two criteria: fluctuation in the cost of living and fluctuation in the peasants' harvests. Wage rates set by township and district soviets must be approved by the *xian* or provincial soviets.

Order to the First Army Group of the Red Army to Launch a General Offensive

(September 1, 1930, 8:00 P.M., at Baitianpu)

1. We have received the following order from Commander-in-chief Zhu and Political Commissar Mao of the Front Army:

... (Omission)[1]

2. Following instructions received, this army group has decided to launch an offensive against the enemy along the entire front, and has made arrangements for attack as follows:

The Twelfth Army will remain in the area of Yanziling, Jingwanzi, Laomiao, and Dongjingpu.

The Third Army should leave enough troops to seize the battlefield slightly behind Shipailing, but its main forces should be concentrated along the Xiangumiao and Mojialong line so as to prevent the enemy from making a surreptitious crossing near Huilongpu.

3. The battle zones of this army group are divided as follows:

To the right of the line along Huangtuling, Lannichong, and Huangnitang (including the line itself) is within the domain of this army group; the Wumeiling, Shiba, and Guitang line is the responsibility of the Twelfth Army; to the left of the Huangtuling, Lannichong, and Huangnitang line is the responsibility of the Third Army.

4. The heavy baggage of this army group, all army clinics for wounded soldiers, as well as all noncombatant units should move tomorrow morning to Bozhutang, stop there and await further orders. All troops and personnel at this location (including the Liu[yang] Seventh Regiment) are under the command of Fan Shude, who will be assisted by Yang Lisan, head of the Twelfth Army's military supplies section, and Wu Hanjie, head of the Fourth Army's military supplies section.

5. Tomorrow we will lead the directly attached units and move to Xujiachong. During the campaign we will be in command from here.

Our source for this order is *Jiangxi dangshi ziliao*, Vol. 6, pp. 110–11.

1. An omission is indicated here in the Chinese text.

Addendum:

Tomorrow all armies must send scouts to reconnoiter targets for attack within their respective battle zones.

Commander-in-chief and	Zhu De
Political Commissar	Mao Zedong

Order to the First Front Army of the Red Army to Surround and Attack Changsha and to Launch a General Offensive

(September 1, 1930, 8:00 P.M., at General Headquarters in Baitianpu)

1. The enemy forces in Changsha are still occupying their fortifications and stubbornly resisting us.

2. The Front Army has decided to launch a general offensive against this enemy along the entire front tomorrow evening (the 2nd).

3. The Third Army Group should move in the evening from its present location to the Dongshan and Litang line, and must complete this shift by tomorrow morning. In addition, it should construct a raft bridge near Dongshan, and take charge tomorrow of attacking the area to the right of the line along Guitang, Shiba, and Wumeiling (including the line itself).

4. The First Army Group (minus the Fourth Army) will be in charge of attacking the area to the left of said line (excluding the line itself). It is to remain in the area of Dongjingpu, Mojialong, Zhoujiaba, and Baitianpu, and must be on guard against an enemy attack from such places as Houzishi, Tantangzi on the other side of the river, and elsewhere. It should construct a raft bridge near Bozhutang. This army group's large baggage should be moved to this place and stored there.

5. It is ordered that the Sixteenth Army of the Third Army Group return to its original unit, and tomorrow from its present location (the Dongtundu and Hujidu line) it should begin to attack along Xinhe toward the northern outskirts.

6. The Fourth Army constitutes the general reserve force, remaining at its present location (the Longjiawan and Zhoujiaba line).

7. After achieving success in their attack, the troops of the First Army Group that will have taken Huangtuling should immediately build on their victory to expand toward the right; the troops of the Third Army Group that will have taken Wumeiling should immediately expand toward Huangtuling along the way behind the enemy's stronghold in Yuhuating; the troops of the Third Army Group that will have taken Erlipai should expand from the enemy's strongholds marked 49 and 50 toward Xinhe to the right, but must leave enough forces in

---

We have translated this order from *Jiangxi dangshi ziliao*, Vol. 6, pp. 112–13.

Yangjiashan, which is between Erlipai and Wumeiling; the troops of the Sixteenth Army that will have taken Xinhe should build on their victory to expand along the railroad towards the enemy stronghold marked 49.

8. At 7:00 tomorrow evening (the 2nd), the First Army Group and the Sixteenth Army will start to attack. At 8:00 the Third Army Group will start to attack.

9. We are now at the position of General Headquarters at Baitianpu. Tomorrow morning we will lead the directly attached units and move to Xujiachong; tomorrow evening the command post will be established there.

Addendum:

1. The Fourth Army, which constitutes the general reserve force, should dispatch capable scouts to places such as Tiaomajian, Tianxinqiao, and Xitangchong, and send Red Guard forces as well as espionage agents to the area between Hengtang and Huilongpu so as to be on guard against an enemy attempt at a secret crossing.

2. The artillery regiment of the Third Army must choose its position near Shiba, so as to be able to fire at the enemy's strongholds in Yuhuating, Wumeiling, and elsewhere.

Commander-in-chief   Zhu De
Political Commissar   Mao Zedong

Order to the First Front Army of the Red Army about Luring the Enemy to Come Out and Attack, and Preparing to Encircle and Destroy Him

(September 4, 1930, 8:00 P.M., at General Headquarters in Baitianpu)

1. The First and Second Brigades, as well as the Supplemental Regiment, the Independent Regiment, the Sixth Regiment, the espionage battalion, and the engineer battalion of the enemy Tao Guang's Division, which launched an attack from Houzishi yesterday, were all driven to the edge of the river by one unit each of our Third Army, Twelfth Army, and Fourth Army. Most of them surrendered, seven or eight hundred were shot dead in the river, and more than a thousand were taken prisoner. We decimated Li Jue's troops, and they retreated back to their enemy stronghold in Houzishi.

The enemy Chen Guangzhong's brigade, which tried to cross the river surreptitiously from Datuopu at 10:00 A.M. yesterday, was met, attacked, defeated, and put to flight by our Fourth Army. They retreated to Yijiawan at 11:00 P.M. yesterday, and we have no reliable report on whether or not they have yet crossed the river. The enemy Luo Lin's division, which launched an attack from Laodaohe at the north gate, was met and attacked by our Sixteenth Army, so they did not succeed either. The forces of Gong Bingfan, Wang Dongyuan, and Luo Shujia were also met and attacked by our Fifth Army and Eighth Army, so they dared not advance.

2. To achieve the goal of luring the enemy out of their strongholds and annihilating them outside their fortifications, this Front Army will remain tomorrow (the 5th) at its present location (from Yangjiachong on the left to Dongsigang on the right along the line of Taohuaduan, Liaojiachong, and Bozhutang), lure the enemy closer, and use our concentrated forces to surround and destroy them.

3. The First Army Group will remain at its present location of the Yangjiachong, Taohua, and Baitianpu area. It should post sentries in the direction of Houzishi, Shimapu, Yijiawan, Tianxinqiao, and Zhuzhou.

The Third Army Group will remain at its present location of the Liaojiachong,

---

Our source for this order is *Jiangxi dangshi ziliao*, Vol. 6, pp. 114–15.

Bozhutang, and Dongsigang area. It should post sentries in the area to the right of Xujiachong to Dongshan, and pay particular attention to the movements of the Gong and Luo divisions, in preparation for an attack on these enemies by this army group. If the enemy approaches our front, each of our guard units should immediately take up their positions, meet and attack the enemy, and await orders to concentrate large forces to surround and destroy them.

4. If the enemy does not come out and attack tomorrow (the 5th), then the entire Front Army is to rest for one day at its present location.

5. We are now at General Headquarters in Baitianpu.

Commander-in-chief   Zhu De

Political Commissar   Mao Zedong

Order to the First Army Group of the Red Army to Concentrate Their Troops and Await the Opportunity to Come Out and Attack the Enemy

(September 4, 1930, 9:00 P.M., at Baitianpu)

1. The following order has been received from Commander-in-chief Zhu and Political Commissar Mao of the Front Army:

(Omission)

2. In accordance with orders, the army group will concentrate its forces at its present location tomorrow (the 5th) and await the opportunity to go out and attack the enemy.

3. The Third Army is to post sentries on the main road in Houzishi (Shipailing) and in the direction of Datuopu and Huilongpu.

The Twelfth Army is to post sentries on the minor road in Houzishi and in the direction of Shimapu.

The Fourth Army is to post sentries in the direction of Guitang and the minor roads in Xujiachong. The right wing is to make sure to establish contact with the Third Army Group's Fifth Army.

4. If the enemy does not come out and attack tomorrow, the army group is to rest for a day in accordance with orders.

5. We are now at the position of General Headquarters in Baitianpu.

Addendum:

1. Each army's wounded soldiers should be carried and transported by members of the Red Guard teams assigned by the aforementioned front army to each army to take responsibility for this.

2. Each sentry unit should send agents beyond the security line, and before dawn they should send out a screen of agents to scout ahead for 5 *li*.

3. The location of this general command headquarters is the location of the Front Army's General Headquarters. It is indicated at night by the suspension of three red lanterns in front of it.

Commander-in-chief   Zhu De
and
Political Commissar   Mao Zedong

We have translated this order from *Jiangxi dangshi ziliao*, Vol. 6, pp. 116–17.

Order to the First Front Army of the Red Army About Luring and Destroying the Enemy Who Is Coming Out by Two Routes to Attack

(September 5, 1930, 11:00 P.M.,
at General Headquarters in Baitianpu)

1. According to the scouts' report, the Duan Xing brigade of the enemy's Nineteenth Division advanced to the other side of the river facing Yijiawan at 3:00 P.M. yesterday (the 4th); the [part of the] Chen Guangzhong brigade routed by our army retreated to the other side of the river facing Datuopu and Huilongpu; and the [part of the] Chen Guangzhong brigade routed by our Fourth Army retreated to the other side of the river facing Dapu and Huilongpu. All of them gave the appearance of intending to make a secret crossing and launch an attack on us from the flank and rear. The remnant forces of He Jian's troops that retreated in defeat to the city of Changsha also have the intention of coming out and attacking along the main road between Huangtuling and Dongjingpu.

2. The Front Army has decided first to lure out and destroy these enemy forces who are coming out by two routes to attack, and then to take advantage of victory and fight our way into Changsha.

3. The First Army Group is to be responsible for destroying the enemy that is coming to attack by making a secret crossing along the line of Datuopu and Yijiawan. Tomorrow morning (the 6th) they must advance from their present location to the area southeast of the Zhujialing and Tianxinqiao line, and await an opportunity to annihilate the enemy along the Datuopu and Yijiawan line.

4. The Third Army Group is to take charge of destroying the enemy that is coming out to attack from the two routes of the city of Changsha and Dongshan. By dusk tomorrow it should seize the opportunity to transfer its entire force (including the Sixteenth Army) to Tongrentang, Baimaotang, Panshiba, Banzhuyu, and all the way to the area on the eastern edge of Zhujialing, and make sure to establish contact with the First Army Group's troops near Zhujialing, the Twelfth Army.

5. The Hunan Red Guard Army should move to the line between Dongsigang, Luzhiling and Zhentoushi, and is to be in charge of transportation in the rear as well as pinning down the enemy in Dongshan.

Our source for this order is *Jiangxi dangshi ziliao*, Vol. 6, pp. 118–19.

6. Once the movement has begun, we will be moving with the First Army Group (if there is no enemy in Yijiawan tomorrow the plan is to camp near Qiantangpo and Tianxinqiao).

Commander-in-chief   Zhu De
Political Commissar   Mao Zedong

Order to the First Army Group of the Red Army to Advance on Tianxinqiao and Exterminate the Enemy in Datuopu and Yijiawan When Opportunity Offers

(September 5, 1930, 12:00 noon,
at General Headquarters in Baitianpu)

1. The following order has been received from Commander-in-chief Zhu and Political Commissar Mao of the Front Army:

... (Omission)

2. According to the order, this army group is to set out from its present location at 3:00 A.M. tomorrow (the 6th), advance to Tianxinqiao, and after arriving at Tianxinqiao, annihilate the enemy in Datuopu and Yijiawan when opportunity offers.

3. The Fourth Army should send capable scouts tonight to set out from the present location and search and advance to Yijiawan by way of Tianxinqiao. They must return to Tianxinqiao and report by tomorrow morning. The rest are to complete their departure from the present location by 2:30 tomorrow morning, advance to Tianxinqiao by way of Daijiachong and Jizhumiao, stop and await further orders (a vanguard should be sent out as well).

4. The General Headquarters espionage team, General Headquarters, and the transportation team should set out from the present location at 3:00 A.M. tomorrow and advance following behind the Fourth Army.

5. The Twelfth Army (which should dispatch a rear guard force) should set out from the present location at 3:00 A.M. tomorrow, advance behind the units directly attached to General Headquarters, and stop to await further orders after arriving near Tianxinqiao.

6. The Third Army should advance from the present location at 3:00 A.M. tomorrow by way of a short cut and arrive near Tianxinqiao, stop there, and await further orders (it should send out sentries on the right flank in the direction of Datuopu).

7. If during the course of its advance the Third Army on the right flank finds enemy troops in the direction of Datuopu, then the Third Army on the right

---

We have translated this order from *Jiangxi dangshi ziliao*, Vol. 6, pp. 120–21.

should immediately occupy an advantageous position from which to attack the enemy. The Fourth Army should rapidly follow the left wing of the Third Army to launch a fierce attack on the enemy's flank. The rest of the forces are to await further orders to provide reinforcements, so that they may be destroyed once for all.

8. The large baggage of the army group (excluding the mess supplies each unit should carry) and the noncombat forces, led by their original commanders, should move tomorrow morning from Tiaomajian to Xinqiao, stop there, and await further orders.

9. During the advance we will be operating at the position of the Fourth Army's army headquarters.

Addendum:

1. Tomorrow each unit (or each company) is allowed to carry along only three or four loads of mess supplies (the rest of the luggage should all be moved to Xinqiao).

2. After arriving at Tianxinqiao, each unit should at once send orderlies to the position of General Headquarters to receive orders.

3. Each column in each army must assign one person to be in charge of the sick and wounded officers and soldiers, and each army should also designate someone to provide unified leadership. Tomorrow morning Director Yang of the General Political Department will guide the Hunan Red Guard forces in escorting [the sick and wounded] from Tiaomajian to the rear in Liuyang.

4. If there is no enemy in Yijiawan and Datuopu tomorrow, the Fourth Army should then move from Tianxinqiao in the direction of Yijiawan and camp there; the Third Army is to arrange to camp in the Jizhumiao and Baimachong area; and the Tenth Army is to arrange to camp in the Louditang and Qiantangpo area. General Headquarters is to encamp near Qiantangpo and Tianxinqiao.

Commander-in-chief   Zhu De
and
Political Commissar   Mao Zedong

Order to the First Army Group of the Red Army to Launch a Forceful Attack on Changsha City

(September 10, 1930, 9:00 A.M., at General Command Headquarters in Tianxinqiao)

1. We have received the following order from the Commander-in-chief and the Political Commissar of the Front Army:

a. The enemy He Jian's forces are still holding the city of Changsha and are resisting us by relying upon their fortifications. Luo Lin's division is now in the Leigongling area.

b. It has been decided that the Front Army will take the said enemy by storm and seize the city walls. A general attack on the enemy in the area of Erlipai, Wumeiling, and Huangtuling has been set to take place at 8:00 tonight.

c. The Third Army Group (minus the Sixteenth Army) is in charge of the attack on the right wing. At around 3:00 P.M. today it should move from its present location (the Banzhutang and Panguba area) to the area near Litang, and must complete its movement by dusk. Tonight it should promptly (at 8:00 o'clock sharp) attack and advance toward the enemy's stronghold in Erlipai, and position its reserve forces near Litang.

d. The First Army Group is in charge of the attack on the left wing. At around 3:00 P.M. today it should move from its present location (the Zhujialing and Tianxinqiao area) to the area of Wumafeng (several *li* beyond Xujiachong), Guitang, and Tianjiling, and must complete its movement by dusk. Tonight it should promptly (at 8:00 o'clock sharp) attack and advance toward the enemy's stronghold in Wumeiling, and dispatch troops to feign an attack on the enemy's stronghold in Huangtuling, positioning its reserve forces near Tianjiling behind Xujiachong.

e. The Sixteenth Army should move this morning (the 10th) from its present location (near Banzhutang) and advance to the area near Langlishi by way of crossing the river in Dongsigang, to pin down the enemy in Leigongling.

f. The heavy baggage of the Front Army is to be concentrated in Dongsigang

---

Our source for this order is *Jiangxi dangshi ziliao*, Vol. 6, pp. 122–24.

(under the direction of the head of the military supplies section of the Third Army, Fan Shude). The First Army Group's mess unit will be positioned on the road between Dongsigang and Xujiachong. The Third Army Group's mess unit will be positioned in Dongshan.

g. During the general offensive tonight we will be on Wumafeng Mountain in front of Xujiachong.

Addendum:

a. Along the way each army group's advance troops attacking the city should pay attention to destroying the enemy's advancing security forces.

b. Darkness is taken to fall at precisely 7:00 o'clock.

c. When attacking the city, all officers and soldiers must march ahead with full courage. Anyone who shrinks and retreats from the battle shall be dealt with by military law.

d. When there is the possibility of attacking an enemy's stronghold, a torch should be lit as a signal.

e. All army groups are to communicate with General Command Headquarters (on top of Wumafeng) by telephone. All armies and army groups, in turn, are to communicate through orderlies or special signals.

f. Command positions at all levels are to be indicated according to originally stipulated torch signals.

g. All night attacks are to be carried out through hand-to-hand combat.

2. According to orders, this army group will take the enemy's stronghold in Wumeiling by storm, and has made the following arrangements:

a. The Fourth Army constitutes the force attacking the city. It should move at 2:00 P.M. today from its present location to the area of Guitang and Shiba, and promptly launch a fierce attack on the enemy's stronghold in Wumeiling.

b. The Twelfth Army will be the reserve force for the attack on the city. It should move from its present location at 4:00 P.M. today and advance following the Fourth Army. Tonight it should dispatch forces (roughly the equivalent of a company) along the main road in Dongjingpu to feign an attack on Shimapu and Huangtuling.

c. The forces attacking the city and the reserve forces for the attack on the city are all under the command of Attack Commanding Officer Lin Biao and Political Commissar Luo Ronghuan.

d. The Third Army constitutes the reserve force of this army group. It should move at 4:30 P.M. today following General Headquarters to the reserve forces position near Tianjiling behind Xujiachong. It should also post a strong security force to stand guard in the direction of places such as Mojialong and Shipailing.

3. The army group's heavy baggage and the mess units of its combatant forces should halt at the positions designated in the Front Army's aforementioned order and begin cooking.

4. During the general offensive tonight we will be atop Wumafeng Mountain.

Commander-in-chief   Zhu De
and
Political Commissar   Mao Zedong

Instruction on Methods for Capturing the Enemy's Weapons[1]

(September 12, 1930)

During the period of guerrilla warfare in the past, our Red Army did not fight any campaigns against big enemies and did not capture large amounts of enemy weapons. As a result, our comrades, officers and soldiers, often ran forward, seized a gun in their hands, and asked the enemy to give it to them. Once they got the gun, they slung it on their back. This habit has been maintained down to the present day. During our attack on Changsha this time, one detachment of the Fourth Army had pursued a regiment under Chen Guangzhong to the point where it was willing to surrender its weapons voluntarily. As in the past, however, our officers and soldiers wanted to carry all these guns themselves, and this was simply impossible, for they were few and the enemy's guns were many, so they naturally could not carry them all. As a result, while they were struggling with this problem, the enemy launched a counterattack, and all the guns of this entire regiment were taken back again by the enemy. This was truly a pity. From now on, every one of us should understand the methods for fighting big campaigns and capturing large numbers of weapons. Whenever the enemy troops raise their banners or hands and wave, or play a salute, or raise their guns and indicate that they are willing to give up their weapons and surrender, we should, on the one hand, be on guard with arms, order them to put their guns in piles (stack their rifles), or order them to put their guns on the ground and move a few steps backward. Afterward, officers should be sent to gather these captives together and lead them away from the battlefield, and the necessary number of troops should be sent to guard them to the rear. As regards all the weapons (whether lying on the ground or piled up in stacks), we should send someone else (it is best to send an adjutant) to lead a few soldiers to escort them to the nearest place in the rear and give them to the empty-handed people to transfer to the rear (removing the triggers if necessary). We absolutely must not carry large amounts of captured enemy weapons ourselves, for this will reduce our fighting strength.

Our source for this document is *Mao Zedong junshi wenji*, Vol. 1, pp. 167–68, where it is stated that the text has been reproduced from the original document in the Party archives.

1. This is Instruction No. 2 of the General Headquarters of the First Front Army.

Particular attention must be paid to this point. The people sent should run back to their units immediately, to deal with the enemy elsewhere. While gathering up the weapons surrendered by the enemy, we should act swiftly and guard them with extreme caution, so as not to give the enemy the opportunity to launch a counterattack. While the guns are still in the enemy's hands, in order to reduce their fighting capacity and accomplish our fighting tasks, we should kill them without the slightest compunction. Conversely, if the enemy has already laid down his weapons and expressed his willingness to surrender, we should not injure him simply because of hatred. This is a very important matter. We hope that all our comrade officers and soldiers will pay special attention to the importance of carrying this out. Be it so ordered.

Commander-in-Chief   Zhu De

Political Commissar   Mao Zedong

Order to the First Army Group of the Red Army to Occupy Places Such as Ping[xiang], You[xian], Li[ling], and Zhu[zhou], and to Await Opportunities

(September 12, 1930, 5:30, at Xinqiao)

1. It is said that Zhang [Fakui]'s troops and those of Guangxi have arrived at Xiangtan, and that there is one unit of the Nineteenth Division in Zhuzhou.

2. To achieve the objective of first eliminating the forces of Zhang [Fakui] and Guangxi, and those of He Jian, and then taking Changsha and attacking Wuhan, the Front Army's intention is to take Ping[xiang], You[xian], Li[ling], and Zhu[zhou] and await opportunities.

3. Our Third Army Group will enter and take Pingxiang today by way of Liling.

4. This army group has received orders to take Zhuzhou tomorrow (the 13th).

5. The Twelfth Army is designated as the vanguard, and it should set out tonight at 4:00 o'clock by way of Longtoupu. If there are enemy forces in Zhuzhou they must destroy this enemy and occupy [Zhuzhou].

6. The unit directly attached to General Headquarters (to set out at 4:00 o'clock) is to march following the vanguard.

7. The Fourth Army constitutes the rear guard. It should set out at 6:00 o'clock and advance following the unit directly attached to General Headquarters.

8. The Third Army should find its own route to advance toward Zhuzhou (on the principle of marching to the right of the Longtoupu road so as not to cross paths with those troops going through Longtoupu).

9. Baggage is to be returned to its original unit.

10. Our movements shall be with the position of General Headquarters.

Addendum:

If there is no enemy upon arrival in Zhuzhou, the Twelfth Army is to be stationed in the direction of Lukou, the Third Army is to be stationed in

---

We have translated this order from *Jiangxi dangshi ziliao*, Vol. 6, pp. 125–26.

Zhuzhou, the Fourth Army is to be stationed in Longtoupu and Zhuzhou, and General Headquarters is to be stationed in the direction of Liling. In other words, they are not to be all stationed in one clump. It is forbidden to sabotage the railroad power lines from Zhuzhou to Liling and Lukou.

It is so ordered.

Front Committee general espionage team leader, He

General Headquarters espionage team leader, Chen

Political Commissar, Liu

Transportation team deputy leader, Yang

Political Commissar, Feng

Headquarters adjutants' section

General Political Department general affairs section, He

Commander-in-chief   Zhu De

Political Commissar   Mao Zedong

Order to the First Army Group of the Red Army to Attack and Take Ji'an

(September 13, 1930, 8:00 P.M., at General Headquarters in Zhuzhou)

1) In accordance with the instructions of the Central Committee of the Chinese Communist Party, and as a prelude to our objective of achieving the initial victory of the revolutionary uprising in Wuhan and the seizure of political power in the whole country, our front army has the tasks of gathering the tens of millions of workers, peasants, and poor people of Jiangxi, and applying a strategy of concentrated offensives to seize Nanchang and the Nanchang-Jiujiang Railroad line as far as Hukou in the fiercest, fastest, and bravest way, destroying Lu Diping and reactionary rule in Jiangxi, blocking and blockading the Yangzi River, attacking Nanjing to the right, and securing the seizure of Wuhan to the left. Our front army has decided on the plan for the first stage of taking Nanchang, which requires the First Army Group to attack Ji'an, and the Third Army Group to plan the seizure of Xiajiang and Xin'gan.

2) This army group has decided to leave here (Zhuzhou) tomorrow (the 14th), and spread out to work along the way, our task being to mobilize the masses, raise funds, and sew clothes and quilts. The duration of the march will be seventeen days in all, and the deadline for the whole army group to reach the township of Yanfu in Ji'an and concentrate its forces there is the 30th of this month.

3) The Twelfth Army should leave here (Zhuzhou) tomorrow, head for the areas of Huangtuling and Youxian, and work along the way, pass through Lianhua and Anfu, and then arrive at the township of Yanfu by the 30th of this month to concentrate its forces. It will also have the responsibility of keeping a close watch in the direction of Hengzhou.

4) The Fourth Army should, starting tomorrow, leave here (Zhuzhou) and scatter its forces to Baiguanpu, Yaojiaba, Lukou, Yutanwan, Shenfuwan, Sifenpu, Shentan, and other places. The working period is eleven days, with a deadline of the 24th for reaching Pingxiang by following the railroad and assembling there (a further order will be issued later regarding the future plans for troop movements of the Third and Fourth Armies and the unit directly attached

---

Our source for this document is *Jiangxi dangshi ziliao*, Vol. 6, pp. 127–29. A slightly less complete text can also be found in *Mao Zedong ji. Bujuan*, Vol. 3, pp. 141–42.

to the General Headquarters), and with the responsibility of keeping a close watch in the direction of Changsha.

5) The Third Army should leave here for Dongchongpu tomorrow morning, work eleven days in Banyupu, Liling, Huangshapu, Chudongqiao, and other places, and then reach Pingxiang by the deadline of the 24th for assembly and further orders.

6) General Headquarters, the directly attached unit and the Workers' and Peasants' Military Commission should leave here tomorrow, advance behind the Third Army, and reach the area between Liling and Pingxiang between the 15th and the 24th.

Addendum:

1. The Fourth Army should send a detachment tomorrow to destroy the main iron bridge within the Zhuchang section of the Guangdong-Hankou railroad, and burn the sleepers of the railway for a distance of ten *li*.

2. After arriving at Youxian, the Twelfth Army should maintain telephone contact with the Fourth Army that has remained here, and the General Headquarters that has gone to Liling. Motor vehicles may be used as the means of transportation between Youxian and Liling.

3. If a large mass of enemy troops from Changsha is pressing upon us, the Fourth Army should move in the direction of Li[ling] and Ping[xiang], remaining in contact with this unit. If a large body of enemy troops appears from the direction of Hengzhou, then the Twelfth Army should also move in the direction of Pingxiang, remaining in contact with this unit.

4. Our Third Army Group is already advancing past Liling in the direction of Pingxiang.

5. Tomorrow morning, when the Third Army and the Twelfth Army set out, they can travel over ten *li* together along the railroad at the beginning of their journey. The Third Army should walk on the left side of the railroad and the Twelfth Army should take the right side of the railroad.

6. During the period when the troops are dispersed, 1 *yuan* in silver for pocket money may be distributed, plus 0.4 *yuan* for buying straw shoes for September.

7. The military uniforms should be lined, and everyone should receive an additional bedsheet.

It is so ordered.

> The Head of the General Services Department of the
> General Political Department, He
>
> The Secretary General of the Workers' and Peasants'
> Revolutionary Committee, Gu
>
> The Head of the Front Committee Espionage Team, He

The Head of the Espionage Team of
General Headquarters, Chen
Political Commissar, Liu
Acting Head of the Communications Detachment, Yang
Political Commissar, Feng
Deputy Head of the Adjutants' Department of This Unit

Commander-in-Chief   Zhu De
and
Political Commissar   Mao Zedong

Report to the Central Committee

(September 17, 1930, at Liling)

To the Provincial Committee, for transmission to the Central Committee:

1) There are three reasons why we failed to take Changsha this time:[1] (1) We were unable to wipe out the main force of the enemy before attacking the fortifications. The enemy had a total of thirty-one regiments, and although we had wiped out more than five regiments of enemy troops in the two campaigns in Wenjiashi and Houzishi,[2] the enemy's main forces retreated behind the city wall before we were able to wipe them out. Thus the enemy had ample strength to defend the city. (2) Various conditions relating to the masses were not met. There was no workers' uprising and no soldiers' revolt inside the city in response [to our action], and the masses along the Guangdong-Hankou Railway line and the Zhuzhou-Pingxiang Railway line, and those of the other side of the river did not rise up. Thus we were unable to cut off the enemy's transportation and communication lines by water or land, and unable to blockade the enemy's economic and military transportation. (3) The technical conditions were not fulfilled. The enemy's fortifications were European-style multilayered works, with eight or nine rings of barbed wire and trenches. We can only fight hand-to-hand campaigns; we do not have heavy artillery to destroy the enemy's fortifications, nor do we have transportation and communication tools such as radios. Thus communications between the two army groups were poor, and as a result, opportunities were missed. The three points noted above account for our failure to take Changsha, and the first cause was the most important. Nevertheless, in the Wenjiashi campaign we wiped out three enemy regiments, and in the Houzishi campaign we wiped out more than two enemy regiments. We captured two thousand rifles and twenty-five machine guns, killed the enemy brigade commander Dai Douheng, injured the enemy brigade commander Chen Wo, captured two enemy regimental commanders, injured two enemy regimental

---

Our source for this document is *Jiangxi dangshi ziliao*, Vol. 6, pp. 132–34. The first section also appears in *Mao Zedong junshi wenji*, Vol. 1, pp. 169–70, where it is stated that the text has been reproduced from the original document in the Party archives.

1. As discussed above, in the Introduction to this volume, the decision to terminate the second attack on Changsha, demanded by Li Lisan, and to retreat toward the southwest, was a crucial turning point in the relations between Mao Zedong and the Central Committee. On August 24, Mao Zedong and Zhu De had issued the order, translated above, to launch the attack; on September 12, they ordered its abandonment. This text contains Mao's own contemporary justification for his actions.

2. On the battle at Wenjiashi, see above, Mao's order dated August 18, 1930. The battle at Houzishi had taken place on September 3, 1930.

commanders, and killed, injured, or captured so many of the enemy's middle- and lower-ranking cadres that we could not keep count. We captured more than two thousand enemy soldiers and killed or injured more than four thousand. We surrounded Changsha for sixteen days and fought hard for several days and nights, on a front extending for more than thirty *li*. On September 3 we routed the attacking enemy troops completely, and thereafter they retreated behind the trenches and did not dare to come out even one step. On September 10 our army's second general offensive failed to achieve its goals, and on September 12 we decided to withdraw to Ping and Li.[3] We had completely demolished the morale and prestige of more than thirty regiments of the enemy troops, to the extent that they did not dare to look the Red Army in the eyes. At the same time, it had a great influence in the entire country, and that constitutes a victory in this war.

This campaign constitutes the first major battle since the founding of the Red Army, and as a result our forces also suffered a considerable number of casualties. According to reports from the First Army Group alone, among the senior cadres Comrades Ke Wudong and Liu Zuoshu were killed on the battlefield, several dozen middle ranking cadres were either killed or injured, and we also lost more than a hundred lower-level cadres and around sixteen hundred soldiers. The losses of the Third Army Group were also not inconsiderable. Although we suffered these losses, generally speaking our morale is still very strong, and there are no problems about going to Jiangxi and continuing our fighting there.

2) The letter to us of early August from the Yangzi Bureau and the Military Commission of the Central Committee was discovered by Zhang Huizan and reported to the national government, which distributed it to the various provinces. He Jian in turn transmitted it to the various *xian*, and consequently we obtained a copy in Zhuzhou. As a result of our discussions, we find the directives of the Central Committee to be entirely correct: seizing Wuhan is a great class battle of national import, and without the existence of revolutionary conditions nationwide, especially in the provinces of Hunan, Hubei, Jiangxi, and Henan, the taking of Wuhan would be quite difficult to sustain and expand upon.[4] The tasks

---

3. The reference is to the two towns of Pingxiang in Jiangxi and Liling in Hunan, located almost immediately across the provincial border from one another, which were on the way to Mao's subsequent destination of Ji'an. Both the order of September 10 to launch yet another assault on Changsha and the order of September 12 to turn away from the city are translated above.

4. This document is not available to us. A directive of the Central Committee to the Yangzi Bureau dated August 10 spoke of the rapid advance of the revolutionary situation, and called for a more aggressive attitude by the Red Army in the battles for Wuhan, Nanchang, Changsha, and Jiujiang. The directive also stressed the importance of rapidly building up Party and workers' organizations to support the coming military offensive. When Nanchang fell, it stated in conclusion, an All-China Revolutionary Committee should be created, with its seat in Nanchang, and Mao Zedong as provisional chairman. The letter from the Yangzi Bureau mentioned by Mao may have reflected or paralleled this directive. See *Central Committee Documents*, 1930, pp. 247–49.

of the First Army Group are to take Nanchang and Jiujiang, occupy the Nan-chang-Jiujiang Railroad, establish political power in Jiangxi and in the whole country, blockade the Yangzi, attack Nanjing on the right, and ensure victory in Wuhan on the left. Resolutely destroying all present enemies, relieving them of their arms and thereby arming the Red Army, the First Army Group should expand its numbers to over a hundred and twenty thousand. At present Ji'an should quickly be attacked and taken, and the millions of revolutionary masses in southwestern Jiangxi led to advance toward Nanchang and Jiujiang from the two routes of Zhangshu and Fuzhou. The Tenth Army should set out from Hukou and Madang; the Twenty-second Army should set out from Fuzhou and Fengcheng; the Twentieth Army should set out from Zhangshu and Linjiang, advance towards Nanchang, and surround it. As for the First and Third Army Groups, one of them is to occupy the Nanchang-Jiujiang Railroad and proceed directly to take Jiujiang, while the other army group is to attack Nanchang. The Third Army Group is to go on to Hunan or Hubei after working for a time in Jiangxi.

3) Both the First and Third Army Groups currently need a monthly cash supply of more than four hundred thousand [*yuan*]. At present the provisioning has run out, and it is necessary to raise funds of approximately two hundred thousand *yuan* in the three *xian* of Ping[xiang], Li[ling], and You[xian] to be able to sustain ourselves for half a month. At the same time, the local work in the various *xian* such as Ping, Li, and You is of crucial importance to seizing politi-cal power in Hunan and opening up connections between Hunan and Jiangxi (these three *xian* are all White areas, and the masses are heavily affected by a sense of defeat). Therefore, beginning on September 14th for a period of twelve days the two army groups are to raise funds in the three *xian*, and help the local Party headquarters mobilize the masses to establish Party and Youth League organizations, establish soviets, and set up Red Guard units. After twelve days, the First Army Group will attack Ji'an from Anfu, and the Second Army Group will attack Zhangshu from Yuanzhou. Around the time of taking Ji'an and Zhangshu, the problem of recruiting new soldiers must be solved, and the Twen-tieth and Twenty-second Army Groups must be transferred to advance northward and, in concert with the broad masses, to mount forceful attacks on Nanchang and Jiujiang, and occupy the Nanchang-Jiujiang Railroad.

4) As regards a Jiangxi provincial committee, three to five capable comrades should be sought to establish one quickly. It would be most suitable for the organ to be set up in Ji'an. The establishment of a Jiangxi provincial committee is of crucial importance to the work in Jiangxi. Last time when we went from Yongfeng through the town of Zhangshu, Shengmijie, and the Niuhang station, there was not a single branch, and there was not a single place where the masses were organized to lend assistance to the Red Army in its actions. The same was true in Ruizhou and other places, and a march of a month's duration was nothing but a purely military action. According to our experience, without the condition

of mass [support], it is very difficult to occupy central cities, and it is also very difficult to destroy the enemy. Naturally, we have no intention of waiting for the provincial committee to prepare the proper conditions among the masses before attacking Nanchang and Jiujiang. Without a doubt it is through such actions as attacking Nanchang and Jiujiang that we will mobilize the masses and create the necessary conditions among the masses. Nevertheless, when there exists a provincial committee it will be easier to attain our goals.

5) For the purpose of commanding the First Army Group and the Third Army Group, the Joint Conference of the Front Committees of the First and Third Army Groups has already decided to organize a General Front Committee with Mao Zedong as Secretary, and openly to organize a General Political Department of the First Front Army General Headquarters, with Zhu De as Commander-in-Chief, Mao Zedong as Chief Political Commissar, and Yang Yuebin as Chief of the General Political Department. Above the Red Army and local political organs will be organized a Chinese Workers' and Peasants' Revolutionary Committee to direct them, with thirty-five committee members and Mao Zedong as Chairman.[5]

6) Comrade Tu Zhennong[6] is relatively familiar with the situation in the First Army Group. After he went with the army from Tingzhou to Ji'an he was to return immediately to the Central Committee. I trust he has already arrived there.

7) The Front Committee of the Third Army Group has a separate detailed report on the situation in the Third Army Group.

Secretary of the Front Committee of the First Army Group   Mao Zedong

---

5. Central Committee Directive No. 47 of July 21, 1930, had called for the creation of such an organ in each battle zone to wield both military and political authority, adding that when victory was won in several provinces, these committees should be immediately combined and transformed into a national organ of revolutionary power. See *Central Committee Documents*, 1930, pp. 178–80.

6. Tu Zhennong (1896–1951) was a native of Jiangxi, who had joined the Guomindang in 1921, and the Chinese Communist Party in 1925. As indicated above, in a note to the text of June 25, 1930, Li Lisan sent Tu to the Jiangxi–Hunan soviet base area as an inspector, to inform Mao of the new policies adopted by the Central Committee in May and June. In this capacity, Tu addressed a number of meetings, and became familiar with the situation in the army. When a Jiangxi Provincial Soviet Government was set up in Ji'an on October 7, 1930, Tu became a member of the Executive Committee. In the early years of the Anti-Japanese War he played an important role in the organization of the Chinese Communist Party, but after being arrested in 1942 he rallied to the Guomindang, which he rejoined in 1943. From then until 1949, he published several anti-Communist books, and helped to train Guomindang special agents. He was executed as a counterrevolutionary in April 1951.

Order for the First Army Group of the Red Army to Leave Pingxiang and Advance Toward Ji'an

(September 23, 1930, 1:00 P.M.,
at General Headquarters in the city of Pingxiang)

1. Orders have been received from the Front Army as follows:

a. The vanguard of the enemy in Hunan (such as the Nineteenth and Thirty-first divisions of He Jian's forces) has reached Liling, and some of the forces of the enemy in Jiangxi (Dai Yue's brigade) have reached Wanzai.
   The city of Ji'an remains under the occupation of Deng Ying's forces.

b. For the purpose of accomplishing its original tasks of taking Nanchang and Jiujiang, eliminating Lu Diping, and then going on to seize Changsha and Wuhan and attack Nanjing, it has been decided that this front army will first take the city of Ji'an. This will cause the forces of the worker and peasant masses of southwestern Jiangxi to progress downstream and cooperate with us, and thus provide a large number of new recruits to expand the ranks of the Red Army.

c. The Third Army Group should set out from here (the city of Pingxiang) tomorrow (the 24th), and then advance toward the town of Zhangshu, first occupying Linjiangfu, mobilize the masses in the Linjiang area, block transportation on the Gan River, and cut off the enemy's reinforcements.

d. The First Army Group should be divided into two routes: the right route via Youxian (Twelfth Army), and the left route via Pingxiang (Third and Fourth Armies) passing through Yuanzhou (the Twentieth Army is also in Yuanzhou), and advancing towards Ji'an. The troops in Anyuan and Pingxiang must set out by the 27th, gather together on arrival at Futian to the north of Ji'an, and coordinate with the local masses in resolutely seizing the city of Ji'an.

2. This Army Group will follow orders to take Ji'an.

3. The General Headquarters, the various directly attached units, and the

---

Our source for this document is *Jiangxi dangshi ziliao*, Vol. 6, pp. 145–47. A fragmentary version of the first four paragraphs appears in *Mao Zedong ji. Bujuan*, Vol. 3, pp. 143–44, where the text is reproduced from a documentary collection published in China in 1980.

Fourth Army will follow the Central Military Commission[1] in moving to Anyuan tomorrow (the 24th) to work for three days. The whole army group (except the Twelfth Army) will advance towards Yichun from both Anyuan and Pingxiang on the 27th and converge in the vicinity of Futian, 90 *li* north of the city of Ji'an, after passing through Yichun (see chart below for details).

Time of arrival at locations shown	General Headquarters Fourth Army	Second Army	Twentieth Army	Twelfth Army
24th–26th	Anyuan	Pingxiang	Arrive 28th to await orders near Linyuan from Yichun by route of own choice. Must arrive at specified place to await orders before October 1	Must gather to await orders before October 1 near Futianjie in Beixiang, Ji'an, coming from Youxian
27th	From Anyuan to Baishapu, from Anyuan to Fenjiepu	From Pingxiang to Xuanfengshi		
28th	From Baishapu, Fenjiepu, to Yichun	From Xuanfengshi to Yichun		
29th	To city of Fenyi	Area around Yantianxin, Lubian		
30th	Arrive at area around Damiaoqian, Yingtangling	Around Fangli, Daijiafang		
31st	Futianjie, Hantang	Around Guojiadian, Pancun		

4. The Twelfth Army, according to the original plan, will come from You-xian, concentrate its forces north of the city of Ji'an, and await orders.

5. After departure, we shall follow the General Headquarters in our movements.

Addendum:

1. Route map to be distributed separately.
2. The destination points for each army are listed tentatively in the chart. Each unit is to judge the actual conditions along the way and adjust its position

---

1. Here our source has "Central Revolutionary Committee" (*zhonggewei*) instead of "Central Military Commission" (*zhongjunwei*) as in the *Bujuan* version. We take the former for a misprint.

slightly backwards or forward, to the left or right according to circumstances, but must arrive at the assembly point at the scheduled time.

3. After departure, each army must provide a daily written report to the General Headquarters.

General Commander   Zhu De
and
Political Commissar   Mao Zedong

Statutes of the
Red Army Soldiers' Association

(September 25, 1930)

Chapter 1: Purposes

Article 1. Raising the political standards of soldiers, strengthening class consciousness, establishing revolutionary ideas, and increasing capacity for struggle.

Article 2. Uniting the revolutionary spirit of soldiers, uniting the revolutionary forces of workers and peasants, and fulfilling the political tasks of the revolution (overthrowing imperialism, the landlord class and the National Government, and setting up a government of workers and peasants).

Article 3. Representing the interests of soldiers, improving their livelihood (such as provisions, hygiene, treatment, and entertainment), and heightening the revolutionary sentiments of soldiers.

Article 4. Assisting the military and political organs, maintaining revolutionary discipline, expanding the political influence of the Red Army, and winning over the broad masses.

Chapter 2: Functions and Rights

Article 5. The soldiers' association conducts its work under the guidance of the political departments and political committees.

Article 6. Regarding all military and political questions, the soldiers' association may put forward its opinions to military and political organs.

Article 7. When the management of the troops is considered inappropriate, the soldiers' association has the right to put forward protests or complaints to superior organs.

Article 8. The soldiers' association has the right to inspect the economy of the army and supervise the provisioning of the army (i.e., examining expenditures and revenues and catering accounts).

Article 9. As regards punishment of its members, the soldiers' association has the right only to give warnings and to expel them from the association directly.

Our source for this document is *Mao Zedong ji. Bujuan*, Vol. 3, pp. 145–51, where the text is reproduced from a documentary collection published in China in 1979.

When it comes to imprisonment, [X] punishment,[1] execution by firing squad, and so on, it may only make proposals to the responsible officers for them to handle.

Article 10. The soldiers' association has the right to select and send representatives to participate in the soviet organization.

Chapter 3: Organization

Article 11. The soldiers' association is a mass organization of soldiers, so its organization should be based on the criterion of the conditions of the masses. The political department of the Red Army is the organ of political power in the army. All the units above the division or column level have political departments. Therefore, the committee of the soldiers' association should not be set up in the units above divisions and columns. Organizations of the soldier masses should be established in all units below the level of regiment. Various levels of directly attached army units may also organize soldiers' associations. The soldiers' associations of regiments are subordinate to the political departments of their respective armies and divisions. The soldiers' associations of the directly attached army units at all levels should be under the direct guidance of the respective political departments.

Article 12. All Red Army officers, noncommissioned officers, soldiers, and laborers may become members of the soldiers' committee.

Article 13. All Red Army officers, noncommissioned officers, soldiers, and laborers have the right to elect and to be elected, but the number of officers elected should not exceed one-third of the committee members.

Article 14. The methods of forming the executive committee of the soldiers' committee at all levels:

> 1) The executive committees at the company level should be composed of seven to nine persons elected by the general meetings of all the soldiers of the respective companies. The executive committee should elect three persons to form a standing committee and recommend one person among them to be the chairman. All military and political administrations have the discretion to increase or decrease the number of those elected.

> 2) The executive committees of the soldiers' associations at the regiment and battalion level should be composed of nine to eleven persons elected by the representative conferences of the entire regiments or battalions. The executive committee should elect three to five persons to form a standing committee and recommend one person among them to be the chairman. (The same applies to the attached units.) The number of representatives is determined by the number of people in each company, with one representative being elected from among every five or ten persons.

---

1. The missing word is presumably "corporal."

Article 15. The organizational systems of the soldiers' associations at all levels are as follows:

1) Soldiers' associations in companies

General Meeting of All Soldiers				
Executive Committee				
Standing Committee				
Chairman				
Member for organization	Member for propaganda	Member for entertainment	Member for health matters	Member for economic affairs

2) Soldiers' associations in divisions and regiments. (This also applies to the soldiers' associations in the directly attached units.)

Representative Conference				
Executive Committee				
Standing Committee				
Chairman				
Secretary	Organization section	Propaganda section	Entertainment section	Health section

Article 16. Below the level of company, small groups should be formed within the units of platoons or squads and have one group leader and one deputy group leader. Group leaders are designated by the executive committees. (The soldiers' associations in military and political administrations may form small groups among ten or twenty persons in light of the conditions of their respective units.)

Article 17. The soldiers' associations of companies may have one member responsible for organization, one for propaganda, one for entertainment, one for health, and three for economic affairs. The members responsible for organization, propaganda, entertainment, and health should all be appointed from the members of the soldiers' associations. The director of the economic committee should also be a member of the soldiers' association and the other two members may be appointed by the executive committee or elected by the general meeting of all the soldiers.

Article 18. The soldiers' associations at the level of regiments and battalions and of the directly attached units may set up sections of organization, propaganda, entertainment, and health. The heads of the four sections should all be members of the soldiers' associations of the regiments and battalion, and a section may be composed of one to three persons appointed by the executive committee.

Article 19. The soldiers' associations at the level of regiments and battalions and of the directly attached units may have one secretary (concurrently held by a member or held by a person hired for the purpose).

Article 20. Tenure of the members of the executive committee:

1) The members of the executive committee of the soldiers' associations in a company are reelected every two months;

2) The members of the executive committee of the soldiers' associations at the level of regiments and battalions and of the directly attached units are reelected every three months and may be reelected consecutively.

Article 21. The time of various meetings:

1) The general meetings of the member of the soldiers' associations in companies should be held every two weeks, the executive committees hold their meetings every week and the standing committees hold their meetings every five days. (The above various sections may hold meetings at any time in case of special circumstances.) Small groups hold meetings every seven days.

2) The general meetings of the soldiers' associations at the level of regiments and battalions and of the directly attached units are held once in a month; the executive committees hold meetings every ten days; and the standing committees meet every five days. (Meetings may be held at any time in case of special circumstances.)

Article 22. Discipline:

1) Members of the associations must abide by the three main rules of discipline of the Red Army [1] Do not take anything from the workers, peasants, and small merchants; [2] When attacking the local bullies, turn over [whatever you take from them]: [3] Obey orders in all your actions) and the eight points for attention ([1] Put back the doors; [2] Bundle up the straw; [3] Speak politely; [4] Pay fairly for what you buy; [5] Return everything you borrow; [6] Pay for anything you damage, and protect public property; [7] Do not shit all over the place; [8] Do not search the pockets of enemy soldiers).[2] Violation of any one of the above-mentioned rules should be reported to responsible officers for appropriate punishment.

2) Decisions of the majority must be obeyed by all members of the association without exception.

3) Those who do not call meetings in a timely fashion, do not attend meetings on time, and disobey the resolutions of the associations shall be

---

2. As indicated above, in a note to the order of March 21, 1930, the rules and points for attention were still evolving in 1930. Although the order of the Three Main Rules is different here from that given in the note to the March 21 document, the wording is the same except for the addition of small merchants to the list of those whose property must not be taken.

punished, warned, or expelled by the associations at all levels according to the circumstances.

4) Members who do not pay dues for three months consecutively without reasons are expelled.

Chapter 4: The Work of the Association

Article 23. Under the guidance of the political departments and the political commissars, the work of agrarian revolution must be carried out with great efforts ([1] Constructing political régimes; [2] Redistributing land; [3] Arming workers and peasants).

Article 24. Revolutionary propaganda must be conducted with great earnestness to expand the political influence of the Red Army in such ways as holding mass meetings to welcome new soldiers and captured soldiers and to send off soldiers on leave and other meetings. Declarations may be distributed and representatives may be sent to attend mass meetings in the name of the soldiers' associations. . . .

Article 25. Close relationships should be established with local mass organizations at all times, and local mass organizations should be set up in places where no mass organizations exist.

Article 26. The literary standards of soldiers should be raised by running literary movements and youth schools, publishing newspapers of soldiers, discussing political issues and practicing speech making, and so on and so forth.

Article 27. Social conditions should be investigated.

Article 28. Suitable amusements for soldiers should be provided, such as organizing clubs, fraternity groups, racing, singing, games, dancing, acting, speeches, martial arts, soccer, and so on.

Article 29. Supervision of supplies and catering accounts.

Article 30. Matters of hygiene should be dealt with, for example, paying attention to the hygiene of tea and drinking water, food, clothes and barracks, keeping fit, installing latrines for the garrisoned troops, putting on more clothes, and covering well with quilts in the mornings and evenings and washing clothes and feet.

Article 31. The soldiers and officers who are ill and wounded should be comforted (sending people to carry and assist the wounded and ill officers and soldiers, fetching water for them to wash their faces, boiling tea and water for them, cleaning houses, raising funds, donating clothes and money, and helping the wounded and ill officers and soldiers). In light of actual conditions, methods of providing special treatments to them should be proposed to the military and political administrations for handling.

Article 32. Investigation and registration should be conducted of comrades who have died, and ways should be found to assist the families of those who have given their lives.

Chapter 5: Finances

Article 33.

1) The expenses of the soldiers' associations of companies are 5 *yuan* each month, those of the associations at the level of regiments, battalions, and directly attached units are 10 *yuan* each month, and funds for all these purposes shall be issued by the Political Department.

2) Members who violate the rule against gambling will have their property confiscated; 80 percent of it shall belong to the soldiers' associations of companies, and 20 percent shall belong to the associations of regiments and battalions. Every member of the soldiers' associations should hand in dues of one copper cash per month.

Chapter 6: Supplementary Articles

Article 34. If the charter of the Soldiers' Association is not satisfactory, it may be revised by the political departments upon the recommendation of over one-third of the members and the opinions of the soldiers' associations and take effect upon the approval of the general political department.

Article 35. This charter will go into force on the day of issuance.

Printed and distributed by the General
Political Department of the First Front
Army of the Red Army

Order of the First Army Group of the Red Army to Leave Yichun, Go to Futian, and Concentrate Its Forces There

(September 29, 1930, 6 P.M., at Yichun)

1. The Hunan enemy is still in the area of Laoguan, Liling, and Huangtuling, and the Dai brigade of the Jiangxi enemy[1] is already retreating from Wanzai toward Nanchang. There are reports that the troops of Deng Ying are being moved from Ji'an back to Nanchang, that the town of Ji'an is being defended by the battalion of Ma Kun moved there from Ganzhou,[2] and that one of the guards regiments near Nanchang has been sent to Ji'an. We are continuing to investigate whether or not this is true.

2. In accordance with the original plan, this army group (minus the Twelfth and Twentieth Armies) is to leave here (Yichun Town) tomorrow (the 30th), and advance past Fenyi toward Ji'an, with the intention of reaching the vicinity of the town of Fenyi (80 *li*) on the 30th, of reaching the vicinity of Lukou (60 *li*) on October 1, and of reaching the vicinity of Futian (55 *li*) on the 2nd, to assemble there.

3. The Fourth Army should have completed its departure from its present location (Xiapu) by five o'clock tomorrow morning, advance through Binjiang to Fenyi, and encamp before the town of Fenyi.

General Headquarters, the General Political Department, and the units directly under them, following after the Revolutionary Military Commission, should get up tomorrow morning at 3:30, assemble at 4:30 on the main road, and start off in this order, directly after the advancing Fourth Army.

The Third Army (minus one column), should set out tomorrow morning at

---

Our source for this document is *Jiangxi dangshi ziliao*, Vol. 6, pp. 148–149. This version is more accurate than that in *Mao Zedong ji. Bujuan*, Vol. 9, pp. 331–32, where the text is reproduced from *Dangshi ziliao* No. 3, July 1978.

1. The reference is to the forces of Dai Yue (1888–1971), *zi* Xipeng, a native of Hunan. As indicated above, in a note to the "Order to Seize the Niuhang Railway Station" of July 29, 1930, he was at this time the commander of the Fifty-second Brigade of the Eighteenth Division of the Guomindang Ninth Route Army.

2. Deng Ying was at this time the commander of the Thirteenth Division of the Nationalist army, and Ma Kun was the commander of the Thirty-fourth Brigade of the Twelfth Division of the Nineteenth Route Army. Apart from these bare facts, little is known about either of these men.

five o'clock, immediately after the units directly under the General Headquarters, reach Fenyi, and encamp in the vicinity.

4. The Third Army should send a force of column strength to Cihua to meet the personnel coming from the Yangzi Bureau of the Chinese Communist Party, and the returning company that the Third Army had previously sent to Liuyang to escort the wounded. After they meet, they should come quickly to the vicinity of Futian, and all return to their units.

5. After setting out, we shall be traveling with the General Headquarters.

Addendum:

1. Along the way, all units should listen for news of the enemy's dispositions.

2. The location of all encampments along the way shall be determined by Commander Lin Biao of the Fourth Army.

3. After the advance units reach Futian, they should mount a surprise attack and take the city of Ji'an when the opportunity offers.

Order for the First Army Group to Attack Ji'an

(October 2, 1930, 8:00 P.M., at General Headquarters in Futian)

1) Ji'an remains under the occupation of Deng Ying's forces. Ma Kun's battalion is still in Ganzhou and has not arrived in Ji['an].

2) This Army Group has decided to launch a general assault on the city of Ji'an at dawn on the 4th. It is scheduled to advance on the line of Baizitang, Sanjiaotang, and Huajia tomorrow (the 3rd), finish preparations, and wait for orders to attack the city of Ji'an. (Orders to attack and supplementary maps will be issued separately tomorrow.)

3) The Fourth Army should complete its departure from here (Futian) tomorrow morning at 6:00 o'clock, pass through Qinghu, Jiekaoxie, Qishanmiao, Huangluping, Cangkeng, Xin'an, Shentang, Zhoujiashan, and Sanheping, and take up quarters in the vicinity of Baizitang. Upon arrival at the place of encampment, officers should immediately be dispatched to reconnoiter the terrain near the Luozi Mountains outside the north gate of the city of Ji'an and prepare for the attack on the morning of the 4th.

4) The Twentieth Army should set out tomorrow morning from its current location (Nanyuan, also known as Linyuan), and advance toward the area of Hujia, Sanjiaotang, and Huajia to set up camp. Officers must be sent to reconnoiter the terrain on the line of the Zhenjun Mountains and the Tianhua Mountains west of the city of Ji'an, and prepare for the attack on the morning of the 4th.

5) The Third Column of the Third Army and the units directly attached to the General Headquarters should set off tomorrow morning (arising at 4:30) from here (Futian) at 5:30, pass through Junziting, Huyuan, Pantang, Jiangzishang, Fenggangqiao, and Tongshuping, and arrive near the front of the mountains to make camp (the place of encampment is to be designated by the adjutants of this Headquarters). The Third Column of the Third Army should also dispatch personnel to reconnoiter the terrain between the Tianhua Mountains and the

---

Our source for this document is *Jiangxi dangshi ziliao*, Vol. 6, pp. 150-51. It also appears in *Mao Zedong junshi wenji*, Vol. 1, pp. 171-72, under the title "Order for the First Army Group to Stand By to Attack Ji'an," where it is indicated that the text is reproduced from the original document in the Party archives. The two versions are virtually identical except that the names of the officers listed in this one before the signatures of Zhu and Mao are omitted from the other text.

Shen'gang Mountains, and the area around the southwest of the city, and prepare for the attack on the morning of the 4th.

6) The army headquarters of the Third Army and the First Column should hasten tomorrow (the 3rd) to encamp in the vicinity of Mawugang in front of Tongshuping, and prepare for the attack on the morning of the 4th.

7) The Twelfth Army should advance towards the Shen'gang Mountains tomorrow morning, watch for an opportunity to encamp, and prepare to attack towards the Shen'gang Mountains on the morning of the 4th. (Having accomplished this they are to attack the south gate along the river.)

8) During the advance, we shall be with the vanguard of the general headquarters.

Addendum:

1) After arriving at the place of encampment tomorrow, each unit must immediately prepare equipment for attacking the city.

2) After reconnoitering the terrain, each unit must sketch a rough map and submit it to headquarters.

3) Each unit must effectively cut the lines of communication.

4) Tomorrow each unit must find its own guides.

It is so ordered.

Team leader   Chen Shuxiang

General Headquarters espionage team
Political Commissar   Liu Guangwan
Deputy team leader   Huang Zhijin

Communications team
Political Commissar   Feng Wenbin
General Political Department, General Affairs chief   He
Central Revolutionary Committee espionage team
    chief   He Xinyun
Headquarters Adjutant Section, adjutant   Liu Jinding

Commander-in-Chief   Zhu De
and
Political Commissar   Mao Zedong

Order for the First Army Group of the Red Army to Launch a General Assault on Ji'an

(October 3, 1930, 2:00 P.M.,
at General Headquarters in Shanqian)

1) The enemy troops of Deng Ying (fewer than three regiments) are still strongly defending themselves with the help of fortifications in the suburbs of the city of Ji'an. Their position has been arranged along the line of the Luozi Mountains, the Zhenjun Mountains, the Tianhua Mountains, and Shen'gang Ridge.

2) This army group has the tasks of seizing Ji'an, destroying Deng Ying's troops, uniting the forces of the masses in southwest Jiangxi, advancing straight toward Nanchang and Jiujiang to establish political power in Jiangxi, blockading the Yangzi River, and attacking Nanjing and safeguarding the victory of the Wuhan uprising. It has been decided to launch a general assault on the city of Ji'an at dawn on the 4th, and to take the city of Ji'an before dawn on the 5th.

3) The Fourth Army constitutes the left flank, which is to attack the enemy position between the Luozi Mountains and the Zhenjun Mountains. With the road from Daxiaochang to Pantang as the demarcation line, the left side of the line (including the road) belongs to the Fourth Army and the right side of the line belongs to the Twentieth Army.

4) The Twentieth Army constitutes the main force, and is to launch feigned attacks against the enemy along the line of the Zhenjun Mountains and the Tianhua Mountains, establishing contact on the left with the Fourth Army and on the right with the Third Army. It will be under the orders of the commander of the Fourth Army, Lin Biao.

5) The Third Army (minus one column) and the Twelfth Army together constitute the right wing, and are to attack the enemy along the line of the Shen'gang Ridge and the Tianhua Mountains. With the road along the river and Taiping Bridge as the demarcation line, the area to the left belongs to the Third Army, and that to the right belongs to the Twelfth Army (not including the line). The Third Army is to secure contact to the right with the Twelfth Army and to the left with the Twentieth Army, and the Twelfth Army is to establish contact to the left with the Third Army.

Our source for this document is *Jiangxi dangshi ziliao*, Vol. 6, pp. 152–53. A less complete and less accurate version, reproduced from a collection published in China in 1980, appears in *Mao Zedong ji. Bujuan*, Vol. 3, pp. 155–56.

6) After each army has successfully carried out the attack on enemy positions, a small portion of the forces should keep watch on the enemy inside the blockhouses, and the main forces should attack the city and cut off contact between the enemies inside the city and those on the front.

7) The army group has no general reserve units and all armies should prepare their own reserve forces.

8) We are now in the Shanqian General Headquarters. At dawn on the 4th, we shall be at the mouth of the the the road near Datang (north of the Zhenjun Mountains), and on the afternoon of the 4th we shall move to the side of the river (south of the Tianhua Mountains).

Attention:

1. Each unit is to attack in the direction of the city immediately after storming the enemy positions. If there are still enemy fortifications around the city, then all surface features should be put to use, and simple bunkers should be constructed as support points, where an opportunity may be awaited to attack the city again.

2. At night all officers and soldiers attacking the city are to wear white towels or white handkerchiefs wrapped around their heads. The rest of the sentry signals, signal calls, and passwords will all be used according to the signals originally fixed by the staff office.

3. In attacking at night, bayonets should be used, so that soldiers need not open fire before enemy positions. Special attention should be paid so as not to get confused with one's own men.

4. After seizing an enemy position, a torch should be immediately raised as a signal.

5. At night, ditches should be used as much as possible to advance.

6. All troops attacking the city should go forward with all their might, and must pay no attention to the enemy's encirclement.

7. All units must strive to move forward at all times.

8. After entering the city, all officers and soldiers must strictly observe discipline, and must not take things arbitrarily.

9. After entering the city, it is forbidden to destroy communications equipment left in the city such as radios, telephones, electric lights, automobiles, and so on.

Commander-in-Chief   Zhu De

Political Commissar   Mao Zedong

A Secret Order to the First Army Group of the Red Army to Carry Out Household by Household Inspections

(October 12, 1930, at 12:00 noon, in Ji'an City)

Although we have now captured this city, there are still reactionary armed forces, as well as the AB Corps of the local bullies and bad gentry, hiding in the vicinity of the city. In order to eliminate these reactionaries completely, it is hereby ordered that household by household inspections should be carried out this night (October 12). The arrangements are as follows:

1. Inspection time: All the inspection personnel involved must be in their positions by 2:30 A.M. this night (the 12th) [i.e., on the morning of the 13th]; the inspection will commence everywhere simultaneously at 3:30 A.M.

2. Partition of the inspection area (divided into 7 districts):

a. The city proper.

b. The area that lies north of Tianhou Temple and Laifu alley, south of Xixi Bridge, and east of South Lake Bridge and Salt Bridge and along the Rivulet.

c. The area that lies south of Tianhou Temple and Laifu Alley, north of Zhupai Alley and Bansu Alley, and east of Jingfu Bridge, Wangjia Bridge, and Xiao Bridge along the rivulet.

   The abovementioned three districts are the responsibility of the Fourth Army, and constitute a single district.

d. The area that lies south of Zhupai Alley and Bansu Alley, and east of Xiao Bridge and Tiegou Bridge along the river, up to the vicinity of Malan Pagoda.

e. The area that lies west of Salt Bridge, Jingfu Bridge, Wangjia Bridge, and Xiao Bridge along the rivulet, and south of the Salt Bridge Electricity Bureau.

   The above-mentioned two districts are the responsibility of the Third Army.

f. The area that lies north of the Salt Bridge Electricity Bureau, and west of Xixi Bridge, South Lake Bridge and Salt Bridge, up to the border of the city proper.

Our source for this document is the text in *Jiangxi dangshi ziliao*, Vol. 6, pp. 158–60. No earlier version appears to be available.

This district is the responsibility of one column of the Twelfth Army.

(The water craft on each segment of the river are to be dealt with by the army unit responsible for the district bordering it.)

3. Inspection personnel. Each inspection group, composed of one squad from the army, and personnel dispatched by the General Political Department of the Government of Jiangxi Province, shall inspect the households in the district assigned to it.

4. The targets of inspection:

Reactionaries and suspected persons.

Arms and military materials.

Reactionary documents.

5. Procedures

a. Vigilance should be exercised while the inspection is taking place:

Guards are to be posted by the Fourth Army at the entry to all roads at Sansi Shoal, North Gate Bridge, Tung Tree Stockade, XX and Long Pond. Traffic is to be cut off beginning at nightfall tonight.

b. Subdivision of the inspection area.

The terrain of each district should be reconnoitered by high-ranking officers sent out by the relevant division, who further subdivide the district into smaller areas and designate those units which are to be responsible for them.

c. Beginning the inspection.

All the teams sent out by each unit should arrive at the areas for which they are responsible by 2:30 A.M., wait until 3:30 A.M., and commence the inspection simultaneously.

6. Point for attention during the inspection:

No seizure of property is allowed. Upon completion of the inspection, the company commander and the political instructor of each company shall make a body search of their officers and soldiers.

Houses in which inspection has been completed should be marked "checked" with chalk on the door, in order to avoid repeated inspection.

Commander-in-chief	Zhu De
Political Commissar	Mao Zedong

Order to the First Army Group of the Red Army to Move Its Forces to the North and Concentrate Them in Qingjiang

(October 13, 1930, 1:00 P.M., at General Headquarters in Ji'an City)

1. The main force of our enemy in Jiangxi Province, the troops of Lu Diping, is located near Nanchang; the main force of Deng Ying's troops is in Zhangshu, and Dai Yue's troops are in Gaoan. Our Third Army Group is in the region of Qingjiang and Sanhu.

2. Our army group has the mission of attacking Nanchang and Jiujiang, annihilating the enemy army of Lu Diping, seizing political power in the whole of Jiangxi Province, safeguarding the victory of the uprising in Wuhan to the left, and attacking Nanjing to the right, so as to promote a direct revolutionary [situation] in the whole country. We have decided to begin moving our forces northward tomorrow, and in four days' travel, by two routes, to arrive in the vicinity of Qingjiang and concentrate our forces.

3. The Third Army will take the left route, via Futian–Pengpo–Anhe–Pengjiazhou (cross the river to Luofang), and concentrate its forces in the vicinity of Shanqianjie.

The Fourth Army will take the right route, via Sanqutan–Xiajiang *xian*–Changpai–Jiefu, arriving in Qingjiang to concentrate its forces. The above two armies should set out from here (Ji'an) tomorrow morning (the 14th), and must arrive at their destinations by the 17th. (Marching plans are to be made independently.)

The Twelfth Army (minus the Second Column) and all organs of units directly attached to General Headquarters will set out on the right route, following the Central Revolutionary Military Commission, on the morning of the day after tomorrow (the 15th). The intention is to spend the night at Sanqutan on the first day, to stop in Xiajiang *xian* on the second day, to reach the vicinity of Changpai and Jiefu on the third day, and to arrive at the *xian* seat of Qingjiang on the fourth day (times of departure will be communicated separately by the Staff Office). The Second Column of the Twelfth Army will cross the river from Jishui to Sanqutan on the west bank on the 15th, and march ahead of General

---

Our source for this order is *Jiangxi dangshi ziliao*, Vol. 6, pp. 161–62.

Headquarters and the Twelfth Army. The Twentieth Army will follow behind.

4. During the march, our position will be that of General Headquarters.

Addendum: General Headquarters of the Third Army is in charge of allocating areas of encampment at Qingjiang.

It is so ordered.

> Acting brigade leader of the transportation brigade of General Headquarters   Huang Zhijin
>
> Brigade leader of the engineering brigade of General Headquarters   Yang Zaikui
>
> Director of the general affairs office of the General Political Department   He Ducai
>
> Leader of the espionage team of General Headquarters   Wang Jie
>
> Leader of the espionage team of the Front Committee   He Jinliang
>
> Adjutant of General Headquarters   Liu Jinding
>
> Commander-in-chief   Zhu De
>
> Political Commissar   Mao Zedong

Letter to the Central Committee

(October 14, 1930, at night, in the city of Ji'an)

To the Southern Bureau, for transmission to the Central Committee:

1. I expect you have already received the letter sent on September 17th from the Front Committee of the First Army Group in Liling to the Central Committee via the Hunan Provincial Committee and the West Fujian Special Committee, and the letter sent on September 26th from the Front Committee of the First Front Army in Anyuan to the Central Committee via the Hunan Provincial Committee, which recounted the course of the attack on Changsha, together with our assessment of the situation, and plans for action. On the way from Anyuan to Yuanzhou, we have conducted a few more discussions regarding problems of the actions [to be taken], and have once again determined that [the goal of] our current actions is to seize political power in Jiangxi, to occupy the Nanchang-Jiujiang Railroad and attack Nanchang and Jiujiang, and then to blockade the Yangzi River, to attack Nanjing on the right, and to guarantee victory in Wuhan on the left. Just as we were all packed up and about to set out from Yuanzhou, Comrade Zhou Yili, who had been sent by the Yangzi Bureau, arrived there. After hearing Comrade Zhou's report, we had another detailed discussion that resulted once more in the decision to seize political power in Jiangxi. The First Army Group is to attack and take Ji'an within a very short time, establish the Soviet Government of Jiangxi Province, recruit new soldiers, procure provisions, and so on. For its part, the Third Army Group is to occupy the *xian* seat of Qingjiang and its vicinity, blockade the Gan River, procure funds, mobilize the masses, reorganize and replenish its ranks, and so on.

2. The entire First Army Group reached the vicinity of Ji'an on October 3rd, and before dawn on October 4th, with the collaboration of over 100,000 of the masses from western Jiangxi Province, it began to attack Ji'an. The forces besieged in the city of Ji'an—Deng Ying's troops, a brigade of Jiangxi Provincial police, and others—amounting to approximately four brigades, retreated that same evening under cover of night, and our army broke through the barbed wire fence that evening and entered the city. As a result, we failed to wipe out the enemy and capture their arms, and this is most regrettable. Although from a military point of view, the victory of the Ji'an uprising on this occasion did not

---

Our source for this letter is *Jiangxi dangshi ziliao*, Vol. 6, pp. 163–66. No other version appears to be available.

lead to the destruction of the main force of the enemy army or to the capture of a large quantity of guns (we did, however, seize over a hundred guns in the river), from a political point of view the achievements were nevertheless not inconsiderable. The victory of the Ji'an uprising undoubtedly marks the final destruction of rule by the despotic gentry, the warlords, and the Guomindang in southwest Jiangxi, the completion of a local uprising in southwest Jiangxi, the beginning of initial victory in the whole of Jiangxi Province, and an excellent occasion for the bold expansion of the Red Army. The first day we entered the city, the Revolutionary Committee of Chinese Workers and Peasants put up posters promulgating the significance of the victory of the Ji'an uprising. As regards the tasks of the revolutionary masses in Jiangxi Province, more than ten provisional regulations were promulgated by the Southwest Jiangxi Soviet Government (the content is to call upon the masses to eliminate the reactionaries and so on). The Southwest Jiangxi Soviet Government also issued regulations for the enforcement of martial law. Plans to pursue the retreating enemy were also immediately discussed, and troops were sent out immediately to pursue the enemy along the two routes of the Jishui and the Xiajiang. As for procuring funds, the Financial Administration Committee of the Southwest Jiangxi Soviet Government was put in charge. Positions were filled equally by personnel from the General Political Department of the First Front Army and personnel from the local governments. The method employed for procurement is that, based on investigation by the Financial Administration Committee, stores with assets in excess of 2000 *yuan* are enlisted for contribution, the amount based on their progressive taxes (those with assets of less than 2000 *yuan* are exempt). The total amount of the procurement will be over 600,000 *yuan* (however, it cannot all be collected quickly, and to date, only 240,000 *yuan* have been received). Regarding the elimination of the reactionaries, relatively comprehensive work has been done this time, and no reactionaries hanging around in the town of Ji'an have been able to flee, although they haven't all been completely rooted out so far. Now we are still actively mobilizing urban workers to carry out this task.

3. As for the establishment of the Soviet Government of Jiangxi Province, the General Front Committee convened an enlarged session of the Southwest Jiangxi Special Committee to decide on a list of names, which was then approved by a mass meeting. There were fifty-three nominees in all, including local revolutionary leaders as well as those from the Red Army, and leaders of the Ji'an workers (relatively few leaders of the workers of Jingdezhen and Jiujiang, and revolutionary leaders from Northeast Jiangxi are included, for we are less familiar with them). The Provincial Soviet was already established on October 7th, and various resolutions were passed by the meeting, including the following: (1) Launch attacks on Nanchang and Jiujiang, (2) Enlarge the Red Army to 1,000,000. (3) Resolutely oppose the rich peasants, and guarantee the success of land redistribution. The following documents were issued: (1) A letter to the Soviet Union. (2) A letter to the proletariat of the whole world. (3) A letter to the revolutionary

masses of the whole country about striving for the victory of the revolution throughout the country. Moreover, in response to instructions in the letter of August 29th from the Central Committee for us to issue a proclamation to those outside [the Party], the Government issued another proclamation, announcing its establishment, and proclaiming thirteen articles of its political program. We are sending a clean copy of each of these documents upward [to the Central Committee]. Please let us know your directives. (Note:[1] only the letter regarding resolutely launching attacks on Nanchang and Jiujiang and the proposal to all revolutionary masses in the country to strive for the nationwide victory of the revolution were received.)

4. As for the arrangement of the work in the province after the Ji'an uprising, the Jiangxi Provincial Action Committee, made up of Comrade Li Wenlin and 12 other people, set up at an enlarged session convened by the General Front Committee, with the participation of local Party branches, will deal with this. It has been decided to establish West Jiangxi, South Jiangxi, East Jiangxi, Northeast Jiangxi, and Northwest Jiangxi action committees. The Provincial Action Committee and the Provincial Soviet will advance northward with the army. In addition to the action committee within the Party in west Jiangxi, a west Jiangxi office of the Provincial Soviet has also been set up to direct the work in Jiangxi. For the purpose of rooting out residual counterrevolutionary forces, continuing to recruit new soldiers, and so on, about 200 additional people have been organized to go northward to carry out this work, and to cooperate with the Red Army in its uprising.

5. Recently the entire Party in southwest Jiangxi has been showing signs of a very serious crisis. The entire Party leadership is dominated by the rich peasants' line, and the slogan about transforming the consciousness of the peasants is being exploited by the rich peasants and landlords to oppose the poor peasants and farm laborers, or even to undermine the trend of equal land distribution in southwest Jiangxi. A large number of AB Corps members have been found in the organs of the Special Committees of both the Party and the Youth League, the Soviet Government of southwest Jiangxi, and the Red Army School respectively. A majority of the leading organs at all levels, both internal and external, are leading organs filled with AB Corps members and rich peasants. Thus, the equal distribution of land means merely "taking from the plentiful to make up for the scarce," but not "taking from the fat to make up for the lean."[2] As a result, the rich peasants have obtained good land, and the farm laborers and poor peasants remain oppressed. So the land is being redistributed once again, to serve the

---

1. In the Chinese text, this note is attributed to *xin* ("heart"). We do not know whether this is a code word for the Central Committee, the Yangzi Bureau, or some other editor.

2. As indicated above, in a note to the land law of August 1930, Mao himself had only very recently discovered this second principle. In February 1930 he had called only for quantitative redistribution.

interests of the farm laborers and poor peasants, to repress the rich peasants, to eliminate rich peasant leadership, and to get rid of the AB Corps. Without a basic transformation of the Party in southwest Jiangxi, this crisis can assuredly not be overcome. At present the General Front Committee is engaged in planning this work but, because of obstacles to our action, the task may not be accomplished very well. The Central Committee must pay careful attention to this matter, and offer assistance.

6. The Twentieth Army in west Jiangxi has recruited over 3,000 men, with more than 1,700 guns. Recently, the Twenty-second Army in south Jiangxi has also developed substantially. We are preparing to have the whole Twentieth Army work in Ji'an for a short time before advancing northward. The Twenty-second Army will attack Ganzhou, or make arrangements for an uprising in Ganzhou, and then proceed northward.

7. This time, while we were in Ji'an, we enlisted 8,000 new soldiers. This reinforcement is far from adequate, and because the local party branches are carrying out a rich peasant line, the number previously set cannot be achieved. This problem is extremely serious. After our departure, we left an office in Ji'an to continue enlisting new soldiers. It is predicted that by the end of this year, at least twenty independent regiments can be recruited to send to the front. This plan is closely linked to correct leadership by the Party in southwest Jiangxi. This goal can be realized only after the Party in southern Jiangxi has undergone a transformation.

8. We are convinced by experience that the more imminent the decisive battle between the classes, the more indispensable is preparation in terms of military technology. Because there was no one to use the radios captured during the occupation of Changsha by the Third Army Group and during the attacks on Ji'an by the First Army Group, we have lost numerous opportunities to wipe out the enemy. In addition, we must request the Central Committee to give us assistance in obtaining military equipment and trained personnel for items such as guns to shoot to high altitudes (used against airplanes), cannons, poisonous gases and masks against them, and so on, for only thus can we successfully prepare for this decisive class war against the imperialists and the Nationalist warlords.

9. The decision of the Politburo of the Central Committee in June and the letter from the Central Committee to the Front Committee of the Fourth Army were not received until recently.[3] We have discussed them in detail, together with the political report presented by Comrade Zhou,[4] and the letter from the

---

3. The reference is to the resolution of June 11, which constitutes the fullest and most extreme expression of the Li Lisan Line, and the letter of June 15, 1930, to the Fourth Army. For summaries of these two documents, see above, the Introduction to this volume.

4. The reference must be to Zhou Enlai's report to the Politburo on August 22 and 24, 1930, immediately after his return from Moscow. For a summary of the report and the discussion which followed it, see Jin Chongji, *Zhou Enlai*, pp. 219–20.

Central Committee dated August 29th.[5] We consider that all the instructions from the Central Committee are completely correct, and we accept them all.[6] Decisions (which will be sent in a few days) have already been made to carry them out. We have also read lately, in the Western Fujian *Red Report*, the recent declaration of the Central Committee. The Front Committee considers that the twenty-nine political principles put forward by the Central Committee are entirely correct and will carry them out immediately.[7]

10. The Third and Fourth Armies of the First Army Group set out from Ji'an today. General Headquarters and the Twelfth Army will have completed their departure tomorrow. They can be expected to arrive at Qingjiang by October 18th, where they will be joined by the Fifth and Eighth Armies, seize the Nanchang-Jiujiang Railroad, and launch an attack on Nanchang. In that area, there will be a great decisive battle.

11. As regards fund-raising by the Central Committee, we have decided to pay 100,000 *yuan* in gold and 50,000 *yuan* by cash remittance.

General Secretary of the Front Committee of
the First Army of the Red Army   Mao Zedong

---

5. The full text of this letter, addressed to the Yangzi Bureau, for transmittal to the Hunan Provincial Committee, does not appear to be available. For a summary of the contents, see *Jiangxi dangshi ziliao*, Vol. 6, p. 286.

6. This statement is perplexing, to say the least. The first two documents Mao mentions, the resolution of June 11 and the letter of June 15, are marked by unqualified optimism and radicalism. In them, Mao's tactics of creating base areas are stigmatized as entirely erroneous, and there is a call for an offensive against Wuhan, to take advantage of the crisis of world capitalism, and achieve rapid victory. Zhou Enlai's report of August 22–24, and the letter of August 29, marked the first stage in Zhou's efforts, following the instructions which he had received in Moscow, to rein in Li Lisan's revolutionary extravagance. In them, Li's previous condemnation of establishing bases as a conservative tactic is explicitly condemned, and it is laid down that for the time being, an attack against Wuhan would be premature. These two pairs of documents were not totally contradictory, but it is hard to understand how Mao could regard all four of them as "completely correct." Perhaps this should be taken as one more instance of Mao's skill at understanding only those aspects of the documents he received which it suited his purposes to understand.

7. The reference is to the declaration issued by the Central Committee on August 14, and published in *Hongqi ribao* on the following day. (For the text, see *Central Committee Documents*, 1930, pp. 250–65.) The twenty-nine points listed in paragraph 5 of this document, under the heading "The Demands of the Chinese Revolution," range from overthrowing imperialism and the Guomindang, establishing a nationwide soviet government, and repudiating unequal treaties to creating peasant cooperatives, establishing equality between men and women, and instituting free public education.

Letter to the Eastern Hunan Special Committee

(October 19, 1930)

To the Eastern Hunan Special Committee:

Your letter of September has been received today at Xiajiang.[1] In all, we have received three letters from you dated prior to September. We made a general reply on the 15th, and hope that you will have received that letter.[2]

Your September letter says that the Central Committee, the provincial committee, and the Yangzi Bureau all sent us letters which were delivered to us. But we have not received them to date, and do not know where they were sent from and went astray.[3] We are most concerned. If you have kept copies, we hope you will copy them again and send them to us as soon as possible.

As for the problem of new soldiers, it would be best if you could send five thousand by the end of this month. We hope that you will step up your efforts at propaganda and agitation, so as to recruit this number of new soldiers or even more. As regards the method of transportation, you should also correspond with the office of the Revolutionary Committee of the Workers and Peasants in Ji'an. We have set up an office in Ji'an, with Mao Zetan as the director and Wan as his deputy. Internally, a Committee of the Rear has been established with Mao Zetan as secretary. The task of the Committee of the Rear is to recruit and transfer new soldiers and to make clothes. You should correspond with the Committee of the Rear concerning the issue of sending new soldiers.

Our source for this document is *Mao Zedong ji. Bujuan*, Vol. 3, pp. 157–58, where the text is reproduced from a documentary collection published in China in 1981. The letter can also be found in *Jiangxi dangshi ziliao*, Vol. 6, pp. 169–70.

1. The reference may be to a missive accompanying the text of a letter from the Central Committee dated September 4, which had been sent to the Yangzi Bureau with the request that it be transmitted to the Front Committee. This letter indicated that, if it had proved impossible to carry out the plans outlined in the Central Committee's directive of August 29 for taking Changsha and destroying He Jian's main force, the Red Army could turn toward Jiangxi and develop its action there. (See the summary in *Jiangxi dangshi ziliao*, Vol. 6, pp. 287–88.)

2. The reference is probably to the letter to the Central Committee translated above, written on the night of October 14.

3. As indicated above, in the Introduction to this volume, Zhou Yili, the emissary of the Yangzi Bureau, had brought to Mao and Zhu on September 29 the letter of August 29 from the Central Committee ordering a renewed attack on Changsha. Thus Mao and his comrades had in fact received at least one letter from higher Party authorities "dated prior to September," but no information is available about the other two letters which had "gone astray."

The General Front Committee arrived at Xiajiang on the 17th of this month, held a plenary meeting here, and adopted resolutions on the assessment of the situation, the question of action, the land question, and the question of capital. As regards the situation, we believe that the chaotic fighting among the warlords of the ruling class will definitely not subside or stop for the time being, but it will also not continue to expand to the extreme. This is to say that under the increasingly tense conditions of the Chinese revolutionary situation, all factions of the reactionary ruling class feel the necessity for a reformist political program. But the question of the leadership of this reformist political régime certainly cannot be resolved by peaceful means. In the near future, a warlord war will undoubtedly break out cruelly. But on the other hand, we should never depart from class analysis and believe that the fighting of the warlords will expand further and continue to the end. It should be understood that when class contradictions surpass the internal contradictions of the ruling class, the reactionary ruling class will inevitably unite to attack the revolution. But we must absolutely not give way to pessimism, because this is a manifestation of the revolutionary high tide. Therefore, our task is to win initial victory in one province, continue to develop and expand such victories, and break through and destroy the allied offensives of the reactionaries before the ruling class settles the issue of the leadership of the reform. Our action at present is to go forward and occupy the Nanchang-Jiujiang Railroad, attack Nanchang and Jiujiang, and annihilate the enemy. The whole army group is scheduled to set out from Xiajiang tomorrow and the day after tomorrow and advance toward the Nanchang-Jiujiang railroad. As regards the land question, we maintain that complete and equal redistribution must be carried out, and that this is the only correct policy. Only by confiscating everything and redistributing it equally can the broad masses of poor peasants be won over, feudal exploitation be overthrown completely, and a future advance toward the victory of socialism be guaranteed. As for the problem of capital, we hold that it is wrong at present to confiscate all factories and shops unconditionally. We should confiscate the shops of counterrevolutionaries, and the factories and shops of warlords and bureaucratic capital. In dealing with capital that does not violate the labor laws of the soviet régime, we should use the method of workers supervising capital to restrict it and overcome its plots and conspiracies (transferring capital, going slow, and not fulfilling orders). These are a few simple words of explanation. For a detailed explanation, please consult the letter of Comrade Zhou Yili, representative of the Yangzi Bureau.[4]

> Secretary of the General Front Committee of the First Front Army
>
> Mao Zedong
>
> Xiajiang *xian*, on the night of October 19.

---

4. For the text of this letter, likewise dated October 19, 1930, see *Jiangxi dangshi ziliao*, pp. 171–73.

Resolution on the Land Problem of the Joint Conference of the General Front Committee and the Jiangxi Provincial Action Committee

(October 19, 1930)[1]

1. The Land Problem Is the Main Content of the Chinese Revolution at Present

The present democratic stage of the revolution consists mainly in opposition to the feudal forces. The land revolution thoroughly destroys the economic basis of feudalism. We must make the land revolution penetrate deeply, for only thus will it be possible to eliminate the domination of the warlord system and of imperialism, only thus can the broad masses of the bitterly poor peasantry be liberated, only thus will the proletariat be able to draw the hundreds of millions of bitterly poor peasant masses into a solid alliance, and win victory for the Chinese revolution. The Red Army was born from the struggles of the land revolution, and it will assuredly assume responsibility for the whole of the proletarian revolution, but if at present it becomes divorced from the land revolution, to the point of

Our source for this document is *Mao Zedong ji. Bujuan*, Vol. 9, pp. 333–45, where the text is reproduced from a documentary collection published in China in 1981. It also appears in *Jiangxi dangshi ziliao*, Vol. 6, pp. 174–84.

1. In the *Mao Zedong ji. Bujuan*, this text is dated October 19; in the *Jiangxi dangshi ziliao*, it is dated simply October. The "joint conference" mentioned in the title took place from October 25 to November 1, 1930. (See the note to the text of October 26, 1930.) It was preceded by a conference of the Front Committee alone, convened by Mao on October 17. This gathering adopted resolutions on several of the same topics discussed at the joint conference, and a chronology in *Jiangxi dangshi ziliao*, Vol. 6, p. 292, indicates that the line taken on the peasant question was entirely in harmony with the text translated here. A plausible explanation for the problem of the date is therefore that the present text was adopted on October 17, issued on October 19, and then laid before the joint conference the following week in the same or very similar form. In any case, one of Mao's primary concerns in October 1930 was to justify his own line regarding the land problem. This accounts for the very sharp attacks on the Party organs in southwestern Jiangxi, which were dominated by Li Lisan's supporters. The statement, in section 2 of this resolution, that two-thirds of their leading personnel are members of the AB or Anti-Bolshevik Corps marks a further escalation of the conflict. (On the AB Corps and the political context in general see above, the Introduction to this volume.)

neglecting the correct implementation of the land revolution, it will no longer be the Red Army, and it will be even more difficult to enlarge the Red Army and to create a Red Army of steel. It is only the liquidationists who, lacking a basic understanding of the antifeudal forces, would want to discard the land revolution.

2. The Crisis in Revolutionary Work

The present soviet districts include many places where the insurrections are not yet complete or which can only be occupied temporarily by guerrilla actions. In southeastern Hubei, even today, we do not have a single *xian* town, and the phenomenon of opposing White and Red forces is a serious situation everywhere. Not only is this true, but there are even many Red districts in which the masses are revolutionary today and defect tomorrow. In the soviet district of eastern Hubei, the Reorganization Clique has developed in a big way, and has put down the uprising. In southwestern Jiangxi, the AB Corps has filled the special committees of both the Party and Youth League, to the point that two-thirds of the personnel of the leading organs of the southwestern Jiangxi soviet government and of the technical workers are AB Corps elements. All levels of the Party and Youth League and soviets, and even the Red Army schools, the Red Guards, and the Red postal service, are filled with the organizations of the AB Corps, carrying out assassinations, preparing to make contact with the army of Deng Ying, and plotting a revolt to eliminate the soviets and the various revolutionary organizations—these problems have become so serious that they merit the close scrutiny of every one of our comrades. We must analyze the origins of these crises and resolutely overcome them. The major causes of these crises are the rich peasant line and opportunism within the land revolution.

3. The Rich Peasant Line and Opportunism Within the Land Revolution

A. Dividing the Land and Not Dividing the Land

The facts have taught us that wherever the land is really divided equally, it is possible to arouse the broad popular masses and firmly establish a revolutionary base. In most cases, it is possible to complete the local uprisings, as in western Fujian and in such *xian* as Yongxin and Xingguo (the second time was more thorough). Whenever the mistake is made of following the rich peasant line and not dividing the land, not only are the local uprisings not completed but it is even impossible to eliminate the opposition between White and Red. In Guangji, in eastern Hubei, the land has not been divided, and the Communist Party and local bullies peacefully coexist in the revolutionary district, with the result that as soon as the White terror arrives, the defections are really terrible. In Anfu, rich peasant elements saw to it that the land was not divided, with the result that most people defected, bringing about a grave betrayal of the revolution. In only two districts, District One and District Three, which were close to and influenced by the land division at Yongxin and did divide the land, did the peasants stoutly resist the counterrevolutionary attacks. In those places in Yongxin and Xiajiang *xian* where the land was completely divided, there are very few from the AB Corps. In Taihe, Xingguo, Jishui, and even in Dayi and Yangxin of the Longxian district of eastern Hubei, wherever the land was not divided completely, if it didn't give rise to a serious AB Corps, then the Reorganization Clique emerged; wherever the land was divided completely, large Red Armies were formed, as in Yongxin, otherwise they could not be mobilized. Why is it that not completely dividing the land equally is so serious? Because the main policy of the antifeudal forces is the land revolution. At present the land revolution must divide the land, and divide it equally and quickly. Only in the struggle to divide the land truly equally can the feudal forces be completely eliminated, and a revolutionary base be established. But how is our land revolution carried out? Brandishing the Red flag, and not dividing the land for three years, for one year, for half a year, is a more or less universal phenomenon in the Red districts of southwestern Jiangxi, of the East River area, of eastern Hubei, of western Hubei, of western Hunan, and even of Jiangsu and Zhejiang. A large number of Red Army and guerrilla units have not paid attention to this problem. This is not just opportunism, it is quite simply the landlord line. By not standing on the side of the poor suffering peasants and representing their desire to divide the land, such failure to divide the land in reality preserves the landlord system. They even go so far as to use the excuses that there must be a detailed investigation with full statistics, that the land that has been planted with young rice plants cannot be divided, and that if it is divided, then the peasant who originally planted it should receive two-thirds of the grain, and the poor peasant who has been given the field should receive one-third, the two and one split (as in Daye). Or they just allocate a bit of the land any old way (in part of Yangxin), or carry out only drawing on the plentiful to make up for the scarce, but not drawing on the fat to make up for the lean. Wherever such rich peasant lines as these exist, they are an obstacle to the progress of the land revolution. Thus, not only can the broad masses of the impoverished peasants not be mobilized to complete the local uprising but also, when the land revolution makes the despotic gentry and landlords run away, eliminates high rents and heavy interest rates, and does away with harsh fees and miscellaneous taxes, if the land is not completely redistributed, in reality those who profit the most are just the rich peasants. Consequently, it is impossible to promote class confrontation between the broad masses of the bitterly poor peasants and the rich peasants, and impossible to establish the revolutionary authority of the poor suffering peasant masses, recognize the true face of the vicious plots of the rich peasants, and suppress the reactionary actions of the rich peasants. On the contrary, the right to lead the land revolution is taken over by the rich peasants. The rich peasants take over the soviets, the Red Guards, and the Party, and use them for the interests of the rich peasant class, to oppress the poor peasants, and then go on to organize the AB Corps, the Reorganization Clique, and the Third Party, to put down the uprisings and betray the revolution. This is precisely the main root cause for not dividing the land equally and resolutely opposing the rich peasants, thus leaving behind a foundation for the activities of the counterrevolutionaries, and of the serious crises that have occurred in the soviet districts.

B. The Opportunist Line

Formulations of the rich peasant line mentioned above, such as the "land allocation method" or the "two and one split," are clearly and obviously proposals of the rich peasants for obstructing the land revolution, and could have been rejected. But because the Party itself fell prey to the formulas of the opportunist line and rationalized them—a very subtle rich peasant line—it not only could not reject these rich peasant proposals but, on the contrary, lent its assistance to developing the proposals of the rich peasants. What kind of opportunist line is this? It makes use of the argument that dividing the land corresponds to peasant consciousness to oppose dividing the land equally. Dividing the land [they argue] is a capitalist fantasy that goes against the socialist future. If you divide the land, this will contribute to the concept of private ownership among the peasantry and is incompatible with the objectives of communism. Therefore, do not put forward the proposal to divide the land or listen to peasant self-determination. Using developing production as their argument, they oppose dividing equally according to population and propose using the criterion of labor power in distributing the land. Using the principle of the democratic stage of the revolution, they oppose all confiscation, because any confiscation would threaten the middle peasant. If these arguments do not come from those who consciously stand on the right (the rich peasant elements in the villages who use the excuse that the Sixth Congress of the Communist Party criticized equal distribution as a petty bourgeois fantasy to oppose equal distribution), then they are empty theoretical speculations that ignore reality. These empty unrealistic speculations seem on the surface to be an ultraleftist defense of socialism, but in reality, being rationalizations for the rich peasants, they constitute the ultrarightist rich peasant line.

C. The Roots of the Errors of This Line

They lie in not understanding that, in China, with its backward semifeudal agricultural economy, the land revolution must go through the process of redistribution, that the Chinese agricultural economy is mainly a small peasant economy, and that whether farmed by tenant farmers or by those who own the land themselves, it is cut up into extremely small economic units and tilled by peasant masses of several hundred millions using Chinese plows. There is virtually no (European-style) landlord economy, and capitalist-type farms are few indeed. It is for this reason that the land revolution does not immediately join all these very small economic units together to carry out socialist collective farm production.

Economic conditions do not allow this, and consequently it must be recognized that when the land revolution begins, the small peasant economy will still be the main form of production, and that the land must be redistributed to the peasants. Furthermore, because those among the peasant masses who have no land or very little land everywhere constitute the vast majority in the countryside, in the south over 70 percent, when the movement for land revolution begins, this kind of redistribution must start with complete confiscation and equal redistribution. Only this will satisfy the needs of the masses. Therefore, the last congress[2] already pointed out that in those places where there were a lot of unemployed and poor suffering peasants, it was necessary to have a movement to "divide the land equally," and that when this slogan was supported by the majority of the peasant masses, the Communist Party should defend it, because this is a slogan for thoroughly eliminating all vestiges of feudalism, and also directly undermines private ownership. All this was resolved theoretically long ago. The Chinese land revolution has already been in progress for two or three years, and we should make further use of the actual lessons of these two or three years to understand this problem.

In fact, so long as the peasants do not rise up and divide the land, things can remain like this, but when they do rise up they will everywhere demand that it be divided equally.

In fact, it is not enough just to confiscate the land of the landlords, it is essential to confiscate all the land even of the rich peasants, because the amount of land they hold, in the various southern provinces, is barely less that of the landlords, and furthermore, most of it is very fertile land. If it is not totally confiscated it is not possible to satisfy the demands of the broad masses of bitterly poor peasants. Thus, in the Northern Route area of Xiajiang and Ji'an, the land was divided several times, but it was only when, finally, all the rich peasant lands had been confiscated and there was an equal distribution that it could be considered completed. In fact, it is a characteristic of the Chinese rich peasant that he engages in severe semifeudal exploitation, no different from the landlord class. From their first cunning tricks until their betrayal is crushed, from beginning to end, they are counterrevolutionary. Unless the land is divided equally, it is impossible from the very beginning to separate a village along a class line of fire in which the impoverished peasant masses are opposed to the rich peasant class, and there is no way to set up a leadership of farm laborers to suppress the reaction of the rich peasants. Any so-called firm opposition to the rich peasants that does not confiscate their land is just empty talk. The fact is that the masses are already marching forward, and that they want everything to be confiscated, while the Party is still mired in the principle of the democratic stage, confiscating only the land of the landlord class, not daring to suggest confiscating everything. But the masses are already confiscating everything, so the Party also says that when the masses demand that everything be confiscated, the Party should not

---

2. I.e., the Sixth Congress of June 1928.

oppose it. How liquidationist this is, not even grasping the tail, just letting the rich peasants lead without fighting for the more than 70 percent constituted by the impoverished peasant masses. In fact, not only will complete confiscation not upset the middle peasants but most of the middle peasants will, on the contrary, receive a share of the land to be divided, as was the case in the Xingguo Tenth District. Although in some places a small number of the middle peasants will inevitably have to give up a little bit, in the face of the revolutionary prestige of the broad masses of the bitterly poor peasants who want to confiscate everything, the middle peasants will feel that all oppressive exploitation has already been eliminated, that the rich peasants can do nothing, much less the landlords, that everyone is equal, and that giving up a little bit is right (as with the middle peasants of Jinjiang in Yangxin *xian*). In other words, it is only the great authority possessed by the impoverished peasant masses that can lay hold of the middle peasants under the conditions of mounting a fierce attack on the landlords, and it is only dividing the land equally that is the best technique for doing so. If the bitterly poor peasant masses are still eking out a living under the rich peasants, and the rich peasants can still exercise power over them, you cannot even think of forming or consolidating an alliance with the middle peasants.

In fact, there are at least two kinds of so-called peasant consciousness: rich peasant consciousness and poor peasant consciousness. Rich peasant consciousness advocates not dividing, while the poor peasants demand dividing equally. To say that dividing the land equally corresponds to peasant consciousness, and that if you want to oppose peasant consciousness, just don't divide the land, is precisely to oppose poor peasant consciousness and to represent rich peasant consciousness. Dividing the land equally is, of course, not socialist consciousness, but at present it truly plays a great revolutionary role and is historically significant in shattering the feudal system and in moving toward socialism. In the past, the Russian Mensheviks criticized Lenin for advocating equal land distribution, saying that this went against socialism. Lenin replied, "Equal distribution has an historical revolutionary role to play that the Mensheviks do not understand." The Sixth Congress pointed out that equal distribution is a petty bourgeois fantasy of socialism that must be criticized by the Party, but it definitely did not reject equal distribution, or oppose it. The Sixth Congress put it very clearly: "We should support the slogan of equal distribution of land but should also criticize it . . . in order to make the peasants understand fully that under the present capitalist system true peace is absolutely impossible. Only after the victory of the proletariat will true socialist reconstruction be possible."[3] This means

---

3. This is a quotation from the "Resolution on the Peasant Question" adopted by the Sixth Congress of the Chinese Communist Party on July 9, 1928. For a nearly complete translation of this document, see Saich, *Rise to Power*, Doc. C.12, pp. 369-76. Mao's citation is accurate, except that equality (*pingdeng*) has been replaced by peace (*heping*) in the statement ". . . under the present capitalist system true equality is absolutely impossible." This must be a copyist's error.

that the job of equal distribution must be done, while at the same time it is necessary to do the job of criticism. The opportunist gentlemen just sit there wasting their breath criticizing. Since they have not yet carried out equal distribution, what are they are criticizing? As for the opposition to expanding the Red Army, the opposition to expanding outward, and the failure to concentrate military forces, all these are the rich peasant ideology. It is the poor peasants who are thoroughly toppling the feudal forces, who are actively expanding outward. At present, to smash conservative ideas, we must concentrate on "opposing rich peasant consciousness"; we definitely cannot sweepingly oppose peasant consciousness and suppress that part of the consciousness of the poor peasants that is very revolutionary (dividing the land equally and opposing the rich peasants). Of course, the Communist Party must establish the leadership of proletarian consciousness (such as criticizing equal distribution) and cannot become bogged down in poor peasant ideology.

In fact, using the so-called development of production and labor power as the criteria for distributing the land is precisely the demand of the rich peasants. The rich peasants count farm implements, fertilizer, seed, and ox power as labor power, and it is only the rich peasants who have the most labor power, who have the best conditions for developing production. The rich peasants say that the poor peasants don't have anything, that if they are given more fields they will lie idle, and therefore the rich peasants use the revolutionary placard of developing production best to obtain a lot of land, while the poor peasants, who are most urgently in need of land, are still unable to solve the problem of a shortage of land. Furthermore, using labor power as a criterion permits not counting capital, but the elderly, the young, and women, having little or no labor power, would be given little of the land distributed. But they certainly do not consume less, and at times they even have to hire peasants to till the fields, and even though they don't have enough to eat they have to pay the wages. How are they to maintain their livelihoods? In the present struggle developing production is not the main thing; only winning over the popular masses is an urgent necessity. It is only by arousing the broad poor peasant masses, thoroughly overthrowing the feudal forces, and winning victory for the revolution nationwide that we can talk about developing production. In reality, the poor peasants divide the land in order to eat. When the entire labor power of a family, male and female, young and old, is used on the land, not only does the land not lie idle but its productivity is already increased—as proved by the harvest this year in western Fujian, which was 20 percent higher than before the revolution.

In fact, when concrete proposals for confiscating and distributing the land are not put forward, in accordance with what is called letting the masses decide, the result usually is that they are manipulated by the rich peasants, and not only is the land not divided equally, it is not even divided at all. This was the case in Anfu. What is called letting the masses decide means to accept the correct demands of the masses. Everywhere the masses have already demanded confiscation of all the land and its equal redistribution. Thus the Party should firmly suggest confiscating all the land and dividing it equally, and see to it that the broad popular masses get resolute leadership, and the rich peasants are not able to carry out their cheating schemes. The Communist Party no longer has any reason to say that distributing the land is not an ultimate objective of the Communist Party, and just sit back and let the peasants divide it. If we do not come out and actively assume the leadership of this present great struggle then, as in the past, we'll just be playing a passive role.

The facts listed above teach us that we should recognize the land problem. The Central Committee instructs us to confiscate according to the principle of the democratic stage, that confiscating from the rich peasants is political, that when the poor peasant masses demand confiscation of all the land, then of course all the land will be confiscated. Regarding redistribution, two methods are also proposed, dividing equally according to population, and division according to labor power. This means working flexibly according to the actual facts of different locations. At present, the facts everywhere teach us to demand complete confiscation and equal distribution. Thus, from among the two methods proposed by the Central Committee, we should select one realistic task. This is the only way to implement the Central Committee line flexibly and correctly. Those who say that confiscating everything and dividing equally is a peasant ideology contrary to the Central Committee directives do not misunderstand the directives of the Central Committee; they purposely give them a distorted interpretation to bolster the rich peasants.

4. The Persistent Historical Development of Opportunism Regarding the Land Problem

In regard to the land problem, the Communist Party has persistently committed the error of the opportunist line. Before the great revolution, the land problem was never raised within the Party. During the period of the great revolution, when the peasant movement of Hunan, Hubei, and Guangdong entered a high tide of dividing the land equally, not only was the Party unable to offer a correct proposal in regard to the land problem, it simply cursed the peasant movement for being excessive. During the Nanchang uprising, knowing that the land revolution was very serious, it still fell into the pit of opportunism and said not to confiscate the land of small landlords who had less than 50 *mu*. This was one grave reason for the failure of the Great Revolution. During the period of adventurism, it engaged in peasant uprisings, but never paid attention to solving the land problem. The Sixth Congress pointed out that the land revolution is the main content of the Chinese revolution, and that we should confiscate the land of the landlord class and support distributing it equally. When the time came to carry out this policy, however, many soviet districts once again followed a grave rich peasant line, and if they divided the land at all they did not divide it thoroughly. And today the broad masses of impoverished peasants have already demanded that all land be confiscated, while we are still saying that this violates the principle of the democratic stage and are still arguing with the masses, putting the popular masses in last place. This cannot even cut off the tip of the tail of opportunism. If we do not resolutely propose confiscating all the land and redistributing it equally, we will not be able to lead the high tide of the peasants' agrarian revolution and establish a strong alliance with the proletariat. The consequence is the phenomenon prevailing today: the slow development of the Red districts, a serious stand-off between the Red and White masses in the soviet border areas, the shrinking of the Red districts and the defection of the masses, and the inability to enlarge the Red Army aggressively. It can be seen that this once again threatens to render the Chinese revolution abortive. Thus the present struggle to oppose the rich peasant opportunist line in the land revolution, on the eve of the high tide of the revolution, is the most important task in mobilizing the hundreds of millions of poor suffering peasant masses to complete their local uprisings and to fight with the proletariat to win victory first in one or several provinces.

5. Eliminating Rich Peasant Elements and Opportunist Elements from Organizations

At present, the Communist Party, especially the Party branches in the countryside, is filled with rich and middle peasant elements, and the proletarian base is extremely weak. This is the organizational source of the grave development of the rich peasant line and opportunism. Thus to oppose firmly the rich peasant line and opportunism in the land revolution, it is necessary, during the struggle, firmly to carry out dividing the land equally, to expel rich peasant elements from the organizations, and to clean out all opportunist elements, because these elements, not having a class viewpoint, are totally divorced from the popular masses and do not recognize the demands of the popular masses. They even use the Party branches and the revolutionary organs of the soviets to suppress the masses and impede the deepening of the land revolution. This must be done in order to guarantee the implementation of the correct strategy of the land revolution.

6. Confiscate All the Land, and Distribute It Equally

Confiscate without exception all land belonging to the landlord class, to public shrines and temples, and even to rich peasants—confiscate without exception and divide it equally. All buildings and wooded hills, such as bamboo or tea-oil growing hills that can be divided and that the poor peasants want to divide, shall be equally distributed without exception. The land must be divided according to population, carrying out drawing on the plentiful to make up for the scarce, and drawing on the fat to make up for the lean, to be completed in seven days at most. Of these three principles, drawing on the fat to make up for the lean is the first that must be done, to avoid having to redistribute the land equally again later, or causing trouble for the poor peasants.

7. The Question of Distributing the Land to All Kinds of People

In principle, land is not distributed to farm laborers; a labor protection law is applied to guarantee their livelihood. When, however, farm laborers ask to be included in the redistribution, they should be given a share. As for porcelain industry workers and semiunemployed workers and unemployed independent laborers, if they cannot be encouraged to join the Red Army, and the government cannot organize production to solve the problem of their livelihood, they will likewise be given land in order to win over the popular masses. Vagabonds are also to be given shares of land. They should be removed from under the ruling class's policy of making use of them, and forced to toil. In order to provide special treatment for Red Army soldiers themselves, they should be given land and the soviet governments should also delegate persons or else force the rich peasants to till it for them, using mutual assistance or other organizations. Rich peasants and landlords who submit to the laws and decrees of the soviets and who do not engage in counterrevolutionary plots shall likewise receive shares of land and be forced to labor.

8. The Question of Organizing Cooperatives

Organize cooperatives for agricultural production and confiscate the draft animals and farm implements of counterrevolutionaries and the surplus oxen and farm implements of rich peasants, to help the poor hired peasants till and plant. Confiscate the wealth of the landlord class and counterrevolutionaries and collect loans of rich peasant monies, organize loan cooperatives that will provide low-interest loans to the poor peasants, and organize trading cooperatives. Collective farms run by the government should be a present propaganda slogan, and whenever possible the soviet governments may run collective farms that use socialist production techniques to compete with capitalist production methods and lead the peasants toward socialist collective production. But at present the political authority of the soviets is characterized by political struggle and does not have the economic and managerial capabilities that can easily run collective farms, and if they are not well operated, the peasants will lose faith in collective production. At present, generally speaking, it is still mainly production cooperatives which should be organized.

9. Nationalization of the Land

At present this is a propaganda slogan. In reality, the ban on buying and selling land and on renting land, and turning the land over to the soviets for redistribution, already constitutes nationalization. It is only when carrying out active propaganda for socialism that we criticize dividing the land equally as insufficient (but when criticizing, it must first be admitted that dividing the land equally is a great victory in overthrowing the several-thousand-year-old feudal system and liberating the peasants). [In carrying out such propaganda, we explain] that the land and farm implements cannot be improved, that fertilizer and seed cannot be managed well, and that insect plagues and flood and drought cannot be prevented [on the basis of equal distribution alone]. Only by cooperating with the proletariat to overthrow totally the rule of the imperialists and of the warlords, and winning the victory of the soviets nationwide, by abolishing the capitalist system and establishing a socialist society, by implementing collective farms, by bringing electrification to the countryside, and by making use of new-style mechanized planting and harvesting, and of scientific fertilization and scientifically improving the fields, and by preventing natural disasters, can the full victory of the land revolution be attained, and thereby the greatest peace and happiness for mankind. This is the real educational task of leading the poor peasants and winning over the middle peasants to the march toward socialism. If nationalization is proclaimed mechanically, it goes against the present demand of the peasants that the land be distributed to them for private ownership, and it will not have a good influence.

10. Cancel All Debts

From the day of the land revolution, all debts, whether as loans or as outstanding bills, including the interest on all kinds of grain loans, shall be totally cancelled. This is because in the countryside, all loans, except for those few friendly loans between one poor peasant and another poor peasant, are by their very nature feudal and exploitative. Their total cancellation is an urgent demand of the broad masses of the poor suffering peasants, but because the rich peasants and the landlord class, for special reasons, have borrowed against the accounts of the poor and hired peasants, they definitely want the loans to be repaid. Debts among the rich peasants and landlords will be turned over to the soviets to provide capital for loans to the cooperatives.

11. Establishing Soviet Political Power

In the struggle of the land revolution, it is essential that the popular masses be resolutely mobilized and that the masses slaughter the despotic gentry, the landlords, and all counterrevolutionaries with their own hands. It is only by ruthlessly eliminating the counterrevolutionaries that the masses can be made to rise up and seize the arms of the landlords, and to establish soviet political power and Red Guard units that are firmly under the leadership of the farm laborers and poor peasants.

Order to the First Front Army of the Red Army to Attack Gaoan

(October 19, 1930, 7:00 P.M., at General Headquarters
beneath Bamboo Hill outside the town of Xiajiang)

1. The enemy situation is as before, and it is reported that Gaoan is under the domination of Dai Yue's brigade.

2. Given the Front Army's task of directly occupying the Nanchang-Jiujiang Railroad and then awaiting the opportunity to seize Jiujiang and Nanchang, the plan for the first step is to destroy the enemy presently in Gaoan, and then to occupy it.

3. The Third Army Group should complete all preparations by the 19th of this month, set out on the 20th from its present location, and go to the right of the line of Qingjiang, Qushuiqiao, Luojia, Heshujia, Huangshagang, and Lianglukou. The journey is to take place over a period of five days, and the town of Gaoan must be occupied on the 24th. Having accomplished this, a close watch must be kept in the direction of Nanchang and Fengxin.

4. The Fourth Army of the First Army Group should set out tomorrow (the 20th) on a five days' journey by way of Renhe, Tiangang, Yongfang, Hamojie, Tuohujie, Dapingjie, Shanqian, and Miaoqian to the line along Gongmiao, Taiyangyu, Guanzigang, Shanghupu, and Zhangjiadu to help the Third Army Group destroy the enemy in Gaoan. If there is no trace of the enemy in Gaoan, then they are to be stationed along the line of Wulipei and Qiliqiao to await further orders. The Third Army should set out on the 21st for a journey of five days by way of Sixi, Dongxibian, Luofang, Wupingyu, Taiheyu, Liyu, Quangang, Qianjialing, Shangxiafang, Longcun, Lujiadian, Guantangfang, Taojia, Luojia, Huibu, and Shinaoyu to Huangpoqiao, stop and await further orders. The said army must dispatch a vanguard tomorrow (the 20th) to destroy the enemy remaining in Dongxibian and Luofang. Along the way they must pay attention to keeping a close watch to the left in the direction of Yuanzhou.

The Twelfth Army, along with the Workers' and Peasants' Revolutionary Committee, the Provincial Soviet government, and General Headquarters and its directly attached units should set out on the 21st for a five-day journey by way of Guantian, Tankou, Wangjiadian, Yaoxijie, Huangtujie, Luogang, Zhanxi,

---

Our source for this order is *Jiangxi dangshi ziliao*, Vol. 6, pp. 167–68.

Yinggangling, Taiyangyu, Wulichen, and Shanghupu to Xiaojia, stop, and station themselves in the area to the rear of the temple.

5. Upon arrival on the 22nd at the line along Qingjiang, Dapingjie, Huangtujie, and Luofangyu, each route must immediately establish contact with General Headquarters. Along the way they must also maintain contact with each other.

6. During the march our position is that of General Headquarters.

Addendum:

1. Each unit (with the exception of the Second Army) is to make its own detailed plans for the march and they are to be reported together.

2. General Headquarters will encamp on the 21st near Huangjiadian, on the 22nd at Huangtujie, on the 23rd near Zhanxi, on the 24th at Wulichen, and on the 25th at the rear of the temple at Xiaogongmiao.

3. Everyone must carry enough rice for two days.

4. Along the way, all units must pay attention to raising funds and strictly maintaining discipline.

5. Upon arriving at the town of Gaoan, the Third Army Group is to be stationed in the northeast outskirts of the city, the First Army Group in the southwest. It is best not to station troops within the town.

Commander-in-chief   Zhu De

Political Commissar   Mao Zedong

Order to the First Front Army of the Red Army to Work Between the Yuan River and the Ruizhou River and to Await Opportunities

(October 24, 1930, 2:30 P.M., at General Headquarters
in Laojia on the northern edge of Huangtujie)

1. The entire enemy division of Tan Daoyuan has already reached Nanchang. Xu Kexiang's forces[1] and the vanguard troops of Xiong Shihui's Fifth Division arrived in succession in Jiujiang on the 19th of this month. According to newspaper reports it is said that the forces of Jin Handing and those of Mao Bingwen[2] continue to make their way towards Jiangxi. The division of Gong (Bingfan) is now in Nanchang; the division of Zhang (Huizan) is now on the Zhangshu and Fengcheng line; the division of Deng (Ying) is now in Fuzhou; in Yuanzhou there are now Luo Lin's forces[3] (the Hunan enemy); in Fenyi there is approximately one battalion of their vanguard forces.

2. The Front Army has the tasks of striving for further victory in the wake of the victory in Ji'an, mobilizing the masses, destroying enemy forces, expanding the Red Army, taking Nanchang and Jiujiang in a planned, collaborative, step-by-step manner, and striving for victory in the entire province of Jiangxi. It has been decided to begin by arranging the work between the Yuan River and the Ruizhou River, deploying the main forces along the Yuan River, mobilizing the masses in this area to raise money for provisions, and making every effort to create the conditions for a decisive battle with the enemy. The provisional time limit is seven days (there will be a separate order in case of extension).

3. The Third Army Group is to undertake the work in the area to the east of the Huangtujie, Zhanxi, Yinggangling, Guantangxu and Huifu line (including the line itself), and should dispatch advance forces to the main roads of Yinggangling and Bojiaxu to threaten and pressure the enemy in Gaoan.

4. The First Army Group is to undertake the work in the area to the west of the same line (excluding the line itself). The Third Army is to be positioned in

---

Our source for this order is *Jiangxi dangshi ziliao*, Vol. 6, pp. 185–86.

1. Regarding Xu Kexiang see above, the relevant note to the text of July 4, 1927. At this time, he was commander of the Guomindang Twenty-fourth Division.

2. Mao Bingwen (1891–1970), a native of Hunan, was at this time the commander of the Eighth Division of the Guomindang Sixth Route Army.

3. Regarding Gong Bingfan, Zhang Huizan, Deng Ying, and Luo Lin see above, the relevant notes to the orders of July 29, August 24, and August 31, 1930.

Fenyi *xian* and to be in charge of the work in the vicinity of the *xian* seat and on both shores of the Yuan River. Special attention must be paid to keeping a close watch in the direction of Yuanzhou. The Twelfth Army is to be positioned in Xinyu *xian* and to undertake the work in the vicinity of the town seat and on both shores of the Yuan River. The Fourth Army is to be positioned in Luofang, and should dispatch advance troops to Qianxu to press on towards Gaoan. Their work area would also tend to be on both shores of the Yuan River.

5. All army groups should set out tomorrow (the 25th).

6. All units should concentrate their main forces on the left wing. The degree to which forces are dispersed is to be decided based upon the enemy's situation.

7. Along the north shore of the Yuan River, on the route from Qingjiang *xian* via Huangtujie, Luofang, and Xinyu *xian* to Fenyi, a main communication line is to be constructed by making use of existing electricity poles, with Luofang as the center (construction to the east of Huangtujie goes to the Third Army Group, and to the west to the First Army Group.)

8. General Headquarters moves tomorrow (the 25th) to Luofang.

Attention:

1. All units stationed along the river (the Yuan River) must set up as many floating bridges as possible and locate as many fording spots as possible.

2. In the area where the First Army Group is to set up electric lines, the Third Army and the Twelfth Army together are to construct the lines between the *xian* seats of Xinyu and Fenyi, and the Fourth Army and the General Headquarters transportation team are to construct the lines from west of Huangtujie to the *xian* seat.

3. All units should as much as possible avoid encampment on the streets, especially in the case of high-level organizations.

4. The amount of funds each army must raise for itself in a week should be enough for a month's provisions.

5. Troops must be sent along the electrical power lines to safeguard them effectively.

6. In the course of this work particular attention should be paid to the work on the borders between Red and White areas.

Above are eight orders and six points for attention.

Commander-in-chief   Zhu De
Political Commissar   Mao Zedong

The Present Political Situation and the Tasks of the First Front Army and of the Party In Jiangxi

(Resolution of the Joint Conference of the General Front Committee of the First Front Army and the Jiangxi Provincial Action Committee)[1]

(October 26, 1930)

I. The Victory of Ji'an and the New Revolutionary Upsurge

Changsha has been occupied, and heavy offensives are still going on. The First and Third Army Groups have converged, and the major city of Ji'an has been seized. These vigorous developments of the forces of the Red Army in coordination with the sharp struggles of the proletariat in all major cities throughout the country and the development of the soviet régime in the countryside have already ensured that the revolutionary high tide in China will soon take the form of a general outburst. In particular, the seizure of Ji'an is the culmination of a local uprising with the greatest mass support and the strongest foundations, carried out by millions of organized masses in southwest Jiangxi, and by over twenty *xian* soviet governments. The victory of Ji'an is the beginning of victory in the whole province of Jiangxi. This victory is the first seizure of a major city by the Red Army and the masses in the course of several years of fighting. It not only provides a more solid foundation to assist the further development of the Red Army, and it is not merely a call to the revolutionary masses of all Jiangxi to complete the recent general uprising in Jiangxi. It is also of the greatest significance in giving an impetus to the revolutionary forces of the whole country and achieving nationwide revolutionary victory. Beyond a doubt, we must continue to build on the victory at Ji'an and seek victory first in Jiangxi.

Our source for this document is *Mao Zedong ji. Bujuan*, Vol. 3, pp. 159–74, where the text is reproduced from a documentary collection published in China in 1980, after checking with a version in the Chen Cheng collection.

1. This conference took place in Luofang, Xinyu *xian*, northeast of Ji'an, from October 25 to November 1, 1930. The purpose was to discuss strategic options in the wake of the retreat from Changsha. See *Zhongguo gongchandang huiyi gaiyao* (A Summary Account of Chinese Communist Party Meetings) (hereafter *Party Meetings*) (Shenyang: Shenyang chubanshe, 1991), pp. 120–22; see also *Nianpu*, Vol. 1, p. 321.

II. The International Situation and the Development
of the World Revolution

Recent developments in the international situation, such as the preparations for war by Italy and France, the breakdown of the naval negotiations between Italy and France, the active expansion of naval forces by France, the anti-German riots in Czechoslovakia, the forceful British denunciation of the U.S. policy of tariff increases, and the organization by seventeen South American republics of the South American Alliance, a movement to resist the United States, are all manifestations of the tensions of a second imperialist world war. The United States has incited Europe and the Americas to impose an economic boycott of the Soviet Union. The recent Soviet dumping of wheat in the United States, in particular, has caused the price of American wheat to collapse and made it more difficult to prevent the panic resulting from its agricultural overproduction, thus increasing U.S. hatred of the Soviet Union. The suppression of the Communist parties and the arrest of their leaders in various countries further demonstrate the intensification of the attack on the Soviet Union. But the irreconcilable contradictions in the era of the imminent demise of imperialism have already urged forward the torrent of world revolution. The French Communist Party has won a big victory in the recent election. Opposing the government's 8 percent cut in the wages of the metallurgical workers, 140,000 workers have waged a big strike in Berlin. The strike of the ship-building workers of Malaga, Spain, has led to a general sympathy strike in Vitoria, causing a situation of rebellion.[2] Although the government has adopted severe measures, it cannot clamp down effectively. Fifty thousand Hungarian workers have taken to the streets, and the Czechoslovakian Communist Party has also staged big anti-German demonstrations. The capital of Poland has witnessed general strikes, protesting the government's arrests of opposition leaders. In southern Chile, revolution broke out suddenly. The strikes of silk workers in Japan have developed into armed confrontations with the police. There have been rebellious riots of the inhabitants in India. The socialist construction of the Soviet Union has been further consolidated and developed. For example, agricultural production has become superior to that of the United States. All this shows that the world revolution is developing in great surges. This situation is very advantageous to the Chinese revolution. It will turn the offensive wars against the Soviet Union into a war for the victory of the world revolution.

---

2. More than four hundred strikes, mainly under Communist and Anarcho-Syndicalist leadership, took place in Spain during the year 1930. Malaga was one of the centers affected by the first big wave of strikes, which began in June. The locality transcribed *Weiduoli* by Mao, which we assume to be Vitoria, a small city in northern Spain, may well have been involved too, but there is no reason to believe that there was any direct influence between two places so different and so far apart. Probably Mao is simply making the point that the strikes swept across the whole country, from North to South.

III. Several Events That Have Occurred in the Chaotic Wars among the Warlords

A. After Chiang Kaishek seized Ji'nan, Zhang Xueliang issued a clever telegram, proposing peace and unification, while waiting for the Nanjing government to take action.

B. Zhang Xueliang led his armies south of Shanhaiguan, and occupied Beiping and Tianjin. Recently, he published a telegram, calling for the convening in Beiping of a reconstruction conference to discuss the so-called question of "striving to save the country."[3]

C. Chiang Kaishek published two important telegrams: (1) asking the Guomindang government to issue an amnesty for all political crimes, excluding Chen Jiongming and Yan Xishan and the Communist Party. (2) convening the Fourth National Congress of the Guomindang to decide on the meeting of a national assembly for the promulgation of a provisional constitution. A proclamation to the citizens contained five items, including eliminating the Communists (within a time limit of three to six months, with regional responsibilities, on the one hand, and comprehensive joint repression, on the other hand), sorting out financial affairs, streamlining the bureaucracy, developing the economy, and practicing self-rule.

D. It was carried in the newspapers that Liu Luyin, the head of the Central Propaganda Department in Nanjing, stated in a report regarding current affairs, "The Japanese language newspapers have created various rumors about Zhang Hanqing [Zhang Xueliang] and the authorities of northeast China. . . . The diplomats of the Japanese government in China go so far as to instigate the Japanese language newspapers to sow discord inside our country, thus making people wonder whether the Japanese government is engaging in deliberate manipulation." He also said, "Englishman Simpson has helped Yan to seize the customs, committing the crime of creating disorder in another country. No response has been made to the several protests of our country and we believe that the British diplomatic authorities in China are irresponsible and that the British government no longer amounts to anything."

E. Chiang Kaishek has occupied Zhengzhou. It is reported that some of the forces of Feng Yuxiang have been captured by Chiang Kaishek, some have surrendered to Chiang, and still others have retreated to northern Henan. There are also reports of an attack on Shanxi.

---

3. In February 1930, Yan Xishan had called for Chiang Kaishek's resignation, and in April he had launched an offensive against Chiang in alliance with Feng Yuxiang. After some initial successes, the dissident forces were decisively defeated in August. It appeared that only Zhang Xueliang could save the northern coalition, and Yan Xishan, on assuming office as chairman of the state council in Beiping on September 9, sought Zhang's collaboration. Instead, Zhang Xueliang issued a call on September 18 for a "reconstruction conference" (*shanhou huiyi*, literally, "a conference so that things will be better afterward") to bring peace to the country and sent his forces into North China.

F. Chiang Kaishek has dispatched Xu Yuanquan, Wang Jinyu, Chen Cheng, Xia Douyin, Cai Tingkai, Jiang Guangnai, Ye Weijun, Xiao Zichu, and others back to Henan and dispatched Tan Daoyuan, Jin Handing, Xu Kexiang, Peng Qilong, Mao Bingwen, Li Yunjie, Tang Yunshan, and other army units to Hubei to suppress the revolution.

IV. The Evaluation of These Events

A. The wars among Chiang, Yan, and Feng are wars among Britain, Japan, and the United States. Exploiting the tensions which have resulted from the clashes between Britain and the United States, Japan has occupied a pivotal position. Seizing the opportunity of the compromise between the United States and Chiang, Japan has caused her lackey Zhang of Fengtian to obtain a sphere of influence in Hebei. As expected, both Britain and the United States have had to make concessions to Japan, and this has been followed by Chiang and Yan's reluctant recognition of the advance made by the forces of Zhang of Fengtian. Chiang especially wants to use this move to deal with Yan.

B. The occupation of Changsha and the continuing heavy attacks [of the Red Army], as well as the seizure of Ji'an, have not only led to widespread changes in the Chinese revolutionary situation but have, at the same time, transformed the relationships among the ruling classes. That is to say that the development of the revolutionary forces and the fundamental contradictions among classes have prompted the imperialists and the Chinese ruling classes to try desperately to moderate the conflicts among themselves and unite in dealing with the revolution. Even the U.S. imperialists feel that this is necessary because the Nanjing government under its control has been increasingly threatened by the revolutionary forces. The Japanese imperialists also naturally feel that the victory of the Chinese revolution is detrimental to Japan first and foremost. Therefore, there is the possibility of temporary compromise between Japan and the United States. Chiang also has to win over Zhang, so as to end the wars speedily. The suppression of the Chinese revolution is urgently necessary to British imperialism as well. With the alliance between Japan and the United States, and the disastrous defeats of Feng and Yan, they have no alternative but to yield temporarily. The temporary alliance of imperialism and the warlords against the revolution makes it necessary and feasible for Chiang Kaishek to remove large numbers of troops from the front to attack the revolution. Meanwhile, suppressing the Chinese revolution requires the employment of new policies of reformism and deception. So, Chiang Kaishek, taking advantage of the military victories after the occupation of Kaifeng and Zhengzhou, published several telegrams which put forward policies of reform and deception and attempted to establish reactionary leadership. The so-called amnesty of political prisoners and convening of a national assembly are in fact acceptance of the programs of the reformists and attempts to seek the support of the middle and petty bourgeoisie. At the same time, he attempts to draw the subordinates of Feng over to his side to oppose Yan and organize an anti-Communist alliance under the leadership of the Chiang faction, that is to say, under the leadership of the United States, for the purpose of crushing the Chinese revolution. This is an effort to achieve leadership in opposing the Chinese revolution, as well as to seek leadership in attacking the Soviet Union and opposing the world revolution.

C. This counterrevolutionary alliance will inevitably disintegrate in the face of the revolutionary upsurge. This can be predicted in advance by the contradictions, vacillations, and collapse of the ruling classes and the vigorous development of the revolutionary forces. Despite their desperate efforts to unite, the internal conflicts among the imperialist warlords have become more acute. Zhang Xueliang's proposal of holding a reconstruction conference obviously clashes with Chiang Kaishek's national assembly. In the chaotic wars among Chiang, Feng, and Yan, the Japanese imperialists and their running dog Zhang Xueliang have actually gained the territories of Beijing and Shandong, thus further intensifying the conflicts between Japan and the United States, and between Zhang and Chiang. The report of Liu Luyin has already provided a clue. Chiang Kaishek has dispatched his troops to the south in a great hurry, setting the deadline of eliminating the Communist bandits within three to six months. These are signs of the tensions of the war between Chiang and Zhang. In particular, because the politics and economy of the ruling class are completely bankrupt, financial disorder has become a nationwide phenomenon, the rural economy is seriously bankrupt, and the peasants' uprisings against the landlords in various southern provinces have been taking place for several years in succession. The fact that no faction of the Guomindang can resolve this situation indicates how much more serious the problem has become. Under the threat of imperialist production, national industries have closed down and collapsed in great numbers, intensifying the crisis of unemployment. Although Feng and Yan have been defeated, the bankrupt in Shanxi and Shaanxi can no longer survive, and a war for territory will naturally take place. In order to extricate themselves from the industrial crisis, the British imperialists will certainly exert all their efforts to regain the influence and political leadership in China they have lost. This proves that, because of their fundamental economic and political bankruptcy, the imperialists and the Chinese ruling classes are no longer capable of stabilizing their future, or of having a solid alliance, and that new fighting among the warlords will certainly occur in the near future and further accelerate their downfall. Chiang Kaishek's so-called peace and unification is nothing but deceptive and ridiculous nonsense. Even lackey Wu Zhihui has said, "One is afraid that there will be no 120 percent guarantee for the hope of eternal peace." On the basis of the facts set out above, the revolutionary movement of the proletariat and the broad masses has, under the leadership of the Chinese Communist Party, moved toward a resolute struggle to overthrow the rule of the Guomindang. What the masses demand is not the national assembly of the warlords, bureaucrats, despotic gentry, landlords, and bourgeoisie, but the soviet assembly of the workers, peasants, soldiers, and broad masses of the oppressed toilers, which is scheduled to be held on November 7. What the masses demand is not the constitution and laws that maintain the oppression and exploitation of the ruling classes, but the soviet laws, ordinances, and programs that guarantee the dictatorship of the proletariat and the interests of the workers, peasants, and toiling masses. What the masses demand is not the local autonomy of the political régime of the despotic gentry and landlords, but the soviet politics of the dictatorship of the workers and peasants. Why are the reformists and the Chiang Kaishek faction putting forward these tricks at this time? Precisely because the revolution is moving toward its high tide and striving for the thorough overthrow of the ruling classes, and because they see the masses waging resolute struggles for the above demands, they have to propose so-called national assemblies, constitution, and laws to attract the middle and petty bourgeoisie in jointly suppressing the demands and the revolution of the workers and peasants. These conspiracies and tricks further lay bare the increasing collapse of the ruling classes and their ugly features of fright and helplessness. The counterrevolutionary alliance of the imperialists and warlords is formed in the present situation of a raging tide of revolution throughout the world and the vigorous development of the Chinese revolution. The nature of these attacks is that the ruling classes are trying to save themselves from crisis and doom. It is not at all the case that the ruling classes are trying to destroy the revolutionary forces at the low ebb of the revolution, as in the past, when they conducted the campaigns of joint suppression against the Jinggangshan. We must reply to the massive offensives of the warlords of the Chiang faction with a nationwide revolutionary uprising. In the present situation where on the one hand the imperialists and warlords are forced to compromise, and on the other hand they are not able to reconcile their contradictions, so that they are tottering on the brink of collapse, we must confirm our victory in this decisive class struggle by obtaining not just victory in one province, but the victory of the revolution in the whole country.

D. There are two incorrect evaluations concerning the fighting among the warlords. The first is a nonclass and unrealistically optimistic evaluation, which holds that the chaotic struggles among the warlords will become forever larger and larger until the destruction of the warlords themselves, and that they will never unite to oppose the revolution. This is a totally wrong and nonclass evaluation. It shows a lack of the understanding that when the class contradictions supersede the internal contradictions of the ruling classes, the ruling classes must inevitably wage last-ditch struggles, abandon their own contradictions for the time being, and unite to oppose the revolution. The consequence of this evaluation will be relaxation in the arrangement of the revolutionary work, a purely military viewpoint, which can easily lead to separation from the masses in our concrete actions, and helplessness whenever we face a reactionary alliance. These empty optimistic evaluations will certainly lead to extreme pessimism.

The other evaluation is pessimistic in believing that the enemies are united against us, and therefore the revolution is faced with great difficulties. This is another nonclass analysis, for it does not understand the revolutionary high tide. The last-ditch joint struggle of the ruling classes is directed at meeting the offensives of the revolutionary forces, and this proves that the revolution has reached high tide. If the revolution is about to destroy the ruling classes, why should not the ruling classes unite and save themselves from dangers and destruction? When the revolution is still developing within one province, the ruling classes use the forces of one province to deal with the revolution every time. This is also the case in the period of guerrilla warfare. On the other hand, when the ruling classes are forming a nationwide alliance, this undoubtedly proves the existence of a nationwide revolutionary high tide. Those who do not recognize this point are incapable of truly understanding the revolutionary high tide and will develop pessimism, evasion, and shameful capitulationism. The correct understanding is that the victory of the Chinese revolution will encounter the brutal wars not only of the domestic warlords but of the international imperialists. As the revolution begins to be victorious, the imperialists and warlords must and can set aside the contradictions among themselves and join forces in dealing with the revolution. This requires us to step up the arrangement of our work throughout the country, pay attention to the balanced development of the four major revolutionary forces, and get ready for the final brutal struggle. The fundamental economic and political bankruptcy of the Chinese ruling classes can no longer be salvaged, and the revolutionary forces are expanding vigorously. We must definitely seek the victory of the Chinese revolution under the conditions of coordinating the work of the whole nation and the smooth development of the world revolution. At present, while the ruling classes are uniting in confronting the revolution, the rightists are easily pessimistic, and those who always used to be optimistic have also turned pessimistic. Therefore, correctly pointing out the vacillation and collapse of the ruling classes, the brewing of new wars, the vigorous development of the revolutionary forces, and the struggle against pessimistic ideas constitutes the necessary preliminary work in order to carry out decisive class struggles and achieve victory in one province.

V. Opposing the Guerrilla Line in Seizing Political Power in One Province

Today, the task of seizing political power in one province actually confronts us. To fulfill this task requires modifications in the guerrilla line inherited from the guerrilla period of the Red Army in the past, that is, changes in the line of lightly armed raids based on the purely military viewpoint. Because this line does not include a correct evaluation of the chaotic wars among the warlords and does not understand that seeking victory in one province is work contributing to the decisive class struggle, it leads to a divorce from the masses and pays no attention to winning over the masses, establishing work among the masses, or expanding the Red Army and strengthening the forces of the Red Army. With regard to military tactics, it still employs only guerrilla warfare and does not know the conditions that are necessary in preparing for the final decisive battle between the classes. Superficially, purely military lightly armed raids (the raids mentioned here refer to the strategic line of seeking victory in one province; it is not a matter of opposing surprise attacks in military tactics) appear as a result to correspond to the left-wing line of resolute attacks, but in fact they delay the coming of the initial victories of the revolution, thus becoming an extremely right-wing line. The events of Changsha and Ji'an have abundantly educated us on this point. The inability to hold Changsha firmly and continue to occupy it the first time resulted mainly from inadequate preparations among the masses, and the fact that the Red Army forces were still not the backbone forces of the Red Army. The second time, because conditions among the masses and contacts with enemy soldiers were still inadequate, it became simply an attack of the Red Army. As a result, half a month of ferocious attacks did not lead to victory. In Ji'an, conditions were quite different; there was a broad mass base, so it could be truly seized. As for the seizure of Changsha the first time, the enemies then had no reinforcements and no fortifications. Only under such circumstances was there the possibility of employing lightly armed raids. At present, as the enemies greatly reinforce their forces and Nanchang and Jiujiang consolidate their fortifications, the Red Army's lightly armed raids on Nanchang and Jiujiang, with the considerable lack of supplies and provisions for the Red Army and the seriously inadequate conditions of transportation, will unquestionably become guerrilla attacks. The consequence is that the Red Army cannot seize the cities and will have to move to other places, thus putting off the victory in one province instead. Therefore, such guerrilla ideas of lightly armed raids run completely counter to the systematic and planned strategy of seeking victory in one province and should be firmly corrected. The Central Committee has recently pointed out that the Red Army needs intensified training and promotion of cadres from among the good elements of peasants and the workers to become the backbone of the Red Army and turn the Red Army into an iron army. It has stated that thirty to fifty thousand backbone troops of the Red Army are required to secure victories in big cities and establish the confidence of the masses in the Red Army. Fighting must be based on the systematic and planned use of strategy. This has given greater depth to our arrangements for seeking victory in one province. We believe that this instruction is very clear. Of course, using the lack of coordination with the masses as a pretext not to launch strong offensives by the Red Army, scattering the work aimlessly, refusing to attack even when success is assured, and lacking understanding of the importance of supplies, reinforcements, and training are problems that can be solved only in the course of struggles waged according to a plan. Naturally, abandoning the task of achieving victory in one province is also a serious right-wing viewpoint, which should be guarded against. Another problem which should be pointed out is the inability to employ strategies and tactics flexibly. Strategies are determined by both objective conditions and subjective forces, whereas tactics involve the use of all available means in the light of various actual conditions at a particular time to realize the objectives of a strategy. So without contravening the strategy, the tactics may change frequently. To take Ji'an first in the task of seizing Nanchang is a very correct strategy. One should not mechanically ask why Ji'an should be attacked first, since it was originally planned to attack Nanchang. For example, under the strategy of occupying the Nanchang-Jiujiang Railroad, the tactics of either moving into the city with attacks or destroying the main forces of the enemy at appropriate places on the two banks of the Gan River and then trying to seize the city depend on the objective and subjective conditions at that time; there are no rigid rules. This should be especially understood by the lower-ranking cadres and the soldier masses of the Red Army. Otherwise, if the masses know only the general objective, they will be suspicious and wavering once they encounter strategic and tactical changes, and will even require the superior leading organs to adapt to the backward thinking of the masses and hinder the flexible use of strategies and tactics. This issue deserves attention.

VI. To Achieve Victory in Jiangxi First Is the Current Task of the First Front Army and the Party Headquarters of Jiangxi

Basing ourselves on the premise that victory must first be won in the provinces and regions surrounding the center of Wuhan, we must now strive for victory in Jiangxi and then to go on to realize victory in Wuhan. Naturally, victory in Jiangxi cannot be separated from the nationwide revolutionary upsurge. Nevertheless, the conditions for victory are more likely to exist in Jiangxi. Jiangxi has over sixty *xian* soviets, and the peasants' uprising has become a widespread revolutionary upsurge. The convergence of the forces of the First and Third Army Groups, the continuous attack on Hukou and Panyang by the Tenth Army of the Red Army and the recent occupation of Ji'an, in particular, have combined all revolutionary forces and seriously threatened Nanchang. The economic bases of the bourgeoisie and landlords in the countryside of Jiangxi have been basically destroyed and are shaking and collapsing further under the increasingly serious threat against Nanchang. The Red Army has been carrying out propaganda from the other side of the river, targeting the Eighteenth Division of the enemy forces. One platoon of their soldiers have come over with their guns and joined the Red Army. The enemy soldiers and we have agreed that we will not fire arms in attacking Nanchang, and the enemy officers are greatly alarmed, gathering the soldiers and reprimanding them in the middle of the night. Not long ago, there were soldiers who came over to the Third Army Group with guns. In May, when they were not paid a single cash, the soldiers were all unwilling to fight, and the officers were often assassinated. It was discovered that there were frequent calls among the troops to go to the Red Army, and they feel that Red

Army soldiers are not oppressed. This situation demonstrates that the tools which the ruling classes use for the desperate struggle are not reliable. Besides, the experience of the enemy soldiers wavering and unwilling to fight in the past further indicates to us that we should not be frightened by the large numbers of enemy troops. At present, although the warlords of the Chiang faction have dispatched many troops to Jiangxi, the struggle among the ruling classes for the counterrevolutionary leadership has by no means been resolved, and new clashes are brewing. Chiang Kaishek is merely using a temporary compromise to deal with the revolution. Furthermore, after the prolonged and chaotic fighting, the soldiers are extremely exhausted and wavering. So long as we step up political and organizational leadership, we can undoubtedly destroy the main forces of the enemy's offensives. Therefore, the tasks of the Party in Jiangxi, and of the First Front Army, are undoubtedly to coordinate their actions with the masses of Jiangxi to carry out the decisive class struggle in a planned and systematic way and to strive resolutely for an initial victory in Jiangxi.

VII. The Line of the First Front Army and of the Party in Jiangxi for Work in Accordance with This Task

1. Intensify propaganda to promote resistance to the warlords' suppression of the revolution, support the armed uprisings to seize political power in Jiangxi, expand propaganda regarding the victory at Ji'an and regarding the establishment of the soviet government in Jiangxi Province and the laws and ordinances issued by it, and raise the slogans of "opposing the suppression of the revolution by the warlords" and "carrying out armed uprisings to seize political power in Jiangxi." We must inspire the masses to fight for the soviet régime, and to reply to the enemy's attacks with a resolute and decisive class struggle and the achievement of initial victory in Jiangxi. Before the high tide of the revolution, increased efforts should be made to oppose the deceptive policies of the reformists, the Reorganizationists, the Third Party, the AB Corps, the liquidationists, and recently of Chiang Kaishek's national assembly, fully exposing all their crimes and eliminating their influence among the masses. This has become a serious political task in smashing the enemy's plots to weaken the revolution during the period of the decisive class war.

2. Make arrangements for work in Nanchang and Jiujiang, and on the Nanchang-Jiujiang Railroad. Today the proletarian uprising has become the principal and indispensable force in seizing the major cities. The last desperate struggle of the enemy is to rely on strong fortifications to hold the cities. The events in Changsha teach us that it is impossible to achieve victory in one province if work in the main cities is lacking. Now we should correct the pessimism and neglect of the work in cities and overcome all difficulties in setting up the work in cities. The main line of the trade union movement is the direct organization of armed uprisings and strengthening the political alliance in preparation for strikes. Red trade

unions of the masses, pickets, and the Red vanguards, which are the core force at the time of the uprisings, should be established. The daily economic struggle should naturally not be abandoned and should be linked to the armed struggle.

3. Carry out local uprisings. First of all, local uprisings should be carried out in such *xian* as Anfu, Taihe, Xinyu, Fenyi, and Yuanzhou in western Jiangxi, Jishui, Yongfeng, Le'an, and Xin'gan in eastern Jiangxi, and Ganzhou in southern Jiangxi. In the White regions, guerrilla wars should be resolutely initiated, and preparations made for uprisings so as resolutely to eliminate the situation of confrontation between the Reds and Whites and join together all the Red regions. Then, Fujian, Hunan, and Hubei should be connected, and we must prepare to use the flame of the mass uprisings to destroy the advancing forces of the enemies and complete the local uprisings. It is imperative to learn the lessons of the past, and confiscate all the land rapidly, for only thus can thorough equalization of the land be carried out. In this struggle, it is necessary to establish the leadership of the farm laborers and set up independent trade unions of farm laborers. When poor peasant committees and soviet Red Guards are set up, rich peasant elements should be strictly prohibited from joining them. Farm laborers and poor peasants should be resolutely selected as leaders. From the beginning of the rural struggle, not only should the landlord class be fiercely attacked, but at the same time the redistribution of land and refusal to pay land rent and debts should also take place. All exploitation and oppression of the poor peasants by the rich peasants should be opposed, and the impoverished peasant masses should be mobilized to combat the rich peasant class, thus laying a solid revolutionary foundation for the thorough destruction of the feudal forces.

4. Mobilizing the broad masses to participate in the fighting and the expansion of the soviet régime. We should point out the development of the national revolutionary situation and the inevitability of a political victory. On this occasion when the warlords are repressing the revolution, we must summon the masses and mobilize all the people, men and women, old and young to cooperate with the Red Army, carry out the final decisive class struggle, destroy the main forces of the enemy, and achieve initial victory in Jiangxi. In all the regions subjected to the attacks of the enemy forces, such as Xiajiang, Xinyu, Fenyi, Yuanzhou, Anfu, and Lianhua, and in Ji'an, Jishui, Yongfeng, Le'an, and other *xian*, the Red Guards and Young Pioneers need to be concentrated. Military and political training should be strengthened and the command should be unified. The main routes used by the enemies should be reconnoitered, and the rear of the enemies and their transportation systems should be disrupted. In addition, capturing the enemies' arms, cutting off their supplies, launching surprise attacks everywhere, and engaging in all sorts of rioting and terrorist activities will entrap the enemies in the Red regions and immobilize them, leading to their total destruction. The Red Guards ought to help the Red Army in guarding and reconnoitering, transportation, and first aid. All *xian* need to get organized and prepared. The arms of all *xian,* including spears and home-made cannons and

ammunition, should be fully prepared by the districts and townships with all possible means. The work described above must employ agitation, the mass line, and soviet mass meetings held in every district and *xian* to enable the masses themselves to decide on the concrete actions and preparations involved in their participation in the struggle. Only the initiation of spontaneous and enthusiastic participation constitutes a political victory. Therefore, commandism (abandoning persuasion and agitation, and forcing the masses to implement the line without understanding the situation) and the parochial line (the Party and the soviet régime do not play the role of agitation and leadership; major issues are not decided by the mass meetings, and an atmosphere of commandism of the few is formed in which the masses feel that they are working only for the sake of individual destinies) must be opposed. On the other hand, the brutality of the warlords in suppressing the revolution, killing villagers, and burning forests must also be exposed. The voluntary confession of betrayals and conspiracies [should be encouraged], and class hatred should be heightened. The slogan of "fighting for the class to the end, and never surrendering" should be put forward to inspire determination in the struggle. In noncombat soviet regions, similar mobilization should also be conducted, and forcefully expanded outward, in order to eliminate the confrontation between Red and White [areas], and win over the masses in carrying out joint attacks against the despotic gentry and landlords. The Red masses need to be persuaded to restrain their vengefulness,[4] and to redistribute the land equally and resolutely. During the considerable time of occupation of the White regions, the masses should be helped to divide up the land and to set up Red Guard units in order to eliminate the serious obstacle of confrontation between Red and White.

5. Stepping up the movement among the White soldiers. Because of brutal sacrifices in the confused fighting, the unbearable oppression and misery of life, and the influence of the revolutionary upsurge of the workers and peasants, the White soldiers are wavering in the extreme. In recent times, incidents of surrendering to the Red Army with guns have been happening incessantly. The conditions for soldiers' uprisings are entirely ripe. The fact that not many uprisings have taken place results from the lack of organization and leadership by the Communist Party. Local Party headquarters and army Party committees must address the past neglect of this work and pay great attention to it. It must be understood that unless the enemy forces disintegrate, the revolution will assuredly not be victorious. This work line is aimed at establishing a broad political base and strict organizational leadership. In the process of turning the wars of warlords into the revolutionary wars of defeating the warlords and the wars of killing workers and peasants into wars of assisting the liberation of workers and peasants, the class consciousness of the soldiers and their uprisings should be raised and organized, the past parochial opportunist line and purely military

---

4. *Baofuzhuyi*, literally "revengeism."

mutinies (a few people running away with guns) should be corrected. Local Parties and political departments of the Red Army must set up the committees of the soldiers' movement, and dispatch large numbers of people to take advantage of all opportunities to penetrate into the enemy forces to conduct this work. Especially at present, propaganda and agitation should be intensified among the White soldiers and the low-ranking officers who have come to Jiangxi. The key is to seize upon the fact that they fought long and hard in Shandong and Henan, and the result was only that massive numbers of people died and were wounded in vain, and that now they are again to be ordered back to fight the workers and peasants. They need to understand the crimes of the warlords, the present development of the revolutionary situation, and that their only way out lies in joining the revolution of the workers and peasants. They should be encouraged to rebel and mutiny. In the regions under the attack of the enemy, a mass movement of soldiers should be carried out. Taking the opportunity of the soldiers barracking in the area, women, children, and old men should be mobilized to approach them and agitate among them by washing clothes for them and selling things to them (but no staple food is to be supplied). The Red Guards should, on the one hand, boldly capture the weapons of the enemy and, on the other hand, try hard to treat the captured White soldiers well, so as to win over the masses of White soldiers, and smash the rumors propagated by the enemy side about the brutal killing of White troops by the Red Guards, and other rumors and deceptions that make the soldiers afraid to mutiny.

VIII. The Serious Tasks in Western Jiangxi, Southern Jiangxi, and Other Soviet Regions

1. Uniting the poor peasants and farm laborers to confront the rich peasants. In the areas where the rich peasants control fertile land, another redistribution of the land on the basis of quality should be carried out rapidly to implement the principle of drawing on the fat to make up for the lean. This is necessary to eliminate classes in the countryside and satisfy the needs of the broad masses. It is also the most effective policy for suppressing completely the counterrevolutionary conspiracies of the rich peasant class. Regarding the places where the redistribution has been thorough in quantity (drawing on the plentiful to make up for the scarce) and in quality (drawing on the fat to make up for the lean), the victory of the land redistribution should be safeguarded and the original redistribution is not allowed to be disrupted. Our slogan is "Fair distribution should not be touched, and unfair distribution should be redone."

2. Reforming the organization of the whole Party and reestablishing the organization of the Youth League. No rich peasant counterrevolutionary element (AB Corps member) is permitted to remain in the Party and the [Youth] League, because the Party and the League in southwestern Jiangxi are full of rich peasant counterrevolutionaries now. This transformation can be carried out only by a

thorough egalitarian redistribution of the land, and by inciting the farm laborers and poor peasants to wage a class struggle against the rich peasants and mobilizing them to purge the rich peasants and other go-slow and vacillating elements, in the course of the final decisive class struggle against counterrevolutionary attacks. Only thus will it be possible to select and promote the activists among the poor peasants and farm laborers. Meanwhile in the local cities (various *xian* towns, especially Ji'an), the will of the poor workers should be carried out thoroughly, and the slogan of workers supervising capitalists and implementing the laws of labor protection should be used to combat exploitation by capitalists. Those workers who are close to capital, and the strata which are not directly exploited, should be guarded against organizationally. All petty bourgeois wavering elements must be purged from urban and rural branches and resolute proletarian elements selected.

3. Putting forward the slogans of "replacing committee members violating the interests of the poor and suffering workers and peasants" and "replacing the committee members opposing the soviet conferences," and reelecting all members of the soviet governments. The poor peasants, farm laborers, and genuine leaders of the masses should be reelected as members of the soviet committees. No rich peasant counterrevolutionary element (AB Corps member) is allowed to remain anywhere, at any level in the soviet governments. The reason is that all levels of the soviet governments in southwestern Jiangxi are full of rich peasant counterrevolutionaries. The soviet government ought simultaneously to root out new-style bureaucratism and commandism, which are suicidal policies of departing from the masses and ruining the soviets. The key tactic in consolidating the soviet régime is to invite the broad masses to participate in management of the soviets and to discuss and solve all major issues through representative conferences. The government shall present work reports to the representative conferences and hear the criticisms of the conferences. This requires regular soviet mass meetings in villages and townships, and representative conferences above the level of township. The fixed system of representation should be opposed, and "the election of the leaders of the poor peasants and workers as representatives" by mass meetings in villages and townships should be proposed. In places where the population under a township government is too large, and its territory too extensive, village soviets must be set up. Government employees may not leave production and are not paid. This is the only way to prevent the occurrence of new-style bureaucratism, enable all soviet administrations to meet the needs of the masses, win the support of the masses, and consolidate the soviets.

4. Pointing out various deceptive schemes of the AB Corps politically, eliminating their influence among the masses, rigorously suppressing the AB League, and executing all activists of the AB League.

5. Establishing, in cities, genuine trade unions of the class, implementing workers' supervision of capital, and strengthening the organization and training of pickets.

6. Setting up independent trade unions of farm laborers, which are extremely important organizations in establishing the leadership of the proletariat in the villages. Branch activities of the trade unions of farm laborers should be initiated, strengthening class education and leading the struggle against the rich peasants. In order to win over the basic masses of the poor peasants and launch the class struggle against the rich peasants, poor peasants' committees should be established, composed of the poor peasants who were exploited by high rent and interest in the past, and the poor peasants who are still poor after the present redistribution of the land. Attention should be given to selecting activists as leaders.

7. Using the method of persuasion and agitation in the vigorous expansion of the reserves of the Red Army, resolutely opposing commandism and deceptive methods which do not contribute to expanding the Red Army, but hinder its development. The reserves must pay attention to military and political training and taking the lead in participating in the work of the masses.

IX. The Present Work of the First Front Army

A. Military strategy: The First and Third Army Groups believe that the situation in which the enemy is advancing toward us after massive reinforcements presents the most excellent opportunity to replenish the weapons of the Red Army, expand the Red Army, and create an iron Red Army. The present strategy is, given the general objective of occupying the Nanchang-Jiujiang Railroad, Nanchang, and Jiujiang, to build on the victory at Ji'an, and achieve further victories. That is to say that we must mobilize the broad masses in the areas between Ji'an and Nanchang and prepare supplies, while at the same time stepping up the mobilization of the masses and the preparation of supplies in the rear, so as to be ready for a large scale decisive battle with the enemy, to destroy his main forces and realize victory in the whole province.

B. Strengthening political training in the army. At present, attention should be concentrated on carrying out the decisive class struggle. The political agitation for achieving initial victory in Jiangxi may point out the inevitable collapse of the counterrevolutionary alliance, the excellent opportunity posed by the massive offensive for creating an iron Red Army and strengthening the determination of the soldiers and officers. At the same time, the army should give attention to opposing the AB Corps and the Reorganizationists, conducting general political education of new soldiers, and establishing soldiers' committees and Party organizations. Special attention should be paid to strengthening the leadership capacity of the Party and enlarging its organization. The number of Party members in each army should double within a month. In addition, emphasis should be placed on planned propaganda on Communist theory and on various questions of revolutionary tactics. Literacy lessons ought also to be conducted in a planned way, in an effort to raise the political level of the Red Army, and the soldiers should be led in doing mass work frequently. Resolute worker and peasant elements should be absorbed in the course of mass struggles, and the Red Army should be expanded, in order to fulfill the task of creating an iron Red Army.

C. Strengthening practical military training is one of the important tasks of an iron Red Army. This applies in particular to the numerous new soldiers. It cannot be neglected in carrying out the decisive class struggle. Inappropriate, formalistic methods of physical culture (such as training in posture) must be abolished. In addition to conducting drills, all time for activity and rest should be used to fulfill this task. The officers of all armies must supervise and inspect the implementation of this work in a planned way.

The Front Committee of the First Front Red Army
The Action Committee of Jiangxi Province

Reproduced on October 26, 1930

Order to the First Front Army of the Red Army to Extend Its Work for Three Days in the Original Location

(October 29, 1930, in front of Luofangyuan)

1. The Jiangxi enemy has not made any significant movements, every single one of the Hunan enemy has returned to Hunan, and there are no enemies in Shanggao, Wanzai, and Yuanzhou.

2. The plan is for this front army to remain in its present location and extend its work for three days until November 2.

3. Points for attention in the work of all units:

a. Each unit should raise enough funds to supply itself with provisions for one month or longer.

b. Make efforts to capture weapons from the landlords and reactionaries, arm reliable peasants to the extent possible, or concentrate forces to organize Red Guard units.

c. Thoroughly distribute all farmland within each work area.

d. Each unit must find ways to purchase bullets (because in the local villages a large quantity of bullets are being hidden.)

e. Pay attention to internal political and military training.

4. General Headquarters remains with the Central Revolutionary Military Committee in the original location.

Attention:

a. The work area should be expanded as much as possible according to circumstances.

b. Transportation and communications during the period of operations should be carried out in compliance with the communications network diagram and the regulations issued by the Staff Office of this headquarters.

c. Each unit must submit a daily report to this headquarters documenting in detail the following items:

(i) Reconnaissance results. (ii) Espionage and transportation arrangements. (iii) Captured arms and their allocation. (iv) Situation and process

---

We have translated this order from *Jiangxi dangshi ziliao*, Vol. 6, pp. 203–204.

of land distribution. (v) Amount of funds collected and the process. (vi) Drilling of the unit itself. (vii) Other. (viii) Comments and suggestions.

d. During this period of work, all units of the First Front Army should operate in accordance with the principles decided upon at the education conference of the whole army group in Ji'an. All must use the new troop formations based on the newly formulated tactics, and must undertake training in the construction of fortifications.

Commander-in-chief   Zhu De

Political Commissar   Mao Zedong

The Problem of the Rich Peasants after Land Redistribution (The Situation in Yongxin and Beilu)[1]

Report by Wang Huai and Chen Zhengren, as noted by Mao Zedong[2]

(October 1930)

Exploitation by the rich peasants in the Red areas in Yongxin is carried out, first, through hoarding grain and, second, by selling industrial products. There are two ways of hoarding grain: (1) hoarding one's own surplus grain and (2) buying poor peasants' grain at cheap prices. This year's serious spring famine was caused in this way. Since rich peasants will hoard grain, and the government sets the maximum grain prices, they hide away their grain altogether, to the point where once the poor residents and workers in the cities ate rice gruel for a whole week. Unable to get rice, the farm laborers and poor peasants in the countryside also went hungry. Later, the leadership of the *xian* soviet led a spring famine struggle, fought the rich peasants resolutely, and made no concessions to them, in a determined effort to bring down grain prices. The Party played a role in each district and township, organizing young pioneers to dig out the hidden grain; they found a large amount of grain concealed by rich peasants in wine barrels, hollow walls, straw huts, clay-brick yards, and underneath their beds. As a result, there was not only enough grain to eat, but even a surplus. When new grain was harvested, rich peasants, one after another, hauled the old grain to the cities for sale. In the small business of selling industrial products, rich peasants make an enormous profit, mainly from salt, machine-knitted socks, towels, sugar, soap, and so on. They have capital and all kinds of old social connections. Rich peasants can do things that poor peasants and farm laborers cannot.

Our source for this report is *Mao Zedong nongcun diaocha wenji*, pp. 252–53, which reproduces the text as it appears in the 1941 Yan'an edition of *Nongcun diaocha*, with helpful annotations.

1. In March 1930, the Southwest Jiangxi Special Committee had set up Eastern, Western, Southern, and Northern Route action committees, under its own control, to help in the task of leadership. The reference here is to the area controlled by the Beilu or Northern Route Action Committee.

2. This observation was added by Mao himself to the text as published in 1941.

(The above is reported by Wang Huai; what follows is reported by Chen Zhengren.)[3]

Not only is it like this in Yongxin, it is the same in Beilu. There, too, a spring famine struggle was waged this year. Rich peasants made money in business, just as in Yongxin. In Futian there is a shop called the Jiuru Tang; the owner is a small capitalist. When there was a shortage of salt in Beilu, he went to Nanchang to buy salt. When there is no ink or paper, he can also get them in Nanchang. Because he has been able to establish contact with the head of the Guomindang's self-defense corps,[4] he has old social connections. The salt and other goods he sells are all very high-priced. During June and July, his salt is sold for as much as six hundred cash per *jin*. He has two sewing machines, which have deprived the tailors in Futian of work, so they are all against him. Moreover, because his prices are too high, the municipal soviet of Futian, at the demand of the masses, arrested him and fined him one thousand *yuan*. Having paid the fine, he continues to do business in Futian. After Ji'an was liberated, his business grew even bigger. At the time of the spring famine in Beilu, rich peasants sold grain to the White areas. The spring famine struggle was to stop grain from flowing into the White areas, and allow it to circulate only between the Red areas.

---

3. Wang Huai (1906–1932) was a native of Jiangxi, who had joined the Chinese Communist Party in 1926. He was a member of the Standing Committee of the Southwest Jiangxi Special Committee from March to October 1930. Chen Zhengren (1907–1972), a native of Jiangxi, had joined the Chinese Communist Party in 1925. In October 1928, he became deputy secretary of the Hunan-Jiangxi Border Area Special Committee. He was secretary of the Northern Route Action Committee of Southwest Jiangxi from May to October 1930; in October, he became head of the Propaganda Department of the Jiangxi Provincial Action Committee.

4. The "self-defense corps" [*shouwang dui*] was an organization that the landlords forced the peasants to join for the purpose of sabotaging the Red areas.

Xingguo Investigation

(October 1930)

In September 1930, the First Front Army of the Red Army returned from the attack on Changsha to Jiangxi. At the beginning of October, it fought its way into Ji'an and advanced into the Yuan River basin. Xingguo sent a large number of peasants to join the Red Army, and I took advantage of this opportunity to conduct an investigation of the Xingguo tenth district, that is, the Yongfeng District. I located eight persons—Fu Jiting, Li Changying, Wen Fengzhang, Chen Zhenshan, Zhong Dewu, Huang Dachun, Chen Beiping, and Lei Hanxiang—and held an investigation meeting. The investigation was conducted at the end of October 1930, the meeting place was Luofang in Xinyu *xian*, and the investigation meeting lasted one week.[1] Yongfeng is located at the juncture of the three *xian* of Xingguo, Gan, and Wan'an, and is divided into four townships [*xiang*]. The old Lingyuan District is the first township, Dongjiang District is the second township, the Shankeng District is the third township, and the Jiangtuan District is the fourth township; Yongfeng Town in the second township is the political and economic center of the district. The population distribution is: the first township, 3,000; the second township, 800; the third township, 3,000; and the fourth township, 2,000; making a total of 8,800. Since the borders of this district cut across Xingguo, Gan, and Wan'an *xian*, it is clear that this district is not much different from the two *xian* of Gan and Wan'an and not much different from the land struggle situation in all of southern Jiangxi. Real policy decisions must definitely be based on the concrete situation. Things

---

Our source for this investigation is *Mao Zedong nongcun diaocha wenji*, pp. 182–251, which reproduces the text as it appears in the 1941 Yan'an edition of *Nongcun diaocha*. The version in *Mao Zedong ji*, Vol. 2, pp. 185–252, is taken from the 1947 Jin-Cha-Ji edition of Mao's works. The content is exactly the same, except that the 1947 edition confuses the date of Mao's preface to this work, which was written on January 26, 1931, with the date of the investigation itself, which was completed in October 1930.

1. These peasants had come a substantial distance, for the Yuan River basin is north of Ji'an, and Xingguo *xian* is to the south, well over 100 kilometers away. Presumably these men were members of the Red Army Reserve Corps from the Xingguo Tenth District, whose participation in the Xinyu campaign is mentioned below in Section VII 5 of this text. As indicated above, in a note to the text dated October 26, 1930, a Joint Conference of the General Front Committee of the First Front Army and the Jiangxi Provincial Action Committee took place in Luofang from October 25 to November 1, 1930, to discuss strategy after the retreat from Changsha. Since Mao says his investigation meeting lasted one week, he was evidently engaged in these two activities simultaneously.

imagined sitting in a room and things reported and written down in rough outline in a book are certainly not the concrete situation, and to determine policy according to what you "think ought to be" or from reports that do not reflect reality is dangerous. A great many mistakes that the Red districts made in the past were the result of Party directives' not being in accord with the real situation. Therefore, detailed, scientific, real investigations are extremely necessary. This investigation, generally speaking, does not probe very deeply, but it is rather more thorough than my previous investigations. First, I have never before investigated eight households, and actually, without this kind of investigation, you do not have a basic concept of the village. Second, investigating the reactions of the various classes in the land struggle is something I did in the Xunwu survey, but it was not done fully. The weakness of this investigation is that it did not investigate the conditions of children and women, that it did not investigate trade conditions or make price comparisons, and that it did not investigate the conditions of agricultural production after land redistribution had been carried out, nor did it investigate the cultural situation. Originally these were supposed to be investigated but, because of the enemy attack on Luofang, the Red Army decided to use the tactic of luring the enemy deep, so we had no choice but to terminate our investigation meeting. This is how the materials that appear below were obtained: From the investigation outline that I suggested, questions were asked and discussed, and all the conclusions were obtained from suggestions that I made on which the eight comrades agreed, which were then written down. There were some things about which no conclusions were made, but which are recorded as their responses. Our investigation meetings were lively and interesting. We met two or even three times every day, sometimes late into the night, yet they never felt tired. I would like to express my deep thanks to these comrades. A few of them were Party members, but most were not.

Mao Zedong

Revised January 26, 1931, in Xiaobu Town, Yudu

I. Observations of Eight Households

1. Fu Jiting:

Resident of the tenth district, first township; ran a small slaughterhouse, had no capital. Fed five persons. Had rice fields yielding 23 *dan*, 3 *dan* to be paid in rent, leaving 20 *dan*. With five people eating 7 *dan* each, altogether they needed 35 *dan*, so they were short 15 *dan*, and relied on their slaughterhouse business to make up the deficiency. For each pig killed, they could receive about 1.30 *yuan* (now there are no large pigs for slaughter, so they can get only 0.50 *yuan* per pig). The five people include: the father (aged eighty),[2] the wife (who cooked, raised pigs, got firewood, did the laundry, and could not till the fields), a son (aged five), a daughter (aged one), and himself (aged thirty-nine, tilled the fields and slaughtered the pigs). In addition to his own fields, he rented fields with a yield of 5 *dan* from someone else, and every year he had to hire a temporary laborer for one month to help him work the fields. His mother died five years ago, and when she died they spent over one hundred *yuan*.[3] In addition to what his brothers put up, he himself borrowed 50 *yuan*, a debt which accumulated interest on the interest, and now already amounted to 150 *yuan*. Of the 23 *dan* of rice from the fields, 17 *dan* were his own. Six *dan* were "absentee fields" belonging to public lands of the Zhong clan over in Bailu (in Gan *xian*, some 10 *li* away). Of these 6 *dan*, each *dan* carried a security deposit of 6 *yuan*, for a total of 36 *yuan*, in addition to which he paid rent of 3 *dan* (50 percent).

In the third [lunar] month of last year, when the revolution failed, he fled to the mountains of Juncun to help work in the mountains. In the ninth month, when the Red Army arrived in Xingguo, he returned to his home, the pacification defense corps dogs went into the hills, and the land was not redistributed. In the second month of this year (March by the solar calendar), the Red Army attacked Ganzhou, and in the second month redistributed the land, but though the redistribution had not got this far, he did not have to pay the rent of 3 *dan*, and the debt of 150 *yuan* was cancelled. At the same time, the security deposit of 36 *yuan* was also not collected. For three months, beginning in the second month, acting as land section chief in the village government, he has helped the people divide the land. Beginning in the fourth month, he has been head of a Red Guard detachment that has spears and no guns. After holding this position for three months, on the 15th of the sixth month, he led the detachment in an attack on the pacification defense corps dogs of Xingguo *xian*. Since the sixth month, the Red Guard detachment has been reorganized as a Red Army reserve brigade, and after being a platoon chief for more than one month, he became company commander. At this time the first township organized two companies. In the eighth month, in the attack on Qifang, he led his forces in the attack, and the attack was successful. At present (October), in the Xinyu campaign, he has been made battalion commander. It is not good for him to be away from the fields, and he has received nothing from the butchering

---

2. All ages in this text are given according to the Chinese system of *sui*.

3. The text specifies that these were *xiaoyang yuan*, literally, "small foreign dollars." These coins, also referred to as "subsidiary silver currency," were 10- and 20-cent silver pieces, which were discounted significantly as compared with the large one-*yuan* coins called *dayang yuan*. Such coins, and the paper money based on them, constituted in fact the normal unit for all day-to-day transactions in the countryside at this time, so in the balance of this text the term has been translated simply *yuan*. Regarding the monetary system at this time, see Roger Thompson, *Report from Xunwu*, Appendix A.

which has been turned over to someone else. He wants to return home and does not want to be in the Red Army.

With six years of schooling, he can, with some difficulty, read newspapers.

2. Li Changying:

From Pengwudong of the first township, tenth district.

Family of six. He, himself, aged forty-eight, tilled the fields. Wife is also forty-eight, has a weak heart, can only cook, wash the clothes, and feed the pig. Son, aged twenty, tilled the fields, very stupid, cannot do calculations. Bride, aged twenty, every day gathers firewood, cannot till the fields. Daughter, aged twelve, was married off in the sixth month of this year, married to a child of the Wu family in Sishili. The second son, aged three, died this year in the fourth month, so now they have only four mouths to feed.

He himself had rice fields yielding 30 *dan* and borrowed the 20 *dan* of fields of his younger brother, Li Changfen. Because his fields were not good enough to cover expenses, Li Changfen had gone to Taihe and Luokeng to work as a fieldhand. If water could be obtained for Li Changfen's 20 *dan* of fields, they would produce only 13 *dan* of rice, of which 9 went for the rent in kind. Li Changfen had a debt of 120 *yuan*, so the 9 *dan* in rent amounted to paying the interest for Changfen. Because his own 30 *dan* of fields were on hillsides where the terraces easily collapse, in reality he could harvest only 17 *dan*, and together with Changfen's fields, which actually brought in only 4 *dan*, his total yield was 21 *dan*. All of this was wet (unhulled) rice, which with a reduction of 30 percent amounted to 15 *dan* of dry hulled rice, and only 17 *dan* in a good year. The annual consumption of rice for six people is 40 *Dan*.[4] Having less than half of what they needed, he relied on sweet potatoes to help out, of which he harvested roughly 30 *Dan* per year. By raising one pig and selling it in the twelfth month, he got enough to buy oil and salt. Ordinarily, they could not eat meat. They bought meat to eat only on the holidays of the Bright and Clear Festival [*qing-ming*] (0.40 *yuan*), the Transplanting Festival [*shitian*] (1.50 *yuan*), Double Five [*duanwu*] (0.30 *yuan*), Eat-New Festival [*chixin*] (1 *yuan*), Mid-Seventh Month Festival (0.20 to 0.30 *yuan*), Mid-Autumn Festival (0.20 to 0.30 *yuan*), Harvest Festival [*gehe*] (2 *yuan*), Double Ninth Festival [*chongyang*] (0.20 to 0.30 *yuan*), and the New Year's Festival (3 *yuan*). On the Eat-New Festival he had to buy 1 *yuan* worth of meat because he had to hire workers to plant the sweet potatoes. At the Transplanting Festival and the Harvest Festival he also had to hire work-ers. Every year he had to hire workers for twenty days. In addition to doing their own work, the father and son also had to help out on the 20-*dan* fields of his

---

4. As indicated above, in a note to chapter III of the Xunwu Investigation, we distin-guish between the two characters read *dan*, one being a unit of weight and the other a unit of volume, by capitalizing the transcription when it refers to the first of these.

second brother, on which every year they had to spend eighty workdays (every *dan* of rice fields required three workdays for good fields, and four workdays for poor fields). Because his second brother had died, leaving behind his wife, Changying's second son has been given to them to continue the family line. Eighty workdays with no pay, so after doing their own work and the work for the second brother's wife, they had no energy left over to work for anyone else.

The debt of 120 *yuan* was owed to the public granary and bore an annual interest payment of 7.5 *dan* (every 16 *yuan* borrowed attracted interest of one *dan* of grain, each *dan* being worth 2.40 *yuan*). At the end of every year, the sale of a pig brought something over 20 *yuan*, and except for buying 6 or 7 *yuan* of salt and oil, all the rest was turned over to pay back the interest to the public granary. The new and the old public granaries in this village each had something over 30 *dan* of rice, for a total of 70 *dan*.

With the redistribution of the land in the third month of this year the six persons each received shares of seven *dan* in fields, for a total of 42 *dan*, and that piece of land owned by Changfen was turned over totally to Changying; the interest that Changying had been paying on Changfen's debt was cancelled, and the debt of 120 *yuan* to the public granary was also cancelled. The 42 *dan* of land is poor land that can give a yield of only 60 percent, about 25 *dan*, more or less, which, together with the sweet potatoes, gives them just enough to get by on.

In the eighth month of this year, there was a development in southwestern Jiangxi. The land was redistributed yet again, [applying the principle] of drawing on the fat to make up for the lean. One of his sons had died and one of his daughters had been married off, leaving only four persons in the family, each of whom received a share of 6 *dan* and 1 *tong* (4 *tong* make 1 *dan*), for a total of 25 *dan* of rice fields. A piece of his poor fields was given to someone else and a piece of someone else's good fields was given to him. This time the land distribution shares were evenly balanced. Why was it that in the third month distribution everyone received shares of 7 *dan* and in the eighth month distribution only 6.25 *dan*? Because after the victory of the revolution, twelve peasants from Pengwudong who had earlier gone to farm in Taihe now returned. The revolution had not yet reached Taihe, and, hearing that there had been a revolution in Xingguo and that the land was being distributed, they all returned so that the shares of everyone in this village were now somewhat smaller.

There are only four surnames in Pengwudong, Yi, Li, Qiu, and Zheng, with a total population of over 130 persons, and there is no village government.

He has not taken any part in affairs of the township government. His son, Li Quanpo, has been in charge of weapons for Pengwudong (spears, shotguns, knives, etc.). His son joined in the attacks on Xingguo and Liangkou, and for the attack on Nanchang it was his turn. He was willing to join the Red Army, but he wanted a one-month leave to return to buy an ox, for only then could he plow the fields, because his ox had fallen down and died[5] on the 27th of the third month, this year. An ox he had bought for 23 *yuan* the year before last, fell and died, and and he was able to sell it for beef for 10 *yuan*. In the sixth month, he spent 12 *yuan* to buy an ox that fell down and died in the seventh month, which sold for beef for 8 *yuan* (which he still has not yet collected). He must buy yet another ox in order to till the fields, and so he wants a month off to return home, after which he will rejoin the Red Army.

"Thanks to the blessings of the Red Army," an ox that cost 70 *yuan* in the past can be bought today for only 20 *yuan*. "Thanks to the blessings of the Red Army," everything is cheaper. Oil that in the past cost 23 *yuan* per *Dan* (100 *jin*), now cost only 20 *yuan* a *Dan*. Unhusked rice that in the past cost 4 *yuan* a *dan* is now 1 *yuan* a *dan* (three coppers[6] per *sheng* of husked rice). Firewood that in the past cost 20 copper cash [*wen*] per *jin* is now 8 copper cash per *jin*. Pork that in the past was 530 copper cash per *jin* is now 320 copper cash per *jin*. Only such items as salt and cloth have become especially expensive. Salt that in the past was 320 copper cash per *jin* is now 800 copper cash per *jin*, while cloth that in the past was, for white cotton cloth, 140 copper cash per foot[7] is today 320 per foot.

3. Wen Fengzhang:

From the fourth township (Houjing) of the tenth district. Houjing has over three hundred persons and a village government.

Four mouths to feed.

The father, aged fifty-six, has sore feet and cannot do any work at all. The mother, aged forty-six, has poor eyesight and, except for feeding the pig, cannot do anything else. He himself is twenty-two, and he tilled the fields. Since the third month of this year, he has been the commander of a detachment, and since the seventh month he has been on the finance committee of the township government. In the tenth month he joined the attack on Nanchang, as company commander of the Red Army Acting Reserves. His wife is sixteen, and she does the cooking, gets firewood, looks after the ox, and does not help in the fields.

He himself had 8 *dan* of absentee landlord fields. He does not know how much security deposit his father put down on them, but every year he still had to pay rent of 2.5 *dan* (dry hulled rice). These were originally 8-*dan* wet [unhulled] paddy fields, and, since they were good fields, they could yield 8 *dan* of dry hulled rice. The four persons needed 28 *dan* per year, or a minimum of 20 *dan*.

---

5. *Diesi*. It has not been possible to identify this disease. Presumably it is some virulent malady such as anthrax, which kills the cattle very quickly.

6. *Tong pian*, modern one-cent copper pieces of which 21 equaled 0.1 *yuan* in silver, according to Mao's Xunwu investigation. The copper to small silver exchange rate, like that between large and small silver coins, varied according to time and place.

7. The reference is to the Chinese foot (*chi*), equivalent to approximately 14.1 English inches, or 0.358 meters.

From a landlord, he rented 120 *dan* of rice fields, with no security deposit and rent in kind. The 120 *dan* of fields were all flood-plain fields. In reality, only 90 *dan* of wet rice could be harvested (there was one harvest a year). After a 20 percent reduction, this made 72 *dan* of dry rice, of which 55 *dan* went to pay the rent (at a rate of 75 percent), leaving 17 *dan*, which was not enough to feed them. After the harvest in the sixth to seventh months, although he had reaped the grain, after paying the rent, and paying back the cost of the grain he had borrowed[8] last year, they had nothing to eat. Then in the eighth to ninth months he again needed to borrow grain. He borrowed from a rich peasant, repaying 1.5 *dan*[9] for each *dan* borrowed for one year. Every year he needed to borrow over 10 *dan* of grain. This year, "thanks to the Red Army," he did not have to pay back last year's 12 *dan* of grain borrowed. He had a debt of 60 *yuan* that he owed to the landlord, Liu Huarang, on which the interest was 1 *dan* of rice for every 10 *haoyang* dollars.[10] Now he does not have to repay this. Fortunately, he was able to harvest 40 *Dan* of sweet potatoes, and with 3 *Dan* of sweet potatoes being the equivalent of 1 *dan* of rice, this was equivalent to a total of 13 *dan* of rice.

In the third month of this year, the four persons received shares in the distribution of the fields totaling 32 *dan* of fields; in addition to their 8 *dan* of absentee landlord fields, they received an additional 24 *dan* of fields. The method of dividing the fields was to take the 128 *dan* that he had originally tilled (120 *dan* as a tenant, plus the 8 *dan* of his own) and to carve out 96 *dan* to give to other people, leaving him with 32 *dan*. As much as possible, the fields given to others were poor fields, while the fields they retained were all good fields. In the second redistribution in the eighth month, it was discovered that he had been given too much, and that his land was too good, so 2 *dan* were cut away, leaving him with 30 *dan*. Some of his good fields were also taken away, and he was given others that were poorer. "The township government distributes the land very equitably."

In the past, when tilling 120 *dan* of rice fields, he was desperately busy, and for the three seasons of transplanting, harvesting, and planting the sweet potatoes, he had to hire workers. At transplanting time he would hire workers for six or seven workdays, and at harvesting time he needed over thirty workdays of help. At sweet potato planting time (twice, for early and late plantings) he needed over thirty workdays, for a total of over seventy workdays of help, not counting the more than ten workdays of friendly exchange (I help you work and you help me work) for transplanting and sweet potato planting. Now he tills only 30 *dan* of rice fields. Not only does he not have to hire outside help, or do friendly exchanges, but his work is not so difficult as it was in the past. Com-

---

8. *Shenggu*, loan-grain; see below.

9. The text actually reads "3 baskets" (*luo*); two such measures were equivalent to one *dan*.

10. *Haoyang* is another name for *xiaoyang*, used in southern China.

pared with the past, his work is only one-third as difficult, and he has a lot of spare time, which he uses to do things in the financial administration of the township government. He has participated in the attack on Xingguo, the attack on Liangkou, and the present attack on Nanchang.

He has four years of schooling. He can make out about half of a poster, and he can keep accounts.

4. Chen Zhenshan:

From the second township (Zhigesi) of the tenth district.

The second township has a total population of eight hundred persons, with the township government at Yongfeng Town.

Seven mouths to feed, three brothers, each with a wife, and the daughter of the eldest brother. The eldest brother is twenty-nine. Chen Zhenshan, the second oldest, is twenty-four, and the third brother is eighteen. The eldest brother had a salt and oil stall that was set up outside the entrance to a store. He sold the salt and oil only in small amounts. He borrowed 130 *yuan* from someone as capital, lost it, and "linked up with the revolution." He did not want to repay the debt, so he could not reopen his stall, and he is now a soldier with the Twentieth Army. The second brother has eight years of schooling. Up until the age of nineteen, he was at home looking after the ox. Beginning at nineteen, he learned how to "look after the land,"[11] and he has been "looking after the land" for five years. He is a propagandist in the township government. In this mobilization he was a company-level political committee member. The third brother was an apprentice to a bamboo carpenter. He had been studying this trade for three years and is now a soldier in the Twentieth Army. The eldest brother's wife cooks, gathers firewood, and grows vegetables. The second brother's wife does the same things and is now head of the women's Red Guard unit of the township government. The third brother's wife is only nine years old. The eldest brother's daughter is aged two.

They had 20 *dan* of rice fields of their own, and rented another 10 *dan* (on which they paid rent of 5 *dan*), under the direction of his eldest brother. The market at Yongfeng Town lasted three days. When the market was open, the eldest brother would go to sell oil and salt, and when the market was over, he would return home to till the fields. In addition to tilling the fields himself, the eldest brother annually hired workers for eighty workdays to help with the work.

On a debt of 130 *yuan*, they had to pay interest of 10 *dan* of rice. Of the 30 *dan* of rice harvested annually they paid 5 *dan* in rent and 10 *dan* in interest,

---

11. The expression translated "to look after the land" (*kan di*) is strictly parallel to that in the previous sentence, *kan niu* (to look after the ox). Since the character used for land is *di*, meaning land in general, or place, rather than *tian*, meaning cultivated field, the sense is apparently "to mind the farm," or "to look after the place." By putting the expression in quotation marks, Mao suggests that it has such a loose or broad meaning.

leaving only 15 *dan*. Of the seven persons, except when the third brother was away helping others to make things from bamboo splints, the six of them needed 42 *dan* to feed themselves, so they are short 23 *dan*, and they relied on the supplement of the little bit of money that came from the eldest brother's oil and salt business, and what the second brother earned looking after the land. The third brother was still in his apprenticeship term, during which he did not earn anything.

In the second month of last year, with the coming of the revolution, both the eldest and second brothers joined the revolution, the eldest brother acting as head of the food supplies office of the peasant association, and the second brother doing propaganda. All the women support the revolution because the creditor of their debt was always pressing them and making life impossible for them. When they heard about resisting rents, resisting service, resisting special fees, resisting grain taxes, and resisting debt payments, they were delighted and thus supported the eldest brother and second brother joining the revolution. The third brother is very naive. He does whatever anyone tells him to do, and this time he did not join the revolution. When the revolution failed in the fourth month, the Pacification Defense Corps dogs came and the eldest brother fled to Juncun and worked in the mountains, while the second brother fled to Guanchao in Taihe to act as a caretaker of someone's property, where he earned 70 to 80 *yuan*. In the twelfth month of last year, the Red Army again occupied Xingguo, and the eldest brother and second brother returned home to again participate in the revolution. When the revolution failed, six of their buildings were burned down by the Pacification Defense Corps dogs.

In the land distribution of the third month this year, in addition to their own 20 *dan* of land, they also received shares of 29 *dan*, giving them a total of 49 *dan*, or 7 *dan* per person. When the women saw that the land had been distributed and that they did not have to pay the rent or return the debt, they were overwhelmed with joy. The wife of the second brother was delighted to go to the township government, where she acted as leader of the women's Red Guard brigade. The land shares received in the third month redistribution were all good fields. When in the eighth month the land was redistributed again to balance the good and poor fields, half their good fields were taken away and replaced with poor fields, so that they still had 7 *dan* per person. Nevertheless, the women remained content, because they were working in the government where they frequently talked about the fact that the good and poor fields of other people should be balanced, so when it came time to balance their own fields, they also agreed.

The eldest brother, the second brother, the third brother, and the wife of the second brother all left home to work for the revolution, leaving at home only the three women, the wife of the eldest brother, the daughter of the eldest brother's wife, and the child wife. Since none of them had the ability to till the fields, the township government delegated people to till the fields for them. The extra manpower delegated by the township government to till their fields tilled the Chen family's fields first, before tilling their own, and did it very well. Those sent to till their fields ate with the Chen family. Of the seven in the family, four were away eating elsewhere, so the 7 *dan* that each of these four would have consumed became a surplus that was then sold, and with the money they bought oil and salt and cloth.

5. *Zhong Dewu:*

From the third township (Shankeng) of the tenth district.

The family has eleven persons. He himself is aged twenty-eight, has had seven years of schooling, and has a position as a gentleman[12] (accounts manager) for Wang's General Store in Bailu (30 *li* from Shankeng), with an annual salary of 60 *yuan*. From the time he began there as an apprentice to becoming store manager, it had been a total of thirteen years. In the third month of last year, when the Red Army came to Bailu, he returned to live at home. The mother is an old woman of fifty-seven, and she takes care of the little children. His older brother, the eighth brother, is thirty-one and tilled the fields. His eighth brother's wife is thirty-two, and she cooks, gathers firewood, does the laundry, and does not work in the fields. He has two nephews, one aged nine, who is studying, and the other aged three. His own wife, who is twenty-eight, cooks, gathers firewood, and tends the pig. He has two sons, one, aged seven, who is studying, and one who is two. His older nephew is married to a girl of nine, who takes care of the little children. There is one niece aged two. Of the above total of eleven persons, only the eighth brother was able to till the fields, while he himself was able to engage in business. None of the others had any productive abilities.

They themselves had only 30 *dan* of rice fields, and they rented from others another 36 *dan*, for a total of 66 *dan* of rice fields. On the rented land they paid rent of 60 percent, or 21.6 *dan,* which they paid in cash, and kept the rice for themselves. They were able to harvest 40 *Dan* of sweet potatoes annually. Eleven persons need 77 *dan* of rice to eat. Such items as raising ducks and a pig, making wine, hiring workers, entertaining guests, and so forth, took another 20 *dan* more or less. Thus, they needed a total of about 100 *dan*, of which their relatively low income left them 20 *dan* short. Annually, the entire family needed a total of 150 to 160 *yuan* for salt, cloth, labor, for buying grain, and all social obligations, including 20-plus to 30 *yuan* for salt, 30-plus *yuan* for cloth, and 25 to 26 *dan* for grain at about 3 *yuan* per *dan* for a total of over 70 *yuan*. In addition, they needed over 20 *yuan* for social obligations. The source of this 150

---

12. For a detailed discussion of the system under which employees in stores at this time progressed from the status of apprentices to that of "gentlemen" (*xiansheng*) see, above, the relevant passage in Mao's Xunwu investigation, Chapter III, the section on "general stores," and the note thereto.

to 160 *yuan* was the 60 *yuan* salary from the general store in Bailu, plus a bonus of 20 *yuan*; 10 or more *yuan* from miscellaneous produce that they grew, such as beans; something over 10 *yuan* from selling the meat that was left over from what they themselves ate of the pig they raised; and 10 or more *yuan* from pine firewood sold annually. This makes a total of approximately 120 *yuan*, to which must be added an annual debt of 30 to 40 *yuan*. The family formerly had a total indebtedness of over 200 *yuan*.

In the past, they had 46 *dan* of rice fields. Ten years ago, they sold 7 *dan* of fields (at a price of 10 *yuan* per *dan*), and the year before last they sold another 9 *dan* of fields (at 12 *yuan* per *dan*), leaving them with only 30 *dan*. The eighth brother did not have enough strength to till them alone, so every year they had to hire over 120 workdays of labor, at 240 cash per workday, for a total of twenty-eight strings of cash for labor annually.

In the second month of this year (March by the solar calendar), with the success of the revolution, each person received 5.5 *dan* of rice fields, giving the eleven persons a total of 60.5 *dan* (including their own 30 *dan*). Because that time the township did not balance good versus poor fields, they now are about to have a new redistribution, which has yet to be carried out. This township has a large population and a shortage of rice fields. A 5.5 *dan* share per person is not enough to live on. In the past, their family needed about 100 *dan* of rice to eat annually, plus miscellaneous funds of 150 to 160 *yuan*. The result of the land redistribution left them with 60.5 *dan*, 6 *dan* less than the 66 *dan* they had before the revolution. But they do not need to pay the 22 *dan* in rent (corresponding to over 60 *yuan* in cash), nor do they have to pay the 40 *yuan* in interest on their loan of over 200 *yuan* (20 percent interest rate). This is the good side. On the bad side is the fact that with the failure of Wang's General Store in Bailu, he is out of a job, so they have 80 *yuan* less in annual income (salary of 60 *yuan*, plus bonus of 20 *yuan*). Taking both aspects into account, they are about the same after the revolution as before. But after the revolution, their miscellaneous expenses are considerably diminished, and although they will still have expenses for entertaining hired workers, these will be somewhat less. Because they can be more economical in their clothing, they can also save a little on cloth. Since they do not have enough rice to eat, they will still have to buy rice, but the price of rice is much lower, 70 cents per *dan*. Their social obligations will be reduced considerably. Thus, the 150 to 160 *yuan* that they formerly needed for miscellaneous expenses will be cut in half, so that 80 *yuan* per year will be sufficient (in Xingguo money is always calculated in *haoyang*).[13]

The land distribution in the third month followed the principles: "take the original tiller as the standard, and draw on the plentiful to make up for the scarce." Taking the village as the unit, since in this village there is a larger

---

13. As noted above, the meaning of *haoyang* is essentially the same as that of the more common *xiaoyang*; presumably Mao is simply indicating which term is in use here.

population and less land, in practice they could only apply letting the original tillers keep their lands and did not draw on the plentiful to make up for the scarce. The further redistribution that is planned to take place will take land from other villages, so that probably each person will be able to receive 7 *dan*. If this is possible their food grain will be about right.

In the fifth month, he accepted responsibility in the land office of the township government for distributing hillside forest lands (as one of the four person committee on distributing the hillsides) and distributed all the hillside forest lands of the third township. Using a model that had been decided upon by the township representative assembly, he then went out and called a mass meeting in each village separately and carried out the distribution of the hillsides in each village. Larger hillside shares were given to those with less in fields, while those with more fields received less in hillside plots. While some with fields received no hillside plots, no one was given just hillside plots and no fields. Those with hillside plots are all given a little in fields. In the fifth month, he became brigade leader of the Red Guard reserve brigade. In the sixth month, he became a propaganda worker in the Independent Brigade. For this latest Xinyu mobilization, he was again a propaganda worker. He participated in the seventh and eighth attacks on Ji'an.

He wants to be a propaganda worker in the Red Army.

6. *Huang Dachun:*

From Chagan Village of the first township, tenth district.

This village has over 390 people.

Four mouths to feed. Aged thirty-six, he worked for someone else making firecrackers. His mother, aged fifty-four, has been ill for nine years and cannot do any work. His wife, aged thirty-one, cut firewood, which she carried to Bailu town to sell (Bailu is 10 *li* from Chagan), and with the money she would buy rice for the table. She also did the cooking, grew vegetables, and did the laundry, a very difficult life. His younger brother, aged thirty-two, was a bamboo craftsman. Last year, in the third month, he went to the Second Regiment and joined the Red Army. There has been no word from him since he left.

The family had 5 *dan* of rice fields that they tilled themselves, and they did not rent land from anyone else.

He helped someone else make firecrackers, working as a hired hand at the rate of 14 cents a day. If he worked every day, he could earn 4 *yuan* per month. His brother, the bamboo craftsman, made 11 cents a day, from which, after tobacco and clothing, he had no money left over.

After the revolution, firecrackers were no longer made, and his younger brother also no longer did the bamboo work and joined the army.

In the past, relying on his job making firecrackers and on the wife selling cut firewood, they never had enough to eat, from the beginning of the year to the end. With the land distribution, they have enough to eat. He owed a debt of 40 *yuan* to a rich peasant named Chen, for which his 5 *dan* of fields was the security deposit. This rich peasant was extremely evil, and during the revolution the masses beat him to death. Last year in the third month, a secret peasant association was organized, and the Chagan Village peasant association had fifty-six members. He was responsible for liaison. In the eleventh month of last year he became leader of the Red Guard brigade. This year, in the fourth month, he was the land cadre; in the sixth month, he became platoon leader in the Red Army Reserve Corps; in the eighth month, he became company commander in the Reserve Corps, and this time he led the corps in the action at Xinyu.

In the third month land redistribution, they received only 6.5 *dan* of fields each, all of which was poor land. Also, because the original tiller had already sown the seeds, the original tiller received 60 percent of the harvest and the new household received only 40 percent. In the new redistribution carried out in the seventh month (August by the solar calendar), each person received 7 *dan* and this time half of it was in good fields.

Since he was an unemployed firecracker worker and his brother was a bamboo worker who had joined the Red Army, both were given shares of land. Other workers who had employment also received shares of land, and furthermore, in the same amounts as the peasants. This was because even if the workers are presently employed, their jobs are not secure and they are always in fear of losing their jobs, so they requested that they be given shares of land. Also, because workers who received shares of land could not farm the fields themselves, they had to hire others to till the fields, and thus they needed the same amount of land as the others. In the beginning the peasants agreed only to let the workers have half shares. When the workers said that if they got only half shares they would have to raise the price of their labor, only then did the peasants say, "We will let you have full shares of land if you do not raise the price of your labor."

When the workers received shares of land, they did not have oxen and had to borrow oxen from friends or relatives, and having no plows they had to borrow plows as well, so they felt this was rather difficult.

Has had no schooling at all and can only write out a bill.

7. Chen Beiping:

From the third township (Shankeng) of the tenth district.

Eleven people. Three brothers, each with a wife. Two nephews, one father and one mother, and one paternal grandmother. The eldest brother, aged thirty-eight, was a bricklayer. The second brother, aged thirty-one, farmed the fields. The third brother, Chen Beiping, aged twenty-four, has had six and a half years of schooling, having studied for one and a half years at the higher elementary school. He has taught in the township elementary school for five years. The father is sixty-five and the mother is sixty-two. The wives of the three brothers stay at home doing the cooking, cutting firewood, growing vegetables, and doing the laundry, and they do not work in the fields. One nephew is aged two, and the other aged three. The grandmother is ninety-one.

They themselves had 32 *dan* of fields and rented from someone else another 20 *dan*, on which they paid 10 *dan* in rent. Of the eleven people, two ate at work, and since the young and the elderly ate somewhat less, 60 *dan* of rice annually would have been enough for them to eat, but their income was only 42 *dan*, so they were short about 20 *dan*. In addition, there were miscellaneous necessities such as entertaining, craftsmen, miscellaneous items such as salt and oil and cloth, gifts for marriages and funerals and seasonal holidays, and so on, for which they needed about 120 *yuan*. They relied on the eldest brother's wages of about 50 *yuan*, on the teaching salary of about 50 *yuan* of the third brother, on about 20 *yuan* they made on items they took from the hills, like palm fiber, firewood, bamboo, and lumber, and on the calf that the female ox gave birth to every year that they were able to sell for about 20 *yuan*, for a total of about 140 *yuan*, which was not enough both to pay for their miscellaneous necessities and to supplement their supply of table rice.

They had a debt of 80 *yuan*.

Last year, the grandmother, mother, and the two nephews all died, leaving behind the three brothers, the wives of the second and third brothers, plus the eldest brother's mother-in-law, so they now have six mouths to feed.

In the third month land redistribution, based on nine persons (at that time, there was one newly born son, one newly born nephew, and the eldest brother's new wife, but in the second half of this year they all died) at 5.5 *dan* of fields each, they were allotted a total of 50.5 *dan*. In addition to their own 32 *dan* of fields they received 18.5 *dan*, all of which were poor fields. In the present reallotment, the survey has already been made clear, but the redistribution has not yet been carried out.

With the fall of the landlords and rich peasants, people no longer build houses, so the eldest brother is out of a job and has turned to farming. The third brother continues to teach, at the newly founded Village People's School, and like the government workers he is paid 10 cents per day for food expenses and receives no salary. In the third month, the third brother (Chen Beiping) became a member of the political committee of the standing reserve corps; in the fourth month, he became a propagandist for the township government; in the fifth month, he became head of the cultural bureau of the township government; in the sixth month, he became a secretary in the township government; in the intercalary sixth month, he returned home to teach; in the ninth month, he went to Xinyu to become a member of the political committee of the Second Company of the army reserves.

Both the eldest brother and the second brother participated in the attacks on Wangtang and Langcun.

8. Lei Hanxiang:

From the third township (Shankeng) of the tenth district.

Five mouths to feed. Three brothers, a mother, and the wife of the eldest brother. The eldest brother, aged forty-three, worked part-time helping others as a hired farm hand, and part-time tilling their own fields. The second brother, aged thirty-nine, worked part-time as a hired farm hand and part-time tilling their own fields. Lei Hanxiang, the third brother, is aged twenty-five, and is a second-year brickmason's apprentice who had returned home to work as a hired farm hand. The mother is seventy. The eldest brother's wife, aged thirty-four, does the cooking, gathers firewood, and grows vegetables.

They had 7.5 *dan* of fields of their own, and they rented 44 *dan* of fields from the public domain [*gongtang*], on which they paid the public domain 60 percent in rent.

They had a debt of 120 *yuan* at 20 percent interest that was borrowed from a rich peasant of their own village named Lei Zurong.

The eldest brother and the second brother did odd jobs for other people. The eldest brother worked at home two-thirds of the time and the second brother no more than one-third of the time. The third brother worked practically all the time doing odd jobs for other people. The eldest brother is head of the household.

In a lean year, the harvest on their own 7.5 *dan* of fields could yield only 6 *dan*, and the 44 *dan* of public domain land they tilled could yield only 70 percent, or 30 *dan*. Even when the harvest was smaller, the rent was not reduced, and they still had to pay 60 percent of the 44 *dan* as rent, which came to 26 *dan*. For all their work in the fields, they then could keep only 4 *dan*. Together with the 6 *dan* from their own fields, this gave them a total of no more than 10 *dan*, which was much less than they needed just to eat. Also, they still had to pay 24 *yuan* in interest, so that the entire family was in really desperate straits.

The way that they supplemented their livelihood, first of all, was with the money that the eldest brother and the second brother, and especially the third brother, earned working for other people. The third brother hired out for about 220 days per year, while the eldest brother hired out for about 30 to 40 days per year, and the second brother helped other people with their work for about 170 to 180 days per year. All together they hired out to work for other people a total of about 420 to 430 days a year. Ordinarily, this kind of work paid 200 copper cash a day. Harvesting and wood cutting paid 500 coppers per day. Their total annual wages came to about 40 *yuan*. Second, they relied on growing sweet potatoes, of which they got over 40 *Dan* annually, which is the equivalent of more than 10 *dan* of rice. Third, they relied on *fandao*, that is, late rice, of which they harvested over 10 *dan* a year. They did not have to pay rent on this. When they planted late rice they could not grow other miscellaneous crops. Fourth, they relied on raising pigs, raising two each year, getting 20 *yuan* or more for each, for a total of over 40 *yuan,* which, subtracting the half that they ate themselves, left them with something over 20 *yuan.*

The above figures show a total income of more than 30 *dan* of rice, and over 60 *yuan* in money. On the expense side, they had only three mouths to feed (about two-thirds of the time the three brothers ate at work, so there was only one mouth to feed at home, plus the two women, for a total of three), plus the 24 *yuan* in interest, so that their expenses were fairly low and they could use the rest of their income on oil and salt and miscellaneous expenses, and their livelihood should not have been too difficult. Why is it then that their family still suffered badly (they really never had anything good to eat, just rice mixed with sweet potatoes every day, and they also had no decent clothes to wear)? The first reason is that all three brothers liked to gamble, especially the second brother, who was always losing at gambling. The second reason is that the wife of the eldest brother liked to eat but was too lazy to cook, and was always storming around the house, so that the three brothers did not want to work, and she killed the pig. The third is that two oxen died one after the other, one from drinking nitric acid, and the other from falling down. The family had bad luck and nothing seemed to go right. For these three reasons, their family was always having problems.

In the third month land distribution, each person received a share of 6.5 *dan* of fields, for a total of 32.5 *dan.* From the 51.5 *dan* they originally tilled (the 7.5 *dan* of their own fields plus the 44 *dan* they rented), 19 *dan* of fields were given to someone else, and the rest became their own. However, the 19 *dan* that were given to someone else were all very poor hillside fields that could yield only one crop a year, while the fields they kept were good fields that could be double-cropped.

The survey for the new redistribution has been completed but not yet carried out.

Since the 19 *dan* of fields taken out in the third month redistribution were then farmed by the new household, the 19 *dan* of rice harvested then belonged to the new household. From those fields that have been given to another family, they will get part of the harvest, 60 percent to the original tiller and 40 percent to the new household. Since the new family does not have to plant the new crop and the fertilizer has already been put in by the original tiller, when it comes time for the harvest, the new household is willing to give 60 percent to the original tiller and the original tiller is willing to let the new household keep 40 percent, just as if the new household was renting it from the original tiller for 40 percent of the yield.

The eldest brother is a soldier in the Red Guard brigade of this village. He participated in the attacks on Qifang and Wangtang. The second brother is a squad leader in the Red Guards. The third brother began as a soldier in the Red Guards and then became a platoon leader, and in the recent campaign at Xinyu was a company commander.

II. The Old Land Relations in This District

A. Distribution of the Land

According to the land situation in the Xingguo tenth district, that is, in the Yongfeng Town area, the old land distribution was as follows:

Landlords:	40 percent	
Public land: [gongtang]	10 percent	(owned in common by landlords and rich peasants)
Rich peasants:	30 percent	
Middle peasants:	15 percent	
Poor peasants:	5 percent	

B. As Percentage of the Population

Landlords:	1 percent
Rich peasants:	5 percent
Middle peasants:	20 percent
Poor peasants:	60 percent
Farm laborers:	1 percent
Handicraftsmen:	7 percent
Small merchants:	3 percent
Vagrants:	2 percent

According to the above data, the truly exploiting class (landlords and rich peasants) constituted no more than 6 percent of the population, while they owned 80 percent of the land, of which the rich peasants owned 30 percent, and the rich peasants also had control over a good amount of the public domain. If the lands of the rich peasants had not been divided equally, it would have been difficult to solve the problem posed by the fact that the majority of the people did not have enough land. The middle peasants were 20 percent of the population, but they had only 15 percent of the land. The middle peasants needed equal distribution of the land because they did not have enough land, and equal distribution added to their lands, rather than decreasing them. Those who say that equal distribution will hurt the middle peasants are wrong.

For the analysis of population distribution here, the household was the unit, not the individual. The 1 percent listed as farm laborers refers to those who were solely hired farm laborers. Those poor peasants who also hired out as farm laborers are not included in this category. The 3 percent small merchants refers to those who were solely small merchants and does not include those who were part-time peasants and part-time small merchants. The 2 percent vagrants refers solely to that group of people who were unemployed and who made a living by gambling, as bandits, and the like, and does not include those who were partially unemployed.

Why did the landlords constitute only 1 percent of the population? Because most of the landlords who had land in this district lived in the Bailu and Tiancun districts of Lingxian and in the *xian* town of this *xian*. If all of these were to be included here the landlord class would probably constitute 2 or 3 percent of the total population.

C. The Conditions of Exploitation

The first category, land rent exploitation.

In the first township (Lingyuan Hamlet), second township (Yongfeng Town), and fourth township (Houjing), all land rents were 50 percent, while in the third township (Shankeng) some were 60 percent and a small portion were 50 percent. Because the first, second, and fourth townships are subject to both flooding and drought, the harvests were often bad, and so the rents were comparatively low. Because the third township does not have floods or droughts, the rents were comparatively high.

Why are the first, second, and fourth townships subject to flooding and drought, while the third township is not? Because fields of the first, second, and fourth townships are alluvial. The hills in that area are all of shifting sands with no trees. All the sand in these hills has been rinsed by the river. The river is higher than the fields, and a section of the river levies are breached by the flood waters, and then when there is no rain for a long time they also have drought. The third township comprises mostly hillside fields. The fields are higher than the river, and although the plots are very small, they do not fear flooding when it rains, nor do they fear drought when it is dry.

There is no way to plant trees on hills of shifting sands.

The fields in this district are planted once a year, and less than 5 percent can grow a second crop of rice. Rent is not collected on the small second rice crop or on other crops.

The second category, high interest exploitation.

1) Money interest: divided into two stages. Before 1927, interest was 30 percent (30 *yuan* interest per 100 *yuan*). But not everyone could get loans. Only those with fields or hillsides or homes to put up as security could get loans. After 1927 (the world had begun to change), very few loaned out their money.

There were very few residing in this district who were strictly landlords. Most of the landlords lived in the Bailu and Tiancun area of Ganxian, and they simply owned land in this district. There were a lot of rich peasants. For this reason, in this district none of the poor peasants borrowed money from the landlords. Eighty percent of the loans came from the rich peasants, with 20 percent coming from the public domain [*gongtang*]. The middle peasants did not want to borrow money, and the hired farm hands could not borrow money. It was only the poor peasants who both wanted to borrow money and had something to put down as collateral. On the other hand, it was mainly the rich peasants who had money to lend, and for this reason confrontation between the poor peasants and the rich peasants in the land revolution unquestionably was inevitable. The rich peasants also sometimes borrowed money from the landlords, several hundred or a thousand *yuan* at a time, at very low interest rates of 15 to 18 percent. This is how the rich peasants got plenty of loan money that they then loaned out to the peasant people in loans of several tens of *yuan* against security items, squeezing out high interests. In this way the rich peasants were the middlemen for the landlord exploitation of the poor peasants, and it is for this reason that the interests of the landlords and rich peasants were inseparable.

The public domain in this district was mostly in the hands of the bad gentry. The greater part of these bad gentry had some fields, but not enough to live on, so they were neither rich peasants nor landlords. They were bad gentry. Because they did not have enough to live on, they wanted to control and exploit the public domain. Sixty percent of the public domain in the first, second, and fourth townships was controlled by the bad gentry; 40 percent was controlled by the rich peasants. In the third township, before the establishment of the Republic of China, most of it was controlled by the bad gentry because at that time the public domain could be managed only by someone with an official degree. With the advent of the Republic, most of it was managed by the rich peasants. The situation was just the opposite of that which prevailed in the first, second, and fourth townships; 60 percent was controlled by the rich peasants, and 40 percent by the bad gentry. When the poor peasants borrowed money from the public domain, the interest rate was slightly less than from the rich peasants. Interest on loans from rich peasants was 24 percent, and public domain interest was 20 percent. Public domain loans likewise required security deposits. The demand for repayment on public domain loans was even more peremptory than for rich peasant loans. If the interest was not paid on time, your ox and pigs were confiscated, and they came into the fields and cut the grain. They could do any of these things. On a rich peasant loan, if the interest was not paid on time, it was possible to explain it to him and pay interest on the interest, to be repaid together next year. Or he could take the fields used as collateral and rent them out to someone else to farm, taking the interest owed from the rent. The purpose of the rich peasant was just to get the interest, so at times they could be flexible with the payment schedule.

Of all the forms of interest, the most outrageous was monthly interest. This was the rate at which vagabonds borrowed money to gamble. The payment period was one month, after which a 1 *yuan* loan required a 2 *yuan* repayment. But this was not common.

2) Interest in rice: a loan in rice was called "living rice" [*shenggu*]. The rich peasants charged very heavy interest, while the interest from the public domain

granary was relatively light. When the rich peasants loaned rice to the poor peasants, no matter whether the loan was made in the eleventh month or twelfth month of the previous year, or in the first month, second month, or third month of the current year, it had to be repaid at the seventh month harvest, and always required 50 percent interest, that is, for each *dan* borrowed, the repayment was 1.5 *dan*. A loan borrowed in the eleventh month and repaid in the seventh month is less than one year; a loan borrowed in the first month or second month and repaid in the seventh month is only half a year; a loan borrowed in the third month and repaid in the seventh month is only four months. Why was the interest so high (30 percent more than money interest)? Because in the winter and spring seasons, the price of rice was very high, twice the price in the fall. In the fall, it was 1.5 *yuan* per *dan*, but in the winter and spring it generally was 3 *yuan*. For this reason, the rich peasant wanted to add his loss in the price of the rice to the interest. Furthermore, he only wanted to sell rice. He did not want to lend rice, because even though the interest rate had risen to 50 percent it was still more profitable for him to sell it in the winter and spring seasons. For a poor peasant to borrow rice from a rich peasant at all, they had to have very close relations. Of 100 *dan* of rice, a rich peasant would sell over 90 percent and lend less than 10 percent. In Chagan (in the first township) there was a rich peasant, Chen Fengwu, who lent grain to a poor peasant, Huang Dachun (in the fourth month of 1920). He did not want to make the loan. He was only willing to lend the money that would then be used to buy the grain from him.

Eighty percent of the money that the poor peasants borrowed was lent to them by the rich peasants, and 20 percent was borrowed from the public domain granaries. They did not borrow any money from the landlords directly. Ninety percent of the rice that the poor peasants borrowed came from the public domain granaries and 10 percent from the rich peasants. From this it can be seen that the rich peasants were purely exploitative and that the public domain granaries actually did give a little relief.

The public domain granaries were also largely exploitative. In the first township, 80 percent of the public domain rice was sold and 20 percent was lent out. In the second, third, and fourth townships, all the rice was sold and virtually none was lent. Only the grain that belonged solely to the welfare granary was all lent out with none of it being sold. Each of the townships in this district had welfare granaries. The first township (population 3,000) had four welfare granaries with 800 *dan* of rice. The second township (population 800) had five welfare granaries with 500 *dan* of rice. The third township (population 3,000) had six welfare granaries with 400 *dan* of rice. These three townships had a total of twenty welfare granaries, with a total of 1,700 *dan* of rice, practically one welfare granary for each village. It was only township four (population 2,000) that had but one welfare granary with 100 *dan* of rice. During the lean months, all the poor peasants of this district relied on borrowing a little cooking rice from the public granaries. It would have been futile to rely on the rich peasants to lend them rice. Interest on rice borrowed from the public granaries was 30 percent, and although this was less than what the rich peasants would charge, a security deposit was very strictly required. Iron implements (plows), tin utensils, silver items, quilts, curtains, clothing, and so on, could all be used for the security, but there had to be something. Only the Yangfang Village public granary in the first township did not require some security deposit for borrowing rice, and required only a "guarantor's note" [*dingpiao*] signed by a neighbor who would guarantee that the interest would be paid. The grain in the public granaries came from contributions made by the landlords, rich peasants, and middle peasants. Their contributions to set up a granary and the relief given to the poor peasants in lean and explosive times were a fraudulent reformist policy to appease riots by the poor people. Those who do not understand this stand there and praise their generosity. The public granary rice, except for the landlords and rich peasants and middle peasants who could not and did not want to borrow it, could be borrowed by poor peasants, hired farm laborers, by workers, and vagrants, as long as they had something to put up as security or could provide a "guarantor's note."

"Living rice" was terrible, but "picking up new rice money" was worse. In the second, third, fourth, and fifth months, when the poor peasants had nothing to eat and "picked up new rice money" from the rich peasants, the price of rice was 3 *yuan* a *dan* while picking up new rice money was 3.50 *yuan*. In the seventh and eighth months, when they repaid the rice loan the price of rice was generally about 2 *yuan*. If they could have borrowed at the market price at this time, it would not have been so bad, but the problem was that the poor peasants turned over their rice at the low price, and then in the spring and summer of the next year would look to the rich peasants who sold at a high price of 3 *yuan* per *dan*. The rich peasants would buy at 1.50 *yuan* and sell at 3 *yuan*, a profit of 100 percent. Wasn't this even worse than the 50 percent interest on "living rice"?

3) Interest on pigs: not applicable in this district.

4) Interest on oxen: seen in all the townships, but not to a great extent. The rich peasants took their female oxen and loaned them to the poor peasants, and the poor peasants fed these oxen and used them to till their fields, for which the rich peasant received a yearly interest of 1.5 *dan* (3 *luo*) of rice. If the ox gave birth to a calf, the rich peasant and poor peasant each owned half of it. Three out of the ten rich peasant families in the first, second, and fourth townships, rented oxen which were called "tax oxen" [*shuiniu*]. In the third township, only one out of ten rich peasant families had oxen that they rented out. The oxen might die of disease or of falling down, so this kind of interest on oxen was not necessarily reliable, and the rich peasants did not make much of an effort to get this kind of interest. They were also afraid that the poor peasants might not feed the oxen well, might starve them or work them too hard, or that they would be stolen by thieves. Thus there had to be a close relationship between the two families for a poor peasant to rent an ox from a rich peasant.

5) Oil interest.[14] When those poor peasants who had hills on which oil crops were grown had no rice to eat in the fifth and sixth months, they would borrow money from the rich peasants by selling new oil in order to buy rice for the table. In the fifth and sixth months, when the price of oil was 25 *yuan* per *Dan* (100 *jin*), they sold new oil for 12 *yuan*, or for as little as 10 *yuan*. In the ninth month, when they turned over the cooking oil, it must not be short. Thus, for 12 *yuan* borrowed from the rich peasants in the sixth month, they had to turn over one *Dan* of oil in the ninth month. The price of oil in the ninth month was generally 18 *yuan* per *Dan*, but might be as high as 20 *yuan* or as low as 15 *yuan*. If 12 *yuan* was borrowed in the sixth month and in the ninth month the price of oil was 18 *yuan*, the interest over four months was the difference of 6 *yuan*, an interest rate of 50 percent. If in the ninth month the price of oil was 20 *yuan*, then the interest of 8 *yuan* equals a rate of interest of 80 percent. When the rich peasants received the oil in the ninth month, they put it into storage and waited until the fourth through eighth months of the next year, when the oil has settled, and ship it to Jiangkou or to Ganzhou City, where they would sell it for at least 25 to 26 *yuan* per *Dan*. There were even times when it sold for as high as 40 *yuan* per *Dan*. In the sixth month of the year before last, when peasants from the first township went to Bailu to buy oil, 1 *yuan* (10 *mao*) would only buy 1 *jin* 12 *liang*. Although this was the retail price on small quantities, if put together, it would have taken 57 *yuan* to buy just 1 *Dan* of cooking oil. In the sixth month of last year, 1 *yuan* would buy 2.5 *jin*, which is 40 *yuan* per *Dan*. Using this figure for the calculation, the 12 *yuan* that a poor peasant would have received from a rich peasant against 1 *Dan* of new oil, by the sixth month of the next year, would mean a loss of over 28 *yuan*, or a rate of interest of over 200 percent. Not only was this form of oil interest very heavy, it was also very reliable. From the ninth to the twelfth month is the time period during which the poor peasants press the oil, and the rich peasants had no fear that the peasants would "run out on them" so they could just sit back and let the poor peasants bring the oil to their doorsteps. If they were afraid that a poor peasant might "run out on them," they could go in person to the poor peasant's house to collect the pressed oil and take it back themselves.

This form of interest on oil, from the poor peasant's point of view, was called "picking up new oil money," and from the rich peasant's point of view it was called "giving out new oil money." The lending of oil by rich peasants (not giving out new oil money) was extremely rare, but did occur occasionally. If a poor peasant borrows 1 *Dan* of oil from a rich peasant in the twelfth month of this year, he will buy it for 20 *yuan*, and next year when the price of oil is high, and he will return the 1 *Dan* of oil or pay in cash at the market price without

---

14. This refers to the "tea-oil" which played such a large part in the economy of Xunwu. For a vivid account of the same type of loan, see above, the "Xunwu Investigation," Chapter IV, section on exploitation.

interest. This was the same as the poor peasant storing 1 *Dan* of oil for the rich peasant, so there was not a heavy interest payment. Only those with close relations to the rich peasants and who could be relied upon to return the oil the next year could get such loans. A poor peasants would get this kind of oil loan upon the death of a parent, or when taking a wife, or for some other emergency at which time he would ask a rich peasant he knew well for a loan in money, to which the rich peasant would reply that he had no money, only oil (or he would say that he only had rice). So the poor peasant would borrow the oil and sell it for cash to meet the emergency expenses. The next year, when the price of oil was high, if the lender wanted oil, the borrower would buy oil from the market to return to him. If the lender wanted cash he would have to repay him in cash at the current market rate. This method of oil borrowing was called "grabbing oil."

Neither the former form of "picking up oil money" nor the latter form of "grabbing oil" was used often. These occurred only in those areas where there were oil crop hills. In the areas that did have oil crop hills, such as the eleventh district of Xingguo (the area around Juncun), many of the poor peasants farmed oil crop hills (very few of the poor peasants had their own oil crop hills, most were rented from landlords and rich peasants). Of one hundred poor peasant families that farmed oil crop hills, twenty of them picked up new oil money. The rich peasants in the Juncun area severely exploited the oil interest loans. In that area, no more than one or two out of a hundred poor peasant families who farmed oil crop hills "grabbed oil" from the rich peasants.

6) Interest on pawning: of two kinds, big pawns and small pawns. There were no big pawns in this district, only in Tiancun and Bailu, where the monthly interest rate was 5 percent. On 100 coppers the monthly interest was 5 coppers, on 1,000 coppers the monthly interest was 50 coppers, and on 1 *yuan* the monthly interest was 5 cents, all calculated in small foreign dollars. The term of a pawn loan was ten months. If the money was not returned by the end of the term, after an extension of one month the item pawned was forfeit. A monthly interest of 5 percent is 60 percent annual interest. This was a particularly severe form of exploitation. A great many poor peasants, hired farm laborers, workers, and vagrants went to the pawnshops. Among these four categories of people, sixty out of a hundred families were in hock to the pawnshops. Iron, tin, or silver utensils, mosquito netting, quilts, or clothing could all be pawned.

A great many people in this district ran over to Bailu to pawn things, some 60 percent of the poor destitute masses. The owner of the pawnshop in Bailu was someone from the Xingguo *xian* town. After eleven months and default, the owner of the pawnshop would send the pawned items to the Xingguo *xian* town to be sold at auction. An item worth 3 *yuan* was pawned for 1.50 *yuan*. But the objective of the pawnshop owner was the interest, not auctioning off the items pawned.

Small pawning took place in all the townships of this district. The rich peasants who gave out pawn loans did not do so openly, nor did they do it often. It was only when an impoverished worker or peasant was really destitute that he picked up something and ran over to a rich peasant's house and begged him to accept it as security for a little cash. This did happen occasionally. Ten out of a hundred impoverished worker and peasant families got small pawn loans this way. Why is it that many went to the regular pawnshops and few pawned things elsewhere? Because engaging in this kind of activity gave one an extremely bad name, and furthermore, the people here in this township knew each other too well, and even if something were accepted as security, the poor peasants would always beg for a few more pennies on the item pawned, and it was not easy for the rich peasants to put up a stiff argument. It is for this reason that most of the rich peasants were not really willing to engage in this activity. The interest rate for small pawns was the same as for big pawns but the time period was very short. It was up to the rich peasant—one month, two months, three months, four months—and if the money was not repaid by the time the period was up, the pawn was forfeit.

Of the eight persons who participated in this survey meeting, the families of four of them, Chen Beiping, Zhong Dewu, Fu Jiting, and Chen Zhenshan, had never pawned anything. The four families of Wen Fengzhang, Lei Hanxiang, Huang Dachun, and Li Changying had all pawned things. Wen Fengzhang pawned something once a year. In the fourth or fifth month he pawned something in order to buy rice for the table, and he also did this once last year. In the fourth month of last year he pawned one iron plow and two wine jars at the Hengxing Pawnshop in Bailu for 2.40 in small foreign dollars, with which he bought and brought back 1 *dan* of rice. In the twelfth month he repaid it. Lei Hanxiang's family also pawned something every year. In addition to things pawned by the eldest brother and second brother, the third brother, Lei Hanxiang, himself, in the first month of last year got one loan in which he pawned one long gown for 1 *yuan*, and two hoe blades for 60 cents, that he has not yet repaid. In the sixth month, he again borrowed money by pawning one trowel for 30 cents and one "*yang touzi*" for 50 cents (both of which are tools that the third brother uses in his masonry work), which also have not been retrieved. Before last year, Li Changying had never pawned anything, but when the revolution began in the second month of last year, he went to work with the large guerrilla corps, and when the White bandits arrived he fled to Bailu, and since his wife at home had nothing to eat he pawned one cotton padded jacket for 1.20 *yuan*. The revolution returned, but he has not yet reclaimed the jacket. Before last year, Huang Dachun had never pawned anything but in the fifth month of last year, since firecrackers were not selling, no one would hire him to make firecrackers, so he had nothing to eat and pawned one quilt for 1.50 *yuan* to a rich peasant in his village named Zhong Kuaizi. When revolution took place in the entire *xian* in the seventh month of this year, the Bailu guerrilla team came to his village, and the poor people rose in revolt. They arrested Zhong Kuaizi, took him to Bailu and killed him, and Huang Dachun got his quilt back. The father of this Zhong Kuaizi was a good man who wanted to help the poor people, so the masses did not kill him. Zhong Kuaizi had had a fireworks shop in Tangjiang, had learned fighting with one hand,[15] and had wounded several dozen people. Everyone was glad to see him dead. His fields were distributed, and three fines, amounting to several hundred *yuan,* were imposed on his family.

7) Interest on salt: Really terrible, because in Xingguo all the salt came from Guangdong and also because quite a few poor peasants engaged in the salt trade. Ten out of a hundred poor peasant families in this district were also salt carriers. Having no capital, they would borrow from the rich peasants to buy ducks, which they then carried to Jiayingzhou (in Meixian, Guangdong). They would carry a load of ducks there and return with a load of salt. For the 1 foreign dollar they borrowed they paid interest of one *jin* in salt. The time period was no more than twenty days to one month. The price of one *jin* of salt was 12 or 13 cents, so in one month, they paid 12 or 13 cents interest on a loan of 1 *yuan.* Since 1927, as the revolution has spread day by day, interest rates have generally come down, falling to 24 percent, but the interest on salt has not fallen.

D. The Third Form of Exploitation: Taxes and Fees

In this district, aside from the grain tax, there were no direct taxes or fees on the peasants.

Three *dan* of rice fields equaled 1 *dan* of "seedling-rent," on which the grain tax payment was 0.044 *yuan* (in silver). For the grain tax, one ounce of silver equaled 3.60 big foreign dollars, so 0.044 *yuan* amounted to 0.1584 big foreign dollars, which was the grain tax on 1 *dan* of seedling-rent.[16] Since 1 *dan* of seedling-rent fields was currently equal to 3 *dan* of ordinary fields, the current grain tax on 1 *dan* of ordinary rice fields was 0.0528 big foreign dollars. Last year, the price of rice in this district was 3 small foreign dollars per *dan*, the equivalent of six copper *yuan* or strings of cash. With 1 *yuan* in big foreign dollars equal to 2.80 *yuan* copper, 0.0528 *yuan* in big foreign dollars, the equivalent of 148 copper cash, could buy slightly less than 2.5 *sheng* of rice.[17] This means that currently in Xingguo, for one *dan* of rice fields the annual grain tax was 2.5 *sheng*. But in this district, the actual grain yield per 1 *dan* of rice fields was only 0.7 *dan* (70 percent), and so this means that for every 0.7 *dan* of rice harvested 2.5 *sheng* were paid in grain tax, a total of about 3.5 percent.

Although in this district there was no other direct tax exploitation, those who go from this district to Guangdong to engage in the salt business have been

---

15. *Yishou da,* apparently a martial art of some kind.

16. The *liang* or ounce of silver (often translated "tael") was no longer an officially recognized monetary unit, but was in fact widely used at this time. Regarding the difference between "big" and "small" foreign dollars, see above, the Note on Sources and Conventions.

17. One *sheng* is equivalent to 1 liter, or 0.01 *dan*.

exploited by various taxes and fees along the way. Middle or poor peasants who engage in the salt trade buy 70 *jin* of ducks in this township at 0.32 *yuan* per *jin*. In the past, a carrying-pole load of ducks taken to Jiayingzhou would bring a little over 0.3 ounces of silver per *jin*, and sometimes as much as 0.4 ounces per *jin*. This year the price has gone up to 0.48 ounces per *jin*. Each 0.74 ounces of silver is equal to one big foreign dollar, so 0.48 ounces of silver is equal to 0.65 big foreign dollars, or 0.91 *yuan* in small foreign dollars. Subtracting the 0.32 *yuan* in capital outlay, each *jin* of ducks could earn 0.59 *yuan* in small foreign dollars, so 70 *jin* of ducks could earn 41.30 *yuan*. Why is the price of ducks so especially high in Jiayingzhou this year? Because of the revolution, few ducks from the various *xian* of southern Jiangxi have been taken there, so they have become very expensive.

From the 41.30 *yuan* net earnings, it is necessary to subtract the expenses incurred along the way. First is wages. In past years, one could get to Jiayingzhou in ten days, but at present it is necessary to make detours in many places that lie between the Red and White districts, so it takes at least fifteen days. At 0.25 *yuan* for a day's work, fifteen days makes a total of 3.75 *yuan*. Second is the expense for food, tobacco, tea, and straw sandals, which comes to at least 0.45 *yuan* per day, or for fifteen days a total of 6.75 *yuan*. Third is the cost of feed for the ducks. Each day 70 *jin* of ducks will eat 0.30 *yuan* in grain, a total of 4.50 *yuan* for fifteen days. Fourth is the *lijin*.[18] From Xingguo to Menling there are no fees, but when you reach Menling there is a *lijin* fee of one *yuan* in big foreign dollars per load of ducks (equal to 1.40 *yuan* in small foreign dollars). After Menling, there are no fees. Fifth, expenses incurred in this district for each load of ducks must be added in, including three days of wages and food and buying the duck cages, for a total of 2 *yuan*. The expense account for the above five items comes to a total of 19.40 *yuan*.[19] Subtracting 19.40 *yuan* from 41.30 *yuan* leaves real earnings per load of ducks of 21.90 *yuan*.

One load of ducks going, and one load of salt coming back again. This year, 1 *yuan* in big foreign dollars can buy only 14 *jin* of salt in Jiayingzhou, and the same was true last year. This year, as the revolution has developed, the consumption of salt has stagnated, so salt has become cheaper. One load of 80 *jin* costs 4.50 *yuan* in big foreign dollars, or 6.30 *yuan* in small foreign dollars. When the salt was carried back to Xingguo, in the fifth and sixth months of this year, salt was very scarce and so the price had risen to the point that 1 *yuan* in small foreign dollars could buy only 2.5 *jin*. Using the market price at this time, 80 *jin* of salt could be sold for 32 *yuan* in small foreign dollars. Subtracting the outlay

---

18. The road tax on goods moved from one locality to another. For a detailed discussion of its impact by Mao, see, in Volume II, his article of July 11, 1923, "The Beijing Coup d'État and the Merchants."

19. These figures do not add up, as the Japanese edition emphasizes by placing the annotation "thus" opposite the total of 19.40 *yuan*, and opposite the profit of 21.90 *yuan* below.

of 6.30 *yuan*, this would leave earnings of 25.70 *yuan* in small foreign dollars.

But from the 25.70 *yuan* net earnings, it is necessary to subtract expenses. First, wages for 15 days, amounting to 3.75 *yuan*. Second, for food, tobacco, tea, straw sandals, 6.75 *yuan*. Third, *lijin* fees in six places, Jitan, Menling, Baibu, Diaoyutan, Huichang, and Huaqiao, a transit fee [*guoli*] at Menling, and inspection stations [*jianpiao*] at the five other places. In the past the transit fee was 0.60 to 0.70 *yuan* per load of salt, but it is now 1 *yuan* in big foreign dollars. At each of the inspection stations the charge is 0.20 *yuan* in big foreign dollars,[20] for a total of 2 *yuan* in big foreign dollars (equal to 2.80 *yuan* in small foreign dollars). The three expenses above total 13.30 *yuan*. Subtracting 13.30 *yuan* from 25.70 *yuan* leaves a remainder of 12.40 *yuan*.

Taking one load of ducks earns 21.90 *yuan* and bringing one load of salt back earns 12.40 *yuan*, for total earnings of 34.30 *yuan* in one month's time. In the past, trade in the two items of ducks and salt was not as lucrative as it is now, but it was more reliable, it was not necessary to make detours, and the round trip took only twenty days. Now you can make more money, but the road is not safe, the militia and the pacification defense forces frequently take any cash that travelers are carrying (after selling the ducks only a small portion of the cash is needed to buy the salt, and most of it is carried on your person). Although they do not want the salt, they will frequently take ducks to eat. They just don't go as far as killing people. Even so, the number of people who go out and engage in trade has by no means diminished.

In the fifth and sixth months salt was expensive, 1 *yuan* for 2.5 *jin*. Now (the tenth month), salt is a somewhat cheaper, 1 *yuan* for 3 *jin* 12 *liang*. This is because the two areas of Jiangkou and Dahujiang have been opened up and salt can be brought to Ganzhou. In comparison to the prerevolution times, it is very expensive. Before the revolution, 1 *yuan* could buy 6 *jin* 4 *liang*, which is about half the price it is now (the tenth month), and about one-third the price of what it was in the fifth and sixth months of this year.

III. The Various Classes in the Struggle

1. Landlords

All the landlords of the first township lived in Xingguo Town and in Bailu, not in their own villages, and the rents had to be sent to Xingguo Town or Bailu. Four or five of the big landlords who owned land in this township lived in Bailu, and each family received rents on over 1,000 *dan*. Some had stores in Bailu, and some did business in Nanchang and in Ganzhou. The one family that lived in Xingguo Town and received rents on 1,000 *dan* owned the Hengchunhao foreign goods store in the town and also had a store in Ganzhou.

---

20. The text reads "small foreign dollars," but this appears to be an error.

In the second township there were three landlord households, each receiving rents of over 300 *dan*, all living in their original villages. Liu Yuelin, with 300 *dan* in rentals, did not himself farm. During the revolution two members of his family were killed, the first and third sons of Yuelong, both of whom were branch commanders in the Pacification Defense Corps. After the revolution, their household still had ten mouths to feed. They were given land shares and submitted to the government. Du Xiyou farmed 200 *dan* of fields himself and received rent on 300. The household numbers over twenty persons. Du Xiyou is aged forty, and in the second month of last year joined the revolution. In the second month of this year when the Red Army arrived, on his own initiative he voluntarily took the land deeds and burned them and distributed the land. Du works in the government, in propaganda. Xie Wenlin, with a household of thirty, farmed 500 *dan* of fields himself and received rent on 100. He is related to Du Xiyou, and he voluntarily burned his land deeds and distributed the land. He is now head of the office of finance in the township government. There are six brothers in his family, five of whom farmed; they also employed four permanent workers, and were the richest in the village. No one in his household can read, and he is very honest and forthright. (Actually, Xie Wenlin was a big rich peasant.)

In the third township there were two landlord families. Ceng Xiqun had five households that received rent on a total of over 1,000 *dan*. He himself did not farm. The five households totaled over twenty persons. He was a famous big landlord and counterrevolutionary. The men have all fled, leaving behind five or six women and little children, each of whom has received land distribution shares. Their house was burned. No one in his family has yet been killed. Two people with the same surname who acted as running dogs for him have been killed. Xie Yuanxiang rented out over 400 [*dan*]. He himself did not farm. Over twenty persons, counterrevolutionaries, have fled. None were killed.

In the fourth township, Wang Runlan, a big landlord, rented out 400 *dan*, and he himself farmed another 200 in rice fields. He had many oil-producing hillsides, all of which he farmed himself. A counterrevolutionary and head of the Pacification Defense Corps, he killed a great many workers and peasants, burned a large number of workers' and peasants' homes, and has now fled. Liu Jiahong had 300 *dan* of fields, of which he farmed 100 himself and rented out 200. Five people, counterrevolutionary, started the Pacification Defense Corps with Wang Runlan and Ceng Meixi. Liu Jiahong and his son were both killed. Ceng Meixi received rent on 100 *dan*, and himself farmed over 100 in rice. A rich peasant, his family comprised five persons, and as second in command of the Pacification Defense Corps he killed many workers and peasants. When he killed the poor peasant Gao Laogou, "his spirit made a ruckus in their house, and the ghost strangled to death Ceng Meixi and his father." Xie Chuanzhen rented out 600 *dan*, and did not do any farming himself. [His family comprises] five or six people. Xie Chuanzhen was arrested by the third district and turned over to the government for detention. He has not yet been killed. The family wealth has been confiscated.

2. Rich Peasants

The first township had a total of twelve families, of which seven were counter-revolutionary. Of these seven families, the heads of household of two of them have been killed. The adult males of all the other five families have fled. The property of the families of those who have fled has been confiscated, including all their cooking pots and pans. The properties of those families whose family heads were killed have not been confiscated. None of the women, old people, or children of the seven families have fled and land has been distributed to all of them. Several of the women have remarried. Liu Nengchang, one of the family heads who was killed, has a son, Liu Shuyao, aged twenty, who joined the revolution and was a squad leader in the Xinyu campaign. The house of one of the families, that of someone called Chen Fengming, was burned down. Five of the twelve families were not counterrevolutionary. They were fined and land was distributed to them. They have joined the Red Guards, and have also made great efforts in revolutionary work. Among them, Xu Changhan had 400 *dan* of rice fields, most of which he farmed himself, a small portion of which were rented out. There are ten people in the household. He also had a lot of cash on which he received interest. The guerrilla team fined him 700 *yuan*. His household goods were not confiscated. His rice was not divided, but his fields were. Xu Changhan, aged twenty-six, joined the revolution in the second or third month of last year, and beginning in the third month of this year acted as a director in the Youth Vanguard Corps and then went to work in the southwestern Jiangxi government (position unknown). In the eighth month he returned home and again went to work in the district government as director of the Youth Vanguard Corps. He was accused of belonging to the AB Corps and arrested. Ling Yuepo had 400 *dan* of rich fields, all of which he himself farmed. With twelve people in the family, his son, Ling Leihan, is a "graduate" who has been a secretary in the village government. He was fined over 100 *yuan* but still continued to act as secretary until people accused him of being part of the AB Corps, when he was detained by the district government for over two months. He was allowed to confess, and then released. Xie Zhongjie, with over 200 *dan* of rice fields, farmed most of them himself and rented out some fields. Eight people. Recently the township government arrested him and will impose a fine in money. Not yet released. Seven of the above twelve rich peasants actively opposed the revolution. Although five of them ostensibly joined the revolution, two were plotting reactionary members of the AB Corps, leaving three families, one of which has been arrested.

There were nine rich peasants in the second township: Chen Xianwei, Mei Jiasheng, Yang Zulian, Xie Zhongyu, Xie Wenlin, Chen Gunwei, Wang Zhengke, Zou Xiangchun, and Xie Liangci. Chen Xianwei had 200 *dan* in fields, of which he himself farmed 120 and he rented out 80. He had money to lend out. Over ten people. He engaged in extremely harsh exploitation and was a counterrevolutionary. Chen Xianwei fled, his three sons were killed, and the family's possessions were confiscated. Mei Jiasheng was actually a small landlord with over 100 *dan* of fields, all of which he rented out. He had money to lend out, was in the cloth business, and was a counterrevolutionary who supervised the Pacification Defense Corps. Mei Jiasheng and his mother, as well as one of their long-term farm laborers, were killed by the guerrilla team, and their household was confiscated. Yang Zulian had over 100 *dan* of fields, half of which he farmed himself and half of which he rented out. A counterrevolutionary and head of the AB Corps assassination team. Executed by the district government in the seventh month. Xie Zhongyu was also a small landlord who rented out all his land and had money to lend. A counterrevolutionary and head of the AB Corps. Generally speaking, he was a member of the evil gentry, and he was executed on the 16th of the eighth month by the district government. Xie Wenlin had 600 *dan* of rice fields, all of which he rented out, and he owned a general merchandise store in Yongfeng Town. At the beginning he joined the revolution and was in charge of finances for the government of the second township. He embezzled over 80 *yuan*, was fired and fined 150 *yuan*. One day at a mass meeting he wrote out somebody's ready-made slogans, "Convince the soviet authorities of the necessity for the AB Corps reform group" and "Defend the necessity for the AB Corps reform group in Ganzhou and Ji'an." He was arrested and beaten. Seven of the above nine rich peasants (three of whom were small landlords while one was a small merchant) were counterrevolutionaries, and only two were revolutionary.

In the third township, there were nine rich peasants: Xie Jiuzhang, Mao Shiji, Lei Yongxia, Chen Fengming, Jiang Taoshu, Qiu Futian, Qiu Shili, Qiu Zhikui, and Xie Yixing. Xie Jiuzhang had over 400 *dan* of fields, of which he farmed over 200 himself and rented out 200. Eight people. He charged high interest rates and was a counterrevolutionary. In the village he was called a despot, and was a local bully. When the revolution started, the entire family fled. Mao Shiji had over 200 *dan* of fields, all of which he farmed himself. He lent money. Some time ago, there were twenty-three people in the household, but now it is divided into four. The grandson, Mao Zhangping, aged twenty-two, a middle school student and a team leader in the AB Corps, has been arrested. Lei Yongxia had over 200 *dan* in fields, of which he farmed 50 himself and rented out over 100. He had money that he lent out. He ran away some time ago. The township government fined him over 200 *yuan*. When he returned home the township government ordered him to go to the Red Army school, and when he failed the entrance examination, the township government told him to go to the Xingguo *xian* training unit. Aged twenty-one. Graduated from higher primary school. Chen Fengming had over 100 *dan* of fields, all of which he farmed himself. Seven people. He had no money to lend out because his son needed money for school in Ganzhou. A counterrevolutionary and secretary of the AB Corps, he was killed and his possessions confiscated. Jiang Taoshu had over 100 *dan* in fields, all of which he farmed himself, and had money to lend out. Ten people.

He joined the revolution, and they fined him 120 *yuan*. Qiu Futian had over 100 *dan* in fields that he farmed himself. Had a little money to lend out. Five people. A counterrevolutionary, he fled, and his wife went off with somebody else. Qiu Shili had 130 *dan* of fields, of which he cultivated 40 *dan*, and rented out 90 *dan*. He smoked opium, and had no money to lend. He was a counterrevolutionary, and he himself fled. The township government told his wife to remarry. His house has been turned into offices of the township government. Qiu Zhikui had 150 *dan* of fields that he farmed himself, and he had money to lend. Six people. He joined the revolution, and his son enlisted in the Red Guards. He was fined 60 *yuan*. Xie Yixing had two hundred *dan* of fields, half of which he cultivated himself, and half of which he rented out. He had money to lend. Twelve people. A member of the AB Corps, he was arrested. His fourth son fled, leaving three sons still at home. Six of the nine rich peasants in the third township were counterrevolutionaries, leaving only three who are not counterrevolutionaries.

In the fourth township, the two rich peasants, Liu Jiahong and Ceng Meixi, were both counterrevolutionaries (see the above section on landlords).

In the four townships of this district, the first township had twelve rich peasants, nine of whom were counterrevolutionaries; the second township had nine rich peasants, seven of whom were counterrevolutionaries; the third township had nine rich peasants, six of whom were counterrevolutionaries; and the fourth township had two rich peasants, both of whom were counterrevolutionaries. The four townships had a total of thirty-two rich peasants, twenty-four of whom were counterrevolutionaries, and although the remaining eight do not yet appear to be counterrevolutionary, who knows what they will be like in the future.

The rich peasants had very good fields, just as good as those of the landlords and the public domain. When they buy land from the poor peasants, they always want to buy their good fields, and the poor peasants have no choice but to sell them their good fields. If they sell their poor fields they have to sell several *mu* for the price of one *mu*. When they make loans the poor peasants have to put up security, for which they want only good fields, not the poor fields. It is for this reason that day by day the good fields become concentrated in the hands of the rich peasants.

When the revolution first begins, as in the second and third month of this year, quite a few of the rich peasants opportunistically join the revolution. Thirty percent of the positions in the township and district soviets were held by rich peasants and their running dogs. During the fourth and fifth months, with the promotion of Oppose the Rich Peasants Week, they were overthrown. By now there are only two rich peasants active in the affairs of this district (one is Xie Wenlin, who is head of the finance office of the second township soviet, and the other is Zou Lidong, who is director of the cultural department of the district government).

3. The Middle Peasants

The middle peasants gain from the land revolution. First, the middle peasants do not lose in land, but rather most of them gain from the equal distribution of the fields. The middle peasants represented 20 percent of the total population of this district, while they had only 15 percent of the land. Thus, with the equal distribution of fields, most of the middle peasants in this district have come out ahead. Although there are some who ended up with less, they were only a very small proportion.

Second, in the past, taking a wife cost about 200 *yuan*, practically the entire resources of the family, so it was not easy for a middle peasant to get married. A great many are in debt because of getting married. If a wife died, it was extremely difficult to marry again. Now, with freedom of marriage, you do not need a penny, and this is a very big benefit.

Third, in the past when one of the elderly people died in a middle peasant family, they had to spent a minimum of 50 *yuan*, and as much as 100 *yuan*, and more. In the past, it was common for a middle peasant to be bankrupted by the death of a father or mother. Today, with the breaking of superstitious customs, when people die they are just buried without spending a penny.

Fourth, in the past oxen were very expensive. When an ox fell down and died the ox meat could be sold for 10 *yuan* or 8 *yuan*, to which more than 10 *yuan* had to be added to buy another ox. Today, although the meat of an ox that has fallen down and died still brings in 10 *yuan* or 8 *yuan*, you need only 3 or 4 *yuan* more to buy another.

Fifth, with the overthrow of the power of the landlords and rich peasants, the abolition of the ceremonial practices, and the breaking of superstition, it is no longer necessary to send gifts and presents or make temple offerings of paper money and candles, and this saves some money.

Sixth, in addition to the five economic benefits listed above, there is also a political benefit, which may be considered as the most important benefit of all. In the past, under the rule of the landlords and rich peasants, the middle peasants had no "right to voice an opinion on things." They had to do whatever others prescribed. Now, together with the poor peasants and farm laborers, they have the right to speak and to act. In both the township and district soviets, about 40 percent of the work is done by the middle peasants. About 10 percent of them had no debts at all, while 30 percent had small debts that did not really threaten their financial well-being.

The middle peasants have very courageously joined the revolution and have participated in "campaigns" (meaning that, organized as self-defense armies, they have gone out into battle), have gone out on patrol, and held meetings, just like the poor peasants.

The middle peasants in this district were 20 percent of the population and had 15 percent of the land. Although the land of the middle peasants was somewhat better than that of the poor peasants, it was far from that of the rich peasants. Generally, the land of the middle peasants was half good land and half poor land.

4. The Poor Peasants

After the revolution, the poor peasants achieved the following benefits:

First, they received shares of the fields. This was a fundamental benefit.

Second, they received shares of the hills. In the past, few poor peasants owned hill lands. In the first and second townships 30 percent of the poor peasants owned hill land, and 70 percent had none. In the third township (Shankeng) in the vicinity of Juncun, there are a lot of hills so 70 percent of the poor peasants had hill land and 30 percent had no hill land. Most of the hills in that area grow oil-bearing crops. In the fourth township, 50 percent of the poor peasants had hill land, and 50 percent did not. In all townships, even those poor peasants who did have hill land had only very small amounts. Of the hills in this district, in the first and second townships most of the hills are of loose sand, so the landlords want only the fields, leaving the hills to others, so the rich, middle, and poor peasants all had parts of the hills. In the first township, the distribution of the hill land was: rich peasants, 40 percent; middle peasants, 40 percent; poor peasants, 20 percent. In the second township, the hill land distribution was: rich peasants, 50 percent; middle peasants, 30 percent; poor peasants, 20 percent. Because the third township has a lot of oil crop hills, the hill areas are valuable and the landlords wanted the hill lands. But the rich peasants had most of the hill lands. The distribution was: landlords, 15 percent; rich peasants, 50 percent; middle peasants, 20 percent; poor peasants, 15 percent. Above we said that in the third township seventy out of a hundred poor families had hill lands, but the amount of hill land they owned was no more than 20 percent. Each family had only a very little bit. In the fourth township, the distribution was: landlords, 20 percent; rich peasants, 20 percent; middle peasants, 50 percent; poor peasants, 10 percent. Having no hill plots or having too little was one of the big difficulties of the poor peasants. First, they had no firewood or not enough firewood and had to gather reed grasses from other people's hillsides. Second, they could not collect pine firewood to carry to the market to sell for oil and salt. They could only take reed grasses to exchange for oil and salt, and 3 *Dan* of reed straw was worth only 1 *Dan* of pine firewood. Third, they had no wood for making houses or utensils. Fourth, having no oil crop hill land or too little, they had no cooking oil, or not enough cooking oil. Now that the land has been redistributed, and like the fields the hills have been distributed according to population, every family has hill land. Although some towns have more hill land and some have less, so that the shares of hill land in some towns are smaller than in other towns, even in those towns that have less hill land, everyone has received some hill land, thus solving a difficult problem of the poor peasants. Because they needed it, the poor peasants adamantly proposed the redistribution of the hill lands. For production too, it was essential to redistribute the hill lands, because where there was not enough manpower some of the land grew wild and some was not well maintained. The great masses of the poor peasants had plenty of manpower that was left idle because they did not have hill land. With the present redistribution of the hill lands, the great manpower of the poor peasants is put to use on their own hill lands, so production can increase greatly.

Third, in the early days of the revolution, with the distribution of the grain held by the landlords and counterrevolutionaries, the poor peasants were able to get cooking grain free. In Bailu (the area where the landlords were concentrated) the grain was also distributed according to population, and the poor peasants have more than enough to eat right down to harvest time.

Fourth, all debts incurred before the revolution have been cancelled. In the third month, at the beginning of the revolution, the official documents coming down from above said that the bills of merchants or of associations must be paid, and that debts owed among poor peasants and farm laborers must be repaid. On the 19th of the sixth month (July by the solar calendar), Southwest Jiangxi (refers to the soviet government of southwestern Jiangxi) sent another document that said that none of them need be repaid. Originally, beginning with the third month, no debts were repaid, but although they were in fact not repaid, the above-named three forms of debts were in principle (in theory) still supposed to be repaid. After the sixth month, this principle was overturned. The poor peasants fully support this kind of action. Why did the poor peasants propose that even those three kinds of debts should not be repaid? First, as regards the bills to merchants, most of the big merchants had fled (of the thirty-five merchants in Bailu, the ten big merchants have all fled). Although the small merchants (such as the twenty-four small shop owners in Bailu) had some accounts outstanding for merchandise sold to workers and peasants, most of the small merchants owed money to the large merchants, to landlords, and to rich peasants. Although the impoverished workers and peasants did not have to repay bills to the small merchants, at the same time, the small merchants did not have repay debts owed to landlords and to rich peasants. Comparing the two, the small merchants still came out ahead, because the indebtedness of the small merchants to the big merchants, landlords, and rich peasants was somewhat larger than the accounts owed them by the impoverished workers and peasants. Second, association bills. For the purpose of arranging for weddings and repaying bills, friends and relatives would be invited to form an association. If these friends and relatives weren't middle peasants, they were rich peasants, so there was no harm in cancelling association debts. Although these associations had been formed to give friendly support, the poor peasants who had started the associations could not repay, so it is right to cancel their debts. Even if the money of a few of the associations was lent to rich peasants, cancelling the debts makes sense, because those rich peasants who borrowed from the associations took that money to lend to other poor peasants with interest, and now the poor peasants do not have to repay them. Moreover, all their personal property has been turned over to the public, and with one contribution after another their coffers are already empty, so not making them repay is also right. This district does not have any of those associations set up by landlords and rich peasants to exploit the impoverished workers and peasants. Third, accounts owed by one impoverished worker or peasant to another. With the revolution, this question is answered like this, "You are impoverished, and I am impoverished too. What do I have to repay you with?" Thus, it is quite correct simply to cancel all indebtedness.

Fifth, table rice is cheap. In the first and second months of this year, the price of rice was 4.60 *yuan* per *dan*. In the third month, as the revolution began, it was 2.00 *yuan* per *dan*. From the sixth month to the present (September, solar calendar), it has been 0.70 *yuan* per *dan*, or six and a half times cheaper than the 4.60 *yuan* price. Now that fields have been distributed to the poor peasants, and they have planted and harvested the crop, the low price of rice is naturally rather disadvantageous, but for the several months time during the beginning of the revolution and before the harvest, low cost rice benefited the poor peasant.

Sixth, "freely taking" a wife (in Jiangxi, the peasants have turned the character *you* of *ziyou* into a verb to distinguish freedom to choose a marriage partner from the old compulsory buying and selling of marriages,[21] and this term is in common usage among all the peasants in the soviets). In the past, taking a wife required money, and for this reason a great many poor peasants could not get married, and even if they did, they either had to raise a child bride or wait until they were already pretty old. If your wife died it was extremely difficult to marry a second time. Today these difficulties have been totally eliminated.

Seventh, when someone dies it does not cost anything, he or she is just buried.

Eighth, the price of oxen is low. It is easy for those without an ox to buy one or to replace an ox that has died. The poor peasants suffer from a severe shortage of ox-power. Among the poor peasants in this district, only 15 percent of the families had an ox of their own, 40 percent of them shared one ox between two families, 10 percent shared one ox among three families, and 5 percent shared one ox among four families, while 30 percent had no ox at all. Under these circumstances, the low price of oxen benefits the poor peasants.

Ninth, with the elimination of obligatory social events and the breaking of superstition, it is no longer necessary to spend money on these items.

Tenth, since there is no opium or gambling, and at the same time there are no thieves, you won't lose things in the night, even if you don't close your door.

Eleventh, with the redistribution of the land, every family can raise pigs, not just to sell them for cash so that others can eat meat, but so they can eat meat themselves as well. In the past, very few poor peasants went to the butchershop to buy meat to eat. Today, many are beginning to buy meat for the table.

---

21. In the compound *ziyou* (freedom), *zi* has the meaning of "self," *you* has the meaning "to follow," and *ziyou* literally of "to follow one's own inclinations." Thus, for the peasants, if they themselves (*zi*) went out and found a wife, instead of relying on a matchmaker, they would be "*you*-ing" her.

Twelfth, and this is most important, they have taken political power. The poor peasants are the pillars of political power in the countryside, and have become the leading class in the villages. The poor peasants can be divided into five strata according to how much ox-power they have, as indicated in item eight above.

5. Farm Laborers

Farm laborers have been given shares of land, just like the poor peasants, and because the landlords and rich peasants have been overthrown, although some people hire temporary workers, no one hires permanent workers. Thus they insisted on shares of the fields. Having been given fields, they still had no ox-power or farming tools, and also it is very difficult to farm. This is a problem that has yet to be solved. The district and township governments did not give the plow oxen and farm tools confiscated from the landlords and rich peasants to the farm laborers, but rather sold them.

Fu Jiting's nephew, Zhu Daxi, was a farm laborer. There are seven persons in the household: four brothers, father, mother, and his wife (a child bride he is bringing up). He is the eldest brother, aged twenty-two. The second brother is nineteen. The eldest brother was a laborer hired by the year for a rich peasant named Zhong, with an annual wage of 39 *yuan* in small foreign dollars. The second brother watched the ox for another family and was paid 10 *yuan* per year. With a total income of 49 *yuan* they could buy a little more than 16 *dan* of rice, enough food for only two and a half persons. They relied on his mother and wife working, cutting reed straw that they sold to get a little bit of money for food. In the winter they ate two meals a day. They had a debt of over 30 *yuan*. They had no house of their own. They lived in a landlord's mountain shed and took care of the mountain for the landlord. His father was originally a farm laborer and is now over sixty years of age.

In this district, farm laborers could take off fifteen days a year. They began work after the Lantern Festival[22] in the first month. They did not get the special dinners of the 1st and 15th of the month.[23] The boss provided a quilt, but not clothes. When you got sick you had to buy your own medicine. You could be sick for three days without having a deduction taken from your wages, but a deduction from your wages was made after three days. Wages were given in bits and pieces. You worked from dawn to dusk, except for time to eat and rest, at least ten hours a day. In the winter, you split wood and peeled sweet potatoes in the evenings.

Ninety-nine percent of the farm laborers did not have wives, and they were

---

22. A festival on the night of the fifteenth of the first lunar month, when sweet dumplings made of glutinous rice flower were eaten.

23. A meal of meat customarily given to employees on these dates in each lunar month.

the most destitute class in the countryside. Not only did every landlord and rich peasant have a wife, some had several wives. Ninety percent of the middle peasants had wives and 10 percent did not. Seventy percent of the poor peasants had wives and 30 percent did not. Of the handicraft workers, 70 percent had wives and 30 percent did not. Ten percent of the vagrants had wives and 90 percent did not, somewhat more than the proportion of farm laborers who had wives. Only the farm laborers were 99 percent without wives. In the seventh month (August of the solar calendar), the government ordered those men who did not have wives "freely to take" a wife, and ordered those women who did not have a husband "freely to take" a husband. Consequently, there was suddenly an increase in cases of "freely taking an old man" and "freely taking an old woman." Since the seventh month, in the space of two months, most of the middle peasants and poor peasants who did not have wives have got married, so that very few of them do not have wives now. It is relatively difficult for a farm laborer "freely to take" a wife. Women dislike the fact that the farm laborers have no household utensils or equipment, and they also dislike the fact that they are seldom at home. Thus it is difficult for the farm laborer to solve the problem of getting a wife. Fu Jiting lives in Yangfang Village in the first township, where only one of the four farm laborers (two brothers each in two families) has "freely taken" a wife. Originally, another one of them was going to be able "freely to take" one, but the head of the social insurance department of the township government said that the two of them had had an affair in the past, so he would not permit them to register for marriage. Because of this, that woman was "freely taken" away by another man and this farm laborer is still without a wife. In the vicinity of Yongfeng Town, in the second township, there are six farm laborers, four of whom have "freely taken" wives. In Houjing Village where Wen Fengzhang lives, there is only one farm laborer, who today still does not have a wife.

After the redistribution of the land, there are no laborers hired on an annual basis, and temporary work has decreased by 70 percent, leaving only 30 percent. Wages have not increased, and the farm laborers have not requested that wages be raised. "With no work to do, how can you talk of increases!"

The problem of ox-power and farming tools for farm laborers following the redistribution of the land. Of the two families of farm laborers in Yangfang Village, one family with the name Chen has one older and one younger brother, both of whom are farm laborers. The older brother worked for a rich peasant named Chen on an annual basis, for yearly wages of 33 *yuan*. The second brother worked for a rich peasant named Zhong on an annual basis, for wages of 42 *yuan*. The father, now dead, was a tenant farmer, and their mother raised them by begging. As soon as they grew up they became farm laborers. The mother died leaving just the two brothers. The older brother is aged twenty-nine, and the younger brother is aged twenty-three. They have one room, a pot for cooking rice, no table or chairs. The farming tools they used to own in the past were sold off. With the redistribution of land in the second month, the two brothers returned home, and the second brother "freely took" a wife. They have no capital. The second brother used to have over 100 *yuan* in cash, which he loaned to a poor peasant named Zhong. When all debts were cancelled, he could not collect on it, because there was no way that the poor peasant could return it. Fortunately, they have an uncle who is a middle peasant, who has loaned them ox-power and farming tools. The three persons were given shares of fields totaling 16.2 *dan*, which they took over and have been farming themselves since the distribution of the fields in the second month. The entire harvest is their own. After the first crop was harvested they planted a second crop. They had good crops. If they had an ox, one person could farm 100 *dan* of rice fields. Since the two brothers together are farming only something over 10 *dan* of fields, they have a good deal of spare time, in which they do temporary work and transport things for other people to earn a little money.

Yangfang Village also has a farm laborer family named Zhong in which there are also two brothers. The father and mother are dead. Together with a paternal uncle (Zhong Enjiang) and aunt and their two sons, one of whom has a wife, and two granddaughters, the household consists of a total of nine persons. The uncle and his two sons farmed fields that they rented from someone else, since they had no land of their own. They were in debt and every year did not have enough to live on. The two brothers worked for others as farm laborers. The older brother, Zhong Shengpo, is over forty and worked as a laborer for a rich peasant named Zhong on an annual basis. The younger brother, Zhong Shenghuai, aged thirty-six, worked as a laborer for a middle peasant named Zhong on an annual basis. Now that the land has been distributed in the second month, they can farm for themselves. They originally had a female ox that they rented from a middle peasant named Zhong Longtan, and they raised two calves. After the revolution, Zhong Longtan wanted these calves returned to him. The township government said to Zhong Longtan, "According to the method used in all the townships, oxen that were rented out have all been turned over. You alone want it returned. It cannot be returned now." Because of this, these oxen now belong to the family of Zhong Enjiang. After the two brothers were given shares of fields, they had no problem of ox-power, or of farming tools, because their uncle had them.

At this point, let us explain the situation with that middle peasant, Zhong Longtan. Zhong Longtan, over thirty years of age, has a mother aged sixty, and a wife who is over twenty—in all three mouths to feed. He had over 10 *dan* of rice fields of his own, and he rented 34 *dan* of fields from someone else. After paying the rent they had more than enough to eat themselves, and the rest they sold. They had three oxen that they rented out to three poor peasant families for an annual rent of 1.5 *dan*. When a calf was born both parties owned half of it. He has a lot of money to lend out. In the land redistribution of the second month, the three people received 24 *dan* in rice fields (8 *dan* per person), a little more than they had before, but they cannot rent land from someone else and so have no surplus rice to sell, and the renting of oxen and loaning of money to other people have all been eliminated. He is a very straightforward person, is not counterrevolutionary, nor has he taken on any important work responsibilities. He is a kitchen helper in the Red Army Reserve Corps in his village.

After the revolution, the farm laborers did not have power in the government. The middle peasants and poor peasants generally looked upon the farm laborers as "illiterate, inarticulate, unenlightened, unfamiliar with public affairs," and not capable of taking charge of anything. In the district, there is not a single farm laborer on the district or township government committees. There is only one who is a Red Guard team leader.

6. Handicraft Workers

Categories of handicraft workers in this district: carpenters, masons, seamsters, iron workers, barbers, bamboo workers, rice hulling workers, rope-makers, stone cutters, painters, tin workers, loom operators, silversmiths, dyers, vat workers, lacquerware workers, pottery workers, and paper workers—some 18 categories. There were relatively more people in the four categories of carpenters, masons, seamsters, and bamboo workers, followed by those who were barbers, iron workers, and vat workers (who press oil). Then came all the rest. In this district there were no coppersmiths, munitions workers, shoemakers, or leather workers. As for oil vats, there was one in the first township, two in the second township, one in the third township, and twelve in the fourth township. For each oil vat there was one vat worker.

Wages: In the past, for one workday, a carpenter made 20 cents, a mason 20 cents, a seamster 15 cents, a bamboo worker 15 cents. A barber, in the first, second, and fourth townships, got 1 *dou* of rice per year, and in the third township, 15 cents per year, and all were fed where they worked. Iron workers got 25 cents. Vat workers in the second township got 10 *qian* for 1 *jin* of oil pressed, in the third township, 3 *qian* per *jin*, and in the fourth township, 2 *jin* for each *Dan* of oil pressed. Since there was little oil production in the first township, the situation is unclear. The wages in the third township were especially low because there was a lot of oil. Rice-hulling workers got 60 cents per *zuo*; it takes three days to hull one *zuo* of rice. Rope-makers got 22 cents, and stone cutters got 45 cents. Artists were paid per painting, whether of the despotic gentry and landlords, or of the gods. Tinsmiths were paid by the piece. Loom operators were paid 10 cents per *zhang* of summer cloth, and also 10 cents per *zhang* of spring cloth (summer cloth is linen, and spring cloth is 80 percent linen, 20 percent cotton). No one made cotton cloth in this district. Silversmiths were paid by the piece. "False accusations are made against a lot of them." Lacquerware workers were paid by the lot, as were pottery workers. Paper workers got 15 cents (making bark paper, only in the third township).

In the past, the four categories of carpenters, masons, seamsters, and bamboo workers worked at most two hundred days a year, and at a minimum something over a hundred days. Since the revolution, the number of days a year that masons and seamsters can find work has been greatly reduced, to probably only a few dozen. Carpenters and bamboo workers have only a little less work than before, there is not much difference. The barber business has expanded because the women are now all cutting their hair. Since the revolution, tinsmiths, painters, lacquerware workers, and paper workers have all disappeared because they are no longer needed (the paper workers made the fuses for firecracker strings used for weddings).

At the "start of the revolution," handicraft workers were given half shares of fields, but the craftsmen demanded that they be given full shares. The reason was that some had lost their jobs and the work had been reduced for others and could not be counted on. It is only by receiving fields of their own that their lives could be made stable. The peasants said, "At the start of the revolution, you received half shares of fields." To which the workers replied, "With half shares of fields, we will have to raise the price of our labor." The poor peasants and farm laborers did not want wages to rise, because, having received fields in the redistribution, they wanted farm implements made, and so were obliged to hire the craftsmen. The rich and middle peasants already had farm tools so they did not need to hire the craftsmen. It was only the poor peasants who particularly needed to hire craftsmen, so the poor peasants and farm laborers did not want the cost of labor to rise. The poor peasants said, "All right, you will be given shares of the fields, but you must not raise the price of your labor." The craftsmen further said that, after they received their shares of the fields, if they still worked a hundred days a year, they would be willing to turn over 2 *dan* of rice to the public. Barbers were not given land shares, because barbers worked long days at the homes of others where they were given their meals. In Ganxian, workers were given shares of land and lowered their labor charges. Carpenters and masons were willing to have their 20 cent wage reduced to 15 cents, and the bamboo workers were willing to have their 15 cent wage reduced to 12 cents.

Seventy percent of the handicraftsmen had wives. Thirty percent did not have wives. Since the revolution, the majority of those who originally did not have wives have "freely taken" one. Because the handicraftsmen have many acquaintances, and because they have a craft, and also because they are relatively bright and articulate and a great many of them are literate, they are somewhat better off in this respect than the farm laborers.

Craftsmen have a general labor union [*gonghui*] at the district level with branch guilds at the township level and branch offices in the villages. For example, Lingyuan in the first township has an all-crafts labor union with over twenty members who have organized a branch office.

In the country villages craftsmen generally also engage in farming. You cannot find 10 pecent whose sole occupation is their craft and who do not farm at all.

Eighty percent of handicraftsmen are in debt.

7. Merchants

Categories of merchants in this district: owners of oil and salt general stores, rice and fruit sellers (of whom there were a dozen or so different kinds), owners of teahouses, restaurant owners, butchershop owners, beancurd makers, and owners of opium houses. In this district, those who did not also farm, whose sole occupation was running small shops, constituted 3 percent of the population (three out of a hundred families).

In the fourth township of this district, there were in the past only three small merchants with 500 *yuan* of capital, all of whom were in Yongfengyu; there were none in the other towns. Small shops in the whole district: five shops in the first township, thirty-five shops in the second township (all in Yongfengyu), six shops in the third township, and none in the fourth township, for a total of forty-six shops. Of these forty-six shops, four had capital of 500 *yuan*. (Of the three shops in Yongfeng Town, one is a pharmacy run by a person from Zhangshu, and two are foreign-goods stores, branches of a store in Xingguo Town, none of which are landlords in this district. When the revolution broke out, they all fled, the shops were confiscated, and their goods were given to the poor peasants. One shopowner in Shankang was a landlord in his township, and the entire family fled and the shop closed.) One shop had 400 *yuan*. (This was in Shankang, a general store, a two-person partnership. One partner, Han Litao, farmed 20 *dan* of rice fields and the other partner, Han Lidong, farmed 60 *dan* of fields. After the revolution Han Litao fled. Han Lidong pretended to join the revolution, and was land office manager for the government, but has now been accused of being a member of the AB Corps, and is under detention by the district government.) There were three shops of 300 *yuan*. (All of these were in Yongfeng Town. Two were general merchandise and fabric shops, run by people from Xingguo Town; they were all counterrevolutionaries and have fled, and their shops have been turned into teahouses. There was one butchershop owner who also had 70 *dan* of rice fields; he joined the revolution, has kept the shop open, is the chairman of the village government, and is a very straightforward and honest person.) Two shops had 100 *yuan*. (One of these was in Shankang, a general store and inn; [the owner had] no ricefields, was a counterrevolutionary, someone killed him, and the business folded. One was in Xijiang, a general store [owner] and silversmith who farmed some 10 *dan* of fields, is not counterrevolutionary, and is still open for business.) Two shops of 50 *yuan*. (These were in the third township, one pharmacy in Zhukang whose owner had 20 *dan* of fields, is not counterrevolutionary, and the shop is now still open; one pharmacy in Jing'ao, whose owner also had fields, a counterrevolutionary who fled, and the shop folded). Twenty-four shops of 20 *yuan*. (There were four in the first township, two in Wuniangmiao and two in Jiaotianjiang, and twenty in the second township, all in Yongfeng Town.) There were ten shops with 10 *yuan*. (Nine of these were in the second township, all in Yongfeng Town, and one in the third township, in Qilinyi.) The above are those who worked solely as small shopkeepers and did not engage in other occupations.

In the villages, there were many who were primarily farmers and secondarily merchants (who depended 80 percent on farming and 20 percent on commerce), about 40 percent of the entire population (forty out of a hundred households). Most of these people were poor peasants, with a minority of middle peasants. Because they did not have enough to live on, they supplemented their livelihood with a little carrying-pole business, like those who went to Jiangkou, to Ganzhou, or Hukoumian, and brought back salt. They went there usually carrying some oil, which became their capital. There were also a great many who carried ducks to Jiayingzhou (in Meixian) to sell and came back with a little salt.

In this district, there were twelve merchants with capital of 50 *yuan* or more, nine of whom were counterrevolutionaries, and three of whom were not counterrevolutionaries.

Of the twelve merchants who had capital of 50 *yuan* or more, only the four who had 500 *yuan* hired shop clerks. Of these three had hired one shop clerk each, and one had hired two. None of the other eight had hired shop clerks.

The thirty-four that had 20 *yuan* or less were called merchants, but in reality they were poor shopkeepers, and for this reason none of them were counterrevolutionary, and their shops are all still open.

Of the thirty-four so-called shopkeepers with 10 to 20 *yuan* of capital, their businesses were as follows:

Inns	9	
Opium dens	4	
Candy shops	2	
Butcher shops	4	
Rice shops	4	
Wood products	1	
Ironsmith	1	
General stores	4	(all in Yongfeng Town)
Teahouses	5	(four in Yongfeng Town, one in the third township)

In the land distribution this time, among those merchants with a capital of 50 *yuan* or more, leaving aside those who were killed or fled, those who were not killed and did not flee, but whose shops were closed or went out of business were all given land. Only the three shops that were not counterrevolutionary are still open for business. One is that of the butcher in Yongfeng Town with 300 *yuan* in capital, who was billed for a contribution of 220 *yuan*, leaving him only 80 *yuan* in capital. He has fifteen mouths to feed, and he is not counterrevolutionary. Having originally had 60 *dan* of fields, in this land redistribution, the proprietor of the shop, Chen Shaolin, was given a half-share and the other fourteen members of the family were given full shares, so that in addition to what they originally had, they even received a little more. Chen Shaolin's younger brother, Chen Shaoying, is a company commander in the Third Army (originally the Second Regiment), so his family is also revolutionary, and Chen Shaolin is chairman of the village government. One is the pharmacy with 50 *yuan* of capital in Zhukang, the owner of which was also given a half-share of fields while his family members were given full shares. One is the general merchandise and silver store with 100 *yuan* of capital in Xijiang, the owner of which is not counterrevolutionary, and whom the village government billed for a contribution (amount unknown). In the land distribution, the shopowner was given one half-share, and his family members were given full shares. In addition, of the thirty-four shops belonging to poor peasants, because the four inns in the first township and the one teahouse in the third township never had much business, the owners had always relied on farming to maintain their livelihood, so in this latest redistribution of the fields, even the shopowners all received full shares of land. But the twenty-nine shops in Yongfeng Town in the past had been solely engaged in their small business, except for the four opium dens that were closed down, the remaining twenty-five, the candy shops, butcher, the rice store, the wood products shop, the ironsmith's shop, the general stores, teahouses, and inns, and so on, not only continued to exist, but their business was no less than it had been in the past. Even so, they were still given shares of fields, half-shares to the shopowners and full shares to the other members of their households. Those who had no ox-power or farming tools borrowed them from their relatives.

Summarizing the above situation, those stores that had 50 *yuan* or more of capital (in reality, most were small shops), were hard-hit in the revolution, as a result of the overly leftist policies of the local government. The poor people who had small businesses of 20 *yuan* to 10 *yuan* benefited greatly in the revolution. In addition to the shares of fields they received, for all of them, their expenses were greatly reduced, it became easy to get a wife, they did not have to spend a fortune on funerals, and they raised their heads politically, just like the poor peasants. These poor small business people belong to the same class as the poor peasants, and it is for this reason that they received virtually the same benefits as the poor peasants.

8. Vagrants

This district had the following categories of vagrants:

1) Gamblers: some fifty or so in the entire district. There were about ten in the first township, about twenty in the second township, all in Yongfeng Town. The third township had six, and the fourth township had about twenty. In the past, nine out of ten of the gamblers smoked opium, but now they do not smoke opium. Of the more than fifty gamblers in this district, not one is counterrevolutionary. They were extremely happy when they heard that the local bullies were to be overthrown and the land redistributed. In the past, they had nothing to wear

when it got cold, and they were very ragged. Now they are well clothed. In the past, when they had money they would eat fish and meat,[24] and when they had no money they had nothing to eat. Today, although they have nothing fancy to eat, they do have food every day. Eight out of ten of the gamblers had no families. Now, having received shares of fields, they borrow ox-power and farming tools from their relatives. Because the gamblers were generally very generous it is now easy for them to borrow things. Of the ten persons in the first township, there is one who previously was a member of the finance committee of the fourth township government. When he gambled he usually gambled hard and well. His credit was good. When he became a member of the finance committee after the revolution, he did a very good job. Among the twenty gamblers from the second township, the four described below worked in the township government. "Skyman,"[25] Wang Zhenyong, was director of the propaganda office of the district government; he had a house but no family. The year before last, he joined the revolution and his house was burned down by the dogs of the Pacification Defense Corps. Chen Guntong joined the revolution the year before last and was a judge in the district government, and later, company commander of the Third Company of the army reserves. Yang Dahu, who joined the revolution the year before last, and became chairman of the township government during the revolution in the second month of this year, did a very good job. Later he went to work in the district government. Chen Shaoqi joined the revolution the year before last, and in the second month of this year became head of the land office for this township. Of the six gamblers from the third township, Lei Yonghuang has a family, gambled, and sold tobacco. He joined the revolution in the second month of this year and was made head of the finance office for the township government. He is very loyal.

2) Beggars: also called mendicants.[26] Four in the first township, five in the second township, four in the third township, and four in the fourth township, for a total of seventeen. These are people who had absolutely no way out, mostly single people alone who had no family. Of the seventeen, only four had families and in each case their whole families were beggars. Now that the land has been redistributed, they borrow ox-power and farm tools from relatives. Since the revolution none have worked in the government.

3) Water-pipe tobacco sellers: two in the second township, and one in the fourth township, for a total of three. Both of those in the second township have wives and sons. Their families rented fields to farm, but they themselves did not engage in a regular occupation, but rather sold tobacco for water pipes in the gambling halls. The one in the fourth township had no family and did not farm.

---

24. I.e., they would live extravagantly, given their resources.

25. *Tianshangren*, a pseudonym—see below under government offices.

26. *Huazi* (also *jiaohuazi*), a term for beggar commonly used of Buddhist monks or Daoist priests who beg for alms.

Now they have all received shares of the fields. None have worked for the government since the revolution.

4) Diviners:[27] Just one, in the fourth township. Has no family, did not farm, just read the trigrams. Has been given a land share.

5) One who carries the Guanyin boddhisatva: One in the first township. Has received a share of fields.

6) Daoist priests: Three in the first township, all have families, did not farm, religious activities were their occupation. Two in the second township, all without families, did not farm. One in the third township, has a family, did a little farming. A total of sixteen Daoist priests, all of whom have been given land shares. Ceng Yunzhang of the second township is a Daoist priest who joined the revolution the year before last. He had no family and no fields. In the second month of this year, he was the general director of the Xingguo-Ganxian-Wan'an guerrilla forces, "Excellent planning, good execution, his troops have never been defeated." Now made part of the Twenty-second Army.

7) Buddhist monks: Two in the fourth township; each lived in a small Buddhist temple, and lived on rent they received. One from Gaoxing Town returned there after the revolution and was given a land share.

8) Play actor: Performed in the play, "The Wooden Skull." One from the third township. Had a family and farmed. Now a soldier in the Twentieth Army. Two in the fourth township; they have families, farm, and have worked in the village government. All three of the above have received land shares.

9) Fortune tellers:[28] One in the first township who himself has no wife, but has brothers. Last year, he joined the revolution, and since the second month of this year he has been head of the propaganda office of the township government. Two in the second township, one of whom is blind. Both have families and do farming. They themselves tell fortunes. This time they have received land shares. The blind man, Chen Xinpo, "A well-known fortune-teller, who was hired once by a *xian* magistrate to tell his fortune, and when he told it very skillfully was given ten *yuan*." Because he is blind he has been given a double share of fields, 14 *dan* of ricefields. Four in the third township, all of whom have families, of which three farmed the land and one did not. Of those who did farm the land, it was the family head who told fortunes. Three of them work for the government. One, called Zeng Qinglong, has no wife. One, called Qiu Dayang, joined the revolution in the second month of this year, and is now on the propaganda staff of the township government. Altogether there were seventeen fortune-tellers.

The nine kinds of vagrants listed above come to a total of ninety persons, who generally welcome the revolution. Not only is there not a single one of them who

---

27. *Dagua de*, specifically, those who read the trigrams/hexagrams of the *Yi jing* (Book of Changes); distinguish from "*suanming de*," below.

28. *Suanming de* .

is counterrevolutionary, but ten of them have participated in the district and township governments doing leadership tasks, and one was a leader of the guerrilla team. This is well worth noting.

Vagrants have benefited a lot from the revolution.

Other than these nine categories, this district has no other vagrants.

IV. The Current State of the Land Distribution

1. Dividing the Fields

First, the land distribution units: In all four townships, the village (*cun*) is the unit of land distribution. Because the townships are large in area and there are many mountain ranges, if the township were to be taken as the unit for dividing the land, some pieces of land would be far away and difficult to farm. The peasants would rather have a little less land in their own villages than have to move to another village far from their own. In villages that have less in fields and more in hill land each person receives less in fields and more in hill land. In villages that have more fields and fewer hills, each person receives somewhat more in fields and somewhat less in hill plots. "Well, it's close enough."

Second, the method of dividing the fields: the "orders from above" were that the redistribution be completed in three days. Actually, in the first and third townships it was completed in seven days, and in the second and fourth townships it was completed in eight days. (This was too short, too rushed a time period.)

The first township has fifteen villages, the second and fourth townships have seven villages each, and the third township has eight villages. At the start of the land redistribution, the district government sent propaganda personnel to each village to hold large mass meetings. It took the first half-day to get the information out and call the people together. The men all came. The women did not come. Children under ten did not come. The propagandist told the masses about the benefits of burning the old land deeds and of redistributing the fields, and how it would be done. In one day, one propagandist could convene mass meetings in two villages. At the mass meetings held in each village at that time, the feelings of the masses who attended were that the talking was fine, but they didn't know whether the program could be maintained or not. Some said, "Burning the papers (i.e., the land deeds), not having to repay debts, hooking up with (meaning, to trust in) the Red Army to divide the fields, all this is very well, but we're afraid we can't rely on it. If the land is divided now, we're afraid we'll still have to pay rents." At the mass meetings, a chairman of the village government was elected, plus one secretary, one head of the finance office, one head of the land office and two staff people, one head of the organization office, one head of the propaganda office, one head of the food supplies office, one head of the military office, and one liaison person. In the first township, the Yangfang Village government was elected at a mass meeting in the morning of the 25th of the second month of the lunar calendar this year. The propaganda person left to go to another village and the people (out of more than 180 persons, counting men and women, the old and young, in the whole village, 60 or 70 attended the meeting that day) dispersed to eat lunch. In the afternoon it started again, the village government calling them to hold a meeting. The chairman of the village government, Zhong Enming (an independent laborer who had no land, worked as a cook, made and sold beancurd, and when a play performance was held some-place else, would go there to sell rice cakes) chaired the meeting this day. The resolutions were as follows:

1) Request contributions from the wealthy families to pay government expenses, under the responsibility of the finance office.
2) Stop all rice in the entire village from being shipped outside the village, under the responsibility of the food supplies office.
3) Bring together all weapons in the entire village, under the responsibility of the military office.
4) Survey the land and carry out distribution, under the responsibility of the land office.

The 26th to the 29th, a total of four days, was the land survey period. The head of the land office, Fu Jiting (one of those who attended this land survey meeting), was in charge of the land staff, Zhong Ensheng and Zhong Enren (both poor peasants). These two met with the four team leaders (the whole village was divided into four teams, ten families in a team) to look at the fields family by family, and to write down what family in what place had how much in rice fields. The survey was completed in four days, and then they knew how much land in ricefields there was in total. Dividing by the population of the entire village, they obtained the quantity of fields that each person should receive. On the 1st of the third month another mass meeting was called to report to the masses which family had how much land, and how many people, the total amount of fields in the whole village, and how much each person should receive. At the time, there were two people who said that the survey was not fair, that it reported them as having more land than they had. One was Fu Hualong, who had 230 *dan* of rice fields, all of which he farmed himself, had ten mouths to feed, owed a debt of over 300 *yuan*, and hired one person to look after the one large water buffalo he had. His fields were all poor land, and in reality he could harvest only something over 140 *dan*, which, because he had ten mouths to feed, was half surplus, from which over 40 *dan* had to be subtracted for interest payments on his debt and rent on the absentee landlord fields [one part of his fields], leaving about 30 *dan*, making him a middle peasant with a slight surplus. The other was Zhong Xianhui, who had over 70 *dan* of rice fields all of which he farmed himself, and three mouths to feed. In the past he had money that he loaned out, but it was all used up building a new house last year. Every year he hired an agricultural laborer, and he had an annual surplus of rice over and above what they ate of more than 30 *dan*, so he was also a middle peasant. He had five brothers who had set up separate households, of whom, aside from himself, one had enough to eat while three were very destitute. Several dozen poor peasants, farm laborers, and workers all spoke up at the meeting to say that what Fu and Zhong had said was not true, that the survey of the land office was definitely not in error. There were also three rich peasants at the meeting who, upon hearing the judgment of the masses, did not open their mouths. Everyone accepted the results of the survey, and then they dealt with which family would "dig up" how much to give to whom, and which family would "fill in" how much from whom. Those that had to dig up land were themselves responsible for saying which piece of land they would turn over, and so they turned over the bad fields. This time, even though the struggle was not yet thorough, and those who received fields got bad fields, they were extremely happy and did not demand good fields. The meeting that day simply accomplished the task of "taking from the plentiful to make up for the scarce." After the redistribution was completed, the secretary of the village government put it down in the registry book and did not post a notice. From the 25th of the second month to the 1st of the third month, in the space of seven days, the redistribution of the land was completed.

After the redistribution was completed, "immediately turning over the farming" versus "turning over the farming in the fall" again turned into a struggle between the poor peasants and the rich peasants. In all the townships in this district, when the land was redistributed at the end of the second month, the fields had already been sown, it was not yet time for replanting the seedlings, and it was just the time for plowing the fields. Most of the fields were turned over immediately. But there were some rich peasants who thought they would like to take another look at the situation, and hoping that the Pacification Defense Corps would return and reject the redistribution of the fields, they said to the poor peasants: I've already put in the fertilizer and plowed the fields. The fields shouldn't be turned over to you this year. Let me farm them until harvest time and then turn them over. I'll give you 40 percent of the crop harvested. Some of the poor peasants accepted this suggestion of the rich peasants, thinking that getting 40 percent for doing nothing was a good deal. Some of the farm laborers and workers indeed had no way they could take over the land and farm it immediately. For this reason, about 10 percent of the whole district used the "40 percent" method and did not turn over the fields immediately.

2. Dividing the Hills and Forests

The fields were divided at the end of the second month and the beginning of the third month, but the hillsides were not redistributed until the end of the fifth month.

In Yangfang Village, dividing the hillsides began on the 27th of the fifth month. The orders from above did not arrive until this time (note how important the orders from above are). On the 27th of the fifth month, the township government sent a propagandist, Liu Dalun. (He was an intellectual who was an enthusiastic worker, but on the 17th of the eighth month it came to light that he was a secretary of the AB Corps and the district government executed him. On this day eleven members of the AB Corps were executed; I fear that, like Liu Dalun, they were wrongly executed.) He came to this village and again called a large mass meeting to tell them about how to divide the hill lands. The seven newly elected land staff decided to divide the hillsides. On this day, the propagandist also reported on the matter of the poor peasant loan office, and it was resolved to act accordingly.

Redividing the hillsides was even more difficult than dividing the ricefields. There were big hills, and there were small hills. Some had a lot of firewood, and some had very little firewood. Some had big trees, some had small trees, and some had no trees. Thus, to divide them up was difficult. The head of the land office and seven land personnel set out together to hike up every hill in the entire village and hammer out a method for dividing them based not on land area but on tea-oil trees. Taking one *Dan* of "peaches" (1 *Dan* of tea-seeds, worth two strings of cash, is called a 1 *Dan* of peaches)[29] as the standard, 30 big trees make 1 *Dan* of peaches, 60 medium-size trees make 1 *Dan* of peaches, and 120 small trees make 1 *Dan* of peaches. After all the peaches from the hillsides in the whole village had been counted, they were then distributed equally among the entire population and signs were set up marking the boundaries. It took four days to divide this village up clearly. The eight men from the land office had the authority to decide on the redistribution, "You can't go by what every individual says, for if you went by whatever each individual chose to say, it would never be untangled."

In Changjiao Village in the third township, there were five persons in the land office (the head of the land office and four staff personnel). The village government issued 2.20 *yuan* for their food supplies, and it took them over thirty days to divide it up clearly, "You can see, its hard to divide."

Although the hills were divided up, only the branches could be cut for wood; you were not permitted to cut down the tree itself unless you had permission from the government.

3. Dividing the Ponds

Taking the village as the unit, the ponds were divided among teams to raise fish according to their size. For a big pond five families would comprise one team to

---

29. According to a note to *Mao Zedong nongcun diaocha wenji*, "peach" (*tao* or *taozi*) was a term commonly used for the seeds of the tea-oil tree.

fish it, and for a small pond three families would comprise one team. With one team for one pond, each family would put in the same number of fish at the same time, and when the fish were caught they would be divided equally. In this district most of the ponds are not relied upon for irrigation, so there is only the fish problem, and no water problem. Aside from the fish ponds, there are also a few mountain ponds whose water is used for irrigation. Those mountain ponds that are fished have been divided according to the above method. Those that are not used for fish go with the fields. Whoever owns the field gets the pond.

Before the revolution, the fish belonged to whoever put them in, and there was no dividing them up. This year, the new owners can't really put fish in until after the original owner of the pond catches his fish this winter.

4. Dividing the Houses

It is, in principle, good to redistribute the houses. For poor peasants, it is often the case that one family of ten or more people have only two or three rooms. Generally speaking, 60 percent of the poor peasants do not have enough living space, and the good houses are all occupied by the rich peasants. One after another the poor peasants have said that they want the houses redistributed, but the government replies, "There aren't any directives from above." It is for this reason that the poor peasants don't dare go and occupy the rich peasants' houses. When Yangfang Village held a meeting and the poor peasants demanded that the houses be redistributed, the head of the land office replied, "those who have a lot of housing space should give some to those who have very little," but no resolution was passed. The rich peasants are unwilling to yield and the poor peasants dare not occupy them (this shows the importance of "directives from above").

In redistributing housing, the village should be taken as the unit, and those who have more housing should have their houses divided up and given to those in the vicinity who have less housing.

In this district, it is only the houses of those landlords, rich peasants, and rapacious merchants who have been killed or driven off because they were reactionary which, if they have not been burned (burning them was wrong), have been occupied by the poor peasants. But they have never been formally redistributed to anyone. As for those who have not been killed and who have not fled, even if they have a lot of extra housing, it has not been redistributed.

The houses of counterrevolutionary landlords and rich peasants that were burned (by the guerrilla teams) are: one in the first township, two in the second township, five in the third township, and four in the fourth township, for a total of twelve, three of which had belonged to landlords and nine to rich peasants. The houses of revolutionary workers and peasants that were burned (by the counterrevolutionaries) were: none in the first township, seven in the second township, eight in the third township, and eight in the fourth township, for a total of twenty-three, of which one belonged to a middle peasant, twenty to poor peasants, one to a small merchant, and one to a vagabond.

5. Public Fields

In the second month redistribution, in all the villages of all the townships, some fields were retained as public fields. In the first township, Yangfang Village retained over 10 *dan* of fields, and Chagan Village kept over 30 *dan*. In the second township, Zhige Village retained 11 *dan*. In the third township, Changjiao Village has retained no fields because it doesn't have much land and there are still sixteen persons who have not yet received shares of fields, but the other villages have all retained fields. In the fourth township, Houjing Village has retained over 100 *dan* of rice fields, all of which are in the flood plain. Why should public fields be retained? One reason is that the remnant of fields left over after redistribution was not easy to divide up, so it was retained. For example, if each person's share was 7 *dan*, and 10 or more *dan* were left over, which if divided up would amount to less than 1 *tong*[30] per person, so redistribution was not convenient, and the residue was retained as public fields. Second, they could be used to provide government expenses. Third, they could be used as land shares for children born next year. When the land was redistributed again in the eighth month, there was a directive from above that the fields must all be thoroughly distributed, so they divided up the public fields too.

Actually, it is just as well not to retain public fields, first because although there will be births, there will also be deaths, so there need be no fear that, if sons are born, there will be no fields for them. Second, by collecting a land tax the government will have money to use and need not rely on public fields for its expenses. Furthermore, in the case of the second month distribution, the fields retained were all poor fields that were not very usable. Thus, it is better to divide them all and benefit the peasants more.

6. The Amounts of Fields Distributed

The villages were all different. For example, in the first township, in Yangfang Village, each person received 5.6 *dan* (in the second month distribution the shares were 8 *dan*, but actually they could only give out 5.6 *dan*), and in Chagan Village each person received 8 *dan*. In the second township, in Zhige Village each share was 7 *dan*. In the third township, in Changjiao Village, the shares in the eighth month were different from those in the second month. In the second month, there were four different amounts of land distributed in this village: some got 7 *dan*, some got 6.5 *dan*, some got 5.5 *dan*, and some got 4 *dan* 1 *tong*. Family surnames were taken as the unit of division, because those surname

---

30. A *tong* was about 1/2 *dou*.

groups with more land were not willing to give away fields to surname groups that had less land. Not until the eighth month was the village taken as the unit, at which time each person received 6 *dan*. In the fourth township, in Houjing Village, each person received 8.5 *dan* in the second month. In the redistribution in the eighth month, poor land that nominally produced 2 *dan* but actually yielded only 1 *dan* was counted as 1 *dan*, and also there were some persons who had returned from the outside, so the shares were only 7.5 *dan* per person.

In Xingguo, there is only one crop a year, and the amounts of fields listed above can yield enough to just get by on, if the young and the elderly give some to the others. Add to this the planting of various other crops and the raising of pigs, and they can also meet their oil and salt and cloth and miscellaneous household needs.

The major other crop grown in this district is sweet potatoes, which on average accounts for 40 percent of the food supply of the entire population. Breaking it down, relatively less is grown in the first township because the soil will not grow sweet potatoes, so they account for only 20 percent of the food consumption. In the second and third townships, the situation is very different, where on average 50 percent of the food consumed is sweet potatoes, going as high as 70 percent. By the end of the year, everyone adds shredded sweet potatoes to the rice. In the fourth township, on average, 40 percent of the food supply is from sweet potatoes.

V. The Land Tax

What is called the "public welfare fee", has already been collected by early in the eighth month (lunar calendar). Those with shares of 6 *dan* in fields are assessed 1 percent (6 *sheng* per person). Those with shares of 7 *dan* pay 1.5 percent (1 *dou* 1 *sheng*), and those with shares of 8 *dan* pay 2.5 percent (0.2 *dan*), and those with shares of 9 *dan* pay 3.5 percent (0.315 *dan*). There are no 9-*dan* shares in this district, so the highest public welfare tax rate in this district is 2.5 percent. In the first township, in Yangfang Village with a population of 182, each person had one 8-*dan* share (using the figure for the second month distribution); when taxed at the rate of 2.5 percent, this yielded a total of 36.4 *dan*. In Chagan Village with 397 people, each with a share of 8 *dan*, the total tax received was 79.4 *dan*. In the third township, Changjiao Village, where the shares were 5.5 *dan* per person, no tax was assessed (only shares of 6 *dan* or more are taxed). The entire district will probably collect about 1,000 *dan* in taxes.

Most of the taxes collected in the eighth month are still in the individual villages, with a portion having been sent to the township government, and none to the district government. When the eighth month tax was collected, the *xian* government directive stated that those who wanted to send rice could send rice and that those who wanted to pay the money equivalent could send the money equivalent, at the money equivalent rate of 30 cash per *jin* of rice. At the time, the market price was only 20 cash, so the peasants were unwilling to pay in money.

When the public welfare fee was first imposed, about 10 percent of the people disagreed with it, and when staff members arrived at their homes, they said, "First you tell us to resist rents and resist taxes, and now you start collecting taxes." When the public welfare tax was to be collected, the order from above was very abrupt. It gave a limit of three days to turn over the rice to the township governments, and the township governments convened a meeting of all the heads of the village land offices. The first township was divided into nine Red Guard big brigades [*dadui*], and one person from each brigade was to be a land office head. They resolved that there would be a meeting of responsible persons in each village, at the end of which the public welfare fee would be collected, without ever having held a mass meeting. When collecting the fee, the brigade was taken as the unit. For example, the Eighth Big Brigade was organized jointly by the three villages of Yangfang, Lingyuan, and Li'ao. The head of the big brigade, the land office heads, the heads of the three medium brigades, and the heads of the nine branch brigades would split up and go to these three villages to collect the tax (one medium brigade for each village). They would go to a house and weigh the harvest. There are 90 *jin* to the *dan*[31] That household would appoint someone to send the tax to the township government. This big brigade in total collected about 400 dan in public welfare fees. In the first township, Chagan Village sent out letters to all its households two days in advance requesting them to send the public welfare fee to the public granary. On that day all the households, one after the other, carried rice over to the public granary (the former welfare granary), where it was received by the responsible persons of this township (five persons), and within a single day the collection was completed, bringing in a total of over 700 dan of rice. They had said beforehand that any family that failed to bring in their public welfare fee on that day would have to pay the meal expenses for that day of the five responsible persons. Because everyone was afraid of having to put out this bit of money, they all brought in their public welfare fees very promptly.

VI. The Soviets

1. The District Government

Members of the the district government (the second month to the sixth month):

Chairman, Liu Shaobiao (from the second township, did not farm, some education, fairly literate, a tailor but later quit tailoring to take up gambling as his

---

31. The *dan* which appears here is the unit of measure, not the unit of weight (generally written *Dan* in this volume). It is assumed in some other texts that one *dan* or bushel of rice weighs roughly one *Dan* or picul, equivalent to 100 *jin* or Chinese pounds, but in this instance Mao uses the more precise figure of 90 *jin*.

profession; joined the revolution the year before last, house burned by the Pacification Defense Corps; after the seventh month, when a new chairman was installed, he became a tailor).

Military Affairs, Xiao Zhichun (from the second township, did not farm, peddled ducks to Guangdong, gambled, caretaker of an ancestral temple, had no house of his own, not very literate, joined the revolution the year before last; since the seventh month has been chairman of the district government).

Finance, Hou Lixin (from the second township, a tailor, literate, since the seventh month has been head of the district labor union committee).

Organization, Liu Shaoming (from the second township, medical doctor, has no other occupation, a formerly well-situated family, the four brothers of which later set up separate households, he became a medical doctor, owed money; joined the revolution year before last, house was burned down by the Pacification Defense Corps; has been finance officer since the seventh month).

Propaganda, Zou Lisan (from Ganxian, a rich peasant, six brothers, middle school graduate; became head of the propaganda office, left for Ganxian in the seventh month).

Wang Zhenren (from the second township, nickname "Skyman," no job, makes his living by gambling; joined the revolution year before last, house was burned down by the Pacification Defense Corps; since the seventh month has been propaganda officer).

Fang Gongshu (from the eleventh district, a scholar, occupation uncertain, house was burned down by the Pacification Defense Corps, returned to the eleventh district in the seventh month).

Xiao Zhicheng (from the second township, gambler by occupation, fairly literate; joined the revolution the year before last, was attacked by the Pacification Defense Corps; has been in the district government offices since the seventh month, position unknown).

Chen Fangbao (from the second township, tailor and also gambler, illiterate; joined the revolution the year before last, arrested in the eighth month under suspicion of being a member of the AB Corps).

Judge, Zeng Libang (from the second township, a Daoist priest with no other occupation, family in very difficult straits; joined the revolution the year before last, later became director general of the Xingguo-Ganxian-Wan'an guerrilla brigade, now incorporated into the Twenty-second Army).

Culture, Zou Lidong (from the second township, formerly had 600 *dan* of fields, used up for his education, left with 100 *dan*, and a debt of over 300 *yuan*, was a bankrupt big landlord; a college graduate, joined the revolution last year, after the reorganization in the seventh month became culture officer).

Secretary-General, Xie Yingshan (from the *xian* seat, a scholar, aged fifty, with the reorganization in the seventh month became secretary-general).

Squad [*shaodui*] political officer, Xiao Shaowen (from the second township, a gambler by occupation, somewhat literate; joined the revolution the year before last, with the seventh month reorganization went to southwestern Jiangxi.

Squad leader, Xu Changhan (from the first township, a rich peasant, was himself a "graduate"; last year the guerrilla corps forced him to make a contribution, he joined the revolution, and was arrested in the eighth month under suspicion of being a member of the AB Corps).

Huang Guan (a scholar, background unclear, since the seventh month reorganization his activities are also unclear).

Chen Guntong (from the second township, father was a local ruffian [*tugun*], now dead; himself a middle peasant and also gambler, illiterate; joined the revolution the year before last, the Pacification Defense Corps confiscated his fields, in the district government offices since the reorganization in the seventh month).

Yang Dacheng (from the second township, formerly a tailor, later gambled for a profession; joined the revolution the year before last, somewhat literate, following the seventh month reorganization became propaganda officer in the second township government).

Women, Liu Chaoying (from the first township, a working woman, illiterate; after the seventh month reorganization went to southwestern Jiangxi.

Of the eighteen persons listed above, six were gamblers by occupation (two of whom had previously been tailors), one was a tailor and gambler, one was strictly a tailor, one a medical doctor, one a Daoist priest, one a bankrupt big landlord, two rich peasants, one middle peasant, three scholars of unknown backgrounds, and one a working woman of unknown family background.

Of the eighteen persons above, the seven who are best at explaining things and have the most authority are Liu Shaobiao, Xiao Zhichun, Liu Shaoming, Wang Zhenren, Xie Yingshan, Chen Guntong, Zou Lidong, and Zeng Libang.

The district government is located in Yongfeng Town.

Between the second month and the ninth month, over twenty district-wide mass meetings were held, and the district representative congress met twice (representatives were elected at mass meetings held in each village). Before the sixth month, there were few district-wide mass meetings. With the deepening of the struggle since the sixth month, more were held. Since the fourth month, women and children have participated in the mass meetings.

2. The Township Governments

To take the township government of the first township as an example:

Chairman, Xie Jinming (poor peasant and pole-bearer, had an extremely small piece of land of his own).

Finances, Zhong Guochu (middle peasant).

Military Affairs, Yang Tingrong (poor peasant, had an extremely small piece of his own land).

Propaganda, Xie Zhongkai (poor peasant, had his own land, but owed money).

Xie Zhongmei (had his own fields that he farmed himself and also traveled to Guangdong, a middle peasant).

Xie Huahuan (rich peasant and graduate of the Xingguo *xian* School).

Chen Fangpo (poor peasant, farmed other people's fields, and fortune-teller).

Secretary, Yi Yonghong (father is a barber, very poor, he himself is educated).

Judge, Chen Yushu (from Liantang, has an education).

Land, Fu Jiting (poor peasant).

Of these ten persons, six were poor peasants, two were middle peasants, and one was a rich peasant, while one was a scholar who came from the outside.

The township governments have held far fewer mass meetings than the district, no more than ten. Before the fourth month, women and children did not participate, but since the fourth month they have participated.

The township representative meetings have met six or seven times, with thirty or forty persons attending each time, in each township, with one or two representatives from each village, and some nonrepresentatives attending from villages near the township government. Each meeting lasted three to four hours. The representatives attending the meetings talked quite a lot, and a temporary chairman was chosen.

3. *Village Governments*

From the second month to the fifth month there were village governments. A village government is really essential during land distribution.. After the lands are distributed it is possible to do without the village governments. Furthermore, to set one up requires money—even if food allowances are not given, administrative expenses do require some money. Since the deepening of the revolution and the distribution of the land, ten households have been formed into a team [*zu*], and there is a Red Guard brigade. If a village government is not desired, that's all right, too.

4. *Defects of Government Personnel*

First is bureaucratism, putting on airs, and an aversion to getting close to the masses. When one of the common people goes to the government and asks a question about something, are the government staff members happy about it and say a few words in reply, or are they not happy about it, and ignore that person totally, or even accuse him of "stirring up trouble"?

Second is after confiscating the things of the reactionaries, not issuing them to the poor people, but selling them for cash, while those who are not on close speaking terms with those in the government have no chance to buy them, and only those who are on intimate terms and can put in a few words with the government personnel can buy them. Moreover, when they are sold only those with money can afford to buy them, while the farm laborers and the poorest of the poor peasants are left out.

Third is sending women to work in the government. The township governments always have one or two women and the district government always has three or four women. It is good to have women working in the government, but the government's hiring methods are wrong. If a woman is not good-looking, they don't want her even if she is articulate and capable. If a woman is good-looking, they want her even if she is inarticulate and incapable of doing the work. And the same is true when the township government people go down to hold meetings in the villages. They talk with the pretty women and won't say a word to those who are not pretty.

Fourth, and this is the most important item, violating public opinion. Government personnel do what a small minority has decided, and the elections to the representative assemblies are merely a matter of form. On one occasion the chairman said that all those who agreed with a certain person should raise their hands, and when some did not raise their hands, the chairman pointed to one of those who had not raised his hand and called him an AB Leaguer. Once the chairman of the meeting angrily interrogated someone who had not raised his hand as to why he did not do so. And then, sometimes only Communist Party members are allowed to work in the government, and those who are not members of the Communist Party, even if they are leaders of the masses, are not allowed to go work in the government (I have told those attending the meetings: These bad things are the conditions of the early stages of the land revolution, and one of the reasons they take place is because the composition of the district government is not so good, these must all be changed in the future, these bad things are wrong).

VII. Militarizing the Villages

1. The Red Guard Brigades

In the first township, nine companies; second township, three companies; third township, four companies; fourth township, four companies. Structure: eight to fifteen men to a squad; three squads to a platoon; three platoons to one company. In the villages within this district, one company usually has eighty to ninety men. For example, the Eighth Company of the first township is composed of the Yangfang First Platoon, the Lingyuan Second Platoon, and the Li'ao Third Platoon, with a total of more than ninety men.

The Red Guard brigades range in age from twenty-three to fifty.

The Red Guard brigades are all male.

In the beginning, they were divided between the standing Red Guard brigades and the reserve Red Guard brigades; later these were combined and were no longer divided between standing and reserve Red Guards.

Duties: To stand sentry day and night. Every village has sentries. Every village must have a sentry station at the entrance of its main road. Ordinarily, the Children's Corps and the Youth Corps stand sentry during the daytime. The regulations stipulate that there be five persons every day, two girls from the Children's Corps, two boys from the Children's Corps, and one sentry inspector from the Youth Corps. If the person from the Youth Corps can read and write, he must look carefully at the travel passes, and no matter who comes through, all must have a travel pass from village A to village B. At night, the Red Guard brigade takes over sentry duty, usually four men every night, two men to a shift, one shift for the first half of the night, and one shift for the second half of the night. When the situation in the environs is tense (as when the Qifang Pacification Defense dogs attacked the vicinity of Jun Village), the Red Guard unit takes over sentry duty both day and night, and furthermore the number of people on sentry duty is increased considerably. Although in the daytime there are still only four, in the evening there will be ten or more, or even twenty or more.

Each Red Guard company has a company commander, who must be one of the most hard-working persons in that township, and must also have some knowledge of military affairs; and a political officer, who must be one of the most hard-working persons in the township and must also be able to read documents.

Formerly the Red Guard brigades were obliged to conduct drills. When the Red Army reserve brigades were formed in the seventh month, they no longer had drills.

The Red Guard brigades are divided into the men's Red Guards and the women's Red Guards. For example, in the Eighth Company jointly organized by the three villages of Yangfang, Lingyuan, and Li'ao in the first township, there are two units, the men's Eighth Company and the women's Eighth Company. The ages of the women Red Guards are similar to the men Red Guards, but they are fewer in number, because there are fewer women than men, and subtracting pregnant women and women who are nursing, each company usually has only forty persons (the Third Company of the second township) or fifty persons (the Eighth Company of the first township and the Third Company of the third township). There are also some with fewer than forty persons, and there are some with more than fifty persons. The women Red Guards ordinarily do not stand sentry duty. In emergency situations, when the men Red Guards are out on campaigns (out fighting is called "out on a campaign"), then the women Red Guards stand sentry duty. The women's Red Guard brigades must also conduct drills, once a month, two to three hours each time. The company commander and the political officer are both women. When they conduct drills, the men's Red Guard brigade delegates someone to go there and act as drill instructor. Since the sixth month, when the men's Red Guards took their best men and formed them into the Red Army reserve brigades, the men's Red Guards were left with only the elderly and the weak, each brigade having only ten or more people, no more than twenty or thirty, so after this they did not have drills. As for the men's Red Guards, each township has one township brigade leader, and one township political officer, both of whom are not permanently attached to the township government, but who live in their own homes, and go where they are instructed to go when something comes up. When there is an all-township drill, they must also go. In each of the villages, the Red Guards have twice conducted all-township drills.

2. Youth Vanguard Brigade

Wherever there is a Red Guard company, there is also a youth company in which there is no division between male and female, and their ages are sixteen to twenty-three. There is a company commander and a political officer. Each company is divided into three platoons, and each platoon is divided into three squads. It is just that they are fewer in numbers than the Red Guard companies; per company there may be twenty persons (Zhige in the second township), thirty persons (Changjiao in the third township), or fifty to sixty persons (the three villages of Yangfang, etc., in the first township). Those with twenty or thirty persons are called platoons, while those with fifty or sixty persons are called companies. Since the sixth month, those with courage have been picked out to be incorporated into the Red Army reserve corps and the district special agent battalion. The remaining youth brigade members continue to conduct drill exercises, twice a month. It is only the men's Red Guard brigade that, since the incorporation of its most courageous and best men into the Red Army reserve corps, no longer holds drill exercises.

The youth brigades, since their best members have been incorporated into the Red Army reserve corps and district special agent battalion, have been left with only a few persons, and actually some places no longer have a youth brigade (as in the case of the three villages of Yangfang, etc., in the first township, and Zhige in the second township).

3. Children's Brigades

No separation of boys and girls, ages eight to fifteen.

Where there is a Red Guard brigade and a youth brigade, there is also a laborers' children's brigade. There is a brigade leader for each village. There are no township brigade leaders. There is a district brigade leader.

The tasks of the children's brigades are first, to stand sentry duty; second, to inspect for opium and gambling; and third, to get rid of superstition and religion. The children's brigades inspect for opium and gambling and attack religion very forcefully, entirely without mercy, "truly and fairly doing their public duty." When mass meetings are held, they attend. Their weapons are primarily wooden guns, and some among them have spears.

All members of the children's brigades are studying in the people's schools. The people's schools were started in the seventh month, five in the first township, three in the second township, seven in the third township, and one in the fourth township, for a total of sixteen. The district government stipulates that each township have three schools and gives a food allowance for three teachers, 0.10 *yuan* per day in big foreign currency, plus 2.00 *yuan* per month for miscellaneous expenses, for a total of 5.00 *yuan* per month. Because the first township is large in size, it is allowed to run five schools. Because the third township has many mountains, three schools are not enough, so they themselves have added four more schools for a total of seven, but since they have only 15 *yuan* in expense funds, each school receives an average allotment of a little over 2 *yuan*. The number of students in the people's schools is as low as twenty and as high as a hundred students, generally forty or so. In the case of the joint school of three villages of Yangfang, Lingyuan, and Li'ao in the first township, which has over a hundred and twenty children between the ages of eight and fifteen, one building is too small to hold them all, and one teacher cannot teach them all, and consequently many children have not yet started to attend school. Of the hundred and twenty children, only about sixty are attending the school. Originally, the three villages wanted to have three people's schools, but because there are no teachers in these villages and they do not have the funds to pay the living expenses of someone brought in from the outside, they cannot operate three schools. In the third township, the school in Zhuzhaoan Village has only twenty-one students.

Every village has a common people's night school and one teacher for each school—someone from the village who can read a little and is given no living expenses. The teachers do their own work at home during the day and go to the poor people's night schools in the evening to hold classes. Fu Jiting from Yangfang and Zhong Dewu in Changjiao are both teachers. The number of students varies. In Yangfang there are forty. Their ages vary, elderly, middle-aged, and young all attend. Most of the night schools have women students, one third of the total. Some have no women, as in the cases of Chagan Village in the first township and Houjing Village in the fourth township, in neither of which are there any women attending the common people's night school. The children's brigades have exercise drills three times per week, all under the direction of the people's schools. "They drill very well."

4. The Inspection Brigades [jiuchadui]

The workers have organized inspection brigades, one company per township, with one company commander and one political officer. The inspection brigade of the second township has 105 persons. The four villages of Yangfang, Lingyuan, Li'ao, and Chashi (i.e., Chagan) in the first township have one platoon with twenty-six people.

5. Red Army Reserve Corps

Composed of the strong and courageous elements from the two organizations, the Red Guards and the youth brigades. Each township has two companies, eight companies in the whole district. Each company has several dozen to over a hundred people. The two companies from the first township have a little over a hundred persons each. In the recent campaign in Xinyu, all the men of the eight companies from the tenth district were present. After the reserve corps was formed in the seventh month, the attacks on Qifang, Langquan, Ganzhou, and the latest Xinyu campaign were all undertaken by the reserve corps. When the reserve corps goes out on campaigns, the sentry duty of the townships and villages is borne by the Red Guards, the youth brigades, and children's brigades. When the reserve corps returns it again helps out with the sentry duty. The eight companies of the entire district are organized into one regiment, with a regimental commander and a regimental political officer. Ordinarily, battalions are not set up. The first township has the First Company and Second Company. The second township has the Third Company and Fourth Company. The third township has the Fifth Company and Sixth Company. The fourth township has the Seventh Company and the Eighth Company. In the latest Xinyu campaign, they were organized into three battalions, the First, Second, and Third Companies forming the First Battalion, the Fourth, Fifth, and Sixth Companies forming the Second Battalion, and the Seventh and Eighth Companies forming the Third Battalion, with battalion commanders and battalion political officers. A company has four pole-carriers, eight mess staff, one to four dispatchers, one orderly, one bugler (can't play the bugle), and no cavalry. Each company has two propagandists, one public speaker, and one person to write slogans. The battalion staff includes no propaganda personnel, no aide-de-camp, and no dispatchers. The regimental staff includes three propagandists, one aide-de-camp, and two dispatchers. The staffs of the three companies and of the battalion live together and eat together. Their weapons are spears and shotguns.

6. The District Special Agent Battalion

Three companies, formed in the seventh month, also selected from the Red Guards and youth brigades. Formed of younger and more courageous elements selected from the Red Guards and youth brigades, better than those of the reserve corps. They are organized and trained, but are not brought together frequently. Ordinarily, they are at home doing their own work. They are brought together for a big exercise drill three times a month, on the 2nd, 12th, and 22nd of the month. When something takes place, they are ordered to assemble and go out to fight. At present the two companies, the first and third, are out on campaign in the attack on Langquan, and the second company is at home, not mobilized. Their weapons are primarily shotguns, locally manufactured guns, and locally made cannons, no automatic rifles, and a few spears. The battalion staff and district government are together. There is a battalion commander and a battalion political officer.

7. The Red Army Independent Regiment

In the whole of Xingguo *xian* a total of three independent regiments have been formed; all have been given to the Red Army. These too have been selected from the Red Guards and from the youth brigades, and are made up of members who are just as good as those of the special agent battalion. They are all young people and furthermore are volunteer soldiers.

Each regiment has over one thousand men. The regiments, battalions, and companies all have commanders and political officers, and are concentrated in the *xian* town, where they receive training and await deployment to be incorporated into the Red Army. They are all empty-handed, having no weapons.

Order to Lure the Enemy Deep into the Red Area, Wait Until They Are Exhausted, and Annihilate Them[1]

(November 1, 1930, 2 P.M., Yuanqian Village, Luofang, Xinyu *xian*)

1. The two enemy divisions of Gong and Luo are in the area of Gaoan and Shanggao; the two regiments of Zhang Huizan are in Zhangshu; Deng Ying's division is in Fengcheng; there is one enemy division in Wanshougong (whose designation is unclear); Peng Qibiao's battalion [2] is near Nanchang; Xu Kexiang has approached Hukou; the division of Tan Daoyuan and the battalion of Hu Zuyu are on the Nanchang-Jiujiang Railroad; Cai Tingkai and Jiang Guangnai's two divisions have reached south Hubei,[3] and the enemy from Hunan, the Li Jue division, have entered Yuanzhou.

2. The Front Army will carry out its original plan of luring the enemy deep into the Red regions and annihilating them when they are exhausted. It has been decided to move its main force to the east bank of the Gan River, seek opportunities to occupy Zhangshu and Fuzhou, promote work in various *xian* such as Xin'gan, Jishui, Yongfeng, Le'an, Yihuang, Chongren, Nanfeng and Nancheng, prepare supplies, and train troops.

3. The Third Army Group, which constitutes the central route army (commanded by Commander-in-Chief Peng [Dehuai] and Political Commissar Teng [Daiyuan]), should speedily cross the Yuan River and concentrate troops on the south bank. It should cross the river near a place directly opposite Xin'gan, on the 5th of this month punctually, advance toward Zhangshu and seize opportunities to take Zhangshu in accordance with our strategy, raise 200,000 [*yuan*] of funds, and mobilize the masses in the areas near the major roads from Zhangshu

---

Our source for this text is *Mao Zedong junshi wenji*, Vol. 1, pp. 181–83, where it has been taken from a printed document held in the Central Party Archives. It can also be found in *Mao Zedong ji. Bujuan*, Vol. 3, pp. 175–77.

1. This is an order of the First Front Army of the Red Army, issued by Mao Zedong and Zhu De.

2. The reference is to the independent Fourteenth Battalion of the Guomindang, commanded by Peng Qibiao.

3. Cai Tingkai (1892–1968) and Jiang Guangnai (1888–1967) were both natives of Guangdong. At this time, they were commanders respectively of the Guomindang Sixtieth and Sixty-first Divisions, which together made up the Nineteenth Route Army.

to Fengcheng and Xin'gan. After that, the place for concentrating the troops is near Tengtian, Yongfeng.

4. The Fourth Army and the Twelfth Army will be the right route army and should concentrate their forces on the 3rd, inspect their work on the 4th, move to the town of Xiajiang on the 5th, and cross the river (under the command of Lin Biao and Yang Yuebin) on the 6th. They should further advance toward Fuzhou through Chongren, seize opportunities to take Fuzhou in accordance with our strategy, carry out work in Nanfeng, Nancheng, Chongren and Yihuang, raise the sum of 400,000 [yuan], and mobilize the masses there. The next place of concentration is near Zhaoxie city in Le'an. If the central route army is threatened by an enemy with superior forces, then the right route should advance the time for concentration and move toward the central route in order to cope with the enemy.

5. The Third Army (commanded by Huang Gonglue and Cai Huiwen) will be the left route with the task of disrupting the enemy in the areas on the west bank of the Gan River (including Anfu), keeping contact with the Twentieth Army and the central route, pinning down the enemy, and preventing them from attacking Ji'an.

6. The Twentieth Army should carry out work in the area of Jishui, Yongfeng and Xin'gan, and should maintain constant contact with General Headquarters.

7. The time for the work is one month, and all units must complete the work in their respective *xian* and districts on time.

8. The rear liaison line[4] stretches to Ji'an through Xiajiang and the Rear Office in Ji'an still remains.

9. The General Headquarters plans to cross the river at the town of Xiajiang, situated near the main road to Xin'gan opposite the Xiajiang *xian* town. Afterward, it will be with the central route (the Third Army Group).

It is so ordered.

Addendum:

(1) The priority in using work time should be raising funds. Meanwhile, the broad masses should also be mobilized and the training of our own troops should be stepped up.

(2) After the separation of troops, if any password or signal is lost, the unit may design its own, inform neighboring friendly forces, and report to the General Headquarters.

(3) During the work, all sides should use all methods to deliver reports to the General Headquarters.

---

4. Here we follow the text in the *Mao Zedong ji*, which has the character *xian* ("line"), rather than *Mao Zedong junshi wenji*, which has *qi* ("period"), followed by the Chinese equivalent of [sic].

Investigations in Dongtang and Other Places

(November 8, 1930)[1]

On October 30, 1930, the Front Committee of the Red Army decided in Luofang to adopt the strategy of luring the enemy deep into our territory.[2] On November 6, the Red Army crossed the Gan River at Xiajiang, heading for Yongfeng and Nancheng. I traveled from Xiajiang to Ji'an to make arrangements for the withdrawal, and stayed overnight in Dongtang on November 7, arriving in Ji'an the next day. I conducted some brief investigations along the way. The investigation in Lijiafang helped me understand the organization and activities of the soviets at the village and township levels in those places in the land struggle. I had only foggy ideas about such facts before this investigation. This investigation enabled me to find out about the importance of redistribution of land using the village as the basic unit. There are several dozens of *xian* in southwest Jiangxi where land has been redistributed. The land laws promulgated by the higher-level governments call for redistribution taking the township as the basic unit. Officials in most higher-level organs also think that land is being redistributed using the township as the basic unit. They do not seem to know that the real situation is completely different. Everywhere redistribution takes place using the village as the basic unit. There are very few cases of redistribution using the township as the basic unit. The method of redistribution which uses the village as the basic unit favors rich peasants, and is disadvantageous to poor peasants; it should be changed.

1. Investigation in Dongtang

Dongtang Village is in the 15th township of Tongshui district in Jishui *xian*.

There are one thousand households, or three thousand people, in the township.

Land has been redistributed using the village as the basic unit.

Our source for this investigation is *Mao Zedong nongcun diaocha wenji*, pp. 254–63, which reproduces the text as it was originally published in Yan'an in 1941.

1. This date does not appear at the head of the Chinese text, but it is implied by the first paragraph of Mao's own account of his movements, and given in *Nianpu*, Vol. 1, p. 323.

2. I.e., during the Joint Conference of the General Front Committee and of the Jiangxi Provincial Action Committee in Luofang (see, above, the note to the text of October 26, 1930).

There are 290 people in this village.

The village government has its chairman and secretary, both support themselves at their own expense.

During land redistribution, each person received 1 *dou* 3 *sheng* of land that yield about 2.5 *dan* of grain (every *dou* of land yields two *dan* of grain).[3]

In some other villages, each person got two *dou* of land. Two *dou* was the upper limit; nobody got more than two *dou* in this township.

The secretary of the village government, Hu Deshun, 48, also teaches in the community's school. He has eight mouths to feed. In addition to himself, he has five sons, his wife and his daughter-in-law. His eldest son works both as a tailor and a farm hand. He is 25. His second son, aged 19, is learning to be a carpenter, and is apprenticed in Yongfeng *xian*. He does not make any money. His third son is 14 and learning to be a bamboo-smith. He is also an apprentice and makes no money. His fourth son, 7, is going to school. His youngest son is three years old. Previously, he owned 1 *dan* 3 *dou* 8 *sheng* of land and could harvest 27 *dan* of grain, which was not enough to feed the family.[4] [He] relied on growing sweet potatoes, raising pigs, and money earned by his eldest son, as well as his own labor in the fields. He owed three hundred strings of cash. In the land redistribution this time, the eight of them received in all 1 *dan* 4 *sheng* of land, and had to give up 3 *dou* 4 *sheng* of land.

From the city of Ji'an to Jingtan, Tongshui and Futian, almost every family in this area about seventy to eighty *li* in diameter has women employed in weaving cloth; they produce a huge amount, using the yarns (foreign-made) supplied to the peasant families by businessmen, rich peasants and landlords. The process of the capitalist destruction of the family cottage industry is not over yet.

2. Investigation in Daqiao

[Daqiao] is under the jurisdiction of the ninth township of Jingtan district in Jishui *xian*; it is fifty *li* from Ji'an.

The district is divided into thirteen townships.

This township is divided into five villages.

---

3. Here Mao uses the Chinese dry measures *sheng* (approximately a litre), *dou* (approximately a decalitre), and *dan* (approximately a hectolitre). Land in this village is being measured, not in terms of the harvest it will normally yield, but in terms of the amount of seed required to sow it. Thus one *dou* of land, having been sown with one decalitre of seed, will yield one hectolitre of grain at the harvest, or ten times the amount of seed used. In the balance of the text, land is measured sometimes in terms of seed required, sometimes in terms of yield.

4. It can be seen from this example, and others in the present text, that the actual yield of a piece of land does not necessarily correspond to the nominal yield used to measure it, but varies with the quality and location of each plot.

This village is called Daqiao.

The chairman of the township government is Sun Xiu'en.

For the 570 people in the Liu village of Jiaokeng township, each received nine *luo* of land, or four and a half *dan*.[5] For the 110 people in the Tang village of Jiaokeng township, each received land with a yield of nine *luo* of grain. For the fifty people in the Wu village of Jiaokeng township, each also received nine *luo* of land. The three villages, Liu, Tang and Wu, share the same village government, and every person got nine *luo* of land.

In Daqiao Village those surnamed Guo number 1,027, each of whom was given eight *luo*, or two *dou*, of land, which yields four *dan* of grain.[6] In Shenjiangyu, those surnamed Luo in two villages number 210 people, and share the same village government. Eight *luo* of land was redistributed to each person.

For the people of the Guo and Luo villages, each received eight *luo* of land because the quality of the land there is slightly better. The villagers in the three villages, Liu, Tang, and Wu, got nine *luo* of land each because the quality of the land there is a bit poorer. On average, for young and old, each person consumes ten *luo* (or five *Dan*)[7] of grain every year.

Second-crop rice can be grown on one-third of the land in each village; it cannot be grown on two-thirds of the land since there is no water. The land on which the second-crop rice can be grown and the land on which it cannot are packaged together during redistribution, with each person getting a bit of each kind. Getting eight or nine *luo* of land both refer to the combined harvest from the first and second crops of grain. Each person consumes ten *luo* of rice every year. Those who got eight *luo* are short two *luo*; those who got nine *luo* are short one *luo*. The method of making up for the shortfalls is, first, engaging in other employment, such as dying cloth, processing rice, working as carpenters, smiths and tailors. More than three hundred people go to other townships to find employment. Of these, more than 170 to 180 people go to Ganzhou to find jobs. Most of them process rice or work as tailors and small businessmen. About one hundred people go to Ji'an, most of them processing rice and dying cloth. Their families have all received redistributed land. This township does not grow non-rice crops. The second method is for housewives to weave cloth, as they do in most households. Each piece of cloth measures 12 *zhang*, or 130 *chi*, for which

---

5. Here Mao (or local usage) introduces yet another complication, by the use of the unit known as a *luo* (basket), equal to half a *dan*. At the same time, yield (rather than seed required) is being used as the measure of land.

6. Here both criteria (seed and yield) are being used simultaneously, and the grain produced is apparently twenty times the amount of seed.

7. As already indicated, two *luo* or "baskets" are equivalent to one *dan*. There are 100 *jin* or Chinese pounds in the unit of weight written *Dan* in this volume. Here it is apparently being assumed that when dealing with grain, the two measures are roughly equivalent (just as one litre of water weighs one kilogram). In Section V of the Xingguo Investigation, on the other hand, Mao gives the proportion as .9 *Dan* per *dan*.

they get paid 400 cash. It takes ten days for a fast worker to finish one piece. Each worker can make 1,200 cash every month. The slower workers and those hampered by their children cannot finish one piece in ten days. Rich peasants and small businessmen buy foreign-made yarns from Ji'an and distribute them among villages and households. The less-accomplished weavers may get 300 cash, or sometimes 200 cash, for one piece. Some even have to pay for unacceptable products. For one piece of cloth, they also make an additional two *liang* of yarn, which can be woven into two *chi* of cloth. One *chi* of cloth sells for 100–110 cash. Peasants depend on such additional yarn for making their own clothes. The monthly income of the weavers, 1,200 cash, is used as money for salt and cooking oil. The odd jobs and weaving mentioned above make up the main sources to augment the shortfalls in daily living expenses. Now there is not much cloth to be woven, nor are there enough odd jobs to be found. The workers who have gone to Ganzhou have not returned; of the 100 workers who have gone to Ji'an, about 50–60 have come back.

This township does not have a school yet.

Recently the district issued an ordinance that each township produce twenty conscripts as volunteers for the Red Army. Eighteen people from this township joined up. All of them volunteered. There is a send-off party today at the Wugang district government.

3. Investigation in Lijiafang

The nineteenth township in Rufang district of Ji'an *xian* is called Lijiafang (40 *li* from Ji'an).

This township has nine villages and six village governments.

Of the nine villages, six are large ones, and the other three are smaller ones.

Six larger ones are Lijiafang, Shangzhaotang, Cangxia, Xuyuan, Jinbi and Zhouyuan. Three smaller villages are Yejiafang, Xiaolijiafang and Yangpingzhou. The three smaller villages share the same village government as Lijiafang. Each of the remaining five villages has its own village government.

There are four officers in the village government: one chairman, one secretary, one land officer who is also the grain officer, and one messenger who is also the cook. The chairman, secretary and messenger-cook live and work in the village government; they eat at the expense of the government. The land-and-food-clerk lives at home and eats at his own expense. He eats at the government's expense only when he goes to the village government to take care of official business.

The expenditures of the village government consist of (1) the daily cost of food for three and the cost of food for an average of two visitors per day. Each person costs 0.1 *yuan* in big foreign dollars every day; the monthly total cost is fifteen *yuan*, (2) three *yuan* in office expenses for lamps, kerosene, paper and pens, (3) money for straw sandals, hair-cuts and tobacco for the Red Guards and

Young Pioneers when they are sent off on missions; the amounts vary from 500 cash to one string of cash (reimbursed to the full actual cost; extra money is returned and shortfalls are made up). There have been nine attacks on Ji'an. On longer missions they sometimes returned home after more than a month. In the past, such items cost three *yuan* per month. For previous missions the village government also paid for the cost of food. Later, the practice was changed, and the township government pays for the cost of food, with the village government paying only for incidental expenses. Of the three items above, the monthly expenditures amount to a total of 21 *yuan*.

The previous village government employed nine people to run its affairs: chairman, secretary, treasurer, buyer, land officer, food officer, arbitrator, transportation officer, and cook. All nine of them work in the village government and eat at the government's expense. This state of affairs continued between the time the revolution began in January of this year and March 19, between June 4 and September 4. Between March 20 and June 3, the reactionary garrison team occupied [the village] and abolished the village government. The head of the government fled to Futian. Since September 5, the practice has been changed; now four people regularly work in the village government; the expenditures were higher when there were nine people working here.

In the township government, starting on January 10 and ending on March 19, and starting on June 4 and ending on September 5, there were these administrators: chairman, secretary, buyer, treasurer, cultural officer, land officer, food officer, arbitrator, transportation officer and cook. There were also three women, three Young Pioneers (team leader, deputy team leader and instructor-secretary), and the head of the children's league. Altogether there were eighteen people, all of whom ate at the government's expense. Since September 6 the number of administrators has been cut to only seven: chairman, secretary, land and food officer, cultural officer, chairman of the women's committee, head of the Red Guards who is also the cook, and another secretary. The secretary has two jobs to do: act as the "commissar for confiscation" and "go to the countryside to propagandize about and expand the Red Army." The seven people mentioned above regularly work and eat in the township government. There are four members of the women's committee who come to eat in the government only when they have business to do there, and stay home when there is nothing for them to do. The job of the four members of the women's committee is to go down to the countryside to organize working women into the Red Guards, relief teams, and laundry teams, as well as persuade men to join the Red Army.

In February this year, eight people from this township joined the Red Army. On June 18, when the second attack on Ji'an was launched, two people from each village joined the Red Army. Altogether eighteen people joined up. In July, when the seventh attack on Ji'an began, another seven went. On August 13, after the ninth attack on Ji'an was underway, forty-six people went to join the Red Army and were grouped into an independent regiment; they received training at the headquarters of the Second Independent Regiment in Datang. Altogether eighty people from this township have gone to join the Red Army; all of them were encouraged to go. But of the last group of forty-six people, four or five people wept and showed reluctance to join up; they were forced to go.

There are nine villages in this township: Lijiafang, with the surname Hu, 228 people; Xiaolijiafang, with the surname Li, 30 people; Yejiafang, with the surname Ye, 45 people; Yangpingzhou, with the surname Xiao, 24 people. These four villages have a total of 327 people (155 men and 172 women). In Shangzhaotang the surname is Liu, and there are 200 people. In Cangxia, with the surname Yan, there are 315 people (150 men and 165 women). In Xuyuan, with the surname Zhou, there are 300 people. In Jinbi there are 190 people. In Zhouyuan, there are 372 people (176 men and 196 women). In all, there are 1,704 people in the nine villages.

The first four villages, including Lijiafang, have a total of 921.1 *mu* of land.[8] In Lijiafang, each person got 2.7 *mu* of land, with a yield of seven *dan* of grain. In Yejiafang, each person received three *mu* of land, with a yield of six *dan* of grain. In Xiaolijiafang, each person was given two *mu* of land, with a yield of 5.5 *dan* of grain. In Yangpingzhou, each person got 2.5 *mu* of land, with a yield of 5.5 *dan* of grain. Lijiafang has a surplus of 17.9 *mu* of land, six *mu* of which was transferred to Xiaolijiafang; another six *mu* of land was transferred to Yejiafang. The remaining 5.9 *mu* of land is held "in public trust." In Yangpingzhou, the remaining 2.3 *mu* of land after redistribution is being held "in public trust." There is leftover land because it is difficult to redistribute the remaining balance. It is used as the public land of the village government; the grain rent derived from it is used as public funds. The rate of rent is 60 percent.

Shangzhaotang village has a total of 820 *mu* of land; each person was given 2.4 *mu* of land, with a yield of 2.5 *dan* of grain. There is a balance of 29.2 *mu* of land after redistribution; it is held "in public trust."

Cangxia village has altogether 690.3 *mu* of land. Each person received a plot of land with a yield of 7.8 *dan* of grain.

Xuyuan has a total of more than 820 *mu* of land. The method of re-distribution of land was: each person living at home received 3.5 *mu* of land. The land of this village is more fertile and each *mu* can yield five *luo* of grain (two *luo* equal one *dan*);[9] altogether, [this much land] can yield 17 *luo* of grain. Each worker received 1.75 *mu* of land, which is half of what a peasant got. Those who have gone elsewhere received 1.4 *mu* of land.

Jinbi village has a total of 489 *mu* of land. Each person was given 2.7 *mu* of

---

8. Here yet a third system of measurement of land, in terms of area, is introduced. As noted elsewhere in this volume, the *mu*, like most traditional Chinese measurements, varied somewhat, but was equivalent to approximately .15 acre. As will be seen from the figures below, yields varied from approximately 1 to 3 *dan* per *mu*.

9. Here once again it is being assumed that the two *dan* (unit of weight and unit of volume) are roughly equivalent in dealing with grain.

land, with a yield of six *luo*. Those who have gone elsewhere did not get any land.

Zhouyuan village has 510.8 *mu* of land altogether. Each person got 2.2 *mu* of land, with a yield of six *luo*. Those who have gone elsewhere were not given any land.

After the Red Army captured Ji'an, the chief, deputy chief, secretary, and a platoon leader of the reactionary guards detachment of this township, four individuals in all, were caught and sent to their executions at the district government of Tongshuping. Members of the garrison team joined the revolution in this township; none of them went to Ji'an. None of the three platoon leaders and ten squad leaders who stayed at home and did not go to Ji'an were executed. They were permitted to join the revolution.

The chairman of the township government, Yan Chunwen, has eight *mu* of land; each *mu* has a yield of only three *luo* of grain; the total yield is 24 *luo*, enough to feed four people. When land was first redistributed in July, those who worked within the township and outside of the township were all given land, and his family gave up 1.2 *mu* of land; the 6.8 *mu* of land left could yield twenty *luo* of grain, giving each person five *luo*. In August, after Ji'an was captured, another round of land redistribution was carried out. Those who had jobs outside did not get any land. Only those who lived in the township and those who did not have jobs elsewhere had a share of the redistributed land. Each person got 2.2 *mu* of land. His family had eight *mu* of land to start with; this time he also got 0.8 *mu* of land. He owed 500 strings of cash in the past and sold one daughter (seven years old) to somebody in Ji'an (the buyer was from Ganzhou and had the Hemao Bank in Ji'an) for 100 *yuan*, which he used to pay his creditors. He still owes 200 strings of cash. He also gave away another daughter (newborn) to the Catholic Church of Ji'an, for whom he did not get any money.

4. Investigation in Xiyiting

This is one of the villages under the jurisdiction of the 23rd township of Rufang district of Ji'an; it is 15 *li* from Ji'an.

Rufang district has more than thirty townships in all.

This township has nine village governments and a population of approximately six hundred people.

This village, Xiyiting, has a village government with five administrators: chairman, secretary, food officer, land officer and officer for women's affairs. They all eat at their own expense; the village government does not provide food. When they gather on official business (such as having meetings), they eat at the village government's expense.

The public funds of the village temple and other religious groups are pooled together and used by the village government.

The expenditures of the village government consist of the cost of missions of the Red Guards and the Young Pioneers (attacking Ji'an or having large meetings), and the cost of food for the soldiers of the independent regiment when they are sent off on missions (each soldier gets 0.1 *yuan* a day). When they are sent off on missions, they get only money for food, but not for straw sandals, haircuts, tobacco, and so on.

This township's government has 19 administrators: one chairman, two secretaries (one for the township government, the other for the Red Guards), one cultural officer, one buyer, one food officer, one land officer, one officer for the Red Guards, one for social security, two for women's affairs (one chairman of the women's committee, the other for organizational affairs), one cook, one transportation officer, one commander of the Red Guards brigade, three company commanders, one political instructor of the Red Guards and the head of the Young Pioneers. The township government came into existence on June 9 this year. Since the reactionaries in Ji'an often came to the township to make arrests, the township government lacked stability; it moved toward the rear as soon as the enemy came. Only after Ji'an was captured did the work of the township move ahead. The reactionaries took away ten people from the township and killed two of them. Eight were released after Ji'an was captured. After Ji'an was captured, more than twenty local reactionaries from this township in Ji'an were arrested; six serious offenders were executed; some of the rest were fined and released; some were sent to the custody of the district government of Tongshuping. Now they are extremely busy, with things like redistribution of land and grain, debt boycott and setting up schools.

At the moment, the township is redistributing land, using the village as the basic unit. Five villages have already completed the land redistribution. Orders have also come down from above that land must be redistributed once again, using the township as the basic unit. According to the views of different villages, those with more land want to use the village as the basic unit; those villages with less land want to use the township as the basic unit. Of the nine villages in this township, eight villages want to use the village as the basic unit; only one village wants to use the township as the basic unit.

The five villages where land has been redistributed are Tingtang, Banxikeng, Tashui, Xintang, and Duanshang. In Tingtang, each person received two *mu* of land (with a yield of four to five *luo* of grain). In Banxikeng, each person got 2.5 *mu* of land; in Tashui and Duanshang, each person was given two *mu* of land. In Xintang, each person got only 0.8 *mu* of land. Xintang has less land and asks that land be redistributed using the township as the basic unit. Xintang village has about 200 people, with the family name Huang. Although they have less land, it is good land (there is no flood); moreover, it has both mountains and land.

It is more than a month since Ji'an was captured; the land of the township has not yet been fully redistributed; it will take another five or six days to finish the redistribution.

The struggle to resist the payment of debts means to have creditors hand in written receipts to burn. To date, of the nine villages only the village of Guantian has handed in receipts to the township government, and they have not yet been burned.

The chairman of the township government was replaced by the district government. The new chairman, Wang Yutang, has been here for only five days.

The former chairman, Liu Quansheng has 1.8 *mu* of land. He is a carpenter and supports two other people. He became chairman in June.

Previously, Ruhang and Fangguo were divided into two districts. Now they have been merged to form Rufang district. The new chairman of the township is from Ruhang district. The township was previously under the jurisdiction of Fangguo district. Wang Yutang is a carpenter and has five *mu* of land, with a yield of 18 *luo* of grain to feed four people. He himself is a carpenter and a farmer. More than seventy people from this district have gone to join the Red Army. More than forty of them were Young Pioneers. They are very brave teenagers.

The district government is located in Tongshuping. Its chairman is Chen Junbin, who works at the rice mill.

Circular of the Front Committee of the First Front Army of the Red Army and of the Jiangxi Provincial Action Committee

Circular:
The Problem of the Line for Expanding the Red Army

(November 11, 1930)

I. The Bold Expansion of the Red Army Is an Indispensable Condition for the Preparation of a Decisive Class War

At present the revolutionary upsurge in the entire nation is rising higher every day, the reactionary ruling class has gone completely bankrupt politically and economically, and its doom is at hand. When class contradictions transcend the contradictions within the ruling class itself, to save its own life, it is inevitable that the ruling class will temporarily reconcile its internal clashes, allocate some of its military forces to attack the revolutionaries, and make a final effort before its death. At this time there is only one solution, that is, to assemble all the revolutionary forces to prepare for a decisive class war. To achieve this objective, we definitely must expand the Red Army boldly, and call on the broad worker and peasant masses to participate passionately in the Red Army. Only thus can we guarantee victory in this decisive war.

II. One of the Major Tasks of the Party in Southwestern Jiangxi at Present Is to Call on the Worker and Peasant Masses to Join the Red Army

The Red Army's actions in surrounding and attacking Nanchang, occupying Changsha and then attacking it yet again, and occupying Ji'an, have promoted the development of the revolution. At the same time, they must necessarily promote awareness of the revolution on the part of the ruling class, and incite the ruling class to attack the revolution. The victory at Ji'an marks the beginning of victory in one province, Jiangxi, but for the ruling class it is the beginning of failure in one province. It was therefore inevitable that the ruling class should send its armies to attack Jiangxi in an attempt to wipe out the revolutionary

---

Our source for this text is *Jiangxi dangshi ziliao*, Vol. 6, pp. 205–10.

forces, wrest Ji'an from the hands of the workers and peasants, and restore its ruling status in the whole country. At this moment, if we fail to intensify our efforts, initial victory in Jiangxi will certainly be delayed. Therefore we must necessarily step up our efforts of all kinds; we must divide up the land completely and evenly, and carry out resolutely the policy of letting the workers supervise capital, so as to arouse the worker and peasant masses to stand up and join the decisive class war for victory in one province. Apart from these tasks, Party headquarters at all levels must also call on the masses to carry out the work of expanding the Red Army. We must closely integrate our work of expanding the Red Army with the work of opposing rich peasants, opposing the AB Corps, completely and evenly distributing the land, letting the workers supervise capital, transforming the Party and Youth League, and transforming the government. All these actions must be carried on simultaneously.

III. Oppose the Policies of Commandism and Deception

In the past, the new recruits sent by various localities were affected by serious mistakes in the expansion of the Red Army made by the local Party and Youth League organizations. The first mistake was employing the commandist method in levying conscripts, or even forcing people to join the army. A man was sent to the army even if he was the only one to cultivate the land in order to feed a family of nine. Directives from superiors were carried out mechanically. Their only concern was to send a sufficient number, and to send the new recruits beyond the *xian* borders; they were entirely unconcerned about how the masses would react to this behavior. The consequences of having this kind of irresolute and unwilling new recruits in the Red Army extended even to using AB Corps hats to threaten the masses, claiming that those who refused to go were AB Corps elements. This is an extremely dangerous method which will alienate us from the masses. The second mistake was the policy of deception. Many new recruits only learn that they are being asked to join the Red Army when they are assigned to various divisions and regiments. All the new recruits from places such as Xingguo, Ji'an, Jishui, Taihe, and Yongxin declared with one voice that the township, district, and *xian* levels had deceived them. Instead of being told that they were about to become Red Army men, they were only told that they were going to Ji'an to catch reactionaries. Such a policy of deceiving the masses likewise alienates us from the masses. New soldiers recruited by the aforementioned two methods (commandism and deceiving the masses) will either weep and wail, and want to go back home, or, if they do join the ranks, will become deserters in great numbers before long. Using these methods of commandism and deception to expand the Red Army is assuredly a mistake made by Party organizations below the *xian* level, but it is also the case that in the past, the policies of the Special Committee for opposing commandism and deception were inadequate. Sometimes it would simply stipulate that so many men were needed, by such-and-such a date. It seemed that they were not concerned about what methods the local Party organizations used; so long as the new recruits were procured, everything was fine. Comrades! we must be aware that the methods of commandism and deception are extremely dangerous methods which will alienate us from the masses. Not only will they directly provoke the opposition of the masses, and fail to contribute to the expansion of the Red Army, but they will actually obstruct the growth of the Red Army. Moreover, they provide excellent propaganda materials for the rich peasants and the AB Corps. The rich peasants and the AB Corps can bribe backward elements to spread rumors about how Communists are no good, and soviets are no good. Our Party organizations at every level must resolutely oppose this kind of erroneous line, and must make every comrade understand thoroughly that this kind of line is absolutely wrong.

IV. The Correct Line for Expanding the Red Army

First, in political terms, we must show the masses a way out. Our party organization at every level should encourage comrades who work for the government to tell the masses clearly about the present political situation (the different kinds of revolutionary forces in the whole country, the internal contradictions of the ruling class and its situation of collapse, and so on), and let the masses know that the revolution will certainly be victorious. At the same time, we should point out that if they embrace ideas of localism and conservatism, and are unwilling to expand the Red Army or to expand the struggle, they will certainly be defeated. To secure victory in land distribution, and solve the problem of the shortage of salt and the high price of cloth, we must definitely expand the Red Army and attack the enemy. In order to bring about the victory of the revolution in the whole country, and the rapid collapse and death of the enemy, we must proceed in this way to rouse the courage of the masses for struggle, so that they are willing to join the Red Army.

Second, we should point out to the worker and peasant masses that it is the duty of the workers and the peasants to join the Red Army. We must explain that the Red Army is the principal driving force of the Chinese revolution, that it is the armed organ of the workers and peasants themselves, which serves to carry out their class mission. If we want to guarantee the victory of the revolution, if we want to fulfill our task of overthrowing the ruling class, we must definitely join the Red Army, and all armed forces must be in the hands of the workers and peasants. At the moment in Hunan, Hubei, Fujian, Guangdong, Zhejiang and many other places the Red Army is being expanded. If, in Jiangxi, we wish to seize power first in one province, it is even more important to expand the Red Army. We must unite the strength of the several million Red Army men all over the country, and the worker-peasant insurrections, thoroughly liquidate imperialism and the warlord system, and strive for victory in the whole country; only thus can the worker and peasant masses achieve a final solution, and win peace. Therefore, for the worker and peasant masses to join the Red Army is for them to seek a solution themselves, and it is a task which their own classes should carry out.

Third, our comrades in the Party and Youth League have failed to lead the masses actively to join the Red Army. In the past, some comrades have not only been unable to adopt the standpoint of the revolution as a whole to lead the masses to join the Red Army, but have themselves manifested localist attitudes and conservatism. They have been unwilling to come and work in the Red Army, and when they did come to the Red Army they soon deserted. Because of these factors, they have not only been unable to carry out the task of expanding the Red Army, they have even hindered the expansion of the Red Army. This is a kind of extremely shameful flightism and liquidationism, they are criminals against the revolution. Comrades! We should assume our class mission, smash localist ideas, and actively mobilize the masses. If we are to lead the masses to join the Red Army enthusiastically, we must first join the Red Army ourselves. We call on our comrades in the whole Party to overcome these weaknesses of wavering, flightism, and hesitation, arm ourselves, and join the Red Army!

Fourth, we cannot obtain good results from the operation to expand the Red Army if we neglect publicity work aimed at women. In a family, women have an extremely close relationship with the men. If they cannot understand the significance and responsibility of expanding the Red Army, they will surely be unwilling to let the men in the family leave home to join the Red Army. Our Party and Youth League organizations in every locality should intensify propaganda work aimed at women, so that the broad masses of women will warmly support the revolution, recognize that it is a most glorious thing to let their husbands and sons join the Red Army, urge and encourage the men to leave home and join the Red Army, and understand the task of expanding the Red Army.

Fifth, the components of the Red Army reserve (the independent regiments) must be the poorest worker and peasant elements who are bravest and most resolute in combat (we must never let in rich peasants, and strictly guard against the AB Corps). They must be between the ages of sixteen and thirty-five, and the sick and weak should not be admitted.

Sixth, when organizing the Red Army reserves (the independent regiments), we should make it clear that they are being prepared to go to the front, and when the time comes actually to move them to the front, we should tell the masses clearly that now is the time when you are being sent to the front. We should never be unclear or deceptive, because only in this way can we cause the masses to make up their mind from the beginning that the number of recruits they recruit for the Red Army is a solid number.

V. Methods of Propaganda and Encouragement

A. Mobilize All Party and League Members to Carry out the Campaign for Red Army Expansion

After receiving this circular, every local Party organization must call a meeting of district committee leaders, taking the *xian* as a unit, to point out past mistakes and decide future methods. When the meeting is dismissed, each district committee will call a meeting of branch secretaries; after that, assemblies of Party and Youth League members will discuss this issue and take decisions.

B. Expand Propaganda Work

1. Organize propaganda teams: select appropriate people who are relatively good speakers to become propagandists, send them to every village and household to make propaganda, the more the better. They should, however, be trained, and propaganda meetings should be held on a regular basis.

2. Hold speeches in makeup: organize propaganda teams in makeup, and send them everywhere to make propaganda, and to perform all kinds of dramas about the expansion of the Red Army and its revolutionary actions.[1] This kind of organization should be set up on a *xian* or district basis.

3. Hold a propaganda week to promote the expansion of the Red Army. During this week we should hold many mass meetings, distribute many pamphlets, and stick up many posters.

C. Welcome and See off the Red Army

Whenever the Red Army crosses a boundary [between districts], the government should organize the masses and line them up to greet it and see it off. As a result, not only will the masses' belief in and admiration for the Red Army be stimulated, but the courage of the Red Army officers and soldiers will also be strengthened.

D. Set up Offices for Recruiting Volunteer Soldiers for the Red Army

Every township must set up such an office, and encourage the masses to become volunteer soldiers.

E. Increase the Training of and Propaganda Aimed at the Young Pioneers and Red Guards

District and township governments should strengthen this work, and encourage them to join the Red Army.

---

1. At this time, Mao attached considerable importance to such theatricals, which are mentioned several times in this volume, notably in the Gutian Resolution of December 1929. As is well known, he continued to take an interest in drama as a vehicle of propaganda, in Yan'an and after.

F. Give Preferential Treatment to the Family Members of Officers, Soldiers, and Porters

All the people who are now working in the Red Army should be given the normal share of land. If there is no one in the family to cultivate it, the government must send someone to till it for them. Rich peasants are not allowed to join the Red Army, but they must be made to help family members of the Red Army men do the work. The lands of these families must not fall into disuse; moreover, we should be ready to help them solve all kinds of difficulties at any moment, so that those masses who have not joined the Red Army as yet will be willing to join the Red Army after witnessing [all these things].

(Reprinted by the School Commitee of the Third Branch of the Chinese Red Army School)

The Situation Regarding Land Redistribution in Western Jiangxi

(November 12 and 15, 1930)

These are the reports made by the delegates to the enlarged meeting of the Western Jiangxi Action Committee on November 12 and the enlarged meeting of the Provincial Action Committee on November 15, 1930. I made brief notes of them during the meetings. Brief as they are, one may get a glimpse into the land struggle in southwestern Jiangxi.

1. The Situation of Land Redistribution

Chunhua: the distance between townships here can be as great as ten *li*. In a township fertile and less fertile land is packaged together for redistribution. The first round of redistribution was carried out in December last year (1929). The second round was conducted this March. The original tiller was taken as the unit, drawing on the plentiful to make up for the scarce. Now the third round is underway; it will draw on the fat to make up for the lean. The redistribution has just begun; it will take more than ten days to finish it.

Ruyan: The land of landlords and the local gentry was redistributed in December last year (1929), but the public land and the land of rich peasants was not redistributed. All land was confiscated in March this year and redistributed according to labor power. The third round was carried out in May. All land was confiscated, and distributed equally according to labor power, but the distribution was not completely equal. Individuals with more fertile land gave up some fertile land to others, and those with more barren land also gave up some barren land to others, but the redistribution was not equalized by dividing the land into three categories, A, B, and C. In most cases, the redistribution was carried out taking the village as the unit.

Shuidong: All three rounds of redistribution were carried out taking the township as the unit. The first round took place in the first month of this year, according to the principle of drawing on the plentiful to make up for the scarce. The second round was in June; it applied the principle of drawing on the fat to make up for the lean, but still did not carry it out thoroughly, and many people

---

Our source for this text is *Nongcun diaocha* (Yan'an, 1941), pp. 99–106. This text is reproduced with very slight changes in *Mao Zedong nongcun diaocha wenji*, pp. 264–70.

were dissatisfied. Now the third round is being carried out. The land commissioners of all townships gather in the district, organize a land committee, and help each other with the redistribution, using the principle of drawing on the fat to make up for the lean. After Ji'an was taken, more than a thousand people returned to the city, and they received land just the same. The redistribution is almost completed; of the seventeen townships, it has been carried out in thirteen.

Xiqu: Two rounds of redistribution have been carried out. The second round occurred in August this year. Although the land was divided into the three categories of superior, average, and inferior, and good and bad land were distributed equally, in reality this was not done thoroughly. The township served as the unit, and a township is too big. Some land is as distant as six to seven *li*, and peasants do not want it.

The district committee recently issued a circular prescribing that the third round of redistribution must be thorough, drawing on the fat to make up for the lean, and burning the old land titles. The district government sent five roving inspectors to help with the redistribution.

Rufang: The first round occurred in the first month of this year. Good and bad land were distributed equally, but it was not done thoroughly, and public lands were retained. Some places used the township as the unit, while others used the village. The second round took place in May. The masses seized the land of the leaders of the defectors,[1] and redistributed it to the poor. (These people [i.e., the defectors] had received land during the first round.) In the third (current) round, the three categories of land—superior, average, and inferior—are being distributed equally. Redistribution has not yet been finished in the three or four newly liberated townships around Nanyuemiao. It is completed in Xiyiting (?);[2] the village was taken as the unit.

Anfu: Redistribution has not been carried out this time in areas where there were no defections. It is being carried out first in areas where defection has occurred; a limit of ten days has been set for completing the redistribution, and it is being done thoroughly. Half of the land in the Seventh District has been redistributed; two-thirds of the land in the Fifth District has been redistributed; land in other areas of defection has not yet been redistributed. Of the nine districts in the whole *xian*, there were no defections at all in the First District. One-third of the Second District did not defect. Half of the Third District did not defect. One-third of the Fourth District did not defect. Three-fifths of the Fifth, Sixth and Seventh Districts did not defect. Half of the Eighth District did not defect. The whole of the Ninth District, that is to say the urban district, defected.

---

1. Regarding the problem of defections (*fanshui*), see, above, the resolution of October 19, 1930, which argues that it occurs where the land has not been divided up completely and equally.

2. This question mark in parentheses appears in the 1941 Chinese text, and has been retained in the 1982 reprint.

The entire area for thirty *li* around the city defected. The areas that did not defect failed to do so because they are adjacent to the Red areas of Yongxin, Lianhua and Yuanzhou. The areas that did not defect are all populated by "small, weak nationalities"[3] who were oppressed by larger villages. Land has been redistributed in all these places, drawing on the plentiful to make up for the scarce. The principle of drawing on the fat to make up for the lean has, however, not been applied.

Donggu: The township is taken as the unit. Land was redistributed in July last year (1929), drawing on the fat to make up for the lean, and equalizing the distribution by dividing the land into three categories, A, B, and C. There was no second round. Later, because those who had joined the Red Army turned over their land to the government, such land in individual villages is now being given to the people in those villages to till. Disputes arose among the popular masses, so the land was equally distributed in July of last year, under the slogan of "equalizing both [quality and quantity]."

Xiajiang: In January and February of this year, the land of the village bullies and bad gentry was redistributed in the first round. In the second round, which took place in March, public land was redistributed. In the third round, carried out in April and May, the land of rich peasants was redistributed. Only then was redistribution truly carried out thoroughly, drawing on the fat to make-up for the lean. The village served as the unit, and because land was plentiful and the people were few, there was some land that no one wanted. Two rounds of land redistribution were carried out in the newly-developed areas. The first round occurred two weeks ago; it was done rather carelessly. The second round is being carried out at the moment, and is scheduled to be completed within five days. Good and poor land are both being divided equally.

Shuinan: The first round took place in March this year, drawing on the plentiful to make up for the scarce. The second round occurred in August. In the places bordering the White areas, the principle of drawing on the plentiful to make up for the scarce was applied, but not that of drawing on the fat to make up for the lean. In the rest of the district, the principle of drawing on the fat to make up for the lean was applied. But the head of the Party bureau gave himself especially good land, and ordered the peasants to help with farming it.

Rulin: The first round occurred in March this year, drawing on the plentiful to make up for the scarce. In May, the entire district defected. In June, the guard detachment was overthrown, and the second round of redistribution took place.

---

3. The phrase used is *ruoxiao minzu*. In this context and region, Mao most likely is actually referring to small, weak kinship groups or lineages, rather than to actual "nationalities" or non-Han minority peoples. It is also possible that he is referring to weak communities of Hakka minority groups.

In a few townships, distribution was effectively carried out on the basis of drawing on the fat to make up for the lean. In most of the townships, redistribution was carried out in name but not in reality, because the AB Corps was in control there. The township was taken as the unit; only in special cases was the village used as the unit.

Yongxin: In the Special District of Xibei, the aged, minors, and the disabled who are unable to farm are given 50 percent more land than ordinary people. The decision of the first *xian* congress was also along the same lines. In addition, "working personnel" whose families do not have the ability to farm are also given 50 percent more land. This method has been applied in part of the Special District of Xibei, but it was vetoed by the West Route (*Xilu*)[4] working meeting of the Special Committee because it was motivated by ideas of charity. Some people mocked it as the "orphans' and widows' line." In Yongxin, land was redistributed throughout the whole *xian*. Two rounds of redistribution were carried out. The first round took place after Longquankou was taken; the second round was undertaken from the time of the decision by the West Route working meeting in June of this year until September. At present, land redistribution has still not been properly completed in the entire First District (the area of the *xian* town), half of the Fourth District (Nanxiang) and the entire Fifth District (Dongxiang), accounting in all for one-fifth of the *xian*. The peasants of Yongxin are willing to redistribute land using productive capacity as the criterion; this was accepted by the *xian* congress.

Jishui: Land redistribution has been completed in Futian and Fengshui; it has not been completed in Jintan.

"Redistribution based on the recipients." "Good land packaged together with unproductive land." "Distribute poor land first."

"Old Henaners" are a difficult problem.[5] In Gucun township, each person got only two *dan* of land.

Wan'an: The village was taken as the unit. In the second round, the principle of drawing on the fat to make up for the lean was already applied (?).[6]

Fenyi: Land was distributed taking the village as the unit. Redistribution was based on the grain yield, not on the amount of land. More than 2,000 houses were burned down by the counter-revolutionaries. There is not an old house within an area more than 30 *li* across.

---

4. An administrative region created by the CCP in western Jiangxi—its territory lay west of the Gan River and Ji'an city, and included the Jinggangshan area.

5. Old Henaners refers to people from Henan who settled in certain parts of Ji'an, Jishui and Yongfeng *xian*. They were a "problem" because, as indicated in the "Investigation in Mukou Village" dated November 21 which appears below, many of them became involved with bandits, and also because they frequently clashed with their non-Henanese neighbors.

6. As before, this question mark in parentheses appears in the Chinese text, presumably to indicate that Mao was not certain of the facts.

2. The Phenomenon of Abandoned Land

Donggu: The least each person got was 16 *dan* of rice paddies (one *dan* is around 80 *jin*). A great deal of land had no one to till it. Most of the hills were abandoned because the wages for tea-oil pickers were so high that the seeds of the tea-oil plants were left unpicked. There was no excavation[7] in the hills, either.

Chunhua: Rice paddies with a yield of 400 to 500 *luo*[8] were abandoned because: (1) the redistribution of March happened during the busy agricultural season; there was no private property, and the land redistributed was both poor and far away, so much land was abandoned; (2) more than 2,000 people had joined the Red Army or gone elsewhere to work (it is said that there were 2,700 to 2,800 such people); there was not enough manpower.

Shuidong: Abandoned land stretched for several *li* because this is a place—the area near the river—where the Red and White zones border each other. The reactionaries in the city of Ji'an frequently came to harass people; several hundred people were needed for guard duties every day. Three layers of guards were required. Sentries were often killed by the enemy at night.

Shuinan: Rice paddies with a yield of several hundred *dan* were abandoned, because they remained as public land, and peasants did not want to rent it to farm, so the land was left idle. "I have received several *dan* of rice paddies in the distribution; it is enough to eat, and I don't want to farm the public land."

Rulin: More than a thousand *dan* of rice paddies were abandoned, and ripe rice was left unharvested. This is because the land belonged to the guards detachment of the reactionary landlords and rich peasants. After these people were gone, the government did not redistribute the land to the peasants, so they had no responsibility for farming or harvesting there. (Rulin is a district close to the suburbs of Ji'an.)

Anfu: Six thousand *dan* of rice paddies were abandoned in Daopu and Chongwen districts. Because of the policy of retribution and slaughter, the peasants who had rebelled did not dare to return home. Another reason was that the land was not thoroughly redistributed, but was redistributed only in terms of quantity. These two causes both resulted from trouble-making by rich-peasant leaders. There is more land and fewer people in Anfu; people from Hunan, Yongxin and Henan are all farming in Anfu. As long as you fulfill the quota of grain contributed to the government on someone's behalf, that person will let you farm the land. Why are there fewer people here? It is because they do not pay attention to hygiene, so a lot of them die.

Xinyu: Several hundred *dan* of rice paddies were abandoned in three Red

---

7. *Wa.* The digging in question was presumably mining. (See below the reference to "hills with raw materials" and "hills with mineral deposits.")

8. A *luo* or "basket" is a measure of volume equal to half a *dan.*

districts because part of the people had gone to join the Red Army. Some of the land in the places on the border between the Red and White areas was also abandoned.

Fenyi: Several dozen *dan* of rice paddies were abandoned.

Yongxin: Generally speaking, there was no abandoned land here. The total quantity of abandoned rice paddies was less than a hundred *dan*.

Gannan: A great deal of land was abandoned in all the regions bordering on the Red and White areas.

3. The Problem of Land Redistribution to Workers

The peasants in Yongxin opposed the equal redistribution of land to workers. The Yongxin congress did not accept this view.

In one district in Taihe, workers who received redistributed land had their wages cut, but these were later restored.

The workers in Ji'an who worked for less than half the year received the same amount of redistributed land. Those who had worked for more than half the year got half the amount.

4. The Problem of Redistributing the Hills

The Yongxin congress decided that the hills producing tea-oil seeds should be redistributed equally on a per capita basis, taking the township as the unit.

The Ji'an congress (October 1930)[9] decided that the hills producing bamboo and timber should not be redistributed; they were to be managed by the township soviets and used by the peasants. Those who needed bamboo and timber must get permission from the government to cut down bamboo and trees. No permission is needed to harvest on cogon grass hills.

Hills producing tea-oil were redistributed equally in Yongxin, Xiajiang, Yanfu, Ruhang, Donggu, Taihe, and Xiqu. Rufang and Chunhua do not have such hills. Wan'an did not redistribute its hills.

Fenyi: On November 5 of this year (1930), the Provincial Action Committee dispatched Liu Lindong to join the *xian* action committee to work out a method for redistributing the hills, and to put it forward for passage at the second *xian* congress of workers, peasants and soldiers. The method was: "Hills worth more than 300 *yuan* each belong to the soviets; hills worth less than 300 *yuan* remain under the management of the original owners." In May and June of this year, however (before the "second congress"),[10] in obedience to orders from higher

---

9. This congress (*daibiao dahui*) may have been held simultaneously with the conference at which the resolutions of October 19, 1930, on the land problem, translated above, were adopted.

10. I.e., before the Second Congress of the Southwest Jiangxi Special Committee in August 1930.

levels (the Fourth Plenum of the Beilu Action Committee), the hills had already been redistributed equally, taking the township as the unit, even though the *xian* itself had not held any meetings. The decision was reversed in November, and the peasants were very dissatisfied.

There are seven types of hills: (1) tea-oil hills, (2) hills for growing miscellaneous grains, (3) hills with raw materials, (4) bamboo-covered hills (both small and large), (5) hills producing firewood (cogon grass and firewood), (6) hills with mineral deposits and (7) wild hills.

The Mistakes in the Land Struggle in Jiangxi

(November 14, 1930)

On November 14, 1930, the Jiangxi Provincial Committee held a meeting in Ji'an; I attended as the representative of the General Front Committee. After Comrades Chen Yi, Chen Zhengren and Ma Ming had given their reports, it was pointed out that since the "Second Plenum," there had been a consistent line of liquidating the land revolution within the Party in southwestern Jiangxi.[1] After discussion, the meeting unanimously agreed that a resolute struggle must be waged against this erroneous line. The following are the main points I noted down when Comrades Chen Yi, Chen Zhengren and Ma Ming gave their reports. There are many places here only I myself can make sense of.

In Rulin district, loyal comrades were purged while all the dyed-in-the-wool AB Corps elements were kept in place.

In the Red areas, rich peasants controlled the economy.

In Yongxin, rich peasants controlled the grain market. The government's policy of suppressing the rich peasants was correct.

Secretaries of district Party committees did not go down to the townships to make inspection tours.

The views of the Central Committee and the upper levels could not be transmitted to the lower levels.

"Exterminate all rich peasants and landlords."

"Land redistribution must be carried out decisively."

The rich peasants' policy of deceiving the poor peasants is, in terms of the white terror, a "white symbol."

When policies are not clearly pointed out, [the poor peasants] are hemmed in and deceived by the rich peasants, as in the committee of the fourth district of Yongxin (with Ma Ming as secretary).

The land on the Eastern Route has not been redistributed at all.[2]

Our source for this text is *Mao Zedong nongcun diaocha wenji*, pp. 271–74, which reproduces the version originally published in 1941 in Yan'an.

1. As explained above, in the Introduction, the Second Plenum of the Sixth Central Committee, which met in June 1929, adopted a line including the view that "it is still a mistake to oppose rich peasants unconditionally." The reference here is not, however, to that Plenum, but to the Second Plenum of the Southwest Jiangxi Special Committee in August 1930, which likewise advocated less radical tactics than Mao in the land revolution.

2. This refers to areas controlled by the Donglu (Eastern Route) Action Committee, under the Southwest Jiangxi Special Committee.

On the Southern Route,[3] the land has not been redistributed except for Xingguo and Gan *xian*.

Zeng Renchao.[4]

Eighty percent of the Party in Ruijin consists of landlords and rich peasants.

There are over 80 Party members in Shangyou. Landlords and rich peasants account for more than 30 of them, including the head of the pacification corps. Land has not been redistributed for two months; even the confiscated and sealed-off rice of the local bullies has been released.

The masses of young people on the Eastern Route are brave, while the Youth League members are afraid of death.

Women have not joined the struggle.

"Everything must be redistributed represents the peasant mentality."

Rich peasants have more tea-oil hills, and poor peasants have less. It is in the interest of rich peasants not to redistribute the tea-oil hills.

Rural schools for ordinary people also serve the interests of rich peasants; few children of poor peasants go to school, because they have to work.

Rich peasants order the masses to fight battles to protect the interests of rich peasants. The officers of the Red Guards in Xinfeng are all rich peasants. "Keeping titles," "Transferring land," "Beatings," and "Fines."

The rich peasants in Xibei township, Xinfeng *xian*, encouraged Red Army soldiers to desert and return home. Their slogan is protecting the Red areas, but the rich peasants are an obstacle to the expansion of the Red Army.

The problem of preferential treatment for the families of Red Army soldiers. Yongxin does not give preferential treatment to those who voluntarily join the Red Army; they do not help with plowing the land. Only those who are sent out by the government get preferential treatment for their families.

In Xinfeng, preferential treatment is given to local families whose members joined the Red Guards and were killed or wounded in combat. They pay no attention to those who went to join the Twenty-second Army and were killed or wounded in combat. Rich peasants are making trouble.

Only rich peasants oppose freedom of marriage. To say that "peasants oppose it" is the kind of talk that does not make distinctions.

The second plenum negates the peasantry and the land revolution.

When Li Wenlin[5] went to the Southern Route on August 24, he did not give a

---

3. This refers to the area under the control of the Southern Route (Nanlu) Action Committee, under the Southwest Jiangxi Special Committee.

4. Zeng Renchao (1890–1932), born in Jiangxi, had been a primary school teacher. He joined the Chinese Communist Party in 1926, and served as secretary of the Party committee in his native *xian* of Xinfeng in 1928–1929. In October 1930, he became a member of the Southern Jiangxi Action Committee.

5. For details regarding Li Wenlin, see above, the relevant note to the Introduction. In August 1930, as indicated in the letter of October 14 to the Central Committee, he was appointed secretary of the Southwest Jiangxi Special Committee. In October 1930, he became secretary of the Jiangxi Provincial Action Committee.

special report on the land revolution, nor was there any special discussion.

At the Southern Route Enlarged Conference on July 15, Chen Yi put forward eight proposals, such as an immediate redistribution of land and harvesting of crops, drawing on the plentiful to make up for the scarce, drawing on the fat to make up for the lean, unconditional redistribution of houses, redistribution of hills and forests, and redistribution of ponds. The Southern Jiangxi Revolutionary Committee issued a report. The rich peasants in Ruijin and Yudu cited Article 14 of the "Southwest Jiangxi land law," which said that the primary criterion should be the original tiller.[6] They kept saying that the land law must not be violated, and that whoever violated it was a counterrevolutionary. It even came to "fights." The revolutionary committee had no choice but to issue that announcement.

Two laborers played a role at the Enlarged Conference.

"He inherits the position; is he the chairman again?"

If you fear the Communist Party, "Don't just talk about it; cut off their heads."

"You could pay all the rent in the past; how come you are unable to farm this little bit of land!"

Wives of Red Army soldiers and the freedom of marriage.

"Are you going to join the Red Army or not? If you join the Red Army, I'm not going to marry you." "If it is reported that, while serving in the Red Army, you have been killed, am I still supposed to keep my chastity for you?" "Eight *yuan* for 80 *jin* of meat." "Yesterday I married him; today I'll marry the chairman. That is what's called freedom." "Chen Zhizhong's report at the joint meeting in Xihe dissipated Chen Yi's atmosphere." (Chen Yi had been holding meetings for nine days, and decided on a detailed land law. Chen Zhizhong came on the tenth day and abrogated it.)

"To confiscate the land of the landlords and redistribute it equally is a temporary tactic; it is not our goal. We have not yet put forward land laws that are marked by proletarian mentality."

On the Northern Route, Xie Hanchang[7] propagated the view: "It is a poor peasant mentality to use labor power as the criterion."

---

6. The Southwest Jiangxi Soviet Government was dominated by disciples of Li Lisan. The land law it adopted in the spring of 1930 included only drawing on the plentiful to make up for the scarce, but not drawing on the fat to make up for the lean, i.e. giving some of the fertile lands of the rich peasants to the poor peasants. It also adopted labor power as the criterion for redistribution. Article 14, mentioned here, provided that when land under cultivation was redistributed, the harvest should belong to the person who had planted it—another provision advantageous to the relatively affluent peasants. For a detailed summary of this law, see Hsiao Tso-liang, *The Land Revolution in China, 1930–1934: A Study of Documents* (Seattle: University of Washington Press, 1969), pp. 12–14.

7. Xie Hanchang (1907–1931) was a native of Jiangxi, who joined the Chinese Communist Party in 1926 and participated in the peasant movement. In July 1930, he was appointed head of the political department of the Twentieth Red Army. In April 1931, in the wake of the Futian Incident, he was denounced as a member of the AB Corps and killed.

The physical strength of poor peasants is not equal to that of rich peasants (poor peasants have nothing to eat). The sons of poor peasants have no physical strength either.

Li said to Cong,[8] "Nobody was sure about the second plenum, so it is better not to discuss the land question." "The Party in southwest Jiangxi builds on the basis of middle peasants and above."

It was said on the Western Route[9] (by Zhou Gaochao),[10]"Redistributing everything corresponds to a peasant mentality."

An enlarged meeting of the Southern Route Action Committee was convened in Xinfeng on October 28. Guo[11] transmitted [the policy of] "drawing on the fat to make up for the lean, carry out equal distribution thoroughly," but after meeting for a day and half, there was no discussion, and no decision.

There are two lines in southern Jiangxi (said Chen Yi).

"The Yongxin line is not the rich peasant line. I object," said Ma.[12]

"I do not agree about deepening the land revolution," Duan Liangbi[13] said to Chen Zhengren.

"Enlarging and deepening at the same time is peasant consciousness pure and simple. Attacking Ji'an first and then Jiujiang will see off the revolutionary high tide in China," said the report of the Special Committee to the Central Committee.

---

8. Li is Li Wenlin. Cong is Cong Yunzhong, who was at this time the secretary of the Southern Jiangxi Action Committee.

9. The reference is to the area controlled by the Western Route (Xilu) Action Committee, under the Southwest Jiangxi Special Committee.

10. Zhou Gaochao (1903–1932), a native of Jiangxi, was at this time the secretary of the Xilu Action Committee.

11. Guo Chenglu (1906–1931), a native of Jiangxi, was at this time secretary of the Southern Jiangxi Action Committee. In January 1931, he was accused of being a member of the AB Corps and killed.

12. Ma refers to Ma Ming.

13. Duan Liangbi was at this time secretary of the Southwest Jiangxi Special Committee of the Communist Youth League.

The Problems of Dividing Up Green Crops and Renting Land

(November 15, 1930)

On November 15, 1930, the Jiangxi Provincial Action Committee held an enlarged meeting in Ji'an. In addition to the standing committee members of the Provincial Party Committee, the participants included the chairmen of the *xian* soviets from Yongxin, Ji'an, Taihe, Wan'an, Jishui, Anfu, Fenyi and Xiajiang, and Comrade Chen Yi from the Twenty-second Army. I attended the meeting as the representative of the General Front Committee. A distinctive characteristic of this meeting is that it discussed the two problems of dividing up green crops and leasing land. On the problem of dividing up green crops, I advocated supporting the mass basis for dividing up green crops. On the problem of leasing land, I refuted the long-standing "leftist" theory that "rent should not be collected in the soviet areas," which is actually a theory of the rich peasants. I also opposed Jiang Hanbo's[1] method of distribution on the basis of labor power, pointing out that his mistake lay in helping rich peasants and hampering the poor peasants. This meeting was adjourned before it had completed its business because the enemy forces had already reached Xiajiang, and the leaders of the various *xian* had to return to make arrangements for resisting the enemy. As a result, such problems as "hills and forests," "ponds," "houses," "uncultivated land," "unemployment," and "debts," which we had intended to discuss, were not discussed. After the meeting, there were serious attacks by the enemy, and the Futian incident took place. As a result, the Provincial [Action] Committee has not yet issued the resolutions of this meeting. The following are a few brief notes I took myself at that day's meeting. Since they contain some important materials, I have kept them.

1. Chunhua Uses the District as the Unit for Land Redistribution

The third round of land redistribution in Chunhua district [of Ji'an *xian*] (October 1930) progressed to the use of the district as the basic unit. Data on population and productive capacity were gathered to see how much land each person

---

Our source for this text is *Mao Zedong nongcun diaocha wenji*, pp. 275–82, which reproduces the version originally published in Yan'an in 1941.

1. Jiang Hanbo (also known as Zhang Huaiwan) was a Jiangxi provincial Party inspector who became actively involved in a number of intra-party policy disputes in southwestern Jiangxi in 1929–30, including the debate on land policy referred to here. He was expelled from the Chinese Communist Party in February 1930.

should receive, and then land was redistributed within the townships. "Land that could be transferred was transferred; when it could not be transferred, people were moved." At present there are more than 30,000 people in the district of Chunhua as a whole, and each person has received an equal amount of land (everyone got 11 *dan* of rice paddies, each *dan* being taken as equivalent to 44 *jin*).

2. The Disadvantages of Using the Village as the Unit for Land Redistribution

The disadvantages of using the village as the unit for land redistribution are: (1) The larger villages are unwilling to transfer land to the smaller villages. (2) There are too many units, it is not easy for the district and township governments to exercise effective supervision, and many malpractices may emerge surreptitiously. (3) Within a single village, it is easy for landlords and rich peasants to use clan ideology to hoodwink the masses, who then fail to redistribute the land thoroughly or overthrow the local bullies completely. This view merits attention.

3. The Land Struggle Cannot Be Deepened at One Stroke

No matter what, land redistribution cannot be completed without several rounds. The first time, the rich peasants always concealed the good land, and it is impossible to survey the land properly, distinguishing among the three categories of superior, average, and inferior quality. In the first round, rich peasants and middle peasants always exercise leadership, and poor peasants have no power. "When the insurrection has gone on a little longer, the proletariat will rise up." This view is correct.

4. Yang Chengfu's Plan for the "Socialization of Agriculture"

The chairman of the Ji'an *xian* Government, Yang Chengfu[2] (who was originally secretary of the Chunhua District Party Committee, and concurrently chairman [of the district government]), proposed collective farming and collective consumption for the land in Chunhua District. This goal was to be reached in three steps: the first step was to redistribute the land, taking the district as the unit; the second step was to organize cooperatives; the third step was collective farming and consumption. This is completely wrong.

5. Jiang Hanbo's Method of Distribution on the Basis of Labor Power

The disadvantage of redistributing land taking labor power as the unit is that all orphans, widows, old people, young children, and women with bound feet, and

---

2. Yang Chengfu (1895–1932) was born in Ji'an. At this time, he was, as indicated by Mao, chairman of the Ji'an *xian* Soviet Government. In June 1932 he was accused of belonging to the AB Corps and killed.

everyone incapable of tilling the land will not have enough to eat. Poor peasants, who have plenty of labor power, are also no match for rich peasants, since poor peasants cannot compete with the strength of the oxen, farm implements, and capital of rich peasants. Moreover, rich peasants can rent land from orphans, widows, old people, young children, and women with bound feet. Consequently, taking labor as the unit for land redistribution benefits only the rich peasants.

The "Jiang Hanbo Method" for redistributing the land taking labor power as the unit has been carried out in the "border area" between Anfu, Ji'an and Fenyi, and in the township of Yanfu in Ji'an. It has, moreover, been carried out in an absolute fashion. Those who had labor power were given land; those without labor power were not given land, regardless of age. Vagabonds were given a share. In the case of those who had no labor power, it was farmed by those with labor power to produce food for them to eat.[3] A political commissar from the Third Army Group came to Ji'an and said to Wang Huai: the method of land redistribution in the border areas between Hunan, Hubei and Jiangxi is based on labor power. Those who have no labor power are given half as much land; they are not provided for by the government.

When redistribution is based on labor power as the unit, the rich peasants, who get more land, will need their oxen and plows for their own use, so there is no way the poor peasants can borrow them. Only when redistribution is equal can poor peasants borrow the surplus farm implements of the rich peasants. That is why poor peasants demand equal redistribution.

6. The Problem of Dividing up Green Crops

Among the peasants in Ruijin and Yudu, some support the slogan "Divide up green crops unconditionally" put forward at the Tingzhou Conference. Some support the slogan "Do not divide the green sprouts" of the Pitou Conference; the argument of the latter is: "The land law must not be violated."[4]

The *xian* of the Northern Route redistributed land in May. The original tiller was compensated for his initial costs at a rate of 600 cash for each *dan* of rice. In Futian, rich peasants received no compensation for their land. Poor peasants got one string of cash for each *dan* of rice from their land.

Chunhua redistributed land in March. At that time, the rice-seedlings had not yet been transplanted. The land had merely been plowed once, and in some cases a small amount of fertilizer had been applied. After land redistribution, no compensation was paid for the initial investment.

---

3. This sentence appears to refer to the vagabonds just mentioned, and to imply that they received land because they were assumed to be able-bodied, but would be helped in this way if they could not or would not work.

4. I.e., the land law of the Southwest Jiangxi Soviet, discussed in a note to the previous text.

On the Northern Route, compensation for each *dan* of unhusked rice was 600 cash or one string of cash. The *xian* set the price of rice at four strings of cash per *dan* before May; the rate of compensation was one-sixth or one quarter [of the value of the crop]. At that time no land had as yet been redistributed. It was also a time of famine. The intention, in setting the price of rice at four strings, was to help poor peasants to keep down rice prices. But they continued to set the price at four strings per *dan* after the harvest; "This is not right."

Last year in Yongxin *xian*, during the fifth lunar month, the government of the Fifth District of the Xibei Special District stipulated that when land was redistributed at the time rice crops were about to ripen, the person who took over the land must pay the person who gave it up one *yuan* in silver for two *Dan*[5] of rice (200 *jin*, or one *dan*). For large rice paddies that harvest only one crop of rice each year, the fifth month is the month shortly after rice-seedlings are planted but before they have developed fully; the person who gives up such land receives one string of cash for each *dan* (two *Dan* of unhusked rice). The *xian* committee's decision was that land be obtained without compensation. But the Fifth District did not receive the instruction of the *xian* committee, because of difficulties of communication; so it acted according to its own decision.

The rich peasants in Yudu, Dongxiang, and the northwestern part of Ganxian demanded that each *dan* (actually eight *dou*) of unhusked rice be compensated for at the rate of two small foreign dollars (worth four strings of cash). The Party did not allow this, and the land was taken without compensation.

The proper policy should be "get land without compensation; redistribute both land and green crops." The families of landlords receive redistributed land all the same, in the interest of uniformity. Landlords have more money, so an additional levy is imposed on them. Vagabonds also get redistributed land because they are toilers. It is wrong for rich peasants to oppose redistributing green land to vagabonds. Middle peasants do not have much land that is redistributed away, so they are not affected. Although "upper poor peasants" who farm more land are affected, they benefit in other ways which should satisfy them. The majority of lower poor peasants, artisans and farm laborers support this method completely. Cases in which people do not have the ability to farm the land after green crops are redistributed may be handled according to the method of leasing.

7. The Integrated Equal Redistribution of Land

In the past, "villages" redistributed land equally using the "family" as the unit and the original tiller as the standard. As a result, this benefited rich peasants but

---

5. In this text, we distinguish as usual between the character *dan* which is a unit of weight, and the character *dan* (stone), also read *shi*, which is a unit of volume, by capitalizing the first of these. As will be seen yet again from the examples in this text, the meaning of these terms, and the relation between them, were extremely elastic.

not poor peasants. The appropriate policy should be: taking the township as the unit, divide the total amount of land originally farmed by the people of the township by the total population of the township (the total population of the township is calculated by adding together the numbers of those who originally farmed in the township, and those who originally farmed in other townships); draw on the plentiful to make up for the scarce, and draw on the fat to make up for the lean; land that can be transferred should be transferred (villages with more land transfer some of the land to villages with less land); when land cannot be transferred, people are moved (when the distance is too great to transfer the land, only people can be moved). This method is called "the redistribution of the originally tilled total acreage."

8. The Non-Laboring Population and New System of Land Lease

When people without labor power lease their land to those who do have labor power for them to cultivate, the tenants pay rent in kind to the landowners. In Chunhua, Wan'an and Xinyu, tenants pay 40 percent of the crops as rent; in Fenyi and Ningdu, tenants pay 50 percent; in Yongxin, tenants pay one-third. In Futian (a district in Ji'an), land is divided into the three categories of superior, medium, and inferior; rent for superior land is 40 percent; for medium-grade land, it is 30 percent; for inferior land, it is 20 percent. This seems fairly reasonable.

Those who have no labor power and must lease out their land amount to 20 percent of the population throughout Chunhua, Anfu, Taihe, Xinyu, Fenyi, and Xiajiang. They make up more than 20 percent of the population in Ningdu; this is because more of the women there have bound feet. They account for only 5 percent of the population in Yongxin, since all the women there have normal feet. Those leasing out land are mostly orphans, widows, cripples, old people, and young children, as well as those who are engaged in revolutionary work. What has just been said refers exclusively to the population of those who have no one at all in the family with labor power, and must lease out their land. Those who have no labor power themselves, but have someone in their families who does engage in cultivation, so that they do not need to lease out their land, make up a large proportion of the population. Generally speaking, those without labor power account for 75 percent of the population, which is to say that only one out of four people is an able-bodied person with ample strength to do farm work. This is a big problem in China. It must be added, however, that what we have called absence of labor power refers to the inability to do farm work in the full sense. Half of the people just mentioned have some capacity for physical labor, such as herding cattle, chopping fire-wood, cooking rice, doing laundry, and cooking meals. Statistically:

25   percent have full labor power;

37.5 percent have half or some labor power;

37.5 percent have no labor power at all.

Everywhere the "leasing of land and payment in unhusked rice" described above is the so-called "system of dividing the rice." Only in Chunhua is the "system of collecting rent" employed. The defect of the system of dividing the rice is that when the tenants farm the land, they give primary attention to their own land, while treating carelessly or failing to use enough fertilizer on the land belonging to the landowner. When the crops ripen, they divide up the harvested rice equally, or split it 40–60 or according to other ratios. This system is not advantageous to the landowner. The system of collecting rent sets the amount of rent irrespective of the size of the harvest. As a result, the tenant will take care to make an effort, and to use enough fertilizer. That is beneficial, not only to output, but to the landowner.

The defects of the system of collecting rent are: (1) the rent is fixed; this is not advantageous to the tenants when natural disaster strikes; (2) if the Red Guards go out on sorties frequently, and thus reduce the number of days they spend working in the fields, this also hurts the tenants.

In sum, the system of dividing the rice benefits the rich peasants; the system of collecting rent benefits the poor peasants.

The appropriate policy should be as follows:

(1) After the poor peasants, farm laborers, and unemployed persons receive redistributed land, the government should confiscate the surplus draft animals and farm implements of the rich peasants and landlords, and distribute them among the farm laborers, poor peasants, and unemployed persons who lack draft animals, farm implements, and capital, for their private use. At the same time, the collective use of these implements should be encouraged by handing over to the cooperatives the possessions confiscated from the rich peasants and the landlords. There is another method, which is to allow individuals to borrow from rich peasants draft animals and farming tools temporarily, as a form of assistance. The government penalizes those rich peasants who deliberately refuse to lend these things; this is to provide assistance for poor peasants, farm laborers, and unemployed persons.

(2) As for those who are totally incapable of farming, they should be allowed, under the following conditions, to rent their land to rich peasants and middle peasants for farming:

   (a) Abolish the system of dividing the rice; set a fixed rate of rent, which will not be reduced because of natural or man-made disasters.

   (b) Set a minimum rate of rent (50 percent), so that the "exploitation" of the poor peasants and farm laborers by the rich peasants will not be excessive.

(c) Do not allow the rich peasants, under whatever pretext, to farm only their own land, and not that of others. When rich peasants are unwilling to rent land, the township government should allocate the land that must be rented within the township to the township's rich peasants and middle peasants for rental, and force them to till it.

9. The Problem of Unemployed Urban Workers Demanding Redistributed Land

There are more than 200 unemployed masons and carpenters in the city of Taihe, who demanded redistributed land, but did not get any. They were from other *xian*, and the peasants in the urban areas did not allow them to get redistributed land. Moreover, the sugar-cane workers outside the city near the south gate also demanded redistributed land.

Disputes have also arisen over this problem in Xingguo.

This problem merits further careful reflection.

Investigation in Mukou Village

(November 21, 1930)

The Red Army gave up Ji'an on November 18, 1930; on the 19th, Comrades Gu Bo,[1] Xie Weijun[2] and I traveled from Ji'an to Tengtian in Yongfeng *xian* to meet the main force of the Red Army. On the 21st we reached Baisha via Shuinan and had lunch in Mukou village. I investigated the class backgrounds of the members of the village government and the class backgrounds of the reactionary elements executed in the village. This investigation proves that middle peasants did not lose anything during land redistribution, but rather made some gains. Rich peasants and small landlords went over to the counterrevolutionary camp during the fierce struggle waged by the peasantry.

Mukou village is under the jurisdiction of the Eighth Township of Shuinan district of Jishui *xian*.

There are 200 people in the village as a whole.

In all, there are 46 able-bodied men capable of toil, all of whom have been inducted into the Red Guards.

The village government is set up in the ancestral hall.

The village government has nine functionaries: chairman, secretary, land officer, social security officer, Red Guards officer, food officer, arbitrator, officer for women's affairs and officer for youth affairs.

The chairman, Liu Xingnan (a small landlord), with a family of two,[3] had 56 *dan* of land (each *dan* of land yields three *luo* of rice; each *luo* of land yields 40 *jin*). He tilled more than 10 *dan* and rented out 40 *dan*. Because he liked gambling, he did not have money to make loans. Most of his land was redistributed away during the recent land redistribution. There are eight mouths to feed in the

---

Our source for this investigation is *Nongcun diaocha* (Yan'an, 1941), pp. 95–98. *Mao Zedong nongcun diaocha wenji*, pp. 283–85, reproduces the original text with minor corrections.

1. Regarding Gu Bo, see above, the relevant note to the Introduction to this volume.

2. Xie Weijun (1907–1935), a native of Hunan, joined the Chinese Communist Party in 1926. He participated in the uprising in South Hunan in 1928, and went up the Jinggangshan, where he served as a Party representative in a unit of Zhu De's Twenty-Eighth Regiment. At this time, he was head of the Political Department of the First Column of the Fourth Red Army.

3. This and all the subsequent figures for family size correspond to the total number of persons, *including* the head of the household.

family of the secretary, Peng Jiafa (a middle peasant). He had 48 *dan* of land and rented more than 20 *dan*, producing enough to eat. He did not have any debts. During the land redistribution, each of them got 7.8 *dan*, making 64 *dan* in all,[4] with 16 *dan* of redistributed land coming into the family. This is proof that middle peasants got redistributed land. The land commissioner, Liu Xingwen (a poor peasant), with a family of three, had 10 *dan* of land, and did not produce enough to eat. This time, he got more than 14 *dan* of redistributed land. He owed more than 60 *yuan* previously. "Social security commissioner" Wu Kailian (a poor peasant) has four mouths to feed. He had 16 *dan* of rice paddies and did not have enough to eat. He rented more than 20 *dan* of land from others. He got 15.2 *dan* of land this time. He owed debts in the past. Peng Jiaxiong (a middle peasant), the Red Guards commissioner, supported only himself in the past with 12 *dan* of rice paddies. Because he had to pay off high-interest debts, he sold six *dan*, keeping only six *dan*, which produced enough for him to eat. He also did odd jobs for others. He did not have a wife, and was unable to raise pigs. He liked gambling and owed 30 *yuan*. After the revolution, he "freely took" a wife.[5] His wife brought a thirteen-year-old son and a thirteen-year-old daughter-in-law. Now the four of them have received redistributed land, with each of them getting 7.8 *dan*; in all, they received 31.2 *dan*. He himself previously had only six *dan*; now he has 7.8 *dan*, an increase of 1.8 *dan*. This is another proof that middle peasants have received redistributed land. The food commissioner, Xu Chuanzhang (a poor peasant), supported himself. He had only two *dan* of rice paddies. It was not enough, so he worked on odd jobs for others. Now he has received 5.8 *dan*, but he still does not have a wife. The position of commissioner of justice is also assumed by the chairman, Peng Xingnan. The commissioner for women's affairs, Yang Jiuying (a middle peasant), had a family of five. They had 50 *dan* of land. Her husband and her father farmed the land, producing enough to eat, but no surplus. She did not owe any debts. This time she got six *dan* of rice paddies. This is another proof that middle peasants got redistributed land. Of the seven functionaries in the village government described above, there is one small landlord, three middle peasants and three poor peasants. The middle peasants here all got redistributed land.

Revolution began in this village two years ago; land was redistributed in January this year (land redistribution started originally in Donggu; this village was previously under the jurisdiction of Donggu). The members of the village government all eat at their own expense; the government has never provided any meals.

The village has killed a total of seven reactionaries: Peng Jiaguang, Peng

---

4. In the 1982 version, this rounded figure has been replaced by 62.4, and 16 becomes 14.4. We have followed the original, edited by Mao himself.

5. On "freely taking a wife" (*you laopo*), see above, the note to the section of the Xingguo Investigation regarding the poor peasants.

Jiashan, Peng Jiajun, Peng Peijun, Peng Changlong, Peng Changxi, and Wen Zhigui. Peng Jiaguang (a small landlord) supported a family of three, and had more than 30 *dan* of rice paddies. He ran a cloth store in Shuinan and rented his land to others to collect rent. The business of his store was not good, and every year he lost some of his capital. He profited by acting as a middle-man in collecting the taxes of the 38th precinct; he smoked opium and was something of a scholar; he was a notorious member of the bad gentry. Peng Jiashan (a rich peasant) was Jiaguang's younger brother; he supported a family of five. He had more than 40 *dan* of rice paddies, and money to make loans. Because he was grieved at the cancellation of debts, he colluded with bandits from Henan. He and his elder brother were arrested in July last year, and executed. Peng Jiajun (a vagabond) had three mouths to feed; he did not have any land, and owed debts to others. He joined the revolution and became an adjutant in the Donggu guerrilla detachment, where he also acted as quartermaster and supplies officer. Later he deserted, after taking three rifles, and became a bandit who attacked the local bullies for his own purposes. He was captured last year and executed. He generally liked to play cards. Peng Peijun (a rich peasant), with a family of four, had 120 *dan* of rice paddies. He hired two permanent workers to farm his land, and also rented out half of his land to be tilled by others. He had money to make loans. When the masses wanted to burn his land deeds during land redistribution, he wouldn't let them; so he was killed. Peng Changlong (a small landlord) had four mouths to feed, and owned 60 *dan* of land, all of which he rented out for others to farm. He made loans to others to buy oil[6] and hemp. He was a scholar, and taught school in Jishui *xian*. He was involved with the bandits from Henan; he was captured on the battlefront and executed. Peng Changxi (a small landlord) had three mouths to feed, and was the younger brother of Peng Changlong. He owned 60 *dan* of land, and made loans to buy oil and hemp. For each *yuan* he lent he got three *luo* of rice in return. He was executed in March two years ago. Wen Zhigui (a rich peasant) had a family of seven. He [farmed] 30 *dan* of rice paddies, and rented out more than 100 *dan*. He worked himself, and hired a worker on a yearly basis, and many temporary ones. He did not make loans. He also ran some small businesses on the side, transporting ducks and fruit for sale. He was executed because he colluded with the bandits from Henan and leaked information about the revolution. (The so-called bandits from Henan refer to those among the settlers from Henan in Jishui *xian* of Jiangxi who had become bandits.)

Of the above seven reactionary elements who were executed, small landlords and rich peasants accounted for three each; there was one vagabond. This proves that when the land revolution penetrates deeply, many small landlords and rich peasants will move in the direction of counterrevolution. It is a question, however, whether all of these seven people should have been killed.

---

6. The 1982 text has changed *boyou* to *boheyou* ("peppermint oil").

Letter to the Jiangxi
Provincial Action Committee

(November 24, 1930)

To the Provincial Action Committee, for transmittal to the Action Committees of the Left Route Armies and Western Jiangxi, and to the Eastern Hunan Special Committee:

1. On arriving in Shuinan,[1] I learned that preparations for dealing with the enemy in this area have already been carried out to a considerable extent. All townships have held mass meetings, and the whole region has convened meetings of activists. Preparations have also been made for strengthening the defenses and clearing the fields.[2] In particular, the propaganda work toward the White army soldiers has been done well. Slogans, declarations and folk songs are written everywhere inside and outside the buildings along the streets of Shuinan. A committee for the movement among the White soldiers has also been organized. In the light of these facts, the work of preparation for meeting the enemy must be considered as far better in Shuinan than in the district of Rufang, where nothing at all has been done, and in Ji'an, where most of the kerosene has not been moved, the moving of salt has not been completed, and propaganda work has not been actively pursued. Judging from the situation in the Rufang district and Ji'an, the situation of the work of readiness against the enemy in various areas such as the Western district, the Rulin district, the Chunhua district, Taihe, Yongxin, Lianhua, Anfu, Yongfeng, Xingguo, and especially in Yudu in the Eastern Route, has been more or less the same. Now it is time for the Provincial Committee to urge the Western Jiangxi and Eastern Jiangxi Action Committees, as well as the Eastern Hunan Special Committee, to issue another strict directive. This directive must point out that after the seizure of Ji'an, the erroneous notion that there would be peace on earth was widely held.[3] It must list the serious

---

Our source for this text is *Jiangxi dangshi ziliao*, Vol. 6, pp. 224–26. This version is preferable to that in the *Mao Zedong ji. Bujuan*, Vol. 3, pp. 179–81, which is marred by a number of errors and omissions.

1. As indicated in the "Investigation in Mukou Village," translated above, Mao arrived in Shuinan in Jishui *xian* on November 21.

2. *Jianbi qingye*, a traditional phrase meaning to strengthen defense works, evacuate noncombatants, and clear the fields by hiding provisions and livestock.

3. *Tianxia taiping*. As indicated, above, in the text of November 21, the Red Army had evacuated Ji'an on November 18, after holding it for a month and a half.

lessons of the total destruction of the *xian* committee and *xian* government of Fengyi, the heavy losses of the *xian* committee and *xian* government of Xinyu, the breakup of the Xiajiang emergency meeting by the enemy,[4] Ji'an's shortage of salt, and the severe lessons of the falling into the enemy's hands of kerosene and over ten thousand *jin* of salt, and so on.

2. It is reported in the newspapers that the Third Regiment of the Sixtieth Division, coming from southern Hubei, arrived on the 5th, and that the Sixty-first Division is still advancing and attacking western Jiangxi from the direction of Suichuan and Lianhua. Apart from the fact that the *xian* committees and *xian* soviet governments of Yongxin and Anfu should prepare themselves with lightning speed to meet the enemy, the Eastern Hunan Special Committee in particular should also prepare quickly. As regards pinning down the troops of Jiang and Cai (which constitute the main forces of the enemy), the masses and the independent division of Eastern Hunan should assume a great responsibility. As soon as the enemy enters places such as Yongxin, Anfu, Taihe, and Ji'an, the Western Jiangxi Action Committee should guide the local masses everywhere to pin down the enemy. At the same time, the greatest efforts should be made to find a method for pinning down those enemy forces which have already arrived in Ji'an. It is essential that the four divisions of Jiang, Cai, Luo, and Li[5] be prevented from crossing to the east of the river. In this task, the Third Army of the Red Army has very heavy responsibilities. Much of the above-mentioned work should be directed both by the Action Committee of the Left Route and the Headquarters of the Left Route. Hitherto, it really appears that the Action Committee and the Headquarters of the Left Route have failed to carry out their responsibilities. They have issued neither a circular to direct the work, nor a notice to every locality asking them to report on the enemy's situation. This is really an extremely great shortcoming, which must absolutely be corrected in the future. In eastern Hunan, the Action Committee and the Headquarters of the Left Route should issue directions. That is to say that in relations between the Provincial Action Committee and the Eastern Hunan Action Committee, the Western Jiangxi Action Committee and the Eastern Hunan Action Committee, and the area under the jurisdiction of the Eastern and Southern Jiangxi Action Committees, it is also impossible, in this emergency situation, to be strictly confined by territorial divisions, and not to provide guidance. The recent enlarged meeting of the Western Jiangxi Action Committee, the joint meeting of the members of various *xian* committees of western Jiangxi, and the conference of representatives of farm laborers did not invite the representatives of Lianhua, Pingxiang, Xingguo, Ningdu and Yongfeng to attend (they should at least have been invited as auditors). This was truly most inappropriate.

---

4. The reference appears to be to the meeting held in Xiajiang on November 6, 1930, to prepare for the coming enemy campaign of encirclement and annihilation. Guomindang forces attacked on November 7, but did not achieve a significant victory.

5. The reference is to Jiang Guangnai, Cai Tingkai, Luo Lin, and Li Jue.

3. Shuinan district still does not know about the fact that only the money for firewood and vegetables has been issued, and no money for oil, salt, and rice has been distributed. Similar situations exist in other places. No circular concerning the provision of oil, salt, and rice to the Red Army has been received. I asked the financial department to send two men to handle the issue of provisions for the Red Army, one of them to Yongfeng and Ningdu, the other to Chunhua, Shuinan, Pitou, Baisha, and Donggu. The responsible persons in the financial department promised to do it, but in fact completely failed to do it. Two days later, the Red Army arrived in these places and the problem of oil, salt, and rice still could not be resolved. In particular, it was the case that the salt sent to these areas to provide for the Red Army had to come from the salt of the provincial government, and was not bought with money. Regarding the issue of raising money, only 130 thousand *yuan* of the 1.2 million *yuan* has been obtained. (Not a single cash of these 130 thousand *yuan* can be used by anyone without an order from the General Front Committee. Please take note of this point.) Great efforts must be used to make money available. As soon as the Red Army arrives in the Red areas, all provisions must be received from the provincial government, and there is no other way out. It is hoped that the Provincial Committee will make a new plan regarding this matter, exercise strict supervision at all times, and avoid any negligence. This is a most important task! The Provincial Committee should convene a meeting of the responsible persons from the Provincial Soviet every day, so that they can exercise centralized guidance of everything.

4. We may reach Baisha today, and arrive at Tengtian tomorrow. It is hoped that every day the Provincial Committee, the Left Route Committee, the Western and Eastern Jiangxi Action Committees, and the Army Committee of the Twenty-second Army will each send an intelligence report to the General Front Committee. It is essential to make rapid transmission of information a priority. The recent report of the Eastern Hunan Action Committee (concerning issues such as the capture of over 500 weapons by the independent division) has been received here.

Mao Zedong

Order of the First Front Army of the Red Army About Concentrating Our Forces at Donggu, Nanlong, and Longgang, and Preparing to Attack the Enemy

(November 25, 1930, 2:00 P.M., at Shaxi)

1. One brigade of Gong's[1] division of the enemy troops in Ji'an crossed the river and arrived at Zhangjiadu on the 22nd. On the 23rd it advanced directly to the Pitou area (it is not clear whether there are other units following).

The vanguard troops of the enemy forces that invaded Yongfeng on the 19th approached Tengtianjie last night (the 24th); the vanguard troops of the enemy forces at Le'an (the Fiftieth Division) approached Liukeng on the 22nd.

2. The Front Army has decided to change the decision regarding concentration which was issued on the afternoon of the 24th; instead, it has decided to concentrate our forces in the Donggu, Nanlong, and Longgang area, and prepare to attack the enemy.

3. Our troops on the right wing (the Fourth and Twelfth Armies) should leave their present location in the area around Shangxi and Xiaxi tomorrow (the 26th), advance to Longgang, concentrate their forces, and await orders.

Our troops in the center (the Third Army Group), the Twenty-second Army as well as the unit of the Twentieth Army in Donggu (all under the command of the commander-in-chief of the Third Army Group Peng Dehuai and political commissar Teng Daiyuan) should, as soon as they receive this order, choose their own roads and march in different groups to concentrate their forces in Donggu and await further orders.

The Eighth Division of the Third Army should immediately leave its present location (Shanggu), advance to Nanlong, and await further instructions. The Thirty-sixth Division of the Twelfth Army should leave its present location for Longgang, and join its original unit.

Our source for this text is *Jiangxi dangshi ziliao*, Vol. 6, pp. 227–28.

1. The reference is probably to Gong Bingfan (1902–1982), commander of the Guomindang Fifth Army.

4. The General Headquarters is planning to move to Nanlong tomorrow (the 26th), and exercise command there.

It is hereby ordered to act in accordance with the above four points.

Commander-in-chief   Zhu De

Political Commissar   Mao Zedong

Order to the First Front Army of the Red Army About Going to Huangpi and Xiaobu to Concentrate Our Forces

(Issued at the General Headquarters
at Nanlong at 2:00 A.M. on November 27, 1930)

1. The two regiments of enemy troops belonging to the forces commanded by Gong which invaded Pitou on the 24th have retreated to Ji'an city.

The divisions of Jiang and Cai have already arrived in the vicinity of Yongxin.

It looks as if the enemy troops in Tingwujiang and Yongfeng may move to Tengtian.

It is still unclear what Tan Daoyuan's next move will be after he reaches Le'an.

2. The Front Army has decided to concentrate its main forces, launch an attack from the right wing, and wipe out the enemy armies one after another. The plan is for the concentration to be completed along the line from Huangpi to Xiaobu and Luokou by December 1; the date for the advance of each unit, and the localities where it is to concentrate its forces, are shown separately in the table.

3. The task of the Twentieth Army is to pin down the enemy troops on our left wing, so that it will be easier for our troops on the right wing to fight, and to strike a blow at the reactionary army's policy of cleansing the villages. If necessary it should also cooperate with our troops on the right wing to wipe out the enemy; part of it should be dispersed on the west bank of the river. The main forces should, however, be dispersed around Baisha, Shuinan, Zhonghao, Futian, Tantou, Shaxi, Donggu, Longgang and so on; if any enemy troops approach Taihe and Wan'an, forces should also be sent to the vicinity of Taihe and Xingguo. In addition, they should cooperate with the masses in building dummy fortifications on the various mountains near Donggu, so that enemy planes will be given a false impression of where our main forces are located (if a given unit is beyond the control of its commanders, the provincial government should command it directly).

Our source for this order is *Jiangxi dangshi ziliao*, Vol. 6, pp. 229–31. It also appears in Volume 17 of the same series, pp. 80–81.

Table Showing the Plans for the Concentration of the First Front Army of the Red Army in the Vicinity of Huangpi				
Unit	DATES			
	Nov. 28	Nov. 29	Nov. 30	Dec. 1
	LOCALITIES TO BE REACHED			
Third Army (Eighth Division)	From Gaohou leave for Shanggu	Shanggu	Leave Shangu for Nanling via Hanxia	Leave Nanling for Huangpi
Forces of the right wing		Move to an appropriate place between Huangpi, Luokou, and Nantuan convenient to attack Dongchao and Nanyuan		
Twelfth Army (Thirty-sixth Division)		Move from Longgang to an appropriate place between Junfu and Xiaobu	Rejoin original unit	
Units directly attached to General Headquarters		Move from Nanlong to the vicinity of Junfu by way of Longgang	Move from Junfu to Xiaobu	Move from Xiaobu to Huangpi
Forces of the central route (Third Army Group)		Move from Donggu to Longgang	Move from Longgang to the area behind Junfu and Xiaobu	Move to Xiaobu
Forces of the left wing (Third Army)		Move from Futian to Nanlong	Move from Nanlong to Junfu via Longgang	Move from Junfu to Huangpi
Twenty-second Army		Move from Futian to Huangsha	Move from Huangsha to the area behind Junfuyu	Move from the area behind Junfuyu to Huangpi

4. The Eighth Division of the Third Army should move to Shanggu on the 28th, post guards in the direction of Shaxi and Tengtian,[1] and keep a close eye on these places, and assist the concentration of our forces, until it withdraws to Huangpi and rejoins its unit on the 30th.

5. We will be traveling with the General Headquarters.

Addendum:

A. The Third and Twenty-second armies should bring 15,000 *jin* of salt from Futian, and the Third Army Group should bring 15,000 *jin* of salt from Donggu; after the link-up this should be turned in.

B. This order should be kept strictly secret, and should only be transmitted to the division level and above.

C. After arriving at the stipulated destinations for concentrating their forces, the Third, Fourth, and Twelfth armies should send out scouts to the front to reconnoiter the situation of the enemy.

Commander-in-chief   Zhu De
Political Commissar   Mao Zedong

Red Letter Order No. 7 to the First Front Army of the Chinese Red Army to Move the Troops Towards Pingtian, Anfu, and Kanchaiguang, so as to Facilitate the Purchase of Provisions

(December 14, 1930, 10:00 A.M., at Huangpi)

1. Regarding the situation of the enemy, see intelligence reports nos. 1 and 2 by the staff office of General Headquarters.

2. To facilitate the purchase of provisions, the Front Army has decided to move the troops to the area of Pingtian, Anfu, and Kanchaigang.

3. The Third Army Group should leave its present location (Xiaobu) tomorrow (the 15th) and move toward the vicinity of Pingtian. Pay attention to collecting intelligence in directions such as the towns of Nanfeng, Yihuang, and Le'an.

The Fourth Army should leave its present location tomorrow (the 15th) and move to Kanchaigang.

The Twelfth Army and the Twenty-second army (both under the command of the Twelfth Army) should leave their present locations (Yangyi and Huangpi) for Anfu tomorrow (the 15th). The Third Army should remain stationary in its present position.

4. General Headquarters, together with the Workers' and Peasants' Revolutionary Committee, will remain in Huangpi.

Addenda:

A. Those armies which have not fully carried out the plans for the first ten days of training should continue to carry them out, and should moreover make plans for a further ten days of training (this plan should pay attention to exercises at night, as well as emergency exercises at divisional level and above, defending strongholds, and crossing rivers).

B. Every army should call its own officers' meeting, examine the merits and shortcomings in the training during the past ten days, and discuss the matters laid

---

Our source for this letter is *Jiangxi dangshi ziliao*, Vol. 6, pp. 232–33. It also appears in Vol. 17 of the same series, p. 101.

down for discussion in the order issued yesterday (the 13th) by the meeting of senior officers.[1]

Four orders and two supplementary notes are issued as shown above.

Commander-in-chief	Zhu De
Political Commissar	Mao Zedong

---

1. Following on from an enlarged meeting of the Front Committee held in Pitou in early December, General Headquarters convened a meeting of the Military Commission on December 13 to review the ten days of training previously carried out in the Red Army, and to lay down a plan for a further ten days of training.

A Letter of Reply by
the General Front Committee[1]

(December 1930)

The true features of rebellion are now completely out in the open! We pointed out very early that the Futian Incident was a joint rebellion by the AB Corps and the Liquidationists.[2] No matter how that bunch of rebels waved the red flag and talked about revolution there, once the Futian Incident took place, they in fact enticed the White armies to attack Futian and Donggu speedily, thus exposing the masses of the region of Futian and Donggu to the bitter suffering of burning, killing, and oppression. In fact, they dragged the army to the west of the river, splitting the revolutionary forces. In fact, they initiated an uprising in the rear while the front was preparing to fight a decisive war, thus sabotaging the decisive class struggle. In fact, they sent letters and dispatched people everywhere to create rumors and sow discord, scheming to separate the masses from the Red Army. In fact, they undermined the provincial soviet government, and attacked XXXXXXX the facts as a whole. Before a resourceful person of the Liquidationist faction (108 characters are missing here) came to Huangpi as the representa-

---

Our source for this letter is the Chen Cheng Collection, Reel XIX, item no. 11 of the microfilm. We have also consulted the version in *Mao Zedong ji. Bujuan*, Vol. 3, pp. 183–91, and the handwritten copy of the text which appears in Hsiao Tso-liang, *Power Relations within the Chinese Communist Movement, 1930–1934*, Vol. II, *The Chinese Documents*, pp. 264–69. Both of these versions cite the Chen Cheng Collection as their source, but they differ in a number of small but significant points both from the copy cited above, and from one another.

1. This document is a reply to, or refutation of (*dabian*), the letter of the Jiangxi Provincial Action Committee dated December 20, 1930, denouncing Mao for his behavior in connection with events in Futian in early December 1930. Regarding the extremely complicated and controversial issue of the Futian rebellion, see above, the Introduction. There is no evidence that Mao himself wrote this letter, but as the secretary of the General Front Committee, he must have approved it. Two earlier statements by Zhu De, Peng Dehuai, and Huang Gonglue, dated December 17 and December 18, take a very similar line, but if they had likewise produced this letter, their signatures would surely have been on it. (For summaries of the December 17 and 18 texts, see Hsiao Tso-liang, *Power Relations within the Chinese Communist Movement, 1930–1934*, pp. 98–102.) Since no other document arguably reflecting Mao's views regarding the Futian Incident is available outside the Party archives, it seems appropriate to include this letter here.

2. The reference is presumably to the statements of December 17 and 18 by Zhu De, Peng Dehuai, and Huang Gonglue, and possibly to earlier texts not available to us.

tive of the Red School, Cong Yunzhong exhorted him personally again and again to hand over this letter secretly to Comrade Zhu De and Comrade Peng Dehuai. Comrade Zhu De immediately made this letter available.[3] Thus the true features of the rebels were unexpectedly exposed. We must ask:

(1) When you come right down to it, who is framing comrades? The only crime with which Mao Zedong is currently charged by the AB Corps and the Liquidationists who oppose him is betraying comrades. They have created the rumor that "he wants to wipe out in one fell swoop all of the cadres in southwestern Jiangxi," scheming thus to frighten and shake a group of revolutionary comrades into opposing Comrade Mao personally, and to carry out the plot of the AB Corps and the Liquidationist faction to sabotage the revolution. The fact is that all the comrades who understand the Futian Incident in the Eastern Jiangxi Action Committee, the office of the Soviet Government in Eastern Jiangxi, the Southern Jiangxi and Southeast Jiangxi Action Committees, the *xian* committee and *xian* soviet government of Xingguo, the *xian* committee and *xian* soviet government of Wan'an, the *xian* committee and *xian* soviet government of Taihe, the soviet government of Ji'an City, the district committee of Shuinan, the *xian* committee and *xian* soviet government of Yongfeng, and the district committee and district soviet government of Xingtian, Shaxi, are now increasingly standing by the correct line of the General Front Committee, and are united in opposing the Futian rebellion. Comrade Mao has no imperial pretensions. Why should he want to "wipe out in one fell swoop" all the revolutionary comrades? The deception and blackmail of wiping them all out has in fact already failed. This time, over 4,400 members of the AB Corps have been discovered and arrested in the Red Army.[4] The AB Corps had already designated a general director, a commander-in-chief, and a head of the military group of the AB Corps in the Red Army. Five uprisings were launched according to plan, and the uprising flags were all made. If there had not been severe repression, the Red Army might already have ceased to exist. But from the bloody mouths of the AB Corps and the Liquidationists were heard unfounded and malicious accusations that "large numbers of cadres have been massacred." It is quite true that, from the perspective of you members of the AB Corps and of the Liquidationists, these people are really cadres. The confessions of the AB Corps ringleaders Liu Tianyue and Zeng Zhaohan, as well as of Long Chaoqing, Liang Dingyuan, Jiang Kekuan, Zhou Chi and others have proved many-sided confirmation that Duan Liangbi, Li Bofang, Xie Hanchang and others of the provincial general headquarters of the AB Corps of Jiangxi have been installed inside the Provincial [Action] Committee as the chiefs of the AB Corps elements. In order to save the

---

3. The reference is to the "Confidential Letter of the Rebels" of December 20, 1930, which Zhu De immediately made known to all concerned. (See Hsiao, *Power Relations*, p. 102.)

4. These arrests had, in fact, been carried out on Mao's orders at the end of November, a week before the Futian rebellion.

revolution in southwestern Jiangxi from crisis, the General Front Committee sent Comrade Li Shaojiu to Futian to make arrests. When Comrade Li arrived in Futian, Duan Liangbi, Li Bofang, Liu Wanqing, Xie Hanchang, Jin Wanbang, and others were in the midst of convening a joint meeting, from which only Comrades Chen Zhengren and Zeng Shan[5] were absent, so it was possible to capture them all at one stroke. Li Bofang, Duan Liangbi, Jin Wanbang, Xie Hanchang and others confessed in writing that they belonged to the AB Corps, adding that their AB Corps was more progressive and less feudal than the one run by Duan Xipeng.[6] How vicious are the AB Corps and the Liquidationists. They sneak into the revolutionary organs to engage in counterrevolutionary activities. If they are overthrown, they accuse others of framing loyal comrades. The decision to eliminate the ringleaders of the AB Corps in the Provincial Action Committee was made by the General Front Committee, and not by Comrade Mao alone. Furthermore, the General Front Committee at that time only pointed out three persons, Duan Liangbi, Li Bofang, and Xie Hanchang. Who cared to catch Jin Wanbang, Cong Yunzhong, Zeng Xing, Wang Huai, Zhou Mian, Liu Jinghua, Ren Xinshi and the others? According to the written confessions of Duan Liangbi, Li Bofang, and Xie Hanchang at that time, Xie Hanchang said, "Overthrow Zhu and Mao, destroy Li and Duan." This conspiracy was concocted as far back as June last year when Xie Hanchang was a member of the District Committee of the Xing[guo]-Yong[feng] border area. At that time, using the pretext that the troops of Jin Handing were oppressing the revolution in Xingguo and Yongfeng, he put on an outward show of passive resistance to the enemy, but inwardly he was already launching the evil plot of betrayal. He made a false allegation that he had ventured to carry out the conspiracy only after approval by Cong Yunzhong and Xiao Ren. This shows that the conspiracy had been hatched for a long time, and the Futian Incident was merely its open manifestation. If Duan, Li, Jin, Xie and others were loyal revolutionary comrades, then even if they were wronged temporarily, they would sooner or later be cleared. Why should they make false confessions and incriminate other comrades? It is understandable that other people may make false accusations. But how could members of the Provincial Action Committee and directors of army political departments like Duan, Li, and Xie, who have such important responsibilities, behave in this manner? As for the incorrect charge that Cong Yunzhong,

---

5. Chen Zhengren (1907–1972) was a native of Jiangxi. At this time, he was head of the Propaganda Department of the Jiangxi Provincial Action Committee. Zeng Shan (1899–1972) was born in Ji'an, Jiangxi. At this time he was a member of the Standing Committee of the Jiangxi Provincial Action Committee, and chairman of the Jiangxi Provincial Soviet Government.

6. Duan Xipeng (1898–1948), a native of Jiangxi, had been one of the original organizers of the AB Corps in late 1926, as an instrument for combatting Communist influence in the Guomindang. Beginning in 1927, he spent most of his time in Nanjing in the entourage of Chiang Kaishek.

Wang Huai and Li Tianzhu belong to the AB Corps, because they wrote a letter to the Left Route Committee, from today's perspective, it is unfortunately true. The letter was in fact secretly forged by Cong Yunzhong, and Li Tianzhu is a saboteur of the Red Army School.[7] The fact is that the number of positions established by the AB Corps in the Third Army is particularly large. If the Third Army, acting upon the opinion of the Left Route Committee, had not crossed the river for consolidation, the present Third Army would certainly have fallen victim to sabotage by the AB Corps and the Liquidationists! Speaking about it, who would believe that they still want to slander others in order to frame them, and attempt once again to hide under the Red flag to prolong their counterrevolutionary lives? And now what? Currently, the AB Corps and the Liquidationists, in order to overthrow Mao Zedong and undermine the revolutionary forces, have gone so far as shamelessly to forge letters. They forged a letter from Comrade Mao to Comrade Gu Bo, requesting criminal charges against Zhu, Peng, Huang, Teng and other comrades, so as to arrest and execute them.[8] On the other hand, they secretly sent this letter to Zhu, Peng, and Huang, and repeatedly and shamelessly begged Zhu, Peng, Huang and Teng to make a comprehensive arrangement immediately to detain Mao, Zhou (Comrade Zhou Yili, representative of the Central Committee) and their running dogs. With this forgery of letters, sowing of discord and sinister desire of detaining people, who is it that is framing comrades, and seeking to wipe them out at one stroke?

(2) In the final analysis, who are the big conspirators? The second phrase used most often by the Liquidationists and the AB Corps in describing Comrade Mao is calling him a conspirator, alleging that Comrade Mao favors the political tactics of "drawing over one and attacking one." Judging from a petty bourgeois perspective, this phrase does to some extent imply conspiracy. But Bolshevik materialists should judge from facts whether it is correct to draw someone over or to attack someone. If the drawing over, and the attack as well, are for the sake of the revolution, why should this not be done? Formerly, did we not win over the Guomindang and attack Wu Peifu and Zhang Zuolin? Did we not also draw over Wang Jingwei and oppose Chiang Kaishek? Should not the proletariat hold firmly to the allied army of the peasants, in order to seize political power? Are we not seeking right now in the countryside to hold fast the middle peasants in order to oppose the rich peasants? What is wrong with all this? These actions are inevitable, no matter what words are used to describe them. You can call it establishing links, or winning over. They do not analyze the facts or the outcome, but are bent on creating rumors and opposing with subjective intent, and this in itself is enough to show their lack of sincerity. Actually, the AB Corps

---

7. Taking *Hongxiao* to be an abbreviation for *Hongjun xuexiao*, referred to below.

8. Most scholars, including those critical of Mao, regard the letter attributed to him, dated December 10, 1930, as a forgery. See Hsiao, *Power Relations,* pp. 104–105. A copy of this letter was enclosed in that of December 20, 1930, to Zhu De and others.

and the Liquidationists are now shouting the slogans "Down with Mao Zedong" and "Support Zhu, Peng and Huang," but Zhu, Peng, and Huang have already proclaimed that it is not a matter of supporting or rejecting an individual, but only of distinguishing between revolution and counterrevolution. The AB Corps and the Liquidationists now say, "We are ready to present our heads before you (referring to Comrades Zhu and Peng)." Faced by a formidable enemy, they do not use their heads to wage a life and death struggle against the warlords, but beg to die before Comrades Zhu and Peng. They do not work hard to fight the enemy in a final class struggle, but strive mightily to persuade Comrades Zhu and Peng to use extraordinary measures for detaining Mao and Zhou. These are truly most shameless schemes and venomous conspiracies of the AB Corps and the Liquidationists to draw over one, and attack one.

As a matter of fact, they forged a letter from Comrade Mao to Comrade Gu Bo, saying that Comrade Mao asked Comrade Gu Bo to subordinate himself to the AB [Corps], thus deliberately forcing him to confess that Zhu, Peng, Huang and Teng were also ringleaders of the AB Corps in the Red Army, and were cooperating with the White armies in their areas to carry out the arrests and executions. In this way [they sought] to prove that Comrade Mao had defected and was attempting to cause the masses to distrust the Red Army, the Red Army to become isolated from the masses, and the revolution to fail. But [where] is the original manuscript of this letter? They themselves say that they investigated the matter for a whole night and still could not locate it. They cannot find the original letter, but say that they offer their heads as a guarantee that it is authentic and not forged. This is an unforced confession, from which we can see that their efforts, despite all their scheming, lead only to nonsensical utterances. Naturally, such fabrications are not rewarded by a single smile from the readers. Even their technique of fabrication does not seem [X][X][X] believable. At the end of the letter the . . . .finished . . . and the date appears as "10/12." Comrade Mao never writes letters in this way [blank space indicating omission].[9] Sowing discord, they think nothing of alleging on the one hand a desire on Mao's part to force the confession of the crimes committed by Zhu, Peng, Huang, and Teng so as to arrest and kill Zhu, Peng, Huang, and Teng, while themselves seeking on the other hand to incite Zhu, Peng and others to kill Mao and Zhou. Not content with the vicious framing of comrades and "forging of letters", they also dispatched people secretly and passed on letters clandestinely. In the last analysis, who is really the big conspirator here? At present, the AB Corps and the Liquidationists are still rushing hither and thither to cook up rumors and decep-

---

9. An explanation for this rather obscure truncated passage is provided by Peng Dehuai's autobiographical notes, as edited and published after his death. According to Peng, Mao in 1930 wrote dates only in Chinese characters, and never used either Roman letters or Arabic numbers. See *Peng Dehuai zishu* (Peng Dehuai's Own Account) (Beijing: Renmin chubanshe, 1981), pp. 162–67.

tions and frame comrades. Hu Jiaju of the AB Corps and the Liquidationist faction rushed over to Taihe to agitate Comrade Li Senlin, the chairman of the *xian* soviet, and Guo Dexiang, a responsible comrade of the *xian* committee, saying that the General Front Committee wanted to arrest and execute them, in order to frighten them into opposing the General Front Committee. But Comrade Li had participated in the meeting on arresting the AB Corps ringleaders Duan, Li and Xie, and had listened to the report by Comrade Shaojiu. They had no doubts at all. Moreover, Comrade Zeng Quanya put it best when he said, if the General Front Committee wanted to arrest Li and Guo, why should they tell you, Hu Jiaju? To this, Hu had no reply at all. The rumors created by the AB Corps and the Liquidationists to the effect that the General Front Committee wants to wipe out at one stroke all revolutionary comrades in southwestern Jiangxi, like the forgery of letters, is a plot to create doubt and terror in every revolutionary comrade in southwestern Jiangxi, so that they can stir up trouble from within. They fail to understand that genuine revolutionaries will never be fooled by their dirty tricks. The AB Corps and the Liquidationists say, our only hope now is that this letter will be able to reach you (referring to Zhu, Peng and the other comrades). They also say that if this letter cannot reach you, and if unfortunately it falls into the hands of the traitors, we will have no recourse but to shed blood to repay the Party. It is truly unfortunate that this letter once again fell into our hands. You, the AB Corps and the Liquidationists, cannot produce the original of Comrade Mao's letter to Comrade Gu Bo, but we have found your original text, the original text giving full play to your conspiracy. (The original text is now being reproduced photographically.) It is a pity that your only remaining hope at the end of your days has once again been dashed. Are you really "shedding blood"? Or are you "sucking blood"? Conspirators of the Liquidationists and the AB Corps, you should not use the heart of a Liquidationist and AB Corps member to judge the mind of Bolsheviks such as Zhu and Peng!

(3) Are the actions of Liu Di not a conspiracy of the AB Corps? On the very first page, the true features of the Futian Incident are explained briefly and clearly. And yet the argument of the AB Corps and the Liquidationists to the effect that the actions of Liu Di were intended to save comrades was put forward after hearing Comrade Li Shaojiu's statement, "It is a political question." It is as though there was a righteous uprising in Futian, and absolutely no traitorous plot. AB Corps and Liquidationists, once again you are not being very intelligent! If indeed the General Front Committee wrongly arrested Duan, Li, and Xie, why did you not demand the convening of a meeting to conduct a detailed investigation and seek a solution? Even if they were in a hurry to save comrades at that time and had no time for other matters, then the release of the comrades should have meant the end of the issue. Why did you have to drag the troops to the west of the river? Why did you have to capture Army Commander Liu? Why did you have to frame Comrade Li Shaojiu? Why did you want the soviet government to get rid of Comrade Zeng Shan? Why did you have to attack the Red Army

School? Why did you have to send special representatives everywhere to hoodwink the masses into keeping away from the Red Army, saying openly, "We want to oppose Mao Zedong and the First Front Army. If the First Front Army comes, we should tell all the masses to leave, and also ask the organs of political power to leave. The Twentieth Army is the only army we can rely upon." They also say, since we have the masses, we are not worried that the Red Army will not get out of Jiangxi. (This was said by a special representative of the AB Corps and the Liquidationists called Wang Anguo in the District of Shuinan.) Moreover, why did you have to forge letters and stir up discord? Some people say that it was a misunderstanding. But why was one misunderstanding followed by another misunderstanding, and then again by a third, endlessly? We must reject this compromising argument about misunderstandings. Moreover, if they really aim at saving comrades, then why do they talk so much about the tactics of a protracted war and the policy of land redistribution not based on labor (letter from Deng Haochun to Yongfeng *xian*)? If it was a matter of tactics, why did they not hold meetings to discuss it, but insist on using guns and cannons? At present, we do not know whether Comrade Li Shaojiu said "it is a political issue," or not. If he said so, he is absolutely correct. Indeed, the treacherous conspiracy of the AB Corps and the Liquidationists to betray the revolution, to sabotage the Red Army by innumerable schemes, and to abandon the agrarian revolution is a serious political issue. Every comrade should pay attention to this matter, and make an effort to eliminate the rebels. The false display of feeling by the AB Corps and the Liquidationists, who said, "We tried very hard to stop the betrayal," appears to have been exploited by the enemy. When the White armies attacked Donggu in the company of the running dogs, the contribution of the running dogs was already outstanding, so perhaps they should not be too modest.

(4) Was not the Second Plenum[10] manipulated by the AB Corps and the Liquidationists? We pointed out long ago that the Second Plenum might be a plot of the AB Corps and the Liquidationists. Because in reality, if you compare the February 7 Joint Conference (led by Comrade Mao) with the Second Plenum, no revolutionary comrade can fail to be suspicious of the Second Plenum. The February 7 Joint Conference resolutely put forward a proposal to redistribute the land.[11] (In the past, the agrarian revolution in southwest Jiangxi was only a topic of investigation and research for those gentlemen of the Communist Party, and the land to be distributed did not include that of Communist Party members.) The Second Plenum did not say even a single word about the agrarian revolution,

---

10. The Second Plenum in question is that of the Southwest Jiangxi Special Committee in August 1930, which adopted a less radical land policy than Mao's. As already noted in various contexts, this committee, dominated by supporters of Li Lisan, had been in conflict with Mao for nearly a year.

11. See above, the "Land Law" of February 7, 1930, and the "Conclusion of the Joint Conference" of February 16, 1930. (As indicated in the latter document, the conference met in fact from February 6 to 9, 1930.)

the principal problem in the Chinese revolution. What it did talk about was simply opposing the agrarian revolution XXXXXXXXXXXXXXXXXXXXX[12] peasant consciousness, opposing the proposal of the February 7 conference for equal redistribution of the land, and liquidating the agrarian revolution. The February 7 Joint Conference resolutely opposed opportunism, and expelled the representative of opportunism, Jiang Hanbo. The Second Plenum resolutely developed the theories of the Liquidationists, and expelled Liu Shiqi, a representative of the struggle for equal land redistribution in southwestern Jiangxi. The February 7 Joint Conference was followed by the launching of the revolutionary struggle for the redistribution of land in southwest Jiangxi, and the establishment of a foundation for the revolution, whereas after the Second Plenum, the AB Corps and the Liquidationist faction developed, and counterrevolutionary plots were concocted. And now? Xie Hanchang personally admitted that the main purpose of the Second Plenum was to counter the February 7 Joint Conference, and that expelling Liu Shiqi meant opposing the February 7 meeting, and opposing Mao Zedong, for Liu Shiqi carried out the seven struggles in Jiangxi, and resolutely implemented the resolutions of the February 7 conference led by Comrade Zedong. The expulsion of Liu Shiqi was first decided by a secret meeting of Xie Hanchang, Li Bofang and a few other persons, and only then was it proposed at the plenary session. Xie himself confessed that he had the responsibility of persuading people at the plenary session. No wonder Xie and Li were so forceful in opposing Liu at that time. Xie also said that there was no reason which could be advanced for opposing the redistribution of land, so they had to use the pretext of "transforming peasant consciousness," and loudly shout that equal distribution was a concept of private ownership, incompatible with a socialist position. Thus an argument against the redistribution of land was drawn from the most [X] theories of socialism, with the aim of undermining the agrarian revolution. Xie also said that the policy of the Communist Party is to win over the masses of farm laborers and poor peasants, and to consolidate the alliance with the middle peasants, and that our policies are aimed at capturing the rich peasants, landlords and vagabonds. The leading roles at the Second Plenum were played by the chiefs of the AB Corps and the Liquidationists, Li Wenlin, Duan Liangbi, Xie Hanchang, and Li Bofang, who performed the tricks described above. Was the Second Plenum manipulated by the AB Corps and the Liquidationists, or was it a formal meeting of the AB Corps and the Liquidationists? We are afraid that the word manipulation cannot describe the meaning adequately. Of course, we cannot say that all those who participated in the Second Plenum were members of the AB Corps and the Liquidationists. Indeed, some of them are genuine Bolshevik comrades such as Comrade Yang

---

12. The methods used for indicating omissions in this text vary from one version to the other. Here there are twenty X's in the copy in the Chen Cheng Collection. Presumably each X stands for one character.

Chengfu, who was so against the expulsion of Liu Shiqi that he was reduced to tears, because he was so angry that he could not say what he wanted. This proves that the Second Plenum was totally dominated by those so-called Party leaders, who are in fact the leaders of the AB Corps and the Liquidationists. From today's point of view, this is naturally not accidental. Since the February 7 meeting, rich peasants and landlords have been attacked ferociously. Therefore, the rich peasants and landlords have not only been forcefully opposing the redistribution of land in their actions, and developing the organization of the AB Corps and the Liquidationists; they have also been formulating a consistent counterrevolutionary theory. The Second Plenum has carried this task to completion. The February 7 meeting was a fierce attack by the proletariat and poor peasants against the landlords and rich peasants, while the Second Plenum was the counter-attack of the landlords and rich peasants.

(5) Who is causing damage to the middle peasants? We have always held that the task in the countryside is to unite the farm laborers and poor peasants, consolidate the alliance with the middle peasants, and struggle against the landlords and rich peasants. Formerly, the AB Corps and the Liquidationists opposed the equal redistribution of land, and demanded distribution taking labor power as the criterion. (In reality, this method reflects the interests of the rich peasants, for only they have capital and thus more labor power. So the rich peasants will have more shares of land. And how about the poor peasants? Since they have neither draft oxen nor farm implements, and also have little fertilizer and seeds, it goes without saying that they have very little labor [power]. Therefore, they will have a relatively small share of the land. And yet, poor peasant families, too, have old people and children, and their stomachs and mouths, too, need food to eat. Comrades of the Liquidationist faction and the AB Corps, you also engage in revolution, and must know the strange fact that these people also need to eat!) The AB Corps and the Liquidationists know that it won't do to oppose the interests of the poor peasants. So they suddenly take up an ultra-leftist position, saying that the poor peasants and farm laborers should be given good land, and the middle peasants should be given poor land. This is to show their particular support for the interests of the poor peasants and farm laborers. Looking at the matter superficially, it cannot be said that they are not revolutionary. But in essence, this is yet another plot. Is it not the case that, deliberately to give bad land to the middle peasants at present is deliberately to undermine the alliance with the middle peasants, deliberately to force the middle peasants to go over to the side of the rich peasants and aid the counterrevolution, and deliberately to isolate the poor peasants? In reality, a proposal which disrupts the alliance with the middle peasants is a proposal which sabotages the agrarian revolution. Is not giving good land to the poor peasants, just like the Guomindang's support for the interests of the masses, high sounding but devoid of substance? In sum, if they cannot abolish the agrarian revolution from the right, they want to shift to the left to abolish the agrarian revolution. Now a blow has been dealt to them from the

right, and they have also been exposed on the left. They are reduced to creating rumors that we have raised slogans that are opposed by the middle peasants.

Finally, we want to ask why Mao Zedong should be overthrown, and Zhu, Peng, and Huang be supported? Is it because of problems with Comrade Zedong as an individual? No, it most certainly is not. If it is a problem of Comrade Mao as an individual, why should Comrade Zhou Yili be captured? "Even if he has retreated ten thousand *bu*,"[13] Comrade Yili has just arrived in Jiangxi and what political tricks has he played? Whom has he seized? Whom has he beaten? So the Liquidationists and the AB Corps have rushed to concoct rumors. Well then, why should Comrade Mao Zedong be overthrown? Precisely because Comrade Mao represents the correct revolutionary line, and is truly leading the struggle and promoting the Chinese revolution at present. Because the AB Corps and the Liquidationists are scheming to sabotage the Chinese revolution, they must overthrow Mao Zedong. It is precisely because Comrade Yili represents the correct line of the Central Committee that he must also be arrested. Why do the AB Corps and the Liquidationists support Zhu, Peng and Huang? This is not at all a matter of supporting the revolution, for the revolution is not a question of supporting an individual or not. Nor do they loyally support Zhu, Peng, and Huang. Their plot is first to draw in Zhu, Peng, and Huang to overthrow Mao Zedong, first concentrating their forces to overthrow one person, and then overthrowing the others one by one. Comrades, at this crucial juncture of the decisive class struggle, Chiang Kaishek is shouting loudly "Down with Mao Zedong" from without, and the AB Corps and the Liquidationists are shouting "Down with Mao Zedong" from within the revolutionary ranks. How they echo each other's voices and copy each other's tastes!

---

13. It is not clear whether *bu* here means "steps," or whether it refers to the unit of length equivalent to 5 Chinese feet.

Eight Great Conditions for Victory[1]

(December 22, 1930)

I. The International Situation Is Conducive to the Final Class Struggle, and Is Unfavorable for Imperialism

A. The Clashes and Fears of the Imperialists

1. Italy has formed an alliance of seven countries with itself as the center. Italy has fierce clashes with France, so it has gathered together those countries hostile to France—Germany, Greece, Turkey, Bulgaria, Hungary, and the Soviet Union—to form a bloc of seven countries to deal with France. France then became terrified that Italy and Germany might stand on the side of the Soviet Union. Germany says, if you (Britain, France, and the United States) do not cancel my reparations, I shall make friends with the Soviet Union. Italy says, if you do not permit me to build a big navy, I shall also be a friend of the Soviet Union. It is terrible for those big imperialist countries (Britain, France, and the United States) either to agree, or not to agree. All this shows that they have irreconcilable clashes among them.

2. Britain wants to set up a five-man dictatorship. The problems of strikes and unemployment in Britain have become very severe. Its foreign trade is not profitable. Its domestic industries and commerce are all screaming, as if great turmoil is about to burst out. So the British imperialists are in a panic, and want to organize a five-man régime to cope with the turmoil by the use of concentrated power.[2] This shows that the internal problems are indeed considerable! In the United States, goods are piled up and rotting, but seven million workers have no food to eat.

The United States has produced too much wheat, and cannot sell it. The capitalists only shout at the farmers who cultivate the land not to grow any more wheat. But there are seven million workers who have no money to buy wheat to

---

Our source for this text is *Mao Zedong ji. Bujuan*, Vol. 3, pp. 193–200.

1. This document was drafted in the course of the enlarged plenum of the Front Committee held at Huangpi in early to mid December of 1930. It was based on Mao's speeches at this meeting. Thus, the substance is his, though he did not actually draft the text.

2. The reference is presumably to the establishment of an inner cabinet by the British Government to deal with the General Strike of 1926.

eat, and who are unemployed and hungry. On the one hand, the wheat is piled up and rotting, and on the other hand, the workers are starving. You see how strange things are under imperialism. The United States also produces a lot of silver, which is stored and without borrowers. Thus, the price of silver has dropped steeply, and it is really a big disaster. Iron, steel and rubber are also difficult to sell. Therefore, over a hundred and thirty banks have collapsed within seven days. This is the so-called panic of overproduction. Now the whole world is in such a state.

In Japan, a big earthquake has taken place. Japan's industries started to panic a long time ago. They have long demanded a policy of retrenchment (using less money and doing less business). Now the big earthquake has occurred, destroying countless houses, factories, and bridges, and killing many people. With this big blow of an iron hammer, the Japanese imperialists are crying out fearfully in their distress.[3]

B. The Development of the World Revolutionary Tide

1. The German Communist Party is staging uprisings everywhere. The German Communist Party is clashing with the National Socialist Party (the die-hard party of the capitalists) all over the place, and it also has confrontations with the police everywhere. In the streets, shootings with handguns are common occurrences. Clashes have even occurred over a performance in a theater (one opposing the imperialist wars), with the Nazi Party opposing its performance and the Communist Party staging demonstrations in favor of performance. The streets are simply zones of guerrilla warfare. Probably the German proletariat will soon stage an insurrection.

2. The general strike of the mine workers in Britain. Ninety thousand mine workers have already begun to strike in Britain, and conditions are favorable for the expansion of the strike to the whole country. The Communist Party is growing among the striking workers. Over 200,000 representatives of the National Association of Mine Workers are under the leadership of the Communist Party. This situation cannot be taken lightly!

3. The Communist Party of the United States is working with great enthusiasm. In the past the U.S. Communist Party was not up to much. Now, with massive unemployment in the imperialist United States, the Communist Party has developed greatly, and the U.S. imperialists are so frightened that they have

---

3. The great Tokyo earthquake took place, of course, in 1923. A rebuilding festival had been held in March 1930, to celebrate the successful renewal of the city after the disaster, so the years 1923–1930 could have been seen as the period of the earthquake and its aftermath, but that would scarcely have justified the verdict that the Japanese were "crying out fearfully in their distress." Probably, as in the case of the "five-man dictatorship" in Britain mentioned above, Mao and his comrades simply did not know much about the chronology of events outside China.

organized a committee for the investigation of the Communist Party. According to the report of the investigating committee, there are over 500,000 Communist Party members. The Communist Party is already organizing large demonstrations, and working with great enthusiasm.

4. The Soviet Union has proclaimed the crimes of the imperialists. The five-year industrial plan of the Soviet Union is developing day by day. The imperialists are terrified, and are trying to disrupt it from within in collusion with the White Russians. They want to destroy all the machines in factories and on the railroads, thus making Soviet industry bankrupt, and then send troops to intervene. This big conspiracy has been discovered by the Soviet Union. Those criminals have confessed that Britain is an accomplice. The Soviet Union has told the whole world through the wireless about these confessions, and proclaimed the crimes of the imperialists. [People everywhere] have risen up to oppose imperialism, and they are all red in the face [with anger]. Now the Soviet proletariat are more united, and Communist Party members have organized patrols on horseback, which are busy patrolling factories and railroads.

II. The Domestic Situation Is Favorable for the Decisive Class Battle, and Is Unfavorable for Chiang Kaishek and Lu Diping

A. The Clashes within the Ruling Class (Seen from the Following Events)

1. The confrontations between Chiang and Zhang, Yan and Feng. Zhang Xueliang wants to reorganize twenty divisions, and Yan Xishan has reorganized the Tenth Army, handing over the military and political management to Xu Yongchang and Shang Zhen in name, but in reality controlling it in secret. Yan and Zhang sent representatives to hold meetings in Tianjin. Feng Yuxiang nominally wants to transfer Sun Liangcheng, Song Zheyuan and others back to Gansu and to concentrate in Shanxi, [X][X] in fact wants to attack Shaanxi. Zhang Xueliang also tries hard to curry favor with Shi Yousan, and Shi Yousan is meeting with various important personalities of the Zhang faction in Tianjin. What tricks are being played? The trick is that Zhang Xueliang uses great strength in pulling the subordinates of Yan and Feng over to expand his own forces. He also wants to start chaotic fighting among the warlords. Chiang Kaishek is still deploying heavy forces on the Longhai line,[4] and has located one field headquarters in Luoyang with Gu Zhujie as the commander. This is to

---

4. As noted earlier, the Longhai line was a major East-West rail artery extending from Xi'an across Henan to the sea in northern Jiangsu.

counterbalance Feng Yuxiang. A field headquarters was established in Zhengzhou with He Yingqin[5] as the commander, obviously targeting Shi Yousan and the subordinates of Yan. In addition, Sun Lianzhong has been sent to Yanzhou, Wang Jun has been deployed in Xuzhou and Jin Handing has been stationed in Haizhou. All these are reactions against Zhang Xueliang. There are troops all along the Longhai line. What is this trick? This is a preparation for new major fighting. There were Chiang, Feng and Yan in the past, and there is a Zhang Xueliang added now. We must use the decisive class battle to oppose these big chaotic wars that massacre the workers and peasants!

2. The issue of Guangxi remains unsettled. Chiang Kaishek has sent many men and horses of the Eighth Route Army to attack Guangxi. The outcome of the fighting is that the forces of Zhang and Guangxi have gained the upper hand, thanks to the defeat they inflicted on the forces from Yunnan. Chiang Kaishek could do nothing about it, and outwardly negotiated peace with them. Guangxi is, however, still dominated by Huang Shaoxiong of Guangxi, and this issue is still unresolved.

3. The small warlords of Sichuan and Yunnan are also preparing to fight with each other.

B. The Development of the Revolutionary Forces

1. A large uprising of one battalion of soldiers of the forces of Guo Rudong.[6]

Guo Rudong led troops to attack Hubei and by [X][X]. Who could have known that when the troops arrived there, a whole battalion would riot. The large uprising of one battalion of men indicates the extent of wavering and collapsing of the enemy forces. Chiang Kaishek was seized by panic, and had to dismiss Guo Rudong.

2. The revolutionary forces in northeast Hubei cannot be crushed.

The First Army of the Red Army has been in northeast Hubei from the beginning. In the past, Chiang Kaishek ordered Xiu Qianyuan to attack it, and now he will also send Xiao Zhichu, and planes as well. This shows that he has no way to deal with this revolutionary force.

---

5. He Yingqin (1890–1987), *zi* Jingzhi, was a native of Guizhou. He studied military tactics in Japan, and from 1924 on was closely associated with Chiang Kaishek in building up the Guomindang's armed forces, first at the Huangpu Academy and then in the course of the Northern Expedition. In 1929, he became chief of staff of the army, navy, and airforce, and in March 1930 he was named minister of war in the national government. In December 1930, when this document was composed, He had just been appointed to command the first "bandit suppression campaign" against the Communists.

6. Guo Rudong (1892–1958), *zi* Songyun, was a native of Sichuan who had been appointed to the command of the Twentieth Army by the Wuhan government in May 1927.

3. The strengthening of the revolutionary forces in north Hunan.

North Hunan has two armies, the Second and the Sixth Armies of the Red Army. He Jian has dispatched a lot of troops to attack them. But the Second and the Sixth Armies threatened Changde, went through Lizhou, and are now in Shimen. He Jian is again very busy, ordering Li Jue to attack, and also moving part of Chen Cheng's division to Huarong. The reactionary newspapers will certainly not mention the news of the victories of the Red Army. But judging from the fact that the reactionaries have reinforced their offensive forces, it is clear that they cannot beat the Red Army, and have even lost many guns to it.

The above-mentioned clashes within the ruling class, and the efforts of the revolutionary forces everywhere within the country to resist the warlords, are extremely helpful to us in winning battles.

III. Our Strategy Has Been Correct, and We Have Won in All Respects. The Strategy of the Enemy Has Failed in Every Respect

1. Luring the enemy deep into the Red areas. The enemy wants us to come to fight with him in the White areas, and we simply refuse. We want the enemy to come to the Red areas, and there is no way he can avoid coming. If we do not go there, we make all of his ships, trains and fortifications useless. Once he comes to the Red areas, our spears will be more effective. Coming to the Red areas, the enemy is like shrimp falling on the beach. It is immediately obvious that the enemy will be defeated, and we shall win.

2. Adopting the tactics of protracted war. This time, the enemy wants to fight a short war, and we just will not fight a short war. The enemy has internal conflicts. He just wants to defeat us, and then resume the in-fighting. Since he sets a limit of three months for "suppressing the bandits,"[7] we know his weakness, and just try to keep him in a stew. Now he has been stewing for two months or so, and he has made wrong moves every step of the way. We should make him stew until he has internal troubles, and then deliver a mighty blow to him. The uprisings of the AB Corps planted within our armies by the enemy have all been smashed by us. We have killed dozens of the top leaders of the Corps, and have got rid of over four thousand members of the AB Corps.[8] We will not fight a fast war with them, but will take some time to kill many small Chiang Kaisheks, eliminate spies in the Red Army, and unite more closely. The enemy is defeated once again, and we have already won a major victory.

---

7. *Jiaofei*, the official Guomindang designation for the campaign which Chiang Kaishek had just launched.

8. This is, of course, a reference to the Futian Incident, discussed in the previous text, on the eve of which Mao had 4,400 officers and men loyal to the Jiangxi Provincial Action Committee arrested on the grounds that they were members of the AB Corps.

3. Besieging the enemy for a long time in a tight encirclement.

The enemy entertains the vain hope of encircling us tightly and besieging us for a long time, sending several armies to surround us by different routes from the east and west sides of the [Gan] river. That being the case, we should strengthen our defenses and clear the fields, and mobilize the masses to besiege him for a long time in a tight encirclement. When we fired into the enemies in Le'an at night from all sides, they ran into the mountains like rats and dared not come down. Because of our harassment, the enemies in Shijiabian fired their machine guns and rifles till dawn. As a result, they fought each other, killing several hundred of their own men. If we harass the enemies, they will sound the bugle call for assembly, tremble with fear, and dare not sleep for the whole night. If they want to fight us, they cannot see us, and if they don't fight, they fear that we will really fight them. You see who is besieging whom. After the enemies arrive in the Red areas, they will have no firewood, rice, oil, and salt, will have to send troops to search for them in the countryside, and after expending great efforts, they will fail to find enough to eat for one meal. You see once again who is besieging whom. We put up posters in a big way, and also make propaganda among the White soldiers. The enemy is extremely vacillating, so even before the fighting begins, the enemy will be defeated at every step and we will triumph at every step. The enemy is both frightened and wavering, and if we deal him a forceful blow, there is no way we can fail to win.

IV. We Have the Cooperation of the Masses, and the Enemy Does Not

We have obtained the assistance of the masses. Everywhere the revolutionary masses make efforts to help us in organizing stretcher teams, transportation teams and first aid, reporting on the situation of the enemy, and acting as guides and communication links. The enemy does not have all this. He has no one to serve as guides, to deliver letters, or to report the news; there are only those who destroy his transportation, catch his spies, and harass his rear. What is more, as soon as we start fighting, the masses climb the mountains and go everywhere to help us with the fighting. Thus, the enemy does not know how many troops we really have, and becomes terrified. After the defeat of the enemy, the masses rise up everywhere to seize weapons and take captives, so none of the enemy can escape out of the Red areas. That is what we mean when we say that the enemy does not have the masses, and we do have them. The enemy will certainly be defeated, and we will certainly be victorious.

V. Our Forces Are Concentrated and the Enemy's Forces Are Dispersed

This time, our First and Third Army Groups have combined in a big way, and concentrated their forces in a single place. Our strength and combat capacity are adequate for the fight. Although twenty regiments of the enemy are a lot of troops, they are scattered from the west of the river to the east of the river, with a distance of several hundred *li* between them. The weapons of the troops of each route do not exceed 4,000 to 5,000 guns. If we smash a single route with our most concentrated firepower, his other routes will not be able to help even if they come. This is called concentrating our forces to destroy the enemy one by one, and these tactics cannot fail to be victorious.

VI. Our Troops Are United and the Enemy's Forces Are Wavering

The enemy soldiers have long been wavering. To this must be added the fact that, when they come to the Red areas, they will see our slogans reading: "Brothers from the White army, kill all those officers who oppress you," and "We welcome our brothers from the White army to join the Red Army." As soon as their eyes light upon this, they will think it over and become more vacillating. There were several instances in which enemies in Le'an sold their weapons to the people and ran away to find the Red Army. Our Red Army is an army led by the proletariat, conscious of why it is fighting, and united as one. If a Red Army of this class character launches a united attack on such a wavering White army, it cannot fail to win.

VII. Our Preparations Are Adequate, and the Enemy Is Seized by a Financial Panic

The Red Army never takes along a lot of provisions when fighting. The Third Army Group had only enough rice for one breakfast, and yet it smashed its way into Changsha. This is a peculiarity of our Red Army. Now we have prepared provisions for three months, and we can fight the enemies in a big way. This time, our officers, soldiers, and porters have donated money for the fighting, something which can be done only by our Red Army. The reason is that they offer money to fight their own war. The Red Army has this spirit, and large-scale preparations. As for the enemy, he is in a financial panic. Taxes are levied on houses, and also on shops, and then there is the salt tax. Public bonds have likewise been issued. All this money always goes into the pockets of the warlords, and the soldiers have no pay. We should certainly get as many enemy soldiers as possible to come, so we can destroy them in a big way.

VIII. We Have Topographic Advantages, and the Enemy Does Not

The region of Ningdu, Yongfeng, and Xingguo is a Red area. At the same time, there are many mountains and ridges, the roads are narrow, and the terrain is dangerous. Thus the enemy cannot engage in large-scale maneuvers, and his cannons are also useless. The Red Army not only moves fast, but is familiar with the terrain. One of its forces may launch a frontal attack from the front of the mountain, and another force may encircle the mountain and attack from the rear, thus leaving the White armies with no place to go, and eliminating them completely.

The above conditions are the conditions for the certain victory of our decisive class war. We must, however, go bravely forth to fight. If we do not fight bravely, there is certainly no way we can fight victorious battles by sitting at home. If we take account only of one factor, for example that the White soldiers are wavering, we could be victorious. But the White officers are the die-hard running dogs of the warlords, the despotic gentry, the landlords, and the bourgeoisie, and they will certainly fight us, for only thus can they save themselves from death. Therefore, only if we fight against them resolutely and bravely can we win victory. Nevertheless, we have eight great conditions for victory, and the enemy has eight great unfavorable conditions. So we have more assurance of victory. Comrades, advance courageously to carry out your class responsibilities!

An Order to Ambush the Enemy Forces That Are Invading Xiaobu

(December 25, 1930)

1. Today (the 24th) the enemy in Shima has moved to Shangxi (fifty *li* from Xiaobu); the enemy in Zhongcun (note: these two localities are both linked to the forces of Zhang Huizan) has reached the line from Yuantou to Shangchao and Lufengling at 11:00 A.M. today (about two regiments). The prospect is obviously that they will invade Xiaobu tomorrow morning (the 25th). One company of our Third Army is still in Xiaobu. The enemy in Xiaotian (Mao's division)[1] has advanced to Wucun this morning, and the enemy in Yinshui (Tan's division)[2] has advanced to Dongshao this morning. Our Political Guards Regiment has already withdrawn to Matian. The enemy in Donggu has arrived at Nanlong today, but has not yet reached Longgang. The forces we sent to Junfu are still there.

2. The Front Army has decided that tomorrow (the 25th) we will first destroy the enemies that are coming to invade Xiaobu.

3. The Third Army Group will be on the right wing, responsible for attacking Xiaobu from the east and north (that is, the height to the south of Nufeng, the height to the north of Yanshupo, and the line from Younaoshang and Wushan to the vicinity of Hewu). Tomorrow morning (setting out around 6:00 or 7:00), they should reach a point about ten *li* from Xiaobujie by 10:00, and stop there (taking care to conceal their objective). Only after the enemies advancing from Yuantou have entered Xiaobu should we cut off their route from Yuantou, and then launch a fierce offensive and destroy them.

The Third Army will be on the left wing, responsible for attacking Xiaobu from the west (that is, Fujiangping and the area around the height to the south of Shukeng). They should set out at 8:00 tomorrow morning, and by 10:00 reach an area about ten *li* from Xiaobujie, and then stop, taking care to conceal their objective. They should wait till the enemies from Shangxi have entered Xiaobujie, cut off the enemies' route from Shangxi, and then launch a fierce attack and destroy them.

Our source for this text is *Mao Zedong junshi wenji*, Vol. 1, pp. 187–89.

1. The reference is to the Eighth Division of the Guomindang Sixth Route Army, commanded by Mao Bingwen.

2. The Fiftieth Division of the Second Column of the Guomindang Ninth Route Army, under the command of Tan Daoyuan.

The Twelfth Army will constitute the center, responsible for attacking Xiaobu from the south (that is, the line from the height to the south of Hewu to the height to the north of Shuixi). They should set out from their present location at 7:30 tomorrow morning, advancing to attack Xiaobu. If the enemy has not yet entered Xiaobu, they should stop before Xiaobu (that is, the southern extremity of Xiaobu), at a distance of about ten *li*.

The Fourth Army is the general reserve force, and should arrive at Tiandongshi (on the way from Diaofeng to Xiaobu) at 10:00 tomorrow morning, stop, and await further instruction (this is the position to be taken up by the general reserve force).

The Political Guards Regiment of the Central Revolutionary Committee, which remains stationed at Matian, should post guards with great secrecy in the three directions of Dongshao, Luokou, and Nantuan, and pin down the enemy at Dongshao and Wucun, so that our main forces can go out, strike, and achieve complete victory.

4. The heavy baggage of all the armies is to be placed in the vicinity of Huangpi, under the command of the head of our adjutant's department.

5. Every unit should bring the noon meal with them.

6. General Headquarters and the Central Revolutionary Committee will move at 8:00 tomorrow morning from here to Tiandongshi, where the general reserve force will be stationed.

Addendum:

1. With reference to positions, you should use the outline maps drawn by the staff office of the Third Army, and issued by this Headquarters, and the Ningdu route map printed and issued by the staff office of this Headquarters.

2. Each army should decide on the location of its own first aid station. The temporary field hospital is in Laijiaping.

3. The telephone should not be dismantled for the time being. If enemy troops are spotted in Matian, the Political Guards Regiment may dismantle it when necessary, but should inform all units at once.

4. The Third Army Group should keep a close watch in the direction of Nantuan.

It is so ordered.

Commander-in-chief   Zhu De
Political Commissar   Mao Zedong

Red Letter Order No. 10 of the First Front Army of the Red Army

(December 26, 1930)

1. According to reliable reports, the enemy troops in Dongshao have already advanced toward Luokou, and it seems that they are going to march to the *xian* town of Ningdu. There are no enemy forces in Nantuan.

The enemy troops in Yuantou have already moved to Shupo (15 *li* from Xiaobu) this afternoon. Their vanguards are stationed as far forward as the locality of Jiakeng (7 *li* from Xiaobu).

The enemy troops in Nanlong have advanced to Wujinkeng, Xianrenfeng, and Yankeng. The one company sent out by our Third Army is still in Longgang. More than 1,000 bandit-pacification troops have arrived at Shaxi.

There is still one company of our forces from the Third Army in Xiaobu.

2. The Front Army has decided to advance to the vicinity of Xiaobu tomorrow, wait for the enemy troops which are going to invade Xiaobu from Shupo, surround them, and wipe them out.

3. The assignments and combat zones of each army, and of the Third Army Group are the same as those given in the Ninth Red Letter Order.

4. Every army (excluding the reserve forces) should send a small unit of troops tomorrow (the 27th) before dawn to occupy the vital points in its combat zone. The main forces should begin to move at 6:00 tomorrow morning, take up a forward position in the combat zone of their respective armies, and conceal themselves. They should wait till all the enemy troops advancing from Shupo have entered Xiaobu and encountered our Twelfth Army, which constitutes the main front, before launching a general offensive. We hope to destroy the whole of the enemy's forces (the one company from the Third Army should seize the opportunity to withdraw from the battle position of its army and rejoin its unit).

5. The heavy baggage and non-combatant personnel of each army should stop in the area of Yangyi and Huangpi and await further orders. They will be commanded by Deputy Chief Adjutant Yang of this headquarters. Wugongduan on the way to Nankeng[1] will be their rear.

6. The wounded from the left wing (the Third Army) should be transferred to

---

Our source for this text is *Jiangxi dangshi ziliao*, Vol. 6, pp. 236–37; it also appears in Vol. 17, pp. 112–13 of the same series.

1. The text in Vol. 17 reads "Egongduan on the way to Nankang."

the general hospital in Yangji, and all the wounded from the other armies should be transferred to the general hospital in Laijiaping.[2]

7. General Headquarters and the Workers' and Peasants' Revolutionary Committee will continue to advance to Tiandongshi and exercise command from there.

Addendum:

A. The forces of the Twelfth Army in front must wait till all the enemy troops have penetrated well into Xiaobu before launching a powerful counter-attack; above all, we must not wipe out the enemy's advance forces too early, thereby letting the enemy's main forces escape.

B. After the fighting is over, every army must immediately assemble its troops, in order to be prepared for the reinforcement of enemy troops from other places.

C. The Third Army should pay attention to posting guards in the direction of Hanxia and Shangxi.

D. The Political Guards Regiment should be stationed at Matian, and post guards in the direction of Dongshao, Luokou, and Nanjin to protect the right wing of our army.

E. Every unit, on arriving at the position where it is to prepare for battle, should immediately send one superior officer to General Headquarters in Tiandongshi to establish liaison and receive orders.

Commander-in-chief   Zhu De

Political Commissar   Mao Zedong

---

2. The text in Vol. 17 reads ". . . to the general hospital in Changqi."

Red Letter Order No. 11 of the First Front Army of the Red Army Regarding the Decision to Sweep Away the Enemy of the Left Wing, Zhang Huizan, and the Various Divisions of Xu, Gong, and Luo[1]

(December 28, 1930, 9:00 P.M., at Huangpi)

(1) The enemy forces of Tan Daoyuan are still held up in the region of Yuantou, Shangchao, Xiachao,[2] and Shupo, and are not advancing. The two regiments of Mao Bingwen which entered Dongshao have moved to Luokou. Their vanguard reached Pingtian yesterday. The actions of the forces following on behind are not clear, but they are probably advancing towards Ningdu.

The forces of Zhang Huizan have passed Shanhe and Tengtian and reached Tantou. Now they are advancing towards Shanggang and Longgang. The actions of Xu's division are not clear. The forces of Gong and Luo are in various places in Donggu, Nanlong, Fengpian, Futian and Pitou.

(2) The Front Army decides to change objectives, sweeping away the enemies currently on our left flank (the forces of Zhang Huizan and also the various divisions of Xu, Gong and Luo), and annihilating them one by one. It is planned to divide our forces into two routes, with the left route advancing along Junbu and Longgang and the right route advancing along Shanggu and Tantou to attack Donggu in order.

(3) The Third Army Group and the Fourth Army serve as the right route forces (command is entrusted to Commander-in-chief Peng Dehuai and Political

---

Our source for this order is *Jiangxi dangshi ziliao*, Vol. 6, pp. 238–39. The text can also be found in *Mao Zedong ji. Bujuan*, Vol. 3, pp. 201–202, but that version, taken from a documentary collection published in China in 1979, is slightly less complete.

1. As indicated in the communiqué of December 30, 1930, Zhang Huizan, the commander of the Eighteenth Division of the Guomindang Ninth Route Army, was shortly captured and executed. Xu is Xu Kexiang; Gong is Gong Bingfan; Luo is Luo Lin. Regarding these three generals see respectively the notes to the texts of July 4, 1927, August 31, 1930, and August 24, 1930.

2. Here the text in *Jiangxi dangshi ziliao* has Shanghu and Xiahu, while *Mao Zedong ji* has Shangchao and Xiaochao. In the light of the occurrence of Shangchao in the text of December 25, 1930, we conclude that the *Mao Zedong ji* version is probably correct as regards this point.

Commissar Daiyuan[3] of the Third Army Group), attacking Shanggu and Xiagu along Saixia. When they have secured these places, they should continue to advance and to attack in the direction of Tantou. Everywhere they should annihilate the enemies they find in each place, and then advance a bit toward Donggu. Tomorrow (the 29th) they should go into action from their present position. (They may draft the marching plan themselves and report on it.)

The Third Army and the Twelfth Army are the left route army (under the command of this Headquarters), attacking Longgang and then Nanlong along Junbu. After destroying all the enemies in the area, they should advance a little toward Donggu. They should go into action from their present position tomorrow (the 29th). (The plan of march is detailed elsewhere.) The Political Guards Detachment of the Central Revolutionary Military Commission (except the fourth company) will remain in Huangpi, place themselves under the command of the battlefield committee, and pin down the enemies in the Eastern region.

(4) The heavy baggage and noncombatant troops of the whole Front[4] Army are commanded by Chen Zongshi, the chief adjutant of General Headquarters of the Third Army Group, and will advance with the left route armies. (All units must take with them only four poles of food,[5] and necessary small pieces of baggage.) The fourth company of Political Work Troops covers the advance of the heavy baggage, and is commanded by Chief Adjutant Chen.

(5) The medical teams will each march with their respective units.

(6) General Headquarters will march with the left route armies.

Attention:

1. If there are no enemies in Shanggu and Xiagu, the right route armies should coordinate with the left route armies in annihilating the enemies in Longgang, and maintain their guard in the direction of Shaxi.

2. The rear guards of the right route armies should pay attention to the enemies in the direction of Yuantou and Shupo.

3. The important documents of all regiments and companies should be gathered together in the divisional headquarters.

4. At least half of the personnel of the political departments of each army should follow the troops and work in the battlefields; the other half should follow the heavy baggage.

---

3. The reference is to Teng Daiyuan (1904–1974), a native of Hunan, who was at this time Political Commissar of the Third Army Group.

4. Here there is a misprint in the *Jiangxi dangshi ziliao* version, which reads *fangxiang* ("direction") instead of *fangmian* ("front").

5. The character *dan* might be taken here to refer to the unit of weight sometimes translated "picul," and commonly represented in this volume by the word *Dan* written with a capital. It seems more plausible, however, that it has its basic meaning of "to carry on a pole." In other words, each unit could take along only what could be borne by four porters, each with a pole on his shoulder.

5. The Thirty-fifth Division (now in Yuexi) should leave Yuexi on the 30th and advance by shortcut to Nanlong and Longgang, attacking Longgang in coordination with the left route armies, and maintaining their guard in the direction of Nanlong.

It is so ordered.

Commander-in-chief   Zhu De
Political Commissar   Mao Zedong

Red Letter Order No. 12 of the First Front Army of the Red Army to Attack the Forces of Zhang Huizan at Longgang

(December 29, 1930, 8:00 P.M., at Junbujie)

(1) The enemy division of Zhang Huizan is advancing toward us from Nanlong. At 10:00 A.M. today (the 29th), its vanguard (the Hundred and Third Regiment of Dai Yue's brigade)[1] reached Longgangyu, which is thirty *li* from here. The whereabouts of the forces following after are not clear. It is said that enemy forces have arrived in Tantou.

The division of Tan Daoyuan is still in Yuantou, Shangchao and Xiachao.[2]

The division of Mao Bingwen has moved to the region of Luokou, Pingtian and Dongshanba.

(2) The Front Army has decided to attack the enemy in Longgang with the left route armies tomorrow (the 30th), and the right route armies should send forces to assist in the destruction of the said enemy.

(3) The Twelfth Army (except the Thirty-fifth Division but including the Sixty-fourth Division) serves as the left wing. It should set out before 4:00 A.M. tomorrow, and advance towards Biaohu. With part of its forces, it must occupy Nanduan, Shuixi and Xiduan in the Manggong Mountains of Longgang, while the main forces cut the major road that leads to Tongnan (passing through Lanshi and Maoping). All of these positions must be occupied by 10:00 A.M.

The Third Army serves as the right wing. It should set out at 5:00 A.M. tomorrow morning, occupy the areas right of Mukeng and the key positions in Lingziling, and advance towards and attack Longgang (the offensive must start at 9:30 A.M.). The right and left wings should dispatch forces to establish effective contact. If the right wing has not sent troops, then the troops should be moved toward the right side and special attention should be given to the right wing.

(4) The time of the general offensive against Longgang is 10:00 A.M. on the 30th.

Our source for this text is *Jiangxi dangshi ziliao*, Vol. 6, pp. 240–41. Another version can be found in *Mao Zedong ji. Bujuan*, Vol. 3, pp. 203–04.

1. As indicated in a note to the order of July 29, 1930, Dai Yue commanded the Fifty-Second Brigade of the Eighteenth Division of the Guomindang Ninth Route Army.

2. Once again, we follow *Mao Zedong ji* for these names, rather than *Jiangxi dangshi ziliao*, which has Shanghu and Xiahu.

(5) The right route armies should send out a force tomorrow morning, to arrive in the vicinity of Huanpu, after passing through Huilong. They should be in contact with the Third Army on the left and with the Twelfth Army on the right, advance and attack the northwest corner of Longgang (near Zhangjiache). Upon arrival, they should establish liaison with the Third Army and General Headquarters. If there are no enemies in Shanggu, the main forces should advance and attack towards the line of Huanpu and Zhangjiache, while a small detachment posts guards in the direction of Xiagu and Tantou.

(6) The small baggage, the shelters for the wounded, and the first aid posts of all armies may be located in places chosen by the units. The reception posts for captured enemy soldiers will be set up in Xiaobie.

(7) The heavy baggage will remain stationary in Yangzhai, awaiting orders. If an enemy presence is detected in Xiaobu, it will be moved in the direction of Yuexi.

(8) General Headquarters will move to the vicinity of Xiaobie tomorrow morning, and exercise command from there.

Addendum:

1. Before setting out tomorrow, all units should assemble for speeches by officers and soldiers. Political agitation should be well conducted, and the work of political agitation should also be carried out well in the reserves at all times.

2. The Twelfth Army should focus its attention on a forceful effort to cut off the reinforcements for the enemy in Nanlong.

3. Wounded from all armies should be moved to the reception center in Xiaobie.

4. All armies should pay attention to maintaining liaison between them, and to collecting intelligence.

5. All units should pay attention to collecting western medicine, and should not destroy radios.

It is so ordered.

Commander-in-chief   Zhu De
Political Commissar   Mao Zedong

News of the Victory of the Red Army (Extracts)

(December 30, 1930)

The Unprecedented Great Victory at Longgang

. . . The two brigades of the Eighteenth Division of the White army were completely wiped out.

. . . We captured the enemy's division commander Zhang Huizan, and brigade commanders Dai Yue and Wang Jiejun.

. . . We captured 5,000 weapons and took more than 9,000 prisoners .

. . . Unite the workers, peasants, and soldiers to continue our efforts to wipe out the enemy.

To all action committees, all *xian* committees, all *xian* soviets, Party organizations and soviets at every level, and all . . . :

. . . times they undertook to suppress the revolution in a big way, and they gradually closed in and encircled the Red region and the Red Army with a great show of strength, our workers . . . prepared to wipe them out in one breath. Today our First Route Army fought a fierce battle against the Fifty-second [Brigade] . . . and Wang Jiejun's brigade of the division of White Bandit Zhang Huizan. They fought for more than five hours, and of the four regiments . . . they did not let even one escape. We captured a total of more than 5,000 rifles, 30 machine guns. . . . [Of these] battalions, the number of officers, soldiers, and porters captured exceeded 9,000. White Bandit division commander Zhang Huizan, and brigade commanders Dai Yue and Wang Jiejun . . . were captured. This time, with so many captured rifles, not only has the strength of the Red Army been increased, but we can [take] a large number. . . . We captured Zhang Huizan, the most faithful running dog of Chiang Kaishek and Lu Diping. For what we have suffered during the past two years from Lu . . . we [X] took [X][X] revenge.[1]

We have translated this text from *Jiangxi dangshi ziliao*, Vol. 17, pp. 119–20.

1. In this communiqué, dated December 30, "revenge" refers simply to the humiliating defeat inflicted on the enemy forces, but the revenge against Zhang Huizan was subsequently carried much further. On January 28, 1931, he was executed by decapitation, and his head was transported to the Gan River and floated downriver to Nanchang. There the Guomindang leaders recovered it and used it as evidence of the cruelty of the Communists.

. . . (because we cleaned out the AB Corps) the soldiers were in very high spirits during the fighting . . . [Zhang Hui]zan said "the Red Army is both fierce and well disciplined." From this point of view, our plan of luring the enemy deep . . . has already achieved victory in the first stage. From the second stage, all the way to the decisive class war, . . . we can achieve our goal under the condition of hard fighting in the decisive war by the Workers' and Peasants' Red Army.

. . . exerted great efforts to suppress the revolution, it had an ambitious plan, only . . . the White bandits . . . thought, moreover, that they could wipe out the Red Army. Consequently, they laid down a grand plan of campaign, allocated forty-four regiments of forces, divided into many different groups to crush the Red area and to besiege the Red Army. But grand as the enemy's plan was, it became in the end a plan to court death in the face of the Workers' and Peasants' Red Army. We had prepared long ago to wipe them out. The first battle, which took place today, shattered part of the enemy's general plan. The revolutionary workers and peasants must cooperate with the Red Army and continue our efforts. The enemy's doom is assuredly not far away. We have decided that the White bandit troops which have always been engaged in repressing the revolution will be wiped out completely in the Red area in which the decisive class war is being fought. Victory in the whole province, and even in the whole country, is beginning to emerge. We hope that everyone will make an effort to participate in the decisive war.

3. Now that the decisive class war is just beginning, continuous victory undoubtedly depends on the efforts of the revolutionary Workers' and Peasants' Red Army. The Bolshevik Communist Party members, and the poor revolutionary workers and peasants must continue their efforts to attack the AB Corps and the Liquidationists, oppose the Provincial Action Committee and the Provincial Government of the AB Corps,[2] support the Provincial Action Committee and Provincial Government under the leadership of Comrade Zeng Shan, support the General Front Committee. We must strive to participate in the decisive war, carry out the policy of intercepting the enemy, stopping the enemy, harassing the enemy, raising revenue for the Red Army, helping the Red Army in its battles. This is the guarantee of the victory of the revolution. We sincerely hope that everyone will make great efforts!

Long live the victory of the Workers' and Peasants' Red Army Long live. . . .

> Chairman of the Chinese Workers' and Peasants'
> Revolutionary Committee   Mao Zedong
> December 30, 1930, sent from Longgang in
> Yongfeng *xian* at 6:00 P.M.

---

2. The reference is to the rival Party and government organs opposed to Mao in the Futian Incident, which he regarded as animated by, or under the control of, the AB Corps. See above, "A Letter of Reply by the General Front Committee," especially section (1).

Bibliography

As in previous volumes, we include here, for the convenience of the reader, the short titles used for certain works, which are likewise given on the first appearance of each entry in the notes.

Averill, Stephen C., "The Origins of the Futian Incident," in Tony Saich and Hans van de Ven (eds.), *New Perspectives on the Chinese Communist Revolution*. Armonk, N.Y.: M.E. Sharpe, 1995. (Short title: Averill, "Futian Incident.")

Baqi huiyi (The August 7 Meeting). Beijing: Zhonggong dangshi ziliao chubanshe, 1986.

Brandt, Conrad, Schwartz, Benjamin, and Fairbank, John K., *A Documentary History of Chinese Communism*. Cambridge, Mass.: Harvard University Press, 1952. (Short title: *Documentary History*.)

Carr, E.H., *A History of Soviet Russia: Foundations of a Planned Economy 1926–1929*, Vol. 3, Part III. London: Macmillan, 1978. (Short title: Carr, *Foundations*, Vol. 3-III.)

Carr, E.H., *The Interregnum. 1923–1924*. Harmondsworth: Penguin, 1969.

Chen Cheng Collection (sometimes referred to as the Shih Sou Collection). Collection of some fifteen hundred Chinese Communist documents from the Jiangxi Soviet Republic (1930–1934), originally collected by Guomindang general and later vice president of the Republic of China on Taiwan, Chen Cheng. Now held on microfilm at the Hoover Institution at Stanford University and other research libraries in the United States, Western Europe, and Japan. A selected and annotated bibliography of the collection, titled *The Kiangsi Soviet Republic, 1931–1934*, was compiled by Tien-wei Wu and published by the Harvard-Yenching Library (Bibliographical Series III) in 1981.

Ch'en, Yung-fa, "The Futian Incident and the Anti-Bolshevik League: The 'Terror' in the CCP Revolution," in *Republican China* vol. XIX, no. 2, April 1994, pp. 1–51.

Chesneaux, Jean, *Popular Movements and Secret Societies in China 1840–1950*. Stanford: Stanford University Press, 1972.

Dangde wenxian (Documents of the Party), no. 1, 1988; no. 5, 1989. Beijing: Zhonggong zhongyang wenxian yanjiushi, 1988, 1989.

Dangshi yanjiu (Research on Party History). Beijing: Zhonggong zhongyang dangxiao, 1980–. (Short title: *Party History*.)

Degras, Jane (ed.), *The Communist International 1919–1943: Documents*, Vol. III, 1929–1943. London: Oxford University Press, 1965. (Short title: Degras, *Communist International*, III.)

Domes, Jürgen, *Vertagte Revolution. Die Politik der Kuomintang in China, 1923–1937*. Berlin: Walter de Gruyter, 1969. (Short title: Domes, *Vertagte Revolution*.)

Galbiati, Fernando, *P'eng P'ai and the Hai-lu-feng Soviet*. Stanford: Stanford University Press, 1985.

Graham, A.C., *Chuang-tzu. The Seven Inner Chapters and Other Writings from the Book Chuang-tzu*. London: Allen & Unwin, 1981.

Grigor'ev, A.M., "The Comintern and the Revolutionary Movement in China under the Slogan of the Soviets (1927–1931)," in *The Comintern and the East*, ed. R.A. Ulyanovsky (Moscow: Progress Publishers, 1979), pp. 345–88.

Grigor'ev, A.M., *Revolyutsionnoe Dvizhenie v Kitae v 1927–1931 gg.* (The Revolutionary

Movement in China in the Years 1927–1931). Moscow: Izdatel'stvo "Nauka," 1980. (Short title: Grigor'ev, *The Revolutionary Movement in China*.)

Gui Yulin, *Jinggangshan geming douzheng shi* (History of the Revolutionary Struggles on the Jinggangshan). Beijing: Jiefangjun chubanshe, 1986. (Short title: Gui Yulin, *Jinggangshan*.)

Hsiao Tso-liang [Xiao Zuoliang], *Power Relations within the Chinese Communist Movement, 1930–1934*. Seattle: University of Washington Press, 1961. Vol. 2, *The Chinese Documents*, 1967. (Short title: Hsiao, *Power Relations*.)

Hsiao Tso-liang [Xiao Zuoliang], *The Land Revolution in China, 1930–1934: A Study of Documents*. Seattle: University of Washington Press, 1969.

Hung, William, *Tu Fu: China's Greatest Poet*. Cambridge: Harvard University Press, 1952.

International Press Correspondence, Vol. X, No. 14, March 20, 1930.

Jiangxi dangshi ziliao (Materials on Jiangxi Party History). Compiled by the Party History Compilation Committee and the Party History Research Department of the Chinese Communist Party Jiangxi Provincial Committee. N.p.: 1988 (vol. 6), 1990 (vol. 17).

Jiang Hua, "Guanyu hongjun jianshe wenti de yichang zhenglun" (A controversy regarding the problem of building a Red Army), *Dangde wenxian* No. 5, 1989.

Jiang Siyi (ed.), *Zhongguo gongchandang jundui zhengzhi gongzuo qishinian shi* (History of Seventy Years of Political Work by the Army of the Chinese Communist Party), Vol. 1. Beijing: Jiefangjun chubanshe, 1991.

Jin Chongji, *Zhou Enlai zhuan 1898–1949* (Biography of Zhou Enlai, 1898–1949). Beijing: Zhongyang wenxian yanjiushi, 1989. (Short title: Jin, *Zhou Enlai*.)

Jin Chongji, *Zhu De zhuan* (Biography of Zhu De). Beijing: Zhongyang wenxian chubanshe, 1993. (Short title: Jin, *Zhu De*.)

Jinggangshande wuzhuang geju (The Armed Independent Régime on the Jinggangshan). Nanchang: Jiangxi renmin chubanshe, 1979. (Short title: *The Jinggangshan Régime*.)

Jingganshan geming genjudi (The Revolutionary Base on the Jinggangshan). 2 vols. Beijing: Zhonggong dangshi ziliao chubanshe, 1987. (Short title: *The Jinggangshan Revolutionary Base*.)

Jinggangshan geming genjudi shiliao xuanbian (Selected Historical Materials on the Jinggangshan Revolutionary Base). Nanchang: Jiangxi renmin chubanshe, 1986. (Short title: *Jinggangshan Historical Materials*.)

Legge, James, *The Chinese Classics*. Vol. I, *Confucian Analects, The Great Learning, The Doctrine of the Mean*. Hong Kong: Hong Kong University Press, 1960.

Leong, S.T., "The Hakka Chinese of Lingnan: Ethnicity and Social Change in Modern Times," in *Ideal and Reality: Social and Political Change in Modern China, 1860–1949*, ed. David Pong and Edmund S.K. Fung (Lanham, Md.: University Press of America, 1985), pp. 287–323.

Lin Yunhui, "Lue lun Mao Zedong tongzhi dui Lisan luxian de renshi he dizhi" (A Brief Account of Comrade Mao Zedong's Understanding of and Resistance to the Lisan Line), in *Dangshi yanjiu* 4, 1980, pp. 51–59.

Ling Yu, "Mao Zedong tongzhi he Lisan luxian de guanxi taolun zongshu" (A Summary of the Discussion Regarding Comrade Mao Zedong's Relationship to the Lisan Line), in *Dangshi yanjiu* 3, 1982, pp. 78–80.

Liu Xiaonong, "Mao Zedong dierci hunyin neiqing" (Inside information on Mao Zedong's second marriage), in *Jizhe xie tianxia* (Reporters Write about the World) no. 21, May 1992.

Ma Yuqing and Zhang Wanlu, *Mao Zedong gemingde daolu* (Mao Zedong's Revolutionary Way). Xi'an: Shaanxi renmin chubanshe, 1991. (Short title: Ma and Zhang, *Mao's Way*.)

Mao Zedong, *Nongcun diaocha* (Rural Investigations). [Yan'an]: "Internal Party Publication," 1941.

Mao Zedong, *Report from Xunwu.* Translated and with an introduction and notes by Roger R. Thompson. Stanford: Stanford University Press, 1990.

Mao Zedong, "Ruhe yanjiu Zhonggong dangshi" (How to Study the History of the Chinese Communist Party), in *Dangshi yanjiu* (Research on Party History), No. 1, 1980, pp. 2–7.

Mao Zedong, *Selected Works of Mao Tse-tung*, Vols. 1–4. Peking: Foreign Languages Press, 1960–1965.

Mao Zedong ji (Collected writings of Mao Zedong), ed. Takeuchi Minoru. 10 vols. Tokyo: Hokubōsha, 1970–1972; second edition, Tokyo: Sōsōsha, 1983.

Mao Zedong ji. Bujuan (Supplement to collected writings of Mao Zedong), ed. Takeuchi Minoru. 10 vols. Tokyo: Sōsōsha, 1983–1986.

Mao Zedong junshi shengya (Mao Zedong's Military Career), ed. Chinese People's Revolutionary Military Museum. Beijing: Renmin chubanshe, 1993.

Mao Zedong junshi wenji (Collected Military Writings of Mao Zedong), Vols. 1–6. Beijing: Junshi kexue chubanshe and Zhongyang wenxian chubanshe, 1993.

Mao Zedong nongcun diaocha wenji (Collected Writings of Mao Zedong on Rural Investigations). Beijing: Renmin chubanshe, 1982.

Mao Zedong shici duilian jizhu (Annotated Edition of Mao Zedong's Poems and Couplets). Changsha: Hunan wenyi chubanshe, 1991. (Short title: *Shici duilian.*)

Mao Zedong shuxin xuanji (Selected correspondence of Mao Zedong), ed. Zhonggong zhongyang wenxian yanjiu shi. Beijing: Renmin chubanshe, 1983.

Mao Zedong wenji (Collected writings of Mao Zedong), ed. Zhonggong zhongyang wenxian yanjiu shi. 2 vols. (January 1921-June 1937 and August 1937-December 1942). Beijing: Renmin chubanshe, 1993.

Mao Zedong xuanji (Selected Works of Mao Zedong), Vol. 1. First edition, Beijing: Renmin chubanshe, 1951. Second edition, Beijing: Renmin chubanshe, 1991.

Mao Zedong xuanji xubian (Supplement to Selected Works of Mao Zedong). Compiled by the Central Bureau of the Chinese Communist Party for the Jin-Cha-Ji Border Area. N.p.: Jin-Cha-Ji Xinhua shudian, 1947.

Mao Zedong zhuzuo xuandu (jiazhongben) (Selected Readings from the Works of Mao Zedong, Edition A), 2 vols. Beijing: Renmin chubanshe, 1964.

Mif, Pavel Aleksandrovich [Mikhail Aleksandrovich Fortus] (ed.), *Strategiya i taktika Kominterna v natsional'no-kolonial'noy revolutsii na primere Kitaya* (The Strategy and Tactics of the Comintern in the National-colonial Revolution, on the Basis of the Chinese Example). Moscow: Institute of International Economics and International Politics, 1934. (Short title: Mif, *Strategy and Tactics.*)

Pang Xianzhi (ed.), *Mao Zedong nianpu. 1893–1949* (Chronological Biography of Mao Zedong, 1893–1949). 3 vols. Beijing: Zhongyang wenxian chubanshe, 1993. (Short title: *Nianpu.*)

Pak, Hyobom (ed.), *Documents of the Chinese Communist Party 1927–1930.* Hong Kong: Union Research Institute, 1971.

Peng Dehuai zishu (Peng Dehuai's Own Account). Beijing: Renmin chubanshe, 1981.

Qiushou qiyi (The Autumn Harvest Uprising). Beijing: Zhonggong zhongyang dangxiao chubanshe, 1982.

Qu Qiubai, "Ji'an de qude he sangshi" (The Conquest and Loss of Ji'an), in *Shi hua* (True Words) no. 2 (December 9, 1930), pp. 3–4.

Rue, John, *Mao Zedong in Opposition (1927–1935).* Stanford: Stanford University Press, 1966. (Short title: Rue, *Mao in Opposition.*

Saich, Tony (ed.), *The Rise to Power of the Chinese Communist Party. Documents and Analysis, 1920–1949.* Armonk, N.Y.: M.E. Sharpe, 1996. (Short title: Saich, *Rise to Power.*)

Snow, Edgar, *Red Star Over China*. London: Gollancz, 1937.

Sun Gang, "Mao Zedong 'shangshan' sixiang de tichu" (How Mao Zedong Put Forward the Idea of "Going Up the Mountains"), in *Dangde wenxian* no. 1, 1988, pp. 78–80.

Thompson, Roger R. (tr.), *Mao Zedong: Report from Xunwu*. Stanford: Stanford University Press, 1990.

Thornton, Richard C., *The Comintern and the Chinese Communists 1928–1931*. Seattle: University of Washington Press, 1969. (Short title: Thornton, *The Comintern and the Chinese Communists*.)

Tian Yuan, "Zai lun Mao Zedong tongzhi dui Lisan de renshi he dizhi" (More on Comrade Mao Zedong's Understanding of and Resistance to the Lisan Line), in *Dangshi yanjiu* 1, 1981, pp. 65–71.

Topley, Marjorie, "The Great Way of Former Heaven: A Group of Chinese Secret Religious Sects," in *Bulletin of the School of Oriental and African Studies*, Vol. 26, part 2, 1963, pp. 362–92. (Short title: Topley, "The Great Way.")

Watson, Burton (tr.), *The Complete Works of Chuang Tzu*. New York: Columbia University Press, 1968.

Xiao Ke, *ZhuMao hongjun ceji* (Perspectives on the Zhu-Mao Red Army). Beijing: Zhonggong zhongyang dangxiao chubanshe, 1993. (Short title: Xiao Ke, *The Zhu-Mao Red Army*.)

Xue Feng, "Yijian choukuan gonghan" (An Official Fund-raising Letter), in *Wenwu tiandi* no. 3, 1983, p.4.

Yu Boliu and Chen Gang, *Mao Zedong zai zhongyang suqu* (Mao Zedong in the Central Soviet Area). N.p.: Zhongguo shudian, 1993.

Zhonggong zhongyang wenjian xuanji (Selected Documents of the Central Committee of the Chinese Communist Party). Beijing: Zhonggong zhongyang dangxiao chubanshe, 1989–90. Vol. 3 (1927), 1989; Vol. 4 (1928), 1989; Vol. 5 (1929), 1990; Vol. 6 (1930), 1989. (Short title: *Central Committee Documents*.)

Zhongguo gongchandang huiyi gaiyao (A Summary Account of Chinese Communist Party Meetings), ed. Jiang Huaxuan, Zhang Weiping, and Xiao Sheng. Shenyang: Shenyang chubanshe, 1991. (Short title: *Party Meetings*.)

Zhongyang tongxin (Central Correspondence). Organ of the Central Committee of the Chinese Communist Party, August 1927-.

Zhou Enlai xuanji (Selected Works of Zhou Enlai), Vol. 1. Beijing: Renmin chubanshe, 1980. (Short title: Zhou, *Works*.)

Index

AB Corps, 548, 583, 668, 669, 731, 732;
accusations against, 647, 648, 650; in
CCP, lxiii, 554, 555; in Jiangxi,
lxivn112, 559n1, 560, 586, 587; and
land redistribution, 561, 562, 676, 680;
members of, 622, 634, 642; in Red
Army, 588, 670; uprising of, 704–713
passim, 718

Adventurism: within CCP, 154, 197, 207,
241, 244, 566; examples of, 167, 238,
445; failures of, xxxvi, 157, 160, 437;
and idealism, 202, 237; and
investigations, 203, 421–422; Mao
accused of, xxiv; of vagabonds, 453,
454

Age, reckoning of, 297n6

Agrarian revolution, 13–19; AB Corps
attacks on, 710, 711; and Autumn
Harvest Uprising, 37, 38, 41; and Bailu
Conference, xxxvi; calls for, 123, 142,
255; classes involved in, 32, 375,
620–639, 693, 712; and democratic
revolution, 64, 114, 116, 134; effects of,
330, 333, 344, 380, 405; in Fujian, 158;
in Hunan, 27, 34; in Hunan-Jiangxi
Border Area, 67, 68, 70, 74, 83, 84;
investigations of, liii; in Jiangxi, 158,
269, 680–683; Li Lisan on, xli–xlii, lv;
political importance of, 236, 270,
559–569; progress in, 57, 458;
propaganda about, 77, 217, 220; and
Red Army, 124, 243, 248, 540; rich
peasants in, 436, 438, 448, 612; Sixth
CCP Congress on, xxxviii; women in,
415–418; in Xunwu *xian,* 405–409. *See
also* land redistribution

Agriculture: collective, liv, 128, 443, 569;
socialization of, xlvi, 442, 444,
446–447, 685

Aihutuan. See under militia

Air forces (GMD), 699, 717

All-China General Labor Union, 457

All-China Peasant Association, 6n10

All-China Revolutionary Committee, 530n4

America, 401n95, 415; Communist Party in,
715–716; and GMD, 141, 144, 145,
250; imperialism of, 123, 133, 224, 248;
international relations of, 64, 238, 575,
577, 578; workers in, 714–715

Amoy. *See* Xiamen

Amulet Society, 452

An Zhongyuan, 19. *See also* codes, security

Ancestral halls, 326, 403, 691; confiscation
of property of, 15, 16, 256, 257, 503,
504; corporate trusts of, 351–353, 379,
389

Anfu clique, 63n4

Anfu *xian,* 86, 89, 113, 263, 583, 688, 694;
GMD forces in, 584, 695; land
redistribution in, 560, 565, 674, 677,
684, 686; military activities in, 57, 118,
243, 274, 526, 531, 657, 702

Anhui Province, 148, 452

Anti-Bolshevik Corps. *See* AB Corps

Anyi, 474–475, 483

Anyuan City, 52, 300

Anyuan *xian,* 44, 45, 149, 369n79, 396, 417;
CCP in, xxin25, 152, 167, 275, 298;
mentioned, xxin27, 301, 552; military
activities in, 118, 274, 533, 534; miners
from, 60; natives of, 328, 339; workers
of, xxiii, xxivn38, 93; Xunwu's trade
with, 299, 302–305, 307, 310, 317, 321

Apprenticeship, 332, 340, 601, 603, 608, 659

Army Committees, xliv, xlv, 59, 60, 67, 68,
84, 87, 88, 98–99, 113, 117, 126, 127,
160, 177n2, 179, 180n11, 182, 184,
187, 268, 270, 279

Army Party Bureau, 171

Art, 126, 219, 338. *See also* dramatic
productions

Artisans, 75, 112, 202, 260, 330, 423, 451; in
Daqiao, 660; in Dongtang, 659; and
land redistribution, 130, 164, 406, 414,
687; and marriage, 630; in Xingguo,
605, 610, 632–633; in Xunwu, 333,
338, 347, 351

About the Editor

Stuart R. Schram was born in Excelsior, Minnesota, in 1924. After graduating from the University of Minnesota in physics, he took his Ph.D. in political science at Columbia University. From 1954 to 1967, he conducted research at the Fondation Nationale des Sciences Politiques in Paris, and from 1968 until 1989, he was Professor of Politics with reference to China at the School of Oriental and African Studies, University of London. Since 1989, he has worked at the Fairbank Center, Harvard University, on the edition of Mao Zedong's pre-1949 writings of which this is the third volume.

His research has dealt with Leninist theories and their application in Asia, Chinese history and politics in the twentieth century, and the influence of the Chinese tradition on the theory and practice of the state in China. His works include *Mao Tse-tung* (1967), *The Political Thought of Mao Tse-tung* (1969), *Marxism and Asia* (in collaboration with Hélène Carrère d'Encausse) (1969), *Ideology and Policy in China since the Third Plenum, 1978–1984* (1984), and *The Thought of Mao Tse-tung* (1989). He has also edited a volume entitled *Foundations and Limits of State Power in China* (1987). *Mao Tse-tung* and *The Thought of Mao Tse-tung* have been translated into Chinese and published in Beijing. Stuart Schram is a member of the Authors Guild.

About the Associate Editor

Nancy J. Hodes was born in Philadelphia in 1946, and spent her formative years in Beijing, China, where her father taught physiology at the Chinese Academy of Medical Sciences. After graduating from Radcliffe College in Far Eastern Languages, she edited the *Bulletin of Concerned Asian Scholars*, taught Chinese, and worked as a freelance translator. She returned to China in the 1970s to teach English and work on *A Chinese-English Dictionary* at the Beijing Foreign Languages Institute (#1). Later she taught Chinese at Tufts University and Harvard Summer School, worked as a translator for M. E. Sharpe's translation journals and the Mao's Writings Project at Brown University, and served as Assistant Editor of the *Harvard Journal of Asiatic Studies*. After receiving her Ph.D. in Chinese literature from Harvard University, she taught East Asian Civilizations and Chinese at Boston College, and has been working since 1991 with Stuart R. Schram on the present edition of Mao Zedong's pre-1949 writings. Until 1995, she served concurrently as Associate Director of the Boston Research Center for the 21st Century, founded in 1993 by Soka Gakkai International President Daisaku Ikeda. She is now engaged in translating a novel by China's former Minister of Culture, Wang Meng.